Virginia County Records

Please direct all correspondence and orders to:

SOUTHERN HISTORICAL PRESS, Inc.
PO BOX 1267
375 West Broad Street
Greenville, SC   29601
southernhistoricalpress@gmail.com

ISBN #0-89308-884-6

Printed in the United States of America

SPOTSYLVANIA

COUNTY RECORDS

1721 - 1800

Being Transcriptions, from the Original Files at the County
Court House, of Wills, Deeds, Administrators' and
Guardians' Bonds, Marriage Licenses, and
Lists of Revolutionary Pensioners.

EDITED BY

WILLIAM ARMSTRONG CROZIER

Preface

ON the year 1720 an Act was passed by the Virginia House of Burgesses authorizing the formation of a new county, to be composed from territory constituting the then counties of Essex, King William, and King and Queen. The new county, whose boundaries " extended westward to the river beyond the high mountains " —the Shenandoah—received the name Spotsylvania, in honor of Alexander Spotswood, Governor of the colony of Virginia. By the terms of the Act creating it, which became operative the first day of May, 1721, it was made one parish, called St. George. In the year 1730 this parish was divided into St. George's and St. Mark's. The latter parish, lying in the upper portion of the county, became, in the year 1734, the county of Orange, and contained all that is now Orange, Madison, Culpeper, and Rappahannock counties. In March, 1769-70, St. George's parish was again subdivided, and a new parish was formed, known as Berkeley, lying within the bounds of Spotsylvania county.

The seat of justice of Spotsylvania County was, first, Germanna, the residence of the Governor, but by Act of Assembly, passed in 1732, it was removed to Fredericksburg. The town of Fredericksburg, named in honor of Prince Frederick, son of George II, was founded in 1727, and its records were incorporated with those of the county, until the formation of the Corporation Court system in 1782, from which time the two records were separate and distinct. After one or two other removals, the court was finally settled at its present site—Spotsylvania Court House.

The record books of the county have suffered materially from lack of care by early custodians, constant handling, removals of the court house, and vandalism during the Civil War. During this latter period they were only preserved by being boxed and buried. The earliest Will Book, covering the period 1722 to 1749, is in an especially bad state of preservation, and the absence of Will Book C will be noted. This book, taking in the years from 1759 to 1761, was destroyed by the Federal soldiers. It will be found, however, that the wills, administrators' and guardians' bonds covering the period of the lost book are recorded at the end of Will Book B, 1749 to 1759, the last entry in Book B being recorded 7 December, 1761, and the first entry in Book D being also dated 7 December, 1761. The loss of Will Book C, therefore, is not irreparable. Again, though there seems to have been no Deed Book I, no records are missing, because Deed Book J begins where Book H ended. In view of these circumstances, and since the value of a transcription depends entirely upon its exactness and conformity with the original, the greatest care has been taken in the preparation of this volume.

Many instances have been found in which the surname in one document was written in three, and even in four, different ways. In all such cases the first spelling has been strictly adhered to. In no instance has any attempt been made to change or modernize the spelling of proper names.

CONTENTS

WILLS

WILL BOOK A

1722–1749

ROBERTS, JOHN, St. George's Parish, d. Sept. 10, 1724, p. Nov. 3, 1724. Wit. G. Lightfoot, John Brown, Matthew Bailey. Ex. son-in-law Francis Kirkley; son John Roberts. Leg. son John, land on Flatt Run joining Hack Norman; son Benjamin, land joining Roger Abbott; son George; daughter Mary Paten. (Page 9)

BOND, ROBERT, Spotsylvania Co., d. Jan. —, 1723–4, p. July 6, 1725. Wit. Robert Cobbs, Thomas Park. Ex. John Bond. Leg. daughter, Mary Thompson; wife (no name given); son John Bond. (Page 14)

JAMES, JOHN, St. George's Parish, d. Jan. 23, 1725, p. Mar. 1, 1725–6. Wit. John Grayson, Stephen Sharp, John Battaille. Ex. wife Alice James, Charles Taliaferro, Junr. Leg. wife Alice and daughter Mary, and the child my wife now goes with. (Page 24)

MOORE, SAMUEL, Mataponia in King George's Parish, d. Feb. 2, 1725–6, p. Apr. 5, 1726. Wit. John Foster, Richard Parstow, Mary Cook. Ex. wife Rachel Moore. Leg. wife Rachel and son Robert Moore. (Page 29)

SAMMS, JAMES, d. Feb. 22, 1725–6, p. Dec. 6, 1726. Wit. John Corbet, John Nalle, James ———. Ex. Katherine Sams. Leg. sons William and James, my lands to be divided between them as follows: to begin on Pike Run, at the mouth of a spring branch near my house, and to run to a corner white oak of Wm. Bradbourn's, and my son William to have the part lying on Mr. Daniel Brown's land down ye Run, and my son James to have ye upper part. (Page 39)

WALTERS, ISAAC, St. George's Parish, d. June 11, 1726, p. Dec. 6, 1726. Wit. Blanche Wall, Susanna Brown, Abraham Field. Ex. Augustine Smith, Junr. Leg. Thomas Smith and Augustine Smith, Junr. (Page 41)

BOURN, ROBERT, Planter, St. George's Parish, d. ———, 1726, p. May 2, 1727. Wit. William Tapp, William Moore. Ex. wife Elizabeth Bourn. Leg. son Robert, 200 acres of land beginning at Mr. Reves' corner, running to Philemon Cavaners' corner, and from said corner upon Mr. Buckner's line, from thence to the beginning; sons William and John; daughters Tacy, Mary and Elizabeth Bourn; wife Elizabeth Bourn. (Page 52)

WARREN, WILLIAM, King George's Parish, d. Sept. 11, 1726, p. May 2, 1727. Wit. John Foster, Samuel Ham, Rachel Askey. Leg. sons John, William, Samuel and James Warren. (Page 53)

1

STEVENS, CHARLES, Spotsylvania Co., d. June 24, 1726, p. Aug. 1, 1727. Wit. Robert Thomas, Thomas Park, James Stevens. Ex. wife Elizabeth Stevens. Leg. wife Elizabeth, land and plantation in Essex Co.; son Mumford Stevens; daughters Mattie and Elizabeth. (Page 61)

Editor's Note. This will being sworn to by Elizabeth Bledsoe, late ye wife of Charles Stevens, now ye wife of William Bledsoe.

CAMMILL, ALEXANDER, Spotsylvania Co., d. July 10, 1727, p. Aug. 1, 1727. Wit. Isaac Bledsoe, Edward Watts. Ex. wife Agnes Cammill. Leg. wife Agnes; son-in-law William Moore; son William Cammill; son-in-law James Moore; daughter-in-law Mary Moore. (Page 63)

BURBRIDGE, MARY, Spotsylvania Co., d. Feb. 8, 1727-8, p. Mar. 5, 1727-8. Wit. Thomas Withorby, Alice Withorby. Ex. Benjamin Horton, Thomas Burbridge. Leg. Robert Burbridge, Mary Burbridge and Benjamin Horton. (Page 69)

TILLARY, SAMUEL, St. George's Parish, d. Apr. 1728, p. Feb. 4, 1728-9. Wit. Daniel Brown, George Carter, Thomas Hobson. Ex. wife Winifred Tillary. Leg. son John Tillary, all my carpenter's and cooper's tools; daughter Mary Tillary. (Page 90)

TALIAFERRO, ROBERT, d. Feb. 1, 1727-8, p. Feb. 4, 1728. Wit. G. Braxton, Junr., William Taliaferro. Ex. my wife and my brother John Taliaferro. Leg. brother John Taliaferro, all my lands in Spotsylvania Co., either patented or to be patented; wife (no name given) land in Essex Co.; daughters Mary and Elizabeth Taliaferro, "that they will not convey unto Mr. George Braxton the land in King & Queen Co. which I have sold him, that then I give and bequeath in Essex Co. to him and his heirs forever." (Verbatim.) Daughter, Martha Taliaferro; brother Richard Taliaferro. Testator mentions negroes and chattels in Spotsylvania Co., be brought down into Essex Co. on my plantation there. (Page 91)

CHEW, LARKIN, d. May 11, 1728, p. Apr. 1, 1729. Wit. William Russell. Ex. son Larkin Chew. Leg. sons Thomas and John Chew; daughter Nan Johnson, wife of William Johnson; Larkin Chew Junr. son of Larkin and Hannah Chew, every part and parcel of my estate after my debts are paid; my wife Hannah Chew to have her first choice of my estate after the debts are paid, to maintain her and my mother Ruth Green, during their natural lives, afterwards to return to Larkin Chew, my natural son and executor. (Page 98)

THOMSON, WILLIAM, d. Jan. 12, 1727, p. Oct. 1, 1728. Wit. Thomas Thomson, Thomas Little. Ex. brothers John and Thomas Thomson. Leg. my wife and children (names not given); brothers John and Thomas Thomson. (Page 99)

BEVERLEY, HARRY, St. George's Parish, d. Nov. 30, 1730, p. Feb. 12, 1730-1. Wit. John Gordon, John Henderson, William Chapman, Thomas Sellars. Ex. son Robert Beverley. Leg. daughter Elizabeth Stanard, the lower part of my tract of land on the River Ta, in Spotsylvania Co., that lies below the branch that is next to Col. John Robinson's bridge; daughter Mary, the residue of above tract; daughter Margaret; daughter Susanna; daughter Catharine; daughter Judith, 1000 acres adjoining the land I sold to Andrew Harrison; daughter Agatha; son Robert, balance of lands not disposed of. (Page 119)

HORSENAIL, JAMES, St. George's Parish, d. July 30, 1730, p. Mar. 2, 1730-1. Wit. John Smith, Myles Potter, Lewis Murrah. Ex. Francis Thornton, Francis Thornton, Junr. Leg. Francis Thornton, Junr; Mary Abbott and William Abbott, son of the aforesaid Mary; my brother and sister Thomas and Elizabeth Horsenail, of Nazing Parish, in Essex Co., England; Mr. Thomas Griffin, whom I appoint my attorney in London; to Francis Thornton, my two servants Robert Deniston and William Aiken, and likewise the rest of the servitude of William Flowers. (Page 120)

MADISON, AMBROSE, St. Mark's Parish, d. July 31, 1732, p. Tuesday Feb. 10, 1732-3. Wit. James Barbour, Robert Martin, George Penn. Ex. my wife; my brother John Madison; Francis Conway; Joseph Brock. Leg. I give and bequeath unto James Coleman —— hundred acres of land according to survey —— adjoining to the said Coleman's plantation; I give and bequeath unto —— hundred acres of land according as it is laid out —— at the great Mountains to himself and his ——; I bequeath unto Daniel S —— and fifty acres of land —— and Abraham Estridge's line ——; I give unto David Roach one hundred acres of land, to be laid off some part of my land —— Mr. George Braxton, Gentl. and others according ——; I give unto my daughter Elizabeth —— acres of land adjoining to the above mentioned land —— to begin at my upper line and so run down to the lower —— thousand acres of land at the great Mountains, lying —— now belonging to John Camm, Gentl., and my son James —— heirs forever; I give unto my daughter —— one thousand acres of land adjoining to her sister Elizabeth —— little Mountain, and also one thousand acres of land —— Mountains lying between the land of my son James on —— and land —— Abraham Estridge ——; I give unto my son James my lands whatsoever that I am possessed of, to him and —— forever, and that he possess the same when he shall arrive ——teen years of age; I lend unto my dear and well beloved wife Frances all and singular my real and personal estate not —— bequeathed. (Page 172)

PIGG, EDWARD, JUNR. (Nuncupative will). dated Feb. 18, 1725, p. Apr. 3, 1733. Wit. P. Rogers, Lawrence Franklin. Administrator, Edward Pigg, Senr. Bondsmen John Foster and Charles Pigg, Bond recorded Apr. 3, 1733. Leg. brothers John and Henry; mentions mother and father then living (no names given); "to Charles and Ann" all his tobacco to be equally divided. (Page 178)

BEVERLEY, ROBERT, St. George's Parish, d. May 12, 1733, p. June 5, 1733. Wit. Elias Watt, Jerome Armon, Larkin Chew, W. Beverley. Ex. my wife; cousin William Beverley and my brother Benjamin Winslow, in case of my wife's marriage. Leg. Mentions late father, Mr. Harry Beverley; nephew Beverley Stanard 6000 acres of land, part of the tract at the mountains in Spotsylvania Co. called Octonia Land; brother-in-law Benjamin Winslow 300 acres of the same tract; to Anthony Head 200 acres of the same tract to include the plantation the said Head now lives on; to Robert Dearing 200 acres of the Octonia Tract; my only son Harry Beverley, not to be sent to England, but put to school at ye college at the age of ten years. William Beverley to be his guardian; my three unmarried sisters, Mary, Catharine and Agatha, to live in my house at Neroland as previously; wife Ann Beverley; my five sisters; my sister Stanard's two daughters. (Page 188)

SPOTSWOOD, ROBERT, Spotsylvania Co., d. May 5, 1733. Wit. Anth. Rhodes Junr., John Gordon, William Booth, Elizabeth Gordon. Ex. Col. Henry Willis. Leg. to Mr. Edmund Bagge, my horse and saddle; to Col. Henry Willis, my watch; to Mary James, twenty shillings; to Thomas Barnett, my wearing apparel; Mr. Elliot Benger, to be paid the money I owe him; estate, after debts are paid, to go to John Willis, the son of Henry and Mildred Willis. (Page 190)

PROCTOR, GEORGE, St. George's Parish, d. Mar. 23, 1730–1, p. Aug. 7, 1738. Wit. G. Home; Joseph Parker; Matthew Giles. Ex. wife Mary and son-in-law Charles Steward. Leg. wife Mary my manor plantation; son George; son John, half the land I now live on, with the manor plantation when his mother dies; daughters Margaret, Mary and Elizabeth. (Page 193)

HOMES, ROBERT, (Nuncupative will). d. Jan. 14, 1732–3, p. July 3, 1733. Wit. Timothy Johnson, Harry Clockgrove. Admx. Sarah Homes, with Timothy Johnson and David Phillips on bond. Leg. son Joseph Homes; wife Sarah Homes. (Page 194)

PLOWMAN, WILLIAM, Spotsylvania Co., d. July 19, 1733, p. Aug. 7, 1733. Wit. Hn. Ballentyne, Hancock Lee, Zach. Taylor, Thomas Nicholls. Ex. Col. Henry Willis. Leg. loving friend Col. Henry Willis of Spotsylvania Co. to have all my estate, both real and personal. (Page 197)

JOHNSON, JAEL, Spotsylvania Co., d. July 7, 1733, p. Sept. 4, 1733. Wit. Antho. Rhodes, Junr., Wm. Call, Junr. Sarah Garton. Ex. Richard Tutt. Leg. my son Richard Tutt, articles of personal estate, among which is a chest called "Elizabeth Tutt's"; my son James Williams; legacies to William Williams, Betty Marshall, Sarah Cavenaugh, Jael Cavenaugh, James Williams, Richard Tutt, Philemon Cavenaugh. (Page 202)

BROYL, JOHN, d. Mar. 7, 1731–2, p. Feb. 5, 1733–4. Wit. Milsel Sollt, Blankenparker. Leg. Mentions children, male and female, and wife.
Note. The will was proved by Ursley Broyl, widow of John Broyl, and Paultus Blankenparker. (Page 209)

ABNEY, DANNITT, Spotsylvania Co., d. Feb. 5, 1732. Wit. Paul Abney, Abner Abney, William Trusty, Mary Abney. Ex. wife, Mary Abney. Leg. wife, Mary Abney, to whom is given the entire estate, and upon her death she is to give to the children that are most dutiful to her. (Page 209)

TWYMAN, GEORGE, d. Mar. 17, 1733, p. Apr. 2, 1734. Wit. Zachary Taylor, Joseph Mintor. Ex. Thomas Coward and wife Agatha Twyman. Leg. children William, George, Catharine, and Mary Twyman; wife Agatha; son William, 100 acres of land in Essex Co. (Page 210)

CRAWFORD, WILLIAM, St. George's Parish, d. Mar. 16, 1733, p. Mar. —, 1734. Wit. William Crostherait, Richard Winslow, Henry Owens. Ex. George Eastham. Leg. eldest son William and youngest son Burnett, 200 acres of land by the mouth of Elk Run; son Thomas; daughter Ann, 50 acres on Elk Run above Benjamin Coward's land; daughter Elizabeth and her husband Benjamin Coward; wife (no name given). (Page 212)

DAVIS, JOHN, St. Mark's Parish, d. Mar. 14, 1733, p. June 4, 1734. Wit. D. Bryne, John Davison, James Coward. Ex. wife and son John. Leg. wife Elizabeth, son John, son-in-law Leonard Phillips; son William; son Matthew; son Joseph; unmarried daughters Elizabeth and Elinor. (Page 223)

DURHAM, ROBERT, Fredericksville, in the Parish of St. George, d. Apr. 15, 1734, p. Aug. 6, 1734. Wit. Charles Barrett, Adam Gordon, William Wombwell Cliff. Ex. Charles Chiswell, Gentl. Leg. wife Agnes; daughters Hannah and Ann, which I had by the said Agnes. Mentions wages due him from the Fredericksville Company. (Page 230)

BLANTON, RICHARD, Spotsylvania Co., d. Sept. 5, 173-, p. Sept. 3, 1734. Wit. R. Curtis, Junr., Robert Blackburne, Francis Smith, William Lindsey. Ex. wife Elizabeth, son Richard Blanton. Leg. wife Elizabeth; children Richard, Thomas, Priscilla, Elizabeth and Mary Blanton. (Page   )

SHARP, STEPHEN, St. George's Parish, d. Mar. 12, 1735, p. June 3, 1735. Wit. George Pool, Henry Chamble. Ex. Elizabeth Sharp. Leg. wife Elizabeth Sharp; mentions Hoke Grayson; Mary Jones; Elizabeth James; John Grayson. (Page 255)

WILLIAMS, JAMES, Spotsylvania Co., d. May 30, 1735, p. Aug. 5, 1735. Wit. M. Battaley, John Conner, William Spencer. Ex. brother-in-law Richard Tutt. Leg. son, William Williams; son John, 400 acres of land on the fork of Rappahannock River, patented by me May 13, 1726; wife Ann Williams; brother-in-law Richard Tutt, guardian to my sons William and John Williams until they are twenty-one years of age. (Page 257)

BANTON, JOHN, St. George's Parish, d. July 27, 1735, p. Feb. 3, 1735. Wit. William Hansford, Henry Sharkes, William Hollot. Ex. wife Mary Banton. Leg. son William, choice of my whip saws and all my shoe-maker's tools; son John; daughter Elizabeth Elson; daughter Alice Banton; wife Mary Banton. (Page 263)

PRICE, RODERICK, St. George's Parish, d. Apr. 1, 1735, p. Apr. 6, 1736. Wit. Thomas Jarman, William Hutcherson, Arthur Hopes. Ex. John Dawner, Senr. Leg. Sarah Dawner, daughter of John Dawner, Senr., John Oliver; John Oliver, son of John Oliver; Henry Moscow, son of Paul Moscow, Senr; William Emmerson; John Dawner. (Page 269)

HAM, SAMUEL, Spotsylvania Co., d. Mar. 2, 1737, p. May 2, 1738. Wit. John Foster, William Ham. Ex. wife Margaret Ham. Leg. daughter Ann Ham; sons Samuel, William and Edward Ham; wife Margaret. (Page 285)

COFFEY, TIMOTHY, d. Apr. 1, 1728, p. June 6, 1738. Wit. John Holloday, Anthony Golston, James Rawlings. Ex. Adam Gordon. Leg. entire estate to friend Adam Gordon. (Page 286)

SUTTON, AMEY, St. George's Parish, d. Oct. 20, 1738, p. Nov. 7, 1738. Wit. Edmund Waller, William McCarsh, Samuel Brown. Ex. Edmund Waller, son of Col. John Waller. Leg. my son Joseph White; Edmund Waller; Mrs. Anne Lewis, daughter of Zachary Lewis, Gentl; my son William Henry Nathan White; Col. Waller; Robert Wills. (Page 293)

WHARTON, SAMUEL, St. George's Parish, d. Oct. 22, 1738, p. Nov. —, 1738. Wit. Robert Stuart, Joseph Neavill, Thomas Nicholls. Ex. brother,

William Wharton. Leg. sister, Martha Wharton; son-in-law James Williams; brother William Wharton; brother Charles Wharton; brothers Zacheus and Joseph Wharton; sister Ann; mother Ann Turlong. (Page 294)

LONG, SAMUEL, St. George's Parish, d. Feb. 14, 1739–40, p. May 6, 1740. Wit. Thomas Ship; Thomas Morris; William Perry. Ex. my brother James Long. Leg. son Bromfield Long; daughters Mary and Elizabeth Long. (Page 310)

PIGG, EDWARD, St. George's Parish, d. Aug. 15, 1739, p. Apr. 7, 1741. Wit. William Waller, Samuel Brockman, William Brockman. Ex. son Charles Fickes Pigg. Leg. daughter Ann, wife of John Clarke; son Charles Fickes Pigg, 200 acres of land I bought of my brother Henry Pigg, lying in King & Queen Co., and adjoining Edward Smith, and is now claimed by one Hudson Allen; son John Pigg; granddaughter Ann Payne, wife of Barnett Payne, Junr; grandchildren Jane and Mary Haskew. (Page 318)

BOSWELL, JOHN, St. George's Parish, d. Jan. 10, 1740, p. May 5, 1741. Proved on the oath of William Bicknell, who wrote the said will for the said John Boswell. Ex. wife Ann Boswell. Leg. eldest daughter Dorothy; youngest Frances; sons Ransom, George and James Boswell, 980 acres of land to be equally divided among the above named children; my younger children to be educated. I desire that the Court may bind my three eldest sons when they arrive at the age of fifteen years to the following trades,—Ransom and John Boswell to a Joyner and Carpenter and George Boswell to a Blacksmith. Wife Ann. (Page 321)

ROY, JAMES, d. Apr. 16, 1741, p. May 5, 1741. Wit. Edward Herndon, John Gordon, Elizabeth Gordon. Ex. Maj. Francis Thornton. Leg. son Thomas Roy, all my land; daughter Elizabeth Gordon, now wife to John Gordon; daughters Effey, Isabella, Mary, and Sarah Roy; son David Roy. (Page 325)

MORRIS, THOMAS, Spotsylvania Co., d. July 21, 1741, p. Apr. 6, 1742. Wit. M. Battaley, John Sisar; Jane Sisar. Ex. wife Margaret Morris, and Zachary Garton. Leg. Thomas Morris; son William Morris; wife Margaret; daughters Mary and Sarah Morris; daughters Elizabeth and Margaret. (Page 343)

HOLLODAY, JOHN, St. George's Parish, in King William Co., d. Nov. 4, 1742, p. Dec. 7, 1742. Wit. John Waller, Jo. Waller, Junr., Thomas Cartwright. Ex. sons, Joseph and Benjamin Holloday and son-in-law Thomas Pulliam. Leg. son William Holloday, 200 acres of land, where Thomas Certain formerly lived; son John Holloday, 250 acres of land where James Perry Junr., lived; son Daniell Holloday, 200 acres of land; son Joseph Holloday, 300 acres of land; son Benjamin Holloday, 300 acres of land; daughter Elizabeth, now the wife of Patterson Pulliam; daughter Winifred, now the wife of Thomas Pulliam; daughter Sarah, now the wife of James Rollings, 300 acres of land lying in Caroline Co., and joining the tract I sold to Thomas Burch; daughter Susanna Holloday, 200 acres of land adjoining Mr. Wyat's land. (Page 346)

BROCK, JOSEPH, Spotsylvania Co., d. Mar. 3, 1742, p. July 5, 1743. Wit. W. Robinson, Agatha Robinson, William Waller. Ex. wife Mary. Leg. wife Mary, 750 acres of land, together with my mansion house, be-

ginning at a black oak, corner of Bloomfield Longs in sight of Burros
Road, and is also a corner of my patent, thence keeping my patent lines
to Rice Curtis, Junr.'s corner on the north side of Burros Road; thence
keeping said Curtis' line to Thomas Duerson's corner pine on the east
side of the road that leads to Snell's Bridge; then along the said road
by Mattapony Church, to the said Duerson's Corner on Larkin Chew's
land; thence keeping the said Chew's several lines, to a large white oak
in the corner of my patent. Then keeping my patent lines to the Middle
River, thence up the river to John Durrett's lower corner on the river;
thence with his line to his corner white oak; then along a line of
marked trees to the first mentioned place. Son William Brock the rest
of my land not disposed of by me to Rice Curtis, Junr. and Thomas
Duerson, which is part of a patent granted Larkin Chew, decd. for 1600
acres in the year 1722. Son Joseph Brock, 787 acres of land from the
same tract with his mother; son Henry Brock, 650 acres of land including the plantation whereon he now lives; daughter Mary Brock plantation known by the name of Folly, and to include 500 acres joining thereto;
daughter Susanna Brock; grandson Joseph Duerson; grandson, Rice
Curtis; daughter Hannah Duerson. Mentions tract of land of about
4,000 acres lying in Spotsylvania Co., also mentions slaves given to Rice
Curtis, Junr. and Thomas Duerson. (Page 360)

ALLEN, THOMAS, St. George's Parish, d. Nov. 10, 1743, p. Feb. 7,
1743. Wit. John Hawkins, James Jones, Nick Jones. Ex. wife Elizabeth
and son Nathaniel. Leg. son Thomas; son Nathaniel; daughter Elizabeth; grandson Robert Hall; wife Elizabeth; son John. (Page —)

GRAYSON, AMBROSE, St. George's Parish, d. Sept. 6, 1742, p. Mar. 6,
1743. Wit. Robert Lovell, George Nix, Peirce Perry. Ex. brother Benjamin Grayson; my wife Alice Grayson; my son John Grayson. Leg. wife
Alice; son John; son Ambrose; mentions other children, but does not
name them. (Page 379)

TAYLOR, JAMES, Spotsylvania Co., d. Jan. 25, 1743, p. Mar. 6, 1743.
Wit. John Taylor, Thomas Graves, William Johnston. Ex. wife Betty
Taylor. Leg. wife Betty Taylor and daughter Milly Taylor. (Page —)

SAMUEL, ANTHONY, St. George's Parish, p. Apr. 3, 1744. Wit. Eliza-
beth Lovell, Ambrose Porter, George Nix. Ex. my father James Samuel,
Senr., and John Calket, Senr. Leg. James Samuel, son of James Samuel.
Senr. 100 acres of land with the plantatior belonging to the same tract
joining to William Bastin, in Essex Co; sister Hannah Samuel; brother
Mark Samuel; my sister's two children John Martin and Mary Martin,
the debt due me from Joseph Red; my father James Samuel, Senior.
(Page 383)

TALIAFERRO, JOHN, St. George's Parish, d. Apr. 30, 1744, p. Aug. 7,
1744. Wit. John Power, Ann Power, Sarah Power, Susanna Power. Ex.
wife Mary, sons Lawrence and William Taliaferro, William Hunter.
Leg. son Lawrence, land at the Robinson containing 1200 acres,
more or less; son William; to William Hunter, as a portion to my daughter Martha, the land called Rackett, 300 acres out of the Robinson tract;
wife Mary; daughters Lucy and Molly; mentions lands in Orange Co.
(Page 395)

BYRNE, EDMUND, Spotsylvania Co., d. Aug. 17, 1744, p. Sept. 4, 1744. Wit. James Mills, Joseph Hawkins, Edward Ware. Admr. Joseph Hawkins. Leg. my brother (page torn) and Thomas Byrne of the Co. of Kilkenney, in the Kingdom of Ireland, whom I do appoint and constitute my joint heirs. (Page 397)

BLAKE, JOHN, St. George's Parish, d. May 17, 1744, p. Nov. 6, 1744. Wit. Joseph Sterling, William Maer, Humphrey Wallace. Ex. Mr. Benjamin Hubbard and my wife Elizabeth. Leg. wife Elizabeth now with child; daughter Mary. (Page —)

POOLE, GEORGE, Spotsylvania Co., d. Feb. 29, 1743, p. Feb. 5, 1744. Wit. Daniel Duval, Matthew Gale, Sharshall Grasty. Ex. wife and sons Micajah and Thomas Poole. Leg. wife Elizabeth; sons Micajah and Thomas; daughter Mary, wife of William Stevens; daughter Elizabeth, wife of James Brown; granddaughter Mary Brown; daughter Ann, wife of James Walston; granddaughter Mary Walston; daughter Joanna, wife of James Young; daughter Milley; daughter Sarah. (Page 411)

LIVINGSTON, SUSANNA, Spotsylvania Co., d. May 22, 1745, p. June 4, 1745. Wit. Francis Thornton, John Thornton, Robert Jackson. Ex. Philip Rootes, Senr. Leg. Philip Rootes of King & Queen; mentions Philip Rootes, Junr., Lucy Rootes, Betty Rootes, son and daughters of the said Philip Rootes; to Thomas Matthews the large bible for the good of his soul; to Philip Rootes, Senr. the land and plantation whereon I now live. (Page 416)

GRASTY, SHARSHALL, Spotsylvania Co., d. May 27, 1745, p. Oct. 1, 1745. Wit. Elizabeth Poole; Micajah Poole; William McWilliams. Ex. wife Sarah and George Hoomes, Gentl. of Caroline Co. Leg. wife Sarah; son John, who is described by the testator as being afflicted with fitts and scarcely compos mentis; sons Butterworth and Sharshall; son George; daughters Ann Waldo Mansfield, wife of John Mansfield, and Mary Grasty. (Page 420)

ELLIS, ROBERT, Spotsylvania Co., d. Aug. 31, 1745, p. Oct. 1, 1745. Wit. John Thornton, John Hughes, John Willis. Leg. brother William Ellis. (Page 422)

NIX, GEORGE, St. George's Parish, d. Nov. 2, 1745, p. May 6, 1746. Wit. William McWilliams, Edward Leavell, Mary Leavell. Ex. Edward Leavell and William McWilliams. Leg. wife Susanna Nix; sons George and Joseph Nix. (Page 430)

HOLLODAY, WILLIAM, St. George's Parish, d. Dec. 4, 1744, p. May 6, 1746. Wit. William Waller, Matthew Gayle, Henry Rogers. Ex. sons, Charles and Robert. Leg. wife Anne; sons John, Charles, George and Robert Holloday; daughter Elizabeth, wife of Thomas Dillard; grandson John Robinson; grandson William Holloday, son of Robert Holloday, all my land in King William Co; grandson William Holloday, son of John Holloday, remainder of my land in Spotsylvania Co; daughter Ann, wife of John Robinson. (Page 431)

SANDIGE, WILLIAM, St. George's Parish, d. Mar. 11, 1746, p. June 2, 1747. Wit. Thomas White, Betty White. Ex. wife Ann, and sons James and David. Leg. sons, William, John, James and David; wife Ann;

granddaughter Sarah Golson, 100 acres of land adjoining the land my son-in-law Golson lives on; my daughter Golson. (Page 443)

GRAVES, JOHN, St. George's Parish, d. Mar. 30, 1747, p. June 2, 1747. Wit. Joseph Holloday, Benjamin Holloday, B. Lewis, William Webb. Ex. wife Susanna, Joseph Peterson, John Wigglesworth. Leg. wife Susanna, 140 acres of land which I had of Nicholas Randolph; son Thomas Graves, 140 acres of land next his brother Edward; daughter Rebecca, 140 acres of land next her brother Thomas; son Isaac, 140 acres of land next his sister Rebecca; son John, 140 acres of land next his brother Isaac; daughter Jemima, 140 acres of land next her brother John. (Page 444)

HUBBARD, THOMAS, Spotsylvania Co., d. Mar. 11, 1745, p. Feb. 2, 1747. Wit. John Waller, Junr., John Shirley, William Pruit. Ex. wife Christian. Leg. son John; son Matthew, my plantation whereon I now live, and 100 acres of land being the part of my tract which joins Thomas Dillard and Daniel Pruit, after the death or marriage of my wife; son Benjamin 100 acres adjoining to John Farish; wife Christian; daughter Anne Hubbard. (Page 450)

CHAPMAN, GEORGE, (Nuncupative will) d. Bath Towne, Sept. 22, 1747, p. Feb. 3, 1747. Admr. Nathaniel Chapman. Bond £1400, with Francis Thornton and Robert Jackson securities. Leg. To Pearson Chapman, second son to Nathaniel Chapman, real and personal estate; to Nathaniel Gordon, a set of tools and to his mother my wearing apparel; mentions George Thompson, Milley Chapman and Betty Chapman. (Page 463)

COLLINS, THOMAS, (Nuncupative will) St. George's Parish, son of John Collins, decd. in the County of King & Queen, d. Jan. 3, 1748–9, p. Feb. 7, 1748. Leg. brother John Collins and his son Edmund Collins, all my estate. (Page 480)

LEAVIL, EDWARD, St. George's Parish, d. Feb. 23, 1742–3, p. Aug. 1, 1749. Wit. George Nix, Martin True, William Woolbank. Ex. wife Mary Leavil. Leg. wife Mary, sons Joseph and Benjamin Leavil, 200 acres of land, my son Joseph having the manor plantation. (Page 484)

GOODLOE, HENRY, St. George's Parish, d. Nov. 25, 1748, p. May 2, 1749. Wit. John Minor, Diana Goodloe, John Wallace Summers. Ex. Robert Durrett, Robert Goodloe. Leg. wife Elizabeth; son Robert; daughter Elizabeth, wife of Robert Durrett; granddaughter Elizabeth Maulden; daughter Jane, wife of John Maulden; daughter Katherine, wife of John Durrett. (Page 496)

MARTIN, JOHN, Spotsylvania Co., July 20, 1747, p. Dec. 6, 1748. Wit. Thomas Frank, John Turner. Ex. Benjamin Martin, William Oliver, Junr. Leg. wife Amy; son John; daughter Ann. (Page 498)

MARTIN, HENRY, St. George's Parish, d. Apr. 19, 1748, p. Aug. 1, 1749. Wit. Martin True, Robert True, Philip Vincent Vass. Ex. wife Jane, son Benjamin and Martin True. Leg. wife Jane; son Benjamin; grandson John Martin, son of John Martin, decd; son Henry Martin; daughter Sarah, wife of Martin True; daughter Alice, wife of John Moore; daughter Mary, wife of —— Robinson. (Page 508)

WILL BOOK B

1749-1759

THORNTON, FRANCIS, Spotsylvania Co., d. Nov. 11, 1748, p. Sept. 5, 1749. Wit. John Sutherland, Sarah Slaughter, Ann Jackson, James Allen, Robert Jackson. Ex. wife, Frances; father, Francis; brother, John; son, Francis. Leg. wife, Frances; son, Francis; to son George, land in Orange Co., bought of Thomas Meriwether and Moseley Battalay; son, William; son, John; daughter, Mildred Thornton; daughter, Mary Thornton. Codicil dated Mar. 21. Wit. Robert Jackson, James Allen, Ann Jackson, George Hicks. (Page 1)

GORDON, JOHN, Fredericksburg, d. Dec. 13, 1748, p. Feb. 6, 1749. Wit. Thomas Mackie, Alexander Cruikshanks, Roger Dixon. Ex. wife, Margaret; Robert Jackson; Charles Dick; Roger Dixon. Leg. wife, Margaret Gordon; daughters, Catherine and Isabella. (Page 15)

FOX, JOHN, Fredericksburg, d. Jan. 10, 1749, p. Mar. 6, 1749. Wit. M. Battalay, John Sutherland, Richard Tutt, James Sparks. Ex. wife, Mary and my kinsman, James Fox. Leg. wife, Mary Fox, plantation in Prince William Co., whereon Winshott lives. My kinsman, James Fox to convey to John Triplett the land in King George Co. (Page 18)

ALLEN, JOHN, Spotsylvania Co., d. Fredericksburg, Mar. 14, 17–9, p. Apr. 3, 1750. Wit. Pat Connelly, John Simpson, James Allenach, Adam Stephen, Francis Gibson. Ex. Coll. John Waller, Junr. Mr. Archd. Mc-Pherson, William and James Hunter, James Allen, Mr. Archd. Ingram, Merch. in Glasgow. Leg. my natural daughter, Martha, who lives at the house of Henry Willis, Gentl. £1,000, to be paid when she arrives at the age of 21 years, or marries with the consent of Coll. William Waller, Junr.; Mr. Archd. McPherson and William Hunter, who I appoint her guardians. To my mother £400; to my sister Christian £400. Above sums to be remitted to Mr. Archd. Ingram, Merch. in Glasgow. To friend, William Hunter £100; to my brother, James Allen lot 62 in Fredericksburg, my household furniture and merchants goods. To Dr. Adam Stephen ten volumes of Rollings Ancient History; to my aunt, Sarah Blake, in Hamelton, £20. The remainder of my estate to be divided between the children of my aunt, Jane Black, in Hamelton; the children of John Wallson, in Hamelton, in the parish of Glasgow; the children of Mary Struthers, married to Thomas Wallson, in Kirk Bride, and Robert Struthers, in Glasgow. Testator to be buried on Fall Hill plantation. (Page 19)

WARREN, THOMAS, Planter, Spotsylvania Co., d. Apr. 13, 1749, p. Dec. 4, 1750. Wit. Robert Huddlestone, Abram Rogers, Barbara Rogers. Ex. wife, Mary and son, Hackley Warren. Leg. son, Hackley Warren,

95 acres of land which I formerly gave to my daughter Rachel Hasken. Daughter, Elizabeth Brook; daughter Mary Buford; daughter, Roxanna More; son, Lancelot Warren. To my wife, Mary Warren, all the rest of my estate during her life. (Page 56)

GILBERT, JOHN, Spotsylvania Co., d. Nov. 16, 1750, p. Dec. 4, 1750. Wit. James Wait, John Williams. Ex. my cousin, Richard Tutt. Leg. Cousin, Elizabeth Tutt; godson, John Tutt; cousin, Richard Tutt. (Page 58)

WARREN, ELIZABETH, d. Feb. 21, 1750-1, p. Apr. 2, 1751. Wit. James Ham and Mary Ham. Ex. son, Samuel Warren; son-in-law Thomas Burges. Leg. son, James Warren; son, Samuel Warren, the money John Farish is owing me. (Page 61)

CARTER, JOSEPH, St. George's Parish, d. Feb. 19, 1750, p. May 7, 1751. Wit. Robert Huddlestone, Wm. Pruitt, James Younger, Robert Durrett. Ex. wife, Catharine Carter; Mr. John Minor and my son, John Carter. Leg. wife, Catharine; son, Joseph Carter, the tract of land bought of Mark Wheeler; son, John, tract of land bought of Benj. Matthews; daughter Mary Carter; daughter, Elizabeth Carter; son, George Carter; son, Robert Carter, the land where I now live after his mother's decease; daughter, Caty Carter. (Page 64)

LUCAS, ANTHONY, Spotsylvania Co., who died on or about the 28th of Jan. 1750 (nuncupative will) Leg, estate to be divided between his cousins, Adam Lindsay and Caleb Lindsay. This will was proved by the depositions of James Stopp, Hannah Alman and Edward Almond, at Spotsylvania Court, May 7 and June 4, 1751. (Page 71)

SHEPARD, GEORGE, St. George's Parish, d. Jan. 10, 1750, p. Oct. 1, 1751. Wit. John Holloday, Benjamin Holloday, Robert Gregory. Ex. wife, Elizabeth (Note. The executrix's bond gives her name as "Elizabeth May Angelick Shepard") Leg. sons, George, Robert, James and John; daughter Ann; wife, Elizabeth. (Page 78)

MOOR, ROBERT, Spotsylvania Co., d. Feb. 12, 1750, p. Dec. 3, 1751. Wit. Wm. Waller, John Farish, Elizabeth Couzins. Ex. my mother Rachel Moor and my wife. Leg. wife, Roxanna Moor. Land lying in this county to be equally divided among my three eldest sons, Samuel, John and Robert, in case of the death of either of them without issue, the land to go to my son George. Son called Thomas, but not yet baptized. (Page 85)

CHILDS, RICHARD, St. George's Parish, d. Jan. 27, 1750, p. Dec. 3, 1751. Wit. Fielding Lewis, Charles Dick, Mary Dick. Ex. Thomas Turner, Robert Armistead. Leg. son, Richard Childs, daughter Sarah Childs, in Bristol. (Page 85)

GOODLOE, ELIZABETH, widow and relict of Henry Goodloe, Spotsylvania Co., d. Feb. 25, 1750, p. Dec. 3, 1751. Wit. Henry Johnson, Elizabeth Maulden. Ex. Robert Goodloe. Leg. granddaughter, Elizabeth Maulden; son, Robert Goodloe. (Page 87)

STUBBLEFIELD, GEORGE, Gentl., Spotsylvania Co., d. Sept. 11, 1751, p. June 2, 1752. Wit. W. Robinson; Agatha Robinson, Jo. Brock. Ex. brother, Thomas Stubblefield; wife, Catharine Stubblefield; friend, Majr.

Rice Curtis, Junr. Leg. son, George, land and plantation whereon I now live, which I bought of Edward Herndon, Junr., also 100 acres adjoining which I bought of James Riddle; son, Henry, land which I bought of Mr. Joseph Brock; sons, Beverley and Robert; wife, Catharine and the child she now goes with. (Page 109)

LONG, JOHN, St. George's Parish, d. Jan. 31, 1750, p. July 7, 1752. Wit. Philip Vincent Vass, Thomas Merry. Ex. wife, Elizabeth Long. Leg. wife, Elizabeth; grandson John Hawkins; daughter, Elizabeth Hawkins; granddaughter, Elizabeth Hawkins. (Page 116)

COLLINS, THOMAS, St. George's Parish, d. June 3, 1751, p. Sept. 1, 1752. Wit. Thomas Collins, Junr., Benjamin Glaze, William Collins, John Collins. Ex. wife, Elizabeth Collins and brother, Joseph Collins. Leg. wife, Elizabeth, sons Thomas Junr. William, Richard and Joyx. (Page 134)

BARNES, THOMAS, (Note. residence and date of will not given) p. Sept. 4, 1753. Wit. proved on the oath of Zachary Lewis, Gentl. who wrote the same. Leg. brother, William Barnes; brother, John Barnes; my mother (no name given) Note. A letter from Margry Barnes to Mr. Zachary Lewis, dated Sept. 1, 1753, states "I cannot come up to Spotsylvania Court to administer upon my son Thomas Barnes' estate, but I give the administration up to my son John Barnes, to act and do in my behalf." (Page 167)

CURTIS, RICE, Senr., Spotsylvania Co., d. Jan. 22, 1749–50 (nuncupative will). Leg. "A direction or instruction given to me by my father, for the division or disposal of his estate after his death, this 22nd day of Jan. 1749–50. 1st. that the slaves that Mr. Philip Vincent Vass have in his possession to be settled to him and his children as was purposed when delivered, and after my mother's death, to deliver to the said Vass his desk. 2nd. that Mr. Henry Pendleton have the negro slaves that he have in his possession settled to him, together with a young negro wench about fourteen years old, to be bought for that purpose, and to deliver to him his looking glass. 3rd. that fifty pounds be raised by the profits of the estate and that sum laid out for two young negro girls to be settled on my son Rice Curtis. 4th. that my negroes Cate and Little, with their present and further increase, be equally divided among my three youngest daughters, division to be as they come to age or marry, if I think fit or otherwise at my death. Lastly, all the remainder to myself after my mother's death, both real and personal. The above is what I desire to be done by my son or who he shall leave for that purpose. Day and year above written." Sig. "Rice Curtis, Senr."

"I do hereby certify that I resign all my right and title to the administration of my decd. husband's estate, as witness my hand this 5th day of Nov. 1753." X mark of Elizabeth Curtis.

Rice Curtis, Adms. with the will annexed of Rice Curtis, Gentl. decd. with William Waller, his security, bond dated and recorded, Nov. 6, 1753. (Page 171)

PROCTOR, WILLIAM, Spotsylvania Co., d. Aug. 17, 1753, p. Nov. 6, 1753. Wit. M. Battalay, Richd. Bryan. Ex. wife, Ann Proctor and son

George. Leg. wife, Ann; sons, George and Charles; daughter Elizabeth Carter; daughter Mary Proctor. (Page 174)

MUSICK, GEORGE, Senr., St. George's Parish, d. not given, p. Mar. 5, 1754. Wit. Henry Chiles, Henry Marsh, Hezekiah Chiles. Ex. wife, Ann Musick and son, Electious Musick. Leg. son, Daniel; son Ambrose; son George; son, Abraham; daughter, Elizabeth Trusty; daughter, Agnes Lynes, land adjoining William Trusty; son, Electious; daughter Kezia Musick; wife, Ann Musick; son, Ephriam. (Page 181)

POLLARD, ANNE, St. George's Parish, d. Nov. 2, 1748, p. Mar. 5, 1754 Wit. John Graves, Junr., George Shepard, Robin Grigory, Jon. Holloday. Ex. Joseph Peterson. Leg. son-in-law Joseph Peterson. (Page 182)

REEVES, GEORGE, Spotsylvania Co., d. Nov. 20, 1753, p. Mar. 5, 1754 Wit. Henry Buchannan, John Crane, Theodore Monson. Ex. brother, Thomas Reeves, Peter Copeland. Leg. nephew, Thomas, son of Thomas Reeves; nephew Henry, son of Thomas Reeves, my land in Essex Co., and if he should die without issue, then to his brother, John Reeves; niece, Patience Ball, daughter of Joseph Reeves; sister, Elizabeth Allen; niece Sarah Attwood, under eighteen years of age and unmarried; niece, Patience Gatewood and her sister, Elizabeth Copeland; Mr. Peter Copeland, my sword, belt and silver cup; brother, Thomas Reeves. (Page 183)

HUNTER, WILLIAM, Fredericksburg, d. Nov. 5, 1753, p. Mar. 5, 1754. Wit. Jno. Sutherland, Robert Massey, Robert Johnston. Ex. cousin, James Hunter; brother-in-law, Wm. Taliaferro, in Orange; Mr. Fielding Lewis; Mr. Charles Dick. Leg. son, James Hunter, the lots I now live upon, called Ferry lots, with the benefit of the ferry, land adjoining the town known by my name, also tract of land at the Fall Hill, commonly called Silvertown Hill; son William Hunter, 300 acres of land, lying at the Robinson in Orange Co., 400 acres of land, which I bought of Mr. George Hume, lying in Culpeper Co., and the house and plantation where Abram Simpson now lives; daughter Martha Hunter, £1,000 currency. Testator desires that the boys may be educated at the college of William and Mary. (Page 185)

ALLEN, ELIZABETH, St. George's Parish, d. Nov. 13, 1753, p. Apr. 2, 1754. Wit. Edward Collins, Hezekiah Chiles. Ex. son, Thomas Allen and daughter Elizabeth Allen. Leg. daughter Elizabeth Allen. (Page 190)

HAWKINS, NICHOLAS, Spotsylvania Co., d. Feb. 15, 1754, p. May 7, 1754. Wit. Owen Thomas, Benjamin Martin, John Button. Ex. wife, Elizabeth and son, John Hawkins. Leg. son, John; daughter, Cate Macdonel; son, Thomas Hawkins; son, Nicholas Hawkins; son, Alexander Hawkins; daughter, Ann Pritchett; grandson, Hawkins Casel. (Page 198)

WALLER, JOHN, Gentl. Spotsylvania Co., d. Aug. 2, 1753, p. Oct. 1, 1754. Wit. John Semple, Thomas Collins, Larkin Chew, Harry Beverley. Ex. wife; sons, John, Thomas, William, and my son Benjamin Waller to be executor in trust. Leg. son John, five hundred acres of land in the Parish of St. John, in the Co. of King William, also 400 acres of land in Spotsylvania Co., surveyed by Nathaniel Claybourn, Surveyor, and patented in my own name Sept. 28, 1730; grandson, Pomfrett Waller; son, Thomas Waller, the land bought of Majr. William Todd, in Spotsylvania Co. adjoining the lands of Zachary Lewis, Majr. Rice Curtis, Mr. Vass,

William Bradburn and Mr. Stubblefield; grandson John Waller, son of Thomas Waller; granddaughter Dorothy Quarles, daughter of my son Thomas Waller; son, William Waller, 400 acres patented in my name Feb. 21, 1726, now in Spotsylvania Co., formerly in King William Co. adjoining the lands of Zachary Lewis, and after my wife's death, all that tract of land I bought of Majr. William Todd in Spotsylvania Co., whereon I now live, and obtained a patent for Apr. 25, 1726, also my tract of land I bought of Capt. Philip Todd, in Spotsylvania Co., patented in my own name June 3, 1726, adjoining the land I live on, and Mr. Coleman's and Mr. Shackleford's; grandson, William Waller, son of William Waller; grandson, John Waller, son of William Waller; son, Benjamin Waller; son, Edmund Waller; grandson, John Waller, son of Edmund Waller; grandson, Benjamin, son of Edmund Waller; grandson, William Edmund Waller, son of Edmund Waller; granddaughter, Mary Waller daughter of Edmund Waller; daughter, Mary Waller, now the wife of Zachary Lewis; granddaughter, Betty Lewis; granddaughter, Lucy Lewis; granddaughter, Dorothy Lewis; grandson, Waller Lewis; great-grandson, John Zachary Lewis; grandson, John Lewis, my secretare that I left at Mrs. Margaret Gordon's, in the room I used to lie in when there. Unto all the rest of my grandchildren, except my granddaughter, Mary Meriwether, and except those above mentioned, as I have given young negroes apiece in this my will, twenty shillings, to be paid six months after my decease. Wife, Dorothy. To son, William Waller, and grandson, John Waller, son of Edmund Waller, all the residue of my tract of 1,000 acres of land that I took up in my son John's name Sept. 28, 1728, and by him conveyed to me.

Codicil to the foregoing will, dated Aug. 15, 1754, with John Minor and John Sams as witnesses, revokes the clause devising to his son, William Waller, and his grandson, John, son of Edmund Waller, the residue of land patented Sept. 28, 1728, in the name of his son, John, and devises the said land to Leonard James Mourning Waller, son of Edmund Waller. (Page 216)

MATTHEWS, BENJAMIN, St. George's Parish, d. Feb. 4, 1754, p. Feb. 4, 1755. Wit. William Waller, Junr., Mary Pain. Ex. wife Anne, and friend Thomas McNeal. Leg. wife; sons, Joseph, William, Samuel; daughters, Ann, Frances, Sarah, Matilda, Mary. (Page 232)

GARTON, URIAH, St. George's Parish, d. Mar. 5, 1752, p. Aug. 5, 1755. Wit. Benjamin Arnold, Abraham Darnot, David Darnot. Ex. sons, Zachariah, Uriah and Elijah. Leg. son, Zachariah, my land that I hold in Lancaster Co; son, Uriah, plantation whereon I now live; son, Elijah, plantation whereon Ephraim Knight now liveth; wife, Winifred Garton. (Page 255)

MINOR, JOHN, Spotsylvania Co., d. Oct. 28, 1754, p. Sept. 2, 1755. Wit. John Goodloe, David Davenport, Joseph Venable. Ex. wife and son John and in case of John's death, son William. Leg. wife; son John, son, William, tract of land that I bought of Francis and John Strother, adjoining the lands of Capt. Compton, in Culpeper Co., son, Thomas; son, Garrett, land lately bought of Henry Gambell, in Culpeper; son, James, land whereon my plantations now are on James River, in Louisa Co; son, Dabney, land lately bought of Charles Kavanaugh, in Culpeper Co: son Vivian, land whereon my plantation now is in Orange Co; son

Peter, land whereon I now live, after my wife's death; daughter, Mary; daughter, Elizabeth; friends, John Carr, John Waller, Rice Curtis and William Carr; to all my children, but John, a gold ring each. (Page 257)

BULLARD, AMBROSE, Spotsylvania Co., d. July 30, 1754, p. Apr. 6, 1756. Wit. James Mills, Benjamin Pendleton. Ex. wife, Betty Bullard, and brother Richard Woolfork. Leg. son, Richard Bullard, land lying in Caroline Co., wife, residue of estate. Land whereon I now live in Spotsylvania to be sold and the money to be applied to the use of my estate and the bringing up of my children. (Page 288)

CHEW, JOHN, St. George's Parish, d. May 11, 1755, p. July 6, 1756. Wit. Francis Cammack; Jas. Marye. Ex. Joseph Brock. Leg. sons, Robert and John; daughter Mary Beverley Brock; daughter Hannah Chew; Mr. Harry Beverley, guardian to my son, John Chew; Joseph Brock, guardian to my daughter Hannah Chew. (Page 295)

COLEMAN, SPILSBE, Spotsylvania Co., d. Mar. 23, 1757, p. May 3, 1757. Wit. Wm. Davenport, Patterson Pulliam, Isaac Bradburn. Ex. brother, Thomas Coleman. Leg. brother-in-law, William Daniel; brother, Robert Coleman; brother John Coleman; brother, Richard Coleman. The lease bought of Zachary Taliaferro to be sold and proceeds distributed amongst the poor of this parish. To brother, Thomas Coleman, remainder of estate. (Page 311)

RAWLINGS, JAMES, St. George's Parish, d. Apr. 9, 1757, p. June 7, 1757. Wit. John, James and Sarah Pulliam. Ex. son, James Rawlings and son-in-law, John Holloday. Leg. son, James Rawlings, land in Spotsylvania, adjoining Zachary Lewis, Thomas Pulliam and Colo. Thomas Moor; daughter, Hannah Gimber, land in Spotsylvania adjoining that of her brother James, it being the land I bought of Henry Chiles; daughter Martha Gains, land in Spotsylvania; daughter, Elizabeth Holloday. (Page 314)

COLLINS, JOSEPH, Spotsylvania Co., d. Aug. —, 1757, p. Nov. 1, 1757. Wit. Joseph Brock, Robert Gains, Richard Long. Ex. sons, John, James, William, Thomas and Lewis Collins. Leg. granddaughter, Amey Collins; wife, Susannah Collins, to have estate real and personal, during her widowhood, at re-marriage, to be sold at auction and the money arising from the sale to be divided among sons James, William, Thomas, Lewis Collins, and daughters Ann Wisdom, Mary Brockman, Susannah Golson, Tabitha Gatewood, Drucilla Cook and Caty Glass. (Page 329)

WHITE, AGNES, Fredericksburg, d. Aug. 30, 1757, p. Dec. 7, 1757. Wit. Thomas Overton, Mary Hunt, Charles Yates. Ex. husband, Robert White, friend Roger Dixon. Leg. my two sisters in Scotland, Margaret Ray and Jean Macklenham, whose maiden names were Johnson; uncle, William Maxwell, who lives in Rutherglen near Glasgow; Miss Peggy Drummond; husband, Robert White. (Page 336)

TALIAFERRO, FRANCIS, Spotsylvania, d. Feb. 23, 1756, p. Mar. 7, 1758. Wit. James Tutt, John Waller; Humphrey Brooke, Richard Tutt, Junr. Ex. sons, Lawrence, Hay, Francis and John Taliaferro. Leg. daughter, Anne Hay Brooke, land and plantation in Spotsylvania, whereon she now lives, which I purchased of Thomas Turner, of King George Co., Gentl. and Thomas Turner and Mary his wife, late of Spotsylvania;

daughter Elizabeth Taliaferro, 1,000 acres of land in Orange Co., formerly
Spotsylvania, granted to me by my deced. brother, John Taliaferro, by
patent dated Sept. 28, 1728; son, Lawrence Taliaferro, all my estate, both
real and personal, in Caroline Co., also 1,200 acres of land and two plantations in Orange Co., it being one moiety of 2,400 acres taken up by
my father, Lawrence Taliaferro, and my uncle, John Taliaferro, and
adjoining the land where William Taliaferro now lives; son Hay Taliaferro, estate in King George Co., and 2,000 acres of land in Orange Co.,
1,000 acres thereof purchased by my now deced. brother, John Taliaferro,
of Richard and William Taliaferro, and the other 1,000 acres purchased
by me of Thomas Smith; son Francis Taliaferro, land and plantation
whereon I now live in Spotsylvania, and to hold the same according to
the division made between me and my brother John Taliaferro, deced.
also 1,000 acres of land in Orange Co., it being one moiety of land which
was patented by my brother John Taliaferro, deced. and divided between
us; son, John Taliaferro, my land and plantation in Spotsylvania, whereon
my brother, John Taliaferro lived, also 1,000 acres of land in Orange Co.,
being the other moiety of the aforesaid mentioned 2,000 acres, and is
that part whereon Nicholas Christopher lived; brother, William Taliaferro; Elizabeth and Ann Battaley, the two daughters of my friend
Moseley Battaley.

Codicil to the above dated Feb. 25, 1757, witnessed by Robert Jackson,
John Catlett and Thomas Catlett, recites "the testator of this will hath
disposed of some estate in his possession belonging to my brother William
Taliaferro (which I claim as heir apparent to him) to several of my
children, he the said William being found an idiot by a jury convened
for that purpose summoned and sworn and their report recorded among
the records of Spotsylvania Co. Court." (Page 343)

MATTHEWS, WILLIAM, Spotsylvania Co., d. Aug. 11, 17—, p. Mar. 7,
1758. Wit. Thomas Graves, George McNeil. Leg. brother Samuel Matthews; brother Joseph Matthews; sister Ann Matthews; mother (no name
given). (Page 347)

LYNN, WILLIAM, Doctor of Physic, Fredericksburg, d. Oct. 21, 1757,
p. Mar. 7, 1758. Wit. John Holloday, William Houston, Robert Duncanson. Ex. Colo. John Thornton, William McWilliams, Junr., and
Roger Dixon, to whom is given a suit of mourning of the price
of £12 current money, each. Leg. My body to be decently interred in
my garden; daughter Ann Dent, plantation in Culpeper Co. bought
of William Eddings, also tract of land adjoining, bought of Alexander
Waugh, during her natural life, then to the heirs of the said Ann Dent,
and in event of said Ann Dent dying without issue, then to be divided
among the children of my reputed daughter, Mrs. Hannah McCauley, of
her lawfully begotten; to Ann Dent, my house and lot on the Hill in
Fredericksburg. To my reputed daughter, Mrs. Hannah McCauley, use
of my let tenement houses, garden, etc. which I now rent to William
Houston in Fredericksburg, and also a lot of ground bought of Gibson
Berryman, also tract of land in Culpeper Co., which I bought of William
Eddings. To Mary McCauley, daughter of the aforementioned Hannah
McCauley, a tract of land in Culpeper Co. which I hold by deed from
the proprietors of the Northern Neck; children of my brother Charles
in Ireland, his eldest son, William Lynn; Ann daughter of my brother

Audley Lynn, deced; David and William the two eldest children of my sister Elizabeth Hutcherson, in Ireland; kinsman, Moses Lynn, near Strabane in Ireland, and his sister Elizabeth, who first married Samuel Cook; kinswoman Margaret Stuart, living in Augusta Co. Va. and her children by her former husband, the Rev. Mr. Paul; mentions the female issue of Lieut. Matthew Lynn, near Londonderry; mentions wife and children of Francis Cochland, who is sister to Mrs. Cook in Strabane; friend Roger Dixon, land in Orange Co; brother-in-law Charles Colhoun and sister-in-law Rebecca Colhoun, both of Letter-kenny in Ireland; sister Lewis and my nephews Thomas, Andrew, William and Charles Lewis, and Mrs. Margaret Long, all of Augusta Co. Directs his executors to sell three tracts of land in Culpeper Co., and a third tract purchased of John and Edward Daugherty, also two tracts of land in Prince William Co., which I lately agreed with Mr. Isaac Savage, of Boston, in New England, for the purchase of.

A codicil to the above, dated Feb. 16, 1758, and witnessed by William Finnie, William Houston and Lewis Willis, appoints his friend, Col. Fielding Lewis as one of the executors.

At a Court held for Spotsylvania Co. Aug. 2nd, 1758, Ann Dent, widow, (since the wife of James Finnie) having been legally summoned to appear and make objection, if any she had, against the proof of the will of William Lynn, Gentl. deced. to whom she is heir at law, etc. etc. (Page 350)

PULLIAM, THOMAS, St. George's Parish, d. Apr. 17, 1758, p. June 6, 1758. Wit. Joseph Holloday, Benj. Holloday. Ex. sons James and Thomas Pulliam. Leg. sons, James, Thomas and Benjamin; daughters, Winifred, Susannah, Elizabeth, Agnes, Mary; Anna, wife of David Sandige; Sarah, wife of Christopher Dickin. (Page 369)

SPOTSWOOD, JOHN, Spotsylvania Co., d. May 6, 1756, p. Dec. 5, 1758. Wit. Jane Somerville; Dorothea Benger; Lucy Dixon; John Taylor, Junr; Jno. Carter; Joseph Steward, James Taylor. Ex. wife, Mary Spotswood, John Robinson, Esq., Col. Bernard Moore; Col. John Champe; Mr. Edmund Pendleton; Mr. Roger Dixon; Mr. Nicholas Seward. Leg. wife, Mary, use of mansion house, and my coach and six, with coachman and postilion and household goods, etc.; to my daughter Ann, £1,000 sterling; to my daughter Mary £1,000 sterling, in compliance with the authority given me in the will of my deced. father, Alexander Spotswood, Esq. Whereas my father, by his last will, did give to his son, Robert Spotswood £3,000 sterling,—to his daughter Anna Catherina £2,000 sterling, and to his daughter Dorothea £2,000 sterling, to be raised by the sale or mortgage of his lands, and I finding it necessary, in order to raise the said fortunes, to sell divers parcels of land, among the rest I sold and conveyed to Col. John Thornton, 7 tracts containing in the whole 9,048 acres, and afterwards I purchased the said 7 tracts of land of the said Col. John Thornton, I give the said 9,048 acres of land to my son, John Spotswood, also to him that tract of land which I bought of Ambrose Grayson, also all my part of the estate in England which will descend to me and my cousin, John Benger after the death of my mother and her three sisters. To my son, Alexander Spotswood to inherit the property left to Mary Spotswood at her death, or second marriage.

Codicil to the aforegoing, dated May 6, 1756, with the same witnesses as to the will, directs that all his children be maintained and educated out of the growing rents and profits of his estate, until they arrive at the age of twenty-one years, or day of marriage. To his goddaughter, Mildred Dixon, daughter of Roger Dixon, £100 sterling. (Page 389)

Editor's Note. Mary Spotswood, widow of John Spotswood, refused the legacies left her in the above will.

BATTALEY, MOSELEY, Spotsylvania Co., d. Sept. 23, 1757, p. Dec. 5, 1758. Ex. Richard Tutt; Robert Jackson; John Thornton. Leg. sons, Samuel, John, Moseley; daughters, Elizabeth, and Ann; wife Margaret; daughter Frances Bryan. (Page 393)

MINOR, WILLIAM, Spotsylvania Co., d. Dec. 13, 1757, p. May 1, 1759. Wit. Thomas Minor, William Davenport; Ambrose Arnold; Thomas Waller. Ex. my mother and John Waller, Gentl. Leg. my loving mother (no name given). (Page 404)

DAVIS, JOHN, d. March 5, 1759, p. June 4, 1759. Wit. Alex. Wright, T. Goddington, John Sutherland, John Butler. Ex. wife, Anne; son-in-law, Jackson Allen. Leg. wife, Anne; daughter Betty Allen. (Page 417)

WALLER, DOROTHY, Spotsylvania Co., d. Oct. 26, 1758. Wit. John Farish, John Coleman, J. Waller. Ex. son, William Waller. Leg. granddaughter, Dorothy Jemima Waller, daughter of my son Edmund Waller; son, William; sons, Thomas and Benjamin Waller; son-in-law Zachary Lewis; Ann Waller, wife of William Waller; daughter Mary, wife of Zachary Lewis. (Page 427)

HERNDON, EDWARD, Spotsylvania Co., d. Feb. 4, 1759, p. Nov. 5, 1759. Wit. William Ficklin, James Williams, John Herndon. Ex. wife, Mary Herndon, friend George Waller; son, Edward Herndon, Junr., and George Waller, Junr. Leg. wife, Mary Herndon; children, Edward, John and Joseph Herndon and Elizabeth Battaley. (Page 435)

WALLER, WILLIAM, Gentl. Spotsylvania Co., d. Oct. 22, 1756, p. May 6, 1760. Wit. John Wood, W. Wood, James Colquhon, Robert Marsh, John Wynill Sanders, John Beverley Roy, James Hurt, David Woodruff, Robert Goodloe, Thomas Coleman. Ex. wife during her widowhood; brothers, John, Thomas and Benjamin Waller; Joseph Brock; Edmund Herndon, Junr., and sons William and John Waller. Leg. son, William Waller, lands in Spotsylvania Co., bought at different times of John Wynill Sanders, William Smither, William Warren, John Warren, Samuel Warren, Lancelot Warren, John Farish, Jeremiah White; son, John Waller, land in Spotsylvania, given to me by my deceased father's will, John Waller, Gentl., also land adjoining that of my brother Benjamin, and Zachary Lewis, also land which I bought of Ambrose Foster, and my lots of land adjoining the town of Fredericksburg, now in the possession of my tenant William Lewis. Daughter Ann; daughter Dorothy; daughter Mary; daughter Sarah; my wife (no name given). My copper plate of my family arms and my silver seal, with the said arms engraved thereon, I desire may descend to my right heirs forever. My brother Benjamin Waller to be guardian to my sons William and John, and to settle account of affairs with our brother Edmund Waller. My apprentice and nephew John Waller to be immediately free. The tract of land I bought of John Champe, Gentl. whereon the widow Parish lives, lying in this county, and the land I bought of Nicholas Horn in Caroline Co. to be sold, and my executors to make what use they can of Nicholas Horn's mortgage to me, if his land sold me falls short in raising what money I must pay for him to Col. Turner, Mr. Copeland and Mr. Mitchell. (Page 445)

THOMAS, OWEN, Spotsylvania Co., d. Nov. 8, 1759, p. May 6, 1760. Wit. Joseph Brock, William Waller, John Hawkins. Ex. wife, Mildred, son Owen Thomas; William Smith; Thomas Minor and James Stevens, to oversee my executors. Leg. wife, Mildred Thomas; son, Owen; sons, James and Robert; daughter Agatha Thomas. Mentions land bought of James Jackson. (Page 453)

CARR, WILLIAM, Gentl. Spotsylvania Co., d. Aug. 2, 1760, p. Nov. 4, 1760. Wit. A. Foster, William Ellis, John Gordon. Ex. wife, Susannah Carr, Edward Herndon, Joseph Brock. Leg. wife, Susannah, land bought of Thomas Ship and John Quarles; son Thomas; son William, land in Louisa Co., daughter Ann Carr, land adjoining Nicholas Crenshaw; daughter Elizabeth; daughter Phoebe; son, Walter Chiles Carr, land in Louisa Co., son, Charles Brooks Carr; daughter Agnes Brooks Carr; son-in-law Mordacai Hord; son, Charles Carr; daughters Susannah, Sarah and Mary.

Codicil to the foregoing will, dated Aug. 12, 1760.

TALIAFERRO, JOHN, Spotsylvania Co., Gentl. Nuncupative Will. Deposition of William Robinson, of Spots. Co., Gentl., aged 43 years. Deposeth and saith that on Dec. 25, 1750, he was at the house of John Taliaferro, who was very ill of white sickness, and that the same day he died, and that three or four hours before his death he called his brother Francis Taliaferro, of said Co., Gentl., and declared to his said brother to let his sister Brooke have £200 that Christopher Robinson at Urbanna owed him, and for the said Francis to raise another £100 and let her have it; then said John told said Francis that all of the rest of his estate he left to him, the said Francis, etc. Said Robinson made oath to the above at Court held for Spots. Co., Sept. 3, 1751. (Page 80)

GRAYSON, AMBROSE, Nuncupative Will. "To Mr. Thos. Grayson, Spots., Aug. 5th, 1754. I, Ambrose Grayson," etc. "Bills drawn by Col. John Spotswood for £60 ster. be either sold or remitted home, and the money arising therefrom, together with my part of my father's estate, be equally divided between my unmarried brothers and sisters." Wit., John Crosse, Lawrence Dully. Proved Mar. 2, 1756. (Page 286)

WILL BOOK D

1761–1772

RICHARDSON, WILLIAM, Spotsylvania Co., d. Dec. 14, 1761, p. Sept. 6, 1762. Wit. Wm. Woody, William Hutcherson, Joseph Carter. Ex. wife, Sarah; grandson, James Hutcherson. Leg. wife, Sarah; grandson, James Hutcherson; grandson, Richardson Hensley; daughter, Sarah Hensley. (Page 1)

LONG, RICHARD, d. Nov. 11, 1761; p. Aug. 1762. Wit. Charles Harrison; Thomas Page. Ex. wife, Elizabeth Long, son Gabriel Long; John Garrot. Leg. estate to be equally divided among my six sons, Gabriel, James, William, Andrew, Rueben and John. (Page 29)

LONG, GEORGE, Fredericksburg, d. Dec. 20, 1761, p. Sept. 6, 1762. Wit. Nathaniel Stevenson, Lawrence Slaughter. Ex. wife, Martha and John Stewart. Leg. daughter, Ann Long; wife, Martha and infant child yet unchristened. (Page 36)

BROCK, HENRY, Spotsylvania Co., d. July 24, 1762, p. July 4, 1763. Wit. John Wilson, Junr., John Wilson. Ex. brother, Joseph Brock and my son, Joseph Brock. Leg. wife, Barbary; children, Joseph, Mary, Hannah, Elizabeth, Harry, John. (Page 40)

HUTCHERSON, WILLIAM, St. George's Parish, d. Oct. 31, 1762, p. July 4, 1763. Wit. William Wood, James Hutcherson, John Sutton. Ex. my wife and mother. Leg. estate to my wife and mother (no names given). (Page 42) Editor's Note. In the probate Margaret Hutcherson and Sarah Coleman, qualified as executors. The bond states Margaret Hutcherson, Edward Coleman and Sarah, his wife.

FOSTER, ANTHONY, Spotsylvania Co., d. Feb. 4, 1763, p. July 4, 1763. Wit. Isaac Darnett, Thomas Crutcher, Edward Herndon. Ex. my son, Anthony Foster and my son-in-law, James Frasher. Leg. son, Thomas; son-in-law, James Frasher; grandsons, Anthony Bartlett, Edmund Bartlett, and their father, Thomas Bartlett and Mary his wife; grandson, Anthony Crutcher and his father Thomas Crutcher and Martha his wife; grandson, Thomas Crutcher; son, Anthony Foster; granddaughter, Mary Foster, daughter of Edmund Foster; grandson, Henry Foster, son of John Foster; son, John Foster; my wife's daughter, Sarah Sparks; my wife, Sarah Foster; grandson, Robert Foster, son of Thomas Foster. (Page 44)

COLEMAN, JOHN, d. Mar. 17, 1762, p. Aug. 1, 1763. Wit. Edward Cason, Benjamin Hatter, Caleb Coleman. Ex. wife; Richard Coleman; Samuel Haws. Leg. wife, Nice Coleman; Mentions land, whereon John Cason now lives, bought of John Oliver. Mentions "all my children that I have or shall have" (no names given) (Page 47)

LEWIS, WILLIAM, Fredericksburg, d. Jan. 27, 1763, p. July 4, 1763. Wit. Hugh Mercer, Wm. Knox, William Hartwell. Ex. wife, Sarah Lewis; Charles Yates; Joseph Brock; Edward Herndon. Leg. son, James Lewis, the lot which I purchased from Anthony Strother; sons John, William, Benjamin and George; wife, Sarah Lewis. (Page 61)

CHEILES, HENRY, Spotsylvania Co., d. June 10, 1763, p. Aug. 1, 1763. Wit. Milley Webb, Richard Crittenden Webb, Ann Webb, Thomas Wiatt. Ex. my wife and son Waltho Cheiles. Leg. sons, John and Henry; son William, part of land I purchased of Mr. Baylor; son, James; son, Waltho; son, Thomas Carr Cheiles; son, Benjamin; my daughter Susannah Harley and her two children; my daughters, Sarah, Elizabeth and Ann Cheiles. (Page 66)

JACKSON, ROBERT, Fredericksburg, d. Jan. 12, 1764, p. Mar. 5, 1764. Wit. H. Mercer, Fras. Tyler. Ex. John Thornton, Dr. Thomas Walker and Col. Fielding Lewis. Leg. wife (no name given); son, John Jackson, land in Orange Co. and two lots in Fredericksburg, one being in the old town and numbered 54, which I bought of Dicky Swan Edwards, the other being in that part of the town laid off by Col. Willis' executors and numbered 5, which I bought of George Buckner; daughter, Mary, now the wife of Lawrence Taliaferro; son, William, land purchased of Col. Humphrey Hill, and land purchased of William Bowler, which the said Bowler bought of John Allen's executors. (Page 103)

JULIAN, CHARLES, Fredericksburg, d. Mar. 6, 1763, p. Apr. 3, 1764. Wit. Charles Yates; Francis Irwin. Ex. wife Phebe; Fielding Lewis; Charles Dick; Francis Thornton. Leg. wife, Phebe; son, John Julian, lot No. 30, whereon I now live, also lot No. 8, bought of Maj. Rootes, and the plantation by the riverside, containing 150 acres, bought of Maj. Rootes; son, Henry Wilson Julian, lot No. 31, whereon Thomas Overton and John Shirley now live, and at the decease of his mother, Mrs. Phebe Julian, the plantation of 150 acres, which I bought of Mr. Charles Dick; daughter, Esther Julian; daughter, Kitty Julian, and the child wherewith my wife is now pregnant. (Page 111)

FOSTER, THOMAS, Spotsylvania Co., d. Mar. 5, 1763, p. May 8, 1764. Wit. Edward Herndon, Moses Downer. Ex. wife, Dorothy, and James Frasher. Leg. wife, Dorothy; children, Hannah, Robert, Sarah, Edmund, Martha, Dorothy.
Codicil to above will dated Mar. 10, 1763, in which testator mentions that he expects his wife, Dorothy, now to be with child, and provides, in case of its birth. (Page 115)

NELSON, JAMES, Junr., Spotsylvania Co., d. May 6, 1764, p. July 2, 1764. Wit. Gerard Banks, William Rennolds. Ex. brothers, William and Benjamin Nelson. Leg. my father and mother, James and Susannah Nelson; my brothers and sister, John, Joseph, Benjamin, William, Mary Ann Nelson. (Page 132)

LONG, ELIZABETH, St. George's Parish, d. Mar. —, 1760, p. Dec. 4, 1764. Wit. William Poultney, John Gordon. Ex. Nicholas Hawkins, Senr. Leg. grandson, John Hawkins; granddaughter, Elizabeth; grandson, Nicholas Hawkins, Junr; granddaughters, Mary, Nanny and Sarah; Nicholas Hawkins, Senr., father of the above named children. (Page 166)

LEWIS, ZACHARY, Spotsylvania Co., d. July 7, 1764, p. Feb. 4, 1765. Wit. Lewis Shackleford, Mary Shackleford, John Waller. Ex. sons, John, Zachary, Waller, Benjamin, and my wife's brother, Mr. John Waller. Leg. son, John, land in Spotsylvania Co., adjoining where I now live; son, Zachary, lands purchased of Joseph Thomas, Robert Turner and Anthony Golson; son, Waller; son, Benjamin; to sons John, Zachary, Waller and Benjamin, 900 acres of land and grist mill lying in Orange Co., which I purchased of Graves and J. Sneed, also my lands and tenements lying in Culpeper Co., at the Great Mountains; wife, Mary; daughters, Meriwether; Betty Littlepage; Lucy Ford; Dorothea Smith; son-in-law, James Littlepage. (Page 163)

FRASER, GEORGE, St. George's Parish, d. June 28, 1763, p. Apr. 1, 1765. Wit. Robert Duncanson; Edward Stevens. Ex. James Hunter, Andrew Sheperd and my wife, Esther. Leg. wife, Esther; children, Mary and Salley Fraser. Mentions lots in Fredericksburg numbered 23 and 24. (Page 191)

JONES, BARBARA, d. Mar. 19, 1765, p. Apr. 2, 1765. Wit. Alexander Wright, Joseph Wriford. Ex. my brother, George Todd and my son, John Rennolds. Leg. my four children, John Rennolds, Phebe Julian; Katy and Molly Rennolds, equal shares of my estate. (Page 194)

DURRETT, ROBERT, St. George's Parish, d. Nov. 5, 1763, p. July 1, 1765. Wit. William Hodgson, Robert Durrett, Richard Durrett. Ex. George Durrett, George Chapman, Henry Goodloe. Leg. son, George; my next son, Robert; daughter Elizabeth Durrett; daughter Leah; daughter Katherine Durrett; wife, Elizabeth; my seven children, viz. George, Robert, Mary Ann Hoskins, Diana Chapman, Elizabeth, Leah and Katherine Durrett. (Page 203)

STANARD, BEVERLEY, St. George Parish, d. Feb. 20, 1765, p. July 1, 1765. Wit. O. Towles, Bar. Yates, Junr., John Chew. Ex. wife, Elizabeth Beverley Stanard; son William, when he arrives to the age of eighteen years. Leg. wife, Elizabeth Beverley Stanard; son William; son Larkin, my tract of land in this county, called Standford, whereon Ephriam Beazley, my Overseer, now lives. Land in Middlesex Co., to be sold, and the money applied towards purchasing a tract of land for the child my wife now goes with. In case the child should die, then the money arising from the sale of the Middlesex Co. land be divided among my wife and all my children, to wit: William Stanard, Larkin Stanard, Elizabeth Stanard, Mary Stanard and Sarah Stanard. I desire that my sons William and Larkin may be put to schools and continue at them until they are liberally and genteely educated. (Page 207)

SUTHERLAND, JOHN, St. George's Parish, d. July 10, 1751, p. July 1, 1765. Wit. W. Russell, Samuel Hilldrup, Harbin Moore. Ex. Mr. Todd of Caroline Co. and Robert Duncanson of Spotsylvania Co. Leg. my father, James Sutherland of Winbreck in the Orkney Islands of Scotland.

Robert Brent took out letters of administration for the above estate, his securities being Fielding Lewis and Joseph Jones, Gentl. (Page 213)

HENSLEY, SAMUEL, St. George's Parish, d. Jan. 7, 1765, p. Aug. 5, 1765. Wit. Benjamin Johnston, Thomas Hutcherson, Thomas Perry. Ex. wife, Martha Hensley and son John. Leg. daughter Caty Estis; granddaughter Patty Estis; sons John and James Hensley. (Page 217)

BRUCE, MARGARET, d. July 22, 1765, p. Aug. 6, 1765. Wit. John Battaley, John Doncastle. Ex. brother-in-law, Thomas James, of Spotsylvania Co. Leg. my mother (no name given); my sister, Mary James; my sisters Susannah Fickling; Elizabeth Bronaugh; Mary James and Frances Banks. (Page 220)

DAVIS, JAMES, Spotsylvania Co., d. Feb. 15, 1765, p. Oct. 7, 1765. Wit. Thomas Wiatt, Joseph Allen, John Hutcherson, Henry Coleman. Ex. wife and son James. Leg. daughter Elizabeth; wife Mary; son John; son James; son Benjamin; son Charles; my four youngest children, William, Mary, Charles and Thomas. (Page 225)

HERNDON, STEPHEN, who died Oct. 1, 1764. (Nuncupative will) d. Sept. 26, 1764, p. Oct. 7, 1765, on the oaths of Sarah and Elizabeth Gordon. Leg. his mother, Mary Gordon; sister Sarah Herndon; brother Joseph Herndon. (Page 227)

ALMOND or ORMOND, CATHARINE, alias REYNOLDS, who died Aug. 8, 1765. (Nuncupative will) d. Aug. 2, 1765, p. Oct. 7, 1765, on the oaths of William Hartwell and Charles Ross. Leg. niece Katy Julian; rest of estate, real and personal, to Mr. Joseph Wriford. (Page 229)

ELLIS, WILLIAM, Spotsylvania Co., d. May 19, 1766, p. Aug. 4, 1766. Wit. W. Wood, John Gordon, Isaac Wilson, James Dudley. Ex. wife, Elizabeth; sons Hezekiah and William Ellis, Col. Joseph Brock. Leg. daughter Mary Proctor; son Hezekiah Ellis; daughter Elizabeth Hawkins; daughter Ann O'Neal; son William Ellis; son John Ellis; daughter Agnes Ellis. If my wife should die before my son arrives at the age of twenty years, I desire that Robert O'Neal take his estate into his possession. (Page 241)

PETERSON, JOSEPH, St. George's Parish, d. Feb. 5, 17—, p. Sept. 1, 1766. Wit. Joseph Holloday, Benjamin Holloday. Ex. sons, James and George Peterson. Leg. sons, James, Joseph and George Peterson; daughter, Betty, wife of Abram Swinney; daughter Lucy, wife of James Edeston, or Ederton; Sally Rush; grandson, Fendell Peterson. (Page 247)

DUDLEY, ROBERT, St. George's Parish, d. Dec. 27, 1766. Wit. Reuben Thornton, Thomas Poole, Matthew Gale, Junr. Ex. wife, Joice; John Carter and son Robert Dudley. Leg. whole of estate to be kept intact until youngest child comes of age, for the benefit of bringing up my youngest children; then to be equally divided amongst them all. (Page 266)

BENGER, JOHN, d. Aug. 14, 1766, p. Nov. 3, 1766. Wit. None. Ex. Capt. William Johnston and Benjamin Johnston. Leg. my wife (no name given); my two daughters, Ann and Dorothea Brayne Benger. (Page 268)

TUTT, RICHARD, Spotsylvania Co., d. Jan. 22, 1766. Executors Bond dated Mar. 2, 1767. Wit. William Newton, Richard Brooke, Francis Taliaferro. Ex. brother, James Tutt and my sons James and John Tutt. Leg. son, James, 400 acres of land in Culpeper Co., adjoining to a patent of 400 acres granted to my brother, Benjamin Tutt, which is now my said son James's; son Richard Tutt, £200 to purchase that 500 acres of land that Capt. Lewis Davis Yancey and his son Philemon now live on, the

money to be paid out of the money arising from the sale of the land
he lived on in King George Co., to Capt. Yancey; son John Tutt 150 acres
of land in King George Co., which I bought of William and John Smith,
also 919 acres of land in Culpeper Co., the remaining part of the tract of
land that I gave my son James; sons Benjamin and Charles Tutt, all that
tract of land at my lower quarter on Muddy Run, in Culpeper Co., about
1200 acres, to be equally divided between them when they come to twenty-
one years of age. 600 acres of land in King George Co., where my son
Richard Tutt lived, to be made over to the Vestry of Hanover Parish,
upon they paying £750. 40 acres to be reserved for Mary Dorset, and
her daughters to live on during their lives, as per agreement. (Page 283)

MILLER, WILLIAM, St. George's Parish, d. Oct. 21, 1766. Executors
Bond dated July 6, 1767. Wit. Walter Chiles, Mary Bledsoe, William True.
Ex. wife, Jane Miller, Edward Herndon and Joseph Herndon. Leg. wife,
Jane Miller, to have the use of all my estate during her life, then as follows: to grandson, William Miller Bledsoe, land and plantation whereon
I now live, with all the land adjoining I shall have at my death; grandsons, William Miller Bledsoe, Miller Bledsoe and Moses Bledsoe, all my
land in Orange Co., to be equally divided between them; daughters, Mary
and Betty. (Page 293)

GRAVES, THOMAS, d. Oct. 17, 1767. Executors Bond dated June 6,
1768. Wit. Francis Meriwether; James Smith; John Graves Junr., James
Smith, Doctor; William Mackgehee. Ex. son, Thomas Graves; son-in-law,
William Pettus; nephew Joseph Graves. Leg. wife, Ann Graves, land
whereon I now live in Spotsylvania Co., and one-third profits issuing from
my mill, and after her death to all my surviving children or their heirs.
(Page 318)

DURRETT, RICHARD, Spotsylvania Co., d. July 28, 1767, Executors
Bond dated July 4, 1768. Wit. Benjamin Tompkins, John Summers. Ex.
wife, Sarah; son William; William Marshall; John Lewis. Leg. wife
Sarah; lands in Spotsylvania and Caroline Cos. to be divided between all
my boys which I now have, or shall have. Any estate that shall fall to
me by the death of Elizabeth Marshall, or any other person, to be equally
divided amongst all my children. My daughter and younger children to
be supported until they shall marry and come to lawful age. (Page 328)

MARYE, JAMES, Senr., incumbent of St. George's Parish, in Spot-
sylvania Co., d. Apr. 25, 1767, p. July 4, 1768. Wit. Henry Heath, William
Proctor, Joseph Jones. Ex. Joseph Jones and my sons, James and Peter
Marye. Leg. son, James Marye, Clerk, land of Varenville; son Peter
Marye, my land of Delos, and my tract of Gum Branch; granddaughters,
Lucy and Susanna Marshall; daughter Lucy Marshall; grandchildren,
James and Loetitia Heath; granddaughter Loetitia Heath 200 acres of
the Gum Branch tract to be laid off on the east side of the said tract;
daughter Susannah Heath. (Page 330)

DANCIE, THOMAS, Fredericksburg, d. Jan. 29, 1768, Executors Bond
dated Aug. 2, 1768. Wit. John Glassell, Henry Heath, Jonathan Huid,
William McMillan. Ex. wife, and Roger Dixon. Leg. wife Ann Dancie.
(Page 337)

BROCK, WILLIAM, Spotsylvania Co., d. Jan. 26, 1768, Executors
Bond dated Sept. 6, 1768. Wit. J. Lewis, James Chiles, Jeremiah Stevens,

Chas. Gordon. Ex. wife, Mary Brock; Edward Herndon. Leg. wife, Mary Brock; sons, Joseph and William Orree Brock; daughter, Mary Brock. (Page 343)

GRAY, GEORGE, St. George's Parish, d. Fredericksburg, Apr. 24, 1766. Wit. Will Huston, Nicholas Smith, James Brown. Ex. wife, Sarah Gray. Leg. daughter, Ann Hoar, one pound, one shilling and sixpence; wife Sarah, the rest of my estate, both real and personal. (Page 359)

TURNLEY, FRANCIS, St. George's Parish, d. Apr. 11, 1765, Executors Bond dated June 5, 1769. Wit. Hudson Muse; Francis Irwin, William Templeman, Charles Yates. Ex. Col. Fielding Lewis, my son, Francis Turnley, Charles Yates. Leg. eldest son Francis Turnley my large family bible; my children Elizabeth; Ann; John; Grace; Susanna and Elinor. (Page 382)

DUERSON, THOMAS, Spotsylvania Co., d. May 5, 1768, Executors Bond dated Aug. 7, 1769. Wit. Joseph Willoughby, Thomas Bartlett, John Wigglesworth. Ex. wife, Mary; son-in-law Edward Herndon; son Joseph Duerson. Leg. wife Mary; children Joseph, Thomas, William, Lucy, Henry; daughter, Sarah Wigglesworth. (Page 386)

HEAD, HENRY, Planter, Spotsylvania Co., d. Feb. 25, 1765, p. May 7, 1772. Wit. Guy Bell, Charles Proctor, Benjamin Steward. Ex. son, Henry Head. Leg. son, Henry Head; son Alexander Spence Head; son Benjamin Head; daughter Mildred Edwards; wife Frances Head. (Page 404)

COLSON, CHARLES, Spotsylvania Co., d. Aug. 22, 1769, Executors Bond dated June 4, 1770. Wit. James Marye, P. Marye, James Marshall. Ex. nephew, Thomas Colson. Leg. brother, Thomas Colson, of Fredericksburg; my niece, the wife of George Hampton, of Frederick Co; Charles Chester Colson Hampton, son of George and Mary Hampton; nephew, Thomas Colson of Spotsylvania Co. (Page 412)

PAIN, JOHN, St. George's Parish, d. July 25, 1764, Executors Bond dated Sept. 20, 1770. Wit. Daniel, William and Mary Trigg. Ex. sons, Thomas and William Pain. Leg. wife, Frances Pain, all my estate, both real and personal, and after her decease, to be disposed of between my eldest son, John Pain and sons Thomas, Barnett, William, Robert and George. Mentions "all my daughters" (no names given) (Page 421)

BATTALEY, JOHN, St. George's Parish, d. Sept. 7, 1770, Executors Bond dated Sept. 20, 1770. Wit. Hammond, John Lurty, Betty Benger, John Richards. Ex. Edward Herndon; John Herndon; Joseph Herndon. Leg. my wife Elizabeth; brother Samuel Battaley; sister Elizabeth Battaley. (Page 428)

CHEW, LARKIN, Spotsylvania Co., d. Mar. 27, 1770, Executors Bond dated Sept. 21, 1770. Wit. Robert Stubblefield, John Dawson, W. Dawson, Mildred Farish, Larkin Chew, Junr. Ex. sons-in-law Mordacai Buckner and Oliver Towles. Leg. my body to be interred by my deceased father on the land I gave Beverley Stanard, Gentl. Wife, Mary Chew; grandson, Larkin Smith, that part of my tract of land purchased of Bushrod Fauntleroy and others, down to the lower corner of the land whereon Dorothy Foster, widow, now lives, including the small tract I purchased of John Waller, Junr. Joseph Brock and Rice Curtis. In the event of my dying, without issue, then to all the children my daughter, Mary Towles, may leave alive at her death. Grandsons, William Stanard and Larkin Smith; all my grandchildren, meaning those to be born as well as those now alive, of my said two daughters, Elizabeth and Mary. Land in Orange Co., also remainder of my tract of land adjoining Benjamin Johnson in this county, part of which I have sold to William Pemberton, and whereas I have become purchaser of a piece of land in which William Hudson, Blacksmith, had the equitable and Joseph Hawkins, of this county, decd. the legal title therein, which piece of land I have promised the said Hudson again, providing he pay the debt due from him to me, my executors to refer any dispute or controversies, should any arise, to the determination of my friends Col. Fielding Lewis, Mr. Roger Dixon and Mr. Thomas Fox, who are gentlemen in my opinion of great probity and integrity.

A codicil to the above will dated Apr. 6, 1770, and witnessed by Robert Stubblefield, W. Dawson and Larkin Chew, Junr., mentions grandchildren (no names given) and my daughters Elizabeth and Mary; mentions William Dawson, who has lived with me some years as Overseer, a suit of mourning for his fidelity and kindness to me during my illness. (Page 431)

ARNOLD, ISAAC, Berkeley Parish, d. July 24, 17—, Executors Bond dated Oct. 18, 1770. Henry Pendleton, John Carthrae, Isaac Arnold Junr. Ex. son, George Arnold. Leg. daughter Sarah Steward, land whereon my son-in-law John Steward now lives in Spotsylvania Co., grandson, John Steward; grandson, Charles Steward; son George Arnold, remaining part of land on the south side of the main road, together with my estate of every kind in King George Co. to whom I leave the care of his mother Sarah Arnold. (Page 441)

TALIAFERRO, MARY, widow, Spotsylvania Co. d. Jan. —, 1771, Executors Bond dated Mar. 21, 1771. Wit. None. Ex. sons-in-law, Charles Lewis, and Joseph Jones. Leg. daughter Mary Jones; grandson, John Taliaferro Lewis; grandson Charles Augustine Lewis; granddaughter Mary Warner Lewis; my sister Adams; daughters Lucy Lewis and Mary Jones; Mr. Charles Lewis, husband of my daughter, Lucy Lewis; Mr. Joseph Jones, husband of my daughter Mary Jones. (Page 458)

HOUSTON, WILLIAM, Fredericksburg, d. Dec. 21, 1770, Executors Bond dated Apr. 9, 1771. Wit. George Mitchell, O. Towles, John Brock. Ex. Charles Yates and my sons Hugh and William. Leg. my sister, Sarah Stacey of the city of Philadelphia, £250 Va. currency. My two natural sons Hugh Wright, alias Houston, and William Wright, alias Houston, which said Hugh and William were born of the body of my decd. wife Elizabeth before intermarriage with her, and out of lawful wedlock, all the rest of my estate, both real and personal. (Page 475)

BATTALEY, ELIZABETH, Spotsylvania Co., d. Feb. 12, 1771, Executors Bond dated May 16, 1771. Wit. James Tutt, Mildred Fitzsimmons. Ex. James Tutt. Leg. brother Moseley Battaley; sister Levinia Battaley; nephew Samuel Hilldrup; mentions Margaret Owens, wife of John Owens; states "my brother and sister mentioned in my will are my half brother and sister"; mentions "fifty pounds current money left my brother John Battaley." (Page 478)

ROBINSON, HENRY, Spotsylvania Co., d. Oct. 29, 1770, Wit. Hezekiah Ellis, Sherod Horn, W. Wood. Ex. Thomas Colson, Edward Herndon, Joseph Brock. Leg. son, Michael Robinson; my wife Mary and the child or children she now goeth with. (Page 484)

WOODRUFF, GEORGE, Spotsylvania Co., d. Oct. 5, 1769, Executors Bond dated Sept. 19, 1771. Wit. George Carpenter, William Clift, Nathaniel Parrish, Sarah Parrish. Ex. son Richard; Joel Parrish; Thomas Minor. Leg. son Richard; grandson Benony son of my daughter Sarah; daughter Sarah; daughter Jean; daughter Mary. (Page 494)

CLAYTON, JACOB, St. George's Parish, d. Aug. 30, 1771, Executors Bond dated Nov. 21, 1771. Wit. John Harrison. Ex. sons, John, William and Thomas Clayton. Leg. wife, Elizabeth Clayton; son Thomas; mentions John Wood; sons John and William Clayton, leaving to John a tract of land in Orange Co., wife to live in my mansion house and have use of one-half the tract of land I now live on, other half to sons Thomas and William; granddaughter Betty Wood; daughter Milly Stewart; daughter Elizabeth Brock; mentions Benjamin Stewart and Joseph Brock. (Page 498)

LEWIS, SARAH, Spotsylvania Co., d. Oct. 28, 1771, Wit. Daniel Branham, Benjamin Burbridge. Leg. daughter Elizabeth Richards; grandson James Lewis; granddaughter Sarah Richards, daughter of Elizabeth Richards; grandchildren William and Sarah Richards, son and daughter of Winifred Richards. (Page 510)

ELLIS HEZEKIAH, Spotsylvania Co., d. Nov. 7, 1771, Executors Bond dated Apr. 16, 1772. Wit. James Lewis, Robert O'Neal. Ex. my wife; brother William Ellis; James Lewis. Leg. wife Mildred Ellis; mentions "my children," but does not name them. (Page 511)

THOMAS, OWEN, St. George's Parish, d. Feb. 15, 1772, Executors Bond dated Apr. 16, 1772. Wit. Sherod Horn, Nathan Hawkins, John Waller. Ex. wife, Elizabeth Thomas; William Smith; John Halloday; Thomas Colson. Leg. wife Elizabeth and daughter Sarah Kenner Thomas. (Page 513)

SMITH, ELIZABETH, Fredericksburg, d. Dec. 12, 1771, Executors Bond dated Apr. 16, 1772. Wit. Thomas Holmes, John Warner. Ex. James Allen. Leg. James Allen of Fredericksburg, Joyner; John Lawson; son Aaron Akerly alias Smith; son William Smith; son Philip Wilson Smith; Mrs. Alice Allen, wife of Mr. James Allen; Margaret Allen; Alice Riddle. (Page 515)

HAWKINS, JOSEPH, Spotsylvania Co., d. Mar. 30, 1769. Wit. Philm. Hawkins; Charles Cosby; W. Robinson. Ex. wife Jane and sons John and Joseph Hawkins. Leg. wife Jane, the tract of land left me by my father with that part of the back land that I purchased from Bernard Moore, Gentl; son Joseph land adjoining James Jones, Edward Coleman and others; my two daughters Lucy and Sarah Hawkins. (Page 525)

FARISH, ROBERT, Spotsylvania Co., d. Apr. 16, 1769. Wit. Erasmus W. Allen, John McCalley, Abraham Estes. Ex. wife Julia. Leg. wife Julia Farish. (Page 526)

WILL BOOK E

1772–1798

DIXON, ROGER, Fredericksburg, d. Oct. 3, 1771, p. June 18, 1772. Wit. none. Ex. my brother, the Rev. John Dixon. Leg. son, Roger, my dwelling house and four lots adjoining in the town of Fredericksburg, my new mill on the Hazel Run, and the Race and lands I am to have of Mr. Lewis Willis, after the death of his (Roger's) mother. Sons, John and Philip Rootes Dixon; daughters Mildred, Eliza, Lucy, Susannah, Mary; wife Lucy. (Page 8)

MINOR, SARAH, widow, Spotsylvania Co., d. Sept. 25, 1772. Executors Bond dated Nov. 19, 1772. Wit. John Waller, Rebecca Ellis, Ann Waller. Ex. sons John and Garritt Minor. Leg. sons John, Thomas, Garritt, Dabney, Vivian, Peter; daughters Mary Herndon, Elizabeth Lewis; sister Agnes Waller; brother-in-law John Waller. (Page 22)

PENN, JOHN, Spotsylvania Co., d. May 13, 1771. Executors Bond dated Nov. 19, 1772. Wit. William Scott, Jesse Smith, William Perry. Ex. my wife Mary and son John, friend Joseph Brock. Leg. son George, 100 acres of land including the plantation whereon I now live; son John, 100 acres of land; son Thomas, 70 acres of land whereon he now lives; son William; my wife Mary; grandchildren Elizabeth, Martha, William, George and Sarah May; daughter Elizabeth May; daughter Mary Pritchett; daughter Rachel Pettit; granddaughter Susannah Pettit; grandson James Pritchett; mentions "my seven children" John, Thomas, George, William, Mildred, Sally and Francis. (Page 27)

CURTIS, RICE, Spotsylvania Co., d. Aug. 8, 1763, p. Apr. 21, 1774. Wit. Larkin Chew, George Stubblefield, Thomas Powe, John Standly, Ambrose Smith. Ex. Joseph and Edward Herndon. Leg. daughter Jane Curtis, all my right, title and interest which I now have, or hereafter shall or may have in two tracts of land, one lying in Louisa Co., and the other in King William Co., which said lands I purchased of John Waller, Junr. and Elizabeth, his wife, and William Carter and Frances, his wife, it being the land the said Waller and Carter held in right of their wives, under the will of John Benger, Gentl. decd. as by said will proved and recorded in the County Court of King William Co. and by Bond duly executed and bearing date May 27, 1763, from said John Waller, Junr. and William Carter; also I give one negro girl named Jenny, which was given her by her grandfather Rice Curtis, Gentl. decd. children Mary Vass, Martha Pendleton, Rice Curtis, Elizabeth Waller, Frances Carter and Jane Curtis. (Page 63)

SHACKLEFORD, RICHARD, Spotsylvania Co., d. Apr. 5, 1774, p. Aug. 18, 1774. Wit. Cain Acuff, Esther Kenaday. Ex. wife Ann Shackleford and James Wiglesworth. Leg. wife Ann; daughters Molly and Betty Shackleford; brother Ambrose Shackleford. (Page 78)

CRANE, JOHN, Spotsylvania Co., d. June 4, 1773, p. Nov. 17, 1774. Wit. H. Goodloe, George Durrett, Robert Durrett. Ex. sons John and James Crane; son-in-law William Wood. Leg. wife Elizabeth; sons John, James, William; daughter Ann, wife of William Wood; daughter Mary, wife of William Bartlett; daughter Elizabeth, wife of Mordacai Redd; daughter Sarah, wife of Harry Bartlett; daughters Phoebe, Rachel and Frances. (Page 86)

HUTCHERSON, JOHN, Spotsylvania Co., d. Oct. 6, 1774, p. Nov. 17, 1774. Wit. William Hutcherson; Charles Hutcherson. Ex. nephew John Hutcherson, and friend James Coleman of Orange Co. Leg. wife Martha; nephews Robert Hutcherson and Charles Hutcherson, sons of my decd. brother William Hutcherson; William Hutcherson, son of my nephew John Hutcherson, who was son of my said brother William. (Page 89)

DILLARD, THOMAS, Berkeley Parish, d. Oct. 23, 1774, p. Dec. 15, 1774. Wit. David Smith, Robert Wheeler, Nathaniel Dickenson. Ex. wife Sarah, son John Dillard, and Elisha Dismukes. Leg. wife Sarah, the old plantation adjoining Peter Mason and a parcel of land I bought of Robert Stubblefield; son Joseph; daughter Mary; my first wife's children Joseph, John, William, James, Thomas Dillard, Ann Pettes, Jane Devall, Lucy Luck, Hannah Dillard; my wife Sarah's children, Richard, Fielding and Mary Dillard. To son Thomas, 100 acres of land adjoining Richard Taylor; to son James, 100 acres of land I bought of John Williams; to son William, 100 acres of land which I bought of John Adam Linch; to son John, portion of land adjoining that which Ann Matthews lives on; to son Fielding, all the land I own adjoining Robert Coleman, John Coleman and George Shepperd; to son Richard, the land I now live on, adjoining Thomas Poole and Robert Coleman. (Page 94)

PAUL, WILLIAM, Fredericksburg, d. Mar. 22, 1772, p. Dec. 16, 1774. Wit. John Atkinson, Thomas Holmes, B. Johnston. Ex. William Templeman and Isaac Heslup. Leg. my sister Mary Young and her eldest children in Abigton in the Parish of Kirthbeen, in the Stewarty of Galloway, North Britain.

The executors named above refusing to serve, John Atkinson was appointed administrator with John Waller, Junr. his security. (Page 97)

DURRETT, JOHN, Spotsylvania Co., d. July 30, 1773, p. Feb. 16, 1775. Wit. Richard Shackleford, James Watkins, Ambrose Shackleford. Ex. son-in-law James Wiglesworth. Leg. son Richard Durrett; daughter Ann Long and her children Elizabeth, Agatha, Ann, Cathren and Susannah Long; grandson Brumfield Long; granddaughter Mary Skelton; daughter, Elizabeth Chiles and her children Elizabeth, Harry and James Chiles; son-in-law James Chiles; son-in-law James Wiglesworth. (Page 107)

HUTCHERSON, WILLIAM, Berkeley Parish, d. Feb. 27, 1771, p. Feb. 16, 1775. Wit. James Cearnell, Beverley Winslow, Ann Parker, George Stubblefield, Julius Lane. Ex. William Parker and Alexander Parker. Leg. wife Ruth, my plantation and the whole of my estate during her widowhood, and afterwards to be divided thus,—son William and son John one shilling each, as they have already been provided for; son Robert, the half of my land whereon I now live; son Charles, the remainder of the tract whereon I now live; daughter Hannah and daughter Mary Ann, the wife of Henry Coleman. (Page 109)

CARTER, HENRY, Berkeley Parish, d. Feb. 4, 1773, p. May 18, 1775. Wit. Henry Pendleton, Jno. Apperson, John Steward. Ex. wife Elizabeth and sons George and John Carter. Leg. son Henry; daughter Salley Carter; son Charles; my wife Elizabeth; son John; my five children, Ann Stevens, Molly Massey, Elizabeth Davenport, Salley Carter and Charles Carter; son George; all my children, Frances, George, Ann, Molley, John, Henry, Elizabeth, Salley and Charles. (Page 117)

ARNOLD, WILLIAM, Berkeley Parish, d. Sept. 17, 1774, p. May 18, 1775. Wit. Henry Pendleton, Samuel Gibson, George Payn. Ex. kinsman George Arnold. Leg. wife Lydia Arnold, son William; son James; my children William; Catey, Lydia, Sarah; Samuel; John; James and Joseph. (Page 119)

GEORGE, JANE, Spotsylvania Co., widow of Robert George, decd. of Caroline Co. Va., d. Sept. 27, 1774, p. Oct. 19, 1775. Wit. J. Lewis, Z. Lewis. Ex. Lewis Shackleford and John Shackleford. Leg. Mary Lewis, my brother Zachary Lewis's widow, and Mary Littlepage, daughter of Betty Halloday. The children of my sister, Elizabeth Shackleford, viz: Lewis Shackleford, Mary Payton, John Shackleford and Zachary Shackleford. Mentions Rueben Long of Caroline Co. (Page 133)

BARTLETT, WILLIAM, Berkeley Parish, d. Oct. 13, 1774, p. Dec. 21, 1775. Wit. Edward Herndon, Joseph Willoughby, Charles Powell. Ex. Susannah Bartlett and son Harry Bartlett. Leg. son Harry Bartlett; my wife Susannah; my five children, viz: Thomas, William and Harry Bartlett, Ann Montague and Isabel Graves. (Page 139)

CHAPMAN, JOHN, Berkeley Parish, d. Dec. 29, 1775, p. Mar. 21, 1776. Wit. Vincent Vass, Francis Turnley, Thomas Chapman. Ex. sons, William and Benjamin Chapman. Leg. wife (no name given); sons, Edward, James, Benjamin, Thomas, Allen, Robert, Erasmus and Thrashley Chapman; daughter Sarah Chapman. (Page 143)

WALLER, JOHN, Berkeley Parish, d. Feb. 6, 1776, p. Apr. 18, 1776. Wit. Thomas Minor, James Mason, Peter Mason. Ex. sons, Thomas and Pomfrett Waller, nephew John Lewis, son-in-law James Bullock. Leg. wife (no name given), the land whereon I now live; son Thomas Waller, the land after my wife's death; daughter Mary Waller; granddaughter, Agnes Waller; daughter Agnes Johnson; granddaughter Agnes Carr Johnson; grandson William Goodloe Johnson; daughter Ann Bullock; daughter Dorothy Goodloe; son Pomfrett Waller; son-in-law James Bullock; my nephew John Lewis. My executors to sell the tract of 200 acres of land in Orange Co., which I bought of Mr. John Guttridge, and also to sell my tract of land and plantation lying on the Mattapony River in King William Co. To son Pomfrett Waller, the two lots of land containing 200 acres that I purchased from Col. Bernard Moore's lottery. (Page 153)

DICKENSON, NATHANIEL, Spotsylvania Co., d. Oct. 21, 1775, p. May 16, 1776. Wit. Andrew Manning, John Coleman, Hannah Coleman. Ex. wife Elizabeth and sons William and Nathaniel Dickenson. Leg. wife Elizabeth Dickenson, all my estate, real and personal, during her natural life, and then to be divided between the following: sons Nathaniel, Richard and Elijah Dickenson and Betty Pulliam and Fanny Garton, but if the said Fanny Garton should marry, she may enjoy her part during her life, and at her death it shall return to Elijah Garton's children; son William Dickenson. (Page 157)

MERCER, HUGH, Esq., Fredericksburg, d. Mar. 20, 1776, p. Mar. 20, 1777. Wit. John Francis Minor, John Bell, Elias Hardy. Ex. wife Isabella Mercer, Col. George Weedon, Dr. John Tenant, of Port Royal, James Duncanson. Leg. wife Isabella and my children, plantation in King George County, adjoining Mr. James Hunter's land, purchased from Genl. George Washington; son William (now under age) one moiety of plantation; son John, remainder; daughter Ann Gordon Mercer; son William, 2000 acres on Kentucky River, in Fincastle Co., which I purchased of James Duncanson; son George, 2000 acres, part of 5000 acres surveyed for me by warrant from the Governor of Va. in consequence of the Royal Proclamation of 1763; son John, 3000 acres on Ohio River in Fincastle Co., which I purchased from Col. George Weedon; daughter Ann Gordon Mercer, 1000 acres on the Ohio River in Fincastle Co., which I purchased of James Duncanson; also 1000 acres on Ohio River above the Miame River purchased from James Duncanson; to child or children my wife may now be going with, 2000 acres of land the other part of said 5000 acres surveyed for me by Warrant from the Governor. Mentions houses and lots bought of James Hunter, adjoining the lot of Charles Dick, where my family now resides; lot bought of Dr. John Sutherland's estate, and the houses thereon adjoining the lot of Mr. James Allen, all situated in town of Fredericksburg; also tract of land on the Fall Hill near Fredericksburg, containing 300 acres, bought of Allen Wiley, now in tenure of Reuben Zimmerman; also three tracts of land on the River Yohogany, near Stuart's Crossing, called Mercerburg, Fredericksburg and Winchester, containing 900 acres, which I purchased from the Proprietor of Pennsylvania; also lease of house in the Main in Fredericksburg, which I now hold from John Dalton; all the above to be sold by my executors. (Page 169)

MINOR, THOMAS, Spotsylvania Co., d. Apr. 9, 1776, p. Dec. 19, 1776. Wit. Ann Smith, John Jesse, James Redd. Ex. wife, Alice Minor and James Tutt. Leg. son John; daughter Agatha, wife to Mordacai Redd; daughter Lucy, wife to James Crane; son Owen; son Thomas, land leading from Lewis' Bridge to Fredericksburg, and from said bridge to Caroline C. H., whereon are two plantations known by the names of "Pharess" and "Gravilly Run," also my land in Spots. Co; daughters, Ann, Clary and Elizabeth Minor; to wife lands in Spots. Co. (Page 175)

MITCHELL, JOHN, millwright, Spotsylvania Co., d. Feb. 17, 1776, Executors Bond dated May 15, 1777. Wit. Len' d. J. W. Waller, William Brooks, Charles Brooks. Ex. my father-in-law, Mr. Daniel Laine. Leg. wife Nancy Mitchell; brother Barnett Mitchell. (Page 180)

BAGGOTT, JOHN, d. Apr. 3, 1773, Executors Bond dated June 19, 1777. Wit. Thomas Reveley, William Hopson, Nicholas Smyth. Ex. wife, Margaret Baggott and James Went. Leg. wife, Margaret; daughter Ellinor Baggott, lot and houses at the riverside; sons John, James, Thomas and George Baggott. (Page 185)

GATEWOOD, HENRY, Spotsylvania Co., d. Jan. 28, 1777, Executors Bond dated Dec. 18, 1777. Wit. Edward Herndon; Edmund Foster; John Frazer; Henry Crutcher; Anthony Frazer. Ex. son Richard Gatewood.

Leg. wife Tabitha; sons Dudley and Henry; son William and Ann his wife, and their sons William, Austin and Ambrose Gatewood; sons Peter, Larkin and Richard Gatewood; daughter, Keziah Sandidge; daughter Dorothy Foster. (Page 190)

JONES, JAMES, Spotsylvania Co., d. Feb. 25, 1776, Executors Bond dated May 21, 1778. Wit. Jesse Haydon, Mary Haydon, Jarvis Haydon. Ex. son Richard Jones. Leg. my son Nicholas and his son James Jones; son Richard; grandson Gabriel Jones; daughter Ann Waggoner; daughter Jane Collings; daughter Mary Haydon; daughter Elizabeth Davis; granddaughter Elizabeth Merrey; my son James Jones' children; my daughter Polly Smith; my daughter Isabell Head. (Page 203)

CRANE, WILLIAM, Spotsylvania Co., d. July 8, 1777, Executors Bond dated May 21, 1778. Wit. Robert Durret; John Carter; Henry Goodloe. Ex. Henry Bartlett, William Wood. Leg. wife Sarah; daughter Elizabeth Turner; money arising from the sale of land devised to me by will of my late father, Col. John Crane, decd., to my wife and child. (Page 208)

TRIGG, JOHN, Spotsylvania Co., d. Feb. 17, 1776, Executors Bond dated May 21, 1778. Wit. Joseph Herndon, Edward Herndon. Ex. Thomas Duerson. Leg. my sister Ann Carter and brother Thomas Trigg, estate to be equally divided between them. As I have never received my part of my father's estate from my brother William Trigg, I desire my executor to take steps to recover same. (Page 210)

CAMMACK, FRANCIS, Spotsylvania Co., (Nuncupative will) Whereas my father Francis Cammack, late of the Co. of Spotsylvania and Parish of Berkeley, died without disposing of his estate by a will in writing, but as I well know through hearing him in his lifetime say how he intended to dispose of his estate, and being willing his desire in that respect should be complied with, therefore I, John Cammack, eldest son and heir-at-law, do relinquish and give up all right, etc. as heir-at-law to the said Francis Cammack, decd., upon condition that my mother, Ann Cammack, widow of the said Francis, and my brothers and sisters do agree to and divide the estate of the said decd. in the manner he intended, which is as followeth: to John Cammack, two negroes; to Henry Cammack, one negro; to Francis, one negro; to Susanna Cammack, one negro; to Katherine Cammack, one negro; to Ann Cammack, one negro; to Ann Cammack, widow of the said decd. one negro and the land and plantation whereon the said decd. lived together with all the remainder of the estate, and at her death the said land to belong to Francis Cammack, youngest son of the said decd., and the remainder of the said estate to be equally divided amongst the above named six children. Dated this 6th day of May, 1778. Wit. A. Frazer, Thomas Sharp, William Johnson, George Cammack. (Page 212)

CHEW, ROBERT, Spotsylvania Co., d. Apr. 28, 1778, p. Sept. 17, 1778. Wit. Thomas Powell, Joseph Brock, Thomas McGee. Ex. my sons, John, Robert Beverley and Harry. Leg. son John, land lying on N. side of Glady Run, including the mill; daughter Elizabeth; sons Robert Beverley and Henry, rest of the tract of land whereon I now live, and above the piney branch to be equally divided between them; son Joseph, 400 acres of land on S. side of Glady Run, according to the bounds of a purchase made by Dr. Foster of Robert Coleman; to my wife Mary, during her life, my plantation with the land below Piney branch, and after her death, to my son John; my children, John, Robert Beverley, Harry, Joseph and Elizabeth; my executors to sell 3036 acres of land, lying on S. side of Glady Run, according to the bounds of a purchase made by Dr. Foster of Edward Herndon. (Page 231)

STEARS, ABEL, Berkeley Parish, Spotsylvania Co., d. Mar. 20, 1776, Executors Bond dated Sept. 17, 1778. Wit. John Steward, George Arnold, Richd. Stears, Jno. Epperson. Ex. son, William Stears. Leg. daughters, Mar'get, Mary and Beatey Stears; granddaughter, Elizabeth Stears; son William Stears. (Page 234)

ALSOP, WILLIAM, St. George's Parish, Spotsylvania Co. d. July 2, 1773, Executors Bond dated Sept. 17, 1778. Wit. James Hutcherson, Patty Estes, James Hensley. Ex. wife, Sarah Alsop and Thomas Colson. Leg. wife Sarah, estate, real and personal, for support of herself and children; son Benjamin Alsop. (Page 242)

VAUGHAN, ELIZABETH, Spotsylvania Co. d. Nov. 14, 1775, Executors Bond dated Nov. 19, 1778. Wit. Nathan Hawkins, Edward Leavell. Ex. William Pemberton. Leg. my four children which are now alive, and my son Martin Vaughan's four children, his part to be equally divided amongst them, Cornelius Vaughan, Bridget Broadas, Elizabeth Pemberton, Margaret Geter. (Page 251)

ARNOLD, EDMUND, Spotsylvania Co., d. Aug. 22, 1778, Executors Bond dated Nov. 19, 1778. Wit. J. Lewis, William Davenport, Ann Davenport. Ex. Benjamin Waller, Thomas Minor. Leg. to my mother, all my estate, real and personal. (Page 253)

ROGERS, WILLIAM, Spotsylvania Co., d. Dec. 24, 1778, Executors Bond dated Feb. 18, 1779. Wit. Abraham Estes, O. Towles, Frances Edinborough, Elizabeth Estes. Ex. wife, Lucy; Robert Farish; George Rogers and my son John Rogers. Leg. sons, John, Larkin, William; daughter Frances, wife of John Downer; daughter Elizabeth, wife of Rice Carter; daughters Sarah and Catherine. (Page 278)

YOUNG, LAURANCE, Spotsylvania Co., d. Feb. 26, 1778, Executors Bond dated Feb. 18, 1779. Wit. James Hiter, James Wallace, James Williams. Ex. wife, Margaret and Richard Young. Leg. son John; wife Margaret; son Leonard; at wife's death, or marriage, estate to be equally divided between my children, Leonard, True, Nancy, John, Laurance, William, Mary and Catherine Young. (Page 282)

GALE, MATTHEW, St. George's Parish, Spotsylvania Co. d. Jan. 12, 1772, Executors Bond dated Feb. 18, 1779. Wit. Robert Dudley, James Smith, George Tod, Ambrose Dudley. Ex. wife Judith Gale, John Gale, Matthew Gale, Junr., Joseph Gale. Leg. wife Judith Gale, estate real and personal during her natural life, then to son Matthew, Junr., plantation whereon I now live; son Joseph, plantation whereon my daughter now lives; daughter Sarah Edwards Deatherage; son Joseph Gale and his wife Rachel, and John Edwards Gale, son of Joseph Gale. Estate not already disposed of at my wife's death to be divided between my seven children, viz. John Gale, Elizabeth Pool, Joyce Dudley, Judith Barnaby, Sarah Edwards Deatherage, Matthew Gale, Junr. and Joseph Gale. Elizabeth Pool's share to be kept free and clear from all debts due from her husband Thomas Pool, in order to support herself and children. (Page 286)

WALLER, AGNES, widow, Spotsylvania Co., d. May 29, 1777, Executors Bond dated Mar. 18, 1779. Wit. Pomfrett Waller, Martha Waller. Ex. son Thomas Waller; nephew John Lewis. Leg. my four daughters, Mary Overton, Elizabeth Eggleston, Sarah Rodes, and Dorothy Goodloe.

Codicil dated Sept. 27, 1778, directs that share of her daughter Dorothy Goodloe shall after her, said Dorothy's, death, revert to the granddaughter, Agnes Carr Goodloe. (Page 288)

WILKERSON, ROBERT, Spotsylvania Co., d. Dec. 20, 1778, Executors Bond dated Mar. 18, 1779. Wit. James Mason, Joshua Smith, Betey Turnley. Ex. John Lewis, William Duggins. Leg. wife, and after her death the estate to be equally divided amongst the children; son George; William Duggins, guardian to my son George. (Page 299)

HAWKINS, PHILEMON, Spotsylvania Co., d. May 6, 1779, Wit. Joseph Hawkins, Ann Hawkins, Katey Finley. Ex. wife Sarah Hawkins; sons John and Joseph Hawkins. Leg. sons John, Joseph, Philemon; daughter Frankey Thomas; daughter Lucy Craig; wife Sarah Hawkins. (Page 334)

STUBBLEFIELD, CATHERINE, widow, Spotsylvania Co. d. Apr. 14, 1777, Wit. O. Towles, Mary Towles, Beverley Winslow. Ex. sons Harry and Robert Stubblefield; Oliver Towles. Leg. sons George, Harry and Beverley Stubblefield; granddaughter Catherine Stubblefield, daughter of Robert Stubblefield; granddaughters Susanna, the daughter of George, and Catherine the daughter of Robert Stubblefield. (Page 348)

HAZELGROVE, JOHN, Fredericksburg, d. June 13, 1780, Executors Bond dated Sept. 21, 1780. Wit. Wm. Hopson, Jn. Green, John Davis. Ex. Richard Young and Capt. Thomas Bartlett. Leg. wife Frances, estate real and personal until my son Benjamin be twenty-one years of age; to my mother-in-law five hundred pounds; to Linamah Hobby of Stafford Co., five hundred pounds, to be held by Mr. Richard Young of Fredericksburg, and Capt. Bartlett, Inspector at Fredericksburg Warehouse; nephew Jessey Hinson, eldest son of my wife's sister Elizabeth, and to Sarah, her eldest daughter, five hundred and fifty pounds each. (Page 349)

LEWIS, JOHN, St. George's Parish, Spotsylvania Co., d. May 31, 1766, Executors Bond dated Oct. 19, 1780. Ex. my brothers Zachary, Waller and Benjamin Lewis; my brothers-in-law Nicholas, Charles and William Lewis; my friends Fielding Lewis and Joseph Jones, Trustees. Leg. wife, one-third of estate; son John Zachary Lewis, land whereon my mother now dwells; son Robert Lewis, lands in Culpeper and Orange counties, also land whereon I now live purchased of Giles Tompkins and Thomas Hill, and my lot in Fredericksburg joining the Court House No. 2; my son Nicholas Lewis, land which I purchased of the Hon. Philip Grymes and Benjamin Temple, with the mill built thereon and the tract of land I purchased of Thomas Graves and George Woodroof.

Codicil dated Nov. 3, 1776, gives to son Robert tract of land on Glady Run, purchased of John Waller, and Ann, his wife. (Page 558)

WARREN, SAMUEL, Berkeley Parish, Spotsylvania Co. d. Sept. 3, 1779, Executors Bond dated Oct. 19, 1780. Wit. John Mason, John Johnston, Peter Mason. Ex. sons William and Samuel Warren; son William, house and plantation; son James 100 acres of land, including the plantation whereon James Rose now lives; son Samuel, land bought of Thomas Coats; son John land bought of Thomas Graves; daughter Letty Humphries; daughter Elizabeth Rash; daughter Ann Warren; grandson Thomas Shackleford, son of my daughter Rebecca Shackleford, decd. (Page 364)

MARYE, JAMES, St. George's Parish, Spotsylvania Co., d. June 21, 1774, Executors Bond dated Dec. 21, 1788. Wit. William Dangerfield, John Chew, Ann Chew, Sophia Crawford, Jesse Haydon, Susanna Marshall. Ex. Thomas Colson, John Chew, James Marshall. Leg. son James, land on Matapony, known by name of "Lewis River," and tract of land whereon I now live; daughter Lucy Marye; daughter Susanna Marye; daughter Salley Marye; tract of land known as "Motts" to my daughters. The money Dr. William Marshall now owes me, three hundred and fourteen pounds, to be applied towards paying my part of the legacies which my father directed, by his will, should be paid his grandchildren. James Marshall and Dr. William Marshall, guardians to my son James. My brother Peter Marye and Col. Joseph Brock and my executors to be guardians to my daughters. In case any of my land should be sold, I desire it may be part of the tract whereon I live, which lies on the E. side of the Old Mine road.

Codicil dated Oct. 3, 1780, witnessed by Joseph Brock and John Chew, and commencing "I, James Marye, clerk," etc. mentions daughter Sarah, son James, daughter Lucy. Money due me from Col. William Grayson, which bond is in the hand of Mr. John Smith, of Winchester, and the money due from my brother Peter, to be equally divided among my three younger children. (Page 376)

PAGE, MANN, of "Mansfield," Spotsylvania Co., d. Nov. 7, 1780, Executors Bond dated Apr. 19, 1781. Ex. three sons, John, Mann and Robert, and my son-in-law Benjamin Harrison. Leg. wife, Ann Corbin Page; son John, lands in Gloucester, also my part of the Dismal Swamp, also my tract of land known by the name of "Frying Pan" or "Copper Mine" in the Northern-neck, now in the possession of the Hon. Robert Carter, of Nomomy; son Warren, all my lands in Spotsylvania Co. and land in the Northern-neck, known by the name of "Bull Run;" son Robert Carter Page, all my land in Hanover and King William counties, excepting the lots laid off for a town, which I desire sold; son Matthew, one square in the town. As it hath pleased God to deprive me of my daughter Judith Burwell, I give to the executors of Lewis Burwell five hundred and seventy pounds, current money, to be divided between his two daughters Judith and Alice. Daughter Elizabeth Page; daughter Lucy Baylor; son George Page, eight lots in Fredericksburg, which I purchased of Col. Fielding Lewis; two hundred pounds to be paid the Free School of Abbingdon, as my mother's gift; my stock in trade to my two youngest sons. My executors above named to be guardians to my two sons Gwin and Matthew until they attain the age of twenty-one. (Page 387)

EDWARDS, URIAH, Berkeley Parish, Spotsylvania Co., d. Apr. 16, 1781, Executors Bond dated Aug. 17, 1781. Wit. Charles Pemberton, Edward Brasfield, Bennet Pemberton. Ex. Edward Herndon, Joseph Herndon and my son John Edwards. Leg. wife Milley Edwards; son John Edwards; my four youngest children, Benjamin, Moses, Milley and Mary Edwards; my seven children, Uriah, Benjamin, Moses, Milley and Mary Edwards, Rebecca, the wife of Reuben Hawkins, and Elizabeth, the wife of Elisha Hawkins. (Page 404)

HOLLODAY, JOHN, Junr., Spotsylvania Co., d. June 17, 1781, Executors Bond dated Aug. 17, 1781. Wit. Wm. Wood, Richardson Hensley, George Hensley, Harry Chew, James Hutcherson, William Spindle, William Pemberton. Ex. Edward Herndon, Thomas Colson, William Spindle. Leg. estate to be kept together for the maintenance of my wife and children until she shall marry, or my youngest child then living shall arrive at the age of 21 years or marry, at which time the estate to be equally divided between my wife and children. That part or parcel of Mr. George Atkinson's estate which falls to me by a deed of gift made by the said Atkinson and wife to myself and Mr. John Wigglesworth, to be divided in form as above mentioned, also whatever may fall to me by will of Robert Thomas, to be divided in like manner. (Page 406)

(Ed. Note.) None of the executors named above qualified, the will being administered by Mildred Holloday, bond dated Aug. 17, 1781.

DANGERFIELD, WILLIAM, gentleman, St. George's Parish, Spotsylvania Co., d. Oct. 17, 1780, Executors Bond dated Oct. 18, 1781. Wit. Thomas Strachan, James Pervis, Francis Rose. Ex. wife Mary Dangerfield, Lewis Willis, Thomas Colson, Oliver Towles. Leg. wife Mary, plantation, etc. during life, then to sons William and Henry; son John, lands in Essex Co., but in case John dies before twenty-one years of age, then to son William and Spotsylvania lands to son Henry; to wife, equal moiety of all slaves, including slaves held by Mrs. Thornton, widow of Reuben Thornton, and the remainder equally divided among all my children, viz. John, William, Henry, Catherine, Elizabeth, Molly, Ann, and Sarah; daughter Catherine, wife of Capt. George Washington Lewis. (Page 409)

CLEMENTS, JOHN, Fredericksburg, d. Oct. 2, 1781, Executors Bond dated Oct. 18, 1781. Wit. Edward Simpson, John Benson, John Welch, John Stamper. Ex. William Smith, joiner, in Fredericksburg. Leg. As I have no relation to whom I hold myself bound by any tie or obligation to leave them any part of my estate, I give and bequeath same to Mr. William Smith. (Page 415)

SANDERS, HUGH, Spotsylvania Co. dated Aug. 5, 1781, Executors Bond dated Oct. 18, 1781. Wit. A. Frazer, James Frazer, W. Frazer, William Wright. Ex. John Sanders, Lewis Craig, Robert Sanders, Peter Gatewood, Anthony Frazer. Leg. wife Catherine Sanders, land and plantation, together with house wherein I now dwell, then to my son Nathaniel Sanders; sons Robert and Charles my land in Culpeper Co., upon Cedar Run; daughter Catherine Sanders; daughter Rosey Sanders; daughter Abigail Sanders; son John Sanders; my children, namely: Elizabeth Page, Sarah Gatewood, Mildred Jones, Nathaniel Sanders, Robert Sanders, Charles Sanders, Mary Lee, Ann Tally, Catherine Sanders, Rosey Sanders and Abigail Sanders. (Page 418)

HOLLODAY, JOHN, Spotsylvania Co., Apr. 8, 1781, Executors Bond dated Nov. 15, 1781. Wit. John Tankersley, Charles Pemberton, Henry

True, John Pierce, Henry Brock. Ex. brothers Joseph and Benjamin Holloday. Leg. wife Tabithy, land whereon I now live purchased of Thomas McGee and John Cammack, then to son William after wife's death; son Benjamin; daughter Lucy; daughter Anna. Mentions tract of land called "Certains" sold to James Tate, mentions suit pending in Spotsylvania Court against executors of Benjamin Grymes, decd., mentions four children of daughter Elizabeth. (Page 425)

PENN, WILLIAM, Spotsylvania Co., d. Mar. 18, 1781, Executors Bond dated Dec. 20, 1781. Wit. Joseph Brock, Jr., Heny. Brock. Ex. my mother, Mary Penn. Leg. my mother, Mary Penn, during her life the whole of my estate both real and personal, and after her death to my sisters, Milley Penn and Frances Carter.

LEWIS, FIELDING, St. George's Parish, Spotsylvania Co. d. Oct. 19, 1781, p. Jan. 17, 1782. Wit. George Noble, Benj. Ledwick, John Butler, Gerard Alexander, Will. Booth, William Carpenter. Ex. wife and my sons John, Fielding and George. Leg. wife, Betty Lewis, during life use of all my lands in Spots. Co. except that part rented to my son John; son John, after death of his mother, all my lands in Spots. Co. and in Fredericksburg; son Fielding, 1000 acres of my Frederick Co. lands, on which he lives; son George, remainder of Frederick Co. lands bought of Robert Carter Nicholas, except 1000 acres to my son Lawrence; son-in-law Charles Carter, Esqr; son Lawrence, 1000 acres of land in Frederick Co.; son Robert, one-half of 10,000 acres of land located for me in the Co. of Kentucky by Mr. Hancock Lee, and one-half of 20,000 acres located or to have been located for me by Nathaniel Randolph in the Co. of Kentucky; son Howell, the remaining half of above lands in Kentucky; all my lands purchased at the Land Office except what is already disposed of, to my sons Robert and Howell equally; my share in the Dismal Swamp Co. my lands bought of Marmaduke Naughflett in partnership with Genl. Washington; my lands bought of Dr. Wright and Jones in Nansemond Co., in partnership with Genl. Washington and Dr. Thomas Walker, and the 320 acres of land in Frederick Co. bought of George Mercer's estate, also my share in the Chatham Rope Walk at Richmond to be sold by executors and the money arising to be paid to my six sons before mentioned, in equal portions.

Codicil dated Dec. 10, 1781, witnessed by Francis Willis, Jr., Gerard Alexander, Fr. Keyes, George Ogelvie, John Butler and William Carpenter; to son Robert Lewis a tract of land purchased of Francis Willis, Jr., adjoining the tract of 320 acres of land in Frederick Co. also the said tract of 320 acres to son Howell Lewis, and the whole tract of 10,000 acres in Kentucky to son John. (Page 434)

DANSIE, ANN, widow, now residing at New Port, in the Co. of Spotsylvania. d. Dec. 15, 1781, Executors Bond dated Mar. 21, 1782. Wit. Rd. Brooke, R. Wellford, L. Brooke, James Tobine. Ex. my brother William Dandridge and his son Francis Dandridge, and my nephew Alexander Spotswood. Leg. Mentions late husband Thomas Dancie; nephew Alexander Spotswood, and his mother my sister Mary Campbell; mentions being entitled to a share in lands in North Carolina under father's will, and directs the said land to be sold and the money arising divided, viz: one-twelfth part between the children of the late Genl. Hugh Mercer, as shall be living at the time of sale; one-twelfth part to James Duncans, late of Fredericksburg, to be divided among his children; one-twelfth part to each and every one of the following persons, viz: Mrs. Mary Campbell, Mrs. Lucy Dixon, Frances Dandridge, Elizabeth Dandridge and Agnes Dandridge. (Page 443)

ESTES or EASTIS, ABRAM, Spotsylvania Co., d. Jan. 15, 1780, Executors Bond dated Apr. 18, 1782. Wit. M. Buckner, Geo. Madison, James Metchum. Ex. wife Ann and son Richard. Leg. wife Ann, slaves and land on which I now live, during her life, afterwards to be sold and divided among the following persons: Elijah Eastis, Richard Eastis, Moses Eastis, Fielding Eastis, Nancy Eastis; son Thomas Eastis, and Hannah, his wife; son John Eastis and Ann, his wife; son Samuel Eastis; daughter Sarah Hart. (Page 453)

(Ed. Note. The name is spelled both Estes and Eastis in this will)

NELSON, WILLIAM, Spotsylvania Co., d. June 25, 1781, Executors Bond dated July 18, 1782. Wit. Sam Gale, Joseph Allen. Ex. sons John and James Nelson. Leg. wife; son William; son James, land I bought of my brother Benjamin in Louisa Co; two youngest sons Haydon and Nugent, to be educated out of my estate. (Page 471)

LUCAS, PETER, Fredericksburg, d. Nov. 16, 1781, Executors Bond dated July 18, 1782. Wit. John Steward, Michael Robinson, James Hackley. Ex. Zachary Lucas, George Kiger. Leg. my six children, viz: Zachariah Lucas, Nancy Kiger, Fielding Lucas, Sally Lucas, Peter Lucas and Polly Lucas. (Page 473)

HAYDON, THOMAS, St. George's Parish, Spotsylvania Co. d. June 27, 1782, Wit. Richard Young, John Chew, Charles Proctor. Ex. son, Jessey Haydon and Ezekiel Haydon. Leg. son Jervey Haydon, tract of 100 acres, also part of land bought of William Fitzhugh, Esqr; grandson Abner Haydon, son of Jervey Haydon, one negro boy Sam, but if he dies without heirs, then I give the said negro to Jessey Haydon, his brother; son Jessey Haydon; son James Haydon; son Ezekiel Haydon; granddaughters Margaret and Sarah Haydon, daughters of Ezekiel Haydon; daughter Mary Haydon; grandson Ezekiel Haydon, son of John and Mary Haydon; daughter Grace Proctor; grandson John Proctor, son of George Proctor; son John Haydon; son William Haydon; daughter, Sarah Ann Millican; daughter Elizabeth Nelson; grandsons Haydon and William Nelson, sons of William Nelson; daughter Mildred Leavell. (Page 482)

POWE, MARSOM, Berkeley Parish, Spotsylvania Co., d. Sept. 24, 1782, Executors Bond dated Nov. 21, 1782. Wit. Gipson Jenkins, James Abbett, Jno. Jenkins. Ex. son Thomas Powe and friend Beverley Winslow. Leg. daughter, Lucy; son Thomas Powe, "all the land and premises I now live on" etc. balance of estate to be divided among "all my children." (Page 502)

LEWIS, ROBERT, Berkeley Parish, Spotsylvania Co., d. Aug. 13, 1782, Executors Bond dated Jan. 16, 1783. Wit. O. Towles, John Woolfork. Ex. my uncle Zachary Lewis, my brother John Zachary Lewis, Thomas Towles. Leg. my only son, Robert Lewis, all of my estate when he comes to twenty-one years of age. In case of his death under age, to be equally divided amongst all my brothers and sisters. (Page 505)

ALLEN, JOSEPH, Spotsylvania Co., d. Sept. 16, 1782, Executors Bond dated Feb. 20, 1783. Wit. Samuel Gale, William Quarles, Beverley Winslow. Ex. my son Samuel, David Thompson, Samuel Berry. Leg. daughter Rachel; son Joseph; daughter Barbary; daughter Winifred; son Samuel; daughter Susanna. (Page 513)

COYLE, BENJAMIN, d. Dec. 29, 1782, Executors Bond dated Mar. 20, 1783. Wit. John Steward, Henry Glass, John Lowe. Ex. Samuel Hildrup, Michael Coyle. Leg. wife Keziah; daughter Keziah Hildrup; sons James, Michael and William; daughters Polly and Lucy. (Page 519)

McCALLEY, JOHN, St. George's Parish, Spotsylvania Co., d. Jan. 19, 1783, Executors Bond dated Mar. 20, 1783. Wit. James Owen, John Bullock, Frances Rose. Ex. wife Elizabeth, James Tutt. Leg. wife Elizabeth; sons Archibald, Charles and James; daughters Ann, Elizabeth and Mary McCalley. (Page 521)

CAMMACK, WILLIAM, Spotsylvania Co., d. Feb. 3, 1783. Ex. Bond dated Apr. 17, 1783. Wit. John Smith, William Smith, Thomas Colson. Ex. Col. Oliver Towles, Edward Herndon, George Cammack, John Tankersley. Leg. son Francis; son William; son John; daughter Margaret Bucknor; daughter Catherine Colacan; daughter Susanna Tankersley; daughter Mary Hawkins; daughter Ann Sanderson; daughter Elizabeth Holloway; granddaughter Susanna Sanderson; grandson John Miller; grandson John Tankersley; granddaughter Margaret Hawkins; granddaughter Betsy Tankersley; granddaughter Jane Beverley Cammack; son George Cammack; grandson Robert Cammack, son of George Cammack. (Page 525)

DURRETT, ELIZABETH, Spotsylvania Co., d. Apr. 20, 1783, Executors Bond dated May 15, 1783. Wit. Hemp Goodloe, Frances Goodloe, James Colquhoun. Ex. Henry Goodloe, Sr., George Durrett, Robert Durrett. Leg. son Robert Durrett; granddaughters Elizabeth and Sarah Hoskins. In case my said granddaughter Elizabeth Hoskins die without heirs, then my estate given to her to be divided among such of my children as may be living and the issue of such as may be dead, except Mary Kidd, but her children to have their proportionable part. (Page 530)

REDD, MORDECAI, Spotsylvania Co., d. Aug. 23, 1782, Executors Bond dated July 17, 1783. Wit. William Wodd, Philip Dudley Redd. Ex. Harry Bartlet, John Wood, brother Allen Redd. Leg. wife Elizabeth; children, Elizabeth; Lucy; James; Mildred and Susannah; son James, land and plantation as by a deed from my father James Redd to me. (Page 535)

DAINGERFIELD, WILLIAM, d. Jan. 4, 1783, Executors Bond dated July 18, 1783. Alexander Spotswood, Admr. Leg. wife, and after her death, or re-marriage, estate to be divided among my children. William Smith of King William Co., to be employed to assist my wife. I desire my brother, William Allen, to act as an executor. (Page 537)

LEAVELL, JAMES, Spotsylvania Co., d. Oct. 17, 1775. Executors Bond dated Sept. 18, 1783. Wit. Henry Pemberton. Ex. William Pemberton. Leg. my mother; sister Nancy Pemberton; brother John Leavell; and his children, and Edward Leavell; brother William Leavell. (Page 545)

SPINDLE, JOHN, Spotsylvania Co., d. Aug. 31, 1783, Executors Bond dated Oct. 16, 1783. Wit. John Spindle, Jr., Leonard Clark, Salley Damnagin. Ex. wife Bridget Spindle, John Spindle. Leg. wife; daughter Ann; daughter Mary Clark; my six children, William, John, Ann, Sarah, Mary and Elizabeth. (Page 549)

FOWKE, JOHN, late of Fredericksburg, but now in the service of the United and Independent States of America, as Adjutant to the 10th Continental Va. Regt., dated Delaware State, Newcastle Town, Apr. 22, 1777. Leg. all balances due on my books which are now in possession of my sister, Mary Fowke, now in Fauquier Co. Va., shall become her sole property.
Wiley Roy, Admr. of the Will of John Fowke, decd. with William Fowke and John Tankersley, his securities. Bond dated Oct. 16, 1783. (Page 551)

LEWIS, NICHOLAS, Spotsylvania Co., d. Feb. 14, 1783, p. Oct. 16, 1783. Ex. Majr. Thomas Mereweather and Majr. Thomas Towles. Leg. wife Elizabeth Lewis; sons, Thomas M. Lewis and John Lewis. (Page 554)

HERNDON, JOHN, St. George's Parish, Spotsylvania Co. d. May 11, 1782, Executors Bond dated Nov. 20, 1783. Wit. Thomas Allen, Joseph Fox, Robert Cunningham. Ex. brothers, Edward and Joseph Herndon, my friend James Lewis, and my sons Joseph and John Herndon. Leg. wife, Mary Herndon, entire estate until her death or re-marriage, then to be equally divided amongst all my children. (Page 557)

CARTER, JOHN, Spotsylvania Co., d. May 9, 1778, Executors Bond dated Dec. 18, 1783. Wit. M. Buckner, Richard Loury. Ex. sons, William and John Carter, Thomas Colson, Joseph Brock. Leg. wife Hannah; son Robert, one hundred pounds for education; son John in trust for the use of my granddaughter Sarah Kenyon Thomas, two negroes; son-in-law Rice Curtis and Frances, his wife, during their lives 300 acres of land whereon they now live, after their death to be equally divided among all their children; stock and household furniture to be divided among my five younger children; all the rest of my estate to be equally divided among all my children, except that if my daughter Martha should die without issue, her portion to be divided among the other children.
Codicil, Oct. 13, 1783, witnesses Edward Herndon and John Mitchell, recites, "whereas since making the within will, my daughter Elizabeth Matilda has been born, she shall be considered and have an equal share in the division of my estate with my five younger children." (Page 560)

McGEE, THOMAS, Spotsylvania Co., d. Feb. 1, 1782, Executors Bond dated Feb. 19, 1784. Wit. John Chew, Jr., John Jessey, Joseph Ormond, John Brock, Jr. Ex. Edward Herndon, William Smith, my son Thomas McGee. Leg. wife Mary; daughter Mary Horn, and her children, and her portion shall not be subject to the payment of any debts contracted for my son-in-law Sherod Horn; daughter Ann Moore; son Thomas McGee; daughter Dinah Mims. (Page 567)

TUREMAN, IGNATIUS, Berkeley Parish, Spotsylvania Co., d. Feb. 5, 1784, Executors Bond dated Mar. 2, 1784. Wit. Edward Herndon, Henry Gatewood. Ex. John Peirce, grandson Tureman Lewis. Leg. grandson Tureman Lewis; grandson Benjamin Tureman, son of John Tureman;

Mary Peirce and Anne Peirce; Elizabeth Carter, wife of Bernard Carter; John Peirce; five grandchildren, Mary, wife of Benet Pemberton, Thomas Tureman, William Tureman, Tureman Lewis and Benjamin Tureman. (Page 572)

WILLIAMS, JAMES, Spotsylvania Co. d. June 1, 1782, Executors Bond dated July 6, 1784. Wit. Math. Leather, Ann Young. Ex. wife, and Charles Williams. Leg. son Charles Williams, my plantation; wife Elizabeth Williams; children James, Bernard, Charles, Alford, Samuel Williams, and Martha Smith. (Page 600)

ADKINS, ALEXANDER, Spotsylvania Co., d. May 12, 1784, Executors Bond dated Aug. 3, 1784. Wit. John Shelton, Reuben Young, Ann Young. Ex. sons, Silence and Benjamin Adkins. Leg. daughter Betty; son Benjamin; son Goen Adkins; son Silence Adkins, the lease and place I now live on. (Page 605)
(Ed. Note. Executors Bond states Silence Adkinson, Ex. of the last will and testament of Alexander Adkinson, decd. etc. The bond is signed Silence Adkins.)

LEWIS, JOHN, Gentleman, Berkeley Parish, Spotsylvania Co. d. Mar. 7, 1784, Executors Bond dated Sept. 7, 1784. Wit. O. Towles, John Chew, Jr. Ex. Col. Joseph Brock, Augustin Woodfolk, Majr. Thomas Towles. Leg. wife Elizabeth, one-half of my land; to children now born or to be born all the rest of estate and reversion of my wife's part. Mr. Augustin Woodfolk, of Hanover, guardian to my three children, Augustin Lewis, Ann Lewis and Betsey Lewis. Col. Joseph Brock, guardian to my child or children that I may have by my present wife, who is his daughter. (Page 610)
(Ed. Note. This will is signed "Jno. Z. Lewis.")

REDD, JAMES, Spotsylvania Co., d. Oct. 10, 1784, Executors Bond dated Dec. 7, 1784. Wit. John Bulloch, James Owen. Ex. son Philip D. Redd, Thomas Minor. Leg. sons Allen Redd and Philip D. Redd, lands which I now hold in Spots. Co. after the death of my wife Elizabeth; daughter Lucy Redd; daughter Fanny Massey; son-in-law William Massey. (Page 639)

WYATT, JOHN, (Nuncupative will) "Sometime about the 13th day of this month we were at Mr. John Wyatt's house and heard him say that after his decease that he gave everything he possessed to his wife Ann, daughter of John Hartt, during her life, and at her death, to be divided equally among his three children, Elizabeth, Roxany and Theophilus Wyatt."
Proved by oaths of William Howard, Esther Howard and Nancy Wilkinson. Sworn to before Nicholas Payne, Dec. 20, 1784. Ann Wyatt, Admx. gave bond Mar. 1, 1785. (Page 653)

RAWLINGS, JAMES, Berkeley Parish, Spotsylvania Co., d. Nov. 15, 1781, Executors Bond dated Apr. 5, 1785. Wit. Lewis Holloday, Rawlings Pulliam, Sarah Pulliam. Ex. wife and sons Benjamin and Thomas. Leg. wife, Sarah Rawlings; sons Thomas and Joseph; son James; son John; daughter Mary Gains; daughter Agnes Gains; daughter Rebecca; son Benjamin. (Page 661)

PAGE, ANN CORBIN, Admx. Bond dated June 7, 1785, Thomas Hughes, Admr. Leg. Mentions four youngest children, who have had little of their father's estate; grandson Mann; legacies to Betty Harrison, Lucy Baylor, my granddaughter Betty Page; to Gwyn, to Matthew, Betty Kerbey; to Lucy. (Page 668)

HOLLODAY, BENJAMIN, Berkeley Parish, Spotsylvania Co. d. Mar. 18, 1875, Executors Bond dated June 7, 1785. Wit. Joseph Holloday, Jr., Stephen Holloday, William Holloday. Ex. son-in-law Joseph Pulliam. Leg. my wife; grandson Benjamin Holloday; daughter Susanna Holloday; daughters Agnes, Sarah, Martha and Mary Holloday; daughter Elizabeth Pulliam, wife of Joseph Pulliam; daughter Nancy Rawlings, wife of John Rawlings. (Page 670)

BLAYDES, WILLIAM, Berkeley Parish, Spotsylvania Co., d. Mar. 11, 1784, Executors Bond dated Dec. 6, 1785. Wit. William Cason, William Brookes, Clayton Coleman. Ex. wife Mary Ann Blaydes, Joseph Graves, John Blaydes, and Hawes and Spencer Coleman. Leg. wife Mary Ann; son John Blaydes. (Page 704)

DARNABY, WILLIAM, St. George's Parish, Spotsylvania Co., d. Oct. 20, 1780, p. Nov. 1, 1785. Wit. Ann Tutt, Clarissa Minor. Ex. Richard Loury, Thomas Minor. Leg. grandson John Darnaby; grandson Edward Darnaby; Agatha Duvall, wife of William Duvall; granddaughter, Sarah Darnaby; wife Diana Darnaby; grandchildren, James Owen, William Owen, Elizabeth Owen, Sarah Owen, Mary Owen, John Darnaby, Edward Darnaby. (Page 707)

WHITE, BASIL, Spotsylvania Co., d. Aug. 8, 1785, Executors Bond dated Feb. 7, 1786. Wit. Joseph Willoughby, Michael Blunt, Alexander Johnston, Caleb Coleman. Ex. wife Patsey White; my brother John White; Waller Chiles; Thomas Lipscomb. Leg. wife Patsey White; son Daniel Basil White; the child my wife is now carrying. (Page 715)

ROBINSON, JOHN, d. Feb. 5, 1786. Wit. James Dudley, William Ledwidge, Elizabeth Kelley. Ex. Ambrose Dudley, Edmund Bryant. Leg. daughter Betty; son William; daughter Fanny; son Lewis; wife Margaret. (Page 738)

APPERSON, JOHN, Berkeley Parish, Spotsylvania Co., d. June 11, 1785, Executors Bond dated Apr. 5, 1786. Wit. Thomas Coleman, Cornelius Wilson, Evans Long, John Stears, Richard Stears. Ex. wife, Margaret Apperson, son-in-law Peter Stubblefield, Evans Long, James Smith, and my friends William Smith and Edward Herndon. Leg. wife Margaret Apperson; daughter Peggy Stubblefield; daughters Lucy Long, Sally Smith, Polly Harrison Apperson, Fanny Apperson.

Codicil dated Feb. 11, 1786, witnessed by John Stears, Richard Stears, Stapleton Crutchfield. Mentions daughters Lucy Long and Sally Smith; son-in-law James Smith. (Page 740)

PEMBERTON, WILLIAM, St. George's Parish, Spotsylvania Co. d. Oct. 16, 1785, Executors Bond dated June 6, 1786. Wit. Thomas Colson, Sarah Perry, James Hutcherson, John True. Ex. wife Elizabeth; sons Henry and Larkin Pemberton. Leg. wife Elizabeth; sons Henry and Larkin; daughters Nancy Coleman, Elizabeth Pemberton, Mary Pemberton, Sarah Pemberton, Margaret Pemberton. (Page 744)

DARNABY, WILLIAM, St. George's Parish, Spotsylvania Co., d. Jan. 17, 1786, Executors Bond dated July 4, 1786. Wit. James Owen, George

Allsop, William Smith. Leg. wife Mary Ann Darnaby; sons Reuben, Edward and William Plunkett Darnaby. (Page 757)

ARNOLD, ANTHONY, Spotsylvania Co., d. Apr. 7, 1782, p. Sept. 5, 1786. Wit. Joseph Willoughby, Mordacai Mastin, Thomas Mastin. Ex. wife Mary; brother William Arnold; George Shepherd. Leg. wife Mary, at her decease estate to be divided among all my children. (Page 778)

PENN, MARY, St. George's Parish, Spotsylvania Co. d. July 20, 1783, Administrators Bond dated Dec. 5, 1786. Wit. Thomas Colson, Henry Pemberton. Ex. Mildred Penn. Leg. daughter Mildred Penn. (Page 795)

GRAVES, JOSEPH, Spotsylvania Co., d. May 12, 1785, Executors Bond dated Dec. 5, 1786. Wit. Edward Cason, Jr. James Graves, Spencer Coleman. Ex. wife Frankey Graves; son-in-law James C. Goodwin; my wife's brother Hawes Coleman; my sons John C. and Joseph, when they come of age. Leg. daughter Nancy Goodwin; wife Frankey Graves; son John C. Graves, half the land I own in Louisa; son Joseph, when he comes of age, remainder of land in Louisa; sons Benjamin, George, Hawes, and the one my wife is now with child, if a son, land in Spotsylvania Co. to be divided among. Mentions property to be divided amongst all my daughters, except Nancy Goodwin. (Page 798)

ROGERS, LUCY, Spotsylvania Co., d. Sept. 24, 1779, Executors Bond dated Jan. 2, 1787. Wit. Farish Coleman, Mildred Spalding. Ex. my brother, Robert Farish and Mr. George Rogers. Leg. son William Rogers; daughters Sarah and Catherine Rogers. (Page 810)

WALLER, THOMAS, Spotsylvania Co., d. Feb. 9, 1787, Executors Bond dated Apr. 4, 1787. Wit. Jona. Clark, Pomfret Waller, Thomas Minor. Ex. son, Carr Waller; sons-in-law, Joseph Woodfolk, and Sharp Smith. Leg. my wife; sons Carr, Dabney, Pomfret and John Waller; daughter Ann and her heirs; daughters Agnes, Sarah, Dorothy, Elizabeth. (Page 832)

Feb. 4, 1822, Dabney Waller, with Thomas Minor, his security, was granted certificate for obtaining Letters of Administration on the estate of Thomas Waller, decd.

PROCTOR, CHARLES, St. George's Parish, Spotsylvania Co., d. Aug. 15, 1784, Executors Bond dated July 3, 1787. Wit. Charles McCalley, Henry Brown, John Chew. Ex. Jesse Haydon, Michael Robinson. Leg. Lucy Lewis, now Lucy Proctor; children William Proctor; Ann Proctor; and the child my wife now goes with; son William Proctor, land in Albemarle Co; to William Proctor, son of Thomas Proctor, the residue of land in Albemarle Co. (Page 845)

PINES, LEWIS, Jr., Spotsylvania Co., d. Feb. 5, 1787, Executors Bond dated June 5, 1787. Wit. Beverley Overton, William Overton, Richard Brightwell. Ex. my wife; my half brother Thomas Brightwell; my half brother William Hall. Leg. wife Elizabeth; daughter Winey Pines; my five sisters, Peggy Bigers, Sarah Wade, Molly Etherton, Jiney Gains, Nancy Abbett; my half brother Thomas Brightwell; my half brother William Hall. (Page 847)

ROGERS, THOMAS, of Culpeper Co., d. Feb. 13, 1783, p. Aug. 3, 1786. Wit. Armistead White, John Grace. Ex. William Darnaby, Benjamin Plunket. Leg. eldest son, Berges Rogers; my wife, all my personal estate until her death or re-marriage, then to be equally divided among my children. (Page 860)

RAWLINGS, THOMAS, Berkeley Parish, Spotsylvania Co., d. Apr. 5, 1786. Wit. Z. Lewis, Robert Hart, Joseph Holloday, Jr. Ex. Lewis Holloday, Benjamin Rawlings. Leg. brother Benjamin Rawlings; sister Rebecca Rawlings. (Page 861)

LUCK, SAMUEL, Senr. Spotsylvania Co., d. June 16, 1787, Executors Bond dated Oct. 2, 1787. Wit. Thos. Minor, John Waller, Benja. Waller, William Rash. Ex. my sons, Nathan, Samuel and George. Leg. wife Mary, sons, Nathan, Samuel, George; daughters Elizabeth Sea; Ann Wilson; Mary Sorrill; daughter Sarah Morris; daughter Betsey Dillard; son-in-law, John Hill; grandson Garland Hill; grandson George Phillips Luck. (Page 874)

BUCKNER, MARY, Berkeley Parish, Spotsylvania Co., d. June 7, 1787. Wit. Harry Stubblefield, A. Parker, Judy Buckner. Ex. sons John, Mordacai and William. Leg. Mentions her first husband Thomas Buckner, who by his will dated June 2, 1755, devised his estate to me, leaving it to my discretion to divide the same among his youngest children at my death, I divide the same among the following: son John, son Mordacai and son William. "And whereas during the time of my intermarriage with Col. Samuel Buckner, and at the same time holding the estate of my first husband Thomas Buckner, the estate of Samuel Buckner became indebted to the estate of the said Thomas to a considerable amount in moneys, be the amount what it will, the same is to be divided between my three sons above named." (Page 881)

BUCKNER, MORDACAI, Berkeley Parish, Spotsylvania Co., Administrators Bond dated Jan. 1, 1788, William Stanard, Admr. Leg. sons John and Baldwin Buckner, negroes assigned by their grandfather, Mr. Larkin Chew, to be divided between them. (Page 882)

COLEMAN, CLAYTON, Spotsylvania Co., d. Sept. 15, 1787, Executors Bond dated Dec. 2, 1788. Wit. Thomas Wiglesworth, James Wiglesworth, Joseph Wiglesworth, Sally Wiglesworth, M. Buckner. Ex. wife Mary Coleman, Joseph Coleman, James Wiglesworth, Senr. Leg. wife Mary; son William Burwell Coleman, the land I had of Leonard Waller, to occupy same until his youngest sister arrives to lawful age or marry, then to be divided amongst my three youngest daughters and himself; eldest daughter Elizabeth Harris; daughter Molly Harris Coleman; youngest daughter Sally Lindsay Coleman. (Page 892)

JOHNSTON, AQUILLA, Berkeley Parish, Spotsylvania Co., d. Feb. 5, 1784, Administrators Bond dated July 1, 1788, Benjamin Winn, Admr. Wit. Richard Coleman, Jr., Ben Johnston. Ex. my two sons John and Aquilla. Leg. wife Elizabeth; Mary Bird, John, Elizabeth, Robert, Aquilla, Henry and George, children of George Goodloe and his wife Priscilla, who was my daughter; my sons John and Aquilla. (Page 894)

EDWARDS, JAMES, Spotsylvania Co., d. Oct. 13, 1788, Executors Bond dated Dec. 2, 1788. Wit. James Pettus, Joseph Pettus, Lindsay Arnold. Ex. John Graves, Jr., Benjamin Waller, Jr., and John Waller, his brother. Leg. wife Elizabeth; my said wife's four children James, Barbary, Susanah and Betty Arnold; my daughter Judith Arnold. (Page 910)

COLEMAN, RICHARD, Berkeley Parish, Spotsylvania Co., d. Mar. 25, 1784, Executors Bond dated Dec. 2, 1788. Wit. Daniel Lindsay, William Trigg, John Mitchell. Ex. Joseph Herndon; my sons Richard and Robert Spilsby Coleman. Leg. daughter Molly; son Richard; son Robert; daughter Nanny; daughter Lucy; Ann Coleman; son William.

Codicil Mar. 24, 1785, son Robert; son Richard; grandson Richard Coleman; grandson William; grandson Stockley; grandson Robert.

Codicil Feb. 20, 1788, grandson Richard Chiles. (Page 914)

PINES, LEWIS, Spotsylvania Co., d. May 28, 1788. Wit. Long Whartin, Thomas Brightwell, William Quire. Ex. wife Sary Pines, John White, Valentine Long. Leg. wife Sary Pines. (Page 923)

PURVIS, FRANCIS, Spotsylvania Co., d. 1787, Administrators Bond dated Jan. 6, 1789, John Purvis, Admr. Wit. Michael McDonald, Edward Newton. Ex. Capt. Charles Tod, Col. Anthony Thornton, Thomas Buckner. Leg. wife Molly; son John Purvis; daughter Molly Purvis. (Page 927)

CUNNINGHAM, ANN, Spotsylvania Co. d. Apr. 23, 1789, Executors Bond dated Aug. 6, 1789. Wit. Elisha Hall, John Chew, Jesse Haydon. Ex. my brother Edward Elley, friend James Lewis and son James Cunningham. Leg. my children, Elizabeth, Ann, James, Henry, George, Nelly and William, to be equally divided between them that tract of land in the Co. of Fayette on Kentucky River, by Patent bearing date 17th of Aug. 1786. (Page 944)

CRUTCHFIELD, STAPLETON, Berkeley Parish, Spotsylvania Co., d. June 17, 1788, Executors Bond dated Sept. 1, 1789. Wit. Joseph Herndon, John M. Herndon, John Carter, Jr., William Herndon. Ex. Edward Herndon, my sons-in-law Samuel Woodfork and Richard Noel, and Edward Herndon, son of Joseph. Leg. three eldest children, John Crutchfield, Jane Lepscome, Agatha Woodfork; son Robert; son Stapleton; son Thomas; son Achilles, to have the tract of land I hold by two patents in the District of Kentucky and Co. of Fayette, to be equally divided amongst them; wife Sarah Crutchfield the plantation and at her death to be divided amongst my five younger children,—Mary Noel, Robert, Stapleton, Thomas and Achilles. (Page 947)

BARKSDALE, DANIEL, Spotsylvania Co., d. Apr. 23, 1789, Executors Bond dated Dec. 1, 1789. Wit. Joseph Willoughby, Mary White, Richard Jarilsones. Ex. Capt. John White, Capt. Francis Coleman and Mr. Thomas Lipcombe. Leg. son Joseph Barksdale, land in Kentucky located by Capt. Hays; grandsons Daniel Basil White, and Anthony Bartlet, land in Kentucky located by James Howard; daughter Bartlet; daughter Katy Gains; son Daniel; daughter Polly White. (Page 964)

HINCHER, MARY, Executors Bond dated Mar. 2, 1790. Wit. Paul Aperson, John Moore. Ex. Robert True. Leg. grandson Martin A. True; son James Hincher; son John Hincher. (Page 970)

PARTLOW, JOHN, Spotsylvania Co., d. Dec. 11, 1789, Executors Bond dated Apr. 6, 1790. Wit. Thomas Minor, Martin Devenport; Robert Hackney, Carr Waller. Ex. wife Sarah, son Lewis, Benjamin Waller, Thomas Minor. Leg. wife Sarah; son Benjamin Partlow, 250 acres in Culpeper Co; daughter Lucy Yates; daughter Dorothy; son John, land joining

Martin Devenport, Col. Jonathan Clark and Thomas Waller's estate; son Lewis; daughter Sarah Devenport; son Elijah; daughters Polly and Sarah. (Page 975)

ATKINSON, GEORGE, Spotsylvania Co., d. Feb. 27, 1790. Wit. Ambrose Dudley, Jully Whithurst, Harry Chew, re-acknowledged same day by John Herndon, Nathaniel Hawkins, Jr., Jesse Haydon, Jr. Ex. John Welch. Leg. wife Catherine; friend John Welch of Fredericksburg; godson George Welch, son of John; Elizabeth Penn wife of George Penn of Spots. Co. (Page 989)

LEWIS, JAMES, Spotsylvania Co., d. June 12, 1790, Executors Bond dated Sept. 7, 1790. Wit. G. Bell, Benjamin Ballard. Ex. wife Hannah Lewis, John Wright, Sr. Leg. wife Hannah; daughter Betsey Lewis; sons James, Willis, Charles and William Lewis; daughters Becky, Clary and Ann Lewis; daughter Mary Ann Halbert; daughter Judith Newton; daughter Tomesone Claxton. (Page 993)

RITCHIE, ROBERT, Fredericksburg, d. Mar. 27, 1790, Administrators Bond dated Dec. 7, 1790, John Ryburn, Admr. Ex. Thomas Montgomerie. Leg. Thomas Montgomerie, late of Dumfries in Va. all my real estate; sister Elenora. (Page 1006)

WHITE, RODERICK, d. Sept. 23, 1790, Executors Bond dated Dec. 7, 1790. Wit. James Munday, Senr., Jas. Dudley, Jas. Munday, Jr. Ex. Mary White, Fielding Ficklin and Daniel Ficklin. Leg. wife Mary, whole of my estate; two children, Betsey Grant White and Polly Parmil White. (Page 1012)

GOODLOE, ROBERT, Berkeley Parish, Spotsylvania Co., d. Nov. 5, 1790, p. Dec. 1, 1790. Wit. Edm. Chapman, W. Coleman, W. Duerson. Ex. George Rogers, Henry Goodloe, Senr., and my son George Goodloe. Leg. son George Goodloe; son Henry Goodloe; son John Goodloe; kinswoman Phebe Goodloe, daughter of my nephew Henry Goodloe. (Page 1017)

CARTER, ELIZABETH, widow, Berkeley Parish, Spotsylvania Co., d. Dec. 13, 1780, Executors Bond dated Jan. 4, 1791. Wit. James Apperson, Henry Pendleton, James Wilson. Ex. sons Henry and Charles Carter. Leg. children, George, Ann, Molly, John, Henry, Elizabeth, Sally and Charles. (Page 1032)

DAVIS, BENJAMIN, Berkeley Parish, Spotsylvania Co., d. Jan. 23, 1787, Executors Bond dated Mar. 1, 1791. Wit. W. Mills, T. Winslow, Gabriel Warren, Martin Hawkins. Ex. wife and Edward Collins. Leg. wife and after her death estate to be divided between all my children, all of whom are now under age. (Page 1042)

WRIGHT, JOHN, Senr., Spotsylvania Co., d. Sept. 23, 1787, Executors Bond dated July 5, 1791. Wit. John Grant, John Blanton, Alexander Sneed, John Wright, W. Wright. Ex. wife Rosamond, Capt. James Tutt, John Steward, Anthony Frazer. Leg. sons William and John, land purchased of Joseph Porter in Culpeper Co; grandson John Metcalfe; son Winfield; daughter Margaret Fulton; daughter Rosanna; wife Rosamond. (Page 1072)

JOHNSTON, RICHARD W., Spotsylvania Co., d. Mar. 2, 1791, Executors Bond dated Sept. 6, 1791. Wit. William Waller, M. D., William Coleman,

Judith Roy. Ex. My relation Hugh Roy. Leg. my aunt Judith Farish; Miss Jiney Carter, daughter of William Carter; my cousin Judith Roy. (Page 1086)

HAYDON, JARVIS, Spotsylvania Co., d. Sept. 10, 1788, Executors Bond dated Sept. 6, 1791. Wit. William Burbridge, Ester Ficklin, Thomas Haydon, Jesse Haydon Jr. Ex. my brother Jesse Haydon; my son James Haydon; James Lewis. Leg. mentions his father Thomas Haydon, decd; wife Mary Haydon; children, James, Jesse, Abner Haydon, Ann Hawkins and Patty Haydon. (Page 1093)

BURBRIDGE, THOMAS, St. George's Parish, Spotsylvania Co., d. Jan. 16, 1790, Executors Bond dated Nov. 2, 1791. Wit. Hannon Hanor, Senr., Benja. Ellis, Hannon Hanor, Junr., George Ellis. Ex. Robert Smith, Linsfield Burbridge and George Burbridge. Leg. son Thomas Burbridge; daughter Mildred Robinson; daughter Sarah Ealley; daughter Frances Smith; son Linsfield Burbridge; daughter Mary Bullett; son George Burbridge; grandson Thomas Burbridge, son of Robert Burbridge, decd; daughter Elizabeth Branham. (Page 1112)

MONTAGUE, CLEMENT, St. George's Parish, Spotsylvania Co., d. Oct. 28, 1791, Executors Bond dated Dec. 6, 1791. Wit. Thomas Waller, John Wiglesworth, John Waller. Ex. sons Thomas and Clement Montague. Leg. wife Hannah Montague; sons Thomas and Clement; daughter Elizabeth, wife of Jonathan Carpenter, and all her children she had by James Trigg, except her son William Trigg; daughter Isabel, wife of James Ballard; daughter Sarah, wife of Charles Whiting; the children of my daughter Susanna Duerson, wife of Joseph Duerson. (Page 1120)

PARISH, JOEL, Spotsylvania Co., d. Apr. 21, 1791, Executors Bond dated Dec. 6, 1791. Wit. Thomas Minor, William Buchanan, John Whitlock. Ex. son John Parish, Benjamin Waller. Leg. daughter Mildred Jones; her husband William Jones; son-in-law Christopher Terrell; daughter Sarah Ellis; sons Joel and Henry Parish; son Timothy and his wife Mary; daughter Mary Hooper; daughter Susanna Proctor; daughter Nancy Burbridge; son James Parish; son John Parish. (Page 1123)

BALLARD, BLAND, Spotsylvania Co., d. Feb. 28, 1791, Executors Bond dated Jan. 3, 1792. Wit. G. Bell, William Ballard, Suener Tennant. Ex. sons John and Benjamin Ballard. Leg. sons Thomas, John and Benjamin Ballard; daughter Ann Haydon; Betsey Tennant. (Page 1130)

LEDWEDGE, EDWARD, Spotsylvania Co., d. Oct. 24, 1791, Administrators Bond dated Jan. 3, 1792, William Schoolar, Admr. Wit. John DuVal, James Mills. Ex. Capt. Thomas Minor, George French. Leg. grandchildren, Margaret and Robert Schoolar; daughter Elizabeth Rains. (Page 1134)

BATTALEY, ELIZABETH, Berkeley Parish, Spotsylvania Co., d. Nov. 1, 1788. Wit. John M. Herndon, John Herndon, Jr., Zach. Shackleford. Ex. Edward Herndon. Leg. nephew Edward Herndon, son of Edward; niece Sarah Herndon, daughter of John; godson Peter Herndon, son of Joseph; nephew Edward Herndon, son of Joseph. (Page 1139)

CHEW, ROBERT BEVERLEY, Fredericksburg, d. Dec. 28, 1791, p. Feb. 7, 1792. Wit. Beverley Chew, R. Wellford. Ex. my brothers John and

Joseph Chew. Leg. nephew R. S. Chew; brother John, my moiety of the house and lot in company with Mr. William Lovell, in trust for his daughters Polly and Elizabeth Chew; brother Joseph Chew; Beverley Chew. (Page 1143)

GATEWOOD, ANN, wife of Henry Gatewood, of Spotsylvania Co., d. May 10, 1791, Executors Bond dated Feb. 7, 1792. Wit. John Pierce, James Price. Ex. my brother Richard Webb and Edward Herndon, Senr. Leg. husband Henry Gatewood; brother James Crittenden Webb and Elizabeth his wife and their children; kinsman Benjamin Webb, son of James Webb; kinswoman Mildred Delany; Ann daughter of Richard C. Webb; Ann daughter of John C. Webb; Frances daughter of William Webb; Sarah Groome, daughter of William Groome; Susanna Randolph; Ann and Benjamin the daughter and son of John Webb. (Page 1148)

CARTER, EDWARD, Fredericksburg, d. Feb. 21, 1792, Executors Bond dated June 6, 1792. Wit. Charles Carter, Jr., Charles Carter, George Carter, George Gilman. Ex. sons Charles and Edward Carter, William Champe. Leg. wife Sally Carter, house and lots in Fredericksburg, plantation and house in Albemarle Co, known by the name of "Blenheim," also tract of land purchased of Col. William Champe, late of Culpeper, during her widowhood; sons Charles and Edward Carter, land in Amherst Co., near where my son John lives; son John and his wife Apphire Carter; son Charles, and his wife the daughter of Col. Fielding Lewis; son George, land in Amherst Co; sons Whitacre and Hill, land in Amherst Co; son William Champe Carter, plantations called "Dicks" and "Wheelers," and land in Albemarle Co; son Robert Carter, plantation in Albemarle, known by the name of "Gloucester" and "Chathams"; daughters Mary Champe and Ann Williams; daughter Elizabeth Stanard; daughter Jane Bradford, wife of Majr. Samuel K. Bradford, and their children; daughter Sally Carter, wife of George Carter. (Page 1156)

ROBINSON, WILLIAM, Spotsylvania Co., d. May 5, 1792, Executors Bond dated Aug. 7, 1792. Wit. Benjamin Stevens, Uriah Proctor, Thomas Adams. Ex. Beverley Winslow; son Benjamin Robinson. Leg. wife Agnes; daughter Agnes Robinson; sons Benjamin, Francis and Samuel Robinson; daughter Lucy Nelson; daughter Elizabeth Nelson. (Page 1168)

HOWERTON, JOHN, Spotsylvania Co., Wit. David Partlow, Samuel Partlow, Samuel Partlow, Jr. Leg. granddaughter, Frances Carr. (Page 1171)
(Ed. Note. This will is without date, and no bond is filed)

FOX, THOMAS, Spotsylvania Co. Not dated, no date of Probate or Bond indexed. Wit. Charles Pilcher, William Riaden, Charles Oliver. Ex. wife, Col. Joseph Brock, Nathaniel Fox, Thomas Fox, William B. Wallace. Leg. on the 27th of Jan. 1765, I conveyed my estate to Oliver Towles, in trust for certain uses therein mentioned, every part and clause of them to be now null and void. My land in King William Co. called "Fox's Ferry" for which there is a suit now pending between Frazer and myself, should, if recovered of the said Frazer, that the money due for the said land be applied in the first place to discharge a debt I owe William Reid, and the balance divided between my sons Nathaniel and Thomas. Executors to sell 73 acres of land I bought of Nathaniel Fox and money arising therefrom to be divided between my sons Stephen, Edmund and James; son Joseph 200 acres, part of the land called "Seaton's" in case of his death without issue then to my son Stephen; son John 200 acres of same tract; son William remainder of said tract; my wife during her natural life, my lease lands, etc; sons Nathaniel, Thomas, William and Joseph, and in the case of the death of my son Joseph without issue, to the children of John Wiglesworth and Philadelphia his wife; daughter Betty and her children; daughter Philadelphia and her children; grandson Thomas Frazer; daughter Ann and her children; wife Philadelphia, negroes, etc. and after her death to be divided among my children John, Stephen, Edmund, James, Barbary and Molly. Balance of estate to be kept together for support of my wife and youngest children John, Stephen, Edmund, James, Barbary and Molly; daughter Ann Chew; mentions Molly Allen, daughter of Elizabeth Allen. (Page 1186)

McAUSLAND, HUMPHREY, Philadelphia, Oct. 12, 1792, entire estate to my brother Archibald McAusland of Greenoch.

William Drummond and Adam Darby, Admrs. Bond dated Nov. 6, 1792. (Page 1191)

SMALLWOOD, JAMES, King George Co., d. Jan. 15, 1792, Executors Bond dated July 2, 1793. Wit. Charles Clark, Phoebe Clark, Thomas Clark. Ex. Charles Clark, Thomas Clark, Catherine Smallwood. Leg. wife Catherine; Charles Smallwood and William Smallwood; remainder of my property to be equally divided among my children. (Page 1274)

BLAYDES, JOHN, Spotsylvania Co., d. Mar. 3, 1793, Executors Bond dated Dec. 3, 1793. Wit. George Tyler, William McGehee, Jr., J. Pleasants. Ex. Philip B. Johnston and Spencer Coleman. Leg. Clary Blaydes; children Sally, Walker, Stephen and Elizabeth Blaydes. (Page 1281)

WINSLOW, BEVERLEY, Berkeley Parish, Spotsylvania Co., d. Feb. 22, 1793. Executors Bond dated Sept. 3, 1793. Wit. Benjamin Robinson, Henry Winslow, Robert S. Coleman; Christopher Daniel. Ex. sons Thomas and William Winslow. Leg. son Thomas; son William, land in the Co. of Orange; Robert Johnston of Kentucky; nephew Richard Parker, land in Fayette Co., Ky; daughter Elizabeth Winslow; daughter Mary Chew; daughter Catherine Robinson Winslow; daughter Agatha Beverley Nelson and her husband John Nelson; daughter Susanna Parker and her husband William Parker; sons Thomas and William Winslow to be guardians to my daughter Catherine Robinson Winslow. (Page 1293)

BRANHAM, DANIEL, St. George's Parish, Spotsylvania Co., Administrators Bond dated Jan. 7, 1784. Wit. Joseph Jones, Thomas Lewis, Thomas Allen, Joseph Brock, Jr. Ex. wife Elizabeth Branham, Capt. Edward Herndon, James Lewis. Leg. sons Thomas, John, Daniel, Benjamin, Robert, Richard and James Branham; daughters Susanna Brock, Sarah Branham, and Polly Branham; wife Elizabeth.

Elizabeth Branham, wife of Daniel, refused the legacy and plead for dower, under date June 1, 1793. (Page 1297)

PENN, THOMAS, St. George's Parish, Spotsylvania Co., d. Jan. 8, 1793. Wit. John Leavell, William Robinson, Thomas Allen. Leg. wife Susannah Penn and at her death estate to be divided among all my children. (Page 1301)

FARISH, JUDITH, Spotsylvania Co. relict of Robert Farish formerly of Spots Co., d. Sept. 23, 1793, Executors Bond dated Dec. 3, 1793. John Farish, Admr. Wit. E. Breeden, William Coleman, William Smith. Leg. my children in equal shares; Robert Farish; John Farish; Larkin Farish; Ann Farish; Sarah Coleman; Catey Stevens; Dolly Farish; Judith Farish and John P. Smith. (Page 1305)

RAWLINS, PETER, d. Apr. 15, 1793. Wit. James Jones, Thomas Colson. Leg. wife Ann; sons John and Peyton Rawlins, in case of their death, to Ann Rawlins, Ann Sylse Smith and Lucy Smith. (Page 1331)

BRIDGES, WILLIAM, d. Nov. 8, 1792, Executors Bond dated Feb. 4, 1794. Wit. Joseph Brock, D. Simpson and Jean Simpson. Ex. sons Matthew and Thomas, and son-in-law William Vigor. Leg. wife; son Thomas; daughter Mary Bridges; daughter Ann. (Page 1332)

BEVERLEY, HARRY STANARD, Fredericksburg, d. Feb. 26, 1794, Executors Bond dated Apr. 1, 1794. Wit. Philip Fitzhugh, Benjamin Grymes, Jr., William Thomas. Ex. brother Robert Gains Beverley, Larkin Stanard. Leg. nephew Robert Hazlewood Beverley, house purchased of John May in Fredericksburg; nephew Harry Stanard Beverley, lot in the town of Port Royal; my mother; my sister, Jane Willy Beverley; my sister Ann Hazlewood Dudley; godson Charles Champe Stanard, son of William Stanard; sister Jane Willy Beverley, land in Orange Co; brother Robert G. Beverley; Larkin Stanard; Colin Reddick. (Page 1349)

SMITH, WILLIAM, Berkeley Parish, Spotsylvania Co., d. Jan. 4, 1792, Executors Bond dated Apr. 1, 1794. Wit. Reuben Massey, Charles Carter, Edward Massey, Thomas Shirley, Richard Long. Ex. my three sons Oswald, John and James Smith. Leg. son Oswald Smith and his daughter Elizabeth Smith; son John Smith; daughter Franky Stubblefield; her husband Col. Harry Stubblefield, and my granddaughter Catherine Stubblefield; son James Smith; daughter Diana Walker; her husband James Walker, and their daughter Polly Walker; daughter Mary Stevens; her husband John Stevens and their daughter Ann Smith Stevens; daughter Lucy Smith. (Page 1358)

PULLIAM, DAVID, Berkeley Parish, Spotsylvania Co., d. Feb. 7, 1794, Executors Bond dated July 1, 1794. Wit. George Penny, Moses Wheeler, William Penny. Ex. sons Joseph, Nathaniel and John Pulliam. Leg. daughter Mary Pulliam; children Nathaniel, Richard, John, Elijah, James, Nancy, Sally Pulliam; youngest son William when he arrives at nineteen years of age. (Page 1370)

COLEMAN, EDWARD, Berkeley Parish, Spotsylvania Co., d. Nov. 28, 1794, Executors Bond dated Jan. 6, 1795. Wit. Richard Gaines, William Moore, Henry Walker. Ex. sons James and Thomas Coleman, James Powell. Leg. wife Sarah; sons James and Thomas; grandson James Coleman, son of Robert Edward Coleman; other children Caty Waggoner, Phebe Hutchinson, Henry Coleman, John Coleman, William Coleman. (Page 1403)

HANOR, HARMON, Spotsylvania Co., d. Dec. 10, 1794, Executors Bond dated Feb. 3, 1794. Wit. Benjamin Chapman, William Beckham. Ex. James Lewis, Thomas Strachan. Leg. wife Eleanor; children William and Harmon Hanor, Sarah Day, Hannah Graves, Anna Gosney. (Page 1422)

MERCER, JAMES, Fredericksburg, d. May 23, 1791, p. Feb. 3, 1795. Administrators John T. Brooke, James M. Garnett. Leg: whole estate, both real and personal, unto my worthy friends and relations Mr. Muscoe Garnett of Essex Co., and Mr. Benjamin Harrison of the City of Richmond, and I also appoint them sole executors of this will upon Trust, and upon the terms and conditions hereinafter mentioned, etc. 1st. for the payment of my just debts and the maintenance and education of my four children and my niece Martha Mercer, and secondly for the use of my said children and niece to the devises of my will. Lots and houses in town and lands not now worked to be sold if necessary. Daughter Mary Eleanor Dick Mercer, one thousand pounds; daughter Lucinda Mercer, three hundred pounds; niece Martha Mercer; son Charles Fenton Mercer, one moiety of my Bull Run land, containing about 300 acres; son John Fenton Mercer; devise to Muscoe Garnett and Benjamin Harrison every right and power that I have or can have to fulfill the wills of the late Alexander Dick and Charles Dick, and also the Trusts reposed in me by the Act of Assembly respecting my late brother George Mercer; guardianship of my daughter Mary to my sister Mrs. Selden; guardianship of my two sons to Mr. Garnett and Mr. Harrison.

Codicil dated May 26, 1791, my gold repeating watch to my eldest son, it being a family watch. Mentions sons John Fenton Mercer, Charles Fenton Mercer and daughter Mary Eleanor Mercer. (Page 1425)

THORNTON, FRANCIS, Spotsylvania Co., d. Feb. 13, 1794, p. Apr. 8, 1795. Wit. James Tutt, Ann Thornton, Sarah Thornton. Leg. wife Ann; son Francis; daughters Elizabeth Gregory Thornton, Mary Thornton, Dorothea Thornton, Frances Buckner, Mildred Washington Maury. (Page 1448)

HOLLODAY, JOSEPH, Spotsylvania Co., d. Sept. 23, 1785, Executors Bond dated Sept. 1, 1795. Wit. Joseph Pulliam, John Rawlings, Joseph Pulliam. Ex. sons Lewis, James, Joseph and Benjamin. Leg. sons Lewis, James, Joseph, Stephen, Benjamin, John, William and Thomas Holloday; daughters Jemimiah, Betty, Winifred Holloday.

Codicil dated July 17, 1795, mentions sons Stephen, John, Lewis and Thomas, and daughters Jemimiah, Betty and Winifred. (Page 1456)

ROBINSON, BENJAMIN, Spotsylvania Co., d. Aug. 11, 1785, proved Dec. 1, 1795. Wit. D. Turner, George Holloway. Leg. sister Sarah Robinson; brother Charles Carter Robinson. (Page 1484)

QUARLES, WILLIAM, Spotsylvania Co., d. Nov. 2, 1794, Executors Bond dated Apr. 5, 1796. Wit. Samuel Sale, Thomas Winslow, Robert Michie. Ex. Col. Garrett Minor and sons Ralph and William Quarles. Leg. wife Frances; son Ralph; son William, land in Bedford Co. conveyed to him in fee by my brother Roger Quarles; son Charles; son Roger; son John; daughters Ann, Frances, Jane and Patsey; daughter Mary, and after her death to her husband. (Page 1521)

WOODROOF, RICHARD, Spotsylvania Co., d. Sept. 12, 1795. Wit. Curtis Waller, Charles Lewis. Ex. Benja. Waller, Senr., Thomas Minor, Senr. and Waller Lewis. Leg. Benjamin Waller, Senr; Waller Lewis; my wife; daughter Betsey Fruel. (Page 1549)

TURNLEY, FRANCIS, Spotsylvania Co., d. Oct. 13, 1796, Executors Bond dated Feb. 7, 1797. Wit. John Mercer, Larkin Stanard, Hugh Roy.

Ex. sons John and Francis. Leg. sons Francis and John; daughters Ann, Sarah and Betty. (Page 1576)

WHITE, GEORGE, Spotsylvania Co., d. Oct. 4, 1796, Executors Bond dated Apr. 4, 1797. Wit. George William Spooner, John Oliver, Elizabeth Oliver, Edmund White. Ex. wife. Leg. Susanna White and my children. (Page 1603)

NEWELL, WILLIAM, Spotsylvania Co., d. July 9, 1793. Wit. James Richards, O. Towles. Ex. James Lewis, Gentl. Leg. wife Mary Newell; my only child Ann (Nancy) wife of Charles Carter, of Spots. Co. (Page 1605)

BOWLIN, JESSE, Berkeley Parish, Spotsylvania Co., d. Nov. 1, 1793. Wit. Henry Pendleton, John Alsop. Ex. Henry Pendleton, Philip Pendleton. Leg. wife Sally; son Joel Bowlin; sons William and Jesse Butler Bowlin; son James Shirlock Bowlin; daughter Mary Burruss. (Page 1608)

PARKER, WILLIAM, Spotsylvania Co., d. Mar. 12, 1797, Executors Bond dated July 4, 1797. Wit. Joseph Herndon Junr., Richard Dickinson, William Duerson, Junr., Thomas Coleman, Junr. Ex. Thomas Winslow, Benjamin Robinson, James Powell. Leg. son William Parker and his son Beverley Parker; sons Thomas, Richard, Harry, Benjamin Parker; daughter Ann Dudley; daughter Susanna Stubblefield; daughter Mary Thomas; daughter Catherine Robinson; daughter Elizabeth Winslow. (Page 1611)

JINKINS, JOHN, Senr., Spotsylvania Co., d. Mar. 14, 1797, Executors Bond dated Dec. 5, 1797. Wit. Francis Coleman, John Greenhorn, James Coleman. Ex. son Gipson Jinkins, John Carter. Leg. sons Gipson, William, Charles, Robert, John. (Page 1636)

CRAWFORD, JOHN, Spotsylvania Co., d. Apr. 24, 1797, Executors Bond dated Feb. 6, 1798. Wit. Benj. Mason, Joseph Crawford, Garland Lively, Martin Calton. Ex. my father James Crawford, my wife Phebe, Thomas Shirley. Leg. sons John, James and William; daughters Elizabeth, Nancy and Polly; wife Phebe. (Page 1642)

[EDITOR'S NOTE.—The will of Elizabeth Salter, dated Dec. 23, 1771, was found in Deed Book H, page 142. It is recorded in Deed Book H, page 289 in this volume.]

WILL BOOK F

1798–1800

CAMPBELL, MARY, Spotsylvania Co., Dec. 6, 1795. Administrators Bond dated July 3, 1798, John Spotswood, Admr. Wit. John Spotswood, Susanna C. Spotswood. Leg. son Alexander; to my son John Spotswood, of Orange, land in the Co. of Spots. which was devised to me by my late sister Dansie; mentions estate of W. Campbell, my late husband. (Page 3)

DAVENPORT, WILLIAM, Spotsylvania Co., d. June 1, 1795, Executors Bond dated July 3, 1798. Wit. Samuel Hill, Thomas Branan, John Minor. Ex. Thomas Minor, son David Davenport. Leg. wife; sons Augustin, William, John, James; daughter Delpha, during her life and her husband's, and if they die without issue, to Delphia Eddes; daughter Nancy; daughter Sarah; son Thomas; son David.
Codicil June 1, 1795, sons Augustin, William and John, and son-in-law William Arnold. (Page 19)

PURVIS, JAMES, Spotsylvania Co., d. Dec. 18, 1797. Wit. John Stewart, John Carter, John Herndon. Ex. William Lovell, Thomas Minor, Edward Herndon, son of Joseph; Lewis Holloday. Leg. grandson James Dudley; grandson Robert W. Dudley; granddaughters Sally, Nancy, Molly and Kitty Dudley; daughter Ann Dudley; grandson Ambrose Dudley; daughter Molly Lovell.
Codicil Feb. 15, 1798, mentions daughter Molly Lovell. (Page 22)

PETTUS, WILLIAM, Spotsylvania Co., d. Sept. 18, 1795, Executors Bond dated Sept. 4, 1798. Wit. Sharp Smith, Peter Arnold, Charles Dabney. Ex. sons William, Overton Hart, James, Joseph and son-in-law William Graves. Leg. wife; sons Overton Hart, James, Joseph; friends Jonathan Clarke, Edmund Clarke and Samuel Overton Pettus, as trustees; daughter Louisa; my children Barbary Arnold, William, Nancy Graves, Susanna Davenport, Overton Hart, James, Joseph and Louisa. (Page 37)

MITCHAM, LUCY, Spotsylvania Co., d. Jan. 16, 1797. Executors Bond dated Dec. 4, 1798. Wit. Hugh Roy, Bartlett Russell, Will Waller. Ex. son-in-law William Beazley, Richard Estes. Leg. daughter Mary Bates; mentions first husband Ambrose Carlton; three eldest daughters, Caty Estes, Elizabeth Beazley, Mary Bates; my last daughter Dorothy Beazley as provided for by the will of her late father James Mitcham. (Page 46)

GRAVATT, GEORGE, of Spotsylvania Co., d. 1798, Executors Bond dated Dec. 4, 1798. Wit. William Willoughby, James Wheeler. Ex. wife, Caty Gravatt and son John Gravatt. Leg. wife Caty Gravatt; son Robert; son John; granddaughter Caty Fagg. (Page 48)

KEITH, ROSANNAH, Berkeley Parish, Spotsylvania Co., d. Nov. 9, 1796, Executors Bond dated Feb. 5, 1799. Wit. John Carter, Leroy Jinkins, Mary Jinkins. Ex. Gipson Jinkins. Leg. Frees three negroes Fanny and her children Anthony and Kitty. (Page 64)

GRAVES, JOHN, Spotsylvania Co., d. Nov. 17, 1798, Executors Bond dated Mar. 5, 1799. Wit. George Tyler, William Cason, Junr., Joseph Graves, T. Hill, Edward G. Hill. Ex. Joseph Graves, George Tyler, son William Graves, Lewis Partlow. Leg. sons Samuel, John, James and William Graves; daughter Susannah Wiglesworth; daughter Mary Partlow; daughter Elizabeth Graves. (Page 67)

DAVIS, JAMES, Berkeley Parish, Spotsylvania Co., d. July 14, 1793, Executors Bond dated July 2, 1799. Wit. Joseph Nelson, Saml. Sale, John Carter. Ex. wife Sarah, Smith Blakey. Leg. wife Sarah and all my children. (Page 69)

FRAZER, JAMES, Spotsylvania Co., d. Dec. 15, 1798, Executors Bond dated Apr. 2, 1799. Wit. John Herndon, Joseph Chew, John Nelson. Ex. brothers Anthony and William Frazer; brothers-in-law John and James Smith. Leg. wife Lucy, and my children. (Page 73)

POOLE, ELIZABETH, Spotsylvania Co., d. Dec. 15, 1798, Wit. Henry Goodloe, William Buchanan, Thomas Thornton. Ex. George Durrett. Leg. granddaughter Nancy Gale Poole, daughter of Elizabeth Poole; daughters Elizabeth and Judith Poole. (Page 76)

WALLER, POMFRETT, Spotsylvania Co., d. July 2, 1793, Executors Bond dated Sept. 3, 1799. Wit. Sarah Clark, Elizabeth Minor, Jona. Clark. Ex. nephews Carr Waller, Dabney Waller and my friend Jona. Clark. Leg. wife Martha Waller; nephews Carr Waller, Dabney Waller, Pomfrett Waller, John Waller and Waller Bulloch. (Page 80)

HERNDON, EDWARD, Berkeley Parish, Spotsylvania Co., d. Aug. 5, 1793, Executors Bond dated Sept. 3, 1799. Ex. my sons-in-law James Lewis and Anthony Frazer. Leg. wife Mary Herndon; son-in-law James Lewis; my children.
Codicil Mar. 14, 1799, appoints his four sons John, Edward, William and Joseph Herndon executors. (Page 90)

NEWTON, JAMES, Spotsylvania Co., d. Oct. 29, 1798, Proved Sept. 4, 1799, Henry Dickinson, Admr. Wit. Griffen Dickinson, Saml. Newton. Leg. nephew Henry Dickinson, whole of estate. (Page 94)

BONNSEL, MOSES, Spotsylvania Co., d. Feb. 8, 1799, Executors Bond dated Dec. 3, 1799. Wit. Anthony Arnold, Edmund Arnold, John Lahorn. Ex. wife Susanna, George Bronaugh, my wife's brother William Month. Leg. wife Susanna; sons John and James Bonsel. (Page 97)

DANIEL, EDMOND, Spotsylvania Co., d. Oct. 1, 1799, Executors Bond dated Dec. 3, 1799. Wit. George Bronaugh, Anthony Arnold, Sarah Arnold. Ex. son Reuben Daniel, James Robbins. Leg. wife Peggy Daniel; sons Reuben and Tomson Daniel. (Page 103)

ADMINISTRATION BONDS

WILL BOOK A

£100 John Finalson, admr. of John Joseph Abbitt, decd., with Abram Bledsoe and John Roberts, sec. Nov. 6, 1722.

£20 Sarah Edmonds, admx. of Charles Edmonds, decd., with Thomas Burbridge, sec. Feb. 1, 1725.

£50 William Macconico, admr. of John James, decd., with William Eddings and Richard Sharp, sec. Apr. 5, 1726.

£1000 Jael Johnson, admr. of Richard Johnson, decd., with John Grayson and G. Lightfoot, sec. Nov. 1726.

£500 Elinor Thomas, admx. of William Thomas, decd., with Robert Slaughter and Robert Green, sec. Nov. 1, 1726.

£500 Mary Kilgore, admx. of Peter Kilgore, decd., with John Kilgore and William Hackney, sec. May 2, 1727.

£50 Katherine Moxum, admx. of Matthew Moxum, decd., with John Hows and Edmund Birk, sec. May 2, 1727.

£100 Robert Green, admr. of Henry Henderson, decd., with Goodrich Lightfoot, sec. May 2, 1727.

£100 John Arnold, admr. of Thomas Garrison, decd., with Goodrich Lightfoot and Robert Spotswood, sec. May 2, 1727.

£200 John Grame, admr. of John Samm, decd., with Goodrich Lightfoot and Robert Spotswood, sec. May 2, 1727.

£50 John Finleson, admr. of Colling Campbell, decd., with Robert Spotswood and John Waller, sec. Nov. 7, 1727.

£500 Mary Johnson, admx. of William Johnson, decd., with George Carter and John Wiglesworth, sec. June 4, 1728.

£500 Katherine Cooper, admx. of John Cooper, decd., with John Cammell and Edward Southall, sec. Aug. 6, 1728.

£1000 Ann James, admx. of Edward Southall, decd., with John Taliaferro, Francis Conway and Benj. Porter, sec. Oct. 5, 1728.

£500 Dorothy Horton, admx. of Benjamin Horton, decd., with Abram Bledsoe and Richard Cheek, sec. Oct. 5, 1728.

£500 William Burbridge, admr. of Thomas Burbridge, decd., with Thomas Watts and Benjamin Cave, sec. Nov. 5, 1728.

£200 Thomas Grame, admr. of William Norvell, decd., with Rodr. Macculloch and William Frazer, sec. Nov. 7, 1728.

£100 Mary Neale, admx. of William Neale, decd., with John Kilgore and John Asher, sec. Feb. 4, 1728-9.

£200 Susannah Livingston, admx. of William Livingston, decd., with Jno. Finalson and Moseley Battaley, sec. Apr. 1, 1729.

£50 Samuel Wright (her husband), admr. of Mary Wright, decd., with John Kilgore and Thomas Byrn, sec. July 1, 1729.

£50 William Frazer, admr. of David Mitchell, decd., with John Gordon and James Roy, sec. Oct. 6, 1730.

£1000 John Snell (his son), admr. of John Snell, decd., with William Bartlett and Samuel Hensley, sec. Apr. 3, 1733.

£50 Henry Willis, admr. of Bryant Mcleroy, decd., with Joseph Brock, sec. Apr. 3, 1733.

£200 Robert Durham, admr. of Nicholas Nicholas, decd., with John Gordon and James Sleet, sec. Oct. 3, 1733.

£50 Susanna Creagler, admx. of Jacob Creagler, decd., with Michael Clare and George Utz, sec. Apr. 3, 1734.

£100 Frances Frazier, admx. of William Frazier, decd., with John Gordon and Susannah Livingston, sec. Apr. 2, 1734.

£200 Isabella Mirtle, admx. of Peter Mirtle, decd., with John Christopher and Thomas Jackson, sec. May 7, 1734.

£500 Richard Phillips, admr. of William Smith, gent., decd., with Edwin Hickman and John Holloday, sec. July 2, 1734.

£100 Catherine Rice, admx. of William Rice, decd., with Henry Goodloe and John Smith, sec. Sept. 3, 1734.

£100 John Gordon, admr. of Thomas Barnett, decd., with John Greame, sec. Nov. 5, 1734.

£50 Ann Robinson, admx. of William Robinson, decd., with Thomas Witherby and John Jones, sec. Mch. 4, 1734.

£1000 Susannah Grayson, admx. of John Grayson, decd., with Ambrose Grayson and Thomas Hill, sec. Mch. 2, 1735–6.

£100 Stephen Hord, admr. of William Hord, decd., with Edwin Herndon and Joseph Brock, sec. May 4, 1736.

£50 John Gordon, admr. of Robert Pringle, decd., with John Waller, sec. Aug. 1738.

£50 Averilla Sheppard, admx. of Edward Sheppard, decd., with John Tennent, sec. May 1, 1739.

£100 Ellinor Dunn, admx. of James Dunn, decd., with Moseley Battaley and Thomas Hill, sec. Nov. 6, 1739.

£50 John Waller, admr. of Peirce Edge, decd., with William Waller, sec. May 7, 1740.

£2000 Andrew Ross, admr. of Nico. C. Bontrue, decd., with John Frogg, sec. Aug. 5, 1740.

£100 Barnett Pain, admr. of Barnett Pain, Jr., decd., with William Johnston, sec. Dec. 3, 1740.

£1000 Humphrey Hill, admr. of Thomas Hill, decd., with John Waller, sec. July 7, 1741.

£250 Martha Flowere, admx. of William Flowere, decd., with Elliot Benger and Daniel Devall, sec. Dec. 1, 1741.

£25 William Waller, admr. of Mary Markendree, decd., with Edmund Waller, sec. Apr. 6, 1742.

£50 William Thompson, admr. of William Webb, decd., with Thomas Allen, sec. Dec. 7, 1742.

£200 Martha Flowere, admx. of Daniel Flowere, decd., with John Menefe, sec. Mch. 1, 1742.

£200 Thomas Chew, admr. of Hannah Chew, decd., with Anthony Foster, sec. Aug. 3, 1743.

£100 William Hunter, admr. of William Reid, decd., with Elliot Benger, sec. Mch. 6, 1743.

£300 Sophia Dowdall, admx. of Patrick Dowdall, decd., with George Morton and John Blake, sec. Mch. 6, 1743.

£100 William Lynn, admr. of Alexander Hill, decd., with Francis Thornton, sec. May 1, 1744.

£200 Knight Burbridge, admr. of William Burbridge, decd., with Anthony Strother, gent., sec. July 3, 1744.

£100 John McDaniel, admr. of John Webster, decd., with Edward Herndon, sec. Dec. 4, 1744.

£200 Morgan Darnell, admr. of Joshua Thomas, decd., with Charles Morgan and William Blackwell, of Prince Wm. Co., sec. Aug. 16, 1745.

£25 Ann Gibson, admx. of Joseph Gibson, decd., with Francis Thornton, sec. Apr. 1, 1746.

£300 John Blanton, admr. of Francis Smith, decd., with John Parrish and Peter Montague, sec. June 3, 1746.

£50 Joseph Bell, admr. of John Smith, decd., with John Jones, sec. Mch. 4, 1746.

£50 Timothy Sisk, admr. of William Whitehouse, decd., with Bland Ballard and John Wheeler, sec. June 2, 1747.

£1000 Henry Willis, admr. of Mildred Willis, decd., with Anthony Strother, sec. Oct. 6, 1747.

£200 Elizabeth Rogers, admx. of Henry Rogers, decd., with John Menefee and Micajah Poole, sec. Nov. 3, 1747.

£100 Anthony Foster, admr. of John Kirkpatrick, decd., with John Waller, Jr., sec. Feb. 2, 1747.

£100 Margaret Randall, admx. of Nicholas Randall, decd., with William Miller, sec. July 5, 1748.

£1000 William Smith, admr. of Oswald Smith, decd., with John Minor, sec. Aug. 2, 1748.

£100 Tabatha Foster, admx. of Edmund Foster, decd., with Joseph Collins, sec. Aug. 2, 1748.

£100 James Boyd, admr. of David Morrison, decd., with William Hughes and Patrick Connelly, sec. Dec. 7, 1748.

£1000 Ann Bowker, admx. of Parmenas Bowker, decd., with Owen Thomas and Thomas Merry, sec. Feb. 17, 1748.

£150 Sarah Davidson, admx. of Alexander Davidson, decd., with Wm. Ellis and John Gordon, sec. Feb. 7, 1748.

£500 William Elliott, admr. of John Royston, decd., with Conquest Royston and Charles Colson, sec. Feb. 8, 1748.

£100 Betty Head, admx. of James Head, decd., with Conquest Royston and John Holloday, sec. Mch. 7, 1748.

£800 Amey Scott, admx. of David Scott, decd., with Achilles Bowker and John Wood, sec. Apr. 4, 1749.

£200 Avarilla Darnaby, admx. of Edward Darnaby, decd., with William Darnaby, sec. July 4, 1749.

ADMINISTRATION BONDS

WILL BOOK B

£100 Robert Jackson, admr. of Thomas Barry, decd., with Richard Tutt, sec. Oct. 3, 1749.

£500 James Rawlings, Jr., admr. of Thomas Rawlings, decd., with John Holloday and Benj. Holloday, sec. Oct. 3, 1749.

£100 Elizabeth Lewis, admx. of John Lewis, decd., with Larkin Johnston and James Parks, sec. Nov. 8, 1749.

£50 Charles Dick, admr. of Charles Boreman, decd., with Anthony Strother, sec. Dec. 5, 1749.

£100 Sarah True, admx. of John True, decd., with John Holloday and William Miller, sec. Feb. 6, 1749.

£100 Fielding Lewis, admr. of Erasmus Johns, decd., with Richard Tutt, sec. Mch. 6, 1749.

£50 William Lewis, admr. of John Lewis, decd., with Benjamin Davis, sec. Mch. 6, 1749.

£200 John Holloday, admr. of Thomas Cartwright, decd., with Anthony Foster, sec. Apr. 3, 1750.

£500 Mary Wiglesworth, admx. of John Wiglesworth, decd., with Edmd. Waller and Benj. Martin, sec. Apr. 3, 1750.

£200 Mary Steward, admx. of Charles Steward, decd., with Joseph Steward, sec. June 5, 1750.

£500 Mary Whitehouse and William Sutton, admrs. of Margaret Vinton, decd., with Wm. Lynn and Wm. McWilliams, sec. July 3, 1750.

£100 Adam Lindsay, admr. of Antho. Lucas, decd., with George Stubblefield, sec. June 4, 1751.

£1500 Dorothea Benger, admx. of Elliott Benger, decd., with Roger Dixon, sec. Aug. 6, 1751.

£50 Humphrey Wallace, admr. of Jacob Morris, decd., with John Jones, sec. Aug. 6, 1751.

£2000 Francis Taliaferro, admr. of John Taliaferro, decd., with William Robinson, sec. Sept. 3, 1751.

£40 Patrick Connelly, admr. of Nicholas Sullivan, decd., with James Boyd and James Allenack, sec. Feb. 5, 1752.

£500 Barbara Jones, admx. of John Jones, decd., with George Tod and John Sutherland, sec. Feb. 6, 1752.

£50 Larkin Johnston, admr. of John Cunningham, decd., with Robert Dudley and Thomas Collins, sec. June 2, 1752.

£50 Mary Artrup, admx. of Colbert Artrup, decd., with Joseph Steward, sec. July 7, 1752.

£200 Robert Duncanson, admr. of John Smith, decd., with William Carr, sec. Jan. 3, 1753.

£500 Margaret Wood, admx. of John Wood, decd., with William Waller and William Miller, sec. Jan. 2, 1753.

£2000 Mary James and Thomas James, admrs. of George James, decd., with Henry Field and Joseph Steward, sec. Mch. 6, 1753.

£30 Andrew Beatty, admr. of William Brumley, decd., with William Lewis, sec. Apr. 3, 1753.

£4000 Lewis Webb, atty. for Saml. Fox, admr. of James Fox, decd., with Roger Dixon and Charles Dick, sec. June 5, 1753.

£3000 William Cunningham, admr. Thomas Macredie, decd., with John Mitchell, Charles Dick and Robert Duncanson, sec. Aug. 7, 1753.

£50 James Hunter, admr. of James James, decd., with John Champe, sec. Apr. 2, 1754.

£50 James Hunter, admr. of Thomas Fuller, decd., with Anthony Strother, sec. Apr. 3, 1754.

£100 Thomas Allen, admr. of Nathaniel Allen, decd., with Erasmus Withers Allen, sec. July 2, 1754.

£100 Anthony Strother, admr. of Elizabeth Houston, decd., with Moseley Battaley, sec. Aug. 6, 1754.

£1000 Anthony McKittrick, admr. of James McKittrick, decd., with John Mitchell and Wm. Cunningham, sec. Aug. 6, 1754.

£100 Mary Wood, admx. of Lancelot Wood, decd., with Wm. Lewis and John Gordon, sec. Aug. 1, 1754.

£500 Rice Curtis, admr. of Elizabeth Curtis, decd., with Thomas Merry, sec. Apr. 1, 1755.

£50 John Wilson, admr. of Charles Andrews, decd., with Thomas Reeves, Jr., sec. Mch. 2, 1756.

£500 Agnes Pavey, admx. of Adam Pavey, decd., with Wm. McWilliams, Jr., and Roger Dixon, sec. Apr. 6, 1756.

£100 William Lynn, admr. of John Dent, decd., with Roger Dixon, sec. Apr. 6, 1756.

£1200 William McWilliams, the younger, of Fredericksburg, merchant, admr. of Catherine Battaille, spinster, decd., with Robert Jackson of Fredericksburg, merchant, sec. Mch. 1, 1757.

£50 Susannah McKenzie, admx. of Alexander McKenzie, decd., with John Elson and John Ballard, sec. May 3, 1757.

£100 Moseley Battaley, admr. of Eleanor Hogg, decd., with John Semple, sec. June 7, 1757.

£100 Richard Brooks, admr. of Robert Cook, decd., with Robert Jackson, sec. Nov. 2, 1757.

£1000 Mary Scott, admx. of Isaac Scott, decd., with William Smith and William Scott, sec. Dec. 6, 1757.

£200 Est. of Adam Pavey, decd., unadministered on by Agnes Pavey, decd., Roger Dixon, admr., William Waller, sec. Feb. 8, 1758.

£2000 Rachel McWilliams and Roger Dixon, admrs. of William McWilliams, Jr., decd., with Fielding Lewis and Chas. Lewis, sec. Mch. 7, 1758.

£100 John Sutherland, admr. of William Fairfield, decd., with Richard Brooke, sec. Mch. 8, 1758.

£50 John Sutherland, admr. of David Snodgrass, decd., with William Lewis, sec. Mch. 9, 1758.

£100 John Holloday, admr. of Patterson Pulliam, decd., with Joseph Hawkins and Joel Parrish, sec. Apr. 6, 1758.

£100 Rice Curtis, admr. of David Payn, decd., with Edward Herndon, Jr., sec. May 3, 1758.

£300 James Sparks, admr. of James Sparks, decd., with William Lewis and Bland Ballard, sec. Aug. 2, 1758.

£2000 William Brooke, admr. of Dorothea Benger, decd., with Lawrence Taliaferro, sec. Apr. 3, 1759.

£200 Est. of Elliott Benger, decd., unadministered on by Dorothea Benger, decd. Roger Dixon, admr., Richard Tutt, sec. Apr. 3, 1759.

£100 George Long, admr. of Isaiah Barns, decd., with Thomas Reeves, Jr., sec. May 2, 1759.

£400 Sarah True, admx. of Martin True, decd., with Benjamin Martin and John Gordon, sec. Aug. 6, 1759.

£100 Thomas Reeves, admr. of Thomas Reeves, decd., with John Battaley and William Lewis, sec. May 6, 1760.

£100 Thomas Reeves, admr. of Henry Reeves, decd., with John Battaley and William Lewis, sec. May 6, 1760.

£400 John Stewart and Chas. Yates, admrs. of William Simms, decd., with George Frazer, sec. Aug. 4, 1760.

£200 Mary Peacock, admx. of Richard Peacock, decd., with Wm. Grayson and John Rakestraw, sec. Aug. 4, 1760.

£300 Mary Owen and Wm. Darnaby, admrs. of Jacob Owen, decd., with Robert Dudley and James Redd, sec. Sep. 1, 1760.

£50 Mary Willicome, late the wife of Jno. Butler, admx. of John Butler, decd., with Robt. Jackson, sec. Sept. 1, 1760.

£150 Roger Dixon, admr. of Samuel Hildrup, decd., with Joseph Jones, sec. Dec. 2, 1760.

£20 Abraham Simpson, admr. of William Lampton, decd., with Joseph Brock, sec. Dec. 2, 1760.

£200 Alice Hubbard, admx. of John Hubbard, decd., with Thomas Hutcherson and Benj. Head, sec. Feb. 2, 1761.

£200 John Smith, admr. of William Pace, decd., with Edward Herndon, sec. Apr. 6, 1761.

£6000 Mary Smith, admx. of John Smith, decd., with Larkin Chew and Beverley Winslow, sec. Apr. 6, 1761.

£100 Ann Standley, admx. of Moses Standley, decd., with Joseph Jones, sec. July 6, 1761.

£500 Richard Bayn, admr. of John Rakestraw, decd., with William Lewis and John Holloday, sec. Oct. 5, 1761.

ADMINISTRATION BONDS

WILL BOOK D

£300 Hannah Gimbo, admx. of Thomas Gimbo, decd., with Joseph Holloday and James Gimbo, sec. Mch. 1, 1762.

£100 John Patty, admr. of James Fewell, decd., with Robert Coleman, sec. Apr. 2, 1762.

£500 Ann Pannell, admx. of Samuel Pannell, decd., with William Garrett, sec. Apr. 5, 1762.

£1000 Susannah Sharp, admx. of John Sharp, decd., with Thomas Hord, sec. July 4, 1763.

£50 Charles Yates, admr. of John Asborough, decd., with Robert Jackson, sec. July 4, 1763.

£100 David Henning, admr. of Patrick Wayland, decd., with Charles Yates, sec. July 4, 1763.

£200 Mary Willicome, admx. of William Willicome, decd., with Andrew Fraser, sec. July 4, 1763.

£100 Andrew Edwards, admr. of John Regar, decd., with Joseph Herndon, sec. July 5, 1763.

£100 Ushula Gains, admx. of Robert Gains, decd., with Moses Bledsoe, sec. Oct. 3, 1763.

£50 Peter Marye, admr. of Thomas Gibbs, decd., with Joseph Herndon, sec. Oct. 4, 1763.

£200 Jane Carpenter, admx. of Jonothan Carpenter, decd., with William Ball and Jonothan Carpenter, sec. Nov. 7, 1763.

£2000 Elizabeth Hawkins, admx. of John Hawkins, decd., with Robert Chew, John Herndon and James Cunningham, sec. Apr. 2, 1764.

£1000 Elizabeth Pulliam, admx. of James Pulliam, decd., with James Rawlings and John Holloday, sec. May 7, 1764.

£50 Stapleton Crutchfield, admr. of John Andrew, decd., with Joel Parrish, sec. June 4, 1764.

£50 John Stewart, admr. of George Long, decd., with John Waller and William Wood, sec. June 4, 1764.

£1000 John Battaley, John Waller, Peter Marye and Wm. Ellis, admrs. of Moses Bledsoe, decd., with Edward Herndon and Wm. Wood, sec. June 4, 1764.

£300 Elizabeth Sherley, admx. of John Sherley, decd., with Roger Dixon, sec. Aug. 6, 1764.

£100 Thomas Reeves, admr. of Barnett Platt, decd., with Erasmus Withers Allen, sec. Dec. 3, 1764.

£2000 James Duncanson, admr. of Robert Duncanson, decd., with Roger Dixon, Joseph Jones and Chas. Yates, sec. Dec. 3, 1764.

£100 Sarah Crawford, admx. of John Crawford, decd., with John Waller and James Crawford, sec. May 6, 1765.

£6000 Robert Brent, admr. of John Sutherland, decd., with Fielding Lewis and Joseph Jones, sec. July 1, 1765.

£30 Barnabas Williams, admr. of John Leather, decd., with Robert True, sec. July 1, 1765.

£300 Sarah Gordon, admx. of John Gordon, decd., with John Chiles, sec. Aug. 4, 1766.

£500 Elizabeth Salter, admx. of Daniel Carter, decd., with Thomas Blanton, sec. Aug. 4, 1766.

£100 Henry True, admr. of Martin True, decd., with James Fraser, sec. Sept. 1, 1766.

£200 Thomas Colson, admr. of James Lyndsay, decd., with Edward Herndon, sec. Oct. 6, 1766.

£200 Patrick Kennen, admr. of Hugh Wilson, decd., with John Lewis, sec. Nov. 3, 1766.

£200 Lucy Day, admx. of Lucy Day, decd., with John Chandler, sec. Dec. 1, 1766.

£200 James Mercer, admr. of William Gyles, decd., with Charles Dick, gent., sec. Feb. 2, 1767.

£150 Judith Darnaby, admx. of William Darnaby, Jr., decd., with Judith Herndon, sec. July 6, 1767.

£3000 Mary Vass, admx. of Philip Vincent Vass, decd., with Edward Herndon, John Vass and John Carthrae, sec. Aug. 3, 1766.

£500 Winifred Jones, admx. of David Jones, decd., with John Carthrae, sec. July 4, 1768.

£200 John Conner, admr. of Charles Conner, decd., with John Herndon, sec. Sept. 5, 1768.

£500 John Carthrae, admr. of John Vass, decd., with Thomas Colson, sec. Oct. 3, 1768.

£2000 George Tankersley, admr. of John Hind, decd., with John Glassell, sec. Dec. 5, 1768.

£500 Ann Samms, admx. of James Samms, decd., with Peter Marye, sec. Dec. 5, 1768.

£500 Francis Wisdom, admr. of John Wisdom, decd., with Edward Herndon, sec. Feb. 6, 1769.

£1000 Mary Trigg, admx. of Daniel Trigg, decd., with Thomas Duerson, Jr., and Harry Bartlett, sec. Mch. 6, 1769.

£100 Richard Lewis, admr. of John Williams, decd., with William Waller, sec. Mch. 6, 1769.

£50 Jeremiah Smith, admr. of Ralph Smith, decd., with John Smith and James Carter, sec. Aug. 7, 1769.

£1000 Mary Rawlings, admx. of Thomas Rawlings, decd., with John Carter and John Carthrae, sec. Sept. 4, 1769.

£100 Roger Dixon, admr. of Jerrerd Keyton, decd., with George Sheppard, sec. Sept. 5, 1769.

£1000 Benj. Johnston and Robt. Johnston, admrs. of Oliver Towles, decd., with Wm. Underwood and Wm. Wood, sec. May 8, 1770.

£200 James Duncanson, admr. of Andrew Frazer, decd., with John Mitchell, sec. May 8, 1770.

£200 Henry Mitchell, admr. of William Hind, decd., with Joseph Jones, sec. Aug. 7, 1770.

£200 William Garrett, admr. of Thomas Mead, decd., with Vincent Vass, sec. Nov. 5, 1770.

£3000 Susannah Heath, admx. of Henry Heath, decd., with James Marye and Peter Marye, sec. Dec. 20, 1770.

£500 Elizabeth May, admx. of Thomas May, decd., with John Penn, sec. Apr. 19, 1771.

£1000 Joseph Brock, admr. of Abraham Simpson, decd., with John Chew and Edward Herndon, sec. July 18, 1771.

£500 William Darnaby, admr. of Mary Owen, decd., with Michael Robinson, sec. Nov. 2, 1771.

£800 Benjamin Waller, admr. of Edmund Waller, decd., with John Wiglesworth and John Carter, sec. Nov. 21, 1771.

£100 Benjamin Johnston, admr. of Betty Benger, decd., with William Wood, sec. Apr. 16, 1772.

£1000 William Templeman, admr. of Alexander Wright, decd., with John Glassell, sec. Apr. 16, 1772.

£300 Achilles Johnson Stevens, admr. of Jeremiah Stevens, decd., with John Carthrae, sec. Apr. 16, 1772.

ADMINISTRATION BONDS

WILL BOOK E

£200 John Dixon, admr. of Jane Neal, decd., with Oliver Towles, sec. June 18, 1772.

£200 Mary Payne, admx. of John Payne, decd., with Joseph Gale and Rice Curtis, Jr., sec. Sept. 17, 1772.

£300 David Blair, admr. of Jeremiah Stevens, decd., with Andrew Buchannan, sec. June 18, 1773.

£500 Jacob Whitler, admr. of Jane Whitler, decd., with John Baggott, sec. July 17, 1773.

£1000 Chas. Yates, admr. of Philip Somerby, decd., with Alexr. Blair, sec. Aug. 19, 1773.

£100 Charles Dick, admr. of Mary Tomlin, decd., with Andrew Buchannan, sec. Aug. 19, 1773.

£200 John Holloday, admr. of John Foster, decd., with Robert Dudley, sec. Oct. 22, 1773.

£1200 Benjamin McWilliams, admr. of William McWilliams, decd., with Joseph Gale and Chas. Todd, sec. April 21, 1774.

£6000 Fanny Houston, admx. of Hugh Houston, decd., with Benjamin Johnston and Gabriel Jones, sec. June 16, 1774.

£500 Ann Butler, admx. of James Butler, decd., with George Durrett and Wm. Butler, sec. July 21, 1774.

£30 James Ward, admr. of John Maxfield, decd., with Andrew Buchannan, sec. July 21, 1774.

£3000 Ann Roy, admx. of John Beverley Roy, decd., with John Lewis and Richard Johnston, sec. Novr. 17, 1774.

£1500 John Lewis, admr. of John Waller, decd., with Edward Herndon, sec. May 18, 1775.

£300 James Hunter, admr. of George Hill, decd., with John Hardia, sec. Mch. 21, 1776.

£200 Margaret McKay, admx. of James McKay, decd., with Stephen Patterson, sec. April 18, 1776.

£500 Alice More, admx. of John More, decd., with Shadrack Moore and John Herndon, sec. Jany 16, 1777.

£200 Wm. Bonnell, admr. of Jacob Wright, decd., with Henry Coleman and Saml. Bonnell, sec. Mar. 20, 1777.

£200 Ambrose Dudley, admr. of Robert Dudley, decd., with John Holloday, sec. Mar. 21, 1777.

£100 John Dedman, admr. of Philip Dedman, decd., with John Hutcherson, sec. Oct. 15, 1777.

£2000 Mary Burbridge, admx. of Benjamin Burbridge, decd., Danl. Branham and Robert Frank, sec. Nov. 20, 1777.

£100 Susannah Collins, admx. of Thomas Collins, decd., with Harry Bartlett, sec. Nov. 20, 1777.

£100 Mary Dolton, admx. of George Dolton, decd., with James Hutcherson and George Hensley, sec. Nov. 20, 1777.

£1000 Benjamin Johnston, admr. of Benjamin Lohore, decd., with John Herndon and John Holloday, Jr., sec. Apr. 16, 1778.

£200 Elizabeth Jones, widow and relict of Thomas Jones, decd., admx. of sd. Thomas Jones; with Edward Simpson, sec. April 16, 1778.

£1000 Charles Proctor, admr. of William Proctor, decd., with John Haydon, sec. May 25, 1778.

£8000 Robt. Smith, admr. of Chas. Smith, decd., with John Brooks and Jos. Gale, sec. "Letter of Peyton Smith, Junr., to court of Spotsylvania Co., "you will be pleased to grant my brother Robert Smith administration on the estate of our Brother Charles Smith, Decd.," etc., etc. July 16, 1770.

£10 Anthony Frazer, admr. of James Frazer, decd., with Edwd. Herndon and Stapleton Crutchfield, sec. Nov. 19, 1778.

£20,000 Gracy Jones, admx. of Richard Jones, decd., with Richard Young and Jesse Haydon, sec. Nov. 18, 1779.

£8000 Mary Skeats, admx. of John Skeats, decd., with John Martin, sec. April 20, 1780.

£5000 John Wright, admr. of James Fulton, decd., with A. Fraser, sec. Decr. 21, 1780.

£40,000 William Allsup, admr. of Francis ——, decd., with B. Alsop and John McColley, sec. Mar. 15, 1781.

£5000 Barbary Quire, admx. of Raymon Quire, with John Almond, sec. Augt. 17, 1781.

£100 Benjamin Sebastine, admr. of Charles Sebastine, decd., with Edward Simpson and John Welch, sec. Oct. 18, 1781.

£500 William Jackson, admr. of William Dunn, decd., with Harry Bartlett, sec. Nov. 15, 1781.

£1000 Ann Cunningham, admx. of James Cunningham, decd., with Thomas Allen and Richard Young, sec. Jany. 17, 1782.

£50 William Burbridge, admr. of "John and William Burbridge, deceased," with Daniel Branham and Tavener Branham, sec. Apr. 18, 1782.

£100 Wharton Schoolar, admr. of Leanna Schoolar, decd., with Joseph Brock, sec. July 18, 1782.

£500 Rice Graves, admr. of Ann Graves, decd., with Joel Parish, sec. Aug. 15, 1782.

£100 Robert Smith, admr. of Peyton Smith, decd., with Robert Frank, sec. Aug. 15, 1782.

£100 Thomas True, admr. of Henry McDaniel, decd., with Edward Brasfield, sec. Sept. 19, 1782.

£5000 John White and Basel White, admrs. of Thomas White, decd., with Peter Stubblefield and Stephen Johnson, sec. Nov. 21, 1782.

£500 Frances Coleman, admx. of Richard Coleman, decd., with John Nelson, sec. May 15, 1783.

£200 Henry Goodloe, admr. of James Colquhoon, decd., with John Woolfork, sec. Oct. 16, 1783.

£1000 Smith Blakey, admr. of George Blakey, decd., with George Stubblefield, sec. Nov. 20, 1783.

£1000 Abram Simons, admr. of Mary O'Neal, decd., with Thomas Allen, sec. March 2, 1784.

£500 William Biggers, admr. of Charles Stewart, decd., with Meacon Biggers, sec. June 1, 1784.

£500 Thomas Bartlett, admr. of estate of "John Waller, which remains unadministered, deceased," etc., with Benjamin Holloday, sec. March 2, 1785.

£100 James Lewis, admr. of Sarah Lewis, decd., with Andrew Buchannan, sec. May 5, 1785.

£500 Joseph Hoomes, admr. of Benjamin Hoomes, decd., with Daniel Branham, sec. June 7, 1785.

£1000 Henry Lewis, admr. of Henry Lewis, decd., with Lewis Holloday, sec. Novr. —, 1785.

£300 Charles Steward, admr. of John Steward, decd., with George Arnold, sec. Nov. 1, 1785.

£100 Daniel Atkinson, admr. of John Ward, decd., with James Owens and Jack Rains, sec. Nov. 1, 1785.

£1000 Betsy St. John, admx. of Isaac St. John, decd., with John Woodfolk, sec. June 6, 1786.

£3000 Milly Johnston, admx. of Aquilla Johnston, decd., with Aquilla Johnston and Henry Goodloe, sec. July 4, 1786.

£1000 John Legg, admr. of Jabez Legg, decd., with Andrew Buchannan, sec. July 4, 1786.

£4000 James Clark, admr., de bonus non, of Edward Southall, decd., with William Clark and John Clark, sec. Nov. 7, 1786.

£500 William Trigg, admr. of James Trigg, decd., with Micajah Poole, sec. Dec. 5, 1786.

£1000 Henry Goodloe, admr. of George Goodloe, decd., with Thomas Goodloe, sec. Jany. 2, 1787.

£200 Elizabeth Olive, admx. of William Olive, decd., with Daniel Ploile and Rice Corner (Conner), sec. Jany. 2, 1787.

£500 Thomas Dillard, admr. of Moses Morris, decd., with John Waller and Ambrose Shackleford, sec. June 5, 1787.

£2000 William Owen, admr. of Jacob Owen, decd., with Thomas Minor, sec. July 3, 1787.

£2000 William Owen, admr. of Mary Owen, decd., with Thomas Minor, sec. July 3, 1787.

£2000 James Weir, admr. of Sarah Marye, decd., with James Heath, sec. June 3, 1788.

£200 Paul Apperson, admr. of Mary Apperson, decd., with John True, sec. July 1, 1788.

£100 Penny Moxley, admr. of William Moxley, decd., with William Jackson, sec. July 7, 1789.

£400 James Lewis, admr., de bonus non, of James Cunningham, decd., with Edward Herndon, sec. Septr. 1, 1789.

£1000 Edwd. Herndon and William Herndon, admrs. of Jacob Whitler, decd., with Wm. Herndon and Edwd. Herndon, sec. Novr. 3, 1789.

£200 Francis Coleman, admr. of Sarah Pollard, decd., with George Taylor, sec. Nov. 1, 1789.

£6000 Ann Chew, admx. of John Chew, decd., with Joseph Brock, sec. March 5, 1789.

£2000 Richard Dickinson, admr., de bonus non, of Nathaniel Dickinson, with William Willis, sec. Septr. 7, 1790.

£500 Reuben Moore, admr. of John Moore, decd., with Daniel Branham, sec. Dec. 7, 1790.

£1500 "Charles Carter, admr., de bonus non, with the last will and testament of Henry Carter, Deceased," etc., with David Pulliam and John Pierce, sec. Jany. 4, 1791.

£200 Michael Robinson, admr. of Richard Breden, decd., with John Robinson, sec. April 5, 1791.

£10,000 Margaret B. Robinson, admx. of Benjamin Robinson, decd., with James Marye, Michael Robinson and John Robinson, sec. April 5, 1791.

£30 John Bullock, admr. of John Bullock, decd., with Thomas Minor, sec. June 7, 1791.

£200 Mary Ashmond, admx. of Thomas Ashmond, decd., with John Herndon and Edward Herndon, sec. July 5, 1791.

£250 Mary Taylor, admx. of George Taylor, decd., with John Day, sec. Sep. 6, 1791.

£20,000 Richard S. Hackley, admr. of William Jackson, decd., with James Lewis, Berkitt Davenport and Charles Croughton, sec. Septr. 6, 1791.

£200 Elizabeth Williams, admx. of Samuel Williams, decd., with Benjamin Steward, sec. Nov. 1, 1791.

£50 Sarah Dempsey, admx. of Jno. Dempsey, decd., with William Trigg, sec. Nov. 1, 1791.

£200 William Schoolar, admr. of Edward Ledwedge, decd., with John Keegar, sec. Jany. 3, 1792.

£5000 Lawrence Brooke, admr. of Richard Brooke, decd., with Fontaine Maury and John T. Brooke, sec. Nov. 6, 1792.

£50 Jacob Stewart, admr. of Elizabeth Williams, decd., with Benjamin Stewart, sec. Nov. 7, 1792.

£500 Joseph Brock, admr. of John Brock, decd., with John Chew, sec. Decr. 4, 1792.

£1000 James Lewis, admr. of William Lewis, decd., with John Steward, sec. Feby. 5, 1793.

£400 "Jeremiah Morton and Richard S. Hackley, admrs., de bonus non, with the will annexed of Robert Jackson, decd.," etc., with Robert Brooke, sec. Apr. 2, 1793.

£20,000 "Jeremiah Morton (is admitted jointly with Richd. S. Hackley) admrs. of Wm. Jackson, decd., unadministered," etc., with James Somerville and James Lewis, sec. July 2, 1793.

£2000 Mary Daniel, admx. of Christopher Daniel, decd., with Walter Chiles and Thos. Boxley, sec. Sept. 3, 1793.

£3000 Robert S. Coleman, admr. of Richard Coleman, Junr., decd., with Spilsbe Coleman, sec. Dec. 3, 1793.

£1000 Francis Thornton, Junr., admx. of Frances Thornton, decd., with Robert Brooke, sec. Feby. 4, 1794.

£100 Eleanor Martin, admx. of John Martin, decd., with Richard Luck, sec. July 1, 1794.

£300 William Stears, admr. of Abel Stears, decd., with William Trigg, sec. Dec. 2, 1794.

£1000 Jos. Bullock and Jas. Bullock, admrs. of John Bullock, decd., with Thomas Minor, sec. Jany. 6, 1794 (1795).

£600 Tilley Emerson, admr. of Francis Simpson, decd., with Edwd. Herndon, Jr., and Reuben Hudson, sec. Jany. 6, 1795.

£500 Robert Lavender, admr. of William Lavender, decd., with John England, sec. April 8, 1795.

$5500 Elizabeth Young, admx. of Lewis Young, decd., with Nathan Smith, sec. Sep. 1, 1795.

$2000 Nathaniel Fox, admr. of William Fox, decd., with William Bronaugh, sec. Septr. 1, 1795.

£1000 Charles C. Robinson, admr. of Benjamin Robinson, decd., with James Newton, sec. Sep. 1, 1795.

£5000 James Frazer, admr. of John Frazer, decd., with William Frazer and Reuben Frazer, sec. Jany. 5, 1796.

£200 Nathaniel Fox, admr. of Elizabeth Frazer, decd., with Anthony Frazer and Joseph Fox, sec. April 5, 1796.

£50 Benjamin Reynolds, admr. of Thomas Reynolds, decd., with Thomas Towles, sec. Septr. 6, 1796.

£150 John Greenhorn, admr. of Jane Gholson, decd., with Francis Coleman, sec. Feby. 7, 1797.

£1200 Thomas Powell, admr. of Thomas Powell, decd., with Edward Hyde, sec. Feby. 7, 1797.

$2000 John Purvis, admr. of Edmund Newton, decd., with Thomas Minor, sec. Dec. 5, 1797.

$2500 Edward Herndon, admr. of Mary Herndon, decd., with John M. Herndon, sec. Jany. 2, 1797.

ADMINISTRATION BONDS

WILL BOOK F

$100 Mary Word, admx. of Margaret Word, decd., with John Peire, Zachariah Shackleford and Joshua Long, sec. July 3, 1798.

$6000 Elizabeth Carpenter, admx. of Jonathan Carpenter, decd., with William Trigg, James Ballard and Clement Montague, sec. Sept. 4, 1798.

£2000 Hugh Hughes, admr. of Thomas Hughes, decd., with James Lewis, Junr., sec. Dec. 4, 1798.

£300 Susannah Parker, admx. of William Parker, decd., with Thomas Winslow, sec. Dec. 4, 1798.

$200 Elijah Barbe, admr. of Margaret Word, decd., with William Henderson, sec. Dec. 4, 1798.

£50 William Willoughby, admr. of John Sorrell, decd., with John Turnley, sec. Jany. 1, 1799.

$1000 Henry Gatewood, admr. of Henry Gatewood, decd., with John Keeton and Richard Estes, sec. July 2, 1799.

$500 Frances Luck, admx. of Richard Luck, decd., with George Smith, sec. Septr. 3, 1799.

GUARDIANS BONDS

WILL BOOK A

£50 William Thomas, guard. to Benjamin Roberts, orph. of John Roberts, with Augustine Smith, sec. Feb. 1, 1725-6.

£200 William Payton, guard. to Benjamin Roberts, orph. of John Roberts, with William Russell, sec. Dec. 6, 1726.

£200 Rice Curtis, guard. to Thomas Merry, Rice Curtis, Jr. sec. Aug. 4, 1730.

£50 Zachary Taylor, guard. to William Lee, orph. of John Lee, with Thomas Chew, sec. Oct. 5, 1731.

£50 John Key, guard. to James Lee, orph, of John Lee, with Zachary Taylor, sec. Oct. 5, 1731.

£1000 John Chew, guard. to Agatha Beverley, orph. of Harry Beverley, with Rodham Kenner, sec. Nov. 6, 1733.

£100 Thomas Estes, guard. to Abraham Rogers, orph. of Peter Rogers, with Zach. Lewis, sec. Aug. 6, 1734.

£150 Edmund Waller, guard. to Isabella Roy, orph. of James Roy, with William Waller, sec. Oct. 6, 1741.

£150 Richard Ship, guard. to Mary Roy, orph. of James Roy, with Edward Herndon and Thomas Ship, sec. Oct. 6, 1741.

£150 John Gordon, Jr., guard. to Sarah Roy, orph. of James Roy, with Edward Herndon and John Parrish, sec. Nov. 3, 1741.

£200 Mary Brock, guard. to Thomas Lyne, orph. of Ann Lyne, with William Robinson and William Waller, sec. June 7, 1743.

£150 John Thornton, guard. of John Willis, Jr., orph. of Henry Willis, with Francis Taliaferro, sec. June 7, 1743.

£150 Isaac Darnell, guard. to Aphia Roy, orph. of James Roy, with Anthony Foster and Daniel Duvall, sec. July 5, 1743.

£100 Francis Thornton, guard. to John Willis, the elder, orph. of Henry Willis, with Francis Taliaferro, sec. Oct. 4, 1743.

£300 Henry Lyne, guard. to Thomas Lyne, an orph. with John Durrett, sec. Dec. 6, 1743.

£300 James Rollings, Jr., guard. to Susanna Holloday, orph. of John Holloday, with John Holloday, sec. Dec. 6, 1743.

£500 Alice Grayson, guard. to John and Ambrose Grayson, orphs. of Ambrose Grayson, with Wm. Cowne and Wm. Williams, sec. July 3, 1744.

£50 Anthony Golston, guard. to Hannah Durram, orph. of Robert Durram, with Joseph Collins, sec. Oct. 2, 1744.

£100 Hancock Lee, guard. to Ann Willis, orph. of Henry Willis, with Anthony Strother, sec. Dec. 4, 1744.

£700 William Waller, guard. to Joseph Brock, orph. of Joseph Brock, with Larkin Chew, sec. July 1, 1746.

£100 John Holloway, guard. to his son Wm. Holloway, with John Chew, sec. Oct. 7, 1746.

£200 Anne Sandige, guard. to John Sandige, orph. of Wm. Sandige, with Benj. Holloday and Joseph Holloday, sec. July 7, 1747.

£50 Moseley Battaley, guard. to Thomas Morris, orph. of Thomas Morris, with George Wythe, sec. Feb. 2, 1747.

£100 William Twyman, guard. to George Twyman, orph. of George Twyman, with John Wood, sec. June 7, 1748.

£2000 Charles Dick, guard. to Lewis Willis, orph. of Henry Willis, with Benj. Grymes, sec. Sept. 5, 1749.

£400 John Gordon, Jr., guard. to Thomas Roy, orph. of James Roy, with Thomas Blossingham and Benj. Martin, sec. July 4, 1749.

GUARDIANS BONDS

WILL BOOK B

£100 William Proctor, guard. to Thomas Morris, orph. of Thomas Morris, with Martin True, sec. Mch. 6, 1749.

£50 Thomas Blossingham, guard. to Mary Mullin, orph. of Daniel Mullin, with William Ellis and Benj. Martin, sec. Aug. 7, 1750.

£100 John Mansfield, guard. to Sharshall Grasty, orph. of Sharshall Grasty, with William McWilliams, sec. Nov. 6, 1750.

£100 John Long, guard. to Bloomfield Long, orph. of Samuel Long, with Nicholas Hawkins, sec. Apr. 2, 1751.

£100 John Mansfield, guard. of George Grasty, orph. of Sharshall Grasty, with Anthony Strother, sec. Sept. 4, 1751.

£500 John Moore, guard. to Jane Thurston. orph. of John Thurston, with Thomas Turner, Jr., sec. Dec. 3, 1751.

£100 Benjamin Davis, guard. to Thomas Morris, orph. of Thomas Morris, with Martin True, sec. Dec. 4, 1751.

£1000 Mary Taliaferro, guard. to Mary Taliaferro, orph. of John Taliaferro, with John Champe and Anchd. McPherson, sec. July 7, 1752.

£50 Nicholas Hawkins, guard. to Elizabeth Long, orph. of Samuel Long, with James Hawkins, sec. July 7, 1752.

£1000 Mary Wiglesworth, guard. to Esther, Sarah, and John Wiglesworth, orphs. of John Wiglesworth, with John Holloday and Henry Lewis, sec. Aug. 4, 1752.

£1000 Mary Wiglesworth, guard. to William Wiglesworth, orph. of John Wiglesworth, with John Holloday and Henry Lewis, sec. Aug. 4, 1752.

£200 William Ellis, guard. to Alexander Davidson, orph. of Alexander Davidson, with Thomas Blossingham and Wm. Lewis, sec. Oct. 3, 1752.

£100 Joseph Collins, guard. to Joyce Collins, orph. of Thomas Collins, with Henry Gatewood, sec. Apr. 2, 1754.

£500 Samuel Hildrup, guard. to Mary and Sarah Redd, orphs. of Thomas Redd, with Robert Duncanson and Roger Dixon, sec. May 8, 1754.

£500 Samuel Hildrup, guard. to Thomas and Wm. Collins, orphs. of Thomas Collins, with Robert Duncanson and Roger Dixon, sec. May 8, 1754.

£100 Roger Dixon, guard. to Elizabeth Redd, orph. of Thomas Redd, with William Waller, sec. July 2, 1754.

£50 Benjamin Davis, guard. to Frances Boswell, orph. of John Boswell, with Joseph Brock, sec. Feb. 5, 1755.

£100 Roger Dixon, guard. to Thomas Redd, orph. of Thomas Redd, with Moseley Battaley, sec. Apr. 1, 1755.

£200 Joseph Collins, guard. to Thomas and Wm. Collins, orphs. of Thomas Collins, with Wm. McWilliams and Hugh Sanders, sec. Apr. 1, 1755.

£100 William Lewis, guard. to Elizabeth Long, orph. of Samuel Long, with Thomas Haydon, sec. Dec. 7, 1756.

£1000 Joseph Brock, guard. to Elizabeth, Frances and Jane Curtis, orphs. of Rice Curtis, with Thomas Rogers. sec. Apr. 5, 1757.

£50 William Burbridge, guard. to Moses and Aaron Burbridge, orphs. of William Burbridge, with Thomas Burbridge and Wm. Lewis, sec. Apr. 6, 1757.

£2000 Fielding Lewis, guard. to Chas. Washington, orph. of Augustine Washington, with John Thornton, sec. Oct. 4, 1757.

£2000 John Thornton, guard. to Mildred Thornton, orph. of Francis Thornton, with Fielding Lewis, sec. Oct. 4, 1757.

£500 Roger Dixon, guard. to Thomas and Wm. Collins, orphs. of Thomas Collins, with William Waller, sec. Nov. 3, 1757.

£2000 Joseph Steward, guard. to Elizabeth Wallace, orph. with Edward Herndon and John Holloday, sec. Apr. 5, 1758.

£12,000 William Taliaferro, guard. to James, William and Martha Hunter, orphs. of William Hunter, with Edward Rice and Joseph Jones, sec. Aug. 2, 1758.

£600 James Pulliam, guard. to Susanna, Isabella and Agnes Pulliam, orphs. of Thomas Pulliam, with David Sandige, sec. Dec. 5, 1758.

£2000 Lawrence Taliaferro, guard. to Elizabeth Taliaferro, orph. of Francis Taliaferro, with Joseph Jones, sec. Dec. 5, 1758.

£400 James Pulliam, guard. to Mary and Benj. Pulliam, orphs. of Thomas Pulliam, with David Sandige, sec. Dec. 5, 1758.

£2000 Charles Gordon, guard. to Joseph, Stephen, Philadelphis, Benjamin, Mary Ann, and Sarah Herndon, orphs. of Joseph Herndon, with Edward Herndon and John Holloday, sec. Oct. 1, 1759.

£2000 Lawrence Taliaferro, guard. to Hay Taliaferro, orph. of Francis Taliaferro, with Reuben Thornton and Chas. Washington, sec. Nov. 5, 1759.

£2000 Lawrence Taliaferro, guard. to John Taliaferro, orph. of Francis Taliaferro, with Reuben Thornton and Chas. Washington, sec. Nov. 5, 1759.

£1000 Joseph Brock, guard. to William Carter, with Edward Herndon, sec. Dec. 3, 1759.

£200 John Holloday, guard. to his son John Holloday, with Edward Herndon, sec. May 6, 1760.

£2000 Richard Brooke, guard. to Francis Taliaferro, orph. of Francis Taliaferro, with William Brooke, sec. June 2, 1760.

£3000 Susannah Carr, guard. to Charles Brooks Carr, Agnes Brooks Carr, Walter Chiles Carr, Phebe Carr, Thos. Carr, orphs. of Wm. Carr, gentl., with Anthony Foster, John Holloday and Wm. Lewis, sec. Nov. 6, 1760.

£6000 Ann Waller, guard. to Dorothy and Mary Waller, orphs. of William Waller, gentl., with Larkin Chew, Beverley Stanard, Joseph Brock and Edward Herndon, sec. Dec. 1, 1760.

£2000 Ann Waller, guard. to Sarah Waller, orph. of Wm. Waller, gentl., with Larkin Chew, Beverley Stanard, Joseph Brock and Edward Herndon, sec. Dec. 1, 1760.

£200 William Wood, guard. to Hannah Wood, orph. of John Wood, with Robert Coleman and Benj. Johnston, sec. Mch. 2, 1761.

£200 William Wood, guard. to Reuben Wood, orph. of John Wood, with Robert Coleman and Benj. Johnston, sec. Mch. 2, 1761.

£4000 Mary Smith, guard. to Mary, Larkin, Elizabeth, Morris, and John Smith, orphs. of John Smith, gentl., with Larkin Chew and Beverley Winslow, sec. Apr. 6, 1761.

£6000 Larkin Chew, guard. to Larkin Smith, orph. of John Smith, gentl., with Henry Heath and Joseph Brock, sec. May 4, 1761.

£100 Benjamin Johnston, guard. to James Wood, orph. of John Wood, with Francis Coleman, sec. June 1, 1761.

£100 John Semple, guard. to John McKenny, orph. of Alexander McKenny, with Wm. Wood, sec. June 1, 1761.

GUARDIANS BONDS

£1000 Alexander Wright, guard. to Agnes Walsh, orph. of John Walsh, with John Semple, sec. Sept. 6, 1762.

£200 Isaac Graves, guard. to Edward Graves, orph. of John Graves, with James Chiles, sec. Aug. 1, 1763.

£500 John Chiles, guard. to Thomas Carr Chiles and Sarah Chiles, orphs. of Henry Chiles, with Walter Chiles, sec. Oct. 3, 1763.

£500 Susanna Chiles, guard. to Elizabeth and Ann Chiles, orphs. of Henry Chiles, with Thomas Wiatt and James Chiles, sec. Oct. 3, 1763.

£250 Mordacai Redd, guard. to Thomas and Wm. Collins, orphs. of Thomas Collins, with Thomas Redd, sec. Mch. 5, 1764.

£200 Benjamin Hayley, guard. to Larkin and Reuben Hayley, orphs. of Thomas Hayley, with Edward Coleman, sec. Mch. 5, 1764.

£1000 Thomas Pulliam, guard. to Benjamin Pulliam, orph. of Thomas Pulliam, with Henry Lewis and John Penn, sec. Apr. 2, 1764.

£1200 Benjamin Johnston, guard. to Caty, Elizabeth, Ann, and Agnes Hawkins, orphs. of John Hawkins, with Oliver Towles, Jr., and William Wood, sec. June 4, 1764.

£1000 John James, guard. to Joseph, Daniel and Henry James, orphs. of George James, with Anthony Strother and Charles Bruce, sec. Aug. 6, 1764.

£600 Michael Robinson, guard. to John Martin, orph. of John Martin, with Robert Dudley and John Battaley, sec. Dec. 3, 1764.

£1000 William Ellis, guard. to Catherine, Elizabeth, Ann and Agnes Hawkins, orphs. of John Hawkins, with John Waller and Wm. Wood, sec. Mch. 4, 1765.

£200 Benjamin Hayley, guard. to Larkin and Reuben Hayley, with William Cave, sec. Mch. 4, 1765.

£3000 Larkin Chew, guard. to Mary and Elizabeth Smith, orphs. of John Smith, gentl., with Joseph Herndon, Wm. Robinson, and O. Towles, Jr., Apr. 1, 1765.

£500 John Battaley, guard. to Samuel Hildrup, orph. of Samuel Hildrup, with Wm. Wood, sec. June 3, 1765.

£800 Richard Coleman, guard. to Samuel Coleman, orph. of John Coleman, with Edward Herndon, sec. Nov. 4, 1766.

£3000 James Hunter, guard. to William Hunter, orph. of William Hunter, with John Glassell and Adam Hunter, sec. Dec. 2, 1766.

£500 Robert Chew, guard. to Catherine, Elizabeth, Ann and Agnes Hawkins, orphs. of John Hawkins, with John Chew, sec. Dec. 7, 1767.

£500 George Chapman, guard. to Leah Durrett, orph. of Robert Durrett, with George Durrett, sec. Dec. 7, 1767.

£500 George Durrett, guard. to Catherine Durrett, orph. of Robert Durrett, with George Chapman, sec. Dec. 7, 1767.

£700 Thacker Vivion, guard. to Joseph and William O. Brock, orphs. of William Brock, with Benj. Waller and Lewis Craig, sec. Oct. 3, 1768.

£1000 Mary Vass, guard. to Martha, Rice and Rachel Vass, orphs. of Philip Vincent Vass, with John Carthrae and Joseph Herndon, sec. Oct. 3, 1768.

£500 William Davenport, guard. to William Graves, orph. of Jonathan Graves, with John Lewis, sec. Nov. 7, 1768.

£100 Drusilla Wisdom, guard. to Tanner Wisdom, orph. of John Wisdom, with George Yates, Jr., and Benj. Winn, sec. Apr. 3, 1769.

£500 Thomas Minor, guard. to Ann Long, orph. of George Long, with John Stewart, sec. June 5, 1769.

£1000 Henry Heath, guard. to his son James, with Roger Dixon and Charles Yates, sec. June 5, 1769.

£500 Joseph Brock, guard. to Joseph and William Oswald Brock, orphs. of William Brock, with John Carter, sec. Sept. 4, 1769.

£2000 William Marshall, guard. to Ann, Richard, Marshall, James and Sally Durrett, orphs. of Richard Durrett, with John Estes and William Rogers, sec. Sept. 4, 1769.

£500 Mary Trigg, guard. to William, Nancy and James Trigg, orphs. of Daniel Trigg, with Thomas Poole and Thomas Duerson, sec. Sept. 4, 1769.

£12,000 Roger Dixon, guard to John and Mary Spotswood, orphs. of John Spotswood, with Rev. John Dixon and Thomas Fox, sec. Oct. 2, 1769.

£1000 Joseph Graves, guard. to John, Mary Ann, Haws and Spencer Coleman, orphs. of John Coleman, with Richard Coleman and John Carthrae, sec. Nov. 6, 1769.

£1000 John Carthrae, guard. to Rice Vass, orph. of Philip V. Vass, with Edward Herndon and Oliver Towles, sec. Sept. 20, 1770.

£200 William Garrett, guard. to William, Thornton and Minor Mead, orphs. of Thomas Mead, with Vincent Vass, sec. Nov. 16, 1770.

£500 Vincent Vass, guard. to Joseph Samms, orph. of James Samms, with Henry Pendleton, John Carthrae and Wm. Garrett, sec. Nov. 16, 1770.

£500 Charles Gordon, guard. to Nancy Gordon, orph. of John Gordon, with Edward Herndon, sec. Mch. 22, 1771.

£5000 Oliver Towles, guard. to Larkin Smith, orph. of John Smith, gentl. with John Lewis and Joseph Herndon, sec. June 20, 1771.

£1000 Joseph Brock, guard. to John Simpson, orph. of Abraham Simpson, with Edward Herndon and John Chew, sec. July 18, 1771.

£1000 Benjamin Johnston, guard. to Ann and Dorothea Brayne Benger, orphs. of Betty Benger, with William Wood, sec. Apr. 16, 1772.

£1000 John Holloday, guard. to Robert, Thomas and Sally Thomas, orphs. of Owen Thomas, with Benjamin Holloday and Joseph Holloday, sec. Apr. 17, 1772.

GUARDIANS BONDS

WILL BOOK E

£500 Reuben Zimmerman, guard. to William and Judith Carter, orphs. of Daniel Carter, with Jacob Whitler, sec. May 22, 1772.

£600, Reuben Zimmerman, guard. to Charles Carter, orph. of Daniel Carter, with John Pattie, sec. June 18, 1772.

£5000 Hugh Houston, guard. to Wm. Houston, orph. of Wm. Houston, with Jacob Whitler and B. Johnston, sec. June 20, 1772.

£2000 Lucy Dixon, guard. to Mildred Dixon, orph. of Roger Dixon, with John Dixon, sec. Septr. 18, 1772.

£20 Thomas Pettit, guard. to his dau. Susannah, with John Waller, sec. Mar. 18, 1773.

£20 John Pritchett, guard. to his son James, with James Pritchett, sec. Mar. 18, 1773.

£2000 Michael Robinson, guard. to Mary Fraser, orph. of George Fraser, with Thomas James, sec. Apr. 3, 1773.

£100 Henry Johnson, guard. to James and John Stevens, orphs. of Jeremiah Stevens, with George Stubblefield, sec. May 20, 1773.

£100 James Brown, guard. to Henry White, orph. of Wm. White, with Joseph Gale, sec. Sept. 17, 1773.

£50 Elizabeth Kelly, guard. to William, Joseph and Griffin Kelly, orphs. of Edward Kelly, with Thomas Collins and Griffin Jones, sec. Augt. 18, 1774.

£1000 John Milcham, guard. to Michael and Harry Robinson, orphs. of Harry Robinson, with James Milcham and Harry Bartlett, sec. Aug. 18, 1774.

£3000 Ann Roy, guard. to Ann, Judy and Bettey Roy, orphs. of John Beverley Roy, with Richard Johnston and Jno. Lewis, sec. Nov. 17, 1774.

£6000 John Lewis, guard. to Hugh Roy, orph. of John Roy, with Oliver Towles and Richard Johnston, sec. Nov. 17, 1774.

£500 John Dillard, guard. to Fielding Dillard, orph. of Thomas Dillard, with George Sheppard and Thomas Dillard, sec. Dec. 5, 1774.

£200 Thomas Jennings, guard. to Charles Carter, orph. of Danl. Carter, with Jas. Brown, Jno. Green, and Jacob Cumes, sec. Jany. 20, 1775.

£100 Thomas Crutcher, guard. to Henry Foster, orph. of John Foster, with Edward Ellis, sec. June 20, 1776.

£100 Bartlet Matthews, guard. to Frances, Sally and Peter Randolph Crawford, orphs. of John Crawford, with Richard Dillard, sec. July 18, 1776.

£3000 Wm. Gausney, guard. to Ann and Agnes Hawkins, orphs. of John Hawkins, with John Kercheval, Richard Eastin and Robert Collins, sec. Dec. 19, 1776.

£500 Michael Yates, guard. to Molly Butler, orph. of James Butler, with George Yates, sec. Sept. 18, 1777.

£2000 Ambrose Dudley, guard. to William Dudley, orph. of Robert Dudley, with Joseph Gale and John Holloday, sec. April 16, 1778.

£200 Edmond Foster, guard. to Thomas Foster, orph. of Thomas Foster, with Henry Bartlett, sec. May 21, 1778.

£8000 Betty Frasher, guard. to William, Reubin and Martha Frasher, orphs. of James Frasher, with Harry Bartlett, sec. Feby. 18, 1779.

£18,000 Lucy Rogers, guard. to Wm., Sarah and Catharine Rogers, orphs. of William Rogers, with George Rogers, Richard Loury, and John Holloday, sec. Feby. 18, 1779.

£1000 John Ellis, guard. to William, Thomas, Eliza, Mildred, Hezekiah and Sarah Ellis, orphs. of Hezekiah Ellis, with Robert O'Neall, sec. March 18, 1779.

£500,000 George French, guard. to Dorothy Brayne Benger, orph. of John Benger, with Andrew Buchanan and James Somerville, sec. June 15, 1780.

£15,000 John Chandler, guard. to Lewis and Ann Day, orphs. of Lewis Day, with Edward Herndon, sec. Octr. 19, 1780.

£100,000 William Stanard, guard. to Beverley Stanard, orph. of Beverley Stanard, with Larkin Stanard, sec. Dec. 21, 1780.

£20,000 Richard Loury, guard. to Elizabeth and Mary Carlton, orphs. of Ambrose Carlton, with Larkin Stanard, sec. Dec. 21, 1780.

£500 William Jackson, guard. to Benjamin Hazlegrove, orph. of John Hazlegrove, with Thomas Allen and Harry Bartlett, sec. July 17, 1782.

£1000 William Ellis, guard. to Eliza, Thomas, Hezekiah, Mildred and Sally Ellis, orphs. of Hezekiah Ellis, with John Ellis, sec. June 20, 1782.

£500 Harry Bartlet, guard. to George Cammack, orph. of William Cammack, with Benjamin Waller, sec. July 18, 1782.

£1500 William Dawson, guard. to John and Susannah Rawlings, orphs. of Thomas Rawlings, with Thomas Towles, Nicholas Payne and Lewis Holloday, sec. Aug. 15, 1782.

£3000 John Rose, guard. to James Marye, orph. of Revd. James Marye, with Thos. Colson and Thos. Duerson, sec. Sept. 19, 1782.

£5000 Mary Daingerfield, guard. to Elizabeth, John, William, Harry, Mary, Ann, Sarah and Willis Daingerfield, orphs. of Wm. Daingerfield, with Thomas Colson and Larkin Smith, sec. Nov. 21, 1782.

£3000 James Weir, guard. to James Marye, orph. of James Marye, with William McWilliams, sec. Nov. 21, 1782.

£3000 John Z. Lewis, guard. to Robert Lewis, orph. of Robert Lewis, with Thomas Towles, sec. Jany. 16, 1783.

£1000 John Hart, guard. to Fielding Estis, orph. of Abraham Estis, with Thomas Montague and Reuben Straughan, sec. Jany. 16, 1783.

£200 Samuel Allen, guard. to Joseph Allen, orph. of Joseph Allen, with Samuel Sale, sec. Feby. 20, 1783.

£100 Harry Bartlet, guard. to William Cammack, orph. of William Cammack, with John Chew, jr., sec. May 15, 1783.

£6000 John Taliaferro, guard. to Edwin Daingerfield, orph. of William Daingerfield, with A. Spotswood, sec. July 17, 1783.

£2000 Benja. Holloday, guard. to John Rawlings, orph. of Thomas Rawlings, with Stapleton Crutchfield, sec. March 2, 1784.

£400 Sarah Crain (Crane), guard. to Elizabeth Turner Crain, orph. of Wm. Crain, with Phillip D. Redd, sec. May 4, 1784.

£2000 John Chew, guard. to Robert and Elizabeth Matilda Carter, orphs. of John Carter, with Joseph Brock, sec. May 4, 1784.

£2000 Joseph Brock, guard. to Hugh Roy, orph. of John B. Roy, with Edward Herndon, sec. May 5, 1784.

£3000 Richard Stevens, guard. to Lucy, Judith and Margaret Carter, orphs. of John Carter, with H. Goodloe, sec. June 1, 1784.

£3000 Augustin Woodfolk, guard. to Ann, Augustin and Elizabeth Lewis, orphs. of John Zachy Lewis, with John Woodfolk, sec. Sept. 7, 1784.

£3000 Robert Hart, guard. to Henry Richard Boucher, orph. of Henry Richard Boucher, with Joseph Graves, sec. Nov. 2, 1784.

£3000 Gerrard Banks, guard. to James Marye, orph. of James Marye, with John Herndon and John Chew, Jr., sec. Feby. 1, 1785.

£4000 Augustin Woodfolk, guard. to Robert Lewis, orph. of Robert Lewis, with Stapleton Crutchfield, sec. Aug. 2, 1785.

£100 Daniel Atkinson, guard. to Charles, Eliza, John, Mary, Thomas and Fanny, orphs. of John Ward, decd., with James Owen and Isaac Rains, sec. Nov. 1, 1785.

£2000 Stephen Johnston, guard. to Benja. Holloday, orph. of Benja. Holloday, with Stapleton Crutchfield, sec. Nov. 1, 1785.

£2000 James Jones, guard. to William Waller, orph. of John Waller, with Thomas Pritchett, sec. Dec. 6, 1785.

£300 William Ail, guard. to Bettley Shackleford, orph. of Richard Shackleford, with Robert Coleman, Wm. Emerson and Bradley Mathews, sec. Mar. 7, 1786.

£5000 Thomas Posey and Mary Posey, guards. to George W. Thornton, Reubin Thornton and Lucy Thornton, orphs. of George Thornton, with William Jones, sec. Novr. 7, 1786.

£500 George Stubblefield, guard. to Owen Thomas Holloday, orph. of John Holloday, Jr., with Thomas Towles, sec. Dec. 5, 1786.

£2000 Micajah Poole, guard. to George Crow, orph. of William Crow, with William Trigg, sec. Dec. 5, 1786.

£4000 John Rogers, guard. to Sarah Rogers, orph. of Wm. Rogers, with George Rogers, sec. Jany. 2, 1787.

£2000 Farish Coleman, guard. to Catharine Rogers, orph. of Wm. Rogers, with Spilsbe Coleman, sec. Jan. 2, 1787.

£500 Abram Simons, guard. to Sally, Benjamin, and Peggy Holloday, orphs. of John Holloday, with John W. Willis, sec. Feby. 6, 1786 (1787).

£200 John Wood, guard. to Polley Holloday, orph. of John Holloday, with Benjamin Alsop, sec. Feby. 6, 1787.

£200 Vincent Vass, guard. to John Holloday, orph. of John Holloday, with Rice Curtis, sec. Feby. 6, 1787.

£200 John Gibson, guard. to Lucy Holloday, orph. of John Holloday, with Edward Herndon, junr., sec. Feby. 6, 1787.

£500 Lucy Proctor, guard. to Ann, William, Charles and Thomas Proctor, orphs. of Charles Proctor, with Alexander Spence Head and John Wigglesworth, sec. Novr. 6, 1787.

£8000 Beverley Stanard, guard. to John Buckner and Baldwin M. Buckner, orphs. of Mordacai Buckner, with William Stanard, sec. Feby. 5, 1788.

£2000 Joseph Brock, guard. to Richard Johnston, orph. of Richard Johnston, with Edward Herndon, sec. Feby. 5, 1788.

£1000 Gerrard Berryman, guard. to Cyrus Berryman, orph. of William Berryman, with Thomas Bartlett, Senr., sec. Sept. 2, 1788.

£2000 Benja. Waller, guard. to Betty, Barbary and Susannah Arnold, orphs. of Benjamin Arnold, with John Waller, sec. Dec. 2, 1788.

£1000 John Waller, guard. to James Arnold, orph. of Benjamin Arnold, with Benj. Waller, sec. Dec. 2, 1788.

£500 Edward Newton, guard. to Lucy Purvis, orph. of Francis Purvis, with John Purvis, sec. Jany. 6, 1789.

£1000 John Purvis, guard. to Alse and Sarah Purvis, orphs. of Francis Purvis, with Edward Newton, sec. Mar. 3, 1789.

£200 Abram Simons, guard. to Polley Holloday, orph. of John Holloday, with James Frazer, sec. Sept. 1, 1789.

£100 John Herndon, guard. to Henry Cunningham and George Cunningham, orphs. of James Cunningham, with William Herndon, sec. Nov. 3, 1789.

£1500 Mary Ann Blaydes, guard. to Nancey, Mary and William Blaydes, orphs. of William Blaydes, with Hawes Coleman and Spencer Coleman, sec. June 6, 1790.

£500 Mary Ann Blaydes, guard. to John Blades, orph. of William Blades, with Spencer Coleman, sec. July —, 1790.

£1000 Hannah Carter, guard. to Elizabeth Carter, orph. of John Carter, with John Chew and James Frazer, sec. Sept. 7, 1790.

£500 James Lewis, guard. to Rebecca Lewis and Charles Lewis, orphs. of James Lewis, with John Herndon, sec. Sept. 7, 1790.

£2000 George Goodloe, guard. to Robert, Aquilla, Henry and George Goodloe, children of, with Daniel Lindsay and Wm. Herndon, sec. Sept. 7, 1790.

£200 Reubin Daniel, guard. to Martha Pollard, orph. of Haz. Pollard, with Benjamin Haley, sec. Nov. 2, 1790.

£2000 Larkin Stanard, guard. to John Chew Buckner, orph. of Mordacai Buckner, with Hugh Roy, sec. Dec. 7, 1790.

£1000 James Crawford, guard. to Phebe Dismukes, orph. of William Dismukes, with James Crawford, sec. Dec. 7, 1790.

£4000 Thomas Minor, guard. to Augustine Edward Scuddy and John Scuddy, orphs. of John Scuddy, with Benjamin Waller and Jonathan Clark, sec. Sept. 6, 1791.

£100 James Powell, guard. to Joseph Reynolds, orph. of Benjamin Reynolds, with William Winslow, sec. Dec. 6, 1791.

£100 James Thomas, guard. to John Holloday, orph. of John Holloday, with John Steward, sec. Dec. 6, 1791.

£200 Thomas Coleman, guard. to Peggy Pemberton, orph. of William Pemberton, with Henry Pemberton and Clement Montague, sec. Jany. 1, 1793.

£2400 Alexander Spotswood, guard. to Hannah Bassett Daingerfield, orph. of William Daingerfield, with William A. Daingerfield, sec. April 2, 1793.

£4800 William A. Daingerfield, guard. to Bland and Henry Daingerfield, orphs. of William Daingerfield, with Alexander Spotswood, sec. April 2, 1793.

£1000 John Chiles, guard. to Fanny Coleman, orph. of Richd. Coleman, Jr., with Thos. Coleman and Robert S. Coleman, sec. Dec. 3, 1793.

£2000 Robert S. Coleman, guard. to Thomas Wootten Coleman and Rice Coleman, orphs. of Richard Coleman, Jr., with Benjamin Waller and Joseph Coleman, sec. Dec. 3, 1793.

£500 Edward Collins, guard. to James, Lewis, Benjamin, Elijah, Richard and Acy Davis, orphs. of Benjamin Davis, with Edward Herndon, Jr., sec. April 1, 1794.

£1000 John Chiles, guard. to Richard Coleman, orph. of Richard Coleman, with Robert S. Coleman, sec. Nov. 4, 1794.

£1000 Edward Herndon, guard. to Stapleton Crutchfield, orph. of Stapleton Crutchfield, with James Lewis, sec. Dec. 2, 1794.

£1000 Edward Herndon, guard. to Thomas Crutchfield, orph. of Stapleton Crutchfield, with James Lewis, sec. Dec. 2, 1794.

£1000 Edwd. Herndon, guard. to Achilles Crutchfield, orph. of Stapleton Crutchfield, with James Lewis, sec. Dec. 2, 1794.

£3500 James Mercer Garnett, guard. to Charles Fenton Mercer, orph. of James Mercer, with John T. Brooke, sec. Jany. 6, 1795.

£300 Edwd. Herndon, Jr., guard. to Gerrard Simpson, Claiborne Simpson, and Elizabeth Simpson, orphs. of Francis Simpson, with Thomas Strachen and Wm. Simpson, sec. July 7, 1795.

$1000 Nicholas Hawkins, guard. to "James Hawkins, child of the sd. Nicholas Hawkins, and grandson of Francis Simpson, decd.," with Tilley Emerson, sec. Augt. 6, 1795.

$1000 Bartlett Perry, guard. to "James Perry and Delphia Perry, children of the sd. Bartlett Perry, and grand-children of Francis Simpson, decd.," with Clement Montague and Michael Robinson, Junr., Sec. Augt. 6, 1795.

£50 William Smith, guard. to his son, Peyton Smith, with John Hart, sec. Sept. 1, 1795.

£1000 William Bronaugh, guard. to Mary Stevens Lurty, orph. of John Lurty, with Nathaniel Fox, sec. Sept. 1, 1795.

£2600 William McGee, guard. to John Scuddy, orph. of John Scuddy, with George Tyler, sec. Decr. 1, 1795.

£400 Henry Wyatt, guard. to Susanna Redd, orph. of Mordacai Redd, with Thomas Minor, sec. Dec. 1, 1795.

£50 John Day, guard. to George Taylor, orph. of George Taylor, with George Bronaugh, sec. Jany. 5, 1796.

£1000 Anthony Frazer, guard. to Thomas Frazer and John Frazer, orphs. of John Frazer, with William Frazer and Reuben Frazer, sec. Jany. 5, 1796.

£1000 Nathaniel Fox, guard. to Elizabeth Frazer and Philadelphia Frazer, orphans of John Frazer, with Joseph Brock and Joseph Fox, sec. Jany. 5, 1796.

£4000 Margaret B. Robinson, guard. to Charles Bruce Robinson, Wm. Pannell Robinson, and Harriott Robinson, orphs. of Benjamin Robinson, with James Marye and Joseph Christy, sec. Jany. 5, 1796.

£100 Nicholas Hawkins, guard. to his son, James Hawkins, with Wm. Simpson, sec. Feby. 2, 1796.

£30 Charles Clark, guard. to Charles Smallwood, orph. of James Smallwood, with Thos. Clark, sec. April 5, 1796.

£3000 Ralph Quarles, guard. to John, Jane and Patsey Quarles, orphs. of William Quarles, with Samuel Sale and Richard Dickerson, sec. April 5, 1796.

£1200 Daniel Coleman, guard. to Francis Coleman, orph. of Richard Coleman, with Henry Goodloe, John Woolfolk, and William Trigg, sec. April 5, 1796.

£1000 Mathew Harris, guard. to Sally Lindsay Coleman, orph. of Clayton Coleman, with William Threldkeld, sec. Apr. 4, 1797.

$1000 Mary Daniel, guard. to Sally Daniel, orph. of Christopher Daniel, with George Bronaugh, sec. Augt. 1, 1797.

$2000 Frances Quarles, guard. to Patsey Quarles, orph. of William Quarles, with Ralph Quarles and William Winslow, sec. July 3, 1798.

GUARDIANS BONDS

WILL BOOK F

$2000 Frances Quarles, guard. to Jane Quarles, orph. of William Quarles, with Ralph Quarles and William Winslow, sec. July 3, 1798.

$3000 Frances Quarles, guard. to John Quarles, orph. of William Quarles, with Ralph Quarles and William Winslow, sec. July 3, 1798.

$1000 Susannah Parker, guard. to Benjamin Winslow, Catharine Beverley, and Thomas Parker, orphs. of William Parker, with William Winslow and Thomas Winslow, sec. Dec. 4, 1798.

£200 William Wilson, guard. to Polly, Betsy, Peggy and Lucy Wilson, children of the said William Wilson, with Jeremiah Wilson, sec. Jan. 1, 1799.

£50 Wm. Ledwedge, guard. to Obed Gregorie, orph. of Jas. Gregorie, with James Long, sec. Jany. 1, 1799.

$1000 Ann Scott, guard. to Day Scott, Polley Scott, Sarah Scott and William Scott, orphs. of William Scott, with David Scott and Henry Robinson, sec. Sept. 3, 1799.

$400 William Jackson, guard. to John Moxley, orph. of William Moxley, with William Shepherd, sec. Septr. 3, 1799.

£1000 Anthony Frazer and William Frazer, guardians to Elizabeth, Patsey and Sarah Frazer, with John Crutchfield and Joseph Herndon, Jr., sec. Dec. 3, 1799.

MARRIAGE LICENSES

From "An Account of Ye Governor's Dues," Order Book 1

*1722—Octr. 3d, John Quarles.

1723—June 7, Robert Slaughter, junr.

1723—Octr. 12, William Johnsons.

1725-6—Jany. 3d, Zach. Lewis.

1726—October 20, John Catlett and Mary Grayson.

1726—Novr. 22—Benjamin Winslow and Susannah Beverley.

1726—Augt. 5, Richard Phillips and Katherine Smith.

1727—Novr. 25, Alexander Howard and Johna. Trippels.

1727—Xber. 16, George Home and Elizabeth Proctor.

1727—March 3, Samuel Hensley and Martha Snell.

1728—Octobr. 22d, Moseley Battaley and Elizabeth Taliaferro.

1729—April 9, John Ward and Alice Symonds.

1729—June 3, Francis Slaughter and Ann Lightfoot.

1729—June 26, John Chew and Margaret Beverley.

1729—Novr. 28—Johnathan Wood and Elizabeth Barefoot.

1729—Xber. 3d, George Wheatley and Mary Henry.

1729-30—March 3d, Chickeley Thacker and Hannah Clowder.

1729-30—June 1, Rodham Kenner and Judith Beverley.

1729-30—June 27, John Tennant and Dorothy Paul.

1729-30—8ber. 6, Joseph Fox and Susannah Smith.

1731—Mch. 1 [Hen]ry Palmer and Ann Burnett.

1731—Apl. 18 [Thom]as Hill and Elizabeth Grayson.

—— Linton and Susannah Grayson.

1731—Oct. 7 [Rich]ard Tutt and Elizabeth Johnson.

1732—Aug. 3 [Wil]liam Woodford and Elizabeth Cock.

1733—Jan. 4 [Ell]iott Benger and Dorothea Brayne.

1733—Jan. 5 [Jam]es Sleet and Euphan Smith.

1733—Sep. 30 [Lark]in Chew, Gent., and Mary Beverley.

1733—Sep. 28 [Rice] Curtis, junr., and Ann Brock.

1734—Jan. 5 [Han]cock Lee and Mary Willis.

1734—Jan. 9 [Wil]liam Conner and Sarah Rogers.

1734—Jan. 25 [An]thony Murray and Mary James.

1734—Oct. 3, John Jones and Agnes Durham.

1735—October 19, George Webb and Lucy Hinkston.

*In the first four marriage records, the name of the woman is not given.

1736—Sep. 3, Francis Thornton and Frances Gregory.

1737—Feby. 17, William Robinson and Agatha Beverley.

1737—May 5, Thomas Duerson and Hannah Brock.

1737—8ber. 21, John Mansfield and Ann Waldo Grasty.

1737—8ber. 16, John Gregg and Elizabeth Waugh.

1737—Xber. 6, Samuel Wharton and Ann Williams.

1738—May 24, Giles Tompkins and Valentine Chiles.

1738—June 21, William Waller and Ann Beverley.

1739—May 13 [Ja]mes Dunn and Elinor Savage.

1739—Sep. 15, John Gordon and Margaret, daughter of Dorothy Tennant.

1739—Nov. 17, Joseph Calvert and Lucy Webb.

1739—Oct. 17, Rev. James Marye and Elinor Purcel Dun.

1740—July 18, James Martin and Mary Lynes.

1740—8ber. 18, Edmond Waller and Mary Pendleton.

1740—8ber. 28, John Thornton and Mildred Gregory.

1741—Xber. 12, John Blake and Elizabeth Thurston.

1742—March 22, Thomas Minor and Alice Thomas.

1742—Decbr. 23, Henry Elley and Esther Herndons.

1743—April 29, Henry Willis and Eliza. Gregory.

1743—March 17, Wm. Cowne and Eliza. Hill.

1744—April 5, William Hunter and Martha Taliaferro.

1744—June 6, Wm. Hughes and Sophia Dowdall.

1744—July 6, Wm. Johnston, Gent., and Betty Taylor.

1744—Augt. 26, James Stevens and Alice Grayson.

1744—Novr. 29, Parmenas Bowker and Ann Stevens.

1745—Feb. —, Robert Dudley and Joyce Gayle.

1745—July 3, Elijah Morton and Elizabeth Hawkins.

1746—June 18, Patrick Connelly and Ann French.

1746—July 28, James Anderson and Margaret Trogs.

1746—Feby. —, Samuel Hildrup and Eliza. Taliaferro.

1747—Novr. 11, Gregory Grant and Sarah Wharton.

1747—Decr. 26th, Mr. George Wythe and Mrs. Anne Lewis.

1747—Decr. 27th, Mr. Richard Shackleford and Mrs. Mary Lewis.

1747—Jany. 26, Mr. Stephen Pettus, Jr., and Anne Dillard.

1747—March 16, The Revd. Mungo Marshall and Lucy Marye.

1748—April 1st, John Harris and Hannah Stevens.

1748—Jany. 20th, John Jones and Barbara Reynolds.

1748—Jany. 31st, Richard Bryan and Frances Battaley.

1748—March 7th, Chas. Julian and Phebe Wilson.

1748—April 20th, Wm. Smith and Ann Bowker.

1749—Jany 16th, Francis Meriwether and Mary Lewis.

1750—April 19th, Beverley Stanard and Eliza. Beverley Chew.

1750—Septr. 27th, Benjamin Pendleton and Mary Macon.

SPOTSYLVANIA CO. COURT MARRIAGE REGISTER

1795–1800

John Spindle and Lucy Sale, April 13, 1795, Thomas Marston.

Burrell Leavell and Mary Purvis, April 13, 1795, Thomas Marston.

William Smith and Judith Farish, April 13, 1795, Thomas Marston.

Benjn. Givin and Sarah Leavell, April 13, 1795, Thomas Marston.

Robt. Cunningham and Elizabeth Stewart, April 13, 1795, Thomas Marston.

Joseph Anderson and Mary Ann Garner, April 13, 1795, Thomas Marston.

Buckerton Washington to Ann Syls Smith, Dec. 7, 1795, H. Goodloe.

James Haney to Dorothy Waller, Dec. 7, 1795, H. Goodloe.

Martin True and Frances Burges, Nov. 26, 1797, Wm. Cooke.

Wm. Carpenter and Phebe Mitchell, Decr. 21, 1797, Wm. Cooke.

William Holmes and Anne Roberts, Feby. 28, 1798, Wm. Cooke.

John McKenney and Elizabeth Smith, March 15, 1797, Jeremiah Chandler.

John Williams and Agnes Simpson, Nov. 16, 1797, Jeremiah Chandler.

William Hame and Pegga Simpson, Nov. 30, 1797, Jeremiah Chandler.

James McDemeath and Nancy Sutton, Dec. 1, 1797, Jeremiah Chandler.

Benj. Wiltshire and Sally Jones, Dec. 21, 1797, Jeremiah Chandler.

Elijah Halbert and Nancy Edge, Jany. 2, 1798, Jeremiah Chandler.

William Rogers and Sarah Branham, Jany. 17, 1798, Jeremiah Chandler.

Jas. Richason and Susanna McKenna, ——, Thos. Mastin.

Chiles Brown and Martha Cary, ——, Thos. Mastin.

John Hughlett and Milly Keaton, Feby. 5, 1798, Thos Mastin.

Elijah Jones and Mary McHorn, April 6, 1798, Jeremiah Chandler.

J. Edwd. Dickerson and Sarah Chandler, May 19, 1798, Jeremiah Chandler.

Isaac Herren and Hannah Mountague, Oct. 7, 1798, Jeremiah Chandler.

Jesse Bradger and Franky Suliven, Dec. 5, 1798, Jeremiah Chandler.

Moses Burbridge and Fanny Haney, Decr. 24, 1798, Jeremiah Chandler.

Edwd. T. Rowzie and Dorothy Waller, Sept. 20, 1798, Hezekiah Arnold, M. G.

James Cash and Sally Willoughby, Octr. 3, 1798, Henry Pendleton.

Robert Clough and Elizabeth Lewis, Feby. 15, 1799, Hezekiah Arnold, M. G.

Joseph Johnson and Elizabeth Bledsoe, Apr. 8, 1799, Jeremiah Chandler.

Charles Oliver and Nancy Cooper, Augt. 8, 1799, Jeremiah Chandler.

James Coleman and Molly Penny, Feby. 15, 1799, Jeremiah Chandler.

William Dodd and Polly Johnson, Octr. 31, 1799, Jeremiah Chandler.

Benjamin Haney and Elizabeth Johnson, Nov. 15, 1799, Jeremiah Chandler.

John Cash and Mildred Daniel, Nov. 22, 1799, Jeremiah Chandler.

William Magee and Caty White, Nov. 26, 1799, Jeremiah Chandler.

Jesse Wayt and Pegga Ballard, Dec. 24, 1799, Jeremiah Chandler.

George White and Sarah Cooper, Dec. 25, 1799, Jeremiah Chandler.

Alexander Wood and Catherine Goodloe, June 4, 1799, H. Goodloe.

Benjn. Johnson and Ann Turnley, June 4, 1799, H. Goodloe.

William Moore and Franky Wheeler, Aug. 25, 1799, Henry Pendleton.

Daniel Trigg and Sally Abbott, Nov. 15, 1799, Henry Pendleton.

Moses Perry and Betsey Turnley, Feby. 15, 1799, Henry Pendleton.

Isaac Knight and Winney Ann Knight, Dec. 25, 1799, Henry Pendleton.

Joseph Metstead and Catherine Smallwood, Dec. 29, 1799, Henry Pendleton.

Philip Garnett and Elizabeth Dudley, April 3, 1799, Tho. Marston.

John Keegan and Ann Long, April 3, 1799, Tho. Marston.

George Riadon and Sally Owen, April 3, 1799, Tho. Marston.

William Shepherd and Rebecca Moxley, April 3, 1799, Tho. Marston.

William Sutton and Elizabeth Moxley, April 3, 1799, Tho. Marston.

DEED BOOK A

1722-1729

Francis Thornton and Mary his wife of Essex Co. and Anthony Thornton and Mary his wife of Stafford Co. to Elizabeth Tapp of Spts. Co. Dated Augt. 24, 1722: Recd. Septr. 4, 1722. 500 lbs. of tobacco. 450 a. of land in Spts. Co. "on ye ridge that lies between ye branches of Massaponnax and the branches of Mattapony river"—part of a tract granted Fran. and Antho. Thornton by patent April 19, 1720. Witnesses: Fran. Conway and Will. Strother.

John x Roberts of St. Geo. Par., Spts. Co., Va., to son-in-law Francis Kerley of St. Geo. Par., Spts. Co. Dated: May 14, 1722. Recd: Septr. 4, 1722. "100 a. on ye mountain run"—patented July 12, 1718. Witnesses: Augt. Smith, Daniel Huff, Abel Maylard.

Augt. 20, 1722. John Spicer of Sittenbourn Par., King Geo. Co., Va., Gent., to John Blanton and Wm. Bartlett of Spts. Co., planters. 5 shill. 100 a. of land in St. Stephen's Par., in Spts. Co., on N. side Mattapony River, adj. Capt. Larkin Chew.

Whereas Jno. Smith, late of Essex Co., by his last will and testament, did bequeath to his son Francis Smith the tract of land of 100 a. whereon the sd. John then lived—the sd. Francis conveyed the sd. land to the sd. John Spicer, etc. Rec. Sep. 4, 1722. Witnesses: George Payne, Edmund Hazell.

Augt. 18, 1722. Larkin Chew of Spts. Co., Va., Gent., to John Spicer of King Geo. Co., Va., £20 currency. 400 a. tract of land in St. Stephen's Par., Spts. Co., on N. side Mattapony River. Witnesses: Tho. Chew, Fran. Hay, Nicho. Ware. Sep. 4, 1722.

Septr. 4, 1722. Larkin Chew, Gent., of Spts. Co., to Nicho. Hawkins of Spts. Co., planter, £24 ster., 400 a. in Spts. Co. joyning the land of Henry Shackleford—part of a pat. granted Chew June 4, 1722. Witnesses: John Spicer, Samuel Loyd. Rec. Sep. 4, 1722.

July 14, 1722. Augustine Smith of Spts. Co., Gent., to Jno. Catlett, junr., and Richard Buckner of Essex Co., £120 sterl., 4000 a. in St. Geo. Par., Spts. Co. Witnesses: Benja. Grubbs, Ann Reynart, Ann x Bell. Rec. Octr. 2, 1722.

Octr. 2, 1722. Larkin Chew of Spts. Co., Gent., to Wm. Richardson of the same Co., planter. £—— sterl., 400 a. in St. Geo. Par., Spts. Co., joyning Francis Smith and William Bartlett—part of patent granted sd. Chew June 4, 1722. Witnesses: Charles Curtis, George Trible, Law. x Franklin. Rec. Octr. 2, 1722.

Octr. 2, 1722. Larkin Chew of Spts. Co., Gent., to Richard Booker of the same Co., Gent. £16 curr. money, 200 a. of land in St. Geo. Par., Spts.

Co., joyning Benja. Robinson—part of tract granted sd. Chew by patent April 26, 1712. Witnesses: John Quarles, John Taliaferro. Rec. Oct. 2, 1722.

Novr. 5, 1722. Wm. Warren and Elizabeth his wife to Saml. Ham. 800 lbs. of lawfull tob., 100 a. in Spts. Co. on ye South Side of ye midle River of Mattapony—part of 1525 a. of land patented by John Rogers, Peter Rogers, John York, Edwd. Pigg and Thos. Gresham. Witnesses: Edward Franklin, Lawrence x Franklin. Rec. Novr. 6, 1722.

July 18, 1722. William Beverley of King and Queen Co. to the Honorable Alexander Spotswood, Esqr., Governor of Va. "Whereas the sd. Alexr. Spotswood and Robert Beverley of the Co. of King and Queen, Gentle., Decd., and Thomas Jones of Wmburg., Mercht., did enter into a copartnership for the carrying on the design of melting and casting of iron, and for that purpose the sd. Beverley and Jones by patent bearing date Feby. 20, 1719, did obtain a grant of 15,000 a. of land in Spts. Co., formerly part of Essex Co., commonly called or known by the name of the Ironmine Land," etc., Robert Beverley's share be devised and bequeathed to the sd. Wm. Beverley, by his last will and testament, the sd. Wm. Beverley disposing of it by this deed to Spotswood for £180 6s. 8d. ster. and £390 0. 1½d. curr. Witnesses: John Waller, R. Booker, Jno. Quarles. Rec. Decr. 4, 1722.

Novr. 6, 1722. Larkin Chew of St. Geo. Par., Spts. Co., Gent., to Saml. Moore of the sd. Par. and Co. 2500 lbs. tobacco, 250 a. of land in sd. Par. and Co. joining Lawrence Franklin and Harry Beverley—part of land granted sd. Chew, June 4, 1722. Witnesses: Wm. Warren, George Trible, Wm. Lynsen. Rec. Febry. 5, 1722–3.

Nov. 6, 1722. Larkin Chew of Spts. Co., Gent., to Edward Franklin of sd. Co., carpenter. £12 ster., 200 a. in Spts. Co., St. Geo. Par., joining lands of Richard Booker and Thomas Edwards—part of sd. Chew's pat. granted June 4, 1722. Witnesses: James Newton, John Chew, Saml. x Ham. Rec. Febry 5, 1722–3.

Nov. 6, 1722. Larkin Chew of Spts. Co., Gent., to Lawrence Franklyn of the sd. Co., planter. £12 ster., 200 a. joining land of Harry Beverley—part of sd. Chew's patent granted June 4, 1722. Witnesses: Jno. Chew, Saml. x Ham, James Newton. Rec. Feby 5, 1722–3.

March 5, 1722. Larkin Chew of Spts. Co., Gent., to Thomas Butler of the sd. Co. £9 ster., 150 a. in St. Geo. Par. joining Wm. Brandagun—part of sd. Chew's patent granted June 4, 1722. Witnesses: John Waller, James Fontaine, William Bledsoe. Rec. April 2, 1723.

March 5, 1722. Larkin Chew of Spts. Co., Gent., to Wm. Brandagun of same Co., planter. 2100 lbs. tob., 150 a. in St. Geo. Par. joining Benja. Robinson—part of sd. Chew's pat. granted June 4, 1722. Witnesses: Jno. Chew, Wm. Johnson, John x Blanton. Rec. April 2, 1723.

March 5, 1722. Larkin Chew of Spts. Co., Gent., to Phillip Brendegen of the same Co., planter. 5 shill. ster. 150 a. of land in St. Geo. Par., Spts. Co., joining Benja. Robinson and Henry Rogers—part of sd. Chew's pat. granted June 4, 1722. Witnesses: John Chew, John x Blanton. Rec. April 2, 1723.

April 2, 1723. Larkin Chew of Spts. Co., Gent., to Samuel Loyd of the same Co. £21 ster. 350 a. in St. Geo. Par., Spts. Co., adjoining the land of Augt. Smith of Gloucester Co., formerly the land of Augustine Warner, Esqr—part of sd. Chew's pat. granted June 4, 1722. Witnesses: W. Russell, Wm. Johnson. Rec. April 2, 1723.

Novr. 3, 1722. Larkin Chew of Spts. Co., Gent., to George Trible of King and Queen Co., Va. 5 shill. ster. 228 a. in Spts. Co. joining the land of Lawrence Franklyn and Robert King—part of sd. Chew's pat. granted June 4, 1722. Witnesses: Thos. Chew, Lawrence x Franklyn, John Chew. Rec. April 2, 1723.

April 5, 1723. Larkin Chew of Spts. Co., Gent., to Jonathan Clark of St. Margaretts Par., King Wm. Co., Va. 4200 lbs. of tob., 533 a. in St. Geo. Par., Spts. Co., joining Wm. Richardson—part of sd. Chew's pat. granted June 4, 1722. Witnesses: W. Russell, Jno. Chew, Wm. Johnson. Rec. April 2, 1723.

April 2, 1723. Larkin Chew of Spts. Co., Gent., to Danl. Brown of South Farnham Parish, Essex Co., Va. 9600 lbs. of tob., 800 a. in St. Geo. Par., Spts. Co., joining Col. John Robertson—part of sd. Chew's patent granted June 4, 1722. Witnesses: W. Russell, Wm. Johnson, Jno. Chew. Rec. April 2, 1723.

Novr. 6, 1722. Larkin Chew of Spts. Co., Gent., to Wm. Lyndsay of the same Co., planter. £12 ster., 200 a. in St. Geo. Par., Spts. Co., on the North Side of the River Po—part of sd. Chew's pat. granted formerly. Witnesses: Christopher x Bell, Jno. Chew, James Newton. Rec. April 2, 1723.

March 5, 1722. Larkin Chew of Spts. Co., Gent., to Henry Rogers of the sd. Co., planter. £12 curr., 200 a. in St. Geo. Par., Spts. Co., joining Majr. Benja. Robinson—part of sd. Chew's pat. granted June 4, 1722. Witnesses: Jno. Chew, Cha. x Duett, Wm. x Richardson. Rec. April 2, 1723.

Novr. 2, 1722. Larkin Chew and Hannah Chew of Spts. Co. to John Landrom of the same Co. £30 ster., 595 a. in Spts. Co. joining Fran. Smith. Witnesses: Geo. Trible, Law. x Franklyn, Jno. Chew. Rec. April 2, 1723.

April 2, 1723. Robert King of St. Geo. Par., Spts. Co., to Abraham Brown of Southfarnham Parish, Essex Co. £10 ster., 100 a. in St. Geo. Par., Spts. Co., on the South Side the River Po. Witnesses: John Foster, John Huskey. Rec. July 2, 1723.

Novr. 5, 1722. Larkin Chew of St. Geo. Par., Spts. Co., Gent., to Wm. Hutcherson of the same Co., planter. £6 ster., 100 a. in St. Geo. Par., Spts. Co., on the North Side the River Po. joining the land of Edward Franklyn—part of sd. Chew's pat. granted as formerly. Witnesses: Wm. Warren, Saml. Loyd, Saml. Moor. Rec. Augt. 6, 1723.

Augt. 2, 1723. Henry Goodloe of St. Geo. Par., Spts. Co., Gent., to Mark Wheeler of the sd. Co. £10 ster., 100 a. in St. Geo. Par., Spts. Co. Witnesses: Thomas Chew, John Chew, Robert x Evans. Rec. Augt. 6, 1723.

July 8, 1722. Robert Smith of the County of Essex, planter, to Alexander Spotswood of Spotsylvania Co., Esqr. £320 ster., "all those messuages, tennants, plantations and land lying and being on both sides of the mouth of a large creek called Massaponnax, in Spts. Co., formerly part of Rappk. Co.—imputed to be 2000 a. of land," on Rappahannock

River. Witnesses: Jno. Roy, Law. Battaile, Jos. Delaney, Mark Shephord, Rec. Septr. 3, 1723—"at which time likewise Dorothy Roy's power of attorney to Jno. Waller to impower him to acknowledge her right of dower of the above said deed," etc.

Septr. 3, 1723. Ann Barrow, widow of Edward Barrow, late of the Co. of Richmond, Gentl., decd., and Edward Barrow, son and heir of the sd. Edward Barrow, to Hon. Alexander Spotswood of Germanna, Spts. Co., Esqr. £35, 177 a. and 46 perches of land in St. Geo. Par., Spts. Co., "at or near the mines."

"Whereas the sd. Edwd. Barrow, decd., late husband of the sd. Ann Barrow and father of the sd. Edward Barrow, party to these presents, by his last will and testament proved in Richmond Co., 7 March, 1721, amongst other things did impower his executor to sell all that tract or parcel of land at ye mines, etc., and by the sd. will did appoint the said Ann Barrow and Edwd. Barrow, Executors," etc. Witnesses: Jno. Metcalfe, Wm. Keith, Jno. Henderson. Rec. Sept. 3, 1723.

Oct. 1, 1723. Larkin Chew of Spts. Co., Gent., to James Sames of Southfarnham Parish, Essex Co. 3600 lbs. of tob., 300 a. of land in St. Geo. Par., Spts. Co., on S. side Mattapony—part of a tract of land granted the sd. Chew. Witnesses: Saml. Sinclare, Tho. Hammond, junr. Rec. Oct. 1, 1723.

Oct. 7, in the 10th year of King George. Larkin Chew of Spts. Co., Gent., and Hannah, his wife, to Joseph Brock of King and Queen Co., Va., Gentl. £320 curr., 9020 a. in Spts. Co., which lands were granted sd. Chew by patents, June 4, 1722 and June 12, 1723. Witnesses: James Taylor, H. Bowcock, Benja. Needler. Rec. Decr. 3, 1723.

Oct. 6, 1723. Augustine Smith of St. Geo. Par., Spts. Co., to Augustine Smith of Petsworth Par., Glo. Co., Va. £60, "1000 a. of land in St. Geo. Par., Spts. Co., adj. the patent formerly granted to Colo. Augt. Warner and now in the possession of the sd. Augt. Smith of Gloucester." Witnesses: Samuel Clark, Rebekea Cohone, Thomas x Ellis. Rec. Decr. 3, 1723.

Feby. 10, 1723. John Quarles of St. Geo. Par., Spts. Co., to John Blackley of the same Co., planter. 5 shill. ster., 180 a., "all ye land lying on ye north side of Nussaponnax granted to the sd. John Quarles, by patent, Sep. 30, 1723." Witnesses: Danil Huff, Robert Green, Francis x Kerkley. Rec. March 3, 1725.

Decr. 25, 1723. Francis Thornton of Essex Co. and Anthony Thornton of Stafford Co., gentlemen, to Benjamin Morris of Spotsylvania Co., planter. 200 a. in Spts. Co., 530 lbs. of tobacco yearly for 99 years. Witnesses: Law. Battaille, Henry Martin. Rec. April 7, 1724.

Decr. 25, 1723. Francis Thornton of Essex Co. and Anthony Thornton of Stafford Co., Gentl., to James Sparks, planter. 200 a. of land in Spts. Co., 530 lbs. of tobacco yearly for 99 years. Witnesses: Henry Martin, Law. Battaille. Rec. April 7, 1724.

Decr. 25, 1723. Francis Thornton of Essex Co. and Antho. Thornton of Stafford Co., Gentl., to Leonard Night, planter. 140 a. of land in Spts. Co., 530 lbs of tobacco yearly for 99 years. Witnesses: Thos. Smith, John Mulkey. Rec. April 7, 1724.

Feby. 11, 1723. Robert x Slaughter, Senr., of Essex Co., to his son, Robert Slaughter, junr., of Spts. Co. £50 ster., 470 a. in Spts. Co.—granted sd. Slaughter, Senr., by patent Feby. 20, 1719. Witnesses: Fran. Thornton, Jo. Taliaferro, 'Law. Battaile, Tho. Smith. Rec. April 7, 1724.

April 6, 1724. William Skrine of Hanover Par., King Geo. Co., Va., to Richard Barnes of North Farnham Par., Richmond Co. £50 ster. and £50 cur. money of Va. and 20,000 lbs. weight of tobacco, "all that tenement, plantation and tract of land in the fork of Rappa. River in St. Geo. Par., Spts. Co., 1200 a. pat. by the sd. Skrine, Reuben Welch of Southfarnham Par., Essex Co., and Wm. Winstone of St. Ann's Par., Essex Co., Augt. 7, 1720. Witnesses: John Crump, Edward Barrow. Rec. April 7, 1724. . John Waller having proved Margaret Skrine's power of attorney in court acknowledged all her right of dower to the sd. land unto the sd. Richd. Barnes.

May 5, 1724. Francis x Browning of St. Ann's Par., Essex Co., Va., to Edward Rowzee of same Par. and Co. £40 curr., 250 a. on N. side River Poo of Mattapony in Spts. Co., being part of land granted Larkin Chew and adjoining the lands of Francis Smith, John Blanton and Wm. Bartlett, etc., etc. Witnesses: John Waller, John Quarles, John x Blanton. Rec. June 2, 1724.

May 4, 1724. Lawrence x Franklyn of St. Geo. Par., Spts. Co., to Samuel More of the same Par. and Co. £3 ster., 30 a. in Spts. Co., St. Geo. Par., S. side of Barnitt Pains Branch. Witnesses: John Foster, Abraham x Brown, James Estham. Rec. June 2, 1724.

May 5, 1724. Larkin Chew of St. Geo. Par., Spts. Co., Gent., to Henry Martin of the same Co., planter. 3600 lbs. Tob., 300 a. of land in St. Geo. Par., Spts. Co., joining Wm. Lindsay. Witnesses: Saml. Lloyde, R. Bayley. Rec. June 2, 1724.

June 2, 1724. Henry Webber of St. John's Parish, King Wm. Co., Va., Gent., to Henry Chiles and John Chiles, heirs of John Chiles, Gent., decd., of St. Margaretts Par. £100 current. 200 a. in St. Geo. Par., Spts. Co., granted sd. Webber by pat., Octr. 28, 1723. The sd. Henry and John Chiles, heirs at law of John Chiles, decd., are only to have but 1334 a. of the sd. land until the decease of Elender Hickman, wife of Edwin Hickman, and Relict of ye sd. John Chiles, decd. Witnesses: James Cox, Fran. Conway, John Hawkins. Rec. June 2, 1724. Jno. Quarles having first proved Mrs. Jane Webber's power of attorney to him in court, acknowledged all ye sd. Janes right of dower to the above deeded land to Henry and John Chiles.

June 2, 1724. Henry Webber of St. John's Par., King Wm. Co., Va., Gent., to Edwin Hickman and Elender, his wife, of St. Geo. Par., Spts. Co., Gent. 20 shill., 666 a. in St. Geo. Par., Spts. Co., granted sd. Webber by pat., Octr. 28, 1723. "Edwin Hickman and Elender, his wife, relict of John Chiles, Gent., decd." Witnesses: James Cox, Franc. Conway, John Hawkins. Rec. June 2, 1724.

July 7, 1724. John Wilkins of St. Geo. Par., Spts. Co., Planter, to Dannett Abney, Senr., of St. Margaretts Parish, King Wm. Co., cooper, and Dannett Abney, Junr., of St. Geo. Par., Spts. Co., carpenter. 4600 lbs. tob. and 280 a. of land in St. Paul's Par., Hanover Co., 400 a. in St. Geo.

Par., Spts. Co., granted sd. Wilkins by patent. Witnesses: John Kembrow, John x Gamball, John x Dolly. Rec. July 7, 1724. James Conner, by virtue of a power of attorney, did acknowledge "Mary Wilkins' right of dower of her said husband's land."

April 16, 1724. John Quarles of St. George's Par. Spts. Co., to Richard Cheek of the same parish and Co. £13 ster., 70 a. in St. Geo. Par., Spts. Co., being part of a tract granted the sd. Quarles by pat. Sep. 30, 1723. Witnesses, Henry Conyers, Z. Lewis, R. Bayley. Rec. July 7, 1724. John Waller, by power of attorney, acknowledged Ann Quarles' right of dower to the above land.

June 3, 1724. Samuel Loyd of St. Ann's Par., Essex Co., and Larkin Chew of St. Geo. Par., Spts. Co., to William Russell of Drysdale Par., King and Queen Co. £36 ster., 614 a. in Spts. Co., being part of a pat. granted the sd. Chew June 14, 1722, and whereon the sd. Loyd lived for awhile and built a small house. Witnesses: Moseley Battaley, R. Bayley. Rec. July 7, 1724.

April 5, 1724. John Blackley of Spts. Co., planter, to James Atkins of the same Co., planter. 1200 lbs. of tob., 100 a. in St. Geo. Par., Spts. Co., by Nassaponnax Run, joining Francis Thornton. Witnesses: Moseley Battaley, Ja. Conner. Rec. Augt. 4, 1724.

Septr. 4, 1724. John Byram of Southfarnham Par., Essex Co., to Philemon Cavenah of St. Geo. Par., Spts. Co., 4000 lbs. tob., 150 a. on S. Side Rappk. River in St. Geo. Par., Spts. Co.—part of a tract formerly granted John Bowey and since his death reverting to the Crown, was granted Augt. Smith, Gent., by patent, Octr. 22, 1712, the sd. Augt. Smith selling unto Henry Byram, by deeds dated Sep. 6 and 7, 1714, whose son and heir the said John Byram is. Witnesses: M. Battaley, Richard Johnson, George Tilley, James Williams. Rec. 6 of Oct. 1724.

May 6, 1724. John Hannis and Catherine, his wife, late of the Island of Barbadoes and now of Essex Co., Va., to Robert Beverley of Essex Co. £60 ster., 1000 a. of land in Spts. Co. Witnesses, Benja. Robinson, Archd. McPherson, Nicho. Davis. Rec. Octr. 6, 1724.

Septr. 12, 1724. Harry Beverley of Spts. Co., Gent., to Joseph Smith of King and Queen Co., Gent. £5 currt., 32 a. in Spts. Co., St. Geo. Par., about one mile above the falls of a Branch of Mattapony, called Po— being the upper part of sd. Beverley's Tract, patented by him, called Newlands, etc. Witnesses: Danll. Huff, R. Bayley, Thos. Chew. Rec. Octr. 6, 1724.

Septr. 10, 1724. Larkin Chew of St. Geo. Par., Spts. Co., Gent., to James Sames of Southfarnham Par., Essex Co. 480 lbs. tob., 34 a. joining Daniel Brown, Jacob Christopher Zallicoffer, and the sd. Sames, being part of a pat. granted sd. Chew June 4, 1722. Witnesses: Jer. Clowder, Wm. x Bradburn, Thos. x Green. Rec. Octr. 6, 1724.

Octr. 7, 1724. Joseph Waugh of Stafford Co., planter, to Honble. Col. Alexander Spotswood of Spots. Co. £5 currt., 436 a. on S. side of Rappa. River in the fork, in Spts. Co. Witnesses: Fra. Hay, Thos. Smith, John Lee. Rec. Octr. 6, 1724.

Octr. 3, 1724. Larkin Chew of St. Geo. Par., Spts. Co., Gent., to Wm. Bradbourne of Southfarnham Par., Essex Co. 2400 lbs. tob., 200 a. in

St. Geo. Par., Spts. Co.—part of pat. granted sd. Chew June 4, 1722. Witnesses: Jer. Clowder, James Sames, Thos. x Green. Rec. Oct. 6, 1724.

Octr. 31, 1724. Elizabeth x Tap of St. Geo. Par., Spts. Co., Va., widow, to my two sons, William Tap and Vincent Tap, and my daughter, Charity Wood, wife of Bartholomew Wood, all of the said parish and County. £40 ster. To my son Wm. Tap the plantation whereon I now live with 175 a. adjoining, in St. Geo. Par., Spts. Co. To my son, Vincent Tap, 175 a. of land St. Geo. Par., Spts. Co. To my daughter, Charity Wood, 100 a. of land in the sd. parish and county—all the above mentioned land purchased by me of Francis Thornton and Mary, his wife; and Anthony Thornton and Winifred, his wife, as by deeds dated Augt. 5, 1722. Witnesses: Moseley Battaley, Richard Johnson, James Williams. Rec. Nov. 3, 1724.

Octr., 1724. Elizabeth x Tap to her sons, Wm. and Vincent Tap: Goods and chattels and personal property. Same witnesses as to preceding deed. Rec. Novr. 3, 1724.

June 27, 1724. Henry Rogers of St. Geo. Par., Spts. Co., planter, to Larkin Chew of the same parish and county, Gent. £12 curr., 200 a. on S. side River Po,. adjoining Majr. Benja. Robinson, Phillip Brandegun and Joseph Brock. Witnesses: John Snall, John x Pane, William x Hutching, Junr. Rec. Novr. 3, 1724.

Novr. 3, 1724. Thomas Chew of St. Geo. Par., Spts. Co., Gentl., to John Hawkins of St. Anne's Par., Essex Co., Gent. £80 ster., 1280 a. granted to said Chew by patent June 12, 1723, in St. Geo. Par., Spts. Co. No witnesses. Rec. Novr. 3, 1724.

Novr. 3, 1724. Larkin Chew of St. Geo. Par., Spts. Co., Gent., to John Hawkins of St. Anne's Par., Essex Co., Gent. £95 ster., 501 a. in St. Geo. Par., Spts. Co.—part of a pat. granted the sd. Chew June 4, 1722, and joining the sd. Chew, Majr. Wm. Todd and Mrs. Mary Waller. No witnesses. Rec. Novr. 3, 1724.

April 6, 1725. Robert Coleman of King and Queen Co. to George Carter of Spts. Co. £25 ster., 200 a. in Spts. Co. adjoining the land of Col. John Robinson—part of a pat. granted sd. Coleman Decr. 2, 1723. Witnesses: Wm. Johnson, Samuel Moor, Edwd. Franklyn. Rec. April 6, 1725.

May 3, 1725. Robert King of St. Geo. Par., Spts. Co., to Anthony Foster of St. Anne's Par., Essex Co. £10 ster., 100 a. in St. Geo. Par., Spts. Co., on S. side River Po. Witnesses: Samll. Moor, John Foster, Abraham x Brown. Rec. May 4, 1725.

April 6, 1725. Harry Beverley of Spts. Co. to Andrew Harrison of Essex Co. 4600 lbs. of tobacco, 600 a. in Spts. Co. part of a pat. granted sd. Beverley. Witnesses, Moseley Battaley, Richard Bayley. Rec. June 1, 1725.

July 6, 1725. Harry Beverley of Spts. Co., Gentl., to John Hawkins of King Wm. Co., planter. £20 ster., 400 a. on N. E. side of Pamunkey River and on both sides of mouth of Terry's Run, alias Jigging River, part of a pat. granted the sd. Beverley in St. Geo. Par., Spts. Co. Witnesses, John Chew, Richd. Bayley, Zachary Lewis. Rec. July 6, 1725.

May 27, 1725. James Taylor of St. Stephen's Par., King and Queen Co., Va., to John Rucker of the same County. 5 shill. ster., 100 a. in St.

Geo. Par., Spts. Co.—part of pat. granted sd. Taylor July 21, 1722. Witnesses: W. Russell, R. Bayley, Samll. Loyd. Rec. July 6, 1725.

July 6, 1725. William Russell of St. Geo. Par., Spts. Co., to Thomas Chew of the same parish and county. £36 ster., 614 a. whereon Saml. Loyd lived—originally granted one Larkin Chew, by pat., June 4, 1722, and by sd. Chew sold to sd. Loyd, and by the sd. Loyd and Chew sold to Wm. Russell, as by deeds having date July 7, 1724. Witnesses: Moseley Battaley, Zachary Lewis, Richard Bayley. Rec. July 6, 1725.

July 1, 1725. James Taylor of Drysdale Par., King and Queen Co., Gent., to John Taliaferro of St. Geo. Par., Spts. Co., Gent. 5 shill. ster., 1260 a. of land, which is the remaining part of an order of Councill granted to Francis and Anthony Thornton, May 2, 1718, for 4000 a. (which 1260 a. by a noat from under the hands of the said Thorntons directed to me May 1, 1721, ordered to be surveyed for the sd. Jno. Taliaferro, as by the said noat will appear) and is included within the bounds of a patent of 8500 a. granted to the above sd. James Taylor, July 21, 1722 —lying in St. Geo. Par., Spts. Co. Witnesses: W. Russell, Richd. Bayley, Samll. Loyd. Rec. July 6, 1725.

May 27; 1725. James Taylor of St. Stephen's Par., King and Queen Co., to Thomas Rucker of St. Ann's Parish, Essex Co. 5 shill., 100 a. in St. Geo. Par., Spts. Co., part of a pat. granted sd. Taylor May 21, 1722. Witnesses: W. Russell, Richd. Bayley, Samll. Loyd. Rec. July 6, 1725.

May 27, 1725. James Taylor of St. Stephen's Par., King and Queen Co., to Edward Tinsley of the same parish and county. 5 shill., 100 a. in St. Geo. Par., Spts. Co.—part of a pat. granted sd. Taylor July 21, 1722. Witnesses: W. Russell, Richd. Bayley, Samll. Loyd. Rec. July 6, 1725.

July 6, 1725. James Taylor of Drysdale Par., King and Queen Co., Gentl., to Anthony Gholstone of St. Geo. Par., Spts. Co. 50 lbs. tob., 200 a. on ye S. side of Holloday's swamp, St. Geo. Par., Spts. Co. Witnesses: W. Russell, Richd. Bayley, Samll. Loyd. Rec. July 6, 1725.

May 27, 1725. James Taylor of St. Stephen's Par., King and Queen Co. to Thomas Jackson, of the same par. and Co. 5 shill., 100 a. of land, part of pat. granted sd. Taylor July 21, 1722, in St. Geo. Par., Spts. Co. Witnesses: W. Russell, Richd. Bayley, Samll. Loyd. Rec. July 6, 1725.

July 6, 1725. James Taylor of Drysdale Par., King and Queen Co., Gent., to John Davison of St. Geo. Par., Spts. Co., planter. 50 lbs. tob., 100 a. of land in St. Geo. Par., near the South West Mountains in Spts. Co., joining George and Erasmus Taylor. Witnesses: W. Russell, Richd. Bayley, Samll. Loyd. Rec. July 6, 1725.

August 24, 1725. James Bridgeforth of St. Stephen's Par., King and Queen Co., to Gawin Corbin of Stratton Major Par., King and Queen Co., Gent. £50 curr., 400 a. of land in St. Geo. Par., Spts. Co., formerly in Stratton Major Par., King and Queen Co.—granted by pat. to the sd. Bridgeforth Feby. 20, 1719. Witnesses: Z. Lewis, Wm. Flett, Benja. Needler. Rec., Chr. Beverley, Septr. 7, 1725.

August 4, 1725. James Bridgeforth to Col. Gawin Corbin. Bill of Sale for Cattle, etc., on the plantation transferred in the foregoing deed. Same witnesses. Rec. Septr. 7, 1725.

Octr. 1, 1725. William Strother of King George Co., planter, to George Proctor of Spts. Co., planter. £100 ster., 1500 a. in Spotsylvania Co., on ye Branches of ye Hasell Run—"it being the fourth part of a grant to Wm. Cocke, Esqr., Chickley Corbin Thacker, Francis Thornton, junr., and William Strother, party to these presents, in joynt partnership," by patent dated Decr. 20, 1718, joining the lands of Majr. Augustine Smith, Buckner & Rashton, and Mann Page, Esqr. Witnesses: Henry Conyers, Moseley Battaley, William x Hackny. Rec. Oct. 5, 1725.

June 27, 1725. Larkin Chew of St. Geo. Par., Spts. Co., Va., Gent., to Samuel Loyd of the same parish and county. £10 ster., 100 a. in St. Geo. Par., Spts. Co.—part of sd. Chew's pat. granted June 4, 1722. Witnesses: Thos. x Green. Rec. Oct. 5, 1725.

Octr. 2, 1725. Larkin Chew of St. Geo. Par., Spts. Co., Gent., to Nicholas Copland of Essex Co., Va. £16 ster., 284 a. in Spts. Co. Witnesses, William Johnson, Robert King, John Chew. Rec. Octr. 5, 1725.

Octr. 4, 1725. Bond of George x Proctor of Spts. Co. to Walter Francis of the same Co., his heirs, Execr. and Adms. Whereas the sd. Walter Francis by his deed dated Augt. 2, 1714, recorded in Richmond Co. Court, did give unto the sd. George Proctor, after the decease of him, the said Walter, a certain tract of land," etc. Witnesses: Wm. Thornton, Francis x Turnley. Rec. Octr. 5, 1725.

Govr. Alexr. Spotswood's proclamation naturalizing "Jacob Haltxclow, a native of Nassaac Siegen in Germany, having settled and inhabited for several years in the County of Stafford." Dated, "at Williamsburg, this 11th day of July, 1722."

March 30, 1725. Thomas Warrin of Spotsylvania Co. to his daughter Rachell Askew, wife of John Askew, a tract of land containing 95 a. on S. Side Middle River in Spts. Co. Witnesses: Austin Ellis, Jacob x Brooks, John x Elson. Rec. Novr. 2, 1725.

Novr. 1, 1725. Samuel Loyd of St. Geo. Par., Spts. Co., planter, to John Roy of St. Mary's Parish, Essex Co., planter. £12 curr., 121 a. of land in St. Geo. Par., Spts. Co. Witnesses: John Chew, William x Logan, Richd. Bayley, Wm. Johnson. Rec. Novr. 2, 1725. Sarah Loyd, wife of Samuel Loyd, in consideration of 5 shill., relinquished her dower to the above tract of land, to John Roy. Octr. 30, 1725.

Octr. 27, 1725. George x Proctor of Spotsylvania Co., Va., to James Roy of the same Co. 3000 lbs. tobacco, 107 acres in St. George Par., Spts. Co., on Haslee Run. Witnesses: John James, Charlesste Ward, Thomas x Morris. Rec. Novr. 2, 1725.

Octr. 27, 1725. George x Proctor, planter, of St. Geo. Par., Spts. Co., "to my daughter Mary, and Charles Stewart her husband," etc., a tract of land in St. Geo. Par., Spts. Co. Witnesses: John James. G. Home, Thomas x Morris. Rec. Novr. 2, 1725.

Oct. 27, 1725. George x Proctor of Spts. Co. to Thomas Morris of the same Co. 6000 lbs. tob., 200 a. in St. Geo. Par., Spts. Co., on Hazlee Run. Witnesses: John James, James x Roy, G. Home. Rec. Novr. 2, 1725.

February 3, 1725. Lawrence x Franklyn of Spts. Co. to Thomas Graves of the same Co., planter. 3500 lbs. tob., 170 a. of land adjoining the land of Harry Beverley, etc. Witnesses: P. Rogers, Edward Pigg, John Foster. Rec. March 1, 1725-6.

April 5, 1725. George Trible of King and Queen Co., Va., to William Johnson of Spots. Co. £12 ster., 228 a. of land in Spots. Co.—the sd. land bought by the sd. Trible from Larkin Chew June 4, 1722, joining the lands of Robert King, Edward Pigg, Barnett Payne and Lawrence Franklyn. Witnesses: Thos. Chew, John Foster, Richd. Bayley. Rec. April 5, 1726.

Jany. 25, 1725. Edward Rowzee of Essex Co. to Thomas Turner of King George Co. £40 curr. money, 250 a. of land in St. Geo. Par., Spts. Co., formerly bought by the sd. Rowzee of Francis Browning. Witnesses: Mary x Merritt, Edwd. Barradall, Moses x Wrathwell, James Markham. Rec. April 5, 1726.

May 3, 1726. William Hansford of St. Geo. Par., Spts. Co., to William Arven and William Beckman of the same parish and county. 3000 lbs. tob., 400 a. of land granted the sd. Hansford, by pat. dated May 14, 1723, on Massaponnax Branch. Witnesses: Jno. Quarles, Benja. Grayson, Richd. Cheek. Rec. May 3, 1726. Sarah Hansford, wife of Wm. Hansford, by Jno. Quarles, her attorney, relinquished her right of dower to the sd. land to the sd. Arven & Brockman.

Octr. 29, 1725. Augustine Smith of Spts. Co., Gent., to Johnathan Gibson, junr. of Essex Co., Gent. £100 ster., 400 a. of land lying in Spotsylvania Co.—part of a pat. grant. the sd. Smith, Augt. 21, 1719. Witnesses: Jno. Catlett, Wm. Taliaferro, Fran. Slaughter, Jno. Grayson, junr. Rec. Novr. 1, 1726.

August 8, 1726. John Shelton of Spots. Co., planter, to Augustine Smith, of the same Co., Gentl. £50 ster., 800 a. of land in St. George's Par., Spts. Co., in the fork of Rappa. River. Witnesses: Rowland Cornelius, J. Barbour, Abra. Kengan, Thomas x Berry, Edward x Newgant, Thos. Smith. Rec. Novr. 1, 1726.

July 6, 1726. Isaac Walters of Spotsylvania Co., planter, to Thomas Smith and Augustine Smith, junr., Gentl., of the same County. £50 ster., 802 a. of land in St. Geo. Par., Spts. Co. Witnesses: Peter x Kilgore, John x Kilgore, William x Muckleroy, Augt. Smith. Rec. Novr. 1, 1726.

Novr. 1, 1726. Augustine Smith of Spots. Co., Gentl., to his daughter, Mary Slaughter, of the same Co. £80 ster., 432 a. in the Fork of Rappa. River in Spts. Co. on the S. side of "ye Mountain Run." Witnesses: R. Bayley, Robt. Spotswood, Moseley Battaley, John Waller, junr. "Augt. Smith, Gent., acknowledged his deed of Release for land unto his daughter Mary, now the wife of Robert Slaughter," etc. Rec. Novr. 1, 1726.

Augt. 12, 1726. Larkin Chew, Senr., of St. Geo. Par., Spts. Co., to James and Uriah Garton of the same par. and Co. £30 ster., 500 a. in St. Geo. Par., Spts. Co., adjoining Col. John Robinson and Joseph Brock— part of a pat. granted sd. Chew June 4, 1722. G. Home, Thos. Smith, Jno. Grayson, junr. Rec. Nov. 1, 1726.

Decr. 21, 1725. "Alexander Spotswood of the Co. of Spots. but now Residing in London, Esquire," and "John Grame of the Parish of St. James, Clerkenwell in the County of Middlesex, Gentleman," and "John

Mackmath of the Parish of St. Mary's at Rotherhith in the County of Surry, Gent." The sd. Spotswood for and in consideration of the said John Grame's removing with his family to Va. to take the care and management of the sd. Spotswood's estate and effects in the Colony. "Two plantations, called Bear Quarter and Wild Cat Quarter near Germanna on the Wild Cat Run, otherwise the Flatt Run in Spts. Co. These estates to John Grame during his natural life and then to his wife, Katherine Grame; at her decease to go to John Macmath. Witnesses: Benja. Graves, Jno. Macmath, John Dunlop. Rec. May 11, 1726.

Augt. 1, 1726. Daniel Brown of Spts. Co., Gent., to Abell Stears of King William Co., planter. £11 ster.—part of pat. to Larkin Chew granted June 4, 1722, sold by the sd. Chew to the sd. Danll. Brown, in Spts. Co. on N. side Cat-tail Lick Branch, adjoining the lands of the sd. Brown and Joseph Brock, 100 a. Witnesses: John Chew, Ralph Richards, Larkin Chew, junr. Rec. Decr. 6, 1726.

Octr. 6, 1726. Larkin Chew of Spts. Co., to Amey Sutton of the same County. £12 ster., 200 a. of land in St. Geo. Par., Spts. Co. Witnesses: John Waller, junr. Rec. Dec. 6, 1726.

April 3, 1727. George x Proctor of St. Geo. Par., Spts. Co., to Edward Price of the same par. and county. 6000 lbs. tob., 200 a. of land in St. Geo. Par., Spts. Co. Witnesses: G. Home, John Skinner. Rec. May 2, 1727.

April 3, 1727. George x Proctor of Spts. Co. to John Skinner of King George Co. 3000 lbs. tob., 100 a. in St. Geo. Par., Spts. Co., on Hasell Run. Witnesses: G. Home, Edwd. Price. Rec. May 2, 1727.

May 2, 1727. Jacob Wall and Blanch Wall, his wife, of Spts. Co., planters, to Robert Green of the same Co., planter. £40 curr., 760 a. in St. Geo. Par., Spts. Co. Witnesses: Larkin Chew, G. Lightfoot. Rec. May 2, 1727.

Feby. 4, 1726. Francis Smith of King and Queen Co. to Edward Pigg of Spts. Co. 2000 lbs. tob., 100 a. of land in Spts. Co. given sd. Smith by the last will and testament of Peter Rogers, decd., and part of a tract granted John Madison, John Rogers, Peter Rogers, Henry Pigg, Edward Pigg and John York by patent, April 1, 1717, and is the part of John Madison, bought by the sd. Peter Rogers. Witnesses: Jonathan Clark, John Connor, William x Smith, Jno. Rogers. Rec. May 2, 1727. Sarah Smith, wife of Francis Smith, acknowledged her dower right to the said land to the said Edwd. Pigg, by her attorney, John Waller.

May 2, 1726. Thomas x Graves of Spts. Co. to William Johnson of the same county. 700 lbs. tob., 48 a. of land in St. Geo. Par., Spts. Co.—part of a tract granted Larkin Chew, June 4, 1722, on the N. side of Paines Branch. Witnesses: B. Grayson, Benja. Porter, Samll. x Ham. Rec. May 2, 1727.

March 2, 1726. Wm. Payton of St. Geo. Par., Spts. Co., to John Kilgore, of the same par. and county. £10 curr., 50 a. in St. Geo. Par., Spts. Co., on Mountain Run, in great Fork of Rappa. River. Witnesses: W. Russell, Jno. Cook, Edmond x Cook. Rec. May 3, 1727.

May 1, 1727. Abraham x Brown of St. Geo. Par., Spts. Co., to Lawrence Franklyn of the same par. and county. 250 a. of land; the said Abraham Brown transfers to the sd. Franklyn 100 a. of land in St. Geo. Par., Spts. Co., whereon the sd. Brown now lives, on S. side of the River and formerly belonging to Robert King. Witnesses: Danll. Brown, Senr.; Thos. Benson, John Foster. Rec. Jun 6, 1727.

Decr. 6, 1726. William x McConnico of St. Geo. Par., Spts. Co., to William Eddings of the same par. and county. £35 ster., 80 a. of land in St. Geo. Par., Spts. Co., on S. side Rapidan River and S. W. Mountain Run—part of pat. granted sd. McConnico June 3, 1726. Witnesses: John Taliaferro, John x Eddins, John x Finnell. Rec. June 6, 1727.

Jany. 17, 1726. John Blackley of St. Geo. Par., Spts. Co., to Robert Williams of the same par. and county. 3000 lbs. tob. 100 a. of land on north side Massaponnax Swamp—part of a pat. formerly granted John Quarles on Septr. 30, 1723. Witnesses: John Quarles, James Stewart, Stephen x Beckham. Rec. June 6, 1727.

Jany. 31, 1726. Joseph Brock of King and Queen Co., Gent., to John Durret of Spots. Co., planter. £20 ster., 200 a. of land—part of a pat. granted Larkin Chew June 4, 1721, and sold by sd. Chew to Joseph Brock. Witnesses: Larkin Chew, Jno. Webley, Willa. x Logan. Rec. July 4, 1727.

July 4, 1727. Daniel Brown of Spts. Co. to Paul Micou, Mercht., of Essex Co. £90 ster., 800 a. in Spts. Co.—part of a pat. granted Larkin Chew June 4, 1722. Witnesses: Fran. Thornton, Jas. Taylor, junr. Rec. July 4, 1727. Elizabeth Brown came into court and acknowledged her right of dower to the above land unto Paul Micou.

July 4, 1727. Larkin Chew of St. Geo. Par., Spts. Co., Gentl., to Daniel Brown of the same par. and county, planter. £22 ster., 341 a. of land in Spts. Co.—part of a pat. granted sd. Chew June 4, 1721, adjoining Col. Jno. Robinson. Witnesses: Moseley Battaley, John Waller, Jno. Waller, junr. Rec. July 4, 1727.

July 4, 1727. Larkin Chew of St. Geo. Par., Spts. Co., Gentl., to Lazarus Tilley of the same par. and co., planter. £— ster., 183 a. of land—part of pat. granted sd. Chew June 4, 1721, in Spts. Co. Witnesses: Henry Willis, Henry Goodloe. Rec. July 4, 1727.

July 4, 1727. Larkin Chew of Spts. Co., Gent., to John Chew of same co., Gent. £35 ster., 335 a. of land—part of pat. granted sd. Chew April 6, 1712, in St. Geo. Par., Spts. Co., joining the lands of John Lewis and Richd. Buckner. Witnesses: Henry Willis, Henry Goodloe, T. Staige. Rec. July 4, 1727.

July 4, 1727. Majr. Augustine Smith of Spts. Co., to Ambrose Madison of King and Queen Co. 5 shill., 863 a. of land—part of pat. dated Augt. 1, 1719, in Spts. Co. Witnesses: John Chew, Ro. Brooke, P. Greenhill. July 4, 1727.

Augt. 8, 1727. Abraham x Bledsoe and Wm. Bledsoe of Spts. Co., planters, to Augustine Smith of Spts. Co., Gent. £50 ster., 333 a. of land in St. Geo. Par., Spts. Co.—part of pat. granted the sd. Bledsoes May 30, 1726. Witnesses: Thos. Chew, James Taylor. Rec. Augt. 1, 1727.

July 31, 1727. James Taylor of Drysdale Par., King and Queen Co., to James Taylor, junr., of St. Geo. Par., Spts. Co. 5 shill., 1000 a. of land —part of a pat. granted the sd. Taylor July 21, 1721, in St. Geo. Par., Spts. Co., on both sides of Little Mountains and S. side Rapidan River. Witnesses: Thomas Carr, junr., Thos. Chew, Zach. Taylor. Rec. August 1, 1727.

Sept. 5, 1727. Abraham x Bledsoe and William Bledsoe of Spts. Co. to Augustine Smith, junr., of the same co. £100 ster., 333 a. in Spts. Co.—part of a pat. granted the sd. Bledsoes and Augt. Smith, junr., May 30, 1726. Witnesses: Thos. Chew, John Chew, G. Lightfoot. Rec. Sept. 5, 1727.

July 4, 1727. Majr. Augustine Smith of Spts. Co. to Ambrose Madison of King and Queen Co. Recites the sale of the land in Deed dated July 4, 1727, recorded A. p. 248.

Novr. 7, 1727. Ambrose Madison and Frances, his wife, of Drysdale Par., King and Queen Co., to Humphrey Bell of London, Mercht. £170 (pd. by Humphrey Hill, agent of sd. Bell), 863 a. of land in St. Geo. Par., Spts. Co.—part of pat. granted Majr. Augt. Smith Augt. 1, 1719. Witnesses: John Waller, Z. Lewis, Robert Green. Rec. Novr. 7, 1727.

Novr. 7, 1727. Thomas Catlett of St. Mary's Par., Essex Co., to Francis Conway of the same par. and county. £60 ster., 1000 a. of land in St. Geo. Par., Spts. Co., on both sides of the South West Mountains—granted by pat. to sd. Catlett May 21, 1726. Witnesses: John Battaile, G. Home, John Taliaferro. Rec. Novr. 7, 1727.

Novr. 7, 1727. Francis Conway of Essex Co., Gent., to John Taliaferro of Spts. Co. £50 ster., 176 a. in St. Geo. Par., Spts. Co.—pat. by sd. Conway June 30, 1726. Witnesses: John Battaile. Thomas Catlett, John Taliaferro. Rec. Novr. 7, 1727.

Augt. 29, 1727. James Taylor of Drysdale Par., King and Queen Co., surveyor, to Richard Thomas of the same par. and county, overseer. 5 shill., 1200 a. of land—part of a pat. granted sd. Taylor July 1, 1722, in St. Geo. Par., Spts. Co. Witnesses: John Taylor, William Tayloe, James Pendleton. Rec. Novr. 7, 1727. Martha Taylor, wife of James Taylor, released her dower right to above property to Richard Thomas, by her attorney, John Waller.

Augt. 11, 1727. James x Atkins of' Spts. Co., planter, to William Hansford of the same co., planter. £20 curr., 100 a. in St. Geo. Par., Spts. Co. Witnesses: G. Home, Saml. x Short, junr, John Quarles. Rec. Novr. 7, 1727. Sarah Atkins, wife of James Atkins, released her dower right to the above property to the sd. Wm. Hansford.

Octr. 3, 1727. James Taylor of Drysdale Par., King and Queen Co., to Zachary Taylor of St. Geo. Par., Spts. Co. 5 shill., 1000 a. of land—part of pat. granted sd. Taylor July 21, 1722, at the Little Mountains and on ye S. side Rapidan River in St. Geo. Par., Spts. Co. Witnesses: Robt. Pollard, junr.; Jno. Scott, Thomas Slaughter. Rec. Novr. 7, 1727.

Septr. 10, 1727. Collo. James Taylor of King and Queen Co., Gent., to Joseph Roberts of King William Co., Lawyer. £30 ster., 300 a. of land in Spts. Co.—part of pat. granted sd. Taylor July 21, 1721, in Spts. Co., joining the lands of Robert Baylor and Richard Gregory, and on both sides of East North East Run. Witnesses: John Scott, Benja. Cave, Zach. Taylor. Rec. Novr. 7, 1727.

Septr. 30, 1727. Phillip Todd of St. Stephen's Par., King and Queen Co., Gentl., to John Waller of St. Geo. Par., Spts. Co. £25 curr., 500 a. of land granted to sd. Todd by pat. June 30, 1726, in St. Geo. Par., Spts. Co. Witnesses: Z. Lewis, E. Wingfield, Richd. Cheek, John Waller, junr. Rec. Novr. 7, 1727.

Febry. 5, 1727. James Taylor of King and Queen Co. and Martha, his wife: of the first part, George Seaton, son and heir of Henry Seaton and Elizabeth, his wife, now the wife of Augustine Moore of King William Co., Gent. of the second part, and the sd. Augustine Moore of the third part. £114 15s. 0d., 1280 a. on both sides of East North East River in St. Geo. Par., Spts. Co.—part of a tract granted the sd. Taylor by pat, July 21, 1722. This property for the use of the sd. George Seaton, and if in default or failure of lawful heirs then to Lucy Moore, dau. of the sd. Augustine Moore and Elizabeth his wife, and in default or failure of heirs, then to Thomas Moore, son of the sd. Augustine Moore and Elizabeth his wife, and in case of failure of heirs, to Bernard Moore, son of the sd. Augustine and Elizabeth his wife, and in case of failure of heirs, then to the said Augustine Moore, his heirs and assigns, etc. Witnesses: Robt. Baylor, Geo. Moore, Frances Baylor, Thomas Griffith. Rec. Mar. 5, 1727-8.

Mar. 5, 1727. Larkin Chew of Spts. Co., Gent., to Amey Sutton of the same county. £2 ster., 73 a.—part of a pat. granted sd. Chew June 4, 1722, in St. Geo. Par., Spts. Co. Witnesses: John Waller, Moseley Battaley, Jno. Waller, junr. Rec. March 5, 1727.

March 4, 1727. James Taylor of King and Queen Co. and Drysdale Par., Gentl., to Richard Maulden of King William Co. £22 ster., 1000 a. of land—part of pat. granted sd. Taylor July 21, 1722, in Spts. Co., on Rapidan River, "amongst ye Little Mountains," joining the lands of Captn. John Taliaferro, Mr. Richard Thomas and Mr. John Baylor, Decd. Witnesses: John Chew, Thos. Chew, Wm. Johnson. Rec. March 5, 1727-8.

March 5, 1727. Thomas Chew of St. Geo. Par., Spts. Co., Gentl., to John Penn and George Penn of Drysdale Par., King and Queen Co. £40 curr., 614 a. formerly occupied by one Samll. Loyd—part of a pat. granted Larkin Chew June 4, 1722; sold by sd. Chew to sd. Loyd, by sd. Loyd and Chew to one Wm. Russell by deeds July 7, 1724, and by the sd. Russell sold to Thomas Chew, on a branch running into Mattapony River, otherwise called Warner's River, joining the lands of Robt. Hutcherson and the land of Augustine Smith of Gloster Co., late called Augustine Warner, Esqr., Decd., land. Witnesses: Wm. Johnson, John Chew, James Taylor. Rec. March 5, 1727-8. Martha Chew, wife of Thomas Chew, released her dower to the above land to the sd. John and George Penn.

Septr. 7, 1726. Edward x Tinsley of King and Queen Co. to William Croford of Spts. Co. £20 ster., 100 a. of land in Spts. Co., which sd. Tinsley purchased of Colo. Taylor. Witnesses: James Taylor, Robert Green, John Finalson. Rec. March 5, 1727-8.

March 4, 1727. Thomas Rucker of King and Queen Co. to Kendry Downs of St. Geo. Par., Spts. Co. 100 a. of land—part of pat. granted James Taylor May 25, 1722, in St. Geo. Par., Spts. Co. Witnesses: John Rucker, Edward x Tinsley, Thomas x Jackson. Rec. March 5, 1727-8.

March 4, 1728. Richard x Sharp of St. Geo. Par., Spts. Co., to John Finalson of the same par. and county. 4 lbs. tob. and £40 curr., 400 a. in Spts. Co.—part of pat. granted the sd. Sharp June 11, 1726. Witnesses: Moseley Battaley, John Chew, W. Russell. Rec. March 5, 1727-8. Mary, the wife of Richard Sharp, acknowledged her dower to the above land to the sd. Finalson.

March 5, 1727. Thomas Tyler of St. Geo. Par., Spts. Co., Va., to Charles Tyler in Great Britain, in Sallop Co. and Hopton Wafter Parish. £80 ster., 500 a. pat. by the sd. Thos. Tyler June 30, 1726, in St. Geo. Par., Spts. Co. Witnesses: Wm. Johnson, Thos. Chew. Rec. March 5, 1727-8.

March 6, 1727. Jeremiah Clowder of St. Geo. Par., Spts. Co., Gent., "to my daughter, Hannah Clowder." 300 a. of land in Spts. Co. Witnesses: John Waller, Z. Lewis, Jno. Waller, junr. Rec. March 8, 1727-8.

March 6, 1727. Jeremiah Clowder of St. Geo. Par., Spts. Co., Gent., "to my daughter, Joyce Clowder." 1300 a. in Spts. Co. Witnesses: Z. Lewis, Jno. Waller, junr. Rec. March 6, 1727-8.

March 6, 1727. Jeremiah Clowder of St. Geo. Par., Spts. Co., Gent., "to my daughter, Mary Elizabeth Thacker, now the wife of Mr. Henry Thacker, Gentl., of the County of Middlesex." 1300 a. of land in Spts. Co. Witnesses: John Waller, Z. Lewis, Jno. Waller, junr. Rec. March 6, 1727-8.

March 5, 1727. Larkin Chew of St. Geo. Par., Spts. Co., Gentl., to his son, Thomas Chew, of the same parish and county. "Tract of land and plantation whereon the sd. Thomas Chew now lives containing 300 a."— being part of a pat. granted the sd. Larkin Chew. Witnesses: Jos. Brock, W. Smith, Jer. Clowder. Rec. March 6, 1727-8.

June 4, 1728. Samuel Wright of St. Geo. Par., Spts. Co., to John Finalson of the same par. and county. 4000 lbs. tob. and 4000 nails, 400 a. of land in St. Geo. Par., Spts. Co., in the great fork of Rappa. River. Witnesses: Augt. Smith, John Waller, Jno. Waller, junr. Rec. June 4, 1727-8. Elizabeth, wife of Samuel Wright, acknowledged her dower to the sd. land to the sd. Finalson.

May 7, 1728. Aaron x Pinson of Spts. Co., planter, to Augustine Smith of Essex Co. £100 ster., 280 a. in Spts. Co. Witnesses: Z. Lewis, W. Russell, Abraham Field. Rec. June 4, 1728.

June 3, 1728. George x Proctor of St. Geo. Par., Spts. Co., "to my lawfull daughter, Elizabeth, and George Home, her lawfull husband." 180 a. of land in the branches of Deep Run in Spts. Co., St. Geo. Par. Witnesses: Benja. Grayson, Robert Cave.

Septr. 3, 1727. George x Carter of Spts. Co., planter, to Phebee Hobson, widdow, of the same county. £7 ster., 50 a. of land—part of pat. granted Robert Coleman Decr. 2, 1723, and sold unto the sd. Carter, in St. Geo. Par., Spts. Co., joining the lands of Collo. John Robinson and Robert Coleman. Witnesses, Danll. Brown, John Nalle, Winifred W. Tillery. Rec. June 4, 1728.

April 3, 1728. John x Bush and Margaret, his wife, of St. Geo. Par., Spts. Co., planter, to Richard Bayley of St. Margarett's Par., King William Co. £12, 200 a. of land in St. Geo. Par., Spts. Co.—being a pat. granted to the sd. Bush. Witnesses: E. Wingfield, Richd. Cheek, Jno. Waller, junr. Rec. June 4, 1728.

May 7, 1728. Leonard Holms of St. Mary's Par., Caroline Co., to John Quarles of Overwharton Par., Stafford Co. £40 curr., 278 a. formerly granted to Leonard Holms by pat. Octr. 31, 1726, in St. Geo. Par., Spts. Co. Witnesses: Jno. Grayson, junr.; Lewis Davis Yancey, William Brown,

Benja. Grayson. Rec. June 4, 1728. Elizabeth Holms of St. Mary's Par., Caroline Co., wife of Leonard Holms, by her attorney, Moseley Battaley, Gentl., acknowledged her dower in the above land to the sd. John Quarles.

July 3, 1728. George x Proctor of St. Geo. Par., Spts. Co., for the love and affection I bear to my Lawfull begotten daughter, Elizabeth, and George Home, her lawfull Husband, and more especially in consideration of ye celebration of Nuptials between them," etc. 180 a. in St. Geo. Par., Spts. Co., on the branches of Deep Run. Witnesses: Wm. Johnson, John Chew. Rec. July 3, 1728.

Augt. 6, 1728. John Wilkins of Spts. Co. to John Wiglesworth of the same county. £25 curr., 200 a. of land—part of a pat. granted the sd. Wilkins June 16, 1727, in St. Geo. Par., Spts. Co. Witnesses: John Waller, John Snall, Z. Lewis. Rec. Augt. 6, 1728. Mary, the wife of John Wilkins, acknowledged her dower in the above land to the sd. John Wiglesworth.

July 23, 1728. James Taylor of Drysdale Par., King and Queen Co., to Thomas Cartwright of the said par. and county. 140 a. in St. Geo. Par., Spts. Co.—part of pat. granted sd. Taylor July 21, 1722. Witnesses: Zachary Taylor, George Taylor. Rec. Augt. 6, 1728. Martha Taylor, wife of James Taylor, acknowledged her dower in the above land to the sd. Cartwright.

Augt. 6, 1728. William x Smith of St. Geo. Par., Spts. Co., planter, to Francis Thornton of St. Mary's Par., Caroline Co., Gentl. £10 curr., 200 a. in St. Geo. Par., Spts. Co., in the fork of Rappk. River. Witnesses: Robert Slaughter, James Taylor, junr.; Thomas Slaughter. Rec. Augt. 6, 1728. Mary, the wife of Wm. Smith, acknowledged her dower in the sd. land, etc.

April 27, 1728. "James Cannon of St. Margaret in Spts. Co., planter," to "John Thompson of the same county and parish." 5 shill., 100 a. in Spts. Co. "on N. side of North River of the Guard Vine fork." Witnesses: Thomas x Duncomb, Thomas x Little. Rec. Augt. 6, 1728. (Ed. Note. This deed is signed "James Canon, Mary x Canon," "and at the motion of Johanna Thomson, mother of the said John, the same was admitted to record.")

Augt. 7, 1728. Henry Willis of King and Queen Co. to Thomas Beale of Richmond County. £80, 3333 a. on the E. side of the Little Mountains in St. Geo. Par., Spts. Co.—part of a pat. granted the sd. Willis July 23, 1728. Witnesses: Thomas Chew, Ambrose Madison. Rec. Augt. 6, 1728.

Feby. 9, 1727. John Waller of St. Geo. Par., Spts. Co., Gentl., to Richard Fitzwilliam of the city of Williamsburg in the County of York. £100 curr., 1000 a. in St. Geo. Par., Spts. Co., where John Key now lives—by pat. granted the sd. Waller June 5, 1722. Witnesses: Z. Lewis, John Key, Jno. Waller, junr. Rec. Oct. 1, 1728. Dorothy Waller, wife of John Waller, acknowledged her dower in the sd. land, etc.

October 1, 1728. James Taylor, the elder, of Drysdale Par., King and Queen Co., Va., Gentl., and James Taylor, the younger, of St. Geo. Par., Spts. Co., Gentl., son of the sd. James Taylor, the elder, to John Tayloe, John Fitzhugh, Samuel Peachey, Humphrey Pope and Nicholas Minor, Gentlemen, executors of the last will and testament of Daniel McCarty, late of the County of Westmoreland, Esqr., decd." £330 curr., "that tract of land whereon Jas. Taylor, the younger, now lives," in St. Geo. Par.,

Spts. Co., at the S. West Mountains, 1722 a.—part of a pat. granted the sd. Taylor, the elder, July 21, 1722. Witnesses: Edwd. Ripping, Thomas Beale, junr.; Richard Lamb. Rec. Octr. 1, 1728.

Octr. 3, 1727. Joseph x Cooper of St. Geo. Par., Spts. Co., to John Kirk of Overwharton Par., Stafford Co. £35, 400 a. in St. Geo. Par., Spts. Co., in the great fork of Rappk. River, adjoining Roger Abbott's land, formerly granted to Jos. Cooper by patent June 24, 1726. Witnesses: W. Russell, John Finalson, John x Killgore. Rec. Oct. 1, 1728. Barbary Cooper, wife of Joseph Cooper, acknowledged her dower in the above land, etc.

Novr. 5, 1728. Augustine Smith of Spts. Co., Gent., to Robert Slaughter of the same county, Gent. £80 ster., 320 a. in St. Geo. Par., Spts. Co., in the fork of Rappa. River. Witnesses: Larkin Chew, junr.; Robert Green, Thomas Slaughter. Rec. Novr. 5, 1728.

*Decr. 3rd, 1728. Augustine Smith and John Waller, Gentlemen, Directors and Trustees of the town of Fredericksburg in Spts. Co., to Humphrey Hill of King William Co., Gent. £8 5s., two half acre lots in the town, Nos. 23 and 24. Witnesses, James Taylor, Jr.; Moseley Battaley, Z. Lewis. Rec. Decr. 3, 1728.

Decr. 3, 1728. James Taylor, the younger, son of James Taylor of King and Queen Co., Gent., to Augustine Moore of King William Co., Gent. £50 ster., 1000 a. in Spts. Co.—part of a tract granted the sd. Jas. Taylor June 30, 1726. Witnesses: Augtine Smith, Moseley Battaley, Z. Lewis. Rec. Decr. 3, 1728. Alice, wife of James Taylor, junr., Gent., acknowledged her dower in the sd. land, etc.

Dec. 3, 1728. The Feoffees or Trustees of the Town of Fredksburg. in Spts. Co. (by John Waller and Augtine. Smith.) to Moseley Battaley of St. Geo. Par., Spts. Co., Gent. 55s., Lot No. 62 in the town. Witnesses: Z. Lewis, James Taylor, junr.; Jno. Waller, junr. Rec. Decr. 3, 1728.

Decr. 2, 1728. Richard Booker of Bruton Par., James City Co., to Rice Curtis of Christ Church Par., Middlesex Co. £100 curr., 500 a. in Spts. Co. Witnesses: William Booker, Samuel Bartlett, Andrew x Donnason. Rec. Decr. 3, 1728.

Feby. 4, 1728. John Waller and John Taliaferro, Gent., Directors and Trustees for Fredksburg town in Spts. Co., to Augustine Smith of Caroline Co. £5 10s., two lots in the town, Nos. 30 and 32. Witnesses: Z. Lewis, Jno. Waller, junr. Rec. Feby. 4. 1728.

Feby. 4, 1728. Augustine Smith of Caroline Co., Gent., to Thomas Slaughter of the same co., Gent. £100 ster., 300 a. of land in Spts. Co. in the fork of Rappk. River. Witnesses: Jo. Taliaferro, G. Lightfoot, Abraham Field. Rec. Feby. 4, 1728-9.

Feby. 5, 1728. Larkin Chew, the elder, of St. Geo. Par., Spts. Co., to his son, John Chew, "the tract of land whereon the sd. John Chew lives in St. Geo. Par., Spts. Co. 335 a. Witnesses: John Waller, Andw. Harrison. Rec. Feby. 5, 1728-9.

Decr. 31, 1728. Andrew Harrison of Spts. Co. to Richard Fitz William, Esqr., in trust for himself, the Honble. Wm. Gooch, His Majesties Lieut. Governor, Capt. Vincent Pearse, Dr. George Nicholas, and Charles Chis-

*Ed. Note.—First lots sold in Fredericksburg.

well. £70 curr., 600 a. in Spts. Co., the sd. land purchased by the sd. Harrison of Harry Beverley, the sd. land having been granted by pat. to the sd. Beverley. Witnesses: William Wombwell Cliff, Tho. Jarman, Augustine Graham. Rec. Feby. 4, 1728-9. Elizabeth, wife of Andrew Harrison, acknowledged her dower in the sd. land, etc.

Feby. 3, 1728. Thomas Slaughter of Caroline Co.; Francis and Robert Slaughter of Spts. Co., to Augustine Smith of Caroline Co. £100 ster., 288 a. in Spts. Co. on both sides of Black Walnut Run—granted to Robert Slaughter, father of the sd. Thomas, Francis and Robert Slaughter, by pat. June 30, 1726. Witnesses: Jo. Taliaferro, G. Lightfoot, Abraham Field. Rec. Feby. 4, 1728-9.

Feby. 3d, 1729. Winnifred x Tillary of Spts. Co. "for the natural love and affection which I have for my children, John Tillary, my son, and Mary Tillary, my daughter," etc. Goods and chattels. Witnesses: George x Carter, Jno. Adcock, Elizabeth x Carter. Rec. Feby. 4, 1728-9.

Jany. 18, 1728. Thomas Guy of King and Queen Co. to Robert Eastham of the same county. £16 0. 3½d., 1000 a. in St. Geo. Par., Spts. Co., in the fork of Rappa. River. Witnesses: W. Russell, Jno. x Bowmar, Edward x Dillard, junr. Rec. Feby. 4, 1728-9.

Decr. 17, 1728. The Honorable Alexander Spotswood, Esqr., by John Grame, Gentl., his attorney, to Thomas Byrn and Martha, his wife, for certain considerations of tobacco each year, etc., a lease for two adjoining plantations in the fork of Rappa. River in St. Geo. Par., Spts. Co.— part of that land known as New German Town, Nos. 18 and 19, with 200 a. adjoining the sd. plantations. Witnesses: Henry Collins, Elliott Benger, Robt. Macculloch. Rec. Feby. 4, 1728-9.

Decr. 4, 1728. John England of Stafford Co. to William Duff of Hanover Par., King Geo. Co. £50 ster., 1000 a. of land in St. Geo. Par., Spts. Co. granted the sd. England by a patent from Govr. Wm. Gooch Septr. 2, 1728. Witnesses: William Allen, Geo. Williams, Stephen Williams. Rec. Feby. 4, 1728-9.

March 26, 1729. John Taliaferro of Spts. Co., Gent., brother and Devisee of Robert Taliaferro, late of the county of Spts., decd., to James Taylor, the younger, of Caroline Co. Whereas the above named Robt. Taliaferro, decd., by his last will and testament bearing Date Feby. 1, 1727, did give and bequeath unto the sd. John Taliaferro all his lands in Spts. Co. to be sold by the sd. John towards discharging the debts of the sd. Robert, the Testator, etc. £46 curr., 670 a. in St. Geo. Par., Spts. Co., granted the sd. Robt. Taliaferro by pat. Decr. 14, 1726, and known by the name of "Silvania." Witnesses: Wm. Woodford, Jno. Warner, Wm. Strother. Rec. April 1, 1729.

March 27, 1729. James Taylor of Caroline Co. to Francis Wyatt of Gloucester Co. £110 curr., £50 ster., 2600 a. in St. Geo. Par., Spts. Co. Witnesses: John Chew, Jno. Holloday, Larkin Chew. Rec. April 1, 1729. Martha Taylor, wife of James Taylor, acknowledged her dower in the sd. land by John Waller, her attorney, etc.

April 1, 1729. James Taylor of Drysdale Par., Caroline Co., to John Holloday of St. Geo. Par., Spts. Co. £36 curr., 260 a. on the E. side of East North East River, part of pat. granted sd. Taylor July 21, 1722, in

St. Geo. Par., Spts. Co. Witnesses: John Key, Samuel Ellis, George Taylor. Rec. April 1, 1729.

April 1, 1729. Robert Martin of King and Queen Co. to Reverend Theodosus Staige of York Co., Clerk. £5 ster., 1000 a. in St. Geo. Par., Spts. Co. —pat. by sd. Martin Octr. 20, 1727. Witnesses: Richard Cheek, Zachary Taylor, John x Blanton. Rec. April 1, 1729.

Feby. 11, 1728. John x Blanton of Spts. Co. to Thomas Turner of King George Co. £32 curr., 200 a. of land in St. Geo. Par., Spts. Co., adjoining the land bought by sd. Turner of one Edward Rowzee on the River Po, a head branch of Mattapony, between the land of sd. Turner and Wm. Blanton, part of pat. granted Larkin Chew. Witnesses: Edward Rowell, Willm. x Smith, Willm. x Hambleton, Saml. x Green. Rec. April 1, 1729.

March 26, 1729. John Blackley of Overwharton Par., Stafford Co., to Robert Williams of St. Geo. Par., Spts. Co. 3000 lbs. tob., 100 a. on N. side Massaponnax Swamp, part of pat. granted John Quarles, Septr. 30, 1723. Witnesses: Wm. Hansford, Francis x Cholmley, Stephen x Beckham. Rec. April 1, 1729.

Feby. 26, 1728. The Honble. Alexander Spotswood, Esqr., by John Grame, Gent., his attorney, to Thomas Parks of St. Geo. Par., Spts. Co., in consideration of so much tobacco, etc. 100 a. of land in fork of Rappa. River. Witnesses: Elliott Benger, And. Stevenson. Rec. April 2, 1729.

April 2, 1729. John Mulkey, Cooper, of St. Geo. Par., Spts. Co., to Joseph Cottman of Somersett Co., Maryland. £30 curr., 1000 a. of land in St. Geo. Par., Spts. Co. Witnesses: Wm. Johnson, John Robinson, Jos. Parker. Rec. April 2, 1729. Sarah, wife of John Mulkey, acknowledged her right of dower in the sd land, by John Waller, her attorney, etc.

April 7, 1729. Christopher Zimmerman, Cooper, of St. Geo. Par., Spts. Co., to Frederick Cohler, planter, of the same par. and county. £40 curr., 200 a. of land in St. Geo. Par., Spts. Co. Witnesses: G. Home, —— ——. Rec. May 6, 1729.

Feby. 4, 1729. Edward Franklyn of Spts. Co. to Rice Curtis, junr., of Middlesex Co. £36 curr., 200 a. of land, granted Larkin Chew by pat. June 4, 1722, in the par. of St. Geo., Spts. Co. (a part of the sd. pat.) Witnesses: Samuel Bartlett, Batho. x Mackderamat, Rice Curtis, Senr. Rec. May 6, 1729.

May 7, 1729. Henry Willis of King and Queen Co., Gent., to Goodrich Lightfoot of Spts. Co. £60 ster., 200 a. of land in Spts. Co. on S. side of the South West Mountains. Witnesses: Wm. Johnson, Ambr. Grayson, Wm. Hackney. Rec. May 6, 1729.

June 3, 1729. John x Hadocks of St. Geo. Par., Spts. Co., planter, to Francis Thornton of St. Mary's Par., Caroline Co. 5000 lbs. tob., 200 a. in St. Geo. Par., Spts. Co., in fork of Rappa. River. Witnesses: Robert Green, Francis x Micall, John x Pendergrass. Rec. June 3, 1729. Dorothea, wife of John Hadocks, acknowledged her dower in the sd. land, etc.

June 3, 1729. John x Kilgore of St. Geo. Par., Spts. Co., to John Hadocks of the same par. and county. 800 lbs. tob., 81 a. in Spts. Co. Witnesses: Francis Thornton, Robert Green, Francis x Mycell. Rec.

June 3, 1729. Mary, wife of John Kilgore, acknowledged her dower in the sd. land, etc.

June 3, 1729. Augustine Smith and John Waller, Gentl., Directors and Trustees for Fredericksburg Town in Spts. Co., to Susannah Livingston, widow, of Spts. Co. During her natural life, and after her decease to Philip Rootes of King William County. £12 5s. curr. Two lotts in Fredksburg, Nos. 29 and 31. Witnesses: John Chew, Jno. Waller, junr.; W. Waller. Rec. June 3, 1729.

June 3, 1729. John x Kilgore of St. Geo. Par., Spts. Co., to John Haddocks of the same par. and county. 2700 lbs. tob., 50 a. of land in St. Geo. Par., Spts. Co., in the great fork of Rappa. River. Witnesses: Fran. Thornton, Robert Green, Francis x Mycell. Rec. June 3, 1729. Mary, wife of John Kilgore, acknowledged her dower in the above land, etc.

May 11, 1729. Nicholas x Yager of St. Geo. Par., Spts. Co., planter, to Philip Paulitz of the same par. and county, planter. £20 ster., a parcel of ground in St. Geo. Par., Spts. Co. Witnesses: G. Home, Andrew Tullser. Rec. July 1, 1729.

July 1, 1729. Augustine Smith of St. Marie's Par., Caroline Co., Gent., to James Horsnale of St. Geo. Par., Spts. Co. £36 ster., 300 a. in St. Geo. Par., Spts. Co. Witnesses: Natha. Claiborne, James Williams, Robert Cave. July 1, 1729.

May 12, 1729. William Todd of Drysdale Par., King and Queen Co., Gent., to John Minor of Spts. Co., Planter. £40 curr., 328 a. of land in Spts. Co. at the Little Mountains. Witnesses: John Scott, Jas. Barbour, John Buford. Rec. Augt. 5, 1729.

April 8, 1729. John Robinson, Esqr., and John Waller, Gent., Directors and Trustees of Fredksburg., in Spts. Co., to John Robinson, junr., Gent., of King and Queen Co. £5 5s. curr., Lot No. 13 in Fredksburg. Witnesses: Jno. Waller, junr., Thos. Waller, Thomas Davis, W. Waller. Rec. Augt. 5, 1729.

April 8, 1729. John Robinson, Esqr., and John Waller, Gent., Directors and Trustees of the town of Fredericksburg, etc., to Thomas Turner of King George Co., Gent. £2 15s. curr., Lot No. 52 in Fredksburg. Witnesses: Jno. Waller, Junr.; Thos. Waller, W. Waller. Rec. Augt. 5, 1729.

Augt. 5, 1729. Elias Downs, Senr., of King and Queen Co., planter, and Elias Downs, junr., of St. Geo. Par., Spts. Co., planter, to John Parks of St. Geo. Par., Spts. Co., Blacksmith. 1600 lbs. tob., 200 a. in St. Geo. Par., Spts. Co., on head branches of Massaponnax Swamps. Witnesses: Robt. Spotswood, G. Home. Rec. Augt. 5, 1729.

Augt. 4, 1729. Thomas Chew, son and heir of Larkin Chew of Spts. Co., Decd., to Joseph Smith of King and Queen Co. £50 curr., 512 a. on S. side about a mile above the falls of the River Po, a branch of York River, lying in St. Geo. Par., Spts. Co.—part of parcel of land granted Larkin Chew, by pat. April 20, 1712, and by him sold to sd. Smith. Witnesses: Jno. Robinson, Wm. Johnson, Z. Lewis. Rec. Augt. 5, 1729.

Augt. 5, 1729. Joseph Smith of King and Queen Co., Gent., to John Robinson, Esqr., and Ambrose Grayson, Gent., Wardens of the Church of St. George's Parish, in Spts. Co. A purchase of the Glebe for the Rectors of St. Geo. Par. 22,500 lbs. tob., 544 a. of land in St. Geo. Par., Spts. Co., on the S. side, about a mile above the falls of the River Po, a branch of York River. Witnesses: G. Home, Wm. Johnson, Zachary Taylor. Rec. Augt. 5, 1729. Sarah, wife of Joseph Smith, acknowledged her dower in the above land, etc.

Augt. 5, 1729. John Chew of Spts. Co. to Edward Franklyn of the same county. £12 curr., 200 a. in St. Geo. Par., Spts. Co. Witnesses: Wm. Johnson, Thos. Chew, Zachary Taylor. Rec. Augt. 5, 1729.

Augt. 4, 1729. The Feoffees or Trustees for the Town of Fredericksburg (by John Robinson and John Waller) to George Carr of St. Geo. Par., Spts. Co., Taylor. £3 curr., Lot No. 50 in Fredksburg. Witnesses: W. Russell, Jno. Mercer, M. Battaley. Rec. Augt. 6, 1729.

*May 24, 1729. Thomas x Gambrill of St. Margaret's Par., King William Co., to John Graves, Junr., of St. Stephen's Par., King and Queen Co. In consideration of 100 a. of land the sd. Gambrill deeds Graves a tract in St. Geo. Par., Spts. Co., containing as by pat. 200 a. Witnesses: Thomas x Graves, John x Gambrill, Thomas x Crimbro. Rec. Septr. 2, 1729.

Augt. 29, 1729. Charles Taliaferro of St. Marie's Par., Caroline Co., to Francis Conway of the same par. and county. £30 ster., 345 a. of land in St. Geo. Par., Spts. Co., the sd. seat or tract of land granted the sd. Taliaferro, by pat. Septr. 28, 1728, joining the lands of Capt. Lawrence and John Taliaferro. Witnesses: Jno. Battaile, Jas. Taylor, junr.; Nicho. Battaile. Rec. Septr. 2, 1729.

Septr. 2, 1729. Charles Taliaferro of Caroline Co., Gent., to Henry Willis of Spts. Co., Gent. £30 curr., 150 a. on S. side Rappa. River in St. Geo. Par., Spts. Co. Witnesses: A. Smith, M. Battaley, Wm. Bledsoe. Rec. Septr. 2, 1729.

Augt. 30, 1729. Charles Taliaferro of St. Mary's Par., Gent., to William Marshall of St. Geo. Par., Spts. Co., planter. £30 ster., 150 a. in St. Geo. Par., Spts. Co.—part of the sd. Taliaferro's Matt Run tract of land. Witnesses: A. Smith, M. Battaley, Wm. Bledsoe. Rec. Septr. 2, 1729.

Augt. 30, 1729. Charles Taliaferro of St. Mary's Par., Caroline Co., Gent., to Jael Johnson and James Williams of St. Geo. Par., Spts. Co. £200 ster., "unto Jael Johnson, during her Naturall life and then unto James Williams, his heirs and assigns," etc., 420 a. of land in St. Geo. Par., Spts. Co., bought by sd. Taliaferro of one Wm. Smith as by deed dated March 4, 1713, on Hazel Run and the Rappk. River. Witnesses: A. Smith, M. Battaley, Wm. Bledsoe. Rec. Septr. 2, 1729.

Septr. 2, 1729. Henry Willis of Spts. Co., Va., Gent., to Philemon Cavenaugh of the same county. £60 curr., 3277 a. of land in the fork of the Rappa. River in St. Geo. Par., Spts. Co. Witnesses: Wm. Marshall, Wm. Strother, Wm. Cave. Rec. Septr. 2, 1729.

Septr. 1, 1729. Lawrence x Franklyn of St. Geo. Par., Spts. Co., Carpenter, to Thomas Salmon of St. Marie's Par., Caroline Co., planter. 4500 lbs. tob., 100 a. of land in St. Geo. Par., Spts. Co., whereon the sd. Franklyn now lives, on the S. side the River Po, adjoining the lands of Robert King, Anthony Foster and John Foster. Witnesses: Thos. Chew, Jas. Taylor, Junr., Nicho. x Hawkins. Rec. Septr. 2, 1729.

*Ed. Note.—The deed is signed Thomas x Gambrill, Ann x Gambrill.

Octr. 7, 1729. John x Cook of Spts. Co. to Charles Stevens of the same county. £20 curr., 300 a. of land on the S. side of the North Fork of the Northanna River in Spts. Co., and granted the sd. Cook by pat. Septr. 28, 1728. Witnesses: Robert Turner, John Stevens. Rec. Octr. 7, 1729. Ann, wife of John Cook, acknowledged her dower in the sd. land, etc.

Augt. 18, 1729. "Sylvanus Pumphary, Late of the Province of Maryland, now in the Colony of Virginia," to William Russell, one negro slave named Ceaser, for value received. Witnesses: Nathan Pumphary, Edward x Teals. Rec. Septr. 15, 1729.

Octr. 7, 1729. Walter x Frances of the parish of Prince George in the County of Spts., "for ye fatherly love, etc., and affection I bare to my son-in-law, Edward Price." Personal effects. Witnesses: John Price, Thomas Price, Francis x Price. Rec. Octr. 7, 1729.

Octr. 7, 1729. John x Landrum of Spts. Co. to Robert Thomas of St. Mary's Par., Caroline Co. 12,000 lbs. tob., 595 a. of land in Spts. Co.—part of pat. granted Larkin Chew June 4, 1722. Witnesses: Wm. Bartlett, Robert Brown, Jno. Thomas. Rec. Octr. 7, 1729. Mary, wife of John Landrum, acknowledged her dower in the above sd. land, by her attorney, John Waller, etc.

Octr. 7, 1729. William Todd and Martha, his wife, of Drysdale Par., King and Queen Co., to Philip Todd of St. Stephen's Par., same county. £41 10s., 2000 a. of land, part of a tract granted by pat. to John Taliaferro, Jno. Battell and Wm. Todd, in St. Geo. Par., Spts. Co. Witnesses: Wm. Strother, Jos. Smith, James Markham. Rec. Octr. 7, 1729.

Novr. 4, 1729. James Canon of St. Geo. Par., Spts. Co., planter, to Joseph Cottman of Somerset Co., Maryland. £30 curr., 350 a. of land in St. Geo. Par., Spts. Co. Witnesses: G. Home, Thomas x Farmer. Rec. Novr. 4, 1729.

Novr. 5, 1729. George x Proctor, planter, of St. Geo. Par., Spts. Co., to Joseph Parker of the same par. and county. £12 18s. curr., 86 a. of land in St. Geo. Par., Spts. Co. Witnesses: G. Home, Fras. Smith. Rec. Novr. 5, 1729. Mary, wife of George Proctor, acknowledged her dower in the sd. land, etc.

Novr. 5, 1729. John Taliaferro, the younger, and Francis Taliaferro of St. Marie's Par., Caroline Co., to Benjamin Porter of St. Geo. Par., Spts. Co. £10 ster., 10 a. of land in St. Geo. Par., Spts. Co.—part of a pat. granted John Taliaferro, the younger, and Francis Taliaferro, June 30, 1726. Witnesses: John Robinson, Thomas Benson, John Mickel. Rec. Novr. 5, 1729.

Decr. 2, 1729. Isaac x Bledsoe of St. Geo. Par., Spts. Co., planter, to Robert Jones of Hanover Par., King George Co., Gent. £10 ster., 1000 a. of land in St. Geo. Par., Spts. Co., in the little fork of Rappa. River. Witnesses: Thoms. Hill, Thos. Smith, Abram x Bledsoe. Rec. Decr. 2, 1729.

Decr. 2, 1729. John x Thomson of St. Peter's Par., New Kent Co., planter, to Benjamin Cottman of Stepeney Par., Somerset Co., Province of Maryland. £9 10s., 100 a. of land in St. Geo. Par., Spts. Co., "on the little fork in the Gourd Vine back in the woods near the head of Rappa. River"—pat. by one James Cannon and conveyed to sd. Thomson. Witnesses: Lewis Davis Yancey, G. Home. Rec. Decr. 2, 1729.

Decr. 1, 1729.   John x Asher, planter, of St. Geo. Par., Spts. Co., to George Home of the same par. and county.   £50 curr., 400 a. in St. Geo. Par., Spts. Co.   Witnesses: Sam. Ham, And. Landale.   Rec. Feby. 3, 1729–30.

Decr. 1, 1729.   George Home of St. Geo. Par., Spts. Co., to John Asher of the same par. and county.   £30 curr., 380 a. in St. Geo. Par., Spts. Co. Witnesses: Sam. Ham, And. Landale.   Rec. Feby. 3, 1729–30.

Feby. 1, 1729–30.   Richard Cheek of St. Geo. Par., Spts. Co., to John Miller of St. Mary's Par., Caroline Co.   4000 weight of tobacco, 70 a. of land in St. Geo. Par., Spts. Co.—part of a pat. granted John Quarles Septr. 3, 1723.   Witnesses: John Miller, John Parks, Jos. Retterford.   Rec. Feby. 3, 1729–30.   Jane Cheek acknowledged her right of dower in the sd. land by Wm. Bartlett, her attorney, etc.

Jany. 7, 1729.   Richard Cheek of St. Geo. Par., Spts. Co., to John Miller, Senr., of St. Ann's Par., Essex Co.   £25 curr., 1000 a. of land in St. Geo. Par., Spts. Co., granted the sd. Cheek Octr. 13, 1727, joining Chick-eley Corbin Thacker and Catesby Cock.   Witnesses: W. Hansford, Wm. Bartlett, John Parkes, John Miller, junr.   Rec. Feby. 3, 1729–30.   Jane Cheek acknowledged her right of dower in the sd. land by Wm. Bart-lett, her attorney, etc.

Feby. 4, 1730.   John x Purvis of St. Geo. Par., Spts. Co., planter, to Philip Watters, Carpenter, of the same par. and county.   5000 lbs. tob., 770 a. of land in St. Geo. Par., Spts. Co.   Witnesses: Edwin Hickman, Wm. Bledsoe, Samll. Hensley.   Rec. Feby. 4, 1729–30.   Elizabeth, wife of John Purvis, acknowledged her right of dower in the sd. land, etc.

Novr. 22, 1729.   William x Blanton of Caroline Co. to Thomas Turner of King George Co.   £20 curr., 150 a. in St. Geo. Par., Spts. Co., adjoining the land the sd. Turner bought of John Blanton on the River Po, a head branch of Mattapony—part of a tract granted Larkin Chew, and between the land whereon Richard Blanton now lives and that of John Blanton. Witnesses: John x Bell, Elizabeth x Bell, Stephen x Turner.   Rec. March 3, 1729–30.   Margaret, wife of Wm. Blanton, acknowledged her right of dower in sd. land by her attorney, Jno. Waller, etc.

March 3, 1729.   Thomas Guy of King and Queen Co. to John Latham of Caroline Co.   £10 curr., 1000 a. of land in St. Geo. Par., Spts. Co., in the fork of Rappa. River.   Witnesses: Zachary Taylor, Wm. Terrell, William Richerson.   Rec. March 3, 1729–30.

March 3, 1729.   John Latham of Caroline Co. to William Richerson of Spts. Co.   £10 curr., 210 a. of land in St. Geo. Par., Spts. Co., in the fork of Rappa. River.   Witnesses: Zachary Taylor, Wm. Terrell, Thos. Guy. Rec. March 3, 1729–30.   Susannah, wife of John Latham, acknowledged her right of dower in the sd. land, etc.

March 3, 1729.   John Latham of Caroline Co. to Thomas Bowmar of Spts. Co.   750 lbs. tob., 225 a. in St. Geo. Par., Spts. Co., in the fork of Rappa. River.   Witnesses: Zachary Taylor, Wm. Terrell, Thos. Guy.   Rec. March 3, 1729–30.   Sussanah, wife of John Latham, acknowledged her right of dower in the sd. land. etc.

DEED BOOK B

Mar. 23, 1729. John Latham of Caroline Co. to John Chapman of King and Queen Co. 3540 lbs. tob., 295 a. in St. Geo. Par., Spts. Co. Zachary Taylor, Wm. Terrell, Thos. Guy. March 3, 1729–30. Susannah Latham, wife of sd. John, acknowledged her dower, etc.

Decr. 9, 1729. John Grayson of St. Geo. Par., Spts. Co., to Ambrose Grayson of same par. and county. £50 ster., 200 a.—part of Deeds formerly purchased by Jno. Grayson of Wm. Smith of Gloucester, in St. Geo. Par., Spts. Co. Francis Turnley, Henry Rogers, James x Roy. March 3, 1729–30. Susannah, wife of Jno. Grayson, acknowledged her dower, etc.

Decr. 10, 1729. Ambrose Grayson of St. Geo. Par., Spts. Co., to Henry Rogers of same par. and county. £20 ster., 100 a.—part of pat. granted sd. Grayson, in 1727, in St. Geo. Par., Spts. Co. John Chew, Zachary Taylor, Wm. Bledsoe. March 3, 1729–30. Alice, wife of Ambrose Grayson, acknowledged her dower, etc.

Decr. 6, 1727. Henry Fitzhugh of Stafford Co. to William Whitehouse of Spts. Co., John Whitehouse and Sarah Whitehouse, his daughter, or the longest liver of them. Lease of 100 a. in Spts. Co. 530 lbs. tob. yearly, on St. Luke's Day, Oct. 18th. Hugh French, John Mulkay. March 3, 1729–30.

Decr. 6, 1727. Henry Fitzhugh of Stafford Co. to James Wheeler of Spts. Co. John Wheeler, his eldest son, and James Wheeler, Junr., his youngest son, or the longest liver of them. Lease of 100 a. in Spts. Co. 530 lbs. tob. yearly, on St. Luke's Day, Octr. 18th. Hugh French, John Thompson. March 3, 1729–30.

Decr. 6, 1727. Henry Fitzhugh of Stafford Co. to John Thompson, Senr., of Spts. Co., William Thompson, his son, and Mary Thompson, his daughter, or the longest liver of them. Lease of 100 a. in Spts. Co. 530 lbs. tob. yearly, on St. Luke's Day, Octr. 18th. Hugh French, John Mulkay. March 3, 1729–30.

Feby. 10, 1729. Zachary Taylor of Drysdale Par., Caroline Co., Gent., to William Phillips of St. Geo. Par., Spts. Co. 1600 lbs. tob., 100 a.—part of pat. granted James Taylor July 21, 1722, on S. side S. W. mountains on Pamunkey Branches in St. Geo. Par., Spts. Co. David Phillips, James Coward. March 3, 1729–30.

March 3, 1729. Zachary Taylor of Drysdale Par., Caroline Co., Gentl., to George Anderson of St. Anne's Par., Essex Co., planter. £19 curr., 123 a.—part of pat. granted James Taylor July 21, 1722, etc., in St. Geo. Par., Spts. Co. Wm. Cave, Wm. Phillips, Jos. Parker. Mar. 3, 1729–30.

March 3, 1730. Wm. Phillips of St. Geo. Par., Spts. Co., planter, to James Coward of the same Par. and Co., planter. £30 curr., 100 a.—part of tract taken up by sd. Phillips and Nicholas Christopher in St. Geo. Par., Spts. Co. G. Home, Jno. Grayson, Jr. Mar. 3, 1729–30. Anne, wife of Wm. Phillips, acknowledged her dower, etc.

March 3, 1730. Wm. Phillips of St. Geo. Par., Spts. Co., planter, to David Phillips of same Par. and Co., planter. £20 curr., 72½ a. in St. Geo. Par., Spts. Co.—part of tract granted sd. Phillips and Nicholas Christopher, etc. G. Home, Jno. Grayson, Jr. Mar. 3, 1729–30. Anne, wife of Wm. Phillips, acknowledged her dower, etc.

April 4, 1730. Richd. Gregory of King Wm. Co. to John White of same county. £85 curr., 1000 a. in St. Geo. Par., Spts. Co.—granted the sd. Gregory by pat. June 16, 1727. John Waller, Robert Turner, Thos. Waller, Thos. Berch. April 7, 1730. Agnes, wife of Richd. Gregory, acknowledged her dower, etc.

April 7, 1730. George Home of St. Geo. Par., Spts. Co., to John Finalson, Gent., of same par. and county. £30 ster., 400 a. in St. Geo. Par., Spts. Co., in Great Fork of Rappk. River, prchased of Jno. Asher—granted sd. Asher Septr. —, 1728. Wm. Bledsoe, John Williams, Wm. Hackney. April 7, 1730. Elizabeth, wife of George Home, acknowledged her dower, etc.

April 4, 1730. John White of St. John Par., King Wm. Co., Gent., to Thomas Crothers of St. Geo. Par., Spts. Co., planter. '100 a. in St. Geo. Par., Spts. Co. £1 curr. Richd. Gregory, Jos. x Roberts, Thos. White. April 7, 1730. Mary, wife of John White, acknowledged her dower, etc.

Mar. 17, 1730. George Carr and Cordelia, his wife, of Spts. Co. to Benj. Berryman of King Geo. Co., Gent. £6 curr., Lot No. 50 in Fredksburg, etc. Hen. Willis, Thoms. Hill, Thos. Smith. April 7, 1730.

May 4, 1730. Feoffees and Trustees of Fredksburg (by John Waller and Hen. Willis) to David Bray of Williamsburg, Gent. £5 5s. curr., Lot 3, Fredksburg. John Grame, Jno. Mercer, Jo. Waller, Jr. May 5, 1730.

May 5, 1730. Feoffees and Trustees of Fredericksburg (by Hen. Willis and John Waller) to Wm. Todd of Drisdale Par., King and Queen Co., Gent. 55 shill. curr., Lot No. 60 Fredksburg. John Grame, Jno. Mercer, Jno. Waller, Jr. May 5, 1730.

May 5, 1730. Feoffees and Trustees of Fredericksburg (by Hen. Willis & John Waller) to Susannah Livingston of St. Geo. Par., Spts. Co., Widow. £5 5s. curr., Lot 6 in Fredksburg. John Grame, Jno. Mercer, Jo. Waller, Jr. May 5, 1730.

April 7, 1730. Isaac Norman of St. Geo. Par., Spts. Co., to John Read of same par. and county. 3000 lbs. tob., 100 a. in St. Geo. Par., Spts. Co., in Great Fork of Rappk. River—part of pat. granted sd. Norman, June 30, 1726.

Feby. 6, 1729. Christopher Smith of Hanover Co., Merch., to Patterson Pulliam of Caroline Co., planter. £31 5s. curr., 250 a. on N. side Pamunkey River, Spts. Co. Wm. Jennings, Edwd. Moore, Wm. Pulliam, John Snelson. May 6, 1730.

June 2, 1730. Thomas Chew of Spts. Co., Gent., to Larkin Chew, Gent. £100 ster., Land on which sd. Larkin Chew lives—part of two patents granted Capt. Larkin Chew, decd., one dated April 26, 1712, the other Decr. 23, 1714, in St. Geo. Par., Spts. Co., 298 a. G. Lightfoot, Wm. Johnson, Joseph Hawkins. June 2, 1730.

June 24, 1730. John Waller, Junr., of Spts. Co. to John Waller, Senr., of same county, for "300 a. of land gave and made over unto the sd. John Waller, Junr.—being part of a tract of 400 a. of land as the sd. John Waller, Senr., took up and was surveyed, April 3, 1730 * * * (adjoining to a tract of 400 a. of land as his father-in-law Maj. Thomas Carr gave him with his wife) and 700 lbs. tob." All that tract of land in St. Geo. Par., Spts. Co., on N. side Northanna River, 1000 a.—same being pat. granted John Waller, Jr., Septr. 8, 1728. John Mackmath, John Gordon, Michael x Oneale. July 30, 1730.

July 6, 1730. Joseph x Cooper of St. Geo. Par., Spts. Co., planter, to Francis Thornton of St. Marie's Par., Caroline Co., Gent. £20 curr., 202 a. in Great Fork, Rapph. River, one moiety of tract sd. Cooper lives on. John Catlett, Jr., G Home, James Strother. July 7, 1730. Barbary, wife of Joseph Cooper, acknowledged her dower, etc.

July 7, 1730. John x Roberts, son and heir of John Roberts, late of Spts. Co., Decd., and Francis x Kirtley of St. Geo. Par., Spts. Co., to Roger Oxford of same Par. and County. 6000 lbs. tob., 100 a. in St. Geo. Par., Spts. Co., in Great Fork, Rappk. River, formerly granted sd. John Roberts, Decd., by pat. July 12, 1718; conveyed by sd. Roberts, decd., to Francis Kirtley by deed of gift in Spts. Co. Court, Sept. 4, 1722. W. Russell, Robert Green, Samuel Ball. July 7, 1730. Elizabeth Roberts and Margaret Kirtley acknowledged their right of dower, etc.

Augt. 4, 1730. David Cave of Drysdale Par., King and Queen Co., planter, to Daniel Cook of the same county, Lawyer, for consideration of the said Cook paying ½ the charges which the sd. Cave was at in taking up 1000 a. of land—500 a. in fork of Pamunkey River in Spts. Co. G. Home, Wm. Phillips. Augt. 4, 1730.

May 11, 1730. Richard Buckner of Caroline Co., planter, to Lawrence Battaile of the same county, planter. £74 ster., 371 a. in fork of Mattapony River, Spts. Co., purchased by sd. Buckner of one Shackleford. Tho. Catlett, Archd. McPherson, John Watt (Wall?). Septr. 1, 1730.

Septr. 1, 1730. James Sparkes of St. Geo. Par., Spts. Co., Planter, to John Scott, Gent., of same Par. and County. £10 ster., 1000 a. on N. side Rappidan River, in the same par. and county. Larkin Chew, Thos. Slaughter, A. Smith. Septr. 1, 1730. Jane, wife of James Sparks, acknowledged her dower, etc.

March 28, 1730. Wm. Todd of King and Queen Co., Gent., to John Scott of Spts. Co. £20 ster., 1000 a. on S. side Thos. Chew's Mill Creek at the Little Mountains in Spts. Co.—part of pat. granted sd. Todd, ——— ———. Ro. Brooke, Lucy Todd, Jas. Barbour. Septr. 1, 1730.

Sept. 1, 1730. George Penn of Drysdale Par., Caroline Co., Carpenter, to David Williams of St. Geo. Par., Spts. Co., planter. 1000 a. in St. Geo. Par., Sptr. Co., £10 ster. J. Minor, Thos. Chew, W. Sutton. Septr. 1, 1730.

Octr. 5, 1730. John Collier, Jr., of Stratton Major Par., King and Queen Co., to Robert Stubblefield of St. Geo. Par., Spts. Co., for the consideration of two tracts of land in King and Queen Co., to the sd. Collier, as by two deeds in King and Queen Co., bearing date Augt. 22, 1726. Sd. Collier gives sd. Stubblefield 800 a. in St. Geo. Par., Spts. Co., granted by pats. to John Collier, Jr., June 30, 1726. Robt. Dudley, Robt. Goodloe, Tho. Collier. Ann, wife of John Collier, acknowledged her dower, etc.

Octr. 16, 1730. Robert Stubblefield of Spts. Co. to John Collier, Jr., of King and Queen Co. £65 curr., also two tracts of land in Spts. Co., each containing 400 acres, granted to sd. Collier by two patents, both dated June 30, 1726, sd. Stubblefield transfers to sd. Collier £65 curr., and also the two mentioned tracts containing 400 a. each, etc., whereon sd. Stubblefield lives, etc., etc. Robert Dudley, Robert Goodloe, Tho. Collier. Octr. 6, 1730.

Octr. 6, 1730. William Bledsoe of St. Geo. Par., Spts. Co., Gent., to John Taliaferro of same par. and county, Gent. £66 curr., 58 a. in same par. and county—part of tract sd. Bledsoe lives on. Z. Lewis, M. Battaley. Octr. 6, 1730.

Octr. 6, 1730. Augustine Smith of St. Mary's Par., Caroline Co., Gent., to William Fauntleroy of Richmond Co., Gent. £81 8s. curr., 546 a. in St. Geo. Par., Spts. Co.—part of tract granted sd. Smith. Ja. Taliaferro, Larkin Chew, W. Russell. Octr. 6, 1730.

Octr. 6, 1730. John Cook of St. Geo. Par., Spts. Co., to Wm. Bohanan of St. Stephen's Par., King and Queen Co. £1 10s. curr., 200 a. in St. Geo. Par., Spts. Co.—part of tract granted by pat. to sd. Cook Septr. 28, 1728. W. Russell, Robert Cook, Benja. Cave. Octr. 6, 1730. Ann, wife of John Cook, acknowledged her dower, etc.

July 14, 1730. Henry Fox of King William Co. to Samuel Henderson of Hanover Co. £16 ster., 1000 a. in Spts. Co. Wm. Jones, John Malory, Nightingall Dalby. Octr. 6, 1730.

Octr. 6, 1730. John x Ashley of St. Geo. Par., Spts. Co., to Wm. Smith of same par. and county. £10, 50 a. in St. Geo. Par., Spts. Co., great fork Rappk. River—part of pat. granted Jno. Quarles and Jno. Ashley June 6, 1726. W. Russell, Richd x Gill, James McCullaugh. Octr. 6, 1730. Mary, wife of John Ashley, acknowledged her dower, etc.

Octr. 6, 1730. Rowland Thomas of Drysdale Par., King and Queen Co., planter, to Robert Turner of St. Geo. Par., Spts. Co., planter. £5, 100 a. in Spts. Co.—part of pat. granted Rowland Thomas June 16, 1727. Richd. Thomas, John Sutton, Junr., Joseph Williams. Octr. 6, 1730.

Octr. 6, 1730. Philip x Brandegun of St. Paul's Par., Stafford Co., planter, to John Wells of same Par. and County. 5 shill. ster., 150 a.— part of pat. granted Larkin Chew, Gent., of St. Geo. Par., Spts. Co. June 4, 1722, and made over by sd. Chew to sd. Brandegun March 5, 1722 (the year began March 25) in St. Geo. Par., Spts. Co., adjoining the lands of Majr. Benj. Robinson and Henry Rogers. Jno. x Dowds, Henry Collins. Octr. 6, 1730.

Septr. 4, 1730. Thomas Chew and Larkin Chew of St. Geo. Par., Spts. Co., Gentl., to Charles Chiswell of Hanover Co., Gent. £29 17 s. curr., 1000 a. in St. Geo. Par., Spts. Co.—formerly granted to Larkin Chew, Senr., Decd., by pat. Septr. 28, 1728. W. Russell, Jo. Waller, junr., John Grame. Octr. 6, 1730.

Octr. 7, 1730. Henry Willis and John Waller, Gent., Feoffees and Trustees for the Town of Fredksburg, to John Williams of the City of Bristol, Mariner. £2 15s. curr., Lotts 49 and 52. J. Mercer, Jno. Waller, Junr. Octr. 7, 1730.

Octr. 3, 1730. Benjamin Porter of St. George's Par., Spts. Co., to Samuel Henslee of Hanover Par., King Geo. Co. 2000 lbs. tob., 400 a. in St. Geo. Par., Spts. Co.—granted to the sd. Porter by pat. Septr. 28, 1728. Abraham Field, Z. Lewis, Jno. Waller. Nov. 3, 1730. Ann, wife of Benj. Porter, acknowledged her dower, etc.

Novr. 3, 1730. James Pollard, Christ Church Parish, Lancaster Co., to Samuel Ball of St. Geo. Par., Spts. Co. 2000 lbs. tob., 210 a. in St. Geo. Par., Spts. Co., in great fork, Rappk. River—part of pat. granted James Pollard Augt. 17, 1727. Wm. Johnson, John Grame, W. Russell. Nov. 3, 1730. Ann, wife of James Pollard, acknowledged her dower.

Novr. 2, 1730. John x Bush of St. Geo. Par., Spts. Co., to his son-in-law, Robert Andras (Andrews) of the same Par. and County. Fatherly affection to Andrews during his life, then to his first male heir, etc. 120 a. in Glady Fork Run in Spts. Co., St. Geo. Par. Wm. Bartlett, Henry Berry. Novr. 3, 1730.

Novr. 2, 1730. John x Bush of St. Geo. Par., Spts. Co., to his son-in-law, David Bruce, of same par. and county. Fatherly affection to Bruce during his natural life, then to his first male heir, etc. 120 a. in Glady Fork Run in St. Geo. Par., Spts. Co. Wm. Bartlett, Henry Berry. Novr. 3, 1730.

Novr. 2, 1730. John x Bush of St. Geo. Par., Spts. Co., to Philip Bush of the same Par. and County. 200 a.—part of pat. granted John Bush, on Glady Fork Run, St. Geo. Par., Spts. Co. "For and in consideration of fatherly love and affection to my son Philip Bush," etc. Wm. Bartlett, Henry Berry. Novr. 3, 1730.

Octr. 6, 1730. Christopher Zimmerman of St. Geo. Par., Spts. Co., to William Johnson of same county and parish. £20, 280 a. in St. Geo. Par., Spts. Co.—part of tract granted sd. Zimmerman by patent Septr. 28, 1728. W. Russell, Andrew Wilson, Tomas Whiland. Decr. 1, 1730. Elizabeth, wife of Christopher Zimmerman, acknowledged her dower, etc.

Feby. 2, 1731. Isaac Norman and James Turner of St. Geo. Par., Spts. Co., to Robert King of same Par. and County. 3200 lbs. tob. and 11 shill. curr., 634 a. in St. Geo. Par., Spts. Co. Wm. Johnson, J. Foster, Wm. Hansford. Feby. 2, 1730-1.

Jany. 6, 1730. Wm. x Eddings of St. Geo. Par., Spts. Co., to Dunkin Bohannan of St. Stephen's Par., King and Queen Co. £175 curr., 611 a. in St. Geo. Par., Spts. Co. Theopholes x Edings, Thos. Burton, Elliott Bohannon. Feby. 2, 1730. Rebeccah, wife of Wm. Eddings, acknowledged her dower, etc.

Jany. 23, 1730. John x Kilgore of St. Mark's Par., Spts. Co., to John Haddox of same par. and county. 2000 lbs. tob., 126 a. in St. Mark's Par., Spts. Co., in Great Fork Rappk. River—sd. land granted Jno. Kilgore by pat. Sep. 28, 1728. Samuel Ball, William x Smith, Matthew Stanton. Feby. 2, 1731-2. Mary, wife of John Kilgore, acknowledged her dower, etc.

Decr. 13, 1730. George x Proctor of St. Geo. Par., Spts. Co., Planter, to "Charles Burges of St. Mary's, White Chappell, in the county of Lancaster, Merchant." £15, 1000 a. in St. Geo. Par., Spts. Co., as by pat. Sept. 28, 1728. Joseph Parker, Batholomew x Redman, Charles Steward. Feby. 2, 1730–1.

Decr. 13, 1730. Edward Price of St. Geo. Par., Spts. Co., planter, to Charles Burges of St. Mary's, White Chappell, in the County of Lancaster, Merchant. 1000 a. as by pat. Septr. 28, 1728, in St. Geo. Par., Spts. Co. John Blake, Jno. Grayson, Junr., Thos. Phillips, Bryan x Shannon. Feby. 2, 1730–1.

Decr. 13, 1730. John Price of St. Geo. Par., Spts. Co., to Charles Burges of St. Mary's White Chappell, in the County of Lancaster, Merchant. £10, 1000 a. as by pat. dated Septr. 8, 1728, in St. Geo. Par., Spts. Co. J. Taliaferro, Joseph Parker, Richard Hill, Henry x Herronton. Feby. 2, 1730–1.

George x Proctor of St. Geo. Par., Spts. Co., to his daughter, Elizabeth, and George Home, her husband. Deed of Gift, "in consideration of ye celebration of nuptials between them," and 60 lbs. ster., a parcell of land in St. Geo. Par., Spts. Co., on ridge between Deep and Hazel Run. Dated, Jany. 2, 1731. Natha. Claiborne, Edwd. Price. Recorded, Feby. 2, 1730–1.

March 2, 1730. Daniel Brown of St. Geo. Par., Spts. Co., planter, to Griffen Fauntleroy, St. Stephen's Par., Northumberland Co., Gentleman. £45 curr., 100 a. in St. Geo. Par., Spts. Co., in branches of River Ta— granted to sd. Brown by pat. Sept. 28, 1728. John Waller, Jno. Mackmath, Jno. Waller, Jr. March 2, 1730–1. Elizabeth, wife of Daniel Brown, acknowledged her dower.

March 3, 1730. Henry Willis of Spts. Co., Gent., to John Lewis of Gloucester Co., Gent., and Charles Lewis of New Kent Co., Gent. 10 shill. ster., 1465 a. in Spts. Co., formerly Rappahannock, at head of Nassaponax Creek, formerly granted on John Bowsey by pat. Nov. 5, 1673, from whom the sd. land lapsed for not seating the same, then granted by Augustine Smith, who relinquished the same, it then being granted the sd. Willis by pat. April 8, 1729. This land for the use of sd. Henry Willis during his lifetime, then for the use of his wife, Mildred Willis, etc. John Waller, M. Battaley, John Mackmarth. March 2, 1730–1.

March 2, 1730. John x Bond of Spts. Co. to George Whetley of the same county. 3500 lbs. tob., 210 a. in fork of Rappk. River in Spts. Co. G. Lightfoot, La. Chew, Edwin Hickman. March 2, 1730–1. Mary, wife of John Bond, acknowledged her dower, etc.

March 2, 1730. John x Asher of St. Mark's Par., Spts. Co., to Robert Boatman of Christ Church Par., Lancaster Co. 2000 lbs. tob., 200 a. in St. Mark's Par., Spts. Co., in Great Fork of Rappk. River. Andr. Harrison, Mathew Stanton, Peter Russell. March 2, 1730–1.

March 2, 1730. John Downer of St. Margarett's Par., Caroline Co., to Thomas Graves of St. Geo. Par., Spts. Co. £20 curr., 400 a. as by patent granted sd. Downer June 16, 1727. Jas. Barbour, James Williams, Thos. Downer. Mar. 2, 1730–1. Ann, wife of John Downer, acknowledged her dower, etc.

April 6, 1731. Francis x Kirtley of St. Mark's Par., Spts. Co., to Elisha Perkins of same Par. and County. £33 curr., 470 a. in St. Mark's Par., Spts. Co., in great fork Rappk. River—granted to sd. Kirtley by Pat. Septr. 28, 1728. Edwin Hickman, W. Russell, John Christopher. April 6, 1731. Margaret, wife of Francis Kirtley, acknowledged her dower, etc.

April 6, 1731. Thomas Chew of St. Geo. Par., Spts. Co., to Nicholas Hawkins of the same Par. and County. £5 curr. and 2750 lbs. tob., 298 a. in Spts. Co. joining sd. Hawkins, Robt. Thomas, Francis Smith, Augustine Smith of Gloucester, Wm. Richason and Johnathan Clark. G. Lightfoot, Robt. Slaughter, Thos. Slaughter. April 6, 1731.

May 4, 1731. Phillip Watters of St. Mark's Par., Spts. Co., Carpenter, to Henry Rice of Drysdale Par., King and Queen Co., Planter. £10 cur., 3000 lb. tob., 470 a. in St. Mark's Par., Spts. Co. Cha. Goodall, Abraham x Bledsoe, Zach. Taylor. May 4, 1731.

May 4, 1731. John Rouse of St. Geo. Par., Spts. Co., to Wm. Eddings of same Par. and County. £100 ster., 305 a. in St. Mark's Par., Spts. Co. G. Homè, Jno. Rucker. May 4, 1731. Mary, wife of John Rouse, acknowledged her dower, etc.

May 4, 1731. William Bartlett of Spots. Co. to Robert Thomas of St. Mary's Par., Caroline Co. £20 curr., 28 a. in Spts. Co.—part of a parcell of land sold Thomas Bartlett, father of sd. Wm. Bartlett, by Larkin Chew. Witnesses: Thos. Jarman, John Miller, Owen Thomas. May 4, 1731. Susannah, wife of William Bartlett, acknowledged her dower, etc.

April 13, 1731. Edward Price of St. Geo. Par., Spts. Co., planter, to William Fauntleroy of Sittenbourn Par., Richmond Co., Gent. £55 curr., 200 a. in St. Geo. Par., Spts. Co., formerly belonging to George Proctor and conveyed by him, April 3, 1727, to the sd. Price. Walter x Frances, Thomas Price. May 4, 1731. Sarah, wife of Edward Price, acknowledged her dower.

April 29, 1731. Robert Coleman of Drysdale Par., King and Queen Co., Gentl., to Henry Rice of same County and Par., planter. 200 a. in St. Geo. Par., Spts. Co., for consideration of 1600 lbs. tob. John x Davis, Zachary Taylor. May 4, 1731. Mary, wife of Robert Coleman, acknowledged her dower.

May 4, 1731. Augustine Smith of St. Mark's Par., Spts. Co., to Thomas Reeves of St. Geo. Par., Spts. Co. £20 "for the better and more perfect confirming and assureing to ye said Thos. Reeves, 200 a. of land by the said Augustine Smith, sold to his father, Henry Reeves, by deeds * * * * in Essex Court, the 9th Septr., 1714, and by sd. Henry Reeves bequeathed to his son, Thomas Reeves"—the sd. 200 a. in St. Geo. Par., Spts. Co., part of pat. granted sd. Smith, Augt. 21, 1719. Benjamin Berryman, Fran. Thornton, Junr., Zachary Taylor. May 4, 1731.

April 7, 1731. Danl. Brown of St. Geo. Par., Spts. Co., planter, to John Hopson of same Par. and County, Bricklayer. £18 curr., 400 a. on River Ta in St. Geo. Par., Spts. Co., granted by pat. to sd. Brown, Feby. 24, 1730. Z. Lewis, J. Mercer, John Buckner. May 4, 1731. Elizabeth, wife of Danl. Brown, acknowledged her dower.

April 8, 1731. Augustine Smith of St. Mark's Par., Spts. Co., Gent., to Cornelius Saile of St. Ann Par., Essex Co., planter. £19, 200 a. in St.

Andrew's Par., in county aforesaid, about two or three miles above falls of Rappk. River—part of pat. granted sd. Smith Augt. 21, 1719, formerly pat. by sd. Saile Novr. 10, 1714, and acknowledged by sd. Smith in Essex Co. Jany. 13 following, etc. T. Waring, Charles Duett, Ro. Brooke. May 4, 1731.

May 4, 1731. Joseph Hawkins of St. Mark's Par., Spts. Co., planter, to Edward Rouse of St. Margaret's Par., Caroline Co., planter. 4400 lbs. tob., 400 a. in St. Mark's Par., Spts. Co. Cha. Goodall, John Johnson, Jno. Waller, Jr. May 4, 1731.

May 29, 1731. Augustine Smith of St. Mark's Par., Spts. Co., Gent., to George Reeves of Southfarnham Par., Essex Co., planter, for consideration paid by Peter Byrom, decd., of Southfarnham Par., Essex Co., sd. Byrom selling sd. land to Henry Reeves, decd., who by his will devised the same to his son, George Reeves—sd. 100 a. part of a tract formerly granted one John Bowsey als, Bonger (or Benger?) and since his death granted to sd. Smith by pat. Octr. 22, 1719, 100 a. on S. side Rappk. River abt. four miles above the falls in Spts. Co. Thomas Hill, John Leigh, Tho. Reeves. June 1, 1731.

June 1, 1731. Christopher Smith of St. Paul's Par., Hanover Co., Gent., to James Rallings of St. Geo. Par., Spts. Co. £82 10s. curr., 1000 a. on Northanna River, in Spts. Co.—granted sd. Smith by Pat. Sept. 28, 1728, except 250 a. part thereof, etc., etc. William James, William Dickenson, William Wombwell Cliff. June 1, 1731.

June 2, 1731. Batholomew x Wood of St. Geo. Par., Spts. Co., to John Wood of Northumberland Co. 2000 lbs. tob., 133 a. in St. Geo. Par., Spts. Co., "in a line of a patent formerly granted Bathomew Wood," etc. Tho. Reeves, Wm. Hackney. June 1, 1731.

June 2, 1731. Batholomew x Wood of St. Geo. Par., Spts. Co., to John Edwards of the same Par. and County. 3000 lbs. tob., 150 a. in St. Geo. Par., Spts. Co. Tho. Reeves, Wm. Hackney. June 1, 1731.

May 2, 1731. Robert Cave of St. Geo. Par., Spts. Co., to Edwin Hickman of same par. and county. £8 curr., 1000 a. in St. Geo. Par., Spts. Co. Fran. Thornton, R. Curtis, Jr., Robt. Turner. June 1, 1731.

June 2, 1731. Batholomew x Wood of St. Geo. Par., Spts. Co., to John Elson of same par. and county. £8 curr., 100 a. in St. Geo. Par., Spts. Co. Tho. Reeves, Wm. Hackney. June 1, 1731.

May 28, 1731. Henry Thacker of Middlesex Co., Gent., to Jeremiah Clowder of Spts. Co., Gent. £5 curr., 1000 a. in Spts. Co.—granted sd. Thacker by Pat. Septr. 28, 1728. John Waller, Robt. Beverley, Jno. Waller, Junr. June 1, 1731.

Mar. 25, 1731. Henry Haines of Spts. Co., planter, to Thomas Hubard of same county, planter. 1000 lbs. tob., 1720 a. in St. Geo. Par., Spts. Co.— part of pat. granted sd. Haines Septr. 28, 1728, on branches of South River, adjoining lands of Robt. Stubblefield, Robt. Baylor and Wm. Pruetts. Witnesses: Wm. Waller, John Talbert, John Nalle. July 6, 1731. Mary, wife of Henry Haines, acknowledged her dower, etc.

Jany. 4, 1730. John Catlett of Caroline Co., Gent., to his son, John Catlett, Junr., of same county, planter. "one moiety or half part of a tract of land purchased by him, the sd. Jno. Catlett and Richard Buckner,

Gent., of Augustine Smith," containing 4000 a. in St. Geo. Par., Spts. Co. Benjamin x Taylor, Charles x Morgan. July 6, 1731. Mary, wife of John Catlett, Gent., acknowledged her dower, etc.

John Williams of City of Bristol, Merchant, appts. Wm. Fauntleroy of Richmond Co., Va., his attorney, etc., to convey several parts and shares of and in "a certain Copper work intended to be carried on in the great fork of Rappahannock River in Spts. Co., Va. * * * * * * by virtue of one Indenture of Lease granted by one John Findenson," etc., etc., to Lyonel Lyde, John Taylor and Andrew Lewis, one-fifth each, and to John Lewis, Wm. Williams and Cornelius Lyde one-tenth each. Witnesses: Wm. Stevens, Thos. Trenayler. July 6, 1731.

July 5, 1731. Aron x Pinson of Spts. Co. to Richard Johnson of same county. £10 curr., 50 a.—part of pat. granted sd. Pinson Octr. 13, 1727, in Spts. Co. Thomas x Little, Abraham x Little, Benj. Cottman. July 6, 1731. Elizabeth, wife of Aron Pinson, acknowledged her dower.

July 6, 1731. John x Duett of St. Mark's Par., Spts. Co., to William Smith of same Par. and County. £10, 400 a. in St. Mark's Par., Spts. Co., in great fork Rappk. River—granted sd. Duett by pat. Sept. 28, 1728. W. Russell, Francis x Michael, Thomas Byrn. July 6, 1731.

July 6, 1731. William Phillips of St. Mark's Par., Spts. Co., to John Davis of same Par. and County. £10 curr. and 2000 lbs. tob., 100 a.—part of pat. formerly granted James Taylor July 21, 1722, in St. Geo. Par., Spts. Co. John Rucker, Thomas x Jackson, Henry x Downs. July 6, 1731. Ann, wife of William Phillips, acknowledged her dower.

Augt. 3, 1731. George Woods of St. Mark's Par., Spts. Co., to John Huffman of same Par. and County. £6 curr., 196 a. in great fork Rappk. River in St. Geo. Par., Spts. Co. John Johnson, Eiprs Hickman. Augt. 3, 1731. "George Woods, alias Utz, acknowledged this his deed," etc., etc.

Philemon x Cavenaugh of St. Geo. Par., Spts. Co., to his daughter, Winifred, and Lewis Davis Yancey, her husband, for £1 ster., 800 a. in St. Mark's Par., Spts. Co., in great fork of Rappk. River. Z. Lewis, M. Battaley, J. Mercer. Dated, Augt. 3, 1731. Recd. Augt. 3, 1731.

April 14, 1731. Augustine Smith of St. Mark's Par., Spts. Co., Gent., to Philemon Cavanaugh of St. Geo. Par., Spts. Co. £15, 150 a. on Rappk. River, about four miles above the falls, in St. Geo. Par., Spts. Co. Robt. Slaughter, Joseph Henderson, Lewis Davis Yancey. Augt. 3, 1731.

July 28, 1731. George Woodroof of St. Geo. Par., Spts. Co., to Joseph Temple of St. Margaret's Par., King William County, Merchant. £25 curr., 180 a. in St. Geo. Par., Spts. Co.—part of tract granted sd. Woodroof by pat. April 17, 1728. Martin x Davenport, Franke x Arnold, Rachell x Arnold, Benja. x Arnold. Septr. 7, 1731. Jane, wife of George Woodroof, acknowledged her dower, etc.

Sept. 7, 1731. Thomas x Yates of St. Mark's Par., Spts. Co., to Samuel Hensley, Junr., of St. Geo. Par., Spts. Co. £12 curr., 360 a.—granted sd. Yates by pat. Sept. 28, 1728, in St. Mark's Par., Spts. Co. Dunkin Bohannon, Peter Murtle, Susannah x Bohannon, W. Russell, Richard x Sharp, George x Popplewell. Oct. 5, 1731. Sarah, wife of Thomas Yates, acknowledged her dower.

July 7, 1731. John Key of St. Geo. Par., Spts. Co., to Henry Lewis of same Par. and County. £35 curr., 350 a. in St. Geo. Par., Spts. Co.—granted sd. Key by pat. Sept. 28, 1728. Charles Barrett, William Taylor, William Wombwell Cliff. Octr. 5, 1731. Martha, wife of John Key, acknowledged her dower.

Octr. 5, 1731. Joseph Cottman of Somersett Co., Maryland, to Thomas Farmer of Spts. Co., Va. 5 shill., 100 a.—part of a tract formerly granted James Cannon in Spts. Co. James Cannon, Thomas x Little, Aaron x Pinson. Octr. 5, 1731.

Oct. 5, 1731. Thomas x Crethers of Spts. Co. to William Lea of same county, and Robert Baylor of King and Queen Co., Gent. £12 by Lea, £30 by Baylor, 100 a. in St. Geo. Par., Spts. Co., whereon sd. Crethers now lives and bought by Crethers of John White of King William, as pr. deed April 4, 1730. Z. Lewis, Zach. Taylor. Octr. 5, 1731. (Zach. Taylor guard. to sd. Wm. Lea, a minor.)

Septr. 5, 1731. Francis x Michael of St. Mark's Par., Spts. Co., to Samuel Wright of same Par. and county. £15 curr., 400 a. in St. Mark's Par., Spts. Co.—granted sd. Michael by pat. Sept. 28, 1728. W. Russell, John Christopher, Pierce x Cowdey. Octr. 5, 1731. Mary, wife of Francis Michael, acknowledged her dower.

Octr. 2, 1731. Aaron x Pinson of Spts. Co. to John Ashley of same county. 2500 lbs. tob., 101 a. in Spts. Co.—part of tract granted sd. Pinson by Patent. Thomas x Little, Abraham x Little, Benjamin Cottman.

Novr. 2, 1731. Augustine Smith of Spts. Co., Gent., to his eldest son, Thomas Smith, of the same County, Gent. £250 ster. and for sd. Thos. advancement in life, 400 a. in Spts. whereon sd. Thos. now dwells and for some time past has dwelt, etc. M. Battaley, J. Mercer. Novr. 2, 1731.

Novr. 2, 1731. Jeremiah Clowder of Spts. Co., Gent., to Patrick Welch of same county, planter. £45 curr., 210 a. in Spts. Co.—part of pat. granted Henry Thacker, Gent., of Middlesex Co. Septr. 28, 1728. Robt. Green, John Scott. Novr. 2, 1731.

Nov. 2, 1731. Moseley Battaley of Hanover Par., King Geo. Co., to Henry Willis of St. Geo. Par., Spts. Co. £15 curr., Lot 62 and house thereon in Fredericksburg. Jno. Grayson, Jr., James Williams, John Gordon. Novr. 2, 1731.

Novr. 2, 1731. Lazarus x Tilly of St. Geo. Par., Spts. Co., to David More of same Par. and County. £11 ster., 183 a.—part of pat. granted Larkin Chew June 4, 1721, in St. Geo. Par., Spts. Co. Rice Curtis, R. Curtis, Jr., Fra. Smith. Nov. 2, 1731.

Octr. 1, 1731. John x Ashley of St. Mark's Par., Spts. Co., to Robert Slaughter and Francis Slaughter of par. and county aforesd., Gentl., present Church Wardens of ye Parish of St. Mark's. 14,500 lbs. tob., 215 a. in St. Mark's Par., Spts. Co.—part of pat. granted sd. Ashley and John Quarles June 6, 1726. This property was sold the churwardens for The Glebe of St. Mark's Par. Witnesses: Wm. Johnson, W. Russell, William Logan. Novr. 2, 1731. Mary, wife of John Ashley, acknowledged her dower.

Novr. 2, 1731. Richard and Isabella Thomas of Drisdale Par., King and Queen Co., planters, to William Briant of Spts. Co., planter. "A sufficient reward," etc., 300 a.—part of pat. granted sd. Isabella Thomas Septr. 28, 1728, in St. Mark's Par., Spts. Co. Joseph Hawkins, John Young, Frances x Mycall.

Novr. 2, 1731. Dunkin Bohannon of St. Stephen's Par., King and Queen Co., to William Edins of St. Mark's Par., Spts. Co. £175 curr., 611 a. in St. Mark's Par., Spts. Co. Robt. Turner, Tho. Park, Dunkin Bohannon, Junr. Novr. 2, 1731.

Novr. 2, 1731. Wm. Edings and Rebeccah, his wife, of St. Mark's Par., Spts. Co. to Dunkin Bohannon of St. Stephen's Par., King and Queen Co. £47 curr., 312 a. in St. Mark's Par., Spts. Co. Robt. Turner, Dunkin Bohannon, junr., Tho. Park. Nov. 2, 1731.

Thomas Carr of St. Margaret's Par., Caroline Co., Gent., to his daughter, Agnes Waller, wife of John Waller, Junr., of Spts. Co. 400 a. in Spts. Co.—granted by pat. to sd. Carr June 16, 1727. John Waller, Z. Lewis, Fra. Smith. Dated, Novr. 26, 1731. Recd. Feby. 2, 1731–2.

Decr. 4, 1731. Dannitt Abney, Jr., of Spts. Co. to Zachary Lewis of same county. 4120 lbs. tob., 381 a. in Spts. Co.—granted sd. Abney, by Pat. Septr. 28, 1728. John Waller, Charles Goodall, Jno. Waller, junr., John Wilkins. Feby. 1, 1731–2. Mary, wife of Dannitt Abney, Jr., acknowledged her dower.

April 4, 1732. Augustine Smith and John Waller, two of the Trustees and Feoffees, etc., for Fredksburg, to Thomas Smith of King George Co. £8 5s., Lots 21 and 22 in Fredericksburg. Jno. Waller, junr., Robert Thomas. April 4, 1732.

April 4, 1732. Henry Willis, Augustine Smith and John Waller of Spts. Co., Gentlemen, Directors and Trustees, etc., for Fredericksburg, to Robert Thomas of Caroline County. £5 10s. curr., Lots 30 and 32 in Fredksburg. Jno. Waller, Junr. April 4, 1732.

April 4, 1732. James Williams of St. Geo. Par., Spts. Co., to Henry Willis of same Par. and Co., Gent. £10 curr., 1 a. near the town of Fredericksburg. M. Battaley, J. Mercer. April 4, 1732.

April 4, 1732. Edward x Rouse of St. Margaret's Par., Caroline Co., Shoemaker, to Samuel Smith of St. Mark's Par., Spts. Co., Planter. £25. 400 a. in St. Mark's Par., Spts. Co. John Bryantt, Robert Cave, George Smith. April 4, 1732. Frances, wife of Edward Rouse, acknowledged her dower, etc.

April 4, 1732. Goodrich Lightfoot of Spts. Co., Gent., to John Lightfoot of same county, Gent. £100 ster., 300 a. in Spts. Co. Thos. Chew, Wm. Bledsoe. April 4, 1732.

"Philemon x Cavanaugh of St. Mark's Par., Spts. Co., do for the love and affection I bear to Elizabeth Yancy, daughter to Winifred and Lewis Davis Yancey, her husband," etc. £1 ster., 100 a. in Spts. Co. "joining land I formerly gave my daughter Winifred and Lewis Davis Yancey, her husband," etc. No witnesses. April 4, 1732.

April 4, 1732. Peter Russell of St. Mark's Par., Spts. Co., to John Dowdey of same Par. & County. £10 curr., 400 a. in St. Mark's Par., Spts. Co.—formerly granted sd. Russell by Pat. Sept. 28, 1728. Mathew Stanton, Wm. Morgan. April 4, 1732. Sarah, wife of Peter Russell, acknowledged her dower, etc.

April 4, 1732. William x Edings of St. Mark's Par., Spts. Co., to Robert Broadaway of same Par. and County. £20 curr., 150 a. in St. Mark's Par., Spts. Co. Robert Turner, Henry x Blackgrove, Elizabeth x Edings. April 4, 1732. Rebeccah, wife of Wm. Edings, acknowledged her dower, etc.

March 6, 1731-2. Henry Berry of Hanover Par., King Geo. Co., to William Fleet of St. Stephen's Par., King and Queen Co. £20 ster., 720 a.— granted sd. Berry by Pat. Septr. 28, 1728. Wm. Bledsoe, John Leigh, Jr., Robert Cave. May 2, 1732.

June 6, 1732. Francis Thornton and Francis Thornton, junr. Executors of the last will and testament of James Horsnale, decd. [See Will Book A.] and of St. Mary's Par., Caroline Co., to William Grayson of St. Bee's Par., Cumberland Co., in Great Britain. £50 ster., 300 a. in St. Geo. Par., Spts. Co., purchased by James Horsnale of Augustine Smith. Witnesses: John Grame, John Bland, James x Roy. June 6, 1732.

June 6, 1732. Abraham x Bledsoe of St. Mark's Par., Spts. Co., to Thomas Watts of same Par. and County. £50 ster., 400 a. in St. Mark's Par., Spts. Co. John Foster, William Henderson, G. Home. June 6, 1732. Sarah, wife of Abraham Bledsoe, acknowledged her dower.

June 7, 1732. John Henderson of Spts. Co., planter, to Samuel Brockman of King and Queen Co., planter. 1200 lbs. tob., 300 a. in Spts. Co. William Henderson, Robert Bickers, Benja. Cave. June 6, 1732. Sarah, wife of John Henderson, acknowledged her dower.

June 7, 1732. Robert Bickers of Spts. Co., planter, to John Collins of Caroline Co., planter. £5 curr., 200 a.—part of tract formerly granted by pat. to sd. Bickers Sept. 28, 1728, in St. Mark's Par., Spts. Co. Benja. Cave, John Henderson, Samuel Brockman. June 6, 1732. Elizabeth, wife of Robert Bickers, acknowledged her dower, etc.

June 5, 1732. Richard Mauldin of St. Mark's Par., Spts. Co., Gent., to Timothy Johnson of same Par. and County. £10 ster., 100 a.—granted by Pat. to sd. Mauldin Sept. 28, 1728, in Spts. Co. William Johnson, Robert Turner, John Parks. June 6, 1732.

Feby. 21, 1731. Joseph x Cooper of St. Mark's Par., Spts. Co., planter, to John Gordon of Fredericksburg, ordinary keeper. £20 curr., 200 a. in fork of Rappk. River. John Young, Wm. x Eddings, James Porteus. Augt. 1, 1732. Barbary, wife of Joseph Cooper, acknowledged her dower.

May 5, 1732. Thomas Turner of King Geo. Co., Gent., to Charles Chiswell of Hanover Co., Gent. £150 curr., 250 a. in Spts. Co., purchased by sd. Turner of Edward Rowzee of Essex, by deeds, Jany. 5, 1725. Also 200 a. in Spts. Co., formerly purchased by Turner of John Blanton of Spts. Co., as pr. deeds Feby. 10th and 11th, 1728. Also 150 a. in Spts. Co., which sd. tracts are part of tract formerly granted Larkin Chew by patent. Wm. Strother, Z. Lewis, M. Battaley. Augt. 1, 1732. Sarah, wife of Thomas Turner, acknowledged her dower, etc.

Feby. 19, 1731. Aaron x Pinson of Spts. Co. to John Ashley of same county. 2000 lbs. tob., 50 a.—one moiety of tract heretofore granted sd. Pinson. John Hamman, John Carder, Robert Slaughter, A. Smith. Augt. 1, 1732. Elizabeth, wife of Aaron Pinson, acknowledged her dower, etc.

Augt. 5, 1732. Joseph Bloodworth of St. Mark's Par., Spts. Co., Carpenter, to Robert Watts of King Geo. Co., planter. 6000 lbs. tob., 400 a.

in St. Mark's Par., Spts. Co. G. Home, Peter Russell. Augt. 2, 1732. Mary, wife of Joseph Bloodworth, acknowledged her dower, etc.

Novr. 17, 1731. Thomas x Allen of Spts. Co., planter, to William Taylor of same county, Mason. £6 curr., 200 a. in Spts. Co.—granted sd. Allen by Pat. Sep. 28, 1728. Joseph Gibson, William Jones, William Wombwell Cliff. Augt. 2, 1732. Elizabeth, wife of Thomas Allen, acknowledged her dower, etc.

Augt. 4, 1732. Edward Pigg of Spts. Co. to John Pigg, Jr., of same county, on consideration of Bill in Chancery of Spts. Co. Court April 5, 1731, sd. Edward Pigg convey to John Pigg, Jr., 150 a.—being a fourth part of 600 a. in St. Geo. Par., Spts. Co. John Foster, John Rucker, Antho. Foster. Augt. 3, 1732.

Augt. 4, 1732. John Pigg, Jr., of St. Geo. Par., Spts. Co., and Elizabeth, his wife, to William Johnson of same county. £20 curr. and 2000 lbs. tob., 150 a.—a part of 600 a. which sd. Pigg has recovered of Edward Pigg of county aforesd., etc. Z. Lewis, John Foster, Antho. Foster. Augt. 3, 1732.

July 4, 1732. Thomas x Jackson of Spts. Co. to David Tinsley of Caroline Co. 40 shill., 268 a.—formerly granted to sd. Jackson by patent. William Phillips, William Crosthwait, John Rucker. Septr. 5, 1732.

Septr. 2, 1732. William Bohannan and Sarah, his wife, of St. Stephen's Par., King and Queen Co., to Edward Smith of same Par. and County. £10 5s. curr., 200 a. in St. Geo. Par., Spts. Co.—part of pat. granted John Cook Sept. 28, 1728. R. Bell, Robert x Tunwell, Eliza. x Bell. Sept. 5, 1732.

Sept. 5, 1732. George Taylor of St. Mary's Par., Caroline Co., to John Zachary of St. Mark's Par., Spts. Co., for "a valuable consideration," etc., 200 a. in St. Mark's Par., Spts. Co.—part of pat. granted sd. Taylor Sept. 28, 1728, on branches of James River, at foot of Great Mountains, etc. James Taylor, Thos. Slaughter, Zach. Taylor. Sept. 5, 1732.

Mar. 14, 1731. Rice Curtis of St. Geo. Par., Spts. Co., planter, to John Minor of St. Mark's Par., Spts. Co., planter. £60 ster., 600 a. in Spts. Co.—part of pat. granted Thos. Chew June 16, 1727, and sold by sd. Chew to sd. Curtis as by deed Oct. 19, 1727. R. Curtis, Jr., Peter Montague, Robert Elless. Octr. 3, 1732.

March 14, 1731. Rice Curtis of St. Geo. Par., Spts. Co., planter, to John Douglass of St. Mark's Par., Spts. Co., planter. £20 ster., 195 a. in Spts. Co. R. Curtis, Jr., Peter Montague, Robt. x Elless. Octr. 3, 1732.

Nov. 1, 1732. Robert Boatman of Christ Church Par., Lancaster Co., planter, to William Tayloe of Drysdale Par., Caroline Co., Gent. £40 curr., 200 a. in St. Mark's Par., Spts. Co.—part of a pat. granted John Ashley Sept. 28, 1728, and sold by him to sd. Boatman as by deeds March 2, 1730. Robert Martin, Adam x Loving, Zach. Taylor. Nov. 7, 1732.

Nov. 6, 1732. Honble. Alexander Spotswood of Spts. Co., Esqr., to Edmund Bagge of Essex Co., planter, "for and in consideration of friendship and regard and for past services rendered," etc., and also the sum of 5 shill., 2284 a., known as "Indian Field," in St. Mark's Par., Spts. Co., and part of pat. granted Thomas Jones, John Clayton and Richard Hickman June 22, 1722, and renewed by pat. April 11, 1732, "and now actually "belonging" to sd. Spotswood, etc. John Grame, Elliott Benger, James McCullough. Nov. 7, 1732.

Sept. 3, 1732. Zachary Taylor of Drysdale Par., Caroline Co., to James Stodghill of St. Mark's Par., Spts. Co. £20 curr., 200 a. in St. Mark's Par., Spts. Co. Daniel Stodghill, Thomas Callaway, John x Zachary. Nov. 7, 1732.

Nov. 7, 1732. Feoffees or Trustees of the Town of Fredericksbg (by Henry Willis and Ja. Taliaferro, Gent.) to Griffin Fauntleroy of Richmond Co., Gent. £2 15s. curr., Lot 16 in Fredksbg. Robert Turner, Benja. Berryman. Novr. 8, 1732.

Octr. 3, 1732. George x Musick of St. Geo. Par., Spts. Co., planter, to Henry Elly of Hanover Par., King Geo. Co., Founder. £14 curr., 500 a. in St. Geo. Par., Spts. Co., granted sd. Musick and Thomas Allen by pat. Sept. 28, 1728. Tho. Jarman, Joseph Hawkins, William Wombwell Cliffe. Nov. 7, 1732. Ann, wife of George Musick, acknowledged her dower.

Nov. 7, 1732. Thomas Chew of St. Mark's Par., Spts. Co., Gent., to Robert Martin of Drysdale Par., King and Queen Co., "for consideration of sd. Martin's coming to live at the So. West mountains in afsd. Co. 30 a. of land. John Rucker, George Penn, William x Crafford. Nov. 7, 1732.

Feby. 4, 1732-3. Wm. Taylor of St. Geo. Par., Spts. Co., Mason, to Henry Elley of aforesaid par. and co., Founder. £— curr., 200 a. in Spts. Co.—part of Pat. formerly granted Thos. Allen and George Musick Sept. 28, 1728. Chas. Barret, John Jones, William Wombwell Cliffe. Feby. 6, 1732-3.

Feby. 6, 1732. Thomas Rucker of Caroline Co. to John Rucker of Spts. Co. £20 ster., 476 a. St. Mark's Par., Spts. Co.—part of pat. granted sd. Thos. Rucker. Witnesses: Thos. Chew, Joseph Hawkins, Robert Turner. Feby. 6, 1732-3. Elizabeth, wife of Thomas Rucker, acknowledged her dower, etc.

March 1, 1733. John Finalson of St. Mark's Par., Spts. Co., to William Tayloe of Christ Church Par., Lancaster Co. £25, 400 a. in St. Mark's Par., Spts. Co., granted sd. Finalson by pat. Mar. 30, 1733. John Waller, M. Battaley, Robert Turner. Apr. 3, 1733.

April 3, 1733. Richard x Sharp of St. Mark's Par., Spts. Co., planter, to James Barbour of same Par. and County, Gent. £25 curr., 1000 a. whereon sd. Sharp now lives—being a pat. granted sd. Sharp Sep. 28, 1728. Thos. Chew, John Minor, James Taylor. April 3, 1733. Mary, wife of Richd. Sharp, acknowledged her dower.

April 3, 1733. Richard Maulden of St. Mark's Par., Spts. Co., to Nicholas Battaille of St. Mary's Par., Caroline Co., Gent. £22 curr., 177 a. in St. Mark's Par., Spts. Co.—part of a tract bought by Maulden out of "another tract granted James Taylor, Decd., by pat. July 21, 1722," etc. John Waller, M. Battaley, James Taylor. April 3, 1733. Jane, wife of Richard Maulden, acknowledged her dower, etc.

April 3, 1733. Richard Maulden of St. Mark's Par., Spts. Co., to Nicholas Battaille of St. Marie's Par., Caroline Co., Gent. £38 16s. curr., 300 a. in St. Mark's Par., Spts. Co.—part of a tract bought by Maulden out of "another tract granted James Taylor, decd., by pat. July 21, 1722," etc. John Waller, M. Battaley. April 3, 1733. Jane, wife of Richard Maulden, acknowledged her dower, etc.

April 3, 1733. Richard Maulden of St. Mark's Par., Spts. Co., Gent., to Zacharias Gibbs of same par. and county. £12 curr., 100 a. in St. Mark's Par., Spts. Co.,—"part of a tract or seat of land purchased of Colo. James Taylor, Decd," etc. Wm. Phillips, Wm. Turberville, Henry Downs. April 3, 1733. Jane, wife of Richard Maulden, acknowledged her dower, etc.

April 3, 1733. Richard Maulden of St. Mark's Par., Spts. Co., Gent., to John Barnett of same par. and county. £22 curr., 184 a. in St. Mark's Par., Spts. Co., etc. Wm. Phillips, Wil. Turberville, Henry Downs. April 3, 1733. Jane, wife of Richard Maulden, acknowledged her dower, etc.

April 3, 1733. Wm. x Edins of St. Mark's Par., Spts. Co., to Richard Maulden of same Par. and Co. £7 ster., 248 a. in Spts. Co.—whole of a pat. granted sd. Edins Sept. 28, 1728. Wm. Phillips, Will. Turberville, Zacharias Gibbs. April 3, 1733. Rebeckah, wife of Wm. Edins, acknowledged her dower, etc.

April 3, 1733. Thomas Chew (the elder son and heir of Larkin Chew, Gent., Decd.) of Spts. Co. to Rice Curtis (the assignee of Wm. Hansford, Gent., the assignee of Samuel Short) of the same county. £20 ster., 611 a. in St. Geo. Par., Spts. Co.—part of pat. granted Larkin Chew June 4, 1722. Anthony Thornton, G. Lightfoot, John Minor. April 3, 1733.

Nicholas Ware of St. Marie's Par., Caroline Co., "for several good causes and considerations do give grant unto Robert Andress," etc. 500 a. in St. Mark's Par., Spts. Co.—part of a tract granted sd. Ware, etc. Witnesses: Wm. Phillips, Thomas Sarnders. May 1, 1733.

April 3, 1733. Moseley Battaley of St. Geo. Par., Spts. Co., Gent., and Elizabeth, his wife, to Richard Tutt of same Par. and County, Gent. £50 curr., 500 a. in St. Mark's Par., Spts. Co., etc. Abra. Field, Wm. Hackney, William Kelly. May 1, 1733.

May 1, 1733. Ambrose Grayson of St. Geo. Par., Spts. Co., to Matthew Gale of Gloster Co. £12 curr., 300 a. in St. Geo. Par., Spts. Co. Thomas Hill, G. Home, Francis Turnley. May 1, 1733. Alice, wife of Ambrose Grayson, acknowledged her dower, etc.

June 5, 1733. Thomas Carr of St. Margaret's Par., Caroline Co., Gent., to John Minor of St. Mark's Par., Spts. Co., planter. £50 curr., 530 a. in St. Geo. Par., Spts. Co.—part of pat. granted Thomas Carr June 7, 1726. Cha. Goodall, Thomas Carr, junr., Jno. Waller, Jr. June 5, 1733.

June 5, 1733. Thomas Carr of St. Margaret's Par., Caroline Co., Gent., to John Waller, Jr., of St. Geo. Par., Spts. Co. "In consideration of the natural love and affection that he bears unto the sd. John Waller, Jr., and more especially for and in consideration of that 400 a. of land and plantation whereon the sd. John Waller, Jr., lives, made over to him the sd. Thomas Carr," etc. 470 a. in Spts. Co.—part of a tract granted sd. Carr by pat. June 7, 1726. Chas. Goodall, Thomas Carr, Jr., John Minor. June 5, 1733.

June 4, 1733. John Catlett, Junr., of St. Marie's Par., Caroline Co., to Benjamin Taylor of St. Mark's Par., Spts. Co. £10 curr., 100 a. in St. Mark's Par., Spts. Co.—part of a tract granted Augustine Smith by patent and now in tenure and possession of sd. John Catlett, Jr., Jno. Catlett, Senr., and Richard Buckner, etc. Jonath. Gibson, John Taliaferro, James

Taylor. June 5, 1733. Alice, wife of John Catlett, Jr., acknowledged her dower.

April 3, 1733. Goodrich Lightfoot of St. Mark's Par., Spts. Co., to Charles Morgain of same par. and county. £12 curr., 86 a. in St. Mark's Par., Spts. Co. R. Progens, Elisha Perkins. June 5, 1733. Mary, wife of Goodrich Lightfoot, acknowledged her dower, etc.

June 1, 1733. Richard Tutt of St, Geo. Par., Spts. Co., to Moseley Battaley of same par. and county. £60 curr., 500 a. in St. Mark's Par., Spts. Co. Henry Terrett, W. Russell, Robert Turner. July 3, 1733. Elizabeth, wife of Richard Tutt, acknowledged her dower, etc.

Dec. 7, 1732. Elias x Downs of King William Co., planter, to Henry Willis of Spts. Co., Gent. £8, 200 a. in Massaponnax Swamp in Spts. Co.— part of a patent granted sd. Downs, etc. Witnesses: Peter Hedgman, Jno. Lee, Hancock Lee, Robt. Spotswood. July 3, 1733.

July 3, 1733. John x Asher of Spts. Co., planter, to Wm. Rosson of Lancaster Co. £40 ster., 400 a. in great fork of Rappk. River, etc. No witnesses. July 3, 1733.

July 2, 1733. Owen Thomas of St. Marie's Par., Caroline Co., to Henry Willis of St. Geo. Par., Spts. Co. £50 curr., 1 a. in St. Geo. Par., Spts. Co., or Lots 32 and 33 in Fredksburg, etc. G. Home, Sam. Hensley, Robt. Williams. July 3, 1733.

July 3, 1733. Thomas Smith of Spts. Co., Gent., to Thomas Hill of same county, merchant. £8 10s. ster., two lots in Fredksburg, Nos. 21 and 22. Robt. Slaughter, Jas. Barbour, Sampson Darrell. July 3, 1733. Anne, wife of Thomas Smith, acknowledged her dower, etc.

Augt. 2, 1733. George Home of St. George's Par., Spts. Co., Surveyor, and Elizabeth, his wife, to Moseley Battaley of same Par. and Co., Gent. £10 curr., 58 a. in St. Geo. Par., Spts. Co. William Henderson, Robert x Pattersone, Elizabeth x Bryant. Augt. 7, 1733.

Augt. 8, 1733. Thomas x Jackson and Margaret, his wife, of St. Mark's Par., Spts. Co., to "William Crosthwait, late of the province of Pensilvania, but now of the parish, county," etc., aforsd. £50 curr., 100 a. whereon sd. Crosthwait now lives, etc.—part of a pat. granted Colo. James Taylor in Spts. Co. July 21, 1722, and made over to sd. Jackson by sd. Taylor as by deeds July 6, 1725. John Red, Henry Downs, Jno. x Scelton. Augt. 7, 1733.

Augt. 15, 1733. Joseph Parker of St. Geo. Par., Spts. Co., Mariner, to Moseley Battaley of same Par. and Co., Gent. £25 curr., 86 a. in St. Geo. Par., Spts. Co., etc. Frans. Taliaferro, Jno. Curtis, Richd. Tutt. Sept. 4, 1733.

Sept. 4, 1733. John x Hadox of Spts. Co. to Francis Thornton of Caroline Co. £50 curr., 51 a. in fork of Rappk. River, and part of pat. formerly granted William Paton June 11, 1726, transferred by sd. Paton to John Kilgore, and from sd. Kilgore to sd. John Hadox, as by deeds June 3, 1729, etc. James Taylor, Robt. Stuart, John Red. Sept. 4, 1733. Dorothea, wife of sd. John Hadox, acknowledged her dower, etc.

Sept. 4, 1733. William Johnston of Spts. Co. to George Hardin of Middlesex Co. £60 curr., 1020 a. in Spts. Co., etc. Edward Herndon, junr.,

Daniel Gwyn, Robt. Johnston. Sept. 4, 1733. Anne, wife of Wm. Johnston, acknowledged her dower, etc.

Oct. 2, 1733. Dannit Abney, the elder, of Spts. Co., planter, and Mary, his wife, and Dannitt Abney, the younger, of Hanover County, planter, and Mary, his wife, to Humphrey Hill of King William Co., Gent. Whereas John Wilkins was granted 400 a. in King William Co., now Spts. Co., by pat. dated June 2, 1722, and by deed dated July 7, 1724, said Wilkins conveyed to Dannit Abney, the Elder, and Dannit Abney, the Younger, the sd. parcel or tract of land, for consideration therein named, etc. £80 curr., the Abneys convey this land to sd. Humphrey Hill, etc. Witesses: Roderick Gordon, Thomas Hill, Thomas Todd, Joseph Woolfolk, Anthony Rhodes, Junr. Oct. 2, 1733.

July 27, 1733. Dannitt Abney, Junr., and Mary, his wife, of St. —— Par., Hanover Co., to Richard Phillips of St. Geo. Par., Spts. Co. £30 curr., 400 a. in Spts. Co. Witnesses: Thomas Ballard Smith, Elias x Deavenport, Thomas Adams. Oct. 2, 1733.

Oct. 2, 1733. Richard Taliaferro of St. Marie's Par., Caroline Co. and William Taliaferro of Stratton Major Par., King and Queen Co., to John Taliaferro of St. Marie's Par., Caroline Co. £120 ster., 1000 a. in St. Mark's Par., Spts. Co. William Strother, Keamp Taliaferro. Oct. 2, 1733.

Jeremiah Clowder of St. Mark's Par., Spts. Co., Gent., "for and in consideration of the love and affection which I have to John Hyat, who hath served me from his youth," as well as for divers other causes and considerations," etc. 100 a. in Spts. Co.—part of a tract granted sd. Clowder, etc. Witnesses: William x Stevens, Joseph Hawkins, Joseph Keaton. Dated, June 7, 1733. Recd. Oct. 3, 1733.

May 26, 1733. Thomas x Cook of St. Mark's Par., Spts. Co., to John Redd of Drysdale Par., King and Queen Co. £10, 100 a. in St. Mark's Par., Spts. Co.—part of a pat. grant. sd. Cooke Sept. 28, 1728. David Cave, Sarah Cave, James x Fidler. Nov. 6, 1733.

Nov. 6, 1733. Roger Tandy of St. Stephen's Par., King and Queen Co., to William Dyer of St. Geo. Par., Spts. Co. £10 curr., 100 a. in St. Geo. Par., Spts. Co. George Smith, Tallefero Cragg, Philip Bush.

May 6, 1733. Thomas x Cook of St. Mark's Par., Spts. Co., to James Fidler of same par. and county. £10, 100 a. in St. Mark's Par., Spts. Co.— part of a tract granted sd. Cook by Pat. Sept. 8, 1728. David Cave, Sarah Cave, John Red. Nov. 6, 1733.

Sept. 1, 1733. Thomas Jarman of St. Geo. Par., Spts. Co., planter, to Henry Elly of same par. and co., Founder. £4 curr., 87 a. in St. Geo. Par., Spts. Co.—pat. by sd. Jarman June 20, 1733. Robert Turner, Charles Barrett, William Wombwell Cliffe. Nov. 6, 1733. Mary, wife of Thos. Jarman, acknowledged her dower, etc.

Augustine Smith of St. Geo. Par., Spts. Co., Gent., to William Triplett of Brunswick Par., King Geo. Co., Gent. £100 ster., 515 a. in St. Geo. Par., Spts. Co., in Fork of Rappk. River. Elliott Benger, Rogr. Quarles, Tho. Reeves. Nov. 6, 1733.

Feby. 5, 1733-4. Thomas Chew of Spts. Co., Gent., to John Grymes of Middlesex Co., Esqr. £93 10s. curr., 348 a. (part of a tract granted Larkin

Chew, Decd., by Pat. Dec. 3, 1714, and by sd. Larkin Chew conveyed to sd. Thos. Chew, as by deeds, March 4, 1727) in St. Geo. Par., Spts. Co. Wm. Bartlet, Owen Thomas, Frederick Coghill, Junr. Feby. 5, 1733-4. Martha, wife of Thomas Chew, acknowledged her dower, etc.

Dec. 4, 1733. Phillip Politch of St. Mark's Par., Spts. Co., to Nicholas Yager of same par. and co. £20 ster.—a parcel of ground in St. Mark's Par., Spts. Co., "being ye upper part of a parcel of land acknowledged in Spts. Co. by Nicholas Yager to Phillip Politch by deeds July 1, 1729," etc. Robert Turner, William Henderson, John Gordon. Feby. 5, 1733-4.

Jany. 28, 1733-4. Thomas Wright of Spts. Co., planter, to William Hackney of Prince William Co. 2000 lbs. tob., 400 a. in St. Mark's Par., Spts. Co. Francis x Michael, Thomas x Wright, Junr., James McDonald, Feby. 5, 1733-4. Frances, wife of Thomas Wright, acknowledged her dower, etc.

Feby. 5, 1733. John Roy of St. Mary's Par., Caroline Co., to Robert Hucherson of St. Geo. Par., Spts. Co. £10 ster., 121 a. (part of a pat. granted Larkin Chew June 4, 1722) in St. Geo. Par., Spts. Co. Jonath. Gibson, M. Battaley, Z. Lewis, Larkin Chew. Feby. 5, 1733-4. Dorothy, wife of John Roy, acknowledged her dower, etc.

Feby. 5, 1734. Dunkin Bohannan of King & Queen Co. to William Eddings of St. Mark's Par., Spts. Co. £30 curr., 312 a. in Spts. Co. G. Home, James King. Feby. 5, 1733-4.

Feby. 5, 1733. John x Kirkley (Kirtlet) of St. Mark's Par., Spts. Co., lease to John Garth of same par. and county; a tract of land in Spts. Co., "to John Garth, Mary Garth or John Horn," "on the Feast of St. Michael, one Fatt Henn, Capon or Pullet," etc. Witnesses: G. Home, Benja. Powell. Feby. 5, 1733-4.

Nov. 8, 1733. Theophilus x Eddings of Spts. Co. to Alexander Waugh of same county. £40 curr., 230 a. in fork of Robinson River—a pat. granted sd. Eddings August 25, 1731. Robert Turner, Antho. Strother. Feby. 5, 1733-4. Diannah, wife of Theophilus Eddings, acknowledged her dower, etc.

Decr. 4, 1733. William x Carpenter of St. Mark's Par., Spts. Co., to "Michael Cook and Michael Smith, wardens and trustees of the German Church, and people Inhabiting in the fork of Rappahannock River in St. Mark's Par., in the County of Spotsylvania," etc. £20 curr., 193 a. in the first Fork of Rappidan River, in parish and county afrsd.—same granted Carpenter by pat. Sep. 28, 1728, the sd. land "to be set apart for a Glebe and for the only proper use of the Minister of the sd. German people," etc. John Waller, Robert Turner, Edwd. Broughton, James King, William Henderson. Feby. 5, 1733-4.

Decr. 4, 1733. William x Eddings of St. Mark's Par., Spts. Co., to Henry Haws of same par. and county. £88 curr., 705 a. in St. Mark's Par., Spts. Co. John Champe, William Phillips. Feby. 5, 1733-4. Rebeccah, wife of Wm. Eddings, acknowledged her dower, etc.

Feby. 6, 1734. John Rucker of St. Mark's Parish, Spts. Co., to Peter Rucker, Elizabeth Rucker, Peter Rucker, junr., and Ephraim Rucker. £20 curr., 420 a.—remainder of a pat. granted sd. John Rucker, in St.

Mark's Par., Spts. Co. "Peter and Elizabeth Rucker, during their Naturall lives, and afterwards to Peter Rucker, Junr., and Ephraim Rucker," etc. G. Home, Joseph Delaney, John Johnson. Feby. 6, 1733–4.

John Rucker of St. Mark's Pa., Spts. Co., "to my sister, Mary Rucker," love and affection and £1 ster., To "Mary Rucker and William Offall, her lawful husband," etc., etc. 100 a. in St. Mark's Par., Spts. Co. Dated, Feby. 6, 1730. Recd. Feby. 6, 1733–4. Witnesses: G. Home, Joseph Delaney, John Johnson.

Sept. 6, 1733. Henry Fitzhugh of Stafford Co., Esqr., to Susannah Livingston of Spts. Co., widow, lease of 100 a. in Spts. Co. "To Susannah Livingston, Thomas Matthews, her servant, and James Frazier, son of William Frazier, taylor," etc.; on Fest. of St. Luke, Oct. 18th, 500 lbs. of tobacco, etc., yearly rental, etc. Witnesses: Sarah Fitzhugh, Lettice Lee. Recd. March 5, 1733–4.

March 5, 1733. William x Briand (Bryan) of Spts. Co. to Phillip Boush of same county. 800 lbs. tob., 102 a. in St. Mark's Par., Spts. Co. Robert Stuart, Wm. Bartlet, Henry Dongun. March 5, 1733–4.

March 5, 1733–4. Robert Andress of Spts. Co. to Henry Rice of Drysdale Par., King and Queen Co., planter. £20 curr., 500 a. (part of a tract formerly granted Nicholas Ware Sept. 28, 1728, and conveyed by sd. Ware to sd. Andress) in St. Mark's Par., Spts. Co. Edward Broughton, William Henderson, John Gordon. March 5, 1733–4.

Octr. 19, 1733. Richard Buckner of St. Marie's Par., Caroline Co., Gent., to William Strother of Brunswick Par., King George Co. £83 ster., 332 a. in Spts. Co.—part of a pat. granted Augustine Smith and conveyed by him to the sd. Buckner and Col. John Catlett, etc. Witnesses: Tho. Catlett, William Tompkins, Keamp Taliaferro. March 5, 1733–4.

March 2, 1733. Goodrich Lightfoot of St. Mark's Par., Spts. Co., to Richard Wright of same par. and county. £4 curr., 50 a. in St. Mark's Par., Spts. Co.—part of a tract granted sd. Lightfoot by pat. June 26, 1731. Jane x Teele, Anthony Sculthorpe, W. Russell. March 5, 1733–.

Feby. 14, 17—. Henry Willis of Spts. Co., Va., Gent., to Thomas Hill of same county, Gent. Whereas by pat. July 23, 1728, Henry Willis was granted a tract of 10,000 a. of land in St. Geo. Par., Spts. Co.; the sd. Willis has sold to Thomas Beale, 3,333 acres; to Ambrose Madison, 3,333 acres, and to Goodrich Lightfoot, 300 acres of that sd. tract. Now for the sum of £25 curr. and £2 ster., 3034 a., the remainder of the sd. tract of 10,000 acres. Z. Lewis, M. Battaley, Fran. Thornton, Jr., Antho. Rhodes, Junr. March 5, 1733–4.

March 5, 1733. John Rucker of Spts. Co. to Phillip Stockdale of St. Anne's Par., Essex Co. £21 5s. curr. and 6000 lbs. tob., 703 a.—150 a. thereof part of a pat. granted sd. Rucker Augt. 17, 1727, and 553 a. part of pat. granted Thos. Rucker June 16, 1730, and sold and made over to sd. John Rucker, as by Deeds, Feby. 5, 1732. In Spts. Co. Thomas Chew, James Cox, Charles Stevens. March 5, 1733–4. Susannah, wife of John Rucker, acknowledged her dower, etc.

April 2, 1734. John Rogers of King and Queen Co. to Edward Pigg of Spts. Co. Whereas by pat. April 1, 1727, John Madison, John Rogers,

Peter Rogers, Henry Pigg, Edward Pigg and John York were granted 1860 acres of land in King Wm. Co.—now part in Spts. Co. and part in Caroline, a division in which Edward Pigg and John Rogers name their moieties, etc. Witnesses: R. Easham, Thos. Estes, Thos. Guy. April 2, 1734.

March 5, 1733. Charles Stevens of St. Mark's Par., Spts. Co., to John Lightfoot of same Par. and County. £21 curr., 300 a. in St. Mark's Par., Spts. Co.—part of a pat. granted sd. Stevens Sept. 28, 1728. W. Russell, Robt. Turner, Thos. Guy. March 5, 1733-4. Elizabeth, wife of Charles Stevens, acknowledged her dower, etc.

April 2, 1734. John x Asher of St. Mark's Par., Spts. Co., planter, to John Martin and Benja. Martin of St. Geo. Par., Spts. Co., planters. 1500 lbs. tob., 400 a. in St. Mark's Par., Spts. Co. M. Battaley, Wm. Waller, Henry x Martin, Jr. April 2, 1734.

April 2, 1734. William x Smith of St. Mark's Par., Spts. Co., to Charles Morgan of same Par. and Co. £24, 150 a. in St. Mark's Par., Spts. Co. Robert Turner, Charles Stevens, John Cook. April 2, 1734. Mary, wife of William Smith, acknowledged her dower, etc.

April 2, 1733. Charles x Morgan of St. Mark's Par., Spts. Co., to William Smith of same par. and county. £12 curr., 86 a. in St. Mark's Par., Spts. Co., in Little Fork of Rappk. River. Robert Turner, Chas. Stevens, John Cook. April 2, 1734. Hannah, wife of Charles Morgan, acknowledged her dower, etc.

April 2, 1734. Roger x Oxford of Spotsylvania Co., planter, to Joseph Delaney of Prince William Co. £30 curr., 400 a. in fork of Rappk. River in Spts. Co.—taken out by Patent by the sd. Oxford, etc. Wit.: Antho. Strother, Peter Daniel, James Elles. April 2, 1734. Margaret, wife of Roger Oxford, acknowledged her dower, etc.

Feby. 7, 1733. William Hutcherson of St. Geo. Par., Spts. Co., to Rice Curtis of same par. and county. £22 curr., 100 a. (part of pat. granted Larkin Chew, decd., June 4, 1722, and conveyed by sd. Chew to sd. Hutcherson by deeds —— ——) in St. Geo. Par., Spts. Co. R. Curtis, junr., Peter Montague, Alexr. x Cleaveland. April 2, 1734.

March 27, 1734. Richard Mauldin of Spts. Co. to Edward Tinsley of King and Queen Co. £20 ster., 120 a. in Spts. Co. Hen. Downs, Jon. Willson, Wm. Rucker. April 2, 1734. Jane, wife of Richard Mauldin, acknowledged her dower, etc.

March 29, 1734. Roger x Oxford of St. Mark's Par., Spts. Co., to Francis Kirtley of same Par. and county. £5, 500 a. in St. Mark's Par., Spts. Co., in great fork of Rappk. River, etc.—granted sd. Oxford by pat. Sept. 28, 1728. G. Home, James Turner, Benja. Roberts. April 2, 1734. Margaret, wife of Roger Oxford, acknowledged her dower, etc.

March 30, 1734. Richard Maulden of St. Mark's Par., Spts. Co., Gent., to William Daniel, junr., of St. Ann's Par., Caroline Co., planter. £50 curr., 300 a. (part of a pat. granted Col. James Taylor, and sold by sd. Taylor to sd. Maulden, etc.) in St. Mark's Par., Spts. Co. Hen. Downs, Jno. Willson, Wm. Rucker. April 2, 1734. Jane, wife of Richard Maulden, acknowledged her dower, etc.

April 3, 1734. David x Williams of St. Mark's Par., Spts. Co., planter, to Thomas Callaway of same par. and county, planter. 5 shill. curr., 100 a. in St. Mark's Par., Spts. Co.—part of pat. granted George Pen Sept. 28, 1728, and sold by Pen to David Williams, etc. Witnesses: John Waller, Zachary Taylor, Wm. Waller. April 3, 1734. Mary, wife of David Williams, acknowledged her dower, etc.

Dec. 1, 1730. George Home of St. Geo. Par., Spts. Co., Gent., to William Russell of same Par. and County, Gent. Whereas Thomas Chew, Wm. Johnson and sd. George did obtain order of Council June, 1728, to survey and take up 6000 a. of land, and about the same time did obtain the order of Council with Larkin Chew, Joseph Smith and sd. Wm. Russell to survey and take up 10,000 a. of land, etc., etc.; now sd. Home for 1100 lbs. tob. transfers all his right, title, interest, etc., to sd. William Russell. Witnesses: Elliott Benger, John Tennant. Dec. 1, 1730.

DEED BOOK C

1734-1742

March 8, 1733. David x MacMurrin of St. Mark's Par., Spts. Co., to Francis Thornton, junr., of St. Geo. Par., Spts. Co. 400 a. in St. Mark's Par., Spts. Co.—pat. by sd. MacMurrin July 21, 1732. W. Russell, Robert Green, Fran. Slaughter, Robt. Slaughter, Augt. Smith. April 2, 1734.

April 7, 1734. Thomas Chew and Martha, his wife, of Spts. Co., Gent., to Hugh Gwyn of Gloucester Co. 800 a. in Spts. Co. Wm. Bledsoe, W. Johnston, R. Curtis, junr. April 3, 1734.

April 2, 1734. David x Williams of St. Mark's Par., Spts. Co., planter, to William Callaway of same Par. and County, planter. 200 a.—part of a pat. granted George Pen Sep. 28, 1728, and sold by Pen to sd. Williams, in St. Mark's Par., Spts. Co. Zach. Taylor, Wm. Conner, John Waller. April 3, 1734. Mary, wife of David Williams, acknowledged her dower, etc.

May 7, 1734. Thomas x Hubbard of St. Geo. Par., Spts. Co., to John Talbert of same Par. and County. 100 a. in Spts. Co.—part of pat. granted Henry Haines Sept. 28, 1728; 200 a.—part of which pat. was conveyed by Haines to sd. Hubbard by Deeds July 6, 1731. Wm. Waller, Robt. Turner, Wm. Phillips. May 7, 1734. Christian, wife of Thomas Hubbard, acknowledged her dower, etc.

Jany. 30, 1733. Isaac Norman of Spts. Co., planter, to Nathaniel Hillin of Spts. Co., planter. 100 a. in St. Geo. Par., Spts. Co. Augt. Smith, Joseph Stapp, Joseph Henderson. May 7, 1734.

Jany. 30, 1733. Isaac Norman of Spts. Co., planter, to "James Turner, my son-in-law, planter, and Kerenhappuch Turner, my daughter, of ye said County," etc., deed of gift and £50. 100 a. in Spts. Co.—part of a pat. whereon sd. Norman now lives, etc. Augt. Smith, Joseph Stapp, Joseph Henderson. May 7, 1734.

April 30, 1734. William Beverley of St. Ann's Par., Essex Co., Gent., to John Burk of St. Mark's Par., Spts. Co., planter, deed of lease. 100 a. on Elkwood in St. Mark's Par., Spts. Co., whereon sd. John now dwells, etc., "said John, Mary, his wife, and Richard, his son," etc., 430 lbs. tob. yearly. Wit.: W. Russell, Anthony Scott, John Sexton, Edmd. Pagett. May 7, 1734.

William x Crawford of St. Mark's Par., Spts. Co., planter, to Benjamin Coward and Elizabeth, his wife. 100 a. on Elk Run, joining Thos. Jackson, Wm. Crawford, Jr., and Thomas Crawford. Deed of Gift. Dated, March 11, 1733. Wit.: D. Bryne, George x Anderson, William Craford, junr. Recd. May 7, 1734.

May 17, 1734. Benjamin Rush of King George Co. to Anthony Strother of Spts. Co. £40 curr., 387 a. in St. Mark's Par., Spts. Co., in fork of

Rappk. River, granted sd. Rush by pat. May 11, 1726. Frans. Thornton, junr., Robt. Biscoe, Peter Daniell. May 7, 1734. Amey, wife of Benjamin Rush, acknowledged her dower.

May 7, 1734. John Foster of Spts. Co. to Thomas Benson of same county. £16 curr., 200 a. (part of pat. granted sd. Foster, 1733) in Spts. Co. Edwd. Herndon, junr., John Askew, R. Eastham. May 7, 1734.

June 4, 1734. Richard Phillips of St. Geo. Par., Spts. Co., to James Edwards of St. John's Par., King William Co. 2500 lbs. tob. and £18 curr., 400 a. in Spts. Co., formerly granted Dannitt Abney, junr., by pat. June 30, 1726, and sold by Abney to sd. Phillips, as by Deeds, Oct. 2, 1733. Wm. Waller, Roger Quarles, Thos. Waller. June 4, 1734. Catherine, wife of Richard Phillips, acknowledged her dower, etc.

June 4, 1734. William x Eddings of St. Mark's Par., Culp. Co., planter, to William Jordan of Lunenburg Par., Richmond Co., Gent. £60 curr., 349 a. in St. Mark's Par., Spts. Co.—part of two tracts of land, one granted Eddings by pat. June 30, 1726, the other bought by Eddings of Wm. Mc-Connico, the sd. two tracts sold by sd. Eddings to Duncan Buchannan and repurchased from sd. Buchannan by sd. Eddings, as by Deeds, Novr. 2, 1731. G. Home, Zach. Taylor, Jno. Willson. June 4, 1734. Rebecca, wife of Wm. Eddings, acknowledged her dower, etc.

June 4, 1734. John Rucker of St. Geo. Par., Spts. Co., to William Rucker of same par. and county. £20 curr., 200 a. in St. Mark's Par., Spts. Co. Thos. Chew, Will. Crosthwait, Wm. Bartlet. June 4, 1734.

June 4, 1734. Richard Maulden of St. Mark's Par., Spts. Co., to Theofolous Eddins of same par. and county. £15 curr., 248 a. formerly granted Wm. Eddins, by pat. Sep. 28, 1728. John Christopher, Wm. Mackay, Jno. Willson. June 4, 1734. Jane, wife of Richard Mauldin, acknowledged her dower, etc.

June 5, 1734. Philemon x Cavenaugh of St. Mark's Par., Spts. Co., "to my daughter Elizabeth and John Conner, her lawful husband," etc. Deed of gift. £1 ster., 400 a. in sd. Par. and County, in fork of Rappk. River. Wm. Deatherage, R. Eastham, Robt. Bayley.

June 4, 1734. Charles Steward of St. Geo. Par., Spts. Co., to George Home of par. and county afsd. £20 ster., land in St. Mark's Par., Spts. Co. David Kinkead, Thomas Hobson, William x Fields. June 5, 1734.

June 29, 1734. Robert Stubblefield of St. Geo. Par., Spts. Co., to Ralph Williams of parish and county afsd. 2500 lbs. tob., 200 a. in Spts. Co. (first taken up by Nicho. Lanford and by him sold to Jno. Collier, Junr., of King and Queen, and by sd. Collier conveyed to sd. Stubblefield, as by deeds, Oct. 6, 1730)—part of pat. granted Jno. Collier, Junr., June 30, 1726. Benjamin x Matthews, Senr., Benjamin x Matthewes, Junr. July 2, 1734. Anne, wife of Robt. Stubblefield, acknowledged her dower, etc.

May 7, 1734. Robert Stubblefield of Spts. Co., St. Geo. Par., to Benjamin Matthews of county and par. afsd. 4090 lbs. tob., 200 a. in Spts. Co. (first taken up by Nicho. Langford, by him sold to Jno. Collier, Junr., of King and Queen Co., and by him conveyed to sd. Stubblefield, as by Deeds, Oct. 6, 1730)—part of pat. granted John Collier, Junr., June 30, 1726. William Rice, Daniel x Pruit. June 2, 1734. Anne, wife of Robert Stubblefield, acknowledged her dower, etc.

Feby. 23, 1733. Tobias Ingram of Essex Co. and Robert Brooke of same county, Gent. An exchange of land, Tobias Ingram, 333 a. in St. Ann's Par, Essex Co. Robert Brooke, 400 a. in St. Mark's Par., Spts. Co. "The sd. 333 a. before mentioned being part of a certain piece or parcell of land containing 400 a. formerly conveyed by one Wm. Moseley, Decd., unto Tobias Ingram, Decd., grandfather to the sd. Tobias, party to these presents, by Deeds dated Augt. 17, 1657, and afterwards confirmed to Thomas Ingram, father of the sd. Tobias, party to these presents, by Edward Moseley, son and heir of sd. Wm. Moseley, by Deed dated Feby. 12, 1712.

"The sd. 400 a. granted sd. Robert Brooke by pat. June 20, 1733," etc. Witnesses: B. Vawter, Wm. Balware, Henry Motley, July 2, 1734.

June 29, 1734. Joseph Delaney of Hamilton Par., Prince William Co., planter, to Robert Biscoe of Brunswick Par., King Geo. Co. £9 curr., 97 a. in St. Geo. Par., Spts. Co., granted sd. Delaney by pat. Sept. 28, 1728. John Latham, James x Roy. July 2, 1734. Mary, wife of Joseph Delaney, acknowledged her dower, etc.

July 23, 1734. Robert Jones of Prince William Co., Gent., to John Mercer of Stafford Co., Gent. £205, 1000 a. in Spts. Co. Charles Brent, James Porteus, Thomas x Staines, Robert Turner, Js. Mercer. Augt. 6, 1734.

Augt. 6, 1734. John Mercer of Stafford Co., Gent., to Charles Carter of King Geo. Co., Esqr. £200 curr., 1000 a. in Spts. Co. in fork of Rappk. River. John Waller, Jno. Taliaferro, Z. Lewis, M. Battaley, Wm. Waller. Augt. 6, 1734.

Augt. 6, 1734. Thomas Ballard Smith, son and heir of William Smith, Gent., of Spts. Co., Decd., to Richard Phillips of afsd. Co. £20 curr., interest in plantation in St. Geo. Par., Spts. Co.—pat. by Wm. Smith, Decd., afsd., Oct. 31, 1726, and conveyed by him to Phillips as by Deeds, etc. Edwin Hickman, Wm. Waller, Edward Blackley. Augt. 6, 1734.

Augt. 6, 1734. Benjamin Berryman of King George Co., Gent., to Frances Frazer, widow, and James Frazer, her son, of the town of Fredericksburg. £6 15s. curr., Lot 50 in the town of Fredksburg, etc. Thomas Hill, James Sleet, Robert Stuart. Augt. 6, 1734.

Augt. 6, 1734. John Red of St. Mark's Par., Spts. Co., to Lazarus Tilly of St. Geo. Par., Spts. Co. 3000 lbs. tob., 100 a. in St. Mark's Par., Spts. Co., bought by sd. Red of Thomas Cook, and formerly granted sd. Cook in a larger patent Sept. 28, 1728. G. Home, Benj. Henslee, David x Watts. Augt. 6, 1734. Mary, wife of John Red, acknowledged her dower, etc.

John x Smith of St. Geo. Par., Spts. Co., "unto my well beloved grandson, John Tyre," 100 a. in St. Geo. Par., Spts. Co.—part of a pat. granted sd. Smith, etc. Deed of gift. Wit.: Wm. Waller, Henry Haynes, John Stubblefield. Dated July 27, 1734. Recd. Sep. 3, 1734.

July 17, 1734. John x Smith of St. Geo. Par., Spts. Co., to William Dobbs of par. and co. afsd. £10 curr., 100 a. in Spts. Co.—part of pat. granted sd. Smith June 30, 1727(?) Wm. Waller, Wm. x Tyre, Wm. x Smith. Sept. 3, 1734. Margaret, wife of John Smith, acknowledged her dower, etc.

July 6, 1734. Richard Bayley of Drysdale Par., King and Queen Co., to James Elliott of St. Margarett's Par., King William Co., Gent. £36 curr., 720 a. in St. Mark's Par., Spts. Co., formerly granted sd. Bayley by Pat. Sep. 28, 1728. Martha Todd, Roderick Gordon, Edwin Hickman, Humphrey Hill, Benja. Hubbard, Robt. Bayley. Sept. 3, 1734.

Humphrey Hill of King William Co. to his nieces, Susannah and Sarah Hill, several slaves. Deed of gift, "my brother Thomas Hill." Dated Sept. 3, 1734. Witnesses: Roderick Gordon, Thomas Todd, Anthony Rhodes. Recd. Sep. 3, 1734. "Humphrey Hill, Gent., unto his two Nieces at ye motion of their father, Mr. Thomas Hill," etc.

Augt. 6, 1734. William Beverley and Ann Beverley, Executors of the last will and testament of Robt. Beverley of Spts. Co., Esqr., Decd., to Lawrence Battaille of Caroline Co. £110 ster., 1000 a. in Spts. Co. Eliza. Jones, Catherine Beverley, Zach. Taylor. Sept. 3, 1734.

William Rush of Spts. Co. to Peter Weaver of Spts. Co. £10 curr., 100 a. in St. Mark's Par., Spts. Co.—part of tract granted sd. Rush by pat. May 11, 1726. Robt. Turner, Jno. Cook, Tho. Pulliam. Oct. 1, 1734. Mary, wife of Wm. Rush, acknowledged her dower, etc.

Oct. 1, 1734. James Coward, of St. Mark's Par., Spts. Co., planter, to John Zachary of Par. and Co. afsd., planter. £30 curr., 100 a. in St. Mark's Par., Spts. Co.—part of a pat. to Wm. Phillips and Nicholas Christopher. Robt. Slaughter, Zach. Taylor, Benja. Powell. Oct. 1, 1734. Elizabeth, wife of James Coward, acknowledged her dower, etc.

Sept. 28, 1734. Anthony x Gholston of Spts. Co. to Wm. Gaines of King and Queen Co. £23 curr., 442½ a. in St. Geo. Par., Spts. Co.—part of pat. granted sd. Gholston Sept. 28, 1728. Joseph Thomas, Charles Stevens, Jno. Cook. Oct. 1, 1734. Jane, wife of Anthony Gholston, acknowledged her dower, etc.

Sept. 28, 1734. Anthony Gholston of Spts. Co. to James Jones of Caroline. £27 curr., 442½ a. (part of a pat. grant. sd. Gholston Sept. 28, 1728) in St. Geo. Par., Spts. Co. Joseph Thomas, Charles Stevens, Jno. Cook, Oct. 1, 1734. Jane, wife of Anthony Gholston, acknowledged her dower, etc.

Sept. 23, 1734. Richard Phillips and Thomas Ballard Smith of St. Geo. Par., Spts. Co., to George Woodroof of Par. and Co. afsd. 300 a. in St. Geo. Par., Spts. Co. Wm. Waller, Edwd. Herndon, Junr., William Henderson. Nov. 5, 1734. Elizabeth Smith acknowledged her dower, etc.

John Madison of Drysdale Par., King and Queen Co., "unto my well beloved niece, Elizabeth Madison, éldest daughter of my brother, Ambrose Madison, lately Deceased," etc. 1000 a. granted sd. Jno. by pat. Sept. 28, 1728, in St. Mark's Par., Spts. Co., upon condition that after she is 21, or at her decease, her heirs shall deed 200 a. of the sd. land in fee simple to Francis Williams and his heirs. Witness: Roger Tandy. Dated Nov. 4, 1734. Recd. Nov. 5, 1734.

Henry Madison of St. John's Par., King Wm. Co., "unto my well beloved niece, Frances Madison, youngest daughter of my Brother Ambrose Madison, Decd," etc. 1000 a. granted sd. Henry by pat. Sept. 28, 1728, in St. Mark's Par., Spts. Co., upon condition that after she is 21, or at her decease, her heirs shall deed 150 a. of sd. land to Daniel Stodg-hill and his heirs in fee simple. Witness: Roger Tandy. Dated, Nov. 4, 1734. Recd. Nov. 5, 1734.

Octr. 7, 1734. Elisha Perkins of St. Mark's Par., Spts. Co., to Thomas Wright Belfield of Lunenburg Par., Richmond Co. 470 a. in St. Mark's Par., Spts. Co. (whereon sd. Perkins now lives, and purchased by sd. Perkins of Francis Kirtley)—sd. land being granted Kirtley by pat. Sept. 28, 1728. Jno. Christopher, Henry Downs, Jno. Willson, Jos. Morton, Wm. x Morton. Nov. 5, 1734. Margery, wife of Elisha Perkins, acknowledged her dower, etc.

Nov. 5, 1734. Thomas Smith of Prince William Co. and Augustine Smith of Spts. Co., Gentlemen, to Francis Thornton, Junr., of Spts. Co., Gent. 400 a. in Spts. Co., which land was given by sd. Augustin to sd. Thomas, as by Deeds in Spts. Co. Court, Nov. 2, 1731. Jonath. Gibson, Thos. Slaughter, Chas. Taliaferro, Junr. Nov. 5, 1734.

Nov. 5, 1734. Francis Thornton, Junr., of St. Geo. Par., Spts. Co., to Henry Taliaferro of St. Marie's Par., Caroline Co. 400 a. in St. Mark's Par., Spts. Co.—pat. by David McMurrin July 21, 1732. Jonath. Gibson, Thos. Slaughter, Charles Taliaferro, Junr. Nov. 5, 1734.

Nov. 4, 1734. Henry Haynes of Caroline Co., planter, to Thomas Dillard of Spts. Co., planter. 170 a. in Spts. Co. on branches of Mattapony, and part of pat. granted sd. Haynes Sept. 28, 1728. Roger Quarles, John Stubblefield, John Dickenson. Nov. 5, 1734. Mary, wife of Henry Haynes of St. Margarett's Par., Caroline Co., acknowledged her dower, etc.

Nov. 4, 1734. Roger Tandy of King and Queen Co., Gent., to John Jones of St. Geo. Par., Spts., Collier. 420 a. in St. Geo. Par., Spts. Co. —granted sd. Tandy by Pat. Oct. 13, 1727. Anthony x Gholstone, William Wombwell Cliffe. Nov. 5, 1734.

Oct. 23, 1734. Alexander Spotswood, Esqr., to William Wood, planter. Lease of 110 a. in St. Mark's Par., Spts. Co., on S. side Rapidan—part of tract granted Spotswood by pat. and called Spotsylvania tract, etc., "to William Wood and Isabel, his wife, etc." John Grame, Tho. Sims, William x Morton. Nov. 5, 1734.

Oct. 23, 1734. Alexander Spotswood, Esqr., to John Marks, planter. Lease of 100 a. in St. Mark's Par., Spts. Co., on S. side Rapidan—part of tract granted Spotswood and called Spts. tract, etc. "John Marks, Mary, the wife, and Mary, the daughter, of the sd. John," etc. John Grame, Tho. Sims, William x Morton. Nov. 5, 1734.

Oct. 23, 1734. Alexander Spotswood, Esqr., to Thomas Sims, planter. Lease of 108 a. of land in St. Mark's Par., Spts. Co., on S. side Rapidan —part of tract granted Spotswood and called Spts. tract, etc. "Thomas Sims and Rebecca, his wife, and Thomas, ye son of sd. Thomas, Senior," etc. John Grame, John Pattey, William x Morton. Nov. 5, 1734.

Oct. 23, 1734. Alexander Spotswood, Esqr., to James Jones, Senr. Lease of 200 a. in St. Mark's Par., Spts. Co., on S. side Rapidan—part of tract granted sd. Spotswood and called Spts. tract, etc. "Thomas Jones and James Jones sons of sd. James Jones, Senr., etc. John Grame, Tho. Sims, William x Morton. Nov. 5, 1734.

Oct. 23, 1734. Alexander Spotswood, Esqr., to William Croucher, planter. Lease of 100 a. in St. Mark's Par., Spts. Co., on S. side Rapidan —part of tract granted sd. Spotswood and called Spts. tract. John Grame, Tho. Sims, William x Morton. Nov. 5, 1734. "Wm. Croucher, Anne, his wife, and Priscilla, his daughter."

Oct. 23, 1734. Alexander Spotswood, Esqr., to Thomas Pettey, planter. Lease of 100 a. in St. Mark's Par., Spts. Co., on S. side Rapidan, etc., etc. tract granted Spotswood and called Spts. tract. "Thomas Pettey and Katherine, his wife, and Christopher Pettey, his son," etc. John Grame, Tho. Sims, William x Morton. Nov. 5, 1734.

Oct. 23, 1734. Alexander Spotswood, Esqr., to John Petty, planter. Lease of 100 a. in St. Mark's Par., Spts. Co., on N. side Rapidan, etc., etc. tract granted Spotswood and known as Spts. tract. "John Petty and Rebecca, his wife, and Thomas Petty, his son," etc. John Grame, Tho. Sims, William x Morton. Nov. 5, 1734.

Nov. 2, 1734. Alexander Spotswood, Esqr., to Robert Allistone, planter. Lease of 100 a. in St. Mark's Par., Spts. Co., on S. side Rapidan —part of tract granted Spotswood and called Spts. tract. "Robert Allistone and his son, Jacob Allistone," etc. Joseph Delaney, William x Bunting, Thomas Lewis. Nov. 5, 1734.

Oct. 25, 1734. Alexander Spotswood, Esqr., to Simon Miller, planter. Lease of 100 a. in St. Mark's Par., Spts. Co., on N. side Rapidan, etc., etc. "Simon Miller and John Allistone, son of Robt. Allistone," etc. Thomas Lewis, Simon Miller, John Blackeley. Nov. 5, 1734.

Oct. 23, 1734. Alexander Spotswood, Esqr., to William Morton. Lease of 200 a. in St. Mark's Par., Spts. Co., on S. side Rapidan, etc., etc. "William Morton and Jeremiah Morton and Elijah Morton," etc. John Grame, Tho. Sims, John Pettey. Nov. 5, 1734.

Oct. 28, 1734. Alexander Spotswood, Esqr., to Elias Smith, planter. Lease of 100 a. in St. Mark's Par., Spts. Co., on S. side Rapidan. "Elias Smith and Elias Smith, Jr., and William Smith, sons of Elias." Elliott Benger, John Blackaby, Thomas Pitcher. Nov. 5, 1734.

Dec. 3, 1734. Augustine Smith of St. Mark's Par., Spts. Co., to James Roy of St. Geo. Par., Spts. Co. 118 a. in St. Geo. Par., Spts. Co. Frans. Thornton, Junr.; Thos. Slaughter, G. Home, Anthony Rhodes, Jr. Dec. 3, 1734.

Dec. 2, 1734. John x Davis of St. John's Par., King Wm. Co., to William Sandige of St. Margarett's Par., Caroline Co. 150 a. on Northanna River, in Spts. Co. Joseph Thomas, Robert Turner, Wm. Waller. Dec. 3, 1734.

Decr. 1, 1733. Abraham Estes of King and Queen Co., to John Leach of St. Mark's Par., Spts Co. 200 a. in St. Mark's Par., Spts Co., on branches of James River. Joseph Thomas, Robert Turner, Alexr. Freeman. Dec. 3, 1734.

Jany. 8, 1734. Col. Henry Willis of Spts. Co., Gent., to John Gordon of sd. County. Lots 25 and 26, in town of Fredericksburg, etc. John Grame, Larkin Chew, G. Home. Jany. 7, 1734.

Jany. 8, 1734. John Waller of St. Geo. Par., Spts. Co., Gent., to John Trustee, planter, of Par. and County afsd. 108 a. in St. Geo. Par., Spts. Co., on branches of Raccoon Swamp. Robt. Barret, Wm. Waller, B. Waller, Edmd. Waller. March 4, 1734–5.

Mar. 4, 1734. John Waller and John Taliaferro, Gent. Trustees, etc., for the town of Fredericksburg, to John Grymes, Esqr. 55 shill. curr. Lot 61 in Fredksbg, etc. W. Waller. March 4, 1734–5.

March 4, 1734. John x Snell of St. Geo. Par., Spts. Co., to Samuel Hensley, Martha Hensley and Kathren Hensley of par. and co. afsd. 100 a. in St. Geo. Par., Spts Co. G. Home, William Henslee. March 4, 1734–5.

March 1, 1734. Edward Pigg of St. Geo. Par., Spts. Co., to Abraham Rogers of Par. and county afsd. 85 a. on N. side middle fork of Mattapony, in Spts. Co., part of a tract granted John Madison, John Rogers, Peter Rogers, Henry Pigg, Edwd. Pigg and John Yorke, by pat., April 1, 1717. Jno. Rogers, Wm. Conner, Charles F. Pigg. March 4, 1734.

Augt. 27, 1731. Andrew Harrison of Spts. Co., to Wm. Johnson of afsd. county. Harrison stands indebted to sd. Johnson, by cause of a Judgment obtained by Jno. Fox and placed in hands of sd. Johnson as Sheriff. £50. Sd. Harrison makes deed to sd. Johnson, for a negro boy, some furniture, cattle, etc., etc. Witnessed by Antho. Foster. Recd. March 4, 1734–5.

June 3, 1735. Rice Curtis of St. Geo. Par., Spts. Co., to Thomas Merry of Par. and County afsd. 180 a. in St. Geo. Par., Spts. Co., part of pat. granted Larkin Chew, Decd., June 4, 1722, and sold by his son and heir, Thomas Chew, Gent., to sd. Curtis, as by deeds, April 2, 1733, etc. R. Curtis, Junr.; Peter Montague, John Wood. June 3, 1735.

June 3, 1735. Rice Curtis of St. Geo. Par., Spts. Co., to Peter Montague of Par. and Co. afsd. 228 a. in St. Geo. Par., Spts. Co.—part of pat. granted Larkin Chew, Decd., June 4, 1722, and conveyed by Thomas Chew, his son and heir, to sd. Curtis, as by deeds, April 2, 1733. R. Curtis, Junr., Thomas Merry, John Wood. June 3, 1735.

June 3, 1735. Rice Curtis of St. Geo. Par., Spts. Co., to John Wood of Par. and Co. afsd. 100 a. in St. Geo. Par., Spts. Co.—part of pat. to Larkin Chew, decd., June 4, 1722, and conveyed by Thomas Chew, his son and heir ,to sd. Curtis, as by Deeds, April 2, 1733. R. Curtis, Junr., Peter Montague, Thos. Merry. June 3, 1735.

June 3, 1735. Robert Goodloe of St. Geo. Par., Spts. Co., planter, to Joseph Carter of par. and county afsd. 190 a. (part of pat. granted sd. Goodloe, Sep. 28, 1728) in Spts. Co. W. Robinson, Larkin Chew, Wm. Waller. June 3, 1735.

May 28, 1735. John Miller, Junr., of St. Mary Par., Caroline Co., to Samuel Long of St. Geo. Par., Spts. Co. 70 a. in afsd. par. and county, part of pat. to John Quarles, Sept. 3, 1723. Wm. Bartlet, Jno. Curtis, John Wood. June 3, 1735.

June 3, 1735. Henry Goodloe of Spts. Co. to Mark Wheeler, of county afsd. 100 a. in St. Geo. Par., Spts. Co., on branches of North fork of South River, etc. John Minor, Robert Stubblefield, Robert Goodloe, George Goodloe. June 3, 1735.

June 3, 1735. John Waller of Spts. Co., to his son, Wm. Waller. Deed of Gift, 274½ a. in Spts. co., on ridge between Mattapony and Pamunkey

Rivers, etc. Thos. Carr, jr., B. Waller, Edmund Waller, Thomas Robinson. July 1, 1735.

June 13, 1735. Rowland Thomas of King and Queen Co. to Joseph Thomas of Spotsylvania, 900 a. in Spts. Co., St. Geo. Par., on N. side Northanna River—part of a pat. granted sd. Rowland Thomas, June 16, 1727. Thomas Hill, Robert Turner, Wm. Waller. July 1, 1735.

July 1, 1735. Thomas x Sartin of St. Geo. Par., Spts. Co., to Peter Gustavus of Par. and Co. afsd. 600 a. in St. Geo. Par., Spts. Co.—part of a tract granted sd. Sartin by pat. May 6, 1727. Wm. Waller, James Terry, Thomas Estes. July 1, 1735. Mary, wife of Thomas Sartin, acknowledged her dower, etc.

July 1, 1735. Thomas x Sartin of St. Geo. Par., Spts. Co., to James Terry of Par. and County, afsd. 200 a. Wm. Waller, Peter x Gustavus, Thomas Estes, July 1, 1735. Mary, wife of Thomas Sartin, acknowledged her dower, etc.

July 1, 1735. Trustees of the Town of Fredericksburg (by Henry Willis, John Taliaferro and John Waller, Gentl.), to Hancock Lee of Spts. Co., Gent. £8 10s. Lots 35 and 36 in the town of Fredericksburg. T. Turner, Tho. Catlett. July 1, 1735.

July 1, 1735. Edward Franklyn of St. Mark's Par., Orange Co., to George Carter of St. Geo. Par., Spts. Co. 200 a. in St. Geo. Par., Spts. Co.—part of pat. granted John Chew, June 4, 1726, and sold by him to sd. Franklyn, as by Deeds, Augt. 5, 1729. Wm. Waller, Da. Kinkead, Edmd. Pagett, Edwd. Herndon, Junr. July 1, 1735.

July 1, 1735. Thomas Chew, heir-at-law, and Larkin Chew, adms. of the last will and testament annexed of Larkin Chew, Gent., Decd., of St. Geo. Par., Spts. Co., to Abraham Mayfield of par. and county afsd., for £12 ster., pd. by one James Stewart to Larkin Chew, decd., for land herein mentioned; sd. Stewart conveyed sd. land to Anthony Foster, who conveyed it to sd. Mayfield, etc., etc. 200 a. in Par. and County afsd., on S. side River Po—part of a tract granted sd. Larkin Chew, decd., by pat. June 4, 1722, etc. Charles Smith, witness. July 1, 1735.

May 29, 1735. John Parks of St. Geo. Par., Spts., Blacksmith, to John True of Gloucester Co., planter, and Martin True of St. Geo. Par., Spts. Co., 200 a. in St. Geo. Par., Spts. Co., etc. M. Battaley, Henry x Martin, Henry x Martin (Junr. ?), Sept. 2, 1735. Margaret, wife of John Parks, acknowledged her dower, etc.

Sept. 2, 1735. Edward x Herndon of Caroline Co. to his son, Edward Herndon, Junr. Deed of Gift, 400 a. in St. Geo. Par., Spts. Co., granted sd. Herndon by pat. June 16th, 1727. Wm. Waller, Jos. Brock, Sep. 2, 1735.

Decr. 31, 1735. Alexander Spotswood, Esqr., to William Pannell, planter. Lease of 172 a. in St. Mark's Par., Spts. Co., on S. Side Rapidan, part of tract granted Spotswood, and called Spts. tract; "sd. Wm. Pannel and Sarah Pannel, his wife," etc. John Lightfoot, Elliott Benger, Abraham Chambers. Sept. 2, 1735. (Sarah Eagles)

Nov. 30, 1734. Alexander Spotswood, Esqr., to John Ingram, planter. Lease of 172 a. in St. Mark's Par., Spts. Co., on S. side Rapidan, etc., etc.

"John Ingram, Hannah Ingram, his wife, and John Ingram, Junr., his son," etc. And. Landale, James Gibbs, Luke Thornton. Sept. 2, 1735.

Nov. 30, 1734. Alexander Spotswood, Esqr., to Luke Thornton, planter. Lease of 200 a. in St. Mark's Par., Spts. Co., on S. side Rapidan, etc., etc. "Luke Thornton and John Randell, his brother in law," etc. And. Landale, James Gibbs, John x Ingram. Sept. 2, 1735.

Oct. 6, 1735. William x Bradburn of St. Geo. Par., Spts. Co., to James Stevens of St. Stephen's Par., King and Queen Co. 200 a. in St. Geo. Par., Spts. Co.—part of pat. granted Larkin Chew, decd., June 4, 1722, and sold by sd. Chew to sd. Bradburn, as by deeds, Oct. 6, 1724. John Waller, Edward Herndon, junr., Wm. Waller. Oct. 7, 1735. Sarah, wife of Wm. Bradburn, acknowledged her dower, etc.

Oct. 7, 1735. John Holloday, Gent., of Spts. Co., to Thomas Pulliam, planter, of same county. 200 a. in Spts. Co. Joseph Woodfolk, Wm. Waller, John Waller. Oct. 7, 1735.

July 21, 1735. Henry Willis and John Waller, two of the Trustees of the Town of Fredksbg, to John Tennant of Spts. Co. £5 10s. curr. Lots 63 and 64 in the town of Fredksbg. Wm. Waller, Jno. Taliaferro. Oct. 8, 1735.

Oct. 2, 1735. David Woodroof of St. Margaret's Par., Caroline Co., to Joseph Woolfolk of Par. and county afsd. 380 a. in St. Geo. Par., Spts. Co., granted sd. Woodroof by Pat. Dec. 3, 1733. Thomas Dickenson, William Dickenson, John Dickenson, Oct. 7, 1735. Ann, wife of David Woodroof, acknowledged her dower, etc.

Nov. 4, 1735. Anthony Thornton of Stafford Co., Gent., to Sharshall Grasty of King and Queen Co. 270 a. (part of pat. granted Anthony and Francis Thornton, April 19, 1720), now in St. Geo. Par., Spts. Co. Wm. Waller, G. Home, Antho. Strother, Edwd. Herndon, Junr. Nov. 4, 1735. Winifred, wife of Anthony Thornton, acknowledged her dower, etc.

Nov. 4, 1735. Mary x Abney of St. Paul's Par., Hanover Co., to Edwin Hickman of St. Geo. Par., Spts. Co. 209 a., half being part of a tract of land granted Thomas Hill and Dannitt Abney, by pat., Sept. 28, 1728. Z. Lewis, Edwd. Herndon, Junr.; Wm. Waller, Robt. Turner. Dec. 2, 1735.

Oct. 23, 1735. George x Proctor of Spts. Co. to John Proctor and Elias Sharp of county afsd. 230 a. in Spts. Co., on branches of Hasell Run. G. Home, Wm. Moore, John x Manard. Feby. 3, 1735-6.

Oct. 30, 1735. Joseph Brock of St. Geo. Par., Spts. Co., Gent., "for consideration of Rice Curtis, Junr., intermarrying with one of ye sd. Joseph Brock's daughters," etc. Deed of Gift. 865 acres in St. Geo. Par., Spts. Co.,—part of two pat. granted Larkin Chew, decd., one, June 4, 1722, the other, June 12, 1723, conveyed by sd. Chew to sd. Brock, as by Deeds, Oct. 17, 1723. Wm. Bartlett, Anthony Foster, James Stewart. Feby. 3, 1735-6.

Bond of Thos. Butler of Stafford Co. to Samuel Bartlett of Spts. Co. £30 curr. Dated Feby. 15, 1726-7.

Sd. Bartlett having purchased of sd. Butler, 150 a. in Spts. Co., formerly bought of Larkin Chew, adj. the land now in possession of Richard Walker. Witnesses, Wm. Bartlet, Larkin Chew.

Saml. Bartlet assigns sd. Bond to Wm. Bartlet, April 7, 1729. Witnesses, Abram Mayfield, Anthony Foster.

Wm. Bartlet assigns sd. Bond to Rice Curtis, Jr., Dec. 17, 1735. Recd. Feb. 3, 1735-6.

Feby. 7, 1735-6. William Richardson of St. Geo. Par., Spts. Co., to John Wood of Par. and Co. afsd. 50 a. in Spts. Co.—part of tract granted Larkin Chew, Decd., and conveyed by him to sd. Richardson, as by deeds, Oct. 2, 1722. Rice Curtis, Peter Montague, R. Curtis, Junr. March 2, 1735-6.

March 2, 1735. George Home and Elizabeth, his wife, of St. Geo. Par., Spts. Co., to John Gordon of Par. and County afsd. 200 a. in the Par. and County afsd., on branches of Deep Run, being a tract conveyed by deed of Gift from George Proctor, Decd., to sd. Home and wife, July 3, 1728. Joseph Thomas, Richard Tutt, Henry Brock. March 2, 1735-6.

March 17, 1735. Henry Goodloe of Spts. Co. to Augustine Owen of county afsd. 100 a. in St. Geo. Par., Spts. Co. George Goodloe, Robert Durret, John Buford. April 6, 1736.

Henry Martin, "to my well beloved children, William Martin and Benjamin Martin." Deed of Gift of 300 a. on N. side River Po. Samuel Long, Thomas Ship, Witnesses. Dated, April 6, 1736. Recd. April 6, 1736.

April 6, 1736. Henry Willis, Esqr., of Spts. Co., to Thomas Shipp of Essex Co. 400 a. in Spts. Co., formerly granted William Hansford, by pat. May 4, 1723, and lapsed from sd. Hansford for want of cultivation to the sd. Willis. Robt. Turner, Henry Goodloe, Wm. Waller, April 6, 1736.

April 6, 1736. Vincent Tapp of St. Geo. Par., Spts. Co., to John Ellson, of Par. and Co. afsd. 175 a. in Spts. Co., part of a tract granted Francis and Anthony Thornton, by pat. April 19, 1720; 450 a. being sold to Elizabeth Tapp, as by Deeds from Francis Thornton and Mary, his wife, and Anthony Thornton and Winifred, his wife, Sept. 4, 1722, 175 a. of the 450 a. being conveyed by sd. Elizabeth Tapp, as by Deed of Gift, Nov. 3, 1724, to sd. Vincent, etc., etc. Witnesses, Jno. Curtis, Henry Sparkes. April 6, 1736.

Henry Goodloe of St. Geo. Par., Spts. Co., to his daughter Elizabeth, now the wife of Robert Durret, Deed of Gift. 190 a. in St. Geo. Par., Spts. Co. David Kinkead, Jno. Hobson, Wm. Waller. June 1, 1736.

Francis Thornton of St. Maries Par., Caroline Co., Gent., to his son, Francis Thornton, Junr. Deed of Gift. 41 a. at the falls of Rappk. River, pat. by sd. Thornton, Senr., Feby. 25, 1720. Dated, June 1, 1736. Thos. Meriwether, Nicho. Battaille, John Thornton. Recd. June 1, 1736.

Thomas Griffin of Leadenhall Street, London, Merchant, appoints Francis Thornton, the Elder, of Caroline Co., in Rappk. River, Va., Merchant, and Francis Thornton, the Younger, of Spts. Co., Rappk. River, Va., Merchant, his attorneys, etc. Dated, Jany. 13, 1735. Witnesses: T. Dove, Thos. Dove, Jr. Recd. June 1, 1736.

July 6, 1736. William Johnston of Spts. Co., St. Geo. Par., to John Hoard of Essex Co., 223 a. in Par. and County afsd. Anthony Foster, Fran. Smith, Thos. Foster. July 6, 1736. Anne, wife of William Johnston, acknowledged her dower, etc.

July 6, 1736. William Johnston of St. Geo. Par., Spts. Co., to Thomas Red of King and Queen Co. 377 a. in County and Par. afsd. Anthony Foster, Fra. Smith, Thomas Foster. July 6, 1736. Ann, wife of William Johnston, Gent., acknowledged her dower, etc.

July 6, 1736. Joseph Brock of St. Geo. Par., Spts. Co., Gent., to John Durett of sd. county and parish, planter. 64 a. in Par. and County afsd. part of pat. granted Larkin Chew, decd., June 4, 1722, and conveyed sd. Brock, as by Deeds, etc. Witness: Wm. Waller. July 6, 1736.

May 4, 1736. Henry Chiles of Spts. Co., and Mercy, his wife, and John Chiles of King William Co., to Humphrey Hill of St. Margaret's Par., King William Co., Merchant. 400 a. in St. Geo. Par., Spts. Co., part of a Pat. granted Henry Webber, Oct. 28, 1723, etc. John Waller, Wm. Waller, Thomas Robinson, Wm. Hansford, Chs. Barrett. July 6, 1736.

Augt. 3, 1736. Edward Pigg of St. Geo. Par., Spts. Co., to his daughter Ann, now the wife of John Clark. Deed of Gift. 130 a. in St. Geo. Par., Spts. Co., on N. side River Tay. Archd. McPherson, Anthony Foster, John Ward. Augt. 3, 1736.

July 6, 1736. Philemon Cavenaugh to Henry Willis, Esqr. 150 a. in St. Geo. Par., Spts. Co., and 275 a. granted sd. Cavenaugh part pat. on lower side of Wilderness Run, etc. Jno. Taliaferro, Z. Lewis, Jno. Tennent, James Porteus. Augt. 3, 1736.

Oct. 1, 1736. George Woodroof and Jane, his wife, of St. Geo. Par., Spts. Co., to William Davenport, and Anne, his wife, of St. Martin Par., Hanover Co. 200 a. in Spts. Co., part of pat. granted sd. Woodroof, April 17, 1728. John Minor, Jno. Waller, Junr., Myles Potter, Wm. Waller. Oct. 5, 1736.

Oct. 5, 1736. William Davenport and Anne, his wife, of St. Martin's Par., Hanover Co., to Francis Arnold and Rachel, his wife, of St. Geo. Par., Spts. Co. Deed of Lease of 100 a. in Spts. Co. John Minor, Wm. Spencer, Wm. Wilson Hollmes. Oct. 5, 1736.

Sep. 7, 1736. John Jones of Spts. Co. to Wm. Hensley of same county, a tract of land in St. Geo. Par., Spts. Co. Adam Gordon, Sam. Hensley, Robert King. Oct. 5, 1736. Agnes, wife of John Jones, acknowledged her dower.

Oct. 6, 1736. Robert Slaughter of Orange Co., Gent., to George Doggett of Lancaster Co., planter. 470 a. in Spts. Co., granted Robert Slaughter of Essex Co., father to sd. Robert Slaughter, partie to these presents, by pat. Feby. 20, 1719. Thos. Slaughter, Fras. Thornton, junr., Fras. Taliaferro. Oct. 5, 1736. Mary, wife of Robert Slaughter, acnowledged her dower, etc.

Dec. 6, 1736. John Foster of St. Geo. Par., Spts. Co., to Cornelius Vaughan and Martin Vaughan (the two youngest sons of Cornelius Vaughan, late Decd.) of Drysdale Par., King and Queen Co. £25 curr. pd. Foster by sd. Vaughan, decd. sd. Foster deeds 465 a. in St. Geo. Par., Spts. Co., part of pat. granted sd. Foster, Oct. 19, 1736. Anthony Foster, John Chapman, Ignatius x Tureman. Dec. 7, 1736.

Dec. 4, 1736. John Waller of Spts. Co., Gent., to Zachary Lewis of same county, Gent. 414 a. in Spts. Co. 397 a. part thereof of pat. granted Jno. Waller, Junr., Sept. 28, 1728, and conveyed by him to sd. Jno. Waller as by Deeds June 23 and 24, 1730—residue thereof, part of a tract granted sd. Waller, Feby. 21, 1720, then in King William Co. Wm. Waller, Thomas Robinson, Edmund Waller. Dec. 7, 1736.

April 5, 1737. David Moore and Sarah, his wife, ot Spts. Co., to George Carter of sd. county. 183 a. in St. Geo. Par., Spts. Co.—part of pat. granted Larkin Chew, decd., and by him sold Lazarus Tilly, as by deeds, July 4, 1722, and conveyed by sd. Tilly to sd. Moore as by deeds Nov. 2, 1731. Wm. Waller. April 5, 1737.

April 9, 1737. William Johnston of Spts. Co., Va., Gent., to John Wiglesworth, of same county. £27 10s. curr. 519 a. in St. Geo. Par., Spts. Co.— granted sd. Johnston by pat. March 15, 1735. Peter Montague, Anthony Foster, Edwd. Dickinson. May 3, 1737.

May 3, 1737. Henry Rice of St. Mark's Par., Orange Co., Gent., to William Bradburn of St. Geo. Par., Spts. Co., planter. £20 ster. 200 a. in St. Geo. Par., Spts. Co., Edwd. Franklyn, Timothy x Dolton, John Gordon. May 3, 1737. Margaret, wife of Henry Rice, acknowledged her dower, etc.

March 12, 1736. John Anderson of King William Co. to Robert Williamson of Caroline Co. £30 curr. 400 a. in Spts. Co., grant sd. Anderson by pat. Jany. 10, 1735. John Haley, Thos. Sparkes, Thos. x Holcomb. June 7, 1737.

June 7, 1737. Robert Goodloe of St. Geo. Par., Spts. Co., to Robert Brown of same par. and county. £8 curr. 89 a. in St. Geo. Par., Spts. Co., joining lands of Thomas Hill and Joseph Carter; part of tract pat. by sd. Goodloe, etc. Chr. Curtis, Wm. Conner. June 7, 1737.

June 6, 1737. John Miller of Essex Co. to William Miller of Spts. Co. £50 ster. 260 a. in Spts. Co., on branches of Massaponnax, etc. John Parrish, Peter Mountague. June 7, 1737.

June 7, 1737. John Tennent of St. Geo. Par., Spts. Co., Gent., to Francis Thornton, Jr., of Par. and Co. afsd., Gent. £5 7s. 6d. Lots 63 and 64, in town of Fredksburg. Jno. Taliaferro, Anthony Francis Duttond. June 7, 1737.

March 24, 1736. John Rogers of Drysdale Par., King and Queen Co., to Abraham Rogers of St. Geo. Par., Spts. Co. £10. 228 a.—part of tract granted John Madison, John Rogers, Peter Rogers, Henry Pigg, Edward Pigg and John Yorke, by pat. April 1, 1717, lying part in Spts. and part in Caroline Counties, and "also all that tract or parcel of land given by my brother, Peter Rogers, Decd., in his last will and testament unto his son, John Rogers, Decd. Wm. Conner, William Smither, Junr., Walter x Fitzgarrell, Jr. June 7, 1737.

June 7, 1737. Trustees of Fredksburg, etc. (by Henry Willis and John Waller), to Joseph Hawkins of Spts. Co., Gent. 55 shill. curr. Lot 38, in Fredksbg, etc. (No witnesses.) June 7, 1737.

June 7, 1737. William x Tapp of St. Mark's Par., Orange Co., and Christian, his wife, to William McWilliams of St. Geo. Par., Spts. Co. £60 curr. 716 a. on Gravel Run, in St. Geo. Par., Spts. Co., pat. by sd. Tapp, "by vertue of his Majesty's grant to the settlers of the County of Spts., before May 1, 1728." Edward Herndon, Jr., Jos Neavill, Joshua Thomas. June 7, 1737.

March 1, 1736. William x Tapp of St. Mark's Par., Orange Co., planter, and Christian, his wife, to George Nix of St. Geo. Par., Spts. Co. £20 ster. 175 a. in St. Geo. Par., Spts. Co., the same having been given sd. Tapp by his mother, Elizabeth Tapp, as by deed, Oct. 31, 1724, etc., etc. (No witnesses.) June 7, 1737.

Augt. 2, 1737. Trustees, etc., of town of Fredksbg (by Henry Willis and John Waller) to John Rucker of Orange Co., Gent. £5 5s. curr. Lot No. 5, in Fredksbg. Wm. Waller. Augt. 2, 1737.

Augt. 2, 1737. George x Proctor, at this time of the County of King George, planter, to John Proctor and Elias Sharpe, both of Spts. Co. £100 ster. "that parcel of land whereon my father, George Proctor, did dwell at the time of his death. 436 a. in Spts. Co., on Hasel Run, residue and remainder undisposed of by my father and by myself since his death, of 1500 a., purchased by sd. father of Wm. Strother of King George; sd. 436 a. being designed by my father to be given to his son, John Proctor, one party to these presents, and his daughter, Margaret Proctor, wife of Elias Sharpe, the other party to these presents," etc. David Bronaugh, John Steward, James Strother, Jno. Hobby. Augt. 2, 1737.

July 5, 1737. George Poole of Spts. Co. to James Brown of same county. £15 9s. curr. 140 a. in Spts. Co. G. Home, William Stevens. Sept. 6, 1737. Elizabeth, wife of George Poole, acknowledged her dower, etc.

Oct. 4, 1737. Abraham Mayfield of Spts. Co., planter, to Blomfield Long of Essex Co., Blacksmith. £35 curr. 200 a. in Spts. Co., part of a tract granted Larkin Chew, Decd., by pat., June 4, 1722. Wm. Bartlet, Jno. Parrish, A. Foster. Oct. 4, 1737. Elizabeth, wife of Abraham Mayfield, acknowledged her dower, etc.

Oct. 4, 1737. Trustees of town of Fredksbg (by Henry Willis and John Waller) to Matthias Gale and William Gale of Whitehaven, Merchants. £7 5s. curr. Lot. No. 2 in Fredksbg, formerly bought by Henry Willis, at outcry, etc. John Chew, Wm. Waller, Edmund Waller. Oct. 4, 1737.

Oct. 1, 1737. John Gordon and Elizabeth, his wife, of St. Geo. Par., Spts. Co., to Thomas Hill of same Par. and County. £90 curr. 200 a. in Par. and Co. afsd., on Deep Run. G. Home, Wm. Cowne, And. Rosse. Oct. 4, 1737.

Nov. 1, 1737. John x Snall of St. Geo. Par., Spts. Co., to Anthony Foster of Par. and Co. afsd. £100 curr. 200 a. in Par. and Co. afsd., on River Po, part of land bought by John Snall ye Elder, Decd., of Larkin Chew, Decd., etc. Wit., William Johnston, Tho. Graves, John Walden. Nov. 1, 1737.

Oct. 10, 1737. James Terry of St. Geo. Par., Spts. Co., to John Holliday, Senr., of county and par. afsd. £20 curr. 200 a. Thos. x Seartin, Wm. Holliday, Ed. Lankford. Dec. 6, 1737.

Feby. 6, 1738. John x Proctor and Sarah, his wife, of Spts. Co., to Thomas Hill of Spts. Co., Gent. £50 curr. 116 a. in Spts. Co., part of a tract acknowledged by Wm. Strother to George Proctor, in Spts. Court, Oct. 1, 1735, the sd. 116 a. being sd. Jno. Proctor's part left sd. John by the last will and testament of George Proctor, etc. G. Home, William Marshall, James Nelson. Feby. 7, 1737.

Feby. 7, 1737. George Carter of St. Geo. Par., Spts. Co., to Isaac Darnell of same par. and co. £23 curr. 200 a. in St. Geo. Par., Spts. Co., part of a pat. granted Jno. Chew, June 4, 1726, and by sd. Chew sold to Edwd. Franklyn, as by Deeds, Augt. 5, 1729, and by sd. Franklyn to sd. Carter, as by Deeds, July 1, 173—. Joseph Adcock, John Stubblefield, Edmund Waller. Feby. 7, 1737. Elizabeth, wife of Geo. Carter, acknowledged her dower, etc.

Jany. 1, 1737. John Chew of Spts. Co., to Henry Martin, Junr., and John Colquit, Junr., of afsd. County, planters. £20 curr. 400 a., part of pat. granted sd. Chew, June 4, 1726, in Spts. Co., St. Geo. Par., joining the lands of John Bush and Michael Guaney. Witnesses: Henry Martin, Martin x True. Feby. 7, 1737.

Decr. 15, 1737. Henry Willis of St. Geo. Par., Spts. Co., Gent., to Francis Thornton of same par. and county, Gent. £25 ster. 150 a. in St. Geo. Par., Spts. Co., part of a tract called Biranis. Witnesses, Jams. Belsches, John Gordon, Elisha Gordon. Mar. 7, 1737.

March 7, 1737. Amey x Sutton of St. Geo. Par., Spts. Co., to John Talbert of same Par. and Co. £12 curr. 73 a. in St. Geo. Par., Spts. Co., part of tract granted Larkin Chew, decd., by pat., June 4, 1722, and by sd. Chew sold to Amey Sutton as by deeds March 5, 1727. Edmund Waller, Wm. Waller. March 7, 1737.

Dec 6, 1737. John Wilkins of Spts. Co., to John Wiglesworth of same county. £70 curr. 220 a., remainder of a pat. granted sd. Wilkins, June 16, 1727, etc. Z. Lewis, Wm. Waller. May 2, 1738. Mary, wife of John Wilkins, acknowledged her dower, etc.

May 2, 1738. Trustees of Town of Fredksburg, etc. (by Jno. Taliaferro and John Waller), to Adam Read of Falmouth, in King Geo. Co., Mercht. 55 shill. curr. Lot 14, in town of Fredksbg. Joshua Thomas, John Gordon. May 2, 1738.

April 6, 1738. Thomas Benson and Sarah, his wife, of St. Geo. Par., Spts. Co., to Edward Levill (Leavell) of Drysdale Par., King and Queen Co. £30 curr. 200 a. in Spts. Co., on branches of Massaponnax. George Nix, Matthew Gayle, Martin x Trew. June 6, 1738.

April 29, 1738. William Fantleroy of Lunenburg Par., Richmond Co., Gent., to Thomas Edmondson of St. Anne Par., Essex Co., Gent. £170 10s. 10d. curr. 200 a. in Spts. Co., purchased by sd. Fantleroy of one Edward Price; *also* 546 a. in St. Geo. Par., Spts. Co., purchased by sd. Fantleroy of Augustine Smith, and part of a tract granted sd. Smith, by pat. Hannah Fantleroy, John Lewis, James x Samuell. June 6, 1738. Mrs. Apphia Fantleroy, wife of Wm. Fantleroy, Gent., acknowledged her dower. July 21, 1738.

April 25, 1738. Anthony x Golston of Spts. Co. to William Crosthwait of Orange Co. £8 curr. 115 a. in Spts. Co. Richard Pickering, James Rallings, Adam Gordon. July 5, 1738.

July 30, 1738. William Coleman of St. John Par., King William Co., son and heir to Darbey Coleman of King and Queen Co., Decd., to Edward Pigg of St. Geo. Par., Spts. Co. £12 6s. 10d. curr. 100 a. in Spts. Co., on branches of middle River of the Mattapony. Wm. Johnston, Charles Filkes Pigg, Barnet x Paine. Augt. 1, 1738.

Augt. 1, 1738. Trustees, etc., of Town of Fredksburg (by Hen. Willis, John Waller), to Thomas Dowdall of Spts. Co. £3 15s. curr. Lot 18, in Town of Fredksbg. Edmd. Waller. August 1, 1738.

Sept. 5, 1738. Achilles Bowker of St. Stephen's Par., King and Queen Co., to Robt. Coleman of St. Geo. Par., Spts. Co. £40 curr. 400 a., being a pat. formerly granted Ralph Bowker, Feby. 20, 1719, and since renewed by Bird Bowker, by pat. July 20, 1736. Arth. Watts, William Johnston, Larkin Chew. Sept. 5, 1738.

Sept. 5, 1738. Joseph Brock, Gent., and Mary, his wife, of St. Geo. Par., Spts. Co., to Ignatius Tureman, of Par. and Co. afsd. £35 curr. 350 a. in St. Geo. Par., Spts. Co., part of pat. granted sd. Brock, in 1738. Thos. Duerson, William Cowne, R. Curtis, Jr. Sept. 5, 1738.

Sept. 4, 1738. Anthony Foster of St. Geo. Par., Spts. Co., to John Snell of Par. and Co. afsd. £50 ster. 100 a. in St. Geo. Par., Spts. Co., on River Po, a parcel of land purchased by Foster of Robt. King. Witnesses: William Johnston, Charles Filkes Pigg, Isabell x Foster. Sept. 5, 1738.

Jany. 27, 1737. Thomas Grayson of Deal, in Kent, eldest son of John Grayson of Spts. Co., colony of Va., lately deceased, to Thomas Turner of King George Co., Va., Gent. £250 ster. 500 a., lying in the colony of Va., in Spts. Co., near the falls of the Rappk. River and near adjoining the lands of Francis Taliaferro and Mann Page, Esqr., decd. Witnesses: James Hume, John Graham, John Moncure, Ignats Semmes, Peter Simms, Henry Donaldson, John Bean. July 4, 1738.

John Word of St. Geo. Par., Spts. Co., mortgage to Joseph Woolfolk of St. Margaret's Par., Caroline Co. £22 9s. 2d. curr., and 60 lbs. Tob. Witnesses: John Holladay, Chas. Stevens, John x Roberts. Dated, Augt. 25, 1728. Recd., Oct. 4, 1738.

Oct. 4, 1738. Trustees of Town of Fredksbg, etc. (by Henry Willis and John Waller), to John Waller, Junr., of Spts. Co., Gent. 55 shill. curr. Lot 56 in Fredksbg. Witness: Edmund Waller. Oct. 4, 1738.

Nov. 30, 1738. John Waller, Jr., of St. Geo. Par., Spts. Co., Gent., to Henry Downs of St. Mark's Par., Orange Co., Gent. £2 15s. curr. Lot No. 56, in town of Fredksburg. John Waller, Edwd. Herndon, Jr.; Robt. Huddleston, Z. Lewis. Feby. 6, 1738.

Nov. 24, 1738. Edward Pigg and Abraham Rogers of Spts. Co., planters, to William Hawkins of Orange Co., Planter. £20 curr. 100 a. [formerly sold to sd. Pigg by Wm. Coleman, as by Deeds, July 30, 1738], and 10 a. [part of a tract belonging to Abraham Rogers] in St. Geo. Par., Spts. Co., on branches of middle river of Mattapony. John Chew, Charles Filks Pigg, Barnet x Paine, Wm. x Paine. Feby. 6, 1738.

March 6, 1738. Thomas Chew of St. Mark's Par., Orange Co., to Nicholas Hawkins of St. Geo. Par., Spts. Co. £5 curr. and 2750 lbs. tob. 298 a. in Spts. Co., joining the lands of sd. Nicholas Hawkins, Robt. Thomas, Francis Smith, Augustine Smith of Gloucester Co., William Richason, Johnathan Clark, John Pen and George Pen, having been acknowledged to sd. Hawkins by sd. Chew, as by Deeds, April 6, 1731, sd. Hawkins being advised sd. Deeds were defective, is the reason for making this deed, etc. John Waller, A. Foster, Edmund Waller. Mar. 6, 1738.

April 3, 1739. Henry Willis of St. Geo. Par., Spts. Co., to John Allen of same Par. and County. £105 curr. Lots 30 and 32, in town of Fredksbg. Witness: Edmd. Waller. April 3, 1739.

Mar. 19, 1738. John Hobson of Chas. Co., Province of Maryland, to Griffin Fantleroy of St. Stephen's Par., Northumberland Co., Va., Gent. £20 curr. 400 a. at head of River Ta, in St. Geo. Par., Spts. Co., formerly granted Daniel Brown of Spts. by pat. Feby. 24, 1730, etc. William Johnston, John Waller, A. Foster, Edmund Waller, Benjamin Waller. April 3, 1739.

May 1, 1739. Henry Willis and John Waller, Gentmn., Trustees, etc., of Fredksbg., to Harry Turner of King Geo. Co. £8 curr. Lot. No. 4 in Fredksbg. Witness: Edmund Waller. May 1, 1739.

April 28, 1739. Joseph Brock of St. Geo. Par., Spts. Co., Gent., and Mary, his wife, to Joseph Penn of Drysdale Par., Caroline Co., planter. £36 1s. 6d. curr. 350 a. (part of pat. granted Larkin Chew, decd., June 4, 1722, and by him sold to sd. Brock, as by Deeds, Oct. 17, 1723, and repatented by sd. Brock, Sept. 2, 1738), in Spts. Co. Thomas Duerson, Mary Lyne, R. Curtis, Junr. May 1, 1739.

May 1, 1739. Joseph Brock of St. Geo. Par., Spts. Co., Gent., and Mary, his wife, to James Lee of St. Stephen's Par., King and Queen Co., planter. £21 1s. 6d. curr. 200 a. in Spts. Co. Witness: Edmund Waller. May 1, 1739.

April 28, 1739. Joseph Brock of St. Geo. Par., Spts. Co., Gent., "in consideration of Thomas Duerson, planter, intermarrying with one of sd. Brock's daughters," etc. Deed of Gift. 720 a. in St. Geo. Par., Spts. Co. R. Curtis, Jr.; John x Wells, Phillemon x Richards. May 1, 1739. Mary, wife of Joseph Brock, acknowledged her dower, etc.

May 1, 1739. John x Smith of St. Geo. Par., Spts. Co., planter, to Thomas Dillard of same Par. and County, planter. 1200 lbs. tob. and 3 bbls. Indian corn. 200 a. in St. Geo. Par., Spts. Co.—part of pat. granted sd. Smith, Sept 28, 1728, joining lands of John Tyre, Ralph Williams, Thomas Hubbard, William Pruet, and near adjoining lands of Thos. Carr, Gent., decd., and John Robinson, Esqr., now Humphrey Bells, etc. Witnesses: Robert Holloway, Mary x Asmon. May 1, 1739. Margaret, wife of John Smith, acknowledged her dower, etc.

July 3, 1739. Trustees, etc., of Town of Fredericksburg (by Jno. Taliaferro and John Waller) to George Chapman, of the Town, Sadler. £4 10s. curr. Lot 49, in Fredksbg. Witness: Edmund Waller. July 3, 1739.

June 1, 1739. James Garton's mortgage or sale to Col. Henry Willis, 2 negroes for £14. Witnesses: John Allan, Alexr. Cumings. Recd. July 3, 1739.

June 1, 1739. Peter x Gustavus and Mary, his wife, of Amelia Co., to William Sandige of Spts. Co. £25 curr. 450 a. in St. Geo. Par., Spts. Co. Thomas Cartwright, George x Willcox, George Sheppard. June 1, 1739.

April 29, 1739. Peter x Gustavus and Mary, his wife, of Amelia Co., to Joseph Peterson of Spts. Co. £16 curr. 150 a. in St. Geo. Par., Spts. Co. Thomas Cartwright, George x Willcox, George Shepperd. July 3, 1739.

Augt. 7, 1739. Trustees, etc., for Town of Fredksbg. (by Jno. Taliaferro, John Waller and Hen. Willis) to Lawrence Washington of Prince William

Co., Gent. £6 15s. curr. Lots Nos. 37 and 39, in town of Fredksbg. Elliott Benger, Wm. Woodford, Dan. Crump, John Pagan. Augt. 8, 1739.

Augt. 7, 1739. Anthony Foster and Martha, his wife, of Spts. Co., to John Snall of Orange Co., planter. £50 ster. 100 a. in Spts. Co., part of pat. granted Larkin Chew, Decd., and by him conveyed to Robert King and by sd. King conveyed to sd. Foster, etc., etc. R. Curtis, Jr.; Henry Rogers, Jo. Foster. Augt. 7, 1739.

Augt. 7, 1739. John Foster of Orange Co., planter, and Isabella, his wife, to Rice Curtis of Spts. Co. £25 4s. curr. 84 a. in Spts. Co.—part of pat. granted Larkin Chew, Decd., April 26, 1712, and by him conveyed to Robert King, etc., and by sd. King conveyed to sd. Foster, as by Deeds, Dec. 2, 1721, etc. Wm. Bartlet, Jas. Beuford, R. Curtis, junr. Augt. 7, 1739.

Augt. 8, 1739. Susanna Livingston of Spts. Co. to John Allan of Fredksburg, Mercht. £10 curr. Lot. No. 6 in town of Fredksburg. Witness: Edmund Waller. Augt. 8, 1739.

Augt. 7, 1739. John x Snall of Orange Co., and Philadelphia, his wife, and Anthony Foster of Spts. Co. and Martha, his wife, to John Taliaferro of Caroline Co., Gent. £100 curr. 200 a. in St. Geo. Par., Spts. Co., on River Po, part of a tract purchased by John Snall, the elder, father of above sd. John Snell, of Larkin Chew, Gent., Decd., and also one acre, granted John Snall, the father, etc. Witnesses: R. Curtis, Jr., Henry Rogers, Jno. Foster. Augt. 7, 1739.

Augt. 4, 1739. John Snall of St. Mark's Par., Orange Co., and Philadelphia, his wife, to Rice Curtis of St. Geo. Par., Spts. Co. £30 curr. 100 a. in Spts. Co. Thos. Merry, John Wood, Peter Mountague. Augt. 7, 1739.

Francis x Arnold, mortgage to Humphrey Bell of London, etc. Witnesses: Larkin Chew, John Blake. Dated, Augt. 8, 1739. Recd. Sep. 4, 1739.

John Hobson, Bricklayer, mortgage to Francis Thornton of Spts. Co., etc. Witnesses: Z. Lewis, Anthony Strother, W. McWilliams. Dated Augt. 7, 1739. Recd. Sept. 4, 1739.

Nathaniel Holland of Spts. Co., Carpenter, to Col. Henry Willis of Spts., Gent. Bill of Sale of Goods, etc. Witnesses: Willi. Reid, Gabriel Cleaton. Dated, Augt. 21, 1739. Recd., Sept. 4, 1739.

August 7, 1739. Trustees, etc., of Town of Fredksbg (by Henry Willis and Jno. Taliaferro) to John Waller of Spts. Co., Gent. £2 15s. curr. Lot 40, in Fredksbg. Witnesses: Elliott Benger, Andr. Craig, John Pagan. Sept. 4, 1739.

Oct. 1, 1739. John Talbert of St. Geo. Par., Spts. Co., planter, to Thomas Hubbard, of sd. Par. and county, planter. £14 curr. 100 a. in St. Geo. Par., Spts. Co., part of pat. granted Henry Haines, Sept. 28, 1728, and conveyed by him to Thomas Hubbard, as by Deeds, and by sd. Hubbard conveyed to sd. Talbert, as by Deeds, May 7, 1734, and now conveyed back to sd. Hubbard, by sd. Talbert, etc. Witnesses: Edmund Waller, John Waller. Oct. 2, 1739. Margaret, wife of John Talbert, acknowledged her dower, etc.

Oct. 2, 1739. Thomas Smith of Prince William Co. to George Reeves of South Farnham Par., Essex Co. £12 curr. 50 a. of land. Jos. Reeves, Tho. Reeves, Kezia Wise. Oct. 2, 1739.

Nov. 6, 1739. Thomas x Sertain of St. Geo. Par., Spts. Co., to John Holloday, Senr., of sd. Par. and County. £25 curr. 200 a., with plantation sd. Sertain now lives on, and part of pat. granted sd. Sertain May 6, 1727. Joseph Thomas, Daniel Holloday, Elizabeth Holloday. Nov. 6, 1739. Mary, wife of Thomas Sertain, acknowledged her dower, etc.

Nov. 6, 1739. Thomas Salmon of St. Geo. Par., Spts. Co., Planter, to William Salmon of sd. Par. and County, 4500 lbs. tob. 100 a. in St. Geo. Par., Spts. Co., whereon sd. Thomas now lives, on S. side River Po—joining land of Robert King, John Snall and John Foster, which land formerly in Possession of Robert King and sold by him unto Abraham Brown and by sd. Brown to Lawrence Franklyn. Witnesses: Edmund Waller, Peter Montague. Nov. 6, 1739. Mary, wife of Thomas Salmon, acknowledged her dower, etc.

Sept. 25, 1739. Rice Curtis of St. Geo. Par., Spts. Co., to William Johnston of sd. Par. and County. 40 shill. curr. 2 acres in Spts. Co. and St. Geo. Par. Philip Vincent Vass, Jos. Stevens, George Moore. Nov. 6, 1739.

Nov. 6, 1739. Humphrey Hill of St. Stephen's Par., King and Queen Co., from John Chiles of Hanover Co. £200. 1000 a. in St. Geo. Par., Spts. Co.— part of a pat. granted Henry Webber, Oct. 28, 1723, etc. Edwin Hickman, Elizabeth Hill, John Blake. Nov. 6, 1739.

April 1, 1740. Henry Willis, Esqr., and John Waller, Gent., Trustees, etc., of Town of Fredksburg, to William Beverley of Essex County, Gent. £5 5s. curr. Lot No. 15 in Fredksbg. Witnesses: Jos. Brock, Wm. Johnston, W. Robinson. April 1, 1740.

Plat of division of land of a tract of which Henry Chiles and John Chiles, are seized in fee simple, as by Deeds to them from Henry Webber, in Spts. Co. Court. Petition of sd. Henry and John Chiles for division as per plat attached. Dated Nov. 6, 1739, and Recd. Nov. 6, 1739.

Henry Willis of Spts. Co., Gent., to his son, Lewis Willis. Deed of Gift— several negroes. Dated April 1, 1740. Recd. April 1, 1740.

Joseph Brock to his grandsons, Giles Curtis and Rice Curtis ("their father Rice Curtis, Junr."), deed of Gift—two negroes. Dated April 1, 1740. Recd. April 1, 1740.

Feby. 4, 1739. James Garton of Spts. Co. to William Bell of same county. £50 curr. 250 a. in Spts. Co., part of a tract formerly sold by Larkin Chew to sd. James Garton and Uriah Garton, as by Deeds, in Spts. Court, etc. Jno. Parrish, Nathll. Holland, Alexr. Cumings. April 1, 1740.

Feby. 22, 1739. Anthony x Gholstone of Spts. Co. and Jane, his wife, to Zachary Lewis of same county. £30 curr. 200 a. in Spts. Co., on S. side Holliday's Swamp—part of pat. granted James Taylor, Gent., Decd., July 21, 1722, and conveyed by sd. Taylor to sd. Gholstone, as by Deeds, July 6, 1725. Joseph Thomas, Charles Barrett, John Holloday, John Bowles. April 1, 1740.

Decr. 18, 1739. Joseph Thomas of Spts. Co., Gent., and Sarah, his wife, to Zachary Lewis of same county. £220 curr. 900 a. on N. side Northanna

River, in St. Geo. Par., Spts. Co., part of a pat. granted Rowland Thomas (father of the sd. Joseph), June 16, 1727, and conveyed to sd. Joseph as by Deeds, June 13, 1735. Tho. Tompkins, Chs. Barrett, Henry Lewis. April 1, 1740.

May 6, 1740. Margaret x Hamm and Samuel x Hamm of St. Geo. Par., Spts. Co., to Richard Couzens of same Par. and Co. £16 10s. 9d. curr. 100 a. in St. Geo. Par., Spts. Co., which land and plantation was devised by the last will and testament of Samuel Hamm, Decd., to his wife, Margaret Hamm, during her life, and at her death to Samuel Hamm (his son one of the parties to these presents, etc.), and part of a tract formerly granted John Rogers and others, etc. Witnesses: John Waller, Sharshall Grasty, Wm. Waller. May 6, 1740.

May 6, 1740. Thomas Turner of King George Co. to Benjamin Winslow of Essex Co. £20 10s. curr. Lot 52 in town of Fredkbg. Jos. Brock, John Thornton, R. Curtis, Jr.; M. Battaley, Dav. McCulloch. May 6, 1740.

Jany. 29, 1739. Robert Brown of St. Geo. Par., Spts. Co., to Joseph Carter of Par. and County afsd. £8 curr. 89 a. in St. Geo. Par., Spts. Co.—adjoining lands of Thomas Hill and sd. Carter. George Goodloe, Isaac Darnell, George Carter. May 6, 1740.

April 30, 1740. Joseph Brock of St. Geo. Par., Spts. Co., Gent., and Mary, his wife, to Philip Sanders of Drisdale Par., King and Queen Co., planter. £41 1s. 6d. 400 a. in St. Geo. Par., Spts. Co.—formerly granted Larkin Chew, Decd., by pat., June 4, 1722, and by him conveyed to sd. Brock, as by Deeds. Oct. 17, 1723, and repatented by sd. Brock, Sep. 17, 1738. Wm. Bartlet, Thos. Merry, Thomas West. May 6, 1740.

March 5, 1739. Francis Thornton, Jr., of St. Geo. Par., Spts. Co., Gent., to Larkin Chew of same Par. and Co., Gent. 500 lbs. tob. Lot 64 in Town of Fredksbg. Wm. Johnston, Nathll. Chapman, Augustine Washington. May 6, 1740.

Mildred Willis, late Mildred Gregory, now the wife of Henry Willis of Spts. Co., Gent. By Indenture Jany. 5, 1733. Between sd. Henry Willis of first part, sd. Mildred of second part, and John Washington of Gloucester Co. of third part, reciting a marriage was to be speedily solemnized between sd. Henry and sd. Mildred, etc.; sd. Mildred in persuance of authority reserved by sd. Indenture, etc.; my son, Lewis Willis, etc.; sd. Henry Willis, my husband, etc.; my three daughters, Frances, wife of Francis Thornton, Jr.; Mildred and Elizabeth. Witnesses: Augustine Washington, Jno. Taliaferro. Dat. Dec. 15, 1739. Recd. May 6, 1740.

John Becket, acknowledges himself servant to Col. Henry Willis, for 13 mos. May 6, 1740. Recd. May 6, 1740.

May 7, 1740. Trustees, etc., of Town of Fredksburg (by Henry Willis and John Waller), to Nathaniel Chapman of Stafford Co., Gent. £4 5s. Lot No. 20 in town of Fredksbg. Edmund Waller. May 6, 1740.

Feb. 11, 1739. John x Dobbs of St. Geo. Par., Spts. Co., to John Smith of Par. and Co. afsd. £20 curr. 100 a. in Spts. Co.—part of a tract granted sd Jno. Smith by pat. June 30, 1726. John Bowles, Isaac Darnell, Ralph x Williams, Samuel x Matthews, Robert Huddleston. May 6, 1740.

Oct. 6, 1739. Joseph Brock of Spts. Co., Gent., and Mary, his wife, to William Bartlet of Spts. Co., planter. £34 13s. 6d. curr. 336 a. in Spts. Co.—granted Larkin Chew, Decd., by pat., June 4, 1722, and conveyed by him to sd. Brock, as by Deeds, Oct. 7, 1723, and repatented by sd. Brock, Sept. 12, 1738. R. Curtis, Junr.; Ann Curtis, John Mountague. May 6, 1740.

April 30, 1740. Joseph Brock of Spts. Co., Gent., and Mary, his wife, to John Boswell of sd. county, planter. £100 curr. 980 a. in Spts. Co.—part of pat. granted Larkin Chew, Decd., June 4, 1723 (1722?), repatented by sd. Brock, Sept. 12, 1738. R. Curtis, Jr.; Ann Curtis, Mary Lynes. May 6, 1740.

June 3, 1740. Trustees of Fredksbg (by John Taliaferro and John Waller), to Benjamin Winslow of Essex Co., Gent. £9 5s. curr. Lot No. 55, in Fredksbg. Jno. Edwards, Edmund Waller. June 3, 1740.

June 3, 1740. Bartholomew Wood and Charity, his wife, of Prince William Co., to Richard Chiles of Spts. Co. £11 curr. 100 a. in Spts. Co. John Gordon, Wm. Spencer, Joshua Thomas. June 3, 1740.

June 3, 1740. Anthony Foster of St. Geo. Par., Spts. Co., to Hugh Sanders of same Par. and County. £200 curr. 1657 a., in Spts. Co., formerly bought by sd. Foster of sd. Sanders. A. Bowker, Parmenas Bowker. June 3, 1740.

July 1, 1740. John Chew and Margaret, his wife, of St. Geo. Par., Spts. Co., to Anthony Gholstone of same Par. and County. £40 curr. 400 a. in Spts. Co. John Waller, Wm. Waller, M. Battaley. July 1, 1740.

June 30, 1740. Robert Turner of Spts. Co. and Catherine, his wife, to Zachary Lewis of same county. £14 3s. 6d. curr. 58 a. in St. Geo. Par., Spts. Co., on Northanna River, part of pat. granted Rowland Thomas, June 16, 1726, and by him conveyed to sd. Turner, as by Deeds, Oct. 16, 1730. Thomas x Durham, Thomas x Gibson, Edmund Waller, John Bowles. July 1, 1740.

Augt. 5, 1740. John Rogers of Drysdale Par., King and Queen Co., of the first part; Edward Pigg of St. Geo. Par., Spts. Co., of the second part; Thomas Gresham of St. Martin's Par., Hanover Co., of the third part, and Robert Johnston and Elizabeth, his wife, and Frances Rogers of St. Margarett's Par., Caroline Co., and Thomas Warren, John Winill Sanders, John Warren, William Warren, Samuel Warren and Richard Couzens of St. Geo. Par., Spts. Co., of the fourth part. Whereas John Rogers, Peter Rogers, Edward Pigg, John York and Thomas Gresham, pat. 525 a., part in Caroline and part in Spts. Co., June 16, 1714, since which sd. Peter Rogers and John York departed this life, since which no legal division made, etc., and by several conveyances, and the last wills and testaments of sd. Peter Rogers and John York, sd. Robt. Johnston and Elizabeth, his wife, Frances Rogers, Thomas Warren, John Winell Sanders, John Warren, William Warren, Samuel Warren, and Richard Couzens are possessed of several parts and parcels of said tract, etc., etc. Witnesses: John Askew, Matthew Brooks, John x Paine. Augt. 5, 1740.

Augt. 5, 1740. Trustees of Fredksbg (by John Waller, Fra. Thornton, John Allen) to Henry Willis, Gent. £5 10s. curr. Lots 41 and 43, in Town of Fredksbg. Augt. 5, 1740.

Augt. 5, 1740. Trustees, etc., of Fredksbg (by John Waller, Fra. Thornton, John Allen) to Henry Willis, Gent. £2 15s. curr. Lot No. 8 in Fredksbg. Augt. 5, 1740.

Augt. 5, 1740. Trustees of Fredksbg (by John Waller, Fra. Thornton, John Allan) to Mildred Willis, Henry Willis and their son, John Willis. £5 10s. curr. Lots 47 and 48, in Fredksbg. Augt. 5, 1740.

Augt. 5, 1740. Trustees of Fredksbg (by John Waller, Fra. Thornton, John Allan) to Henry Willis and Mildred, his wife, and Lewis Willis. £6 15s. curr. Lots 45 and 46, in Fredksbg. Augt. 5, 1740.

Augt. 5, 1740. Trustees, etc., of Fredksbg (by John Waller, Fras. Thornton, John Allan), to Henry Willis, Gent. £10 15s. curr. Lots 33 and 34, in Fredksbg. Augt. 5, 1740.

Augt. 5, 1740. Trustees of Fredksbg (by John Waller, Fras. Thornton, John Allan), to Henry Willis, Gent., £5 curr. Lot 59, in Fredksbg. Augt. 5, 1740.

Augt. 5, 1740. Trustees of Fredksbg (by John Waller, Fras. Thornton, John Allen), to Gawin Corbin, Esqr. £5 5s. Lot 17, in Fredksbg. Augt. 5, 1740.

July 6, 1740. Rice Curtis of St. Geo. Par., Spts. Co., to Peter Montague of St. Geo. Par., Spts. Co. (son of Thomas Montague.) £60 curr. 182 a. in Spts. Co. Witnesses: William Johnston, Thos. Merry, Ann Johnston. Augt. 5, 1740.

July 1, 1740. Henry Goodloe and Elizabeth, his wife, and Robert Goodloe, of St. Geo. Par., Spts. Co., to John Scandland Crane of St. Stephen's Par., King and Queen Co. £72 curr. 554 a. in St. Geo. Par., Spts. Co. David x Ramsey, Elizabeth x Durret, Aniclina x Serles (?). Augt. 5, 1740.

Sept. 2, 1740. Trustees, etc., of Fredksbg (by Jno. Taliaferro, John Waller, Fras. Thornton) to John Edwards of Spts. Co., Gent. £5 curr. Lot 54, in Fredksbg. Witness: Edmund Waller. Sept. 2, 1740.

Augt. 21, 1740. George x Dowdy of St. Geo. Par., Spts. Co., to Wm. Marsh of Par. and Co. afsd. £45 curr. 600 a., remaining part of pat. granted sd. Dowdy. Witnesses: James x Jones, John Howaton, Jos. Collins. Oct. 7, 1740.

Oct. 7, 1740. Wm. x Dyer of St. Geo. Par., Spts. Co., to Robert Spilsbe Coleman of Essex Co. £10 curr. 100 a. in St. Geo. Par., Spts. Co., on branches of Pammkey River, part of a pat. granted Roger Tandy, Oct. 13, 1727. Wm. Waller, Edmund Waller. Oct. 7, 1740. Mary, wife of Wm. Dyer, acknowledged her dower, etc.

Augt. 5, 1740. James x Roy of St. Geo. Par., Spts. Co., Planter, to Thomas Edmondson of St. Ann's Par., Essex Co., Gent. £24 curr. 107 a. in St. Geo. Par., Spts. Co., purchased by sd. Roy from one George Proctor. Witnesses: John Waller, John Gordon, John Wigglesworth, Willi. Reid, Andr. Craig. Oct. 7, 1742. Elizabeth, wife of James Roy, acknowledged her dower, etc.

Oct. 6, 1740. Joseph Brock of St. Geo. Par., Spts. Co., Gent., and Mary, his wife, to Thomas West of sd. Par. and Co. £21 1s. 6d. 250 a. in Spts. Co. John Durret, William Long, George Trible. Oct. 7, 1740.

Oct. 6, 1740. Robert King of St. Geo. Par., Spts. Co., and Mary, his wife, to Edward Cason of St. Mary's Par., Caroline Co. £57 15s. curr. 231 a. in Spts. Co. Rice Curtis, Thos. Merry, Thomas West. Oct. 7, 1740.

May 2, 1740. Ralph x Williams of St. Geo. Par., Spts. Co., to William Williams of Par. and Co. afsd. £30 curr. 100 a. in Spts. Co.—formerly taken up by Nicholas Lankford and by him conveyed to John Collier, Jr., of King and Queen, and by sd. Collier to Robert Stubblefield, and by sd. Stubblefield to sd. Ralph Williams, as by Deeds, July 2, 1734. Robt. Huddleston, Thomas Dillard. Oct. 7, 1740.

May 2, 1740. Ralph x Williams of St. Geo. Par., Spts. Co., to John Williams of Par. and Co. afsd. £10 curr. 100 a. in Spts. Co. Robert Huddleston, Thomas Dillard. Oct. 7, 1740.

Sept. 12, 1740. Edward Pigg of St. Geo. Par., Spts. Co., to Charles Filkes Pigg of Par. and county afsd. £5 curr. 150 a. in St. Geo. Par., Spts. Co. Wm. Johnston, Robert Johnston, James Atkins, Wm. Power. Oct. 7, 1740.

Oct. 4, 1740. Hugh Sanders of St. Geo. Par., Spts. Co., planter, to Dudley Gatewood of sd. Par. and County. £24 10s. curr. 235 a. in Spts. Co.—formerly granted Nathaniel Sanders, Decd., and by him given to sd. Hugh Sanders, by his last will and testament. Robt. King, Jr.; William Long, William x Malding. Oct. 7, 1740. Caty, wife of Hugh Sanders, acknowledged her dower, etc.

Oct. 7, 1740. Mary Hawkins, widow of John Hawkins, late Decd., and Joseph Hawkins, George Smith and Elizabeth, his wife, and Phebe Hawkins to Philemon Hawkins. £50 curr. 132 a. on Northanna River, in St. Geo. Par., Spts. Co., and all personal estate of sd. John Hawkins, Decd., in the possession of sd. Philemon. Thos. Chew, Jos. Morton, Charles x Smith. Oct. 7, 1740.

October 7, 1740. Robert Biscoe of Lancaster Co. to James Brown of Spts. Co. £6 curr. 97 a., granted by Pat. to Joseph Delanie, Sep. 28, 1728, and conveyed by him to sd. Biscoe, as by Deeds, June 29, 1734, in Spts. Co. Matthew Gayle, Francis Turnley. Oct. 7, 1740.

Nov. 1, 1740. Griffin Fauntleroy of Northumberland Co., Gent., to Peter How and Richard Kelsick of Whitehaven, Merchants. £20 curr. Lot 16, in Town of Fredksbg. Jno. Taliaferro, Richard Griffith, Jno. Hobby. Dec. 2, 1740.

Dec. 1, 1740. Robert Turner and Katherine, his wife, of St. Geo. Par., Spts. Co., to James Rawlins of sd. Par. and County. £20 curr. 40 a. in Spts. Co.—part of tract conveyed to sd. Turner by Rowland Thomas, and part of pat. granted sd. Thomas, June 16, 1727. Edmund Waller, Z. Lewis, George Woodroof. Dec. 2, 1740.

Augt. 5, 1740. Trustees, etc., of Fredericksburg (by John Waller, Fras. Thornton and John Allan) to Henry Willis, Gent. £8 curr. Lots 9 and 10, in town of Fredksburg, "purchased by Francis Willis, Gent., and by him assigned." Wit.: Edmund Waller. Dec. 3, 1740.

Augt. 5, 1740. Trustees, etc., of Fredericksburg (by John Waller, Fras. Thornton, John Allen), to Henry Willis and John, the son of Henry and Mildred Willis. £8 curr. Lot 11 and 12, in town of Fredksbg—"purchased by Wm. Gooch, Esqr., and by him assigned." Witness: Edmund Waller. Dec. 3, 1740.

Augt. 5, 1740. Trustees of Fredericksburg (by John Waller, Fras. Thornton, John Allan) to Henry Willis, Gent. £4 10s. curr. Lot 53 in town of Fredksbg—purchased by Francis Willis, and by him assigned. Witness: Edmund Waller. Dec. 3, 1740.

Augt. 5, 1740. Trustees, etc., of Fredericksburg (by John Waller, Fras. Thornton, John Allan) to Henry Willis, Gent. £5 10s. curr. Lots 57 and 58, purchased by Coll. John Taliaferro and by him assigned. Witness: Edmund Waller. Dec. 3, 1740.

Dec. 2, 1740. Thomas Ship of Spts. Co. to Richard Ship of Caroline Co. £20 5s. curr. 194 a. in Spts. Co.—purchased by sd. Thomas of Henry Willis, Gent., as by Deeds, April 6, 1736. Jno. Parrish, Thomas West, Patrick Dowdall. Dec. 2, 1740.

Dec. 2, 1740. Parmenas Bowker of St. Geo. Par., Spts. Co., to James Gardener of St. Stephen's Par., King and Queen Co. £65 curr. 500 a. Witnesses: Wm. Allcock, A. Foster, Saml. Hensley. Dec. 2, 1740.

Feby. 6, 1740. Edmund Waller of Spts. Co. and Mary, his wife, to Zachary Lewis, of same county. £7 6s. 4d. curr. 61 a. in Spts. Co.—part of pat. granted sd. Waller, Sept. 28, 1728. Thos. Cowper, Ann Lewis, John Lewis. March 3, 1740.

Jany. 23, 1740. Edmund Waller of St. Geo. Par., Spts. Co., and Mary, his wife, to John Wigglesworth, of same Par. and county. £12 10s. curr. 110 a. in St. Geo. Par., Spts. Co.—part of a pat. granted sd. Waller, Sept. 28, 1728. John Waller, John Cockburn, George Atkinson. April 7, 1741.

April 7, 1741. Henry Elley of Spts. Co., planter, to Robert Spilsbe Coleman of Essex Co. 5 shill. curr. 200 a. in St. Geo. Par., Spts Co., on Plentiful Run, part of a pat. granted Thomas Allen and George Musick, Sept. 28, 1728, and by sd. Allen sold to Wm. Taylor, and by sd. Taylor sold to sd. Elley, Feby. 3, 1732. Edwd. Herndon, Thos. Stubblefield. April 7, 1741. Mary, wife of Henry Elley, acknowledged her dower, etc.

April 7, 1741. Henry Elley of Spts. Co., founder, to Robert Spilsbe Coleman of Essex. £5 curr. 87 a. in St. Geo. Par., Spts. Co., on both sides Plentiful Run, being a pat. granted Thomas Jarman, June 20, 1733, and sold by sd. Jarman to sd. Elley, Augt. 31, 1733. Edwd. Herndon, Thomas Stubblefield, April 7, 1741. Mary, wife of Henry Elley, acknowledged her dower, etc.

Thomas Hill of St. Geo. Par., Spts. Co., Mercht., mortgage to Humphrey Bell of London, Mercht. £382 16s. 2d. Witnesses: Wm. Cowne, John Blake, Benja. Hubbard. Dated Feby. 6, 1740. Recd. April 7, 1741.

Feby. 6, 1740. Thomas Hill of St. Geo. Par., Spts. Co., Mercht., to Humphrey Bell of London, Mercht. £250. Mortgage of lands and plantations in Orange Co. Witnesses: Wm. Cowne, John Blake, Benja. Hubbard. April 7, 1741.

April 14, 1741. Thomas Hill, Gent., and Elizabeth, his wife, of Spts. Co., to Humphrey Hill of King and Queen Co., Gent. £50. Lots 21 and 22, in town of Fredksbg. Wm. McWilliams, Rob. Jackson, John Blake. May 5, 1741.

Nov. 25, 1740. Hugh Sanders of Spts. Co., planter, and Katy, his wife, to Joseph Pen of Caroline Co., planter. £15 15s. curr. 105 a. in Spts. Co., part of a pat. granted Nathaniel Sanders, Decd., and by his last will and testament given sd. Hugh., and by sd. Hugh sold to Anthony Foster, and by sd. Foster conveyed to sd. Hugh, by Deeds, June 3, 1740. Thos. Merry, Dudley Gatewood, John Hoskins. May 5, 1741.

May 5, 1741. Larkin Chew of St. Geo. Par., Spts. Co., Gent., to John Allan of same Par. and county, Gent. £25 10s. curr. Lot 64, in Town of Fredksbg. Witness: Edmund Waller. May 5, 1741.

April 14, 1741. John Robinson of Stratton Major Par., King and Queen Co., Esquire, to Joseph Collins of Spts. Co., planter. £20 curr. 400 a. in Spts. Co., in Forks of River Po, etc. Humphrey Hill, Benja. Hubbard, Thomas Collins. June 2, 1741.

June 2, 1741. Peter Mountague of St. Geo. Par., Spts. Co., Planter, to John Blake of Fredericksburg, Mercht. £40 curr. 242 a. in St. Geo. Par., Spts. Co.—purchased by sd. Mountague of Rice Curtis, Senr., as by Deeds, June 3, 1735. Edmund Waller, William Barber. June 2, 1741. Elizabeth, wife of Peter Mountague, acknowledged her dower.

May 4, 1741. Rice Curtis of St. Geo. Par., Spts Co., to John Parrish of sd. Par. and County. £50 curr. 200 a. in Spts Co. Philip Vincent Vass, Thos. Merry, R. Curtis, Junr. June 2, 1741.

Francis x Arnold, for £25 curr. mortgage, 100 a. of land, whereon he now lives, etc., etc., to Thomas Graves, Richard Phillips and John Minor. Dated, June 1, 1741. Witnesses: Thomas Graves, Jr., John Graves. July 7, 1741, Recd.

Robert Coleman, the Elder, of Drysdale Par., King and Queen Co., to his son, Robert Coleman, the Younger, of St. Geo. Par., Spts. Co. Deed of Gift. 440½ a. in Spts. Co. granted sd. Coleman, the Elder, Sept. 7, 1723. Witnesses: Z. Lewis, Wm. Waller, E. Pendleton. July 7, 1741.

July 7, 1741. John Robinson, Esqr., of Essex Co., to William Robinson, Gent., of Spts. Co. £150 ster. 500 a. in the fork of the River, in St. Geo. Par., Spts. Co., part of a pat. granted sd. John Robinson, April 23, 1718, and known by the name of Clesby. Witness: Edmund Waller. July 7, 1741.

June 2, 1741. John x Smith of St. Geo. Par., Spts. Co., and Margaret, his wife, to John Farish of St. Stephen's Par., King and Queen Co. £60 curr. 400 a. in Spts. Co., a patent, June 30, 1726. Robert Farish, Jas. Martin, Samuel Poe. July 7, 1741.

July 7, 1741. George Carter of Spts. Co. to his son, Henry Carter, of same county, Deed of Gift. 183 a. in St. Geo. Par., Spts. Co.—purchased by sd. George of David Moore and Sarah, his wife, as by Deeds, April 5, 1737. Wm. Waller, Jos. Adcock, Edwd. Ware. July 7, 1741.

July 5, 1741. Trustees, etc., of Fredericksburg (by John Waller, Fras. Thornton) to Augustine Moore of King Wm. Co. and John Baylor of Caroline Co., Gentlemen. £5 5s. curr. Lot No. 19, in town of Fredksbg. Edmund Waller, Henry Pendleton. July 7, 1741.

Augt. 4, 1741. William x Marsh of St. Geo. Par., Spts. Co., to Erasmus Withers Allen of St. Ann's Par., Essex Co. £18 curr. 304 a. in Spts. Co.

Larkin Chew, Tho. Reeves. Augt. 4, 1741. Elizabeth, wife of William Marsh, acknowledged her dower, etc.

Augt. 3, 1741. James Edwards, Senr., of St. John's Par., King William Co., to his son, James Edwards, of same Par. and county. Deed of Gift. 200 a. on Northanna River, in St. Geo. Par., Spts. Co., adjoining lands of Thomas Graves, John Graves and Humphrey Hill, and part of a tract sd. Edwards, Senr., purchased of Richd. Phillips, as by Deeds, June 4, 1734. John Waller, Edmund Waller, Z. Lewis, Henry Pendleton. Augt. 4, 1741.

June 4, 1741. Honble. John Grymes of Middlesex Co., Esqr., and Francis Willis of Gloucester, Esqr., executors of the last will and testament of Henry Willis, late of Spts. Co., Esqr., Decd., to John Allen of Spts. Co., Mercht., and Nathaniel Chapman of Stafford Co., Gent. Whereas Henry Willis by his last will and testament bearing date July 27, 1740, among other things, did appoint sd. Jno. Grymes and Francis Willis, executors, etc. £141—by Allen and Chapman paid—they receive (as highest bidders) a tract of land partly in the town of Fredksbrg and partly in Spts. Co. Witnesses: Benja. Hubbard, William Hunter, Thos. Wood, John Thornton. Augt. 4, 1741.

June 4, 1741. John Grymes of Middlesex, Esqr., and Francis Willis of Gloucester, Esqr., execrs. of last will and testament of Henry Willis of Spts. Co., Esqr., Decd., to William Hunter of Spts., Mercht. £250 10s. A tract of land adjoining the town of Fredericksburg. Witnesses: John Allan, Nathaniel Chapman, John Thornton, Thos. Wood. Augt. 4, 1741.

June 4, 1741. John Grymes of Middlesex Co., Esqr., and Francis Willis of Gloucester Co., Esqr., execrs. of last will and testament of Henry Willis, Esqr., Decd., to John Thornton of Spts. Co., Gent. £288 curr. Lots 41 and 43, in Fredksbg—purchased by Rev. Mr. Staige and assigned by him to Henry Willis and conveyed to him by Deeds of the Trustees, Dated Augt. 5, 1740. Nathll. Chapman, Benja. Hubbard, William Hunter, Thos. Wood, John Allan. Augt. 4, 1741.

June 5, 1741. John Grymes of Middlesex Co., Esqr., and Francis Willis of Gloucester Co., Esqr., executors of the last will and testament of Henry Willis of Spts. Co., Esqr., Decd., to Philip Rootes of King and Queen Co., Gent. £12 curr. Lot No. 8 in Town of Fredksburg. Augustine Washington, John Thornton, Henry Willis. Augt. 4, 1741.

June 5, 1741. John Grymes of Middlesex Co., Esqr., and Francis Willis of Gloucester Co., Esqr., execrs. of the last will and testament of Henry Willis of Spts. Co., Esqr., Decd., to Andrew Craig of Spts. Co., Chirgeon. £35 10s. curr. Lot 62 in town of Fredksbg. Jno. Taliaferro, John Thornton, Henry Willis, Thomas Wood, Augustine Washington. Sep. 1, 1741.

June 4, 1741. John Grymes of Middlesex Co., Esqr., and Francis Willis of Gloucester Co., Esqr., execrs. of the last will and testament of Henry Willis of Spts. Co., Esqr., Decd., to Benjamin Hubbard of King William Co., Merchant. £11 10s. curr. Lot 53 in Fredksbg. John Allan, Nathll. Chapman, Thos. Wood, John Thornton. Sept. 1, 1741.

June 5, 1741. John Grymes of Middlesex Co., Esqr., and Francis Willis of Gloucester Co., Esqr., Execrs. of the last will and testament of Henry Willis of Spts. Co., Esqr., Decd., to Augustine Washington of King Geo. Co.,

Gent. £40 curr. Lots 33 and 34 in Fredksbg. Jno. Taliaferro, John Thornton, Henry Willis, Thomas Wood, Andr. Craig. Sep. 1, 1741.

Oct. 6, 1741. James Jones, planter, and Mary, his wife, of St. Geo. Par., Spts Co., to Joseph Hawkins, planter, of same Par. and county. £10 curr. 200 a. in Spts. Co. Larkin Chew, Isaac Darnell. Oct. 6, 1741.

July 7, 1741. Trustees, etc., for Fredericksburg (by Jno. Taliaferro, John Waller, Fras. Thornton), to John Allan, Mercht. £5 curr. Lot. No. 7 in Town of Fredksburg. Witness: Edmund Waller. Oct. 6, 1741.

Oct. 6, 1741. Joseph Hawkins, now of Hanover Co., Gent., and Jane, his wife, to Robert Jackson of Fredericksburg, Gent. £25 curr. Lot 38 in Fredksbg. John Thornton, Wm. Bartlett, John Word, William Pollard. Oct. 6, 1741.

Sept. 29, 1741. John Wiglesworth of Spts. Co., carpenter, and Mary, his wife, to Benjamin Waller of the City of Williamsburg, Gent. £8 12s. curr. 50 a. in St. Geo. Par., Spts. Co.—part of a tract granted one John Wilkins by pat., June 16, 1727, and by him sold to sd. Wiglesworth. Witnesses: John Waller, Edmund Waller, Thos. Cowper, Henry Pendleton, Beery Lewis. Oct. 7, 1741.

June 4, 1741. John Grymes of Middlesex Co., Esqr., and Francis Willis of Gloucester, Esqr., Execrs. of the last will and testament of Henry Willis of Spts. Co., Esqr., Decd., to Humphrey Hill of King and Queen Co., Gent. £15 10s. curr. Lot No. 59 in town of Fredksbg. John Allan, Nathl. Chapman, John Thornton, Thos. Wood. Oct. 6, 1741.

Nov. 3, 1741. John Hord, Junr., of Hambleton Par., Prince William Co., to Joseph Redd of Drisdale Par., King and Queen Co. £30 curr. 123 a. in St. Geo. Par., Spts. Co.—between branches of the Ny and Massaponnax. Thomas Dickenson, John Carter. Nov. 3, 1741. Sarah, wife of John Hord, Junr., acknowledged her dower, etc.

Nov. 3, 1741. Anthony Thornton of Stafford Co., Gent., to Richard Childs of Spts. Co. £5 ster. 50 a. in St. Geo. Par., Spts. Co. Witness, Edmd. Pendleton. Nov. 3, 1741.

Oct. 10, 1741. Thomas Dillard of St. Geo. Par., Spts. Co., to Robert Huddleston of same Par. and County. £9 10s. curr. 113 a. in St. Geo. Par., Spts. Co.—part of a tract granted John Smith by Pat. Sept. 28, 1728. Thos. x Hubbard, Catherine x Hubbard, Janet x Hubbard. Nov. 3, 1741. Elizabeth, wife of Thomas Dillard, acknowledged her dower, etc.

Nov. 3, 1741. Joseph Brock of Spts. Co., Gent., and Mary, his wife, to George Stubblefield of County afsd., Gent. £54 6s. curr. 538 a. in Spts. Co.—part of a pat. granted sd. Brock, Sept. 12, 1738. No witnesses. Nov. 3, 1741.

Nov. 28, 1741. James Stevens of St. Geo. Par., Spts. Co., and Mary, his wife, to Jeremiah Stevens of St. Geo. Par., Spts. Co., planter. £15 curr. 71 a. in St. Geo. Par., Spts Co.—part of pat. granted sd. James, Dec. 13, 1738. Thos. Duerson, John Talbert, Samuell Brown. Dec. 1, 1741.

Nov. 19, 1741. Phebe Hobson of St. Mark's Par., Orange County, widow, to Robert Coleman, the Younger, of St. Geo. Par., Spts. Co. £20 curr. 50 a. in St. Geo. Par., Spts. Co.—part of a pat. granted Robert Coleman, Senr. (father of the above named Robt. Coleman), Dec. 2, 1723, and by him conveyed to one George Carter, and by sd. Carter to sd. Phebe Hobson. Witnesses, Joseph Adcock, George Carter, David Roy. Decr. 1, 1741.

Feby. 2, 1741. Benjamin Winslow of Essex Co., Gent., to John Allan of Spts. Co., Mercht. £22 10s. curr. Lot 52 in town of Fredksburg. Rob. Jackson, William Hunter, John Thornton, Andr. Craig. Feby. 3, 1741.

Dec. 9, 1741. Bernat (Barnett) x Paine of Drysdale Par., King and Queen Co., to John Farish of St. Stephen's Par., King and Queen Co. £103. 350 a. in Spts. Co.—on North side Middle River. Witnesses, Robert Farish, James Martin, John x Warren. Feby. 2, 1741.

Feby. 28, 1741. Charles Filks Pigg of St. Geo. Par., Spts. Co., to William Johnston of Par. and county afsd. £32 15s. curr. 131 a. in St. Geo. Par., Spts. Co. John Chew, Larkin Chew, A. Foster. March 2, 1741. Sarah, wife of Charles Filkes Pigg, acknowledged her dower, etc.

March 1, 1741. John Waller, Junr., of Spts. Co., Gent., and Agnes, his wife, to James Shackleford, of same county. £55 curr. 400 a. in Spts. Co., which sd. land was granted Thomas Carr, Jr., of King William Co., by pat., June 16, 1727, and by him conveyed to sd. John and Agnes Waller, by Deed of Gift. Nov. 6, 1731. Z. Lewis, Anne Lewis, Mary Lewis. April 6, 1742.

Feby. 26, 1741. Johnathan Gibson of Orange Co. to John Allan, Mercht., of Spts. Co. £218. 400 a. in Spts. Co., granted sd. Gibson by Deeds from Augustine Smith, Oct. 29, 1726. George Chapman, Henry Willis, Jno. Blake, John Edwards. April 6, 1742.

April 6, 1742. Nicholas x Copeland of Orange Co. to Benjamin Martin of Spts. Co. £20 curr. 100 a. in St. Geo. Par., Spts. Co.—part of the land formerly bought by sd. Copeland of Larkin Chew. Witnesses, John Chew, Archd. McPherson, John Allan. April 6, 1742.

April 6, 1742. Nicholas x Copeland of Orange Co. to John Sutton of Spts. Co. £20 curr. 100 a. in St. Geo. Par., Spts. Co.—formerly purchased by sd. Copeland of Larkin Chew. Witnesses, John Chew, Wm. Lindsay, Benjamin Martin. April 6, 1742.

May 4, 1742. Robert Coleman, Jr., of St. Geo. Par., Spts. Co., to George Carter of same Par. and County, Whereas Robt. Coleman, Senr., father to sd. Robt., party to these presents in the year 1725, for consideration of 25 pounds Sterling, sold sd. George Carter 200 a. of land, as by Deeds, April 6, 1725. A resurvey shows that the sd. tract contains only 165 a., and Robt. Coleman, Senr., being desirous that the balance of 35 a. be conveyed to sd. Carter; but sd. Robt., Senr., having conveyed the adjoining land to his son Robt., party to these presents, by Deed of Gift, June 12, 1741, etc., sd. Robt., Jr., party to these presents, conveys to sd. George Carter, 35 a., in consideration of the sum as before mentioned to sd. Coleman, Senr. Witnesses, Thos. Duerson, Edmund Waller, John Carter. May 4, 1742.

May 15, 1741. George Stubblefield of St. Geo. Par., Spts. Co., and Catherine, his wife, to George Cook of sd. Par. and County. £21 10s. curr. 100 a. in Spts. Co.—part of pat. granted Harry Beverley, Decd., and by the last will and testament of the sd. Beverley, it is bequeathed that his daughter Catherine have this tract, etc. No witnesses. May 4, 1742.

April 15, 1742. Francis Thornton of King Geo. Co., Gent., and Elizabeth, his wife, to John Lewis of Gloucester Co., Gent. £500. 812¼ a. in St. Geo.

Par., Spts. Co.—purchased by sd. Thornton of Thomas Hawkins and Ann, his wife, as by Deeds, April 26, 1738, recd. in General Court of the Colony, etc. No witnesses. April 6, 1742.

May 4, 1742. John Sartin of St. Geo. Par., Spts. Co., and Anna, his wife, to George Cook of afsd. Par. and County. £12 curr. 200 a. in Spts. Co.—part of pat. granted sd. Sartin, Sept. 28, 1728. No witnesses. May 4, 1742.

June 1, 1742. Philip x Sanders of Drysdale Par., King and Queen Co., and Mary, his wife, to Mary Curtis of St. Geo. Par., Spts. Co. £20 10s. curr. 200 a.—part of pat. granted Larkin Chew, Decd., June 4, 1722, and by sd. Chew sold to Joseph Brock, by Deeds, Oct. 17, 1723, and repatented by sd. Brock, Sept. 17, 1728, and sold by him to sd. Sanders, as by Deeds, April 30, 1740. R. Curtis, Junr., Philip Vincent Vass, John Graves. June 1, 1742.

June 1, 1742. Philip x Sanders of Drysdale Par., King and Queen Co., and Mary, his wife, to Richard Coleman of Caroline Co. £20 10s. curr. 200 a. in Spts. Co.—part of a pat. granted Larkin Chew, Decd., June 4, 1722, and by him sold to Joseph Brock, Gent., as by Deeds, Oct. 17, 1723, etc., and by sd. Brock sold sd. Saunders, as by Deeds, April 30, 17—. Rice Curtis, R. Curtis, Jr., Philip Vincent Vass. June 1, 1742.

May 31, 1742. Edmund Waller and Mary, his wife, of St. Geo. Par., Spts Co., to Samuel Brown of same Par. and County. £—. 170 a. in St. Geo. Par., Spts. Co.—part of a tract granted sd. Waller by pat., Sept. 28, 1728. Henry Pendleton, Michael Lawless. June 1, 1742.

July 3, 1742. Hugh Sanders and Catey, his wife, of Spts. Co., to Henry Gatewood of King and Queen Co. £11. 207 a. in St. Geo. Par., Spts. Co., on branches of Mattapony. Witnesses, Robert Coleman, Henry Gatewood, Sarah Coleman. July 6, 1742.

July 6, 1742. Thomas x Allen of St. Geo. Par., Spts. Co., to Thomas Allen, Jr. [son of sd. Thomas Allen.] Deed of Gift. 100 a. (part of a pat. granted sd. Thomas Allen and George Musick, Sept. 28, 1728) in St. Geo. Par., Spts. Co.—joining Robert Spilsbe Coleman, Edward Ware and Edward Coleman. Witnesses, Edmund Waller and Henry Pendleton. July 6, 1742.

Feby. 22, 1741. John x Wells of St. Geo. Par., Spts. Co., planter, and Frances, his wife, to Bloomfield Long, Senr., of Par. and county afsd. £20 curr. 150 a. in Spts. Co.—joining lands of John Walker and Bloomfield Long, and formerly granted to Larkin Chew, Gent., by pat., June 4, 1722, and by him made over to Philip Brandegon, as by Deeds, March 5, 1722-(1723), and by sd. Brandegon to sd. Wells, as by Deeds, Oct. 6, 1730. Larkin Chew, A. Foster, John Durret, Igs. x Turman. July 6, 1742.

July 5, 1742. Daniel Brown of St. Mark's Par., Orange Co., to Thomas Brown of Par. and County afsd. £40 curr. Tract of land whereon sd. Daniel formerly lived, in St. Geo. Par., Spts. Co.—on S. side Pike Run, and part of a tract purchased by sd. Daniel of Larkin Chew, Decd., and part of a tract granted sd. Chew, June 4, 1722. Jas. Pendleton, Philip Clayton, John Nalle, John Parks. July 6, 1742.

DEED BOOK D

*Mary x Gresham of Spts. Co., to her "loving children," Mary Johns, William Gresham and Rachael Gresham. Deed of Gift. Goods and chattels. Witnesses, John Waller, John Gordon, James Allan. July 7, 1742.

June 5, 1742. Andrew Craig of Spts. Co., Chirgeon, to John Allan of same county, Mercht. £32 curr. Lot No. 6, in town of Fredksburg. John Thornton, Henry Willis, Wm. Barber, Thos. Wood, Roger Malory. July 7, 1742.

March 3, 1741. John Waller of Spts. Co., Gent., to Augustine Washington of King George Co., Gent. £26 17s. 6d. curr. Lot 40 in town of Fredksbg. John Allan, Geo. Chapman, Henry Willis, Roger Malory, James Allan. July 7, 1742.

July 3, 1742. George Musick of Spts. Co., and Ann, his wife, to Nicholas Randall of Spts. Co., Planter. £10 curr. 170 a. in St. Geo. Par., Spts. Co. Witnesses, Francis Gouldman, W. Russell, John Wetherall. Augt. 3, 1742.

Augt. 3, 1742. Francis Thornton of St. Geo. Par., Spts. Co., to David Alexander of Petsworth Par., Gloucester Co., Gent. £27 curr. Lot 63, in town of Fredksbg. John Waller, Philip Rootes, Jno. Sutton. Augt. 3, 1742.

August 16, 1742. Robert Williams of St. Thomas Par., Orange Co., to Thomas Haydon of Brunswick Par., King Geo. Co. £40 curr. 100 a., part of pat. granted John Quarles, Sept. 30, 1723—in St. Geo. Par., Spts. Co. Lincefield Sharpe, Wm. x Burbadge, Thomas x Morris. Sept. 7, 1742.

Sept. 7, 1742. Thomas Ship and Elizabeth, his wife, of Orange Co., to William Carr of Caroline Co. £70 curr. 357 a. in St. Geo. Par., Spts. Co.— part of a tract granted Henry Willis, Gent., Decd., etc. Witnesses, Thos. Roy, Geo. Taylor, Wm. Burnett. Sept. 7, 1742.

Sept. 7, 1742. Abraham Rogers and Barbary, his wife, of St. Geo. Par., Spts. Co., to Abraham Estes, Junr., of St. Stephen's Par., King and Queen Co. 2228 lbs. tob. 83 a. in Spts. Co. Abraham Estes, Senr., Matthew Brooke, Robert Johnston. Sept. 7, 1742.

July 15, 1742. Robert King of St. Geo. Par., Spts. Co., to his son, Robert King, Jr., of same Par. and County. Deed of Gift. 150 a. in St. Geo. Par., Spts. Co. Witnesses, William Johnston, James Taylor, Thos. Minor, Wm. Logan. Sept. 7, 1742.

Nov. 16, 1742. Joseph Hawkins (son and heir of John Hawkins, Late Decd.) of Spts. Co., to Philemon Hawkins of sd. County. Whereas, John Hawkins, father of the sd. Joseph and Philemon Hawkins, parties to these presents, by his last will and test. recorded in King William Co., by which certain lands were given to sd. Philemon Hawkins, and others, the children

*This deed is signed "Mary x Grayson."

160

of the sd. John Hawkins, Decd., it being doubted what lands were meant to sd. Philemon Hawkins and others, the children of the sd. John, Decd., and the sd. Philemon having lately bought several parts or shares of the lands of others, his mother and sisters, to whom the same was devised, and sd. Philemon Hawkins, is now possessed of the sd. shares or parts of Mary Hawkins, his mother, George Smith and Elizabeth, his wife, and Phebe Hawkins, amounting to 200 a., in St. Geo. Par., Spts. Co. The sd. Joseph Hawkins, knowing the intent of his father, the sd. John Hawkins, deeds to sd. Philemon Hawkins the afsd. lands, etc., under agreement that sd. Philemon will deed his interest in lands in Caroline Co. (sold by sd. Joseph to Augustine Moore, Gent.), and also pay Mary Hawkins (mother of the sd. Philemon), yearly during her natural life, 500 lbs. tob. and 5 bbls. of Indian Corn, etc. Witnesses, Edwd. Herndon, W. Miller, Thos. Pritchett. Nov. 2, 1742.

Nov. 2, 1742. William Johnston of St. Geo. Par., Spts. Co., Gent., and Ann, his wife, to Thomas Minor of same Par. and County, Planter. £44 curr. 220 a. in St. Geo. Par., Spts. Co., same being formerly granted to Wm. Johnston. Sept. 28, 1728. No witnesses.

Nov. 2, 1742. Henry Elley of Hambleton Par., Prince Wm. Co., to Edward Ware of St. Geo. Par., Spts. Co. £21 curr. 300 a. in St. Geo. Par., Spts. Co., part of tract formerly granted Thomas Allen and Geo. Musick, Sept. 28, 1728, etc. Edward Herndon, Robert Huddleston, Edmund Foster. Nov. 2, 1742.

Nov. 2, 1742. Henry Elley of Hambleton Par., Prince Wm. Co., to Edward Coleman of St. Geo. Par., Spts. Co. £14 curr. 200 a. in St. Geo. Par., Spts. Co., part of a tract granted Thomas Allen and Geo. Musick, Sept. 28, 1728, etc. Edwd. Herndon, Robt. Huddleston, Edmund Foster. Nov. 2, 1742.

Novr. 1, 1742. William Hawkins of St. Thomas Par., Orange Co., planter, and Mary, his wife, to Abraham Estes of St. Stephen's Par., King and Queen Co. £24 curr. 110 a., part of land sold by Edward Pigg, Decd., and Abraham Rogers, both of Spts. Co., to sd. Hawkins. Lark. Chew, George Smith, Richd. x Bradley. Nov. 2, 1742.

Dec. 7, 1742. Joseph Brock of St. Geo. Par., Spts. Co., Gent., and Mary, his wife, to Henry Lines of Drisdale Par., King and Queen Co. £107 10s. curr. 1075 a., part of pat. granted sd. Brock, Sept. 12, 1738. No witnesses. Dec. 7, 1742.

Feby. 1, 1742. Thos. x Allen of St. Geo. Par., Spts. Co., to his son, John Allen of same par. and county. Deed of Gift. ⅓ profits, etc., of a grist mill and 100 a. whereon sd. Thomas now lives, etc., after death of sd. Thomas and Elizabeth, his present wife, Land adjoining Hon. Wm. Gooch, James Jones, and Thomas Allen, Junr. Witnesses, Edmund Waller, Henry Pendleton. Feby. 1, 1742.

Feby. 1, 1742. Richard Ship of Spts. Co. to William Carr of Caroline Co. £30 curr. 194 a. in Spts. Co., being a tract of land purchased of Thomas Ship, etc. Witnesses, Lark. Chew, Robt. Seayres, Patrick Dowdall. Feby. 1, 1742. Elizabeth, wife of sd. Richard Ship, acknowledged her dower, etc.

Dec. 30, 1742. William Reid of Fredksburg, in Spts. Co., to John Gordon of same place, in trust for John Thornton, John Allan, John Parrish,

William Picket, John Edwards, Rd. Tutt, and Jos. Calvert, above sd. Reid's Securities in a bond payable (for £80 curr.) to John Grame of Williamsburg. Mortgage. Witnesses, Dorothy Tennant, James Allenach, Alexander x Lamb. Red. Feby. 2, 1742.

Feby. 23, 1742. Charles Filks Pigg of St. Geo. Par., Spts. Co., planter, and Sarah Pigg, his wife, to Bloomfield Long of Par. and County afsd. £30 curr. 118½ a. in St. Geo. Par., Spts. Co., formerly belonging to Edward Pigg, Decd., and adjoining the land of John Clerk. Witnesses, William Johnston, A. Foster, Jos. Stevens, Larkin Johnston. March 1, 1742.

March 1, 1742. Francis Thornton of Spts. Co., Gent., to Abraham Darnell of sd. County, planter. Deed of lease. 180 a. in Spts. Co. "Abraham Darnell, and Elizabeth his wife, and David Darnell, his son," etc. Witnesses, G. Home, Jno. Parrish. March 1, 1742.

March 1, 1742. Francis Thornton of Spts. Co., Gent., to John Proctor of same county, planter. Deed of lease. 169 a. in Spts. Co. "John Proctor, Sarah Proctor, his wife, and John Proctor, Junr.," etc. Witnesses, G. Home, Abraham x Darnell. March 1, 1742.

May 3, 1743. Robert King and Mary, his wife, of St. Peter's Par., Orange Co., to John Carter of St. Geo. Par., Spts. Co. £35 curr. 140 a. in St. Geo. Par., Spts. Co. Robt. King, Junr., George Moore, Jno. Parrish. May 3, 1743.

April 26, 1743. William Lindsey of St. Geo. Par., Spts. Co., to Nicholas Hawkins of Par. and county afsd. £55 curr. 200 acres. Parmenas Bowker, John x Hutcheson, William x Martin, John x Sutton, James Hawkins, Nathan Hawkins, Alexander Hawkins. June 7, 1743.

June 4, 1743. Diana Goodloe, executrix of the last will and testament of George Goodloe, late of St. Margaret's Par., Caroline County, Gent., Decd., to Robert Goodloe of St. Geo. Par., Spts. Co. £16 curr. 160 a. in St. Geo. Par., Spts. Co., granted sd. Goodloe, Decd., March 12, 1739. John Durrett, Wm Long, Jno. Crane. June 7, 1743.

Nathaniel Sanders of Northampton Co., in North Carolina, bond to Robert Coleman of Spts. Co., Va., dated Jany. 26, 1742, sd. Nathniel Sanders had left him by his deceased father, Nathaniel Sanders, 400 a. in Spts. Co., and for non payment due his majesty sd. Coleman petitioned and was granted the same. Witnesses, Jno. Wynill Sanders, George x Chapman, June 7, 1743.

Charles Filks Pigg of St. Geo. Par., Spts. Co., to his wife, Sarah Pigg, and his daughter, Jane Pigg. Deed of Gift. Dated Feby. 22, 1742. Witnesses, Wm. Waller, J. Brock, Junr. June 7, 1743.

June 7, 1743. Daniel Holloday and Agnes, his wife, of St. Geo. Par., Spts. Co., to Thomas Pulliam of same Par. and county. £59 3s. 6d. curr. 197 a. in sd. Par. and County on East North East River, being devised to sd. Daniel, by the will of his father, John Holloday, Decd., dated Nov. 4, 1742. Josias Baker, Pattersn. Pulliam, Anthony Gholston. June 7, 1743.

June 7, 1742. Anthony Gholston, Junr., of Spts. Co., planter, to William Lea of King and Queen County. £50 curr. 500 a. in St. Geo. Par., Spts. Co. Saml. Coleman, Antho. Strother, Robert Goodloe. June 7, 1743. Mary, wife of Anthony Gholston, acknowledged her dower, etc.

June 7, 1743. Thomas Todd of St. Stephen's Par., King and Queen Co., Gent., to Richard Todd of sd. county. £15 curr. "To sd. Richard Todd, etc., all his part of a lot of ground in the Town of Fredericksburg described in the plat of the sd. town by the figures 60, which was devised to him by the last will and testament of his father, Colo. William Todd, Decd.," etc. Witnesses, John Latane, Patrick Dowdall, Joshua Thomas. June 7, 1743.

July 5, 1743. John Sartin and Anna, his wife, of Spts. Co., to The Revd. James Marye, Clerk, of same county. £70 curr. 800 a. whereon sd. Sartin lives, and is part of pat. granted the sd. Sartin, Sept. 28, 1728, in St. Geo. Par., Spts. Co., etc. John Waller, Richd. Tutt, Wm. Hughes. July 5, 1743.

July 5, 1743. Lawrence Washington of Fairfax Co., Gent., to Robert Jackson of Fredericksburg, Gent. £42 10s. curr. Lot 37 in town of Fredksbg. Hancock Lee, Archd. McPherson, Thos. Slaughter. July 5, 1743.

April 21, 1743. John Wiglesworth of St. Geo. Par., Spts. Co., to William Johnston of same Par. and County. £103 curr. 519 a. in St. Geo. Par., Spts. Co. Jas. Taylor, Stephen Johnston, John Mountague. June 7, 1743.

June 20, 1743. Charles Filks Pigg of St. Geo. Par., Spts. Co., to William Johnston of Par. and Co. afsd. £35 curr. 94 a. in Par. and county afsd. Robt. King, Junr., Thos. Estes, Junr., Larkin Johnston, Robert Farish, Samuel x Warren. July 5, 1743.

June 9, 1743. Humphrey Hill of King and Queen Co. and Frances, his wife, to William Lynn of Fredericksburg, Doctor of Physic. £310 curr. Lot No. 22 in town of Fredksbg. John Champe, George Morton, Wm. Hughes, John Taliaferro, Junr. July 5, 1743.

June 8, 1743. Elizabeth Hill of Fredericksburg, Va., widow and relict of Thomas Hill, late of Fredericksburg, Gent. Decd., to Humphrey Hill of King and Queen Co., Gent. 5s. ster., and other causes her thereunto moving, etc. Lotts Nos. 21 and 22 in town of Fredksbg, which sd. Humphrey purchased of sd. Thomas, Decd., during his lifetime, etc. No witnesses. July 5, 1743.

Augt. 1, 1743. Robert Hutcherson of St. Mark's Par., Orange Co., and Ann, his wife, to Peter Montague of St. Geo. Par., Spts. Co. £—. 120 a. in St. Geo. Par., Spts. Co., part of a pat. granted Larkin Chew, Decd., June 4, 1722, and by him sold to John Roy, etc. Witnesses, John Wood, William x Richerson, Thos. Merry. Augt. 2, 1743.

Augt. 2, 1743. William Holloday of St. Geo. Par., Spts. Co., and Judey, his wife, to John Holloday, of same Par. and county. £30 curr. 200 a. in Par. and County afsd., part of pat. granted Thomas Sertain (Sartin), May 6, 1727, and by him conveyed to John Holloday, Gent., Decd., father of the sd. William, as by Deeds, Nov. 6, 1739, and sd. John, Decd., devised sd. tract to his sd. son William, as by his last will and testament appeareth, etc. Edmund Waller, H. Pendleton, Reuben Daniel. August 2, 1743.

Augt. 2, 1743. George Doggett of Orange Co. to William Ellis of Gloucester Co. and Robert Ellis of Spts. Co. £100 curr. 470 a. in Spts. Co., formerly granted Robert Slaughter of Essex Co., Feby. 20, 1719, and conveyed to his son, Robert Slaughter, Gent., of Orange Co., and by him conveyed to sd. Doggett, by Deeds, etc. Witnesses, H. Pendleton, Joel Parrish, John Gordon. Augt. 2, 1743. Ann, wife of George Doggett, acknowledged her dower, etc.

July 1, 1743. John Williams of St. Geo. Par., Spts. Co., and Jannet, his wife, to Thomas Dillard of same Par. and county. £10 curr. 100 a. in St. Geo. Par., Spts. Co., part of a tract belonging to Ralph Williams that he had of Robert Stubblefield. Witnesses, Robert Huddleston, Thomas x Shurley. Augt. 2, 1743.

John Allan of Fredericksburg to George Chapman of the same place. £2 10s. curr. Lot No. 7 in town of Fredksbg. No witnesses. Augt. 2, 1743.

Sept. 6, 1743. George Cook and Sarah, his wife, of St. Geo. Par., Spts. Co., to Revd. James Marye, Clerk, of same county. £13 curr. 200 a. in St. Geo. Par., Spts. Co., part of pat. granted John Sertain, Sept. 28, 1728, etc. Cuthbert Sandys, Cs. Boreman. Sept. 6, 1743.

Sept. 6, 1743. Robert King, Junr., and Mary, his wife, of Spts. Co., to John Carter of same county. £80 curr. 150 a. in Spts. Co. Robt. Dudley, George Moore, Thomas Watts. Septr. 6, 1743.

Sept. 6, 1743. George Cook and Sarah, his wife, of St. Geo. Par., Spts. Co., to Henry Lewis of sd. Par. and county. £12 curr. 400 a. in St. Geo. Par., Spts. Co., granted sd. Cook, by pat., Feby. 12, 1742. No witnesses. Sept. 6, 1743.

Octr. 4, 1743. John x Clarke and Ann, his wife, of St. Margaret's Par., Caroline Co., to Abraham Estis., Junr., of St. Stephen's Par., King and Queen Co. £32 curr. 130 a. in St. Geo. Par., Spts. Co., on N. side River Ta. Henry Brock, Wm. Bartlet, A. Foster.

Oct. 1, 1743. Thomas Edmundson, Gent., of Essex Co., and Dorothy, his wife, to James Garnett, Gent., of same Co. £230 curr. 853 a. in St. Geo. Par., Spts. Co.; "500 a. thereof purchased of Wm. Fantleroy of Augustine Smith," etc.; "200 a. part thereof of Edward Price by sd. Wm. Fantleroy," etc.; "107 a.," etc.; first two parts bought by sd. Edmundson of sd. Fantleroy, and the last by sd. Edmundson of one James Roy, etc. Witnesses, John Seayres, Jas. Davis, Jno. Levingston. Oct. 4, 1743.

Oct. 4, 1743. William Hansford and Sarah, his wife, of St. Geo. Par., Spts. Co., to Revd. James Marye, Clerk, of same Par. and County. £200 curr. 400 a. in St. Geo. Par., Spts. Co., whereon sd. Hansford now lives, granted James Canne, by pat., July 15, 1717; also 100 a. in same Par. and Co., purchased by James Atkins from John Blackle, as by Deeds, April 4, 1724, and by sd. Atkins sold to sd. Hansford, as by Deeds, Augt. 11, 1727, etc. Jos. Morton, George Morton, Jno. Edwards. Octr. 4, 1743.

Octr. 4, 1743. Edward Herndon, Junr., of St. Geo. Par., Spts. Co., and Elizabeth, his wife, to George Stubblefield, of afsd. Par. and county. £41 1s. 6d. curr. 400 a. granted to Edward Herndon of King and Queen Co. by pat., June 16, 1727. No witnesses. Oct. 4, 1743.

Decr. 5, 1743. Joseph Red of King and Queen Co. to James Red of same county. £35. 223 a. in Spts. Co. Saml. Hipkins, Margaret Hipkins, Suca Jones. Decr. 6, 1743.

August 22, 1743. William Smither of Essex Co., planter, to William Waller of Spts., Gentl. £9 16s. 9d. curr. 61½ a. in Spts. Co. Wm. Smither,

Junr., Robt. Smither, Joseph Foster, John Wynill Sanders, John x Warren.
Decr. 6, 1743.

Decr. 5, 1743. Thomas x Red of King and Queen Co. to Joseph Red of
same county. £125. 177 a. in Spts. Co., on branches of Massaponnax.
Saml. Hipkin, James Red, Suca Jones. Dec. 6, 1743.

Jany. 27, 1743. Nicholas x Randolph and Margaret, his wife, of Spts.
Co., to John Graves of sd. county. £25 curr. 170 a., part of a tract granted
Musick by pat., and by him sold to sd. Randolph. Witnesses, Henry Chiles,
Ambrose x Musick, John x Davis. Feby. 7th, 1743.

Feby. 7, 1744. Henry x Martin, Junr., of St. Margaret's Par., Caroline
Co., planter, and Susanna, his wife, to Alexander Spence Head of St. Geo.
Par., Spts. Co., planter. £12 7s. 9d. curr. 166 a. in St. Geo. Par., Spts. Co.,
part of pat granted John Chew, Gent., June 4, 1726, and by him sold to sd.
Henry, Jr., and John Collier, Junr., as by deeds, Jany. 31, 1737. Joseph
Hawkins, Isaac Darnell, Martin True. Feby. 7, 1743.

March 1, 1743. Lawrence Washington, now of Fairfax Co., Gent., to
Francis Thornton of Spts. Co., Gent. £42 10s. curr. Lot 39, in town of
Fredksbg. Mildred Willis, John Thornton, Henry Willis, March 6, 1743.
Ann, wife of Lawrence Washington, acknowledged her dower, etc.

March 6, 1743. James White and Sarah, his wife, of Hanover Co., to
Thomas White of Spts. Co. £29 curr. 300 a. (devised to sd. James White
by the will of his father, John White, Decd., recorded in King William
Co.) in Spts. Co., adjoining the land of sd. Thomas White, William Lea and
Chilion White. Witnesses, John Graves, William Lea. March 6, 1743.

Thomas Sanders of St. Geo. Par., Spts. Co., Mason, to Charles Coulson
(Colson) of same par. and county. Mortgage, personal estate. £53 3s. curr.
Witnesses, Joseph Steward, Joshua Thomas. Dated, Feby. 10, 1743-4.
Recd. March 6, 1743.

April 2, 1744. Edmund Waller and Mary, his wife, of St. Geo. Par.,
Spts. Co., to John Sartin of same par. and county. £6 curr. 200 a. (part of
a pat. granted sd. Edmund, Nov. 25, 1743) on Devils Ditch, in same par. and
county. Thos. Duerson, H. Pendleton. April 3, 1744.

May 1, 1744. Thomas Foster of St. Mark's Par., Orange Co., to Thomas
Solman of St. Geo. Par., Spts. Co. "400 a. in afsd county, amongst the
Branches of Mattapony River," etc. Ignatius x Tureman, Edmund Fos-
ter. May 1, 1744.

May 1, 1744. Thomas West and Catherine, his wife, of Overwharton
Par., Stafford Co., to William Long of St. Geo. Par., Spts. Co. £30 curr.
250 a. in St. Geo. Par., Spts. Co., part of a pat. granted Joseph Brock,
Gent., Decd., and by him conveyed to sd. West, etc. Witness, Edmund
Waller. May 1, 1744.

June 5, 1744. Edward Ware of St. Geo. Par., Spts. Co., and Lucy, his
wife, to Erasmus Wethers Allen of St. Ann's Par., Essex Co. £55 curr. 300
a. in St. Geo. Par., Spts. Co., part of a pat. granted Thomas Allen and
George Musick, Sept. 28, 1728. Benja. Winslow, Hugh Sanders, Richd.
Phillips. June 5, 1744.

July 28, 1744. Cornelius Sale of Essex Co. to Francis Thornton of Spts.
Co. £50 curr. 200 a. in Spts. Co., and purchased by sd. Sale of Augustine

Smith, as by Deed, April 8, 1731. Richard Childs, James Sale, Anthony Sale. Augt. 7, 1744.

Augt. 6, 1744. Peter Mountague, Jr., of St. Geo. Par., Spts. Co., to Roger Cason of Caroline County. £40 curr. 84 a. in Spts. Co., formerly belonging to John Foster, etc. Witnesses, William Johnston, Robt. King, Junr. Augt. 7, 1744. Authorit, wife of Peter Mountague, Jr., acknowledged her dower, etc.

Augt. 6, 1744. Peter Mountague, Jr., of St. Geo. Par., Spts. Co., and Authorit, his wife, to William Johnston of same Par. and county. £40 curr. 98 a. in Spts. Co., Augt. 7, 1744. Augt. 5, 1746, "Authorit Mountague, late the wife of Peter Mountague, Decd.," etc., acknowledged this said deed, etc.

Sept. 4, 1744. Henry Chiles of St. Geo. Par., Spts. Co., planter, and Mercy, his wife, to George Seaton of St. John's Par., King William Co., Gent. £180 curr. 600 a. in St. Geo. Par., Spts. Co., part of a tract granted Henry and John Chiles, as joint tenants, etc. Witnesses, George Morton, William x Sandige, John x Graves. Sept. 4, 1744.

Sept. 4, 1744. Patterson Pulliam of Spts. Co., planter, and Elizabeth, his wife, to Henry Chiles of sd. Co., planter. £90 curr. 250 a. in St. Geo. Par., Spts. Co. George Seaton, George Morton, John x Graves. Sept. 4, 1744.

August 25, 1744. James Taylor of St. Stephen's Par., King and Queen Co., and Martisha, his wife, to Joseph Temple of St. Margaret's Par., King William Co. £40 curr., and a tract of land on Branches of Beaver Dam Swamp, Hanover Co. 593 a., formerly granted sd. Temple, March 12, 1739. 800 a. in St. Geo. Par., Spts. Co., on both sides Arnolds Run, granted John and James Taylor, by pat., June 30, 1726. Michael Wharton, William Temple, Hannah Temple. Sep. 4, 1744.

Sept. 4, 1744. Edward Herndon, Jr., of St. Geo. Par., Spts. Co., to Thomas Foster, Surgeon, of county and Par. Afsd. £26 6s. curr. 337 acres. William Lynn, Wm. Smith, Charles Boreman. Sept. 4, 1744. Elizabeth, wife of Edward Herndon, acknowledged her dower, etc.

Oct. 2, 1744. William Lea of King and Queen Co. to Anthony Garnett of Spts. Co. £55 10s. curr. 500 a. in St. Geo. Par., Spts. Co. Jos. Brock, Thos. Foster, John Coffey. Oct. 2, 1744. Rachael, wife of William Lee, acknowledged her dower, etc.

Oct. 2, 1744. Robert Williamson of Caroline Co. to John Haley of Hanover Co. £50 curr. 400 a. in Spts. Co., pat., Jany. 10th, 1735. Wm. Barber, William Rolfe, Jos. Collins. Octr. 2, 1744. Elizabeth, wife of Robert Williamson, acknowledged her dower, etc.

Oct. 2, 1744. John Thornton of Fredksburg, Gent., to David Bell of Henrico Co., Mercht. £290 curr. Lots No. 41, "whereon the long Ordinary now stands," and Lot 43, in town of Fredericksburg, purchased of sd. Thornton of Henry Willis, Esqr., late Decd., as by Deeds, June 4, 1741. William Hunter, Thos. Prestwood, Junr., Tully Choice. Oct. 2, 1744.

Oct. 2, 1744. Griffin Fantleroy, Junr., of Northumberland Co., Gent., to Henry Lewis of Spts. Co., planter. £40 curr. 400 a. in St. Geo. Par., Spts.

Co., on the River Ta, granted Daniel Brown, by pat., Feby. 24, 1730, etc. Wm. Hughes, John Holloday. Octr. 2, 1744.

Octr. 2, 1744. Henry Lewis of Spts. Co. and Martha, his wife, to Patterson Pulliam of same county, planter. £55 curr. 400 a. at head of River Ta, in St. Geo. Par., Spts. Co., granted Daniel Brown, by Pat. Feby. 24, 1730, etc. John Holloday, Wm. Hughes.

Anthony x Gholston and Jane, his wife, of St. Geo. Par., Spts. Co., to William Pollard of St. Thomas Par., Orange Co. £55 curr. 120 a., part of the tract whereon sd. Anthony lives, formerly bought of John Chew. Witnesses, Edwd. Herndon, A. Foster, Edmd. Foster. Oct. 2, 1744.

Nov. 6, 1744. William Gains of St. Thomas Par., Orange Co., and Isbell, his wife, to Joseph Hawkins of St. Geo. Par., Spts. Co. £7 curr. and 2600 lbs. tob. 442½ a. in St. Geo. Par., Spts. Co., part of a tract granted Anthony Gholston, Sept. 28, 1728, by pat. James Mills, James x Jones, Jos. Collins, William Collins. Nov. 6, 1744.

Decr. 4, 1744. John Menefee and Mary, his wife; James Stevens and Alice, his wife; James Kennerley and Elizabeth, his wife, Planters, to James Ball, of the Parish of White Chapel, Lancaster County, Gent. £70 curr. 850 a. granted John James, by pat., June 30, 1726, in St. Geo. Par., Spts. Co. No witnesses. Dec. 4, 1744.

Dec. 4, 1744. John Menefee and Mary, his wife; James Stevens and Alice, his wife; James Kennerley and Elizabeth, his wife, planters, to James Ball of Parish of White Chappel, Lancaster Co., Gent. £10 curr. 249 a. in St. Geo., Spts. Co. No witnesses. Dec. 4, 1744.

Nov. 6, 1744. Joseph x Roberts of Spts. Co. and Susanna, his wife, to Wm. Sandage of same county. £140 curr. 512 a. in St. Geo. Par., Spts. Co., 300 a. purchased by sd. Roberts of Coll. James Taylor, the other 212 a. part of a pat. to sd. Roberts, Sept. 28, 1728. Thos. Cowper, John Holloday, Isaac Bradburn. Nov. 6, 1744.

Dec. 4, 1744. Francis Thornton, Gent., of Spts. Co., to George Head of sd. County, planter. Deed of Lease. 200 a. in Spts. Co., joining John Proctor and Abraham Darnell and the division line of the sd. Francis and Anthony Thornton and Humphrey Bell of London. "George Head and Elizabeth, his wife," etc. John Waller, Richard Tutt, Wm. Waller. Decr. 4, 1744.

Decr. 4, 1744. William x Samms and Mary, his wife, of St. Geo. Par., Spts. Co., to John Pain of same Par. and County. £25 curr. 100 a. in sd. Par. and county, devised the sd. William, by his father. Witnesses, Thos. Duerson, Felix Gilbirt, Isaac Davis. Dec. 4, 1744.

Novr. 17, 1744. William x Prewett of Caroline Co., planter, to John Shirley of Caroline Co., planter. £25 curr. 200 a. in Spts. Co., part of a pat. granted sd. Prewett. Witnesses, William Emmerson, George Stubblefield, Henry Williamson. Dec. 4, 1744.

Jany. 12, 1744. George Woodroof of St. Geo. Par., Spts. Co., and Jane, his wife, to Henry Pendleton of same Par. and county. £33 curr. 300 a. granted by pat. to William Smith, Gent., Decd., Sept. 28, 1728, in St. Geo. Par., Spts. Co. Edwd. Jones, Wm. Searcy, Wm. Woodroof. Feby. 5, 1744.

Nov. 17, 1744. George Woodroof of St. George Par., Spts. Co., planter, and Jane, his wife, "for the naturall love and affection that they bear to George Woodroof, Junr.," and 5 shill. curr. 100 a. Spts. Co., part of pat. granted sd. George Woodroof, June 24, 1726. Witness, Benjamin Woodroof. Feby. 5, 1744.

Decr. 20, 1744. John Farish of Spts. Co. to William Waller of sd. County. 5 shill. curr. 1½ a. on N. side River Ta. Lark. Chew, William Johnston, John Mitchell, William Login, Jos. Brock. Feby. 5, 1744.

Nov. 15, 1744. Edward Coleman and Lucrea, his wife, of St. Geo. Par., Spts. Co., to Samuel Waggoner of Essex Co., and Southfarnham Par. £12 curr. 100 a. in St. Geo. Par., Spts. Co. James Waggoner, Joseph Reynolds, Kerenhappuch Reeves. Feby. 5, 1744.

John x Elson of St. Geo. Par., Spts. Co., mortgage to Anthony Strother of sd. Par. and Co., Gent. £100. 175 a. in Spts. Co., St. Geo. Par., and goods and chattels as security, etc. Wit., Z. Lewis, Wm. Waller. Feby. 6, 1744.

William Potter of Fredericksburg, barber, mortgage to Anthony Strother of Fredksburg, Mercht. £10 7s. 11d. curr. Goods and chattels as security, etc. Witnesses, Frans. Tyler, John Prince.

March 4, 1744. George Cook and Sarah, his wife, of St. Geo. Par., Spts. Co., to Joseph Allen of Southfarnham Par., Essex Co. £47 curr. 200 a. in St. Geo. Par., Spts. Co., part of pat. granted Harry Beverley, Decd., who by his will and testament bequeathed part of this sd. patent to his daughter Catherine, being now the wife of George Stubblefield, and the afsd. 200 a. was transferred by sd. Stubblefield and Catherine, his wife, to sd. Cook, in the year 1742. Witnesses, James Waggoner, John Evans, Leonard x Young. March 5, 1744.

March 4, 1744. Robert King, Junr., and Mary, his wife, of Spts. Co., to Edward Cason of same county. Sd. Cason by Deed of Gift, July 16, 1729, in County Court of Caroline, did give, etc., unto his daughter, Mary Cason, several negroes, after the death of sd. Cason. Since making which Deed the sd. Mary, on Feby. 28, 1741, intermarried with sd. Robert. This deed conveys certain negroes, the increase of those deeded sd. Mary, back to sd. Cason. Witnesses, Wm. Waller, William Johnston, Edmund Foster, John Mitchell. Mar. 5, 1744.

Feby. 21, 1744. George Woodroof of Spts. Co., planter, and Jane, his wife, "for consideration of the natural love and affection they bear unto * * George Woodroof, Junr.," and for sum of £5 curr. 100 a. in Spts. Co. John Minor, George Willson, Thos. x Graves. March 5, 1744.

March 28, 1745. George Woodroof of St. Geo. Par., Spts. Co., and Jane, his wife, "in consideration of the natural love and affection that they bear unto * * Benjamin Woodroof, planter," etc., and for sum of 5 shill. curr. 200 a. on both sides Arnolds run in Spts. Co. John Parrish, Wm. Miller, John Carter. April 2, 1745.

Sept. 8, 1744. John Allan of Spts. Co., mercht., to Charles Dick of sd. County, mercht. £25 curr. Lot 51 in town of Fredksbg. John Thornton, George Chapman, Alexn. Wright. April 3, 1745.

April 1, 1745. Edmund Waller of St. Geo. Par., Spts. Co., to Alexander Hume of sd. Par. and county. Deed of Lease, "said Alexander Hume and

Mary, his wife, etc." 90 a. whereon sd. Edmund now lives, and granted by pat. to sd. Edmund, Sept. 28, 1728. Josias Baker, Edmund Foster. April 3, 1745.

May 7, 1745. Augustine Owen of Middlesex Co., planter, to William Baskett of Caroline Co., planter. £50. 100 a. in St. Geo. Par., Spts. Co. John Hughes, Wm. x Martin. May 7, 1745.

May 7, 1744-(1745?). William x Sandige and Ann, his wife, of Spts. Co., to Anthony Gholston, Junr., of sd. County. £35 curr. 200 a. in St. Geo. Par., Spts. Co. No witnesses. May 7, 1745.

May 7, 1745. Nicholas x Hawkins of St. Geo. Par., Spts. Co., to Nathan Hawkins of Par. and county afsd. £60 curr. 200 a., part of a grant to Larkin Chew, and by sd. Chew sold to William Lindsay, as by Deed, Nov. 5, 1722, and sold by sd. Lindsay to sd. Nicholas Hawkins, as by Deeds, April 26, 1743. Parmenas Bowker, Alexander Hawkins, Thomas Cartwright. May 7, 1745.

April 26, 1745. Anthony Thornton, Gent., and Winifred, his wife, of Stafford Co., to Sharshall Grasty of Spts. Co. £27 15s. curr. 222 a. granted sd. Anthony and Francis Thornton, by pat., April 19, 1720, in St. Geo. Par., Spts. Co. Wm. Waller, John Farish, Wm. McWilliams. May 7, 1745.

April 20, 1745. Anthony Thornton, Gent., and Winifred, his wife, of Stafford Co., to Wm. McWilliams of Spts. Co. £43 8s. curr. 434 a. granted sd. Anthony and Francis Thornton by pat., April 19, 1720, in St. Geo. Par., Spts. Co. Wm. Waller, John Farish, Sharshall Grasty. May 7, 1745.

June 3, 1745. Dudley Gatewood of St. Geo. Par., Spts. Co., planter, and Sarah, his wife, to Henry Gatewood, Senr., of Par. and County afsd. £8 10s. curr. 83 a. (part of a tract bought by sd. Gatewood of Hugh Sanders) in Spts. Co., on Glady Fork Run. Robert Coleman, Henry Gatewood, Junr., Wm. Gatewood. June 4, 1745.

Robert Coleman of St. Geo. Par., Spts. Co., and Sarah, his wife, to Henry Gatewood, Senr., of Par. and County afsd. £31 6s. 6d. curr. 174 a. in Spts. Co., on Glady Fork Run. Henry Gatewood, Junr., Dudley Gatewood, Wm. Gatewood. June 4, 1745.

Nicholas x Hawkins, Senr., of St. Geo. Par., Spts. Co., to his son, James Hawkins. Deed of Gift. A negro and 100 a. of land in St. Geo. Par., Spts. Co. Dated, June 4, 1745. Witnesses, John Parrish, Jacob Fox. Recd., June 4, 1745.

June 4, 1744 (1745?). William x Samms and Mary, his wife, of St. Geo. Par., Spts. Co., to James Samms of Par. and County afsd. £10 curr. 18 a. in St. Geo. Par., Spts. Co., devised to sd. Wm. by his father. Witnesses, Wm. Carr, John Bigger, John Carr, Junr. June 4, 1745.

June 4, 1745. James x Samms and Anne, his wife, of St. Geo. Par., Spts. Co., to William Samms of same Par. and county. £10 curr. 34 a. in St. Geo. Par., Spts. Co., devised the sd. James, by his father. Witnesses, Wm. Carr, John Bigger, John Carr, Junr. June 4, 1745.

June 4, 1745. Robert Coleman and Sarah, his wife, of St. Geo. Par., Spts. Co., to Thomas Foster, Surgeon, of Par. and county afsd. £50 curr. 400 acres. A. Foster, John Gordon, Jno. Parrish. June 4, 1745.

May 14, 1745. John Robinson of Stratton Major Par., King and Queen Co., Esqr., to Thomas Collins of Spts. Co. £36 curr. 300 a. in St. Geo. Par., Spts. Co., part of a pat. granted sd. Robinson. Witnesses, Humphrey Hill, Jos. Collins, Wm. Collins, G. Braxton, Junr. June 4, 1745.

May 14, 1745. John Robinson of Stratton Major Par., King and Queen Co., Esqr., to Joseph Collins of Spts. Co., planter. £15 curr. 254 a. in Spts. Co. and fork of River Po, part of a pat. granted sd. Robinson. Witnesses, Humphrey Hill, Thos. Collins, Wm. Collins, G. Braxton, Junr. June 4, 1745.

May 14, 1745. John Robinson of Stratton Major Par., King and Queen Co., Esqr., to William Collins of Par. and county afsd. £24 curr. 200 a. in St. Geo. Par., Spts. Co., etc., etc. Humphrey Hill, G. Braxton, Junr., Jos. Collins, Thos. Collins. June 4, 1745.

July 2, 1745. William Hunter of Spts. Co., Gent., and Martha, his wife, to John Allan of Spts. Co., Gent. £16 13s. 4d. curr. 10 a. and 20 perches near the town of Fredericksburg, joining the lands of Humphrey Hill, Henry Willis, Decd., and John Royston. Witness, Edmund Waller. July 2, 1745.

July 2, 1745. William Hunter of Spts. Co., Gent., and Martha, his wife, to Humphrey Hill of King and Queen Co., Gent. £16 13s. 4d. curr. 10 a. and 20 perches, near town of Fredksbg, and joining the land sold John Allan, etc. Witness, Edmund Waller. July 2, 1745.

July 2, 1745. William Long and Ann, his wife, of Spts. Co., to Thomas Duerson of St. Geo. Par., Spts. Co. £37 curr. 250 a. in St. Geo. Par., Spts. Co., part of pat. granted Joseph Brock, Gent., Decd., and by him sold to Thomas West, and by sd. West conveyed to sd. Long. Witness, Edmund Waller. July 2, 1745.

June 29, 1744. Bloomfield Long of St. Geo. Par., Spts. Co., and Mary, his wife, to Anthony Foster of Par. and county afsd. £60 curr. 331 a. in county and parish afsd. Henry Brock, Thomas Duerson, Hannah Duerson, W. Miller, Peter Montague, Junr. July 2, 1745.

Augt. 6, 1744. William Marshall of Caroline Co., planter, to Richard Durrett of Orange Co., planter. £5 curr. 400 a. in Spts. Co., granted by pat. to Thomas Allen, and by him sold to sd. Marshall. Witnesses, Han. Lee, John Willis, Jno. Madison. Augt. 6, 1745.

July 16, 1745. Richard x Couzens of Spts. Co., planter, and Elizabeth, his wife, to William Waller of sd. Co., Gent. £20 curr. 100 a. in St. Geo. Par., Spts. Co., on Middle River of Mattapony, part of a tract granted to John Rogers and others, by patent. Jos. Brock, Nicholas Horn, Margaret x Ship. Augt. 6, 1745.

Augt. 6, 1745. John x Pain and Frances, his wife, of St. Geo. Par., Spts. Co., to John Talburt of same co. and parish. £26 5s. curr. 100 a., part of a tract devised Wm. Samms by his father, in Par. and county afsd. Jos. Brock, James Lea, John Graves. Augt. 6, 1745.

June 25, 1745. John Talburt of St. Geo. Par., Spts. Co., and Margaret, his wife, to Jeremiah Stevens of same Par. and county. £12 curr. 36 a. in St. Geo. Par., Spts. Co., on Cattail Swamp, of Mattapony River (joining

Joseph Brock and the Orphans of James Samms, near the Samms plantation), part of a tract granted Larkin Chew, by pat., June 4, 1722, and by him conveyed to Amey Sutton, and by sd. Sutton to sd. Talburt. Witnesses, Robt. Huddleston, Matthew Hubbard. Augt. 6, 1745.

Plat of Land. The sd. land devised to William Wiat, Edward Wiat, Thomas Wiat, each 667 acres, and John Thurston (in right of Ann, his wife), the remainder, by the will of Francis Wiatt, Decd. A division of the land. Dated, August 29, 1745. Witnesses, Wm. Waller, Jos. Brock, Nicholas Horn. Recd., Septr. 3, 1745.

Oct. 1, 1745. Edwin Hickman of Albemarle Co. to Giles Tompkins of Spts. Co. £22 curr. 209½ a. in Spts. Co. Chrisr. Tompkins, Henry Chiles. Oct. 1, 1745.

Robert Coleman of Drysdale Par., Caroline Co., to his son, Thomas Coleman, of par. and county afsd. Deed of Gift. 346 a. in Spts. Co., part of two patents granted sd. Robt. Coleman, Decr. 2, 1723, and June 16, 1727, on N. side Robinson Run. Dated, Augt. 9, 1745. Witnesses, Thos. James, Richard Coleman, Joseph Ray. Recd., Oct. 1, 1745.

Sept. 21, 1745. George Woodroof, Jr., of St. Margaret's Par., Caroline Co., planter, and Ann, his wife, to Thos. Graves of St. Geo. Par., Spts. Co., planter. 200 a. in Spts. Co., "a part of the lands made over to the sd. George Woodruff, Junr., by his father, George Woodroof. Witnesses, Jno. Parrish, Wm. McWilliams, A. Foster. Octr. 1, 1745.

Oct. 1, 1745. Richard Todd of King and Queen Co., Gent., to William Lynn of town of Fredericksburg, Doctor of Physic. £40 curr. Lot 60, in town of Fredericksburg. "Devised by the last will and testament of Collo. William Todd, formerly of the county of King and Queen, and since Decd., to his son, Thomas Todd, who by Deeds, June 7, 1743, did sell the same to sd. Richard Todd, etc. W. Kelly, Edwd. Herndon, Wm. Hughes. Oct. 1, 1745.

Oct. 1, 1745. Adam Reid of town of Urbanna, Middlesex Co., Mercht., to John Tayloe, Junr., of Richmond Co., Esqr. £141 curr. Lot 14, in town of Fredksburg. Robert Burwell, John Champe, James Hunter, William Black. Octr. 1, 1745.

June 3, 1745. John Martin of King and Queen Co. to Robert Farish of St. Geo. Par., Spts. Co. 5 shill. ster. 400 a. "in county afsd." William Johnston, John Coleman, Henry May, Richd. Coleman. Oct. 1, 1745.

July 2, 1745. Robert Spilsbe Coleman of Essex Co. and Sarah, his wife, to Richard Couzens of Spts. Co. £25 curr. 100 a. whereon Wm. Dyer formerly dwelt, in St. Geo. Par., Spts. Co., on branches of Pamunkey River. John Edmondson, Richd. Coleman, John Willson, Richard Shipp.

Octr. 31, 1745. Thomas Cartwright of St. Geo. Par., Spts. Co., and Rachel, his wife, to George Sheppard of Par. and County afsd. £25 curr. 140 a. whereon sd. Cartwright now dwells, and which he bought of Colo. James Taylor. Witnesses, Edmund Waller, Mary Waller, Ephraim Musick. Nov. 5, 1745.

Nov. 4, 1745. Peter Mountague of St. Geo. Par., Spts. Co., and Elizabeth, his wife, to John Long of Essex Co. £70 curr. 100 a. in "par. and county afsd." Owen Thomas, Nicholas Hawkins, Jr., Nicholas x Hawkins, Senr. Nov. 5, 1745.

Nov. 5, 1745. William Baskett and Elizabeth, his wife, of Spts. Co., to Jeremiah White of Spts. Co. £23 curr. 100 a. in St. Geo. Par., Spts. Co. Witness, Edmund Waller. Novr. 5, 1745.

Feby. 4, 1745. George Carter of St. George Par., Spts. Co., and Elizabeth, his wife, to John Lea of the co. afsd., and Ann, his wife, "in consideration of the natural love and affection they, the sd. George and Elizabeth, bear unto the sd. John Lea; their son-in-law, and Ann, his wife, their daughter," etc. Deed of gift. 185 a. in St. Geo. Par., Spts. Co. No witnesses. Feby. 4, 1745.

Robert Coleman of Drysdale Par., Caroline Co., to his son, John Coleman. Deed of Gift. 316 a. in Spts. Co., part of a pat. granted sd. Robt., Dec. 2, 1723. Witnesses, Ed. Wiat, Samuel Hawes, Thomas Coleman, Wiat Coleman. Recd. Feby. 4, 1745. Dated —— —, 1745.

Nov. 5, 1745. Benjamin Woodroof of St. Geo. Par., Spts. Co., and Mary, his wife, to William Davenport of St. Mark's Par., Louisa Co. £40 curr. 200 a. in St. Geo. Par., Spts. Co., on both sides Arnold's Run, and joining lands of Capt. Joseph Temple and Thomas Hill, and part of a pat. granted George Woodruff June 24, 1726, and given sd. Benja. by his father, George Woodroof, as by deeds, Mar. 28, 1745. Witnesses, Jno. Minor, Benja. Arnold, Ambrose Arnold, John Davenport. Feby. 4, 1745.

William Searcy of Spts. Co., Innkeeper, mortgage to Edmond Waller of sd. County, Gent., Goods and Chattels. £22 curr. Witnesses, Edmund Foster, Thos. Foster, Wm. Hughes. Dated, Dec. 4, 1745. Recd. April 1, 1746.

Nicholas x Hawkins of St. Geo. Par., Spts. Co., Planter, to his daughter, Ann Pritchett, wife of James Pritchett, a negró and 15 a. in Par. and Co. afsd. Dated, Nov. 5, 1745. Witnesses, James Hawkins, Nicholas Hawkins, Alexander Hawkins, John Hawkins. April 1, 1746.

Nicholas x Hawkins of St. Geo. Par., Spts. Co., planter, to his son, Nicholas Hawkins, a negro and 100 a. on N. E. side of Germanna Road. Dated Nov. 5, 1745. James Hawkins, James Pritchett, Alexander Hawkins, John Hawkins. April 1, 1746.

May 6, 1746. Joseph Holloday of Spts. Co. to Thomas Pulliam of Spts. Co. £5 curr. 22 a. in St. Geo. Par., Spts. Co. John Holloday, James Edwards. May 6, 1746.

Feby. 27, 1745. James Shackleford and Elizabeth, his wife, of St. Geo. Par., Spts. Co., to Edward Jones of same Par. and county. £10 7s. curr. 69 a. in St. Geo. Par., Spts. Co. John Wiglesworth, Edmund Waller, Isaac Bradburn. May 6, 1746.

May 6, 1746. William Woodford of Caroline Co., Gent., and Anne, his wife, to John Champe of King George Co., Gent. £640 curr. (mortgage). 1600 a. in Spts. Co., purchased by sd. Woodford of Richard Taliaferro and Charles Taliaferro, to whom it was conveyed by the brother, Francis Taliaferro, by deed Dated Sept. 28, 1682, and part of a pat. granted their father, Robert Taliaferro, and one Lawrence Smith, March 26, 1666; also slaves. Witnesses, T. Turner, Peter Daniel. May 6, 1746.

May 6, 1746. Henry Downs of St. Thomas Par., Orange Co., Gent., to Francis Thornton of St. Geo. Par., Spts. Co., Gent. £43 curr. Lot 56 in town of Fredksburg, etc. John Chew, Richd. Tutt, Thos. Slaughter. May 6, 1746.

June 3, 1746. Thomas Brown of Orange County, to Richard Stears. £58 curr. 258 a. in Spts. Co. Jno. Parrish, Wm. Long, Richard Phillips. June 3, 1746.

June 30, 1746. Thomas Salmon of St. Thomas Par., Orange Co., to Thomas Cook of Spts. Co. £50 curr. 300 a. in St. Geo. Par., Spts. Co., part of a pat. lately granted Thomas Foster, June 1, 1741. Wm. Collins, Thomas Collins, Jos. Collins. July 1, 1746.

Jany. 27, 1745. William x Samms and Mary, his wife, of St. Geo. Par., Spts. Co., to James Stevens of same Par. and county. £8 curr. 34 a., part of a tract devised James Samms by his father, James Samms, Decd., and by sd. James Samms conveyed to sd. Wm. Samms, June 4, 1745. Jeremiah Stevens, John Talbert, James x Samms. July 1, 1746.

July 1, 1746. Luke x Hambleton of Fredericksvil Par., Louisa Co., and Susanna, his wife, to Anthony Foster of St. Geo. Par., Spts. Co. £60 curr. 135 a. in St. Geo. Par., Spts. Co., part of a pat. granted Larkin Chew, June 4, 1722. Witnesses, Lark. Chew, W. Robinson, Edmund Foster. July 1, 1746.

June 7, 1746. David Bell of Henrico Co. to Charles Colson of town of Fredericksburg, Innkeeper. £370 curr. Lots No. 41 and 43, in Town of Fredericksburg. John Allan, Alexr. Scott, Peter x Lucas, Patrick Connelly, William Thompson. July 1, 1746.

July 1, 1746. Joseph Holloday of Spts. Co., to Zachary Lewis of same county. £110 curr. 120 a. in Spts. Co., part of the lands devised sd. Joseph, by the last will and testament of his father, John Holloday, Decd. Witnesses, M. Battaley, Jos. Brock, Jon. Holloday. July 1, 1746.

William x Bell of Spts. Co., planter, to his daughter, Lydia Arnold, "plantation whereon her husband, William Arnold, now lives, with 70 a. adjoining. Dated, Augt. 5, 1746. Witnesses, Jno. Parrish, Philip Vincent Vass. Recd. Sept. 2, 1746.

William x Bell of Spts. Co., planter, to his daughter, Bathsheba Bell, "the plantation whereon I, Wm. Bell, now live," with 100 a. adjoining, mentions "privilege reserved to Lydia Arnold," etc. Dated, Augt. 5, 1746. Witnesses, Jno. Parrish, Philip Vincent Vass. Recd. Sept. 2, 1746.

Sept. 16, 1746. Benjamin Winslow, Gent., and Susannah, his wife, of Essex Co., to Revd. James Marye, Minister of the Parish of St. George, Spts. Co. £28 curr. Lot 55 in town of Fredksbg. John Nicholas, Thos. Walker, Rob. Jackson, Geo. Taylor, Hen. Downs, Taverner Beale, John Willis, Jas. Barbour, Thos. Scott. Oct. 7, 1746.

Oct. 7, 1746. Henry Lewis of Spts. Co. to John Parrish of same county. £30 curr. 400 a. in Spts. Co., granted by pat. to George Cook, Feby. 12, 1742, and conveyed by him to the sd. Lewis. Witness, Edmund Waller. Oct. 7, 1746. Martha, wife of Henry Lewis, acknowledged her dower, etc.

Sept. 17, 1746. Mary Belfield, widow, and John Belfield and Wm. Jordan, Gent., all of the County of Richmond, in Va., executors of the Last will and testament of Thomas Wright Belfield, Gent., Decd., to Charles Dick of Fredericksburg, Spts. Co., Mercht. Recites—Trustees of Fredksburg, by Deed, Augt. 2, 1737, sold to John Rucker of Orange Co., Gent. Lot No. 5, in town of Fredksbg, sd. Rucker by his last will and testament devised the sd. lot to Thomas Wright Belfield, and his heirs, etc., sd. Belfield taking possession thereof at sd. Rucker's death, sd. Belfield making his last will and testament, Dated Dec. 6, 1743, and stated for his excrs. to dispose of such land as they should think fit for the payment of his debts, etc., etc. Witnesses, T. Turner, Thos. Turner, Junr., James Dun, Archd. Gordon. Oct. 7, 1746.

*Oct. 7, 1746. Edward Wyat of Gloucester Co. to Joseph Peterson of Spts. Co. £17 10s. curr. A tract of land in St. Geo. Par., Spts. Co. Thos. White, John x Graves, Thomas x Fagg (Tagg). Oct. 7, 1746.

Sept. 6, 1746. William Williams of St. Geo. Par., Spts. Co., and Elizabeth, his wife, to John Williams of same Par. and county. £35 curr. 100 a. in St. Geo. Par., Spts. Co., part of a tract taken up by Nicholas Lankford, and by him sold to John Coller (Collier), Junr., of King and Queen Co., and by sd. Coller sold to Robert Stubblefield and Ralph Williams, by Deeds, in Spts. Co. Court, and afterwards acknowledged to Wm. Williams, etc. Witnesses, Robt. Huddleston, Danl. x Pruit, John Huddleston. Nov. 4, 1746.

Nov. 4, 1746. Bloomfield Long of St. Geo. Par., Spts. Co., to Reubin Long, his son, of same parish and county. 118½ a. in St. Geo. Par., Spts. Co. Witnesses, Thomas Graves, Robt. Moor, William Johnston. Nov. 4, 1746.

March 3, 1746. Benjamin x Matthews and Ann, his wife, of Spts. Co., to Joseph Carter of same county. £8 curr. 100 a. in St. Geo. Par., Spts. Co., joining lands of Humphrey Bell of London, Mercht. Robt. Goodloe, Thomas Dillard, and others. Witnesses, Abraham Estes, Tho. Magee, Edmund Foster. Mar. 3, 1746.

March 3, 1746. Richard Phillips of Louisa Co., Gent., and Katherine, his wife, to Oswald Smith of Orange Co. £200 curr. 380 a. in Spts. Co. and a mill thereon, formerly granted Wm. Smith, Gent., by Pat., Octr. 31, 1726. John Waller, John Minor, Edmund Waller. April 7, 1747.

April 7, 1747. Taliver x Cragg and Mary, his wife, of St. Geo. Par., Spts. Co., to Joseph Hawkins of sd. Par. and county. £5 curr. 200 a. on both sides of Terrys run, in Co. and Par. afsd., left by the last will of John Hawkins, Decd., to be divided between Mary, his wife, and four of his children (vizt.), Elizabeth Smith, Philemon Hawkins, Phebe Smith, and the sd. Mary Cragg. Witnesses, A. Foster, Edmund Foster, Larkin Johnston. April 7, 1747.

Feby. 12, 1746. Margaret x Morris of Spts. Co., widow, to Moseley Battaley of same co., Gent. Deed of lease. 200 a. in Spts. Co., whereon sd. Margaret now lives. Witnesses, John x Wheeler, J. Battaley, Joseph x Brooks. May 5, 1747.

May 4, 1747. Henry Goodloe of St. Geo. Par., Spts. Co., Gent., to his son, Robt. Goodloe of same Par. and Co., planter. Deed of Gift. 150 a. in

* Ed, Note.—This deed is signed Edward Wiatt.

St. Geo. Par., Spts. Co., part of à pat. granted sd. Henry, May 21, 1726. George Eastham, John Spalding. May 5, 1747.

April 30, 1747. Henry Goodloe of St. Geo. Par., Spts. Co., to Thomas Coats of St. Margaret's Par., Caroline Co. £37 curr. 303 a. in Spts. Co. Robert Stubblefield, John Crane, Richard Stubblefield. May 5, 1747.

Dec. 19, 1746. Thomas Chew of St. Thomas Par., Orange Co., Gent., and Martha, his wife, to John Penn of Drysdale Par., Caroline Co. £25 curr. 307 a. in Spts. Co., on south branches of Mattapony, called Lewis' River. John Ray, Joseph Hoomes, Eusebius Stone, Augustin Muse, Moses Penn. June 2, 1747.

Decr. 19, 1746. Thomas Chew of St. Thomas Par., Orange Co., Gent., and Martha, his wife, to George Penn of Drysdale Par., Caroline Co. £20 curr. 307 a. in Spts. Co., on south Branches of Mattapony, called Lewis' River. John Ray, Joseph Hoomes, Eusebius Stone, Augustin Muse, Moses Penn. June 2, 1747.

Joseph x Venable, for £15 15s. 8d. curr., to John Minor of Spts. Co., mortgage, Goods and Chattels, June 2, 1747. Witnesses, Peter Daniel, James x Sparks. Recd. June 2, 1747.

June 2, 1747. Beverley Randolph of Kingston Par., Gloucester Co., Gent., to James Garnett of St. Anne's Par., Essex Co., Gent. £45 5s. curr. Lot. No. 3, in town of Fredksbg. John Livingston, jr.; Cha. Dick, Alexr. Wright. June 2, 1747.

June 2, 1747. William Wiat, Mariner, to Joseph Herndon of Caroline Co. £133 8s. 667 a. in Spts. Co., devised by the last will and testament of Francis Wyatt, Decd., to his son, the sd. William, etc. Witnesses, James Taylor, Joseph Russel, Richard Todd. June 2, 1747.

Augt. 4, 1747. William x Hensley and Jane, his wife, of St. Geo. Par., Spts. Co., to Robert Spilsby Coleman of Southfarnham Par., Essex Co. £35 curr. 420 a. in St. Geo. Par., Spts. Co., part of a tract granted Roger Tandy, by pat., Oct. 13, 1727. Witnesses, A. Bowker, Thomas Coleman, Hugh Sanders.

Augt. 4, 1747. John Allan of Fredericksburg, Mercht., to Charles Dick of same town, Mercht. £20 curr. Lots Nos. 5 and 6, in town of Fredericksburg, etc. No witnesses. Augt. 4, 1747.

Augt. 4, 1747. John Allan, Gent., of Spts. Co., to Revd. Robert Rose of Essex Co., Clerk. £20 curr. Lots 3 and 4 in Spts. Co., near town of Fredksbg. No witnesses. Augt. 4, 1747.

William Bartlet of St. Geo. Par., Spts. Co., Planter, to "my son-in-law, Clement Mountague, and Ann, his wife," etc. Deed of Gift, "my grand-daughter, Susanna Mountague," etc. 56 a. in par. and county afsd., granted sd. Bartlet, by pat., March 12, 1739. Dated, Sept. 21, 1747. Witnesses, Francis Miller, Edmund Foster. Recd. Sept. 1, 1747.

June 3, 1746. George x Musick, Senr., and Ann, his wife, of St. Geo. Par., Spts. Co., William x Sandidge and Ann, his wife, of same Par. and county, to William Trustee of same Par. and county, "sd. George Musick, Senr., and Ann, his wife, to William Trustee, their son-in-law, and Elizabeth, his wife, their daughter." Deed of Gift. 50 acres, and sd. Wm. Sandidge and Ann, his wife, for consideration of £4 curr., to them by sd. Wm. Trustee paid, convey 15 acres adjoining the afsd. 50 acres. Witnesses, Thos. White, William Lea, Phillip Ballard. June 3, 1746.

May 4, 1746. George x Musick, Senr., and Ann, his wife, of Spts. Co., to Robert Beadles of sd. county. £7 curr. 50 a. in St. Geo. Par., Spts. Co. [same being part of the tract whereon sd. Geo. Musick, Senr., liveth and by him given to his son, George Musick, Junr., but never acknowledged, to him, and by the sd. George, Junr., sold to the sd. Beadles]. Witnesses, Thos. White, William Lea, Phillip Ballard. June 3, 1746. Further proved, Oct. 6, 1747.

April 17, 1747. Alexander Scott, late of town of Fredksbg., power of attorney to friend Charles Colson of Fredksbg. Witnesses, Samuel Ritchie, Saml. Martin, W. Woodward. Octr. 6, 1747.

Oct. 6, 1747. John Allan of Spts. Co., Gent., to Revd. John Thompson of Orange Co., Clerk. £10 curr. Lot near the town of Fredksbg. Witnesses, Z. Lewis, Charles Colson, Thos. Howison. Oct. 6, 1747.

Oct. 6, 1747. George Woodroof of Spts. Co. and Jane, his wife, to Zachary Lewis of same county. £33 15s. curr. 135 a. in Spts. Co., on Arnolds run, part of a pat. granted sd. George Woodroof, June 24, 1726. William Taliaferro, Harbin Moor, Anne x Sandige. Oct. 6, 1747.

Octr. 30, 1747. Edmund Waller of St. Geo. Par., Spts. Co., and Mary, his wife, to Phillip Ballard, now of the sd. County and Parish. £13 curr. 352 a., part of a pat. granted sd. Waller, Nov. 25, 1743, on Devils Ditch, in Par. and County afsd. Witnesses, H. Pendleton, Richard Phillips, Junr. Novr. 3, 1747.

Oct. 4, 1747. Benjamin Holloday and Susanna, his wife, of Spts. Co., to Zachary Lewis of same county. £180 curr. 295½ a. in Spts. Co., devised the sd. Benjamin by the last will and testament of his father, John Holloday, Decd. Witnesses, George Wythe, A. Bowker, Edmund Waller. Nov. 3, 1747.

Nov. 17, 1747. Jeremiah White of Spts. Co. and Mary, his wife, to William Waller of same county, Gent. £23 curr. 100 a. in Spts. Co. Edmund Waller, George Wythe, Benja. Davis. Feby. 2, 1747.

Feby. 3, 1747. John Allan of Fredericksburg, Mercht., to John Mitchell of the same town, Mercht. £20 curr. Lot 1 and 2 in a plan of lots lately laid out by sd. Allan. Witnesses, Archd. Gordon, Patrick Mitchell, James Miller. Feby. 3, 1747.

Feby. 2, 1747. William Marshall of St. Margaret's Par., Caroline Co., planter, to Charles Dick of Fredericksburg, Mercht. £66 curr. 150 a. in St. Geo. Par., Spts. Co., formerly belonging to Chas. Taliaferro, and called Motts Run Tract, and by sd. Taliaferro transferred to sd. Marshall, etc. Witnesses, Anthony Strother, Alexr. Wright, John Jones. Feby. 2, 1747.

Feby. 2, 1747. Edward Wiat of Gloucester Co. to Benjamin Holloday of Spts. Co. £110 curr. 597 a. in Spts. Co., part of a tract conveyed by James Taylor, Gent., to Francis Wiat, Decd., who by his last will and testament devised the sd. tract to his son, Edward Wiat, party to these presents, etc. No witnesses. Feby. 2, 1747.

May 3, 1748. John Holloday of St. Geo. Par., Spts. Co., and Elizabeth, his wife, to John Wiglesworth of same Parish and county. £45 curr. 200 a. in Par. and county afsd., part of a pat. granted Thomas Sartin, May 6, 1727, and by him sold to John Holloday, Gent., Decd., father of the sd. John Holloday. Witnesses, Joel Parrish, Benja. Martin, Thoms. Stubblefield. May 3, 1748.

May 3, 1748. Robert Coleman of St. Geo. Par., Spts. Co., and Elizabeth, his wife, to John Pain of same Par. and county. £45 curr. 140 a. whereon sd. Robert Coleman now liveth, 50 a. thereof bought by sd. Coleman of Phebe Hobson, and the remaining part given to him by his father, Robert Coleman, Decd. Witnesses, Edmund Waller, Richd. Phillips, Junr. May 3, 1748.

Feby. 5, 1748. Abraham Rogers and Barbary, his wife, of St. Geo. Par., Spts. Co., planters, to Henry Bartlet of Par. and county afsd. £30 curr. 100 a. in St. Geo. Par., Spts. Co., and part of a pat. granted Peter Rogers. Witnesses, Owen Thomas, William Rogers, John Griffen, junr. May 3, 1748.

Oct. 9, 1747. William Hawkins of Essex Co., St. Ann's Par., Gent., and Margaret, his wife, to Rice Curtis, Junr., of St. Margaret's Par., Caroline Co. £50 curr. 501 a. in Spts. Co., part of pat. granted Larkin Chew, June 4, 1722, and by him sold to John Hawkins of Essex Co., Gent., Decd., as by Deeds, Nov. 3, 1724, and devised by sd. John Hawkins, Decd., to sd. Wm., party to these presents, as will appear by sd. will recorded in Essex Co. Witnesses, Wm. Conner, Thos. Scott, Jas. Dismukes, John Garrett, John Hudgens, John Boutwell. Nov. 3, 1747.

July 5, 1748. Robert Coleman of Orange Co. and Sarah, his wife, to William Hutcheson of St. Geo. Par., Spts. Co. £31 curr. 226 a. in Spts. Co., on S. side Glady Run, part of pat. granted sd. Coleman, Augt. 30, 1744. John Chew, Samll. Major, A. Foster. July 5, 1748.

Henry Goodloe, Gent., of Spts. Co., as by Deed, May, 13, 1736, conveyed unto George Goodloe of Caroline Co., Gent., now decd. 800 a. in Caroline and Spts. Co., which sd. 800 a. of land is devised by the sd. George Goodloe, Decd., in his last will and testament, Dated, Octr. 4, 1741, unto his three sons, Henry, George and Robert, etc. Witnesses, Edmund Waller, John Fox, Nichl. x Hawkins, Rob. Jackson, Thos. Turner, Junr., Benjamin Woodward. Augt., 1748.

Septr. 3, 1748. Mary Brock, widow and executrix of Joseph Brock, Late of Spts. Co., Gent., Decd., to Henry Brock, their son, of same county, planter. 650 a. of land in Spts. Co., Va. Witnesses, Elizabeth Blake, W. Robinson, Zachary Boughan. Septr. 6, 1748.

Sept. 6, 1748. John Allan of Spts. Co., Gent., to Elliott Benger of same county, Esqr. £10 curr. Lot No. 8 in Spts. Co., near the town of Fredericksburg. Ambrose Bullard, W. Russell. Sept. 6, 1748.

Decr. 6, 1748. Pattison Pulliam of Spts. Co. to Joseph Pulliam, his son. Deed of Gift. 130 a. in Spts. Co. Edmund Waller, Jno. Holloday, Benjamin Pulliam. Decr. 6, 1748.

Dec. 6, 1748. Pattison Pulliam of Spts. Co. and Elizabeth, his wife, to John Holloday of county afsd. £22 10s. curr. 150 a. in Spts. Co. Edmund Waller, Benjamin Woodward. Dec. 6, 1748.

Dec. 6, 1748. Pattison Pulliam and Elizabeth, his wife, of Spts. Co., to George Wilcocke of same county. £25 curr. 114 a. in Spts. Co. Edmund Waller, Jno. Holloday. Decr. 6, 1748.

May 20, 1748. Thomas Chew of Orange Co., Gent., to William Waller of Spts., Gent. £10 15s. curr. 171 a. in Spts. Co. Stephen Chenault, Edmund Waller, Jos. Redd, Ambrose Foster. Sept. 6, 1748.

Feby. 8, 1748. Thomas Chew of Orange Co., Gent., son and heir of Larkin Chew, late of Spts. Co., Gent., Decd., and Larkin Chew of Spts. Co., Gent., son and Devisee of the sd. Larkin Chew, Decd., to John Thruston of Gloucester Co., Gent. Sd. Larkin Chew, Decd., in his lifetime, April 2, 1721, for consideration of £100 curr., by his deeds of Lease and Release acknowledged in General Court of Va., April 29 last, conveyed to Wm. Dolton of Gloucester Co., 996 a. in Spts. Co., sd. Dolton dying intestate, the sd. land descended to his son, Wm. Dolton, who being possessed thereof, by his will, dated Dec. 8, 1733, made the same land to his wife, Sarah Dolton, and the heirs male of her body, and in case of no issue, after her death to my brother, Michael Dolton, etc., then to my sister, Margarett Dolton, sd. Wm. dying soon thereafter his will was proved in Co. court of Gloucester. It appears that sometime after, the sd. John Thurston, party to these presents, intermarried with Sarah Dolton, widow and relict of the testator of the afsd. mentioned will. It appears by a recent survey that the land intended to be conveyed in the deed afore-mentioned was not contained within the bounds therein laid, etc.; the sd. Chews hereby convey the sd. Property to sd. Thruston. Witnesses, Wm. Carr, Roger Dixon, A. Foster, Edmund Waller. March 7, 1748.

Grant of the King (George II) by Wm. Gooch, Gov. of Va., to Church wardens of St. Geo. Par., Spts. Co. 570 a. in Spts. Co., on S. side River Po, 512 a. being a part of a pat. to Larkin Chew, Gent., April 26, 1732, the residue, part of a pat. granted Harry Beverley, Gent., March 23, 1715, and by divers conveyances now vested in the sd. churchwardens. 1s. yearly for every 50 a. on St. Michael and All Angels' Day. Dated, Sept. 29, 1748. Recd. March 8, 1748, on motion of Zachary Lewis, Gent., one of the church wardens.

Henry Chew, late of Calvert Co., Maryland, to his daughter, Jane Chew, "for and in consideration of her going to North Carolina with me." Deed of gift. 3 negroes and 2000 lbs. sterling. Dated, Nov. 6, 1748. Recd. Dec. 6, 1748. Witnesses, Lark. Chew, Jos. Brock, Jno. Spooner, Patrk. Carey.

Feby. 13, 1748. Henry Brock and Barbara, his wife, of St. Geo. Par., Spts. Co., to Thomas Brooks of Par. and county afsd. £25 curr. 150 a. in Spts. Co. Witnesses, George Trible, Wm. Waller, Nicho. Horn, Martin True. April 4, 1749.

April 4, 1749. Thomas Wyatt of Essex Co., and Sukey, his wife, to Henry Chiles of Spts. Co. £153 curr. 667 a. in Spts. Co. Jo. Brock, Thos. Estes, Nicho. Horn. April 4, 1749. (Signed, Thomas Wiat.)

July 22, 1748. John Corbin of Essex Co., Gent., and Lettice, his wife, to Anthony Foster of Spts. Co. £30 curr. 223 a. in St. Geo. Par., Spts. Co. Witnesses, Samll. Major, John Carter, James Zachry. Sept. 6, 1748.

May 2, 1749. John Haley of Spts. Co. and Mary, his wife, to John Faulconer of Orange Co. £50 curr. 200 a. in Spts. Co., part of a pat. granted,

Sept. 10, 1735. Henry Rains, Jr., Thomas Massey, James Debrise. May 2, 1749.

Nov. 30, 1748. Wm. Davenport of Louisa Co. and Ann, his wife, to George Woodroof of Spts. Co., in consideration that George Woodroof and Jane, his wife, will, jointly with the sd. Davenport and wife, make and convey to Joel Parrish, 200 a. of land formerly sold by Benjamin Woodroof to sd. Davenport. 94 a. in Spts. Co. Ambrose Arnold, Benja. Woodroof, Jane Woodroof, Rachel x Arnold. June 6, 1749.

Nov. 30, 1748. William Davenport of Louisa Co. and Ann, his wife, and George Woodroof of Spts. Co. and Jane, his wife, to Joel Parrish. £38 curr. 200 a. in Spts. Co. Ambrose Arnold, Benjamin Woodroof, Jane Woodroof, Rachel Arnold. June 6, 1749.

June 6, 1749. John Healey of St. Geo. Parish, Spts. Co., to Ambrose Healey of St. Thomas Parish, Orange Co. £30 curr. — acres in St. Geo. Par., Spts. Co. Wm. Barber, Geo. Wells, James Stevens. June 6, 1749. Mary, wife of John Healey, acknowledged her dower, etc.

June 6, 1749. Thomas Cartwright of Spts. Co. and Rachel, his wife, to Joseph Holloday of sd. county. £43 curr. 80 acres in St. Geo. Par., Spts. Co. Witnesses, John Crittenden Webb, Wm. x Gholeston, Henry Sparks. June 6, 1749.

July 4, 1749. Henry Chiles of Spts. Co., planter, and Marcy, his wife, to James Rawlings, Senr., of the sd. county, planter. £90 curr. 250 a. on N. side Pamunkey River, in St. Geo. Par., Spts. Co. Ben. Johnson, John C. Webb, Jos. Brock. July 4, 1749.

July 4, 1749. Henry Chiles of Spts. Co. and Marcy, his wife, to William Webb of same county. £23 curr. 100 a. in Spts. Co. Ben. Johnson, James Rallings, Jo. Brock. July 4, 1749.

July 4, 1749. Henry Chiles of Spts. Co. and Marcy, his wife, to John Crittenden Webb of same co. £23 curr. 100 a. in Spts. Co. Ben. Johnson, James Rawllings, Jos. Brock. July 4, 1749.

July 2, 1749. John Farish of Spts. Co. and Sarah, his wife, to Nicholas Horn of same county. £120 curr. 400 a. in Spts. Co., on both sides south fork of South River. Jeremiah White, Junr., James Younger, John Farish, Junr. July 4, 1749.

Novr. 1, 1748. Robert Stubblefield and Ann, his wife, of St. Geo. Par., Spts. Co., to Richard Baylor of King and Queen, Co., Mercht. £100 curr. 400 a. in St. Geo. Par., Spts. Co., granted by pat. to John Collier, Junr., June 30, 1726, and by him conveyed to sd. Stubblefield, as by Deeds. Oct. 5, 1730. Joseph Hawkins, Richd. Woolfolk, Richd. Dobson, Humphrey Wallis, Wm. Barber.

Nov. 17, 1748. John Robinson, Junr., of King and Queen Co., Esqr., to John Allan of Spts. Co., Gent. £65 curr. 1000 a. in Spts. Co., on head branches of Mattapony. Nathal. Harrison, Wm. Waller, Henry Willis, Chas. Dick, Jr. Feby. 7, 1748.

July 20, 1749. John Willis of Culpeper Co., son of Henry and Mildred Willis, Decd., and Nanny, his wife, to Henry Willis of Spts. Co., Gent. £50 curr. Lots 11 and 12, in town of Fredksburg, etc. Will. Lynn, John Willis, Geo. Livingston, Humphrey Wallis. Augt. 1, 1749.

July 20, 1749. John Willis of Culpeper Co., son of Henry and Mildred Willis, Decd., and Nanny, his wife, to Henry Willis of Spts. Co., Gent. £50 curr. Lots 47 and 48, in town of Fredericksburg. Will. Lynn, John Willis, George Livingston, Humphrey Wallis. Augt. 1, 1749.

June 16, 1749. Thomas x Howell of Fredericksburg, Blacksmith, to John Fox of Fredericksburg, etc. £9 curr. Goods and chattels. Witnesses, David Mitchell, John Innis, John Simpson, Wm. Hughes. Augt. 1, 1749.

April 25, 1728. James Shackleford of St. Geo. Par., Spts. Co., to Richard Shackleford and Mary, his wife, of the same Par. and county, the tract of land whereon sd. Richd. now lives, etc. Edmund Waller, Richd. Phillips, Junr. Sept. 5, 1749.

Sept. 5, 1749. William Golson and Susanna, his wife, of St. Geo. Par., Spts. Co., to George Blakey of sd. Par. and county. £65 curr. 500 a. in St. Geo. Par., Spts. Co., joining the lands of Anthony Garnett and Joseph Hawkins, and remaining part of a pat. of land granted Anthony Golson and sd. Wm. Golson, Sept. 28, 1728. Lark. Chew, Larkin Johnston, Ambrose Foster, John Waggoner. Sept. 5, 1749.

John Skinner of Brunswick Par., King Geo. Co., to Mical Skinner of Washington Par., Westmoreland Co. Deed of Gift. 100 a. in St. Geo. Par., Spts. Co., on Hasel Run. Dated, June 21, 1749. Witnesses, Richd. Griffith, Anthony Griffith, William Marders. Sept. 5, 1749.

Benjamin Woodward of Spts. Co. to his daughter, Mary Woodward. Deed of Gift. One negress and goods and chattels. Dated, Sept. 5, 1749. Witnesses, Roger Dixon, William Strother, Anthony Strother. Sept. 5, 1749.

Octr. 2, 1749. Richard Coleman of Hanover Co. to John Sanders of Caroline Co. £30. 200 a. in Spts. Co. John Sanders, Junr., Robin Sanders, junr., John Jeter, junr. Oct. 3, 1749.

June 6, 1749. Richard x Chiles of St. Geo. Par., Spts. Co., to Nicholas Seward of same Par. and county. £50 curr. 150 a. (100 a. purchased by sd. Childs of Bartholomew Wood and Charity, his wife, as by Deeds, June 3, 1740, and 50 a. purchased by sd. Childs of Anthony Thornton, Gent., as by Deeds, Nov. 3, 1741.) George Gray, William Cunningham, John Gordon, Thomas Foster. Oct. 3, 1749.

Octr. 2, 1749. Matthew Hubbard and Martha, his wife, of St. Thomas Par., Orange Co., Planters, to John Adam Link of St. Geo. Par., Spts. Co. £30 curr. 100 a. in St. Geo. Par., Spts. Co., part of pat. granted Henry Haines, Sept. 28, 1728, and by sd. Haines conveyed to Thomas Hubbard, etc. Witnesses, W. Miller, Hen. Brock. Nov. 7, 1749.

Novr. 7, 1749. George x Wilcock and Mary, his wife, of Spts. Co., to Robert Beadles of same county. £28 curr. 114 a. in Spts. Co. Joseph Gale, George x Shepherd. Nov. 7, 1749.

Nov. 6, 1749. George x Shepperd of St. Geo. Par., Spts. Co., and Elizabeth Mary Angelicke, his wife, to Benjamin Holloday of same par. and county. £25 curr. 60 a., part of land whereon sd. Shepperd lives, etc. Witnesses, Joseph Holloday, William x Miller, Margaret x Randolph. Nov. 7, 1749.

Nov. 7, 1749. Thomas Turner, Junr., Gent., and Mary, his wife, of Spts. Co., and Francis Conway, Gent., and Sarah, his wife, of Caroline Co., to John Allan of Fredericksburg, Mercht.

Whereas Charles Taliaferro, the Elder, late of the Co. of Caroline, died, seized and possessed of a tract of land in a place called Motts, and by his last will and testament, dated March 2, 1734, bequeathed the same to his granddaughters, Mary and Sarah Taliaferro, the sd. Mary intermarried with Thomas Turner, Junr., and the sd. Sarah intermarried with sd. Francis Conway, etc., sd. parties for £120 curr. sell the 570 a. to the sd. Allan, etc. No witnesses. Nov. 7, 1749.

Augt. 21, 1749. John Allan of Fredericksburg, Mercht., to John Mitchell of same town, Mercht. £140 curr. Lot. No. 32, in town of Fredksburg. Chas. Dick, John Gordon, Adam Stephen, James Miller, William Cunninghame, Wm. Waller. Nov. 7, 1749.

Dec. 5, 1749. George Carter of St. Geo. Par., Spts. Co., and Elizabeth, his wife, to John Pain of same Par. and county. £12 10s. curr. 25a., whereon sd. George Carter's son Benjamin now liveth, etc., part of the tract whereon sd. George dwells, etc., etc. Witnesses, Thos. Duerson, Edmund Waller, Richd. Phillips, Junr. Dec. 5, 1749.

Augt. 15, 1749. John Willis (the younger son of that name of Col. Henry Willis, Decd.,) of Culpeper Co. and Nanny, his wife, to Joseph Stevens of St. Margaret's Par., Caroline Co. £270 curr. Two tracts of land in Spts. Co., on Massaponax Run, one containing 200 acres, the other 1465 acres, made by Collo. Henry Willis, Decd., as by Deed of gift to the sd. John Willis. Witnesses, Anthony Strother, Roger Dixon, Kemp Taliaferro, George Buckner, Thoms. Slaughter. Sept. 5, 1749.

Decr. 19, 1749. John Allan of Fredericksburg, Mercht., to Robert Duncanson of the same town, Mercht. £150 curr. Lot 30, in town of Fredksburg. William Lynn, Thomas Mackie, John Sutherland, Jas. Fleming, Wm. McWilliams, junr. Feby. 6, 1749.

Jany. 31, 1749. John Quarles of Prince Wm. Co., Gent., to Charles Col. son of Fredericksburg, Ordinary Keeper. £100 curr. 278 a. in Spts. Co., granted Leonard Helms, by pat., Oct. 31, 1726, and by him conveyed to John Quarles, father of the sd. John Quarles, party to these presents, etc. Witnesses, M. Battaley, John Dent, John Jones, William Lynn, Thomas Mackie. Feby. 6, 1749.

Sept. 23, 1749. John x Trusty of Spts. Co. to Zachary Lewis of same county. £35 curr. 108 a. in Spts. Co., purchased by sd. Trusty of John Waller, Gent., as by Deeds, Jany. 4, 1734, etc. William Phillips, Robert x Beadles, Jno. Lewis, Zachary Lewis, junr. March 6, 1749.

March 6, 1749. Robt. x Beadles of Spts. Co. and Dilly, his wife, to John Trusty of same county. £25 curr. 50 a. in Spts. Co., purchased by sd. Beadles of George Musick, Senr., as by Deeds, May 4, 1746. Edmund Waller. March 6, 1749.

Feby. 9, 1749. Benjamin Martin of St. Geo. Par., Spts. Co., to Edmund Waller of sd. Par. and county. Deed of Lease. 150 a., part of the tract whereon Henry Martin, Decd., did live, joining Revd. James Marye and John Thornton, son of Collo. Francis Thornton, Decd., on Hazel Run, in the par. and county afsd., etc., etc. Witnesses, Charles Snead, James Wiglesworth, Richd. Phillips, Junr. Mar. 6, 1749.

Jany. 5, 1749. Mark Wheeler and Sarah, his wife, of Spts. Co., to Joseph Carter of same county. £28 curr. 100 a., conveyed to sd. Wheeler by Henry Goodloes, Gent., Decd., as by Deeds, June 3, 1735. Robt. Durrett, James Younger, James x Ham, Patrick Kennedy. April 3, 1750.

Feby. 3, 1749. James Jackson of Albemarle Co., planter, and Susanna, his wife, to Owen Thomas of Spts. Co. £86 curr. 300 a. in St. Geo. Par., Spts. Co. Nicholas x Hawkins, John Cuningham, Mumford Stevens, Isaac Scott. April 3, 1750.

April 3, 1750. John Allan and Margarett, his wife, of Spts. Co., to Richard Hudnall of Northumberland Co. £14 curr. 358 a. in Spts. Co., a tract granted the sd. Allan, by pat., April 1, 1749. No witnesses. April 3, 1750.

May 1, 1750. Henry Pendleton of King William Co. and Martha, his wife, to James Dyer of Caroline Co. £27 curr. 70 a. in St. Geo. Par., Spts. Co. (joining lands of Zachary Lewis, Daniel Prewitt, John Shirley and Nicholas Horn), and part of tract purchased by sd. Pendleton of George Woodroof, and known as Woodroofs Ordinary, etc. No witnesses. May 1, 1750.

May 1, 1750. Robert True of Spts. Co., planter, and Margarett, his wife, to Edward Kelley of afsd. County. £30 curr. 150 a. in Spts. Co. Philip Vincent Vass, Robert Dudley, John Menefee. May 1, 1750.

Jany. 16, 1749. John Holloday of St. Geo. Par., Spts. Co., and Elizabeth, his wife, to Thomas Magee of Par. and county afsd. £46 curr. 150 a. in St. Geo. Par., Spts. Co. Philip Vincent Vass. Edwd. Herndon, junr.; Benjamin Holloday. May 1, 1750.

May 1, 1750. Erasmus Wethers Allen of St. Geo. Par., Spts. Co., to James Waggoner of same Par. and county. £30 curr. 300 a. in Spts. Co. Nathaniel x Allen, Thomas x Allen. May 1, 1750. Sarah, wife of Erasmus Wethers Allen, acknowledged her dower, etc.

April 28, 1750. William x Mash of St. Mark's Par., Culp. Co., to Obediah Howerton of St. Geo. Par., Spts. Co. £30 curr. 300 a., being a reversion of a tract taken up by George Dowdey, etc. Erasmus Wes. Allen, James x Jones, John Faulconer. May 1, 1750.

Decr. 5, 1749. John Allan of Fredericksburg, Mercht., to Robert Todd of Borough of Norfolk, Mercht. £300 curr. Lot 52, etc., in town of Fredksburg, whereon sd. John Allan lives, etc. M. Battaley, William Hunter, Andr. Rosse, Chas. Dick, Robt. Duncanson, James Allan. June 5, 1750.

June 5, 1750. Joseph Redd of St. Geo. Par., Spts. Co., carpenter, and Betty, his wife, to James Redd of King and Queen Co., planter. £32 8s, curr. 108 a. in Spts. Co. Larkin Johnston, John Crane, John Carter. June 5, 1750.

June 5, 1750. Cornelius Vaughan of Caroline Co. and Frances, his wife, to William Darnaby of Spts. Co. £40 curr. 247 a. in St. George Par., Spts. Co. Jno. Battaley, W. Miller. June 5, 1750.

William Crawford, mortgage, to Edmund Waller of Spts. Co., whole of estate. £10 curr. Witnesses, Richard Phillips, junr.; Elizabeth Williams. June 5, 1750.

May 1, 1750. Hancock Lee of King George Co., Gent., and Mary, his wife, to Anthony Strother of same Co., Mercht. £175 curr. Lots 35 and 36, in town of Fredksburg, etc. James Hunter, Geo. Taylor, Valentine Peyton, junr. June 5, 1750.

June 5, 1750. John Farish of Spts. Co. and Sarah, his wife, to Wm. Waller of Spts. Co., Gent. £49 10s. curr. 34½ a., part of a pat. to Bernard Pain, Jany. 22, 1717, in Spts. Co. John Carter, John Hoskins, Richd. Pollard. July 3, 1750.

July 4, 1750. Archibald McPherson, William Hunter and James Hunter, execrs. of the last will and testament of John Allan, late of the town of Fredericksburg, Decd., to James Allan of the sd. town, Joyner. Under certain conditions named in the will of sd. John Allan, Decd., Dated, March 14 last. Lot No. 64, sold to sd. James Allan, for £152 curr. Witnesses, Alexander Campbell, William McWilliams, Junior. July 3, 1750.

Augt. 6, 1750. Edward Jones of Spts. Co. and Sarah, his wife, to Francis Meriwether of Louisa County. £34 curr. 69 a. in Spts Co., purchased by sd. Jones of James Shackleford and Elizabeth, his wife, as by Deeds, Feby. 27, 1745. Jno. Lewis, Zachary Lewis, Junr. Augt. 7, 1750.

Oct. 2, 1750. Joseph Redd of Spts. Co., carpenter, and Bettey, his wife, to James Redd of King and Queen Co., planter. Whereas Thomas Redd of King and Queen Co., by deed, Dec. 5, 1743, conveyed to Jos. Redd, party to these presents. 370 a. in Spts. Co., and whereas sd. Joseph and Bettey, his wife, by their Deed, June 5, 1750, conveyed to sd. James Redd (a party to these presents), 108 a., part thereof of the sd. 370 acres, etc. For the sum of £130 curr., Joseph and Bettey Redd afsd. convey to James Redd afsd., remainder of the sd. tract, etc., etc. Robert Huddleston, Jos. McWilliams, Alexander Guill. Octr. 2, 1750.

Wm. Beverley of Blandfield, Essex Co., Esqr., guardian of Harry Beverley, son and heir of Robert Beverley, late of Spts. Co., Esqr., Decd. Power of attorney to William Waller "of sd. county, Gentl., Dated, June 20, 1750. Witnesses, R. Tunstall, W. Russell. Recd. Oct. 2, 1750.

Sept. 20, 1750. Thomas Duerson of Spts. Co. and Hannah, his wife, to Joseph Brock of sd. county. £250 curr. 720 a. in Spts. Co., having been conveyed to sd. Duerson by Joseph Brock, Decd., as by Deeds, April 28, 1739. Thomas Estes, Patterson Pulliam, Ephraim Knight. Octr. 2, 1750.

Oct. 2, 1750. John Grayson of St. Mark's Par., Culpeper Co., and Barbary, his wife, to Martin True of St. Geo. Par., Spts. Co. £20 curr. 331 a. in Spts. Co. Robert Huddleston, John x Elson. Octr. 2, 1750.

Sept. 20, 1750. Joseph Brock of Spts. Co. to Thomas Duerson of sd. county. £200 curr. 600 a. in Spts. Co. Thomas Estes, Patterson Pulliam, Ephraim Knight. Oct. 2, 1750.

Wm. Smither of Spts. Co., mortgage, to Wm. Waller of same county. £6 5s. 1d. curr. Goods and chattels. Witnesses, Harry Beverley, Thomas McNiell, Johnathan Gibson. Oct. 2, 1750.

Oct. 24, 1750. Wm. x Martin of St. Geo. Par., Spts. Co., to Benjamin Martin of Par. and county afsd. £53 curr. 100½ acres, in Par. and co. afsd. Thomas Collins, Nathan Hawkins, Nichos. Hawkins, Junr., John Hutcherson, Jeremiah Smith. Nov. 6, 1750.

Decr. 4, 1750. John Champe of King Geo. Co., Gent., to Wm. Waller of Spts. Co., Gent. £60 curr. 200 a. in St. Geo. Par., Spts. Co. No witnesses. Dec. 4, 1750.

Dec. 4, 1750. Abraham Rogers of St. Geo. Par., Spts. Co., and Barbary, his wife, planters, to George Rogers of Drysdale Par., King and Queen Co., joyner. £60 curr. 10 a. in St. Geo. Par., Spts. Co., and sd. Abraham's right and title in a water grist mill, etc. Robert Huddleston, Lancelot x Warrin, Hackley Warrin. Dec. 4, 1750.

Dec. 3, 1750. George x Nix of Orange Co. and Elizabeth, his wife, to John Calahan of Spts. Co. £12 curr. 87½ a. devised sd. Nix by the last will and testament of his father, George Nix, Decd. Edmund Waller, R. Phillips, Jr., Alexander x McKenny. Dec. 4, 1750.

William Sutton of Spts. Co., planter, power of Attorney to Mary Whitehouse of same county. Dated, Sept. 28, 1750. Cuthbert Artrip, William Grayson. Dec. 4, 1750.

Decr. 4, 1750. Fielding Lewis of Spts. Co., Gent., and Betty, his wife, to Charles Dick of Fredericksburg, Gent. £50 curr. Tract of ground adjoining the town of Fredksbg and adj. Lots 51 and 52 of the sd. town, etc. John Spotswood, Richd. Tutt, Robt. Armistead. Dec. 4, 1750.

Dec. 4, 1750. Fielding Lewis of Fredericksburg, Gent., and Bettey, his wife, to John Mitchell of Fredksbg, Mercht. £30. Tract of ground adjacent to the town of Fredksbg, and joining Lots 31 and 32 of the sd. town. John Spotswood, Richard Tutt, Robert Armistead. Dec. 4, 1750.

Feby. 4, 1750. William Bledsoe, Gent., to his son, "Moses Bledsoe, during his natural life to his son, William Bledsoe," etc. Deed of Gift. 100 acres on north side of mill branch of Hunting Run. Robert Coleman, Thomas Brown, John Gore. Feby. 5, 1750. Elizabeth, wife of William Bledsoe, acknowledged her dower, etc.

Sept. 4, 1750. Patrick Connelly of the town of Fredksbg, hatter, to William Thomson of the town afsd. £28 curr. Goods and Chattels. Robert Croker, Broadbent McWilliams. April 2, 1751.

April 2, 1751. John x Tyre of Albemarle County, Va., to John Williamson of Spts. Co. £16 curr. 100 a. in St. Geo. Par., Spts. Co., part of a pat. granted John Smith, Sept. 28, 1728. Robert Huddleston, William Matthews, Andrew Caddle, Edward Land. Apr. 2, 1751.

Jany. 31, 1750. Thomas Warrin, son and heir at law of Thomas Warrin, late of Spts. Co., Decd., to Lancelot Warrin, son of the sd. Decd. Thoms. Warrin, Decd., was at the time of his death seized of a tract of 210 a. of land in St. Geo. Par., Spts. Co., and by his will, Dated April 13, 1749, etc., etc. The grantor in this deed believing the testator of the will intended leaving the property herein conveyed, to Lancelot Warrin (after the death of sd. testator's wife, and she being now dead), etc., etc., for the sum of 5 shill. curr., conveys 210 a. of land to sd. Lancelot Warrin and his heirs and assigns, etc., etc. Witnesses, Wm. Waller, Hackley Warrin, Robert Moor, James x Ham. April 2, 1751.

Dec. 13, 1750. Obediah x Howerton of St. Geo. Par., Spts. Co., to John Waggoner of county and Par. afsd. £40 curr. 300 a. Witnesses, Erasmus Wrs. Allen, George Blakey, Samuell Waggoner. April 2, 1751.

Oct. 24, 1750. Thomas Estes of Spts. Co. to Thomas Merry of county afsd. £40 curr. Three negroes. Mortgage. Witnesses, John Cunningham, Charles x Robins, Elizabeth x Sutton. April 2, 1751.

April 2, 1751. Joseph Brock of Spts. Co. to Larkin Chew of Spts. Co., Gent. £52 17s. curr. money. 150 a. in Spts. Co. W. Miller, Wm. Waller, Wm. McWilliams. April 2, 1751.

April 2, 1751. John Chew of Spts. Co., Gent., to Larkin Chew of afsd. Co., Gent. £300 curr. 528 a. in St. Geo. Par., Spts. Co. W. Miller, Joseph Steward, Jos. Brock, Wm. McWilliams, A. Foster. April 2, 1751.

Decr. 4, 1750. George Woodroof of Spts. Co., Planter, and Jane, his wife, to Rice Graves of sd. County, planter. £10 curr. 100 a. in Spts. Co. Robt. Huddleston, John Smith, James Fox. Decr. 4, 1751.

May 7, 1751. Nathaniel Chapman of Stafford Co., Mercht., to Benjamin Grymes of Spts. Co., Gent. £300 curr. A lot in the town of Fredericksburg, purchased by sd. Chapman and John Allan, in partnership of the executors of Henry Willis, Decd., etc., the sd. Allan being now Dead, the whole of the lot is rested in st. Chapman, etc., etc. Witnesses, Peter Hedgman, Robt. McLaurine, Wm. McWilliams, Junr. May 7, 1751.

May 7, 1750. Nathaniel Chapman of Stafford Co., Mercht., to Benjamin Grymes of Spts. Co., Gent. £450 curr. Lot No. 20, in town of Fredericksburg. Peter Hedgman, Robt. McLaurine, William McWilliams, Junr. May 7, 1751.

Samuel Kennerly of Over, in the County of Chester, joiner, eldest son and heir of Samuel Kennerly, late of St. Mark's Par., Orange Co., Va., Joiner, Decd., power of attorney to Francis Thornton of Caroline Co., Rappk. River, in Va., Gent. Witnesses, Thos. Word, William Quinney. Dated, Jany. 31, 1750. Recd. May 7, 1751.

June 4, 1751. Benjamin Hubbard, Gent., and Elizabeth Blake (widow and Legatee), executors of the last will and testament of John Blake, late of Spts. Co., Mercht., Decd., to John Wood of same county, tailor. 240 a. in Spts. Co. June 4, 1741.

May 13, 1751. William Bell, Senr., of St. Geo. Par., Spts. Co., to Uriah Garton, Junr., of sd. par. and county. £15 curr. 100 a. in Spts. Co. Ephraim Knight, Wm. Arnold, Abraham x Darnal. June 4, 1751.

June 5, 1751. Lancelot Warren of Spts. Co. and Margaret, his wife, to William Waller of Spts. Co., Gentl. £100 curr. 210 a. on s. side Middle River of Mattapony, in St. Geo. Par., Spts. Co. Richd. Tutt, Geo. Stubblefield, Robt. Mickleborough. Augt. 6, 1751.

July 2, 1751. William Ellis and Elizabeth, his wife, of St. Geo. Par., Spts. Co., to Ambrose Bullard of Par. and County afsd. £100 curr. 470 a. in St. Geo. Par., Spts. Co., formerly granted by pat. to Robert Slaughter of Essex Co., Feby. 20, 1719. Wit., Jno. Battaley. Augt. 6, 1751.

Augt. 6, 1751. Richard Wyatt Royston of Petsworth Par., Gloucester Co., and Anne, his wife, to William McWilliams, the younger, of Fredericksburg, Mercht. £350 curr. Lots 27 and 28, in Fredksbg., whereon the public warehouses, called Roystons, are situated.

Robert Glen of City of Glasgow, Mercht., power of Attorney to Alexander Campbell of Falmouth, upon the Rappk. River, Va., Mercht. Witnesses, James Allen, Gavin Roger, Wm. Williamson. Dated, Glasgow, March 6, 1751. Recd., Spts. Co. Court, Sept. 3, 1751.

Margaret Black, alias Allan, widow of the deceased James Allan, Mercht., in and late Baillie of Hamilton, and mother of John Allan, Mercht., in Hamilton, eldest Lawfull son of the Deceased James Allan, thereafter of Spts. Co., Va., Decd. Whereas sd. Jno. Allan of Spts. Co., Va., Mercht., Decd., did by his will devise to his mother, the sd. Margaret Black, alias Allan, £400 ster., etc., etc., Sd. Margaret Black, alias Allan, power of attorney to Samuel Ritchie, Archibald Ritchie and John Miller, on Rappk. River, Essex Co., Va., Merchants. Witnesses, Gavin Roger, Wm. Williamson, James Allan. Dated, March 1, 1750-1. Recd. Septr. 1, 1751.

Christian Allan, daughter Lawfull of the deceased James Allan, Mercht., in and late Baillie of Hamilton, and sister German of John Allan, Mercht., in Hamilton, eldest Lawfull son of the decd. James Allan, thereafter of Spts. Co., in Colony of Va. Power of attorney to Samuel Ritchie, Archibald Ritchie and John Miller of Rappk. River, Essex Co., Va., Merchants. Witnesses, James Allan, Gavin Roger, Wm. Williamson. Dated, March 1, 1750-1. Recd., Sept. 3, 1751.

Sarah Black, Residenter in Hamilton, Aunt of John Allan, Merchant, in Hamilton, Eldest lawfull son of the Deceased James Allan, Mercht., in and late Baillie of Hamilton, thereafter of Spts. Co., Va., now also Deceased. Whereas sd. John Allan, by his last will and testament, devised certain legacies to his sd. Aunt, Sarah Blacks, power of attorney, to Samuel Ritchie, Archibald Ritchie and John Miller of Rappk. River, Essex Co., Va., Merchts. Witnesses, James Allan, Gavin Roger, Wm. Williamson. Dated March 1, 1750-1. Recd. Sept. 3, 1751.

Jean Morison in the shire of Aberdeen, North Britain, Lawfull daughter to the Deceased John Morison, Mercht., in Stonehaven. Procreate betwixt him and Patience Wallace, his spouse, who was the only surviving sister of the Deceased David Wallace, planter, on James River, Virginia. Power of attorney to Capt. John Thomson, commander of the Ship Anne, of Aberdeen. This power of attorney mentions Colo. Thomas Turner of King Geo. Co., Va. Dated, March 3, 1750. Witnesses, George Trail, Alexander Morison, Andrew Thomson. Acknowledged before Alexander Robertson, Esqr., Provost of the City of Aberdeen, March 14, 1750. Recd. Spts. Co., Va., Septr. 3, 1751.

May 21, 1751. Edmund Waller of Spts. Co. (in trust for John, Benjamin, Mary, and Wm. Edmund Waller, his children) to John Waller, the elder, of the same County, Gent. £110 curr. Plantation whereon sd. Edmund Waller lately lived, in St. Geo. Par., Spts. Co. Witnesses, Thomas Dickinson, Zachary Lewis, Junr., Benjamin Waller. Septr. 3, 1751.

Septr. 3, 1751. William Brock and Larkin Chew, Gentlemen, of Spts. Co., to Moseley Battaley and Wm. Waller, Gentlemen, Churchwardens of St. Geo. Par., Spts. Co. £4 curr. 16,384 super final feet, a square of 128 feet on each side lately laid off for a church yard at Mattapony, including the said Church, etc., etc. No witnesses. Septr. 3, 1751.

August 31, 1751. James Allan of Fredericksburg, brother and heir at law of John Allan, late of the sd. town, Mercht., Decd., to Charles Dick of the same town, Gentl. Under direction in the will of sd. John Allan the following lot is sold. £46 10s. curr. 5½ a. of land, part of a tract the sd. Jno. Allan purchased of the executors of Henry Willis, Decd. Witnesses, Archibald McPherson, William Hunter, James Hunter, Roger Dixon, Robt. Huddleston. Septr. 3, 1751.

Augt. 31, 1751. Archibald McPherson, James Hunter and James Allan, acting executors of the will of John Allan, late of the town of Fredericksburg, Mercht., Decd., to William Hunter. £350 10s. curr. 400 a. in Spts. Co. Witnesses, Charles Dick, Roger Dixon, Robt. Huddleston. Septr. 3, 1751.

April 31, 1751. Archibald McPherson, William Hunter, James Hunter, and James Allan, acting executors of the last will and testament of John Allan of Fredericksburg, Mercht., Decd., to Charles Julian of the Borough of Norfolk, baker, £245 curr. Lot No. 30, in town of Fredericksburg, now in tenure of Saml. Hildrup, and all that part of the sd. lot not conveyed by sd. John Allan in his deed to Robt. Duncanson, Decr. 19, 1749. Witnesses, Charles Dick, Robt. Halkerston, Roger Dixon. Septr. 3, 1751.

March 7, 1750. Andrew Crawford of Fredericksburg to Charles Dick of the sd. town, Merchant. Mortgage. £36 16s. 3½d. Goods and Chattels. Witnesses, Jno. Battaley, Edward Herndon, Junr. Sept. 4, 1751.

Augt. 31, 1751. Benjamin Holloday of Spts. Co. and Susanna, his wife, to George Shepherd of same county. Sd. Holloday having sold to one George Sheperd 108 a. of land in Spts. Co. for £19 curr., and whereas the sd. George Sheperd departed this life before a conveyance of sd. land was made him, sd. Shepherd, by his last will and testament, dated Jany. 10, 1750, devised the sd. land to his two sons, George and Robert Shepherd, to be equally divided between them. Under these conditions sd. Holloday and wife convey the sd. property to George Shepherd, son of George Shepherd, decd., etc., etc. Witnesses, Zachary Lewis, John Battaley, John Payton. Octr. 1, 1751.

Octr. 1, 1751. William Collins of Southfarnham Par., Essex Co., to James Haley of St. Thomas Parish, Orange Co. 5 shill. curr. 200 a. in St. Geo. Par., Spts. Co., part of a tract granted John Robinson, etc. Witnesses, Edward Collins, Lewis Collins, John x Collins. October 1, 1751. Elizabeth, wife of William Collins, acknowledged her dower, etc.

DEED BOOK E

1751-1761

Augt. 31, 1751. Benjamin Holloday of Spts. Co. and Susanna, his wife, to Robert Shepherd of same county. Whereas sd. Benjamin Holloday had sold unto one George Shepherd a tract of 108 a. in Spts. Co. and before conveying same the sd. George Shepherd died and by his will dated Jany. 10, 1750, devised the sd. land to his sons, George Shepherd and Robert Shepherd, party to these presents. Sd. Holloday and wife convey to sd. Robt. Shepherd his share of the sd. land as under the will of the decd. George Shepherd, etc., etc. Zachary Lewis, John Battaley, John Payton. Octr. 1, 1751.

Augt. 6, 1751. William Davenport and Ann, his wife, of Spts. Co. to George Woodroof of same County. In consideration that sd. George Woodroof and Jane, his wife, shall jointly with sd. Davenport and Ann, his wife, deed to Joel Parrish, 200 a. of land, purchased by sd. Davenport of Benja. Woodroof, and als. 5 shill. Curr. The sd. Davenport and Ann, his wife, convey 94 a. in Spts. Co. Witnesses, Phillip Vincent Vass, John Holloday, John Davenport. Augt. 6, 1751.

Augt. 6, 1751. William Davenport and Ann, his wife, of Louisa Co., and George Woodroof and Jane, his wife, of Spts. Co., to Joel Parrish of Spts. Co. £58 curr. 200 a. in Spts. Co. Philip Vincent Vass, Jno. Holloday, John Davenport. Octr. 1, 1751.

Oct. 1, 1751. John Grayson and Barbary, his wife, of Culpeper Co., to Alexander Hawkins and Benjamin Martin of Spts. Co. £103 curr. 245 a. in St. Geo. Par., Spts. Co. Witnesses, Jno. Battaley, Rob. Dudley, Richard Blanton. Oct. 1, 1751.

July 11, 1751. Nicholas Horn of Spts. Co. and Mary, his wife, to Robert Hall of Caroline Co. £140 curr. 400 a. in Spts. Co. Wm. Waller, Richd. Murrey, Wm. Dyer. Dec. 3, 1751.

Octr. 1, 1751. John Quarles of Chesterfield Co. and Susanna, his wife, to William Carr of Spts. County. £70 curr. 350 a. in Spts. Co., part of a pat. granted John Quarles, Decd., Sept. 30, 1723. Witnesses, John Battaley, Wm. Miller, A. Foster, Rob. Dudley. Dec. 3, 1751.

Nov. 4, 1751. John Adam Link of St. Geo. Par., Spts. Co., planter, and Sarah, his wife, to Thomas Dillard of same Par. and co. £20 curr. 100 a. in St. Geo. Par., Spts. Co., part of pat. granted Henry Haines, Sept. 28, 1728. Witnesses, Robt. Huddleston, Benja. x Hubbard, Rice Graves. Dec. 3, 1751.

Dec. 3, 1751. James Allan of Fredksbg., Brother and heir at law of John Allan, late of the sd. town, Mercht., Decd., and Archibald McPherson, William Hunter, and James Hunter, three execrs. of the last will and testament of the sd. John Allan, etc., Decd., to William Allcock of Caroline Co.

£61 10s. 1000 a. in Spts. Co., on head branches of Mattapony, purchased by sd. John Allan, Decd., of John Robinson, Junr., of King and Queen Co., Esqr., as by Deeds, Novr. 17, 1748. No witnesses. Decr. 3, 1751.

Decr. 12, 1751. Bowker Smith of Southam Par., Cumberland Co., and Judith, his wife, to Thomas McGee of Spts. Co. £32 10s. curr. 150 a., part of a pat. granted Ralph Bowker, Clerk, of St. Stephen's Parish, King and Queen Co., and bequeathed by him to his daughter, Anna Smith, and renewed to Bird Bowker of Co. and Par. afsd., by pat., May 10, 1729, and bequeathed by the sd. Bird Bowker to the sd. Bowker Smith, etc. Witnesses, A. Bowker, Jo. Bowker, Isaac Scott, Wm. Smith. Feby. 4, 1752.

May 5, 1752. James Stevens and Alice, his wife, of St. Geo. Par., Spts. Co., to James Sams of same Par. and Co. £10 curr. 34 a., part of a tract Devised to James Sams and by the sd. James conveyed to his brother, William Sams, and by sd. William sold and released, as by Deeds, June 4, 1745, etc. James Lea, James x Chapman. May 5, 1752.

May 3, 1752. Larkin Chew of Spts. Co., Gent., and Mary, his wife, to Beverley Stanard and Elizabeth, his wife, the daughter of the sd. Larkin Chew and Mary, his wife. Deed of Gift. 528 a. in St. Geo. Par., Spts. Co. 193 a., part thereof being granted to John Chew, Gent., by Pat., June 4, 1726, the remaining 335 a. conveyed to sd. John Chew by his father, Larkin Chew, Gent., Decd., as by Deeds, July 4, 1727. Wm. Robinson, Thos. Stubblefield, Wm. Smith. June 2, 1752.

June 2, 1752. Rice Curtis, Junr., of St. Geo. Par., Spts. Co., to Henry Pendleton of same Par. and county. £5 curr. 151 a. in St. Geo. Par., Spts. Co. No witnesses. June 2, 1752.

June 2, 1752. Rice Curtis, Jr., of St. Geo. Par., Spts. Co., to Philip Vincent Vass of same Par. and county. £231 curr. 462 a. in Spts. Co., granted by pat. to sd. Curtis, Dec. 13, 1738. No witnesses. June 2, 1752.

June 2, 1752. Daniel x Pruett of Spts. Co. and Sarah, his wife, to Christopher Dicken of Spts. Co. £70 curr. 200 a. in Spts. Co. John Crittenden Webb, Joel Parrish, John Dent. June 2, 1752.

Feby. 13, 1752. James Wiglesworth, son and heir of John Wiglesworth, Decd., and Mary Wiglesworth, widow and relict of the sd. John Wiglesworth, Decd., of Spts. Co., to John Wood of the sd. County. £18 curr. 130 a. in St. Geo. Par., Spts. Co. John Waller, Samuel x Brown, William Wiglesworth. June 2, 1752.

Jany. 16, 1752. William Williams of Culpeper Co. and Lucy, his wife, to Roger Dixon of the said County. £1000 curr. Whereas, Charles Taliaferro, late of Caroline Co., Gent., Decd., was in his lifetime seized of a tract of land of 420 a. in St. Geo. Par., Spts. Co., which he purchased of one Wm. Smith., sd. Taliaferro, as by Deed, Augt. 30, 1729, conveyed the sd. land to Joel Johnson and James Williams unto the sd. Joel Johnson, during her natural life and then to the sd. James Williams, his heirs, etc., and sd. James Williams surviving the sd. Joel, became seized of the sd. tract of land, and being thereof seized, was lawfully suited of 90 a. or thereabouts of the sd. tract by Henry Willis, Gent., who obtained a judgment in the general court of this Colony, April 26, 1735, against the sd. Williams, whereby the sd. Williams became seized of the residue of the tract, only containing 330 a., and being so thereof seized made his (Williams') last will and testament, Dated May 30, 1735, devising the sd. tract to his son, William Williams, party to these presents, etc., etc. Witnesses, Pat. Connelly, Robert Halkerston, James Fox, Gabriel Throckmorton. June 2, 1752.

June 2, 1752. Henry Pendleton of Spts. Co., James Dyer of Caroline Co., and Eleanor, his wife, to John Davenport of Hanover Co. £30 curr. 70 a. in Spts. Co. No witnesses. June 2, 1752.

Richard Wiatt Royston of Petsworth Par., Gloucester Co. and Ann, his wife, to Fielding Lewis of Spts. Co., Gent. £861 curr. 861 a. in St. Geo. Par., Spts. Co., joining the town of Fredericksburg (surveyed by Geo. Washington), part of a pat. granted John Buckner and Thomas Royston, grandfather of the sd. Richd. Wiatt Royston, and given to the sd. Richd. Wiatt Royston by the will of his father, John Royston, son to the sd. Thomas Royston, etc. Witnesses, Samuel Buckner, James Baytop, Daniel Fitzhugh, Alexr. Cruikshanks, James Allan, Charles Lewis. June 2, 1752.

June 17, 1752. Lawrence Washington of Fairfax Co., Gent., to his brother, George Washington, of King Geo. Co., Gent. Deed of Gift. All rights, titles, interests, etc., sd. Laurence Washington (as heir at law unto Augustine Washington, late of King Geo. Co., Gent., Decd.), in Lotts Nos. 33, 34 and 40 in the town of Fredericksburg. Witnesses, Mary Washington, Martha Posey, W. Fairfax, Saml. Washington, John Washington, Charles Washington. July 7, 1752.

May 28, 1752. Thomas Duerson of Spts. Co. to Edwd. Herndon, Jr. £50 curr. 100 a. in Spts. Co. Jos. Brock, Jno. Battaley. July 7, 1752.

July 7, 1752. James Marye of St. Geo. Par., Spts. Co., clerk, to George Stubblefield of Par. and county afsd. 100 a. in Spts. Co. No witnesses. July 7, 1752.

June 19, 1752. Thomas Brooks of Spts. Co. to Edward Herndon, Junr. £4 16s. 9d. curr. 9 a. in Spts. Co. Jos. Brock, Thos. Duerson, Hannah Duerson, William Brock. July 7, 1752.

June 22, 1752. Benjamin Grymes of Spts. Co., Gent., and Betty, his wife, to Archibald McPherson of Fredericksburg. £234. Lot No. 20 in town of Fredksbg. Dorothy Tennent, Margaret Gordon, Chs. Dick. July 7, 1752.

July 7, 1752. Isaac Darnal and Frances, his wife, late Frances Frasher, and James Frasher, her son, of Spts. Co., to James Hunter of Fredericksburg, Mercht. £53 15s. curr. Lot No. 50, in Town of Fredksbg. No witnesses. July 7, 1752.

Dec. 13, 1751. Susanna Winslow of Spts. Co. to her son, Beverley Winslow of Spts. Co. Deed of Gift and for half profits of a water mill and of the Benefit of the Orchards, etc., on a plantation known as Lanches Quarter. 595 a. in Spts. Co., part of a tract devised the sd. Susanna by the last will and testament of Harry Beverley, Gent., Decd., etc., etc. Witnesses, Lark. Chew, Jos. Brock, Benja. Winslow, Mary Chew. July 8, 1752.

July 15, 1752. Robert x Bruce of Spts. Co. to Ambrose Foster of the same county. £20 curr. 120 a. in the Branches of Glady Fork, and is the same land given by John Bush (grandfather of the sd. Robert) to David

Bruce (father of the sd. Robert) during his natural life, then to his first male heir. The land conveyed to David Bruce from John Bush, as by Deeds (in Spts. Co. Court) Nov. 2, 1730. Wm. Waller, Harry Beverley, John Hoskins, Johnathan Gibson. Augt. 4, 1752.

May 1, 1752. Joseph Brock of Spts. Co. to Rice Curtis, Junr., of Spts. Co., Gent. £260 curr. 278 a. in St. Geo. Par., Spts. Co. Lark. Chew, Samuel Hawes, Junr., Robert Goodloe. Augt. 4, 1752.

June 3, 1752. James Stevens of St. Geo. Par., Spts. Co., planter, and Alice, his wife, late relict and legatee of Ambrose Gresham (Grayson?), late of Par. and county afsd., Planter, Decd., to Thomas Turner of same Par. and county, Gentl. £35 curr. Deed of lease. The plantation whereon the sd. Ambrose dwelt and 200 a. in the par. and county afsd. Witnesses, Thomas Macredie, John Dent, George James, Richard x Turnley. Augt. 4, 1752.

Augt. 4, 1752. John Lea of Orange Co., North Carolina, and Anne, his wife, to Thomas McNeal of St. Geo. Par., Spts. Co., Va. £24 curr. 185 a. whereon sd. McNeal now dwells and formerly being a pat. granted George Carter and given by sd. Carter to the sd. John Lea, his son-in-law, by Deed of Gift. Said land joining the lands of Humphrey Bell of London, John Williamson, Robert Huddleston, Colo. John Waller and Richard Coleman, etc., etc. No witnesses. August 4, 1752.

Sept. 1, 1752. William Lea of Spts. Co. and Frances, his wife, to Thomas White of the same county. £55 curr. 100 a. whereon sd. Lea, lives and part of a pat. belonging to sd. Thomas White in Spts. Co. Chilion White, Milisent x White. Septr. 1, 1752.

May 6, 1752. Hugh Sanders of St. Geo. Par., Spts. Co., planter, and Catey, his wife, to Dudley Gatewood of par. and county afsd. £45 7s. 9d. curr. 267 a. on Glady Fork Run, in Spts. Co. Edwd. Holmes, John Hoskins, Micajah Chiles. Oct. 3, 1752.

Oct. 3, 1752. Ransone Boswell of St. Geo. Par., Spts. Co., and Mary, his wife, to Peter Gatewood of Par. and county afsd. £40. 100 a. in Spts. Co., being part of the land belonging to John Boswell, Decd., etc. Witnesses, Edward Holmes, Hugh Sanders, John Word. Oct. 3, 1752.

Octr. 3, 1752. Ransone Boswell of Spts. Co. and Mary, his wife, to John Holloday of county afsd. £50 curr. 149 a. in county afsd. Wm. Waller, H. Tyler, John Word. Oct. 3, 1752.

Octr. 20, 1752. Abraham Rogers of St. Geo. Par., Spts. Co., planter, and Barbara, his wife, to Wm. Rogers of St. Margaret's Par., Caroline Co. £340 curr. 240 a. in St. Geo. Par., Spts. Co., part of a pat. granted Peter Rogers, Decd. Wm. Connor, John Couch, Dority x Couch, William Crisp, Sarah Bartlett. Nov. 7, 1752.

Nov. 5, 1752. Charles Colson and Elizabeth, his wife, of St. Geo. Par., Spts. Co., to George James of Stafford Co. £500 curr. Lotts 41 and 43, in town of Fredericksburg. Anthony Strother, Andr. Rosse, Jno. Battaley, Thomas James. Novr. 7, 1752.

Nov. 7, 1752. James Haley of Spts. Co. to Daniel Gardner of Caroline Co. £40 curr. 200 a. in St. Geo. Par., Spts. Co. Daniel Trigg, John Sandidge, Jerema x Smith. Novr. 7, 1752.

Oct. 2, 1752. Edmund Waller of Spts. Co. to Wm. Waller of Spts. Co., Gent. Sd. Wm. Waller having become security to Benjamin Waller of Williamsburg, Esqr., on a certain Bond, he is secured by a deed for 5 negro slaves, and goods and chattels, etc. John Waller, John Temple, Johnathan Gibson. Nov. 8, 1752.

Octr. 6, 1752. Richard Collins of King and Queen Co. to Joy Collins, William Collins and Thomas Collins. 5 shill. curr., and in compliance with the will of Thomas Collins, Decd. "All that tract and separate parcels of land devised to them by the will of the sd. Thomas Collins, Decd., to be divided according to the direction of Joseph Collins, Gent., and Richard Collins," party to these presents, etc. Witnesses, Wm. Waller, Samuel Brown, Johnathan Gibson, John Temple (Semple?). Nov. 9, 1752.

Decr. 5, 1752. Giles Tompkins of Albemarle Co. and Valentine, his wife, to John Lewis of Spts. Co. £80 curr. 209 a. in Spts. Co., conveyed by Mary Abney, as by Deeds, Nov. 4, 1735, to Edwin Hickman, and by sd. Hickman to sd. Giles Tompkins, as by Deeds, Octr. 1, 1745. M. Battaley, Z. Lewis, Jonathan Gibson. Decr. 5, 1752.

Dec. 14, 1752. Benjamin x Hubbard and Mary, his wife, of Spts. Co., to Mary Hall, widow of Robert Hall, Decd., and Robert, John, Ann, Margaret, Elizabeth, and Mary, children of the sd. Robert Hall, Decd., of Caroline Co. £15 curr. 100 a. in Spts. Co., which was devised the sd. Benjamin by his father, Thomas Hubbard, Decd. Witnesses, Wm. Waller, John Temple (Semple?), Ambrose Foster, John Shirley, Jonathan Gibson. Jany. 3, 1753.

Feby. 6, 1753. Francis x Wisdom of Spts. Co. and Sarah, his wife, to Joseph Brock of Spts. Co. £110 curr. 1000 a. in Spts. Co. No witnesses. Feby. 6, 1753.

Octr. 6, 1752. Robert Smith of St. Geo. Par., Spts. Co., and Sarah, his wife, to Garnett Keaton of same Parish and county. £40 curr. 150 a. in Spts. and Caroline Counties. Wm. Waller, Robert x Jackson, William Ellis. Feby. 6, 1753.

Dec. 2, 1752. Henry Bartlett of Spts. Co. and Sarah, his wife, to Benjamin Watts of Caroline Co. 100 a. in St. Geo. Par., Spts. Co., part of a pat. formerly granted Peter Rogers, etc. Peter Copland, Walter Clark, James Samuell. Feby. 6, 1753.

Octr. 31, 1752. Anthony Garnett of Spts. Co., bricklayer, to Edward Collins of afsd. co., planter. £30 10s. curr. 200 a. Wm. Howard, Nicholas Jones, Lancelot x Warrin. Feby. 6, 1753. (Ed. Note. This deed is also signed by "Amey x Garnett.")

March 5, 1753. James Lea of St. Geo. Par., Spts. Co., and Ann, his wife, to John Chapman of afsd. Par. and Co. £80 curr. 200 a. in Spts. Co. No witnesses. March 6, 1753.

Septr. 16, 1752. Wm. Bell, Jr., of St. Geo. Par., Spts. Co., to Uriah Garton, Jr., of same Par. and co. £25 curr. 100 a. in Par. and co. afsd. Zachariah Garton, Ephraim Knight, Abraham x Darnal, David x Darnal. March 6, 1753.

March 6, 1753. Nathaniel x Allen to Chilion White. £46 curr. 120 a. in Spts. Co., whereon sd. Allen dwells. No witnesses. March 6, 1753.

April 3, 1753. Martin x True of St. Geo. Par., Spts. Co., planter, to Richard Turnley of the Par. and Co. afsd., planter. £25 curr. 50 a. in St. Geo. Par., Spts. Co. No witnesses. April 3, 1753. Sarah, wife of Martin True, acknowledged her dower, etc.

April 3, 1753. George Washington of King Geo. Co., Va., Esqr., to Andrew Cochrane, John Murdock, William Crawford, junr., Allan Dreghorn, Robt. Bogle, junr., of Glasgow, in the Kingdom of Great Britain, Merchants and Partners. £280 curr. Lots 33 and 34, in town of Fredericksburg. No witnesses. April 3, 1753.

March 7, 1753. William Williams and Lucy, his wife, of Culpeper Co., to John Schooler of Spts. Co. £138 curr. 484 a. in St. Geo., Spts. Co., on Mattapony River. Lark. Chew, Wm. Carr, Joseph Steward, A. Foster, John Holloday. April 3, 1753.

Jany. 3, 1753. Fielding Lewis of Fredericksburg, Gent., and Betty, his wife, to Alexander Cruikshanks of the same town, carpenter. £30 curr. A lot of land adj. Fredksbg. John Moor, Ben. Johnson, Adm. Pavey. June 5, 1753.

March 12, 1753. Thomas Chew, Larkin Chew of Spts. Co., Gent., and Mary, his wife, and Beverley Stanard of the same county, Gent., and Elizabeth Beverley, his wife, to Benjamin Grymes of Spts. Co., Esqr. For the consideration that the sd. Benjamin Grymes and Betty, his wife, shall convey to sd. Beverley Stanard 60 a. in Spts. Co., convey 240 a. adjoining the lands of John Lewis, Esqr., and the sd. Grymes, part thereof being formerly given and conveyed John Chew, Gent., by Larkin Chew, Gent., Decd., in Spts. Co. Witnesses, James Butler, Thos. Maxwell, Stephen Bright, Jno. Thornton, W. Robinson, Harry Beverley, Wm. Smith. June 5, 1753.

June 5, 1753. Edward Herndon and Mary, his wife, of Spts. Co., to Joseph Herndon of sd. county. £10 curr. Lot No. 3 in Spts. Co., adjoining lot No. 56 of the town of Fredksbg. Benjamin Davis, Isaac Scot, Richard Blanton. June 5, 1753.

Robert x Marsh of Spts. Co. to Wm. Waller, for his being security in a suit of Peter Copland and others in Caroline Co. vs. sd. Marsh, pending in Spts. Co. Court. Goods and Chattels Conveyed. Dated, Nov. 6, 1752. Witnesses, John Carter, Jonathan Gibson. June 5, 1753.

June 24, 1753. Thomas Turner of King Geo. Co., Gent., and Thomas Turner, the younger, of Spts. Co., Gent., and Mary, his wife, to Francis Taliaferro of Spts. Co., Gent. £1150 ster. 500 a. in Spts. Co., near adjoining the sd. Taliaferro, part of a tract sold by Wm. Smith, late of Abingdon Par., Gloucester Co., unto John Grayson, late of Christ Church Par., Lancaster Co., Decd., as by deeds, in General Court, April 22, 1714, which sd. land descended to Thomas Grayson, late of Deal, in Kent Co., in Great Britain, from his father, the sd. John Grayson, Decd., who died intestate, and was by the sd. Thomas Grayson conveyed to the sd. Thomas Turner of King Geo. Co., Gent., as by Deeds, Jany. 27, 1727. Witnesses, Rd. Brooke, Edward Dixon, James Tutt, Robt. Brooke, jr.; Hy. Brooke, jr.; John Catlett, Lawrence Taliaferro. July 3, 1753.

Jany. 16, 1753. Lyonel Lyde of London, Mercht., power of attorney, to Samuel Lyde and James Hunter of Fredericksburg, Va., Mercht. Before

Abraham Ogier of London. Not. Pub. Witnesses, John Gaitshill, Archd. Crawford. July 3, 1753.

June 6, 1753. Micajah Poole and Betty, his wife, of Culpeper Co., to John Thornton of Spts. Co. £60 curr. 300 a. in Spts. and Caroline Counties, devised the sd. Micajah by the last will and testament of his father, George Poole, Decd. Witnesses, Henry Willis, David Williamson, Reuben Thornton, Richard Peacock, James Allan. July 3, 1753.

June 8, 1753. John Tayloe of Richmond Co., Esqr., to William Lewis of Spts. Co. Deed of Lease. Lots 14 and 15, in town of Fredericksburg. £15 curr. yearly. Witnesses, Anthony Strother, Ralph McFarlane, Ann Farley. July 4, 1753.

Augt. 7, 1753. Chilion White and Millicent, his wife, of Spts. Co., to Henry Lewis of the same county. £43 10s. curr. 300 a. in co. afsd. Ed. Herndon, jr.; Jo. Brock, Thos. White. Augt. 7, 1753.

Sept 4, 1753. Peter Gatewood of Spts. Co. to John Holloday. £40 curr. 100 a. in Spts. Co., on forks of Bushes and Mine Roads, part of the land belonging to John Boswell, Decd., and conveyed to sd. Gatewood by Ransom Boswell and Mary, his wife, as by Deeds, Octr. 3, 1752. Ed. Herndon, junr.; Thos. Bartlett, Thos. Crutcher, junr. Sept. 4, 1753.

Septr. 4, 1753. Ambrose Haley of St. Thomas Par., Orange Co., to David Cave, Senr., of Par. and Co. afsd. £15 curr. 200 a. in St. Geo. Par., Spts. Co., which sd. Ambrose purchased of John Haley. Witnesses, John Haley, Benjamin Cave. Septr. 4, 1753. Temperance, wife of Ambrose Haley, acknowledged her dower, etc.

Sept. 14, 1753. Thomas Dowdall of Spts. Co. to Mary James of Fredericksburg, Innkeeper. £65 curr. Lot No. 18, in town of Fredericksburg. Joseph Steward, Charles Colson, Adam Pavey. Octr. 2, 1753.

Nov. 5, 1753. Elizabeth x Curtis, widow and relict of Rice Curtis, the Elder, late of Spts. Co., Gent., Decd.; to her son, Rice Curtis; her part of water grist mill, the Dam and appurtenances belonging in St. Geo. Par., Spts. Co., on River Po, etc., late the property of Rice Curtis, Decd. Witnesses, Philip Vincent Vass, Anthony Samuell, Senr.; Henry Pendleton, Greensbe Waggoner, Mary Samuell. Novr. 6, 1753.

Nov. 5, 1753. John Holloday of Spts. Co. and Elizabeth, his wife, to Joseph Peterson of Spts. Co. £80 curr. 140½ a. in Spts. Co., devised sd. Holloday by the will of his father, John Holloday. Witnesses, Joseph Holloday, Abraham Sweney, Benja. Holloday, Edward Herndon, Junr. Nov. 6, 1753.

Nov. 5, 1753. John Holloday of Spts. Co. and Elizabeth, his wife, to Joseph Holloday of Spts. Co. £30 curr. 100 a. in Spts. Co., devised sd. Holloday by the will of his father, John Holloday. Witnesses, Wm. Holloday, Abraham Sweney, Benjamin Holloday. Nov. 6, 1753.

Nov. 6, 1753. William Brown and Elizabeth, his wife, of St. Paul Par., Stafford Co., to Nathaniel Price and Jane, his wife, of sd. Par. and county. 150 a. in St. Geo. Par., Spts. Co., purchased by one Thomas Butler of Larkin Chew, Gent., Decd., as by Deeds, March 4, 1722. Sd. Thomas Butler, dying, seized of the sd. tract, intestate leaving two daughters (to wit), Jane, who intermarried with Nathaniel Price, and Elizabeth, who intermarried with William Brown, both as afsd., etc., etc. Witness, M. Battaley. Novr. 6, 1753.

Feby. 23, 1754. Thomas White and Betty, his wife, of Spts. Co., to John Thornton and Wm. Waller, Gent., Church Wardens of St. Geo. Par., Spts. Co. 640 lbs. tob. "144 sq. poles, being a square of 12 poles on each side, being lately laid off for a church yard at the New Church at East North East, including the sd. Church, which stands in thé centre thereof," etc., in trust for the Par. James Lea, John Sandidge, Richard Poindexter. March 6, 1754.

Sept. 3, 1753. Ambrose Foster of Spts. Co. to Wm. Waller, Gent., of the co. afsd. £11 2s. 9d. curr. 120 a. in Spts. Co. Witnesses, Jo. Brock, Edwd. Herndon, Junr.; Robt. Chew. April 2, 1754.

March 18, 1754. Thomas Duerson of Spts. Co. and Hannah, his wife, of Spts. Co., to William Bartlett of Spts. Co. £50 curr. 200 a. in Spts. Co. Ed. Herndon, Jr.; Jo. Herndon, Jo. Brock. April 2, 1754.

March 12, 1754. William Fitzhugh and Francis Thornton, Gent., executors of the last will and testament of Gilson Berryman of Stafford Co., Gent., Decd., to William Lynn of Fredericksburg, Doctor of Physic. Whereas sd. Berryman in his lifetime agreed, for the consideration of £7 12s. 8d., to convey to the sd. Lynn, Lot No. 13 in the town of Fredksburg, which he, the sd. Berryman, purchased of Francis Willis, Esqr., and John Grymes, Esqr., Execrs. of the last will and testament of Henry Willis, Gent., Decd., etc. (Will of Gilson Berryman, dated, July 28, 1743.) Witnesses, Charles Yates, Alexander Woodrow, Thomas James. April 2, 1754.

April 3 1754. John Allen of St. Geo. Par., Spts. Co., to Thomas Allen of Par. and County afsd. £40 curr. 100 a. in Spts. Co. Pat. Connelly, James Collins, Jon. Collins. April 3, 1754.

April 3, 1754. Larkin Chew of Spts. Co., Gent., and Mary, his wife, to Anthony Foster of county afsd. £12. 183 a. in St. Geo. Par., Spts. Co., part of a pat. formerly granted John Bush. Witnesses, Joseph Hawkins, J. Brock, Thos. Foster. April 3, 1754.

March 2, 1754. Thomas Poole of Culpeper Co., planter, to James Ball of Lancaster Co., Gent. £76 curr. 400 a. in St. Geo. Par., Spts. Co. Matthew Gayle, John Menefee, Philip Vincent Vass. May 7, 1754. "Thomas Poole and Elizabeth, his wife* * * * and Elizabeth Poole, widow," acknowledged this their deed to James Ball, Gent.

May 6, 1754. Charles Smith of St. Martin's Par., Louisa Co., and Ann, his wife, to Thomas Wiatt of St. Mark's Par., Spts. Co. £150 curr. 446 a. in St. Mark's Par., Spts. Co. Joseph Smith, John Gordon, Edward Wiatt. May 7, 1754.

May 6, 1754. Archibald McPherson and James Hunter, execrs. of the last will and testament of John Allan, Decd., and James Allan, brother and heir at law of the sd. John Allan, to John Sutherland of Fredericksburg. Doctor of Physic. £400 curr. 570 a. in Spts. Co., at a place called Motts, on the S. side of Rappk. River, purchased by sd. John Allan, Decd., from Thomas Turner, Jr., and Mary, his wife, and Francis Conway and Sarah, his wife, as by Deeds, Nov. 7, 1749. No witnesses. May 7, 1754.

William Robinson of Spts. Co. to his son, John Robinson. Deed of Gift. A negro child, etc. Dated, Feby. 4, 1754. Witnesses, John Clayton, Rubin x Banghan. July 2, 1754.

July 2, 1754. Martin x True of St. Geo. Par., Spts. Co., and Sarah, his wife, to James Ball of Christ Church Par., Lancaster Co., Gent. £35 curr. 331 a. on Massaponnax Swamp, in Spts. Co., conveyed by John Grayson and Barbary, his wife, to sd. True, as by indenture dated Oct. 2, 1750. John Ballandine, James Pollard, Jas. Glendining. July 2, 1754.

July 2, 1754. John Crittenden Webb and Mary, his wife, of Spts. Co., to Joseph Herndon of Caroline Co. £30 curr. 100 a. in Spts. Co. Z. Lewis, Roger Dixon, Richard Woolfolk. July 2, 1754.

June 4, 1754. William Bartlett of St. Geo. Par., Spts. Co., to Susanna, wife of Thomas Collins of sd. County. 336 a. in Spts. Co. Jo. Brock, Henry Bartlett, Thos. Brooks. July 2, 1754. "William Bartlett acknowledged this deed of Gift of land unto his daughter, Susanna Collins, wife of Thos. Collins," etc.

August 6, 1754. William Johnston of Caroline Co., Gent., to William Waller of Spts. Co., Gent. £10 10s. 31 a. in St. Geo. Par., Spts. Co. John Minor, George Frazer, Jo. Brock. Augt. 6, 1754.

Augt. 6, 1754. Wm. Waller of Spts. Co., Gent., to his god-daughter, Betty Johnston, daughter of William Johnston of Caroline Co., Gent., Deed of Gift. 171 a. in Spts. Co. Witnesses, John Minor, George Frazer, Jo. Brock. Augt. 6, 1754.

April 29, 1754. Before John Wennington, N. P., in Whitehaven and one of the Masters of Chancery Extraordinary, personally appeared Richd. Laybrone of Cockermouth, County of Cumberland, Hatter, who acknowl- edged power of atty. to Edward Dixon of Port Royal, Rappahannock River, Va., Mercht. Witnesses, Edward Rothery, John Hodgson. Recd. Augt. 6, 1724.

Samuel Hildrup of Spts. Co. to Robert Duncanson of sd. County, two servant men, Oliver Moules and John Smith, and one negro man, Berk- shere, and goods and chattels. Mortgage. £100 curr. Witness, George Frazer. Dated, Jany. 8, 1754. Recd., Augt. 6, 1754.

Augt. 6, 1754. Benjamin Martin of St. Geo. Par., Spts. Co., to Benjamin Davis of same Par. and county. £40 curr. 100 a. on N. side River Poe, in Spts. Co. John Holloday, John Hawkins, Jos. Collins. Augt. 6, 1754.

July 15, 1754. William Crawford to Edmund Waller of Spts. Co. Mort- gage. £10 curr. Goods and chattels. Witnesses, Wm. Waller, Wm. Wood. Augt. 7, 1754.

Septr. 3, 1745. John Durritt of St. Geo. Par., Spts. Co., to Henry True and Martin True of Par. and county afsd. £30 curr. 200 a. in St. Geo. Par., on s. side River Ta. Benja. Davis, Alexr. Hawkins, James Sparkes. Sept. 3, 1754.

Richard Peacock of town of Fredericksburg, Blacksmith, to Lewis Webb, Gent., Adms. of James Fox. £16, owing to him for "the shop and house wherein I dwell," etc., Blacksmith's tools. Dated, Sept. 3, 1754. No witnesses. Recd., Sept. 3, 1754.

Sept. 3, 1754. Richard Peacock of town of Fredericksburg, Blacksmith, to Roger Dixon of King George Co. Whereas one Colburt Artrup, late of Spts. Co., Decd., died intestate, leaving an estate worth £50, and leaving a widow, Mary Artrup, and three infant children, vizt., John Artrup, Wm. Artrup and Anne Artrup. Administration granted Mary Artrup, his widow, who soon afterwards intermarried with sd. Peacock, for the sum of 5 shill. curr. Goods and chattels. No witnesses. Sept. 3, 1754.

Augt. 24, 1754. Henry Pendleton to Coll. Wm. Waller and Majr. Rice Curtis, Gentlemen., sd. Waller and Curtis being responsible for the sd. Pendleton to Wm. Cowne of King Wm. County for the balance due of a judgment obtained by Humphrey Bell of London, Merch., against sd. Pendleton for £72 14s. 2d. Bond for £100. Five negroes as security. Witnesses, Wm. Wood, Richd. Tutt, junr. Octr. 1, 1754.

March 16, 1754. Gawin Corbin of Westmoreland Co., Esqr., and Hannah, his wife, to Thomas Brooks of Spts. Co. £17 10s. curr. 175 a. in St. Geo. Par., Spts. Co. Jas. Steptoe, Wm. Flood, Thomas Crutcher, Thos. Bartlett, Wm. Crutcher, Jo. Brock. Oct. 1, 1754.

March 16, 1754. Gawin Corbin of Westmoreland Co., Esqr., and Hannah, his wife, to Anthony Foster of Spts. Co. £55 curr. 550 a. in St. Geo. Par., Spts. Co. Jas. Steptoe, Wm. Flood, Thos. Crutcher, Thos. Bartlett, Wm. Crutcher, Jos. Brock.

March 16, 1754. Gawin Corbin of Westmoreland, Esqr., and Hannah, his wife, to Thomas Crutcher of Caroline. £92 10s. curr. 925 a. in St. Geo. Par., Spts. Co. Jas. Steptoe, Wm. Flood, Samuel Oldham, Thos. Bartlett, Wm. Crutcher, Jo. Brock. Oct. 1, 1751.

March 16, 1754. Gawin Corbin of Westmoreland Co., Esqr., and Hannah, his wife, to Joseph Brock of Spts. Co. £100 curr. 550 a. in St. Geo. Par., Spts. Co. Jas. Steptoe, Wm. Flood, Thos. Crutcher, Thos. Bartlett, Wm. Crutcher. Oct. 1, 1751.

Sept. 9, 1754. John Callahan of St. Geo. Par., Spts. Co., to Anthony Foster of same Par. and county. £20 curr. 95 acres in county and parish afsd. Wm. Waller, John Semple, Richard Tutt, junr.

Oct. 1, 1754. Rice Graves of Spts. Co. to Thomas Graves of same county. 5 shill. curr. 100 a. in Spts. Co. Z. Lewis, Chas. Colson. Oct. 1, 1754.

Augt. 17, 1754. Samuel Waggener and Bettie, his wife, of St. Geo. Par., Spts. Co., to Edward Coleman of Co. and Par. afsd. £40 curr. 100 a. in St. Geo. Par., Spts. Co. Joseph Allen, Richd. Long, Mossom x Poe. Oct. 1, 1754.

Oct. 1, 1754. James Allan and James Hunter, surviving executors of the last will and testament of John Allan, Decd., etc., to Charles Dick of Fredericksburg, Mercht. £43 curr. Lot. No. 7, in town of Fredericksburg. No witnesses. Oct. 1, 1754.

Nov. 5, 1754. Richard x Couzens of Orange Co. to Richard Coleman of Essex Co. £19 curr. Tract of land in Spts. Co., purchased by sd. Couzens of Robt. Sp. Coleman of Essex Co. Jo. Brock, Robt. Sp. Coleman, George James. Nov. 5, 1754.

Nov. 5, 1754. Joseph Collins of St. Geo. Par., Spts. Co., to John Collins of afsd. Par. and county. 270 a. on both sides Robinson River, in Spts. Co. Ths. Collins, Lewis Collins. Nov. 5, 1754.

June 28, 1754. Joseph Martin and Joseph Pulliam of Louisa Co. to James, William, David and John Sandige and Anthony Gholson. Bond. £300 curr. "Joseph Martin is now going to be married to Ann Sandige," etc. Witness, John Semple. Recd. Nov. 5, 1754.

Anne Martin, wife of Joseph Martin, of Louisa Co. Whereas Wm. Sandige, late of Spts. Co., decd., was seized of several tracts of land in Spts. Co., and made his last will and testament, March 11, 1746, and by the sd. instrument did leave to the sd. Ann, party to these presents, then his wife, three negroes, etc., and the balance of his property to be divided between the sd. Ann, and his three sons, James, David and John, etc., etc., and his daughter, Mary Golson, wife of Anthony Golson, Junr., etc. Dated, Nov. 4, 1754. Z. Lewis, George Atkinson, Robert x Gregory. Novr. 5, 1754.

Nov. 10, 1754. Achilles Bowker of Spts. Co. and Martha, his wife, to Robert Chew of Co. afsd. £150 curr. 400 a. in St. Geo. Par., Spts. Co. John Chew, Harry Beverley, Jos. Brock, Francis Cammack. Decr. 3, 1754.

Novr. 5, 1754. Thomas Foster of Cumberland Co. and Elizabeth, his wife, to Robert Chew of Spts. Co. £200 curr. 737 a. in St. Geo. Par., Spts. Co. John Chew, Benja. Martin, Thos. Estes, Francis Cammack. Dec. 3, 1754.

Jany. 4, 1755. Wm. Bartlett of Spts. Co. to his son, Thomas Bartlett. Deed of Gift. 273 a. in St. Geo. Par., Spts. Co. No witnesses. Feby. 4, 1755.

Feby. 4, 1755. George Washington of Fairfax Co., Esqr., to John Thornton, an infant (son of Fran. Thornton, Late of Spts. Co., Gent., Decd., and Frances Thornton, his widow and relict.) Deed of Gift. "Consideration of the Natural love, good-will and affection which he beareth to the sd. John Thornton, his cousin," etc. Lot 40, in town of Fredksbg. No witnesses. Feby. 4, 1755.

Jany. 1, 1728. Rice Curtis of Spts. Co., Gent., to Richd. Kewen of same Co., Shoemaker. Deed of lease. 50 a. in Spts. Co. £1 10s. curr. yearly. W. Stephen, Rice Curtis. Feby. 4, 1755.

Decr. 5, 1754. Fielding Lewis of Spts. Co., Gent., and Betty, his wife, to Wm. Waller of sd. Co., Gent. £20 curr. A lot in town of Fredksbg., adj. land bought by sd. Waller of the executors of Henry Willis, Gent., Decd. Cuthbert Sandys, Benj. Baron, Jacob x Clayton. Feby. 5, 1755.

March 28, 1755. William x Richerson of St. Geo. Par., Spts. Co., planter, to his son-in-law, Thomas Hutcherson, then to his son, James Hutcherson. Deed of Gift. 95 a. in St. Geo. Par., Spts. Co. Witnesses, Henry Pendleton, Owen Thomas. April 1, 1755.

March 3, 1755. William x Richerson of St. Geo. Par., Spts. Co., planter, to his daughter, Sarah Hensley, my grandson, Richerson Hensley, after the death of George Hensley, his father, and Sarah Hensley, his mother. Deed of Gift. 110 a. in Spts. Co. Witnesses, Henry Pendleton, Owen Thomas. April 1, 1755.

Feby. 19, 1755. Wm. Bartlett and Susanna, his wife, to Edwd. Herndon, junr. £28 5s. curr. 113 a. in Spts. Co. Thos. Duerson, Jo. Brock, Joseph Herndon, William x Burbridge. April 1, 1755.

Feby. 19, 1755. Thomas Duerson of Spts. Co. to Edwd. Herndon, Junr., of same co. £19 16s. curr. 99 a. in Spts. Co. Jo. Brock, Wm. Bartlett, Joseph Herndon, William x Burbridge. April 1, 1755.

April 1, 1755. Ransom Boswell, John Boswell and William Gatewood and Ann, his wife, to Peter Gatewood. £46 curr. 125 a. in Spts. Co. Henry Gatewood, junr. Ignatius Tureman, Dudley Gatewood. April 1, 1755.

April 1, 1755. John Boswell of Spts. Co. to John Holloday of sd. county. £25 curr. 120 a. in county afsd. Jo. Brock, Thomas Foster, Peter Gatewood. April 1, 1755.

Jany. 7, 1755. Anthony Foster of Spts. Co. to James Frazier and Betty, his wife, the daughter of sd. Anthony Foster. Deed of Gift. 234 a. in Spts. Co. No witnesses. April 1, 1755.

Jany. 7, 1755. Anthony Foster of Spts. Co. to his son, Thomas Foster. Deed of Gift. 230 a. in Spts. Co. No witnesses. April 1, 1755.

Nov. 12, 1754. Isaac Bradburn of Spts. Co., mortgage to Wm. Bradburn. £40 curr. Horses, cattle, etc. Witnesses, Spilsbe Coleman, William Pace, Luke Burford. April 1, 1755.

Feby. 3, 1755. Alexander Cruikshanks to Benjamin Pipeman, tailor, both of Spts. Co. £10 15s. curr. ¼ of a. of land in Fredksbg town. Peter Lucas, John Ladd, George Hicks. April 2, 1755. Mary, wife of Alexander Cruikshanks, acknowledged her dower, etc.

May 7, 1755. Robert Farish of St. Geo. Par., Spts. Co., and Judith, his wife, to Thomas Minor of Par. and county afsd. £150 curr. 400 a. in afsd. co. Jos. Collins, Nicholas Hawkins, Thos. Rogers. May 7, 1755.

Nov. 16, 1754. John Williams and Jane, his wife, and Wm. x Williams of Granville Co., North Carolina, to Charles Kennedy of Hanover Co. £21 curr. 100 a. in Spts. Co., conveyed by Ralph Williams to the afsd. Wm. Williams and by him conveyed to the afsd. John Williams. John Woolfolk, James Wiglesworth, James Crawford, Wm. Davenport. June 3, 1755.

Oct. 4, 1754. Mary James of Spts. Co., widow, and Thomas James, eldest son and heir at law of George James, decd., late husband of the sd. Mary. Articles of Agreement. Said Mary to release her dower in lands, etc., in Prince Wm. Co. 900 a. on Deep Run, to sd. Thomas James. Said Thomas James to execute to sd. Mary, a deed for lots in town of Fredksbg, which sd. George James purchased of Charles Colson, etc., mentions Mary James, Dianah James, Joseph James, Daniel James, and Henry James, youngest children of sd. George James and Mary, his wife. Witnesses, Z. Lewis, Wm. Waller, Joseph Hawkins, Francis x Kerkley. June 3, 1755.

June 3, 1755. Thomas James of Prince Wm. Co. (eldest son and heir of George James, late of the town of Fredksbg, Decd.) and Jenny, his wife, of the first part; Henry Field of Culpeper Co., Gent., and Esther, his wife, of the second part; Mary James, widow, late wife of the sd. George James, Decd., of the third part., and Mary James, Dianah James, Joseph James, Daniel James, and Henry James, youngest children of sd. George James,

Decd., of the fourth part. Deed of Lease. Lots of land and tenements in town of Fredericksburg, commonly known as the Long Ordinary, etc., etc., considerations and conditions, etc. Witnesses, Joseph Steward, George James, Ann x Kenny. June 3, 1755.

March 3, 1755. John x Talburt of St. Geo. Par., Spts. Co., and Margaret, his wife, to John Ballard of same par. and county. £25 10s. curr. pd. to Richd. Coalman, for 100 a. of land, which sd. Talburt and wife sold sd. Coalman and sd. Coalman sold the land to the sd. Ballard, before it was acknowledged to the sd. Coalman, being the tract sd. Talburt bought of John Pain and Frances, his wife, as by deeds, Augt. 6, 1745, sd. land on s. side Pike Run in Co. and Par. afsd. Henry Carter, John Coleman, James Sames. Oct. 7, 1755.

June 2, 1755. Wm. Waller of Spts. Co., Gent., to Samuel Brown of co. afsd., planter. £12 18s. curr. 92 a. in St. Geo. Par., Spts. Co., part of a tract devised sd. Waller, by the will of his father, Jno. Waller, Gent., Decd., etc. Nicho. Horn, William Smith, Thos. x Graves. June 3, 1755.

June 5, 1755. William Russell and Robert Green of Culpeper Co., Gent., to John Forman of town of Fredericksburg, Leather Breeches Maker, and Ordinary Keeper. £10 15s. Lot No. 7, near the town of Fredksbg, purchased of the executors of Henry Willis, Decd., as by Deeds, Oct. 20, 1745, by the sd. Russell and Robert Green, Decd., father of the sd. Robt., party to these presents, etc. M. Battaley, J. Brock, John Field, Saml. Battaley, George Sames. Augt. 5, 1755.

Augt. 5, 1755. William Holloway of Caroline Co. and Mary, his wife, to Robert Dudley of Spts. Co. £50 curr. 250 a. in St. Geo. Par., Spts. Co. Witness, J. Brock. Augt. 5, 1755.

Augt. 5, 1755. Henry Pendleton of St. Geo. Par., Spts. Co., and Martha, his wife, to John Davenport of St. Martin's Par., Hanover Co. £18 curr. 230 a., part of a pat. granted Wm. Smith, Gent., Decd., in St. Geo. Par., Spts. Co., and just below the ordinary belonging to the sd. John Davenport, on Pamunkey Roling Road., sd. land purchased by sd. Pendleton of George Woodroof and Jane, his wife, as by deeds, Feby. 5, 1744. No witnesses. Augt. 5, 1755.

Joseph Martin of Louisa Co., Gent., and Anne, his wife, late wife of Wm. Sandige, late of Spts. Co., Decd., to Francis Meriwether of Spts. Co., Gent. ⅓ part of a tract of 150 a., called Elk Neck, in Spts. Co., purchased by sd. Wm. Sandige in his lifetime of John Davis of King Wm. Co., and by sd. Wm. devised to his son, Wm., who sold it to the sd. Meriwether. Witnesses, Benja. Holloday, James Pulliam, Joseph Rash. Dated, Sept. 1, 1755. Recd. Sept. 2, 1755.

Augt. 13, 1755. John Battaley of Culpeper Co. to Mary, wife of Edward Herndon, Jr. £5. A negro child. Witness, Joseph Herndon. Sept. 2, 1755.

Oct. 7, 1755. James Reynolds of St. Geo. Par., Spts. Co., and Elizabeth, his wife, to Aquilla Johnson of St. Margaret's Par., Caroline Co. £24 curr. 300 a., situated in St. Geo. Par., Spts. Co. Witness, Jo. Brock. Oct. 7, 1755.

Benjamin Grymes of Spts. Co., Gent., power of attorney to Fielding Lewis of same Co., Gent. Dated, Augt. 19, 1755. Witnesses, Tho. Rogers, James Butler. Recd., Oct. 7, 1755.

Augt. 13, 1755. Benjamin Grymes of Spts. Co., Gent., and Betty, his wife, to John Champe of King Geo. Co., Mercht. £3103 curr. 1750 a. in Spts. Co., whereon the sd. Grymes lives; also 700 a. in Spts. Co., purchased by sd. Grymes, formerly belonging to Edmund Smith; also lots in town of Fredericksburg, purchased by sd. Grymes of Nathaniel Chapman, etc., and 51 slaves. Mortgage. Witnesses, J. Mercer, Fielding Lewis, James Butler. Oct. 7, 1755.

Dec. 2, 1755. John Ballard and Ann, his wife, of St. Geo. Par., Spts. Co., to Henry Pendleton of same Par. and Co. £28 curr. 100 a. in St. Geo. Par., Spts. Co., on s. side Pike Run. No witnesses. Dec. 2, 1755.

Oct. 21, 1755. William Smither of Spts. Co. and Ann, his wife, to Wm. Waller of co. afsd., Gent. £35 curr. 69 acres. John Semple, Ed. Herndon, junr.; Jo. Brock, John Waller. Dec. 2, 1755.

Oct. 9, 1755. Charles Lewis of Spts. Co., Gent., to Fielding Lewis of Fredericksburg, Gent. £650 curr. 1800 a. on or near Mattapony River, in Spts. Co., devised the sd. Charles, by the will of his father, Honble. John Lewis, Esqr., Decd., and part of a tract called Warners, etc.; also several slaves. Mortgage. Witnesses, James Strachan, Danl. Fitzhugh, Henry Heath. Dec. 2, 1755.

Dec. 2, 1755. James Stephens of St. Geo. Par., Spts. Co., and Alice, his wife, to Philip Vincent Vass of Par. and Co. afsd. £140 curr. 107 a. in Spts. Co. Greensbe Waggoner, Wm. Brock. Dec. 2, 1755.

Dec. 2, 1755. John Schooler and Martha, his wife, of Spts. Co., to Richard Tutt of Spts. Co. £69 curr. 242 a. in St. Geo. Par., Spts. Co., part of a tract granted Thomas Elzey of Stafford Co., by pat., Jany. 22, 1717. Witnesses, Charles Washington, Francis Thornton, James Tutt, Richard Tutt, junr. Dec. 3, 1755.

Feby. 2, 1756. Henry Chiles and Susanna, his wife, of Spts. Co., to John Chiles of same county, second son of the sd. Henry Chiles, etc. Deed of gift. 150 a. in co. afsd. Witnesses, Thomas Wiat, Wm. Webb, John Holloday. March 2, 1756.

March 1, 1756. James Allen to Peter Lucas, both of Spts. Co. £80 curr. Lot No. 62 in town of Fredericksburg. No witnesses. March 2, 1756.

Augt. 22, 1755. Uriah Garton to William Brock. £90 curr. 300 a. on N. side River Ta, in Spts. Co. Edwd. Herndon, Junr.; Thos. Estes, Joseph Herndon. March 2, 1756.

March 2, 1756. John Carter of Spts. Co. to Thomas McNeil of same county. £10 curr. 100 a. in St. Geo. Par., Spts. Co. No witnesses. March 2, 1756.

Nov. 15, 1753. Nicholas Horn of Caroline Co. to Col. Wm. Waller and David Allen of Spts. Co. £100 ster. 3 negroes. Mortgage. Witnesses, John Semple, Michael Yates, Wm. Wood. Recd. March 1, 1756.

John Word of St. Geo. Par., Spts. Co., to Wm. Waller of same county. £10 curr. Mortgage. Goods and chattels, horses and cattle, etc. Witnesses, Richd. Tutt, junr.; Wm. Wood. Dated, Jany. 13, 1756. Recd. March 3, 1756.

Feby. 20, 1756. William Waller of Spts. Co. to William Lewis of Fredericksburg. Deed of Lease. House and lots in Fredksbg. £15 curr. yearly. Jos. Brock, Wm. Carr, Wm. Wood. Mar. 3, 1756.

April 6, 1756. Aquilla Johnson and Elizabeth, his wife, of Caroline Co.. to John Beazley of Caroline Co. £30 curr. 300 a. in Spts. Co. Richd. Woolfolk, Wm. Wood, Ben. Boughan. April 6, 1756.

April 29, 1755. John Thornton, Gent., and Mildred, his wife, of Spts. Co., to Charles Colson of same county. £64 10s. curr. Part of Lot. No. 43, in town of Fredericksburg. Henry Willis, Hugh Lenox, Charles Yates, Robt. Philips, James Nelson. May 4, 1756.

Lawrence Taliaferro of Spts. Co., power of attorney to Richard Brooke. Dated, May 29, 1756. W. Robinson, Nathaniel x Stephens, Hay Taliaferro, Richd. Tutt, Wm. Brooke, John Benger. May 4, 1756.

Jany. 2, 1756. James Edwards, the Elder, of St. John Par., King Wm. County, planter, to James Edwards, the Younger, of St. Geo. Par., Spts. Co. 400 a., out of which 200 had already been given sd. James, the younger, and is the tract whereon he lives, sd. 400 a. purchased by sd. James, the Elder, of Richd. Phillips, as by deeds, June 4, 1734, on N. side Northanna River, in Spts. Co. Ambrose Edwards, John Waller, Thos. Waller, John x Gooch, John Waller. June 1, 1756.

Oct. 4, 1755. Benj. x Watts and Mary, his wife, of Spts. Co., to Jesse Harper of Caroline Co. £65 curr. 100 a. in St. Geo. Par., Spts. Co. Peter Copland, Jas. Martin, John Goodloe, John Daniel. June 1, 1756.

April 7, 1756. Reuben Thornton of Caroline Co., Gent., to John Spotswood of Spts. Co., Esqr. Whereas, Francis Willis of Gloucester Co., Esqr., only surviving Execr. of the last will and testament of Henry Willis, late of the Co. of Spts., Decd., and John Thornton of the last mentioned Co., Gent., atto. in fact for John Land and Ann Land, his wife, of St. Leonard, Middlesex Co., Gt. Britain, by their deed, April 25, 1754, conveyed to sd. Reuben Thornton, two lots in Fredksbg, Nos. 57 and 58; now sd. Reuben Thornton for the sum of £65 5s. transfers the sd. lots to sd. Spotswood. Witnesses, Robt. Jackson, James Hunter, Antho. Strother, Antho. Walke, Fra. Wroughton. June 1, 1756.

John Tayloe of Richmond Co., Esqr., releases to William Lewis of Fredksbg, Lots 14 and 15 in Fredksbg. £15 curr. yearly. Dated, April 14, 1756. Fielding Lewis, Antho. Strother, Wm. Waller, Jos. Jones, Edwd. Pendleton. June 1, 1756.

March 1, 1756. John Chew of Spts. Co., Gent., to his daughter, Mary Beverley Brock. Deed of gift. Negroes. Witnesses, John Chew, junr.; John Semple. July 6, 1756.

March 1, 1756. John Chew of Spts. Co., Gent., to his daughter, Hannah Chew. Deed of Gift. Negroes. Witnesses, J. Brock, Mary Beverley Brock, John Semple. July 6, 1756.

March 1, 1756. John Chew of Spts. Co., Gent., to his son, John Chew, junr. Deed of Gift. Negroes. Witnesses, Jo. Brock, Mary Beverley Brock, John Semple. July 6, 1756.

March 19, 1756. Zachary Lewis of Spts. Co., of the first part; Richard Shackleford of same co. and Mary, his wife, of the second part; and Mary

Shackleford, dau. of James Shackleford of the same county, of the third part. Whereas, Zachary Lewis, by letter dated May 29, 1755, did give to Mary, daughter of sd. James Shackleford, and Elizabeth, his wife, sister of the sd. Zachary; sd. Zachary now deeds the sd. negro to the sd. Richd. Shackleford and Mary, his wife, for the use of the sd. Mary, dau. of James; the third party to these presents. Witnesses, Z. Lewis, Junr.; Waller Lewis, Betty Lewis, Dorothea Lewis. Augt. 3, 1756.

Sept. 7, 1756. Samuel Matthews and Joseph Matthews of Louisa Co. to William Matthews of Spts. Co. Benja. Matthews, Decd., father of the sd. Samuel, Joseph and William Matthews, was possessed of a tract of 100 a. of land, and by his last will and testament directed the sd. land sold and the proceeds divided among his three sons, the parties to these presents; therefore in consideration of £20 curr. the land is deeded the sd. Wm. Matthews. No witnesses. Oct. 5, 1756.

Sept. 7, 1756. Gawin Corbin of Westmoreland Co., Esqr., and Hannah, his wife, to Thomas Brooks of Spts. Co. 50 shill. curr. 25 a. in Spts. Co. J. Brock, Edwd. Herndon, junr. Sept. 7, 1756.

Sept. 7, 1756. Gawin Corbin of Westmoreland Co., Esqr., and Hannah, his wife, to Anthony Foster of Spts. Co. £11 14s. curr. 234 a. in Spts. Co. Wm. Waller, Jo. Brock, Ed. Herndon, junr. Sept. 7, 1756.

Sept. 7, 1756. Gawin Corbin of Westmoreland Co., Esqr., and Hannah, his wife, to Edward Herndon, junr., of Spts. Co. £26 8s. curr. 264 a. in St. Geo. Par., Spts. Co. Wm. Waller, Jo. Brock, A. Foster. Sept. 7, 1756.

Augt. 21, 1756. Roger x Cason of Spts. Co. and Elizabeth, his wife, to William Johnston, Gent., of Caroline Co. £23 curr. 84 a. in Spts. Co. Wm. Waller, William Wood, Thos. Cason, Benjamin Watts. Sept. 8, 1756. A letter from Roger Cason saying his wife cannot come to the court to acknowledge her dower, "as it will be prejudicial to us in preventing our intended removal to the province of North Carolina," etc.

Oct. 5, 1756. Michael Yates and Martha, his wife; Daniel May and Alice, his wife; John Jones and Ann, his wife, to James Nelson of Spts. Co. £57 12s. curr. 670 a., part of a pat. granted Michael Ginney, June 30, 1726, in Spts. Co. No witnesses. Oct. 5, 1756.

Nov. 1, 1756. Thomas Brooks of Spts. Co. and Rachell, his wife, to William Brock of Spts. Co. £50 curr. 141 a. in Spts. Co. John Holloday, Ed. Herndon, junr.; Jos. Herndon. Nov. 2, 1756.

Dec. 7, 1756. Joseph Collins and Susannah, his wife, of Spts. Co., to Aaron Quesenburey of Caroline Co. £50 curr. 275 a. in Spts. Co. W. Wood, Thomas Coleman, Philip Vincent Vass. Dec. 7, 1756.

April 29, 1756. Henry Willis, Gent., of Spts. Co., to Peter How, Esqr., of Whitehaven, in Kingdom of Gt. Britain. £74 10s. 3½d. curr. A negro slave. Witness, Charles Yates, William Steward. Dec. 7, 1756.

Feby. 25, 1757. Fielding Lewis of town of Fredksbg, Gent., and Betty, his wife, to John Thornton of the sd. town, Gent. £450 curr. Lots on N. side Caroline St., in Fredksbg. Chas. Dick, Hugh Lenox, Thos. Rogers. March 1, 1757.

April 2, 1757. Philip Vincent Vass of Spts. Co. and Mary, his wife, to Ignatius Tureman of afsd. Co. £20 curr. 200 a. in St. Geo. Par., Spts. Co. No witnesses. April 5, 1757.

March 2, 1757. Aaron Grigsby of King Geo. Co., planter, and Margaret, his wife; John Proctor of Spts. Co., planter, and Sarah, his wife, to John Mitchell of Fredksbg., Mercht. £35 curr. 150 a. in St. Geo. Par., Spts. Co., devised by the last will and testament of George Proctor, Decd., to his daughter, Margaret, now the wife of Aaron Grigsby, and to John Proctor, son and heir at law of the sd. George, the testator. M. Battaley, Jno. Sutherland, Hugh Lenox. May 3, 1757.

May 3, 1757. Henry Pendleton of St. Geo. Par., Spts. Co., and Martha, his wife, to Elizabeth Curtis, Frances Curtis and Jean Curtis of Par. and co. afsd. £30 curr. 150 a. in St. Geo. Par., Spts. Co., part of a tract belonging to Rice Curtis, and formerly acknowledged in Spts. Co. by sd. Curtis to sd. Pendleton, etc. No witnesses. May 3, 1757.

April 30, 1757. Thomas Duerson of St. Geo. Par., Spts. Co., and Mary, his wife, to Stapleton Crutchfield of same Par. and co. £12 10s. curr. 50 a. in St. Geo. Par., Spts. Co. Ed. Herndon, junr.; John Herndon, John Collins. May 3, 1757.

May 30, 1757. Humphrey Hill of King and Queen Co., Gent., and Frances, his wife, to Humphrey Bell of London, Mercht. £8 5s. curr. Two lotts in town of Fredksbg., purchased by sd. Hill of Feoffees of the town as by deeds, Decr. 3, 1728. Ambrose Camp, John Hill, Robt. Baylor, John Smith. June 7, 1757.

Feby. 24, 1757. James Wiglesworth of Spts. Co. and Mary, his wife, to Wm. Wiglesworth. 5 shill. curr. 200 a. in Spts. Co., formerly belonging to John Wiglesworth, Decd., and fell to the sd. James, as heir at law to the Decd., etc. Edmund Waller, Jno. Waller, junr. June 7, 1757.

April 1, 1757. Rice Curtis of Spts. Co., Gent., to Robt. Jackson of Fredksbg, Mercht. £162 17s. 6d. Mortgage. Slaves. Witnesses, George Walker, James Tutt, Lewis Willis. June 7, 1757.

March 23, 1757. Francis Taliaferro of Spts. Co., Gent., to his daughter, Ann Hay Brooke. Deed of Gift. A negro girl. Witnesses, Humphrey Brooke, Law. Taliaferro. June 7, 1757.

Jany. 15, 1757. Francis Taliaferro of Spts. Co., Gent., to his son, Lawrence Taliaferro. Deed of Gift. Slaves. Witnesses, Rd. Brooke, John Catlett, M. Battaley. June 7, 1757.

June 20, 1757. Edward Watkins and Sally, his wife, of Culpeper Co., to Mrs. Margaret Gordon of Spts. Co £50 curr. 150 a. in St. Geo. Par., Spts. Co., which descended to sd. Sally, party to these presents, from her father, Thomas Hill. Adam Menzies, John Strother, W. Brown, P. Clayton, Thos. Lendrum. July 6, 1757.

Jany. 6, 1757. Dorothea Benger of Spts. Co., widow, and admx. of Elliott Benger, late of the County of Spts., Decd., Esqr., to Roger Dixon of sd. county, Attorney at Law. Whereas sd. Dixon became security for sd. Dorothea, on her Bond as Admx., etc., and since it appears that the sd. Elliott Benger's debts far exceed the value of his personal estate, and whereas sd. Dixon assumed numerous debts and agreed to assume others, all of which amount to £420, etc., and whereas judgment has been obtained against sd. Dorothea, by Amy Cary, widow; Henry Stevens and Edward Woockck, Esqr., Execr. of Robt. Cary of London, Esqr., Decd., etc., sd. Dixon standing responsible for this debt, sd. Dorothea deeds him, as by an agreement, the personal estate of the sd. Elliott Benger, in Spts. and Albemarle Counties, etc. Witnesses, Margaret Morten, James Hume. July 6, 1757.

June 11, 1757. James Tennent of Whitehaven, Cumberland Co., Mason, and Elizabeth, his wife (which sd. Elizabeth is the only sister living of William Russell, late of Philadelphia, Mercht., Decd.), power of atty. to William Bragg of Whitehaven afsd. Witnesses, Christr. Wilson, Joseph Collin. Recd., Oct. 4, 1757.

James Tennent of Whitehaven, Cumberland Co., Mason, and Elizabeth, his wife, having formerly appointed Samuel Bowman, Thomas Price, Phillip Walker, their attorneys, having decided to send their friend, Wm. Bragg, of Whitehaven, afsd., to Phila., to see as to the will of Wm. Russell, late of Phila., the sd. Tennent and Elizabeth, his wife, revoke their power of atto. to the sd. Bowman, Price & Walker, etc. Dated, June 11, 1757. Witnesses, Christr. Wilson, Joseph Collin. Recd., Oct. 4, 1757.

Augt. 2, 1757. Robert Chew of Spts. Co. and Mary, his wife, to Harry Beverley of Caroline Co., Esqr. £25 curr. 262 a. in St. Geo. Par., Spts. Co. Richd. Tutt, junr.; Wm. Wood, Jos. Brock. Octr. 4, 1757.

Sept. 30, 1757. William Bartlett of Spts. Co. to his sons, William Bartlett and Harry Bartlett. To sd. Wm., 100 a. off the upper part my land, adj. Edward Herndon; To sd. Harry, 100 a. off the lower part my land, adj. William Allen, Esqr., and Thomas Bartlett, etc. Witnesses, Ed. Herndon, Jr.; Joseph Herndon. Oct. 4, 1757.

Oct. 3, 1757. Isaac Darnell of St. Geo. Par., Spts. Co., to his son, Henry Darnall. 50 a. in St. Geo. Par., Spts. Co. Jos. Holloday, Jacob Owen, Thomas Crutcher.

Oct. 4, 1757. Henry Brock and Barbara, his wife, of Spts. Co., to John Holloday of afsd. Co. £85 curr. 521 a. in Spts. Co. John Phillips, Thomas Crutcher. Octr. 4, 1757.

Oct. 4, 1757. Bloomfield [Brumfield] Long of Spts. Co. to Samuel Simpson of Louisa Co. £20 curr. 70 a. in St. Geo. Par., Spts. Co. Anthony Foster, John Holloday, Ed. Herndon, junr. Nov. 1, 1757.

Augt. 2, 1757. Benjamin Martin of Spts. Co. and Elizabeth, his wife, to Charles Colson of Fredksbg. £30 curr. 260 a. in Spts. Co. (save one hundred acres, part thereof which by the will of Henry Martin, Decd., father of the sd. Benjamin, was devised to John Martin, son of John Martin of Spts. Co.). William Allcock, Benjamin Davis, Tho. Rogers. Nov. 6, 1757.

Oct. 15, 1757. Harry Beverley of St. Geo. Par., Spts. Co., Gent., to Warner Lewis of Abigdon Par., Gloucester Co. £300 ster. 1500 a. in St. Geo. Par., Spts. Co. No witnesses. Dec. 6, 1757.

May 23, 1757. John Brumskitt, junr., of Pr. Wm. Co., to Wm. McWilliams, Junr., of Spts. Co. £168 12s. 6d. Negroes. Witnesses, George Neavill, T. McClanahan, Robert Massey. Dec. 6, 1757.

Nov. 3, 1757. Robt. Jackson of Fredksbg., Gent., and Ann, his wife, to Benjamin Grymes of Spts. Co., Gent. £60 curr. Lot No. 17, adj. town of Fredksbg, purchased by sd. Jackson of John Grymes, Esqr., and Fran. Willis, Esqr., Execrs. of the last will and testament of Henry Willis, Decd., as by Deeds, April 20, 1744. Jas. Tutt, David Meriwether, Jos. Jones. Dec. 6, 1757.

Augt. 2, 1757. Wm. McWilliams of Fredksbg. to Richard Lewis of King Geo. Co. Deed of Lease. A lot in Fredksburg, formerly Mr. Royston's, and whereon the warehouse stands, and adj. Mrs. Gordon's dwelling place, etc. £3 curr. yearly. James Nelson, junr.; Robert Phillips, John Stewart. Dec. 7, 1757.

Nov. 16, 1757. Bloomfield Long of St. Geo. Par., Spts. Co., Blacksmith, to his daughters, Molly, wife of John Payne, junr., and Sarah Long. Deed of Gift. 118½ a. in Spts. Co., whereon the sd. Bloomfield Long lives. Wm. Waller, John Estes, Jonathan Gibson, James Colquhoun, Jo. Waller. March 7, 1758.

March 6, 1758. Anthony Street of Spts. Co. to Micajah Cox and Samuel Street. 165 a. in Co. afsd. £30 curr. No witnesses. March 7, 1758.

April 4, 1758. Ignatius Tureman to William Pace. £10 curr. 100 a. in Spts. Co. William Crutcher, Peter Gatewood. April 4, 1758.

March 17, 1758. Frances Thornton of Spts. Co., widow; John Thornton of same Co., Gent., and Mildred, his wife, and Reuben Thornton of same Co., Gent., and Elizabeth, his wife, to Lewis Willis of Fredksbg., Gent. Whereas, Mildred Willis, late the wife of Henry Willis, late also of the Co. afsd., Gent., Decd., and mother of the sd. Lewis Willis, Frances Thornton, Mildred, wife of John Thornton, and Elizabeth, wife of Reuben Thornton, Parties to these presents, did by her deed of Dec. 15, 1739, grant to the sd. Lewis Willis, at her death, slaves, stocks, plate, goods and chattels. The sd. Mildred Willis and Henry Willis, her husband, both being long since dead, the sd. parties of the first part, to better perfect the above mentioned Deed, hereby deed to Lewis Willis, the sd. mentioned articles, etc. Witnesses, Charles Yates, Edward Carter, William Champe. April 4, 1758.

March 2, 1758. Philip x Ballard of Orange Co. and Ann, his wife, to John Hubbard of Culpeper Co. £43 curr. 434 a. in Spts. Co. Ann x Head, Peggy x Bruce, Robt. Sharman, Joseph Hawkins, Robt. x Beagles, Dilly x Beagles, Thos. Wiatt. April 4, 1758.

April 4, 1758. Thomas x Graves and Eleanor, his wife, of Spts. Co., to John Waggener of sd. County. £30 curr. 120 a. in St. Geo. Par., Spts. Co., whereon sd. Graves lives, bounded by lands of Beverley Stanard, John Farish, Wm. Johnston and the late Samuel More. Witnesses, Lark. Chew, Robert Goodloe, Joseph Herndon. April 5, 1758.

April 1, 1758. John Collins of Spts. Co. to Richard Collins of same county. 5 shill. curr. 100 a. in St. Geo. Par., Spts. Co. Edwd. Herndon, junr.; James Cunningham, Joseph Herndon. April 5, 1758.

May 2, 1758. Mary x Steward to her two sons, Benjamin and William Steward. Deed of Gift. 200 a. in Spts. Co., sd. land given the sd. Mary Steward by her father, George Procvor, by Deed, Nov. 2, 1725. Witness, M. Battaley. May 2, 1758.

May 2, 1758. Gawin Corbin of Westmoreland Co., Esqr., and Hannah, his wife, to Uriah Garton of Spts. Co. £24 curr. 300 a. in Spts. Co. No witnesses. May 2, 1758.

May 2, 1758. Gawin Corbin of Westmoreland Co., Esqr., and Hannah, his wife, to Anthony Foster of Spts. Co. £21 12s. curr. 541 acres. No witnesses. May 2, 1758.

May 2, 1758. Gawin Corbin of Westmoreland Co., Esqr., and Hannah, his wife, to Joseph Brock of Spts. Co. 40s. curr. 50 a. in Spts. Co. No witnesses. May 2, 1758.

May 2, 1758. Gawin Corbin of Westmoreland Co., Esqr., and Hannah, his wife, to Joseph Brock of Spts. Co. £20 8s. curr. 510 a. in Spts. Co. No witnesses. May 2, 1758.

May 2, 1758. Gawin Corbin of Westmoreland Co., Esqr., and Hannah, his wife, to John Herndon of Spts. Co. £16 13s. curr. 416 a. in Spts. Co. No witnesses. May 2, 1758.

May 2, 1758. Gawin Corbin of Westmoreland Co., Esqr., and Hannah, his wife, to James Moore of Spts. Co. £5 6s. 8d. curr. 133 a. in Spts. Co. No witnesses. May 2, 1758.

May 2, 1758. Gawin Corbin of Westmoreland Co., Esqr., and Hannah, his wife, to John Proctor of Spts Co. £12 curr. 200 a. in Spts. Co. No witnesses. May 2, 1758.

May 2, 1758. Gawin Corbin of Westmoreland Co., Esqr., and Hannah, his wife, to James Stevens of Spts. Co. £40 curr. 400 a. in Spts. Co. A. Foster, John Herndon, Jos. Brock. May 2, 1758.

April 27, 1758. Joseph x Venable of Spts. Co. to James Townsend of Orange Co. £17 curr. Goods and chattels. Mortgage. Witnesses, James Edwards, junr.; Thomas Waller, Wm. Minor. May 2, 1758.

April 9, 1755. Andrew Cochran, John Murdock, William Craufurd, junr.; Allan Dreghorn and Robert Bogle, junr., of the City of Glasgow, Merchts., power of attorney to William Cuningham and John Stewart, on Rappahannock River, Virginia, Merchts. Provd. in Caroline Co. (Va.), July 10, 1755, and Recd. in Spts. Co., May 3, 1758.

April 15, 1758. Joseph Brock of Spts. Co. and Mary Beverley, his wife, to Larkin Chew of same Co., Gent. £100 curr. 40 a. in Spts. Co. No witnesses. May 3, 1758.

March 20, 1758. George x Boswell to Patterson Pulliam. £10 curr. 50 a. in Spts. Co. John Holloday, Dudley Gatewood, Henry Brock, Ed. Herndon, junr. May 3, 1758.

Dec. 29, 1757. Rice Curtis of St. Geo. Par., Spts. Co., Gent., to Joseph Herndon of Par. and Co. afsd. Deed of lease. 250 a. in St. Geo. Par., Spts. Co Jo. Brock, Francis Whelchel, George Trible. May 3, 1758.

May 17, 1758. Anne Fauntleroy of Northumberland Co. to John Gale of Spts. Co. £62 curr. 800 a. in Spts. Co. Henry True, Mathew Gale, junr.; Walter Jameson, James x Boswell. June 6, 1758.

June 5, 1758. William Waller of St. Geo. Par., Spts. Co., to Robert Marsh of Par. and County afsd. Deed of Lease. 100 acres. William Wood. June 6, 1758.

July 3, 1758. William Waller of Spts. Co., Gent., to John Page of same co. £30 curr. 100 a. in Caroline and Spts. Counties. No witnesses. July 4, 1758.

Dec. 2, 1757. William Robinson of Spts. Co. to his daughter, Catharine Robinson of sd. Co. Deed of Gift. Negros. No witnesses. July 4, 1758.

July 4, 1758. Roger Dixon of Fredksbg, Gent., and Lucy, his wife, to William Sim of Fredksbg, baker. £40 curr. One lot opp. house and lot where Saml. Hildrup lives. Wm. Williams, James Hume, Addison Day. July 4, 1758.

July 6, 1758. Fielding Lewis of Fredksbg, Esqr., and Betty, his wife, to Alexander Kennedy, late of Philadelphia, Penn., mariner. £185 curr. Two lots in town of Fredksbg. Chas. Dick, William Scott, Daniel Sturges. July 5, 1758.

July 4, 1758. Joseph Herndon and Philadelphia, his wife, of Spts. Co., to William Waller of same Co., Gent. £20 curr. Lot No. 3 in Spts. Co., adj. Fredksbg. No witnesses.

July 4, 1758. George x Boswell and Ann x Gatewood of Spts. Co. to Martin True of sd. county. £7 2s. curr. 27 a. in Spts. Co. James Chiles, James Pulliam, Henry True. July 4, 1758.

Augt. 1, 1758. Roger Dixon of Spts. Co., Gent., and Lucy, his wife, to Thomas Blanton of same county, carpenter. £40 curr. A lot near Fredksbg. Thos. Minor, James Hume. Augt. 1, 1758.

May 22, 1758. William Robinson of Spts. Co. to John Robinson of sd. Co. £100 curr. Negroes. Witnesses, Beverley Winslow, Benja. Winslow. Augt. 1, 1758.

Sept. 5, 1758. Joseph Brock of Spts. Co. and Mary Beverley, his wife, to Thomas White of Co. afsd. £57 curr. 400 a. in Spts. Co. Jno. Carter, Jno. Herndon, A. Foster. Sept. 5, 1758.

Sept. 5, 1758. John Herndon of Spts. Co. to Abraham Simpson of Co. afsd. £21 13s. curr. 416 a. in Spts. Co. Witness, Wm. Carr. Sept. 5, 1758.

Augt. 23, 1758. William x Salmon and Mary, his wife, late of Spts. Co. £30 curr. 100 a. in Spts. Co. Robt. Goodloe, Wm. Waller, Ed. Herndon, junr.; Joseph Herndon. Sept. 5, 1758.

Oct. 3, 1758. James Stevens of Culpeper Co. and Alice, his wife, to John Davis of Spts. Co. £40 curr. 400 a. in Spts. Co. Jos. Brock, Ed. Herndon, junr.; Joseph Herndon, John Goodloe. Oct. 3, 1758.

Oct. 3, 1758. Achilles Bowker and Martha, his wife, of Cumberland Co., to Michael Roberson [Robinson] of Spts. Co. 200 a. in Spts. Co., formerly King William, on S. side Mattapony River, and part of a pat. of 400 acres, etc. Witnesses, Joseph Steward, Wm. Miller, Benjamin Martin, Wm. Carr, Peter x Lucas, Thos. Colson. Oct. 3, 1758.

May 9, 1758. John Champe of King Geo. Co., Gent.; Nicholas Battaille of Caroline Co., Gent., and Wm. Woodford of Caroline Co. [son and heir of Col. William Woodford, late of Caroline Co., Decd.], execrs. of the sd. William Woodford, Decd., to Benjamin Grymes of Spts. Co., Gent. Whereas, William Woodford, by his last will and testament, dated June 8, 1755, recorded in Caroline Co., did direct the sale of certain lands, etc., and appointed sd. John Champe, Nicholas Battaille, John Taliaferro, Junr. (since Decd.), and William Woodford, his son, Executors; Under the conditions of the sd. Will the sd. Executors convey to the sd. Grymes, for £400 curr., 6300 a. in St. Geo. Par., Spts. Co., called Nassaponnax Lands, and formerly granted Robt. Taliaferro and Lawrence Smith, Gentlemen, by Pat., March 6, 1666. Witnesses, Catesby Cooke, Jno. Taliaferro, Danl. Payne, Danl. Sanford, Jos. Jones. Octr. 3, 1758.

Oct. 3, 1758. John x Proctor and Sarah, his wife, to Thomas Crutcher of Caroline Co. £21 10s. curr. 200 a. in Spts. Co. Peter Gatewood, Hugh Crutcher, Anthony Foster, junr.; John Proctor, junr.; Thomas Crutcher, junr. Dec. 5, 1758.

May 16, 1758. John Gawith, mariner, Master of the Ship Johnson, belonging to Liverpool, in Gt. Britain, power of atto. to Robert Jackson of Fredksbg, Va., Mercht. Witnesses, Geo. Stalker, James Tutt, Joseph Smith, David Meriwether, John Whitfield. Dec. 5, 1758.

April 6, 1758. John Forman of Spts. Co., leather breeches maker, and Mary, his wife, to Richd. Peacock of Fredksbg., Blacksmith, and his son, Richd. Peacock, junr. £23 13s. Lot No. 7, near the town of Fredksbg, in Spts. Co., formerly belonging to Henry Willis, Gent., Decd., and by his Executors sold to Wm. Russell, now of Culpeper Co., Gent., and Robt. Green, then of Orange Co., Gent., now decd., and purchased of sd. Russell and Robt. Green, son of Robt. Green, Decd., by the sd. Forman, as by Deed, June 5, 1755. Moses Bledsoe, William Ellis, Wm. Lewis. Dec. 5, 1758.

Nov. 7, 1758. Thomas McNeil of St. Geo. Par., Spts. Co., to Thomas Graves, junr., of Par. and Co. afsd. £14 curr. 100 a. in Par. and Co. afsd. Witnesses, John Semple, Wm. Waller, W. Wood. Dec. 5, 1758.

Sept. 25, 1758. Larkin Chew of Spts. Co., Gent., and Mary, his wife, of the first part; Joseph Brock and Robt. Chew, Gentlemen, of the second part; John Smith of King and Queen Co., Gent., and Mary, his wife, of the third part. Larkin Chew and Mary, his wife, to their daughter, the sd. Mary Smith, etc. Deed of Gift. 1042 a. in Spts. Co., part of a pat. granted Harry Beverley, Gent., Decd., Dec. 24, 1723, and by the sd. Beverley devised in his last will and testament to his daughter, the sd. Mary, now the wife of the sd. Larkin Chew. Witnesses, Robt. Goodloe, Jno. Crane, George Stubblefield. Dec. 5, 1758.

Feby. 3, 1759. Joseph Hannis of province of North Carolina, Gent., to Wm. Waller of Spts. Co., Va., Gent. Whereas a decree of the Court of Chancery, April 13, 1758, in a suit pending between Joseph Hannis, Pltf., vs. Wm. Waller and Ann, his wife, and Harry Beverley, Gent., Defds., etc., mentions Slaves and Sale and lease of lands, etc.; also principal of a debt due from Joseph Hannis, Decd. (father of the sd. Joseph, party to these presents), to Robert Beverley, Decd., father to the sd. Harry, a party to these presents, etc., of £181 8s. 4d. Ster. Joseph Hannis, party to these presents, agrees to sell certain slaves to sd. Waller. £501 10s. 6d. Curr., etc., etc. Witnesses, James Mills, Jno. Waller, Wm. Wood. Feby. 6, 1759.

Sept. 14, 1758. Sarah Hicks of Whitehaven, in Cumberland Co., Executrix and Admx. of the late Wm. Hicks, Esqr., of Town and county afsd., po. of atto. to Col. John Carlyle of Alexandria, Fairfax Co., Va., Mercht., to receive from Jeremiah Aderton of Chicamaxen, in province of Maryland, or any other persons, sums, etc. Witnesses, Thos. Benson, Deckar Thompson. Feby. 6, 1759.

George Woodroof of St. Geo. Par., Spts. Co., to Wm. Waller of sd. Co., Gent. £100 curr. Mortgage. Tract of land in Spts. Co., goods, chattels, etc. Dated July 31, 1758. W. Taliaferro, Wm. Wood. Feby. 7, 1759.

Jany. 11, 1759. Wm. Woodroof of Spts. Co. to George Woodroof of same Co. Mortgage. £30 curr. Goods and chattels. Witnesses, Edmund Waller, Jack Waller, Ben. Waller, junr., Jno. Waller. Feby. 7, 1759.

Bond of George Woodroof of Spts. Co. to Wm. Waller of same Co., Gent. £200 curr. As the sd. Waller has become security to Wm. Spiller of King William Co. for the sd. Woodroof and Wm. Woodroof, etc. Dated Feby. 5, 1759. Test, Wm. Wood. Recd. Feby. 7, 1759.

Feby. 7, 1759. Rice Curtis of Spts. Co., Gent., to Benjamin Grymes of same Co., Gent. £200 curr. 400 a. in St. Geo. Par., Spts. Co. Rice Curtis, junr., Joseph Herndon, Moses Handley, Jno. Carter. April 3, 1759.

May 1, 1759. Uriah Garton of Spts. Co. and Mary, his wife, to James Pritchett of the Co. afsd. £50 curr. 300 a. in St. Geo. Par., Spts. Co. John Battaley, Wm. Brock, Richard Holt. May 1, 1759.

May 1, 1759. James x Davis of Spts. Co. and Mary, his wife, to Mossom Poe of County afsd. £30 curr. 100 a. in Spts. Co. No witnesses. May 1, 1759.

May 1, 1759. Richard Tutt of Spts. Co. to Jacob Clayton of afsd. Co. £120 curr. 240 a. in St. Geo. Par., Spts. Co. Erasmus Wrs. Allen, Robt. Dudley, Ed. Herndon, junr. May 1, 1759.

April 30, 1759. William Bledsoe of Spts. Co. to his son, Joseph Bledsoe. Deed of Gift. Negro. Witnesses, Joseph Brock, Moses Bledsoe, William x Lampton. May 1, 1759.

April 30, 1759. William Bledsoe of St. Geo. Par., Spts. Co., to his son, Moses Bledsoe. Deed of Gift. Negroes. Witnesses, Joseph Brock, Joseph Bledsoe, William x Lampton. May 1, 1759.

Jany. 8, 1759. James Collins of North Carolina, eldest son and heir at law of Joseph Collins, late of Spts. Co., Decd., to Thomas Collins. £20 curr. Interest in landed estate of the sd. Joseph Collins, Decd. Witnesses, Wm. Collins, John x Collins, Ann x Collins. May 1, 1759.

April 30, 1759. Thomas Cooke of St. Geo. Par., Spts. Co., to Thomas Page of Par. and Co. afsd., and daughter Sarah Page. 100 a. in St. Geo. Par., Spts. Co. Wm. Collins, John x Collins, Thomas Collins. May 1, 1759 Recd.

Jany. 19, 1759. John Robinson, Humphrey Hill, Philip Rootes, Thomas Reade Rootes and John Rootes of King and Queen Co., Gentlemen, Executors of the last will and testament of Philip Rootes, late of the sd. County, Gentl., Decd., to Charles Julian of Fredksbg., Tavernkeeper. Whereas, sd. Philip Rootes, Decd., by his will Dated Augt. 13, 1756, directed his three lots in town of Fredksbg. sold for payment of debts, and legacies by the sd. will, etc. The sd. Executors for the sum of £98 curr., convey Lots 31 and 38 in town of Fredksbg. to sd. Julian, etc. Witnesses, Fielding Lewis, Daniel Fitzhugh, Henry Heath, Thomas Colson, junr., Roger Dixon. May 1, 1759.

Novr. 7, 1758. Charles Dick of Fredksbg., Mercht., an executor and devisee in trust named in the last will and testament of Archibald McPherson, Gent., Decd., to Henry Heath of Fredksbg., Doctor of Physick. £200 curr. Lot No. 20 in Fredksbg. Witnesses, Richard Brooke, Charles Yates, Lawn. Taliaferro. May 1, 1759.

May 1, 1759. Erasmus Withers Allen and Sarah, his wife, of St. Geo. Par., Spts. Co., to Edward Coleman of Par. and Co. afsd. £106 curr. 300 a. in Spts. Co. Joseph Allen, Thos. Collins. May 1, 1759.

April 16, 1759. Rice Curtis of Spts. Co., Gent., to Larkin Chew of same Co., Gent. £5 8s. and 47 a. of land; 59 a. in Spts. Co. Joseph Herndon, Robert Chew, Joseph Brock, Robert Goodloe. May 1, 1759.

Augt. 15, 1758. Anthony Bacon of City of London in Gt. Britain, Mercht., to Benjamin Grymes of Spts. Co. Whereas, by an agreement, Jany. 9, 1756, sd. Bacon and Grymes agreed to be jointly concerned in consignments of Tobacco from Va. to London, the sd. Bacon and Grymes dissolve partnership, etc. Witnesses, Fielding Lewis, Edward Carter, Joseph Jones. June 4, 1759.

Octr. 14, 1758. Thomas Waller of St. John's Par., King Wm. Co., Gent., and Elizabeth, his wife, to Isaac Bradburn of St. Geo. Par., Spts. Co. £5 curr. 25 a. in St. Geo. Par., Spts. Co. Witnesses, John Waller, James x. Samms, Samuel x Brown. June 4, 1759.

March 21, 1759. Benjamin Waller of Williamsburg, James City Co., Esqr., and Martha, his wife, to John Coleman of Spts. Co. £258 12s. 6d. curr. 1034½ a. in Spts. Co. B. Grymes, Fielding Lewis, James Hunter, Wm. Waller, Z. Lewis. June 4, 1759.

March 9, 1759. Anthony Bacon and Gilbert Franklyn of the City of London, Merchts. and partners, po. of atto. to Fielding Lewis of Fredksbg., Spts. Co., Va., Mercht. Witnesses, J. Mercer, Jas. Mercer. June 4, 1759.

June 16, 1759. John Clayton, Junr., of St. John's Par., King Wm. Co., to William Gholston of St. Geo. Par., Spts. Co. £110 curr. 250 a., partly in Spts. Co. and Orange Co. W. Robinson, Ed. Herndon, junr., John Robinson, Edward Collins. Augt. 6, 1759.

May 18, 1759. James Moore of Spts. Co. and Mary, his wife, to Samuel Dyer of Co. afsd. £15 curr. 133 a. in Spts. Co. Joseph Brock, Robert Chew, William Simson. Oct. 1, 1759.

Septr. 3, 1759. Henry Lyne, of King and Queen Co., Gent., and Lucy, his wife, to William Smith of Spts. Co., Gent. £215 curr. 1075 a. in Spts. Co. William Harris, Robt. Harris, Miles Kanty. Octr. 1, 1759.

Octr. 1, 1759. George Nelson, Esqr., Alderman of London, in Gt. Britain, and Mary, his wife; Latham Arnold and John Maynard of London, Merchts., to Thomas Coleman of Spts. Co., Va. Whereas, Humphrey Bell, late of Clapham, in Surry County, and of Old Swanlane, in the City of London, Mercht., by his last will and testament dated Feby. 12, 1757, recd. in Prerogative Court of Archb. of Canterbury, and thereby did leave his property in Va. to sd. Nelson, Arnold and Maynard, in trust for purposes stated in the sd. will; and whereas, by Deeds dated April 19, 1757, recd. in King Wm. Co., the sd. Bell did convey to sd. Arnold and Maynard, his lands and plantations, etc., in King Wm., King and Queen, Caroline and

Spts. Counties, Va., in trust to sell, convey, etc., sd. Bell was seized and possessed of a tract of 1395 a.· in Spts. Co. which Humphrey Hill, Gent. (as agent), did sell to the sd. Thomas Coleman for £299 curr.; sd. Nelson, Arnold and Maynard, now by this deed convey the sd. estate to sd. Coleman. No witnesses. Oct. 1, 1759.

Oct. 1, 1759. George Nelson, Esqr., Alderman of London, and Mary, his wife, Latham Arnold and John Maynard of London, Gt. Britain, Merchts., to Daniel Trigg of Spts. Co., Va. Whereas, etc. [as in above deed]; etc., sd. Bell was possessed of a tract of 500 a. in Spts. Co. which Humphrey Hill, Gent., [as agent] did sell to Daniel Trigg for £80; sd. Nelson, Arnold and Maynard, now by this deed, convey the sd. Estate to the sd. Trigg. No witnesses. Octr. 1, 1759.

Octr. 1, 1759. George Nelson, Esqr., Alderman of London, and Mary, his wife, Latham Arnold and John Maynard of London, Gt. Britain, Merchts., to Robert Coleman of Spts. Co., Va. Whereas, etc. [as in above deed] sd. Bell was possessed of a tract of 2680 a. in Spts. Co. called Iron Pan, which Humphrey Hill, Gent. [as agent] did sell to sd. Robert Coleman, for £550; sd. Nelson, Arnold and Maynard, now by this deed convey the sd. Estate to sd. Coleman. No witnesses. Oct. 1, 1759.

Oct. 1, 1759. George Nelson, Esqr., Alderman of London, and Mary, his wife; Latham Arnold and John Maynard of London, Gt. Britain, Merchts., to Thomas McNeil of Spts. Co., Va. Whereas, etc. [as in preceding deeds] sd. Bell was possessed of a tract of 141 a. in Spts. Co. which Humphrey Hill, Gent. [as agent] did sell to Thomas McNeill for £42 curr.; sd. Nelson, Arnold and Maynard, now by this deed convey the sd. Estate to sd. McNeill. No witnesses. Oct. 1, 1759.

Richard Brooke of Spts. Co. to Francis Taliaferro of sd. Co. Bond. £400 curr. Dated, Jany. 15, 1757. Witnesses, John Catlett, M. Battaley, Lawrence Taliaferro.

Lawrence Taliaferro of Spts. Co. to Francis Taliaferro of sd. Co. Bond. £400 curr. Dated Jany. 15, 1757. Witnesses, M. Battaley, Richard Brooke, John Catlett.

Sept. 1, 1759. Abraham Simpson of Spts. Co. and Ann, his wife, to James Cuningham of same Co. £12 12s. curr. 150 a. in Spts. Co. John Battaley, John Herndon, Joseph Brock, Robt. Richards, Thomas Blanton, William Smith. Octr. 1, 1759.

Nov. 3, 1759. John Beazley of Caroline Co., Husbandman, to his son, Charles Beazley of Spts. Co. Deed of Gift. 100 a. in Spts. Co. Witnesses, John Sutton, Margaret Sutton, Gedion Coghill. Nov. 5, 1759.

Oct. 2, 1759. George Nelson and Mary, his wife, Latham Arnold and John Maynard of London, to John Roan of Essex Co. Whereas, Humphrey Bell of London, Mercht., by will dated Feby. 14, 1757, appointed sd. Nelson, Arnold and Maynard, his executors, and divided his whole estate thereby to his executors in trust and the residue to the sd. Mary Nelson, his daughter. Sd. Bell, by Deed April 19, 1757, conveyed the whole of his Va. estates to sd. Arnold and Maynard; the sd. Nelson, Arnold and Maynard taking upon themselves the Executorship of the sd. will, did by po. of atto. executed before the Lord Mayor of London, July 19, 1758, and recd. in King Wm. Co., Va., impower Humphrey Hill, of King and Queen Co., Va., Gent., to sell and dispose of the whole of the estates in Va.; sd. Hill for the sum of £600 curr. sold the tract of 1075 a. (admitting a claim of Thos. Reeves of Spts. Co. to 19 a.) to the sd. John Roan. The sd. Nelson, Arnold and Maynard, by this deed convey the sd. land to the sd. Roan, etc. No witnesses. Oct. 2, 1759.

Nov. 5, 1759. Robert Coleman and Elizabeth, his wife, of Spts. Co., to Richard Coleman of sd. Co. £107 15s. curr. 552 a. in Spts. Co., St. Geo. Par. Witnesses, Robt. Goodloe, Henry Pendleton, Benjamin Tompkins. Nov. 5, 1759.

Nov. 5, 1759. Robert Coleman and Elizabeth, his wife, of Spts. Co. to John Coleman of same county. £164 curr. 470 a. in St. Geo. Par., Spts. Co. Robert Goodloe, Henry Pendleton, Benjamin Tompkins. Nov. 5, 1759.

Oct. 30, 1759. Robt. Coleman of Spts. Co. and Elizabeth, his wife, to Thomas Dillard of same Co. £62 10s. curr. 250 a. in Spts. Co. J. Lewis, Isaac Bradburn, Fras. x Watts. Nov. 5, 1759.

Nov. 5, 1759. Chilion White and Millicent, his wife, of King and Queen Co. to John Corthorn of St. Geo. Par., Spts. Co. £50 curr. 120 a. in Spts. Co. purchased by sd. White of Nathaniel Allen and Eliza., his wife. Witness, Edward Collins. Nov. 5, 1759.

Nov. 5, 1759. John Gale of Spts. Co. and Sarah, his wife, to Henry Gatewood of same Co. £20 curr. 112 a. in Spts. Co. Peter Gatewood, John Sanders, Thomas Crutcher, junr. Nov. 5, 1759.

Octr. 2, 1759. Zachary Lewis, Wiliam Robinson, Richard Tutt, William Waller, Robert Jackson, Fielding Lewis, Rice Curtis, Joseph Brock, Richard Brooke, Roger Dixon, Charles Lewis, and John Carter, Gentlemen, the Present Vestrymen of St. Geo. Par., Spts. Co., to Erasmus Withers Allen of Par. and Co. afsd. 499 a., part of the Glebe land. Witnesses Philip Vincent Vass, Edwd. Herndon, Joseph Herndon. Nov. 5, 1759.

Oct. 2, 1759. Zachary Lewis, William Robinson, Richard Tutt, William Waller, Robt. Jackson, Fielding Lewis, Rice Curtis, Joseph Brock, Richard Brooke, Roger Dixon, Charles Lewis and John Carter, Gentlemen, Vestrymen of St. Geo. Par., Spts. Co., to Abraham Estes of same Par. and Co. £23 6s. curr. 78 a., part of the Glebe land. Witnesses, Philip Vincent Vass, Edwd. Herndon, Joseph Herndon. Nov. 5, 1759.

Nov. 5, 1759. John x Payne, junr., and Mary, his wife; Bloomfield x Long and Mary, his wife, to Abraham Estes. £25 curr. 59¼ a. in Spts. Co. Wm. Waller, Wm. Wood, Jno. Bev. Roy, J. Waller, John Waller, junr. Nov. 5, 1759.

June 14, 1759. Benjamin Hubbard of Caroline Co., Gent., and Elizabeth, his wife, to Richard Brooke of Spts. Co., Gent. £40 curr. Lot No. 53 in town of Fredksbg.; also Lot No. 6 adj. the town of Fredksbg. Thomas Lendrum, Z. Lewis, John Semple. Dec. 3, 1759.

Nov. 6, 1759. Thomas Coleman of Spts. Co. and Sarah, his wife, to John Payn of sd. Co. £135 curr. 500 a. in Spts. Co. Henry Pendleton, John Coleman, John Brammer, Robert Coleman. Dec. 3, 1759.

Dec. 3, 1759. Thomas Coleman of Spts. Co. and Sarah, his wife, to Isaac Arnold of King George Co. £60 curr. 500 a. in Spts. Co. No witnesses. Dec. 3, 1759.

Nov. 30, 1759. William Oliver of St. Geo. Par., Spts. Co., to his children, William Edmund Oliver, John Oliver, Turner Oliver and Ann Oliver. Deed of Gift. Goods and Chattels. Witness, John Battaley. Dec. 3, 1759.

July 11, 1759. John Robinson, Humphrey Hill, Philip Rootes and Thomas Reade Rootes of King and Queen Co., Gentlemen, executors of the last will and testament of Philip Rootes, late of the sd. County, Gentl., Decd., to Charles Colson of Fredksbg., Tavernkeeper. Whereas, sd. Philip Rootes, Gentl., Decd., by his last will and testament, dated Augt. 13, 1756, and recd. in King and Queen Co., did thereby direct the sale of his three lots in the town of Fredksbg., and did thereby appoint the sd. Robinson, Hill, Philip Rootes and Thomas Reade Rootes, Execrs., and also his son, John Rootes, when he should come of age, etc. These sd. Execrs. for the sum of £145 curr. convey lot No. 29 in Fredksbg. to the sd. Colson. Witnesses, James Hunter, John Stewart, Reuben Thornton. Feby. 4, 1760.

Feby. 4, 1760. Edward Herndon of Spts. Co. to John Herndon of Co. afsd. £30 curr. 264 a. in St. Geo. Par., Spts. Co. Joseph Brock, William Miller, Joseph Herndon. Feby. 5, 1760.

Oct. 12, 1759. Anthony Foster of Spts. Co. to his son, Anthony Foster, junr., of sd. Co. Deed of Gift. 787 a. in Spts. Co. Withers Conway, William Wiglesworth, John Sanders, John Foster. Feby. 5, 1760.

July 12, 1759. George Boswell to Richard Blanton. Deed of Lease. 160 a. in Spts. Co. "sd. Richard Blanton and Joanha, his wife, and James Blanton, his son," etc. 55 shill. yearly. Witnesses, Benja. Martain, junr., Benjamin Martain, Henry Martain. Feby. 5, 1760.

Dec. 4, 1759. William Wiglesworth of St. Geo. Par., Spts. Co., and Mary, the wife of James Wiglesworth of the same Co., to John Pulliam of Par. and Co. afsd. £57 curr. 200 a. in Par. and Co. afsd. A. Foster, Wm. Miller, Edward Herndon, William Lewis. May 6, 1760.

Feby. 1, 1760. John Holloday and Elizabeth, his wife, of Spts. Co. to Alexander Spence Head of same Co. £100 curr. 419 a. in Spts. Co. Robt. Chew, Thos. Megee, Joseph Brock, William Smith, A. Foster, Wm. Bartlett, junr., John Herndon. May 6, 1760.

March 5, 1760. Joseph Brock of Spts. Co. and Mary Beverley, his wife, to Samuel Dyer of Co. afsd. £20 8s. curr. 510 a. in Spts. Co. John Waller, Wm. Wood, William Hutcherson. May 6, 1760.

May 5, 1760. Thomas x Page of Spts. Co. and Sarah, his wife, to Samuel Dyer of Spts. Co. £7 curr. 100 a. in Spts. Co. May 6, 1760.

Nov. 21, 1759. William Bledsoe and Elizabeth, his wife, of the first part; Moses Bledsoe of Spts. Co., of the second part; and Joseph Bledsoe (son of sd. Wm. Bledsoe and Elizabeth, his wife) of the third part. Wm. and Elizabeth Bledsoe, deed of gift, to their son, Joseph Bledsoe. 100 a. in St. Geo. Par., Spts. Co. Witnesses, Joseph Brock, James Cunningham, Abraham Simpson, William Lampton, George Gibson. May 6, 1760.

Feby. 13, 1760. Achilles Bowker of Cumberland Co., Gent., and Martha, his wife, to William Cammack of Spts. Co. £200 curr. 400 a. in St. Geo. Par., Spts. Co. Francis Cammack, Wm. Bartlett, junr.; George Cammack, Ralph Bowker. May 6, 1760.

Feby. 26, 1760. Zachary Garton and Elijah Garton and Frances, his wife, to Ephraim Knight. £36 curr. 165 a. in Spts. Co. Uriah Garton, John Smith, John Knight, Uriah Knight, Edwd. Herndon, Henry Carter, A. Foster, Harry Bartlett. May 6, 1760.

May 6, 1760. Daniel Trigg and Mary, his wife, of Spts. Co., to Joseph Hewel of Co. afsd. £26 curr. 150 a. in Spts. Co. No witnesses. May 6, 1760.

April 5, 1760. Phillip x Ballard of Orange Co. and Ann, his wife, to William May of Spts. Co. £9 7s. 6d. curr. 100 a. in Spts. Co. John Penn, Alexr. Spence Head, Peter Gatewood. May 6, 1760.

April 7, 1760. John Waller of Spts. Co., planter, to Henry Johnson of same Co., carpenter. £120 curr. 400 a. in Spts. Co. Z. Lewis, Edwd. Herndon, Benja. Holloday. June 2, 1760.

June 2, 1759. John Gale of Spts. Co. and Sarah, his wife, to John Detherage of Spts. Co. £25 curr. 330 a. in Spts. Co. William Gatewood, George Perry, William Chiles. June 2, 1760.

June 2, 1760. Taliaferro Crag of Spts. Co. and Mary, his wife, to their son, Lewis Crag. Deed of Gift. 276 a. in Spts. Co. No witnesses. June 2, 1760.

June 2, 1760. Taliaferro Crag of Spts. Co. and Mary, his wife, to their son, John Crag. Deed of Gift. 87 a. in Spts. Co. No witnesses. June 2, 1760.

May 5, 1760. Charles Beazley, Spts. Co., and Susanna, his wife, to Charles Curtis of Co. afsd. £35 curr. 100 a. Z. Lewis, Joseph Brock, Edwd. Herndon, Jam. Redd. June 2, 1760.

Dec. 13, 1759. Thomas x Allen and Sarah, his wife, of Spts. Co., to Robert Sp. Coleman of Essex Co., Southfarnham Par. £13 7s. 9d. curr. 47 a. in Spts. Co. Witnesses, Bevy. Winslow, Benjamin Winslow, Richd. Coleman, Robt. Eastham, junr. June 2, 1760.

Nov. 26, 1759. John Coleman and Nice, his wife, of Spts. Co., to Robert Goodloe. £87 curr. 250 a. in Spts. Co., St. Geo. Par. Thomas McNeill, Robert Coleman, Richard Coleman. June 2, 1760.

June 2, 1760. Robert Baylor and Molly, his wife; Gregory Baylor and Mary, his wife, of King and Queen Co., to Henry Chiles of Spts. Co. £150 curr. 1100 a. in St. Geo. Par., Spts. Co. No witnesses. June 2, 1760.

Augt. 1, 1760. George Woodroof of Spts. Co. and Jane, his wife, to John Lewis of same Co. £43 curr. 107½ a. in Spts. Co. Z. Lewis, junr., John Waller, Chas. Lewis, Benjamin Lewis. Augt. 4, 1760.

Augt. 1, 1760. Thomas x Hill of Spts. Co., planter, and Barsheba, his wife, to John Lewis of same Co., Attorney at Law. £38 5s. curr. 124 a. in Spts. Co. Z. Lewis, junr., Chas. Lewis, Benjamin Lewis, John Waller. Augt. 4, 1760.

Jany. 25, 1760. Thomas x Graves of Spts. Co. and Ann, his wife, to John Lewis of same Co., Attorney-at-Law. £35 curr. 200 a. in Spts. Co. Z. Lewis, junr., Charles Lewis, Benja. Lewis. Augt. 4, 1760.

June 9, 1760. Alexander Wright of Fredksbg., Mercht., to James Hunter and George Frazier of Fredksbg., Merchts. ⅔ interest in Lots 23 and 24 in Fredksbg. Anthony Strother, Richard Holt, William Knox, William Strachen. Augt. 4, 1760.

June 4, 1760. Humphrey Hill of King and Queen Co., Gent., as well for himself as for George Nelson, Esqr., Latham Arnold and Jno. Maynard, Execrs. of the last will and testament of Humphrey Bell, late of London, Mercht., Decd., to Alexander Wright of Fredksbg., Mercht. £300 curr. Lots Nos. 23 and 24 in town of Fredksbg. Witnesses, Archd. Hunter, Hugh Lenox, Chas. Dick, John Semple, Roger Dixon, John Miller, James Mills, Wm. Knox, George Frazer, William Strachan, Edward Foster. Augt. 4, 1760.

Dec. 3, 1759. Edward x Cason of St. Geo. Par., Spts. Co., planter, and Joanna, his wife, to John Benger and Bettey, his wife, of Par. and Co. afsd. £150 curr. 231 a. in St. Geo. Par., Spts. Co. Edwd. Herndon, Joseph Brock, Joseph Herndon. Augt. 4, 1760.

June 23, 1760. Henry Darnell of Spts. Co. to Dudley Gatewood of same Co. £9 curr. 50 a. in Spts. Co. John Penn, John Holloday, Jas. Frasher, John Holloday, junr. Augt. 4, 1760.

Feby. 4, 1760. Mary James of Spts. Co. to Peter Marye of the sd. County. £180 curr. Lot No. 18 in town of Fredksbg. Witnesses, John Semple, Henry Foote, Wm. Murray. Augt. 5, 1760.

Augt. 6, 1750. John Waller of Spts. Co., son and Devisee of Wm. Waller, late of the sd. Co., Gent., Decd., to Zachary Lewis of same Co., Gent. 10 shill. curr. 185 a. in Spts. Co., granted John Waller, Gent., Decd., by pat. Feby. 21, 1720, and by him devised to his son, William Waller, decd., and by sd. Wm. Waller, Decd., devised to his son, sd. John Waller, party to these presents, etc. No witnesses. Augt. 5, 1760.

May 30, 1760. Charles Dick of Fredksbg., Mercht., and Mary, his wife, to Charles Julian of Fredksbg. £150 curr. 150 a. in St. Geo. Par., Spts. Co. J. Sutherland, Alexander Cunison, Daniel Sturges. Augt. 5, 1760.

April 26, 1760. Mary x Butler of Fredksbg. to Thomas Butler and Thomas Willicome. Deed of Gift. Goods and Chattels, etc. John Battaley, Andr. x Frazer, Susanna x Frazer. Sept. 1, 1760.

Sept. 1, 1760. William Robinson and John Robinson and Lucy, wife of the sd. John Robinson, of St. Geo. Par., Spts. Co., to Richard Coleman of Par. and Co. afsd. £44 4s. curr. 110½ a. in St. Geo. Par., Spts. Co. No witnesses. Sept. 1, 1760.

Sept. 1, 1760. William Robinson and John Robinson and Lucy, wife of the sd. John Robinson, of St. Geo. Par., Spts. Co., to Beverley Winslow of Par. and Co. afsd. £44 4s. curr. 110½ a. on E. side. No witnesses. Sept. 1, 1760.

May 31, 1760. James Cave of St. Thomas Par., Orange Co., to John Faulconer of St. Geo. Par., Spts. Co. £20 curr. 200 a. in St. Geo. Par., Spts.

Co. Witnesses, Tolefor Craig, John Craig, Lewis Craig, Philm. Hawkins, Antho. Golson. Sept. 1, 1760.

May 2, 1758. Gawin Corbin of Westmoreland Co., Esqr., and Hannah, his wife, to Thomas Breedlove of Spts. Co. £25 16s. 6d. curr. 369 a. in Spts. Co. A. Foster, Jno. Herndon, Joseph Brock. Sept. 1, 1760.

Sept. 1, 1760. Thomas x Breedlove of Orange Co. and Sarah, his wife, to James Pritchett of Spts. Co. £25 16s. 6d. curr. 369 a. in Spts. Co. Wm. Miller, A. Foster, Edwd. Herndon. Sept. 1, 1760.

Nov. 3, 1760. Francis Meriwether of Spts. Co. and Mary, his wife, to James Crawford of same Co. £28 curr. 69 a. in Spts. Co. Samuel Ragland, Wm. McGehee, William Davis. Nov. 3, 1760.

Nov. 3, 1760. James Shackleford of St. Geo. Par., Spts. Co., and Alice, his wife, to John Crawford of same county. £25 curr. 100 a. in Spts. Co. Wm. Brock, Antho. Gholston, Ephraim Musick. Nov. 3, 1760.

April 5, 1756. Phillip x Ballard of Orange Co. and Ann, his wife, to John Penn of Spts. Co. £10 curr. 200 a. in Spts. Co. Peter Gatewood, Alexr. Spence Head, John Tureman. Nov. 3, 1760.

Sept. 22, 1760. Thomas Moore of King William Co., Gent., x Joanna, his wife, to John Graves of Spts. Co. £90 curr. 338 a. in Spts. Co. Wm. Webb, Wm. x Davis, Jos. Graves. Nov. 3, 1760.

Nov. 3, 1760. Alexander Spence Head of St. Geo. Par., Spts. Co., and Sarah, his wife, to James Rousey of Par. and Co. afsd. £18 curr. 160 a. in St. Geo. Par., Spts. Co. Joseph Steward, Michael Robinson, W. Bartlett, junr. Nov. 3, 1760.

Octr. 6, 1760. Bushrod Fauntleroy and Elizabeth, his wife, of St. Stephen's Par., Northumberland Co., to Larkin Chew and John Smith of St. Geo. Par., Spts. Co. £250 curr. 700 a. in Spts. Co. Witnesses, George Stubblefield, W. Robinson, James Frasher, James Harris, Ralph Smith, William White, James Chapman. Nov. 3, 1760.

Oct. 21, 1760. John Robinson of King and Queen Co., Esqr., and William Robinson of Spts. Co., Gent., to Henry Carter of Spts. Co. £25 curr. 52 a. in St. Geo. Par., Spts. Co. Lark. Chew, Edwd. Herndon, Jno. Waller. Nov. 3, 1760.

Sept. 5, 1760. Rice Curtis of St. Geo. Par., Spts. Co., Gent., to Jos. Herndon of co. and par. afsd. £50 curr. 250 a. in Spts. Co. Henry Pendleton, Edwd. Herndon, Elizabeth Curtis. Nov. 3, 1760.

Nov. 3, 1760. Anthony Strother of King Geo. Co., Gent., and Mary, his wife, to William Lewis of Fredksbg. £300 curr. Lots No. 35 and 36, in town of Fredksbg. Witnesses, William Smith, William Brock, Edwd. Herndon. Nov. 4, 1760.

Nov. 4, 1760. Abraham Simpson of Spts. Co. and Ann, his wife, to William Page of King and Queen Co. £4 curr. 100 a. in Spts. Co. Decr. 1, 1760.

Decr 1, 1760. William Bledsoe of Spts. Co. to his son, Joseph Bledsoe. Deed of Gift. "Sd. Wm. Bledsoe and Elizabeth, his wife." A Negro Boy. Joseph Brock, Abraham Simpson, Moses Bledsoe. Dec. 1, 1760.

Nov. 29, 1760. Benjamin Arnold, now in the Co. of Spts., to Abel Steers, junr. £30 curr. 100 a., conveyed by Wm. Bell to his dau., Bathsheba, the wife of Benjamin Arnold, by Deed of Gift, Aug. 5, 1746. Henry Pendleton, John Steward, Richard x Steers. Dec. 1, 1760.

Nov. 3, 1760. John Clayton, Junr., of St. John Par., King Wm. Co., and Elizabeth, his wife, to William Gholson of St. Geo. Par., Spts. Co. £25 curr. 150 a., partly in Orange and partly in Spts. Co. Humphrey Hill, John Waller, Robert Baylor, John Hill, John Semple. Dec. 1, 1760.

Nov. 29, 1760. Thomas Moore of King William Co., Gent., and Joanna, his wife, to Bernard Moore of same Co., Gent. Whereas, Augustine Moore of the Co. of King Wm., Gent., Decd., father of the Parties to these presents, did by his will, dated Jany. 6, 1742, devise a part of a tract of land in Spts. Co. to his son, Augustine Moore, Junr., and in case of the death of the sd. Augustine, Junr., without children, then to his sons, Bernard and Thomas Moore, afsd., the sd. Augustine, junr., dying without issue, the sd. Bernard and Thomas entered into possession of the sd. tract. Now, the sd. Thomas Moore for the sum of £360, pd. by the sd. Bernard, does convey to him all that moiety or half part of the Fork Tract devised sd. Thomas by his father, etc., containing 1855½ a. in Spts. Co., etc. Frans. Muneas, William Stanard, Abram Fargeson. Decr. 1, 1760.

Sept. 23, 1760. Betty Seaton, widow, and Augustine Seaton of King William Co., to Edward Cason of Spts. Co. £135 curr. 600 a. on East North East River, in Spts. Co. Witnesses, Wm. Webb, Guy Smith, John Brasfield. Dec. 1, 1760.

Novr. 27, 1760. Bernard Moore of St. John's Par., King William Co., Gent., and Anna Catharina, his wife, to Patrick Belschers of St. Martin's Par., Louisa Co., Gent. £300 curr. 1385 a. in St. Geo. Par., Spts. Co. No witnesses. Dec. 1, 1760.

Decr. 1, 1760. Bernard Moore of Williamsburg, James City Co., and Anna Catharina, his wife, to William Quarles of Caroline Co. £150 curr. 500 a. in Spts. Co. No witnesses. Dec. 1, 1760.

Novr. 11, 1760. Joseph x Allen and Sarah, his wife, of Albemarle Co., to Owen Thomas of Spts. Co. £41 2s. Curr. 400 a. in Spts. Co. Witnesses, Willm. Smith, Elie Grifin, Wm. Wood, Agnes Thomas, Peter Marye. Dec. 2, 1760.

Feby. 2, 1761. Fielding Lewis, Esqr., and Betty, his wife, of Spts. Co., to William Bartlett of co. afsd. £125 curr. 300 a. in Spts. Co., on E. side Chiswells Mine Road. John Leach, William x Darnaby. Feby. 2, 1761.

Feby. 2, 1761. Fielding Lewis, Esqr., of Spts. Co., and Betty, his wife, to Clement Mountague of same county. £125 curr. 300 a. on upper side of Chiswells Mine Road, in Spts. Co. Witnesses, John Leach, William x Darnaby. Feby 2, 1761.

Nov. 3, 1760. John Clayton of Hanover Co. and Elizabeth, his wife, to William Hutcherson of Spts. Co. £65 16s. curr. 329 a. in Spts. Co. Andw. Manner, John Hutcherson. March 2, 1761.

Jany. 7, 1761. William Wood and Ann, his wife, of Spts. Co., to George Hensley, Jr., of same Co. £15 15s. curr. 63 a. in Spts. Co. William Hutcherson, Margaret Hutcherson, Richardson Hensley. March 2, 1761.

April 6, 1761. Richard Coleman and Ann, his wife, of Spts. Co., to John Carter of co. afsd. £50 curr. 320 a. in Spts. Co. No witnesses. April 6, 1761.

Oct. 4, 1760. John Fisher of Cockermouth, in Cumberland Co., Gent.; Joseph Glaister of Whitehaven, in sd. Co., Mercht., and Stanley Leathes of Aylsham, in Norfolk Co., Clerk, execr. of the last will and testament of Thomas Leathes, his late father, Decd. (who was execr. in trust of the last will and testament of John Winder of Cockermouth afsd., Decd., po. of atto. to Isaac Fletcher of Underwood, in Co. Cumberland. By authority of the po. of atto. to Isaac Fletcher, he, the sd. Fletcher, appts. David Briggs of Virginia, Mercht., as attorney, etc. Recd. Feby. 2, 1761.

Novr. 7, 1760. John Page of Caroline Co. and Elizabeth, his wife, to Robert Goodloe of Spts. Co. £45 curr. 100 a. in Caroline and Spts. Counties. Benja. Tompkins, H. Goodloe, Wm. Emerson. April 6, 1761.

Nov. 13, 1760. William Collins, Thomas Collins and Lewis Collins, sons of Joseph Collins, late of Spts. Co., Decd., to John Collins of Spts. Co. £85 curr. All est., right, title or interest held by sd. Wm. Thomas and Lewis Collins in est. of sd. Joseph Collins, Decd., after the death or marriage of his relict, Susanna Collins, etc. Witnesses, Z. Lewis, Zy. Lewis, junr.; John Collins, Waller Lewis, Elijah Garton, George x Perry. April 6, 1761.

Oct. 6, 1760. William x Gholson and Susanna, his wife, of Spts. Co., to Edward Herndon of Co. afsd. £50 curr. 300 a., partly in Spts. Co. and partly in Orange Co. Witnesses, W. Robinson, W. Miller, Edwd. Coleman, Anthony Gholson, Jos. Brock, Willm. Smith, Jos. Herndon, Hugh Lenox, Michael Robinson, Jno. Marshall, Peter x Lucas. April 6, 1761.

April 6, 1761. John x Collins and Ann, his wife, of Spts. Co., to John Mastin of Co. afsd. £75 curr. 275 a. in Spts. Co. Witnesses, Edwd. Herndon, John Carter, H. Goodloe. April 6, 1761.

April 6, 1761. Martin Vaughan of Caroline Co. and Elinor, his wife, to John Bullock of Spts. Co. £35 curr. 233 a. in Spts. Co., part of a tract purchased by Cornelius Vaughan, Decd., of John Foster, and by the sd. Foster conveyed to Cornelius and the sd. Martin Vaughan, sons of Cornelius Vaughan, Decd., as by Deed, June 5, 1750. Edwd. Herndon, John Holloday, Rice Graves. April 6, 1761.

April 6, 1761. Christopher Dicken of Culpeper Co. and Sarah, his wife, to Richard Tyler of Spts. Co. £80 curr. 200 a. in Spts. Co. No witnesses. April 6, 1761.

April 6, 1761. Joseph Hewell of Spts. Co. and Frances, his wife, to Ephraim Beasley of same Co. £35 curr. 150 a. in Spts. Co. No witnesses. April 6, 1761.

April 4, 1761. Anthony x Gholstone of St. Geo. Par., Spts. Co., to Joseph Hawkins, junr., of same Par. and Co. £60 curr. 280 a. in Spts. Co. Witnesses, Lark. Chew, George Stubblefield, Willm. Waller, Benjamin Winslow. April 6, 1761.

Feby. 18, 1761. Thomas Roy of St. Geo. Par., Spts. Co., and Margaret, his wife, to John Gordon of Par. and Co. afsd. £6 10s. curr. 118 a. in

Par. and Co. afsd. Witnesses, Ephraim Musick, Abraham x Darnall. April 6, 1761.

May 9, 1749. Williäm Strother of Culpeper Co. to Kemp Taliaferro of Caroline Co. £20 ster. All right, title, interest or claim which sd. Strother has himself or by right of his wife, Mildred, under the will of Zachary Taliaferro, Decd. Witnesses, John Field, Reuben Long. April 6, 1761.

March 15, 1761. Benjamin Davis of St. Mark's Par., Culp. Co., to Benjamin Martin, Junr., of Spts. Co. £60 curr. 101 a. in St. Geo. Par., Spts. Co. Chs. Linch, John Leavell, James Davis. April 7, 1761.

Jany. 24, 1761. Edmund Waller of Spts. Co. and Mary, his wife, to their daughter, Mary, and William Wiglesworth, her husband. Deed of Gift. 200 a. in Spts. Co. Wm. Woodroof, Alice x Hicks. May 4, 1761.

Dec. 19, 1760. Edmund Waller of St. Geo. Par., Spts. Co., to his son, John Waller, of the same Par. and Co. Deed of Gift. 100 a. in St. Geo. Par., Spts. Co. Wm. Wood, Saml. x Brown, Martha x Brown. May 4, 1761.

May 4, 1761. Richard Blanton and Hannah, his wife, to Henry Martin. £26 5s. curr. 150 a. in Spts. Co. Guy Bell, James Cunningham, John Moore. May 4, 1761.

Augt. 28, 1760. Robt. Coleman and Elizabeth, his wife, of Spts. Co., to Thomas Coleman of same Co. £150 curr. 600 a. in St. Geo. Par., Spts. Co. Witnesses, John Coleman, James Watkins, Niell Coleman. May 4, 1761.

May 3, 1761. Rice Curtis, junr., of Spts. Co., to Rice Curtis, Gent., of the same Co. Whereas, Rice Curtis was seized of a certain tract of land containing 865 a., which was conveyed to him by Joseph Brock, Gent., Decd., as by Deeds, Octr. 30, 1735, being so seized the sd. Curtis, about 20 yrs. ago, did make a deed conveying the sd. land to his two only sons by his second wife, the afsd. Rice Curtis, junr., and Giles Curtis (since decd. intestate and leaving no issue), then infants of very tender years. The sd. Rice Curtis, however, remained in possession of the sd. land, and soon after making the conveyance to his two sd. sons, did cancel and destroy the same. Whereas, the sd. Curtis, junr., having lately made claim to the sd. land, as heir of his decd. brother, Giles Curtis, and in his own right. As differences and disputes seem to be arising, sd. Curtis deeds to sd. Curtis, junr., 324 a., in consideration whereof the sd. Curtis, junr., promises deed of release on the afsd. 865 a., etc., etc. Witnesses, Henry Pendleton, James Chapman, Mary Ann Mountague, John Chapman, Charles Walden. May 4, 1761.

May —, 1761. Jackson x Allan of Frederick Co. and Betty, his wife, to Samuel Dyer of Spts. Co. £44 curr. 400 a. in Spts. Co. No witnesses. May 4, 1761.

March 16, 1761. Joseph Brock of Spts. Co. and Mary Beverley, his wife, to Thomas White of same Co. £20 curr. 200 a. in Spts. Co. Roger Lipscomb, Abraham x Darnel, John White. May 4, 1761.

Feby. 23, 1761. Thomas Poole of Spts. Co. to Robert Coleman of afsd. Co. £147 curr. Mortgage. Negroes. Witnesses, Wm. Wood, B. Johnston. May 4, 1761.

May 4, 1761. Robert Coleman and Elizabeth, his wife, of Spts. Co., to Thomas Poole of same Co. £140 curr. 560 a. No witnesses. May 4, 1761.

Oct. 21, 1760. Bernard Moore of Williamsburg to Joseph Hawkins of Spts. Co. £90 curr. 310 a. in Spts. Co., in N. fork of the North Anna River. Witnesses, Alexr. Wright, Erasms. Allen, Larkin Chew, J. Waller, Edwd. Herndon. May 4, 1761.

June 1, 1761. William Bartlett of Spts. Co. to his son, William Bartlett. Deed of Gift. A negro woman. Edward Herndon, John Crane. May 4, 1761.

June 1, 1761. William Robinson of Spts. Co. to his son, Harry Robinson, of sd. Co. Deed of Gift. Four negro slaves. No witnesses. June 1, 1761.

Nov. 21, 1760. Robert Sp. Coleman and Sarah, his wife, of Southfarnham Par., Essex Co., to Richard Coleman of St. Geo. Par., Spts. Co. £300 curr. 200 a. in St. Geo. Par., Spts. Co., on Plentiful Run; also 87 a. on Plentiful Run, in St. Geo. Par.; also 47 a. in St. Geo. Par., Spts. Co. Archibald Ritchie, Andrew Crawford, Robinson Dangerfield. June 1, 1761.

June 1, 1761. Richard Coleman and Ann, his wife, of St. Geo. Par., Spts. Co., to James Coleman of Essex Co. £30 curr. Parcel of land sd. Richard purchased of Richd. Couzens, as by Deeds, Novr. 5, 1754, in Spts. Co., on Pigeon Run. No witnesses. June 1, 1761.

July 29, 1760. Joseph Temple and Mary, his wife, of St. Stephen's Par., King and Queen Co., to Robert Baylor and John Semple of Par. and Co. afsd. £80 curr. 400 a. in St. Geo. Par., Spts. Co., part of a tract granted Joseph Temple of King William Co., Gent., Decd., and by him devised to the sd. Joseph Temple, his son, etc. Witnesses, Lark. Chew, John Smith, Rd. Tunstall, Humphrey Hill, Baylor Walker. June 1, 1761.

April 1, 1761. Thomas Wiatt of St. Geo. Par., Spts. Co., and Sukey, his wife, to Nathaniel Gordon of Par. and Co. afsd. £50 curr. 109 a. in St. Geo. Par., Spts. Co. Saml. Pannill, Robt. Coleman. June 1, 1761.

April 2, 1761. Daniel x Musick of St. Geo. Par., Spts. Co., and Elizabeth, his wife, to Thomas Wiatt of Spts. Co., St. Geo. Par. £10 10s. curr. 61½ a. in St. Geo. Par., Spts. Co. Jas. Chiles, John Pulliam. June 1, 1761.

June 1, 1761 Fielding Lewis of Fredksbg, Esqr., and Bettey, his wife, to Lewis Willis of same town, Gent. £20 curr. Lot 121 in extension of the town of Fredksbg. No witnesses. June 2, 1761.

June 1, 1761. Fielding Lewis of Fredksbg, Esqr., and Betty, his wife, to Charles Yates of same town, Mercht. £80 curr. Lot 121 in extension of the town of Fredksbg. No witnesses. June 2, 1761.

June 2, 1761. Fielding Lewis of Fredksbg, Esqr., and Bettey, his wife, to Robert Duncanson of town, Mercht. £40 curr. Lots 133 and 134 in extension of the town of Fredksbg. No witnesses. June 2, 1761.

June 2, 1761. Fielding Lewis of Fredksbg, Esqr., and Bettey, his wife, to Charles Dick of same town, Mercht. £40 curr. Lots 135 and 136 in the extension of the town of Fredksbg. No witnesses. June 2, 1761.

June 2, 1761. Fielding Lewis of Fredksbg, Esqr., and Bettey, his wife, to James Allan of same town, joiner. £20 curr. Lot 124 in extension of the town of Fredksbg. No witnesses. June 2, 1761.

June 2, 1761. Fielding Lewis of Fredksbg, Esqr., and Bettey, his wife, to George Washington of Fairfax Co., Esqr. £40 curr. Lots 111 and 113 in extension of the town of Fredksbg. No witnesses. June 2, 1761.

May 14, 1761. Benjamin Smith, Miles Brenton, Thomas Middleton and Samuel Brailsford of Charlestown, Province of So. Carolina, po. of atto. to John Champe and James Hunter of Virginia. Witnesses, William Lowe, Thos. Etherington. July 7, 1761.

May —, 1761. Samuel Wragg, surviving co-partner of Joseph Wragg, Junr., of the Province of So. Carolina, po. of atto. to James Hunter of Fredksbg, Va. Witnesses, Thos. Etherington, John Wragg. July 1, 1761.

June 10, 1761. Roger x Gains of Spts. Co. and Martha, his wife, to James Rallings of same Co. £45 curr. 100 a. in Spts. Co., devised sd. Roger Gains and Martha, his wife, by the last will and testament of James Rallings, Decd., and part of a greater tract held by the sd. Jmes Rallings, Decd., and devised to his other children, etc. Witnesses, Wm. Garrett, Jas. Chiles, James Pulliam, Edwd. Herndon. July 6, 1761.

July 6, 1761. Thomas Brooks of Caroline Co. and Rachel, his wife, to John Battaley of Spts. Co. £65 curr. Two tracts of land, one containing 175 a., and the other 25 a. No witnesses. July 6, 1761.

Augt. 3, 1761. Warner Lewis of Gloucester Co., Esqr., and Eleanor, his wife, to Charles Washington of Spts. Co., Gent. £80 curr. Lots 87 and 88, in extension of the town of Fredksbg. No witnesses. Augt. 3, 1761.

Augt. 2, 1761. Warner Lewis of Gloucester Co., Esqr., and Eleanor, his wife, to James Davis of Spts. Co. £41 14s. curr. 139 a. in Spts. Co. No witnesses. Augt. 3, 1761.

Augt. 3, 1761. Wm. x Hutcherson of Spts. Co. and Ruth, his wife, to Richard Gatewood. £80 curr. 126 a. in Spts. Co., on S. side Glady Run, part of a pat. granted Robt. Coleman of Culpeper Co., Augt. 13, 1744, etc. John Herndon, James Cunningham, Dudley Gatewood. Aug. 3, 1761.

April 11, 1761. James Boswell, Ransom Boswell and William Gatewood and Ann, his wife, to Peter Gatewood of Spts. Co. £24 curr. 81 a. in Spts. Co. Dudley Gatewood, James Gatewood, George Humphries, Uriah Edwards. Augt. 3, 1761.

Augt. 3, 1761. Thomas Coleman of Spts. Co. and Sarah, his wife, to Hugh Lenox & Co., Merchts. £50 curr. 170 a. in St. Geo. Par., Spts. Co., part of a pat. granted John Robinson, Esqr., Nov. 2, 1720, and recovered by sd. Coleman of David Kinkead and John Robinson, Esqr., by petition of non-payment of quitrents, etc. Isaac Bradburn, William Wiglesworth, Richard Coleman, John Carthrae. Augt. 3, 1761.

Augt. 3, 1761. Isaac Bradburn of Spts. Co. and Mary, his wife, to Hugh Lenox & Co., Merchts. £125 curr. 150 a. in St. Geo. Par., Spts. Co. Thomas Coleman, William Wiglesworth, Richard Coleman, John Carthrae. Augt. 3, 1761.

June 12, 1761. Benjamin Hubbard of Caroline Co., Gent., and Elizabeth, his wife, to Richard Brooke of Spts. Co., Gent. £50 curr. Lot 53 in adj. town of Fredksbg. Witnesses, Rob. Jackson, Ths. Lendrum, Jno. Harrison, John Sherley, John Miller, junr. Augt. 3, 1761.

DEED BOOK F

June 6, 1761. Jos. Brock and Edward Herndon, execrs. of the last will and testament of Wm. Waller, late of Spts. Co., Decd., to Benjamin Grymes of Spts. £50 curr. Whereas by his last will and testament, dat. Oct. 4, 1756, the sd. Wm. Waller, Decd., directed the sale of a certain tract of land, and dying Jany. 10, 1760, the sd. Execrs. proceed to sell and convey to sd. Grymes "200 a. in Spts. Co.; whereon the widow Parrish lives." Witnesses, Ch. Robinson, Ludwell Grymes, A. Foster. Augt. 3, 1761.

June 15, 1761. Thomas Moore of King Wm. Co. and Joanna, his wife, to Francis Meriwether of Spts. Co. £1— 10s. 240 a. in Spts. Co., devised by Augustine Moore of King Wm. Co., Decd., to the sd. Thos. Moore. Witnesses (names erased). Augt. 3, 1761.

Septr. 7, 1761. Roger Dixon of Fredksbg, Mercht., to Benjamin Grymes of Fredksbg. £5 curr. Lot 17 in town of Fredksbg. No witnesses. Septr. 7, 1761.

Sept. 7, 1761. Benjamin Grymes of Fredksbg to Roger Dixon of Fredksbg, Mercht. £5 curr. Lot 17 in Fredksbg. No witnesses. Sept. 7, 1761.

June 1, 1761. Wm. Garrett and Elizabeth, his wife, of Spts. Co., to Lewis Day of sd. Co. £50 curr. 300 a. on Pigeon Run, Spts. Co. Witnesses, Wm. Pannell, junr.; Wm. Taylor, Job. Harris. Septr. 7, 1761.

June 1, 1761. Wm. Garrett of Spts. Co. and Eizabeth, his wife, to John Day of Hanover. £250 curr. 1300 a. in Spts. Co. Witnesses, Wm. Garrett, junr.; Wm. Taylor, Lewis Day. Septr. 7, 1761.

Sept. 7, 1761. Wm. Garrett of Spts. Co. and Elizabeth, his wife, to Thomas Lane of same Co. £30 curr. 200 a. in Spts. Co. John Penn, James Sandidge, Stapleton Crutchfield. Sept. 7, 1761.

June 1, 1761. Wm. Garrett and Elizabeth, his wife, of Spts. Co., St. Geo. Par., to Wm. Brooks of St. Martin's Par., Hanover Co. £30 curr. 300 a. in St. Geo. Par., Spts. Co. Wm. Garrett, junr.; Wm. Taylor, Lewis Day. Septr. 7, 1761.

June 1, 1761. Wm. Garrett and Elizabeth, his wife, of Spts. Co., to Alsop Yarbrough of Hanover Co. £135 curr. 600 a. in Spts. Co. Wm. Garrett, junr.; Wm. Taylor, Lewis Day. Septr. 7, 1761.

June 1, 1761. Wm. Garrett and Elizabeth, his wife, of Spts. Co., to John Chandler of St. Martin's Par., Hanover Co. £60 curr. 300 a. in St. Geo. Par., Spts. Co. Wm. Garrett, junr.; Wm. Taylor, Lewis Day. Sept. 7, 1761.

June 1, 1761. Wm. Garrett and Elizabeth, his wife, of Spts. Co., St. Geo. Par., to Job Harris of sd. Co. and Par. £30 curr. 300 a. on Douglasses Run, in Par. and Co. afsd. No witnesses. Sept. 7, 1761.

Septr. 7, 1761. Roger Dixon of Fredksbg, Mercht., and Lucy, his wife, to Alexander Kennedy of Fredksbg, Mariner. £30 curr. ½ a. on Hazel Run. No witnesses. Sept. 7, 1761.

Septr. 7, 1761. Roger Dixon of Fredksbg, Mercht., and Lucy, his wife, to James Hunter of King George Co., Gent. £140 curr. 1 9-10 a. on the river side at Fredksbg; also part of a lot on Main Street, in Fredksbg, adj. Thomas Blanton. No witnesses. Sept. 7, 1761.

Sept. 7, 1761. Roger Dixon and Lucy, his wife, of Fredksbg, to Wm. Houston of sd. town, Sadler. £75 curr. Lots 255 and 265 in Fredksbg. No witnesses. Septr. 7, 1761.

Septr. 7, 1761. Roger Dixon of Fredksbg, Mercht., and Lucy, his wife, to Andrew Frazier of sd. town, Mason. £25 curr. Lot 227 in Fredksbg. No witnesses. Sept. 7, 1761.

Septr. 7, 1761. Joseph x Penn of Spts. Co. and Elizabeth, his wife, to John Penn of sd. Co. £5 curr. Tract of land in Spts. Co. Wm. Garrett, Thomas Lane. Septr. 7, 1761.

Septr. 7, 1761. Thomas Blanton of Fredksbg, Carpenter, and Ann, his wife, to Roger Dixon of sd. town, Mercht. £36 curr. Lot 258 (a part thereof), in additional lots of town of Fredksbg. No witnesses. Septr. 7, 1761.

Sept. 7, 1761. Wm. Waller of Spts. Co. to Beverley Stanard of Co. afsd., Gent. £35 curr. 200 a. in Spts. Co. No witnesses. Septr. 7, 1761.

July 27, 1761. Patterson x Pulliam to John Holloday. £10 curr. 50 a. in Spts. Co. John Penn, James Chiles, Ransom Boswell, Jno. Anderson, Geo. x Anderson. Septr. 7, 1761.

March 7, 1761. Anthony Foster of Spts. Co. and Sarah, his wife, to John Foster, their son. Deed of Gift. 320 a. on Glady Run, in St. Geo. Par., Spts. Co., whereon sd. Anthony Foster lives, part thereof conveyed sd. Foster by Hugh Sanders, as by Deeds, April 14, 1740, the other part thereof conveyed the sd. Foster by John Corbin and Lettice, his wife, as by Deeds, July 20, 1748. Ignatius Tureman, Henry Gatewood, junr.; Charles Tureman. Sept. 7, 1761.

Oct. 1, 1761. Thomas x Cooke and Elizabeth, his wife, of Spts. Co., planters, to John Craig of sd. Co., planter. £10 curr. 60 a. in Spts. Co. John Faulconer, Lewis Craig, George x Criste. Octr. 5, 1761.

Octr. 5, 1761. Roger Dixon and Lucy, his wife, of Fredksbg, to James Swain of sd. town. £40 curr. Lot 245 in town of Fredksbg to sd. James Swain during his natural life, then to his three daughters, Eleanor, Catharine and Elizabeth Swain, etc. Octr. 5, 1761.

July 30, 1760. Harry Gaines of St. David's Par., King Wm. Co., Gent., and Martha, his wife, to James Gatewood of Spts. Co. £27 10s. curr. 200 a. in Spts. Co., bequeathed to Humphrey Bate by the last will and testament of Nathaniel Saunders, late of King and Queen Co., decd., dated August 4, 1731, and confirmed to the sd. Gaines by a decree of the General

Court, etc. Lark. Chew, Beverley Stanard, John Smith, John Semple, Saml. Garlick, Harry Beverley, Robert Gaines. April 5, 1762.

Septr. 8, 1761. James Compton of Soho Square, City of London, Gt. Britain, now in Virginia, Esqr., po. of atto. to Fielding Lewis of Fredcksbg, Esqr. Mentions a tract of 10,000 a. in Culpeper Co., granted sd. Compton by Honble. Thomas, Lord Fairfax, and also that Compton intends leaving the Colony. Witnesses, Cha. Dick, Wm. Scott, John Marshall. Oct. 5, 1761.

Oct. 15, 1761. "Thos. Waller of King Wm. Co. to my grandson, Thomas Waller, son of John Waller, my son." Deed of Gift. A Negro Girl. Jno. Waller, Jno. Farish, James Edwards. June 7, 1762.

Nov. 3, 1761. George x Carter of Caroline Co. and Sarah, his wife, to Philemon Jones of afsd. Co. £50 curr. 129 a. on Robinson River, in Spts. Co. Benja. Tompkins, John Cannon, Joseph Carter. Decr. 7, 1761.

Decr. 7, 1761. John Waggoner of St. Geo. Par., Spts. Co., to Robert Bradley of same Par. and Co. £30 curr. 300 a., remainder of a tract taken up by George Dowdy, etc. Andrew Waggoner, Ann x Waggoner, Sophia Waggoner. Decr. 7, 1761.

Nov. 27, 1761. Rice Curtis of Spts. Co. to his son, Rice Curtis, junr. Deed of Gift. 350 a. in Spts. Co. Jos. Brock, Wm. Carter, Elizabeth Curtis, James Chapman. Decr. 7, 1761.

Nov. 27, 1761. Rice Curtis of Spts. Co., Gent., and Rice Curtis, junr., of Co. afsd., to Wm. Carter, who intermarried with Frances, dau. of the sd. Rice Curtis, etc. Deed of Gift. 157 a. in Spts. Co. Jos. Brock, Rice Curtis, junr.; Elizabeth Curtis, James Chapman. Dec. 7, 1761.

Oct. 26, 1761. Benjamin Waller of Williamsburg, Gent., to John Waller of Spts. Co. £20 curr. 133 a. in St. Geo. Par., Spts. Co. Edwd. Herndon, Roger Dixon, Wm. Brock, Jas. Mercer. Decr. 7, 1761.

Octr. 22. Wm. Croswert (Crosthwart) and Mille, his wife, of Culpeper Co., to Paul Macclarna of St. Geo. Par., Spts. Co. £— curr. 115 a. in St. Geo. Par., Spts. Co. Jon. Jones, Alexr. Wright, Charles Harrison. Decr. 7, 1761.

Decr. 7, 1761. Wm. Robinson and John Robinson and Lucy, wife of sd. John Robinson of St. Geo. Par., Spts. Co., to Philemon Hawkins of sd. Par. and Co. £40 curr. Tract of land in Spts. Co. Geo. Stubblefield, James Tolbert, Jno. Battaley. Decr. 7, 1761.

Decr. 8, 1761. Fielding Lewis of Fredksbg, Esqr., and Bettey, his wife, to John Mitchell, Hugh Lenox and Wm. Scott of same town, Merchts. £120 curr. Lots 68, 77 and 78 in extension of town of Fredksbg. No witnesses. Dec. 8, 1761.

Decr. 8, 1761. Fielding Lewis of Fredksbg, Esqr., and Betty, his wife, to Anthony McKetrick, of same town, Mercht. £80 curr. Lots 91 and 92, in extension of town of Fredksbg. No witnesses. Dec. 8, 1761.

Dec. 8, 1761. Fielding Lewis of Fredksbg, Esqr., and Betty, his wife, to George McCall, of same town, Mercht. £80 curr. Lots 79 and 80, in extension of town of Fredksbg. No witnesses. Dec. 8, 1761.

Decr. 8, 1761. Fielding Lewis of Fredksbg, Esqr., and Betty, his wife, to Margaret Gordon of same town, widow. £80 curr. Lots 81 and 82, in extension of town of Fredksbg. No witnesses. Dec. 8, 1761.

Dec. 8, 1761. Fielding Lewis of Fredksbg, Esqr., and Betty, his wife, to John Smith of Middlesex Co., Esqr. £80 curr. Lots 99, 100, 101 and 102 in extension of town of Fredksbg. No witnesses. Dec. 8, 1761.

Octr. 13, 1761. Fielding Lewis of Spts. Co. and Betty, his wife, to Michael Robinson of sd. Co. £250 curr. Lots 107 and 108 in extension of town of Fredksbg. No witnesses. Dec. 8, 1761.

May 27, 1761. A letter of Benj. Waller, referring to a mortgage referred to in the will of his brother, Colo. Wm. Waller, which was owing the sd. Wm. from their brother, Edmund Waller, etc. Mentions "younger children of the sd. Edmund," etc. Witnesses, John Waller, John Waller, junr. March 1, 1762.

April 4, 1762. John Waggoner and Rachel, his wife, of Spts. Co., to John Pitts of Caroline Co. 300 a. in St. Geo. Par., Spts. Co. No witnesses. April 5, 1762.

Sept. 4, 1761. Henry Heath of Fredksbg, Doctor of Physic, to Revd. James Marye of Spts. Co., Clerk, and Revd. James Marye, junr., of Orange Co., Clerk. In consideration of love and affection for his wife, Susanna, and for the advancement of and provision for his family," and 5 shill. Lot No. 20 in town of Fredksbg, where the sd. Heath now liveth, also two negroes, etc. For the use of sd. Henry Heath during his natural life, then to his wife, Susannah, and at her death to any child or children he, the sd. Henry, has or may have by the sd. Susannah, etc. Witnesses, Peter Marye, Isaac Huly, John Stewart. April 5, 1762.

———, 1762. Wm. Garrett of Spts. Co. and Elizabeth, his wife, to Wm. Pigg of New Kent Co. £140 curr. 350 a. in Spts. Co. Wm. Garrett, junr.; Job Harris, George Pettie. April 5, 1762.

April 5, 1762. Wm. Garrett and Elizabeth, his wife, of Spts. Co., to John Jenkins of Hanover Co. £90 curr. 500 a. in Spts. Co. Wm. Garrett, junr.; Job Harris, George Pettie. April 5, 1762.

April 6, 1762. John Semple of King and Queen Co., surviving partner of Robt. Baylor, Gent., Decd., and the sd. John Semple, late Merchts. and partners, and Elizabeth, his wife, to Wm. Cunningham of town of Falmouth, John Stuart of Fredksbg, and Alexander Cunningham of Falmouth, Merchts. and partners. £250 10s. curr. Tenement and store known by name of New Market and 400 a. in St. Geo. Par., Spts. Co., adjoining. No witnesses. April 6, 1762.

June 26, 1762. John Graves and Susannah, his wife, of Spts. Co., to John Page of same Co. £30 curr. 100 a. in St. Geo. Par., Spts. Co., on branches of N. fork of South River, conveyed to Mark Whealer by Henry Goodloe, Gent. (since decd.), as by Deeds, June 3, 1735, etc. Henry Goodloe, Wm. Marsh, George Goodloe, Benj. Woodroof, W. Hodgson, Robt. Goodloe, George Durrett. Septr. 6, 1762.

Octr. 31, 1761. John x Graves, Senr., and Frances, his wife, of St. Geo. Par., Spts. Co., to John Graves, junr., of St. Martin's Par., Louisa Co. £50 curr. 238 a. in St. Geo. Par., Spts. Co. Fras. Meriwether, Jos. Graves, Wm. x Davis, James Mackgehee. June 7, 1762.

June 2, 1762. John x Graves, Senr., of Spts. Co., and Frances, his wife, to Joseph Graves of same Co. £10 curr. 100 a. in Spts. Co. Wm. Kimbrow, John Graves, junr.; Wm. Wright. June 7, 1762.

Jany. 23, 1762. Wm. x Davis of Culpeper Co. and Sarah, his wife, to Francis Meriwether of Spts. Co. £148 10s. 6d. curr. 114¼ a. in Spts. Co. John Graves, junr.; Jos. Graves, Wm. Mackgehee, junr.; Wm. Mackgehee. June 7, 1762.

Nov. 16, 1761. James Shackleford of Spts. Co. and Alice, his wife, to Richard Shackleford of Spts. Co. £70 curr. 231 a. in Spts. Co. Witnesses, Joseph Herndon, John Waller, Edwd. Herndon, John Waller, junr.; Z. Lewis. June 7, 1762.

June 7, 1762. Joseph Leavell and Sarah, his wife, of St. Geo. Par., Spts. Co., to Wm. Darnaby of same Par. and Co. £20. 100 a. in Spts. Co. Witnesses, Joseph Herndon, Laurence Campbell. June 7, 1762.

Septr. 1, 1762. Thomas Hill, Gent., and Eleanor, his wife, of King Geo. Co., to Stephen Johnson of Essex Co., Carpenter. £110 curr. 400 a. purchased by Paul Micou of Danl. Brown, as by Deeds, July 4, 1727, in Spts. Co. Frans. Robinson, Jeoffery x Marriner, Susannah x Marriner, Francis Stone, Joseph x Right. Septr. 6, 1762.

Jany. 19, 1762. Wm. Waller of Spts. Co., Gent., to Thomas Page and Sarah, his wife, of sd. County. Deed of Lease. 100 a. in Spts. Co. 5 shill. curr. yearly, etc. Jno. Bev. Roy, Richd. Johnston. Septr. 6, 1762.

July 27, 1762. Benjamin Temple of King William Co. to William Davenport of Spts. Co. £42 curr. 84 a. in Spts. Co., on East North East River, granted by pat. to George Woodroof and sold to Joseph Temple of King Wm. Co., and by his last will and testament devised to his son, the sd. Benjamin Temple. Moses Bledsoe, Wm. Lewis, Jas. Lewis. Augt. 2, 1762.

July 2, 1762. Thomas Cook of Spts. Co. to his daughter, Joanna Cook, of Co. afsd. Deed of Gift. 150 a. in Spts. Co. Witnesses, John Read, Wm. Gaines, Thomas Collins. Septr. 6, 1762.

June 7, 1762. Joseph Hewell and Frances, his wife, of Spts. Co., to John Mitchell of same Co. £37 curr. 100 a. in Spts. Co. James Chiles, James Lewis, Joseph Herndon. Sept. 6, 1762.

Septr. 6, 1762. Phillip Penn of Caroline Co. and Martha, his wife, to Thomas May of Spts. Co. £65 curr. 220 a. in St. Geo. Par., Spts. Co. No witnesses. Septr. 6, 1762.

July 15, 1762. Ephraim Beazley of Spts. Co. and Winne, his wife, to John Partlow of Caroline Co. £35 curr. 150 a. in Spts. Co. Wm. Allen, Andrew Waggener, David Partlow, Saml. Partlow. Septr. 6, 1762.

*July 4, 1763. Robert Coleman of Spts. Co. and Elizabeth, his wife, to Thomas Coleman of same Co. £150 curr. 600 a. in St. Geo. Par., Spts. Co., part of a tract purchased by sd. Coleman of Humphrey Hill, Gent., etc. James Pulliam, John Talbert, George Woodruff, John Carthrae. July 4, 1763.

*Note.—Deed Signed, Robt. Coleman, Senr.

July 4, 1763. Francis x Wisdom of Spts. Co. and Sarah, his wife, to Richard Quinn of Culpeper Co. £125 curr. 500 a. in St. Geo. Par., Spts. Co. No witnesses. July 4, 1763.

Feby. 11, 1763. William x Hutchason and Ruth, his wife, of St. Geo. Par., Spts. Co., to their son, John Hutchason, junr. Deed of Gift. 100 a. in St. Geo. Par., Spts. Co. John Tureman, Edwd. Coleman, Edwd. Collins, Wm. Gardner, Henry Coleman, Sarah Coleman. July 4, 1763.

July 4, 1763. Sarah x Foster, widow and relict of Anthony Foster, Decd., to John Foster. £20 curr. 333 a. in Spts. Co., dower of the sd. Sarah, under the will of her late husband, Anthony Foster, Decd., etc. No witnesses. July 4, 1763.

April 10, 1763. John Foster of Spts. Co. to Sarah Foster, widow and relict of Anthony Foster, late of sd. Co., Decd. Deed of lease. 350 a. on West side of Pamunkey River, whereon sd. John Foster now lives, etc., "until Henry Foster, son of sd. John Foster, comes of age," etc. 7s. 6d. yearly. John Battaley, Thomas Crutcher, Gaydon Branham. July 4, 1763.

Nov. 10, 1762. John Holloday of Spts. Co. and Elizabeth, his wife, to Uriah Edwards of Co. afsd. £60 curr. 120 a. in Spts. Co. Joseph Herndon, John Allinder, Phillip Penn, Joseph Holloday. July 5, 1763.

Decr. 23, 1762. Joseph Brock of Spts. Co. and Mary Beverley, his wife, to Abraham Darnal of Co. afsd. £40 curr. 400 a. in St. Geo. Par., Spts. Co. James Pritchett, John Pritchett, Saml. Dodson. July 5, 1763.

Decr. 6, 1762. Thomas x Coates of St. Geo. Par., Spts. Co., and Elizabeth, his wife, to Samuel Warren of same par. and county. £60 curr. 303 a. in Spts. Co. Robt. Goodloe, John Waller, Edwd. Herndon, Joseph Herndon. July 5, 1763.

April 23, 1763. Peter Marye of Fredksbg, Mercht., to Wm. Hall and Edwd. Fletcher of Whitehaven, Gt. Britain, Merchts. and Partners. £350 6s. 7d. curr. Lot No. 10 in Fredksbg, whereon Peter Marye keeps store, etc. Mortgage. Hudson Muse, Francis Irwin, Isaac Heeyslop. (Signed, Chas. Yates, for Hall & Fletcher.) July 4, 1763.

July 4, 1763. Isaac x Arnold and Sarah, his wife, late of King Geo. Co., to Wm. Arnold of St. Geo. Par., Spts. Co. £13 curr. 100 a. in St. Geo. Par., Spts. Co. No witnesses. July 4, 1763.

Nov. 11, 1762. Benjamin Hubbard to Joseph Willoughby of Spts. Co. £18 curr. 196 a. in Spts. Co., granted sd. Hubbard by pat., July 20, 1753, Chs. Robinson, John Penn, B. Johnston, O. Towles, jr.; Jos. Jones, Edwd. Herndon. July 4, 1763.

July 5, 1762. George x Boswell, Ransom Boswell and Wm. Gatewood and Ann, his wife, of Spts. Co., to Richard Blanton of same Co. £60 curr. 154 a. in Spts. Co. Jos. Holloday, junr.; Jno. Gayle, Henry True, Alexr. Spence Head. July 4, 1763.

Augt. 1, 1763. Wm. Johnston of Caroline Co., Gent., to his son, Richard Johnston, of Spts. Co. £500 curr. 618 a. in St. Geo. Par., Spts. Co. No witnesses. Augt. 1, 1763.

July 30, 1763. Rice Curtis of Spts. Co., Gent., to John Carter of same Co., Gent. £200 curr. 594 a. in Spts. Co. Joseph Brock, John Beverley Roy. Augt. 1, 1763.

April 14, 1763. Edmund Waller of St. Geo. Par., Spts. Co., Gent., and Mary, his wife, to their son, John Waller, junr., of Par. and Co. afsd. Deed of gift. 200 a. in Spts. Co. Wm. Wright, James Parish, Robt. Hall, Wm. Ed. Waller. Augt. 1, 1763.

Nov. 1, 1762. Robt. x Beadles of St. Geo. Par., Spts. Co., and Dilley, his wife, to Thomas Wiatt, of par. and co. afsd. £50 curr. 114 a. in St. Geo. Par., Spts. Co. Geo. x Perry, Patterson x Pulliam, Richard x Foreacres, Jos. Willoughby, Lark. Chew, O. Towles, jr.; John Chew. Augt. 1, 1763.

May 9, 1763. Rice Curtis, Senr., of Spts. Co., Gent., to his grandson, John Waller (son of Edmund Waller, his son in law). Deed of Gift. 200 a. in Spts. Co., 47 a. of which the sd. Curtis bought of Larkin Chew, Gent., etc. Witnesses, Jane x Curtis, W. Buckner, Vincent Vass, Joseph Herndon, James Colquhoun, John Benger, Thos. Bartlett. Augt. 1, 1763. Also a deed May 9, 1763, from Rice Curtis of St. Geo. Par., Spts. Co., Gent., to John Waller, junr. Deed of Gift. Negro children, etc. Recd. Augt. 1, 1763.

Augt. 1, 1762. Samuel Rice and Elizabeth, his wife, and Joseph Pollard and Frances, his wife, to Nathaniel Dickinson. £50 curr. 120 a. in Spts. Co. Z. Lewis, John Robinson, John Forman. Augt. 1, 1763.

Augt. 1, 1763. Stephen Johnston of Essex Co. and Phebe, his wife, to James Sams of Spts. Co. £150 curr. 400 a., which sd. Johnston bought of Thomas Hill and Eleanor, his wife, as by Deeds, Septr. 1, 1762. Henry Johnston, Thos. Bartlett, James Cunningham. Augt. 1, 1763.

March 2, 1763. John Waller of St. Geo. Par., Spts. Co., Gent., and Ann, his wife, to John Coleman of same par. and co. £21 curr. 133 a. in St. Geo. Par., Spts. Co. Witnesses, Nicho. Horn, George Goodloe, Will. Waller, Edmund Waller. Augt. 1, 1763.

July 30, 1763. Daniel x Musick of Spts. Co. and Elizabeth, his wife, to John Chiles of same Co. £8 curr. 30 a. in Spts. Co. Richd. Crittenden Webb, Joseph Venable. Augt. 1, 1763.

March 10, 1763. Thomas Crutcher and Sarah, his wife, of Caroline Co., to their son, Thomas Crutcher, junr. Deed of Gift. 225 a. in Spts. Co. John Penn, Hugh Crutcher, Chs. Tureman, Henry Gatewood, junr. Augt. 1, 1763.

—— 5, 1763. Wm. x Hutcherson of Spts. Co. to his son, Wm. Hutcherson, junr. Deed of Gift. 100 a. in Spts. Co. O. Towles, jr.; Edwd. Herndon, Joseph Herndon. Sept. 5, 1763.

Feby. 6, 1763. Wm. x Trusty of St. Geo. Par., Spts. Co., and Elizabeth, his wife, to Daniel Musick of Par. and Co. afsd. £12 curr. 50 a. in St. Geo. Par., Spts. Co. Witnesses, Henry Chiles, John Chiles, Joseph Venable. Augt. 1, 1763.

July 11, 1763. Isaac Fletcher of Underwood, in Par. of Brigham, Co. Cumberland, yeoman, po. of atto., Octr. 4, 1760, to David Briggs of Va., Mercht., mentions firm of Joseph Glaister & Co., mentions one John Fisher, mentions Adms. of Wm. McWilliams, Decd., Agt. for the Company, etc. Before Joseph Dixon, Bailiff and Chief Magistrate of the Borough of Cockermouth. Recd. Oct. 3, 1763.

—— —, 1763. Samuel Street and Lurana, his wife, of St. Geo. Par., Spts. Co., to Lewis Pines of same Par. and Co. £10 curr. 100 a. in St. Geo. Par.,

Spts. Co., adj. lands of John Howerton, John Pitts and Antho. Street. Witnesses, Thos. Standard, Thos. Street, Thos. Brightwell, Caty Street. Septr. 5, 1764.

April 4, 1763. John Waller, Clerk of Spts. Co. Court, to Zachary Lewis of same Co. £9 19s. curr. 35 a. in Spts. Co. Witnesses, John Waller, K. W.; Richd. Shackleford, Z. Lewis, Jr.; Waller Lewis. Sept. 5, 1764.

Feby. 6, 1763. John x Trusty of Spts. Co. to John Chiles of sd. Co. £12 curr. 50 a. in Spts. Co., purchased by sd. Trusty of Robt. Beadles, as by Deeds, March 6, 1749. Henry Chiles, Thomas Wiatt, Ths. White, Joseph Venable. Augt. 1, 1763.

Augt. 1, 1763. John Gayle of Spts. Co. to John Penn of Co. afsd. £5 2s. curr. 17 acres of land. Augt. 1, 1763. No witnesses.

Jany. 5, 1763. Wm. Waller of St. Geo. Par., Spts. Co., Doctor of Physick, to John Waller of same Par. and Co., Gent. In trust. All lands and tenements in Par. and Co. afsd., devised the sd. Wm. and John Waller, parties to these presents, by the last will and testament of their father, Wm. Waller, Gent., Decd.; also several slaves, etc. The rents, hires and issues, etc., from the above to be applied to debts now due and which shall hereafter be due from the sd. Wm. Waller, etc., etc. Witnesses, Jno. Beverley Roy, Geo. Goodloe, Jos. Matthews, Willm. Smith, Cain Acuff. Augt. 1, 1763.

June 23, 1762. John Robinson of Spts. Co. to John Robinson of King and Queen Co., Esqr. £200 curr. 4 negroes. Witnesses, Elijah Morton, Uriah Garton, Wm. Dickinson. Augt. 1, 1763.

May 11, 1763. Edmund Waller of St. Geo. Par., Spts. Co., to Hugh Lenox & Co. £136 1s. 6d. Mortgage. Slaves, goods and chattels. Witnesses, John Carthrae, Thos. Bartlett, Henry Pendleton. Augt. 1, 1763.

Augt. 9, 1763. John Benger of Spts. Co. to Larkin Chew of same Co., Gent. Mortgage. Several slaves. Witnesses, Thos. Powe, George Stubblefield, Richd. Johnston, John Roy. Nov. 8, 1763.

Septr. 5, 1763. Henry Martin, junr., and Elizabeth, his wife, to Thomas Colson. £40 curr. 149 a. in Spts. Co. No witnesses. Septr. 5, 1763.

Augt. 29, 1763. John Waller of St. Geo. Par., Spts. Co., Gent., and Ann, his wife, to George Atkinson of same Par. and Co., Wheelwright. £45 curr. Two lots in town of Fredksbg, joining lots 59 and 56. Witnesses, Edmund Waller, John Waller, Owen Minor. Septr. 5, 1763.

Septr. 5, 1763. James x Samms and Anne, his wife, of Spts. Co., to Wm. Smith of same Co. £60 5s. curr. 120½ a. in St. Geo. Par., Spts. Co. Jos. Brock, Robt. Chew, Thos. Wiatt. Septr. 5, 1763.

Sept 5, 1763. Bettsworth Grasty of Caroline Co. and Elizabeth, his wife, to Mordacai Redd of Spts. Co. £30 curr. 164 a. in Spts. Co. No witnesses. Septr. 5, 1763.

Septr. 5, 1763. James Brown and Elizabeth, his wife, to Mordacai Redd of Spts. Co. £40 curr. 237 a. in Spts. Co. No witnesses. Sept. 5, 1763.

Augt. 4, 1763. Wm. Waller of Spts. Co. to John Waller of same Co., Gent. £500 curr. in hand and £40 curr. annually, during the natural life of the sd. Wm., etc. All lands, tenements, etc., devised the sd. Wm. by the will of his late father, Wm. Waller, Gent., Decd., etc. Witnesses, Wm. Wood, Ann Waller, Owen Minor, John Gardner. Sept. 5, 1763.

Augt. 28, 1763. Philip Vincent Vass of St. Geo. Par., Spts. Co., to his son, John Vass. Deed of Gift. 2 negroes. Witnesses, Edwd. Herndon, John Waller. Septr. 5, 1763.

Septr. 5, 1763. Anthony Foster of Culpeper Co. and Rose, his wife, to John Harrison of Spts. Co. £110 curr. 671 a. in St. Geo. Par., Spts. Co. Jos. Brock, James Cunningham, John Somerville. Sept. 5, 1763.

Sept. 5, 1763. Anthony Foster and Rose, his wife, of Culpeper Co., to John Battaley of Spts. Co. £13 10s. curr. 113 a. in Spts. Co. Jos. Brock, Jas. Cunningham, John Somerville. Sept. 5, 1764.

Nov. 22, 1763. Wm. Hudson of Spts. Co. to Larkin Chew of sd. Co., Gent. Mortgage. £20 curr. 110 a. in Spts. Co. (adj. lands of Capt. Jos. Hawkins, James Jones, Paul McClary, and Robt. Bradley); also goods and chattels, etc. Thos. Powe, John Chew, Joseph Brock. Dec. 5, 1764.

July 5, 1764. John Waller (Clerk) of Co. of Spts. to Larkin Chew, Gent., of same Co. Mortgage of 1200 a. in Spts. Co., whereon sd. Waller lives, and known as "Newport"; devised sd. John by the last will and testament of his late father, Wm. Waller, Gent., Decd., etc.

Feby. 2, 1764. Anthony Strother of Fredksbg, Mercht., and Mary, his wife, to Honble. John Tayloe of Richmond Co., Esqr. £827. 322 a. on Branches of Deep Run, in Fauqueir Co., adj. lands of Robt. Jones, Wm. Brooks and Jno. Ferguson; also several slaves and effects, etc. Witnesses, Chs. Yates, Wm. Templeman, Jos. Jones. Oct. 1, 1764.

Feby. 11, 1764. John Waller, Clerk of the County of Spts., to David Pinn of afsd. Co., Shoemaker. Deed of Lease. 50 a. in Spts. Co. "The sd. David and Averilla, his wife." Quitrents. Richd. Coleman, Edmund Waller, Benja. Waller, jr. Oct. 1, 1764.

Septr. 29, 1764. John Pitts and Ann, his wife, of St. Thomas Par., Orange Co., to Paul McClary of Spts. Co. £10 curr. 100 a. in St. Geo. Par., Spts. Co. Wm. Nelson, Edwd. Collins, John x Collins. Octr. 1, 1764.

Octr. 1, 1764. Bland x Ballard, Senr., of Spts. Co., to his daughter, Ann Ballard, "now called Ann Haydon," etc. Deed of Gift. A negro. Witnesses, G. Bell, Thos. Reeves. Oct. 1, 1764.

Septr. 12, 1764. Thomas x Haydon of Spts. Co. to his son, William Haydon, and his wife, Ann Haydon. Deed of Gift. A negro. Witnesses, Guy Bell, Wm. Nelson. Octr. 1, 1764.

April 20, 1764. Gabriel Penn of Amherst Co. and Sarah, his wife, to John Penn of Spts. Co. £60 curr. 130 a. in Spts. Co. Wm. Ellis, John x Sutton, Jno. Penn, jr.; Jerimh. x Smith, Thos. Penn, Benja. Johnston. Octr. 1, 1764.

Octr. 1, 1764. John Gale and Sarah, his wife, of Spts. Co., to Joseph Tankersley of Caroline Co. £145 curr. 240 a. in Spts. Co. John Penn, Thos. Croutcher, Thos. Minor. Oct. 1, 1764.

Octr. 3, 1763. James Boswell and Sarah, his wife, and Ransom Boswell of Spts. Co., to John Penn of sd. Co. £27 15s. curr. 111 a. (which was left sd. James Boswell by his father.)   Edwd. Herndon, John Chiles, Uriah Edwards. Oct. 3, 1763.

Octr. 3, 1763. James Boswell and Sarah, his wife, of Spts. Co., to Uriah Edwards of Co. afsd. £10 curr. 39 a. in Spts. Co. Edwd. Herndon, Benja. Martin, junr.; Ransome Boswell. Oct. 3, 1763.

Oct. 3, 1763. Ephraim Musick and Isabel, his wife, to Jno. Smith of Spts. Co. £10. 125 a. in Spts. Co. Jos. Brock, John Waller, James Cunningham. Oct. 3, 1763.

Sept. 19, 1763. Joseph Penn of Spts. Co. to John Taylor of Caroline Co., in trust for the purposes hereinafter named. Slaves, lands, stocks, etc. For the sd. Joseph Penn, during his natural life, then to his son, Philip Penn; son Moses Penn; son Thomas Penn; daughter Catharine, wife of Larkin Gatewood; daughter Mary Penn; daughter Frances Penn; wife, Elizabeth Penn; "John, Philip, Moses, Thomas, Catharine, Mary and Frances, children of sd. Joseph." Witnesses, Uriah Edwards, James Chiles, Joseph Holloday, Thomas Green. Octr. 3, 1763.

July 11, 1763. Dickey Swan Edwards of Northumberland Co., Va., to Robert Jackson of Fredksbg, Mercht. £25 curr. Lot 54 in town of Fredksbg. James Buchanan, John Whitfield, Dekar Thompson. Oct. 3, 1763.

Augt. 7, 1763. Abraham x Darnal of Spts. Co. to Larkin Chew of sd. Co. £30 curr. Mortgage. Tract of land in Spts. Co., St. Geo. Par., bought of Jos. Brock, and goods and chattels. Thomas Powe, Henry Stubblefield. March 5, 1764.

March 5, 1764. Jos. Bledsoe of Spts. Co. to Moses Bledsoe of Co. afsd. 40 shill. curr. 1 a. in Spts. Co. Mentions mill dam formerly belonging to "Wm. Bledsoe, father of the parties," etc. Benja. Pendleton, Owen Minor, John Battaley. March 5, 1764.

Decr. 5, 1763. John Robinson of Spts. Co. to Edwd. Herndon of Co. afsd. £4 10s. curr. 9 a. in Spts. Co., in fork of Terrys and Beverleys Run. Jos. Brock, Wm. Wood, Benja. Johnston. March 5, 1764.

Nov. 7, 1763. John Waggener of St. Geo. Par., Spts. Co., and Rachel, his wife, to Ephraim Beazley of same Par. and Co. £60 curr. 122 a. in Spts. Co., purchased by sd. Waggener of Thos. Graves and Eleanor, his wife, as by deeds, April 4, 1758. Thomas Coleman, Andrew Waggener, Robt. Goodloe. Nov. 7, 1763.

Novr. 3, 1763. Wm. Robinson of Spts. Co., Gent., to his son, John Robinson. (Whereas the sd. Wm. is tenant by courtesie of England in a certain tract of land in Spts. Co., containing 1190 a., devised to Agatha, late wife of the sd. Wm. Robinson, by Harry Beverley, Gent., Decd.) Deed of Gift. Rights in above mentioned tract, etc. Witnesses, Jos. Brock, Bevy. Winslow, Richard Coleman. Nov. 8, 1763.

March 2, 1763. Wm. Smither of St. Geo. Par., Spts. Co., to Larkin Chew of same Co. and Par., Gent. £50 curr. Several negroes, devised sd. Smither by his father, Wm. Smither, Decd., of Essex Co., as by his will recd. in Essex Co. Court, etc., "sd. negroes now in possession of his mother, Elizabeth Smither of Essex Co.," etc. Witnesses, Beverley Stanard, Thomas Powe. Nov. 8, 1763.

Nov. 7, 1763. James Townsend of Orange Co. and Patience, his wife, to John Shephard of Spts. Co. £20 curr. 100 a. in Spts. Co., adj. lands of John Champe and Daniel Musick. Witnesses, James Sandidge, Joseph Venable. Nov. 7, 1763.

—— —, 1763. Joseph Venable and Lucy, his wife, to John Davis of Spts. Co. £8 10s. curr. 100 a. in Spts. Co. No witnesses. Nov. 7, 1763.

Nov. 1, 1763. John Waller, Clerk of Spts. Co., to Zachary Lewis of Spts. Co. £61 17s. 6d. curr. 247½ a. in Spts. Co., part of a tract of land devised sd. Waller by his father, Wm. Waller, Decd. Witnesses, Wm. Wood, Zachary Lewis, junr.; Isaac Bradburn. March 5, 1764.

Octr. 1, 1763. Richd. Blanton and Joanna, his wife, of Spts. Co., to Wm. Scott of same Co. £75 curr. 162 a. in Spts. Co. David Anderson, Alexr. Spence Head, Henry True. March 5, 1764.

March 3, 1764. John Waller, Clerk of Spts. Co., to Richd. Coleman of Co. afsd. £3 11s. curr. 29 a. in Spts. Co. Witnesses, Owen Minor, George Shepherd, Seth Cason. March 5, 1764.

Decr. 1, 1763. James Garnett of Essex Co., Gent., to Charles Curtis of Spts. Co. £22 4s. curr. 148 a. in St. Geo. Par., Spts. Co. Wm. Ellis, Isaac Willson, Moses x Wheeler. March 5, 1764.

March 5, 1763. Daniel x Gardner of Spts. Co. and Isabell, his wife, to Thomas Pettit. £30 curr. 200 a. in St. Geo. Par., Spts. Co. No witnesses. March 5, 1764.

Augt. 29, 1763. John Gardner of Louisa Co. and Mary, his wife, to Joseph Allen of Spts. Co. £80 curr. 206 a. in St. Geo. Par., Spts. Co. Witnesses, Benjamin Winslow, John x Byrd, Richard Byrd, Samuel Allen, Hezekiah x Chiles, Robr. Silvey. March 5, 1764.

Novr. 5, 1763. Reuben Straughn of Spts. Co. to Larkin Chew of sd. Co., Gent. £50 curr. Mortgage. Goods and chattels. Witness, Thomas Powe. March 5, 1764.

March 6, 1764. Henry Lewis to son-in-law, Alexander Johnson, "and my daughter, his wife, Mary Johnson," etc. Deed of.Gift. 358 a. in Spts. Co. No witnesses. March 5, 1764.

Feby. 5, 1764. Thomas Ballard Smith of Trinity Par., Louisa Co., to his grandsons, vizt.: Thos. Ballard Wyatt, Francis Wyatt and John Wyatt, sons of John Wyatt of St. Geo. Par., Spts. Co. 330 a. in St. Geo. Par., Spts. Co. Thomas Fox, Thos. Hughes, junr.; Sarah Fox. March 5, 1764.

March 6, 1764. Wm. Johnston of Drysdale Par., Caroline Co., to Benjamin Johnston of St. Geo. Par., Spts. Co., for five shill. and "for the natural love and affection that he, the sd. Wm., hath and beareth unto the sd. Benja." 403 a. in St. Geo. Par., Spts. Co., part of a pat. granted Larkin Chew, Gent., Decd., June 4, 1722, and by the sd. Chew conveyed to Johnathan Clark, as by Deeds, March 13, 1723, for 533 a., 130 a. thereof now in possession of Wm. Wood and George Hensley, etc. Regranted sd. Wm. Johnston by pat. from Govr. Gooch, March 15, 1735. No witnesses. April 3, 1764.

April 2, 1763. Charles Dick of Fredksbg, Mercht., and Mary, his wife, to Charles Yates of same town, Mercht. £40 curr. Lots in Fredksbg, formerly Allanstown, Nos. 5 and 6. No witnesses. April 2, 1764.

April 4, 1764. John Waller of Spts. Co., Gent., and Ann, his wife, to John Battaley of co. afsd., Gent. £100 curr. Lot 1, adj. town of Fredksbg., purchased by Wm. Waller, Gent., Decd., of Fielding Lewis, Gent., etc. Wm. Wood, John Vass. May 8, 1764.

Septr. 6, 1763. Benjamin Leavell of Spts. Co. and Mildred, his wife, to James Redd of same Co. £20 curr. 100 a. in Spts. Co., one-half or mostly of a tract purchased by Edwd. Leavell from Thomas Benson, etc. Witnesses, John Bulock, Thos. x Haydon, Mary x Ballard, Sarah x Haydon. May 7, 1764.

May 7, 1764. James Chiles and Jemima, his wife, of St. Geo. Par., Spts. Co., to Barnabas Williams of Par. and Co. afsd. £15 10s. curr. 168 a. in St. Geo. Par., Spts. Co., having been devised to the sd. Jemima by her father, John Graves, and to be laid off adj. the land of John Graves, son of sd. John Graves, Decd., as by his will dated, March 30, 1747. No witnesses. May 7, 1764.

April 2, 1764. Thomas Colson of Spts. Co. and Frances, his wife, to Clement Mountague of same Co. £35 curr. 70 a. in St. Geo. Par., Spts. Co. Lewis Willis, James Allan, Peter Marye. May 7, 1764.

April 2, 1760. Clement Mountague of Spts. Co. and Ann, his wife, to Thomas Colson of Spts. Co. £92 curr. 85 a. in Spts. Co. Lewis Willis, James Allan, Peter Marye. May 7, 1764.

April 10, 1764. James Carter of Spts. Co. to George Hensley of same Co. Mortgage. Goods and Chattels. Witnesses, Richardson Hensley, Charles Goodman, Barnabas Williams. May 7, 1764.

May 8, 1764. John Waller of Spts. Co., Gent., and Ann, his wife, to George Shepherd of Co. afsd. £60 curr. 141 a. in St. Geo. Par., Spts. Co. John Battaley, Wm. Wood. May 8, 1764.

May 8, 1764. Wm. Johnston of Caroline Co., Gent., to his son, James Johnston. Deed of Gift. 188 a. in St. Geo. Par., Spts. Co.; also 50 a. in same Par. and Co. bounded by lines of Richd. Johnston, John Benger, and others, on W. side Tarkiln Branch, remainder of the tract whereon sd. Wm. Johnston lived, and now divided between his sons, Richard and James Johnston, etc. No witnesses. May 8, 1764.

May 7, 1764. John Bullock and Elizabeth, his wife, of Spts. Co., to Samuel Bullock of same Co. £13 3s. 4d. curr. Tract of land in Spts. Co. No witnesses. May 7, 1764.

March 3, 1764. Thomas x Hill of Spts. Co. and Barsheba, his wife, to John Lewis of same Co. £63 curr. 86 a. in Spts. Co. Witnesses, Robert Goodloe, John Crane, Zachary Lewis, junr.; Chas. Lewis, junr. June 4, 1764.

Jany. 3, 1764. Thomas Moore of King Wm. Co. and Joanna, his wife, to John Carpenter of sd. Co., son and heir of Jonathan Carpenter, late of Spts. Co., Decd. £200 curr. 500 a. in Spts. Co., part of which was devised sd. Moore by his father, Augustine Moore, Decd., the other part purchased by sd. Thomas Moore of George Seaton, etc. Witnesses, Wm. Ball, John Brasfield, Jonathan Carpenter. June 4, 1764.

June 4, 1764. John x Payn and Frances, his wife, of Spts. Co., to Wm. Payn, son of the sd. John Payn, etc. Deed of Gift. 100 a. of land in Spts. Co. Witnesses, Thomas Powe, Henry Stubblefield. June 4, 1764.

June 1, 1764. John x Payn of Spts. Co. and Frances, his wife, to Thomas Coleman of Spts. Co. £13 5s. 7d. curr. 49 a. on N. side Rilay River, in Spts. Co. Edwd. Herndon, Daniel Trigg, Isaac Bradburn, Andrew Waggener. June 4, 1764.

—— —, 1764. John Carpenter, son and heir of Jonathan Carpenter, Late of Spts. Co., Decd., to Wm. Ball of Spts. Co. £200 curr., pd. by Jonathan Carpenter, in his lifetime to Thomas Moore of King Wm. Co., etc., "to sd. Wm. Ball and his heirs by his late wife, Ann," etc. 200 a. in Spts. Co., part of a tract purchased by sd. Jonathan Carpenter, Decd., during his lifetime of sd. Thomas Moore and Joanna, his wife, and by them conveyed to sd. John Carpenter, party to these presents, etc. No witnesses. June 4, 1764.

—— —, 1764. John Carpenter of King Wm. Co. (son and heir of Jonathan Carpenter, late of Spts. Co., Decd.) to Jonathan Carpenter of Spts. Co. £200 curr., paid by sd. Jonathan Carpenter, Decd. during his lifetime to Thomas Moore and Joanna, his wife, etc. 150 a. in Spts. Co., part of a tract purchased by sd. Carpenter, Decd., of sd. Moore and wife, and by them conveyed to sd. John Carpenter, party to these presents, etc. No witnesses. June 4, 1764.

May 7, 1764. Isaac Bradburn of Spts. Co. to Hugh Lenox & Co., Merchts., of same Co. £100 19s. 5d. curr. 75 a., whereon sd. Bradburn now lives, etc. Mortgage. O. Towles, junr.; Edwd. Herndon, James Lewis, John Lewis. June 4, 1764.

June 4, 1764. Anthony Gholson and Mary, his wife, of Spts. Co., to Peter Marye of sd. County. £61 0s. 6d. curr. 200 a. in St. Geo. Par., Spts. Co. George Mitchell, Thos. Walker, James Brown. June 4, 1764.

May 10, 1764. Richard Coleman of Spts. Co. and Ann, his wife, to John Waller of afsd. Co. 5 shill. curr. 29 a. in St. Geo. Par., Spts. Co. Zachy. Lewis, Junr.; Cain Acuff, Barnard x Carter. June 4, 1764.

April 26, 1764. John Waller, Clk., and Ann, his wife, to Wm. Waller of Spts. Co. and John Beverley Roy of Caroline Co. £120 10s. curr. 241 a. in St. Geo. Par., Spts. Co. Richard Johnston, Owen Minor, Barnett x Carter. July 3, 1764.

March 9, 1764. John Kendrick of Spts. Co. to Robert Fleming of Louisa Co. Goods and Chattels. Witnesses, Robert Fleming, junr.; Mary Fleming. July 2, 1764.

Jany. 5, 1764. Patrick Belsches of St. Martin's Par., Louisa Co., Gent., and Judith, his wife, to Charles Cosby of same par. and co., planter. £200 curr. 500 a. in Spts. Co., on Northanna River, part of tract purchased by sd. Belsches of Colo. Bernard Moore. Witnesses, Richmond Terrell, John Jones, Richd. Anderson, jr. July 2, 1764.

April 2, 1764. Thomas Ward of Liverpool, Lancaster Co., Mercht., po. of atto. to James Hunter of Fredksbg, Mercht., and Wm. Quincey of Liverpool afsd., Mariner. Witnesses, John Breakhill, Saml. Davies, Henry Silvester, John Brew, James Richardson, Jas. Benn Rowe. July 2, 1764.

May 4, 1764. Elizabeth x Grant, widow and relict of John Grant, and late widow and relict of Charles Bruce of King Geo. Co. Whereas, Wm. Pannell, Decd. (father of sd. Elizabeth Grant), by his will, recorded in Richmond Co., did devise to the sd. Elizabeth a negro wench and her issue, and the negro now has two living children, which were with other negroes by the will of Chas. Bruce (late husband of sd. Elizabeth Grant) given to be divided amongst his children, which division hath since been made setting apart the sd. negro to Mary Bruce, now Mary James; another negro to Frances Bruce, now Frances Banks; and another negro to Margaret Bruce., sd. Elizabeth Grant "of the natural love and affection I bear unto my well beloved daughters, the sd. Mary James, Frances Banks and Margaret Bruce," etc., confirming the legacies of the negroes from sd. Charles Bruce, etc. Witnesses, Wm. Nelson, James Nelson, junr.; Gerard Banks. July 2, 1764.

July 2, 1764. John x Elson and Mary, his wife, of Spts. Co., to Charles Lewis of Spts. Co. £20 curr. 87½ a. in St. Geo. Par., Spts. Co., purchased of Joseph and George Nix, and adjoining the land of George Moore, William Darnaby, Collo. James Ball and John Callaham. Witnesses, Wm. Darnaby, junr.; James Chiles, John Bullock. July 2, 1764.

Nov. 16, 1763. John Page and Elizabeth, his wife, of Spts. Co., to Wm. Perry of same Co. £30 curr. 100 a. in St. Geo. Par., Spts. Co. Witnesses, Jno. x Johnson, Jno. x Reany, Joanna x Reany, Jno. x Perry, junr.; John x Peary, Jno. Waller, Robt. Coleman, Senr.; John Pottey. July 3, 1764.

July 2, 1764. Abraham x Darnal of Spts. Co. to Abraham Darnal, junr., of Co. afsd. £30 curr. 220 a. in Spts. Co., "immediately after the death of the sd. Abraham Darnal and Elizabeth, his wife, to the sd. Abraham Darnal, junr.," etc. Witnesses, Larkin Chew, Wm. Smith, Jos. Brock. July 3, 1764.

Dec. 9, 1763. Benjamin Temple of King Wm. Co. to John Woolfolk of Spts. Co. £56 curr. 112 a. in Spts. Co. Joel Parrish, Edmund Waller, John Hill, Wm. Davenport. Augt. 6, 1764.

Dec. 7, 1763. Thomas Minor of Spts. Co., from Benjamin Temple of King Wm. Co. £162 10s. 250 a. in Spts. Co., part of a tract purchased by Joseph Temple (father of the sd. Benjamin) of James Taylor, and by his will devised to the sd. Benjamin Temple, etc. Witnesses, Wm. Davenport, John Pulliam, John Woolfolk. Augt. 6, 1764.

Jany. 23, 1764. Wm. x Davis of Culpeper Co. and Sarah, his wife, to Francis Meriwether of Spts. Co. £148 10s. 6d. curr. 114¼ a. in Spts. Co. John Graves, junr.; Jos. Graves, Wm. Mackgehee, junr.; Wm. Mackgeehee. June 7, 176–.

Augt. 6, 1764. Thomas McNeil of King and Queen Co., talior, and Ann, his wife, to John Waller of Spts. Co., Gent. £130 curr. 326 a. of land, 185 a. thereof conveyed to sd. McNeil by John Lee, as by deeds, Augt. 4, 1752, and 140 a. thereof conveyed the sd. McNeil by George Nelson, Esqr., and others, Executors of Humphrey Bell, late of the City of London, Decd. No witnesses. Augt. 6, 1764.

March 15, 1764. Hannah x Gimber of St. Geo. Par., Spts. Co., to Larkin Chew of Par. and Co. afsd. £11 8s. 8d. curr. 150 a. in Par. and Co. afsd., adjoining the lands of James Rawlins, Colo. Thomas Moore, "which sd. land the sd. James Rawlins, Decd., bought of Henry Chiles, Decd., and gave her by her father's last will and testament, bearing date April 9, 1757," etc. Thos. Powe, Martha x Oliver, James Gimber, John Sanders, Henry Stubblefield, Robt. Stubblefield. Augt. 6, 1764.

Jany. 16, 1764. James x Rowsy and Elizabeth, his wife, of Spts. Co., to John Sutton, Senr., of Co. afsd. £12 curr. 160 a. in Spts. Co., part of a pat. granted John Chew, Gent., June 4, 1726, and sold to Henry Martin, junr., and John Colquit, junr., as by Deed, Jany. 31, 1737, and sold to Alexander Spence Head, as by Deeds, Feby. 7, 1744, etc. Witnesses, Thomas Powe, Larkin Chew, Will. Waller, Wm. Smither, John x Smither. Augt. 6, 1764.

March 31, 1764. George x Perry of Spts. Co. to Larkin Chew, Gent., of sd. Co. £10 curr. Mortgage. 53 a., which is pd. for by the sd. Perry to John Gayle of sd. Co., as by sd. Gayle's bond to the sd. Perry, Dec. 4, 1763, for conveyance thereof, etc., and part of a tract whereon sd. Gayle lives, and adj. the lands of John Deathridge, John Penn and Wm. Gatewood; also goods and chattels, etc. Witnesses, Thos. Powe, Jos. Pulliam, James Pulliam. Augt. 6, 1764.

Augt. 7, 1764. Wm. Page of King and Queen Co. and Usiller (Usurla), his wife, to Joseph Brock, junr., of Spts. Co. £10 curr. 100 a. in Spts. Co. Joseph Brock, Mary Beverley Brock, John Harrison, Thomas Crutcher. Septr. 3, 1764.

Augt. 29, 1764. Wm. Garrett of Louisa Co. and Elizabeth, his wife, to John Day of Hanover Co. £100 curr. 452 a. in Spts. Co. Witnesses, George Pottie, Chs. Gordon, Walter Chiles. Septr. 3, 1764.

Septr. 4, 1764. Phebe Julian of Fredksbg to John Herndon of Spts. Co. Deed of lease. 30 a. in Spts. Co., on road from Fredksbg to Germanna, with houses, etc., thereon lately built by Charles Julian, Decd., etc. £5 curr. yearly. Witnesses, Joseph Brock, John Battaley, Alexr. Wright, Larkin Chew. Septr. 4, 1764.

Augt. 10, 1764. Thomas x Haydon to his son in law, Wm. Nelson, and his wife, Elizabeth, dau. of sd. Thos. Haydon. Deed of Gift. A negro girl. Witnesses, Gerard Banks, Benja. Nelson, Joseph Rennolds, Daniel Branham. Septr. 3, 1764.

July 2, 1764. Joseph Bledsoe of Spts. Co. and Elizabeth, his wife, to Abraham Simpson of same Co. £20 curr. 58 a. in Spts. Co. Benja. Johnston, John Harrison, John Herndon, Joseph Brock. Septr. 3, 1764.

Septr. 3, 1764. Roger Dixon and Lucy, his wife, of Fredksbg, to John Thompson of St. Mark's Par., Culpeper Co., Clerk. £28 10s. curr. Lot 275 in town of Fredksbg. No witnesses. Oct. 1, 1764.

Oct. 1, 1764. Roger Dixon of Fredksbg, Mercht., and Lucy, his wife, to Charles Mortimer, Doctor of Physick, and Robt. Fargeson, Gent. £24 curr. Lot No. 202 in town of Fredksbg. No witnesses. Oct. 1, 1764.

Oct. 1, 1764. Roger Dixon of Fredksbg, Mercht., and Lucy, his wife, to Philip Rootes of King and Queen Co., Gent. £87 10s. curr. Lot 187, Lot 211, and Lots 230 and 231 in town of Fredksbg. No witnesses. Oct. 1, 1764.

Octr. 1, 1764. Roger Dixon of Fredksbg, Mercht., and Lucy, his wife, to Wm. Thompson of London, Mariner, Captain of the Ship John and Presley. £25 curr. Lot 251 in town of Fredksbg (opposite Dwelling house and garden of sd. Dixon, etc.). No witnesses. Octr. 1, 1764.

Oct. 1, 1764. Roger Dixon of Fredksbg, Mercht., and Lucy, his wife, to Thomas Walker of sd. town, Watchmaker. £25 curr. Lot 274 in town of Fredksbg, adj. lot of Revd. John Thompson, etc. No witnesses. Octr. 1, 1764.

Octr. 1, 1764. Roger Dixon of Fredksbg, Mercht., and Lucy, his wife, to Oliver Towles, junr., of Spts. Co., attorney-at-law. £25 curr. Lot No. 216 in town of Fredksbg. No witnesses. Octr. 1, 1764.

Octr. 1, 1764. Roger Dixon of Fredksbg, Mercht., and Lucy, his wife, to John Rootes of Gloucester Co., Gent. £21 10s. curr. Lot 212 in town of Fredksbg. No witnesses. Octr. 1, 1764.

Octr. 1, 1764. Roger Dixon and Lucy, his wife, of Fredksbg, to Nicholas Winterton of Borough of Norfolk, Mariner. £22 curr. Lot No. 261 in town of Fredksbg. No witnesses. Octr. 1, 1764.

Octr. 1, 1764. Roger Dixon of Fredksbg, Mercht., and Lucy, his wife, to Colo. William Peachey of Richmond Co. £19 curr. Lot No. 249 in town of Fredksbg. No witnesses. Octr. 1, 1764.

Octr. 1, 1764. Roger Dixon of Fredksbg, Mercht., and Lucy, his wife, to Jacob Wray of Hampton, Elizabeth City Co., Mercht. £25 curr. Lot 225 in town of Fredksbg. No witnesses. Octr. 1, 1764.

Octr. 1, 1764. Roger Dixon of Fredksbg, Mercht., and Lucy, his wife, to David Chevies of Borough of Norfolk, Mercht. £25 curr. Lot No. 243 in town of Fredksbg, adj. the lot on which sd. Dixon store house stands, etc. No witnesses. Oct. 1, 1764.

Septr. 3, 1764. Roger Dixon of Fredksbg, Mercht., and Lucy, his wife, to Dr. Thomas Walker of Albemarle Co. £25 curr. Lot No. 217 in town of Fredksbg. No witnesses. Octr. 1, 1764.

Sept. 3, 1764. Roger Dixon of Fredksbg, Mercht., and Lucy, his wife, to John Dixon of Kingston Par., Gloucester Co., Clerk. £125 curr. Lots Nos. 253, 263, 271 and 235. No witnesses. Octr. 1, 1764.

Septr. 3, 1764. Roger Dixon of Fredksbg, Mercht., and Lucy, his wife, to Capt. Thomas Dixon of City of Bristol, Gt. Britain, Mariner. £25 curr. Lot 234 in town of Fredksbg. No witnesses. Oct. 1, 1764.

Oct. 1, 1764. Roger Dixon of Fredksbg, Mercht., and Lucy, his wife, to John Waller, Clerk of the Co. Court of Spts. £50 curr. Lots Nos. 196 and 198 in town of Fredksbg. No witnesses. Oct. 1, 1764.

Oct. 1, 1764. Roger Dixon of Fredksbg, Mercht., and Lucy, his wife, to Dr. Hugh Mercer and Capt. George Weedon of Fredksbg. £75 curr. Lots Nos. 203, 240 and 250 in town of Fredksbg. No witnesses. Oct. 1, 1764.

Oct. 1, 1764. Roger Dixon of Fredksbg, Mercht., and Lucy, his wife, to Wm. Neale of King Wm. Co., Gent. £25 curr. Lot No. 215 in town of Fredksbg. No witnesses. Oct. 1, 1764.

Nov. 20, 1764. Richard Lewis and Ann, his wife, of King Geo. Co., to Peter Lucas of Spts. Co. £100 curr. Lot No. 76 in town of Fredksbg. John Dolton, Thos. Jennings. Dec. 4, 1764.

Nov. 5, 1764. Wm. Allcock of Caroline Co. to Abram Mitchell of Spts. Co. £40 curr. 400 a., partly in Orange Co. and partly in Spts. Co., part of a tract purchased by Allcock of Allens Estate, etc. Witnesses, Edwd. Herndon, Thomas James, Benjamin Martin, Jno. Battaley. Decr. 3, 1764.

Dec. 3, 1764. John x Payn and Frances, his wife, of Spts. Co., to his son, John Payn. £23. 100 a. in Spts. Co. No witnesses. Decr. 3, 1764.

June 5, 1764. Fielding Lewis of Fredksbg, Esqr., and Betty, his wife, to John Tayloe of Richmond Co., Esqr. Whereas, sd. Lewis, in the year 1760, sold to Anthony Strother of Stafford Co., Gent., two lots, Nos. 67 and 25, in an extension of the town of Fredksbg, the sd. Strother having obtained as yet no legal title to the sd. lots, and desiring to dispose of the same to the sd. Tayloe, sd. Lewis at request and approbation of sd. Strother and the sd. Strother for the sum of £430, the sd. lots are deeded the sd. Tayloe, etc. Witnesses, James Allan, Edmund Taylor, Jos. Jones. Dec. 3, 1764.

Oct. 16, 1764. Richard Corbin, Esqr., to Edwd. Herndon of St. Geo. Par., Spts. Co. £15 curr. 450 a. in St. Geo. Par., Spts. Co. Henry Carter, Henry True, James Frasher. Dec. 3, 1764.

Septr. 6, 1764. Abel x Steers of Spts. Co., planter, to his youngest son, Achilles Steers. Deed of gift. A negro boy. Witnesses, John x Donnaldson, John Wynell Sanders. Feby. 4, 1765.

Septr. 15, 1764. Messrs. Wm. Cunninghame, John Stewart & Co., Merchts., from Richard Johnston of Spts. Co. £103 8s. 6d. curr. Mortgage. Slaves. Witnesses, Colen Troup, John Benger, Alexr. Horsburgh. Feby. 4, 1765.

Octr. 22, 1764. Susannah Winslow of St. Geo. Par., Spts. Co., to her son, Benjamin Winslow. Deed of gift. 595 a. in St. Geo. Par., Spts. Co., given sd. Susannah by her father, Harry Beverley, Decd. Mentions "having formerley given the other and upper half of the sd. land to my son, Beverley Winslow," etc. Witnesses, Wm. Parker, Harry Winslow, James Younge, Hy. Stubblefield. Feby. 4, 1765.

Septr. 6, 1764. John x Sutton and Elizabeth, his wife, of St. Geo. Par., Spts. Co., to Edwd. Straughan of same Par. and Co. £60 curr. 100 a. in St. Geo. Par., Spts. Co., part of a tract purchased by sd. Sutton of Nicho. Copland. Witnesses, Larkin Chew, Thomas Powe, Reuben Straughan. March 4, 1765.

Septr. 22, 1764. Thomas x Haydon of Spts. Co., "for and in consideration of the natural love and affection which I have and doth bear unto Benjamin and Mildred Leavell," etc. Deed of Gift. A Negro Girl. Witnesses, Wm. Nelson, Wm. Haydon. March 4, 1765.

March 4, 1764. John Foster of Spts. Co. and Elizabeth, his wife, to James Frasher of same Co. £200 curr. 323 a. in St. Geo. Par., Spts. Co., whereon the sd. Frasher now lives, and of which Anthony Foster, Late of Spts. Co., died possessed, having first by deed of bargain and sale conveyed the same to his son, the sd. John Foster, party to these presents, etc. No witnesses. March 4, 1765.

Septr. 3, 1764. Roger Dixon of Fredksbg and Lucy, his wife, to Anthony Walke, junr., of Princess Anne Co., Mercht. £12 10s. curr. Lot No. 268 in town of Fredksbg. No witnesses. March 5, 1765.

Septr. 3, 1764. Roger Dixon of Fredksbg and Lucy, his wife, to Wm. Fleet of King and Queen Co., Gent. £25 curr. Lot No. 206 in town of Fredksbg. No witnesses. March 5, 1765.

Septr. 3, 1764. Roger Dixon of Fredksbg and Lucy, his wife, to Wm. Fitzhugh of "Marmion," Stafford Co., Esqr. £25 curr. Lot No. 260 in town of Fredksbg. No witnesses. March 5, 1765.

Septr. 3, 1764. Roger Dixon of Fredksbg and Lucy, his wife, to Jane Neale and John Somerville of sd. town. £25 curr. Lot 244 in town of Fredksbg. No witnesses. March 5, 1765.

March 2, 1765. Ephraim Knight of St. Geo. Par., Spts. Co., to Hugh Lenox & Co., Merchts. £28 18s. 11d. curr. Mortgage. 165 a. in Par. and Co. afsd., purchased by sd. Knight of Zachary and Elijah Garton, etc. Witnesses, Wm. Wood, James Crane, Jos. Herndon. March 5, 1765.

March 4, 1765. Benja. x Martain and Elizabeth, his wife, to Thomas Colson. £40 curr. 149 a. in Spts. Co. Edwd. Herndon, James Crane, Jos. Herndon. March 5, 1765.

Nov. 5, 1763. John Collins of St. Geo. Par., Spts. Co., and Catharine, his wife, to John Wheeler of Par. and Co. afsd. £50 curr. 200 a. in Spts. Co., part of a pat. of 400 a. granted sd. John Collins, Feby. 12, 1742, the sd. John Collins hath given and granted to his sons, Richard and John, 200 a., part thereof, or 100 a. each, etc. Witnesses, Nathan Hawkins, Thos. Ashman, An. Waggener, John Collins, junr. April 1, 1765.

Nov. 22, 1763. John Collins and Catharine, his wife, of Spts. Co., to Thomas Roy of same Co. £12 curr. Tract of land in Spts. Co. James Chiles, David Anderson, Thos. Ashman, Richd. Collins, Nathan Hawkins, Benja. Poe. April 1, 1765.

Nov. 5, 1764. Wm. Robinson of Spts. Co. and Agnes, his wife, to John Robinson of King and Queen Co., Esqr. £208. 228 a. in St. Geo. Par., Spts. Co., and goods and chattels. Mortgage. O. Towles, jr.; Beverley Stanard, Elizabeth Beverley Stanard. April 1, 1765.

Dec. 3, 1764. Samuel Brown of St. Geo. Par., Spts. Co., and Martha, his wife, to James Wigglesworth of same Par. and Co. £12 5s. curr. 24 a. in St. Geo. Par., Spts. Co. April 1, 1765.

Septr. 17, 1764. Wm. McWilliams of Spts. Co. to Jos. Minor of sd. Co. Deed of Lease. Land in Spts. Co. 1000 lbs. tob. yearly. Thos. Minor, Benjamin McWilliams, Owen Minor. April 1, 1765.

Nov. 27, 1764. John Pitts of Spts. Co. and Ann, his wife, to David Darnell of Culpeper Co. £15 curr. 400 a. in Spts. Co., purchased of John Wagner, etc. Witnesses, John x Collins, Abram x Darnall, Senr.; Wm. x Ganes, Abraham x Darnall, junr. April 1, 1765.

Septr. 13, 1764. Jacob x Young of Spts. Co. to James Duncanson of Fredksbg, Mercht. £25 16s. 8d. Goods and Chattels. Witness, Wm. Scott. April 1, 1765.

March 13, 1765. Richard Coleman and Ann, his wife, of St. Geo. Par., Spts. Co., Planters, to James Lindsay of St. Maries Par., Caroline Co. £175 curr. 200 a. in St. Geo. Par., Spts. Co. James Wiglesworth, Robt. Coleman, Senr.; Daniel Lindsay. April 1, 1765.

Jany. 9, 1765. Benjamin x Pipeman and Rebecca, his wife, of Fredksbg, to Charles Yates of same town, Mercht. £27 15s. 5d. Lot in addition of town of Fredksbg, which sd. Pipeman now lives on and which he purchased of Alexr. Cruikshanks and Mary, his wife, etc. Mortgage. Witnesses, Wm. Templeman, Hudson Muse, Francis Irwin. April 1, 1765.

Octr. 1, 1764. Nicholas Jones of Spts. Co. to Hugh Lenox, Scott & Co., of Spts. Co., Merchts. £59 14s. 8d. curr. A Negro and horse. Witnesses, John Marshall, Wm. Gregory. April 2, 1765.

May 7, 1765. John x Dyer of Spts. Co. to Nicholas Hawkins of same Co. £82 curr. 400 a. in Spts. Co. No witnesses. May 6, 1765.

Septr. 24, 1764. Henry True of Spts. Co. to Lenox, Scott & Co., Merchts. £21 5s. 7d. curr. Mortgage. 210 a. in Spts. Co. Edwd. Herndon, Saml. Sparks, Wm. Duerson. May 6, 1765.

April 11, 1765. John Gayle and Sarah, his wife, of King and Queen Co., to Martin True of Albemarle Co. £10 15s. curr. 53 a. in Spts. Co. Larkin Chew, O. Towles, junr.; Thos. Coleman, Henry True, Mathew Gale. May 6, 1765.

Nov. 7, 1764. Edmund Waller of Spts. Co. and Mary, his wife, to their son, Benjamin Waller, of same Co. 191 a. of land in Spts. Co. Jno. Waller, junr.; Wm. Edmund Waller, Wm. Davenport, Jas. Crawford, Wm. x Bruce. May 6, 1765.

May 6, 1765. John Herndon of Spts. Co. to John Foster of same Co. £65 curr. 264 a. in St. Geo. Par., Spts. Co. No witnesses. May 6, 1765.

May 5, 1765. Alexander Hawkins and Mary, his wife, of Culpeper Co., and Benjamin Martin of Spts. Co., to Thomas Blanton "of Co. afsd." £250 curr. 245 a. in Spts. Co. Jno. Carter, Rob. Dudley, Thos. Minor. May 6, 1765.

Nov. 26, 1764. Michael Skinner of Westmoreland Co. and Dinah, his wife, to John Battaley of Spts. Co., Gent. £58 curr. 100 a. in St. Geo. Par., Spts. Co. Wm. Rowley, Richd. Vowles, Burdett Skinner, James Rowlin, Wm. Marders. May 7, 1765.

Augt. 6, 1764. Sharshal Grasty and Ann, his wife, then of Fairfax Co., and George Grasty to Mordacai Redd. £85 curr. 492 a. in St. Geo. Par., Spts. Co. Jno. Battaley, Jos. Brock, Thos. Powe. Augt. 6, 1764.

June 3, 1765. John x Collins of Spts. Co., planter, and Ann, his wife, to John Mitchell, Wm. Scott and Hugh Lenox of Fredksbg, Merchts. £90 curr. 700 a. in branches of Po River, in Spts. Co. Whereas, Joseph Collins, late of Spts. Co., Decd., by his will, dated Augt. 7, 1757, among other things, loaned unto his wife, Susanna Collins, his whole estate, etc., during her widowhood, and after her marriage or death the executors of sd. will were to dispose of the estate and the sd. will directed the money arising from sale of land to be equally divided between his four sons, to wit: James, William, Thomas and Lewis Collins, and whereas sd. James, by deed, —— —, 17—, conveyed unto sd. Thomas his share and the sd. Wm., Thomas and Lewis Collins have since by their deed Nov. 13, 1760, conveyed to the sd. John, party to these presents, the whole land devised as aforesaid by the will afsd., etc. Witnesses, Jos. Jones, John Sanders, Wm. Gregory. June 3, 1765.

June 3, 1765. John x Collins and Ann, his wife, of Spts. Co., to Wm. Gholson. £30 curr. 123 a. in Spts. Co. Hugh Lenox, Wm. Gregory. June 3, 1765.

Octr. 2, 1764. Susannah Winslow of St. Geo. Par., Spts. Co., to her son, Benjamin Winslow. Deed of gift. 595 a. in Spts. Co., remaining and lower half of a tract of land given sd. Susannah by her father, Harry Beverley, Decd. "I having formerly given the other and upper half to my son, Beverley Winslow," etc. Witnesses, Wm. Parker, Harry Winslow, James Young, Hy. Stubblefield. Feby. 4, 1765.

June 3, 1765. Charles Colson of Spts. Co. to James Duncanson of Fredksbg, Mercht. £100 curr. Lot No. 29 in town of Fredksbg. Edwd. Herndon, Jos. Herndon, Thomas Colson. June 3, 1765.

May 31, 1765. John Waller of Spts. Co. and Elizabeth, his wife, to John Carter of Co. afsd., Gent. £90 curr. 200 a. in St. Geo. Par., Spts. Co. Wm. Wood, Jno. Beverley Roy, O. Towles. June 3, 1765.

May 31, 1765. John x Graves of Spts. Co. to his son, Joseph Graves. Deed of Gift. "Sd. Joseph's wife, Franky, daughter of John Coleman, Decd.," etc. 200 a. whereon sd. John now lives; slaves, stocks, etc., etc., sd. tract of land purchased by sd. John of Thomas Gambrill and Ann, his wife, as by deeds, May 24, 1729, etc. "Sd. John Graves and Frances, his wife, during their lives," etc. Witnesses, J. Lewis, Nice Coleman, Wm. Wigglesworth, Samuel Coleman. June 5, 1765.

June 3, 1765. George Sharp and Mary, his wife, of Spts. Co., to Thomas James of Fredksbg. £35 curr. 150 a. in Spts. Co., part of a tract of land devised by George Proctor, Decd., to his daughter, Margaret, who intermarried with Elias Sharp, father of the sd. George Sharp, who is eldest son and heir at law of sd. Elias, who dying intestate, whereby sd. land descended to the sd. George, party to these presents, etc. Witnesses, J. Lewis, Chs. Robinson, Geo. Stubblefield, Francis Taliaferro, John Chew. June 3, 1765.

March 30, 1765. John x Dyer of Spts. Co. to his brother, Samuel Dyer, of same Co. Deed of Gift. 510 a., conveyed by Jos. Brock and wife to Samuel Dyer, Decd., March 5, 1760. Robt. Chew, John Harrison, Daniel Branham, James Cunningham. July 1, 1765.

—— —, 1765. George x Hensley and Sarah, his wife, of Spts. Co., to Roger Dixon of afsd. Co., Mercht. £50 curr. Mortgage. 40 a. in Spts. Co., lately purchased by sd. Hensley of Thos. Morris, and whereon James Carter lately lived, and adj. the land which sd. Dixon lately purchased of sd. Thomas Morris. Witnesses, John Stewart, Colin Troup, Jno. Battaley.

March 9, 1765. George x Hensley of Spts. Co. and Sarah, his wife, to Roger Dixon and Wm. Wood of same Co. £65 curr. Mortgage. 205 a. in Spts. Co., one tract lately purchased by sd. Hensley of James Hutcherson, the other whereon sd. Hensley lives, etc. John Stewart, Colen Troup, Jno. Battaley. July 1, 1765.

June 3, 1765. George Kenner of Caroline Co. and Margaret, his wife, and John Beverley Roy of Spts. Co., and Ann, his wife, to Francis Jerdone of Louisa Co., Mercht. £275 curr. 1194 a. in Spts. Co., which sd. tract is part of a tract devised by the last will and testament of Harry Beverley to be divided among his five daughters, to wit: Margaret, Susannah, Katherine, Judith and Agatha, etc., the sd. 1194 a. was allotted to the sd. Judith (who afterwards intermarried with the Revd. Rodham Kenner, by whom she had issue, the George Kenner, her eldest son and heir at law) and hath since departed this life, without having disposed of the same by will or otherwise, etc. Witnesses, J. Lewis, Jno. Glassell, junr.; James Lewis, Geo. Pottie, Patrick Robb, O. Towles. June 3, 1765.

Feby. 25, 1765. Benja. Johnston of St. Geo. Par., Spts. Co., to Oliver Towles, junr., of same Par. and Co. Consideration of 5 shill., and sd. Towles being a security to indemnify the sd. Towles, the sd. Johnston deeds him as mortgage certain Slaves, goods, debts, etc. "As the sd. Benja. Johnson is now intending a voyage to Gt. Britain," etc. Witnesses, J. Lewis, Richard Johnston, Jas. Johnston. July 1, 1765.

Feby. 25, 1765. Benjamin Johnston of Spts. Co., po. of atto. to Oliver Towles, junr., of Same Co., Gent. "During my absence I intending on a voiage to Great Britain," etc. Witnesses, J. Lewis, Richard Johnston, Jas. Johnston. July 1, 1765.

Decr. 15, 1764. Anthony Strother of King Geo. Co., Gent., to Charles Carter of same Co., Esqr., and Joseph Jones of Spts. Co. Whereas, sd. Carter and Jones became sd. Anthony Strother's security for his faithfully discharging the office of High Sheriff of King George Co., and sd. Strother having failed to settle with the Treasurer of the Colony for public collection for years 1762 and 1763, whereby it is feared sd. Carter and Jones may be in danger of suffering, etc. Whereby sd. Strother deeds as mortgage to sd. Carter and Jones 400 a. of land, whereon sd. Strother lives; also negroes, horses, cattle, etc. Witnesses, John Thornton, George Taylor, Jos. Butler, James Clark, jr.; Mordacai Lanton, John x Kelley, James Mullin. Augt. 5, 1765.

Feby. 14, 1765. Wm. Gale of Whitehaven, in Cumberland Co., Gt. Britain, Mercht., po. of atto. to John Thornton of Fredksbg, Esqr. Witnesses, Andw. Green, Joseph Nicholson, Thomas Hodgson, Isaac Sakeld. Augt. 5, 1765.

June 28, 1765. John Waller, Clerk of the Co. of Spts., Gent., and Ann, his wife, to John Beverley Roy of same Co. £372 15s. curr. Tract of land on which Mrs. Ann Waller now lives, same being conveyed the sd. John Waller by Deed from his brother, Wm. Waller, son of Wm. Waller, Gent., Decd., who did by his will devise the same to the sd. Wm., etc. Witnesses, Richard Johnston, James Wood, John True, J. Lewis, Wm. Prockter, Wm. Waller. Augt. 5, 1765.

Augt. 4, 1764. George x Hensley of Spts. Co. to Roger Dixon. Mortgage. £50. Goods and chattels. Witnesses, Thos. x Perry, John Somerville. Augt. 5, 1765.

Augt. 6, 1765. Harry Ellison of Whitehaven, Mercht., from Bartholomew x West of Spts. Co. Mortgage. £18 10s. 11d. Curr. Goods and chattels. Witnesses, Francis Irwin, Wm. Templeman, Chas. Yates. Augt. 6, 1765.

March 4, 1765. John Waller, Clerk of Spts. Co., and Ann, his wife, of the first part; Larkin Chew of same Co., Gent., of the second part, and Oliver Towles, junr., of the same Co., Atto. at Law, of the third part. Whereas, John Waller, Gent., late of Spts. Co., Decd., being seized of several tracts of land, did by his will, dated Augt. 2, 1753, devise to his son, Wm. Waller, Gent., late of the sd. Co., Decd. (and father to the sd. Jno. Waller, party to these presents), the afsd. tracts of land in fee simple, to wit: 400 a. of land, which sd. Jno. Waller, Decd., patented in his own name, adjoining the lands of Zachary Lewis, and his, the sd. Waller's home plantation (except 19 a. thereof the sd. Waller, Decd., sold Zachary Lewis, etc.); also that part of 1000 a. tract on the S. side Robinson Run, adj. the sd. 400 a. tract, and also 500 a. adj. the lands sd. Jno. Waller, Decd., lived on, and the same two tracts already described the sd. Jno. Waller, Decd., purchased of Capt. Philip Todd, etc. And whereas the sd. Wm. Waller after the death of his father, sd. Jno. Waller, Decd., by virtue of the devise, etc., entered into possession of the sd. lands, sd. Wm. Waller did by his will, dated Octr. 24, 1756, devise to his son, the sd. Jno. Waller, party to these presents, the sd. several tracts of land, etc., etc. Sd. John Waller and Ann, his wife, in consideration of the sum of £233 2s. curr., pd. by sd. Oliver Towles, junr., conveys to the sd. Towles the sd. tracts, and Larkin Chew, Gent., a party to these presents, holding a mortgage on the sd. estate from under the sd. Jno. Waller's hand, releases to sd. Towles, right, title and interest in the sd. Estate, etc. This deed alludes to pat. of Col. Jno. Waller, Decd., Feby. 21, 1720, pat. to Wm. Waller, Decd., April 20, 1726, and pat. to Philip Todd, June 30, 1726, and also a pat, to Robt. Coleman, etc. Witnesses, Robert Chew, Bartho. Yates, jr.; John Battaley. March 4, 1765.

Augt. 3, 1765. Wm. Brooks, Senr., of Spts. Co., to Johnston & Co., of City of Glasgow. £21 curr. Mortgage. 300 a., whereon sd. Brooks lives, etc. Witnesses, John Garrett, Geo. Lumsden, John Brooks. Octr. 7, 1765.

Augt. 17, 1765. Wm. Garrett and Elizabeth, his wife, of Spts. Co., to James Rawley of Hanover Co. £30 curr. 200 a. in St. Geo. Par., Spts. Co. George Pottie, Stephen Tatom, John Garrett, Lewis Day, Thomas Lane. Octr. 7, 1765.

April 2, 1765. Barnabas Williams of Spts. Co. and Hannah, his wife, to John Mitchell, Hugh Lenox and Wm. Scott. Mortgage. £20 curr. Whereas, James Chiles and Jemima, his wife, by deed, May 7, 1764, sold to sd. Barnabas Williams and his heirs, etc., 160 a. in St. Geo. Par. Spts. Co. being the same devised the sd. Jemima, by the will of her father, Jno. Graves, as by his will dated March 30, 1747. Sd. Williams and Hannah, his wife, convey the sd. land to Mitchell, Lenox and Scott, etc. Witnesses, James Allan, Wm. Strachan, Wm. Gregory. Augt. 6, 1765.

Augt. 15, 1765. Joseph Temple of King and Queen Co. to Joel Parrish of Spts. Co. £95 curr. 200 a. in Spts. Co. Joseph Hawkins, junr.; George Woodroof, Nathaniel Parrish. Oct. 7, 1765.

Oct. 4. 1765. Thomas Lane and Ann, his wife, of Spts. Co., to Stephen Tatom of same Co. £26 curr. 150 a. in St. Geo. Par., Spts. Co. John Garrett, George Pottie, James Young. Oct. 7, 1765.

Oct. 7, 1765. John Faulconer and Joyce, his wife, of Spts. Co., planters, to John Craig, of same Co., planter. £12 curr. 100 a. in Co. afsd. and is part of land whereon sd. Faulconer lives, etc. No witnesses. Octr. 7, 1765.

Augt. 19, 1765. Bernard Moore of St. Jno. Par., King Wm. Co., Gent., and Anna Catharine, his wife, to John Clark, of Caroline Co., planter. £304 16s. curr. 508 a. in Spts. Co. Benja. Pendleton, Thomas Fox, Frans. Thornton, Chas. Washington. Oct. 7, 1765.

Octr. 5, 1765. Benjamin Temple of King Wm. Co. to John Lewis of Spts. Co. £50 12s. 6d. curr. 81 a. in Spts. Co. conveyed by Geo. Woodroof and others to Joseph Temple, who by his last will and testament devised it to his son Benjamin Temple, party to these presents, etc. Witnesses, Waller Lewis, Charles Gordon, Benja. Lewis, John Woodfolk, Joel Parrish, John Waller, junr. Octr. 7, 1765.

Octr. 5, 1765. Thomas Waller of King Wm. Co., acting Executor of last will and testament of Thomas Waller, Gent., late of the sd. Co., Decd., to Oliver Towles, Junr., Atto-àt-Law, of Spts. Co. Whereas, Thomas Waller, by his last will and testament, dated Septr. 19, 1764, did among other things devise that part of a tract of land in Spts. Co. (adj. lands that formerly belonged to his brother William Waller, Zachary Lewis and Vincent Vass) to his son John Waller and the remainder to be sold, as by the sd. will of record in King Wm. County, etc. Sd. Thomas Waller, as executor, conveys to sd. Towles, 312 a. in Spts. Co. for £90 10s. 10d. curr. Witnesses, John Waller, K. W.; William Steers, Cain Acuff. Octr. 7, 1765.

Augt. 14, 1765. Richard Johnston of Spts. Co. and Dorothy, his wife, to Mary Dawson, widow and relict of Revd. Musgrave Dawson, decd. Whereas, Revd. Musgrave Dawson by his last will and testament, Dated Feby. 24, 1764, directed his executors to sell all or any part of his estate and to lay out the same in any manner they should think fit for the advantage of his children and the sd. Mary, his wife, and whereas the sd. Dawson departed this life, leaving a very considerable estate in slaves without any lands whereon to work them, and it being thought well that a tract of land be purchased as well for a residence of the sd. Mary Dawson and her surviving child John Dawson as for the occupation of the sd. slaves, and whereas Wm. Johnston, by his deed dated Augt. 1, 1763, conveyed to his son Richard Johnston, party to these presents 618 a. in Spts. Co., the sd. Richard conveys the same to the sd. Mary Dawson, as executrix afsd. for the sum of £450. Witnesses, Joseph Brock, John Bevy. Roy, Alexander Waugh, junr. Oct. 7, 1765.

Septr. 2, 1765. Hugh Lenox and Wm. Scott, Merchts., in Fredksbg., from Abell Steers and Mildred, his wife. £100 1s. curr. Mortgage. 100 a. in Spts. Co. whereon sd. Steers lives and by him purchased of Daniel Brown, also cattle, etc. Witnesses, O. Towles, jr., J. Lewis, John Woodfolk. Octr. 7, 1767.

Octr. 17, 1765. Peter Gatewood and Sarah, his wife, of Culpeper Co., to Uriah Edwards of Spts. Co. £60 curr. 162½ a. of land. John Waller, K. W.; John Penn, Wm. Bartlett. Octr. 7, 1765.

Octr. 7, 1765. Joseph Holloday of Spts. Co. and Elizabeth, his wife, to Benjamin Lewis of sd. County. £20 curr. in hand pd. by Zachary Lewis, Decd., etc. 69 a. on East North East River in Spts. Co. and part of a tract devised sd. Joseph Holloday, by his father John Holloday, etc. No witnesses. No date of record.

Octr. 7, 1765. Benjamin Martin, Senr., of Spts. Co., and Elizabeth, his wife, to Lenox and Scott & Co., Merchts., of Spts. Co. £141 15s. curr. 400 a. in St. Marks Par., Culpeper Co. As by pat. granted Jno. Asher Augt. 25, 1721. Peter Marye, Thos. Colson, Thos. x Hutcherson. Octr. 7, 1765.

May 1, 1765. Edmund Waller of Spts. Co., Gent. and Mary, his wife, of the first part, John Semple, surviving partner of Robt. Baylor, Gent., Decd., of second part, and Robt. Wilkinson of Spts. Co., Blacksmith, of third part. Sd. Edmund Waller and Mary, his wife, for £50 15s. curr. convey to sd. Robt. Wilkinson, 151 a. in Spts. Co., residue of a tract of land whereon sd. Edmund Waller and several of his children now live and in which sd. Edmund remains seized in fee simple of the several parts allotted to each of his children that were entitled by the will or settlement heretofore made thereof by John Waller, Gent., Decd. (father to the sd. Edmund), in his lifetime, etc. And the sd. tract having been mortgaged by indenture Augt. 22, 1764 to the above named John Semple as surviving partner of Robt. Baylor, Gent., Decd., in order to secure payment due from sd. Edmund to sd. Semple, and as by mutual agreement the land was sold, the sd. Semple entering in this conveyance, etc. Witnesses, O. Towles, jr.; Jno. Bevy. Roy, W. Wood. Octr. 7, 1765.

Octr. 7, 1765. Benjamin x Martin, Senr. of St. Geo. Par., Spts. Co. & Elizabeth, his wife, to Lenox, Scott & Co., of sd. County, Merchts. £141 15s. curr. 100 a. in St. Geo. Par., Spts. Co., given the sd. Benjamin Martin by his father, Henry Martin, etc. Mortgage. Witnesses, Peter Marye, Thomas Colson, Thomas x Hutchinson, Septr. 5, 1765.

Augt. 6, 1765. John Mitchell, Hugh Lenox, and Wm. Scott, Merchts., in Fredksbg to John Battaley of Spts. Co., Gent. £40 curr. 1 a. and 11 sqr. yds. No witnesses. Octr. 7, 1765.

Octr. 7, 1765. John Mitchell, Wm. Scott and Hugh Lenox of Fredksbg., Merchts., to John Carthrae of Spts. Co., Mercht. £225 curr. 322 a., the plantation whereon sd. Carthrae now lives, in St. Geo. Par., Spts. Co. No witnesses. Octr. 7, 1765.

Sptr. 2, 1765. Richard Collins of Spts. Co. and Sarah, his wife, to Hugh Lenox & Co., of same county. £50 curr. 100 a. in Spts. Co. No witnesses. Octr. 7, 1765.

Septr. 25, 1765. Benjamin x Martin, Senr., of Spts. Co., to Lenox, Scott & Co., of Fredksbg. Merchts. £141 4s. 6d. Mortgage. Negroes, etc. Witnesses, Edwd. Herndon, Thomas x Perry. Septr. 6, 1768.

Septr. 21, 1765. Joseph Willoughby and Elizabeth, his wife, of Spts. Co., to Charles Robins, of afsd. Co. £12 curr. 96 a. in Spts. Co. Edwd. Herndon, Wm. Mastin, Lewis Craig, James Frasher. Octr. 7, 1765.

March 11, 1750. Charles x Evans, a mulatto, agrees to serve Wm. Taliaferro of Orange Co., Gent., for the term of sd. Taliaferro's natural life, etc. Witnesses, Roger Dixon, Margt. Gordon. Sd. Evans agrees,

Octr. 7, 1765, to serve Wm. Walker of Fredksbg as he served under the above contract, etc. Recd. Octr. 7, 1765.

Octr. 11, 1765. John Waller of Spts. Co. to George Pottie. £500. Mortgage. Negroes. Witnesses, George Stubblefield, John Garrett. April 7, 1766.

Septr. 11, 1765. Wm. Pigg of Spts. Co. to George Pottie of Louisa Co. £63 curr. Mortgage. 400 a. whereon sd. Pigg resides. Witnesses, John Garrett, Wm. Garrett, jr., Harry Garrett. April 7, 1766.

May 3, 1766. Edward x Cason of Spts. Co. to his son, Wm. Cason, of sd. Co. 200 a. in Spts. Co. Deed of Gift. W. Underwood, Henry Johnson, Francis Meriwether. May 5, 1766.

May 1, 1766. Edward x Cason of Spts. Co. to his daughter-in-law, Susannah Cason. Deed of Gift. 200 a. in Spts. Co. Witnesses, W. Underwood, George Stubblefield, John Carthrae, Henry Johnson. May 5, 1766.

Octr. 15, 1765. Henry Ellison, Esqr., of Gt. Britain, from John Penn, Senr., of Spts. Co. £188 16s. 5d. curr. Mortgage. Negroes. Witnesses, Hudson Muse, Francis Irwin, George Penn. June 2, 1766.

May 13, 1766. Wm. Bartlett of Spts. Co. to Joseph Herndon of Co. afsd. £170 curr. 400 a. in St. Geo. Par., Spts. Co., purchased of Fielding Lewis, etc. Witnesses, James Crane, Stapl. Crutchfield, Thos. Bartlett, Edwd. Herndon. June 2, 1766.

Octr. 9, 1765. Hannah x Gimbo of Spts. Co. and Larkin Chew of same Co., Gent., to James Rawlings, Jr., of Co. afsd. £75 curr. 150 a. in Spts. Co. whereon sd. Hannah lives, and devised by the last will and testament of James Rawlings, Senr., Decd., to the sd. Hannah, the then wife of Thomas Gimbo, since Decd. The sd. Chew holding a mortgage on the sd. property releases it in favor of sd. James Rawlings, Junr., etc. Witnesses, Larkin Chew, junr., John Holloday, John Talbert, O. Towles, junr. June 2, 1766.

July 10, 1765. John Waller of Spts. Co. to Joseph Brock of Co. afsd. Mortgage. Slaves. The sd. Brock being the sd. Waller's Security on a bond of £100 payable to Benja. Waller, Esqr. This deed of slaves to indemnify the sd. Brock, etc. Witnesses, Robt. Chew, John Foster. Augt. 4, 1766.

July 7, 1766. David x Jones of Spts. Co. to his son-in-law, Wm. Allsup, and Sarah, his wife, dau. of the sd. David Jones. Deed of Gift. 5 slaves, etc. Witnesses, W. Wood, James Crane. Augt. 4, 1766.

Octr. 23, 1765. Benjamin x Martin of Spts. Co. and Elizabeth, his wife, to George Atkinson of sd. Co. £70 curr. 136 a. in Spts. Co. Joseph Brock, Robert Chew, John Simmons. Augt. 4, 1766.

Octr. 23, 1765. Benjamin x Martin of Spts. Co. and Elizabeth, his wife, to John Simmons of sd. Co. £53 curr. 100½ a. in Spts. Co. Jos. Brock, Robert Chew, George Atkinson. Augt. 4, 1766.

March 4, 1766. John Simmons of Spts. Co. to John Benger of sd. Co. £52 curr. Tract of land in Spts. Co. adj. Robt. Chew, Benja. Martin, Nathan Hawkins and John Waller, on River Po. opposite to where John Waller now lives, which sd. land sd. Simmons purchased of Benja. Martin, as by

Deeds, —— — 1765, etc. Also two negroes, hogs, cattles, etc. Mortgage. Witnesses, Benja. Johnston, Thos. x Hutcherson, Geo. Hutcherson. Augt. 4, 1766.

Augt. 4, 1766. John Benger of Spts. Co., son and heir of Elliott Benger, Esqr., Decd., and Benjamin Johnston of sd. Co. to Gabriel Johnston of sd. Co., son of the sd. Benja. Johnston, etc. Whereas, sd. Benger in right of his father is possessed of a lot of Land in the town of Fredksbg. and whereas sd. Benger did give po. of atto. to sd. Benja. Johnston, as by indenture, Octr. 24, 1764, and the sd. Benger having sold to the sd. Gabriel Johnston, for £15 curr., the sd. lot, the sd. Benger being willing to ratify and confirm the same unto the sd. Gabriel with the consent of the sd. Benja. as under the aforementioned Indenture; witnesseth, the sd. Benger and Johnston convey to the sd. Gabriel Johnston Lot No. 8 in town of Fredksbg. Witnesses, W. Wood, James Crane, J. Lewis. Augt. 4, 1766.

July 4, 1766. John Benger of Spts. Co. to Benjamin Johnston of afsd. Co. £500 curr. Mortgage. 12 negroes, also cattle, etc. Witnesses, W. Wood, James Crane, J. Lewis. Augt. 4, 1766.

Feby. 4, 1766. Benjamin Johnston of Spts. Co. to Wm. Johnston of Caroline Co. Mortgage. To indemnify sd. Wm. who stands security on sd. Benjamin's bond to John Gray of Port Royal, Mercht., in sum of £555 15s. 2d. Curr. Negroes, horses, etc. No Witnesses. Augt. 4, 1766.

June 20, 1766. Abram Mitchell of Orange Co. to Wm. Allcock of Caroline Co. £40 curr. 400 a. on head branches of Mattapony River, partly in Spts. and partly in Orange Counties. Witnesses, Nicholas Ware, Reuben Ware, Reuben Samuell. Augt. 4, 1766.

July 7, 1766. Harry Robinson of Caroline Co. and Elizabeth, his wife, to John Apperson of Caroline Co. £72 10s. Curr. 145 a. in Spts. Co. Jno. Waller, Richard Johnston, W. Underwood, Beverley Stubblefield, Edwd. Herndon. Augt. 4, 1766.

July 7, 1766. Harry Robinson of Caroline Co. to Henry Carter of Spts. Co. £25 curr. 50 a. in Spts. Co. John Waller, Richard Johnston, W. Underwood, Beverley Stubblefield, O. Towles, junr.; Edwd. Herndon, Augt. 4, 1766.

July 7, 1766. Harry Robinson of Caroline Co. & Elizabeth, his wife, to John Wilson of Spts. Co. £107 10s. curr. 215 a. in Spts. Co. John Waller, Richard Johnston, W. Underwood, Bevy, Stubblefield, O. Towles, Edwd. Herndon, Augt. 4, 1766.

Octr. 7, 1765. Roger Dixon of Fredksburg and Lucy, his wife, to Joseph Royle of Williamsburg, Va., Gent. £24 curr. Lot 197 in town of Fredksbg. No witnesses. Augt. 4, 1766.

Octr. 7, 1765. Roger Dixon of Fredksbg. and Lucy, his wife, to Wm. Smith of Hampton, Elizabeth City Co., Mercht. £25 curr. Lot 252 in town of Fredksbg. and opp. the dwelling house of the sd. Dixon, etc. No witnesses. Augt. 4, 1766.

Octr. 7, 1765. Roger Dixon of Fredksbg. and Lucy, his wife, to Maximilian Calvert of Borough of Norfolk in Norfolk Co., Mercht. £110 curr. Lots 210, 224, 218, 220 and 269 in town of Fredksbg. No witnesses. Augt. 4, 1766.

Octr. 8, 1765. Roger Dixon of Fredksbg. and Lucy, his wife, to John Lyne of King and Queen Co. £25 curr. Lot 201 in Fredksbg. No witnesses. Augt. 4, 1766.

Octr. 9, 1765. Roger Dixon of Fredksbg, and Lucy, his wife, to William Williams of Culpeper Co., Gentl. £25 curr. Lot 195 in town of Fredksbg. No witnesses. Augt. 4, 1766.

Octr. 7, 1765. Roger Dixon of Fredksbg. and Lucy, his wife, to Joseph Herndon of Spts. Co. Lot 204 in town of Fredksbg. No witnesses. Augt. 4, 1766.

Oct. 7, 1765. Roger Dixon of Fredksbg. and Lucy, his wife, to Thomas Jemison (or Jameson) of Orange Co. £25 curr. Lot 219 in town of Fredksbg. No witnesses. Augt. 4, 1766.

Octr. 8, 1766. Roger Dixon of Fredksbg. and Lucy, his wife, to James Hunter of King Geo. Co., Mercht. £40 curr. Lot 267 in town of Fredksbg. No witnesses. Augt. 4, 1766.

Octr. 7, 1766. Roger Dixon of Fredksbg. and Lucy, his wife, to Wm. Fitzhugh, junr., of Stafford Co., Esqr. £25 curr. Lot 239 in town of Fredksbg. No witnesses. Augt. 4, 1766.

April 30, 1766. John Waller, Clerk of Spts. Co., to John Roan of Spts. Co. £71 10s. 6d. Curr. Mortgage. 14 negroes. Witnesses, Gabriel Jones, jr., B. Johnston. Augt. 4, 1766.

July 30, 1766. Jane (or Jean) Curtis, single woman, of Orange Co. to Rice Curtis of Orange Co., Gent. £20 curr. 50 a. in St. Geo. Par., Spts. Co., part of the sd. Jane's part of a tract of land given by the sd. Rice Curtis to his three daughters, Elizabeth, Frances and the sd. Jane, as by Deed recd. in Spts. Co. Court, etc. Witnesses, Joseph Herndon, Charles Powell, Thoms. Bartlett. Augt. 5, 1766.

April 8, 1766. John Waller of Spts. Co. to Wm. Wood and John Battaley of Co. afsd. £350 curr. Mortgage. 200 a. in Spts. Co. which sd. Waller purchased of Thos. McNeill; also 7 negroes, Goods and Chattels. Witnesses, Joseph Brock, Larkin Chew, jr., Edwd. Herndon. Augt. 5, 1766.

Augt. 4, 1766. George x Hensley and Sarah, his wife, of Spts. Co. to Roger Dixon of same Co. £55 curr. 40 a. in Spts. Co. purchased by sd. Hensley of one Thos. Morris, as by Deed, Octr. 7, 1763, in General Court Recorded. No witnesses. Augt. 4, 1766.

Septr. 12, 1765. John Waller to John Bevy. Roy and Richard Johnston of Spts. Co. £45 curr. Mortgage. Slaves, hogs, cattles, etc. Witness, George Stubblefield. Augt. 5, 1766.

Augt. 3, 1766. Robert Wilkinson of Spts. Co. and Alce (Alice?) his wife, to James Wiglesworth of Spts. Co. £44 2s. 6d. Curr. 101 a. in Spts. Co. purchased of Edmund Waller, and is part of 151 a., the residue of the tract of land whereon sd. Edmund Waller and several of his children live and in which sd. Edmund has a fee simple right, after the several shares allotted to each of his children that were entitled by the will or settlement heretofore made of the afsd. tract by John Waller, Decd., father of the sd. Edmund Waller, etc. Witnesses, W. Underwood, Joseph Herndon, Henry Pendleton, Jno. Waller, jr. Septr. 1, 1766.

Septr. 1, 1766.   John Schooler of Spts. Co. and Martha, his wife, to their son, Wharton Schooler. 100 a. in Spts. Co. Edwd. Herndon, John Tutt, James Lewis. Septr. 1, 1766.

Septr. 4, 1766.   John x Graves, Senr., of St. Geo. Par., Spts. Co., to his son, John Graves, junr., of Par. and Co. afsd. Deed of Gift. Slaves. Witnesses, O. Towles, jr., Seth Cason, Jonathan Carpenter. Octr. 6, 1766.

June 10, 1766.   John Waller, Clerk of Spts. Co., Gent., to Jno. Mitchell, Hugh Lenox and Wm. Scott, Merchts. and partners, of Fredksbg. Whereas, sd. Scott on behalf of himself and partners became bound, etc., to Thos. Graves of Spts. Co. in sum of £357 3s. 5d. Curr. as security for sd. Waller, for which sd. Graves has entered suit agst. sd. Waller and Scott and his partners, and the sd. Scott & Co. being liable for the sd. debt, and whereas sd. Waller is indebted to the sd. Scott & Co. in the sum of £310 10s. 1d., and for advancing the sd. Waller £200 at or before the sealing of these presents to meet debts, vizt., John Stewart of Fredksbg., Mercht., £120; to the Executors of Wm. Marshall's Estate, £50; and the remaining £30 to John Semple, surviving partner of Robt. Baylor, Gent., Decd., in consequence of the preceeding the sd. Waller deeds to sd. Scott & Co. every fee and benefit to be gained by him, the sd. Waller as Clerk of Spts. Co., etc., for space of five years, if not exceeding £200 with interest from date, etc., balance to be applied to debt due the sd. Mitchell, etc., by the sd. Waller, etc., etc. Witnesses, O. Towles, junr., Richard Johnson, Jn. Bevy. Roy, W. Wood. Septr. 1, 1766.

June 29, 1766.   Benjamin Temple of King Wm. Co. to Robert Hill of same Co. £150 8s. curr. 376 a. in St. Geo. Par., Spts. Co., on Pamunkey River, and adj. lands of Colo. Humphrey Hill, Thos. Minor, John Woolfolk, the widow of the late Jno. Minor, Gent., Wm. Davenport and Jno. Lewis, Atto. at Law, which sd. land is remainder of a tract devised to the sd. Benjamin Temple by his father, the late Joseph Temple, Gent. Witnesses, John Camm, James Semple, jr., John Semple, Rd. Tunstall, jr. Septr. 6, 1766.

Septr. 6, 1766.   John Penn, Senr., of Spts. Co. and Mary, his wife, to Thomas Colson of sd. Co. £20 curr. 130 a. in Spts. Co. John Chew, Thos. Bartlett, Joseph Herndon. Nov. 3, 1766.

Octr. 4, 1766.   Thomas Graves of Culpeper Co. and Sarah, his wife; John Graves and Ann, his wife, of sd. County; Isaac Graves and Mildred, his wife, of Orange Co., to George Humphreys of Spts. Co. £12 curr. 120 a. in Spts. Co. Witnesses, Jno. Chiles, Saml. Bullock, Jos. Dicken, Forest Webb. Nov. 3, 1766.

Nov. 3, 1766.   Samuel Bullock and Mildred, his wife, of Spts. Co. to Wm. Darnaby of same Co. £12 curr. Tract of land in Spts. Co. No witnesses. Nov. 3, 1766.

Octr. 3, 1766.   Thos. Graves of Culpeper Co. and Sarah, his wife; John Graves and Ann, his wife, of sd. Co., and Isaac Graves and Mildred, his wife, of Orange Co., to John Chiles of Spts. Co. £13 curr. 200 a. in Spts. Co. devised the sd. Thos., John and Isaac Graves by their father, John Graves, Decd. Witnesses, James Chiles, George Humphries, Samuel Bullock, Joseph Dicken. Nov. 3, 1766.

March 15, 1766. John Davis of St. Geo. Par., Spts. Co., and Martha, his wife, to Ambrose Shackleford of Par. and Co. afsd. £10. 100 a. in St. Geo. Par., Spts. Co., and bounded by lands of Jos. Venable, Jas. Townsend, John Shackleford and Wm. Thurston, it having been purchased by sd. Davis of Jos. Venable, etc. Witnesses, Thos. Wiatt, Morgan Murray, Jos. Venable, Francis Browning. Nov. 3, 1766.

Octr. 3, 1766. Thos., John and Isaac Graves, and their wives, of Spts. Co. to Samuel Bullock of Co. afsd. £5 10s. curr. 136 a. in Spts. Co. John Chiles, George Humphries, Forest Webb, Joseph Dicken. Nov. 3, 1766.

Decr. 5, 1764. John Williamson of St. Geo. Par., Spts. Co., and Susannah, his wife, to James Watkins of same Par. and County. £35 curr. 100 a. in St. Geo. Par., Spts. Co., part of a pat. granted John Smith Septr. 27, 1728, etc. Robert Goodloe, Richard Coleman, John Regney. April 1, 1765.

May 2, 1766. Samuel Faulconer and Mary, his wife, of St. Geo. Par., Spts. Co., to James Bowler of Par. and Co. afsd. £18 10s. Curr. 185 a. in St. Geo. Par., Spts. Co., part of a tract sd. Faulconer lives on, etc. Witnesses, John Collins, Lewis Craig, Elijah Craig. Nov. 3, 1766.

DEED BOOK G

1766–1771

Nov. 3, 1766. James x Jones and Mary, his wife, of St. Geo. Par., Spts. Co., to Marsom Poe of Par. and Co. afsd. £30 curr. 48½ a. in St. Geo. Par., Spts. Co. Jos. Herndon, Joseph Allen. Nov. 3, 1766.

Nov. 3, 1766. James x Jones and Mary, his wife, of St. Geo. Par., Spts. Co., to John Jinkins of Par. and Co. afsd., in consideration of a tract of land and £5 curr. 21 a. in St. Geo. Par. Spts. Co. Jos. Herndon, Joseph Allen. Nov. 3, 1766.

May 31, 1766. Antony Ben of Rensingham, Par. of St. Bees, Co. Cumberland, Gt. Britain; po. of atto. to Charles Yates of Fredksbg., Va., Mercht. Witnesses, Thomas Falcon, Stephen Chambers. Nov. 3. 1766.

Dec. 1, 1766. John x Dyer and Elizabeth, his wife, of Spts. Co., to Andrew Ross of Caroline Co. £10 curr. 100 a. in Spts. Co. John x Sills, Phebe x Sills. Dec. 1, 1766.

Dec. 2, 1766. James Finnie and Ann, his wife, to James Duncanson of Fredksbg. £90 curr., life interest of sd. Ann Finnie in Lot 22 in town of Fredksbg., etc., Whereas, Dr. Wm. Lynn, by his will dated Oct. 1, 1752, did devise his daughter Ann, then wife of Jno. Dent, now party to these presents, a life interest in a lot dwelling house etc., etc., in town of Fredksbg, etc. No witnesses. Dec. 2, 1766.

Augt. 7, 1764. John Roane of Spts. Co. and Susanna, his wife, to Michael Robinson of Co. afsd. £198 curr. 198 a. in Spts. Co Wm. Templeman, George Thornton, Hudson Muse, Wm. Thornton. Augt. 7, 1764.

June 11, 1766. John Mitchell of Spts. Co. to John Holloday of same Co. £15 1s. 1d. 100 a. in St. Geo. Par., Spts. Co. Thomas Poole, John Allinder, Joseph Roy. Feby. 4, 1767.

July 14, 1766. John Lawson of Caroline Co. to Wm. Crutcher of Spts. Co. £40 9s. 1d. Slaves. Witnesses, Thos. James, James Brown. Feby. 4, 1767.

Sept. 4, 1766. William Grayson of Spts. Co. to Henry Allison of Whitehaven, Mercht. £13 7s. 10d. curr. Mortgage. Goods and Chattels. Witnesses, John Battaley, Hudson Muse. Feby. 4, 1767.

Feby. 5, 1767. Benjamin Grymes of Spts. Co., Gent., and Priscilla, his wife, to Honble. Presley Thornton of Northumberland Co., Esqr., and Wm. H. Fitzhugh of Stafford Co., Esqr. Whereas, by Indenture Dated Decr. 21, 1764, the sd. Grymes conveyed to the sd. Thornton and Fitzhugh sundry tracts of land, etc., in St. Geo. Par., Spts. Co. and also lots and houses in town of Fredksbg. and forges, furnaces, slaves, stocks, etc., in trust for uses stated therein, as by the afsd. Ind. recorded in the

General Court to avoid the arising of differences, difficulties, etc., this present Ind. is made, etc. The sd. Benjamin Grymes and Priscilla, his wife, in consideration of the purposes mentioned in the recited Ind., etc., convey to sd. Thornton and Fitzhugh, the tract of land whereon the Furnace stands, containing 1650 a.; also tract of land purchased by sd. Grymes of Wm. Woodford, containing 1600 a.; also tract purchased of Smith's Executors containing 700 a.; also the land purchased of Williams and Tompkins containing 500 a.; also the tract of land given the sd. Benjamin Grymes by his father, The Honbl. John Grymes, Esqr., Decd., lying on Mattapony River, containing abt. 1900 a.; also tract of land whereon the forge stands purchased of Rice Curtis, containing 400 a.; also tract purchased of Jos. Herndon containing abt. 250 a.; also tract purchased of Executors of Wm. Waller, Decd., containing abt. 250 a.; also Lots and houses in town of Fredksbg., etc. Slaves, Stocks, Vessels, Goods, Chattels, etc. In trust to indemnify the sd. Thornton and Fitzhugh from loss, on ac. of various sums they have or may advance sd. Grymes, etc. Witnesses, Jos. Jones, Ben. Gwinn, Wm. Menefee. Feby. 5, 1767.

Feby. 5, 1767. Benjamin Grymes of Spts. Co. to Presley Thornton and Wm. Fitzhugh, Esqrs. £800. Slaves. Witness, Ben. Gwinn. Feby. 5, 1767.

Septr. 10. 1766. Wm. White of Spts. Co., Va., to Henry Ellison of Whitehaven, Mercht. £32 curr. Mortgage. Goods and Chattels. Hudson Muse, Chs. Yates. Feby. 5, 1767.

Augt. 2, 1766. John Waller of Spts. Co. to John Carthrae, of sd. Co., Mercht. £20 curr. Mortgage. A slave. Witness, J. Lewis. March 2, 1767.

March 2, 1767. John x Jinkins and Nanny, his wife, of Spts. Co., St. Geo. Par., to their son Charles Jinkins of Par. and Co. afsd. Deed of Gift. 112 a. in St. Geo. Par., Spts. Co. No witnesses. March 2, 1767.

Feby. 24, 1767. John Mitchell of Spts. Co. to Richard Johnston of same Co. £40 curr. 100 a. in Spts. Co. No witnesses. March 2, 1767.

Nov. 29, 1766. Anthony Street of Spts. Co. and Elizabeth, his wife, to Thomas Brightwell of Co. afsd. £22 10s. curr. 235 a. in St. Geo. Par., Spts. Co. Witnesses, Jno. Hutcherson, James Hutcherson, Thos. Allen. March 2, 1767.

Feby. 10, 1767. John Penn of Spts. Co. and Elizabeth, his wife, to John Holloday of same Co. £15 curr. 200 a. in Spts. Co. purchased by Penn of Philip Ballard and joining the lands the sd. Holloday bought of John Sartin, and the lands of Wm. Mays, and the patent granted Edmund Waller, etc. Witnesses, Jno. Holloday, junr.; Edwd. Chapman. March 2, 1767.

July 28, 1766. John Davenport of St. Geo. Par., Spts. Co., to George Lumsden of Trinity Par, Louisa Co. £200 curr. Mortgage. 300 a. in St. Geo. Par., Spts. Co. and negroes. Witnesses, Jacob Higgin, Wm. Pettics, Wm. Edmund Waller. Feby. 2, 1767.

Sept. 18, 1766. George Carter of Buckingham Co. to his brother John Carter of Spts. Co. £30 curr. 95 a. in Spts. Co. on both sides Robinson's Swamp. Robt. Huddleston, Daniel Lindsay, John x Johnston, John x Pain, John Huddleston. Feby. 2, 1767.

Feby. 9, 1767. James Crap of Stafford Co. to Warner Lewis of Gloucester Co., Esqr. £1000 curr. Mortgage. Slaves. Witnesses, Fielding Lewis,
Charles Washington, Edmund Taylor. March 3, 1767.

Jany. 31, 1767. John Waller, junr., and Elizabeth, his wife, of St. Geo.
Par., Spts. Co., to Larkin Chew of Par. and Co. afsd. £12 curr. 92 a.
in St. Geo. Par., Spts. Co., which sd. land was allotted the sd. Elizabeth
(now wife of sd. Jno. Waller) being her part of a tract of land sold to
the sd. Elizabeth, Francis Curtis and Jean Curtis by Henry Pendleton and
Martha, his wife, the sd. Pendleton having purchased sd. land of Rice
Curtis, Senr., as by Deeds, May 3, 1757, etc. Jno. Bevy. Roy, Robt. Wilkinson, W. Wood, O. Towles, jr. March 3, 1767.

Feby. 28, 1767. Robert Wilkinson of Spts. Co. and Alce, his wife, to
Joseph Talbert of Spts. Co. £40 curr. 50 a. in Spts. Co. Witnesses, Geo.
Stubblefield, James Crawford, James Wiglesworth, Thos. Wheeler. March
3, 1767.

March 4, 1767. Roger Dixon of Fredksbg. and Lucy, his wife, to Wm.
Houston of same town, Saddler. £40 curr. Lot 273 in town of Fredksbg.
No witnesses. March 4, 1767.

March 4, 1767. Roger Dixon and Lucy, his wife, of Fredksbg. to Dr.
Henry Heath of same town. £60 curr. Lots 256 and 266 in town of
Fredksbg. No witnesses. March 4, 1767.

Nov. 3, 1763. John Robinson of Spts. Co. and Lucy, his wife, to William
Robinson of Co. afsd., Gent. £140 curr. 228 in St. Geo. Par., Spts. Co.,
part of a pat. granted Harry Beverley, Gent., Decd. Witnesses, Bevy.
Winslow, Jos. Brock, Richd. Coleman. Nov. 8, 1763.

Nov. 7, 1763. John Robinson and Lucy, his wife, of Spts. Co. to Nathaniel Dickenson, of sd. Co. £20 curr. 68 a. in Spts. Co. Jos. Brock, W.
Parker, B. Johnston. Nov. 8, 1763.

Nov. 7, 1763. John Robinson and Lucy, his wife, of Spts. Co. to Wm.
Parker of Caroline Co., Gent. £322 15s. 6d. 581 a. in St. Geo. Par., Spts.
Co. whereon sd. John Robinson lives, and is part of a tract granted Harry
Beverley, Gent., Decd., and by him devised to his daughter Agatha, etc.
Witnesses, Joseph Brock. Edwd. Herndon, Joseph Herndon, Moses Bled-
soe, Richard Johnston. Nov. 8, 1763.

March 30, 1767. John Farish and Robert Farish of Spts. Co. to Ambrose
Carlton of Caroline Co. £150 curr. 309 a. in Spts. Co. whereon sd. Jno.
and Robt. live, adjoining lands of John Beverley Roy, Mary Dawson,
Ephraim Beasley, etc., reserving to the sd. Jno. Farish and heirs 1 a., in-
cluding the sd. Farishes family burying ground, etc. O. Towles, jr.; Jno.
Bevy. Roy, Wm. Wood. April 6, 1767.

April 6, 1767. Oliver Towles, Junr., Atto. at Law, of Spts. Co., and
Mary, his wife, to Thomas Coleman of same Co. £14 9s. curr. 50 a. in
Spts. Co., part of a tract lately purchased by sd. Towles of Thos. Waller,
Execr. of Thos. Waller, Decd. No witnesses. April 6, 1767.

April 6, 1767. Robert Goodloe of St. Geo. Par., Spts. Co., to his son
George Goodloe of sd. Par. and Co. Deed of Gift. 350 acres. Jo. Carter,
Edwd. Herndon, John Chew. April 6, 1767.

Oct. 8, 1766. Thomas Moore of King Wm. Co. and Joanna, his wife, to Francis Meriweather of Spts. Co. Whereas sd. Moore being seized of a tract of 500 a. in Spts. Co. abt. March 18, 1761, bargained and sold the same to Nathaniel Pope of Louisa Co. for £250 curr., but before the sd. land was conveyed, the sd. Pope sold it to the sd. Meriweather, for 20,000 lbs. tob. The sd. Moore and wife, in consideration of the premises, etc., convey sd. 500 a. of land known as Rich Neck, which was devised the sd. Thomas, by the will of his father, Augustine Moore, Decd. Witnesses, Go. Weedon, Jno. Roane, O. Towles, jr. April 6, 1767.

Augt. 22, 1766. Wm. White of Spts. Co. to Isaac Heslop, Mercht. £23 18s. 7d. curr. Mortgage. Negro slave. Witnesses, Jno. Battaley, John Herndon. April 6, 1767.

Augt. 22, 1766. Nicholas Smyth of Spts. Co. to Isaac Heslop, Mercht. £10 7s. 10d. Goods and Chattels. Mortgage. Witnesses, John Battaley, John Herndon. April 6, 1767.

Septr. 13, 1766. William Smither and Ann, his wife, of Spts. Co., to Patrick Cary of same Co. £17 7s. 6d. Curr. 34¾ a. in Caroline and Spts. Counties, known by lines of lands purchased by Lawrence Anderson of Wm. Smither, father to sd. Wm. Smither, and land purchased by Colo. Wm. Waller, Decd., of sd. Wm. Smither, now the property of Jno. Beverley Roy, etc., remainder of 200 a. devised by Wm. Smither of Essex Co. to sd. Wm. party to these presents, etc., as the records of Essex Co. will show, etc. Witnesses, Lark. Chew, Thomas Powe, John x Smither. April 8, 1767.

April 29, 1767. Ursley x Gains of St. Geo. Par., Spts. Co., to her daughter, Mary Gains. Deed of Gift. Goods and Chattels. Witnesses, W. Robinson, Thomas Powe. May 4, 1767.

April 29, 1767. Ursley x Gains of St. Geo. Par., Spts. Co., to her son, Robert Gains, of Par. and Co. afsd. Deed of Gift. Goods and chattels. W. Robinson, Thomas Powe. May 4, 1767.

March 16, 1767. William x Simpson of Spts. Co. to Roger Dixon. £20 curr. Mortgage. Goods and chattels. John McCally, James Hume, Richard Brock Williams. May 5, 1767.

July 5, 1766. John x Rouzie of Amherst Co. and Mary, his wife, to James Frasher of Spts. Co. £20 curr. 183 a. in Spts. Co., part of pat. formerly granted John Bush, etc. Witnesses, John Sanders, John Penn, Henry True. Augt. 4, 1766.

March 4, 1767. Fielding Lewis of Fredksbg., Esqr., and Betty, his wife, to James Duncanson of same town, Mercht. £80 curr. Lots 91 and 92 in the sd. Lewis' addition to the town of Fredksbg. No witnesses. July 6, 1767.

March 24, 1767. John Davies of City of Chester, Mason, only son and heir at law of Thomas Davies, late of County of Prince Wm., in Va., Gent., Decd., po. of atto. to Thomas Triplett of Fairfax Co., Va., Gent. "Whereas I am entitled by virtue of the last will and testament of my sd. late father after the death of Judith, his late wife," etc. Witnesses, William Quinney, George Davidson, Robert Hare, James Richardson, James Young, Wm. Jones. July 6, 1767.

April 27, 1767. Philip x Sanders and Mary, his wife, of Drysdale Par., Caroline Co., to John Sanders, Senr., of St. Marys Par., Caroline Co. £25 curr. 200 a. in Spts. Co. Reuben Sanders, Prittyman Sanders, Richard Sanders, Thomas Reynolds. July 6, 1767.

April 27, 1767. John Sanders, Senr., of St. Marys Par., Caroline Co., to his grandson, John Stern, son of Francis Stern of Par. and Co. afsd. Deed of Gift. 206 a. in Spts. Co. Reubin Sanders, Prittyman Sanders, Richard Sanders, Thomas Reynolds. July 6, 1767.

June 1, 1767. Daniel x Musick and Thomas Wiatt of Spts. Co. to Benjamin Johnston of Co. afsd. £10 curr. 100 a. on East North East in Spts. Co., joining lands of George Humphries, Francis Aravin, and the sd. Musick, and it being the land the sd. Musick inherited from his father, George Musick, Decd. Witnesses, Wm. Wood, Rd. Johnston, James Johnston. July 6, 1767.

July 6, 1767. Michael Robinson and Mary, his wife, of Spts. Co., to Thomas Colson of same Co. £100 curr. 127 a. in Spts. Co. No witnesses. July 6, 1767.

May 3, 1767. Thomas Duncanson of town and Parish of Forress, Co. Murray, Scotland, Surgeon, to Henry Mitchell of Fredksbg., Va., Mercht. Whereas, Robert Duncanson of Fredksbg., Decd., in his lifetime was seized of certain lots, etc., in town of Fredksbg. and being so seized died intestate, whereby the sd. lots descended to the sd. Thomas Duncanson, his heir at law, and whereas the sd. Thomas by his letter of attorney, dated July 7, 1764, constituted and appointed James Duncanson of Fredksbg., Mercht., his lawful attorney, etc. The sd. Thomas Duncanson, by the sd. James Duncanson, his attorney, for the sum of £66, conveys to the sd. Henry Mitchell, lots 133 and 134 in town of Fredksbg. No witnesses. July 7, 1767. Also deed from sd. Thos. Duncanson, etc., to sd. Henry Mitchell, for lot No. 30 in Fredksbg. Dated May 1, 1767. No witnesses. Recd. July 7, 1767.

May 30, 1767. Wm. Webb of Spts. Co. to his daughter, Milley Webb. Deed of Gift. A negro. Witness, Richard Crittenton Webb. Augt. 3, 1767.

Feby. 2, 1767. Benjamin Grymes to John Holloday, Senr. Deed for Slaves. Witnesses, Robt. Clark, Joseph Reeves. Augt. 3, 1767.

July 7, 1767. Henry Mitchell of Fredksbg., Mcht., to James Duncanson of sd. town, Mercht. £250. curr. Lot No. 30 in town of Fredksbg., purchased by sd. Mitchell of Thos. Duncanson, as by Deed, May 1, 1767, etc. No witnesses. Augt. 4, 1767.

July 8, 1767. Henry Mitchell of Fredksbg., Mercht., to James Duncanson of same town, Mercht. £66 curr. Lots 133 and 134 in Fredksbg., formerly purchased by sd. Mitchell from Thos. Duncanson, as by Deed, May 3, 1767. No witnesses. Augt. 4, 1767.

June 29, 1767. William Garrett and Elizabeth, his wife, of Louisa Co., and Nathaniel Gordon and Elizabeth, his wife, of Spts. Co., to Francis Jerdone of Louisa. 5 shill. to Garretts, and £500 curr to Gordons. 456 a. in Spts. Co. with a water grist mill. Witnesses, J. Lewis, George Pottie, Thomas x Cayson. July 6, 1767.

Augt. 3, 1767. Richard Gatewood of Culpeper Co. to Daniel Branham of Spts. Co. £54 7s. 16d. curr. 226 a. in Spts. Co. whereon Martin True now lives as tenant to the sd. Gatewood. Witnesses, Henry Elly, Junr.; John Foster, Hezekiah Brown. Augt. 3, 1767.

April 27, 1767. Whereas David Jones, by deed Dated July 7, 1766, conveyed to his daughter, Sarah Allsup, and her husband, William Allsup, five slaves, etc., this writing witnesseth, that the sd. Wm. Allsup and Sarah, his wife, for natural love, etc., convey the sd. slaves, etc., to Martha, wife of Wm. Leathers, and Catharine Jones, daughters of the sd. David Jones, and sisters of the sd. Sarah Allsup. etc. Witnesses, Jno. Carter, Wm. Wood, P. Stubblefield. Augt. 3, 1767.

April 27, 1767. David x Jones of Spts. Co. to son-in-law, Wm. Leathers, and Martha, his wife, and Catharine Jones, daughters of the sd. David Jones. Deed of Gift. All estate real and personal, after "my wife's death," etc. Witnesses, Jno. Carter, Wm. Wood. Augt. 3, 1767.

Feby. 21, 1767. Edmund Waller of Spts. Co., Gent., and Mary, his wife; John Waller, jr., Wm. Edmund Waller and Benja. Waller, to John Wigglesworth of Spts. Co. £29 12s. 6d. curr. 79 a. in Spts. Co. "part of a greater tract whereon sd. Edmund Waller, etc., now lives," etc. Witnesses, John Woolfolk, Jas. Wigglesworth, Wm. Wigglesworth. Augt. 3, 1767.

Augt. 3, 1767. Charles Colson of Spts. Co. to Wm. Walker of Fredksbg. £500 curr. Lot 29 in town of Fredksbg. Jos. Herndon, Edwd. Herndon, Thomas Colson, jr. Augt. 3, 1767.

Augt. 3, 1767. John Davenport of Spts. Co. and Mary, his wife, and George Lumsden of Louisa, to Andrew Cochrane, Wm. Cunninghame, John Stewart & Co. of City of Glasgow, Merchts. £120 curr. to sd. Davenport and wife and 5 shill. to sd. Lumsden. 320 a. in Spts. Co., first granted Wm. Smith by pat. and the sd. Smith, dying intestate the tract descended to Thomas Ballard Smith, his eldest son and heir at law, who, together with Richard Phillips, conveyed the sd. land, by Deeds, Septr. 24, 1734, to George Woodruff, and by the sd. Woodruff conveyed to Henry Pendleton, who conveyed the same to John Davenport. No witnesses. Augt. 3, 1767.

April 7, 17—. Wm. Fitzhugh of Somerset, and Benjamin Grymes, Gentleman, to Benjamin McCoy, Shoemaker and Saddler. Deed of lease. "The house where James Lindsey lately lived on the lot formerly granted Susanna Livingston, with 20 a. to be laid off, etc. £1 cash and four hens, etc., on Feast of St. Lukes. Witness, Robert Clerk. Augt. 4, 1767.

Augt. 4, 1767. Charles Lewis of Caroline Co., Gent., and Lucy, his wife, to Fielding Lewis of Spts. Co., Esqr. £1500. 1000 a. in Spts. Co., whereon sd. Charles Lewis lately dwelt, bounded by the road leading from Thos. Minor's plantation to Lewis' bridge, the land of sd. Minor, James Redd, Wm. Dangerfield, and Mattapony River. Witnesses, Hugh Mercer, Jos. Jones, John Lewis. Augt. 5, 1767.

Augt. 4, 1767. Fielding Lewis of Fredksbg., Esqr., and Betty, his wife, to John Baggot of sd. Town, Bricklayer. £40 curr. Lot 179 in town of Fredksbg. Hugh Mercer, Jos. Jones, John Lewis. Augt. 5, 1767.

July — 1767. Betty Benger, Widow, of Caroline Co., to James Johnston of Spts. Co. £100 curr. 231 a. in Spts. Co. B. Johnston, Jno. Bevy. Roy, Richard Johnston. Octr. 5, 1767.

July 20, 1767. George Durrett and Elizabeth, his wife, of Spts. Co., to Robert Durrett of Spts. Co. 5 shill. 190 a. in St. Geo. Par., Spts. Co., which was conveyed to Robt. Durrett and Elizabeth, his wife, by Henry Goodloe, Deed., as by Deed of Gift, recd. in Spts. Co. Witnesses, William Crane, William Durrett, John Summers. Octr. 5, 1767.

Octr. 5, 1767. Anthony Benn of Co. Cumberland, Gt. Britain, Esqr., to James Ritchie & Co. of Glasgow, Gt. Britain, Merchts. Whereas sd. Benn, granted po. of atto. to Charles Yates of Fredksbg., Mercht., to act for him, the sd. Yates by virtue of the sd. power of attorney, having contracted with sd. Ritchie & Co. for the sale of a lot belonging to sd. Benn, Witnesseth, that for £500 ster. sd. Benn, conveys by sd. Yates, his attorney, Lot 16 in town of Fredksbg. to sd. Ritchie & Co. Witnesses, Hudson Muse, Edward Moor, Octr. 5, 1767.

Augt. 28, 1767. John x Howerton of Spts. Co. and Mary, his wife, to James Floyd of Caroline Co. £11 curr. 50 a. in Spts. Co. Robert Goodloe, George Goodloe, Daniel Lindsay. Octr. 5, 1767.

July 23, 1767. John Waller, Clerk of Spts. Co. Court, to Wm. Wood. £200. Goods and Chattels. Witnesses, Peter Stubblefield, Jonathan Clark. Dec. 7, 1767.

March 16, 1767. Thomas Roy and Margaret, his wife, of Spts. Co., to James Chiles of same Co. £12 curr. 100 a. in Spts. Co. Joel Lewis, Thos. Ashman, Nathaniel x Haggard, John Waller, Andw. Waggener, Lewis Young, Lewis Shackleford. Decr. 7, 1767.

Septr. 1, 1767. Judy Belches, James Belches and Francis Jerdone, Executors of last will and testament of Patrick Belches, Decd., to John Minor of Caroline Co. £200 curr. 885 a. in N. Fork Northanna River, in Spts. Co., purchased by sd. Patrick Belches of Bernard Moore, Esqr., etc. Whereas, Patrick Belches, by will dated Dec. 29, 1763, did constitute and appt. Judy Belches, James Belches and Francis Jerdone, executors therefor, and therein directed the sale of lands in Spotsylvania and Hanover Counties, etc. Witnesses, Fielding Lewis, John Stewart, William Knox, James Somerville, Gavin Lawson, George Pottie, Garritt Minor, Geo. Lumsden, Jo. Graves. Dec. 7, 1767.

Dec. 7, 1767. John Waller of Spts. Co. and Mary Ann, his wife, and Elizabeth Waller, widow of Thomas Waller, of King William Co. to Joseph Duerson of Spts. Co. Whereas, the sd. Thos. Waller, late husband of the sd. Elizabeth and late father of the sd. John Waller, being seized of a tract of land in Spts. Co. by his last will and testament dated Septr. 19, 1764, devised to his said son, John Waller, that tract of land whereon sd. John did then and now doth live, adj. the lands formerly belonging to his brother, Wm. Waller, Zachary Lewis, and Phillip Vincent Vass, etc. Witnesseth, sd. John Waller and Mary Ann, his wife, for the sum of £65 12s. 9½d. curr., convey to sd. Duerson, 199 a. in Spts. Co. Witnesses, Jas. Wigglesworth, Fras. Meriweather, James Edwards, Augustine Edwards. Decr. 7, 1767.

Octr. 10, 1767. John Waller of Spts. Co. to James Edwards. In consideration of sd. Edwards standing security for sd. Waller, etc. Mortgage. Five negroes. Witnesses, O. Towles, jr., Jo. Graves. Decr. 7, 1767.

Octr. 7, 1767. Wm. Daingerfield, jr., of Spts. Co., Gent., and Mary, his wife (late Mary Willis, daughter and heiress of Jno. Willis, Gent., Decd., also Niece and heiress of Henry Willis, Gent., late of Spts. Co., Decd.) to Larkin Chew, Junr., of Spts. Co.

Whereas, John Smith, Gent., of Gloucester Co., in his lifetime being seized of a certain tract of land containing 3333 a. (whereon sd. Wm. Daingerfield and Mary, his wife, now live) and being so seized did by his last will and testament, Dated, May 10, 1735, by a residuary clause did devise as follows, "Item, I give and bequeath unto my grandmother, Anna Alexander, all my other lands not bequeathed, negroes, money and stocks of what kind soever during her natural life and after her decease to my brother, Henry Willis, and his heirs, but in case he should die without heir, then my will and desire is that my brother, John Willis, enjoy the whole gift of the sd. Anna Alexander, to him and his heirs or assigns, forever," as by will recorded in Gloucester Co. Whereas, soon after making the sd. will the sd. John Smith departed this life and the afsd. tract being comprehended in the devise aforesaid and not before by the sd. will specifically or particularly devised, the sd. Anna Alexander possessed and enjoyed the same during her life and after her death the sd. Henry Willis, by virtue of the devise to him entered into the sd. tract, and whereas the sd. Henry Willis having departed this life without leaving or having heir or heirs of his body, etc., and the sd John Willis, to whom this estate was left (in case of failure of heirs in the sd. Henry Willis, Decd.) having died without disposing of the sd. Estate, the sd. Estate has descended to the sd. Mary Willis, now Mary Daingerfield, daughter and heiress in fee simple of the sd. John Willis. The sd. Wm. Daingerfield and Mary, his wife, deed the sd. tract of 3333 a. to sd. Larkin Chew, jr., in trust for the benefit of the sd. Wm. and Mary, during their natural lives and then to their right heirs, etc. Witnesses, O. Towles, jr., Walter Chiles, John Crittenden Webb. Decr. 7, 1767.

Decr. 2, 1767. Nathaniel Gordon of Spts. Co. and Elizabeth, his wife, to Nancy Gordon, daughter of John Gordon, Decd. (brother of sd. Nathaniel Gordon) and Sarah, his wife, of Spts. Co. Deed of Gift and £90 10s. 109 a. in Spts. Co. purchased by sd. Nathaniel Gordon of Thomas Wiatt, etc. Witnesses, Henry Chiles, Jos. Herndon, John Chiles. Decr. 7, 1767.

April 30, 1767. Ralph Bowker of Cumberland Co. to his couzin, Ann Waller, daughter of John Waller, Clerk of Co. Court of Spts. Co. 1400 a. in Spts. Co., known as Blakeley Park, devised by the last will and testament of Ralph Bowker, Gent., Decd. (as recorded in King and Queen Co.) to his son, Byrd Bowker, and in case the sd. Byrd should die without issue, etc., the sd. land to be devided between his (the sd. Ralph's) other four children, vizt: Achilles Bowker (father of Ralph Bowker, party to these presents), Parmenas Bowker, Catharine Lewis and Anne Smith, etc. Witnesses, B. Johnston, Mary x Horn, Sherod Horn, Owen Thomas. Decr. 7, 1767.

Augt. 14, 1767. Henry Elley of Culpeper Co. to son-in-law, John Foster. Deed of Gift. 7 negro slaves, with stocks of horses, cattle, etc., "sd.

Henry Elley and Esther, his wife," etc. Witnesses, Joseph Brock, Joseph Bledsoe. Decr. 8, 1767.

Decr. 8, 1767. Thomas Reeves and Sarah, his wife, of Spts. Co., to James Hunter of King Geo. Co., Esqr. £358 15shill. 350 acre tract of land whereon sd. Thomas Reeves now lives, in St. Geo. Par., Spts. Co., being sales out of a larger tract formerly granted John Bowsey, 1680 a. in Freshes of Rappk. River opp. the falls, which after the death of sd. Bowsey was granted Augustin Smith, by pat., Octr. 22, 1712. The first sale being 200 a. conveyed by sd. Smith to Henry Reeves, by Deeds (recd. in Essex Co.) Septr. 9, 1714. The second sale 100 a. conveyed by Peter Byrom to Henry Reeves, the Elder, as by Deeds in Essex Co., May 19, 1719. The third sale of 50 a. conveyed by Thomas Smith to George Reeves, as by Deeds in Spts. Co., Octr. 2, 1739, now, by several conveyances legally vested in the sd. Thomas Reeves, etc. Witnesses, Rd. Corbin, Mann Page, Wm. McMillan, Geo. Weedon, Henry Mitchell, John Stewart, David Briggs, Chas. Yates, Chas. Dick, David Blair, Philip Somerby, Andrew Shepherd, Adam Hunter. Decr. 8, 1767.

Nov. 19, 1767. Joseph Hawkins of Spts. Co., St. Geo. Par., to Larkin Chew, Gent., of sd. Co. and Par. £5 5s. curr. 120 a. on a branch of Plentiful Run, in Spts. Co., joining lands of James Jones, Robt. Bradley and the sd. Hawkins. Witnesses, Jos. Hawkins, jr., Wm. Stanfield, Wm. Wood, John Herndon, John Foster, Jonathan Clark. Decr. 8, 1767.

Dec. 8, 1767. George Lumsden of Louisa Co. to Andrew Cochrane, Wm. Cunningham & Co., Merchts., in Glasgow. Transfers any interest he may have in a certain tract of land lately mortgaged to him by John Davenport of Spts. Co., etc. No witnesses. Decr. 8, 1767.

Augt. 12, 1767. Samuel Battaley of Spts. Co., po. of atto. to his brother, John Battaley. Witnesses, Frans. Tyler, Wm. Wood, Wm. Crutcher. Dec. 9, 1767.

Feby. 1, 1768. Charles Colson of Spts. Co. from Wm. Walker of Co. afsd. £500 curr. Lot 29 in town of Fredksbg., etc., slaves, goods and chattels. Mortgage. Witnesses, George Stubblefield, John Walker, Thomas Colson. Feby. 1, 1768.

Augt. 22, 1767. Edward Coleman of Spts. Co. to Thomas Walker of Albemarle and John Hawkins of Hanover Co. £141 12s. curr. Mortgage. 300 a. in Spts. Co. bought by Coleman of E. W. Allen, also 200 a. whereon sd. Coleman lives; also slaves, stocks of horses, cattle, etc. Witnesses, Beverley Winslow, Ben. Winslow, Thos. Powe. Feby. 1, 1768.

Augt. 1, 1767. Isaac Darnall of Spts. Co. to James Frasher. Bill of Sale. Goods and Chattels. Sd. Frasher standing as sd. Darnall's security to George Stubblefield, etc. Witnesses, Wm. Mastin, Molly x Darnall. Feby. 1, 1768.

Augt. 14, 1767. Thomas Lane of Spts. Co. to Andrew Johnston of Louisa Co. £40 curr. Mortgage. 50 a. whereon sd. Thomas Lane now lives, etc. George Pottie, John Garrett, James Overton, Wm. Garrett, junr. March 7, 1768.

March 5, 1768. Wm. Garrett and Elizabeth, his wife, of Trinity Par., Louisa Co., to John Glen of St. Geo. Par., Spts. Co. £20 curr. 200 a. in

Spts. Co. Wm. Garrett, junr., Jno. Garrett, Robt. Fleming, George Pottie. March 7, 1768.

Feby. 27, 1768. Wm. Garrett and Elizabeth, his wife, of Spts. Co., to Michael Blunt of Louisa Co. £10 curr. 104 a. in Spts. Co. Jno. Garrett, Wm. Garrett, Jr., Robt. Fleming, Geo. Pottie. Mch. 7, 1768.

March 7, 1768. Edward Graves of Spts. Co. to John Chiles of sd. Co. £13 curr. 200 a. in Spts. Co. devised the sd. Edwd. by the will of his father, John Graves, Decd. No witnesses. March 7, 1768.

Octr. 3, 1766. Thomas, John and Isaac Graves and their wives, of Spts. Co. to Francis Irwin of sd. Co. £12 curr. 268 a. in Spts. Co. James Chiles, Forest Webb, Joseph Dicken. March 7, 1768.

March 2d, 1767. Wm. Webb of Spts. Co. to his daughter, Ann Webb. Deed of Gift. Negro slave. Mentions his "daughter, Milley Webb." Witnesses, Edwd. Herndon, Chs. Gordon. March 7, 1768.

March 7, 1768. Wm. Wigglesworth and Mary, his wife, of Spts. Co., to John Wigglesworth of Spts. Co. £13 13s. 9d. curr. 36½ a. in Spts. Co., part of a tract of land formerly given by Capt. Edmund Waller to his daughter, Mary, the wife of Wm. Wigglesworth, parties to these presents, etc. No witnesses. March 7, 1768.

Nov. 9, 1767. Wm. Waller, Doctor, to Ann Waller, daughter of Jno. Waller, Clerk of Spts. Co., brother to the sd. Wm. Waller. Deed of Gift. Slaves, etc., that will be his at the "death of Ann Waller, his mother." The provision is that in case the sd. Wm. Waller should marry, then the sd. Ann Waller does not inherit the slaves, etc. Witnesses, Frances Colson, Sarah x Buckner, Catharine x Hawkins, Nathan Hawkins, Tho. Megee, Senr., Thomas Megee, Jr. March 8, 1768.

Decr. 31, 1767. Fielding Lewis of Spts. Co., Esqr., to Charles Lewis of Caroline Co., Gent. Whereas Charles Lewis, by Indenture, abt. the year 1755, mortgaged to sd. Fielding, certain lands, etc., to secure a debt owing the sd. Fielding, and whereas the sd. debt having been settled the sd. Fielding grants the sd. Charles, this quit claim. Witnesses, Chs. Carter, Wm. Woodford, Jos. Jones. March 9, 1768.

June 12, 1766. John Waller, Clk. of Spts. Co., and Ann, his wife, to James Frazier of afsd. Co. £18 curr. 120 a. in Spts. Co. conveyed by one John Bush to David Bruce, during his natural life, then to his first male heir, etc., and afterwards conveyed by Robert Bruce to Ambrose Foster, who conveyed it to Wm. Waller, Gent., Decd., who by his will devised the sd. land to the sd. John, party to these presents, etc. Witnesses, Sherod Horn, Richard Blanton, Wm. x Morris, John Penn, Wm. Wood, James Crane, Robt. Chew. Augt. 4, 1766.

July 18, 1767. Elizabeth x Martin and Henry Martin (her son) and Elizabeth, his wife, to Thomas Colson. £25 curr. 2 a. of land on River Po. etc. Thos. Blanton, James Williams, George Carter. Septr. 5, 1768.

Nov. 3, 1767. John Smith of Middlesex Co. to Michael Robinson of Spts. Co. £272 10s. Curr. 545 a. in Spts. Co., part of a pat. granted George Warner, etc. Witnesses, Fielding Lewis, Jno. Thornton, Seth Thornton, John Glassell, James Somerville. Augt. 3, 1768.

June 6, 1766. James Hunter of King Geo. Co. to Hugh Mercer of town of Fredksbg. £480 curr. Lot in town of Fredksbg. No witnesses. June 6, 1768.

June 6, 1768. John Foster of Spts. Co. and Elizabeth, his wife, to John Herndon of same Co. £100 15s. curr. 264 a. in St. Geo. Par., Spts. Co. No witnesses. June 6, 1768.

June 6, 1768. Thomas James of Fredksbg. but now of Fauqueir Co. (son and heir of George James, Decd., of the afsd. town), and Mary, his wife, to Wm. Houston of afsd. town. £150 curr. Part of Lot No. 41 in town of Fredksbg,, known as the Long Ordinary, formerly conveyed by Chas. Colson to George James and by him to his son, the sd. Thomas James, etc. No witnesses. June 6, 1768.

Octr. 5, 1767. Charles Lewis of Caroline Co., Gent., and Lucy, his wife, to Thomas Minor of Spts. Co., Gent. £500 curr. 700 a. in St. Geo. Par., Spts. Co. Fielding Lewis, Chas. Dick, J. Lewis. June 6, 1768.

June 4, 1768. Nathaniel Dickinson and Elizabeth, his wife, of St. Geo. Par., Spts. Co., to Wm. Hutcherson of Par. and Co. afsd. £14 2s. 6d. curr. 28¼ a. in St. Geo. Par., Spts. Co. Jno. Hutcherson, junr., Richard Dickinson, Robert Hutcherson. June 6, 1768.

April 29, 1768. Ambrose Ranes and Sarah, his wife, of Spts. Co., to Francis Purvis of Caroline Co. £120 curr. 300 a. in St. Geo. Par., Spts. Co. No witnesses. June 6, 1768.

May 2, 1768. Thomas Duerson and Joseph Duerson of Spts. Co. to Edward Herndon. £60 curr. 250 a. in Spts. Co. Jos. Herndon, J. Lewis, Thomas Colson, O. Towles, jr., Wm. Wood, Jonathan Clark. July 4, 1768.

Nov. 27, 1767. Thomas Wiatt of St. Geo. Par., Spts. Co., and Sukey, his wife, to Thomas White of Par. and Co. afsd. £16 curr. 300 a. in St. Geo. Par., Spts. Co., joining lands of Wm. Mays, Jno, Bowie, and the sd. White, etc. Witnesses, Wm. Webb, Jno. Wiatt, Alexr. x Johnson, Wm. Howard. July 4, 1768.

Jany. 6, 1768. Whereas by the will of my late husband, Joseph Collins, Decd., he lends to me during life or widowhood all estate both reall and personal and after my marriage or decease to be disposed of as by the sd. will directed, etc. Having formerly given consent to sale of lands, etc., do hereby now give consent to sale of personal effects, etc., the money arising from such sale to be divided amongst all my children, etc., in case of my death or marriage, etc., etc. Signed, Susannah x Collins. Witnesses, Richd. Thomas, Reubin Daniel, Vivion Daniel, Thos. Merry. July 4, 1768.

July 4, 1768. John Deatheridge of Spts. Co. to George Gravitt of afsd. Co. £15 curr. 125 a. in Spts. Co. No witnesses. July 4, 1768.

July 4, 1768. John Deatherage of Spts. Co. and Sarah Edwards Deatherage, his wife, to Edward Brasfield of Caroline Co. £70. 200 a. in Spts. Co., bought by sd. Deatherage of John Gale and Sarah, his wife, etc. No witnesses. July 4, 1768.

March 18, 1768. John Waller, Clk. of Spts. Co. to Wm. Wood and John Battaley. Mortgage. Witnesses, Thomas Megee, Thomas Megee, Junr., July 4, 1768.

Feby. 13, 1768. Jesse Harper and Dianna, his wife, of Spts. Co. to William Rogers of afsd. Co. £60 curr. 100 a. in St. Geo. Par., Spts. Co., part of a pat. formerly granted Peter Rogers, etc. Witnesses, Robert Goodloe, Jno. Bevy. Roy, Benjamin Waller. July 4, 1768.

Decr. 31, 1767. Reuben Thornton and Elizabeth, his wife, of Caroline Co., to Wm. Dangerfield of Spts. Co., Gent. Whereas, Henry Willis, Gent., former husband to the sd. Elizabeth, was in his lifetime and during the coverture of the sd. Elizabeth, seized of a tract of land in Spts. Co., containing 3333 a. and is the same tract whereon sd. Dangerfield now lives, the sd. Elizabeth being entitled to ⅓ part thereof, after the death of sd. Henry Willis, etc., the sd. Elizabeth, having remained seized thereof ever since, etc. Sd. Thornton and Elizabeth, his wife, convey to sd. Dangerfield the sd. Elizabeth's dower in the sd. tract, in consideration of £200 curr. Witnesses, James Taylor, Junr., Anthony Thornton, Richard Buckner. July 4, 1768.

Augt. 1, 1768. Wm. Pigg of New Kent Co., Joiner, and George Pottie of Louisa Co., Mercht., to Francis Jerdone of Louisa Co., Mercht. £45. 176 a. in Spts. Co., formerly mortgaged by sd. Pigg to the sd. George Pottie, etc. No witnesses. Augt. 1, 1768.

Feby. 20, 1768. Nathaniel Stevenson of Fredksbg., "being on an Intended voyage to Britain," etc., po. of atto. to Benjamin Johnston. Witnesses, Wm. White, Benjamin Johnston. Augt. 1, 1768.

Jany. 20, 1768. John Battaley of Spts. Co. to Andrew Cochrane, Wm. Cunninghame & Co., Merchts., in Glasgow. £280 curr. Mortgage. Slaves. Witnesses, Wm. Reid, Alexr. Horsburgh. Augt. 3, 1768.

Augt. 1, 1768. Thomas Reeves and Sarah, his wife, of Frederick Co., Va., to James Cunninghame of Spts. Co. £20 curr. Lot 127 in town of Fredksbg. No witnesses. Augt. 1, 1768.

March 30, 1768. Catharine Stubblefield of Spts. Co., widow, to Hugh Lenox, John Mitchell & Co., Merchts., and Henry Mitchell of Fredksbg., Atto. in Fact for George McCall, Mercht. Mortgage. £209 1s. 4d. Curr. 956 a. on Pamunkey River in Spts. Co. Witnesses, Jos. Herndon, George Stubblefield, John Herndon, Harry Stubblefield. Augt. 1, 1768.

Augt. 1, 1768. Wm. Gale of Whitehaven, Gt. Britain, Mercht., by John Thornton, his attorney in fact, to Charles Yates of Fredksbg. £233. Lot No. 2 in town of Fredksbg., formerly conveyed by Trustees of sd. Town, as by Deed, Octr. 4, 1737, to Wm. Gale and Matthias Gale, etc. Witnesses, Wm. Wood, John Chew, J. Lewis, W. Underwood, Jonathan Clark. Augt. 2, 1768.

May 9, 1768. Pearson Chapman of the Province of Maryland, Esqr., to John Dalton of Fredksbg., Va., Tailor. Deed of Lease, "the sd. John Dalton and Elizabeth, his wife, and Walker Dalton, his son," etc. Tenement in town of Fredksbg., late in tenure and occupation of Barbary Jones, widow, now decd., etc. £20 curr. on Nov. 16 annually, etc. Witnesses, Jonathan Hind, Thos. Walker, Robt. Maitland. Augt. 2, 1768.

Jany. 21, 1768. Henry Heath, Gent., Practitioner of Physick, in Fredksbg., to Charles Yates of Fredksbg., Mercht. £128 15s. 11d. Ster. Mortgage. Lot 20 in town of Fredksbg. Hudson Muse, James Duncanson, John Stewart, William Templeman. Augt. 3, 1768.

July 26, 1768. Joseph Peterson of Orange Co., North Carolina, and Lucy, his wife, to John Pulliam of Spts. Co., Va. £55 curr. 147½ a. in Spts. Co. Lark. Chew, Jno. Carter, Stephen Johnson. Septr. 6, 1768.

Septr. 5, 1768. John Mitchell of Fredksbg., Mercht., and partner of Hugh Lenox & Co., to Thomas Ashman of Spts. Co. £9 curr. 100 a. in Spts. Co. James Somerville, Jos. Herndon, John x Collins. Septr. 5, 1768.

Augt. 29, 1768. Waller Lewis of Spts. Co. to Benjamin Waller of same Co. £16 10s. curr. 55 a. in Spts. Co., part of a pat. granted Zachary Lewis, Septr. 28, 1732, etc. John Chew, J. Lewis, Oliver Towles. Septr. 5, 1768.

Septr. 5, 1768. Samuel Dyer of Caroline Co. to Aquilla Johnston of Caroline Co. £20 curr. 510 a. in Spts. Co. Wm. Wood, Harry Robinson, James Lewis, Jonathan Clark. Sept. 5, 1768.

Septr. 5, 1768. Joseph Bledsoe of Spts. Co. and Elizabeth, his wife, to Abraham Simpson of sd. Co. £140 curr. 156 a. in St. Geo. Par., Spts. Co., given sd. Joseph Bledsoe by his father, Wm. Bledsoe, and whereon the sd. Jos. lately lived, bounded by lands of Wm. Hunter, Decd. John Schoolar, Alexander Spotswood and Moses Bledsoe, Decd., etc. No witnesses. Septr. 5, 1768.

Feby. 2, 1768. Benjamin Winslow of Spts. Co. to Beverley Winslow of same Co., Gent. Mortgage. 595 a., part of the tract whereon sd. Beverley now lives, and given the sd. Benjamin by his mother, Susanna Winslow, etc. Also several negroes. Witnesses, O. Towles, jr., Thomas Powe, Jos. Herndon, Harry Winslow. Septr. 6, 1768.

Feby. 20, 1768. John Mitchell of Spts. Co., having bought 300 weight of pork from Estate of Wm. Miller, Decd., gives mortgage to Jane Miller and Joseph Herndon, Execrs. of the last will, etc., of sd. Wm. Miller, Decd. Witnesses, Jno. Carter, Wm. Wood. Septr. 6, 1768.

Septr. 5, 1768. John Waller of Spts. Co., Gent., and Ann, his wife, to Wm. Waller of same Co. In consideration that sd. Wm. Waller releases sd. John Waller from the payment of £40 annually on land and slaves deeded sd. John by sd. Wm. Waller, the sd. John Waller and Ann, his wife, deed to sd. Wm. Waller 240 a. in Spts. Co., purchased of Thomas McNeal, etc. Also one negro, etc. Witnesses, Tho. Megee, Sherod Horn, Tho. Megee, junr., Oswald Smith. Septr. 7, 1768.

Nov. 14, 1766. Hugh Sanders of Spts. Co. to his son in law, Lewis Craig, of same Co. Deed of Gift. 300 a. in Spts. Co. Witnesses, John Sanders, Jno. Robinson, John x Collins, Thos. Gholson. Octr. 3, 1768.

Octr. 3, 1768. Edward Coleman and Sarah, his wife, of St. Geo. Par., Spts. Co., to Samuel Alsup of Drysdale Par., Caroline Co. £80 curr. 300 a. in branches of Pamunkey River in Spts. Co. No witnesses. Octr. 3, 1768.

Septr. 28, 1768. Elizabeth x Hawkins, widow and relict of Nicholas Hawkins, decd., to her daughter, Ann Pritchett, wife of James Pritchett. Deed of Gift. "One negro girl * * * * * which I bought of my son, John Hawkins, Decd.," etc. Witnesses, Wm. Wood, John Pritchett, Jonathan Clark. Nov. 7, 1768.

Nov. 7, 1768. John Lewis of Spts. Co. and Waller Lewis of same Co. Whereas sd. John and Waller Lewis have mutually agreed to change lands, sd. John Lewis to convey the sd. Waller Lewis 49 acres purchased by sd. John of Thomas Hill, etc., sd. Waller Lewis to convey to sd. John Lewis 49 acres, part of a tract devised sd. Waller by the will of Zachary Lewis, Decd., etc., etc. No witnesses. Nov. 7, 1768.

Decr. 1, 1768. Henry Elly of Culpeper Co. to his son, Henry Elly, junr., of Spts. Co. Deed of Gift. Negroes and interest in a tenement of land whereon sd. Elly, junr., lives, which was purchased by sd. Elly, Senr., of the executors of Col. John Spotswood, Decd. Witnesses, Tavener Branham, Samuel Sparks, Thomas Burbridge. Decr. 5, 1768.

Nov. 14, 1768. Mildred Thomas of Spts. Co. to her two children, Agnes (wife of Thos. Merry) and my son, James Thomas, etc. Deed of Gift. Right or title she may have under the will of her husband, Owen Thomas, Decd., after her decease, etc. Witnesses, O. Thomas, Jno. Holloday, junr. Dec. 5, 1768.

Augt. 2, 1766. Jno. Waller, Clk. of Spts. Co., and Ann, his wife, to Peter Taliaferro of Culpeper Co. £30 curr. Lots 196 and 198 in town of Fredksbg. Harry Bartlett, Richard Johnston, James Chiles, Robert Chew, B. Johnston. Augt. 6, 1766.

July 5, 1768. Thomas Reeves, late of Augusta Co., to John Herndon of Spts. Co. £100 curr. Mortgage. Slaves. Test, Joseph Brock. Feby. 6, 1769.

June 12, 1768. John Waller, Clk. of Spts. Co., to Richard Johnston of Culpeper Co. £35 curr. All the sd. John Waller's interest in slaves that may be coming to him at the death of his mother, Mrs. Ann Waller, as devised in the will of his father, Col. Wm. Waller, Decd. Witnesses, W. Buckner, Lark. Chew, Jno. Bevy. Roy. Feby. 6, 1769.

Feby. 6, 1769. Benjamin Martin of Orange Co. and Sarah, his wife, to George Atkinson of Spts. Co. £21 2s. 5d. curr. 91 a. in Spts. Co. sold by Benjamin Martin, Decd., to Benjamin Davis and by him conveyed to Benjamin Martin, party to these presents, etc. Witnesses, Joseph Brock, junr., Thomas May. Feby. 6, 1769.

Augt. 3, 1768. John Battaley of Fredksbg. to Joseph Brock and Joseph Herndon of Spts. Co. Mortgage. 400 a. of land in Spts. Co. and three lots in town of Fredksbg., whereon sd. Battaley now lives, etc.: also goods and chattels. Witnesses, Ben. Winslow, George Stubblefield, Joseph Minor. March 7, 1769.

March 6, 1769. Thomas Merry of Orange Co. and Agnes, his wife, and Reuben Daniel of Orange Co. and Elizabeth, his wife, to John Holloday of Spts. Co. £25. 170 a. in Spts. Co. Wm. Wood, Jno. Crane, Willm. Smith, Jona. Clark. March 6, 1769.

Feby. 6, 1769. Benjamin Johnston of Fredksbg to Wm. Wood of Spts. Co. Lease. 360 a. in Spts. Co., formerly Bells Ordinary. £11 5s. curr. annually. Jno. Bevy. Roy, Jonathan Clark, Harry Robinson, W. Underwood. March 6, 1769.

July 12, 1768. Joanna x Cook of Spts. Co. to Michael Yates of Caroline Co. £10 curr. 150 a. in Spts. Co. given and sold the sd. Joanna by her father, Thomas Cook, joining lands of Taliaferro Craig, John Craig, Samuel Dyer and the heirs of Thomas Collins and Thomas Salmon, Decd.

Witnesses, John McDonald, Wm. Stears, Susannah x Conell. March 6, 1769.

Octr. 15, 1768. William McWilliams of Spts. Co. "for the natural love and affection wch. he hath and beareth unto * * * * Benjamin McWilliams." Deed of Gift. 934 a. in Spts. Co. whereon sd. Wm. McWilliams now lives, etc.; also several slaves, etc. "The sd. Wm. McWilliams and Ann McWilliams, his wife, after their decease," etc. Witnesses, Owen Minor, Joseph Minor, Igns. Rains, John Estes, jr., James Mills. March 6, 1769.

Octr. 7, 1768. Wm. x Gholson of Spts. Co. and Susannah, his wife, to John Mitchell of Fredksbg., Mercht. £35 curr. 60 a. in St. Geo. Par., Spts. Co. Jos. Brock, Mary Gordon, Wm. Thompson, Geo. x Brudwell. April 3, 1769.

March 31, 1769. Benjamin Johnston of Fredksbg. to Wm. Johnston of Caroline. £555 curr. Mortgage. Goods and chattels. To indemnify sd. Wm. Johnston, who stands security on a bond of the sd. Benjamin Johnston, etc. No witnesses. April 3, 1769.

Augt. 25, 1768. John Roane of King Wm. Co., Gent., and Susanna, his wife, to William Champe of King Geo. Co., Esqr. £600 curr. 1075 a. in Spts. Co., purchased by sd. Roane of Humphrey Hill, atto. in fact for Humphrey Bell of London, Mercht., etc. Witnesses, Geo. Mitchell, Henry Mitchell, Fras. Thornton. April 4, 1769.

March 24, 1769. Wm. Dangerfield of Spts. Co. and Mary, his wife, to Charles Yates of Fredksbg., Gentl. £130. Lots 11 and 12 in town of Fredksbg. Walter Chiles, William Hutson, Michael Ludwidge. April 4, 1769.

Augt. 10, 1768. Henry Pendleton of Spts. Co. to James Somerville of Fredksbg., Mercht. £133 6s. 3d. curr. Mortgage. Slaves, etc. Witnesses, Edward Stevens, Hugh Stewart. April 4, 1769.

May 29, 1769. John x Durrett and James Chiles of St. Geo. Par., Spts. Co., and Elizabeth, wife, of sd. James Chiles, to Abram Larew of New East Jersey. £90 curr. 233 a. in St. Geo. Par., Spts. Co., part of a pat. granted sd. John Durrett. Witnesses, James Wigglesworth, John x Rainey, Jno. Wigglesworth, junr., Mary Long. June 5, 1769.

July 7, 1764. Thomas Duncanson, Surgeon, of Forres, Co. Murray, North Britain, and brother german to the Decd. Robert Duncanson of Fredksbg., Va., Mercht. Whereas the sd. Robert Duncanson sometime since departed this life in town of Fredksbg., Va., leaving neither letter, will or testament or disposition of his estate, by which the sd. Thos. Duncanson is heir to the sd. Robert as nearest of kin, etc., and po. of atto. to James Duncanson of Fredksbg., Va., Mercht., etc. Witnesses, John Frazer, Alexr. McSween. No date of record.

June 5, 1769. John x Durrett, James Wigglesworth and Mary, his wife, of St. Geo. Par., Spts. Co., to Abram Larew of New East Jersey. £34 curr. 340 a. in St. Geo. Par., Spts. Co., part of pat. granted sd. Durrett. Witnesses, James Chiles, Mary Long. June 5, 1769.

June 3, 1769. Robert Coleman of St. Geo. Par., Spts. Co., and Elizabeth, his wife, to Benjamin Steward of Westmoreland Co. £65 curr. 125 a.

in St. Geo. Par., Spts. Co., purchased by sd. Coleman of Humphrey Hill, atto. in fact for Humphrey Bell, etc., now in possession and occupied by Paul Apperson on Pawpaw Swamp, etc. Witnesses, Thos. Dillard, Paul Apperson, John Steward. June 5, 1769.

Feby. 28, 1769. Richard Clay and Thomas Midgley of Liverpoole, Co. Lancaster, Gt. Britain, Merchts. and copartners, etc., po. of atto. to Henry Parry of Liverpoole, Master and Mariner, etc. Witnesses, John Southward, Isaac Tully, Stephen Backhouse. Augt. 7, 1769.

April 13, 1769. Gregory Baylor and George Brooke, acting executors of last will and testament of Robert Baylor, late of King and Queen Co., Gent., Decd., to Benjamin Tompkins of Caroline Co. Whereas, sd. Robt. Baylor was in his lifetime and at his death seized in fee simple of 2 tracts of land in Spts. Co. (which descended to him from his brother, Richard Baylor, Decd.) and being so seized in and by his last will and testament among other things did direct the sd. land to be sold and of his said will appointed his wife, Molly Baylor (who renounced the executorship and all benefit of sd. will), Gregory Baylor and George Brooke, Executors; and whereas, by a decree of the County Court of King and Queen, made July 8, 1765, in a suit in Chancery there depending between Frances Baylor, Molly Baylor, Elizabeth Baylor, Hannah Baylor and Ann Baylor, younger children of sd. Robert Baylor, Decd., Pltfs., and John Baylor, son and heir, and Gregory Baylor and George Brooke, Execrs. of sd. Robt. Baylor, Decd., Defds., it was among other things decreed and ordered that the sd. Executors should sell the sd. lands and apply the money arising therefrom towards paying the sd. Robt. Baylor, Decd., debts, etc. Witnesseth, sd. Baylor and Brooke, as Executors, for sum of £204 curr. convey to sd. Tompkins 1019 a. in Spts. Co., etc. Witnesses, Richard Stevens, Josiah Samuel, Robt. Dudley, Isaac Graves. June 5, 1769.

Septr. 29, 1768. John x Beazley of Caroline Co. to Wm. Chowning of Caroline Co. £12 curr. 200 a. in Spts. Co. Witnesses, Wm. Hill, junr., Wm. x. Stevens, Micajah Stevens. June 5, 1769.

June 5, 1769. Nicholas Hawkins, junr., of Spts. Co., to Richard Keown of same Co. £30 curr. 100 a. in Spts. Co., which said land was devised by the last will and testament of John Long, Decd., to his wife, Elizabeth Long, and since by the last will and testament of sd. Elizabeth Long, Decd., devised to her grandson, the sd. Nicholas Hawkins, junr., which sd. wills are recorded in Spts. Co. Court, etc. Witness, Nicholas Hawkins. June 5, 1769.

March 2, 1769. William Scott and Ann, his wife, of Spts. Co., to Alexander Spence Head of same Co. £100 curr. 162 a. in Spts. Co. Chs. Tureman, Benjamin Johnston, jr., Uriah Edwards, Sherod Horn, Nicholas Hawkins, Nicholas Hawkins, junr.

June 5, 1769. Thomas Colson of Spts. Co. to John Penn of same Co. £20 curr. 130 a. in Spts. Co. No witnesses. June 5, 1769.

June 5, 1769. John Penn, Senr., of Spts. Co., and Mary, his wife, to Sherod Horn of same Co. £20 curr. 130 a. in Spts. Co. No witnesses. June 5, 1769.

April 8, 1769. James Johnston of Caroline Co. and Mary, his wife, and Richard Johnston and Dorothy, his wife, to John McCauley of Spts. Co. £145 7s. 1d. 279 a. in Spts. Co.; also 48 a. called Farkiln Branch Tract, adjoining the lands of Mrs. Dawson, Beazley and Betty Benger. Witnesses, Henry Crutcher, B. Johnston, Geo. Mitchell, Hugh Stewart. June 5, 1769.

Jany. 1, 1759. John Hawkins of St. Geo. Par., Spts. Co., to his mother, Elizabeth Hawkins. £19 curr. A negro slave. Witnesses, Nathan Hawkins, Randile Macdaniel, Willm. Smith. July 3, 1769.

Jany. 26, 1769. John Glenn of Spts. Co. to Richard Coleman of Co. afsd. £21 5s. 3d. curr. Mortgage. 200 a. in St. Geo. Par., Spts. Co., adjoining lands of James Davis, Jno. Jinkins, Massom Powe and Garretts, which land sd. Glenn purchased of Wm. Garrett, etc. Witnesses, Bevy. Winslow, John Chew, John Gadbery. Augt. 7, 1769.

Feby. 18, 1769. Hugh Sanders and Katharine, his wife, of Spts. Co., to Benjamin Mastin of sd. Co. £25 curr. 101 a. in Spts. Co. John Sanders, Wm. Ellis, Lewis Craig. July 3, 1769.

Augt. 7, 1769. John Taliaferro of King Geo. County, Gent., to Wm. Allsup of Spts. Co. Lease., "sd. Wm. Allsup and Sarah, his wife, etc." 600 a. in Spts. Co. 1200 lbs. tob. yearly. Witnesses, Wm. Wood, Andr. Buchannan. Augt. 7, 1769.

Augt. 7, 1769. Roger Dixon of Fredksbg., Mercht., and Lucy, his wife, to William Smith of same town, Mercht. £55 curr. Lots 252 and 262 in town of Fredksbg. No witnesses. Augt. 7, 1769.

Septr. 4, 1769. Charles Cosby of Spts. Co. to John Minor of Caroline Co. £8 8s. curr. 21 a. in Spts. Co., part of a tract purchased by sd. Cosby of Patrick Belches, etc. No witnesses. Septr. 4, 1769.

Septr. 4, 1769. Charles Cosby and Elizabeth, his wife, of St. Geo. Par., Spts. Co., to William Quarles of same Co. £40 curr. 50 a. in Par. and Co. afsd. No witnesses. Septr. 4, 1769.

Jany. 31, 1769. Thomas Crutcher of Caroline Co. and Sarah, his wife, to Francis Simpson of Spts. Co. £20 curr. 200 a. in Spts. Co. Jos. Brock, John Harrison, Thomas Crutcher, junr. Septr. 4, 1769.

Septr. 4, 1769. Francis Turnley and Mary, his wife, and Ann x Turnley, widow of Richard Turnley, Decd., to James Redd of Spts. Co. £10 curr. 50 a. sold unto the sd. Richard Turnley by Martin True, etc. No witnesses. Septr. 4, 1769.

Jany. 6, 1769. Samuel Simpson and Mary, his wife, of Albemarle Co., to Peter Marye of Spts Co. £40 curr. 70 a. in St. Geo. Par., Spts. Co. James Marshall, Ann Waller, Ellis Carr, Merriman Marshall, George Waller, William Carr, Lodowick Oneale, Richard x Wilson. Septr. 4, 1769.

Septr. 5, 1769. Wm. Allsup of Spts. Co. to James Hutcherson of Co. afsd. Lease. 100 a. to be laid off on part of tract sd. Allsup leased of John Taliaferro, etc., "sd. James Hutcherson and Margaret, his wife, sd. William Allsup and Sarah, his wife," etc. £3 curr. yearly. No witnesses. Septr. 5, 1769.

Sept. 4, 1769. Fielding Lewis of Fredksbg., Esqr., and Betty, his wife, to James Mercer of same town, attorney-at-law. £92. Lot whereon sd.

Mercer dwelling stands and the two lots occupied by his study in the town afsd. No witnesses. Sept. 6, 1769.

May 1, 1769. Henry Heath of Fredksbg., Surgeon, and Susanna, his wife, to Charles Yates of same town, Mercht. £110 curr. Lots 256 and 266 in town of Fredksbg. P. Marye, Beverley Winslow, James Purvis. June 5, 1769.

Octr. 2, 1769. James Chiles and Elizabeth, his wife, of Spts. Co., to David Anderson of Spts. Co. £10 curr. 100 a. in Spts. Co. No witnesses. Octr. 2, 1769.

June 28, 1769. James Bowlere (Boulwer) of Essex Co. to Abraham Darnal of Spts. Co. £10 curr. 185 a. in St. Geo. Par., Spts. Co. James Nelson, Thomas x Page. Octr. 2, 1769.

Septr. 13, 1769. James Lindsay of Caroline Co. to his son, Daniel Lindsay, of Spts. Co. Deed of Gift. 200 a. in St. Geo. Par., Spts. Co. Robt. Gilchrist, Wm. Bogle, Wm. Dickson. Octr. 2, 1769.

Octr. 2, 1769. Robert Goodloe of Spts. Co., Gent., to his son-in-law, Daniel Lindsay. Deed of Gift. 200 a. in Spts. Co. James Lindsay, Wm. Walker. Octr. 2, 1769.

Novr. 6, 1769. James Chiles of Spts. Co. and Jemima, his wife, to Thomas Lipscomb of Albemarle Co. 244 a. in Spts. Co., devised to the sd. James Chiles by his father, Henry Chiles, Decd., etc. No witnesses. Novr. 6, 1769.

June 8, 1769. Phillip Jones and Jane, his wife, of Caroline Co., to Robert Coleman of Spts. Co. £70 curr. 129 a. in St. Geo. Par., Spts. Co., on Robinson River, etc. Thomas Coleman, Jacob Daniel, Elisha Dismukes. Novr. 6, 1769.

Octr. 23, 1769. Aaron Marders and Elinor, his wife, to John Frederick Baker of Fredksbg. £13 6s. 8d. curr. Right, title and Interest in a certain lot in town of Fredksbg., purchased by James Swain of Roger Dixon, Gent., and by him conveyed to the sd. James Swain, during his life, and afterwards to the sd. Swain's three daughters, vizt: Elinor (party to these presents), Catharine and Elizabeth. Witnesses, Jno. Battaley, Jno. Richards, Christopher x Ward. Nov. 6, 1769.

Nov. 2, 1769. Charles Lewis and Lucy, his wife, of Caroline Co., to Edward Lutwitch (Ludwidge?) of Spts. Co. £15 curr. 87½ in St. Geo. Par., Spts. Co., adjoining lands of George Moore, Wm. Darnaby, Colo. James Ball and John Callahan, and part of a tract purchased of Joseph and George Nix, etc. Witnesses, Jos. Jones, Aust. x Terrell, Jno. Robinson. Novr. 7, 1769.

June 21, 1769. John Davenport and Wm. Davenport, junr., to Wm. Davenport. £33 curr. Slaves. Witnesses, J. Lewis, O. Towles, jr. Novr. 8, 1769.

Septr. 12, 1769. John Lurtey of Fredksbg., Mariner, to Hunter & Glassell of same town, etc., Merchts. £55 curr. A slave. Witnesses, Robert Brown, John Swan. Decr. 5, 1769.

Augt. 1, 1769. Andrew x Fraser of Spts. Co. to James Duncanson of Fredksbg., Mercht. £52 7s. 1d. Curr. A slave and goods and chattels, etc. Wm. Walker, Adam Walker. Decr. 5, 1769.

Octr. 13, 1769. George Washington of Fairfax Co., Esqr., and Martha, his wife, to James Mercer of Fredksbg., Attorney-at-Law. £50. Two lots in town of Fredksbg. adjoining the two lots purchased by sd. Mercer of Fielding Lewis, Esqr., etc. Witnesses, Chs. Dick, Chs. Washington, John Lithgow. Decr. 5, 1769.

Augt. 28, 1769. Aaron Quisenberry of Spts. Co. and Joyce, his wife, to John Mitchell of sd. Co. £170 curr. 275 a. in St. Geo. Par., Spts. Co. Fielding Lewis, James Somerville, Wm. Nelson, Richard Lewis. Decr. 5, 1769.

June 8, 1769. Thomas Reeves to James Somerville, atto.-in-fact for John Mitchell, Hugh Lenox, Scott & Co. Agreement, etc. Witness, Chas. Bruce. Decr. 5, 1769.

Feby. 22, 1770. Alexander Spotswood of Spts. Co. to Thomas Fox of sd. Co. Lease. 300 a. of land and the houses wherein Mr. Benger formerly lived, etc. £16 curr. yearly. Wm. Marshall, James Tutt, Benjamin Tutt. March 5, 1770.

Octr. 9, 1769. George Humphries of Orange Co. and Eleanor, his wife, and Edward Graves of Culpeper Co. and Sarah, his wife, to John Chiles of Spts. Co. £10 curr. 120 a. in Spts. Co., part of a tract willed by John Graves, Decd., to his sons, the sd. Edward and Thomas, John and Isaac Graves, etc. Witnesses, Henry Chiles, Ben. Chiles, Chas. Powell, Joseph Dicken. May 7, 1770.

Septr. 28th, 1769. Henry Terrell of Spts. Co. to Wm. Ware & Son of City of Bristol. Mortgage. To secure payment of £62 3s. 7½d. Negroes. Witnesses, Richard Terrell, Garritt Minor. May 7, 1770.

May 7, 1770. James Ware and Agnes, his wife, to John Chick of Hanover Co. £1 5s. curr. 100 a. in Spts. Co. Wm. Crow, Francis Baber, Nicho. Ware. May 7, 1770.

May 7, 1770. James Ware and Agnes, his wife, of Caroline Co., to Nathaniel Hill of Hanover Co. £2 10s. curr. 100 a. in St. Geo. Par., Spts. Co., which sd. land sd. Hill drew as a prize in Ware's Lottery, etc. Francis Baber, John Chick. May 7, 1770.

May 7, 1770. James Ware and Agnes, his wife, of Caroline Co., to James Riddle of sd. Co. £1 5s. curr. 100 a. in Spts. Co., in St. Geo. Par., which sd. land was drawn in Ware's Lottery, etc. Wm. Crow, Nicho. Ware. May 7, 1770.

May 7, 1770. James Ware and Agnes, his wife, of Caroline Co., to Ezekiah Mitchell of sd. Co. £1 5s. curr. 100 a. in St. Geo. Par., Spts. Co., which sd. land was drawn in Ware's Lottery, etc. John Chick, Wm. Crow, Francis Baber. May 7, 1770.

May 7, 1770. James Ware and Agnes, his wife, of Caroline Co., to Humphrey Haley of sd. Co. £2 10s. curr. 100 a. in St. Geo. Par., Spts. Co., drawn in Ware's Lottery, etc. John Chick, Francis Baber, Wm. Crow. May 7, 1770.

May 7, 1770. James Ware and Agnes, his wife, of Caroline Co., to Thos. Upshaw of Essex Co. £1 5s. curr. 100 a. in St. Geo. Par., Spts. Co., drawn in Ware's Lottery, etc. John Chick, Francis Baber. May 7, 1770.

May 7, 1770. James Ware and Agnes, his wife, of Caroline Co., to Wm. Crow of King and Queen Co. £2 10s. Curr. 100 a. in St. Geo. Par., Spts. Co., drawn in Ware's Lottery, etc. John Chick, Francis Baber, Nicho. Ware. May 7, 1770.

May 7, 1770. James Ware of Caroline Co. and Agnes, his wife, to Francis Baber of same Co. £1 5s. curr. 100 a. in St. Geo. Par., Spts. Co., drawn in Ware's Lottery, etc. Wm. Crow, John Chick. May 7, 1770.

April 23, 1770. Dudley Gatewood and Sarah, his wife, of Amherst Co., to Francis Cammack of Spts. Co. £90 curr. 150 a. in Spts. Co. Henry Gatewood, jr., George Cammack, Henry Cammack, Wm. Cammack. May 7, 1770.

May 7, 1770. John Herndon of Spts. Co. and Mary, his wife, to Thomas May of same Co. £90 curr. 264 a. in St. Geo. Par., Spts. Co. Ambrose Raines, Wm. Wigglesworth, Robert Richards. May 7, 1770.

Feby. 12, 1770. John Penn and Elizabeth, his wife, of Amherst Co., to John Holloday of Spts. Co. £130 curr. 275 a. in Spts. Co. Henry Gatewood, junr., John Tureman, Benjamin Holloday, jr., Benjamin Perrye. May 7, 1770.

Jany. 13, 1770. Joseph Wharton of Orange Co., son of Samuel Wharton of King Geo. Co., Decd., to Wharton Schooler of Spts. Co. £10 curr. Title, interest and right in the est. of his decd. father, Samuel Wharton, etc. Witnesses, Reuben Young, John Schooler, Samuel Schooler. May 7, 1770.

April 2, 1770. Thomas Graves and Ann, his wife, of St. Geo. Par., Spts. Co., to Samuel Warren of Par. and Co. afsd. £35 curr. 100 a. in Par. and Co. afsd., adjoining lands formerly Humphrey Bell's and Robert Goodloe and Thomas Dillard's land, etc. Witnesses, Roger Dixon, Chs. Yates, Wm. Wood, Jona. Clark. May 8, 1770.

Nov. 25, 1760. Isaac Darnall of Spts. Co. to Nicholas Darnall of Caroline Co. £45 curr. 150 a. in Spts. Co. Benja. Powe, Jos. Willoughby, Wm. Mastin, Benja. x Mastin, John Mastin. No date of Record.

June 4, 1770. Thomas May and Elizabeth, his wife, of Spts. Co., to Wm. Scott of Spts. Co. £100 curr. 220 a. in Spts. Co., whereon sd. May now dwells, etc. Robt. Collins, Thos. Poole, Henry Johnston. June 4, 1770.

April 10, 1770. William Fitzhugh of Stafford Co., Esqr., and Ann, his wife, to Thomas Burbridge, junr., of Spts. Co. £40 curr. 85 a. in St. Geo. Par., Spts. Co. B. Johnston, Phillip Somerby, Jno. Brock. June 4, 1770.

June 4, 1770. Wm. Fitzhugh of Stafford Co., Esqr., and Ann, his wife, to Isaac Willson of Spts. Co. £50 curr. 174 a. in St. Geo. Par., Spts. Co. No witnesses. June 4, 1770.

April 10, 1770. Wm. Fitzhugh of Stafford Co., Esqr., and Ann, his wife, to John Chew of Spts. Co. £110 curr. 232 a. in St. Geo. Par., Spts. Co., known as "New Lick." B. Johnston, Phillip Somerby, Jno. Brock, Jos. Brock. June 4, 1770.

April 10, 1770. Wm. Fitzhugh of Stafford Co., Esqr., and Ann, his wife, to Thomas Burbridge of Spts. Co. £145 curr. 450 a. in St. Geo. Par., Spts.

Co. (except one acre reserved for a church yard, etc.); B. Johnston, Phillip Somerby, Jos. Brock, Jno. Brock. June 4, 1770.

June 4, 1770. Wm. Fitzhugh of Stafford Co., Esqr., and Ann, his wife, to William Ficklin of Spts. Co. £50 curr. 250 a. in St. Geo. Par., Spts. Co. No witnesses. June 4, 1770.

Octr. 5, 1769. Wm. Fitzhugh of Stafford Co., Esqr., and Ann, his wife, to Daniel Branham of Spts. Co. £68 curr. 150 a. in St. Geo. Par., Spts. Co. Chas. Carter, James Benson, Ben Guinn, B. Johnston, Phillip Somerby, Jno. Brock, Jos. Brock. June 4, 1770.

April 10, 1770. Wm. Fitzhugh of Stafford Co., Esqr., and Ann, his wife, to John Moore of Spts. Co. £69 curr. 345 a. in St. Geo. Par., Spts. Co. B. Johnston, Jos. Brock, Jno. Brock, Phillip Somerby. June 4, 1770.

June 4, 1770. Wm. Fitzhugh of Stafford Co., Esqr., and Ann, his wife, to John Shelton of Spts. Co. £40 curr. 150 a. in St. Geo. Par., Spts. Co. No witnesses. No date of Record.

April 10, 1770. Wm. Fitzhugh of Stafford Co., Esqr., and Ann, his wife, to John Herndon of Spts. Co. £192 curr. 635 a. in St. Geo. Par., Spts. Co. B. Johnston, Jno. Brock, Phillip Somerby, Jos. Brock. June 4, 1770.

Octr. 5, 1769. Wm. Fitzhugh and Ann, his wife, of Stafford Co., to Bland Ballard of Spts. Co. £65 curr. 143 a. in St. Geo. Par., Spts. Co. Chs. Carter, Ben. Gwinn, James Benson, B. Johnston, Phillip Somerby, Jno. Brock, Jos. Brock. June 4, 1770.

April 10, 1770. Wm. Fitzhugh of Stafford Co., Esqr., and Ann, his wife, to Thomas Haydon of Spts. Co. £150 curr. 503 a. in St. Geo. Par., Spts. Co. B. Johnston, Phillip Somerby, Jno. Brock, Jos. Brock. June 4, 1770.

Octr. 5, 1769. Wm. Fitzhugh of Stafford Co., Esqr., and Ann, his wife, to James Cunninghame of Spts. Co. £87 curr. 218 a. in St. Geo. Par., Spts. Co. Chs. Carter, Ben Gwinn, James Benson, B. Johnston, Phillip Somerby, Jno. Brock, Jos. Brock. No date of record.

June 4, 1770. Wm. Fitzhugh of Stafford Co., Esqr., and Ann, his wife, to Peter Marye of Spts. Co., Gent. £275 curr. 1500 a. in St. Geo. Par., Spts. Co., known as "Chatham." No witnesses. No date of Record.

Octr. 5, 1769. Wm. Fitzhugh of Stafford Co., Esqr., and Ann, his wife, to James Marye of Spts. Co., Clerk. £170 curr. 700 a. in St. Geo. Par., Spts. Co. Chas. Carter, Ben. Gwinn, James Benson, B. Johnston, Phillip Somerby, Jno. Brock, Jos. Brock. No date of Record.

April 10, 1770. Wm. Fitzhugh of Stafford Co., Esqr., and Ann, his wife, to Wm. Riaden of King Geo. Co. £44 10s. curr. 245 a. in St. Geo. Par., Spts. Co. B. Johnston, Phillip Somerby, Jno. Brock, Jos. Brock. June 4, 1770.

April 10, 1770. Wm. Fitzhugh of Stafford Co., Esqr., and Ann, his wife, to Robert Oneale of Spts. Co. £50 10s. curr. 118 a. in St. Geo. Par., Spts. Co. B. Johnston, Phillip Somerby, Jno. Brock, Jos. Brock. No date of record.

April 10, 1770. Wm. Fitzhugh of Stafford Co., Esqr., and Ann, his wife, to John Mitchell of Spts. Co. £260 curr. 1121 a. in St. Geo. Par., Spts. Co. B. Johnston, Phillip Somerby, Jno. Brock, Jos. Brock. June 4, 1770.

April 10, 1770. Wm. Fitzhugh of Stafford Co., Esqr., and Ann, his wife, to James Lewis of Spts. Co. £120 curr. 290 a. in St. Geo. Par., Spts. Co. B. Johnston, Phillip Somerby, Jno. Brock, Jos. Brock. June 4, 1770.

April 10, 1770. Wm. Fitzhugh of Stafford Co., Esqr., and Ann, his wife, to John Price of Spts. Co. £17 10s. curr. 150 a. in St. Geo. Par., Spts. Co. B. Johnston, Phillip Somerby, Jno. Brock, Jos. Brock. June 4, 1770.

June 4, 1770. Wm. Fitzhugh of Stafford Co., Esqr., and Ann, his wife, to John Mitchell of Spts. Co. £85 curr. 400 a. in St. Geo. Par., Spts. Co. No witnesses. June 4, 1770.

Octr. 5, 1769. Wm. Fitzhugh of Stafford Co., Esqr., and Ann, his wife, to Hezekiah Ellis of Spts. Co. £90 curr. 190 a. in St. Geo. Par., Spts. Co. Chs. Carter, Ben. Gwinn, James Benson, B. Johnston, Philip Somerby, Jno. Brock, Jos. Brock. June 4, 1770.

June 4, 1770. Bland x Ballard of Spts. Co. to his son, Benjamin Ballard, of Spts. Co. Deed of Gift. 143 a. in St. Geo. Par., Spts. Co. No witnesses. June 4, 1770.

June 4, 1770. John Mastin, jr., and Elizabeth, his wife, of Spts. Co., to John Mitchell of sd. Co., Mercht. £80 curr. 275 a. in St. Geo. Par., Spts. Co. Jos. Brock, Isaac Willson. June 4, 1770.

June 2, 1770. Thomas Minor of Spts. Co. and Mary, his wife, to Robert Hill of King and Queen Co.. Whereas, Benja. Temple of King Wm. Co. sold to Thomas Minor 250 a. in Spts. Co. for £162 10s. curr. (same being part of a tract devised sd. Benja. Temple by the will of his father, Jos. Temple, Decd., etc.), and did make and execute a deed to the sd. Minor, Dec. 7, 1763, by which the sd. land was described as within certain bounds, and from a recent survey was found to include 56 a. above the sd. 250 purchased by the sd. Minor; and whereas the sd. Benja. Temple after selling and conveying several parcels of land devised him as aforesd., having bargained and sold to the sd. Robt. Hill all the residue of sd. land containing 376 a. including the sd. 56 a. as conveyed in the sd. Minor's deed, hath by a deed, June 29, 1766, conveyed all right, title, interest, etc., to the sd. Hill, in fee, etc. Witnesses, J. Lewis, Jno. Todd, Jno Z. Lewis, O. Towles, Geo. Stubblefield. No date of Record.

May 17, 1770. John Waller of Spts. Co., po. of atto. to John Arnold of sd. Co. Witnesses, James Edwards, Will. Waller, Wm. Wood, Jona. Clark. June 4, 1770.

Feby. 28, 1770. John Glinn and Elizabeth, his wife, of Berkeley Par., Spts. Co., to Edward Coleman of Par. and Co. afsd. £50 curr. 200 a. in Par. and Co. afsd., in branches of Plentifull Run. James Davis, John Gadbery, Robert Edward Coleman. June 4, 1770.

June 4, 1770. John x Gordon of Spts. Co. and Elizabeth, his wife, to James Gordon of Co. afsd. £31 curr. 127 a. in St. Geo. Par. Spts. Co. No witnesses. June 4, 1770.

Augt. 16, 1770. Thomas Blanton and Jane, his wife, of Spts. Co., to Wm. Paul of Co. afsd. £120 curr. Lot 258 in town of Fredksbg., purchased by sd. Blanton of Roger Dixon, Gent., etc. Witnesses, Richd. Young, John Atkinson. Augt. 16, 1770.

Augt. 16, 1770. Wm. Plumr. Thurston and Frances, his wife, of Louisa Co., to Clayton Coleman of Spts. Co. £140 curr. 578 a. on East North East River in Spts. Co. No witnesses. Augt. 16, 1770.

Augt. 2, 1770. Archibald Dick of Caroline Co., Clerk, and Susanna, his wife, to John Holloday, junr., of Spts. Co. £80 curr. 504 a. in Berkeley Par., Spts. Co. Anthony New, John Baynham, Erasmus Allen. Augt. 16, 1770.

Augt. 16, 1770. John Holloday and Elizabeth, his wife, of Spts. Co., to their son, John Holloday, junr. Deed of Gift. 150 a. in Berkeley Par., Spts. Co. No witnesses. Augt. 16, 1770.

August 15, 1770. John Holloday and Elizabeth, his wife, of Spts. Co., to Charles Pemberton of Caroline Co. £100 curr. 200 a. in Spts. Co. No witnesses. Augt. 16. 1770.

Feby. 23, 1770. Fielding Lewis of Spts. Co., Esqr., "for and in consideration of the natural love and affection which he hath and beareth unto" John Lewis of Spts. Co., Esqr., as also in pursuance of an agreement made with John Thornton of Caroline Co., Esqr., in consideration of a marriage then intended to be solemnized between the sd. John Lewis and Lucy Thornton, daughter of sd. John Thornton (which marriage has lately been solemnized), etc. All those lands whereon sd. Jno. Lewis now lives, purchased by sd. Fielding Lewis, Esqr., of Charles Lewis, Esqr., in Spts. Co., for and during the lifetime of the sd. Fielding Lewis, etc. Witnesses, Chs. Washington, Geo. Weedon, Henry Crutcher. Augt. 16, 1770.

April 6, 1770. Wm. x Gholson of Spts. Co. to James Somerville, for John Mitchell and Hugh Lenox, surviving partners of Lenox & Scott, of Fredksbg., Merchts. £101 5s. Curr. Negroes, etc. Witnesses, Robert Slaughter, junr., John Swan, James Somerville. Augt. 18, 1770.

Septr. 20, 1770. Benjamin Steward (Stuart) and Sarah, his wife, of Westmoreland Co., to Thomas Dillard of Berkeley Par., Spts. Co. £70 curr. 125 a. in Berkeley Par., Spts. Co. John Carthrae, George Shepperd, John Dillard. Septr. 2, 1770.

Augt. 21, 1770. Owen Thomas of Spts. Co. to James Pritchett of same Co. Lease. 100 a. in Spts. Co. £3 curr. yearly after first two years. Wm. Wood, George Hensley, junr., Jona. Clark. Septr. 30, 1770.

Septr. 21, 1770. Benjamin Lewis and Martha, his wife, of Louisa Co., to Stephen Johnston of Spts. Co. £55 curr. 84 a. in Spts. Co., purchased of Thomas Pulliam of Culpeper, etc. No witnesses. Septr. 21, 1770.

Decr. 28, 1769. John Waller (commonly called John Waller of King William), of first part; Oliver Towles, attorney at law, of the second part; George Stubblefield of Spts. Co. of third part. For trusts hereafter mentioned the sd. Jno. Waller conveys to the sd. Oliver Towles 252 a. in Spts. Co., which joins the lands of the sd. Towles, Mary Lewis, widow, land belonging to the est. of Philip Vincent Vass, decd., and land sold by sd. Waller to Joseph Duerson, and which sd. land is remainder of a tract devised to sd. Jno. Waller by the will of his father, Thomas Waller, Decd., that was left and by the sd. John Waller reserved to himself, etc. In trust that the sd. Jno. Waller and his heirs may have the use and occupation of the sd. land, etc., the land is given sd. Towles in trust and as security for a debt due George Stubblefield by sd. Waller, etc. Witnesses, Jno. Robinson, Harry Robinson, Thomas Towles, John Chew, Harry Stubblefield, Beverley Stubblefield. No date of Record.

Octr. 13, 1770. Joseph Graves of Spts. Co. and Frankey, his wife, to Nice Coleman of same Co. £70 curr. 184 a. in Spts. Co. James Watkins, Wm. Blaydes, James Shackleford. No date of Record.

June 5, 1770. Joseph Temple of King and Queen Co. and Mary, his wife, to David Woodroof of Spts. Co. £60 curr. 200 a. in Spts. Co., part of a tract devised sd. Jos. Temple by the will of his father, Joseph Temple, etc. John Z. Lewis, Benja. Waller, Richd. Owen. Octr. 18, 1770.

June 5, 1770. Joseph Temple of King and Queen Co. and Mary, his wife, to Richard Mauldin Owen of Spts. Co. £60 curr. 200 a. in Spts. Co., part of a tract devised sd. Joseph Temple by the will of his father, Joseph Temple, etc. John Z. Lewis, Benja. Waller, D. Woodroof, John Todd. Octr. 18, 1770.

June 5, 1770. Joseph Temple of King and Queen Co. and Mary, his wife, to Robert Wilkinson of Spts. Co., Blacksmith. £58 2s. 6d. curr. 195 a. in Spts. Co. Richd. Owen, Jno. Z. Lewis, Benja. Waller, John Todd. Octr. 18, 1770.

Octr. 18, 1770. Thomas Colson and Frances, his wife, of Spts. Co., to Geo. Mitchell of Fredksbg., Mcht. £400 curr. Lot 43 in town of Fredksbg. No witnesses. Novr. 15, 1770.

Nov. 15, 1770. Job Harris and Susanna, his wife, of St. Geo. Par., Spts. Co., to Wm. Duerson of sd. Par. and Co. £25 curr. 227 a. on Douglass Run, in Par. and Co. afsd. No witnesses. Novr. 15, 1770.

Novr. 15, 1770. Michael x Blunt of Spts. Co. and Elizabeth, his wife, to Walter Chiles of Co. afsd. £14 10s. curr. 104 a. in Spts. Co. No witnesses. Novr. 15, 1770.

Novr. 11, 1770. James Sandidge and Jane, his wife, and David Sandidge and Anne, his wife, to Phillip Day of Spts. Co. £56 18s. 8d. curr. 122 a. Spts. Co. No witnesses. No date of record.

June 25, 1770. Wm. Garrett of Louisa Co. and Elizabeth, his wife, to John Day of Hanover Co. £60 curr. 200 a. in Spts. Co. Wm. Garrett, junr., Thomas Poindexter, His. Cosby Dickason. Novr. 15, 1770.

Novr. 15, 1770. James Sandidge and Jane, his wife, of Louisa Co., to John Shepperd of Spts. Co. £20 curr. 400 a. in Spts. Co. No witnesses. Novr. 15, 1770.

Augt. 18, 1770. Benjamin Grymes of Spts. Co., Esqr., in his own right and as Executor of the late Honble. Phillip Grymes, Esqr., of the first part; the Honble. John Tayloe of Richmond Co., Esqr., in his own right and as executor of the Honble. Presley Thornton, Esqr., of the second part; Joseph Herndon of Spts. Co., Gent., of the third part, and Thomas Poole of same Co., of the fourth part. Whereas sd. Poole hath contracted with sd. Benjamin Grymes, with consent of sd. Tayloe, for the purchase of a forge called Grymeses Forge, with bellows, plates, etc., etc., together with tracts of land bought of Col. Rice Curtis, the sd. Herndon and Executors of the late Colo. Wm. Waller. The sd. Benjamin Grymes, in consideration of £1250 curr., etc., conveys to the sd. Thomas Poole the forge, lands, about 400 a., etc., purchased of Curtis and 200 a purchased of Herndon, etc., and abt. 200 a. purchased of Colo. Wm. Waller's Estate, etc. The sd. Tayloe also releases right, etc. Witnesses, John Mitchell, Wm. Rash, George Shepherd, John Kennedy, Benjamin Grymes, junr. Novr. 15th, 1770.

June 5, 1770. Robt. Wilkinson of Spts. Co. to Benjamin Waller of Spts. Co. 5 head cattle as security for a debt sd. Wilkinson owes Jos. Temple, Gent., and which sd. Waller has assumed, etc. Witness, Edmund Waller. No date of Record.

Novr. 8, 1770. Thomas Wiatt of Berkeley Par., Spts. Co., and Susannah, to David Pulliam of Par. and Co. afsd. £40 curr. 114 a. in Par. and Co. afsd. Charles Gordon, John Holloday, Ambrose Shackleford, Sarah Gordon. No date of Record.

Novr. 15, 1770. Owen Thomas of Spts. Co. to Thomas Colson of Co. afsd., Gent. £23 8s. curr. 52 a. in St. Geo. Par., Spts. Co. James Went, Erasmus W. Allen, Ambrose Dudley. Novr. 16, 1770.

April 10, 1770. Wm. Fitzhugh of Stafford Co., Esqr., and Ann, his wife, to Lawrence Young of Spts. Co. £19 curr. 180 a. in St. Geo. Par., Spts. Co. B. Johnston, Phillip Somerby, Jno. Brock, Jos. Brock, O. Towles, Edwd. Herndon. Decr. 16, 1770.

Augt. 20, 1770. Thomas Poole of Spts. Co. to Honble. John Tayloe of Richmond Co., Esqr. Whereas by an Indenture bearing date the day before the presents [see Indenture, dated Augt. 19, 1770, Benja. Grymes, etc., of first part; Jno. Tayloe, etc., of second part; Joseph Herndon of third part, and Thomas Poole of fourth part, etc.], Benjamin Grymes, etc., conveyed to Thomas Poole the sd. Grymeses Forge, etc., now the sd. Poole, in consideration of £1250 curr. conveys the same to the sd. John Tayloe, etc. Mortgage. Witnesses, John Mitchell, Wm. Rash, John Kennedy, Josiah Gale. Novr. 16, 1770.

July 3, 1770. Jno. Waller, Clk. of Spts. Co., and Ann, his wife, to John Lewis, Oliver Towles and John Chew of same Co. In trust. 600 a. in Spts. Co., remainder of a larger tract, which sd. tract sd. John and Ann Waller hold in right of the sd. Ann, which sd. tract descended from Parmenas Bowker to his son, Ralph Bowker (his eldest son and heir) and on the death of sd. Ralph, which occurred before he arrived at age and without any issue, was vested in his (Ralph's) sister, Ann (now Ann Waller, etc.), the remainder of sd. tract being held by Wm. Smith and Ann, his wife, in right of the sd. Ann Smith, for her dower as widow of sd. Parmenas Bowker, etc., the sd. tract is whereon the sd. Jno. Waller now hath his plantation and slaves, with his overseer, Bernard Carter, living thereon, etc. Also slaves, horses, cattle, goods and chattels, etc. In trust for indemnifying the sd. Lewis, Towles and Chew, etc., etc. Mentions debts, etc. Witnesses, Jos. Brock, Robert Chew, Sherod Horn. Novr. 17, 1770.

Octr. 19, 1770. John Waller, Clk. of Spts. Co., to Wm. Wood of same Co. Bill of Sale. Witnesses, Edwd. Herndon, J. Lewis. Novr. 17, 1770.

Octr. 19, 1770. J. Lewis to Jno. Waller, Clk. Releases a negro to sd. Waller, etc. Test, Edward Herndon. No date of Record.

Novr. 17, 1770.   James Cunninghame of Spts. Co. and Ann, his wife, to Robert Smith of same Co.   £60 curr.   150 a. in St. Geo. Par., Spts. Co. No witnesses.   Novr. 17, 1770.

Dec. 12, 1770.   Erasmus Withers Allen of Spts. Co. to John Chapman of same Co.   Po. of atto.   Witnesses, Abraham Estes, Jona. Clark, William Spindle.   No date of Record.

Novr. 14, 1770.   Harry Stubblefield of Berkeley Par., Spts. Co., to George Stubblefield, Gent., of Par. and Co. afsd.   Lease.   Tract of land 100 a., bounded by lands of Jno. Chapman, Wm. Smith and Jno. Wheeler, and land where Thomas Ashman formerly lived to be included, etc. 40 shill. curr. annually, etc.   Witnesses, Beverley Stubblefield, Abraham Larew, O. Towles, Beverley Winslow, Willm. Smith.   Decr. 20, 1770.

Decr. 18, 1770.   Oliver Towles of Spts. Co., Gent., and Mary, his wife, to Harry Stubblefield of same Co.   In trust.   Whereas, Larkin Chew, Gent., and Mary, his wife, in right of sd. Mary, were seized, etc., of a tract of land in Spts. Co. containing 1042 a., and by indenture Septr. 25, 1758, conveyed the sd. land to Jno. Smith, Gent., and Mary, his wife, and their heirs, etc. (which sd. Mary was daughter of sd. Larkin Chew and Mary, his wife, etc.), and whereas since the sd. Indenture was made, the sd. John Smith, Gent., has died and the sd. Mary, his wife, has inter-married with the sd. Oliver Towles, and the sd. Larkin Chew being also dead, the sd. Oliver Towles and Mary, his wife, in her right and by force of the sd. Indenture, etc., in trust for the use of the sd. Mary Chew, the mother, and the sd. Mary Towles, etc., and the sd. Oliver Towles and Mary, his wife, being desirous to make a settlement to provide for the children of the sd. Mary by both marriages.   This Indenture Witnesseth, for carrying sd. intention into execution, and the love and affection sd. Oliver Towles and Mary, his wife, bear to Larkin Smith, Mary and Elizabeth Smith (son and daughters of the sd. Mary Towles by her former husband, John Smith), and to the children begotten or to be begotten, between the sd. Oliver and Mary, the sd. Towles and wife deed to sd. Stubblefield in trust the reversion and inheritance expectant on death of the afsd. Mary Chew, of and in the sd. 1042 a. of land, etc.   Witnesses, Geo. Stubblefield, Jno. Carthrae, Beverley Stubblefield, Jas. Minor, Vincent Vass.   Decr. 20, 1770.

Novr. 29, 1770.   Wm. Smith, of Spts. Co., Gent., and Ann, his wife, and Jno. Waller, Clk. of Spts. Co., and Ann, his wife.   Whereas sd. Wm. Smith and Ann, his wife, in right of the sd. Ann are entitled to and now hold dower in a tract of land in Spts. Co., containing 900 a. and is the tract whereon sd. Jno. Waller and Ann, his wife, now live, the reversion in fee of which sd. dower as well as the fee simple estate in possession of the other two thirds are in the sd. Ann Waller, and whereas the sd. Ann Smith, being formerly the widow of Parmenas Bowker, who, having died intestate, the sd. Ann thereby became entitled to dower in the sd. Bowker's slaves as well as of the land afsd., and the sd. Wm. and Ann, his wife, are now in possession of and hold certain slaves, held as the dower of sd. Ann, in the estate of the sd. Bowker, the reversion in fee, etc., of which slaves, etc., are in the sd. Ann Waller, the dau. and heiress of the sd. Bowker, and whereas the sd. Wm. and Ann Smith and the sd. John and Ann Waller have agreed to make an exchange of the dower in land afsd. and the reversion in fee in the slaves afsd., etc.   Witnesseth, that the sd. Wm. and Ann Smith for consideration of all right, title, etc., of sd. Jno. and Ann Waller in the afsd. slaves, the sd. Wm. Smith and Ann, his wife, do by these presents relinquish, etc., the dower of the sd. Ann Smith in afsd. tract of land, etc., etc. Witnesses, O. Towles, Thomas Towles, John Carthrae, Jeremiah Stevens, G. Sims, Robert Chew. Decr. 20, 1770.

Octr. 5, 1769. Wm. Fitzhugh of Stafford Co., Esqr., and Ann, his wife, to Jno. Patty of Spts. Co. £80 curr. 175 a. in St. Geo. Par., Spts. Co. Chs. Carter, James Benson, B. Johnston, Phillip Somerby, Jno. Brock, Jos. Brock. Dec. 20, 1770.

April 10, 1770. Wm. Fitzhugh of Stafford Co., Esqr., to Reubin Young of Spts. Co. £26 10s. curr. 78 a. in St. Geo. Par., Spts. Co. B. Johnston, Phillip Somerby, Jno. Brock, Jos. Brock. Decr. 16, 1770.

Septr. 3, 1770. Thomas Coleman of Spts. Co. and Sarah, his wife, to Richard Coleman of same Co. £25 curr. 100 a. in Spts. Co. Geo. Stubblefield, O. Towles, Willm. Smith. No date of record.

Octr. 17, 1770. John Davis of Mecklenburgh Co. to James Davis and Benja. Davis of Spts. Co. £50. 400 a. on Plentifull run, Spts. Co., "whereof their father, James Davis, decd., died seized and possessed," etc. Beverley Winslow, Wm. Parker, Jno. Glinn, Robt. Evans. April 18, 1771.

Jany. 17th, 1770. Benjamin Davis and Elizabeth, his wife, of Berkeley Par., Spts. Co., of the first part; James Davis of same Par. and Co., of second part, and John Nelson of sd. Par. and Co. of third part, Whereas John Davis of Mecklenburg Co., being seized of reversion in fee, etc., in a certain tract of land in Spts. Co., expectant in the death of his mother, who holds a Life estate therein, which sd. land is particularly described in the last will and testament of James Davis, Decd., recd. in Spts. Co. Court, and by Indenture dated Octr. 17, 1770, the sd. Jno. Davis conveyed the sd. land and all other lands the sd. James Davis, Decd., died possessed of, to James and Benjamin Davis, parties hereto, by which conveyance they were seized as joint tenants, and the sd. James hath consented that the sd. Benjamin, out of his undivided moiety may sell and convey unto sd. John Nelson 102 a. of land, for the sum of £45 curr., etc. Witness, Tho. Comb. No date of Record.

April 10, 1770. Wm. Fitzhugh of Stafford Co., Esqr., and Ann, his wife, to Alexander Walden of Spts. Co. £40 curr. 185 a. in St. Geo. Par., Spts. Co. B. Johnston, Phillip Somerby, Jno. Brock, Jos. Brock. April 18, 1771.

Octr. 2, 1770. James Duncanson of Fredksbg. and Mary, his wife, to Robert Walker of Stafford Co. £200 curr. Lots 91 and 92 in a plan of the town of Fredksbg. made after the extension of its limits as by act of Assembly, made 32d George 2d, etc. No witnesses. Jany 17, 1771.

Octr. 5, 1769. Wm. Fitzhugh of Stafford Co., Esqr., and Ann, his wife, to Hezekiah Ellis of Spts. Co. £47 curr. 94 a. in St. Geo. Par., Spts. Co. Chs. Carter, Ben. Gwinn, James Benson, B. Johnston, Phillip Somerby, Jno. Brock, Jos. Brock. No date of Record.

March 21, 1771. Mann Page of "Mansfield," Spts. Co., Esqr., to his son, Mann Page, the younger. Deed of Gift. 500 a. in Spts. Co., known as Massaponax or New Quarter on Massaponax Run. No witnesses. No date of Record.

Feby. 25, 1770. Wm. Waller, Doctor, of Spts. Co., to Cain Acuff of sd. Co., planter. £60. 240 a. in Berkeley Par., Spts. Co., known as McNeale's Tract. Witnesses, Vincent Vass, Jno. Waller, K. W.; John Carnahan, Jno. Carter, Lewis Young, Wm. Steers. March 21, 1771.

Decr. 21, 1770. Henry Gatewood of Spts. Co. and Tabitha, his wife, to Benjamin Head of sd. Co. £30 curr. 112 a. in Spts. Co. Alexr. Spence Head, David Head, James Head. No date of Record.

Jany. 4, 1771. Catharine x Carter, widow of Joseph Carter, late of Spts. Co., Decd., to Jno. Carter of Spts. Co., planter. £10 curr. "All her right, title, dower as widow of sd. Jos. Carter, in and to 215 a. whereon the sd. Jos. Carter, decd., formerly lived in Spts. Co., on Robinson's Swamp. Witnesses, Wm. Woodroof, Joseph Hewell, John Conner, Daniel Lindsay, Wm. Trigg, John x Johnson. March 21, 1771.

March 6, 1770. Sherod Horn and Mary, his wife, of Spts. Co., to Wm. Scott of sd. Co. £75 curr. 130 a. in Spts. Co. Isaac Willson, Henry Robinson, George Willson. March 21, 1771.

June 12, 1770. Joseph Hawkins of Spts. Co. and Margaret, his wife, to Benjamin Robinson, son of Wm. and Agness Robinson of same Co. £50. 100 a. in upper end of Spts. Co. Beverley Winslow, Andw. Manning, Wm. P. Thurston. March 21, 1771.

March 21, 1771. James Redd of Spts. Co. to his son, Mordacai Redd. Deed of Gift. 300 a. in Spts. Co., joining lands of Messrs. Thomas Minor and Jno. Lewis, junr. No witnesses. No date of record.

March 20, 1771. Charles Yates of Fredksbg. to John Glassell. £200 ster. and £100 curr. Lots 11 and 12 in town of Fredksbg. No witnesses. March 21, 1771.

March 20, 1771. Abraham Darnall and Elizabeth, his wife, of Berkeley Par., Spts. Co., to Thomas Tabbit of Par. and Co. afsd. £15. 185 a. in Par. and Co. afsd. Abraham Darnall, Wm. Nelson, Joseph Roy, John Smith, Hy. Winslow. No date of record.

March 21, 1771. Edwd. Herndon, John Herndon, Jos. Herndon, Executors of the last will and testament of John Battaley, Decd., and Elizabeth Battaley, relict of Jno. Battaley, to Charles Yates of Fredksbg. By right of authority given them in the will of late Jno. Battaley, Decd. £126 curr. Lot No. 1 in a plan of an addition to town of Fredksbg., etc. Wm. Wood, Stapleton Crutchfield, James Cunninghame, Jona. Clark, March 21, 1771.

March 20, 1771. Edwd. Herndon, Jno. Herndon, Jos. Herndon, Executors of the last will and testament of John Battaley, Decd., and Elizabeth Battaley, relict of John Battaley, Decd., to Ewen Clements of Fredksbg. £60 curr. Lots 1 and 2 as in a plan of the town made by Col. Wm. Waller, and formerly property of John Allen, Decd., etc. Witnesses, Wm. Wood, Stapleton Crutchfield, James Cunninghame, Jona. Clark. No date of record.

March — 1771. John x Dyer and Elizabeth, his wife, of Spts. Co., to John Mitchell of Co. afsd. £35 curr. 133 a. in Spts. Co. No witnesses. March 21, 1771.

Decr. 19, 1770. Fielding Lewis of Fredksbg., Esqr., to Jno. Lewis of Spts. Co., Gent. Whereas, previous to the marriage of sd. Jno. Lewis with his late wife, Lucy, dau. of John Thornton of Caroline Co., Gent., etc., etc., whereas, a marriage is shortly to be had between the sd. John Lewis and Elizabeth, daughter of the late Honble. Presley Thornton, Esqr., to the sd. John, the tract of land purchased of Charles Lewis, and whereon sd. John Lewis now lives, for and during the term of the natural lives of sd. Fielding Lewis and Betty, his wife, etc., also from and after the deaths of sd. Fielding and Betty Lewis, all that part of the tract of land adjoining the town of Fredksbg.; also ten slaves, etc., etc. Witnesses, John Glassell, Alexr. Wright, Beverley Daniel. March 21, 1771.

March 20, 1771. George Mitchell of Fredksbg. to John Atkinson of Fredksbg. £150 curr. Part of lot 43 in town of Fredksbg. purchased of Thomas Colson and Frances, his wife, as by Deed, Octr. 18, 1770, etc. B. Johnston, H. Steward, Jno. Brock. March 21, 1771.

March 21, 1771. Thomas Walker of Fredksbg., Watchmaker, and Jane, his wife, to John Mitchell of sd. town. £31 curr. Lot 274 in town of Fredksbg. H. Stewart, Wm. Templeman, B. Johnston. March 21, 1771.

Octr. 5, 1769. Wm. Fitzhugh of Stafford Co., Esqr., and Ann, his wife, to Wm. Robinson of Spts. Co. £105 curr. 237 a. in St. Geo. Par., Spts. Co. Chs. Carter, Ben. Gwinn, James Benson, B. Johnston, Phillip Somerby, Jno. Brock, Jos. Brock. March 21, 1771.

April 18, 1771. Wm. Forson of Spts. Co. and Milley, his wife, to Wm. Chiles of sd. Co. £40 curr. 200 a. in Spts. Co., part of a tract devised sd. Forson by Michael Guinny, Decd. Witnesses, Richd. Vernon, John White. April 18, 1771.

Octr. 16th, 1770. John Huddleston of Johnston Co., North Carolina, son and heir at law of Robert Huddleston, late of Spts. Co., Va., Decd., to Robert Huddleston, now of Berkeley Par., Spts. Co., Va. Whereas, Robert Huddleston, Decd., did, by his last will and testament, desire that a tract of 113 a. in Spts. Co., whereon he formerly lived, should be sold and the money arising therefrom equally divided amongst all his children, and the sd. Robt., party to these presents, having purchased the shares of all the sd. children; and the sd. John, being satisfied with his proportionable part and being desirous that the will of his decd. father should be carried out, etc., by this Indenture, conveys the sd. Robert, 113 a. in Berkeley Par., Spts. Co. Witnesses, John Waller, junr., Lewis Craig, James Chiles, Andrew Tribble. No date of record.

Decr. 28, 1770. Wm. x Gholson and Susannah, his wife, of Spts. Co., to John Larew of Frederick Co. £150 curr. 563 a. in St. Geo. Par., Spts. Co. Jos. Brock, John x Schooler, Jno. Brock, Jno. Chew, junr. No date of record.

April 18, 1771. John Partlow and Sarah, his wife, of Caroline Co., to Jeremiah Willson of Spts. Co. £45 curr. 150 a. in Spts. Co. Thomas Coleman, Senr., Daniel Trigg, Thos. Wheeler, Wm. Trigg. No date of record.

April 18, 1771. James Lewis of Spts. Co. and Elizabeth, his wife, and Sarah Lewis, widow of Wm. Lewis, of Co. afsd., to Jacob Whitley of Fredksbg. [Whereas, sd. Sarah Lewis is entitled to ⅓ part of 2 lotts, etc., for life as a Tenant in Dower and the inheritance of sd. ⅓ expectant on the death of sd. Sarah Lewis is in the sd. James Lewis, as well as the other ⅔ part in possession; the sd. James Lewis and Sarah Lewis have both agreed to sell and convey their sd. interests, etc.] £400 curr. Lots 35 and 36 in town of Fredksbg., purchased by sd. Wm. Lewis, father of sd. James Lewis, of Anthony Strother, etc. Witnesses, Jos. Brock, Robert Chew, John Herndon, Daniel Branham, James Cunningham. April 18, 1771.

April 9, 1771. Charles Yates of Fredksbg., Mercht., to Col. Edward Carter of Albemarle Co. £128 curr. Lots in town of Fredksbg. Numbered 129, 130, 131 and 132, purchased by sd. Yates of Fielding Lewis, etc. No witnesses. No date of record.

April 9, 1771. John Waller, K. W.; of Spts. Co., and Mary Ann, his wife, and Oliver Towles, atto.-at-law, of the same Co., to George Stubblefield of sd. Co. Whereas, John Waller, being seized of a tract containing abt. 252 a., part of a tract given him by his father, Thomas Waller, Gent., Decd., and the sd. John, being so seized, conveyed the same, in trust, to Oliver Towles, as by Indenture, Decr. 28, 1769, etc. The sd. John Waller and Mary Ann, his wife, and Oliver Towles, convey the sd. land to sd. Stubblefield, for £147, etc., etc. James Stevenson, Z. Lewis, Beverley Stubblefield, Susanna Parker, Mary Stubblefield, Lewis Young, Edwd. Herndon, Jos. Herndon, Thomas Colson, Owen Thomas, Robert Chew. April 18, 1771.

March 22, 1771. Dudley Gatewood of Spts. Co. to Benjamin Craig of sd. Co. £25. 50 a. in Spts. Co. Jos. Brock, Daniel Branham, Henry Gatewood, junr., John Sanders. April 22, 1771.

April 19, 1771. Paul x McClarney of Spts. Co. to John Mitchell & Co. of Spts. Co., Merchts. £10 0s. 5d. Mortgage. 208 a. in Spts. Co. whereon sd. McClarney lives; purchased of Wm. Crosthwait and John Pitts. Witnesses, Jos. Herndon, George Stubblefield, James Somerville. April 19, 1771.

Jany 26, 1771. Wm. x Leathers and Patty, his wife. £7 7s. curr. "All our title and interest and claim of and to all that part of the Estate of David Jones, Decd., which we shall be entitled to at the death of Winifred Jones, widow of the sd. David Jones, Decd.," etc. Witnesses, Sarah Leathers, O. Towles, G. Stubblefield. No date of record.

Jany. 14, 1771. Sarah x Gardner of Hanover Co., St. Pauls Par., and John Gardner of Louisa Co., to Francis Ford of Spts. Co. £50 curr. 200 a. in Berkeley Par., Spts. Co. Wm. Gardner, Peter Schooler, Thomas x Gardner. No date of record.

May 16, 1771. Benjamin Tompkins and Elizabeth, his wife, of Caroline Co., to Leonard Young of Spts. Co. 300 a. in Spts. Co. No witnesses. May 16, 1771.

May 8, 1771. John x Durrett of Spts. Co. to his grandson, John Crutchfield, and grand-daughter, Agatha Crutchfield. Deed of Gift. Negro. Witnesses, Edwd. Herndon, Jos. Herndon, Jas. Wigglesworth. No date of record.

March 25, 1771. Wm. Dangerfield of Spts. Co., Esqr., and Mary (late
Mary Willis), his wife, to Henry Mitchell of Fredksbg. Mercht. Whereas,
Henry Willis, late of Spts. Co., Decd., in his lifetime and at the time of
his death being seized of two lots in Fredksbg. (half of square on which
Lewis Willis, Esqr., now lives, etc.), and being so seized died intestate
leaving Elizabeth, his relict, and the afsd. Mary, his niece and heiress,
on which Mary the inheritance of the sd. two lots descended in fee; the
sd. Elizabeth, the widow, being entitled to ⅓ part thereof for her lifetime as tenant in dower, and whereas the sd. Elizabeth, being so entitled,
intermarried with Reuben Thornton, now decd., which sd. Reuben (during his lifetime), with the sd. Elizabeth, sold sd. Eliza. dower to Richard Lewis, for the life of the sd. Elizabeth, by which means the sd. Wm.
Dangerfield, by right of the sd. Mary, is now dependent on the life of
the sd. Elizabeth, etc. Witnesseth, the sd. Wm. Dangerfield and Mary,
his wife, for the sum of £187 10s., convey the two lotts afsd. thus, that
is to say, ⅔ according to the bounds thereof, etc., from day of date of
these presents, and the remaining ⅓ from the death of the above named
Elizabeth, etc., etc. Witnesses, John Glassell, John Steward, John Terrie.
May 17, 1771.

DEED BOOK H

April 19, 1771. Roger Dixon of Fredksbg., Spts. Co., Gentl., and Lucy, his wife, to Thomas Walker of same town. £300 curr. Lots 246 and 237 in town of Fredksbg. No witnesses. April 19, 1771.

May 16, 1771. Joseph Hawkins and Margaret, his wife, of Berkeley Par., Spts. Co., to George Blakey of same Par. and Co. £10. 100 a. in afsd. Par. and Co. No witnesses. May 16, 1771.

May 13, 1771. Robert Foster and Agatha, his wife, of Spts. Co. to Wm. Gholson of same Co. £50 curr. 144 a. in St. Geo. Par., Spts. Co. John Herndon, Jos. Herndon, John Foster. No date of Record.

May 16, 1771. Wm. x Gholson and Susanna, his wife, of Spts. Co., to Robert Smith of afsd. Co. £42 5s. Curr. 64 a. in St. Geo. Par., Spts. Co. No witnesses. May 16, 1771.

May 16, 1771. James Marye of St. Geo. Par., Spts. Co., Clerk, to Wm. Blyth of Fredksbg. £40 curr. Lot 55 in town of Fredksbg., purchased by Benj. Winslow of the Trustees of the Town, by Deed, June 3, 1740, and by the sd. Winslow conveyed to Revd. James Marye, Minister of St. Geo. Par., etc., as by deed, Sept. 16, 1746, and by the sd. James Marye devised to his son, William Marye, since decd., and from whom it descended to James Marye, his brother and heir, etc. No witnesses. May 16, 1771.

Augt. 10, 1771. John Berryman and Martha, his wife, of Stafford Co., to James Duncanson of Fredksbg. £20 curr. Lot 13 in town of Fredksbg. Peter Scott, Thomas Kerr, Wm. Walker. Augt. 15, 1771.

July 17, 1771. Benjamin Tompkins of Caroline Co. and Elizabeth, his wife, to John Mason of Spts. Co. £150 curr. 400 a. in Spts. Co., part of a tract purchased of the Executors of Robt. Baylor, etc. No witnesses. July 18, 1771.

June 5, 1771. Elizabeth Waller of King Wm. Co., widow, and her son, John Waller, K. W. of Spts. Co., to George Stubblefield. Right, title and dower of sd. Elizabeth in 250 a. of land whereon sd. John now lives, etc. Witnesses, Thomas Waller, Harry Stubblefield, Solomon Quarles. June 21, 1771.

Jany. 14, 1771. John Waller, K. W. of Spts. Co., to Thomas Waller of King Wm. Co. £50 curr. Goods and chattels, stocks, etc. Aaron Quarles, Solo. Quarles, Tunstall Quarles, Wm. Stark. June 21, 1771.

May 18, 1771. Ludwell Grymes of Orange Co. and Mary, his wife, to Thomas Walker of Fredksbg. £37 curr. Lot 236 in town of Fredksbg. Willm. Prestidge, Zach. Burnley, Garland Burnley, Charles Bruce. June 21, 1771.

Decr. 12, 1770. Benja. Pulliam and Lucy, his wife, of Culpeper Co., to Joseph Holloday of Spts. Co. £100 curr. Tract of land in Spts. Co. Jos. Brock, Lewis Holloday, Jas. Holloday. June 20, 1771.

June 20, 1771. Waller Lewis of Berkeley Par., Spts. Co., Gent., and Sarah, his wife, to John Waller, Junr., of same Par. and Co. £14 14s. curr. 49 a. in sd. Par. and Co. No witnesses. No date of Record.

May 11, 1771. Mary x Lewis, widow of Zachary Lewis of Spts. Co. and daughter of John Waller, Decd., to her sons, Zachary Lewis and Benjamin Lewis. Deed of Gift. Negroes. Witnesses, O. Towles, Waller Lewis. No date of Record.

June 20, 1771. Ambrose Shackleford of Spts. Co. and Margaret, his wife, to Clayton Coleman of same Co. £20. 85 a. in Spts Co. No witnesses. June 20, 1771.

May 16, 1771. John Herndon of Spts. Co. to Joseph Scrogham of sd. Co. Lease. 100 a. in St. Geo. Par., Spts. Co. "Sd. Joseph Scrogham and Mary, his wife," etc. £4 curr. yearly. No witnesses. June 20, 1771.

June 5, 1771. Wm. Fitzhugh of Stafford Co., Esqr., and Ann, his wife, to Henry Elley of Spts. Co. £55 curr. 128 a. in St. Geo. Par., Spts. Co. Chs. Carter, James Benson, Ben. Gwinn, B. Johnston, Philip Somerby, Jno. Brock, Jos. Brock. No date of Record.

June 19, 1771. John Lewis and Ann, his wife, of Spts. Co. to Charles Yates, of Fredksbg., Gent. £30 curr. Lot No. 2 in town of Fredksbg., in that portion laid out by Jno. Allan, Decd., etc., which descended to sd. John Lewis as heir at law of his father, Zachary Lewis, Decd., etc. Witnesses, John Davenport, James Davenport, Jno. Z. Lewis, David Woodroof. June 21, 1771.

June 21, 1771. Wm. Fitzhugh of Stafford Co., Esqr., and Ann, his wife, to Francis Simpson of Spts. Co. £55 curr. 115 a. in St. Geo. Par., Spts. Co. Chs. Carter, Ben. Gwinn, James Benson, Jno. Brock, B. Johnston, Phillip Somerby, Jos. Brock. June 21, 1771.

May 12, 1771. Phillip Bush, Senr., and Phillip Bush, Junr., of Orange Co. to Benjamin Craig of Spts. Co. £50 curr. Tract of land in Spts. Co. Tolever Craig, John Craig, James Haydon, Richard Cave. No date of Record.

June 20, 1771. Francis Turnley and Mary, his wife, of Spts. Co. to James Redd of same Co., planter. £20 curr. 111 a. in St. Geo. Par., Spts. Co. John Wright, Wm. Templeman, Jno. Chew, Jacob Whiteley, Wm. Smith. July 18, 1771.

Feby. 1, 1771. Bartlett x Matthews of Berkeley Par., Spts. Co., to John Waller, junr., and James Crawford of same par. and Co. Whereas, sd. John Waller and James Crawford sometime in the yr. 1765 entered into bond in sum of £100 curr. as securities for Sarah Crawford, then the widow of John Crawford, late of sd. Co., Decd., for her due administration of the sd. Decd's. Estate, and whereas the sd. Sarah has since intermarried with the sd. Bartlett Matthews who hath taken the sd. Estate into his custody, etc. Witnesseth, sd. Matthews to indemnify sd. Waller and Crawford, instead of giving counter security, etc. Mortgage.

Goods and chattels. Witnesses, Edmund Waller, Peter Mason, Jos Talbert, Ben. Waller. July 18, 1771.

May 10, 1771. John Carter, late sheriff of Spts. Co., Gent., to Wm. Champe of King Geo. Co., Esqr. £1590 curr. 1122 a. contained in several tracts of land. Whereas by decree of Honble. Genl. Court, between Jane Champe, Wm. Champe, and John Champe, executors of late John Champe, of King Geo. Co., Decd. Pltffs. and Benjamin Grymes, Deft., it was decreed, etc., that the sheriff of Spts. Co. sell at public auction in the April next following, sundry lands and slaves, and whereas the sd. John Carter, then sheriff of Spts. Co. in obedience to the sd. decree did sell among other things three several tracts of land, etc., part of those mentioned in sd. decree, to Wm. Champe, etc., etc. No witnesses. July 19, 1771.

—— ——, 1771. John Carter, late sheriff of Spts. Co., Gent., to Lewis Willis, Esqr., and Charles Yates, Mercht., of Fredksbg. £500. 1062 a. of land. As under a decree of the General Court as recited in foregoing deed, etc. No witnesses. July 19, 1771.

July 19, 1771. John Carter, late sheriff of Spts. Co., Gent., to John Glassell, of Fredksbg., Mercht., £220. Lots in town of Fredksbg., known by name of Fredksbg. Warehouses, purchased by Benja. Grymes of Nathl. Chapman, Decd., as under a decree of General Court as recited on preceding deeds, etc. No witnesses. July 19, 1771.

May 17, 1771. Wm. Champe and Mary, his wife, of King Geo. Co., to John Wright, of Spts. Co. £116 4s. curr. 258 a. in St. Geo. Par., Spts. Co. No witnesses. July 19, 1771.

May 17, 1771. Wm. Champe and Mary, his wife, of King Geo. Co., to Francis Purvis, of Spts. Co. £178 16s. curr. 394 a. in St. Geo. Par., Spts. Co. No witnesses. No date of Record.

July 19, 1771. Wm. Champe, of King Geo. Co., Esqr., and Mary, his wife, to Wm. Dangerfield, of Spts. Co., Esqr. £1000 curr. 369 a. in Spts. Co. No witnesses. No date of Record.

Augt. 15, 1771. John McKenney, of Spts. Co., to George Moore, of same Co. £5 curr. 175 a. in Spts. Co., which sd. land sd. McKenney recovered by a decree in Chancery, from Jno. Ellson, July 7, 1761. Jno. Bullock, Nathaniel Stevens, Edwd. Ledgen. No date of Record.

Sept. 9, 1771. John Holloday, junr., of Berkeley Par., Spts. Co., and Mildred, his wife, to Peter Stubblefield, of Co. afsd. £160 curr. 150 a. in Berkeley Par., Spts. Co. Wm. Wood, James Gordon, Richardson Hensley, Jona. Clark. Septr. 19, 1771.

June 6, 1771. John Foster, of Spts. Co., to Edward Elly. Deed of Gift. A negro boy. Witnesses, John Herndon, John Sills. No date of Record.

July 31, 1771. Fielding Lewis, of Fredksbg., Esqr., and Betty, his wife, to Richard Lewis, of Fredksbg. £50 curr. Lots No. 76 in plan of an extension of town of Fredksbg., etc. No witnesses. No date of Record.

Augt. 1, 1771. Richard Lewis, of Fredksbg., sadler, and Ann, his wife, to Charles Washington, of Fredksbg., Esqr. £50 curr. Lot 76 in addition of town of Fredksbg., etc. No witnesses. No date of Record.

July 19, 1771. Thomas Poole, of Spts. Co., to John McCauley, of Spts. Co. £86 curr. A negro. Witnesses, Ambrose Raines, J. Holloday, junr., Thomas Allen, John Chew. No date of Record.

April 18, 1771. James Johnston and Mary, his wife, of Caroline Co., to Betty Benger, of Spts. Co. Tract of land in Spts. Co., whereon sd. Johnston, lately lived. Witnesses, Jona Clark, Thomas Farish, B. Johnston. No date of Record.

April 18, 1771. Benjamin Johnston, Execr. of the last will and testament of John Benger, Decd., to George Atkinson, of Spts. Co. Whereas, one John Simons, did by his Indenture, mortgage to the sd. Jno. Benger, Decd., in his lifetime a tract of 100 a. of land in Spts. Co., and the sd. Johnston in right of the sd. Benger, obtained decree in court of Spts. Co. in 1770, foreclosing the sd. Mortgage, and among other things the decree directed that Thomas Colson and Wm. Wood, of sd. Co., should see the sd. decree complied with; the sd. Colson and Wood making sale thereof, the sd. Atkinson became highest bidder, etc., etc. No witnesses. No date of Record.

Nov. 21, 1771. John Spotswood, of Spts. Co., and Sarah, his wife, to Nathaniel Stevens, of Spts. Co. £45. 200 a. in St. Geo. Par., Spts. Co. No witnesses. No date of Record.

Novr. 21, 1771. John Pattie and Susanna, his wife, of Spts. Co., to Joel Parish, of sd. Co. £120 curr. 175 a. in St. Geo. Par., Spts. Co. B. Grymes, Henry Johnson. Nov. 22, 1771.

Nov. 21, 1771. Stephen Tatom (or Tatum), and Mourning, his wife, of Spts. Co., to Richard Blanton and George Anderson, of same Co. £45 curr. 150 a. in Spts. Co. David Anderson, James Wheeler, John Smith. Novr. 21, 1771.

June 19, 1771. Joseph Pulliam, of Spts. Co., to David Pulliam, of Spts. Co. £55 curr. 130 a. in Spts. Co. David Sandage, Lewis Holloday, Austin Sandage, James Holloday. No date of Record.

Novr. 21, 1771. John Pulliam and Sarah, his wife, of Spts. Co., to Wm. Smith, of same Co. £200 curr. 347½ a. in Berkeley Par., Spts. Co. Conveyed by Wm. Wigglesworth and Mary, wife of James Wigglesworth, to the sd. Pulliam, Decr. 4, 1759, etc., also a part conveyed the sd. Pulliam by Joseph Peterson and Lucy, his wife, July 26, 1768, etc. Witnesses, Jno. Holloday, junr.; Jos. Pulliam, William Hutcherson, Sherod Horn. Novr. 21, 1771.

Nov. 21, 1771. James Duncanson and Mary, his wife, of Spts. Co., to Michael Robinson, of same Co. £90. Lots 133 and 134 in town of Fredksbg. No witnesses. Novr. 21, 1771.

May 7, 1771. Wm. Wood, of Spts. Co., to Andrew Cochrane, Wm. Cunningham & Co., Merchts. £239 15s. 8d. curr. Mortgage. 414 a. in Co. afsd., given sd. Wood by his father, John Wood, Decd. Witnesses, Alexr. Spence Head, David Head, James Hensley. Nov. 21, 1771.

March 29, 1765. John Campbell, of Spts. Co., Bond to Lenox, Scott & Co., Merchts. £201 16 2d. curr. Test, Wm. Gregory. April 16, 1772.

Jany. 27, 1765. Thomas Fox, of St. Geo Par., Spts. Co., to Oliver

Towles, Junr., attorney-at-law, of same Par. and Co. In trust. "For the natural love and affection which he hath and beareth to Nathaniel, Thomas, Junr., Wm., and Joseph Fox, and Philadelphia, Ann, and Polly Fox, sons and daughters of the sd. Thomas Fox," etc. All sd. Fox's land in King Wm. Co. being 500 a. on Mattapony; 672 a. in Spts. Co., purchased of George Seaton; also 27 slaves, etc., etc. Witnesses, John Stewart, Francis Tyler, Jno. Battaley, Wm. Reid. March 5, 1765.

Augt. 5, 1765. James Hutcherson and Margaret, his wife, and Edward Coleman and Sarah, his wife, of St. Geo. Par., Spts. Co., to George Hensley, of same Par. and Co. £50 curr. 95 a. in Spts. Co., part of a tract purchased by Wm. Richason, Decd., of Larkin Chew, Decd., and by the last will and testament of the sd. Wm. Richason, decd., devised to his grandson, James Hutcherson, which sd. land is bounded by the lands of Jno. Taliaferro, Decd.; John Wood, Decd., and the sd. Hensley, etc. No witnesses. Sept. 1, 1766.

Sept. 23, 1771. John x Sutton, Senr., and Elizabeth, his wife, of Orange Co., to Benjamin Poe, of Berkeley Par., Spts. Co. £12 curr. 164 acres. Jos. Willoughby, Edward Brasfield, Leonard Brasfield. No date of Record.

June 18, 1771. Robert Goodloe and Sarah, his wife, of Bute Co., North Carolina, to Henry Goodloe, of Caroline Co. £35 curr. 200 a. in Berkeley Par., Spts. Co., given sd. Goodloe by his father, George Goodloe, Gent, Decd., by his last will and testament, etc. Witnesses, Robt. Goodloe, Wm. Durrett, James Colquohoon, W. Emmerson. No date of Record.

Septr. 28, 1771. Joel Parish to his daughter, Sarah Parish, now Sarah Ellis, of Spts. Co. Deed of gift. "Sd. Sarah Ellis and John Ellis, her husband," etc. Two negroes. Witnesses, Agness Ellis, Wm. Grayson. No date of Record.

April 16, 1772. Paul x McClary and Rose, his wife, of Orange Co., to Peter Roswell, of Berkeley Par., Spts. Co. £20. 115 a. in Berkeley Par., Spts. Co. Beverley Winslow, Frans. x Wisdom, Edward Chapman. April 16, 1772.

April 13, 1772. John Pitts and Ann, his wife, of St. Thomas Par., Orange Co., to Paul McClanney, of St. Geo. Par., Spts. Co. £10 curr. 100 a. in St. Geo. Par., Spts. Co. Francis x Wisdom, Robert Bradley, Peter Rozell. No date of Record.

July 7, 1771. Alexander Wright, of Fredksbg., to Charles Yates, of sd. town. £165 curr. A negro woman, goods and chattels, etc. Witnesses, Wm. Templeman, Danl. Payne, John Meals. No date of Record.

Jany. 18, 1772. George Hensley, junr., and Martha, his wife, of Spts. Co., to George Hensley, Senr., of same Co. 5 shill. curr. 63 a. in Spts. Co. Jona Clark, Wm. Wood, John Estes, junr.; Ambrose Dudley. No date of Record.

April 16, 1772. Edwd. Herndon, John Herndon, and Joseph Herndon, Executors of the last will and testament of John Battaley, Decd., and Elizabeth, widow of the sd. John Battaley, Decd., to Wm. Hord, Junr., of Caroline Co. £100 curr. 313 a. in Spts. Co. No witnesses. April 16, 1772.

Jany. 20, 1772. George Hensley, Senr., and Sarah, his wife, of Spts. Co., to George Hensley, junr., of same Co. 5 shill. curr. 95 a. in Spts. Co., part of a tract purchased by Wm. Richardson, Decd., of Larkin Chew, Decd., and by the last will and testament of sd. Richardson devised to his grandson, James Hutcherson, and by the said Hutcherson sold to the sd. George Hensley, Senr., etc. Witnesses, Wm. Wood, Jona. Clark, John Estes, Junr.; Ambrose Dudley. April 16, 1772.

March 19, 1772. Nathaniel Hill, of Hanover Co., to Joseph Ball, of Northumberland Co. £18 curr. 100 a. drawn by sd. Hill in a lottery of James Ware, etc. Henry Johnson, Wm. Wood, B. Johnston. No date of Record.

March 28, 1772. Thomas Pettit and Rachel, his wife, of Spts. Co., to John Mitchell & Co., of county afsd., Merchts. £16 curr. 200 a. in St. Geo. Par., Spts. Co. Jos. Brock, Robert Chew, Jno. Brock, Jno. Chew, jr. No date of Record.

March 28, 1772. Francis x Simpson and Mary, his wife, of Spts. Co., to Thomas Pettit, of same county. £25 curr. 200 a. in Spts. Co. Jos. Brock, Robt. Chew, Jno. Brock, Jno. Chew, jr.

Novr. 25, 1771. Beverley Winslow, of Berkeley Par., Spts. Co., to Wm. Mills, of Hanover Co. £220 curr. 350 a. in Berkeley Par., Spts. Co. Rd. Taylor, Wm. Quarles, Hy. Winslow. April Court, 1772.

Nov. 21, 1771. John Holloday, Senr., of Spts. Co., and Elizabeth, his wife, to Wm. Spindle, of same Co. £45 curr. 170 a. in St. Geo. Par., Spts. Co. Robert Dudley, John Estes, junr.; Jona. Clark. No date of Record.

Novr. 22, 1771. Wm. Fitzhugh, of King Geo. Co., Esqr., and Ann, his wife, to Thomas Allen, of Spts. Co. £42 curr. 106 a. in St. Geo. Par., Spts. Co. Ger. Banks, James Cunningham, Charles Bruce, John Simpson, Jos. Brock. April 17, 1772.

March 4, 1772. Wm. Fitzhugh, of Stafford Co., Esqr., and Ann, his wife, to George Wilson, of Spts. Co. £50 curr. 165 a. in St. Geo. Par., Spts. Co. Jno. Carter, Jno. Harrison, Benja. Tompkins, Jos. Brock. May 21, 1772.

Octr. 23, 1771. John x Gordon, Senr., of Spts. Co., and Elizabeth, his wife, to James Ritchie & Co., of Glasgow. £87 7s. 4½d. curr. Mortgage. 200 a. in Spts. Co., joining lands of James Marye, Peter Marye, and James Gordon, etc. Witnesses, Peter Crawford, Robert Maitland, Niel McCoull. No date of Record.

Novr. 22, 1771. Wm. Fitzhugh, of King Geo., Esqr., and Ann, his wife, to John Gordon, of Spts. Co., planter. £14 curr. 56 a. in St. Geo. Par., Spts. Co. Ger. Banks, James Cunningham, Charles Bruce, John Simpson, Jos. Brock. May 21, 1772.

May 25, 1772. James Coleman, of Spts. Co., and Betty, his wife, to Joel Lewis, of same Co. £175 curr. 415 a. on East North East River, in Spts. Co. No witnesses. No date of Record.

Novr. 6, 1771. Nicholas Darnall, of Hanover Co., to George Tureman, of Orange. £60 curr. 150 a. in Spts. Co. Wm. Mastin, John Mastin, Benjamin Craig, Thomas Mastin. May 21, 1772.

March 11, 1772. Benjamin Grymes, of Spts. Co., Esqr., The Honble. John Taylor and Francis Thornton, Executors of the last will and testament of Honble. Presley Thornton, Esqr., Decd., and Wm. Fitzhugh, Esq., trustees of the estate of the sd. Benjamin Grymes, and Peter Presley Thornton, eldest son and heir at law of sd. Presley Thornton, to Lewis Willis, of Fredksbg., Esqr. Whereas, sd. Benjamin Grymes and Priscilla, his wife, by Indenture, dated —— ——, 1767, conveyed to the Honble. Presley Thornton, Esqr., and Wm. Fitzhugh, Esqr., all the est. of the sd. Grymes for purposes therein stated, and amongst other things was a lot No. 61, in town of Fredksbg., which sd. lot the sd. Grymes and Trustees have disposed of to the sd. Willis for £50 curr. Witnesses, James Went, Geo. Bayn, John Talbert, Richd. Parker. May 22, 1772.

Novr. 6, 1771. James Frazer and Elizabeth, his wife, of King Wm. Co., to John Mastin, of Spts. Co. £33 curr. 332 a. in Berkeley Par., Spts. Co. Wm. Mastin, Thos. Mastin, Benj. Johnston, jr. No date of Record.

Novr. 22, 1771. Wm. Hunter, of Spts. Co., to John Simpson, Junr., of same Co. £100 curr. 58 a. in St. Geo. Par., Spts. Co., conveyed by Wm. Bledsoe to John Taliaferro, by Deeds, Oct. 6, 1730, etc. Witnesses, Francis Taliaferro, John Thornton, Jos. Brock, Francis Simpson, John Harrison, D. Simpson. May 21, 1772.

July 26, 1771. Charles Yates, of Fredksbg., Mercht., to Dr. Ewen Clements, of same town. £600 ster. Lots 5 and 6 in town of Fredksbg. Wm. Templeman, John Meals, Joshua Meals, James Allan. May 21, 1771.

Decr. 25, 1771. John Campbell and Mary, his wife, and Alexander Spotswood to Wm. Lampton, of Spts. Co. Lease. 75 acres. "Sd. Wm. Lampton and Martha, his wife, and Wm. Lampton, his son," etc. 450 lbs. tob. yearly. John Spotswood, Mann Page, junr.; R. C. Page, James Lewis, Jos. Brock, Jos. Brock, junr. May 21, 1772.

Decr. 25, 1771. John Campbell and Mary, his wife, and Alexander Spotswood to Daniel Simpson, of Spts. Co. Lease. 119 acres. "Sd. Daniel Simpson, his son, Abraham, and Frederick Gholson," etc. 500 lbs. tob. yearly. Jno. Spotswood, Mann Page, junr.; R. C. Page, James Lewis, Jos. Brock, junr. May 21, 1772.

Jany. 24, 1772. John x Cammack and John x Collins, of Spts. Co., to Francis Cammack, of same Co. 3 negroes. As security to a bond of Benj. Johnston for £30 for John Cammack. Witness, Henry Gatewood, junr. May ——, 1772.

March 2, 1772. Charles Curtis, of Spts. Co., to Wm. Reid, of Fredksbg., Mercht. £60 19s. 4d. curr. Mortgage. 250 a. in Spts. Co., adjoining lands of Wm. Nelson, Garnett, and Beasley, etc. Witnesses, Robert Patton, James Crawford, John Chew. May 22, 1772.

*The will of Elizabeth x Salter, of Fredksbg., Spts. Co. Dated, Dec. 23, 1771. No date of Record. Witness, B. Johnston. "Youngest daughter, called Juda Carter, who is to live with my daughter, Timerman." "My four children, Wm. Carter, Mary Timerman, Charles Carter, and Juda Carter," "daughter, Sarah Jinnings," "son, Wm. Carter, sole executor."

*Ed. Note.—The above will is recorded in Deed Book H, p. 142.

April 18, 1772. Thomas Wyatt and Sukey, his wife, of Essex Co., to James Coleman, of Spts. Co. £175 curr. 415 a. on East North East River, in Spts. Co., formerly purchased by sd. Wyatt of Chas. Smith and Ann, his wife, etc. John Coleman, Spilsbe Coleman, Daniel Lindsay. No date of Record.

Decr. 7, 1771. Thomas Crutcher and Sarah, his wife, of Caroline Co., to John Spindle, of Caroline Co. £75 curr. 300 a. in Spts. Co. Henry Crutcher, John Spindle, junr.; Reuben Landrum, Hugh Crutcher. June 18, 1772.

Nov. 10, 1771. John Thornton, of Caroline Co., Gent., Edwd. Carter, Esqr., and George Todd, surviving executors of Dr. John Sutherland, Decd., Robt. Brent, adms. with the will annexed of the sd. Jno. Sutherland, and Susanna, widow and relict of the sd. Jno. Sutherland, decd., to Robert Bogle & Scott & Co., of London, Gt. Britain. Whereas, sd. John Sutherland, died possessed of Lots 71 and 72 in town of Fredksbg., and by his last will and testament directed the sale of the sd. lots, and whereas, the sd. Sutherland having purchased the sd. lots of the sd. Edwd. Carter (who had purchased them from the sd. John Thornton), yet no deed had been made thereto, and whereas, under the directions of the sd. Sutherland will the sd. lots were sold at public outcry to James Robb, one of the partners of the sd. Robert Bogle, etc., for £520. Witnesseth, that sd. Thornton, the sd. Carter, the sd. Executors and Administrators and the sd. relict of the sd. John Sutherland, Decd., join in deed to the sd. Bogle & Co., etc. Witnesses, James Duncanson, John Glassell, James Somerville, Peter Scott, Archibald McLaine, John Johnston. June 18, 1772.

—— ——, 1771. John Campbell and Mary, his wife, and Alexander Spotswood to John Ellis, of Spts. Co. Lease. 135 acres. "Sd. Ellis and Sarah, his wife, and Wm. O'Neal," etc. 740 lbs. tob. yearly. Jno. Brock, Thos. Fox, Wm. Clayton, Wm. Ellis, Sherod Horn, Jas. Gordon. June 18, 1772.

April 16, 1772. Edmund Pendleton, and Peter Lyons, Gentlemen, surviving Admrs. of the estate of John Robinson, Esqr., Decd., to John Waller, of Spts. Co. Whereas, Bernard Moore, Esqr., being seized of 6000 a. on Pamunkey River in Caroline Co., did by Indenture in Augt. 1767, convey the sd. land to the sd. Pendleton and Lyons by way of mortgage for securing payment of a debt due by sd. Moore to the est. of sd. Robinson, and by consent of the sd. Pendleton and Lyons the sd. Moore divided the sd. tract into smaller lots for Distinct Prizes in a lottery. Since the drawing of which lottery sd. Moore and Anna Catharine, his wife, have executed an Indenture of Release to the sd. Pendleton and Lyons whereby the Equity of Redemption of the sd. Moore and the dower of the sd. Anna Catharine are absolutely released to the sd. Pendleton and Lyons to enable them to convey the prizes drawn in sd. lottery, etc., and whereas, lot No. 56 in plot of sd. Lottery was drawn by a ticket sold to Wm. Champe, Esqr., and by him to the said John Waller, etc. Witnesseth the sd. Pendleton and Lyons convey sd. Waller, 100 acres as drawn by the afsd. ticket, etc. Witnesses, Ch. Sims, J. Waller, Jas. Mercer, Wm. Porter, Isaac Heslop, James Somerville. June 18, 1772.

Decr. 21, 1771. Stephen Johnson, of Spts. Co., to Joseph Holloday, of same Co. £60 curr. 84 a. in Spts. Co. Robt. Patton, Ben. Holloday, Ben. Lewis, Jacob x Young. No date of Record.

Jany. 23, 1772. Benjamin Winslow, of Orange Co., and Mary, his wife, to Hancock Taylor, of same Co. £400. 595 a. on Pamunkey River, Berkeley Par., Spts. Co. Jos. Hawkins, Thomas Bell, Rowland Thomas, James Taylor, Frances Taylor, Andrew Shepherd. June 18, 1772.

June 10, 1772. Alexander Spotswood, of Spts. Co., to Wm. Wood, of sd. Co. Lease. 200 a. 750 lbs. tob. Sherod Horn, Wm. Ellis, James Gordon, Jos. Brock. June 18, 1772.

Dec. 25, 1771. John Campbell and Mary, his wife, and Alexander Spotswood, Gent., to David McQuittie, of Spts. Co. Lease. 130 a. "James McQuittie, Wm. McQuittie, and Mary McQuittie." 500 lbs. tob. Jno. Spotswood, Mann Page, junr.; R. C. Page, James Lewis, Jos. Brock, Jos. Brock, junr. June 18, 1772.

May 16, 1772. Robert Walker, of Fredksbg., to James Duncanson, of same town, Mercht. £200 curr. Two lots in town of Fredksbg. John Wright, Jacob Whitler, Thomas Herbert. No date of Record.

June 20, 1772. George Atkinson and Martha, his wife, of Spts. Co., to Wm. Templeman, of same Co. £32 5s. curr. Lot No. 3 in Fredksbg. No witnesses. No date of Record.

Dec. 25, 1771. Alexander Spotswood, of Spts. Co., Gent., to Joseph Brock, of same Co. Lease. 360 a. in St. Geo. Par., Spts. Co. "Sd. Joseph Brock's three sons, John, Joseph, and Wm.," etc. 1200 lbs. tob. Jno. Brock, Wm. Clayton, Thos. Fox. June 19, 1772.

June 3, 1772. James Mercer, of Spts. Co., Esqr., and Charles Dick, of same Co., Esqr. Whereas, a marriage is shortly intended to be solemnized between the sd. James Mercer and Eleanor Dick, daughter of sd. Charles Dick, who is under age, and whereas, sd Mercer stands seized of a considerable estate of land, slaves, etc., etc. Marriage settlement. Witnesses, Samuel Selden, Alexr. Dick, Francis Taliaferro, Chs. Simms. No date of Record.

Sept. 17, 1771. John Keeton, of Spts. Co., to Benjamin Johnston, Execr. of John Benger. £12 9s. 2d. Mortgage. 50 a. in St. Geo. Par., Spts. Co. John Chew, Thos. Farish. No date of Record.

—— ——, 1771. John Campbell and Mary, his wife, and Alexander Spotswood, to George Rose, of Spts. Co. Lease. 100 a. "Sd. Rose and Mary, his wife, and his son, George," etc. 600 lbs. tob. Sherod Horn, Elizabeth Spotwood, Thos. Turner, Jno. Simpson, junr.; John Simpson, Wm. Clayton, James Gordon, Jos. Brock. June 20, 1772.

June 6, 1772. Dudley Gatewood and Sarah, his wife, and James Gatewood and Frances, his wife, of Amherst Co., to Edward Brasfield, of Spts. Co. £80 curr. 220 a. in Berkeley Par., Spts. Co. (Mentions brother, Peter Gatewood), Joseph Willoughby, Benj. Poe, Leonard Brasfield, Thos. Penn, Jno. Penn, James Coleman, Larkin Gatewood. No date of Record.

May 20, 1772. Alexander Spotswood, of Spts. Co., Esqr., to John Brock, of afsd. Co. Lease. 216 a. in St. Geo. Par., Spts. Co. "Sd. Jno. Brock,

Joseph Brock, and Wm. Brock," etc. 800 lbs. tob. Wm. Clayton, Thos. Fox, Jos. Brock. July Court, 1772.

July 16, 1772. George Wilson and Ann, his wife, of Spts. Co., to James Lewis, of same Co. £50 15s. curr. 35 a. in St. Geo. Par., Spts. Co. No. witnesses. July 16, 1772.

Oct. 14, 1772. Marriage to be solemnized between Michael Robinson and Esther Frazer, Agreement. Witnesses, Jas. Marye, Thomas James, Theophilus Theobald. No date of Record.

Nov. 21, 1771. John Campbell and Mary, his wife, and Alexander Spotswood to John Angle, of Spts. Co. Lease. 100 a. "Sd. John Angle, Mildred, his wife, and George, his son," etc. 600 lbs. tob. Jno. Spotswood, Mann Page, junr.; R. C. Page, James Lewis, Jos. Brock, Jos. Brock, junr. July Court, 1772.

Jany. 1, 1772. John Campbell and Mary, his wife, and Alexander Spotswood to Benjamin Haley, of Spts. Co. Lease. 208 a. "Francis Haley Allen," etc. 1000 lbs. tob. James Lewis, Jos. Brock, Jos. Brock, junr. July 16, 1772.

March 30, 1772. Mary Jarvis, formerly Mary Brown, elict of Wm. Brown, Decd., now of Spts. Co., to James Brown, of Fredksl g. Whereas, sd. Wm. Brown, died leaving several children whereof one is called James, and sd. Mary being desirous to do what she can for the benefit of sd. James, apprentices him to James Brown, the other party to these presents, etc. Term, 13 yrs. Jas. Jarvis, who intermarried with sd. Mary Brown, gives his assent, etc. Witnesses, Chas. Sebastin, Zachariah Lucas. July 17, 1772.

July 17, 1772. Charles Dick, Joseph Brock, John Carter, and Charles Washington, Justices of the Peace for Spts. Co., apprentices Henry White, orphan of Wm. White, to James Brown of Fredksbg., silversmith. Term, eleven years. Test, O. Towles. July 17, 1772.

March 30, 1772. Catharine Green, of Fredksbg., apprentices her son, Benjamin Weeks, unto James Brown, of Fredksbg., for term of 8 yrs. Test, O. Towles. July 17, 1772.

July 17, 1772. Fielding Lewis, surviving executor of Dr. Wm. Lynn, late of Fredksbg., Decd., to James Duncanson of sd. town. £42 10s. Lot 60 in town of Fredksbg., purchased by sd. Lynn of Richd. Todd, of King and Queen Co., etc. July 17, 1772.

July 17, 1772. Margaret Gordon, of Fredksbg., and Hugh Mercer and Isabella, his wife, of same town, to Edward Vass, of St. Geo. Par., Spts. Co. Whereas, sd. Margaret Gordon being seized of two lots in Fredksbg., Nos. 79 and 80, purchased of Fielding Lewis and Betty, his wife, and the sd. Mercer purchased sd. lots of sd. Margaret Gordon and had possession thereof devised to him and by virtue whereof the Equitable right to the sd. lots was in sd. Mercer, and the sd. Isabella, his wife, was in Equity entitled to Dower, etc., sd. Gordon, Mercer and wife, join in deed to sd. Vass, for sum of £120 curr. pd. sd. Mercer, etc. Witnesses, Arthur Hamilton, John Julian, Go. Weedon. No date of Record.

July 17, 1772. Fielding Lewis, St. Geo. Par., Spts. Co., Esqr., and Betty, his wife, to Edward Vass, of St. Geo. Par., Spts. Co. £100 curr. Four lots in town of Fredksbg. "whereon the sd. Edwd. Vass's brick yard is contiguous." No witnesses. No date of Record.

July 17, 1772. Wm. Smith, of Fredksbg., and Ann, his wife, to John Taliaferro, of King Geo. Co. £65 curr. Lots 252 and 262 in town of Fredksbg. Philip Clayton, junr.; James Hunter, junr.; Edward Vass. July 17, 1772.

April 16, 1772. Francis Purvis, of Caroline Co., and Mary, his wife, to James Mercer, of Spts. Co., Esqr. £112 16s. curr. Tract of land in St. Geo. Par., Spts. Co., lately bought by sd. Purvis of Col. Wm. Champe. Witnesses, La. Campbell, Geo. Muir, Charles Simms, Wm. Wiatt. No date of Record.

March 9, 1772. James Howerton, of Brunswick Co., to John Faulconer, of Spts. Co. £15 curr. Tract of land in Spts. Co. James Haydon, Thos. Faulconer, John Faulconer. Augt. Court, 1772.

Augt. 20, 1772. Joseph Venable, of Spts. Co., and Sussie, his wife, to Clayton Coleman, of same Co. £40 curr. 100 a. in Spts. Co. No witnesses. Augt. 20, 1772.

Augt. 20, 1772. Henry Chiles, of Spts. Co., to Joseph Herndon, of same Co. £10 12s. 6d. Tract of land in Spts. Co. No witnesses. No date of Record.

Augt. 20, 1772. David Anderson, of Spts. Co., to Joseph True, of same Co. £20 curr. 100 a. in Berkeley Par., Spts. Co. Henry True, David Head, Alexr. Spence Head. No date of Record.

Augt. 19, 1772. James Watkins, of Berkeley Par., Spts. Co., and Mary, his wife, to Elisha Dismukes, of sd. Par. and Co. £40 curr. 100 a. in Berkeley Par., Spts. Co. Witnesses, James Wiglesworth, Senr.; Samuel x Traynum, James Wiglesworth, junr. August Court, 1772.

Augt. 20, 1772. John Thornton, jr., son of Francis Thornton, of Spts. Co., Decd., to John Baggot, of Fredksbg. £320 curr. Lot in town of Fredksbg., devised sd. Thornton by the last will and testament of his father, Francis Thornton, Decd. Dated, Nov. 11, 1748. No witnesses. Augt. 20, 1772.

April 4, 1772. John Campbell and Mary, his wife, and Alexander Spotswood, Esqr., to Thomas Hutcherson, of Spts. Co. Lease. 200 a. "Sd. Hutcherson, his son, Wm., and his daughter, Sukey Hutcherson," etc. 1000 lbs. tob. Thos. Fox, James Allan, Philip Somerby, Ann Clark, Shadrock Moore, Nathl. Fox, John Taliaferro. Augt. 20, 1772.

April 23, 1772. Paul x McClary and Rose, his wife, of Orange Co., to Peter Roswell, of Berkeley Par., Spts. Co. £20. 100 a. in Plentifull Run in Berkeley Par., Spts. Co. Wm. Bonnel, Jacob Wright, Wm. Hall. Sept., 1772.

Septr. 15, 1772. Alexander Spotswood, of Spts. Co., to Thomas Ficklin, of sd. Co. Lease. 220 a. in St. Geo. Par., Spts. Co. "Sd. Ficklin, his wife, Mary, and his son, Jno. Herndon," etc. 1080 lbs. tob. John Brock, Js. Lewis, Jno. Chew, jr.

Septr. 17, 1772. Moseley Battaley, an infant, apprentices himself to John Wigglesworth, House Carpenter, etc., sd. Battaley now 17 yrs. of age, apprenticed until he reaches the age of 21 years, etc. No witnesses. No date of Record.

Septr. 18, 1772. Michael Robinson, of Spts. Co., and Esther, his wife, to George Washington, of Fairfax Co., Esqr. £275 curr. Lots 107 and 108 in town of Fredksbg., purchased of Fielding Lewis, etc., as by Deed, Oct. 3,̀ 1761. No witnesses. No date of Record.

Septr. 28, 1772. Wm. Fitzhugh of King Geo., Esqr., and Ann, his wife, to John Chew of Spts. Co. £31 15s. curr. 127 a. in St. Geo. Par., Spts. Co. Mann Page, junr.; Patr. Kennan, Andrew Shepherd, Go. Weedon, Benj. Grymes, junr. Novr. 20, 1772.

Novr. 3, 1772. John x Durrett of Spts. Co. to his daughter Mary, wife of James Wiglesworth. Deed of gift. Slaves. Witnesses, James Watkins, Nathan Hawkins. Novr. 20, 1772.

April 13, 1772. Wm. Wood of Spts. Co. to Joseph Herndon of same Co. Mortgage, to indemnify sd. Herndon who is security for sd. Wood to the Revd. James Marye, Decd. Negroes. Witnesses, Ambrose Rains, Reuben Straughan, Jack Estes. Novr. 20, 1772.

Nov. 19, 1772. Wm. Bartlett of Spts. Co. of the first part; Edwd. Herndon, Joseph Herndon, Thos. Bartlett, and Harry Bartlett, of the second part; and Thomas Perry and Sarah, his wife, of the third part, etc. Sd. Wm. Bartlett for and in consideration of the natural love and affection he hath and doth bear unto his daughter the sd. Sarah and her issue conveys to the sd. Edwd. and Jos. Herndon, Thos. and Harry Bartlett, in trust, for the sd. Thos. Perry and Sarah, his wife, during their lives, and then to be sold for the benefit of their children, etc. 153 a. in St. Geo. Par., Spts. Co. No witnesses. Nov. 20, 1772.

May 27, 1772. John Campbell and Mary, his wife, and Alexander Spotswood, Esqr., to Thomas Fox of Spts. Co. Lease. Tuball Plantation, etc. "Sd. Thomas Fox, Joseph Fox, Betty Fox, Molly Fox," etc. 1000 lbs. tob. James Allan, Edwd. Vass, John Herndon, Ann Clark, Shadrack Moore, Nathl. Fox, Thos. Rogers. Novr. 20, 1772.

Nov. 9, 1772. Benjamin Tompkins and Elizabeth, his wife, of Caroline Co. to John Carthrae of Spts. Co. £75 curr. 315 a. in Spts. Co. Wm. Heslop, Jacob Whittler, Jno. Richards. No date of Record.

Septr. 21, 1772. Robert Taliaferro and Jane, his wife, of Caroline Co. to Long Wharton of Co. afsd. £80 curr. 550 a. in Spts. Co. Daniel Starke, Joseph Bridges, James Livingston. Nov. 20, 1772.

Novr. 19, 1772. Robert Chew, Gent., to Martin True of Spts. Co. Lease. 100 a. "Sd. Martin True and his sons John and Larkin," etc. 600 lbs. tob. John Chew, Harry Bartlett, Thos. Megee. Nov. 20, 1772.

Octr. 26, 1772. Alexander Spotswood to James Lewis and Joseph Herndon of Spts. Co., Gentl. Lease. 256 a. in St. Geo. Par., Spts. Co. "Sd. Lewis and Herndon and his son Edwd. Herndon," etc. 1224 lbs. tob. Jno. Brock, Jno. Chew, junr.; Jos. Brock. Novr. 20, 1772.

Novr. 1, 1772. Alexander Spotswood, Esqr., to John Schooler of Spts. Co., planter. Lease. 87 a. in St. Geo. Par., Spts. Co. "John Wharton and his wife Lizzie, and Benjamin Schooler," etc. 480 lbs. tob. Jno. Brock,

Jno. Chew, jr.; Js. Lewis, Jn. Chew, John Smith, Wm. Penn, Nathan Hawkins. Novr. 20, 1772.

Decr. 25, 1770. John Campbell and Mary, his wife, and Alexander Spotswood to Wm. Haydon of Spts. Co. Lease. 95 a. "Sd. Haydon, Jeremiah Craig, Benja. Craig and his son Joseph," etc. 400 lbs. tob. James Lewis, Jos. Brock, Jos. Brock, junr. No date of Record.

Oct. 1, 1772. Alexander Spotswood of Spts. Co. to Sherod Horn of sd. Co. Lease. 67 a. in St. Geo. Par., Spts. Co. 268 lbs. tob. Philip Somerby, Thomas Colson, Js. Lewis. Novr. 20, 1772.

Septr. 25, 1772. Alexander Spotswood of Spts. Co., Esqr., to John Clayton of same Co., planter. Lease. 170 a. in St. Geo. Par., Spts. Co. "Sd. John Clayton, Alexr. Spotswood and Elizabeth Rogers," etc. 880 lbs. tob. Philip Somerby, Thomas Colson, Js. Lewis. Novr. 20, 1772.

Septr. 4, 1772. Joseph Talbert of Spts. Co. and Sarah, his wife, and James Crawford of same Co. and Mary, his wife, to James Wiglesworth of same Co. £97 10s. curr. 112 a. in Berkeley Par., Spts. Co., part of a tract of land granted by Patent to Edmund Waller. Witnesses, Joel Parish, Jonathan Carpenter. Novr. 20, 1772.

Septr. 19, 1772. John Wiglesworth of Berkeley Par., Spts. Co. to James Wiglesworth of same Par. and Co. £150 curr. 300 a. in Par. and Co. afsd., part of two tracts of land patented by John Wilkins and Edmund Waller. Witnesses, Henry Johnson, Wm. Cason. Novr. 20, 1772.

Oct. 5, 1772. Long Wharton and Ann, his wife, of Caroline Co. to Daniel Starke of same Co. £40 curr. 275 a. tract purchased of Robt. Taliaferro of Caroline Co., etc. James Livingston, Reuben Moore. Novr. 20, 1772.

Octr. 1, 1772. Alexander Spotswood of Spts. Co. to Nicholas Hawkins, junr. Lease. 110 a. in St. Geo. Par., Spts. Co. "Sd. Hawkins and Sarah, his wife, and his son Benjamin," etc. 450 lbs. tob. Philip Somerby, Thomas Colson, Js. Lewis. Novr. 20, 1772.

Novr. 1, 1772. Alexander Spotswood, Esqr., to Robert Frank of Spts. Co., planter. Lease. 254 a. in St. Geo. Par., Spts. Co. "Sd. Frank, Robt. Frank, junr.," etc. 1000 lbs. tob. Jas. Brooke, Jno. Brock, Jno. Chew, junr. Novr. 20, 1772.

Oct. 26, 1772. Alexander Spotswood, Esqr., to John Simpson, junr. of Spts. Co. Lease. 105 a. in St. Geo. Par., Spts. Co. "Sd. Simpson and Frances, his wife, and Lewis Sharpe," etc. 400 lbs. tob. Jno. Brock, Js. Lewis, Jos. Brock. Novr. 20, 1772.

Augt. 29, 1772. Alexander Spotswood of Spts. Co. to Taliaferro Craig of sd. Co. Lease. 170 a. in St. Geo. Par., Spts. Co. "Sd. Craig, Jeremiah Craig, Benja. Craig and his son Joseph," etc. 760 lbs. tob. Jno. Brock, Jno. Chew, Jr.; Js. Lewis. Nov. 20, 1772.

Augt. 30, 1772. Alexander Spotswood of Spts. Co., Esqr., to Taliaferro Craig of same Co. Lease. 200 a. "Sd. Craig, Jeremiah Craig, Benjamin Craig and his son Joseph," etc. 800 lbs. tob. John Brock, Jno. Chew, junr.; Js. Lewis. Nov. 20, 1772.

Novr. 5, 1772. Rice Vass of Spts. Co. and Ann, his wife, of first part; Mary Vass, widow and relict of Philip Vincent Vass, of second part, to George Stubblefield of Spts. Co., Gent. Whereas, Philip Vincent Vass at his death was seized of a certain tract of 576 a. in Spts. Co. and dying intestate sd. tract descended to his son John Vass, his eldest son and heir, who sometime afterward died intestate and without issue, by which the same descended to the sd. Rice Vass, as elder brother and heir of the sd. John Vass, and since the sd. Rice Vass has agreed to sell part of the sd. tract to sd. Stubblefield, the sd. Mary Vass, being entitled to dower in the sd. tract, joins in the deed, etc. For the sum of £45 3s. curr. 150 a. of the afsd. tract, etc. Witnesses, Wm. Heslop, Thos. Towles, Harry Stubblefield, Jno. Carthrae, O. Towles, Robt. Stubblefield, Lewis Young, Leonard Young. Novr. 20, 1772.

Septr. 21, 1772. Edward x Straughan x Mary, his wife, to John Brock of Spts. Co. £52 10s. curr. 100 a. in St. Geo. Par., Spts. Co. Robt. Chew, Jos. Brock, R. B. Chew. March 18, 1773.

Decr. 5, 1772. James Ware and Agnes, his wife, of Caroline Co. to John Knight of Spts. Co. £15 curr. 100 a. in Spts. Co. Nathal. Holloway, Thomas Wisdom. March 18, 1773.

Decr. 7, 1772. John Graves of Spts. Co. to his son Joseph Graves. Deed of Gift. Negro, goods and chattels, etc. Witnesses, Wm. Pettus, Samuel Coleman. No date of Record.

Decr. 23, 1772. Ann x Graves to her granddaughter, Barbra Pettus. Deed of Gift. A negro girl. Witnesses, Jo. Graves, Jno. Shackleford, Elizabeth Gregson, Samuel Coleman. No date of Record.

Feby. 10, 1773. Uriah Edwards and Mildred, his wife, of Spts. Co. to John Cammack of Co. afsd. £45 curr. 46½ a. in Berkeley Par., Spts. Co. Henry Gatewood, junr.; Geo. Cammack, Francis Cammack. March 18, 1773.

Septr. 25, 1772. Robert Collins and Elizabeth, his wife, of Spts. Co. to John Waller, K. W. £30 curr. Tract or parcel of land in St. Geo. Par., Spts. Co. which sd. land sd. Collins holds in right of dower by his sd. wife being ⅓ of the tract of land belonging to John Hawkins, Decd., etc. John Chew, John Estes, junr.; Jno. Chew, junr.; Nathan Hawkins. No date of record.

Jany. 25, 1773. Mordacai Buckner and Oliver Towles of Spts. Co., Execrs. of the last will and testament of Larkin Chew, Gent., Decd., to Stapleton Crutchfield of same Co. £151 12s. curr. 379 a. in Spts. Co. Whereas, sd. Larkin Chew did by his last will and testament devise to his grandson Larkin Smith part of his tract of land purchased of Bushwod Fauntleroy, the remainder to be sold by his executors, the remainder contains 445 a. the sd. Executors selling 379 a. thereof to the sd. Crutchfield, etc. Witnesses, Edwd. Herndon, Willm. Smith, Thomas Colson, Wm. Wood, John Herndon. March 18, 1773.

March 18, 1773. Stapleton Crutchfield of Spts. Co. and Sarah, his wife, to Joseph Herndon of same Co. £35 7s. 3d. 62 a. in Berkeley Par., Spts. Co. No witnesses. March 18, 1773.

Decr. 31, 1772. John Julian of Fredksbg., Doctor of Physick, to John Gaspar of same town, Sadler. £78 6s. curr. 150 a. on s. side Rappk. River, conveyed by Francis Willis, Esqr., of Gloucester Co., Executor of Henry Willis, Esqr., late of Spts. Co., and Philip Rootes, son and heir and acting executor of Philip Rootes, late of King and Queen Co., Gent., Decd., by their deed July 17, 1759, to Charles Julian, who by his last will and testament devised the same to his son, the sd. John Julian, etc. Witnesses, Henry Mitchell, John Ferrie, Wm. McWilliams, junr. March 18, 1773.

Jany. 2, 1772. Henry Mitchell of Fredksbg. to George McCall, Archibald Smillie, Richard Smillie, and Henry Mitchell, known by name of McCall, Smillie & Co., of City of Glasgow, Merchts. and Partners. £187 10s. curr. Two lots in town of Fredksbg. in the square where Lewis Willis, Esqr., lives, and conveyed to sd. Mitchell, by Wm. Dangerfield and Mary, his wife, as by their Indenture, March 25, 1771, etc. March 18, 1773.

March 17, 1773. Fielding Lewis of Spts. Co., Esqr., and Betty, his wife, and John Lewis of same Co. to John Thornton, Charles Dick, James Allan, James Hunter, Lewis Willis, Charles Yates, James Mercer, and Charles Washington, Gentlemen, Trustees of Fredksbg. £830 curr. Mortgage. Several tracts of land in St. Geo. Par., Spts. Co. purchased by John Lewis, Esqr. (father of the sd. Fielding Lewis), of Francis Thornton, Gent., and devised to the sd. Fielding by his sd. father, containing 409 a., also the tract containing 886 a. which sd. Fielding purchased of Richard Royston, except so much of the sd. tract as has been settled on sd. John Lewis, party to these presents, etc. Witnesses, George Muir, Benj. Grymes, jr.; B. Johnston, Wm. Wiatt, Harry Bartlett, Joseph Gale, Jno. Carter. March 19, 1773.

Septr. 22, 1772. Robert Wilkinson of Spts. Co., Blacksmith, and Alice, his wife, and Fielding Lewis of Fredksbg., Gent., and Betty, his wife, to James Somerville of Fredksbg., Mercht. Whereas, sd. Alice Wilkinson "whilst sole" purchased of sd. Lewis and wife, a lot in town of Fredksbg., for which she was to pay £75 curr., part thereof she pd. on July 19, 1763, and there remained £20 with interest, etc., and the sd. Lewis having made no conveyance to the sd. Alice, "while sole," or to the sd. Robt. and Alice, since their intermarriage, and the title being still vested in the sd. Lewis, and whereas, the sd. Robt. and Alice having agreed for the sale of the sd. lot to the sd. Somerville, for the sum of £50 curr., etc., the parties all join in this deed to the sd. Somerville, etc. Witnesses, Robert Chew, Charles Washington, Lewis Willis, Michael Robinson, junr.; B. Johntson, John Glassell. March 17, 1774.

March 11, 1773. Mary x Steward, widow, and Benjamin x Steward and Wm. x Steward, her sons, of Spts. Co. to Charles Washington of sd. Co., Gent. £200 curr. 200 a. of land. Whereas, George Proctor, late of Spts. Co., by his deed of Gift, Nov. 2, 1725, gave to his daughter Mary, and her then husband Charles Steward, and to her heirs, one tract of 200 a. of land, which tract sd. Mary Steward, after the decease of her husband Chas. Steward, gave to her two sons the sd. Benjamin and Wm. Steward, as by deed, May 2, 1758, etc. Witnesses, Wm. Triplet, James Tutt, James Hamilton, Ben. Tutt. March 19, 1773.

Feby. 10, 1773. James Mercer of Spts. Co. to John Thornton, Charles Dick, Fielding Lewis, Lewis Willis, James Allan, James Hunter, Chas.

Yates, and Chas. Washington, Gentlemen, Trustees, of Fredksbg. £695. Mortgage. Whereas, sd. Mercer in the month of May or June last being seized of ten lots in town of Fredksbg. and 744 a. of land near the sd. town, and other lands which sd. Mercer intended soon to dispose of, etc., etc. Mentions his agreement with Chas. Dick, relative to sd. Mercer's intermarriage with sd. Dick's daughter, etc., etc. Sd. Mercer mortgages to the sd. Trustees all sd. Mercer's right, title and interest in the sd. 10 lots and the tract of 740 a. in and near the town of Fredksbg., also several slaves, etc. Witnesses, Ch. Simms, Geo. Muir, Benj. Grymes, jr.; B. Johnston, Wm. Wiatt. March 19, 1773.

Feby. 28, 1773. James Mercer of Spts. Co. to Muscoe Garnett of Essex Co., Esqr. Mortgage. In consideration of sd. Garnett being sd. Mercer's security on a bond to John Hessline of the province of Md., and also sd. Garnett, abt. the year 1769, having become security for Mrs. Ann Mercer, late of Stafford Co., in a bond payable to Mrs. Ann Tasker of the province of Md. "Mentions, Col. Geo. Mercer, then at London." Mortgages 36 slaves, etc. Sd. James Mercer mentions himself as sole executor of Mrs. Ann Mercer, etc. Witness, Chs. Simms. March 19, 1773.

Jany. 23, 1773. Samuel Fox of Fauquier Co. to John Welch of Fredksbg. Lease. 50 a. of land joining land of James Mercer, abt. 2 miles from Fredksbg., in Spts. Co. £6 curr. yearly. Nicholas Smith, Philemon Noakes, Bartho. Barrett. March 19, 1773.

July 1, 1771. John Foster of Spts. Co. to James Robb of Fredksbg., Mercht. £25 9s. 10d. curr. Mortgage. Goods and chattels. Witnesses, Rob. Chew, Daniel Branham, Edward Collins, John Penn, junr.; John Chew. No date of Record.

Novr. 20, 1772. Wm. Smith of King Geo. Co. to Cary Selden of Elizabeth City Co. Mortgage. To indemnify sd. Selden who stands security in a bond of the sd. Smith's to James Robb of Fredksbg., Mercht, etc. A negro wench, goods and chattels, etc. Witnesses, John Glassell, Henry Mitchell, James Robb, Danl. Payne. No date of Record.

Octr. 15, 1772. David Darnal and Ann, his wife, of St. Marks Par., Culpeper Co. to Peter Roswell of Berkeley Par., Spts. Co. £30. 300 a. in Berkeley Par., Spts. Co. Wm. Triplet, Lewis Craig, Daniel Triplett. No date of Record.

Decr. 4, 1772. Morgan Alexander of Frederick Co., son and heir of the late David Alexander of Gloucester Co., Decd.; George Todd, surviving executor of Dr. John Sutherland, Decd. Robt. Brent, adms. with the will annexed of the sd. John Sutherland, Decd., and —— Sutherland, widow and relict of the sd. John Sutherland, Decd., to Dr. Hugh Mercer of Fredksbg. Whereas, the sd. Jno. Sutherland purchased of the sd. David Alexander, Lot No. 63 in town of Fredksbg., etc., but before obtaining a deed thereto the sd. Sutherland died, and by his will directed the sale of his estate and appt. Robt. Duncanson, now Decd., and the sd. George Todd, Executors, who refusing the executorship letters of administration with the will annexed were in due form granted the sd. Robert Brent who in pursuance of the sd. Sutherland will the sd. lot No. 63 being exposed to sale was purchased by the sd. Hugh Mercer, for £41 pd. to the sd. Morgan Alexander with the approval of sd. Todd, Brent, etc., etc.

Witnesses, John Meals, Chas. Dick, James Somerville, Jno. Lewis, Charles Taylor, Valent. Peyton, Wm. Jenkins, Wm. McWilliams, jr. No date of Record.

Augt. 17, 1772. Fielding Lewis of Fredksbg., Esqr., and Betty, his wife; George Todd, surviving executor of Dr. John Sutherland, Decd., and —— Sutherland, widow of sd. John Sutherland, and Robert Brent, administrator with the will annexed, of Dr. Jno. Sutherland, to Dr. Hugh Mercer of Fredksbg. Whereas, sd. Lewis and Betty, his wife, sold to Dr. John Sutherland, lot No. 123 in town of Fredksbg., the sd. Sutherland by his will directed the sale of his estate, which being exposed the sd. lot was purchased by the sd. Mercer, for the sum of £20 pd. to the sd. Lewis, no deed for the sd. lot having been formerly made the sd. Jno. Sutherland, etc., etc. Witnesses, Charles Taylor, Valent. Peyton, Wm. Jenkins, Wm. McWilliams, jr. No date of Record.

April 16, 1773. Benjamin Lewis of Trinity Par., Louisa Co. and Martha, his wife, to Betty Littlepage ofBerkeley Par., Spts. Co. £360 curr. 484 a. in Berkeley Par., Spts. Co. devised the sd. Benjamin, by Zachary Lewis, Decd., etc. No witnesses. April 16, 1773.

Feby. 20, 1773. John and Richard Ray of King and Queen Co. to John Craig of Spts. Co. £25 curr. 497 a. in Spts. Co. on branches of Mattapony River. Witnesses, Taliver Craig, John Perry, Margaret Long. No date of Record.

May 20, 1773. John Craig of Spts. Co. and Sarah, his wife, to Daniel Lambert of sd. County. £27 curr. 273 a. in Spts. Co. on branches of Mattapony, etc. No witnesses. No date of Record.

Decr. 17, 1772. Thomas Ashman and Mary, his wife, of Spts. Co. to Joseph Pulliam of same Co. £40 curr. 89½ a. in Spts. Co. James Frazer, Jno. Warner, John Baggott, David Pulliam, Wm. Wood, Harry Bartlett, Jno Chew, jr. No date of Record.

May 19, 1773. Waller Lewis of Spts. Co. and Sarah, his wife, to James Crawford of same Co. £32 5s. curr. 149 a. in Spts. Co. J. Lewis, Jno. Z. Lewis, Robt. Lewis, John x Goodrick, Wm. Davenport, John Arnold. May 20, 1773.

May 18, 1773. Edward Coleman and Sarah, his wife, of Berkeley Par., Spts. Co. to Henry Coleman of Par. and Co. afsd. £50 curr. 200 a. on Plentiful Run in Par. and Co. afsd. John Hutcherson, junr.; John Coleman, Thomas Coleman. No date of Record.

May 18, 1773. John Carpenter of Spts. Co. and Mary, his wife, to Wm. Cason of same Co. £18 curr. 24 a. in Spts. Co. Jo. Graves, John Graves, Jonathan Carpenter. May 20, 1773.

May 18, 1773. Jean Carpenter, Jonathan Carpenter, and Susannah, his wife, of Spts. Co. to Benjamin Waller of same Co. £140 curr. 150 a. in Spts. Co., conveyed the sd. Jonathan Carpenter by John Carpenter, etc. Witnesses, Jo. Graves, John Graves, Wm. Cason. May 20, 1773.

May 20, 1773. Joseph Sams, orph. of James Sams, with the consent of his guardian, Vincent Vass, apprentices himself to Robert Stubblefield of Spts. Co., etc. Witnesses, Rice Vass, Leonard Young. No date of Record.

Jany. 25, 1773. Alexander Spotswood, Esqr., to Amos Jones of Spts. Co. Lease. 250 acres. "Sd. Jones and May, his wife, and Ann, his daughter," etc. £7 10s. curr. yearly, etc. Andrew Shepherd, John Munro, Jona. Wilson. May 20, 1773.

Oct. 1, 1772. Alexander Spotswood of Spts. Co., Esqr., to Wm. Hudson of same Co. Lease. 190 a. in St. Geo. Par., Spts. Co. "Sd. Wm. Hudson, and Reuben and Richard Hudson, his two sons," etc. 880 lbs. tob., etc. Philip Somerby, Thomas Colson, Js. Lewis. May 20, 1773.

May 8, 1773. John Thornton, junr., of Spts. Co. to Daniel Payne of Falmouth, King Geo. Co. £90 curr. Lot 56 in town of Fredksbg., devised by Francis Thornton, Decd., to his son, the sd. John Thornton, etc. Witnesses, Fras. Thornton, Lewis Willis, Wm. Triplet, Daniel Triplet. May 21, 1773.

March 31, 1773. James Hunter of King Geo. Co., Esqr., and Allan Wiley of Spts. Co. and Eve, his wife, to Hugh Mercer of Fredksbg. Whereas, sd. Hunter sold to sd. Allan Wiley, 350 a. in St. Geo. Par., Spts. Co., conveyed by Thos. Reeves and wife, to sd. Hunter, as by deeds, Decr. 8, 1767, etc., etc., and whereas, the sd. Wiley hath since sold the sd. land to the sd. Hugh Mercer, etc. Sd. Allan Wiley and wife, in consideration of £350 curr. 300 a. of the aforementioned tract, etc. Witnesses, Js. Mercer, Chas. Washington, Chs. Dick, Ch. Simms, James Ward. No date of Record.

June 19, 1773. Mary Horn of Fredksbg. to McCall, Smillie & Co., Merchts., in Glasgow. £88 7s. 5½d. Mortgage. Negro, etc., goods and chattels. Jno. Ferrie, Wm. McWilliams, Jr. May 21, 1773.

Decr. 22, 1772. John Mason and Anna, his wife, of Spts. Co. to Peter Mason of Spts. Co. £80 2s. curr. 178 a. in Spts. Co. Witnesses, Elisha Dismukes, John Shurley, John Shackleford, James Mason. June 17, 1773.

Jany. 10, 1773. Nicholas Hawkins, Senr., to his son Nicholas Hawkins, junr. Deed of Gift. 128 a. in St. Geo. Par., Spts. Co. Francis Cammack, Henry Cammack, George Cammack. June 17, 1773.

Octr. 20, 1772. Benjamin Poe and Elizabeth, his wife, of Spts. Co. to Edward Brasfield of same Co. £40. 160 a. in Spts. Co. purchased of John Sutton, etc. Witnesses, Uriah Edwards, Charles Pemberton, Uriah Edwards, junr. No date of Record.

April 17, 1773. Alexander Spotswood, Esqr., to John Sanders of Spts. Co., planter. Lease. 200 a. in St. Geo. Par., Spts Co. "Sd. John Sanders, his son Nathl. Sanders, and Reuben Mastin," etc. 500 lbs. tob., etc. Jno. Brock, Js. Lewis. June 17, 1773.

May 11, 1773. Alexander Spotswood of Spts. Co. to Thomas Allen of sd. Co. Lease. 100 a. in St. Geo. Par., Spts. Co. "Sd. Thomas Allen and Mildred and James Allen," etc. 480 lbs. tob. Witness, John Brock. June 17, 1773.

Novr. 19, 1772. Alexander Spotswood, Esqr., to Benjamin Haley of Spts. Co. Lease. 255 a. in St. Geo. Par., Spts. Co. "Sd. Haley and ——, his wife, and daughter Frances," etc. 630 lbs. tob., etc. Jno. Brock, Jno. Chew, junr.; Js. Lewis. June 17, 1773.

Decr. 25, 1772. John Campbell, Esqr., and Mary, his wife, and Alexander Spotswood, Esqr., to Fielding Lewis and Joseph Brock, Gentl., churchwardens of St. Geo. Par. Lease. 50 a. in St. Geo. Par., Spts. Co. 315 lbs. tob., etc. Jno. Brock, John Munro, Jona. Wilson. No date of Record.

Decr. 25, 1772. Alexander Spotswood, Esqr., to James Butler of Spts. Co. Lease. 240 a. in St. Geo. Par., Spts. Co. "Sd. James Butler, Nan Butler, and Peter Estes," etc. 960 lbs. tob., etc. Witness, Jno. Brock. June 17, 1773.

Novr. 30, 1772. Alexander Spotswood of Spts. Co., Esqr., to Richard Jones of same Co. Lease. 300 a. in St. Geo. Par., Spts. Co. "Sd. Richard Jones and his sons Francis and John," etc. 500 lbs. tob., etc. Jno. Brock, Robert Chew, Ambrose Dudley. June 17, 1773.

May 10, 1773. Alexander Spotswood of Spts. Co. to Thomas Burbridge of same Co. Lease. 165 a. in St. Geo. Par., Spts. Co. "Sd. Thomas Burbridge and Linchfield and George Burbridge," etc. 700 lbs. tob., etc. Jno. Brock, Js. Lewis. June 17, 1773.

Jany. 1, 1773. John Dixon of College of Wm. and Mary, Clerk, to Dr. Charles Mortimer of Essex Co. £600 ster. Four lots in town of Fredksbg. 253, 263, 271 and 235, purchased of Roger Dixon and Lucy, his wife, as by Deeds, Septr. 3, 1764. Witnesses, Wm. Reid, O. Towles, James Douglass, Patr. Kennon, Andrew Shepherd. June 17, 1773.

Jany. 10, 1773. Robert Huddleston of Berkeley Par., Spts. Co. and Elizabeth, his wife, to Elijah Dismukes of Drisdale Par., Caroline Co. £40 curr. 113 a. in Berkeley Par., Caroline Co., conveyed by John Huddleston, heir-at-law of Robt. Huddleston, Decd., to the sd. Robt. Huddleston. Witnesses, Jno. Shurley, George Shepherd, Lewis Shackleford, Elizabeth Shurley, Wm. Graves Ashburn, John Kennedy. No date of Record.

Feby. 13, 1773. John Penn of Spts. Co. to John Chew of same Co. £10 curr. and also in consideration of sd. Chew being security for sd. Penn for the Executorship of his father John Penn, Decd., etc. To indemnify sd. Chew, etc. 100 a. devised sd. Penn by his father Jno. Penn, Decd., in St. Geo. Par., Spts. Co. Jos. Brock, Jos. Brock, jr.; John Brock, Robert Richards. June 17, 1773.

June 17, 1773. Thomas Colson and John Holloday, junr., Executors of the last will and testament of Owen Thomas, late of Spts. Co., Decd., to John Carter of Spts. Co. Whereas, sd. Thomas in his lifetime was seized of 2 tracts of land in Spts. Co., and being so seized did on Feby. 15, 1772, make his last will and testament, directed the sale of the sd. land, etc., whereupon the sd. Colson and Holloday, on Nov. 20, 1772, exposed the sd. land to sale the sd. two tracts containing 357 a. in Spts. Co., for the sum of £160 curr. to the sd. Jno. Carter. No witnesses. No date of Record.

May 28, 1773. Gawin Corbin of Caroline Co., Gent., to Thomas McGee of Spts. Co. £24 10s. curr. 35 a. in Spts. Co. John Young, Thos. McGee, jr.; Shadrack Moore. June 17, 1773.

May 25, 1773. Wm. Fitzhugh of King Geo. Co., Esqr., and Ann, his wife, to John Chew, of Spts. Co. £31 15s. curr. 127 a. in St. Geo. Par., Spts. Co. Joseph Gale, John Meals, B. Johnston. June 17, 1773.

May 22, 1773. Wm. Fitzhugh, junr., to Benjamin Coyle. Lease. 100 a. in St. Geo. Par., Spts. Co., etc., part of the Fall Hill tract and bounded by lands of Wm. Hayden, John Sill, and McField Whiting, etc. "Sd. Benja. Coyle and Kezia Coyle, his wife, and James Coyle, his son," etc. £5 curr. yearly. Benj. Gwinn, McField x Whiting. June 17, 1773.

May 22, 1773. Wm. Fitzhugh, junr., to McField Whiting. Lease. 150 a. in St. Geo. Par., Spts. Co., part of Fall Hill tract and bounded by lands of Allen Wiley and Wm. Hayden, etc. "Sd. McField Whiting, Lettis Whiting, his wife, and Wm. Whiting, his son," etc. £7 10s. curr. yearly. Benj. Gwinn, Benja. Coyle. No date of Record.

Novr. 11, 1773. Benjamin Grymes of Spts. Co., Gent., and Priscilla, his wife, and Honble. John Tayloe, of Richmond Co., Esqr., and Francis Thornton of Stafford Co., Gent., executors of Honble. Presley Thornton, Esqr., Decd., and Wm. Fitzhugh of King Geo. Co., Esqr., to Joseph Jones and Wm. Woodford, Gentlemen; whereas, Benjamin Grymes purchased of the late Roger Dixon, Gent., Decd., 3 lots in additional part of Fredksbg. at the lower end thereof, Nos. 254, 264 and 272 being the lots where the Bloomary was built, etc., but no deed conveying the legal title of the sd. lots was made by sd. Dixon, although sd. Grymes possessed and built upon sd. lots; and whereas, sd. Grymes, did deed in trust all his lands, slaves, etc., to Wm. Fitzhugh and Presley Thornton, to indemnify them, and whereas, sd. Presley Thornton, having departed this life leaving sd. Taylor and Francis Thornton his executors, the sd. executors together with the sd. Fitzhugh have contracted for the sale of the sd. lots to the sd. Jones and Woodford for the sum of £305 curr. Witnesses, Robt. Wormeley Carter, Neill McCoull, David Allison, Anth. Thornton, junr. June 17, 1773.

Jany. 12, 1773. John Penn, jr., of Spts. Co. to Thomas Colson of Co. afsd. £30. Mortgage. 100 a. in Spts. Co., etc. Wm. Wood, B. Johnston, Jno. Chew, jr. June 17, 1773.

May 27, 1773. Wm. Champe of King Geo. Co., Gent., and Mary, his wife, to Edward Carter of Spts. Co., Gent. £858 curr. 1075 a. in Spts. Co., purchased by sd. Champe of John Roane, and by the sd. Roane purchased of Humphrey Hill, Gent., attorney-in-fact for Humphrey Bell of City of London, Mercht., etc. Chas. Washington, Lewis Willis, Fras. Thornton. June 17, 1773.

May 27, 1773. James Hunter, junr., of Spts. Co. to John Stewart of sd. Co. £300 curr. 400 a. in St. Geo. Par., Spts. Co., called "Silverton Hill," formerly conveyed by Augustine Smith to Jonathan Gibson, as by Deeds, Octr. 29, 1726, and by the sd. Gibson to John Allan, as by Deeds, Feby. 26, 1741, and by the sd. Allans executors, to Wm. Hunter, as by Deeds, Augt. 31, 1751, and by the sd. Hunter, devised in his will to his son, James Hunter, party to these presents, etc. Witnesses, Henry Mitchell, James Tutt, Michael Robinson, Jno. Ferrie. June 17, 1773.

Novr. 26, 1772. Ambrose Rains of Spts. Co. to John Herndon of sd. Co. £82 12s. 6d. curr. Mortgage. Goods and chattels, etc. James Cunningham, Thomas Allen, John Wiglesworth. June 18, 1773.

June 19, 1773. Goaring White of King Geo. Co., po. of atto., to Wm. Waddle. Witnesses, John Atkinson, Jas. Fuller. June 19, 1773.

June 1, 1773. Ralph Smith of Spts. Co. to James Robb & Co., of Fredksbg. £30 curr. Mortgage. Goods and chattels. Witnesses, Wm. McWilliams, jr.; John Ferrie, Peter Scott. No date of Record.

June 17, 1773. Mary x Mayfield of Spts. Co. binds her son, John Holloday, aged 9 yrs. 8 mos. 7 da., to Thomas Walker of Fredksbg. Test, John Chew. No date of Record.

July 1, 1773. James Hunter, junr., of Fredksbg. to Wm. Jackson of same town. £300 curr. 10 a. of meadow land in St. Geo. Par., Spts. Co., adjoining town of Fredksbg.; devised the sd. James Hunter by the last will and testament of his father Wm. Hunter, Decd. Witnesses, Jas. Mercer, Chas. Dick, junr.; James Allan, Ch. Simms. July 16, 1773.

Decr. 25, 1772. Alexander Spotswood, Esqr.. to John Estes of Caroline Co. Lease. 205 a. in St. Geo. Par., Spts. Co. 820 lbs. tob. John Munro, Jona. Wilson, John Brock. July 15, 1773.

Decr. 25, 1772. Alexander Spotswood, Esqr., to John Estes of Caroline Co., Planter. Lease. 250 a. in St. Geo. Par., Spts. Co. 1000 lbs. tob. John Brock, Jona. Wilson, Benja. Herndon. July 15, 1773.

Jany. 25, 1773. Philip Penn and Martha, his wife; John Holloday, Senr., and Elizabeth, his wife; Uriah Edwards and Mildred, his wife, of Spts. Co. to Peter Stubblefield of sd. Co. £100 curr. 220 a. in Berkeley Par., Spts. Co. Jno. Holloday, junior.; Francis Cammack, John x Cammack. No date of Record.

Jany. 21, 1773. Philip Penn of Spts. Co. to McCall, Smillie & Co., Merchts., in Glasgow. £77 0s. 5½d. curr. Mortgage. 237 a. left the sd. Philip Penn by his father Joseph Penn, Decd., etc. Witnesses, Jno. Ferrie, W. McWilliams, junr.; Peter Stubblefield. July 15, 1773.

July 16, 1773. Alexander Kennedy of Fredksbg., Mariner, to John Glassell, Mercht., x Charles Mortimer. £30 curr. Lot in town of Fredericksburg, purchased by sd. Kennedy of Roger Dixon, Gent., etc. No witnesses. July 16, 1773.

July 16, 1773. George Atkinson of Spts. Co., wheelwright, and Martha, his wife, to James Duncanson of Fredksbg., Mercht. £32 10s. curr. Lot 119 in town of Fredksbg., etc. No witnesses. July 16, 1773.

May 10, 1772. Alexander Spotswood, Esqr., and Robert Chew, Gent., to Robert Richards of Spts. Co. Lease. 130 a. in St. Geo. Par., Spts. Co. "Sd. Robt. Richards, John Richards, Willm. Richards, and Lewis Terril," etc. 650 lbs. tob. Jno. Brock, Wm. Clayton, Thos. Fox, John Penn, jr. July 16, 1773.

July 16, 1773. Richard Brooke of Spts. Co., Gent., to John Hazlegrove of Fredksbg. £102 10s. Lots Nos. 6 and 53 in town of Fredksbg. No witnesses. July 16, 1773.

Augt. 2d, 1773. George x Hensley, Senr., of St. Geo. Par., Spts. Co. and Sarah, his wife, to Benjamin Johnston of Fredksbg. £20 curr. 63 a. in St. Geo. Par., Spts. Co., conveyed by George Hensley, jr., to sd. George Hensley, Sr., as by Deeds, Jany. 18, 1772, and purchased by sd. Hensley, Jr., of Wm. Wood, etc., and part of a tract inherited by sd.

Wm. Wood from his father John Wood. Witnesses, Wm. Wood, Jno. Brock, Jno. Chew, junr. Augt. 19, 1773.

July 24, 1773. John x Rogers of Fauqueir Co. to Thomas Blanton of Spts. Co. £40 curr. 100 a. in St. Geo. Par., Spts. Co., inherited by sd. John Rogers from his father Henry Rogers, Decd. Witnesses, Thomas Roors, Wm. Darnaby, John x McKenny. Augt. 19, 1773.

March 25, 1773. Alexander Spotswood, Esqr., to Wm. Simpson. Lease. 150 a. in St. Geo. Par., Spts. Co. "Sd. Wm. Simpson, his son John, and daughter Nancy," etc. 750 lbs. tob. John Munro, Jona. Wilson, Jno. Brock. Augt. 19, 1773.

Decr. 25, 1772. Alexander Spotswood, Esqr., to John Estis (Estes) of Caroline Co. Lease. 165 a. in St. Geo. Par., Spts. Co. " Thomas Turner, Lusindy (Lucinda) Turner, and Edward Turner," etc. 660 lbs. tob. Jno. Brock, Jno. Munro, Jona. Wilson. No date of record.

June 17, 1773. Lease assigned to Thos. Turner and his heirs, etc., by sd. Estes, etc.

April 15, 1773. John Gale of Whitehaven, Cumberland Co., Esqr., John Lewthwaite and Robt. Wilkinson, Gent., of same place, Assignees of the Commrs. appt. and acting in and under a Commission of Bankruptcy against Peter How of Whitehaven, Mercht., Decd., po. of atto., to Charles Yates of Fredericksburg, Colony of Va., Esqr. Witnesses, Richard Fletcher, George Spencer. No date of Record.

April 14, 1773. John Sarjeant of Whitehaven, Cumberland Co., Eng., Mercht., and Sarah, his wife, po. of atto., to Charles Yates of Fredericksburg, Colony of Va., Mercht. To sell "one of our Estates or plantations containing 1250 a. * * * situate, lying and being in Culpeper Co. in the Colony of Virginia, aforesaid, commonly called * * * Quakers Land," etc. Witnesses, Richard Fletcher, George Spencer, Jno. Heywood. July 16, 1773.

May 15, 1773. Philip Somerby of Fredericksburg, Va., to Charles Yates of the Kingdom of Gt. Britain, but late of Fredericksburg, Va., Gentl. £73 16s. 6d. curr. A negro man named Gilbert. Witnesses, John Meals, George Spencer, Tuley Whithourst. No date of Record.

Augt. 19, 1773. Wm. Purkins of Spts. Co. apprentices himself to Charles Powell, to learn the trade of Bricklayer and plasterer, etc. Term 5 years, etc. No witnesses. No date of Record.

June 25, 1773. John Taliaferro and Betty, his wife, of King George Co. to Wm. Allsup of Spts. Co. 5 shill. curr. 313 a. in St. Geo. Par., Spts. Co. Ambrose Rains, John Brock, John Steward. Oct. 21, 1773.

June 25, 1773. John Taliaferro and Betty, his wife, of King George Co. to Thomas Colson of Spts. Co. £280 curr. 247 a. in St. Geo. Par., Spts. Co. Ambrose Rains, John Brock, John Steward. Oct. 21, 1773.

July 3, 1773. John x Collins, Senr., of Berkeley Par., Spts. Co. to James Robb & Co. of Fredksbg., Mercht. £27 6s. 7¾d. curr. A negro slave, etc. Witnesses, Peter Scott, Thomas x Gains. Sept. 16, 1773.

Augt. 20, 1773. Jane x Price of Stafford Co. to Henry Pendleton of Spts. Co. 5s. and in consideration of a decree passed against her and others in behalf of sd. Pendleton in Co. Court of Spts., June 22, 1771, sd. Jane Price deeds the sd. Pendleton 150 a. in Spts. Co. Witnesses, Andrew Grant, John x Limmik, Alvin Moxley, A. Strother, Will. Waller, Rice Curtis. No date of Record.

March 24, 1773. Thomas Lane of Spts. Co. to John Glassell of Spts. Co. £14 6s. curr. Mortgage. 100 a. part of the old mine tract, on Douglass Run in Spts. Co., purchased by sd. Lane of Wm. Garret, etc. Witnesses, George Muir, Jno. Ferrie, William Wiatt. Septr. 16, 1773.

Feby. 1, 1773. Robert Walker of Spts. Co. to John Glassell of Spts. Co. £81 2s. 7d. curr. Mortgage. Four slaves. Witnesses, Lachtom Campbell, William Wiatt, George Muir. No date of Record.

Septr. 16, 1773. Benjamin Herndon of Culpeper Co. and Sarah, his wife, to Charles Gordon of Spts. Co. £200 curr. 507 a. in Spts. Co., devised the sd. Benjamin by the last will and testament of his father Joseph Herndon, Decd. John Sanders, Peter Stubblefield, Joseph Gale. Septr. 16, 1773.

May 15, 1773. John ·Miller of Spts. Co., Mercht., po. of atto., to David Blair of Fredksbg., Mercht. Witnesses, Jno. Ferrie, Wm. McWilliams, Jr. Septr. 16, 1773.

Septr. 15, 1773. John Penn of Spts. Co. to Reuben Massey of sd. Co., Planter. £100 curr. 100 a. in St. Geo. Par., Spts. Co., devised the sd. Penn, by the last will and testament of his father, John Penn, Decd. No witnesses. Septr. 16, 1773.

June 7, 1773. Thomas Estes of Spts. Co., Va., to his son, John Estes of Orange Co., Province of North Carolina. Whereas, Thos. Estes, formerly of Caroline Co., Decd., by his last will and testament, among other things did lend to his daughter Barbara Rogers, a negro girl * * * during the life of the sd. Barbara and' after her death the sd. slave to be sold and the money arising from the sale to be equally divided amongst her children (as by the sd. will of record in Caroline Co., etc), etc., and since which the sd. slave having had several children that are now alive and dispersed in the province of North Carolina, etc., and the sd. Thos. Estes, the testator, having made no disposition of the increase of the sd. slave, the sd. Thomas Este, party to these presents, as eldest son and heir of the sd. Decd., deeds his right or title in the sd. increase of the sd. slave, to his son John Estes, etc. Witnesses, Wm. Wood, Jno. Holloday, Jr.; Rice Curtis, junr.; Jno. Chew, jr. No date of Record.

Augt. 12, 1773. John Waller, Clk., and Ann, his wife, and William Waller, his brother, of Spts. Co. to Richard Templeman. £45 curr. Lot in town of Fredksbg., etc. Wm. Wood, Saml. Hilldrup, Robt. Thomas, Harry Beverley, James Taliaferro/ John Mitchell. Septr. 17, 1773.

Augt. 7, 1773. Richard Keown of Spts. Co. to John Carthrae of sd. Co. £75. Mortgage. Stock, Goods and Chattels. Witnesses, J. Lewis, Vincent Vass, John Steward. Septr. ——, 1773.

Octr. 21, 1773. Clayton Coleman of Spts. Co. and Mary, his wife, to Thomas Lipscomb of sd. Co. £205 curr. 670 a. on branches of East North East River in Spts. Co. No witnesses. Octr. 21, 1773.

April 13, 1773. Hancock Taylor of Orange Co. to Wm. Bell of same Co. £300 curr. 600 a. in Spts. Co. Witnesses, James Madison, Zachary Taylor, James Madison, junr.; Ambrose Madison, Alexr. Waugh, jr.; Richd. Barbour. Octr. 21, 1773.

Augt. 25, 1773. Alexander Spotswood of Spts. Co., Esqr., to Benjamin Ballard of same Co. Lease. 160 a. in St. Geo. Par., Spts. Co. "Sd. Ballard, James Ballard and Benj. Ballard, jr.," etc. 680 lbs. tob. Jno. Brock, Js. Lewis. Octr. 21, 1773.

Octr. 21, 1773. Clement x Montague of Spts. Co. to his son, Thomas Montague, of sd. Co. Deed of Gift. 70 a. in Spts. Co. Jos. Brock, jr.; Bartlett Collins. No date of Record.

May 19, 1773. Patrick Cary of Spts. Co. to Patrick Kennan, factor for Dunlop & Crosse of Glasgow, etc. £6 5s. 5d. curr. Mortgage. Goods and chattels. Witnesses, Wm. Stephen, Elizabeth x Cary, John x Cary. No date of Record.

May 17, 1773. Peter Stubblefield of Spts. Co. to his nephew, Benjamin Stubblefield, son of George Stubblefield. "Sd. Peter Stubblefield * * * "his mother, Mrs. Catharine Stubblefield," etc. Deed of Gift. Negro slave. Witnesses, O. Towles, Geo. Stubblefield. Octr. 21, 1773.

Octr. 18, 1773. Richard Chamberlain of Fredksbg., Baker, to Elizabeth Shaw. £50 curr. Goods and chattels. Witnesses, John Heald, Charles Ross, Benjamin x Duncanson. Octr. 21, 1773.

—— ——, 177—.* Edmond Jones and Mary, his wife, to Richard Bullard of Spts. Co. £58 15s. curr. Right and title in tract of 470 a., etc. Whereas, Ambrose Bullard, by his last will and testament, Dated, July 30, 1754, bequeathed the tract of land whereon he lived to be sold and the proceeds to be applied to the bringing up and educating of his children, part thereof of his said children, to wit, Francis, Thomas, and Lucy, having departed this life in their minority and before any disposition of the said land, whereby the sd. land became wholly vested in the sd. Mary Jones and Richd. Bullard, parties to these presents and surviving children of sd. Ambrose Bullard, Decd. The sd. tract containing 470 a. which sd. Ambrose Bullard, Decd., purchased of Wm. Ellis and Elizabeth, his wife, etc. Witnesses, Fielding Lewis, James Ward, Wm. Triplet, Edward West. Octr. 21, 1773.

July 13, 1773. John Waller, K. W., of Spts. Co. to John Lewis, Atto. at Law, of Spts. Co. £100 curr. Two negro slaves. In trust, etc. Witnesses, Jno. Z. Lewis, Robert Lewis, Zachary Meriwether, Geo. Stubblefield. No date of Record.

Septr. 26, 1773. John Clayton of Spts. Co. to his brother, William Clayton of sd. Co. Deed of Gift and "also to comply with the will of his deceased father," etc. 120 a. whereon sd. Wm. Clayton lives in Spts. Co., etc. Jos. Brock, Jos. Brock, jr.; John Schooler, jr. Octr. 21, 1773.

Septr. 26, 1773. John Clayton of Spts. Co. to his brother, Thomas Clayton, of sd. Co. Deed of Gift, and "also to comply with the will of his deceased father," etc. 121 a. in Spts. Co. whereon sd. Thomas Clayton now lives, etc. Jos. Brock, Jos. Brock, jr.; John Schooler. Octr. 21, 1773.

Novr. 18, 1773. Thomas x Payne and Elizabeth, his wife, of Berkeley Par., Spts. Co. to Thomas Coleman, jr., of St. Margarets Par., Caroline Co. £24 curr. 100 a. in Berkeley Par., Spts. Co. No witnesses. No date of Record.

Novr. 18, 1773. Peter Rosell (Roswell) and Ann, his wife, of Berkeley Par., Spts. Co. to Cornelius Donohue of Loudoun Co. £59 curr. 200 a. in Spts. Co., Berkeley Par. on waters of Plentiful Run, etc. No witnesses. Nov. 19, 1773.

March 23, 1773. "We Richard Keown and Mary, my wife, do hereby agree to give unto Jno. Carthrae, junr., son of John Carthrae and Elizabeth, his wife, the tract or parcel of land whereon we now live after our deaths, etc., with all the other Estate . . . both real and personal," etc. Witnesses, John Carthrae, John Steward, George Arnold. No date of Record.

June 24, 1773. Rice Curtis to Wm. Carter, "all my right, title to 50 a. of land which was by Colo. Rice Curtis given unto his daughter (the wife of the sd. Wm. Carter)," etc. Witnesses, John Carter, Junr.; Jno. Brock. No date of Record.

Oct. 16, 1770. Thomas Rogers of Orange Co. to John Ward of Spts. Co. Lease. £3 curr. yearly. 100 a. in St. Geo. Par., Spts. Co. Witnesses, Wm. Plunkett, Junr.; John Plunkett, Wm. Plunkett, Senr. No date of Record.

Octr. 23, 1773. John Mitchell of Fredksbg., Mercht. (surviving partner of John Mitchell, Hugh Lenox, and Wm. Scott, etc.), and Susannah, his wife, to Fielding Lewis of Fredksbg., Gent. £200 curr. Lot No. 68 in town of Fredksbg. Chs. Dick, jr.; James Duncanson, Michael Robinson, James Allen, James Somerville. No date of Record.

Novr. 17, 1773. John Meals of Fredksbg. to Charles Yates of sd. town. £500 curr. 1062 a. purchased by sd. Meals of Lewis Willis and Charles Yates, to whom it was conveyed by John Carter, late Sheriff of Spts. Co. Witnesses, Charles Washington, Frans. Thornton, Geo. Thornton. Novr. 19, 1773.

Novr. 19, 1773. Betty x Ware of Fredksbg. binds her daughter, Nancy Ware, to James Allan of Fredksbg. No witnesses. Novr. 19, 1773.

May 26, 1773. Lucy Dixon, widow and relict of Roger Dixon, late of Fredksbg., Gent., Decd., to Joseph Jones and Wm. Woodford. £50. Whereas, the sd. Roger Dixon, was in his lifetime seized and possessed of Lots 254, 264, 272 in town of Fredksbg., and sold them to Benjamin Grymes, Esqr., who (notwithstanding no deeds were made to him by the sd. Dixon), being possessed thereof, assigned and made over unto Presley Thornton and Wm. Fitzhugh, Esqrs., all his right, title, etc., and whereas, the trustees having agreed with the sd. Jones and Woodford for the sale of the lots, and having also made satisfaction to the sd. Lucy Dixon for her right and claim of Dower therein, the sd. Lucy Dixon makes this deed, etc. Witnesses, Antho. Thornton, junr.; Maria Hume, George McCamock. No date of Record.

April 14, 1773. Catharine Stubblefield of Spts. Co., widow, to Henry Mitchell of Fredksbg., Mercht. Mortgage. Witnesses, George Stubblefield, Thomas Towles, Harry Stubblefield, O. Towles, Jno. Ferrie, James Freedland. March 17, 1774.

Augt. 19, 1773. Wm. Parker of Spts. Co., Gent., and his son, Alexander Parker, junr., of same Co., po. of atto., to Hugh Houston of Fredksbg., "mentions property situated in St. Nicholas Par., Bristol, Gt. Britain." Witnesses, Jos. Brock, W. Buckner, Robt. Chew, John Brock, Thos. Minor, jr. No date of Record.

Octr. 25, 1773. John Mitchell, surviving partner of Hugh Lenox, Scott & Co., Merchts., to Joseph Pulliam of Spts. Co. £23 curr. 168 a. in Spts. Co., devised Jemima, wife of James Chiles, by the will of her father, John Graves, Decd., dated, March 30, 1747, etc. Witnesses, James Somerville, Henry Mitchell, James Duncanson, John Glassell, James Freeland. No date of Record.

Dec. 16, 1773. James Sharp apprentices himself to John Atkinson of Fredksbg., Periwig Maker and Barber, etc. No witnesses. No date of Record.

Novr. 8, 1773. Wm. Champe of King Geo. Co., Esqr., and Mary, his wife, to Charles Yates of Fredksbg. £520 curr. Tract of land in Spts. Co., purchased by sd. Champe of Jno. Carter, Sheriff of Spts. Co. at the sale of Benjamin Grymes' Estate, as by Deeds, May 10, 1771, etc. Witnesses, Geo. Thornton, John Taliaferro, Townshend Dade, Lewis Willis. March 18, 1779.

Novr. 7, 1773. Lewis Willis and Charles Yates of Fredksbg. to John Meals of same town. £500 curr. 1062 a. purchased by sd. Willis and Yates of Jno. Carter, Sher. of Spts. Co., at the sale of Benja. Grymes' Estate, etc. Witnesses, Fras. Thornton, Chas. Washington, Geo. Thornton. No date of Record.

July 19, 1773. Rice Vass of Spts. Co. and Ann, his wife, to George Stubblefield of afsd. Co., Gent. £56 curr. 139 a., of which 57 a. is now held by Mary, widow of Philip Vincent Vass, decd., as tenant in dower, the remainder held by the sd. Rice, etc. Witnesses, Susa. Winslow, Harry Stubblefield, Leonard Young, O. Towles, Reuben Straughan, Robt. Dudley. Octr. 21, 1773.

June 17, 1773. Alexander Spotswood, Esqr., of Spts. Co. to Martin Welch of same Co. Lease. 600 a. £18 curr. Witness, John Brock. No date of Record.

March 15, 1774. Stephen x Jackson of Spts. Co., a free mulatto, of the age of 23 yrs., apprentices himself to Moses Doolittle of Spts. Co., Hatter, etc. Witness, B. Johnston. March 17, 1774.

March 2, 1774. John Waller, Clk., of Spts. Co., having large debts due him by Reuben Vass, who resides in South Carolina, gives po. of atto. to Wm. Arnold of Caroline Co., Va., to collect same, etc. Witness, O. Towles. March 17, 1774.

March 17, 1774. George Mitchell of Fredksbg., Mercht., having a debt due him by John Nall, who resides in one of the Carolinas, gives po. of atto. to Wm. Arnold of Caroline Co., Va., to collect same, etc. Witness, John Wiglesworth. March 17, 1774.

Octr. 13, 1773. Rice Vass and Ann, his wife, of Berkeley Par., Spts. Co. to Joseph Duerson of same Par. and Co. £75 12s. 116 a. in Par. and Co. afsd. George Stubblefield, Henry Stevens, Moses x Wheeler, Susanna Beverley Stubblefield, Jno. Carthrae, Willm. Smith, Edwd. Herndon. April 21, 1774.

Novr. 1, 1773. David Chevis of Caroline Co. and Sarah, his wife, to Charles Mortimer of Fredksbg. £40 curr. Lot 243 in town of Fredksbg. Witnesses, Gawin Corbin, John Buckner, Nathl. Gray, Will. Hamilton, Robt. Maitland, Chas. Mortimer, junr. March 17, 1774.

March 17, 1774. Charles Davis of Berkeley Par., Spts. Co., apprentices himself to Winslow Parker of same Par. and Co., etc. No witnesses. March 17, 1774.

March 18, 1774. Benjamin Johnston of Fredksbg. to George Thornton of Spts. Co. £25. Lot 8.8. in town of Fredksbg., that portion formerly Allanstown, purchased by sd. Johnston of John Benger, son and heir of Elliott Benger, Esqr., Decd., etc. No witnesses. March 17, 1774.

Novr. 30, 1773. Robert Beverley, Esqr., and Mary, his wife, to James Ritchie & Co. of Glasgow, Gt. Britain. £75 curr. Lot No. 15 in town of Fredksbg., etc. Witnesses, Jas. Robinson, Hen. Mitchell, David Blair, Patr. Kennan. March 17, 1774.

Septr. 26, 1772. Wm. Fitzhugh, junr., to Allen Wiley. Lease. 200 a. in St. Geo. Par., Spts. Co., part of Fall Hill tract, etc., bounded by lands of Wm. Hayden and McField Whiting, etc. "Sd. Wiley, Eve Wiley, his wife, and Moses Wiley, his son," etc. £10 yearly. Witnesses, William Haydon, Ben. Gwinn. March 17, 1774.

Feby. 12, 1774. John Waller, Clk., of Spts. Co., po. of atto., to James Somerville of Fredksbg. O. Towles, Mary Towles, John Dawson. March 17, 1774.

March 16, 1774. James Hackley of Spts. Co. to Wm. Walker, James Slaughter, Gabriel Jones, and John Gray of Culpeper Co. Mortgage. Sd. Hackley having purchased of Wm. Walker Lot. No. 29 in town of Fredksbg., etc., for sum of £500 curr. Witnesses, B. Johnston, Joseph Bledsoe, Joel Lewis. March 17, 1774.

Jany. 31, 1774. James Sutherland of Falmouth, Cumberland Co., po. of atto., to his brother, Wm. Sutherland, of So. Ronald Sha., Orkney Isles, Europe, now residing in Fredksbg., Va., mentions, "Our late brother, Dr. John Sutherland, late of Fredksbg., Decd.," etc. Witnesses, Ezra Jordan, George Lowell, John x Collier. March 17, 1774.

April 15, 1774. Samuel x Brown of Spts. Co. and Martha, his wife, to James Wiglesworth of same Co. £29 10s. curr. 59 a. in Spts. Co. James Watkins, Chas. Powell, David Sandidge. April 21, 1774.

Novr. 17, 1774. John Carpenter of Spts. Co. and Mary, his wife, to Wm. Blaydes of same Co. £187 10s. curr. 231 a. in Spts. Co. Jonathan Carpenter, Wm. Cason, Edwd. Cason. April 21, 1774.

April 4, 1774. John Clark of Caroline Co. and Ann, his wife, to Jonathan Clark of Dunmore. £150 curr. 508 a. in Berkeley Par., Spts. Co. O. Towles, Edwd. Herndon, Jno. Chew, jr. April 21, 1774.

April 21, 1774. John Carter and Jean, his wife, of Berkeley Par., Spts. Co. to Richard Coleman of Par. and Co. afsd. £85 curr. 200 acres. No witnesses. April 21, 1774.

Decr. 6, 1773. George Penn and Elizabeth, his wife, of Spts. Co. to John Brock of Co. afsd. £30 curr. 30 a., known as "The Schoolhouse Leavell," etc. Wm. Penn, Jos. Brock, Robt. Chew. April 21, 1774.

March 8, 1774. Thomas Pettit and Rachel, his wife, of Spts. Co. to Sherod Horn of sd. Co. £30 curr. 200 a. in Spts. Co. Jos. Brock, John Brock, Robt. Chew. April 21, 1774.

March 29, 1774. James x Mitcham of Spts. Co. to Ephraim Beazley of same Co. 37s. 6d. curr. 3¾ a. in Spts. Co. Jno. Hart, John True. April 21, 1774.

April 14, 1774. Rice Vass of Spts. Co. to George Stubblefield of same Co. £40 curr. 6 a. in Spts. Co., with mill and dam, etc. Robt. Dudley, Joseph Sames, Moses Wheeler. April 21, 1774.

March 1, 1774. Margaret Gordon, widow and relict and acting Executrix of John Gordon late of Fredksbg., Decd., and Charles Dick of same place, one of the executors named in the will of the sd. Gordon, of the first part; George Weedon of same place and Catharine, his wife, of second part; Dr. Hugh Mercer of same place and Isabella, his wife, of the third part, and Wm. Triplet, of the fourth part, etc. Sd. Margaret Gordon and Charles Dick convey to the sd. Triplet, two lots in town of Fredksbg., whereon sd. Weedon lives, in trust, to convey the same to George Weedon and Catharine, his wife, etc. Whereas, John Gordon, by his last will and testament, dated Decr. 13, 1749, devised his lands and houses in Fredksbg. to the sd. Margaret Gordon during the infancy and discoverture of the afsd. Catharine and Isabella, etc., and did direct that at his sd. Daughters . . . arriving at age or marrying, the sd. lots, etc., should be sold and the money arising therefrom divided between his sd. wife and two daughters, etc., whereas, at the death of the sd. Gordon the sd. Margaret took upon herself the executorship and the sd. Catharine and Isabella, having intermarried with the sd. George and Hugh sometime before the 10th of April, 1764, and the sd. Margaret, George and Hugh, being severally intitled, on April 10, 1764, each to a third part of sd. lots and houses, it was agreed the sd. George should have the whole of the lots to his sole use upon his paying the sd. Margaret and Hugh, a third part of a certain sum which was agreed to be the full value thereof, etc., etc. Witnesses, Geo. Thornton, Frans. Thornton, Edmund Addison. April 21, 1774.

March 24, 1774. Margaret Gordon of Fredksbg. to George Weedon of same place. £100 curr. 150 a. in St. Geo. Par., Spts. Co., moiety of land which descended to Sally, wife of Edwd. Watkins, from her father, Thomas Hill, and by sd. Watkins and wife conveyed to the sd. Gordon, as by Deeds, June 20, 1757, etc. Witnesses, Geo. Thornton, Fras. Thornton, Edmund Addison. April 21, 1774.

March 24, 1774. Wm. Triplet of Spts. Co. to George Weedon of Fredksbg. 25s. curr. Two lots in town of Fredksbg., as by an agreement in deed dated March 1, 1774, between Margaret Gordon and others and the sd. Triplet, etc. Witnesses, George Thornton, Fras. Thornton, Edmund Addison. April 21, 1774.

April 20, 1774. John Simpson, Junr., and Frances, his wife, to George Mitchell of Fredksbg., Mercht. £90 curr. 150 a. in St. Geo. Par., Spts. Co., whereon Robt. Richards now lives, and bounded by lines of Robt. Chew, Jos. Brock, junr., and Robt. Smith, etc. No witnesses. April 21, 1774.

April 17, 1773. Benjamin Johnston of Fredksbg. to Honble. John Tayloe, Esqr., of Richmond Co. £85 18s. 8d. curr. and £333 6s. 8d. ster. Mortgage. Goods and chattels, slaves. Lots 10.10 and 11.11 in town of Fredksbg., etc. Witnesses, Anth. Thornton, junr.; O. Towles, Chs. Mortimer, junr. April 23, 1774.

April 22, 1774. John Campbell and Mary, his wife, and Alexander Spotswood to John Herndon of Spts. Co. Lease. 150 a. "Sd. Herndon and Mary, his wife, and Mary Herndon, their daughter," etc. 800 lbs. tob. Geo. Stubblefield, Alexander Blair, James Brown. April 22, 1774.

DEED BOOK J

1774–1782

Decr. 13, 1770. Alexander Spotswood to Philemon Richards of Spts. Co. Lease. 196 a. in Spts. and Orange Counties. "Ben. Richards, Ben. Richards, Jnr., and Benj. Chapman," etc. 1000 lbs. tob. Js. Lewis, Wm. Richards, Thos. Brooks. June 16, 1774.

May 24, 1774. Alexander Spotswood of Spts. Co. to John Chew of same Co. Lease. 214 a. in St. Geo. Par., Spts. Co. "Sd. Jno. Chew, Beverley Chew, and Jno. Chew, jr.," etc. 1000 lbs. tob. Thos. Colson, jr.; Js. Lewis, Wm. Richards. June 16, 1774.

Nov. 18, 1773. Wm. Arnold and Isaac Arnold of Spts. Co. to George Mitchell of Fredksbg., Mercht. £21 curr. Mortgage. 70 a. on Black Rock Run in Spts. Co. Jno. Chew, Jno. Munro, Jno. Meals. June 16, 1774.

Novr. 16, 1773. John Simpson of Orange Co. to George Mitchell of Fredksbg., Mercht. £30 15s. Mortgage. Goods and chattels, etc. Jno. Meals, Jno. Munro, Rd. Richards. June 16, 1774.

June 2, 1774. Jno. Simpson, junr., of Spts. Co. to Geo. Mitchell of Fredksbg., Gent. Mortgage, etc. Mentions "land whereon Robt. Richards now lives," "land bought by my father of Wm. Hunter, and whereon Robt. Frank now lives," etc. Witnesses, Jno. Brock, Jno. x Simpson, Senr.; D. Simpson. June 16, 1774.

June 10, 1774. Thomas Colson of Spts. Co., Gent., and Frances, his wife, to Robt. Sharewood of Co. afsd. £200 curr. 428 a. in St. Geo. Par., Spts. Co. Anth. Thornton, junr.; Stapleton Crutchfield, Js. Lewis. July 21, 1774.

Decr. 2, 1773. Andrew Ross and Elizabeth, his wife, of Caroline Co. to Coleman Ross of same Co. £10. 100 a. in Spts. Co., formerly Thos. Page's, etc. James Jarrell, Richd. Lewis, Jno. McDonald, Aquilla Johnson. July 21, 1774.

May 25, 1774. Mordacai Redd and Agatha, his wife, of Frederick Co. to Jno. Tayloe and Francis Thornton, Execrs., of Presley Thornton, Esqr., Decd., and Wm. Fitzhugh, Esqr., which sd. Tayloe, Thornton, and Fitzhugh are trustees of the Estate of Benj. Grymes, Gent. £150 curr. 730 a. in Spts. Co. Wm. Reid, Harry Bartlett, Geo. M. Cormack, Thos. Minor, Jno. MacDonald, Angus MacDonald. July 21, 1774.

April 15, 1774. George Hill of Spts. Co. to James Somerville of Fredksbg. £39 1s. 4d. Negroes. Witnesses, Thos. Mitchell, Jno. Phillibrown, Collin Fraser. July 21, 1774.

June 15, 1774. Charles Yates of Fredksbg., Gent., to Susanna Heath of sd. town. £100. Lots 256 and 266 in town of Fredksbg., in addition thereof made by act of assembly 32 George 2d. which sd. Yates purchased of Henry Heath and Susanna, his wife, as by Deeds, May 1, 1769. No witnesses. July 21, 1774.

June 15, 1774. Charles Yates of Fredksbg., Gent., to Susannah Heath of same town. Whereas, Dr. Henry Heath, during his lifetime and by deeds dated Jany. 21, 1768, mortgaged to the sd. Charles Yates Lot No. 20 in town of Fredksbg., sd. Yates by this deed recoveys the sd. lot to Susannah Heath, etc. No witnesses. July 21, 1774.

June 17, 1774. Wm. Parker and his eldest son and heir, Alexander Parker, of Spts. Co., po. of atto., to Messrs. Hart & Marshall., Mercht. Witnesses, B. Johnston, James Marshall. July 21, 1774.

April 11, 1774. James Gildart of Liverpool, Lancaster Co. (Eng.), Mercht., po. of atto., to James Duncanson and James Maury of Fredksbg., Va., Merchts. Witnesses, Jas. Wignell, Richd. Holkerd. July 21, 1774.

March 8, 1774. Richard Coleman of Spts. Co. and Ann, his wife, to Ambrose Smith of same Co. £160 curr. 393 a. in Spts. Co. Samuel Coleman, Wm. Trigg, James Smith. July 21, 1774.

Augt. 13, 1774. Charles Gordon of Spts. Co. and Mary, his wife, to Robert Hart of Hanover Co., Mercht. £400. 600 a. in Berkeley Par., Spts. Co., whereon sd. Gordon lived, devised by the will of Joseph Herndon to his son, Benjamin, of whom sd. Gordon purchased the same, etc., also 300 a. in Berkeley Par., Spts. Co., purchased of one Wm. Garrett, etc. Witnesses, Robt. Grayham, Geo. Stubblefield, Willm. Smith, Franky Smith, Walter Chiles. Augt. 18, 1774.

Decr. 26, 1773. Josiah Bush and Sarah, his wife, of Albemarle Co. to Wm. Mastin of Spts. Co. £17 10s. 125 a. in Spts. Co. Jno. Sanders, Benj. Craig, Geo. Tureman. Augt. 18, 1774.

June 19, 1774. James Marye of St. Geo. Par., Spts. Co., Clerk, to his son, James Marye. Deed of Gift. 10 negroes. Witnesses, Sophia Crawford, Susanna Heath, Robt. True, Peter Marye, Eleanor Marye, James Cunningham. Augt. 18, 1774.

June 19, 1774. James Marye of St. Geo. Par., Spts. Co., Clerk, to his daughter, Susanna Marye. Deed of Gift. 6 negroes. Witnesses, Sophia Crawford, Susanna Heath, Robt. True, P. Marye, Eleanor Marye, Jas. Cunningham. Augt. 18, 1774.

June 19, 1774. James Marye of St. Geo. Par., Spts. Co., Clerk, to his daughter, Sarah Marye. Deed of Gift. 6 negroes. Witnesses, same as in preceding deed. Augt. 18, 1774.

June 19, 1774. James Marye of St. Geo. Par., Spts. Co., Clerk, to his daughter, Lucy Marye. Deed of Gift. 7 negroes. Witnesses, same as in preceding deeds. Augt. 18, 1774.

June 19, 1774. James Marye of St. Geo. Par., Spts. Co., Clerk, to his children, Lucy, Susanna, Sarah, and James. Goods and chattels. Deed of Gift. Witnesses, same as in preceding deeds. Augt. 18, 1774.

Jany. 12, 1773. Henry Pendleton to Edwd. and Joseph Herndon of Spts. Co., Gentlemen. Mortgage. They being security for sd. Pendleton on a bond to Mrs. Mary Vass, widow of Philip Vincent Vass, Decd., etc. Witnesses, Geo. Stubblefield, J. Lewis. Augt. 19, 1774.

July 19, 1774. Wm. Arnold of Spts. Co. from Benjamin Chiles and Mildred, his wife, of same Co. £40 curr. 235 a. in Spts. Co. Jas. Wiglesworth, Ambrose Shackleford. Augt. 18, 1774.

Augt. 18, 1774. Thomas Colson of Spts. Co. from George Atkinson of same Co. £113 7s. 6d. curr. Mortgage. 330 a. on River Po., etc. No witnesses. Augt. 18, 1774.

Augt. 11, 1774. John Frederick Baker and Frances, his wife, of Fredksbg. to James Fulton of same town. £30 curr. Lot in town of Fredksbg., purchased by sd. Baker of Aaron Marders and Elinor, his wife, as by Deeds, Octr. 23, 1769, etc. B. Johnston, Jas. Brown, Jno. Richards. Augt. 18, 1774.

March 8, 1774. Joseph Herndon and Betty, his wife; Charles Gordon and Mary, his wife, of Spts. Co. to Aaron Fontaine. £200 curr. 260 a. in Spts. Co. Wm. Smith, Edwd. Herndon, Peter Stubblefield. Augt. 18, 1774.

March 13, 1774. Wm. Riadon of Spts. Co. to Andrew Cochrane, Wm. Cunningham & Co. £37 6s. 4d. Mortgage. 180 a. in St. Geo. Par., Spts. Co., purchased of Wm. Fitzhugh of "Chatham," Esqr., exclusive of 65 a. sold Richd. Young, etc. Geo. M. Cormack, Chs. Mortimer, junr.; James Douglas. Septr. 15, 1774.

March 4, 1774. Sherod Horn of Spts. Co. to Andrew Cochrane, Wm. Cunningham & Co. £31 14s. 4d. curr. Mortgage. His interest in a tract of land in Spts. Co., which he holds by Lease from Spotswood, etc. Geo. M. Cormack, Chas. Mortimer, jr.; Jas. Douglas. Sept. 15, 1774.

Feby. 24, 1774. Jno. Waller, K. W., of Spts. Co. to Jno. Waller, Clk., of same Co. Whereas, sd. Waller, K. W., was seized in his demense, etc., in 247 a. in Spts. Co., sold the same to Geo. Stubblefield, and when conveying the same, Mary Ann Waller, his wife, refused to relinquish her dower, etc., but proposed that her sd. husband should secure to her a negro, etc., and he so doing she relinquishes her dower in sd. land, etc. Now, this Indenture witnesseth that the sd. Waller, K. W., deeds the sd. Waller, Clk., a negro in trust as by agreement, etc. Witnesses, James Pritchett, Catharine x Gordon, Jno. Waller, junr.; Thos. Pritchett, O. Towles, Jno. Chew, jr. Septr. 15, 1774.

June 15, 1774. Wm. Wood of Spts. Co. to Hannah Wood, Oliver Towles and Jno. Herndon of Spts. Co. £37 curr., justly due the sd. Hannah Wood, and also for the consideration that the sd. Towles and Herndon being his security to Jno. Gray & Co. of Port Royal, to indemnify them, the sd. Wood conveys 230 a. in St. Geo. Par., Spts. Co., which he holds by lease from Spotswood, etc., also goods and chattels, etc. Jos. Herndon, Jas. Lewis, Harry Bartlett, Wm. Crane. Novr. 17, 1774.

Sept. 26, 1774. Elizabeth May, widow of Thomas May, of Spts. Co., Decd., to Daniel Branham of Co. afsd. £20 curr. Right, title or dower the sd. Elizabeth may have in 267 a. in St. Geo. Par., Spts. Co., of which Thos. May, died, seized and possessed, etc. Witnesses, Jos. Brock, Jno.

Wiglesworth, Robt. Smith, Robt. Richards, Wm. Robinson. Novr. 17, 1774.

Septr. 21, 1774. Capt. Thomas Dixon of Gloucester Co. to Dr. Charles Mortimer of Fredksbg. £25 curr. Lot 234 in town of Fredksbg. James Ward, Thos. Walker, Philip Clayton, junr. Novr. 18, 1774.

Novr. 17, 1774. Wm. McCowan (an infant) of Spts. Co. with consent of his mother, Prisiah McCowan (alias Shepherd), apprentices himself to John Green of sd. Co., Saddler, etc. No witnesses. Novr. 18, 1774.

Decr. 15, 1774. Thomas Colson, jr., of Spts. Co. to Wm. Wood and Ann, his wife, of same Co., during their lives, then to their sons, John and James Wood, etc. 5s. curr. A negro slave. No witnesses. Decr. 15, 1774.

March 8, 1774. Jno. Moor of Albemarle Co., Robt. Moor of Augusta, po. of atto., to Robt. Moor of Culpeper Co., to sell to Oliver Towles of Spts. Co. Tract of land in Spts. Co., devised the sd. John, Robt. and Samuel Moor by the will of their deceased father, Robert Moor, etc. Witnesses, Jno. Dawson, Vincent Vass, Wm. Trigg, Wm. Heslop, Thos. Towles. Decr. 15, 1774.

Oct. 19, 1774. Peter Marye and Eleanor, his wife, of Spts. Co. to Benj. Holloday, Senr., of same Co. £195 curr. 1360 a. in Berkeley Par., Spts. Co. Geo. Stubblefield, Jos. Brock, Reuben Straughan, Robt. Dudley, Harry Bartlett. Decr. 15, 1774.

Septr. 14, 1774. John Darnaby, son of Wm. Darnaby, of Spts. Co., Decd., apprentices himself to Ambrose Dudley of Co. of Spts., Joiner and House Carpenter, etc. No witnesses. Decr. 15, 1774.

Octr. 31, 1774. Richard Templeman of Great Bridge, in Norfolk Co. to George Thornton of Fredksbg., Spts. Co. £200 curr. Lot in town of Fredksbg. which Col. Wm. Waller formerly purchased of Jos. Herndon, etc. Jno. Meals, Jona. Wilson, Robt. Forsyth. Decr. 16, 1774.

April 21, 1774. John Keeton of St. Geo. Par., Spts. Co. and Elizabeth, his wife, to George Shepherd of Berkeley Par., same Co. £50 curr. 150 a. in Spts. Co. and Caroline Co., etc. Wm. x Thornton, John x Thornton. Decr. 16, 1774.

Jany. 2, 1775. Jacob Cunes of Spts. Co. to Jno. Wiglesworth, Jno. Brock, Benj. Ballard, Ambrose Rains, Wm. Hudson, Robt. Smith, Francis Simpson and Henry Head. To indemnify them for standing security on a bond, etc. Witnesses, Jno. Chew, junr.; Harry Bartlett, Jno. Holloday, jr. Jany. 19, 1775.

Jany. 4, 1775. Wm. x Gholson and Susanna, his wife, of Spts. Co. to Jacob Cunes of same Co. £40 curr. 80 a. in St. Geo. Par., Spts. Co. Jno. Brock, Ro. B. Chew, Jno. Holloday, jr.; Peter Stubblefield. Jany 19, 1775.

Jany. 18, 1775. Humphrey Haley and Ann, his wife, of Caroline Co. to Capt. John Jones of sd. Co.. 100 a. in Spts. Co. Jno. Richards, Jacob Whitler, Wm. Houston. Jany. 20, 1775.

Jany. 16, 1775. Charles Gordon of Spts. Co., but now living in Louisa Co. and Mary, his wife, to John Lewis of Spts. Co. Sd. Gordon having deposited £100 in the hands of the sd. Lewis for the benefit of sd. Mary

Gordon, etc. Witnesses, Anderson Thompson, Nicholas Lewis, Tho. Minor. Feby. 16, 1775.

Novr. 21, 1774. David x Pinn and Avarilla, his wife of Spts. Co. to Oliver Towles, attorney at law, of same Co. £25 curr. 50 a. called "Newpost," belonging to the sd. Towles, and in which the sd. Pinn and wife hold a life estate which they convey, etc. Edwd. Herndon, Geo. Stubblefield, Thos. Towles. Feby. 16, 1775.

Octr. 12, 1774. Peter Marye and Eleanor, his wife, of Spts. Co. to John Chew of same Co. £65 curr. 158 a. in St. Geo. Par., Spts. Co. Jno. Schooler, Jos. Brock, Jno. Brock. Feby. 16, 1775.

Feby. 16, 1775. James Stevens, orphan of Jeremiah Stevens, Decd., with the consent of Henry Johnston, his guardian, apprentices himself to John Carnahan of Spts. Co. Witness, Jno. Waller, jr. Feby. 16, 1775.

Feby. 16, 1775. Edward Brasfield of Spts. Co. to John Sorrell of same Co. £21 curr. 160 a. in Spts. Co. No witnesses. Feby. 16, 1775.

Augt. 20, 1774. Peter Marye and Eleanor, his wife, of Spts. Co. to John Wiglesworth of same Co. £300 curr. 670 a. in St. Geo. Par., Spts. Co., etc. Wm. Green, Jos. Brock, James Haydon, Joseph Gale. Feby. 16, 1775.

Feby. 16, 1775. James Frazer, orph. of James Frazer, Decd., with consent of his mother, Elizabeth Frazer, etc., apprentices himself to John McCalley of Spts. Co. No witnesses. Feby. 16, 1775.

Novr. 29, 1774. Jno. Holladay, jr., of Spts. Co. and Mildred, his wife, of the first part; Reubin Straughan of same Co., of second part; Oliver Towles of Co. afsd., Atto. at Law. Whereas, sd. Jno. Holladay, jr., is seized of a tract of land in Berkeley Par., Spts. Co., conveyed to him by Archibald Dick, Clerk, and Susanna, his wife, as by deeds Augt. 2, 1770, sd. tract containing 504 acres, etc., but by a recent survey found to contain 450 acres, and whereas, sd. Holladay, jr., has agreed to sell the sd. land to sd. Straughan for the sum of £135 curr. to be pd. in five different payments, sd. Towles being made trustee, etc. Witnesses, John Terrill, Larkin Smith, Bernard x Carter. Feby. 16, 1775.

March 8, 1775. Erasmus Withers Allen and Sarah, his wife, of Province of North Carolina, to Richard Loury of Caroline Co. £250 curr. 499 a. in Spts. Co., Va., bounded by lands of Harry Beverley, Decd., Mrs. Mary Dawson, Abraham Estes, and John McCauley. Witnesses, Vincent Vass, Francis Turnley, Benjamin Chapman, Thomas Chapman. March 16, 1775.

Feby. 24, 1775. John Lewis, Oliver Towles, and John Chew of Spts. Co. to John Waller and Ann, his wife, of sd. County. Whereas, sd. Waller and wife, by their indenture conveyed 600 a. of land, slaves, goods and chattels, to indemnify them the sd. Lewis, Towles, and Chew, who stood security for the sd. Waller, etc. Reconveyance. Larkin Chew, Reuben Straughan, John Holloday. March 16, 1775.

Oct. 29, 1774. Thos. Burbridge of Spts. Co. and Sarah, his wife, to John Wiglesworth of sd. Co. £100 curr. 125 a. in St. Geo. Par., Spts. Co. Jas. Lewis, Hezekiah Ellis, Henry Elley, Jr. March 16, 1775.

Decr. 5, 1774. Jno. Simpson, junr., of Spts. Co. to Robt. Frank of same Co. £25 16s. 9d. curr. Mortgage. Goods and chattels. John Herndon, Jas. Hackley, Benj. Ballard. May 18, 1775.

Nov. 19, 1774. Reuben Massey of Spts. Co. to John Brock of sd. Co. Lease. 100 a. in St. Geo. Par., Spts. Co., purchased of John Penn, etc. £6 curr. Joseph Brock, George Hensley, Richardson Hensley. May 18, 1775.

April 20, 1775. John Wiglesworth and Philadelphia, his wife, of Spts. Co. to Wm. Houston of sd. Co. £100 curr. 540 a. in St. Geo. Par., Spts. Co. Jno. Brock, Reuben Straughan, Ro. Dudley. May 18, 1775.

April 20, 1775. Wm. Houston and Judith, his wife, of Fredksbg. to John Wiglesworth of Spts. Co. £100 curr. Lot 41 in town of Fredksbg., "whereon my father, Wm. Houston, Decd., formerly lived," etc. Jno. Brock, Reubin Straughan, Jno. Richards. May 18, 1775.

May 18, 1775. Wm. Houston and Judith, his wife, of Fredksbg. to Isaac Heslop and David Blair of Fredksbg., Merchts., etc. £192 curr. Lot 273 in town of Fredksbg. Jno. Wiglesworth, Benjamin Burbridge, Lodowick Oneal. May 18, 1775.

Septr. 20, 1774. Lucy Dixon of Fredksbg. to Thomas Dixon of Kingston Par., Gloucester Co. £440 curr. Mortgage. Tract in Spts. Co. which she purchased out of land mortgaged by Roger Dixon to James Harford of Bristol, etc., also 120 a. in Spts. Co., purchased of Thos. Steward, also slaves, etc. Witnesses, Chs. Mortimer, Philip Clayton, junr.; Mildred Dixon. May 18, 1775.

April 19, 1775. Ignatius x Tureman of Spts. Co. to his son, Charles Tureman of same Co. Deed of Gift. 200 a. in Spts. Co. Edwd. Herndon, jr.; Reubin Straughan, Jno. Pierce. June 15, 1775.

Oct. 17, 1774. Richard Ray of King and Queen Co. to John Craig of Spts. Co. £30 curr. 497 a. in Spts. Co. James Gaff, Toliver Craig, Jeremiah Craig, John Pattie. May 18, 1775.

Novr. 17, 1774. John McCalley and Elizabeth, his wife, of Spts. Co. to Ephraim Beazley of same Co. £21 curr. 28 a. in Spts. Co. Wm. McWilliams, Wm. Trigg, John Carter. May 18, 1775.

May 18, 1775. John Taliaferro and Lucy, his wife, to John Hardia. £——. Lots 252 and 262 in town of Fredksbg., purchased from Wm. Smith, as by Deeds. July 17, 1762, etc. John Rose, G. Weedon, Geo. Thornton. May 18, 1775.

Feby. 25, 1775. John Waller and Ann, his wife, of Spts. Co. to John Lewis of Spts. Co. In trust. Whereas, sd. Waller and Ann, his wife, in right of sd. Ann, are seized and possessed of 914 a. whereon they live, they convey the same to the sd. Lewis for purposes specified in this deed, for payment of debts, to indemnify, and for the benefit of the children of sd. Waller and Ann, his wife, etc. Witnesses, O. Towles, Larkin Chew, Thos. Megee. May 18,1775.

Feby. 2, 1775. James Harford of Bristol, Gt. Britain, Mercht., surviving partner of Jos. Robson and James Harford, of the first part; Revd. Jno. Dixon, Clerk, Adms. with the will annexed of Roger Dixon, Gent.,

Decd., of the second part, and Dr. Charles Mortimer of Fredksbg., of the third part. Whereas, sd. Roger Dixon in his lifetime being justly indebted to the sd. James Harford in the sum of £1995 ster., and to secure the sd. debt, did by Deeds convey to the sd. Harford sundry tracts of land, slaves, etc., among which was a tract of 300 a., adjoining the town of Fredksbg., and whereas, the sd. Roger in his lifetime failed to pay the sd. indebtedness, and in his last will and testament did appt. his brother, the sd. John Dixon, to administer upon his estate, and among other things to dispose of his lands and houses (except his dwelling house and four lots adj. in Fredksbg.), and to lay off his wife Lucy's dower, and whereas, the sd. Harford did appt. by his letter Wm. Fisher of Phila., his lawful atto., and the sd. Fisher did by the authority granted him in the sd. letter, appt. as his substitutes Robt. Pleasants and Thos. Bates of Henrico Co., and under an agreement to which the sd. Pleasants and Bates, on behalf of the sd. Harford, came to an agreement with the sd. Dixon for the settling of the sd. claim, etc., and at a public sale of the sd. 300 acres, Dr. Charles Mortimer became purchaser of 64 a. thereof for the sum of £183 curr., etc. Witnesses, Richd. Evers Lee, Robt. Dudley, Ambrose Dudley, B. Johnston, Philip Clayton, junr.; Lachlan Campbell, Wm. Wiatt, O. Towles, Jno. Chew, junr.; Chas. Mortimer, junr. May 18, 1775.

May 31, 1775. James Harford of Bristol, Gt. Britain, Mercht., etc., of first part; Revd.. Jno. Dixon, Clk., Adms. with the will annexed of Roger Dixon, Gent, Decd., of second part; Lucy Dixon, widow, etc., of the sd. Roger, of the town of Fredksbg., of the third part; Dr. Charles Mortimer of Fredksbg., of the fourth part, [see Deed dated Feby. 2, 1775], for the sum of £132 17s. 2d. 15½ a. are conveyed to Dr. Charles Mortimer, etc. Witnesses, Jno. Chew, jr.; Philip Clayton, junr.; Chs. Mortimer, junr. June 15, 1775.

June 15, 1775. John Carthrae of Spts. Co. to Peter Mason of sd. Co. £110 curr. 318 a. in Spts. Co. No witnesses. June 15, 1775.

April 19, 1775. Joseph Hawkins of Spts. Co. and Margaret, his wife, to Wm. Plummer Thurston of sd. Co. £500 curr. 755 a. in Spts. Co. Provided, that the title of Jane Hawkins to that part of the above land left her during her natural life by the will of her late husband, Joseph Hawkins, Decd., shall not be affected, etc. Witnesses, Beverley Winslow, Wm. Parker, Nicholas Taliaferro, John Hawkins, jr.; John Alcock, Wm. Forson. June 15, 1775.

Feby. 2, 1775. James Harford of Bristol, surviving partner of Joseph Robson of sd. City, Mercht, Decd., by his letter of attorney dated May May 24, 1764, constituted and appointed Wm. Fisher of Philadelphia, Mercht., his attorney, etc., and by the power granted him the sd. Fisher, in the sd. letter, the sd. Fisher did appt. Robt. Pleasants and Thomas Bates of Henrico Co., by his letter May 29, 1765, substitutes, etc., the sd. Pleasants and Bates by this their letter appt. and substitutes Oliver Towles of Spts. to act for them, whereas Roger Dixon, Gent., in his lifetime being indebted to the sd. James Harford, etc., in the sum of £1995 ster. with legal interest, from May 2, 1765, and to secure payment thereof did convey in fee by two deeds of mortgage, recd. in General Court of the Colony, sundry tracts of land, slaves, etc. Witnesses, G. Weedon, Fielding Lewis, Wm. Triplet, Lewis Willis. June 15, 1775.

Decr. 20, 1774. Ann Dansie to John Alcock. Lease. 600 a. in Berkeley Par., Spts. Co., in fork of Pamunkey. £25 curr. Rd. Brooke, Mary White, Jane Washington. June 15, 1775.

Novr. 24, 1774. Geo. Peterson and Margaret, his wife, of Spts. Co. to Clayton Coleman of same Co. £65 curr. 144 a. in Spts. Co. Oswald Smith, James Peterson, David Griffin, Wm. Etherton. June 15, 1775.

June 15, 1775. Wm. Stanard of Spts. Co. to his brother, Beverley Stanard, of sd. Co. Deed of Gift. Slave. Witnesses, W. Buckner; Alex. Parker, O. Towles. June 15, 1775.

Novr. 22, 1774. Augustin or Austin Garnett of Essex Co., Gent., and Betty, his wife, to Neil McCoul of Spts. Co., Mercht. £120 curr. 1000 a. in Spts. Co. Whereas, James Garnett, formerly of Essex Co., Gent., by his last will and testament proved in Essex Co., Augt. 19, 1765, did devise to his grandson, sd. Augustin or Austin Garnett and his heirs, a moiety of 2000 a. in Spts. Co., called Glady Fork, and by the sd. will devised the other moiety of the sd. tract to his grandson, Harry Garnett, and whereas, sd. Augustin and Harry came to an agreement by which the sd. land was divided Sept. 28, 1771, etc., each of them becoming seized and possessed of their tracts as by the division, etc. Witnesses, R. Hipkins, Henry Garnett, Wm. Woddrop, Jno. Woddrop. June 15, 1775.

Feby. 1, 1775. James Harford of Bristol, Gt. Britain, Mercht., etc., of the first part; Revd. John Dixon, Clk., Adms. with the will annexed of Roger Dixon, Gent., Decd., of the second part; Lewis Willis of Fredksbg., Gent., of the third part. [See Deed dated Feby. 2, 1775.] For the sum of £324 16s. 90 a. of the tract is conveyed to Lewis Willis, etc. Witnesses, Richd. Evers Lee, Robt. Dudley, Philip Clayton, junr.; Ambrose Dudley, B. Johnston, Ch. Yates, Alexr. Dick, Wm. Triplet, O. Towles, Patr. Lenogan, Larkin Chew. June 15, 1775.

Feby. 1, 1775. James Harford of Bristol, Gt. Britain, Mercht., etc., of the first part; Revd. Jno. Dixon, Clerk, Adms. with the will annexed of Roger Dixon, Gent., Decd., of the second part; Wm. Thompson of Culpeper Co., Gent. [See Deed dated Feby. 2, 1775.] For the sum of £205 11s. 6d. 60 a. of the sd. tract is conveyed to the sd. Wm. Thompson, etc. Witnesses, Richd. Evers Lee, Robt. Dudley, Philip Clayton, junr.; Ambrose Dudley, B. Johnston, Ch. Yates, Alexr. Dick, Wm. Triplet, O. Towles, Patr. Lenogan, Larkin Chew. June 15, 1775.

Decr. 31, 1774. Wm. Blaydes of Spts. Co. and Mary, his wife, to Clayton Coleman of sd. Co. £140 curr. 184 a. in Spts. Co. Jonathan Carpenter, Saml. May, Jno. Coleman. Augt. 17, 1775.

Augt. 2, 1775. John Hall of Caroline Co. and Molly, his wife, to James Crawford of Spts. Co. £115 curr. 200 a. in Spts. Co., part of a tract patented by Smith and bequeathed by Robt. Hall to the sd. John, etc. Witnesses, Robt. Gilchrist, James Miller, James Gordon. Augt. 17, 1775.

Augt. 2, 1775. John Hall of Caroline Co. and Molly, his wife, to John Waller, son of Edmund Waller, of Spts. Co. £110 curr. 200 a. in Spts. Co., part of tract "bequeathed the sd. John Hall by his late father, Robert Hall," etc. Witnesses, Robt. Gilchrist, James Miller, James Gordon. Augt. 17, 1775.

Augt. 17, 1775. Peter Mason and Elizabeth, his wife, of Spts. Co. to Leonard Young of same Co. £27. 80 a. in sd. County. No witnesses. Augt. 17, 1775.

Augt. 17, 1775. Peter Mason and Elizabeth, his wife, of Spts. Co. to John Shackelford of same Co. £30 curr. 50 a. in Spts. Co. No witnesses. Augt. 17, 1775.

Augt. 17, 1775. James x Jones of Spts. Co. to John White of sd. County. £55 curr. 283 a. in Berkeley Par., Spts. Co. Wm. Chiles, Basil White, Richd. Jones. Augt. 17, 1775.

April 29, 1775. Joseph Hawkins and Margaret, his wife, of Berkeley Par., Spts. Co. to John Edwards of same Par. and Co. £25. 100 a. on Plentiful Run, Par. and Co. afsd. Edwd. Collins, John Coleman, Robt. Hutcherson, Beverley Winslow, Thos. x Allen, Richd. Allen. Augt. 17, 1775.

March 17, 1775. Benjamin Johnston of Culpeper Co. and Dorothy, his wife, to John Welch of Fredksbg. £——. Part of lot No. 17 in Fredksbg. Wm. Houston, Wm. Blyth, Jno. Haselgrove. Augt. 17, 1775.

Augt. 17. 1775. David Woodroof and Rachael, his wife, to their daughter, Sarah, wife of Thomas Hackney. Deed of Gift. 50 a. in Spts. Co. No witnesses. Augt. 17, 1775.

Feby. 4, 1775. James Rawlings, Senr., and Sarah, his wife, and John Holloday, Senr., and Elizabeth, his wife, of Spts. Co. to James Rawlings, junr., of same Co. £250 curr. 500 a. in Spts. Co., part of a tract granted by pat. to Christopher Smith, etc. Chas. Gordon, Z. Lewis, Geo. Stubblefield, Moses Wheeler, Richd. Rawlings. Oct. 19, 1775.

Augt. 17, 1775. John Dillard of Drisdale Par., Caroline Co. to his brother, Richard Dillard, of Berkeley Par., Spts. Co. £50 curr. 100 a. in Berkeley Par., Spts. Co., given the sd. Jno. Dillard, by the will of his father, etc. No witnesses. Augt. 17, 1775.

May 9, 1775. Thos. Megee, Sr., to his son, Thos. Megee, Jr., on day he is married. "By a contract of marriage," etc. Tract of land, negroes, 6 head cattle, etc. Witnesses, Shadrach Moore, Jno. Oliver. Sept. 21, 1775.

May 9, 1775. Michael Robinson, Senr., of Spts. Co. to his daughter, Mary, "by contract of marriage Sept. 1, 1775." Several slaves, cattle, goods and chattels. Witnesses, James Freeland, Shadrach Moore. Septr. 21, 1775.

Septr. 15, 1775. Peter Stubblefield and Margaret, his wife, of Spts. Co. to Thomas Megee, junr., of same Co. £80 curr. 210 a. in Berkeley Par., Spts. Co. Jno. Welch, Larkin Chew, Jacob Whitler. Septr. 21, 1775.

Septr. 11, 1775. Alexander Spotswood, Esqr., to Alford Williams of Spts. Co. Lease. 100 a. in Spts. Co. "Sd. Williams, his wife, and his son, John," etc. 600 lbs. tob. Js. Lewis, Thos. Fox, Benja. Burbridge. Sept. 21, 1775.

Novr. 21, 1771. John Campbell and Mary, his wife, and Alexander Spotswood to Benjamin Burbridge of Spts. Co. Lease. 45 a. "John Wiglesworth and Philadelphia, his wife, and Mary Fox," etc. 287 lbs. tob. Js. Lewis, Thos. Fox, Alford Williams. Septr. 21, 1775.

Septr. 11, 1775. Alexander Spotswood, Esqr., to Benjamin Burbridge of Spts. Co. Lease. 170 a. "Benj. Burbridge, Molly Burbridge and Jno. Burbridge, his son," etc. 850 lbs. tob. Jas. Lewis, Thos. Fox, Alford Williams. Sept. 21, 1775.

Septr. 11, 1775. Alexander Spotswood, Esqr., to Jervis Haydon of Spts. Co. Lease. 200 a. "Jervis Haydon, James Jones Haydon, and Jessey Haydon, sons of the sd. Jervis Haydon," etc. 1000 lbs. tob. Jas. Lewis, Thos. Fox, Benja. Burbridge. Septr. 21, 1775.

Septr. 11, 1775. Alexander Spotswood, Esqr., to Thomas Fox of Spts. Co. Lease. 284 a. "Barbara Fox, Lucy Fox, John Fox," etc. 1000 lbs. tob. Jas. Lewis, Benja. Burbridge, Alford Williams. Septr. 21, 1775.

Septr. 11, 1775. Alexander Spotswood, Esqr., to Thomas Fox of Spts. Co. Lease. 230 a. "Thos. Fox, junr.; Wm. Fox, Nathl. Fox," etc. 1150 lbs. tob. Jas. Lewis, Benja. Burbridge, Alford Williams. Septr. 21, 1775.

Feby. 13, 1775. Daniel x Musick and George x Musick of Albemarle Co. and Lurritia and Jean, their wives, to George McNeil of Spts. Co. £15 curr. 68 a. in Spts. Co. Jno. Shepherd, Jno. Musick, Ephraim Musick, Jno. Lewis, Thos. Lipscomb, Francis Irwin, Joel Lewis. Sept. 21, 1775.

Feby. 16, 1775. George x Musick and Lurite, his wife, Daniel x Musick and Jean, his wife, of Albemarle, to Thomas Lipscomb of Spts. Co. £11 curr. 40 a. in Spts. Co. Jno. Lewis, Jno. Shepherd, Jno. Musick, Ephraim Musick, Geo. McNeil, Francis Irwin, Joel Lewis. Sept. 21, 1775.

Septr. 13, 1775. Alexander Spotswood, Esqr., to Churchill Jones. Lease. 262 a. in St. Geo. Par., Spts. Co., on s. side Rapidan River, part of a tract of 40,000 a. left the sd. Alexander Spotswood by his grandfather, etc. "Sd. Churchill Jones, Wm. Jones, and Betty Jones," etc. £13 2s. yearly. Will. Stanard, John Lewis, Jos. Somners, Jno. Rose. Septr. 21, 1775.

Septr. 10, 1775. Alexander Spotswood, Esqr., to Benjamin Grymes, now of Orange Co. Lease. 405 a. in Spts. Co. "Geo. Thornton, Molly Thornton, and George, son of George and Molly Thornton," etc. £20 5s. yearly. Jno. Lewis, Wm. Stanard, Jno. Rose. Sept. 21, 1775.

Octr. 5, 1775. Benjamin Johnston and Dorothy, his wife, of Culpeper Co. to John Holloday, jr., of Spts. Co. £300 curr. 325 a. in Spts. Co. Jos. Brock, Robt. Thomas, Wm. Houston. Oct. 19, 1775.

Septr. 21, 1775. Alexander Spotswood to Thomas Burbridge, Senr., of Spts. Co. Lease. 100 a. 600 lbs. tob. Michael Robinson, Jas. Lewis, Jno. Munro, Jno. Horner. Oct. 19, 1775.

July 10, 1775. John Chapman and Mary, his wife, of Spts. Co., of the first part; Thomas Towles and Mary, his wife, of sd. Co., of second part, and Wm. Dawson of sd. Co., of the third part. Whereas, John Chapman, being seized of a tract in Berkeley Par., Spts. Co., containing, by recent survey, 185 a., sold the same to the sd. Thomas Towles, but before proper conveyance was thereof made the sd. Towles sold the land to the sd. Dawson. The sd. Towles having pd. the sd. Chapman £161 17s. curr. for the sd. tract, etc. These parties now enter in their deed to the sd. Dawson, who having pd. the sd. Towles £200 curr. for the above-mentioned 185 a., etc. Witnesses, O. Towles, Larkin Chew, Wm. Trigg, Harry Bartlett. Oct. 19, 1775.

Oct. 20, 1775. Wm. Houston and Judith, his wife, and Fanny Houston of Fredksbg., widow and relict of Hugh Houston, Decd., to Oliver Towles, atto. at law, of the Co. afsd. £550 curr. Lots 255 and 265 in town of Fredksbg., etc. Whereas, Wm. Houston of afsd. town, Decd., being seized of two lots in the town of Fredksbg. (besides other valuable estate), etc., made his last will and testament, by which he devised all his estate to his two sons, Wm. Houston (party hereto) and Hugh Houston, except a legacy of £250 bequeathed to his sister, Sarah Stacey of Phila., and soon afterwards the sd. testator died, and the sd. Wm. and Hugh, by virtue of the devise, entered into possession thereof, and before a division of the estate was made the sd. Hugh died intestate, whereby the sd. Wm. became entitled to the sd. Hugh's undivided moiety, by survivorship; the sd. Wm. Houston, for the advancement of the sd. Fanny and her child, Sallye, agreed not to take more than a just share, giving to the sd. Fannie the remainder of her decd. husband's moiety, after his just debts paid, etc., etc., the sd. Wm. having agreed to sell certain lots to the sd. Towles, the sd. Fanny joining in this conveyance thereby releasing any right she may have thereto, etc. Witnesses, Jno. Chew, Will. Hamilton, Neil McCoull, Jno. Holloday, Wm. Daingerfield. No date of Record.

March 21, 1775. Benjamin Johnston, now of Culpeper Co. to Oliver Towles of Spts. Co., Atto. at Law. To indemnify the sd. Towles who stands security on the sd. Johnston's bond to Wm. Daingerfield in the sum of £225 curr. Mortgages. Lots and houses, purchased of Hon. Jno. Tayloe and others. 360 a. in Spts. Co., whereon Jno. Holloday, jr., lives, also the 3000 a. in Fincastle Co., purchased of the sd. Daingerfield and for which the sd. Bond was given, etc. Witnesses, Jno. Holloday, jr.; Jos. Pulliam, Mildred Holloday, Robt. Thomas. Novr. 17, 1775.

Nov. 15, 1775. Thomas Colson of Spts. Co. and Frances, his wife, to Wm. Duerson of sd. Co. £100 curr. 148 a. in Spts. Co. No witnesses. Novr. 17, 1775.

Novr. 15, 1775. Thomas Colson of Spts. Co. and Frances, his wife, to Wm. Trigg of Spts. Co. £100 curr. 148 a. in Spts. Co. No witnesses. Novr. 16, 1775.

June 1, 1774. The Revd. Jno. Dixon, Clk., Adms. with the will annexed of Roger Dixon, Gent., Decd., and Lucy Dixon of Fredksbg., widow of the sd. Roger Dixon, etc., to David Blair of Fredksbg., Mercht. £161 curr. Lot in town of Fredksbg. O Towles, Reuben Straughan, P. Clayton, Anth. Thornton, junr.; Wm. Smith, Chs. Yates, Henry Mitchell, Wm. Horner, Danl. Payne, Jno. Rose, Benja. Day, James Marshall. Decr. 17, 1775.

May 31, 1775. Charles Mortimer of Fredksbg., Doctor of Physick, and Sarah, his wife, to John Glassell of Fredksbg., Mercht. £157 18s. 7d. curr. 31 a. in Spts. Co., adj. Fredksbg., purchased of James Harford,

Jno. Dixon, etc. Witnesses, O. Towles, Jno. Chew, junr.; George Muir, Lachlan Campbell. Nov. 17, 1775.

Octr. 14, 1774. Henry Pendleton and Martha, his wife, of Spts. Co.; Rice Curtis and Frances, his wife of same Co. to Oliver Towles of same Co., Attorney-at-Law. Whereas, by a decree of the County Court of Spts. June 22, 1771, it was ordered that Nathaniel Price and Jane, his wife, convey all their right, title, etc., in 150 a. in Spts. Co. to the sd. Henry Pendleton, and whereas, the sd. Pendleton, before such conveyance was obtained, did by his deed, July 3, 1771, convey his right, title, etc., in the sd. land to the sd. Rice Curtis, and whereas, on Augt. 20, 1772, the sd. Henry Pendleton did obtain conveyance of the sd. land from the sd. Jane Price, the sd. Nathaniel being then dead; and the sd. Rice Curtis being seized, etc., of 58 a. in the sd. Co., adjoining the sd. 150 a. and both tracts contiguous to the lands of Larkin Smith, an infant, the sd. Curtis having agreed with the sd. Oliver Towles, guardian to the sd. Larkin Smith, for the sale of the sd. two tracts of land for the sum of £94 curr. The land is conveyed the sd. Towles, as guardian of the sd. Smith, etc. Witnesses, Thos. Towles, Stockley Towles, Jos. Hewell. Novr. 17, 1775.

Augt. 21, ——. Wm. Bartlett, Jr., and Mary, his wife, of Berkeley Co., Va., to Harry Bartlett of same place. £50 curr. 100 a. in Berkeley Par., Spts. Co., devised the sd. Wm. Bartlett by his father, Wm. Bartlett, as will more fully appear by a deed dated Sept. 30, 1757, from the sd. Bartlett, Senr., to the sd. Bartlett, junr., etc. Peter Stubblefield, W. Dawson, O. Towles, Larkin Chew. Decr. 21, 1775.

Decr. 21, 1775. Richard Durrett of Caroline Co. to Wm. Durrett of sd. Co. In consideration of sd. Wm. Durrett, making him absolute right, etc., to a tract of land whereon sd. Richd now lives, etc. 116 a., which fell to the sd. Richd. by lot of his father's estate in Spts. Co., bounded by lines of Elizabeth, George, Marshall, and James Durrett, etc. "Sd. Richd. Durrett and Elizabeth, his wife," etc. No witnesses. Dec. 21, 1775.

Novr. 4, 1775. Dudley Gatewood of Amherst Co. to Jno. Sanders of Spts. Co. £150. 300˙ a. in Spts. Co. Chas. Sanders, Henry Gatewood, junr. March 21, 1776.

Augt. 22, 1775. Benjamin Craig of Orange Co. to Benjamin Perry of Spts. Co. Lease. 200 a. in Spts. Co. 1000 lbs. tob. yearly. Jno. Sanders, David Pulliam, Geo. Moor. March 21, 1776.

Feby. 26, 1776. Lewis Willis, Fielding Lewis, Thos. Colson, Chas. Washington, Michael Robinson, Wm. Dangerfield, and Wm. Wood, Gentlemen, Vestrymen of St. Geo. Par., Spts. Co., to George Thornton of Fredksbg., Gent. Whereas, an Act of the Assembly, passed 12th George 3d, empowered the Vestry of St. Geo. Par. to dispose of so much of the church-yard around the church in Fredksbg., as had not been used as a graveyard, and the sd. land be vested in the vestry of the Parish in Trust, etc., and whereas, the sd. vestry having laid the sd. land off in lots, have sold lot No. 3 in the sd. plan to the sd. Thornton, for £150 curr., etc. Jno. Chew, Jno. Herndon, Jno. Wright. March 21, 1776.

Feby. 24, 1776. Lewis Willis, etc., Vestrymen of St. Geo. Par., Spts. Co. to Jno. Lewis of Spts. Co., Gent. [See preceding deed.] £110 curr.

Lot No. ——, in the Vestry's plan, etc. Jno. Chew, Jno. Wright, Jno. Herndon. March 21, 1776.

March 21, 1776. Henry Elley and Sarah, his wife, of Culpeper Co. to Thomas Burbridge of Spts. Co. £90 curr. 128 a. in St. Geo. Par., Spts. Co. No witnesses. March 21, 1776.

March 21, 1776. Theodore x Buckhanan of Spts. Co. apprentices himself to James Crawford of same Co., Shoemaker. No witnesses. March 21, 1776.

March 21, 1776. John Stevens, shoemaker and servant, belonging to James Crawford. Agreement, sd. Stevens to teach shoemaking to Wm. and Christopher, sons of sd. James Crawford, etc. No witnesses. March 21, 1776.

Feby. 16, 1776. Peter Marye of Spts. Co., Gent., and Eleanor, his wife, to Randal McDaniel of same Co. £52 curr. 138 a. in St. Geo. Par., Spts. Co. Wm. Robinson, George Willson, Leaving Willson. March 21, 1776.

Octr. 23, 1775. Lewis Willis, James Tutt, Chas. Washington, Thos. Colson, Michael Robinson, Wm. Dangerfield, Wm. Wood, Vestrymen of St. Geo. Par., Spts. Co. to Alexander Blair of Fredksbg., Mercht. [See Deed, Feby. 4, 1776, Vestry of St. Geo. Par. to Geo. Thornton, etc.] £130 10s. curr. Lot No. —— in a plan of the sd. Vestry, etc. Witnesses, Geo. Thornton, Jno. Herndon, Jno. Haselgrove, James Cunningham. March 21, 1776.

June 21, 1775. Robert Shearwood and Esther, his wife, of Spts. Co. to Thomas Proctor of same Co. £50 curr. 110 a. in St. Geo. Par., Spts. Co. No witnesses. March 21, 1776.

March 1, 1776. Ann x Graves of Spts. Co. to her granddaughter, Susannah Spencer, of Albemarle Co. Deed of Gift. Slave. Witnesses, Benj. Waller, Jno. Arnold, Thos. Minor. April 18, 1776.

Oct. 18, 1775. Richard Coleman of Berkeley Par., Spts. Co., Carpenter, and Ann, his wife, to their son, Francis Coleman. Deed of Gift. 110½ a. in Par. and Co. afsd. Wm. Parker, Bevy. Winslow, Jno. Smith, Edward Coleman. April 18, 1776.

Dec. 25, 1775. Edward x Cason of Buckingham Co. and Joanna, his wife; and Thomas x Cason of Halifax Co., son of the sd. Edwd., to Wm. Cason of Spts. Co., also son of the sd. Edward. Whereas, sd. Edward Cason did agree with his son, Thomas Cason, to give him 200 a. in Spts. Co. or whatever sum the sd. land should sell for, etc., and whereas, before any conveyance was made to the sd. Thomas, the sd. Edward Cason by his son, Seth Cason, his att. in fact, and with consent of the sd. Thomas, hath sold the sd. tract to the sd. Wm. Cason for the sum of £171 curr. Witnesses, Saml. Coleman, Clayton Coleman, Jonathan Carpenter, James Shackleford, Drury Mims, Peter Ford, Wm x Tupua. May 16, 1776.

Jany. 2, 1776. Edward x Cason of Buckingham Co. to his son-in-law, James Shackleford, of Spts. Co. Deed of Gift. 100 a. in Spts. Co., whereon sd. Shackleford lives, also a negro, goods and chattels, etc. "Which sd. land is part of the tract Susannah Cason hath a lease for during her natural life," etc. Witnesses, Jno. Sanders, Seth Cason, Elizabeth x Sanders. May 16, 1776.

Novr. 15, 1775. Jno. x Shepherd of Spts. Co. and Sarah, his wife, to Wm. Arnold, junr., of same Co. £130 curr. 500 a. in Spts. Co. Witnesses, Geo. McNeil, Thos. Minor, Jno. Sanders, Jno. Arnold. May 16, 1776.

Feby. 10, 1776. Wm. Arnold of Spts. Co. to Benj. Waller and Thomas Minor of sd. Co. To indemnify the sd. Waller and Minor who stand security to Jno. Shepherd in the sum of £61 curr. for the sd. Arnold, etc. Sd. Aronld mortgages to them the sd. 500 a. bought of sd. Shepherd, etc. Witnesses, Jno. Sanders, Geo. McNeil, Jno. Arnold. May 16, 1776.

Feby. 15, 1776. Wm. Daingerfield of Spts. Co., Gent., to Larkin Chew. Whereas, sd. Daingerfield in right of his wife, Mary, is entitled to reversion in fee of all dower slaves held by Elizabeth Thornton, relict of Reuben Thornton of Caroline Co., Gent., Decd., which she recd. as her dower of the slaves of her former husband, Henry Willis, Gent., Decd., which descended to the sd. Mary Daingerfield, as niece and heiress of the sd. Willis who died intestate and without issue. Sd. Daingerfield conveys the sd. reversion in the sd. slaves, to the sd. Chew, in trust, for the use of sd. Daingerfield, his heirs and assigns forever, etc. Witnesses, Thos. Duerson, Tho. Pritchett, Francis Rose. May 16, 1776.

March 2, 1776. Thomas Burbridge, Junr., of Spts. Co. to Thomas Burbridge of sd. Co. £40 curr. 85 a. in St. Geo. Par., Spts. Co. Daniel Branham, Robert Smith, Henry Gatewood, Junr. June 20, 1776.

Novr. 17, 1775. Alexander x Walden and Sarah, his wife, of Spts. Co. to Benjamin Walden of sd. Co. £20 curr. 92 a. in St. Geo. Par., Spts. Co. Jno. Chew, jr.; Michael Robinson, Jno. Welch. June 20, 1776.

Novr. 16, 1775. Alexander x Walden and Sarah, his wife, of Spts. Co. to Thomas White of King Geo. Co. £55 curr. 91 a. in Spts. Co. Michael Robinson, Jno. Conner, Jno. Welch, Jno. Chew, jr. June 20, 1776.

Decr. 12, 1775. Joel Parish and Mary, his wife, of Spts. Co. to Martin Davenport of same Co. £62 10s. 100 acres. Part of a tract purchased by sd. Parish of Joseph Temple, etc. Thos. Minor, Robt. Wilkinson, Wm. Davenport. June 26, 1776.

June 28, 1776. Gawin Corbin of Spts. Co. to Thos. Megee, jr. Lease. 113 a. in Berkeley and St. Geo. Parishes in Spts. Co. "Sd. Thos. Megee, Mary Megee and Thos. Megee Moore," etc. £5 yearly. Witnesses, Jno. Chew, jr.; Danl. Branham, Jno. Frazer, Shadrack Moore. June 20, 1776.

June 19, 1776. Gawin Corbin of Spts. Co. to Thos. Megee of sd. Co. Lease. 105 a. in Berkeley Par., Spts. Co. "Sd. Thos. Megee, Dinah Megee and Margaret Megee," etc. £5 5s. yearly. Jno. Chew, jr., Jno. Frazer, Danl. Branham, Shadrack Moore, Thos. Megee, jr. June 20, 1776.

June 18, 1776. Gawin Corbin to Betty Frasher of Spts. Co. Lease. 150 acres. "Sd. Betty Frasher, John Frasher and Reuben Frasher," etc. £7 10s. yearly. Daniel Branham, Shadrack Moore, Jno. Frazer, Thomas Megee, jr.; Jno. Chew. June 20, 1776.

Feby. 15, 1776. Alexander Spotswood, Esqr., to James Lewis. Lease. 100 acres, etc. "Sd. James Lewis, Ann, his wife, and Willis Lewis, his son," etc. 600 lbs. tob. Jno. Craig, Benja. Burbridge, Allen Wiley, James Lewis, Smyth Tandy. June 20, 1776.

Novr. 10, 1775. Wm. Riadon and Elizabeth, his wife, of Spts. Co. to Richard Young of sd. Co. £20 curr. 66 a. in St. Geo. Par., Spts. Co. Reuben Young, James Adkins, Alexander Adkins. June 20, 1776.

March 20, 1776. Fielding Lewis, Esqr., and Betty, his wife, and John Lewis of Spts Co., Gent., to Edward Carter of Fredksbg., Esqr. £2000 curr. Lots 83, 84, 85, 86, 95, 96, 97 and 98 whereon sd. Carter's house, stables, etc., stand and added to the sd. town by act of assembly, etc., whereon sd. Carter now lives, etc. No witnesses. June 20, 1776.

July 10, 1776. Wm. Wigglesworth of Spts. Co. and Mary, his wife, to Peter Stubblefield of same Co. £210 curr. 170 a. Robt. Chew, Edwd. Herndon, Jno. Carthrae. July 18, 1776.

July 10, 1776. Wm. Edmund Waller and Mildred, his wife, of Spts. Co. to Peter Stubblefield of same Co. £74 curr. 78 a. in Spts. Co. Robt. Chew, Edwd. Herndon, Jno. Carthrae. July 18, 1776.

June 2, 1776. Gawin Corbin, jr., of Spts. Co. to Jno. Buckner of Caroline Co. Lease. 652 a. "Sd. Jno. Buckner, Richd. Buckner and Jno. Buckner, jr.," etc. £32 12s. curr. Catesby Woodford, Henry Woodford, Jno. Chew. July 18, 1776.

May 16, 1776. Jno. Rootes of Gloucester Co., Gent., to Jno. Welch of Fredksbg. £15 curr. Lot 212 in town of Fredksbg. Witnesses, Thos. Walker, Robt. Scott, Thos. Anderson. Augt. 15, 1776.

Feby. 24, 1776. Peter Stubblefield and Margaret, his wife, of Spts. Co. to John Tankersley of same Co. £190 curr. 150 a. in Spts. Co. Ambrose Dudley, Jno. Apperson, Stapleton Crutchfield, Jacob Whitler. Sept. 19, 1776.

Sept. 18, 1776. Jno. Holloday and Elizabeth, his wife, of Spts. Co. to Jno. Tankersley of same Co. £250 curr. 299 a. in Berkeley Par., Spts. Co. Witnesses, Robt. Chew, Edward Herndon, Thos. Megee, jr.; Jno. Holloday, jr.; J. Lewis. Sept. 19, 1776.

Sept. 19, 1776. Philip Day and Franky, his wife, of Spts. Co. to Clayton Coleman of sd. Co. £70 curr. 122 a. in Berkeley Par., Spts. Co. No witnesses. Sept. 19, 1776.

July 22, 1776. Wm. Sandidge and Elizabeth, his wife, of Albemarle Co.; David Sandidge and Ann, his wife, of Spts. Co., and Charles Powell and Sarah, his wife, to Clayton Coleman of Spts. Co. £80 12s. 6d. curr. 115 a. in Spts. Co. Anthony Gholston, Jos. Gholston, Rd. Bishop. Sept. 19, 1776.

Oct. 6, 1775. Jno. Holloday, jr., of Spts. Co. to Benjamin Johnston of Culpeper Co. £100 curr. 325 a. in Spts. Co., etc. Jos. Brock, Robt. Thomas, Wm. Houston. No date of Record.

March 18, 1774. Ewen Clements of Tappahannock, Essex Co., and Ann, his wife, to Wm. Hunter of Spts. Co. and Sarah, his wife. 5s. curr. Lots 1 and 2 in town of Fredksbg., formerly in Allans Town, etc. Thos. Moore, Henry Clements, Mace Clements, Chs. Yates, Jno. Meals, Geo. Thornton. Decr. 19, 1776.

Jany. 2, 1775. Geo. Mitchell of Spts. Co., Mercht., of the first part; Thomas Colson and Frances, his wife, of same Co., of the second part, to Robt. Jardine, late of City of London, now of Spts. Co., Mercht., of third part. Whereas, sd. Mitchell on Oct. 18, 1770, as factor for the sd. Jardine, purchased of Thos. Colson, half a lot, etc., in town of Fredksbg., and for conveniency took a conveyance in his own name, as the sd. deed recorded in Spts. Co. Court, Nov. 15, 1770, and whereas, the sd. Mitchell, on March 20, 1771, sold and conveyed part of the sd. lot to Jno. Atkinson of Fredksbg., and whereas, the sd. Mitchell, having given up his factorship, and the sd. Jardine being now in Colony and being desirous of having a legal title in that part of the lot purchased of sd. Colson which remains after sd. sale, etc., to the intent sd. Jardine may have a clear title, etc., this conveyance is made, etc. Witnesses, Jas. Mercer, Jno. Munro, Jno. Atkinson. Decr. 19, 1776.

May 18, 1775. Wm. Thompson and Sarah, his wife, of Culpeper Co. to Edwd. Vass of sd. Co. £125 curr. Lot 275 in town of Fredksbg. No witnesses. May 18, 1775.

Decr. 6, 1776. Wm. Thompson and Sarah, his wife, of Culpeper Co. to Lewis Willis of Fredksbg., Esqr. £205 11s. 6d. curr. 60 a. in Spts. Co., adj. Fredksbg., which was conveyed the sd. Thompson by James Harford of Bristol, and Revd. Jno. Dixon. Witnesses, Edwd. Carter, Jno. Hardia, Thos. Powell, Robt. Yates. Decr. 19, 1776.

Septr. 28, 1776. James Redd of Spts. Co. to his son, Allen Redd, of sd. Co. Deed of Gift. 111 a. in St. Geo. Par., Spts. Co., purchased of Francis Turnley, etc. Witnesses, Wm. Wood, Wm. Crane, Jno. Hensley, Mordacai Redd. Dec. 19, 1776.

—— ——, 177—. Wm. x Perry of Spts. Co., planter, and Sapphira, his wife, to Jane and Elizabeth Jarrell of sd Co. £40. 100 a. in Berkeley Par., Spts. Co. No witnesses. Decr. 19, 1776.

Decr. 19, 1776. Michael Robinson of Spts. Co. to Michael Robinson, Junr., of sd. Co. Deed of Gift. 198 a. in Spts. Co. Decr. 19, 1776.

Decr. 18, 1776. Peyton Smith of Spts. Co. to his son, Robert Smith. In consideration of the sum of £4 curr. to the sd. Peyton Smith and Ann, his wife, to be pd. yearly, etc. Four negroes. Witnesses, Jos. Brock, Wm. P. Thurston, David Hanson, and Jos. Brock, jr. Decr. 19, 1776.

Augt. 16, 1776. Thomas May of Surry, in North Carolina, to Daniel Branham of Spts. Co. £100 curr. 264 a. in Spts. Co. Witnesses, Robt. Smith, Henry Gatewood, jr.; James Pritchett, Jos. Brock, Jno. Brock, Jos. Brock, jr.; Jno. Schooler, Jno. Harrison, Thos. Crutcher, Anthony Crutcher, Thos. Crutcher, jr.; Thos. Sharp. Decr. 19, 1776.

Jany. 7, 1777. George Atkinson of Spts. Co. and Martha, his wife, to Jno. Holloday, jr., and Jno. Wiglesworth, both of afsd. Co. "For the love and friendship they have and do bear the sd. Wiglesworth and Holloday," etc., and for the trusts hereafter named. All lands, slaves, personal estate of the sd. Atkinson, in trust for them during their lives, and after their deaths, a slave, for the use of Betty Penn, wife of Geo. Penn of Spts. Co., etc. The sd. Holloday and Wiglesworth discharging a debt now due from sd. Atkinson to Thomas Colson, etc. Witnesses, Larkin Chew, O. Towles, Jno. Smith, Robt. Thomas. Jany. 16, 1777.

Novr. 20, 1776. Robert x Shepherd and Sarah, his wife, George Shepherd and Mary, his wife, of Spts. Co. to Benjamin Holloday of Co. afsd. £54 curr. 108 a. in Spts. Co. Chs. Yates, Edwd. Herndon, Jno. Chew, jr.; Anthony Gholston, Clayton Coleman, Jno. Herndon, Jno. Holloday, jr. Jany 16, 1777.

Jany. 14, 1777. Gawin Corbin of Spts. Co. to John Wright of sd. Co. Lease. 454 a. in Berkeley Par., Spts. Co. "Sd. Jno. Wright, Rosamond Wright, and Winfield Wright," etc. £22 14s. yearly. Jas. Marye, Jos. Brock, Geo. Thornton, Danl. Branham, Jno. Williams, Senr.; Jno. Chew. Jany. 16, 1777.

Jany. 14, 1777. Gawin Corbin of Spts. Co. to Col. Lewis Willis of same Co. Lease. 300 a. in Berkeley Par., Spts. Co. "Sd. Lewis Willis, Henry Willis, Wm. Champe Willis," etc. £15. Jas. Marye, Jos. Brock, Geo. Thornton, Danl. Branham, Jno. Chew, Jno. Williams, jr. Jany. 16, 1777.

March 17, 1777. Francis x Wisdom of Spts. Co. and Sarah, his wife, to Thos. Wisdom of same Co. 1 shill. 100 a. on Plentiful Run in Spts. Co. Edwd. Collins, Benj. Quinn, Benj. Davis. March 20, 1777.

March 20, 1777. Isaac Willson and Margaret, his wife, of Culpeper Co. to Wm. Lewis Seaman (or Leaman). £150 curr. 174 a. in St. Geo. Par., Spts. Co., purchased of Wm. Fitzhugh, Esqr. No witnesses. March 20, 1777.

Feby. 17, 1777. Wm. Williams and Lucy, his wife, of Culpeper Co. to Wm. Reid of Fredksbg. £5 curr. Lot 195 in town of Fredksbg. Robt. Patton, Churchill Jones, James Somerville, D. Jameson, jr. March 20, 1777.

Jany. 1, 1777. Alexander Spotswood of New Post, Spts. Co., po. of atto., to James Lewis (present steward of the sd. Spotswood). Witnesses, Chas. Washington, Willm. Smith, Michael Robinson. March 21, 1777.

July 18, 1776. Wm. Houston of Spts. Co. to John Carter, Gent. £41 curr. Mortgage. 4 slaves. Witnesses, Jos. Brock, Jno. Brock. March 21, 1777.

Decr. 9, 1776. Isaac Head (son of Alexander Spence Head), of Spts Co., apprentices himself to Wm. x Hudson of same Co., Blacksmith. Witnesses, Jos. Brock, Alexr. Spence Head, David Hanson. March 21, 1777.

Decr. 7, 1776. Alexander Spotswood, Esqr., to James Hutcherson. Lease. 200 acres in St. Geo. Par., Spts. Co. "Sd. James Hutcherson, Peggy Hutcherson, and his son, Archibald Hutcherson," etc. 1000 lbs. tob. James Lewis, Jno. Meals, Willm. Smith. March 21, 1777.

Feby. 20, 1777. David Blair to George Muir. £150 ster. Lot 247 in town of Fredksbg., bought at sale of Estate of Roger Dixon, etc. No witnesses. March 21, 1777.

March 21, 1777. Benjamin Waldin and Lucy, his wife, of Spts. Co. to Christian Rife of sd. Co. £12. 20 a. in Spts. Co. No witnesses. March 21, 1777.

March 17, 1777. Jno. Carthrae and Mary, his wife, of Spts. Co. to Jno. Apperson of afsd. Co. £250 curr. 322 a. in Berkeley Par., Spts. Co., whereon sd. Carthrae lives, etc. Stapleton Crutchfield, Geo. Arnold, Vincent Vass. April 17, 1777.

Decr. 3, 1776. Jno. Waller of Spts. Co. and Elizabeth, his wife, to Sarah Wiglesworth of Spts. Co. £80 curr. 94 a. in Spts. Co., purchased of John Hall, etc. Witnesses, John Smith, Jos. Duerson, Jas. Wiglesworth, Senr. April 17, 1777.

April 17, 1777. Richard Quinn of Culpeper Co. to Benjamin Quinn of Spts. Co. 1 shill. curr. 500 a. in St. Geo. Par., Spts. Co. No witnesses. April 17, 1777.

Octr. 8, 1776. W. Dawson to Jno. Carthrae and Robt. Stubblefield, to indemnify them, they being sd. Dawson's security on a bond to Thomas Towles for £200 curr., etc. Tract of land in Spts. Co., purchased of sd. Towles, etc. Witnesses, George Arnold, Harry Stubblefield. April 17, 1777.

April 18, 1777. Michael Robinson of Spts. Co. to his son, Wm. Robinson, of same Co. Deed of Gift. 324 a. in Spts. Co. No witnesses. April 18, 1777.

April 18, 1777. Lawrence x Young of Spts. Co. and Margaret, his wife, to Christian Rife of Co. afsd. £80 curr. 180 a. in St. Geo. Par., Spts. Co. No witnesses. April 18, 1777.

March 22, 1775. John Spotswood and Sarah, his wife, of Spts. Co. to Benjamin Johnston of Culpeper Co. £50. Lots 57 and 58 in town of Fredksbg., of which sd. Spotswood became possessed under the will of his father, John Spotswood, Esqr., Decd., etc. Witnesses, James Hackley, Mary Campbell, Uriah Edwards. April 18, 1777.

Novr. 6, 1776. Robert Chew of Spts. Co. to Elizabeth Mitcham. Lease. 100 a. in Spts. Co. £5 yearly. Jos. Brock, Nathan Hawkins, Thos. Bartlett, Jno. Collins, Jno. Schooler. May 15, 1777.

May 15, 1777. Ignatius Tureman (heir at law of Gèo. Tureman, Decd.), and Eleanor, his wife, of Spts. Co. to Thomas Jenkins of same Co. £75 curr. 150 a. in Spts. Co. No witnesses. May 15, 1777.

May 15, 1777. Wm. Arnold and Mary, his wife, of Spts. Co. to Jno. Crawford of Hanover Co. £85 curr. 160 a. in Spts. Co. No witnesses. May 15, 1777.

May 14, 1777. John Simpson, jr., to Jinkins Haney, both of Spts. Co. Lease. 75 a. in St. Geo. Par., Spts. Co., part of land sd. Simpson holds under lease from Alexr. Spotswood, etc. £5 curr. yearly. No witnesses. May 15, 1777.

May 15, 1777. Alexander Spence Head of Spts. Co. to his son, Henry Head, of the sd. Co. Deed of Gift. 100 a. in Spts. Co. No witnesses. May 15, 1777.

May 15, 1777. Benj. x Walden and Lucy, his wife, of Spts. Co. to Benj. McCoy of sd. Co. £55 curr. 72 a. in Spts. Co. No witnesses. May 15, 1777.

April 21, 1777. Wm. Woodford of Caroline Co. and Joseph Jones of King George Co. to George Thornton of Spts. Co. £550. ⅓ interest in Lots Nos. 254, 264 and 272 in town of Fredksbg., "which sd. Woodford and Jones purchased from the late Benjamin Grymes and his trustees," etc., as by Deeds Nov. 11, 1772, and having erected a brewery thereon, have agreed to admit the sd. Thornton a partner, etc. Witnesses, Chas. Washington, Jas. Hunter, jr.; Fran. Taliaferro, Jas. Allan, Jno. Julian, Jno. Legg, Benj. Taylor. May 15, 1777.

April 7, 1777. Wm. Houston of Spts. Co. to Elisha Dickenson of same Co. £200 curr. A negro blacksmith (slave), his tools, etc. Saml. Hildrup, James Williams, Rob. Sharpe. May 15, 1777.

Feby. 22, 1777. John Hensley of St. Geo. Par., Spts. Co., "for love and affection I have and do bear unto Hannah Wood of Par. and Co. afsd." To the sd. Hannah Wood and Nancy Dudley Wood, her daughter, all estate, real and personal, after death of sd. Hensley, etc. Witness, Wm. Wood. May 15, 1777.

March 10, 1777. Wm. Hunter and Sarah, his wife, of Orange Co. to George Thornton of Fredksbg. £440 curr. Lots 1 and 2 in the plot of Fredksbg., formerly Allans Town, etc. No witnesses. May 15, 1777.

May 1, 1777. Jno. Thos, Gwillim, apprentices himself to James Wallace of Fredksbg., Shoe Maker. Witnesses, Wm. Jenkins, Jas. x Slaven. May 15, 1777.

June 18, 1777. Fielding Lewis and Betty, his wife, of Spts. Co. to George Thornton of Fredksbg. £175 curr. Lot of land in Fredksbg., etc. No witnesses. June 19, 1777.

March 31, 1777. David Woodroof and Rachael, his wife, and Richd. Owen and Ann, his wife, of Spts. and Caroline Counties to George Cook of Spts. Co. £100 curr. 220 a. in Spts. Co. Fielding Woodroof, Robt. Chewning, Jno. Hackney, jr.; Nicholas Lewis. June 19, 1777.

June 19, 1777. Peyton Smith and Wm. Robinson of Spts. Co., deed of gift to Ann and Dorothy Peyton Robinson, daughters of the sd. Wm. Robinson, etc. Seven negroes. "After the death of sd. Wm. Robinson and Sarah, his wife," etc. Witnesses, Robt. Smith, Benja. Ballard, Hezekiah Ellis, Jno. Wigglesworth. June 19, 1777.

Feby. 20, 1777. James x Peterson of Spts. Co. and Ann, his wife, to James Stevenson of sd. Co. £70 curr. 74½ a. in Spts. Co. Benj. Holloday, Senr.; Jos. Holloday, Senr.; Lewis Holloday, Jno. Chew, jr.; Edwd. Herndon, Robt. Chew. June 19, 1777.

March 19, 1777. Charles Yates of Fredksbg. to Fielding Lewis of Spts. Co., Esqr. £27 10s. curr. Lot No. 11 in town of Fredksbg. No witnesses. June 19, 1777.

May 2, 1777. Daniel Branham and Susanna, his wife, of Spts. Co. to Gawin Corbin of Caroline Co., Esqr. £165 curr. 264 a. in Spts. Co. Jos. Brock, Robt. Smith, Thos. Colson, Aaron Dinney, Jno. Chew. June 19, 1777.

July 17, 1777. Fielding Lewis of Fredksbg., Esqr., and Betty, his wife, to James Cunningham. £20. Lot 127 in town of Fredksbg., formerly sold Henry Reeves and at his request conveyed to sd. Cunningham, no previous conveyance having been made, etc. No witnesses. July 17, 1777.

April 11, 1776. George Stubblefield of Spts. Co., Gent., to John Carnochan of same Co. Lease. 25 a. in Spts. Co., etc. Witnesses, Vincent Vass, Rice Vass, W. Dawson, Harry Stubblefield, Robt. Stubblefield. Sept. 18, 1777.

June 21, 1777. James Nelson and Susannah, his wife, of Spts. Co. to Wm. Nelson of sd. Co. £145. 451 a. in Spts. Co. Jos. Willoughby, Jno. Sanders, Jno. White, Wm. Mastin, Thos x Jenkins. Sept. 18, 1777.

June 21, 1777. Wm. Nelson and Elizabeth, his wife, and James Nelson and Susanna, his wife, of Spts. Co. to Thomas Sharp of same Co. £80 curr. 225 a. in Spots. Co. Jos. Willoughby, Jno. Sanders, Jno. White, Wm. Mastin, Thos. x Jenkins. Septr. 18, 1777.

July 25, 1777. James Crawford and Mary, his wife, of Berkeley Par., Spts. Co. to Peter Stubblefield of Par. and Co. afsd. £195 5s. 201 a. in Spts. Co., etc. Thomas Towles, Edwd. Herndon, Jno. Apperson, Sept. 18, 1777.

Sept. 18, 1777. Thos. Wisdom of Spts. Co. and Martha, his wife, to Jno. Pattey of Caroline Co. £80 curr. 100 a. in Berkeley Par., Spts. Co. No witnesses. Sept. 18, 1777.

Sept. 6, 1777. Thos. Megee, Jr., of Spts. Co. and Mary, his wife, to Jno. Holloday, Senr., of same Co. £90 curr. 210 a. in Berkeley Par., Spts. Co. No witnesses. Septr. 18, 1777.

Sept. 2, 1777. Edward Vass and Jane, his wife, of Culpeper Co. to James Somerville of Fredksbg., Spts. Co. £350 curr. Lot 275 in town of Fredksbg. John Meals, Wm. Wiatt, James Allan, Richd. Waugh. Sept. 18, 1777.

Feby. 17, 1777. Alexander Spotswood, Esqr., to Wm. Jones. Lease. 642 a. in Orange Co. "Wm. Jones, Betty Jones, and Churchill Jones," etc. £30 curr. yearly. Wm. Stanard, Wm. Smith, Jas. Lewis. Sept. 18, 1777.

May 18, 1777. John Minor and Elizabeth, his wife, of Caroline Co. to Garrett Minor of Louisa Co. £566 5s. curr. 906 a. on N. fork Northanna River in Spts. Co., etc. Eliza Fontaine, Jane Cosby, Peter Minor, Jos. Herndon, Jas. Lewis, Wm. Lewis. Sept. 18, 1777.

Sept. 18, 1777. Wm. Trigg and Ann, his wife, of Spts. Co. to Samuel Gibson of same Co. £34 curr. 68 a. in Spts. Co. No witnesses. Sept. 18, 1777.

Sept. 18, 1777. Wm. Trigg and Ann, his wife, of Spts. Co. to Jeremiah Wilson of King Geo. Co. £31 17s. 6d. 51 a. in Berkeley Par., Spts. Co. No witnesses. Sept. 18, 1777.

Sept. 18, 1777. James Kirby, son of Mary Kirby, now of Stafford Co., apprentices himself to John Green of Fredksbg., Saddler. No witnesses. Sept. 18, 1777.

May 3, 1777. Alexander Spotswood, Esqr., to Jno. Simpson. Lease. 120 a. in St. Geo. Par., Spts. Co. 680 lbs. tob. yearly. Richd. Jones,

Henry Head, Jos. Brock, jr.; Wm. Clayton, Robt. Frank, Danl. Branham. Octr. 16, 1777.

July 26, 1777. Thomas Brown of Falmouth, Stafford Co., to Alexander Kennady of Fredksbg. £300 curr., etc. Mortgage. Lots 73 and 74 in town of Fredksbg., etc. Dorothy Johnston, Ann Benger, Edwd. Simpson. Octr. 16, 1777.

April 12, 1777. James Heslop of Whitehaven, Gt. Britain, and James Blair of Fredksbg., Va., Merchts. and Partners, to Charles Yates of Fredksbg., Mercht. £250 ster. Lot 273 in town of Fredksbg., etc. Gec. Muir, A. Buchanan, Jas. Taylor, Wm. Porter, Jno. Meals. Oct. 16, 1777.

Oct. 15, 177—. Wm. Chapman of Culpeper Co. and Benjamin Chapman of Spts. Co., Execrs. of the estate of John Chapman of Spts. Co., Decd., to Francis Turnley of Spts. Co. £28 curr. 70 a. in Spts. Co., part of a larger tract left by the sd. Jno. Chapman, Decd. (in his will recorded in Spts. Co. Court), to be sold, etc. Witness, Jno. Hume. Oct. 16, 1777.

Oct. 14, 1777. Wm. Chapman of Culp. Co., Executor of Jno. Chapman, Decd., to Benja. Chapman of Spts. Co. £227 5s. curr. 303 a. in Spts. Co., etc. Witnesses, Jno. Hume, Francis Turnley. Oct. 16, 1777.

Oct. 16, 1777. Wm. Chapman of Culpeper Co., Benjamin Chapman of Spts. Co., James Chapman of Roan (Rowan?) Co., N. C., to John Carter of Spts. Co. £153 15s. curr. 205 a. in Spts. Co., etc. No witnesses. Oct. 16, 1777.

Oct. 16, 1777. Wm. Chapman of Culpeper Co. and Benjamin Chapman of Spts. Co., Execrs. of the estate of Jno. Chapman of Spts. Co., Decd., to John Carter of Spts. Co. £313 10s. curr. 425 a. in Spts. Co. No witnesses. Oct. 16, 1777.

Augt. 4, 1777. John Simpson, jr., of Spts. Co. to Henry Gatewood, the Younger, of sd. Co. Lease. 75 a. in St. Geo. Par., Spts. Co. £20 yearly. Joseph Brock, Wm. Clayton, Jno. Schooler. Novr. 20, 1777.

Novr. 12, 1777. James x Jones of Spts. Co., deed of gift to his grandson, Gabriel Jones, the son of Richard Jones, etc. A negro slave. Witnesses, Henry Gatewood, jr.; Reuben Hortor, Richd. Jones. Novr. 20, 1777.

Novr. 20, 1777. Thos. White and Elizabeth, his wife, of Stafford Co. to John West of same Co. £60 curr. 91 a. in Spts. Co. No witnesses. Novr. 20, 1777.

Novr. 20, 1777. Wm. x Payn and Catherine, his wife, of Berkeley Par., Spts. Co. to Jeremiah Wilson of sd. Par. and Co. £75 curr. 100 a., purchased by Jno. Payn of Thos. Colson, and conveyed to his son, the sd. Wm. Payn, etc. No witnesses. Novr. 20, 1777.

Novr. 10, 1777. Lydia x Arnold of Spts. Co. and Wm. Arnold and Susannah, his wife, of Louisa Co. to Henry Pendleton, jr., of Spts. Co. £30 curr. 50 a. in Berkeley Par., Spts. Co., whereon Wm. Arnold, Decd., lived, and devised by him to his son, Wm., etc. Witnesses, Jno. Daniel, Thos. Coleman, jr.; Wm. Phillips, Wm. Pain, Wm. Trigg. Novr. 20, 1777.

July 25, 1777. Alexander Kennedy of Fredksbg. and Ann, his wife, to Thomas Brown of Falmouth, Stafford Co. £400. ½ of Lot No. 74 in town of Fredksbg. Witnesses, Dorothy Johnston, Ann Benger, Edwd. Simpson. Novr. 20, 1777.

May 16, 1778. "Alexander Spotswood of 'New Post,' Spts. Co., Province of Va., Esqr., grandson and h. at law of Butler Spotswood, decd., late wife of Alexander Spotswood, late of Va., afsd. Esqr., decd., and which sd. Butler was one of the four daughters and co-heiresses of Richd. Brayne, late of St. Margarets Par., City of Westminster, Gent., and Anne, his wife, before her marriage called Anne Begnold, Spinster, sometime before and on the 14th Feby., 1775, entitled to lands in the Manors of Greenshall [or Grunshall] Tower hill and Grunshall Netty in Co. Surry, Eng., and in Manor of High Cheer in Co. Berks, in Eng., willing to sell the same, for that purpose made Chas. Mortimer of Fredksbg., Spts. Co., Va., Doctor of Physic, Jno. Hopkins of Paternoster Row, London, Druggist, and Christopher Taddy of same place, Druggist, my true and lawful attorneys," etc., etc. Mentions certain deeds of lease and release made by him, the sd. Spotswood and Elizabeth, his wife, to the sd. Attorneys, for the better perfecting of the sale of the sd. lands, "and whereas, by the advice of the sd. Attorneys, he the sd. Spotswood, did further appt. Thos. Frost, the younger, Yoeman, and James Estone, Cordwainer, both of Shierre, in Co. Surry, Eng., his attorneys, and also appt. Wm. Bray of Gt. Russell Street in St. Geo. Par., Bloomsbury, Middlesex, Esqr., and Richd. Bullock of Cross Street in St. James Par., Westminster, Gent., etc., etc., and whereas, the troubles then existing between Gt. Britain and America interrupted all intercourse, etc., by these several powers of atto., might be affected, etc., during the suspension of Government, etc. Robt. Jardine now of Fredksbg., Va., Mercht., formerly of New Bond Street in London, etc., agreed to purchase all the lands afsd. of the sd. Spotswood for the consideration of £1989 curr. of Va. The sd. Spotswood hereby conveys the sd. lands to the sd. Jardine, etc., etc. No witnesses. May 21, 1778.

Feby. 15, 1776. "Alexander Spotswood of Newpost, Spts. Co., Va., Esqr., grandson and heir at law of Butler Spotswood, decd., late wife of Alexander Spotswood, late of Va., Esqr., decd., which sd. Butler was one of the four daughters and co-heirs of Richd. Brayne, late of St. Marys Par., City of Westminster, Gent., and Ann, his wife," etc., etc., po. of atto., to Wm. Bray of Gt. Russell Street, St. Geo. Par., Bloomsberry, in Co. Middlesex, Esqr., and Richd. Bullock of Cross St., St. James Par., Westminster, Gent., etc., etc., to appear at the next subsequent General or Special Court Baron held for the Manor of High Cheer in Co. Berks., to pray and procure that he be admitted tenant to all part or parts of Lands, tenements, etc., held in Manor of High Cheer as he the sd. Spotswood is entitled to as Grandson, etc., of sd. Butler Spotswood and as nephew and heir at law of Diana Brayne and Ann Brayne, late of St. Margaret's Par., Westminster, afsd., Decd., two other daughters and co-heiresses of sd. Richd. Brayne and Ann, his wife, etc., etc., etc. No witnesses. May 21, 1778.

Feby. 15, 1776. Alexander Spotswood, etc., co-heir at law of Diana Brayne, late of St. Margaret's Par., Westminster, Spinster, one of the four daughters, etc., of Richard Brayme of same place, Gent., and Ann, his wife, daughter and sole heir of James Begnold, heretofore of Shierre,

Co. Surry, Gent., and Anne, his wife, pos. of atto., to Thomas Frost, the younger of Shierre, afsd. Yoeman, and Jas. Elstone of same place, Cordwainer, etc., etc. etc. No witnesses. May 21, 1778.

Septr. 26, 1777. Wm. and Mary Champe of Culpeper Co. to David Pulliam of Spts. Co. £20 curr. 400 a. in Spts. Co. Francis Thornton, Geo. Thornton, Jno. Meals, Chas. Washington, Jas. Tutt, Jno. McCalley. April 16, 1778.

Augt. 9, 1775. Archibald Cary and Richard Randolph, Esqrs., surviving Executors of Honble. Peter Randolph, late of Chatsworth, Henrico Co., Esqr., Decd., to Walker Taliaferro of Caroline Co. £800. 2000 a. Whereas, Benj. Grymes of Spts. Co., Gent., was seized of 2000 a. in St. Geo. Par., Spts. Co. (which was devised him by the last will and testament of his father, The Honble. John Grymes, Esqr., Decd.), and did by indenture Augt. 30, 1755, mortgage the same to the sd. Peter Randolph, now decd., to indemnify him for having become the sd. Grymes' security on bond to Honble. Wm. Nelson and Thomas Nelson, Esqrs., etc., and whereas, the sd. Benj. Grymes, having failed to meet the obligations of the sd. bond, etc., the sd. Randolph having met the same and since died, and by his will appointing the sd. Cary and Randolph, his executors, etc., and whereas, by Decree of Spts. Co. Court April 19, 1771, by which decree and arrangements the mortgage having been foreclosed, the sd. Cary and Randolph, dispose of the sd. tract of land, etc. Witnesses, Mann Page, jr.; Wm. Fitzhugh, Geo. Stubblefield. April 16, 1778.

Dec. 16, 1777. John Harrison and Mary, his wife, of Spts. Co. to Charles Yates of Fredksbg., Mercht. £600 curr. 671 a. whereon sd. Harrison lives, in St. Geo. Par., Spts. Co. Jos. Brock, Robt. Chew, Thos. Crutcher, Jno. Brock, Jos. Brock, jr.; Saml. Estes. April 16, 1778.

Decr. 18, 1777. Peter Taliaferro and Ann, his wife, to Thos. Allen of Spts. Co. £60. Lots 196 and 198 in town of Fredksbg., purchased of Jno. Waller, jr., etc. April 16, 1778.

Feby. 26, 1778. Thos. Blanton and Jane, his wife, of Spts. Co. to Wm. Porter of Fredksbg. £425 curr. Two tracts in St. Geo. Par., Spts. Co., one cont. 245 a., purchased of Alexander Hawkins and Mary, his wife, and Benj. Martin, etc.; the other cont. 100 a. and purchased of Jno. Rogers, etc. Jno. Julian, Ambrose Dudley, James Owen. April 16, 1778.

July 4, 1775. George Mitchell to Robt. Jardine of Fredksbg. £90 curr. 150 a. in St. Geo. Par., Spts. Co., purchased of Jno. Simpson, jr., as by deed, April 20, 1774. Witnesses, Jno. Atkinson, Jas. Brown, Jno. Munro. April 16 1778.

March 21, 1778. Moonin x Coker apprentices herself to Jno. Welch of Fredksbg. Test, Richd. Lucas, Jno. Davis. April 16, 1778.

April 2, 1777. Peter x Lucas of Fredksbg. binds out his son, Fielding Lucas, to Edwd. Simpson of Fredksbg., Saddler, to be taught the trade, etc. Witnesses, James Brown, Jno. Willis. April 16, 1778.

April 16, 1778. Richard Lucas of Fredksbg. binds out his son, Samuel Lucas, to Edward Simpson of Fredksbg., Saddler, to be taught the trade, etc. No witnesses. April 16, 1778.

April 16, 1778. Jacob x Young of Fredksbg. binds out his son, Jacob Young, to Edwd. Simpson of Fredksbg., Saddler, to be taught the trade, etc. No witnesses. April 16, 1778.

Novr. 4, 1777. Shadrack Moore and Ann, his wife, of Spts. Co. to Gawin Moore of sd. Co. £60 curr. 178 a. in St. Geo. Par., Spts. Co. No. witnesses. May 21, 1778.

Novr. 4, 1777. Richard Gatewood of Amherst Co. to Lewis Craig of Spts. Co. £156 curr. 233 a. in Spts. Co. Wm. Mastin, Jno. Saunders, Charles Saunders, Jno. Frazer. May 21, 1778.

Decr. 13, 1777. Tabitha x Gatewood, widow, and x John Holloday, widower, to Wm. x Gholson. Deed their estates to the sd. Gholson, in trust for the use of the Gatewood and Holloday, etc. Witnesses, Jno. True, Anne Stevens, Fredk. Gholson. May 21, 1778.

May 21, 1778. Alexander Spotswood, Esqr., to Benjamin Miller. Lease, 150 a. in St. Geo. Par., Spts. Co. "Sd. Benj. Miller and Margaret, his wife, and his son, Benjamin Miller," etc. 800 lbs. tob. yearly. No witnesses. May 21, 1778.

May 21, 1778. Alexander Spotswood, Esqr., to Jno. Drake. Lease 100 a. in St. Geo. Par., Spts. Co. "James Drake and Winnifred, his wife, and Thos. Drake," etc. 600 lbs. tob. yearly. No witnesses. May 21, 1778.

May 21, 1778. Alexander Spotswood, Esqr., to Geo. W. Spooner. Lease. 104 a. in St. Geo. Par., Spts. Co. "Geo. W. Spooner and Sarah, his wife, and Geo. Wm. B. Spooner," etc. 616 lbs. tob. yearly. No witnesses. May 21, 1778.

May 21, 1778. Alexander Spotswood, Esqr., to John Simpson. Lease. 107 a. in St. Geo. Par., Spts. Co. "John Simpson, his wife, Frances, and his uncle, Francis," etc. 628 lbs. tob. yearly. No witnesses. May 21, 1778.

May 21, 1778. Alexander Spotswood, Esqr., to Jno. Wharton. Lease. 112 a. in St. Geo. Par., Spts. Co. "Jno. Wharton, Jno. Schooler, and Samuel Schooler," etc. 648 lbs. tob. yearly. No witnesses. May 21, 1778.

May 21, 1778. Alexander Spotswood, Esqr., to Henry Head. Lease. 200 a. in St. Geo. Par., Spts. Co. "Henry Head and Mary, his wife, and his son, Wm. Head," etc. £15 curr. yearly. No witnesses. May 21, 1778.

Feby. 23, 1778. Alexander Kennedy of King and Queen Co. and Ann, his wife, to Thomas Brown of Fredksbg. £350 curr. Moiety of Lots 73 and 74 in town of Fredksbg. Witnesses, James Somerville, Geo. Muir, Neil McCoull. May 21, 1778.

Decr. 31, 1777. Wm. McWilliams, Senr., "to my kinsman, Wm. McWilliams, Junr.," of Spts. Co. Deed of Gift. 300 a. in Spts. Co. as by pat. granted Wm. McWilliams, Senr., adj. the plantations of Nathl. Stephens, Benja. McWilliams, Thos. Minor, and James Red, etc. Witnesses, Thos. Brown, Jno. Dalton, Robt. Walker. May 21, 1778.

June 18, 1778. John Wiglesworth and Philadelphia, his wife, of Spts. Co. to Harman Haner of Stafford Co. £200 curr. 125 a. in St. Geo. Par., Spts. Co. No witnesses. June 18, 1778.

June 18, 1778.　Joseph Bledsoe of St. Geo. Par., Spts. Co. and Betty, his wife, to Wm. Porter of Fredksbg., Mercht. £77 5s. curr. 51½ a. purchased by Thos. Blanton of the sd. Bledsoe, and directed by the sd. Blanton to be conveyed to the sd. Porter, etc. No witnesses. June 18, 1778.

June 15, 1778.　Lucy x Edenton of Spts. Co. to Clayton Coleman of same Co. £10 curr. 10 a. in Spts. Co. Benja. Holloday, Jos. Holloday, Jno. Chiles. June 18, 1778.

Decr. 27, 1777.　Wm. Houston of Spts. Co. and Judith, his wife, to Jno. Chew of same Co. £23 10s. curr. 23½ a. in St. Geo. Par., Spts. Co. Jno. Wiglesworth, Thos. Blanton, Thos. Megee, jr.; Jno. McCalley, Jno. Chew, jr. June 18, 1778.

May 10, 1778.　John Sanders and Jane, his wife, of Spts. Co. to Jno. Cammock of same Co. £28 curr. 32 a. in Berkeley Par., Spts. Co. Geo. Cammock, Henry x Cammock, W. Mastin. June 18, 1778.

Feby. 17, 1778.　Thomas x Haydon of Spts. Co. to his son, James Haydon. Deed of Gift. 100 a. in St. Geo. Par., Spts. Co. Lodowich Oneal, Jno. Mullikin, Jessee Haydon. June 18, 1778.

Feby. 17, 1778.　Thomas x Haydon of Spts. Co. to his son, Jessee Haydon. Deed of Gift. 95 a. in St. Geo. Par., Spts. Co. Lodowich Oneal, Jno. Mullikin, James Haydon. June 18, 1778.

Jany. 28, 1778.　Thomas x Haydon of Spts. Co. to his son, John Haydon. Deed of Gift. 154 a. in St. Geo. Par., Spts. Co. Jas. Marye, Chas. Proctor, James Haydon. June 18, 1778.

June 18, 1778.　Abraham Darnall, jr., and Mary Ann, his wife, and Abraham Darnall, Sr., and Elizabeth, his wife, of Spts. Co. to Harman Haner of Stafford Co. £100 curr. Tract of land in Spts. Co. No witnesses. June 18, 1778.

June 15, 1778.　Lewis Holloday and Betty, his wife, of Spts. Co. to Joseph Holloday of same Co. £360 curr. 180 a. on East North East River in Spts. Co. Benja. Holloday, James Holloday, Jeremiah x Holloday. June 18, 1778.

June 18, 1778.　George Shepherd and Mary, his wife, of Spts. Co. to Wm. Emerson, jr., of same Co. £75 curr. 141 a. in Berkeley Par., Spts. Co. No witnesses. June 18, 1778.

June 2, 1778.　Larkin Smith of Spts. Co., Gent., to Stapleton Crutchfield of same Co. £446 curr. 258 a. in Berkeley Par., Spts. Co. Jno. Chew, jr.; Jno. Brock, Larkin Stanard, Reuben Straughan. June 18, 1778.

June 18, 1778.　John x Keen, an orphan, of Spts. Co., apprentices himself to John Coleman of Spts. Co., Wheelwright, etc. No witnesses. June 18, 1778.

June 18, 1778.　James Somerville of Fredksbg., atto. in fact for Hugh Lenox & Co. to Jno. Epperson of Spts. Co. Whereas, Isaac Bradburn, late of sd. Co., being seized of a tract whereon he lived in Spts. Co. 75 a. Mortgaged the same to the sd. Lenox & Co., May 7, 1773, and failing to pay the debt, for which the sd. land stood security, a decree was obtained, under which the sd. land was sold to Jno. Carthrae, but before conveyance was made the sd. Carthrae arranged for the sale of the sd. land to the sd. Epperson, the sd. Somerville conveys the land in consideration of the sums of £10 curr. and £37 10s. curr. No witnesses. June 18, 1778.

June 27, 1778. Peyton Smith of Pitsylvania Co. to his brother, Robert Smith. Deed of Gift. 3 negroes. Witnesses, Jos. Brock, John Brock. July 16, 1770.

Sept. 17, 1778. Thomas x Haydon of Spts. Co. to his son, Ezekiel Haydon. Deed of Gift. 103 a. in St. Geo. Par., Spts. Co. Henry Head, Samuel Hildrup, Jno. Haydon. Septr. 17, 1778.

Augt. 19, 1778. John x Gordon of Spts. Co. and Elizabeth, his wife, to Neil McCoull of Fredksbg. £337 10s. curr. 150 a. in St. Geo. Par., Spts. Co. Jno. Chew, Rob. Frank, Wm. Gordon, Randole McDaniel, Asa x Hall. Sept. 17, 1778.

Augt. 6, 1778. Thos. Towles of Spts. Co., Gent., of first part; Larkin Smith of same Co., Gent., of second part; Oliver Towles of Co. afsd., of third part. Witnesseth, the sd. Larkin Smith (grandson of Larkin Chew, Gent., Decd.), for sum of £6 curr. pd. by Thos. Towles, and the sd. Thomas, for the sum of £100 curr. pd. by the sd. Oliver Towles, they the sd. Larkin and Thomas, do sell and convey unto the sd. Oliver, the reversion, claims, etc., which the sd. Larkin, on behalf of himself and the sd. Thomas, hath in right of his wife Mary (who is a granddaughter of the sd. Larkin Chew), of and in the slaves devised by the will of the sd. Larkin Chew, etc., except the negro boy George, etc. Witnesses, James Trigg, John Davenport. Sept. 18, 1778.

Augt. 5, 1778. Oliver Towles of Spts. Co., Gent., and Larkin Smith of same Co., Gent. Whereas, the sd. Oliver Towles is now seized and possessed of 13 slaves, etc., in right of his wife Mary, as her Dower in slaves of her former husband, John Smith., Gent., Decd., the reversion and inheritance in which are vested in the sd. Larkin Smith, eldest son and heir of the sd. Jno. Smith, etc., sd. Oliver Towles releases to the sd. Smith all dower of the sd. Mary, in 8 of the sd. slaves; the sd. Smith releases all his right in the remaining 5 slaves, also giving the sd. Towles a negro man named Cato, etc. Witnesses, Larkin Stanard, Reubin Straughan, Thos. Towles, James Trigg, Jno. Davenport. Sep. 17, 1778.

Augt. 22, 1778. Benj. Waller of Spts. Co. and Jane, his wife, to Wm. Blaydes of same Co. £150 curr. 150 a. in Spts. Co. Wm. Ball, Mary Straughan, Sarah Morris, Mary Lewis. Novr. 19, 1778.

Novr. 10, 1778. Joseph Brock and Mary Beverley, his wife, of Spts. Co. to Charles Yates of sd. Co. £225 curr. 150 a. in St. Geo. Par., Spts. Co. No witnesses. Novr. 19, 1778.

Novr. 19, 1778. Joseph x True of Spts. Co. to Lovel Perry of sd. Co. £161 curr. 100 a. in Spts. Co. No witnesses. Novr. 19, 1778.

Novr. 19, 1778. Thos. Megee, the younger, of Spts. Co. and Mary, his wife, to Reubin Massey of same Co. £60 curr. 155 a. in Berkeley Par., Spts. Co. No witnesses. Novr. 19, 1778.

Novr. 19, 1778. Alexander Spotswood, Esqr., to Robert Frank. Lease. 101 a. in St. Geo. Par., Spts. Co. "Robert Frank, Elizabeth Frank, and

Robert Frank, his sons," etc.   £5 1s. yearly.   Jas. Lewis, Jno. Meals, Willm. Smith.   Novr. 19, 1778.

Novr. 9, 1778.   Alexander Spotswood, Esqr., to James Parish.   Lease. 188 a. in St. Geo. Par., Spts. Co.   "James Parish, his wife Lucy, and his brother John Parish," etc.   £5 cash and 528 lbs. tob.   No witnesses. Novr. 19, 1778.

Novr. 9, 1778.   Geo. Wilson of Spts. Co. and Ann, his wife, to James Lewis.   £390 curr.   130 a. in St. Geo. Par., Spts. Co., purchased of Wm. Fitzhugh, Esqr., etc.   No witnesses.   Novr. 19, 1778.

Feby. 19, 1778.   Wm. Garrett, Senr., and Elizabeth, his wife, of Trinity Par., Louisa Co. to Susannah Chandler of Berkeley Par., Spts. Co. £20 curr.   100 a. in Berkeley Par., Spts. Co.   Jno. Dedman, Thos. Lane, Geo. Taylor.   Novr. 19, 1778.

Novr. 19, 1778.   John Chew, jr., of Spts. Co. to Geo. Cammack of same Co.   Whereas, Robt. Chew, Gent., Decd., in his lifetime was possessed of a tract of 336 a. of land in Spts. Co., and being so possessed made his last will and testament and thereby appointed the sd. John Chew, Jr.; Robt. Beverley Chew, and Harry Chew, Executors of the sd. will, impowering them to sell the sd. tract of land, etc., sd. Chew sells the sd. land to Cammack for the sum of £400 curr., etc.   No witnesses. Novr. 19, 1778.

Sept. 21, 1778.   Reubin Straughan of Spts. Co. and Catherine, his wife, of first part; Oliver Towles of same Co., of second part; Thomas Henderson of Culpeper Co., of third part.   Whereas, Jno. Holloday, jr., being seized of a tract of 450 a. in Spts. Co., purchased of Archibald Dick, Clerk, conveyed by Deed, Augt. 2, 1770; the sd. Jno. Holloday and Mildred, his wife, by deed, Novr. 29, 1774, did sell the sd. land to the sd. Oliver Towles, in trust, for the sd. Reuben Straughan, etc., the sd. Straughan hereby conveys the sd. land to the sd. Henderson, for the sum of £500 curr, etc.   Witnesses, Jno. x Wilson, James x Head, John Davenport.   Novr. 19, 1778.

Sept. 14, 1778.   Wm. Chiles and Agnes, his wife, of Berkeley Par., Spts. Co. to Clement Mountague of St. Geo. Par., Spts. Co.   £170 curr. 200 a. in Berkeley Par., Spts. Co., devised to Wm. Forson by Michael Guinney, Decd., etc.   Wm. Smith, Edwd. Herndon, John Smith, James Smith.   Novr. 19, 1778.

Novr. 19, 1777.   Clayton Coleman and Mary, his wife, of Spts. Co. to Benjamin Holloday of same Co.   £41 curr.   82 a. in Spts. Co.   No witnesses.   Novr. 19, 1778.

Novr. 17, 1778.   Clayton Coleman and Mary, his wife, of Spts. Co. to Leonard Waller of sd. County.   £20 curr.   184 a. in Spts. Co.   No witnesses.   Novr. 19, 1778.

Novr. 19, 1778.   Benjamin Holloday and Mary, his wife, of Spts. Co. to Clayton Coleman of same Co.   £50 curr.   101 a. in Spts. Co.   No witnesses.   Novr. 19, 1778.

Jany. 18, 1777.   Leonard James Mourning Waller of Spts. Co. to Clayton Coleman of same Co.   £323 curr.   365 a. in Berkeley Par., Spts. Co., devised by Jno. Waller, Gent., Decd., to his grandson, L. J. M. Waller, etc.   Wit-

nesses, Jas. Wiglesworth, Sr.; Benj. Waller, Jas. Wiglesworth, Jr.;
James Shakefoot, Robt. Coleman. Novr. 19, 1779.

Novr. 17, 1778. Joseph Holloday of Spts. Co. and Elizabeth, his wife,
to James Holloday of same Co. £200 curr. 100 a. in Spts. Co. Benj.
Holloday, Clayton Coleman, Joseph Holloday, jr. Novr. 19, 1778.

Augt. 5, 1778. Larkin Smith, Gent., of Spts. Co., Letter of Attorney
to Thomas Towles, Gent., etc. "Whereas, the sd. Larkin Smith, intending soon to join the Grand Continental Army in Defense of the Just
Rights of his Country," etc. Mentions several tracts of land, etc., etc.
Witnesses, Reuben Straughan, James Trigg, John Davenport. Novr. 19,
1778.

Feby. 18, 1779. Benjamin Johnston of Fredksbg. and Dorothy, his
wife, to Peter Dudley of Spts. Co. £250. 150 a. purchased of John True,
as by Deeds, Oct. 8, 1778, whereof the widow and relict of John True,
who since intermarried with Edward Kelly holds ⅓ during her life,
etc. No witnesses. Feby. 18, 1779.

Oct. 23, 1778. Wm. Houston of Spts. Co., in consideration of making
a provision for his wife Judith, deeds in trust, certain goods and chattels, to John Chew, etc. Witnesses, Jos. Brock, Thomas Colson, Jas.
Wallace. Nov. 18, 1778.

Jany. 1, 1779. Benjamin Johnston of Fredksbg. and Dorothy, his wife,
to Elizabeth Wilkerson and Mary Sullivan of same town. £6500 curr.
Lots 17.17 and 10.10 and 11.11, etc., in town of Fredksbg. No witnesses.
April 15, 1779.

April 15, 1779. Anth. Thornton, Junr., as agent for Benj. Grymes,
Gent., Trustees, binds himself to secure from Mrs. Priscilla Grymes,
her relinquishment of dower, in lots, in the town of Fredksbg., sold
unto Benja. Johnston, etc., since sold by sd. Johnston to Mrs. Sullivan
and Wilkerson, etc. "Sd. Priscilla Grymes, relict of the sd. Benj.
Grymes," etc. Witness, Wm. Johnston. April 15, 1779.

Novr. 18, 1778. John x Jenkins of Spts. Co. to Gipson Jenkins of same
Co. 1 shill. curr. 100 a. in Spts. Co. James Abbitt, Jno. Personet, Wm.
Jenkins. Novr. 19, 1778.

Novr. 18, 1778. John x Jenkins of Spts. Co. to John Personet of same
Co. £50 curr. 100 a. in Spts. Co. James Abbett, Gipson Jenkins, John
Musick. Novr. 19, 1778.

Novr. 18, 1778. Marsom x Poe of Spts. Co. to James Abbett of same
Co. £43 curr. 43 a. in Spts. Co., purchased of James Jones, etc. Witnesses, Gipson Jenkins, John Personet, Mary Poe. Novr. 19, 1779.

May 18, 1778. Robert Jardine, Mercht., in London, at this time in
Fredksbg., Spts. Co., Colony of Va. Power of Attorney to James Som-
erville of Fredksbg., Colony of Va., etc., etc. Witnesses, Alexander Blair,
David Blair, Lachlan Campbell. Nov. 19, 1778.

May 25, 1778. Benjamin Head of Orange Co. and Gracey, his wife, to
John Edwards of Spts. Co. £150 curr. 100 a. in Spts. Co. Edwd. Collins,
Uriah Edwards, jr.; Andrew Johnston, Isaac Head. Novr. 19, 1778.

May 28, 1778. John Penn of Amherst Co. to Benjamin Perry and Elizabeth Perry, his mother, of Spts. Co. £33 curr. 128 a. in Spts. Co. Wm. Smith, Thos. Lipscomb, Uriah Edwards, Henry McDaniel. Novr. 19, 1778.

Nov. 19, 1778. Benj. Waller of Spts. Co. and Rachael Arnold to Wm. Davenport of same Co. £60 curr. 18½ acres. J. Lewis, Thos. Minor, Thos. Davenport. Nov. 19, 1778.

Nov. 17, 1778. John Tankersley of Spts. Co. and Susanna, his wife, to Bennett Pemberton. £100. 48 a. in Spts. Co., bounded by lands of Chas. Pemberton, Ignatius Tureman, and Chas. Tureman's Estate, formerly purchased of Jno. Holloday, Sr., etc. Thos. Pritchett, Edwd. Herndon, Richd. Gatewood. Nov. 19, 1778.

Nov. 19, 1778. Wm. Garrett of Louisa Co. to Wm. Ball of Spts. Co. £65 curr. 300 a. in Spts. Co. No witnesses. Nov. 19, 1778.

July 17, 1778. Wm. Houston of Spts. Co. to Edwd. Simpson of Fredksbg. £425 curr. Slave. Witness, Jno. Welch. Nov. 19, 1778.

Feby. 18, 1779. Jeremiah Wilson of King Geo. Co. and Katherine, his Wife, to Wm. Trigg of Spts. Co. £33 10s. curr. 59 a. in Spts. Co. No witnesses. Feby. 18, 1779.

Jany. 10, 1779. Alexander Spotswood of Fredksbg. to his brother, John Spotswood, of Orange Co. Whereas, the sd. Jno. Spotswood is possessed of several slaves it is conjectured the sd. Alexander may be entitled to. Witnesseth, the sd. Alexander makes the sd. John, a clear title thereto, etc. Test, John Rose. Feby. 18, 1779.

Feby. 9, 1779. Mordacai Buckner and Oliver Towles of Spts. Co., Gentl., Executors of the will of Larkin Chew, Gent., Decd., of first part; Wm. x Hudson of Orange Co., of second part; John Lambert of Orange Co., of third part. Whereas, sd. Hudson having contracted formerly with one Jos. Hawkins for 120 a. of land, and being indebted to the sd. Larkin Chew, Decd., in abt. the sum of £20, did mortgage the sd. land to the sd. Chew, etc., etc., the sd. Hudson having paid the debt due the sd. Chew to his Executors, but before release was made him, the sd. Hudson agreed for the sale of sd. land to the sd. Lambert, for the sum of £20 curr. The parties hereby enter in this deed conveying the sd. land to the sd. Lambert, etc. Witnesses, Thomas Towles, Wm. Carter, Larkin Stanard, Reuben Straughan, Ano. Bartlet, Jno. Chew, jr. Feb. 18, 1779.

April 11, 1778. John Hasalgrove of Fredksbg. and Frances, his wife, to Jesse Slaven of Spts. Co. £1000. Lot 53 in town of Fredksbg., purchased of Richd. Brooke, etc. Witnesses, B. Johnston, John Richards, Jno. Jarvis. Feby. 18, 1779.

Oct. 8, 1778. John x Kelly of Granville Co., North Carolina (son and heir of Edwd. Kelly of Spts. Co., Decd.), and Nancy, his wife, to Benjamin Johnston of Fredksbg., Va. £55. 150 a. in Spts. Co., Va. "Fifty acres thereof now held by Edwd. Bryant, Sr., in right of his wife who was the widow and relict of John True, from whom the sd. Edwd. Kelly, father of the present John, purchased, which sd. Edwd. died intestate, and the sd. John, as eldest son and heir at law became proprietor thereof, save the dowers in the land, to wit., that of Sarah, the wife of Edwd.

Bryant, and Elizabeth, the wife and relict of the sd. Edward Kelly," etc., etc. Witnesses, Wm. Handley, James Brakley, Edmund Bryant, Fanny Houston. Feby. 18, 1779.

Augt. 13, 1778. Peyton Smith to his son, Robert Smith. £5 annually, etc. "During my life and his mother's," etc. Right, title, etc., of the sd. Peyton Smith in the estate of his decd. son, Charles Smith, etc. Witnesses, Joseph Brock, Henry Brock. Feby. 18, 1779.

Decr. 18, 1778. John Lewis, son of Richd. Lewis of Stafford (formerly King George Co.), to Wm. Craighill of Fredksbg. £250. Right, title, etc., in houses and lots in Fredksbg. (in possession of Edwd. Simpson, by lease from the widow of Richd. Lewis, and mother of the sd. John), expectant on the death or marriage of the sd. widow of Richard Lewis. Whereas, Richd. Lewis, father of the sd. Jno. Lewis, did by his last will and testament, among other things devise his houses and lots in Fredksbg., for the support of his wife, "during her natural life or widowhood," etc., and "afterwards to be sold and money arising therefrom equally divided among my six surviving children, vizt., John, Elizabeth, Mary, Ann, Sarah, and Hannah;" "since the death of the sd. Richard two of his daughters, Mary and Sarah, are dead, leaving no issue," etc., etc. Witnesses, B. Johnston, Thomas Allen, Jno. Hasalgrove. Feby. 18, 1779.

Novr. 21, 1778. Matthew Gale and Joseph Gale, sons of Matthew Gale, late of Spts. Co., decd., and Executors of the sd. Matthew's will; and Mary Gale, wife of Matthew Gale, and Rachael Gale, wife of Joseph Gale, etc., to Wm. Craighill of Co. afsd. £600 curr. 300 a. in Spts. Co., purchased by the sd. Matthew Gale, Decd., of Ambrose Grayson (and by the sd. Gale, in his last will and testament, dated Jany. 12, 1772, devised to his sons, the sd. Matthew and Joseph), as by deeds, May 1, 1773, etc. Witnesses, Jessey Slaven, Nathl. Craighill, Jas. Frazer, B. Johnston, Wm. Wood, Wm. Richards, Jno. Frazer, Wm. Blyth, S. Waddy, Jacob Whitler. Feby. 18, 1779.

Decr. 17, 1778. "Whereas, my husband, Matthew Gale, Decd., did by his last will will and testament dated Jany. 12, 1772, lend me all his estate, real and personal, during my natural life, and since the same did make unto my son, Joseph Gale, all his the sd. Matthew's Estate, both real and personal," etc. Signed, "Judith Gale." Witness, Wm. Wood. Recd. Feby. 18, 1779.

Feby. 11, 1777. Articles of agreement, Between Matthew Gale of Spts. Co. and Joseph Gale (his son), of the Co. afsd. Sd. Matthew Gale does make over all his estate, real and personal, to the sd. Joseph, for and during the natural lives of the sd. Matthew Gale and Judith, his wife, the sd. Joseph Gale to assume the entire management thereof, etc. Witness, Wm. Wood. Feby. 18, 1779.

—— ——, 177—. Joseph Gale and Matthew Gale of Spts. Co. to Wm. Craighill of Fredksbg. £300 curr. Tract of land leased by Ambrose Rains of Alex. Spotswood, Esqr. 200 a. as by Lease dated, March 20, 1773. Tract of 100 a. held by Aaron Denny, by lease from sd. Spotswood, lying in Orange Co., etc., etc. No witnesses. Feby. 18, 1779.

Novr. 17, 1778. Wm. McWilliams, son of Broadbent McWilliams, to Benjamin McWilliams, son of Wm. McWilliams, the Elder, of Spts. Co. £150 curr. 300 a. in Spts. Co., purchased by Wm. McWilliams, the Elder, of Wm. Tapp, and bounded by lines of John Spotswood, Decd.; Wm. Darnaby, Thos. Minor, and James Redd, etc., "and is the land given by Wm. McWilliams, the Elder, to his son, Broadbent McWilliams, during his natural life, and the fee simple estate thereof to go and descend unto Ann McWilliams, the dau. of the sd. Broadbent, etc., which sd. Broadbent is since dead, whereupon the sd. Ann became entitled, since which the sd. Ann has departed this life without leaving issue as afsd., and by counsel learned in the law, Wm. McWilliams, son of Wm. Mc-Williams of Fredksbg., who was son of Wm. McWilliams, the Elder, and own brother to the sd. Broadbent and uncle to the sd. Ann. That Wm. McWilliams, son of Wm., and cousin to the sd. Ann, has become entitled to the legal and lawful right of the sd. land, which Wm. McWilliams of Fredksbg., the Cousin, etc., has by his certain deed of gift, bearing date ——— ———, 1778, given, granted, etc., the same land unto Wm. McWilliams, the son of the sd. Broadbent, etc., the sd. Wm. McWilliams having sold the same unto his uncle the above named Benjamin McWilliams, etc., etc. Witnesses, B. Johnston, Jno. Welch, Jno. Hasalgrove, Wm. Johnston. Feby. 19, 1779.

Oct. 6, 1778. John Lewis of Spts. Co. (son of Col. Fielding Lewis of Fredksbg.), and Elizabeth, his wife, to John Craig of Spts. Co., and Elijah Craig of Orange Co. £400 curr. ⅓ of that part of the church lot in Fredksbg., ordered sold by act of the assembly, which sd. Lewis purchased from the Vestry, at the sale thereof, etc. Witnesses, Jno. Frazer, Fielding Lewis, Michael Robinson. Feby. 19, 1779.

Septr. 1, 1774. Benjamin Grymes of Spts. Co., Gent., and Priscilla, his wife, of the first part; Wm. Fitzhugh of King Geo. Co., Gent., of the second part; the Honble. John Tayloe, Esqr., and Francis Thornton, Gent., Executors of the last will and testament of Presley Thornton, Esqr., Decd., of the third part; the sd. John Tayloe, of the fourth part; Chas. Dick, Humphrey Hill, John Thornton, James Hunter, Lewis Willis, Fielding Lewis, and James Allan, seven, or any four of the Trustees, etc., of the Town of Fredksbg., of the fifth part, and Benjamin Johnston of Fredksbg., of the sixth part. Whereas, sd. Benjamin Grymes was seized in fee simple of Lots 10.10 and 11.11 in town of Fredksbg., which he purchased of Jno. Smith, who purchased them of John Grymes and Francis Willis, Esqr., Executors of the will of Henry Willis, Esqr., Decd., and was also possessed of Lot 17.17 in same town which he purchased of Robt. Jackson, who purchased the same of the sd. Executors of Henry Willis, Decd., and being so seized the sd. Grymes exchanged the part of the sd. Lot 17.17 with Roger Dixon, Gent., for part of an adj. lot No. 258, the sd. Benj. Grymes was also seized of Lots 9 and 10 between which and the Lot 17.17 a street called Wolf St. was layed off which being stopped in other parts, etc., and rendered useless, the sd. Benjamin Grymes built part of a dwelling house thereon, and by act of assembly for enlarging the towns of Fredksbg., etc., etc., the sd. Trustees, etc., were empowered to sell and convey the sd. Street lying between the sd. lots 9 and 10 and 17.17 at rate of 10 shill. for every foot, etc., between the sd. dwelling house and lots 17.17, which conveyance hath not yet been made, nevertheless the sd. Grymes, by Indenture dated Decr. 25, 1764, mortgaged, etc., the lots 17 and 10.10 and 11.11 to the sd. Presley Thornton and Wm. Fitzhugh, and whereas, the sd. Thornton and Fitzhugh, with consent of the sd. Grymes, did expose to public sale the lots 10.10 and 11.11 and 17.17 with the street adjoining, when the sd. John Tayloe became the highest bidder, etc., but before any conveyance was thereof made the sd. Thornton died, and by his will appointed the sd. Tayloe and Francis Thornton his executors, since which the sd. Tayloe hath agreed to sell the sd. premises to the sd. Benjamin Johnston, for the sum of £500 ster. All parties concerned having given their consent and join in this conveyance to the sd. Johnston, etc. Witnesses, Robert Wormeley Carter, Wm. Randolph, Alexr. Spotswood, Mann Page, jr.; Jas. Mercer, John Lewis, Wm. Wood, Jno. Walker, Jno. Chew, jr. Feby. 19, 1779.

Decr. 30, 1778. Benjamin Quinn of Spts. Co. and Frankey, his wife, to David Chevis of Caroline Co. £1250 curr. 500 a. in Berkeley Par., Spts. Co. Isaac Carrick, James Sullenger, Wm. Benson. March 18, 1779.

Novr. 18, 1779. Randal McDaniel of Spts. Co. and Jane, his wife, to Neil McCoull of same Co. £1000 curr. 138 a. in St. Geo. Par., Spts. Co., purchased of Peter Marye, who formerly purchased the same of Wm. Fitzhugh, Esqr., etc. No witnesses. Novr. 18, 1779.

Decr. 3, 1778. John Pattey of Spts. Co. and Ann, his wife, to David Chevis of Caroline Co. £321 curr. 107 a. in Spts. Co. Benjamin Quinn, Jno. Sanders, Jas. Jones, Jno. White. March 18, 1779.

Sept. 4, 1778. Ann x McWilliams of Spts. Co. to John Ward of same Co. 100 acres. Lease. £4 pr. year Witnesses, John McWilliams, James Campbell. March 18, 1779.

March 18, 1779. Benjamin Craig of Spts. Co. and Ann, his wife, to Thomas Blanton of same Co. £400 curr. 200 a. in Spts. Co., purchased of Philip Bush; also 50 a. in Spts. Co., purchased of Dudley Gatewood, etc. No witnesses. March 18, 1779.

Nov. 18, 1778. Peter Roswell and Anne, his wife, of Berkeley Par., Spts. Co. to Christopher Daniel. £30. 100 a. in Berkeley Par., Spts. Co. Benj. Quinn, John Pattie, jr.; Long Wharton. March 18, 1779.

Novr. 13, 1778. Francis x Wisdom of Spts. Co. to Valentine Long Wharton of Caroline Co. £300 curr. 400 a. in Spts. Co., bounded by lands of John White, Abraham Darnal, Benj. Quinn, and John Pattie. Witnesses, John Pattie, jr.; Peter Rosell, John White, Benj. Quinn. March 18, 1779.

Decr. 20, 1778. James Pritchett of Spts. Co. to John Wiglesworth of same County. £250 curr. 669 a. in St. Geo. Par., Spts. Co. John Brock, Jno. Chew, jr.; Jos. Brock, jr.; Sherod Horn. March 18, 1779.

Feby. 5, 1779. Oliver Towles of Spts. Co., Gent., and Mary, his wife, of first part; John Waller, K. W., of same Co., of second part; Elizabeth Towles, of third part. Whereas, sd. Oliver, being seized in fee of 770 a., called Newport, which he purchased of John Waller, Clerk; also 312 a. purchased of the Executors of Thomas Waller; and also 12 a. on N. side Robinson Run, purchased of Jno. Waller, K. W., but never had any conveyance thereof; the sd. Towles and wife, for the sum of £361 curr., con-

vey the sd. Elizabeth Towles, 250 a. of the Newport tract; 12 a. above
mentioned, and 260 a. of the tract purchased of the Executors of Thos.
Waller, etc. Witnesses, Thos. Towles, Larkin Chew, Larkin Stanard,
R. Wellford. The sd. Jno. Waller, K. W.,* conveys the sd. 12 a., etc.
March 18, 1779.

Feby. 5, 1779. Larkin Smith of Spts. Co., Gent., to Oliver Towles of
same Co., Gent. £570 curr. 460 a. in Spts. Co., etc., etc. R. Wellford,
Larkin Chew, Larkin Stanard, John Waller, K. W. March 18, 1779.

Novr. 17, 1777. Wm. Wood to John Herndon and Oliver Towles of
Spts. Co. To indemnify them for standing security on Bond of sd. Wood
to Jno. Gray & Co. "All the estate and effects . . . devised to my
wife Ann, by the will of her deceased father, John Scandland Crane except one negro," etc. Witnesses, Geo. Stubblefield, Reuben Straughan,
Jos. Herndon, etc. March 18, 1779.

Feby. 8, 1779. Oliver Towles of Spts. Co., Gent., of first part; Elizabeth Towles of same Co., of second part; Thomas Towles of same Co.,
of third part. Whereas, Oliver Towles, being seized in fee of a tract
called Newport, did out of it sell the sd. Elizabeth Towles 331 a., but
before any conveyance was made the sd. Elizabeth, she the sd. Elizabeth,
for the love and affection she bears to her son the sd. Thomas Towles,
gave the same unto him the sd. Thomas. The sd. Oliver and the sd.
Elizabeth now enter into this conveyance to the sd. Thomas, etc. Witnesses, Nicholas Payne, Henry Stevens, John Z. Lewis. March 18, 1779.

Decr. 24, 1774. Samuel Moor of Culpeper Co. and Rachael, his wife;
John Moor of Albemarle Co. and Susanna, his wife, and Robert Moor
of Augusta Co. to Oliver Towles of Spts. Co., Atto. at Law. Whereas,
Robt. Moor, late of Spts. Co., being in his lifetime seized in fee of a
certain tract of land in Spts. Co. afsd., made his last will and testament,
among other things he devised to his wife, Rosanna, all his estate, real
and personal, during her widowhood, and after her death or marriage
his land consisting of 280 a. to be divided among his three elder sons,
the sd. Samuel, John, and Robert; the sd. Samuel, soon after died, and
recently the sd. Rosanna, having died, the sd. sons have entered into
possession of the sd. land, etc., etc., sd. Moors convey to sd. Towles the
aforementioned 280 a. in Berkeley Par., Spts. Co., etc., for the sum of
£66 5s. curr. Witnesses, Lachlan Campbell, Neil McCoull, Chs. Yates,
Henry Mitchell, John Glassell, James Somerville. March 18, 1779.

March 4, 1779. Wm. Woodford of Caroline Co., Esqr., to George
Thornton of Fredksbg., and Joseph Jones of King George. Whereas, a
co-partnership recently existed between the sd. Woodford, Thornton,
and Jones, in carrying on the Brewing business in Fredksbg., under the
name of "The Fredksbg. Brewery," with slaves, stock, implements, etc.,
the sd. Thornton and Jones hath agreed to purchase the interest of the
sd. Woodford, for the sum of £3000. The sd. Woodford hereby conveys
his interest, right, etc., in Lots 254, 264 and 272 in Town of Fredksbg.,
whereon the Brewery stands, and also slaves, implements, etc. Witnesses,
Elisha Dickenson, La. Mackintosh, Thos. Walker, Benja. Day, Thos. Allen.
March 18, 1779.

*The initials K. W., were used to distinguish between John Waller of
King William Co., and John Waller of Spts. Co.

Feby. 9, 1779. Oliver Towles of Spts. Co., Gent. (intending soon to go to the City of New York, being required so to do by the Commander in Chief of the British Army), Power of Atto., "to my Friend, Thomas Towles, of Spts. Co., Gent. Mentions, slaves, lots and houses whereon Capt. George Thornton now dwells, in Fredksbg., etc. Witnesses, Pierce Perry, Larkin Stanard, Bruton x Sullivan. July 15, 1779.

April 12, 1779. Abraham Larew and Sybil, his wife, of Orange Co. to James Head of Spts. Co. £145 curr. 290 a. in Spts. Co. Danl. Branham, Nathan Pulliam, David Head, Henry Head. July 15, 1779.

Novr. 4, 1778. George Atkinson of Spts. Co. and Martha, his wife, to Thomas Allen of same Co. £306 curr. 306 a. whereon sd. Atkinson now lives, etc. Witnesses, Jno. Brock, Hy. Chew, John x Thornton, Reubin x Thornton, B. Johnston, Nathl. Craghill, Wm. Craghill, jr.; Jos. Brock, Allen Wiley, Wm. Johnston. March 18, 1779.

March 29, 1779. Thomas Allen and Mary, his wife, of Spts. Co. to James Ward of Fredksbg. £300 curr. Lot 198 in town of Fredksbg., formerly property of John Waller (since decd.), and by him conveyed to John Mitchell, and by the sd. Mitchell to Peter Taliaferro, and by the sd. Taliaferro to the sd. Thomas Allen, etc. Witnesses, B. Johnston, Nathl. Craghill, T. Waddy, Jno. Richards. April 15, 1779.

March 8, 1779. Lewis Willis and Ann, his wife, of Fredksbg. to Alexander Spotswood of sd. town. £5000. Lots 45 and 46 in town of Fredksbg., inherited by sd. Willis from his father. Lot 121 in same town, conveyed by deed, June 2, 1761, from Fielding Lewis, and lot 61, conveyed by deed, March 11, 1772, from Benj. Grymes etc. John Meals Jno. Frazer Danl. Delozur. April 15 1779.

Novr. 10, 1778. Gawin Corbin of Spts. Co. to Richard Whittle of sd. Co. Lease. 300 a. in St. Geo. Par., Spts. Co. "Sd. Richard Whittle, Delila Whittle, and Richard Whittle, junr.," etc. £15 yearly. John Chew, Thomas Lee. April 15, 1779.

March 17, 1779. Anthony Thornton, Jr., agt. for John Tayloe, Presley Thornton, Wm. Fitzhugh, Esqrs., and others, Trustees for Benjamin Grymes, Gent., Decd., having obtained on April 17, 1773, a deed of Trust from Benjamin Johnston, as security for the payment of certain sums, the sd. Johnston, having on March 12, 1779, pd. the sd. sums, the sd. lands, lots, etc., are hereby released, etc. Witness, Wm. Johnston. April 15, 1779.

Novr. 17, 1778. Jno. Wyatt and Ann, his wife; Thos. Ballard Wyatt and Susanna, his wife, of Hanover Co. to Thomas Chiles of Caroline Co. £500 curr. 330 a. in Spts. Co., bounded by lands of George Luck, James Mason, David Woodroof, etc. Witnesses, Anthony Arnold, John Hackney, jr.; Wm. Mason. July 15, 1779.

Jany. 30, 1779. Wm. Wood of Spts. Co. to his sons, John and James Wood. Deed of Gift. "Slaves, goods, chattels, etc., devised or bequeathed to Ann Wood, wife of the sd. Wm. Wood, by the last will and testament of her decd. father, John Crane," etc. Witnesses, Larkin Chew, Thomas Towles. July 15, 1779.

Feby. 13, 1779. Ambrose x Month of Spts. Co. to Micajah Poole of same Co. "The sd. Month hath by this present indenture bound unto the sd. Micajah Poole, his three children, vizt., two girls and a boy, known by the names of Charity Grymes Penn, David Penn, and Averilla Penn," etc. Witnesses, Thomas Towles, Jno. Poole. July 15, 1779.

Novr. 18, 1778. John Edwards and Dorothy, his wife, of Berkeley Par., Spts. Co. to John Martin. £333. 100 a. in Spts. Co. Leonard Crutcher, James Head, Henry Head, Robt. Lawrence, Sherod Horn, Mathew Pulliam. July 15, 1779.

March 1, 1779. Alexander Spence Head and Sarah, his wife, of Spts. Co. to Henry Head of same Co. £500 curr. 162 a. in Spts. Co. No witnesses. July 15, 1779.

July 15, 1779. Alexander Spence Head of Spts. Co. to his son, David Head. Deed of Gift. 80 a. in Spts. Co. No witnesses. July 15, 1779.

July 15, 1779. George Cammack of Spts. Co. (age 14, March 31, 1776), binds himself to Benjamin Waller of same Co., Millwright. No witnesses. July 15, 1779.

July 15, 1779. Wm. Cammack, jr. (age 13, Augt. 28, 1777), binds himself to Benjamin Waller of Spts. Co., Millwright. No witnesses. July 15, 1779.

April 24, 1779. Wm. Hunter of Orange Co. and Sarah, his wife, to George Thornton of Fredksbg. £440. Lots 5 and 6 in Fredksbg., commonly known as Allan Town, etc. Chs. Yates, Lac. Mackintosh, Jas. Hunter, jr.; Benja. Lewis. July 15, 1779.

April 14, 1778. Honble. John Tayloe, Esqr., of Richmond Co., one of the trustees of Benjamin Grymes, Esqr., etc., and Wm. Smith, Gent., late Sheriff of Spts. Co. to Wm. Spindle of Spts. Co. Whereas, certain lands in Spts. Co. were mortgaged the sd. Tayloe by Thomas Poole, and whereas, a suit to foreclose the sd. Mortgage, and a judgment has been obtained in Spts. Co. Court in June, 1772, failure having been made by the sd. Poole in paying the sd. indebtedness, and in consequence the sd. Smith, as Sheriff, sold the sd. land in lots and parcels, the sd. Poole purchasing 180 a. thereof for the sum of £101 5s. curr. Conveyance of same herein, etc. Witnesses, Anth. Thornton, jr.; Thomas Lomax, Griffin Garland. July 15, 1779.

April 14, 1778. Honble. John Tayloe, Esqr., etc., to Walker Taliaferro of Caroline Co. Whereas, in deed preceding, etc. £200 curr. 700 acres, etc. Anth. Thornton, jr.; Thomas Lomax, Griffin Garland. July 15, 1779.

June 16, 1779. Clement Montague and Ann, his wife, to Thomas Colson. 2000 lbs. Crop tob. 25 a. of tract sd. Montague lives on, etc. Jno. Waller, Jno. Chew, jr.; Harry Bartlet, A. Bartlet. July 15, 1779.

March 29, 1779. Thomas Allen and Mary, his wife, of Spts. Co. to Wm. Wiat of Fredksbg. £350 curr. Lot 196 in town of Fredksbg., formerly property of Jno. Waller (since decd.), and by him conveyed to John Mitchell, and by the sd. Mitchell conveyed to Peter Taliaferro, and by him conveyed to the sd. Thomas Allen, etc. Witnesses, James Somerville, James Robb. July 15, 1779.

Decr. 25, 1775. John Simpson, jr., and Frances, his wife, of Stafford Co. to Minister and Elders of Baptist Church of Spts. Co. £15 15s. curr. 1 a. in Spts. Co. July 15, 1779.

July 13, 1779. Joseph Jones, Fielding Lewis, James Taylor, jr., and George Taylor, Esquires, appt. by law for selling lands whereof John Thornton, died, seized and possessed, to John Taliaferro of King Geo. Co., Esqr. £9 pr. acre. 798 a. called "Long Branch," etc. Geo. Thornton, Chas. Washington, Fras. Thornton, Rd. Brooke. July 15, 1779.

Novr. 30, 1778. Charles Bruce of Orange Co., Executor of the last will and testament of Thos. James, late of Fauqueir Co., decd., of first part; Michael Robinson, jr., and Molly, his wife, of Spts. Co., of second part; Richard Price of Orange Co. and Agatha, his wife, of third part; John Wiglesworth of Spts. Co., of fourth part. Whereas, Thos. James, in his lifetime promised the sd. Michael Robinson, the sum of £250, as portion with sd. Molly, as daughter of sd. James; and also having promised sd. Richd. Price the like sum as portion with the sd. Agatha, another daughter of the sd. James, and in order to provide for the payment thereof the sd. James, by his last will and testament, dated April 9, 1772, directed the sale of those lots in town of Fredksbg., commonly called the Long Ordinary by his Executors, and the respective sums pd. the sd. daughters Molly and Agatha, out of the sale thereof; and whereas, a communication being afterwards had between the sd. Michael Robinson, Richd. Price, and Thomas James, concerning the portions of their wives, it was mutually agreed that the sd. Robinson and Price should accept the sd. Lots and Houses in lieu of the sd. portions, in pursuance of the sd. agreement, in the year 1775, intending to confirm that agreement, had a deed drawn for conveying the sd. lots, etc., to the sd. parties, but as some difference had arisen between the sd. James and Michael Robinson, the Elder (father to the sd. Michael), respecting the fortune promised by him to his sd. son on the marriage afsd., the sd. James, in order to force the Robinson, the Elder, to comply with his promise, undertook to convey the afsd. lands to Richard Price, in trust, as to one moiety, to be held for the benefit of the wife of the sd. Michael, jr., until the sd. Michael, Senr., should comply with his promise, with the understanding that the one retaining the sd. property should pay the other party £250; and whereas, the sd. James died, and by his will, proved in Fauqueir Co., Feby. 26, 1776, appointed Chas. Bruce, Thos. Hord, Gerrard Banks, and John James, Executors, the sd. Charles Bruce alone accepting the Executorship, etc., the sd. Michael Robinson, the Elder, having complied with his agreement aforementioned, etc., the sd. Robinson, jr., and Price, being intitled to the sd. lots, etc., agree for the sale thereof to the sd. John Wiglesworth for the sum of £550 curr., and hereby convey the same, etc. Witnesses, John Steward, Michael Robinson, Stapleton Crutchfield, James Hackley, Richard Young, John Hawkins. July 15, 1779.

May 18, 1779. John Arnold of Caroline Co. from David Pulliam and Betty, his wife, of Spts. Co. £35. 200 a. in Spts. Co. Jos. Pulliam, Reuben Massey, Benj. Perry. Sept. 16, 1779.

April 12, 1779. Abraham Larew of Orange Co. to Henry True of Spts. Co. £25 curr. 50 a. in Spts. Co. Thos. True, Reuben Massey, David Pulliam, Nathan Pulliam, Joseph True. Sept. 16, 1779.

July 12, 1779. George Thornton of Fredksbg., Gent., and Mary, his wife, to Thomas Walker of same Town. £400 curr. An undivided third in Lot 245 in Town of Fredksbg., conveyed by Roger Dixon, Gent., Decd., to James Swain, during his lifetime, then to sd. Swain's three daughters, Elinor, Catharine, and Elizabeth, and the sd. Elinor, with Aaron Marders, her husband, conveyed her ⅓ to Jno. Fredk. Baker who, with his wife, conveyed the same to James Fulton, who conveyed it to Henry Brett who conveyed the same to the sd. George Thornton, etc. Witnesses, Chs. Mortimer, Lac. Mackintosh, John Banks, Edwd. Ross. Oct. 21, 1779.

April 18, 1780. Alexander Spotswood, Esqr., and Elizabeth, his wife, of Spts. Co. to George Thornton of same Co., Esqr. "£307 10s., former currency of Va." 410 a. on Wilderness run in Spts. Co., leased by sd. Spotswood to Benj. Grymes of Orange Co., Esqr., Sept. 10, 1775, and by the sd. Grymes assigned to sd. Thornton on Sept. 13, 1775, etc. No witnesses. April 20, 1780.

April 12, 1779. Abraham Larew of Orange Co. to Thomas True and Henry True of Spts. Co. £100 curr. 218 a. in Spts. Co. Reuben Massey, Joseph True, Nathan Pulliam, David Pulliam. Sept. 16, 1779.

Oct. 29, 1778. George McNeil to Mack McDaniel of Spts. Co. £50 curr. 60 a. in Spts. Co. Edwd. Brasfield, Benj. Perry, Robert Gravit, Micah. Blunt. Sept. 16, 1779.

April 22, 1779. Thomas x Steward and Elizabeth, his wife, of Spts. Co. and Lucy Dixon of Frederick Co. to James Tutt of Spts. Co. £250. 150 a. in Spts. Co., purchased by sd. Steward of Francis Purvis, etc. Witnesses, Rd. Brooke, John McCalley, Francis Rose, John Minor, John Tutt, Ben. Tutt, Mordacai Redd. Octr. 21, 1779.

June 8, 1779. John Craig and Sarah, his wife, and Elijah Craig and Frances, his wife, to Edward Simpson of Fredksbg. £600 curr. ⅓ part of the church lot in Fredksbg., sold by act of assembly and purchased by John Lewis, Gent., who with Elizabeth, his wife, conveyed the same to the sd. John and Elijah Craig, etc. Witnesses, Henry Beattie, Fielding Lucas, John Stamper, James Jarvis, Wm. Craghill, Wm. Hopson, James Brown. Sept. 16, 1779.

Nov. 20, 1778. Thos. Estes and Catherine, his wife, of Spts. Co. to James Hensley of same Co. £50. 64 a. in St. Geo. Par., Spts. Co. Wm. Smith, Thos. Colson, Thos. Montague, Wm. Carpenter, Thos. Bartlett, Charles Goodman. Oct. 21, 1779.

Sept. 10, 1779. John Halladay and Tabitha, his wife, of Spots. Co. to James Tate of Westmoreland Co. £1200. 430 a. in Berkeley Par., Spts. Co. Chas. Pemberton, Edwd. Brasfield, Jno. Tankersley, Benj. Perry, Jno. Halladay, jr. Sept. 16, 1779.

April 3, 1779. Henry Brett and Tabitha, his wife, of Fredksbg. to George Thornton of same Town. £300 curr. ⅓ of a lot in Fredksbg., which sd. Brett purchased of James Fulton and Margaret, his wife, as by Deeds, March 17, 1779, etc., etc. Witnesses, Elisha Dickenson, John Stamper, Thos. Walker. Sept. 16, 1779.

Sept. 15, 1779. Joseph Herndon of Spts. Co. and Mary, his wife, to Christopher Donnelly of same Co. £200. Lot 204 in Town of Fredksbg. Stapleton Crutchfield, James Frazer, Edwd. Herndon, jr. Sept. 16, 1779.

April 10, 1779. Harry Chew, Gent., of Spts. Co. to Robert Smith of sd. County, Gent. £500 curr. 68 a. in St. Geo. Par., Spts. Co. Jos. Brock, Jno. Brock, Jno. Brock, jr.; Danl. Branham, Thomas Crutcher, Jos. Brock, jr. Sept. 16, 1779.

Augt. 17, 1779. Long Wharton and Ann, his wife, of Spts. Co. to James Owen of Spts. Co. £50 curr. 275 a. in Spts. Co., half of a tract of land purchased of Robt. Taliaferro, Gent., of Caroline Co., as by deeds, 21st Sept., 1772, etc. Wm. Darnaby, Jno. Bullock, James Dudley. Sept. 16, 1779.

May 13, 1779. Clement Montague of Spts. Co. and Ann, his wife, to Fielding Lewis, Charles Dick, Beverley Winslow, Jos. Brock, Wm. Smith, and Mann Page, jr., Gent. "In consideration of the Court House being built on the premises and the sum of 5 shill. curr." 2 acres of land in Spts. Co., in trust for the Co. of Spts., etc. Thomas Colson, Thomas Allen, Harry Bartlett, Reuben Straughan, Thomas Towles, Jno. Chew, jr. Sept. 16, 1779.

June 17, 1779. John Wiglesworth of Spts. Co. and Philadelphia, his wife, to Wm. Jackson of Fredksbg. £1050 curr. "Upper part of the lot of ground which sd. Wiglesworth purchased of Wm. Houston," etc., on s. side Caroline Street, joining end of the Long Ordinary, etc. Harry Bartlet, John Warner, Jno. Welch, Reuben Straughan. Sept. 16, 1779.

Feby. 30, 1779. George x Moor and Susanna, his wife, of Spts. Co. to John McKenny of Fredksbg. £200 curr. 175 a. in Spts. Co., joining lands of Edwd. Ludwick, Wm. Darnaby, Benj. McWilliams, and Nathl. Stevens, etc. Witnesses, B. Johnston, Jno. Wiglesworth, Jno. Welch. Sept. 16th, 1779.

Augt. 10, 1779. John Simpson (son of Abram), and Frankey, his wife, of Spts. Co. to Wm. Richards of Orange Co. £3500 curr. 274 a. in Spts. Co., whereon Simpson's Ordinary stands, on main road from Fredksbg. to Orange and Culpeper Counties, and adjoins lands of Col. Alexander Spotswood and Mattapony, and is land formerly patented by Wm. Bledsoe, 58 a. conveyed by the sd. Bledsoe to Jno. Taliaferro and afterwards conveyed to Abraham Simpson, father to the sd. John, the remainder the sd. Abraham purchased of heirs of Wm. Bledsoe, except 100 a. in fork of the runs which was devised to Peachey Bledsoe, son of Moses Bledsoe, who was son and heir of the sd. Wm.; and is all that land possessed by Abram Simpson, father of the sd. John, who claims the same as son and heir at law to the sd. Abram, etc. Witnesses, Jno. Welch, Jacob Whitler, John Robinson, Jos. Craig, Jno. Chew, jr. Feby. 17, 1780.

Augt. 16, 1779. Charles Bruce, Thomas Hord, Gerard Banks, and John James, Executors of the last will and testament of Thomas James, Decd., to Jacob Whitler and Jno. Welch of Fredksbg. Whereas, the sd. Thomas James, Decd., by his will dated Apr. 9, 1772, and proved in Fauqueir Co., directed the sale of certain lands, vizt., "land in Spts. Co., I purchased of George Sharpe, my lots and houses in town of Fredericksburg, known by name of Long Ordinary, and 1000 a. I have purchased of Warner Washington," etc., the tract of 188 a. in Spts. Co., being exposed to sale, the sd. Whitler and Welch purchased the same for the sum of £752 curr., etc. Witnesses, Will. Craghill, Jesse Slaven, Jno. Hasalgrove, Jno. Holloday, jr. Sept. 16, 1779.

Oct. 21, 1779. Thomas Allen and Mary, his wife, of Spts. Co. to Edward Simpson of Fredksbg. £2125 curr. 306 a., formerly purchased of George Atkinson, etc. No witnesses. Octr. 21, 1779.

July 16, 1779. Saml. x Alsup and Ann, his wife, of Berkeley Par., Spts. Co. to Daniel Lambert of Par. and Co. afsd. £2000. 296 a. in Par. and Co. afsd. Jno. Mercer, Jno. Long, George Alsup, jr. Oct. 21, 1779.

Oct. 21, 1779. John Spindle and Bridget, his wife, of Spts. Co. to Charles Yates of Fredksbg. £600. 300 a. in Spts. Co., formerly purchased of Thomas Crutcher and Sarah, his wife, etc. Reuben Landram, Wm. Spindle. Oct. 21, 1779.

May 27, 1779. Edward Vass (or Voss) of Culpeper Co. and Jane, his wife, of first part; Philip Lipscomb of Fredksbg. and Jane, his wife, of second part, to Charles Washington of same town, Gent., of third part. Whereas, sd. Voss and wife, being seized, etc., of lots 79 and 80, in town of Fredksbg., did sell the sd. lots to the sd. Lipscomb, but before any conveyance thereof was made, the sd. Lipscomb agreed for the sale of the sd. lots with the sd. Washington, for the sum of £1000 curr. Conveyance, etc. No witnesses. Oct. 21, 1779.

Augt. 18, 1779. Thomas Montague and Agatha, his wife, to Reuben Straughan. £170 curr. 70 a. in Berkeley Par., Spts. Co. A. Bartlet, B. x Sullivan, Jno. Carter, Jno. Davenport, Harry Bartlett, Thomas Bartlett. Oct. 21, 1779.

March 17, 1779. James Fulton and Margaret, his wife, of Fredksbg. to Henry Brett of sd. Town. £215 curr. ⅓ of a lot in town of Fredksbg., purchased of Jno. Fredk. Baker and Fanny, his wife, as by deeds, Augt. 11, 1774, etc., etc. B. Johnston, Jacob Whitler, Jno. Hasalgrove. Oct. 21, 1779.

Oct. 21, 1779. John Wiglesworth and Philadelphia, his wife, of Spts. Co. to Wm. Jackson of Fredksbg. £400 curr., "all that part of the lower end of the lot in Fredksbg., known as the Long Ordinary," etc. No witnesses. Oct. 21, 1779.

July 4, 1797. Wm. Ellis and Agnes, his wife, of Spts. Co. to John Robinson of same Co. £180 curr. 90 a. in Spts. Co. Jo. Steward, Michael Robinson, Wm. Massey. Oct. 21, 1779.

July 4, 1779. John Smith of Frederick Co. to Wm. Ellis of Spts. Co. £180 curr. 90 a. in Spts. Co. James Somerville, Henry Armistead, Michael Robinson. Octr. 21, 1779.

June 30, 1779. John Dolton of Fredksbg., Tailor, and Elizabeth, his wife, to Michael Robinson of Fredksbg. Lease. Lot in Fredksbg., held by sd. Dolton under lease from Pearson Chapman, etc. £4 annually, etc. Wm. Robinson, Benj. Robinson, Thos. Brown. Oct. 21, 1779.

Oct. 9, 1779. John Dolton of Fredksbg., Tailor, to John Welch of same town, Cooper. Lease. Lot in town of Fredksbg., held by sd. Dolton under lease from Pearson Chapman, then of Maryland, during the lives of sd. Dolton, Elizabeth, his wife, and Walker Dolton, his son, etc. £2500 curr., for the whole term of the sd. Lease, as from Chapman to Dolton, etc. Jacob Whitler, John Atkinson, John Wiglesworth, John Hasalgrove. Octr. 21, 1779.

Augt. 27, 1779. Rice Curtis of Spts. Co. to his children, Nancy, John, Sarah, Elizabeth, Mary, Frances, Margaret, George Bartemeus and James Curtis. Deed of Gift. "Whereas, the sd. Rice Curtis is about to enter into the Continental service as a soldier," etc. All estate, real and personal, after the death of Frances, wife of the sd. Rice Curtis, etc. Witnesses, Wm. Carter, Wm. Heslop, Francis Turnley. Novr. 18, 1779.

July 15, 1779. Richard Pollard of St. Stephens Par., King and Queen Co. and Ann, his wife, to Fielding Lewis of Spts. Co., Gent. £97 10s. curr. 130 a. in St. Geo. Par., Spts. Co., given to the sd. Ann Pollard's mother by her father, Thomas Hill, etc. A. Frazer, Jno. Frazer, Edwd. Hill, Saml. Garlick, John Ware. Novr. 18, 1779.

July 10 1779. John Gardner and Mary, his wife, of Berkeley Par., Spts. Co. to Gilmon Lane of same Par. and Co. £300 curr. 100 a. in fork of Pamunkey River, in Par. and County afsd, etc. Thomas Gardner, Leonard Young, jr.; Hackley Young, Francis Ford, Wm. Taylor. Novr. 18, 1779.

Octr. 23, 1779. Wm. Houston and Judith, his wife, of Spts. Co. to Samuel Todd of same county. £2000 curr. 388 a. in St. Geo. Par., Spts. Co. Jos. Brock, Thomas Colson, John Chew, Jas. Wallace. Novr. 18, 1779.

—— ——, 1779. Richard Dillard of Spts. Co. to John Coats of Caroline Co. £1000 curr. 100 a. in Spts. Co. on N. side Pawpaw Swamp, whereon sd. Dillard lives, etc. No witnesses. Nov. 18, 1779.

Novr. 17, 1779. Ann Mathews and Ann x Shackleford of Spts. Co. to John Coats of Caroline Co. £500 curr. 130 a. in Spts. Co. Elisha Dismukes, Thomas May, Richd. Dillard. Novr. 18, 1779.

—— ——, ——. Robt. Gilchrist of Caroline Co. Bond to Wm. Smith of Spts. Co. £15,000 curr., etc., etc. Henry Woodford, John Woodford, James Robb. Nov. 18, 1779.

Augt. 16, 1779. Taliver x Craig of Spts. Co. to Thomas Almond of same Co. £124 curr. 124 a. in Spts. Co. Benj. Bradley Reubin Emerson. Novr. 18, 1779.

Jan. 13, 1780. James Haydon and Elizabeth, his wife, of Spts. Co. to John Haydon of same Co. £1300 curr. 100 a. in Spts. Co. Jas. Cunningham, Lodowich Oneal, Jesse Haydon, Ezekiel Haydon. Feb. 17, 1780.

Decr. 31, 1779. Col. Fielding Lewis and Betty, his wife, of Spts. Co. to Charles Yates of Fredksbg. £600. Lots 126 and 128 in town of Fredksbg. George Lewis, Hay Battaile, Philip Lightfoot, Jno. Taliaferro. Feby. 17, 1782.

Augt. 6, 1779. Lewis Craig of Spts. Co. and Elizabeth, his wife, to John Skaths of same Co. £72 curr. 250 a. in Berkeley Par., Spts. Co. John Martin, Joseph Brock, Thos. Blanton. Feby. 17, 1780.

Augt. 6, 1779. Lewis Craig of Spts. Co. and Elizabeth, his wife, to John Martin of same Co. £450 curr. 200 a. in Berkeley Par., Spts. Co. John Skaths, Jos. Brock, Thos. Blanton. Feby. 17, 1780.

Septr. 4, 1779.   John Faulconer of Spts. Co. to Samuel Partlow of Caroline Co. £1500. 300 a. in Spts. Co. Wm. Grady, John Martin, Joseph Willoughby, Mary x Rose. Feby. 17, 1780.

Jany. 1, 1780.   Shadrach Moore of Spts. Co. and Ann, his wife, to Richard Young of same Co. £90 curr. 20 a. in Spts. Co. No witnesses. Feby. 17, 1780.

Feby. 17, 1780.   Susanna Collins, Bartlett Collins and Elizabeth, his wife, of St. Geo. Par., Spts. Co. to John Robinson of same Par. and County. £1200 curr. 157 a. in St. Geo. Par., Spts. Co., given and granted the sd. Susanna Collins, etc., by Wm. Bartlett, and half a larger tract belonging to sd. Bartlett, and joining the lands of Wm. Daingerfield, Thos. Strachan, Charles Dick, and Wm. Ellis, as by deed, from Bartlett to sd. Collins, dated June 4, 1754. No witnesses. Feby. 17, 1780.

Jany. 10, 1780.   John Brock of St. Geo. Par., Spts. Co. to Geo. Stubblefield of Berkeley Par., Spts. Co. £2500. 135 a. in St. Geo. Par., Spts. Co., purchased by sd. Brock of Edwd. Straughan and Mary, his wife, etc. Henry Carter, George Stubblefield, jr.; Jno. Wiglesworth, Jno. Chew, jr.; John Chew. April 20, 1780.

Jany. 10, 1780.   Reuben Massey and Molly, his wife, of Spts. Co. to George Stubblefield of same Co., Gent. £225 curr. 100 a. in Spts. Co. Willm. Smith, Thos. Towles, Harry Stubblefield, John Smith, Geo. Stubblefield, jr. April 20, 1780.

Jany. 30, 1780.   John Price and Elizabeth, his wife, of Spts. Co. to Henry Glass of Stafford Co. £3000 curr. 150 a. in Spts. Co. Richd. Young, Robt. Thomas, John Branham. April 20, 1780.

March 1, 1780.   George Weedon and Catherine, his wife, of Fredksbg. to Jacob Whitler of same place. £2664 curr. 222 a. in St. Geo. Par., Spts. Co., moiety of a tract which descended to Sally Watkins, wife of Edwd. Watkins, as one of two co-partners, from her father, Thomas Hill, and conveyed by the sd. Watkinses to Margaret Gordon, as by deed, June 20, 1757, and by the sd. Gordon conveyed to the sd. Weedon, as by deed, March 24, 1774. Edwd. Simpson, Jno. Richards, John Welch, James Hackley. April 20, 1780.

April 20, 1780.   John Martin of Spts. Co. and ——, his wife, to James Marye of sd. Co., Clerk. £800 curr. 100 a. in St. Geo. Par., Spts. Co. No witnesses. April 20, 1780.

Novr. 30, 1779.   John Waller of Spts. Co. and Elizabeth, his wife, to James Crawford of same Co. £121 curr. 131 a. in Spts. Co., part of a tract purchased of John Hall, etc. Ben. Waller, Wm. Wiglesworth, Jno. Hackley, jr.; Wm. Edmund Waller, Elisha Dismukes, Wyatt Hewett, W. Emerson, Christopher Crawford, James Crawford, jr.; John Crawford, John Dempsie. April 20, 1780.

Decr. 1, 1778.   Simon Miller of St. Anns Par., Essex Co., Esqr., and James Hunter, the younger, of Fredksbg., Mercht., and Mary Ann, his wife, to Charles Dick of Fredksbg. £212 pd. to sd. Hunter, and 20 shill. to sd. Miller, etc. Tract of land in Spts. Co., near Massaponax Run, and the lands of Wm. Porter and Wm. Jackson, etc. Jas. Mercer, Paul

Micou, Paul Micou, jr.; Thos. Hill, Alexr. Phillips, Jas. Gordon, jr. April 20, 1780.

Septr. 27, 1779. Edward Cason, Senr., of Prince Edwd. Co., and Seth Cason, attorney for the sd. Edwd Cason, Senr., to Edward Cason, Jr., of Hanover Co., grandson of the son Edwd. Cason, Senr., and son of John Cason, who was son of the sd. Edward Cason, Senr., etc. £20 curr. 200 a. in Spts. Co. William Cason, James Shackleford, Nathl. Lancaster. April 20, 1780.

Novr. 24, 1779. Joseph Dillard of Amherst Co. and Mary, his wife, and James Dillard of same Co. and Sukey, his wife, to Richard Dillard of Spts. Co. £1500 curr. 270 a. in Spts. Co., whereon Thomas Dillard, Decd., lived, and which he devised by his last will and testament to his sd. sons, Joseph and James, etc. Leonard Young, George Luck, Thomas Dillard, Elisha Dismukes, Moses Morris, Bradley Mathews. June 15, 1780.

Jany. 10, 1780. Thomas Bartlett and Mary, his wife, of Spts. Co. to Joseph Herndon of same County. £3200 curr. 273 a. in Berkeley Par., Spts. Co., deeded the sd. Bartlett by his father, Wm. Bartlett, etc. Jos. Brock, Jno. Holloday, jr.; A. Bartlett, Geo. Stubblefield. June 15, 1780.

June 12, 1779. Hawes Coleman of Spts. Co., to Clayton Coleman of same County. £22 curr. 30 a. in Spts. Co. Stapleton Crutchfield, Jno. Holloday, jr.; Rice Vass. Augt. 16, 1781.

April 20, 1780. Charles Washington of Spts. Co., Gent., and Mildred, his wife, to Thomas Strachan of sd. County, Gent. £8000 curr. 759 a. in Spts. Co., purchased of John Smith and Mary, his wife, as by deed, Octr. 29, 1759. Fras. Thornton, Jno. Chew, Rob. Bevy. Chew, Joseph Brock, Jno. Chew, jr. June 15, 1780.

June 5, 1780. Wm. Jackson and Millie, his wife, of Spts. Co. to James Duncanson of Culpeper Co. £65 curr. Lot No. 21 in Fredksbg. Geo. Thornton, Thomas Towles, John Herndon, Jno. Hardia, Chas. Washington, Thomas Bartlett, James Tutt. June 15, 1780.

June 14, 1780. Wm. Thompson of Spts. Co., Gent., to Dr. George French of Fredksbg. and Ann Brayne, his wife. Whereas, the sd. Ann Brayne, jointly with her sister, Dorothea Brayne Benger, as daughters of John Benger, late of Virginia, decd., are intitled to and seized of a moiety or ½ of an Estate in lands in the Co. of Surry, England, which came to them on the death of Ann Brayne, late of the City of London, England, sometime decd.; the other ½ of which estate came or descended to Alexander Spotswood, Esqr.; and whereas, the sd. land is supposed to be liable to an incumbrance of £200 ster., etc., by virtue of a deed of Mortgage, ½ of which money the sd. co-heirs are bound to pay in order to exonerate the land, etc., and whereas, the sd. Ann Brayne, decd., was in her lifetime intitled to the sd. Mortgage money, etc., and made her last will and testament with a codicil thereto by which, after bequeathing some special legacies, she gave the residuum of her Estate to be equally divided between the sd. Wm. Thompson and four other legatees, etc., and whereas, it is the opinion of Council, that the sd. £200 ster. is to be looked upon as part of the residuum of the sd. Ann's estate and as such to be equally divided among the residuary legatees afsd., of whom sd. Thompson is one and intitled to ⅕ part, etc. Witnesseth, the sd. Thompson in consideration of £40 ster., relinquishes any claim, right of title he may have to the sd. mortgage money, to the sd. George French and Ann Brayne, his wife, etc. Witnesses, Andrew Buchanan, George Buckner, James Somerville. June 15, 1780.

Septr. 8, 1779. James Stevenson and Frances A., his wife, of Berkeley Par., Spts. Co. to Clayton Coleman of Par. and Co. afsd. £100 curr. 74½ a. in Spts. Co. Wm. Mastin, Richd. Littlepage, Willm. Smith, Thomas Towles. June 15, 1780.

June 15, 1780. John x Barlayan, orphan of John Barlayan, Decd., binds himself to James Frazer of Spts. Co., etc. Witness, John Chew. June 15, 1780.

March 6, 1780. John Chiles and Mary Ann, his wife, of Spts. Co. to Wm. Dawson of same County. £6050 curr. 550 a. in Spts. Co., etc., in five tracts, etc. Vincent Vass, John Scott, Robert Dawson, Thomas Montague. Sept. 21, 1780.

Sept. 21, 1780. Samuel Coleman of Caroline Co. to Aquilla Johnson, Senr., of Spts. Co. £420 curr. 13 a. in Spts. Co., bounded by lands of George Goodloe, Mrs. Roy and Warrens' Swamp, etc. No witnesses. Sept. 21, 1780.

Oct. 14, 1777. Samuel Coleman of Caroline Co. and Sarah, his wife, of first part; Ambrose Smith and Isabella, his wife of Spts. Co., of second part; Thomas Towles of Spts. Co., of third part. Whereas, Robert Coleman of Caroline Co., being seized, etc., of a tract of land in Spts. Co., granted him by pat. dated Decr. 2, 1723, did by deed dated Dec. 28, 1745, grant unto John Coleman of Spts. Co., his son, 316 a., part thereof bounded by lands of Richard Coleman and Robt. Coleman, jr., which tract of land John Coleman, died, seized and possessed, did by his last will and testament, among other things, direct all his land equally divided among all his children, the sd. tract or parcel of land was allotted to sd. Samuel Coleman, son of the sd. John Coleman, decd., etc., and whereas, Richd. Coleman, being seized of another tract, part of the same patent abt. 320 a. did convey the same to Ambrose Smith, 140 a., part thereof sd. Smith sold to sd. Saml. Coleman, but made no conveyance, since which the sd. Thos. Towles hath purchased of the sd. Samuel Coleman, the two sd. tracts, 316 a. and 140 a. for the sum of £190 curr., sd. Smith agreeing to make conveyance, etc. Anthony Winston, Saml. Winston, Eliza Winston, Thomas x May, James Smith, John x Smith. Sept. 21, 1780.

Sept. 21, 1780. Joseph Willoughby of Spts. Co. and Elizabeth, his wife, to Benjamin Perry and Elizabeth Perry, his mother, of Orange Co. £2000. 100 a. in Spts. Co. Anthony Arnold, Henry Macdaniel, Ben. Mastin. Sept. 21, 1780.

Augt. 17, 1780. Sherod Horn and Mary, his wife, of St. Geo. Par., Spts. Co. to Peter Crawford of Trinity Par., Louisa Co. £300 curr. 200 a. in St. Geo. Par., Spts. Co., bounded by lines of Gawvin Corbin, Capt. Thomas Crutcher, and Jno. Wiglesworth. Witnesses, Thos. Magee, jr.; A. Frazer, Jas. Raines, Harry Bartlet. Sept. 21, 1780.

Augt. 1, 1780. Wm. Clayton, deed of gift, to his brother, John Clayton. A mulatto girl, etc. Witnesses, James Jones, Thos. Clayton. Sept. 21, 1780.

Sept. 21, 1780. Wm. Chiles of Spts. Co. and Agnes, his wife, to Caleb Coleman of same County. £2000 curr. 262 a. in Spts. Co., part of a tract purchased by Henry Chiles of Geo. Baylor, etc. No witnesses. Sept. 21, 1780.

March 20, 1780. James Pritchett of Spts. Co. to Clement Montague of same county. £350 curr. 19 a. in Spts. Co. John Waller, K. W.; Thos. Waller, jr.; Clement Montague, jr. Sept. 20, 1780.

Feby. 2, 1780. Richard Loury and Betty, his wife, of Spts. Co. to John McCauley of same Co. £800 curr. 100 a. in Spts. Co. Joseph Perry, John x Pruett. Sept. 21, 1780.

Augt. 29, 1780. Alexander Spotswood, Esqr., to Thomas Allen. Lease. 100 a. in St. Geo. Par., Spts. Co. "Sd. Thomas Allen, Mary Allen, and his son, James Allen," etc. 600 lbs. tob. yearly. Edwd. Herndon, jr.; Richd. Young, A. Frazer, Jas. Lewis. Oct. 19, 1780.

Oct. 16, 1780. Thomas x Almond and Ann, his wife, of Spts. Co. to Wm. Shelton of Stafford Co. £1000 curr. 124 a. in Berkeley Par., Spts. Co. John Hawkins, Thomas Magee, jr.; Danl. Branham, John Almond, Wm. Duval, Richd. Estes. Oct. 19, 1780.

June 15, 1780. John x McKenny and Mary, his wife, to Wm. Moore. £1100 curr. 175 a. in Spts. Co., bounded by lands of Wm. Darnaby, Nathl. Stephens, Benja. McWilliams, and Edwd. Leddage, etc., formerly purchased of George Moore, etc. Witnesses, Jno. Rose, Robt. Brooke, Willm. Welch, John Robinson. Octr. 19, 1780.

Sept. 21, 1780. John Mastin and Elizabeth, his wife, of Spts. Co. to Anthony Arnold of same County. £1000 curr. 203 a. in Spts. Co. Benj. Perry, Benj. Mastin, Henry Macdaniel. Novr. 16, 1780.

March 20, 1780. Wm. x Floid of Caswell Co., N. C., to Thomas Brightwell of Spts. Co. £100. 50 a. in Spts. Co., bounded by lands of Thos. Brown, Wm. Gains, Jno. Howerton, and Lewis Pines, etc. Witnesses, Charles x Jenkins, James Abbett, John x Jenkins.

Sept. 8, 1780. Larkin Stanard of Spts. Co. and Elizabeth, his wife, to Ephraim Beasley of same county. £4000 curr. 30 a. in Berkeley Par., Spts. Co. Jno. Brock, Jas. Mitcham. Novr. 16, 1780.

Nov. 16, 178—. Larkin x Straughan (orph. of Edwd. Straughan, decd.), of Spts. Co., binds himself to Jesse Smith of Culpeper Co. Witness, Jno. Brock. Novr. 16, 1780.

Dec. 2, 1780. Henry Coleman and Mary Ann, his wife, of Spts. Co. to Thomas Sharpe of same county. £14,000 curr. 200 a. in Spts. Co. Bevy. Winslow, Willm. Mills, Benj. Robinson, Benj. Davis. Dec. 21, 1780.

Oct. 5, 1780. Isaac Head of Spts. Co. to Rhodam Bigbee of same county. ———. 100 a. in Spts. Co. Richd. Young, Wm. Massey, Jno. Green. Dec. 21, 1780.

April 12, 1779. Jacob Cunes to Wm. Golson. £31 curr. 80 a. in St. Geo. Par., Spts. Co. Robt. Smith, Hy. Chew, John Brock. Dec. 21, 1780.

March 15, 1781. Gabriel x Long and Lucy, his wife, of Culpeper Co. to John Estige of Caroline Co. 6000 lbs. tob. 500 a. in Berkeley Par., Spts. Co. No witnesses. March 15, 1781.

Novr. 28, 1780. James x Pritchett of Spts. Co., deed of gift to his daughter, Elizabeth Hawkins. A negro slave. Tavener Branham, Letty Tibbetts, Elizabeth x Branham. March 15, 1781.

Oct. 28, 1780. Charles Kennedy and Crosha, his wife, of Hanover Co. to Ambrose Shackleford of Spts. Co. £110. 100 a. in Spts. Co. Thos. Minor, Elisha Dismukes, Cain Acuff. March 15, 1781.

March 15, 1781. John Wiglesworth and Philadelphia, his wife, of St. Geo. Par., Spts. Co. to Richard Todd. £3500 curr. 424 a. in St. Geo. Par., Spts. Co.

March 15, 1781. George French of Spts. Co., po. of atto., to "my beloved friend, Robert Forsyth, of Spts. Co." Wm. Wiatt, John Hall, Abner Vernon.

March 15, 1781. Israel Myers of the City of Philadelphia, po. of atto., to Wm. Wyat of Fredksbg., Va., etc. Witness, Robert Forsyth. March 15, 1781.

March 14, 1781. Gregory Baylor of King and Queen Co., Gent., and Mary, his wife, to Wm. Ed. Waller of Spts. Co. £125 curr. 200 a. in Spts. Co., etc. Theod. Noel, Wm. Harrison, Thomas Wafford, Jno. Waller, Nathan. Holloway, Thos. Faulkner. April 19, 1781.

Novr. 10, 1780. Francis Meriwether and Mary, his wife, of Spts. Co. to Wm. Blaydes of same county. £5340 curr. 228 a. in Spts. Co. Jas. Wiglesworth, Nicholas Payne, Jno. Webber. April 19, 1781.

Novr. 10, 1780. Francis Meriwether and Mary, his wife, of Spts. Co. to Joseph Graves of same county. £2160 curr. 72 a. in Spts. Co. Jas Wiglesworth, Nicholas Payne, Jno. Webber. April 19, 1781.

May 10, 1781. Alexander Spence Head of Berkeley Par., Spts. Co. to his son, Isaac Head, of same Par. and Co. £3000 curr. 100 a. in Spts. Co. Michael McDaniel, David Head. May 17, 1781.

Novr. 10, 1780. George Stubblefield of Spts. Co., Gent., and Sally, his wife, to John Carnochan of same Co., Mechanoc (mechanic or Merchant?). £300 curr. 30 a. in Spts. Co. Rice Vass, Jos. Duerson, Wm. Trigg, Clayton Coleman, Thomas Coleman. May 17, 1781.

April 17, 1781. Joseph Sams of Spts. Co. and Nanny, his wife, to Thomas Shurley of same county. £3000. 70 a. in Spts. Co. No witnesses. May 17, 1781.

May 17, 1781. John Carter of Spts. Co. to John Johnson of same county. £3000 curr. 25 a. whereon sd. Johnson now lives, etc. No witnesses. May 17, 1781.

May 16, 1781. Charles Yates of Fredksbg. to Philip Evans of same town. £30 *specie*. Lot 141 in that part of Town of Fredksbg., added by Col. Fielding Lewis, etc. Jno. Welch, Jno. Clements, Jno. Davis, Wm. Jackson, Edwd. Herndon, jr. May 17, 1781.

Decr. 20, 1780. Fielding Lewis of Spts. Co. and Betty, his wife, of Spts. Co. to David Galloway, jr., of same county. £400 curr. Lot 143 in Town of Fredksbg. Edwd. Herndon, Laurence Ashton, Jno. Frazer. May 17, 1781.

March 30, 1781. John Mitchell of Spts. Co., Gent., and Susannah, his wife, and Robert Gilchrist and James Somerville, Gentl., two of the trustees of the sd. Mitchell and wife, to Richard Kenny of Fredksbg. £800 curr. Lots 77 and 78 in town of Fredksbg., purchased of Fielding Lewis by Jno. Mitchell, Hugh Lenox, and Wm. Scott (the two latter now decd.), as by deeds, Dec. 8, 1761, etc. Jno. Frazer, Thos. Kenny, Geo. Buckner, jr. May 17, 1781.

March 30, 1781. John Mitchell of Spts. Co., Gent., and Susannah, his wife, to James Somerville of Fredksbg., Mercht. £125 curr. ½ of lot No. 274 in town of Fredksbg., purchased of Thos. Walker and wife, as by deed, March 21, 1771, etc. Jno. Frazer, Thos. Kenny, Geo. Buckner, jr. May 17, 1781.

March 30, 1781. John Mitchell of Spts. Co., Gent., and Susannah, his wife, to Robert Johnston of town of Port Royal, Mercht. £125 curr. ½ of lot 274 in town of Fredksbg., etc. Jno. Frazer, Thos. Kenny, Geo. Buckner, jr. May 17, 1781.

April 12, 1781. John Wright and Rose, his wife, of Spts. Co. to Wm. Moxley of same county. £8400 curr. 258 a. in St. Geo. Par., Spts. Co. Harry Bartlet, Thos. Bartlett, James Tutt, Robert Smith, Thos. Minor. May 17, 1781.

Sept. 20, 1780. Jno. Wiglesworth and Philadelphia, his wife, of Spts. Co. to Richard Garner of same county. £5000. 143 a. in St. Geo. Par., Spts. Co. Witness, Jno. Brock. May 17, 1781.

Jany. 3, 1780. John Herndon of Spts. Co., Gent., and Mary, his wife, to John Wiglesworth of same county. £3492 curr. 292 a. in Spts. Co. Jno. Chew, Sam. Todd, Jas. Jarvis. May 17, 1781.

Jany. 11, 1781. John Herndon of Spts. Co., Gent., and Mary, his wife, to Thomas Jennings of same county. £1000 curr. 135 a. in Spts. Co., whereon Joseph Scroghan now lives, etc. Sam. Todd, Jno. Wiglesworth, James Jarvis, James Cunningham. May 17, 1781.

March 10, 1781. Charles Mortimer of Fredksbg. and Sarah, his wife, to Saml. Selden of Stafford Co., Gent. 4000 lbs. tob. Lot 202 in Fredksbg., formerly purchased of Roger Dixon and Lucy, his wife, as by deeds, Oct. 1, 1764. John Benson, John Welch, Edwd. Herndon, John Hardia. May 17, 1781.

May 15, 1781. Fielding Lewis of Fredksbg., Esqr., and Betty, his wife, and John Lewis, Gent. (son and heir of the sd. Fielding, etc), Elizabeth, his wife, to Dr. Thomas Powell of Spts. Co. £12,000 curr. 1243 a. in Spts. Co., formerly deeded the sd. John Lewis, as by deed, Dec. 19, 1770, etc. Thos. Strachan, Robt. B. Chew, Jno. Legg, John Rose, Richd. Littlepage. May 17, 1781.

Nov. 17, 1780. Fielding Lewis of Fredksbg. and Betty, his wife, to Wm. Stanard of Orange Co. £4492 curr. 416 a. in Spts. Co., part of tract called Warner's Patent, etc. Thos. Allen, Joseph Holloday, jr.; Jno. Frazer. May 17, 1781.

July 19, 1781. James Calaghan of Spts. Co., apprentices himself to Tully Whithurst of Fredksbg., Tailor. No witnesses. July 19, 1781.

July 16, 1781. John x Wheeler and Elizabeth, his wife, of Spts. Co. to George Stubblefield of same County. £2000 curr. 80 a. in Spts. Co. Nicholas Payne, Peter Stubblefield, Harry Stubblefield. July 19, 1781.

Decr. 20, 1780. Fielding Lewis of Fredksbg., Esqr., and Betty, his wife, to Joseph Herndon of Berkeley Par., Spts. Co. £2070 curr. 172½ a. in St. Geo. Par., Spts. Co. Richd. Young, Edwd. Simpson, Edwd. Herndon. Decr. 21, 1780.

May 17, 1781. Fielding Lewis of Spts. Co., Esqr., and Betty, his wife, to John Carpenter of same county. £1944 curr. 162 a. in St. Geo. Par., Spts. Co. Edwd. Herndon, jr.; Richd. Young, Thos. Kenny. May 17, 1781.

May 17, 1781. Fielding Lewis of Spts. Co., Esqr., and Betty, his wife, to Henry Duerson of same county. £2985 curr. 248¾ a. in St. Geo. Par., Spts. Co. Edwd. Herndon, jr.; Richd. Young, Thos. Kenny. May 17, 1781.

Augt. 1, 1780. Wm. Dawson and Mary, his wife, of Spts. Co. to Zachariah Billingsly of St. Mary's County, Maryland. £3300 curr. 185 a. in Spts. Co., purchased of Thos. Towles and Mary, his wife, as by deed, July 10, 1775. David Pulliam, Jas. King, Jos. Pulliam. May 17, 1781.

May 3, 1781. Richard Dillard of Spts. Co. and Susanna, his wife, to James Humphreys of same county. £500 curr. 73 a. in Spts. Co., whereon Thos. Dillard, decd., lived, etc. John Waller, Thos. Sherley. Wm. Rash. May 17, 1781.

June 8, 1781. Larkin Smith, Gent., and Mary, his wife, of Spts. Co. to Oliver Towles of same county, Gent. Sd. Towles having this day granted and conveyed fee simple estate in 2 lots in Fredksbg., the sd. Smith paying £250 specie, and hereby deeding to sd. Towles 550 a. in Spts. Co., devised sd. Smith, by his grandfather, Larkin Chew, decd., etc. Larkin Stanard, Jno. Chew, jr.; Nancy Turnley, March 21, 1782. Deed of conveyance for lots, May 8, 1781. Recd. March 21, 1782, etc.

Augt. 29, 1781. John Haydon of Spts. Co. and Lucy, his wife, to David Galloway, jr., of same county. £5500 curr. 154 a. in St. Geo. Par., Spts. Co. Andrew Buchanan, James Taylor, Wm. McWilliams, Thos. Kenny. March 21, 1782.

Feby. 19, 1780. John Wiglesworth and Philadelphia, his wife, of Spts. Co. to John Welch of Fredksbg. £10,000 curr. Lot 41 in Fredksbg., purchased of Wm. Houston, etc. Richd. Young, Saml. Todd, James Cunningham. Augt. 20, 1780.

Augt. 7, 1780. Hugh Sanders of Spts. Co. and Catherine, his wife; John Sanders and Jane, his wife; Wm. Mastin and Lucy, his wife, to Thomas Bartlet of Spts. Co., Gent. £6000 curr. 900 a. in Berkeley Par., Spts. Co. Edwd. Herndon, Wm. Wood, Thos. Sharpe, A. Frazer, A. Bartlet, W. Frazer, Jno. Chew, jr.; Jos. Brock, Peter Gatewood, Thos. Montague, Thomas Colson. Sept. 20, 1780.

Feby. 10, 1781. Peter Marye and Eleanor, his wife, of Culpeper Co. to Robt. Forsyth of Fredksbg. £350 ster. Lot 18 in Fredksbg., purchased from Mary James, as by deed, Feby. 4, 1760, etc. John Hall, Frans. Tate, Wm. Wiatt. March 15, 1781.

June 30, 1781. Taliaferro x Craig of Orange Co. and Mary, his wife, to Wm. Wiatt of Spts. Co. £20,000 curr. 500 a. in Berkeley Par., Spts.

Co. Jos. Brock, Willm. Smith, Danl. Branham, Benony Williams. July 19, 1781.

Augt. 30, 1781. Wm. Ficklin of Spts. Co. to James Julian of same county. £44 5s. Lgd. Curr: 124 a. in St. Geo. Par., Spts. Co. George Burbridge, Jacob Muselman, —— ——, (written in German). Oct. 18, 1781.

Decr. 14, 1780. Wm. x Webb of Spts. Co. to David Sandidge of same county. £1000 curr. 100 a. in Spts. Co. Henry Gatewood, Sr.; David Sandidge, jr.; James Sandidge. July 19, 1781.

—— ——, 1781. John Edwards of Spts. Co. to Uriah Edwards of same county. £7000. 100 a. in Spts. Co. Jos. Willoughby, Jno. Tankersley, Wm. x Palmer. Augt. 16, 1781.

April 10, 1781. James Pritchett, Senr., of Spts. Co. to his son, Thomas Pritchett of same county. Deed of Gift. Slaves, lands, stocks, etc. Benj. Ballard, James Pritchett, Jeremiah Long, Reuben Hudson. Augt. 16, 1781.

Feby. 24, 1781. Wm. Wood of Spts. Co. to Wm. Scott of same county. To indemnify sd. Scott who stands as security for sd. Wood in several matters, etc. Tract of land whereon sd. Wood resides, etc. Wm. Pemberton, James Pritchett, James Wood, Larkin Pemberton. Augt. 16, 1781.

Augt. 15, 1781. John Craig of Spts. Co. and Sarah, his wife, to James Somerville of Fredksbg. £35,000 curr. paper. 471 a. on Robinson Run, in Spts. Co., whereon sd. Craig lives, etc. No witnesses. Augt. 16, 1781.

Augt. 16, 1781. Thomas Lipscomb and Mary, his wife, of Spts. Co. to Francis King of the state of Maryland. £4000 curr. 400 a. in Spts. Co. No witnesses. Augt. 16, 1781.

June 6, 1781. James Head and Sarah, his wife, of Spts. Co. to Francis King of Maryland. £1595 curr. 290 a. in Spts. Co. Thomas Terry, Thomas Turner, James King. Augt. 16, 1781.

Augt. 16, 1781. James King of Spts. Co. and Susannah, his wife, to Wm. Hewell of same county. £10,000 curr. 300 a. in Spts. Co. No witnesses. Augt. 16, 1781.

April 10, 1781. John Zachary Lewis, Robert Lewis, Nicholas Lewis, Zachary Meriwether in behalf of Jane, his wife; David Meriwether in behalf of Mary, his wife; Zachary Lewis, Waller Lewis, Benjamin Lewis, to Mary Stears of Spts. Co. 5 shill. curr. Two negroes, part of increase of those negroes lent by the last will and testament of Zachary Lewis, decd., to his wife, Mary Lewis, during her life, etc. Witnesses, John Woolfolk, Mary Straughan. Augt. 16, 1781.

March 15, 1781. Richard Estes and Caty, his wife; Richd. Lowry, guardian of Elizabeth and Mary Carlton, orphans of Ambrose Carlton of Spts. Co., decd., to James Mitcham of Spts. Co. £6010 curr. 280 a. in Spts. Co. Whereas, sd. Ambrose Carlton, died, seized and possessed of a tract of 280 a. in Spts. Co., and by his last will and testament, devised the sd. land to his three daughters, viz., Caty (who has since intermarried with the sd. Richd. Estes), Elizabeth and Mary, etc., the sd. Estes in behalf of his sd. wife and the sd. Lowry, in behalf of his sd. Wards, conveys the sd. land, etc. Benj. Alsop, Edmund Foster, Jno. Chew, jr. Augt. 16, 1781.

Augt. 16, 1781. Clement Montague and Ann, his wife, of St. Geo. Par., Spts. Co. to Michael Blunt of Berkeley Par., Spts. Co. £600 curr. 200 a. in Berkeley Par., Spts. Co., part of a tract devised to Wm. Forson, by Michael Guinney, decd. No witnesses. Augt. 16, 1781.

Augt. 29, 1780. Wm. Ball and Mary, his wife, of Spts. Co. to James King of same county. £1000 curr. 300 a. in Spts. Co., purchased of Wm. Garrett, Senr., of Louisa County, etc. Jas. Wiglesworth, Wm. Ashley, W. Dawson. Augt. 16, 1781.

Oct. 18, 1781. Joseph Herndon of Berkeley Par., Spts. Co. and Mary, his wife, to Thomas Sharpe of same par. and county. £56 specie. 28 a. in St. Geo. Par., Spts. Co., part of a larger tract purchased of Wm. Bartlett, etc. No witnesses. Octr. 18, 1781.

Oct. 18, 1781. Joseph Herndon of Berkeley Par., Spts. Co. to Thomas Sharpe of same par. and county. Lease. 237 a. in St. Geo. Par., Spts. Co., part of a tract purchased of Wm. Bartlett, etc. "Sd. Thomas Sharpe and Judith, his wife, and Wm. Sharpe, his eldest son," etc. £14 16s. 3d. specie yearly. No witnesses. Oct. 18, 1781.

Decr. 21, 1780. Wm. Craghill and Elizabeth, his wife, of Stafford Co. to Jonathan Nixon, jr., of Maryland. £3000 curr. 300 a. in St. Geo. Par., Spts. Co. Harris Hooe, Wm. Craghill, jr.; Betty Craghill, John Chew, Lodowick Oneal, John Haydon, Jno. Welch. May 17, 1781.

Oct. 18, 1781. Thomas White of Spts. Co. to his son, Basil White of same county. Deed of Gift. 200 a. on East North East River in Spts. Co., bounded by lands of Caleb Coleman, Thomas Lipscomb, Johnson, and Bowie, etc. Witnesses, Thos. Sharpe, Wm. Chiles, Jno. Chiles. Oct. 18, 1781.

Oct. 18, 1781. "Thomas White of Spts. Co. to my granddaughter, Betty Lipscomb, the daughter of Wm. Chiles, by my daughter, Agness," etc. Deed of Gift. Slave. "Sd. Betty and her husband, Joel Lipscomb," etc. Witnesses, Basil White, Thomas Sharpe. Oct. 18, 1781.

Augt. 23, 1781. Robert Oneal of Spts. Co. and Ann, his wife, to Abram Simons of same county. £500,000 curr. 118 a. in St. Geo. Par., Spts. Co. Jos. Brock, Jno. Chew, jr.; Thomas Waller, jr.; Lodowich Oneal, Wm. Ellis. Octr. 18, 1781.

Oct. 18, 1781. John Sanders and Jane, his wife, of Spts. Co. to John Wright of same county. £3000 curr. 203 a. in Berkeley Par., Spts. Co. No witnesses. Octr. 18, 1781.

Augt. 29, 1781. Lewis Craig of Spts. Co. to James Jones of same county. £200 curr. 233 a. in Spts. Co. Henry Brock, Wm. Mastin, Edwd. Brasfield, Job Shadrack, John Sanders. Oct. 18, 1781.

Nov. 15, 1781. Lucy x Etherton, widow, of Spts. Co. to Clayton Coleman of same county. £10 specie. 15 a. in Spts. Co. No witnesses. Novr. 15, 1781.

Nov. 15, 1781. Benjamin Perry and Mary, his wife, and Elizabeth x Perry, mother of the sd. Benja. of Spts. Co. to John Davenport of same county. £3000 curr. 128 a. in Spts. Co. Jno. Tankersley, Jno. Edwards, Henry MacDaniel, Thomas True. Novr. 15, 1781.

April 16, 1781. Thomas White of Spts. Co. to Leonard J. Waller and Agnes, his wife, of same county. Deed of Gift. Slave. Witnesses, Wm. Chiles, John Chiles. Novr. 15, 1781.

Augt. 23, 1781. Benjamin Robinson and Mildred, his wife, of Spts. Co. to Reuben Hudson of sd. Co. £1200 curr. 32 a. in Spts. Co., dower of the sd. Mildred Robinson, in estate of lands of her former husband, Hezekiah Ellis. [Ed. note, see will of sd. Ellis.] Witnesses, Jos. Brock, Jno. Chew, jr.; Thos. Waller, jr.; Lodowick Oneal, Wm. Ellis. Novr. 15, 1781.

Sept. 3, 1781. Mack McDaniel and Lucy, his wife, of Spts. Co. to Jno. Mastin of same county. £10,000 curr. 60 a. in Spts. Co. Michael x Blunt, Thomas Lipscomb, Nathan Lipscomb. Nov. 15, 1781.

Oct. 22, 1781. Alsey Hubbard and Matthew Hubbard of Pitsylvania Co. to David Chives of Caroline Co. £108 10s. specie. 434 a. in Spts. Co. Long Wharton, Peter Rosell, Thos. Jones, Jno. White. Novr. 15, 1781.

Augt. 27, 1781. James Rawley of Albemarle Co. to Wm. Emerson of Spts. Co. £400 curr. 100 a. in Spts. Co. Job Harris, jr.; Thomas Turner, James Harris. Novr. 15, 1781.

Augt. 27, 1781. James Rawley of Albemarle Co. to James Jarrell of Caroline Co. £400 curr. 100 a. in Spts. Co. Job Harris, jr.; Thomas Turner, James Harris. Novr. 15, 1781.

Sept. 20, 1781. Wm. Mastin and Lucy, his wife, of Spts. Co. to Richard Luck of same county. £40 specie. 125 a. in Spts. Co. (except 25 a. formerly sold Capt. Thos. Bartlett), etc. Jno. Chew, jr.; Thomas Bartlett, Jos. Brock, Peter Gatewood, Thomas Montague. Novr. 15, 1781.

Augt. 11, 1781. Sarah x Hawkins, relict of Philemon Hawkins, decd.; Philemon Hawkins and Catherine, his wife, of Berkeley Par., Spts. Co. to Beverley Winslow of same par. and county. £30,000 paper curr. and £110 specie. 300 a. in same par. and county whereon sd. Sarah, etc., now live. Edwd. Herndon, Willm. Mills, Richd. Coleman, Richd. Dickinson, Edwd. Coleman. Dec. 20, 1781.

Feby. 28, 1782. Jno. Wiglesworth and Philadelphia, his wife, of Spts. Co. to Wm. Smith of Fredksbg. £200 specie. Part of lot in Town of Fredksbg, etc. Wm. McWilliams, James Taylor, John Welch. June 20, 1782.

Augt. ——, 1782. Daniel Lambert and Hannah, his wife, of Berkeley Par., Spts. Co. to Richard Coleman of same par. and county, Carpenter. £20,000 curr. 250 a. in par. and county afsd. Bevy. Winslow, Wm. Mills, Francis Coleman, Thos. x Allen. Sept. 20, 1782.

Augt. ——, 1781. Daniel Lambert and Hannah, his wife, of Berkeley Par., Spts. Co. to Thomas Allen of same par. and county. £100 curr. 50 a. in Spts. Co., etc. Bevy. Winslow, Wm. Mills, Francis Coleman, Richard Coleman. Dec. 20, 1781.

Jany. 8, 1782. John Personet and Ann, his wife, of Spts. Co. to John White of same county. £6 curr. 1½ a. in Berkeley Par., Spts. County. Long. Wharton, Christopher Daniel. Jany. 17, 1782.

May 22, 1779. Robert Bogle, the elder; Robt. Bogle, the younger, and Wm. Scott, all of Love Lane, East Cheap, London, and James Robb of Orange Co., Va., Merchts., and partners, of first part; Jno. Hyndman of London, Mercht, and Thomas Bell of Clement Lane, London, Broker, and Joseph Stanfield of Foster Lane, London, Iron Monger, assignees of estate, etc., of aforenamed Robt. and Robt. Bogle & Scott, of second part; Gawin Corbin of Caroline Co. [Va.], Esqr., and Elizabeth, his wife, of third part, and Wm. Smith of Spts. Co. [Va.], Mercht., of fourth part. Whereas, the sd. Robt., for the sd. Bogles & Scott, did purchase of the representatives of Dr. Jno. Sutherland [viz., Jno. Thornton and Edwd. Carter, Gentlem.], Lots No. 71 and 72 in Fredksbg., Va., and the sd. Robt. being concerned in partnership with the sd. Bogles & Scott, and being their sole agent and atto., etc. [the sd. Scott possessing the same powers except when they may be abridged by the commission of Bankrupt awarded and issued agst. sd. Bogles & Scott], recd. the conveyance of the afsd. two lots, in behalf of the sd. Bogles & Scott, as by Ind., dated Novr. 10, 1771, whereby the fee simple estate in sd. lots was conveyed to aforementioned Bogles & Scott and the sd. Robt., in company, and whereas, the afsd. being so interested and a commission of Bankrupt having been duly awarded, etc., Thos. Lane, Augustine Greenland, and Joseph Eyre, Gentlm., being a major part of the commissioners, etc., etc., by their deed, dat. Jany. 1, 1774, assigned, etc., the right, title and estate of the sd. Bogles & Scott & Co. [particularly describing their interests in America, among which was their interest in the aforementioned lots], unto the afsd. Jno. Hyndman, Thomas Bell and Joseph Stanfield, upon trust to sell and convey to any purchasers the real estates, etc., etc., and whereas, these sd. trustees, being thus interested, etc., etc., by their certain letter of atto., dated Feby. 1, 1774, nominated and appted. [and thereby did confirm the po. hereinbefore vested in him by the Bogles & Scott, etc.], him, the sd. Robb, their lawful attorney, together with Robert Gilchrist of Caroline Co., Mercht., and whereas, the sd. Robb and Gilchrist, being thus vested with po. to act, did on —— ——, 1776, sell the two aforementioned lots to the sd. Gawin Corbin, Esqr., etc., and the sd. Corbin having now sold the same to the sd. Wm. Mills, etc., etc. All of the parties of the first, second, and third parts join in conveyance of the sd. lots, by this Indenture, to sd. Mills; the Corbin acknowledging recpt. of £5900 curr., which sd. Smith pd. for the sd. Lots, etc., etc. Witnesses, Henry Woodford, Jno. Woodford, James Bowie, jr.; Wm. Buckner, jr.; Jno. Miller, Thos. Bromfield, Jas. Somerville, Saml. Roddy, James Taylor, Richd. Young, Jno. Welch. Jany. 17, 1782.

Decr. 18, 1781. John Martin and Elizabeth, his wife, of Spts. Co. to Thomas Sharpe of same county. £150. 100 a. in Spts. Co. Jno. Bradley, Jno. White, Jno. Personet, Wm. Hall. Jany. 17, 1782.

Jany. 15, 1781. Wm. Parker of Berkeley Par., Spts. Co. to his son, Winslow Parker, of same par. and county. Deed of Gift. 113 a. in Spts. Co., Berkeley Par., on Terry's Run. Bevy. Winslow, Benj. Robinson, Wm. Parker, jr.; Francis Coleman, Jno. Hutcherson. Jany. 17, 1782.

Augt. 23, 1781. John Haydon of Spts. Co., planter, and Lucy, his wife, to Richard Kenny of Fredksbg., Mercht. £130 specie. 100 a. in St. Geo. Par., Spts. Co., conveyed by deed, dated April 10, 1770, from Wm. Fitzhugh, Esqr., to Thomas Haydon, father of the sd. John Haydon, etc., sd. Thomas Haydon conveying the same to his son, James Haydon, and by the sd. James Haydon, etc., conveyed to his brother, the sd. John Haydon, as by deed, dated Jany. 13, 1780, etc. Witnesses, Wm. McWilliams, James Taylor, Andrew Buchanan, Edwd. Herndon, Thomas Kenny, Jno. Legg. Jany 17, 1782.

Feby. 21, 1781. Reuben Young of Spts. Co. and Ann, his wife, to Christian Rife of same county. £125 curr. 78 a. in St. Geo. Par., Spts. Co. No witnesses. Feby. 21, 1782.

Feby. 20, 1782. Peter Stubblefield of Spts. Co. and Peggy, his wife, to John Waller (Baptist). £680 *gold* and *silver*. 279 a. in Spts. Co., purchased of James Crawford and Wm. Edw. Waller, etc. Robt. Lewis, Zachy. Meriwether, Geo. Stubblefield, Joel May, Thomas Ashman, Benj. Waller, Wm. Edw. Waller. Feby. 21, 1782.

Sept. 9, 1781. Robert Lewis of Spts. Co. to Joel Parish of sd. county. £1269 12s. 8 a. in Spts. Co. Tho. Minor, Thos. Montague, Zachy. Meriwether. Feby. 21, 1782.

June 5, 1778. George Muir of Fredksbg., po. of atto., to James Somerville of Fredksbg. "Sd. Muir fully intends in short time to go to the West Indies," etc. Witness, James Kemp. March 21, 1782.

May 1, 1779. Wm. Wiatt, in behalf of George Muir and Esther, his wife, both of Spts. Co. to George French of same county. £150 ster. Lot 274 in Fredksbg. Wm. Porter, Richd. Kenny, James Julian. March 21, 1782.

March 8, 1782. Francis Thornton, Esqr., surviving executor of the last will and testament of the Honble. Presley Thornton, Decd., and Wm. Fitzhugh, Esqr., surviving trustee of Benjamin Grymes; Priscilla Grymes, widow of the sd. Grymes, and Benj. Grymes, jr., son and heir at law of the sd. Grymes to James Somerville of Fredksbg. £1346. 1600 a. in Spts. Co., purchased of executors of Col. Wm. Woodford of Caroline, decd., etc., etc. Witnesses, Thos. Smith, Lewis Willis, James Weir, Wm. Arnold, Edwd. Herndon, James Heath, Edwd. Simpson, Wm. McWilliams. March 21, 1782.

March 8, 1782. Francis Thornton, Esqr., surviving executor of Hon. Presley Thornton, decd., and Wm. Fitzhugh, Esqr., surviving trustee of Benj. Grymes to James Somerville of Fredksbg., Mercht. £276 curr. 730 a. in Spts. Co. Thos. Smith, Lewis Willis, Jas. Weir, Wm. Arnold, Edwd. Herndon, Jas. Heath, Edwd. Simpson. March 21, 1782.

Feby. 22, 1782. George Stubblefield of Spts. Co., Gent., and Sally, his wife, to Peter Stubblefield of same county, Gent. £680 specie. 230 a. in Spts. Co., in three tracts, etc. Jno. Chew, jr.; Thomas Montague, Thomas Towles, Nicholas Payne. March 21, 1782.

Sept. 6, 1781. Lewis Craig and Elizabeth, his wife, of Spts. Co. to John Mitchell of same county. £7 curr. Reversion in abt. 50 a., commonly called Gardner's, in Spts. Co., etc. James Somerville, Antho. Arnold, Jno. Skeaton, John Sanders, Benj. Mastin, Wm. Wiatt, Wm. Strother. March 21, 1781.

Sept. 6, 1781.   Lewis Craig of Spts. Co. and Elizabeth, his wife, to John Mitchell of same county. £10 curr. 108 a. in Spts. Co., part of a tract purchased by Taliaferro Craig of Corbin, etc. James Somerville, Antho. Arnold, John Keaton, Wm. Strother, Jno. Sanders, Benj. Mastin, Wm. Wiatt. March 21, 1782.

Sept. 5, 1781.   Daniel Lambert and Hannah, his wife, of Spts. Co. to James Somerville of Fredksbg. £8000 Va. paper money. 273 a. in Spts. Co., purchased of John Craig, as by deeds, May 20, 1773, and by sd. Craig purchased of Richard Ray, in a larger tract, etc. Witnesses, Mourning Pigg, Job Shadrack, Jno. Mitchell, Susanna Mitchell, Wm. Wiatt. March 21, 1782.

Sept. 1, 1781.   Lewis Craig of Spts. Co. and Elizabeth, his wife, to Wm. Strother. £120 curr. 168 a. in Spts. Co. Jno. Ellis, George Cammack, Robt. Smith, Daniel Branham, Antho. Arnold, Tavener Branham. March 21, 1782.

March 21, 178—.   Wm. Strother of Orange Co. and Ann, his wife, to David Pannill. £1—— curr. 168 a. in Spts. Co. No witnesses. March 21, 1782.

April 15, 1782.   Larkin Stanard of Spts. Co., Gent., and Elizabeth, his wife, to Oliver Towles of same county, Gent. £580 specie. 240 a. in Spts. Co. Peter Stubblefield, Geo. Stubblefield, Thomas Towles. April 18, 1782.

Nov. 17, 1781.   Wm. Dillard of North Carolina, to Thomas Dillard of Spts. Co., Va. £35 specie curr. 100 a. in Spts. Co., bequeathed sd. Wm. Dillard by the last will and testament of his father, Thomas Dillard, decd., and adjoins lands of Capt. Nicho. Payne, Jno. Shirley, Jas. Crawford, James Humphreys, Richd. Dillard, and sd. Thomas Dillard. Witnesses, Elisha Dismukes, Jas. Crawford, Sr.; John Shirley, Moses Morris. April 18, 1782.

April 18, 1782.   George Cook and Mary, his wife, of Spts. Co. to Benoni Woodroof of same county. £56 specie. 70 a. in Spts. Co., joining lands of David Woodroof and Harry Terrell, etc. Jno. Hackney, Wm. Cook, Thomas Hackney, Mary Straughan. April 18, 1782.

April 18, 1782.   George Cook and Mary, his wife, of Spts. Co. to Thomas Hackney of same county. £——. 40 a. in Spts. Co., etc. Jno. Hackney, Wm. Cook, Benoni Woodroof, Mary Straughan. April 18, 1782.

March 26, 1782.   Wm. Daingerfield, Wm. Fitzhugh, Mann Page, John Francis Mercer, Gentlemen, to Alexander Spotswood, Esqr. Whereas, an act of assembly passed Dec. 27, 1781, directing certain lands whereof Burgess Ball, is seized as tenant, to be vested in Trustees, whereby 1583 a. in Spts. Co., and 600 a. in Stafford Co., and the sd. lands are vested in the sd. Daingerfield, Fitzhugh, Page, Mercer, and Spotswood, in trust, that they or any three of them should sell and convey the same to purchaser and invest the money arising therefrom in other lands to be conveyed to the sd. Trustees for the benefit of the sd. Ball, during his life, and after his death to such child or children, etc., as he by his will shall think fit to direct, etc., in consideration of £1200, the sd. Trustees convey to the sd. Spotswood 1583 a. in Spts. Co., etc., etc. Witnesses, Jas. Mercer, Jno. Lewis, Henry Armistead. April 18, 1782.

May 16, 1782. Michael Robinson and Esther, his wife, of Spts. Co. to their son-in-law, Thomas Magee, of same county. Deed of Gift. 207 a. in Spts. Co., etc. Thomas Allen, Robt. Smith, Hezekiah Ellis, Wm. Price, Abraham Simons. May 16, 1782.

April 8, 1782. Thomas Powell of Spts. Co., Gent., and Elizabeth, his wife, to George Stubblefield of same county, Gent. £4000 specie. 1243 a. in Spts. Co., whereon sd. Powell now lives, and purchased of Fielding and Jno. Lewis, Esqrs., etc. Witnesses, Larkin Stanard, Peter Stubblefield, Beverley Stanard, Thomas Towles, Nicho. Payne, Thomas Minor, Henry Duerson. May 16, 1782.

April 18, 1782. Thomas Crutcher and Sarah, his wife, of Caroline Co. to Henry Crutcher of Spts. Co., son of the sd. Thomas, etc. Deed of Gift. 336 a. in St. Geo. Par., Spts. Co., etc. Wm. Sneed, Thomas Crutcher, jr.; Richard Blanton. May 16, 1782.

April 15, 1779. Alexander Spotswood of Fredksbg., Gent., and Elizabeth, his wife, to Charles Yates of same town, Gent. £270. 180 a. in St. Geo. Par., Spts. Co. No witnesses. April 15, 1779.

Feby. 5, 1782. Wm. Daingerfield of Spts. Co., Esqr., and Sarah, his wife, to James Mercer of same County, Esqr. £1000 ster. 1300 a. on Snow Creek in Spts. and Caroline Counties, inherited by sd. Sarah, from her father, Lawrence Taliaferro, and her grandfather, John Taliaferro, late of Spts. Co., Decd., etc. Mann Page, James Taylor, Wm. Smith. May 16, 1782.

March 1, 1782. James Mercer of Spts. Co., Esqr., to Wm. Daingerfield of same county, Esqr. £1000 ster. 1300 a. on Snow Creek in Spts. and Caroline Counties, etc., etc. [as in preceding deed, etc.]. Witnesses, Wm. McWilliams, John Lewis, Thomas Brown, James Maury, Sam Roddy, Jno. Welch, Zacharias Lucas. May 16, 1782.

Augt. 20, 1781. Edward Simpson of Fredksbg. and Catharine, his wife, to John Welch of same town. 20,000 lbs. tob. ⅓ of land sold by the Vestry of St. Geo. Par. to Jno. Lewis, and by the sd. Lewis sold to John and Elijah Craig, and by the sd. Craigs sold to the sd. Simpson, and being a lot in town of Fredksbg., etc. Jno. Chew, jr.; Saml. Lucas, Jno. Tinsley. May 16, 1782.

Augt. 20, 1782. Wm. Ellis and Agnes, his wife, of Spts. Co. to George Lewis of same county. £600 curr. 300 a. in Spts. Co. Thos. Colson, Jas. Lewis, Jno. Chew, jr.; Daniel Branham, Thos. Strachan, Hezekiah Ellis. Sept. 19, 1782.

DEED BOOK K

1782–1785

May 15, 1782. Aaron Fontaine and Barbara, his wife, to David Sandidge of Spots. Co. £225 curr. 260 a. in Spots. Co. No witnesses. June 20, 1782.

May 19, 1780. Jno. Wiglesworth and Philadelphia, his wife, to Wm. Clutton. £1520 curr. 95 a. in Spots. Co., etc. Jas. Jarvis, Richd. Todd, Richd. Garner. June 20, 1782.

May 17, 1782. Henry Crutcher of Spots. Co. to Anthony Bartlett of same Co. £180 curr. 336 a. in St. Geo. Par., Spots. Co., etc. Bennet Pemberton, Jno. Tankersley, Jno. Edwards, Harry Bartlett, Thomas Montague, Jno. Chew, jr. June 20, 1782.

April 17, 1782. Henry Chiles of Spots. Co. to David Sandidge of same Co. £1000 curr. 100 a. in Spots. Co., etc. Austin Sandidge, David Sandidge, jr.; James Sandidge, Jno. Rawlings, Thomas Rawlings. June 20, 1782.

Decr. 17, 1780. Wm. Nelson and Elizabeth, his wife, of Spts. Co. to Nathl. Sanders of same Co. £5000. 207 a. in Spots. Co., etc. Henry McDonald, Alexander Johnston, Mordacai Mastin. June 20, 1782.

June 20, 1782. Lewis Willis of King Geo. Co., Gent., and Ann, his wife, and Benj. Johnston of Washington Co., Penna., and Dorothy, his wife, to Robt. Forsyth of Fredksbg., Va. Whereas, sd. Willis, being seized of a tract of land adj. the town of Fredksbg., Spots. Co., which he purchased of the Est. of Roger Dixon, Gent., Decd., did sell 15 a. thereof to the sd. Johnston, but before any conveyance was made to him the sd. Johnston agreed for the sale of the sd. 15 a. to the sd. Forsyth for £55 curr. No witnesses. June 20, 1782.

May 21, 1782. Wm. Bledsoe of Lincoln Co., Va., and Elizabeth, his wife, to Wm. McWilliams of Spots. Co. £100 curr. 260 a. near Fredksbg., Spots. Co., formerly property of Capt. Wm. Miller, decd. Witnesses, Moses Bledsoe, Jno. Floyd, Antho. Gholson, Lawrence Long, Wm. Ellis. June 20, 1782.

March 9, 1782. John Hutcherson of Spots. Co. and Mary Stears of same Co. "Whereas, as marriage is shortly intended to be had and solemnized between the sd. parties," etc., and whereas, sd. Mary Stears being possessed in her own right of 2 slaves, and sundry cattle and goods and chattels, liberty is granted her to dispose of the same without hindrance of the sd. Hutcherson, etc. Witnesses, Jas. Wiglesworth, Senr.; Jos. Duerson, Jno. Steward. June 20, 1782.

July 15, 1782. Jonathan Nixon, jr., of Province of Maryland, to Bartlett Collins of Spots. Co. £75 curr. 300 a. in St. Geo. Par., Spots. Co., etc.

A. Bartlett, Jno. Curtis, Benja. Alsop, Jno. Wood, Jas. Wood. July 18, 1782.

April 5, 1782. George Stubblefield and Sally, his wife, of Spots. Co. to Jno. Chew, jr., of same Co. £1296 gold and silver. 426 a., and 6 a. in Spots. Co., etc. Witnesses, Thomas Towles, Nicho. Payne, Benja. Stubblefield, Peter Stubblefield, Thomas Powell. July 18, 1782.

Feby. 16, 1781. Whereas, Henry Brock, late of Spots. Co., did by his last will, etc., lend unto his wife, Barbara Brock, all his est., real and personal, during her life or widowhood, and after her death or marriage to be equally divided among his children, viz., Joseph, Mary, Hannah, Elizabeth, Henry, and John Brock, and whereas, the sd. Barbara, with the consent of her sd. children above mentioned (and now all being of lawful age), has agreed to divide the slaves of the sd. Henry Brock, decd., among his children in the following manner, to wit: To Joseph Brock, 1 negro; to Jno. Bourn (who intermarried with Mary), 3 negroes; to Henry Cammack (who intermarried with Hannah), 1 negro; to Elizabeth Brock, 1 negro, etc.; to Henry Brock, 1 negro; to John Brock, 1 negro; the sd. Barbara Brock to keep one negro during her lifetime and after her death to be divided, etc. Witnesses, Jos. Brock, Edwd. Herndon, Jno. Estes. July 18, 1782.

Feby. 22, 1781. Henry x. Cammack of Spots. Co. to his wife, Hannah Cammack. Deed of Gift. 1 negro. And after sd. Hannah's death, to her children or in case of failure in issue then to the sd. Hannah's brothers and sisters, etc. Witnesses, Henry Gatewood, jr.; Jno. Cammack. July 18, 1782.

July 15, 1782. Jno. Chew, jr., of Spots. Co. and Elizabeth, his wife, to Robert Lewis of same Co. £1000 specie. 348 a. in Spots. Co., etc. Jos. Sams, Leo Young, Jno. Carnochan, Geo. Stubblefield. July 18, 1782.

Feby. 19, 1782. Nicholas Lewis of Spots. Co. and Elizabeth, his wife, to Benja. Waller of same Co. £3500 curr. 120 a. in Spots. Co., etc. Thos. Minor, Joel Parish, Wm. Pettus, Geo. Stubblefield, B. Stubblefield, Peter Stubblefield. July 18, 1782.

Feby. 19, 1782. Nicholas Lewis and Elizabeth, his wife, of Spots. Co. to Joel Parrish of same co. £3500. 90 a. in Spots. Co., etc. Thos. Minor, Benja. Waller, Wm. Pettus, Geo. Stubblefield, B. Stubblefield, Peter Stubblefield. July 18, 1782.

July 4, 1782. Robert Lewis of Spots. Co. to Benjamin Waller of same co. £32. 32 a. in Spots. Co., bequeathed the sd. Robt. Lewis by his father, Jno. Lewis, decd., etc. Jno. Z. Lewis, Peter Mason, Saml. Longan, Fielding Woodroof, Geo. Stubblefield, B. Stubblefield, P. Stubblefield. July 18, 1782.

Sept. 4, 1781. Mathew Gale of Orange Co., po. of atto., to Stapleton Crutchfield of Spots. Co., etc. Witnesses, Edwd. Herndon, Thomas Herndon. Augt. 15, 1782.

July 4, 1782. Richard Young and Mary, his wife, of Spots. Co. to Wm. Smith, Gent., of Fredksbg. £90 curr. 66 a. in St. Geo. Par., Spots. Co. Wm. Price, Jas. Lewis, Thomas Allen. Augt. 15, 1782.

Augt. 2, 1782. Bartlett·Collins and Elizabeth, his wife, of Spots. Co. to Wm. Porter of same co. £125 curr. 300 a. in St. Geo. Par., Spots. Co., etc. Harry Bartlett, Benja. Alsop, A. Fraser, J. Wood. Augt. 15, 1782.

July 24, 1782. Thomas Allen and Mary, his wife, of Spots. Co. to Thomas Jennings of same county. £58 curr. 58 a. in Spots. Co., etc. Richd. Young, Jno. Herndon, Jos. Brock, Jno. Wiglesworth, Wm. Fox. Augt. 15, 1782.

June 11, 1782. Rawlins Pulliam (heir at law of James Pulliam, Decd.), of Spots. Co. to Stephen Johnston of same co. £150 curr. 200 a. in Spots. Co., etc. Phil. B. Johnson, Thomas Rawlins, Jno. Rawlins. Augt. 15, 1782.

Augt. 13, 1782. George Stubblefield and Sally, his wife, of Spots. Co. to Clayton Coleman of same county. £40 curr. 80 a. in Spots. Co., etc. Leonard Young, Rice Vass, Molly Kenniday. Augt. 15, 1782.

—— ——, 1782. Nicholas Hawkins, jr., and Mary, his wife, of Spots. Co. to Wm. Gholson, jr. £30 curr. 133 a. in Spots. Co. No witnesses. Augt. 15, 1782.

Augt. 15, 1782. Nicholas Hawkins and Elizabeth, his wife, of St. Geo. Par., Spots. Co. to Larkin Perry of Par. and co. afsd. £30 curr. 120 a. in Spots. Co., etc. No witnesses. Augt. 15, 1782.

May 5, 1729. James Mercer of Fredksbg., Atto. at Law, to George Weedon, Esqr., of same town. £600 curr. "Lots 240 and 250 on each side of Main St. in Fredksbg., and below the houses where the late Mr. Roger Dixon lived," etc. Jno. Lewis, R. B. Chew, Jno. Legg, Jas. Taylor, Wm. McWilliams, Larkin Smith. Augt. 15, 1782.

April 28, 1779. George Weedon of Fredksbg., Esqr., and Catherine, his wife, of first part; the sd. Geo. Weedon, Jno. Tennant of Caroline Co., Doctor of Physic, and Isabella Mercer, widow and relict of Brigadier Hugh Mercer, late of Fredksbg., decd., execrs. of the will of the sd. Mercer, of the second part, to Samuel Selden of Stafford Co., Esqr. Whereas, the sd. George Weedon and Hugh Mercer were seized, as joint tenants, of three certain lots in Fredksbg., there being no division, and the sd. Mercer, dying, did direct in his will the sale of certain property in which was included the within named lot, and did by his will appt. the sd. Weedon, Tennant, and Isabella Mercer, as afsd., his executors, etc. This Ind. witnesseth the sd. Geo. Weedon and his wife, Catharine, in consideration of the premises and 20 s. ster., and the sd. Executors for the sum of £80 curr., convey to the sd. Seldon, Lot 203 in Fredksbg., purchased by sd. Weedon and Mercer in 1764, of Roger Dixon, Gent., etc., etc. Witnesses, Jno. Lewis, Wm. McWilliams, R. B. Chew, Larkin Smith, Jno. Legg, Jno. Rose. Augt. 15, 1782.

April 28, 1779. Geo. Weedon of Fredksbg., of the first part; sd. Weedon, Jno. Tennant of Caroline Co. and Isabella Mercer of Fredksbg., widow, Execrs. of the will of Brigadier Hugh Mercer, late of Fredksbg., decd., of second part, to James Mercer of Fredksbg., atto. at law. Whereas, etc., etc. [as in preceding deed]. This Ind. witnesseth the sd. Weedon, etc., in consideration of £300 curr., being one moiety of the purchase money, etc., and the sd. Executors in consideration of the like sum of

£300, convey to the sd. Jas. Mercer Lots 240 and 250 in town of Fredksbg., purchased by sd. Weedon and Mercer of Roger Dixon, Gent., etc., etc. Witnesses, Jno. Lewis, R. B. Chew, Jno. Legg, Jas. Taylor, Larkin Smith, Wm. McWilliams, Jno. Rose. Augt. 15, 1782.

Augt. 2, 1782. James Redd and Elizabeth, his wife, and Allen Redd and Susannah, his wife, of Spots. Co. to Edwd. Dannaby [Darnaby], planter. £20 curr. 111 a. in St. Geo. Par., Spots. Co., etc. Philip Dud. Redd, Jno. Bullock, Marmaduke x Holesworth. Augt. 15, 1782.

Augt. 14, 1783. Edwd. Simpson and Catherine, his wife, and James Durand and Molly, his wife, to Mary Sullivan. £153. 306 a. in Spots. Co., which sd. Simpson, etc., did by deed, dated Novr. 14, 1780, sell and convey to sd. Durand, and the sd. Durand for divers causes, etc., relinquished all claim and title to the sd. Simpson, etc. Jno. Wiglesworth, Thomas Allen, Jno. Rose. Augt. ——, 1782.

Augt. 13, 1782. Robt. Lewis of Spots. Co., Gent., to Nicholas and Jno. Lewis of same Co., Gentl. Whereas, sd. Nicho. and Jno. having become bound in several bonds to Geo. Stubblefield of same Co., amounting to £1000 curr., and the sd. Robert Lewis to indemnify them the sd. Nicho. and Jno. Lewis, etc. 848 a. in Spots. Co., etc. O. Towles, Jno. Woolfolk, Zachary Meriwether. Sept. 19, 1782.

Augt. 26, 1782. Benjamin Johnston of Washington Co., Penna. (formerly of Fredksbg., Va.), and Dorothy, his wife, to Wm. Dawson of Spots. Co., Va. £20 curr. 100 a. on East North East River in Spots. Co. Witnesses, Peter Stubblefield, Larkin Stanard, Jno. Chew, jr.; Nicholas Payne. Sept. 19, 1782.

Sept. 19, 1781. Thomas Duerson of Spots. Co. and Sarah, his wife, to James Crawford of same Co. £1100 curr. 94 a. in Spots. Co., conveyed by Jno. Hall to Jno. Waller, and by sd. Waller to Sarah Wiglesworth, now the wife of the sd. Thomas Duerson, etc. No witnesses. Sept. 19, 1782.

Feby. 21, 1782. Wm. Ball and Mary, his wife, of Halifax Co. and Jno. Ball (son of sd. Wm. Ball by his former wife Ann), and Nancy, his wife, of same co. to Wm. Bladyes of Spots. Co. £1750 curr. 200 a. in Spots. Co., conveyed by deed, dated June 4, 1764, by Jno. Carpenter to the sd. Wm. Ball and his heirs by his former wife Ann, etc., etc. Witnesses, Wm. Cason, Jno. Knight, Jno. Blaydes. Sept. 19, 1782.

Sept. 19, 1782. Henry Duerson and Sarah, his wife, of Spots. Co. to Thomas Duerson of same co., in consideration of 90 a. in Spots. Co., this day conveyed by sd. Thos. Duerson and Sarah, his wife, to James Crawford, at the request of the sd. Henry Duerson, the sd. Henry hereby conveys to sd. Thomas his right in undivided moiety of 354 a. in a tract bequeathed sd. Henry by his father, Thomas Duerson, Decd., etc. No witnesses. Septr. 19, 1782.

June 20, 1782. Richard Loury and Betty, his wife, of Spots. Co. to John Hart of same county. £1000 curr. 100 a. in Spots. Co., etc. Elijah Estes, Moses Estes. Septr. 19, 1782.

Sept. 19, 1782. Wm. Ellis, jr., of Spots. Co. to Abraham Simons of same co. £60 curr. 96 a. on Lewis's River in Spots. Co., etc. Danl. Branham, G. Bell, Jno. Thornton, Robt. Smith, Henry Carter, Reuben Hudson, Richd. Estis. Sept. 19, 1782.

Oct. 17, 1782. Garritt Minor to Joseph Wharton. Lease. 100 a. in Berkeley Par., Spots. Co. "Sd. Joseph Wharton and Mary, his wife, and Samuel Wharton, his son," etc. 600 lbs. tob. yearly, etc. Jas. Nelson, jr.; Beverley Winslow, Benja. Robinson. Oct. 17, 1782.

Oct. 17, 1780. Garritt Minor to Peter Schoolar. Lease. 100 a. in Berkeley Par., Spots. Co. "Sd. Peter Schoolar and Ann, his wife, and Ann, his daughter," etc. £5 curr. yearly, etc. Beverley Winslow, Benja. Winslow, Jas. Nelson, jr.; Wm. Mills. Oct. 17, 1782.

Sept. 20, 1782. James Jones and Mildred, his wife, of Spots. Co. to John Penny of same co. £200 curr. 233 a. in Spots. Co., etc. Henry Brock, Jas. Bartlett, Wm. Mills, Bevy. Winslow. Oct. 17, 1782.

Oct. 12, 1782. Wm. Emerson of Spots. Co. to Thomas Goodloe of same co. £141. 141 a. in Spots. Co., etc. No witnesses. Sarah Emerson also signing the deed. Oct. 17, 1782.

Augt. 13, 1782. Elizabeth x Lawless of Spots. Co., po. of atto., to Reuben Straughan of same co. Witnesses, Bennet Pemberton, Benja. Masten, John Greenhow. Oct. 17, 1782.

Oct. 8, 1782. Fielding Woodroof of Spots. Co., deed of gift to his daughter, Catharine. 3 slaves. Witnesses, Thomas Towles, Peter Stubblefield, Nicholas Payne, Nicholas Lewis. Oct. 17, 1782.

Feby. 14, 1783. Michael Robinson of St. Geo. Par., Spots. Co. to his his son, Michael Robinson, jr. Deed of Gift. 5 negroes. Witnesses, Danl. Branham, Jno. Wiglesworth. Feby. 20, 1783.

March 18, 1783. Michael Robinson of St. Geo. Par., Spots. Co. to his son, William Robinson. Deed of Gift. 2 negroes. Witnesses, Edwd. Darnaby, Thomas True. March 20, 1783.

Sept. 19, 1783. Anthony Bartlett of Spots. Co. to George Stubblefield of same co. £152 specie. Mortgage. 336 a. in St. Geo. Par., Spots. Co., purchased of Henry Crutcher, etc. O. Towles, David Woodroof, B. Stubblefield. Sept. 19, 1783.

Nov. 19, 1782. Francis x Cammack and Clary, his wife, of Spots. Co. and Ann x Cammack [mother of the sd. Francis], to Anthony Frazer of same co. £20 10s. curr. 20½ a. in Berkeley Par., Spots. Co., etc. Benj. Holloday, jr.; Benj. Perry, Jno. Jesse. Novr. 21, 1782.

Jany. 3, 1783. Joel Parish of Spots. Co. to James Lewis of same co. £200 curr. 175 a. in St. Geo. Par., Spots. Co., etc. Edwd. Herndon, Jos. Herndon, Thoms. Herndon, Thomas Towles, Nicho. Payne. Jany. 16, 1783.

Feby. 20, 1783. George Carter, an orphan, apprentices himself to James Crawford, jr., of Spots. Co. No witness. Feby. 20, 1783.

Dec. 31, 1783. Thomas Strachan of Spots. Co. and Mary, his wife, to James Pervis of Loudoun Co. £15,000 curr. 308 a. on River Ny in Spots. Co., etc. Harry Bartlet, Jona. Johnston, James Dudley, Jos. Jones. Feby. 20, 1783.

Feby. 20, 1783. Richd. Dillard of Spots. Co. and Susannah, his wife, to James Hicks of Caroline Co. £150 curr. 124 a. in Spots. Co., whereon Thos. Dillard, Decd., lived, etc. Thos. Shearly, John Shearly, Joel May. Feby. 20, 1783.

Feby. 20, 1783. Rice Vass of Spots. Co., son and heir-at-law of Philip Vass, decd. (dying intestate), to David Sandidge, jr., of same co. £1750 curr. Right, title and interest in two negroes "now possessed by my mother, Mary Vass, widow of my sd. father," etc. Geo. Mason, Leonard Young, Aaron Higgin, Wm. Brown. Feby. 20, 1783.

Oct. 30, 1782. Charles Yates of Fredksbg. to Thomas Casson [Cason] of Stafford Co. £900 curr. 1301 a. in Spots. Co., purchased of Jno. Harrison, Alexander Spotswood, Jos. Brock, and Jno. Spindle, etc. Witnesses, Jas. Somerville, James Taylor, Wm. Lovell, Edwd. Simpson, Jno. Rose. Feby. 20, 1783.

Feby. 20, 1783. James Davis, orph. of James Davis, decd., apprentices himself to John Carter. No witnesses. Feby. 21, 1783.

June 10, 1779. James Pritchett, Senr., of Spots. Co. to his daughter, Sarah Pritchett. Deed of Gift. A negro slave. Witnesses, Thomas Strachan, A. Frazer, Jno. Holladay, jr. March 20, 1783.

Novr. 21, 1782. Harry Chew of Spots. Co. to Jno. Chew, Senr., of same co. £10 specie, and 10,000 weight tob. Mortgage. 160 a. Witnesses, Thos. Allen, Wm. Fox, Thomas Waller, jr. March 20, 1783.

Augt. 23, 1782. Peter Marye and Eleanor, his wife, of Culpeper Co. to Lodowick Oneal of Spots. Co. £228 10s. curr. 1140 a. in St. Geo. Par., Spots. Co., etc. Jno. Brock, Benj. Grayson, Thomas Stewart. March 20, 1783.

March 17, 1783. Edwd. Herndon, Jos. Herndon, Thomas Bartlett and Harry Bartlett of Spots. Co. to James Pervis of same co. Whereas, Wm. Bartlett by his deed, dated Nov. 19, 1772, did convey 153 a. of land to the sd. Herndons and Bartletts, in trust, for the use of Thomas Perry and Sarah, his wife, for the time of their natural lives and afterwards to be sold, the sd. Thomas Perry and Sarah, his wife, having relinquished their right, etc., in the sd. land by signing their names hereto, etc. This indenture Witnesseth, for the sum of £154, the sd. persons convey the sd. land to the sd. Pervis, etc. Witnesses, Jo. Brock, Jno. Estes, Jno. Smith, jr.; James Mitcham, Wm. Beasley, Jno. Crutchfield. March 20, 1783.

March 17, 1773. Bond of Thomas, William, Milley, Larkin, Salley, Bartlet, Molly, Suckey, and Nancy Perry, to Edward Herndon, Jos. Herndon, Thomas Bartlett and Harry Bartlett, to indemnify them against the claim of Edmond Bartlett Perry, an infant son of Thomas and Sarah Perry, etc. The bond recites, whereas, Wm. Bartlett, by his deed, did convey to Edwd. and Jos. Herndon, Thos. and Harry Bartlett, 154 a. in St. Geo. Par., Spots. Co., in trust for Thomas Perry and Sarah, his wife, during their lives and after their deaths to be sold and the money arising from the sale thereof to be equally divided among the surviving children of sd. Perry and Sarah, his wife, and whereas, sd. Thomas Perry and Sarah, his wife, relinquished their right to the sd. land and the sd. Trustees sold the same to Jas. Pervis for £154, and by consent of the children of the sd. Thomas Perry and Sarah, his wife, to wit, Wm. Perry, Milley Perry, Larkin Perry, Salley Perry, Bartlet Perry, Molly Perry, Suckey Perry, and Nancy Perry, etc., etc. Witnesses, Jos. Brock, Jno. Estes. March 20, 1783.

—— —— ——. Thomas x Perry of St. Geo. Par., Spots. Co., for the sum of £154 curr., conveys to his children, viz., Wm. Milley, Larkin Salley, Bartlet, Molly, Suckey, Nancy, and Edmund Perry, whole of estate both real and personal, to be taken possession of after the deaths of sd. Thomas Perry and Sarah, his wife. Witnesses, Jos. Brock, Jno. Estis. March 20, 1783.

Dec. 10, 1782. Lodowick Oneal and Susannah, his wife, to John Wiglesworth of Spots. Co. £90. 90 a. in St. Geo. Par., Spots. Co., etc. Geo. Stubblefield, James Purvis, Jno. Smith, jr. March 20, 1783.

April 17, 1783. Joseph Herndon, Gent., and Mary, his wife, of Spots. Co., and his son, Edwd. Herndon, jr., Gent., and Margaret his wife, to George Stubblefield of same co., Gent. Whereas, the sd. Jos. Herndon did give to his son, the sd. Edwd. Herndon, jr., a certain tract of land, and the sd. Edwd., without having had a conveyance of the same in writing, did sell the sd. 172½ a. in St. Geo. Par., Spots. Co., to the sd. Stubblefield for the sum of £300 curr., the sd. parties enter into this deed of conveyance to the sd. Stubblefield, etc. Witnesses, Jno. Brock, Jno. Chew. April 17, 1783.

Novr. 22, 1782. Jno. Graves of North Carolina, eldest son and heir at law of Thos. Graves of Spots. Co., Va., to Wm. Pettus of Va. Whereas, sd. Thos. Graves, decd., by his last will and testament, after certain legacies were paid, directed the remainder of his estate equally divided among all his children or their heirs, but did not empower his executors to convey the same, the title so far, therefore, remains vested in the sd. Jno. Graves, as eldest son and heir at law, etc., and it being found necessary to sell and convey certain tracts of land in Spots. Co., whereof sd. Thos. Graves died, seized, etc., this indenture witnesseth, the sd. Jno. Graves, for the sum of £451, gold or silver, to be pd. by the sd. Pettus to the Executors of the sd. Thomas Graves, the sd. John hereby conveys to the sd. Pettus 399 a. in Spots. Co., etc., etc. Witnesses, Joseph Graves, Jno. Graves, Wm. Graves, jr.; Jno. Arnold, Jno. W. Pettus. April 17, 1783.

Dec. 9, 1779. Wm. Arnold and Mary, his wife, of Randolph Co., North Carolina, to John Arnold of Louisa Co., Va. 5 s., and the love and good will they bear the sd. John Arnold, convey to him 230 a. in Spots. Co., etc. Wm. Graves, Wm. Pettus, Wm. Pettus, jr.; Jno. Z. Lewis, Robert Lewis. April 17, 1783.

April 16, 1783. Robert Payne and Rachel, his wife, of Spots. Co. to Robert Coleman of same co. £50 curr. 100 a. in Spots. Co., devised by Jno. Payne, decd., to be divided between sd. Robt. Payne and his brother, Barnet Payne, etc., etc. Witnesses, Micajah Poole, Jos. Hewell, Barnet x Payne. April 17, 1783.

Novr. 25, 1782. Wm. Wiatt, on behalf of George Muir and Esther, his wife, both of Spots. Co. to George French of same co. £150 ster. Lot 247 in town of Fredksbg., conveyed by Roger Dixon (since decd.), to David

Blair and by the sd. Blair to the sd. George Muir, etc. Witnesses, Jno. Julian, Jas. Julian. April 17, 1783.

Decr. 7, 1782. John Colquitt of Spots. Co. to David Pulliam of same county. £175 curr. 163 a. in Spots. Co., etc. Henry True, Benj. Perry, Benj. Mastin, Thomas True, Martin True, Joseph Pulliam. April 17, 1783.

March 28, 1783. Thomas Allen and Mary, his wife, of Spots. Co. to John Chisum of same co. £200 paper curr. 50 a. in Spots. Co., etc. Thomas Jennings, Benj. Ballard, Jos. Hoomes. April 17, 1783.

Nov. 1, 1782. Francis Irwin and Ann, his wife, of Spts. Co. to Dennis Wright of same county. £100. 268 a. in Spots. Co., etc. Walter Chiles, Jno. Mastin, Benj. Perry, David Pulliam. April 17, 1783.

April 17, 1783. Thomas Dillard and Richard Dillard of Spots. Co. to James Crawford of same county. £150 curr. 75 a. in Spots. Co., "formerly belonging to their father, Thomas Dillard, decd.," etc. No witnesses. April 17, 1783.

Oct. 7, 1782. Wm. Jones of Spots. Co. to Joseph Hoomes of Charles City Co. Lease. "Parcel of land commonly called the Wilderness," etc. £30, gold or silver, yearly, etc. Witness, Jno. Brock. April 17, 1783.

July 2, 1783. Thomas Carr of Spots. Co. to Benj. Robinson of Fredksbg. £85 10s. 85½ a. in St. Geo. Par., Spots. Co., etc. Jas. Julian, Wm. Robinson, Jno. Mitcham. July 17, 1783.

March 25, 1783. Wm. Dawson, of first part; Denis Wright, of second part; John Mastin, of third part; Joel Lewis, of fourth part. An agreement between them to establish certain lines between their several properties in Spots. County, etc., etc. Witnesses, Walter Chiles, Jno. Harlan, Michael Blunt. April 17, 1783.

Sept. 9, 1782. Richd. Stevens of Caroline Co. to George Shepperd of Spots. Co. £200 curr. 200 a. in Spots. Co., known by name of Downes, and now occupied by Wm. Darnaby, etc. Witnesses, Wm. Johnston, jr.; G. Baynham, Charles Tod, Joseph Brock, Thos. Towles. April 17, 1783.

May 25, 1783. Lodowick Oneal and Susannah, his wife, to their daughter, Catherine, wife of Jno. Rogers. Deed of Gift. 400 a. in St. Geo. Par., Spots. Co. No witnesses. May 15, 1783.

April 17, 1783. Lodowick Oneal and Susannah, his wife, of Spots. Co. to Thomas Carr of same Co. £40 specie. 85 a. in St. Geo. Par., Spots. Co., etc. Jno. True, Wm. Mead, Jos. Stewart. May 15, 1783.

May 14, 1783. Henry Head and Nancy, his wife, of Spots. Co. to Samuel Alsop of Caroline Co. £162. 162 a. in Spots. Co., etc. Hy. Crutcher, Alexr. x Moor, Thomas Henderson. May 15, 1783.

May 15, 1783. George Kiger of Frederick Co. and Nancy, his wife, to Zachariah Lucas of Fredksbg., Spots. Co. £322 curr. Lot 76 in town of Fredksbg., purchased by sd. Kiger of sd. Lucas, as executor of his father, Peter Lucas, decd., etc. Witnesses, Jas. Jarvis, Thos. Strachan, Jas. Hackley, Tully Whithurst. June 19, 1783.

June 19, 1783. Jno. White and Mary, his wife, of Spots. Co., to Basil White of same county. "Good will and affection and £50 specie." 800 a. in Spots. Co., etc., etc   No Witnesses. June 19, 1783.

Octr. 26, 1782. Wm. x Arnold of Spots. Co. to Joseph Willoughby of same county. £1000. 300 a. in Spots. Co., etc., etc. Basil White, Jno. Langley, Edlyne Willoughby, Wm. Willoughby, Michael Blunt. June 19, 1783.

June 17, 1783. George Cook and Mary, his wife, of Spots. Co. to George Mason of Caroline Co. £80 curr. 114 a. in Spots. Co., etc., etc. Jno. Carles, Thos. Goodloe, Wm. Wiglesworth, James Mason. June 19, 1783.

June 19, 1783. Wm. x Owens of Spots. Co., apprentices himself to Charles MacCalley of same co., Carpenter, etc. No witnesses. June 19, 1783.

June 3, 1783. Lodowick O'Neal and Susannah, his wife, to John Rogers. 630 a. whereon sd. O'Neal now lives and eleven slaves, in trust, three of the sd. slaves, etc., for the use of the sd. Susannah, during her life and then afterwards for the benefit of those claiming under the will of Capt. Wm. Carr, decd., the sd. 630 a. of land and the remainder of the slaves, for the use of the sd. Lodowick, his heirs., etc., forever, etc. Witnesses, Jno. True, Danl. Scrugham, Wm. Mead, Wm. Steward. June 19, 1783.

July 17, 1783. Henry Johnston and Agnes, his wife, of Spots. Co. to Ann Shackelford, widow. £20 specie. 20 a. in Spots. Co., etc. No witnesses. July 17, 1783.

June 30, 1783. Benj. Chapman of Spots. Co. and Elizabeth, his wife; George Stubblefield and Sally, his wife, of same co. to Thomas Powell of same co. Whereas, sd. Chapman did sell to sd. Stubblefield 303 a., formerly belonging to Jno. Chapman, decd., and the sd. Stubblefield before the same was conveyed agreed for the sale of same to the sd. Powell, the sd. Powell paying the sd. Chapman £330 specie and the sd. Powell paying the sd. Stubblefield the like sum, etc. Conveyance. Larkin Chew, O. Towles, Harry Bartlet. July 17, 1783.

July 11, 1783. John Waller and Elizabeth, his wife, of Spots. Co. to Benj. Chapman of same co. £160 specie. 150 a. conveyed to sd. Waller, by Peter Stubblefield, in Spots. Co. Thos. Towles, Nicho. Payne, Bennet Pemberton. July 17, 1783.

July 17, 1783. Jno. Z. Lewis of Spots. Co., Gent., to Haws Coleman of same co. £198 curr. 220 a. in Berkeley Par., Spots. Co., etc. No witnesses. July 17, 1783.

July 17, 1783. Jno. Zachary Lewis of Spots. Co. to Clayton Coleman of same co. £150 curr. 123 a. in Spots. Co., etc. Jno. Brock, Haws Coleman, Spencer Coleman. July 17, 1783.

Novr. 29, 1782. Jno. Herndon and Mary, his wife, of Spots. Co.; Jno. Wiglesworth and Philadelphia, his wife, of same co., and James Jarvis and Mary, his wife, of Fredksbg. to Samuel Roddy of Fredksbg. Whereas, sd. Herndon and wife, for a valuable consideration, did sell to sd. Wiglesworth 108 a. in St. Geo. Par., Spots. Co., the sd. Wiglesworth, etc., being seized and possessed thereof, but having no deed of conveyance, did sell the same to the sd. Jarvis, and the sd. Jarvis, being seized and possessed thereof, but having no deed, did sell the same to the sd. Roddy. All the sd. parties do herein acknowledge the receipt of the considerations to each other paid and join in this conveyance, etc., etc. Saml. Todd, Richd. Garner, Jos. Fox, Benony Williams. July 17, 1783.

Augt. 13, 1782. Jno. Rogers and Caty, his wife, of Spots. Co. to Thomas Pollard of Fairfax Co. £1200 curr. 640 a. in Spots. Co., on Middle River, branch of Mattapony, etc. (except dower of Lucy Rogers, widow of Wm. Rogers, decd., who is now in actual possession, etc.). Witnesses, Lodowick Oneal, Wm. Rogers, Geo. Rogers, Jas. Brown, Jno. Welch. March 20, 1783.

July 16, 1783. Wm. Miller Bledsoe of Lincoln Co. and Elizabeth, his wife, to Wm. McWilliams of Fredksbg., Spots. Co. £100 curr. 261 a. in Spots. Co., devised sd. Bledsoe, by his grandfather, Wm. Miller, decd., part of a pat. granted Jno. Miller, Feby. 9, 1737, and by him conveyed the sd. Wm. Miller, etc., etc. No witnesses. July 17, 1783. [Sd. Wm. Miller Bledsoe, son of Joseph Bledsoe, etc. Bond dated July 16, 1783.]

July 17, 1783. Aquilla Johnston and Elizabeth, his wife, of Caroline Co. to David Galloway, jr., of Spots. Co. £5 curr. 510 a. in St. Geo. Par., Spots. Co., formerly Col. Gawin Corbin's, and adj. lines of Nicho. Hawkins, Jas. Pritchett, Jno. Mitchell, Thomas Pettit, Thos. Crutcher, and Alex. Spotswood, etc., etc. Witness, Jno. Miller, Jno. Brock, Beverley Stanard. July 17, 1783.

Augt. 8, 1783. Thomas Strachan and Mary, his wife, of Spots. Co., of first part; John Hull and Ann, his wife, of Northumberland Co. to Jno. Willis of Spots. Co. £1200 curr. 440 a. in St. Geo. Par., Spots. Co. Witnesses, Thos. Towles, Nicho. Payne, Jno. Chew, jr.; Geo. Stubblefield, Wm. Barret, Larkin Chew, Mathew Carpenter, Thomas Bartlett. Aug. 21, 1783.

May 1, 1784. Thomas x Oliver and Martha, his wife, of Spots. Co. to Reuben Straughan of same co. £40 curr. 100 a. in Spots. Co., etc., etc. Jno. Crutchfield, Elisabeth Straughan, Jas. Straughan. May 5, 1784.

June 1, 1784. Reuben Straughan and Catharine, his wife, of Spots. Co. to George Pottie of Louisa Co. £60 curr. 100 a. in Spots. Co., purchased of Thos. Oliver, etc. No witnesses. June 1, 1784.

Sept. 16, 1782. Wm. Robinson, Senr., and Sarah, his wife, of Spots. Co. to Thomas Strachan. In consideration of 4 slaves, etc., and £20 curr. Conveyance. 237 a. in Spots. Co., purchased of Wm. Fitzhugh, etc., of Stafford Co., Esqr. Witnesses, Jas. Lewis, Nicho. Hawkins, jr.; G. Bell, Harmon Haner. Augt. 21, 1783.

July 26, 1784. John Thornton and Jane, his wife, of Culpeper Co. to his brother, Francis Thornton, of Spots. Co. £800 curr. 836 a. in Spots. Co., devised sd. Thornton by his father, Francis Thornton, decd., part of pat. granted Dec. 20, 1718, to Wm. Cocke, Chickeley Corbin Thacker, Francis Thornton, jr., and Wm. Strother. Witnesses, Wm. Fleming, Mary Champe, Wm. McWilliams, Jno. Legg, Edwd. Simpson, Saml. Hilldrup. Sept. 7, 1784.

July 26, 1784. Francis Thornton and Ann, his wife, of Spots. Co. to Gabriel Jones of Rockingham Co. £800. 836 a. in Spots. Co., purchased of Jno. Thornton [as in preceding deed], to whom it was devised by his father, Francis Thornton, decd., etc. No witnesses. Septr. 7, 1784.

Augt. 21, 1783. Wm. Leavel of Caroline Co., po. of atto., to John Smith of Spots. Co. No witnesses. Augt. 21, 1783.

Augt. 20, 1783. Uriah Edwards and Betsy, his wife, of Spots. Co. to Thomas Oliver of sd. county. In consideration of 1 negro boy. Conveyance. 100 a. in Spots. Co. Witnesses, Jno. Edwards, Jno. Pierce. Augt. 21, 1783.

June 26, 1783. Mary x Skeaths of Spots. Co., widow of Jno. Skeaths, decd., to her son, Jno. Penny. Deed of Gift. 250 a. of land, two negroes, etc., etc., certain articles in trust for Mary, the dau. of the sd. Jno. Penny, etc., making reservations for a marriage of herself and one Jno. Pottet, and any issues by that marriage, etc. Witnesses, Edwd. Herndon, Chas. Pemberton, Henry Brock, A. Frazer, Jno. Brock, Jno. Bourn. Augt. 21, 1784.

June 30, 1783. Mary x Skeaths, mentions deed of gift to her son, Jno. Penny; "marriage is intended shortly to take place between Jno. Pottet and myself." Sd. Pottet doth consent to the sd. deed, etc. Witnesses, James Livingston, Jno. x Rains. Augt. 21, 1783.

Augt. 29, 1783. Clement Montague and Ann, his wife, Thomas Montague and Agnes, his wife, to Thomas Colson. £800 curr. 150 a. where sd. Thomas Montague lives, in St. Geo. Par., Spots. Co., known as Court House Tract, etc., etc. Reuben Straughan, Benj. Alsup, Clement Montague, George Hensley, Francis x Cammock. Sept. 18, 1783.

Augt. 23, 1783. Nicholas Lewis and Elizabeth, his wife, of Spots. Co. to Wm. Blades of same co. £1500 curr. 500 a. on Pamunkey River, Berkeley Par., Spots. Co., devised the sd. Nicholas by his father, Jno. Lewis, Esqr., decd., etc., etc. Thomas Towles, Nicho. Payne, Rice Vass, Thos. Davenport. Sept. 18, 1783.

Sept. 18, 1783. Wm. x Moor and Elizabeth, his wife, of Spots. Co. to Wm. Darnaby, jr., of same co. £85 curr. 175 a. in Spots. Co. No witnesses. Sept. 18, 1783.

Feby. 10, 1783. Wm. Wiglesworth and Mary, his wife, of Caroline Co. to Henry Chandler of Spots. Co. £100. 100 a. in Spots. Co., etc. Benja. Waller, Thomas Turner, Wm. Edmd. Waller. Sept. 18, 1783.

April 12, 1783. Joseph Sams of Spots. Co. and Nancy, his wife, to Jno. Sams, brother of the sd. Joseph Sams, etc. "To fulfill the desire of his father, James Sams, who died intestate," etc., plantation whereon sd. James Sams formerly lived [in Spots. Co.], adj. lands of Jeremiah Stevens, decd., and Henry Pendleton, etc., etc. Witnesses, Vincent Vass, W. Dawson, Anne Sams, Mary Dawson. Oct. 16, 1783.

Sept. 20 (?), 1783. Thomas Montague of Spots. Co., po. of atto., to Harry Bartlet of same Co. Witnesses, B. Stubblefield, Jas. Hutcherson, Jno. Chew, jr.; Benja. Holladay, jr. Oct. 17, 1783.

Augt. 29, 1783. Thomas Sharp and Judith, his wife, of Orange Co. and Thomas Montague and Agnes, his wife, of Spots. Co. to Thomas Colson of Spots. Co. £500 curr. 28 a. in St. Geo. Par., Spots. Co. Witnesses,

Reubin Straughan, Benj. Alsup, Clement Montague, George Hensley, B. Stubblefield, Thos. Brown, Harry Bartlet, Nicho. Payne. Oct. 16, 1783.

June 7, 1783. Agreement between John Lewis of Spots Co., Esqr., son and heir at law of Fielding Lewis, late of same place, Esqr., and Betty Lewis, widow and relict of the sd. Fielding Lewis. An agreement for lease of certain land, heretofore leased by the sd. Fielding Lewis, during his lifetime to the sd. Jno. The sd. Jno. paying annually to the sd. Betty 175 Bbls. Indian Corn, to continue to the end of the year the sd. Betty may die, etc., etc. Witnesses, Elisha Dickerson, Zachariah Lucas, Wm. Lorman. Nov. 20, 1783.

Nov. 20, 1783. Robt. x Bradley of Spots. Co. to John Bradley of same co. £100 curr. 300 a., the remainder of a tract taken up by George Dowdy, etc. No witnesses. Novr. 20, 1783.

Oct. 16, 1783. Jno. Apperson of Spots. Co. "to my son-in-law, James Smith my daughter Salley," etc. Deed of Gift. 230 a. in Spots. Co., etc. Witnesses, Robt. Hart, Jno. Smith, jr.; Jno. Smith, A. Bartlett. Dec. 17, 1783.

Novr. 29, 1783. Thomas Colson of Spots. Co., Gent., and Frances, his wife, to John Willis of same co., Gent. £1000, gold or silver, and ammt. of £1000 of certificates, granted by the Assembly of Va., for arrears of pay and depreciation due the Continental officers, etc., the sd. Colson, etc., convey to the sd. Willis 545 a. in St. Geo. Par., Spots. Co., purchased of Jno. Smith and Mary, his wife, as by Ind., dated Sept. 17, 1772, etc. O. Towles, George Lewis, Lark. Chew. Dec. 18, 1783.

Nov. 28, 1783. Thomas Colson and Frances, his wife, of Spots. Co. to Thomas Sharpe of same Co. £1500 in gold and silver, etc. "143 a., known by name of Court House tract, and whereon the Court House stands," etc., etc., and the sd. Sharpe to insure the payment of the sd. sum to be made at several stated periods, conveys to the sd. Colson several slaves and certain goods and chattels, etc., etc. Witnesses, Wm. Fontaine, O. Towles, Henry Pemberton. Dec. 18, 1783.

June 28, 1783. Benjamin Johnston of Washington Co., Penna., to Mildred Holladay, widow and executrix of John Holladay, late of Spots. Co., Va., decd. Whereas, the sd. Jno. Holladay, in his lifetime purchased of the sd. Johnston a tract of 324 a. whereon the sd. Mildred Holladay now lives, and whereas, the sd. Jno. Holladay, by deed, dated Oct. 6, 1775, conveyed to sd. Johnston, in fee the sd. land with the provision, that upon the sd. John Holladay's paying the sd. Johnston the sum of £100 curr., the sd. deed should become void, which sd. sum, the sd. Mildred, as executrix aforesd., hath duly paid, by virtue of which the sd. Johnston hath agreed to release all right and title in the sd. land to the sd. Mildred, in trust for the several children, etc., of sd. Jno. Holladay, who are thereto entitled under his will, etc., and whereas, one Jno. Clarke of Caroline Co., claims the same land and threatens suit to recover same, and upon the payment of the sd. sum by the sd. Mildred Holladay to the sd. Johnston it was one of the stipulations that the sd. Mildred should be indemnified from loss, the sd. Johnston doth by these presents convey all his right and title in the sd. 325 a. to the sd. Mildred, and also 3 negroes, with the understanding that the 3 sd. negroes are for the sole purpose of indemnifying the sd. Mildred and the heirs, under the will of the late Jno. Holladay from loss, etc., etc. Witness, Oliver Towles. Feby. 19, 1784.

Nov. 7, 1783. Robert Cunningham of Spots. Co. to Ann Cunningham of same co. All his right, title, etc., in a certain part of a dwelling house as well as other houses, etc., where the sd. Ann now lives, etc., in consideration whereof sd. Ann releases all her ⅓ part in a lot in Fredksbg., this day sold by sd. Robert to Jno. Frazer, Mercht., of Fredksbg., etc., etc. Witnesses, Jno. Chew, Geo. W. Spooner, Wm. Robinson.

July 15, 1783. James Hicks and Mary, his wife, of Spots. Co. to James Humphries of same co. £100 specie. 124½ a. in Spots. Co. Witnesses, Elisha Dismukes, Ambrose Shackelford, Moses Morris, Thos. Dillard. Feby. 19, 1784.

Sept. 3, 1783. Thomas Carr of Spots. Co., Gent., to Oliver Towles of same co., Gent. £1600 curr. 600 a. in St. Geo. Par., Spots. Co., etc. Geo. Stubblefield, Thomas Towles, Jno. Chew, jr. Feby. 19, 1784.

Dec. 9, 1783. Barnet x Pain and Nancy, his wife; George x Pain and Lizzie, his wife, of Spots. Co. to Robt. Coleman of same co. 55 curr. 125 a. in Spots. Co., etc. Thos. Coleman, jr.; Jno. Daniel, Wm. Phillips, Micajah Poole, Spilsbe Coleman. Feby. 19, 1784.

Decr. 2, 1783. Saml. Roddy of Fredksbg. to Harry Bartlet, Deputy Sheriff of Spots. Co., to indemnify him. Conveys to sd. Bartlet ⅔ ds. of lot in Fredksbg., etc. Wm. Carter, Thoms. Bartlet, Robt. Thomas. March 2, 1784.

Jany. 10, 1784. Rice Curtis of Spots. Co. Release of any right, title or interest he may possess in a tract of land purchased by Jno. Carter, Gent., decd., "of my decd. father, Rice Curtis, Gent.," etc. Witnesses, O. Towles, Zach. Burnley, Jno. Curtis, Jona. Carter. Feby. 19, 1784.

Jany. 9, 1784. Wm. Heslop of Spots. Co., deed of gift, to his daughter, Ann Graham Heslop. 1 negro slave. Witnesses, O. Towles, Harry Bartlet, Feby. 19, 1784.

Feby. 19, 1784. Wm. Lewis Callahan apprentices himself to Norcut Slaven of Fredksbg., Tailor, etc. No witnesses. Feby. 19, 1784.

Feby. 19, 1784. James Callahan apprentices himself to Norcut Slaven of Fredksbg., Tailor, etc. No witnesses. Feby. 19, 1784.

Feby. 19, 1784. Thomas Carr of Spots. Co. to John Benson of same co. £300 curr. 140 a. purchased of Moseley Battalay, known as Chalkey Levell in St. Geo. Par., Spots. Co., etc. Jno. Brock, Henry Brock, Wm. Heslop. Feby. 19, 1784.

Feby. 19, 1784. Thomas Carr of Spots. Co. to Norcut Slaven of same co. £30. 10 a. in St. Geo. Par., Spots. Co., etc. Jno. Brock, Henry Brock, Wm. Heslop. Feby. 19, 1784.

Jany. 21, 1784. Mary x Pottet, now the wife of John Pottet, did give to my son, John Penny, by deed, dated June 26, 1783, a tract of land and other estate, with certain provisions; confirms the sd. deed and gives immediate possession of the sd. estate, etc., to the sd. Penny. A bed, etc., to be held in trust by sd. Jno. Penny for his dau., Mary Penny, etc. Witnesses, James Hawkins, Jno. Martin, Lucy Martin. Feby. 19, 1784.

—— ——, ——. Henry Head, jr., of Spots. Co. to Alexander Spence Head of same co. £100. Mortgage. 2 negroes. Witnesses, Geo. Stubblefield, Jno. Wiglesworth, jr.; Jno. Chew. March 2, 1784.

March 2, 1784. Wm. Dawson and Mary, his wife, of Spots. Co. to Benj. Holladay. £40 1s. 65 a., dower of sd. Mary Dawson in the land of Thos. Rawlins, Decd., etc. No witnesses. March 2, 1784.

Octr. 1, 1783. David Galloway, jr., of Fredksbg. and Margaret, his wife, to Elizabeth Blair. "£154 curr., which money recd. in part of the sd. Margaret's proportion for land sold unto Thacker Washington, Esqr., and by agreement of the sd. Galloway, jr., with Margaret, his wife, before her giving consent to the sale of the sd. land, was to be laid out in property to be settled on her children by the sd. Galloway, jr., for which purpose this deed is made to the sd. Elizabeth Blair in order that she may convey to the children of the sd. D. Galloway, jr., the land mentioned therein." etc., etc., "by these presents doth grant, etc., confirm forever all that tract., etc., etc., situate, etc., in par. of St. Geo. Co. of Spots., etc. 154 a. formerly belonging to John Haydon," etc., etc. No witnesses. "I hereby oblige myself, etc., to reconvey the within mentioned tract of land to my sister, Margaret Galloway, and to her son, James Blair Galloway," etc., signed, "Elizabeth Blair." Recd. March 2, 1784.

Oct. 27, 1783. Henry Chiles of Spots. Co. to Leonard Waller of same co. £300 specie. 300 a. in Spots. Co., etc. Harry Bartlet, A. Bartlet, Jno. Waller, Rice Vass, Jos. Brock, jr. March 2, 1784.

Sept. 18, 1783. Henry Head of Spots. Co. to Timothy Conner of Spots. Co. 1 negro, in trust, for the use of Ann, wife of the sd. Henry Head, during her life and then to whom she may direct, etc., etc. Witnesses, Ben. Holladay, jr.; Jos. Brock, A. Bartlet. May 4, 1784.

March 3, 1784. Lodowick Oneal and Jno. Rogers of Spots. to James Julian of same co. £461 13s. 4d. 554 a. Jos. Brock, Jno. Wiglesworth, Benja. Robinson, Wm. Robinson, James Jarvis. May 4, 1784.

Feby. 19, 1784. Francis Purvis and Mary, his wife, of Spots. Co. to Wm. More of same co. £50 specie. 200 a. on n. side Granveley Run, in Spots. Co. No witnesses. Feby. 19, 1784.

Decr. 11, 1783. Peter Stubblefield and Pegge, his wife, of Spots. Co. to John Herndon of same co. £460 curr. 235 a., being the same sd. Stubblefield purchased of his brother, George Stubblefield, as by deed, Feby. 22, 1782, etc., etc. Jas. Lewis, George Atkinson, Catherine x Atkinson, Thomas Colson. May 4, 1784.

Septr. 7, 1783. Leonard Young, jr., and Mary, his wife, of Spots. Co. to Thomas Gaddass of the same co. £30 specie. 50 a. in Spots. Co., etc. Jas. Crawford, Christopher Crawford, Thomas Shearley. May 4, 1784.

Septr. 29, 1783. Vincent Vass and Elizabeth, his wife, of Orange Co. to Richard Dickerson. 550 lbs. tob., etc. "For and during the life of Elizabeth Vass (now the wife of the sd. Vincent), a certain tract of land," etc., etc. Witnesses, Edwd. Thomas, Elijah Carter, Benj. Robinson. May 4, 1784.

Sept. 29, 1783. Vincent Vass and Elizabeth, his wife, of Orange Co. to Benjamin Robinson. 500 lbs. tob. "During the life of the sd. Elizabeth Vass, now the wife of the sd. Vincent), a certain tract of land," etc., etc. Witnesses, Edwd. Thomas, Richard Dickerson, Elijah Carter. May 4, 1784.

Novr. 21, 1783. Thomas Chiles and Mary, his wife, of Caroline Co. to James Parish of Spots. Co. £600. 140 a. in Spots. Co., etc., etc. Rice Vass, P. Mason, James Crawford, jr. May 4, 1784.

Jany. 1, 1784. Thomas Sharpe of Orange Co. to Wm. Willoughby of Spots. Co., and his heirs, etc. Lease. [99 years.] 244 a. in Spots. Co., etc. 500 lbs. tob. yearly during first three years, and then 750 lbs. tob. yearly until expiration of lease, etc., etc. James Livingston, A. Sorrell, Henry x Willoughby. June 1, 1784.

May 22, 1784. Jacob Whitler and Jane, his wife, of Spots. Co. to Jno. Welch of same co. £800 curr. 188 a. in Spots. Co., being tract purchased by sd. Whitler and Welch in partnership of Charles Bruce, Thos. Howard, Gerard Banks, and Jno. James in pursuance of trust reposed in sd. Bruce, Howard, Banks, and James under the last will of Thomas James, Decd., etc., etc. Witnesses, Rd. Johnston, Jno. Wiglesworth, Edwd. Herndon. June 1, 1784.

Jany. 13, 1784. James Cowden of Henry Co., atto in fact for Jane Hawkins of same co., widow of Joseph Hawkins, decd., to Wm. P. Thurston of Spots. Co. £50. Tract of land on Pamunkey River in Spots Co., held by sd. Jane under the will of her decd. husband, etc., etc. Witnesses, Bevy. Winslow, Richd. Coleman, Thomas Winslow. June 1, 1784.

Dec. 3 ,1783. Richard Dillard and Susannah, his wife, of Spots. Co. to John Coats of same county. £250 curr. 250 a., adj. lands of sd. Coats, Micajah Poole and Jno. Coleman in Spots. Co., etc. Witnesses, Jno. Waller, Wm. Rash, Wm. Coats, Jno. Shackelford. June 1, 1784.

June 1, 1784. James Pritchett to his sons, Benjamin Pritchett and Alexander Pritchett, when of age, one negro slave each, etc. No witnesses. June 1, 1784.

Novr. 29, 1783. Richard Dillard and Susannah, his wife, of Spots. Co. to Wm. Rash of same co. £20 specie. 40 a., formerly part of the land of Thos. Dillard, decd., and purchased by sd. Richard Dillard of Joseph and James Dillard, etc., etc. Jno. Mason, Jeremiah Wilson, James Jarrill. June 1, 1784.

Augt. 5, 1783. John Dawson Grymes, Mariner, po. of atto., to John Dawson of Caroline Co., to land in Henry Co., formerly Lunenburg Co., conveyed by deed dated Augt. 10, 1764, to sd. Grymes, Thomas B. Dawson, and sd. Jno. Dawson, by Jno. Dawson of Caroline Co., Decd., etc. Witness, James Bates. June 1, 1784.

June 1, 1784. Francis x Cammock and Clary, his wife, of Berkeley Par., Spots Co., to Jno. Cammock of same par. and co. £50 curr. 140 a. on Stony Run, in same par. and county, etc., etc. Anth. Bartlet, Wm. Hewell, James Metchum. June 1, 1784.

March 27, 1784. Wm. Blaydes and Mary Ann, his wife, of Spots. Co. to James Coleman Goodwin of same county. £350 curr. 200 a., formerly conveyed by Jno. Carpenter to Wm. Ball and his heirs in Spots. Co., etc., etc. Wm. Cason, jr.; Wm. Cason, Agatha x Cason. July 6, 1784.

May 22, 1784. Thomas Sharpe of Spots. Co. and Judith, his wife, to Joseph Whitehead of Dinwiddie Co. £400 curr. 495 a. in Berkeley Par., Spots. Co., etc., etc. Jno. Z. Lewis, Jno. Brock, Jno. Chew, jr. July 6, 1784.

May 20, 1784. "Whereas, Jno. Chiles of Caroline Co. and Lucy Coleman of Spots. Co., are now abt. to solemnize the state of matrimony," etc., etc., conveys to the sd. Lucy, etc., two negroes, etc. Witnesses, Richard Coleman, Spil. Coleman, Robt. T. Coleman. July 6, 1784.

Decr. 7, 1784. Thomas Sharpe of Spots. Co., Inn Keeper, and Judith, his wife, to Robert Scott, now of Fredksbg. £400. 225 a., on branches of Mattapony River, in Spots. Co., formerly property of Wm. Nelson, etc., etc., also 224 in Spots. Co., and also 200 a. in Spots. Co., etc., etc. Jno. Nelson, jr.; John Estes, Jos. Wood, jr.; Charles Carter. Decr. 8, 1784.

May 21, 1784. Thomas Strachan and Mary, his wife, of Spots. Co. to Mary Daingerfield, Thomas Colson, and Oliver Towles, acting executors of Wm. Daingerfield, decd., and to Thomas Walker, jr., and Matthew Maury of Albemarle Co. Whereas, the sd. Wm. Daingerfield, during his lifetime, the sd. Walker, jr., and Maury became security for the sd. Strachan for a debt due by him to the sd. Colson, the sd. Strachan to perform and fulfil the covenants and agreements comprised in certain articles drawn, then the sd. Obligation to be void, but the sd. Strachan being now greatly in arrears, and the sd. Walker and Maury and the estate of the sd. Daingerfield, decd., being liable therefor, the sd. Strachan, etc., deeds to the sd. Executors and the sd. Walker and Maury 237 a. whereon sd. Strachan lives in St. Geo. Par., Spots. Co., purchased of Wm. Robinson, and also several slaves, in trust, to indemnify the sd. parties from loss by their standing as security for the sd. Strachan, etc., etc. Witnesses, Jno. W. Willis, Jno. Mathews, Jno. Julian. July 6, 1784.

Jany. 21, 1775. Wm. Triplett of Fredksbg., Mercht., and George Thornton of same town, Mercht. Whereas, the sd. Triplett and Thornton, having been partners in merchandising, having had stores in Falmouth and Fredksbg., by agreement dissolved the sd. partnership Dec. 19 last, under agreement that sd. Triplett should take all goods, wares, etc., amtg. in value £540 ster., and allowed his sole use of all debts due to the Fredksbg. store (except a certain balance due on sd. Thornton's acct.), in consideration whereof the sd. Triplett undertook to pay all the debts due, etc., from the sd. partnership and to allow the sd. Thornton, to his sole use all the debts due the Falmouth store, etc., pursuant to which agreement the sd. Triplett and Thornton have executed mutual assignments, and whereas, it is reasonable that the sd. Thornton, who still remains equally chargeable with the sd. Triplett for the debts due from the sd. partnership, should be fully indemnified against the same, wherefore, the sd. Triplett, to indemnify the sd. Thornton from loss, deeds him in trust for that purpose, 300 a. in King Geo. Co., on Rappa River, abt. five miles above Leedstown, and also several slaves, etc., etc., also appts. sd. Thornton his attorney, etc. Witnesses, John Fowke, Christopher Edrington, Alexr. Dick. Augt. 3, 1784.

Decr. 27, 1783. Robt. Hutcherson of Spots. Co. to Wm. Lotspietch of Stafford Co. £87. 75 a. in Spots. Co. Mortgage, etc. Bevy. Winslow, Wm. Winslow. Augt. 13, 1784.

July 27, 1784. Richard Tyler of Caroline Co. and Catherine, his wife, to Nicholas Payne of Spots. Co. £200 curr. 200 a. in Spots. Co., etc. Thos. Towles, Jno. Waller, Geo. Mason, Henry Chiles, Moses Higgin, Filding Estes. Augt. 3, 1784.

July 30, 1784. Nicho. Payne and Elizabeth, his wife, of Spots. Co. to Samuel Luck of same co. £225 curr. 200 a. in Spots. Co. Witnesses, Thomas Towles, Jno. Z. Lewis. Augt. 3, 1784.

Dec. 17, 1783. Benjamin Robinson of Fredksbg. to Thomas Walker of same town. £85 curr. 84½ a. in Spots. Co., etc. Jno. Legg, Thos. Sharpe, Wm. McWilliams, Jas. Julian. Augt. 3, 1784.

Augt. 3, 1784. Jno. White and Mary, his wife, of Spots. Co. to Thomas Sharpe of same co. £30 curr. 30 a. in Spots. Co., etc. Jno. Brock, Richd. Todd, Robt. Farish. Augt. 3, 1784.

Augt. 2, 1784. Jno. Sorrell and Sarah, his wife, of Spots. Co. to Ashman Sorrell of same co. £20 curr. Tract of land in Spots. Co., etc. Wm. Willoughby, James Sorrell, James Wheeler, Thos. Dillard, Moses Morris, Augt. 3, 1784.

March 13, 1784. Bennet Pemberton and Mary, his wife, of Spots. Co. to Wm. Duvall, junr., of same co. £52. 48 a. in Spots. Co., etc., etc. Jno. Price, George Hutcherson. Augt. 3, 1784.

July 2, 1784. Leonard Young and Mary, his wife, of Spots. Co. to Daniel Coleman of Caroline Co. £300. 339 a. in Spots. Co. No witnesses. Augt. 3, 1784.

May 17, 1784. John x Smith of Orangeburg Dist., South Carolina, Planter, eldest son and heir at law of Jno. Smith, late of the same place, decd., to Thomas Carr, late of Spots. Co., Va. £600 ster. 4000 a. in Berkeley Par., Spots. Co., Va., sd. tract invested by entailment in Lawrence Smith, after his death in John Smith, heir of the sd. Lawrence, and at death sd. John, descended unto sd. Jno. Smith, party to these presents, etc., etc. Peter Stubblefield, James Dawson, B. Dawson, Walter Carr, George Henning, John Brag. Sept. 7, 1784.

May 17, 1784. Jno. x Smith of Orangeburg Dist., South Carolina, po. of atto., to Thos. Carr, late of Spots. Co., Va., Esqr. Witnesses, Peter Stubblefield, W. Dawson, Walter Carr, Jas. Dawson, George Henning. Septr. 7, 1784.

Sept. 4, 1784. Richard Loury, Gent., and Elizabeth, his wife, of Spots. Co. to George Stubblefield, same county. £343 17s. 6d. curr. 227¼ a. in Berkeley Par., Spots. Co., etc. Jno. Brock, O. Towles. Sept. 7, 1784.

Augt. 11, 1784. David Woodroof of Spots. Co. to George Stubblefield of same co. £84 1s. 5½d. Mortgage. 130 a. and 3 slaves, etc. Thomas Towles, Nicho. Payne, B. Stubblefield. Septr. 7, 1784.

Sept. 6, 1784. Henry True of Berkeley Par., Spots. Co., to Joseph True of same par. and co. £40 curr. 100 a. in Berkeley Par., Spots. Co. No witnesses. Sept. 7, 1784.

Novr. 4, 1783. Thomas Jennings and Sarah, his wife, of St. Geo. Par., Spots. Co., to John Wiglesworth of par. and co. afsd. £104 2s. 6d. curr. 59½ a. in par. and co. afsd., etc. Jos. Brock, Jno. Brock, Jno. Chisum, Thomas Haydon. Septr. 7, 1784.

Sept. 28, 1784. Wm. Gosney and Elizabeth, his wife; Thomas Jones and Ann, his wife; Benja. Haley and Agatha, his wife, of Frederick Co. to Clement Montague, Senr., of Spots. Co. £400 curr. 325 a. in Spots. Co., being the land devised by Nicholas Hawkins to his son, John Hawkins, and at the death of sd. John Hawkins, descended to his three daughters, Elizabeth, who intermarried with Wm. Gosney; Ann, with Thomas Jones, and Agatha with Benja. Haley, etc., etc., except 190 a. of sd. land laid apart to Elizabeth, widow of sd. Jno. Hawkins, decd., who has since intermarried with Robt. Collins, who sold the sd. 190 a. to John Waller, K. W., for the lifetime of the sd. Elizabeth, then to revert to the sd. Montague, etc. Witnesses, Sam. Clagett, jr.; Anth. Bartlet, Clement Montague, Ann Haley.

Sept. 7, 1784. Wm. Edmd. Waller and Mildred, his wife, of Spots. Co. to Wm. Wiglesworth of Caroline Co. £150 curr. 200 a. in Spots. Co., etc., etc. Jno. Waller, Jas. Crawford, Benja. Waller, Geo. Mason, Henry Chandler. Novr. 2, 1784.

Oct. 28, 1784. Henry Pendleton, Senr., and Matthey [Martha], his wife, and Rice Vass and Peggy, his wife, of Spots. Co. to Leonard Young of same co. £60 curr. to Pendleton and wf., and 5s. to Vass and wf. 110 a. in Spots Co. [100 a. thereof purchased of Jno. Ballard and Ann, his wife, and 10 a. purchased of Rice Vass and Peggy, his wife, but had no conveyance therefor], etc., etc. Geo. Stubblefield, Harry Stubblefield, Jno. Chew, jr.; Jno. Wiglesworth, jr. Novr. 2, 1784.

Augt. 28, 1784. Margaret x Tureman, widow and relict of Charles Tureman, decd., and Bennet Pemberton and Mary, his wife, of Berkeley Par., Spots. Co. to Edmund Foster of same par. and co. Whereas, Chas. Tureman, decd., by his last will and testament, did leave to his wife the sd. Margaret "all his estate, real and personal, during her natural life," etc., and after her death the same to be sold and the money arising from such sale divided amongst his children, and the sd. Margaret, being abt. to remove to the Western waters of this State, and believing it to be advantageous to herself and children to sell sd. land, therefore, she, the sd. Margaret (on behalf of herself and two sons, Thos. and Wm. Tureman, both under age), and the sd. Pemberton and Mary, his wife, do for the sum of £100 curr., convey 200 a. in Berkeley Par., Spots. Co., to the sd. Foster, etc., etc. Witnesses, Wm. Duvall, Jas. Rains, Chas. Pemberton, Jno. Jesse. Novr. 2, 1784.

June 5, 1784. John Mastin and Elizabeth, his wife, of Berkeley Par., Spots. Co., to his son, Thomas Mastin, of Par. and Co. afsd., etc. Deed of Gift. 100 a. in Berkeley Par., Spots. Co., etc. Jno. Waller, W. Dawson, Betty Mastin, Agnus Blanton. Novr. 2, 1784.

Novr. 1, 1784. Thomas Carr of the State of Georgia, and at present in Spots. Co., Va., to Robert Hart of Spots. Co., Va. 20s. "A small parcel of land on Douglass Run, part of a larger tract which sd. Carr lately purchased of Jno. Smith," etc., etc. Henry Lane, Thomas Terry, Thomas Turner, Wm. Brock, Thos. x Brooks. Nov. 2, 1784.

July 4, 1784. Thomas Clayton and Frances of Orange Co. to Wm. Bridges of Spots. Co. £135. 125 a. in Spots. Co., devised the sd. Thomas Clayton by his father, Jacob Clayton, decd., etc., etc. Jos. Brock, Bennet Pemberton, Daniel Branham, Richd. Collins, Henry Gatewood, jr.; John Edwards, Benja. Head. Novr. 2, 1784.

—— ——, ——. Tavener Branham deeds John Brock one negro slave, to indemnify the sd. Brock, who stands security for the sd. Branham, etc. Witness, A. Frazer. Novr. 2, 1784.

Oct. 1, 1784. John x Raidon of Spots. Co. to his brother, Wm. Raidon, of same co. Deed of Gift. 100 a. in Spots. Co., etc. George Sharpe, Silence Atkins, Isaac Palmer. Novr. 2, 1784.

Decr. 7, 1784. John Tankersley and Susannah, his wife, of Spots. Co. to Nicho. Payne and Jno. Chew, jr., of same co. £487 6s. 3d. curr. 422 a. in Spots. Co., etc. No witnesses. Dec. 7, 1784.

June 1, 1784. Whereas, Henry Head by Indenture dated Sept. 18, 1783, conveyed to Timothy Conner one negro slave in trust for Ann, the wife of the sd. Henry Head, the sd. parties being desirous to make sale of sd. slave, they do sell him to Henry Bartlet, for the sum of £85, etc., etc. Jno. Langley, Jas. Berry, Jas. Ballard. Decr. 9, 1784.

Jany 4, 1785. Peter Stubblefield of Spots. Co., but Intending to the State of Georgia, po. of atto., to his brother, George Stubblefield of Spots. Co., etc., etc. Witnesses, Jno. Carnahan, Jno. Chew, jr.; Benj. Holladay, jr. Jany. 4, 1785.

Decr. 10, 1783. Morda. Buckner of Spots. Co. to Peter Stubblefield of same co. Whereas, sd. Buckner is in possession of 2 tracts of land under leases from Alexander Spotswood, and the sd. Buckner has leased to the sd. Stubblefield 125 a. thereof, 100 a. part for and during the lives of Jno. Brock, Jos. Brock, and Wm. Brock, and 25 a., part thereof for and during the lives of Jno. Chew, Beverley Chew, and John Chew, jr., etc., etc. Witnesses, Clayton Coleman, Joel Lewis, Robt. Stubblefield. Jany. 4, 1785.

Novr. 7, 1784. Thomas Carr of the State of Georgia, but at present in Spots. Co., Va., to George Stubblefield of Spots. Co., Va. £300 ster. ½ of a tract of 3450 a. in Berkeley Par., Spots. Co., purchased by sd. Carr of Jno. Smith, etc., etc., and the sd. Carr and Stubblefield both being desirous of selling the whole tract, and the sd. Carr, being in the State of Georgia, etc., gives po. of atto. to sd. Stubblefield, to act for him, etc., etc. Witnesses, John Whitaker Willis, Harry Stubblefield, Richd. Lowry, B. Stubblefield. Jany. 4, 1785.

Oct. 10, 1784. Saml. Allen, David Thompson, and Saml. Berry, Executors of the last will and testament of Joseph Allen, decd., to Thomas Boxley of Spots. Co. £100 curr. 206 a. on Pamunkey River in Spots. Co., directed by the sd. Jos. Allen, decd., to be sold by his executors, and the money arising from sale thereof to be divided with his other estate, etc., etc. Witnesses, Bevy. Winslow, Jno. S. Boxley, Wm. Winslow, Thomas Winslow. Jany. 4, 1785.

Jany. 4, 1785. Peter Stubblefield and Peggy, his wife, and Wm. Davenport and Mary, his wife, of Spots. Co. to John Webber. £30 curr. to the sd. Stubblefield, etc., pd. 164 a. in Spots. Co., and £10, to sd. Davenport, etc., pd., 18 a. joining the aforementioned tract, etc., etc. No witnesses. Jany. 4, 1785.

Novr. 3, 1784. Wm. Arnold, Senr., of Caroline Co. to George Arnold of Spots. Co., in trust for his two children, William and Nancy. Deed of Gift. 3 negroes, cattle, goods and chattels, etc., etc. Witnesses, Jno. Waller, Ambrose x Smith, James Smith. Feby. 1, 1785.

Augt. 3, 1784. John Mason of Spots. Co. and Anna, his wife, of first part; Peter Mason of same co. and Elizabeth, his wife, of second part; John Hawkins of Caroline Co., Gent., and Anna Gabriela, his wife, of third part, to Thomas Towles of Spots. Co., of fourth part. Whereas, sd. Jno. Mason, being seized and possessed of a certain tract of land of 222 a. [purchased of Benjamin Tomkins, who purchased same of the Excrs. of Robt. Baylor of King and Queen Co., Gent., Decd.], did sell the same to the sd. Jno. Hawkins for the sum of £222 curr., but before making conveyance thereof, the sd. Hawkins sold the sd. land to the sd. Thomas Towles, and whereas, the sd. John Mason and Peter Mason having exchanged some low ground, and the sd. Peter never having made any conveyance thereof, and the sd. low ground being included in the sd. land purchased by sd. Hawkins, the sd. parties making this conveyance to the sd. Towles, etc., etc. Witnesses, Jno. Carter, Spilsbe Coleman, Meredeth Anderson. Augt. 3, 1784.

Sept. 9, 1784. James True and Sarah, his wife, of Caroline Co., of the first part; Peter Dudley and Susannah, his wife, of Spots. Co., of the second part; Edmund Bryant and Sarah, his wife, of Spots. Co., of the third part, to Edward Marsh of Spots. Co., of fourth part. Whereas, the sd. Peter Dudley, being seized in fee in a certain tract of land containing 150 a. for a consideration sold the same to the sd. James True, but before conveyance of same was made, the sd. James sold the same to the sd. Marsh for £150 curr., and whereas, the sd. Sarah Bryant, who was formerly the widow of John True, late of Spots Co., decd., and now wife of sd. Edmund Bryant, was entitled to ⅓ part of sd. land during her life as for her dower in the same of the endowment of her former husband, the sd. Jno. True, who was in his lifetime seized of sd. land, which right of dower was never relinquished, but which she, in conjunction with her sd. husband, Edmund Bryant, have now agreed to release to the sd. Marsh, etc., etc. Witnesses, Jas. Lewis, Mathew Carpenter, Thomas Colson. Novr. 2, 1784.

Decr. 7, 1784. John Welch of Fredksbg., Trader, and Eleanor, his wife, to Wm. Jackson of same place, Stone Mason. £225 12s. 188 a. in Spots. Co., etc., formerly the property of Thomas James, decd., etc., etc. Witnesses, Jno. W. Willis, Robt. B. Chew, O. Towles, Jno. Benson, Jos. Wood, jr. Decr. 7, 1784.

Novr. 22, 1783. Wm. Dawson and Mary, his wife, of Spots. Co. to Thomas Towles of sd. co. £250. Mortgage 702 a. Edmd. Foster, Jno. Chew, jr.; Rice Vass. Jany. 4, 1785.

Feby. ——, 1785. Thomas Gaddis of Spots. Co., of the first part; Thomas Coleman and Robert Coleman of same co., of the second part, to Thomas Towles of same co., Gent., of third part. Sd. Gaddis in consideration of £20 curr., conveys 60 a. in Spots. Co., purchased of Leonard Young, and whereas, sd. Robt. Coleman sold to the sd. Thomas Coleman a tract of land in fork of Robinson and Horse Pen Runs, but never made any conveyance therefor, which sd. Thomas has lately sold to sd. Thomas Towles for 21s. Conveyance of above named property to the sd. Towles, etc., etc. Witnesses, Jeremiah Wilson, Rice Vass, John Chew Buckner, Merideth Anderson. March 1, 1785.

July 23, 1784. Peter Rosell [or Roswell] and Ann, his wife, of Albemarle Co. to Benjamin Dawson of Spots. Co. £150. 215 a. purchased of Paul McClery and Rose, his wife, in Spots. Co., etc., etc. John White, Long Wharton, Benja. Wharton, W. Dawson. March 1, 1785.

October 11, 1784. Wm. Garrett and Ann, his wife; Henry Garrett and Mary, his wife, of Louisa Co. to Beverley Winslow of Berkeley Par., Spots. Co. £200. 800 a. in Berkeley Par., Spots. Co., etc., etc. Francis Coleman, Thomas Lipscomb, John Alcock, Wm. Quarles, Wm. Trigg. March 1st, 1785.

Septr. 3, 1784. Peter Mason of Spots. Co. to John Shackelford of same county. £50 curr. Mortgage. 50 a., "part of tract I had of Jno. Mason," etc., etc. Wm. Warren, Elisha Dismukes, Ambrose Shackelford. March 1, 1785.

Decr. 17, 1784. Wm. Lewis and Sarah, his wife, of Spots. Co. to James Lewis of same co. £243 12s. 174 a. in St. Geo. Par., Spots. Co. No witnesses. Decr. 17, 1784.

Dec. 6, 1770. Harry Beverley of Caroline Co. and Jane Wiley, his wife, to Richd. Johnston of sd. County. £25 curr. 262 a. purchased of Robt. Chew in Berkeley Par., Spots. Co., etc. Jno. B. Roy, O. Towles, Geo. Stubblefield. March 1, 1785.

Octr. 10, 1784. Owen Minor of Culpeper Co. to his two daughters, Ann Minor and Judith Minor, "for 5s. to me in hand pd. by Hugh Roy and Saml. Scott, their friends and trustees," etc. Deed of Gift. "Reversion in and of the slaves that I might claim at the death of Mrs. Ann Waller, under the will of Col. Wm. Waller, decd.," etc. Witnesses, Wm. Johnston, jr.; Wm. Coleman, Wm. Waller, Richd. Johnston, jr. March 1, 1785.

Jany. 3, 1785. "Whereas, our mother, Barbary Brock, did on the 16th day of Feby., 1781, by consent of us, divide the slaves bequeathed to her for life by her Late husband, Henry Brock, decd.," in consideration that the sd. Barbary should keep one negro and that the undersigned heirs pay her £3 specie, each, annually, etc. The sd. Barbary, now in consideration of the sd. undersigned releasing all their right, title, etc., in sd. negro, to her, she releases them from the yearly payment as aforesaid, etc. Signed, "Joseph Brock, Clk.; Jno. Brock, jr.; Elizabeth x Brock, Henry x Cammock, John Bourn." Witnesses, Mary Beverley Brock, Jos. Brock, Elizabeth Lewis, Susannah Brock, Tureman Lewis, Harry Bartlet, A. Frazer. March 2, 1785.

Decr. 14, 1784. John Edwards to Mildred Edwards, his mother, relict of Uriah Edwards, decd., both of Spots. Co. In consideration of sd. Mildred's relinquishing her right in part of a tract of land, held by her for widowhood, under the will of her late husband, Uriah Edwards, decd., etc., also a negro man, the sd. John conveys to the sd. Mildred, all remainder of the sd. tract, devised by the will of the sd. Edwards, decd., etc., including the plantation and houses, etc., etc. Witnesses, Edwd. Herndon, John Herndon, Wm. Herndon, Thomas Colson, Jos. Willoughby. March 2, 1785.

Novr. 10, 1783. Benja. Nelson of Spots. Co. to Joseph Nelson of same co. £10,000 curr. 290 a. in N. fork Pamunkey River, Spots. Co., etc., etc. Jos. x Harper, B. Poindexter, Wm. Tate. April 5, 1785.

April 5, 1785. John Coats of Spots. Co. and Ann, his wife, to Bradley Mathews of same co. £130 curr. 130 a. in Spots. Co., etc., etc. Christopher Crawford, Benja. Chapman, James Crawford. April 5, 1785.

April 5, 1785. John Coats and Ann, his wife, of Spots. Co. to Benja. Winn of Caroline Co. £——. 128 a. in Spots. Co., etc. Benja. Chapman, James Crawford, Christ. Crawford. April 5, 1785.

Jany. 15, 1785. Peter Minor of Dinwiddie Co. to John Partloe of Spots. Co. £300 curr. 400 a. in Spots. Co., devised the sd. Peter by the last will and testament of his father, John Minor, decd., etc., etc. Tho. Minor, Christopher Crawford, Jas. Crawford, Geo. Mason, Jas. Crawford, jr. Augt. 2, 1785.

April 4, 1785. Michael x Blunt and Elizabeth, his wife, of Spots. Co. to James Arnold of Caroline Co. £25 curr. 25 a. in Spots. Co., etc., etc. Jno. Sorrell, Benj. Perry, Jas. Robins, Chas. Sanders. April 5, 1785.

April 5, 1785. John Sorrell and Sarah, his wife, of Spots. Co. to James Robbins of same co. £25 curr. 50 a. in Spots. Co., etc. John Waller, James Arnold, Benja. Perry. April 5, 1785.

July 10, 1784. Whitehead Coleman of Essex Co. to Wm. Plunkett of Orange Co. £200 curr. 400 a. in upper end of Spots. County, etc., etc. John Nelson, Francis Coleman, Edwd. Herndon, jr.; Jno. Nelson, jr.; Jas. Coleman, Robt. S. Coleman. April 5, 1785.

April 5, 1785. Thomas x Hutcherson of Spots. Co. to his son, George Hutcherson. Deed of Gift. 100 a. of land, etc. Jos. Brock, Clk.; B. Stubblefield. April 5, 1785.

—— ——, ——. Thomas Turner of Spots. Co. to Griffin Jones of same co. Lease. 80 a. in Spots. Co. "Sd. Griffin Jones and Agness, his wife, and Joseph Jones, his son," etc. 380 lbs. tob. yearly. Witnesses, B. Stubblefield, Jno. Brock, jr. April 5, 1785.

April 6, 1785. Wm. Coleman of Spots. Co., po. of atto., to friend, Wm. Robbins of Gloucester Co. "Share of estate of my father, Robt. Coleman, decd., his last will and testament recd. in Gloucester Co.," etc., etc. No witnesses. April 6, 1785.

Sept. 29, 1784. Richardson Hensley and Minney, his wife, and Sarah Hensley of Spots. Co. to John Carter of same county. £200 curr. 110 a. in St. Geo. Par., Spots. Co., etc. James Hutcherson, James Cully, Geo. Hensley. Septr. 29, 1784.

Septr. 9, 1784. Reuben Straughan of Spots. Co. to Harry Bartlett of same co. Whereas, sd. Bartlett was security for the sd. Straughan to the Sheriff of Caroline Co., to indemnify the sd. Sheriff for selling a negro, supposed to be the property of John Ellis of North Carolina; the sd. Straughan to indemnify the sd. Bartlett, deeds him 70 a. of land, etc., etc. Witnesses, Geo. Stubblefield, Jno. Chew, jr.; Benja. Rawlings. April 6, 1785.

March 7, 1785. Clement Montague of Spots. Co. to son, Clement Montague. Deed of Gift. 1 negro, etc. Witnesses, Thomas Waller, Thomas Montague, Benja. Pritchett. April 6, 1785.

April 6, 1785. Thomas Swinney of Spots. Co. to Thomas Montague of same co. Sd. Swinney binds himself to sd. Montague to learn Carpenter's trade, etc., etc. Witness, Jno. Brock. April 6, 1785.

Decr. 23, 1780. James Pritchett of Spots. Co. to his sons, Benjamin Pritchett and Alexander Pritchett. Deed of Gift. A negro to each. Witnesses, Tavener Branham, Thos. Estis, Eliza x Branham, John Robinson. April 6, 1785.

Sept. 4, 1784. Peter Mason of Spots. Co. to Nathl. Sanders. To indemnify sd. Sanders, etc. 376 a. in Spots. Co., etc., etc. Thos. Sharpe, Benj. Alsop, Robt. Coleman. April 6, 1785.

Dec. 6, 1784. Edwd. Herndon, Jr., of Spots. Co. to John Shelton. 1 negro and £31 curr. Conveyance of four negroes. Witnesses, V. Long Wharton, Jno. Crutchfield, Harry Chew. April 6, 1785.

March 6, 1785. Ann x Waller of Spots. Co. to her son, Wm. Waller, of same county. 5s. Stocks of Cattle, horses, sheep, etc. Witnesses, James Jones, Sam. Scott, Wm. Coleman, Hugh Roy. April 6, 1785.

April 6, 1785. Wm. Waller of Spots. Co. to his nephew, Hugh Roy. Deed of Gift. All right, title, etc., in slaves and other estate in possession of my mother, Mrs. Ann Waller, etc., etc. Jno. Brock, Wm. Coleman. April 6, 1785.

May 4, 1785. Stephen White, orphan of Wm. White, decd., apprentices himself to Goodlove Heiskell, Blacksmith, etc. Witness, John Chew, jr. May 4, 1785.

March 7, 1785. Churchill Jones of Spots. Co., Gent., to Mann Page of same county, Esqr. £2000. Mortgage. 33 slaves. Witnesses, Jos. Wood, jr.; R. Brooke, Benja. Leavell. May 4, 1785.

Feby. 21, 1785. John Personet and Ann, his wife, to Gip Jenkins. £31. 100 a. in Spots. Co., etc., etc. Wm. Hall, Daniel Baldwin, Jas. Abbitt, Charles x Jenkins. May 4, 1785.

Jany. 10, 1785. Nathl. Sanders of Spots. Co. to Wm. Jenkins of same county. £100. Wagon and team. Witnesses, Jno. White, Gibson Jenkins, Charles x Jenkins. May 4, 1785.

May 4, 1785. Thomas Foster of Spots. Co. to Edmund Foster of same co. 8000 lbs. tob. and £25 specie. 2 negroes. Witness, Harry Bartlett. May 5, 1785.

April 6, 1785. Wm. x Moor and Elizabeth, his wife, of Spots. Co. to Adrian Fellier of same co. £100 curr. 200 a. in Spots. Co. No witnesses. April 6; 1785.

June 6, 1785. Elisha Dismukes and Ann, his wife, of Spots. Co. to James Gimbo of same co. £60 curr. 60 a. in Spots. Co., etc., etc. Jno. Waller, Nancy Waller, Phebe Waller. June 7, 1785.

June 7, 1785. Clement Montague of Spots. Co. to his son-in-law, John Estis, of same county. Deed of Gift. 1 negro. Witnesses, Jos. Brock, Clk.; Robt. Frank. June 7, 1785.

June 7, 1785. Wm. Duerson and ——, his wife, of Spots. Co. to Benjamin Haley of same county. £75 curr. 227 a. conveyed to sd. Duerson by Job. Harris and Susannah, his wife, as by Indenture dated Novr. 15, 1770, in Spots. Co., etc., etc. Witness, John Brock. June 7, 1785.

Oct. 7, 1784. Jno. Larue and Mary, his wife, of Frederick Par., Frederick Co. to David Blair of Spots. Co. £300 curr. [pd. by Edm. Taylor for sd. Blair]. 563 a. in Spots. Co., etc., etc. David Hunter, Jabez La Rue, Wm. Stribling, Michael Everhart, James Young, D. Norton, Edmd. Taylor. June 8, 1785.

June 6, 1785. Dennis x Wright and Ellender, his wife, of Spots. Co. to Peter Stubblefield of the State of Georgia. £100. 268 a. in Spots. Co., Va., etc. Wm. Owen, Thos. Sharpe, Stapleton Crutchfield, Geo. Stubblefield. June 8, 1785.

April 15, 1784. Richd. Johnston and Ann, his wife, of Caroline Co. to Beverley Winslow of Spots. Co. £131. 262 a. in Berkeley Par., Spots. Co., etc. Harry B. Towles, Thos. Bron, Geo. Stubblefield. June 7, 1785.

July 5, 1785. Chapman x Gordon, with consent of his mother, Caty Gordon, apprentices himself to Benja. x Haley of Spots. Co. Witness, Jno. Brock. July 5, 1785.

April 2, 1785. Saml. x Brown and Martha, his wife, and George Penn and Elizabeth, his wife, of Spots. Co. to James Wiglesworth of same county. £20 curr. 25 a. in Spots. County, etc., etc. Benja. Chapman, James Gimber, Thos. Wiglesworth. July 5, 1785.

July 5, 1785. George Penn and Elizabeth, his wife, of Berkeley Par., Spots. County, to James Trigg of same par. and county. Whereas, Jno. Penn, decd., during his lifetime and at his death was seized and possessed of a tract of land in St. Geo. Par., Spots. Co., and being so seized, made his last will and testament, and thereby directed that 170 a., part of the land whereon he lived, be equally divided between his widow, Mary Penn, and his son, George, and at the death of the sd. Mary, the whole of the sd. 170 a. to be vested in sd. George, and after the sd. division was made the sd. George sold to Jno. Brock 30 a. of his dividend, leaving 55 a. remaining, and the reversion of the 85 a. alloted the sd. Mary, the sd. George Penn hereby conveys the fee simple estate of 55 a. and the reversion of the sd. Mary's 85 a. to the sd. Trigg for £150 curr., etc., etc. Witnesses, Jno. Brock, Harry Bartlett. July 5, 1785.

March 25, 1785. Wm. Ccats of Spots. Co. from John Carter and Susannah, his wife, of Orange Co. £103 2s. 6d. 165 a. in Spots. Co., part of a tract purchased by Jos. Carter, father of the sd. Jno. Carter of Robt. Goodloe, etc., etc. Witnesses, Bevy. Winslow, Wm. Mills, Will. Winslow. July 5, 1785.

June 2, 1785. Samuel x Brown of Spots. Co. and Martha, his wife, to George Penn of same co. £80 curr. 153 a. of land and a negro, etc. Jno. Waller, Jas. Wiglesworth, Sarah Wiglesworth, Ann Fleeman. July 5, 1785.

April 15, 1785. John Carter and Susannah, his wife, of Orange Co. to Merideth Anderson of Spots. Co. £50 curr. 60 a. in Spots. Co., etc., etc. Bevy. Winslow, Wm. Mills, Will. Winslow. July 5, 1785.

April 9, 1785. Norcut Slaven and his wife, Ann Thomas, of Fredksbg. to James Frazee of Spots. Co. £90 curr. 10 a. in Spots. Co., St. Geo. Par., purchased of Thomas Carr, etc. Witnesses, R. Stubblefield, Jno. Benson, Jno. W. Welles, Jas. Wood. Augt. 2, 1785.

April 5, 1785. Wm. P. Thurston and Lucy Mary, his wife, of Spots. Co. to Richard Dickerson of Spots. Co. £20 curr. 22 a. in Berkeley Par., Spots. Co., etc. Bevy. Winslow, Wm. Mills, Ben. Robinson. Augt. ——, 1785.

April 12, 1785. Reuben Straughan and Catherine, his wife, of Spots. Co. to Oliver Towles of same county. To indemnify sd. Towles, who stands security for sd. Straughan in several matters, the sd. Straughan conveys him 73 a. of land in Spots. Co., goods and chattels, etc., etc. Witnesses, Sarah x Pemberton, Elisabeth Straughan, Fanny Straughan. Augt. 4, 1785.

March 29, 1785. John Carter and Susannah, his wife, of Orange Co. to David Lively of Spots Co. £70 curr. 95 a. in Spots Co., etc. Bevy. Winslow, Wm. Mills, Will. Winslow. Augt., 1785.

July 20, 1785. Peter Crawford and Julia, his wife, of Mecklenburg Co. to John Waller of Spots. Co. £50 curr. 100 a. in Spots. Co., which devolved on the sd. Peter Crawford, as heir at law to his father, John Crawford, decd., etc., etc. Witnesses, Thomas Shearley, Dise x Cockrom, John Kennaday. Augt. 2, 1785.

Decr. 11, 1784. Wm. Dawson and Mary, his wife, of Berkeley Par., Spots. Co. to Wm. Mills of par. and county afsd. £150. 150 a. in same par. and co., etc., etc. Benja. Davis, James Davis, Robert Sp. Coleman. March 1, 1785.

Augt. 3, 1785. Daniel Branham and Susannah, his wife, of Spots. Co. to Wm. Carter of same county. £162 curr. 216 a. in Berkeley Par., Spots Ca., purchased of Richd. Gatewood, etc. Witness, Jno. Brock. Septr. 6, 1785.

Feby. 22, 1785. George Penn of Spots. Co. to Thomas Waller, jr., of same county. Lease. "Tract of land sd. Penn's mother lives on exclusive of her Thirds," etc., etc. £1 15s. curr. yearly. Witnesses, Jno. Waller, K. W., Jno. Stears. Septr. 6, 1785.

Augt. 22, 1785. Mary x Aldiss [or Alders], who was formerly widow and relict of Jno. Paine, decd., and John Paine, eldest son and heir at law of the sd. John Paine, decd., to Thomas Coleman of Spots. Co. Whereas, the sd. John Paine, decd., being in his lifetime possessed of a certain tract of land in Spots. Co. and departed this life intestate, being so seized, whereby the sd. Jno. Paine became possessed of the sd. land with the exception of his mother's dower; the sd. Paine, with consent of his, the sd. Mary Alders (his mother), has agreed to sell to the sd. Coleman the sd. tract containing 100 a. for sum of £120 curr. Conveyance. Witnesses, Richd. Coleman, Spils. Coleman, Richd. Coleman, jr.; Wm. Coleman. Sept. 6, 1785.

Sept. 6, 1785. Richd. Garner and Ann, his wife, of Spots. Co. to Richard Todd of same co. £100 curr. 134 a. in St. Geo. Par., Spots. County, etc. Jno. Brock, D. S.; Joseph Hoomes, Robt. Frank. Sept. 6, 1785.

Sept. 6, 1785. Hawes Coleman of Spots. Co. to Oswald Smith of same county. £112 15s. 110 a., part of the tract purchased of John Z. Lewis, etc., etc. No witnesses. Septr. 6, 1785.

Septr. 4, 1783. Edward Darnaby and Elizabeth, his wife, of Spots. Co. to Mark Davis, planter. £50 curr. and £61 curr. 111 a. in St. Geo. Par., Spots. Co., etc., etc. Philip D. Redd, Jos. Robinson, Edmund Bryant. Septr. 7, 1785.

Feby. 18, 1785. Ephram Musick and Isabel, his wife, of Albemarle Co. to Danl. Baldwin of Spots. Co. £55 curr. 236 a. in Spots. Co., etc. James Abbitt, Gipson Jenkins, Jno. Musick, Charles x Jenkins. Septr. 6, 1785.

Septr. 1, 1785. Charles Cosby and Elizabeth, his wife, of Berkeley Par., Spots. Co. to Wm. Quarles of same par. and county. £480 curr. 378½ a. in Berkeley Par., Spots. Co., bought of Patrick Belsches, etc., etc. Witnesses, Fortunatus Cosby, Wm. Mills, Charles Tate. Septr. 6, 1785.

Septr. 10, 1785. John Shearley and Elizabeth, his wife, of Spots. Co. to Samuel Luck of same county. £10 curr. 9 a. of land, etc., etc. Nicho. Payne, Thomas Shirley, Francs. Hodges. Novr. 1, 1785.

Novr. 1, 1785. Joseph Holladay and Elizabeth, his wife, of Spots. Co. to James Holladay of same co. £100 curr. 146 a. in Spots. Co., etc., etc. Lewis Holladay, Jos. Holladay, jr.; Benj. Holladay, Stephen Holladay. Novr. 1, 1785.

Novr. 1, 1785. James Holladay and Suffier, his wife, to Joseph Holladay of same co. £100 curr. 100 a. in Spots. Co., etc. Lewis Holladay, Jos. Holladay, jr.; Benj. Holladay, Stephen Holladay. Novr. 1, 1785.

Jany. 8, 1785. John Mastin of Spots. Co. to Ashman Sorrel of same county. £40 curr. 64 a. in Spots. Co., etc. Jas. Willoughby, John Sorrel, Royall Thompson, Thomas Sorrell. Novr. 1, 1785.

Sept. 1, 1785. David Pulliam and Betty, his wife, of Spots. Co. to John Fagg of same county. £40 curr. 200 a. in Spots. County, etc., etc. Joseph Pulliam, Joseph Pulliam, jr. No date of record.

June 16, 1784. Robert G. Beverley and Elizabeth, his wife, of Caroline Co. to George Stubblefield of Spots. Co. Whereas, sd. Beverley stands seized in reversion in fee of 828 a. of land in Spots. Co., expectant on the death of Mrs. Ann Waller, widow, who holds same as part of her dowry of the lands of her former husband, Robert Beverley, decd., grandfather to the sd. Robert, party to these presents, etc., the sd. Beverley, etc., in consideration of £1656 curr., conveys the afsd. reversion to the sd. Stubblefield, etc. Witnesses, Reuben Straughan, J. Dawson, Jeremiah Wilson, Jno. Wiglesworth, O. Towles, Ben. Holladay, jr. Septr. 7, 1784.

Septr. 10, 1784. Robert Gaines Beverley and Betsy, his wife, of Caroline Co. to Thomas McKenny of Spots. Co. £1700. 115 a., part of a tract called "Newland" in Spots. Co., etc.. etc. W. Buckner, Tavener Branham, Jno. Brock. Decr. 7. 1784.

Octr. 1, 1785. Thomas Chiles and Mary, his wife, of Caroline Co. to Harry Terrell of Spots. Co. £20 and 127 a. in Caroline county, etc. 150 a. in Spots. Co., part of tract formerly the property of Thomas Ballard Smith, etc., etc. Witnesses, Joel Yarbrough, Chas. Terrell, Jas. Mason, Wm. Cook. Novr. 1, 1785.

June 17, 1785. Shadrach Moore and Ann, his wife, of Spots. Co. to Wm. Smith of same county. £5 curr. 22 a. in St. Geo. Par., Spots. County, etc. Witnesses, Joseph Ficklin, Lodowick Oneal, Samuel Todd. Novr. 1, 1785.

Novr. 1, 1785. George Stubblefield and Sally, his wife, of Spots. Co., Va. and Thomas Carr of the State of Georgia, to Beverley Stubblefield of Spots. Co. £225. 225 a. in Berkeley Par., Spots. County, etc. No witnesses. Novr. 1, 1785.

June 6, 1785. Clayton Coleman and Mary, his wife, of Spots. Co. to Moses Wheeler of same county. £15 curr. 80 a. in Spots. Co., etc. No witnesses. Nov. 1, 1785.

Novr. 1, 1785. George Mason of Caroline Co. to Thomas Turner of Spots County. £84 15s. 113 a. in Spots. Co., purchased of George Cook, etc., etc. James Mason, John Waller, Henry Terrell. Novr. 1, 1785.

Novr. 1, 1785. Wm. Warren and Catherine, his wife; Saml. Warren and Betty, his wife of Spots. Co. to Wm. Durrett of Caroline County. £20. 195 a. in Spots. Co. No witnesses. Novr. 1, 1785.

March 15, 1785. John x Gordon and Elizabeth, his wife, of Culpeper Co. to Lodowick Oneal of Spots. Co. £30 curr. 60 a. in Spots. Co., etc., etc. Isaac Wilson, Wm. Gordon, Alexander Wilson, George Wilson. Novr. 1, 1785.

Novr. 1, 1785. Joseph Herndon and Mary, his wife, of Spots. Co. to Thomas Colson of same county. £97 10s. curr. 75 a. in Spots. county, etc., etc. No witnesses. Novr. 1, 1785.

Octr. 8, 1785. John Allen of Surry Co., Esqr., to Stapleton Crutchfield of Spots. County. £616 5s. 6d. curr. 435 a. in Berkeley Par., Spots. Co., etc. Henry Pemberton, Thos. Colson, Wm. Wiatt, Jno. Anderson, Robt. Gregg. Novr. 1, 1785.

Oct. 8, 1785. John Allen of Surry Co., Esq., to Stapleton Crutchfield of Spots. Co. £616 5s. 6d curr. 435 a. in Berkeley Par., Spts. Co., etc. Henry Pemberton, Thos. Colson, Wm. Wiatt, Jno. Anderson, Robt. Gregg. Nov. 1, 1785.

Octr. 8, 1785. John Allen of Surrey Co., Esqr., to Thomas Colson of Spots. Co. £699 3s. 9d. curr. 490 a. in Berkeley Par., Spots. Co., etc., etc. Henry Pemberton, Stapleton Crutchfield, Wm. Wiatt, Jno. Anderson, Robt. Gregg. Novr. 1, 1785.

Oct. 8, 1785. John Allen of Surry Co., Esqr., to Tho. Colson and Stapleton Crutchfield of Spots. Co. £684 10s. 9d. curr. 480 a. in Berkeley Par., Spots. Co., etc., etc. Wm. Wiatt, Jno. Anderson, Robt. Gregg, Henry Pemberton, James Straughan. Novr. 1, 1785.

March 2, 1785. Wm. Blaydes and Mary Ann, his wife, of Spots. Co. to John Blaydes of same co. £112 10s. curr. 75 a. in Spots. Co., etc., etc. Spencer Coleman, Hawes Coleman, John Chew, jr. Novr. 1, 1785.

Decr. 26, 1785. John x Cary and Frances, his wife, of Spots. Co. to John Estes of Caroline Co. £35 curr. 67 a. in Spots. and Caroline Counties, etc., etc. No witnesses. Novr. 1, 1785.

June 11, 1785. Wm. Warren of Spots. Co. and Katey, his wife, to John Waller of same county. £33 curr. 78 a. in Spots. Co., part devised the sd. Wm. by the last will and testament of his father, Samuel Warren, decd., and part devolved upon him as heir of his brother, Jno. Warren, decd., etc., etc. Witnesses, Benja. Waller, Jno. Shackleford, Merideth Anderson, Wm. Rash. Novr. 1, 1785.

Novr. 1, 1785. Wm. Warren of Spots. Co. and Katey, his wife, to John Lahone of same county. £20 curr. 25 a. of land whereon sd. Lahone lives, etc., etc. No witnesses. Novr. 1, 1785.

Octr. 8, 1785. Thomas Carr of the State of Georgia and George Stubblefield and Sally, his wife, of Spots. Co. to John Chandler of Spots. Co. £115 10s. 283 a. in Berkeley Par., Spots. Co., etc., etc. T. Dawson, Jno. Day, Wm. Moore, Wm. Taylor. Novr. 1, 1785.

Septr. 7, 1785. Mark Davis and Susannah, his wife, to George Stubblefield. £80 curr. 111 a. in St. Geo. Par., Spots. Co., etc., etc. Jno. Brock, Edwd. Darnaby, Ambrose Dudley, B. Stubblefield. Septr. 7, 1785.

DEED BOOK L

1785–1788

Septr. 20, 1785. Jno. Robinson and Margt., his wife, to George Stubblefield. £314 curr. 314 a. in St. Geo. Par., Spots. Co., etc. Thos. Powell, Peter Dudley, Benj. Stubblefield, Bevy. W. Stubblefield, Nicho. Payne. Dec. 6, 1785.

June 12, 1785. Wm. Richards and Elizabeth, his wife, of Culpeper Co. to Henry Gatewood, jr., of Spots. Co. £700 specie. 440 a. in Spots. Co., etc., etc. Jos. Brock, Jno. Bridges, Richd. Blayle, Judith McDaniel, Elizabeth Clayton. Novr. 3, 1785.

June 12, 1785. Henry Gatewood, jr., of Spots. Co. to Wm. Richards and Robt. Slaughter of Culpeper Co. £700 specie. 440 a. in Spots. Co., etc., etc. Mortgage. Jos. Brock, Jno. Bridges, Richd. Blayle, Judith McDaniel, Elizabeth Clayton. Novr. 3, 1785.

Novr. 5, 1785. Hugh Roy of Spots. Co. to his neice, Balinda Scott. Deed of Gift. 1 negro. Witnesses, Jos. Brock, Thos. Pritchett. Dec. 6, 1785.

Dec. 6, 1785. Jno. Edwards of Spots. Co., po. of atto., to friends, Jno. White and Long Wharton, of same co., etc. Witnesses, Edwd. Herndon, Robt. Hart, Bevy. Winslow. Decr. 6, 1785.

June 16, 1785. Ann x Waller of Spots. Co., po. of atto., to her grandson, Wm. Johnston, jr., of Caroline Co., etc. Witnesses, Richd. W. Johnston, Judith Roy. Decr. 6, 1785.

Decr. 6, 1785. James Hensley and Catharine, his wife, of St. Geo. Par., Spots. Co. and John Hensley and Hannah, his wife, of same Par. and Co. to Wm. Spindle of Caroline Co. £60 specie. 105 a. sold by Jno. Snell to Saml. Hensley in 1734, also 60 a. bought by sd. James Hensley of Thos. Estes in Spots. Co., etc. No witnesses. Decr. 6, 1785.

Sept. 8, 1785. Geo. Stubblefield and Sally, his wife, and Thos. Carr, to Thos. Powell of Spots. Co. £582 10s. curr. 776 a. in Berkeley Par., Spots. Co. Larkin Stanard, Richd. Loury, Ben. Holladay. Decr. 6, 1785.

Octr. 6, 1785. Thos. Carr, George Stubblefield and Sally, his wife, to Thomas Powell. £145 curr. 222¾ a. in Berkeley Par., Spots. Co., etc. B. Stubblefield, Benj. Stubblefield, W. Dawson. Decr. 6, 1785.

Octr. 12, 1785. Thos. Carr of the State of Ga. and Geo. Stubblefield and Sally, his wife of Spots. Co., Va., to John Wren of King George Co. £100. 100 a. in Spots. Co., etc. Jno. Robinson, B. Stubblefield, Benj. Stubblefield. Decr. 7, 1785.

Octr. 6, 1785. Thos. Carr, Geo. Stubblefield and Sally, his wife, to Wm. Dawson. £102 curr. 170 a. in Spots. Co., etc., etc. B. Stubblefield, Benja. Stubblefield, Thos. Blanton, Thos. Powell. Decr. 7, 1785.

Oct. 11, 1785. Thos. Towles of Spots. Co., Gent., to Wm. Dawson of same co. Release of land mortgaged to sd. Towles by sd. Dawson, etc., etc. Jno. Brock, Jas. Sandidge, Nich. Payne. Decr. 7, 1785.

Novr. 1, 1785. John Wiglesworth and Philadelphia, his wife, to Richd. Garner of Spots. Co. £180. 90 a. in Spots. Co., etc., etc. Saml. Todd, Robt. Cunningham, McField Whiting. Feby. 7, 1786.

Decr. 29, 1785. Jno. Waller and Elizabeth, his wife, of Spots. Co. to Wm. Durrett of Caroline Co., Gent. £19 curr. 35 a. Elisha Dismukes, Peter Mason, Thomas Sorrell. Feby. 7, 1786.

Feby. 4, 1786. Thos. Hackney and Sarah, his wife, of Spots. Co. to Thomas Turner of same county. £100 curr. 100 a., part purchased of Geo. Cook; part given sd. Hackney by David Woodroof (as by deed in Spots. Co.), near New Market in Spots. Co., etc., etc. Jno. Waller, Benoni Woodroof, Jno. Turner, Thos. Turner, jr. Feby. 7, 1786.

Jany. 30, 1786. David Woodroof and Rachel, his wife, of Spots. Co. to Thomas Hackney of same co. £100 specie. 130 a. Thos. Turner, Jno. Turner, Benoni Woodroof. Feby. 7, 1786.

Decr. 13, 1785. Henry Willis of King Geo. Co. to his neice, Mary Champe Willis, dau. of John Willis, Gent. Deed of Gift. 1 slave. Witnesses, Thos. Colson, Hay Battaile, O. Towles. Feby. 7, 1786.

Septr. 26, 1785. Chas. Cosby and Elizabeth, his wife, of Spots. Co. to Benj. Nelson of same co. £50 in gold. 50 a. in Berkeley Par., Spots. Co., etc., etc. Bevy. Winslow, Wm. Mills, Saml. Sale, Jos. Holladay. Feby. 7, 1786.

Feby. 7, 1786. Owen Thomas Holladay, orph. and son of Jno. Holladay, decd., aged 16 yrs. Septr. 13 last, apprentices himself to Thos. Herndon, house carpenter, etc., etc. No witnesses. Feby. 7, 1786.

July 23, 1784. Wm. Thompson promises to let Saml. Hildrup build an house, one tenement occupied by Mrs. McCoile, etc., etc. Witnesses, Z. Lucas, Jno. Wiglesworth, Saml. Todd. March 7, 1786.

March 7, 1786. Leonard Waller and Agness, his wife, of Spots. Co. to Spencer Coleman of same co. £240 curr. 184 a. in Berkeley Par., Spots. Co., etc., etc. W. Dawson, Hugh Roy, Jno. Waller. March 7, 1786.

Feby. 10, 1786. Jno. Dawson of Spots. Co. to Ephraim Beazley of same county. £75 curr. 50 a. in Berkeley Par., Spots. Co., etc., etc. Jas. Mitchim, Richd. Coleman, Ephraim Beazley, Micajah Poole. March 7, 1786.

Novr. 12, 1785. Wm. Dawson of Spots. Co. to Messrs. Smith, Young and Hyde of Fredksbg., Merchts. £260 specie. Mortgage. 170 a. in Spots. Co., etc., etc. O. Towles, Jno. Benson, Peter Lucas. March 7, 1786.

Feby. 7, 1786. Nathl. Stevens of St. Geo. Par., Spots. Co. to his sons, Nathl. Stevens, James Stevens, and John Stevens of same Par. and county. Deed of Gift. 200 a. whereon sd. Nathl. Stevens lives in Spots. Co., to be equally divided amongst them. Witnesses, Wm. Bullock, Jno. Bullock, Wm. Schooler. March 7, 1786.

Oct. 13, 1785. Wm. Heslop of Spots. Co. to George Stubblefield of same county. £231. Mortgage. 303 a. in Berkeley Par., Spots. Co., etc., etc. Jno. Brock, Jno. Davenport, Thos. Brown. March 7, 1786.

Feby. 9, 1786. Anthony Bartlett of Spots. Co. to George Stubblefield of same county. £200. 336 a. in St. Geo. Par., Spots. Co., etc., etc. Harry Bartlett, Jno. Davenport, Geo. W. B. Spooner, Wm. Herndon, Benj. Stubblefield, B. Stubblefield. Mar. 7, 1786.

March 5, 1785. Henry x Head to Alexander Spence Head. Mortgage. 4 negroes, etc. Witnesses, Jno. Herndon, Jno. Wiglesworth. March 7, 1786.

Augt. 16, 1785. David Pannill of King Wm. Co. to David Partlow, jr., of Spots. Co. £150 curr. 168 a. in Spots. Co., etc., etc. Thomas Jones, Jas. Faulconer, Saml. Partlow, jr. March 7, 1786.

March 7, 1786. Nathaniel Ch. Gordon of Wilkes Co., North Carolina, and Nancy, his wife, to Wm. Estes of Spots. Co., Va. £40 curr. 95 a. in Spots. Co. No witnesses. March 7, 1786.

Decr. 6, 1785. Peter Mason and Eliza., his wife, of Berkeley Par., Spots. Co., to Samuel Hawes of Caroline Co. £296. 370 a. in Spots Co., etc., etc. No witnesses. Decr. 6, 1785.

Decr. 11, 1785. John White and Mary, his wife, of Spots. Co. to James Bartlett of same county. 300 a. in Spots. Co. "In consideration of good will and affection they bear the sd. James and also the sum of £10," etc., etc. Jos. Willoughby, Long Wharton, Jos. Barksdale. April 4, 1786.

April 3, 1786. Elizabeth Towles of Spots. Co. to Thos. Towles of Berkeley Par., Spots. Co. £150 13s. curr. 131 a. in par. and co. afsd., on Robinson Run, etc., etc. B. Stubblefield, Nicho. Payne, Jno. Chew, jr. April 4, 1786.

April 3, 1786. Elizabeth Towles of Spots. Co. to John Chew, jr., of same county. £196 10s. curr. 131 a. in Berkeley Par., Spots. Co., etc., etc. B. Stubblefield, Nicho. Payne, Thos. Towles. April 4, 1786.

Augt. 9, 1795. Mordacai Buckner of Spots. Co., Gent., to Oliver Towles of same county, Gent. Whereas, the sd. Towles was sec. for executorship of Mrs. Elizabeth Stanard of the last will, etc., of Beverley Stanard, Gent., Decd., and whereas, the sd. Mordacai Buckner by intermarrying with the sd. Elizabeth Stanard became vested with sd. Executorship during the life of the sd. Elizabeth, whereof he became liable for the execution of the sd. will, and being desirous of saving harmless the sd. Towles, etc., deeds to him several slaves, in trust, etc., etc. Witnesses, Jno. Brock, Thos. Towles, Jno. Chew, jr. Apr. 4, 1786.

Jany. 3, 1786. Lodowick Oneal of Spots. Co. to Goodlove Heiskell of Fredksbg. Mortgage. Several slaves, etc., etc. Witnesses, O. Towles, Jno. Anderson, Robt. Gregg. Apr. 4, 1786.

March 24, 1786. Wm. Smithers, Harry Rains, Jno. Smithers, James Smithers, and Elizabeth Smithers of Spots. Co. to Edwd. Ledwedge of same county. £16 curr. 187 a., formerly property of Jno. Calahan, decd., in St. Geo. Par., Spots. Co., etc., etc. Wm. Schooler, Jno. Stephens, Jno. Bullock. April 5, 1786.

April 8, 1785. Wm. Dawson of Spots. Co. to Thomas Towles. Mortgage. To indemnify sd. Towles for being sd. Dawson's security on two bonds amounting to £350, etc., etc. 2 slaves. Witnesses, Eliza. Chew, Nancy Towles, Jno. Chew, jr. April 5, 1786.

Oct. 11, 1785. Wm. Dawson and Mary, his wife, of Spots. Co. to Wm. Bronaugh of same county. £700 curr. 650 a. in Spots. Co., etc., etc. Jno. Brock, Thos. Towles, Nicho. Payne, Jas. Sandidge. June 6, 1786.

Septr. 17, 1785. Thomas Carr, Geo. Stubblefield and Sally, his wife, to Robt. Hart. £24 curr. 69 a. on Douglass Run, Spots. Co., etc., etc. V. Minor, Jas. Byars, Elizabeth Minor. June 6, 1786.

Octr. 12, 1785. Thomas Powell and Elizabeth, his wife, of Spots. Co. to Wm. Heslop of same county. £331. 303 a. in Spots. Co., etc., etc. Geo. Stubblefield, Francis Turnley, jr.; Jas. Stevens. June 6, 1786.

Septr. 8, 1785. Geo. Stubblefield and Sally, his wife, of Spots. Co. and Thomas Carr of the State of Georgia, to Richd. Loury of Spots. Co. £375 curr. 500 a. in Berkeley Par., Spots. Co., etc., etc. Jno. Brock, D. S.; Larkin Stanard, Ben. Holladay, Thomas Powell. June 6, 1786.

June 1, 1786. Thomas Powell and Elizabeth, his wife, of Spots. Co. to Richd. Loury of Caroline Co. £134 8s. curr. 224 a. in Spots. Co., etc., etc. Harmon Anderson, Wm. Heslop, Francis Turnley, Senr. June 6, 1786.

June 6, 1786. Jno. Wiglesworth, Gent., and Philadelphia, his wife, of Spots. Co. to Joseph Jones of Caroline Co., Gent. £450 curr. 300 a. on both sides of the town of New Holland, in St. Geo. Par., Spots. Co., etc., etc. No witnesses. June 6, 1786.

Octr. 27, 1779. Wm. Trigg of Spots. Co. of first part; James Trigg of King and Queen Co., of second part; Mary Trigg, widow, of Spots. Co., guardian of Thomas Trigg, of third part. The sd. Wm. Trigg releases to James Trigg one equal moiety in two slaves, and to Mary Trigg, in trust for Thos. Trigg, the other moiety in sd. slaves, etc., etc. Witnesses, Wm. Duerson, Anne Stevens. July 4, 1786.

June 23, 1786. Genl. Alexander Spotswood to Joseph Brock, Clk. Lease. 82½ a. in St. Geo. Par., Spots. Co. "Sd. Jos. Brock, Thomas Brock, and Robert Brock, etc., etc. 421 lbs. tob. yearly, etc. Witnesses, Danl. Branham, Jno. Clayton, John McWhirt, Henry Gatewood, jr. July 4, 1786.

April 18, 1785. Harry Bartlett of Spots. Co., Gent., to George Stubblefield of same county, Gent. £715 specie. ⅔ ds. of a lot and improvements in town of Fredksbg., deeded to sd. Bartlett by one Saml. Roddy, to indemnify him, etc., and the sd. Roddy failing to pay the debt for which sd. Bartlett stood his security, the sd. land is sold to satisfy the claim of sd. Bartlett, etc., etc. Witnesses, Thomas Towles, Nicho. Payne, Jno. Chew, jr.; B. Stubblefield. July 4, 1786.

July 4, 1786. Henry True and Jane, his wife, of Spots. Co. to Saml. Alsup of same Co. £12 3s. specie. 27 a. in Berkeley Par., Spots. Co., etc., etc. No witnesses. July 4, 1786.

Mar. 15, 1786. Thomas Blanton and Jane, his wife, of Spts. Co. to Saml. Alsup of same Co. £200 curr. 250 a., purchased of Benj. Craig, in

Berkeley Par., Spots. Co., etc., etc. Willm. Smith, Harmon Haner, Geo. Cammack. July 4, 1786.

Mar. ——, 1786. Wm. Thompson of Spots. Co. to Danl. Branham of same Co. £——. 2 negroes. Witness, Henry Gatewood, jr. July 4, 1786.

May 6, 1786. Jos. Willoughby of Spots. Co. to Francis Coleman of same co. £12 10s. 100 a. in Spots. Co. No witnesses. July 4, 1786.

March 7, 1785. Gilmon Lane and Susannah, his wife, of Berkeley Par., Spots. Co. to Wm. Moore of same par. and county. £60. 100 a. in par. and co. afsd., etc. Bevy. Winslow, Wm. Mills, Jno. Nelson, jr. Mar. 7, 1786.

Augt. 1, 1786. Nicho. Payne and Elizabeth, his wife, and Jno. Chew, jr., and Elizabeth his wife, of Spots. Co. to Stockly Towles of Goochland Co. £487 6s. 3d. 422 a., purchased by sd. Payne and Chew of Jno. Tankersley in Spots. Co., etc., etc. No witnesses. Augt. 1, 1786.

Feby. 10, 1786. Thomas Allen of Spots. Co. to Edwd. Herndon and Jacob Whitler of Fredksbg. Mortgage. 103 a. and also 100 a. leased from Alexander Spotswood, etc., etc. R. Thornton, F. Brooke, Jno. Minor, Wm. Carter, Thos. Duerson. Augt. 1, 1786.

July 25, 1786. Adrien Tellier of Spots. Co. to John Joseph Combs of Fairfax Co. £225 specie. 200 a. in Spots. Co., etc., etc. Jas. Julian, Sebastian Losh. Augt. 1, 1786.

July 31, 1786. Mildred x Edwards of Spots. Co. to Stockly Towles of same co. £56 10s. curr. 83¾ a. in Spots. Co., etc., etc. Saml. Allsop, Jno. Crutchfield, Edmd. Foster. Augt. 1, 1786.

July 28, 1786. Thomas Brightwell and Molly, his wife, of Orange Co. to Sarah Wade of Spots. Co., Berkeley Par. £3. 50 a. in Berkeley Par., Spots. Co., etc. No witnesses. Augt. 1, 1786.

Augt. 1, 1786. Benja. Holladay and Sally, his wife, to Wm. Dawson. £5. 5 a. of land, etc., etc. No witnesses. Augt. 1, 1786.

Augt. 1, 1786. Wm. Dawson and Mary, his wife, to Smith, Young & Hyde. £161 17s. 6d. 120 a., purchased of Stubblefield & Carr, in Spots. Co., etc., etc. Jas. Julian, Jos. Woolfolk, Jno. Sunderland. Augt. 1, 1786.

Augt. 1, 1786. Thos. Colson, Gent., and Frances, his wife, of Spots. Co. to James Hutcherson of same county. £38 4s. specie. 26 a. in St. Geo. Par., Spots. Co., etc., etc. Jno. Herndon, Thos. Towles, Wm. Frazer, Geo. Hutcherson. Augt. 1, 1786.

June 19, 1786. James Frazer and Sally Kyon, his wife, of St. Geo. Par., Spots. Co. to John Welch of Par. and Co. afsd. £200. 10 a. in Spots. Co., etc., etc. Abram x Simons, Jas. x Culley. Augt. 1, 1786.

March 1, 1786. Ambrose Dudley and Ann, his wife, of Spots. Co. to Wm. McWilliams of same co. £900. 375½ a. in Spots. Co., etc., etc. Benj. Stubblefield, Peter Dudley, Edmund Bryant. Augt. 1, 1786.

July 25, 1784. Geo. Pottie of Louisa Co. to Wm. Bruce of Spots Co. Lease of a tract of land purchased of Reubin Straughan, during lifetime of sd. Bruce and wife, etc., etc. Witness, Archd. Dick, Senr. Augt. 1, 1786.

Augt. 1, 1786. Tureman Lewis and Marg., his wife, of Spots. Co. to Jno. Pierce of same co. £15 10s. curr. 15 a. in Spots. Co. No witnesses. Augt. 1, 1786.

April 8, 1786. Geo. Stubblefield and Sally, his wife of Spots. Co. and Thos. Carr of the State of Georgia, to Benja. Holladay of Spots. Co. £180 curr. 150 a. in Berkeley Par., Spots. Co., etc., etc. Jno. Brock, D. S., S. C.; Larkin Stanard, Richd. Loury, Thos. Powell. Augt. 2, 1786.

July 26, 1786. Peter Stubblefield of the State of Georgia [at present in Spots. Co., Va.], to Geo. Stubblefield of Spots. Co., Va. £150 curr. 1 negro, horses, wagons, etc., etc. Jno. Chew, jr.; B. Stubblefield. Augt. 2, 1786.

Jany. 5, 1786. Thomas Ballard Wyatt and Francis Wyatt to James Parish of Spots. Co. £150 curr. 140 a., part of a tract conveyed by Deed from Thomas Ballard Smith to his grandchildren, the sd. Thos. B. Wyatt and Francis Wyatt, in Spots. Co., etc., etc. Jno. Waller, Benj. Waller, Thos. Wyatt, Eliza. Wyatt. Augt. 2, 1786.

Decr. 12, 1774. Wm. Daingerfield of Spots. Co. Deed of Gift to Sally Daingerfield in the Co. of King and Queen, widow of Robinson Dainger-field of the sd. county. "All the negroes that came by the sd. Sally, and their increase," etc., etc. "And in consideration of sd. Sally's giving up her dower in the land and other est. of sd. Robinson Daingerfield," etc., etc. Witnesses, Wm. Cuming, Richd. Ray, Thos. Loury. Augt. 2, 1786.

Jany. 3, 1786. Thomas Foster to Sarah Hensley. Mortgage. 1 negro. Witnesses, Jos. Herndon, Jona. Clark. Augt. 3, 1786.

July 18, 1786. Edwd. Marsh and Eleanor, his wife, of Spots. Co. to Abraham Simons of same co. £200 curr. 150 a. in Spots. Co., etc., etc. No witnesses. Septr. 5, 1786.

Septr. 5, 1786. Henry Foster of Fayette Co. and Mildred, his wife, to Robt. Smith of Spots. Co., Gent. £30 curr. 401 a. in St. Geo. Par., Spots. Co., etc., etc. Jos. Brock, Hy. Crutcher, Wm. Jones, Richd. Collins, Wm. Herndon. Septr. 5, 1786.

March 20, 1786. Thomas Mastin and Priscilla, his wife, of Spots. Co. to Edmund Daniel of Caroline Co. £87 curr. 100 a. in Spots. Co., etc., etc. Wm. Cannon, Elizabeth Keith, Jno. Mastin. Septr. 5, 1786.

Sept. 5, 1786. Jos. Brock, act. executor of the last will, etc., of Jno. Zachary Lewis of Spots. Co., Gent., Decd., to Nicho. Payne of same co., Gent. £660 curr. 415 a. in Spots. Co., etc., etc. No witnesses. Sept. 5, 1786.

Sept. 5, 1786. Nicho. Payne of Spots. Co., Gent., and Elizabeth, his wife, to Joseph Duerson of same co., Gent. £206 18s. 90 a. in Berkeley Par., Spots. Co., etc., etc. No witnesses. Sept. 5, 1786.

Sept. 2, 1786. Alexander Parker of Caroline Co., po. of atto., to Robt. Beverley Chew of Fredksbg. "Mentions property in St. Nicholas Par., City of Bristol, Gt. Britain," etc., etc. Witnesses, Larkin Stanard, Edwd. Peyton, Geo. Scott. No date of Record.

Feby. 21, 1786. Thomas Thorpe of Spots. Co. binds himself to Larkin Stanard of same county.' Witnesses, Edwd. Peyton, Jno. Chew. Sept. 5, 1786.

Septr. 5, 1786. John Edwards of Spots. Co., po. of atto., to Capt. Francis Coleman of same county. Witnesses, Edwd. Herndon, Wm. Mills, Edwd. Herndon, jr. Sept. 5, 1786.

Sept. 4, 1786. Thomas Henderson and Mary, his wife, of Spots. Co. to Wm. Smith of same co., Gent. £56 10s. curr. 113 a. in Berkeley Par., Spots. Co., etc., etc. No witnesses. Sept. 5, 1786.

Augt. 10, 1779. Agreement between John Coleman and Francis Coleman, both of Spots. Co. "The sd. Jno. and Francis having agreed to purchase a quantity of land in the new country," etc. Each putting in £200 curr. The sd. Jno. to go and secure the land, the warrant, etc., in his name; then sd. Jno. is to deed ½ of the same to the sd. Francis or his heirs, etc., etc. Witnesses, Jno. Hutcherson, Henry Coleman, Robt. Ed. Coleman. Oct. 3, 1786.

March 30, 1786. David Partlow of Spots. Co. to Edwd. Ballenger. £168 curr. 168 a. in Spots. Co., etc., etc. Wm. Strother, Jno. Penny, Saml. Partlow, Saml. Partlow, jr. Oct. 3, 1786.

June 1, 1786. Richd. Loury and Betty, his wife, of Caroline Co. to Thomas Powell of Spots. Co. £374 curr. 374 a. in Spots. Co., etc., etc. Harmon Anderson, Wm. Heslop, Francis Turnley, Senr. June 6, 1786.

April 24, 1786. Thos. Ballard Wyatt, Francis Wyatt, and Thos. Chiles to Henry Terrell of Spots. Co. £180 curr. 150 a., part of tract conveyed by deed from Thos. Ballard Smith to his grandchildren, Thos. Ballard Wyatt and Francis Wyatt, in Spots. Co., etc., etc. Theop. Wyatt, Jno. Arnold, Benoni Woodroof, Eliz. Wyatt. Novr. 7, 1786.

May 2, 1786. Abram Simons and Mildred, his wife, of St. Geo. Par., Spots. Co., to Edwd. Herndon of same par. and county. £4000 curr. 214 a. in St. Geo. Par., Spots. Co., etc., etc. Jno. W. Willis, Danl. Branham, Thomas Colson, Jos. Herndon, Wm. Jones. Novr. 8, 1786.

July 18, 1786. George Stubblefield and Sally, his wife, of Spots. Co. to Thos. Adams of same county. £150. 149 a. in Berkeley Par., Spots. Co., etc., etc. Richd. Loury, Benja. Stubblefield, John Cary. Novr. 7, 1786.

March 2, 1786. Richd. Loury of Caroline Co. to John Wren of Spots. Co. £10. 2 a. in Spots. Co., etc. Geo. Stubblefield, Benja. Stubblefield, Susanna B. Stubblefield. Novr. 7, 1786.

June 19, 1786. Saml. Coleman and Sally, his wife, of Caroline Co. to James Wiglesworth of Spots. Co. £12 5s. curr. 49 a. in Spots. Co., etc., etc. Spencer Coleman, Jas. x White, Clayton Coleman, Elizabeth Coleman. Decr. 5, 1786.

Decr. 5, 1786. Geo. Penn of Spots. Co. to Jas. Wiglesworth, Sr., of same co. £9 13s. 4d. specie. 9⅔ a. in Spots. Co., etc., etc. Nicho. Payne, Beverley Stubblefield, John Crutchfield. Dec. 5, 1786.

Decr. 5, 1786. Wm. x Golson and Joan, his wife, of Spots. Co. to Robt. Smith of same co., Gent. £20 specie. 80 a. whereupon Thos. Perry now lives in Spots. Co., etc., etc. No witnesses. Novr. 5, 1786.

Sept. 19, 1786. Abraham x Simons and Mildred, his wife, of Spots. Co. to George Stubblefield of same county. £200. 150 a. in Spots. Co., etc., etc. Saml. Roddey, Stephen Johnson, Jno. Herndon. Decr. 5, 1786.

Sept. 26, 1786. James x Warren and Mary, his wife, of Spots. Co. to Thomas Towles of same co., Gent. £50 curr. 100 a., bounded by lands of sd. Towles, Capt. Wm. Durrett, Jno. Lehone, Wm. Coats, and Jno. Crane, and devised sd. Warren by the last will of his father, Saml. Warren, decd., in Spots. Co., etc., etc. Wm. Smith, Nicho. Payne, Jno. Chew, jr. Decr. 5, 1786.

Decr. 5, 1786. Thomas Colson of Spots. Co. to Wm. McCloud of same co. Lease. 100 a. in St. Geo. Par., Spots. Co. "Sd. Wm. McCloud and Elizabeth, his wife, and his son, Richd. McCloud," etc., etc. £3 specie rent. No witnesses. Decr. 5, 1786.

Decr. 5, 1786. Thos. Colson of Spots. Co. to James Cully of same co. Lease. 70 a. in St. Geo. Par., Spots. Co. "Sd. James Culley and Susannah, his wife, and his son," etc., etc. 500 lbs. tob. rent. No witnesses. Decr. 5, 1786.

Augt. 22, 1786. Wm. Carter and Frances, his wife; John Carter and Mary, his wife; Rice Curtis and Frances, his wife; Margaret Marshall, Wm. Heslop and Ann, his wife; Wm. Sutton and Sally, his wife; Richd. Stevens and Mary Beverley, his wife; Joseph Sutton and Judy, his wife; Lucy Carter ——; Robert Carter and ——, to Wm. Duerson. £10 to each of above parties. 200 a. in Berkeley Par., Spots. Co., etc., etc. Witnesses, Thos. Pritchett, Benj. Ballard, Jno. Davenport, Thos. Bartlett, Jno. Parrish, Jno. Chew, jr.; Nicho. Payne, Jas. Stevens, Edwd. Herndon, Benj. Stubblefield, Jo. Brock, Jno. Carter, jr.; Wm. Carter, Rice Curtis, James Mitchem. Jany 2, 1787.

June 23, 1786. Robt. Hutcherson of Spots. Co. to Francis Coleman. £15. "Legacy given me by my uncle, Jno. Hutcherson, decd., as by his last will and testament," etc., etc. Jno. Hutcherson, Wm. Hutcherson. Saml. Wharton. Jany. 2, 1787.

Novr. 7, 1786. James x Humphries and Letty, his wife, of Spots. Co. to Wm. Rash of same co. £50 specie. 62¼ a. in Spots. Co., etc., etc. B. Stubblefield, Thos. Coleman, Jno. Waller. Jany. 2, 1787.

Novr. 7, 1786. E. Callender and David Henderson of Fredksbg., Merchts., and Elizabeth Callender and Mildred Henderson, their wives, to Beverley Winslow, Joseph Brock, Wm. Smith, and Edwd. Herndon, Gentlm. £15. 11,682 sq. ft. in Spots. Co., "in trust for the use of Spots. Co.," etc., etc. Witness, Wm. Waddle. Jany. 2, 1787.

Decr. 1, 1786. Joseph Hewell and Frances, his wife, of Halifax Co. to Spilsby Coleman of Spots. Co. £125. Tract of land in Spots. Co., etc., etc. Jno. Poole, Jos. Hewell, jr.; Barnet Payne. Jan. 2, 1787.

Septr. 12, 1786. Peter Stubblefield and Peggy, his wife, of the State of Georgia; Evans Long and Lucy, his wife, of Spots. Co., Va.; James Smith and Sally, his wife, of same county; Zachariah Lucas and Polly Harrison, his wife, of the same co.; Richd. Long and Fanny, his wife, of same co., to Thomas Coleman, jr. Whereas, John Apperson, decd., did by his last will and testament devise to his daughter, Peggy, wife of the above named Peter Stubblefield, 200 a., part of a tract purchased by sd. Apperson of Jno. Carthrae and Jas. Somerville for her natural life, and in case the sd. Peggy should die without issue, the sd. land to be equally divided amongst his other children, viz., the sd. Lucy, wife of Evans Long; the sd. Sally, wife of James Smith; sd. Polly Harrison (who has since intermarried with Zachariah Lucas), and sd. Fanny (who has since intermarried with Richd. Long), or the survivors, etc., etc., and whereas, the sd. Evans Long and wife, James Smith and his wife, Zachariah Lucas and his wife, Richd. Long and his wife, having agreed to relinquish to the sd. Peter Stubblefield and Peggy, his wife, all their right, title, etc., as aforementioned, and so do by their being parties to these presents, etc., etc., the sd. Peter Stubblefield and Peggy, his wife, for the sum of £——, convey the sd. land   (with the other parties, they being pd. 5s. each) to the sd. Coleman, etc., etc. Witnesses, Stapleton Crutchfield, Jos. Duerson, Wm. Henderson, Jno. Chew, jr.; Nicho. Payne, Henry Pendleton, jr. Jany. 2, 1787.

Oct. 21, 1786. Larkin Smith and Mary Elenor, his wife, of King and Queen Co. to Stapleton Crutchfield of Spots. Co. £160 curr. 68 a. in Spots. Co., etc., etc. Saml. Woolfolk, Jno. Crutchfield, Harry B. Towles. Feby. 6, 1787.

Jany. 27, 1787. Susannah Holladay to John Rawlings. £40. 65 a., which descended to sd. Susannah from her father, Benj. Holladay, and which he purchased of Wm. Dawson and Mary, his wife, who was the late widow of Thos. Rawlings, decd., in Spots. Co., etc., etc. W. Dawson, Rawlings Pulliam, Austin Sandidge. Feby. 6, 1787.

Feby. 6, 1787. George Hensley and Martha, his wife, and Sarah x Hensley to Thomas Colson of Spots Co. £98 specie. 95 a., part of a larger tract purchased by Wm. Richardson, decd., of Larkin Chew and by sd. Richardson devised to his grandson, James Hutcherson, and by him conveyed to the sd. Geo. Hensley, etc., in Spots. Co., etc., etc. No witnesses. Feby. 6, 1787.

Octr. ——, 1786. Evans Long and Lucy, his wife, of Spots. Co. to Wm. Henderson of same co. £125 curr. 150 a. in Spots. Co., etc., etc. Thos. Towles, Nicho. Payne. Feby. 6, 1787.

Sept. 27, 1785. Jno. Arnold of Spots. Co. to Ashmond Sorrell of same co. £20. 30 a. in Spots. Co., etc., etc. Jos. Willoughby, Edwd. Brasfield, Jno. Sorrell. Feby. 6, 1787.

Jany. 23, 1787. Wm. Pettus of Spots. Co., po. of atto., to his son, Wm. Pettus, etc., etc. Witnesses, Jno. Arnold, Jas. Pettus. Feby. 6, 1787.

June 23, 1786. Genl. Alexander Spotswood of Spots. Co. and Elizabeth, his wife, to John Clayton of same co. £125 curr. 253 a. in Spots. Co., etc., etc. Danl. Branham, Jno. McHurt, Henry Gatewood, jr.; Jos. Brock, Clk. Feby. 6, 1787.

Decr. 21, 1786. Zachariah Lucas and Polly Harrison, his wife, of Fredksbg to Joseph Herndon and John Wilson of Berkeley Par., Spots. Co. £240 curr. 240 a., devised the sd. Polly Harrison Lucas by her father, Jno. Apperson, decd., in Berkeley Par., Spots. Co., etc., etc. Edwd. Herndon, Thos. Strachan, Jno. Crutchfield, Fieldg. Lucas. Feby. 6, 1787.

Septr. 23, 1786. Margaret Marshall of Caroline Co.; Wm. Sutton and Sarah, his wife, of same co.; Richd. Stevens and Mary Beverley, his wife, of same co.; Lucy Carter of Spots. Co.; Wm. Heslop and Ann, his wife, to Wm. Carter of Spots. Co. £210 curr. 208 a. in Berkeley Par., Spots. Co., etc., etc. Witnesses, Nicho. Payne, Wm. Smith, Jno. Brock, Richd. Stevens, Rice Curtis. Feby. 6, 1787.

Jany. 31, 17——. Jno. Benson and Eleanor, his wife, of Spots. Co. to David Simons of same co. £300 curr. 140 a., known as Chalkey Level, purchased of Thos. Carr in St. Geo. Par., Spots. Co., etc., etc. Jno. Chew, jr.; Jos. Chew, Fontaine Maury. Feby. 6, 1787.

Jany. 29, 1787. John Welch and Eleanor, his wife, of the State of Maryland, Baltimore Co., to David Simons of Fredksbg., Va. £200 curr. 10 a., conveyed by Thos. Carr to Norcut Slaven and by sd. Slaven to James Frazer and by sd. Frazer to the sd. Welch, etc., in Spots. Co., etc., etc. John Chew, jr.; Jos. Chew, Fontaine Maury. Feby. 6, 1787.

Jany. 4, 1787. Henry Willis of King Geo. Co., Gent., to his niece, Mary Champe Willis, dau. of Jno. Whitaker Willis, of Spots. Co., Gent. Deed of Gift. 1 slave. Witnesses, O. Towles, Larkin Stanard, A. Dick. Feby. 6, 1787.

Feby. 6, 1787. Jno. Frazer (son of Andrew Frazer, late of Fredksbg., decd.), aged 17 yrs. Oct. 4th last, apprentices himself to Thomas Herndon of Spots. Co., house carpenter. No witnesses. Feby. 6, 1787.

Decr. 30, 1786. John Tankersley of Richmond County, Georgia, po. of atto., to Edwd. Herndon of Spots. Co., Va., etc., etc. Witnesses, Geo. Cammack, Wm. Orril Brock. Feby. 6, 1787.

Oct. 16, 1787. Henry Lewis and Ann, his wife, of Culpeper Co. to Robt. Hart of Spots. Co. £230. 350 a. in Spots. Co., purchased by Henry Lewis, the elder, of Jno. Key, who patented same in 1728, and descended to the sd. Henry Lewis, party to these presents, as heir at law of his father, Henry Lewis, the elder, decd., etc., etc. Witnesses, R. Brooke, Robt. Taylor, Jno. Minor. Feby. 6, 1787.

Augt. 14, 1786. Larkin Stanard and Elizabeth, his wife, of Berkeley Par., Spots. Co., to James Mitcham of same par. and co. £80 curr. 80 a. in same par. and co., etc., etc. A. Parker, Wm. Heslop, Ephraim Beazley, Jno. Brock. Septr. 5, 1786.

March 7, 1787. Ann x Waller of Spots. Co., po. of atto., to Hugh Roy of same county, etc. Witnesses, Robt. Smith, Wm. Waller, M. D. March 10, 1787.

Septr. 5, 1786. Wm. P. Thurston of Spots. Co. to Wm. Mills of same co. Mortgage. Three slaves, etc., etc. Witnesses, Robt. Taylor, Edwd. Herndon, jr.; Wins. Parker. March 8, 1787.

April 3, 1787. Thomas x Allen and Sarah, his wife, of Berkeley Par., Spots. Co., to Robt. Edward Coleman of same par. and co. £100 curr. 50 a., purchased of Danl. Lambert, in Berkeley Par., Spots. Co., etc., etc. Jos. Chew, Edwd. Coleman, Edwd. Herndon, jr. March 3, 1787.

Octr. 7, 1786. Evans Long and Lucy, his wife, of Spots. Co. to Henry Pendleton, jr., of same Co. £106 curr. 106 a. in Berkeley Par., Spots. Co., etc., etc. Thos. Towles, Wm. Smith, Nicho. Payne. April 3, 1787.

March 2, 1787. Nathaniel Sanders and Sally, his wife, of Spots. Co. to James Somerville and Henry Mitchell of Fredksbg., Merchts. Whereas, Hugh Sanders, late of Spots. Co., decd., by his last will, etc., devised to his wife, Catherine, his plantation in Spots. Co., during her life, and then to his son, Nathaniel Sanders, he first paying to the Excrs. of the sd. Testator ½ the value thereof in specie to be applied to the testator's debts contracted before the Revolution, and whereas, the sd. Nathl. hath accounted with the sd. Executors and hath agreed to sell the same and the reversion thereof after the death of his mother, for the sum of £620 curr. to the sd. Somerville and Mitchell, etc., etc. Conveyance. Witnesses, David Blair, John Miller, Geo. Hutcherson. April 3, 1787.

March 9, 1787. James Mercer of Fredksbg., Esqr., devisee and trustee of Alexander Dick, late of same place, decd., to George Weedon of same place, Esqr. Whereas, Charles Dick, late of Fredksbg., Esq., decd., did by his last will and testament devise his whole estate to his only son and heir, the sd. Alexander Dick, Decd., subject to the payment of the sd. Chas. Dick's debts, and whereas, after the death of the sd. Chas. Dick, the sd. Alexander Dick entered into possession of the sd. estate and departed this life March 17, 1785, having made his will, and therein devised his whole estate and Interest, to the sd. James Mercer, in fee and upon trust; first, for the payment of the debts, etc., of the sd. Charles Dick, and secondly, for the payment of the proper debts of the sd. Alexander Dick, etc., etc., and under the sd. will the sd. Mercer, for the sum of £290, conveys to the sd. Weedon 290 a. in St. Geo. Par., Spots. Co., purchased by sd. Charles Dick of Simon Miller of Essex Co., as by deed, Decr. 1, 1778, etc., etc. Witnesses, Chs. Yates, Jas. Lewis, Mann Page, J. Dawson, Jno. Chew, jr.; R. Brooke, Gust. B. Wallace. April 3, 1787.

May 9, 1786. John Anderson of Spots. Co., Va., to Charles Stewart of New Jersey, and Ephraim Blain of Penna. In trust, the sd. Anderson being indebted with one Wm. Wiatt to the sd. Stewart and Blain, conveys to them 190½ a. in Westmoreland Co., Penna. [purchased of Jno. Montgomerie and Sarah, his wife, as by Ind. dated May 30, 1777]; also being entitled to ¼ part of sundry tracts of land in Westmoreland Co., Penn. [which he holds in partnership with Wm. Parr, Owen Biddle, and Clement Biddle], also entitled to ⅓ part of abt. 3000 a. [held in partnership with James Milligan and Hugh Lenox], being so entitled the sd. Anderson deeds in trust, to cover the indebtedness afsd., the afsd. tracts of land to the sd. Stewart and Blain, etc., etc. Witnesses, Jos. Herndon, James Hutchinson, Reubin Straughan, Robt. Stubblefield. April 3, 1787.

June 23, 1786. Alexander Spotswood and Elizabeth, his wife, of Spots. Co. to Joseph Brock, Clk., of same co. £40 curr. 200a. in Spots Co., etc., etc. Danl. Branham, Henry Gatewood, jr.; Jno. McHurt, Jno. Clayton. July 4, 1786.

Novr. 7, 1786. Joseph Tankersley and Catherine, his wife, and George Green Tankersley of Caroline Co. to Henry Pendleton of Spots. Co. £318 2s. 440 a. in Berkeley Par., Spots. Co., etc., etc. Danl. Branham, A. Frazer, Geo. Cammack, Wm. Estes. April 3, 1787.

Jany. 4, 1787. Henry Willis of King Geo. Co., Va., "about to depart . . . and go to the State of Georgia," po. of atto., to Lewis Willis of

Spots. Co., Gentl. Witnesses, O. Towles, A. Dick, Larkin Stanard. April 3, 1787.

Decr. 1, 1786. Leonard Waller and Agnes, his wife, of Spots. Co. to Wm. Bronaugh of same county. £300 specie. 296 a. in Spots. Co., etc., etc. Nicho. Payne, Wm. Dawson, Austin Sandidge, Lewis Holladay, Beverley Stubblefield. April 3, 1787.

Sept. 12, 1786. Thomas Burbridge of Fayette Co., Kentucky District, po. of atto., to Danl. Branham of Spots. Co., Va. Witnesses, Danl. Branham, Jos. Brock, Clk.; Jno. Brock, jr. April 3, 1787.

March 12, 1787. Susannah x Bartlett, for a sum to be pd. her annually by the legatees, relinquishes her right, title, etc., in any estate of her decd. husband, Wm. Bartlett, as under his will, etc., etc. Witnesses, Edwd. Herndon, Thos. Colson, Jos. Herndon. April 4, 1787.

April 3, 1787. Beverley Stubblefield to Wm. Dawson. In consideration of 1 bald-face Horse, conveys a small tract of land in Spots. Co., etc., etc. No witnesses. April 3, 1787.

March 10, 1787. Geo. Weedon of Fredksbg., Esqr., to James Mercer of same place, Esqr. Whereas, the sd. Weedon purchased of the sd. Mercer, a tract of land of the estate of Charles Dick, decd., for the sum of £290, payable in installments, the sd. Weedon finding it inconvenient to meet the payments and being desirous of relinquishing the same, and the sd. Mercer consenting therto, the sd. Weedon hereby reconveys the sd. land, 290 a. in St. Geo. Par., Spots. Co., etc., etc. Witness, Chs. Yates. April 3, 1787.

March 6, 1787. Jno. x Jenkins, jr., and Elizabeth, his wife, of Spots. Co. to Henry Mitchell of Fredksbg. £100 curr. 200 a. in Spots. Co., etc., etc. Wm. Wiatt, Thos. Sharpe, Geo. Stubblefield. April 3, 1787.

Oct. 6, 1786. Charles Washington and Mildred, his wife; Geo. Augustine Washington and Frances, his wife, to George French. Whereas, the sd. Chas. Washington, etc., did for affection they bore the sd. Geo. Augustine, give him a tract of 145 a. in Spots. Co., purchased of Mary, Benj., and Wm. Steward, and never having made the sd. Geo. Augustine conveyance thereof, and the sd. Geo. Augustine, etc., for the sum of £200, conveys the said land to the sd. French, the sd. Charles Washington and wife joining in the conveyance, etc., etc. Witnesses, Chas. Mortimer, Fran. Thornton, Zachariah Lucas, R. B. Chew. April 3, 1787.

Augt. 18, 1786. Alexander Spotswood of Spots. Co., Esqr., to Joseph Brock of same co. £12 curr. 60 a. in Spots. Co., etc., etc. Wm. Frazer, Jos. Hoomes, Edwd. Herndon, jr.; Jno. Bridges, Danl. Branham, O. Towles. Apr. 4, 1787.

Jany. 19, 1787. Jno. Downer and Frances, his wife, of Caroline Co.; Rice Corner (or Conner) and Elizabeth, his wife; Wm. Rogers and Martha, his wife, of Spots. Co.; Sarah Rogers and Catherine Rogers, which sd. Frances, Elizabeth, Sarah, Catherine, and Wm. are the children of Wm. Rogers, late of the sd. County of Spots., Decd., to John Rogers of Spots. Co., son of the sd. Wm. Rogers, decd. Whereas, the sd. Wm. Rogers in his lifetime, did sell to Thos. Pollard of Fairfax Co., a certain tract of land, and it has been suggested that the heirs as afsd., might have an interest in the same, therefore, they have agreed to release all their right, title, interest which they may have in or to the sd. land, to the sd. Jno. Rogers, etc., etc. Witnesses, Atwell Coghill, Jno. Yates, Jno. Pollett, jr.; Jno. x Pollett, Sr.; Danl. Playle, Jesse x Coats, Elizabeth x Oliff, Mary x Playle. April 3, 1787.

Novr. 3, 1786. David Galloway, jr., and Margaret, his wife, of Spots. Co. to Richd. Garner of same co. £45 curr. 30 a. in St. Geo. Par., Spots. Co., etc., etc. Valentine Garland, Wm. White, Robt. Frank. May 1, 1787.

Novr. 25, 1786. George Stubblefield, Gent., High Sheriff of Spots. Co., to Robt. Smith, Gent., of same county. Sale of lands of the estate of Wm. Howard, decd., and of Henry Foster, late of Spots. Co., for taxes, etc., etc. Benja. Stubblefield, Richd. Loury, Stephen Johnson, Thos. Herndon. May 3, 1787.

Sept. 15, 1786. Wm. Hewell and Susannah, his wife, of Spots. Co. to Wm. King of same co. £30 curr. 20 a. in Spots. Co., etc., etc. Zachariah Billingsly, James King, Clement Burroughs. May 3, 1787.

June 5, 1787. Ambrose Shackelford and Margaret, his wife, of Spots. Co. to Benja. Waller, jr., of same co. £60 specie. 100 a., purchased of Chas. Kennadey, in Spots. Co., etc., etc. Jno. Estes, Thos. Goodloe, Micajah Poole, Jno. Waller. June 5, 1787.

Jany. 27, 1788. Cain x Acuff and Esther, his wife, of Henry Co. to Thomas Goodloe of Spots. Co. £30 curr. 135 a. in Spots. Co., etc., etc. Thos. Towles, Jas. Wiglesworth, jr.; Benj. Waller, Wm. Durrett, Wm. Hewell, Jno. Shirley, jr.; Jno. Waller, Ambrose Shackelford. June 5, 1787.

Jan. 27, 1787. Cain x Acuff of Henry Co. to Jno. Waller of Spots. Co. £100 specie. 105 a. in Spots. Co., etc., etc. Thos. Towles, Wm. Hewell, Jas. Wiglesworth, jr.; Jno. Shirley, jr.; Benj. Waller, Thos. Goodloe, Wm. Durrett, Ambrose Shackelford. June 5, 1787.

May 12, 1787. Wm. Porter, Mercht., and Margaret, his wife, of Fredksbg. to Chas. Yates and Danl. Payne., Merchts. £225 ster. 300 a. in St. Geo. Par., Spots. Co., etc., etc. Wm. Jackson, Jas. Blair, Wm. Lovell. June 5, 1787.

Oct. 18, 1786. Jno. Gains of Spots. Co. to Lewis Hyett of same co. £35 Mortgage. Wagon, horses, harness, etc., etc. Witnesses, Jno. Carter, David Allen. June 5, 1787.

Novr. 7, 1786. Caleb Coleman of Spots. Co. and Hannah, his wife, to Edwd. Brasfield of same co. £222 10s. curr. 262 a. in Berkeley Par., Spots. Co., etc., etc. Jos. Brock, Robt. Hart, W. Buckner, Geo. Stubblefield. June 5, 1787.

Apr. 2, 1787. Henry x Cammock of Spots. Co. to Joseph Brock, Clk. In trust for Hannah, wife of the sd. Cammock, during her life, and then for benefit of Elizabeth, Beverley, Wm. and Polly, children of the sd. Henry Cammock; 1 negro slave. Witnesses, Tureman Lewis, Jno. Brock, jr. June 5, 1787.

Oct. 23, 1786. Jno. x Overton of Spots. Co. to Wm. Overton of same co. £5. 100 a. of land, etc., etc. Wm. Hall, Thos. x Brightwell, Capel Murray. June 5, 1787.

April 13, 1787. Thomas Sharpe and Judith, his wife, to Thomas Colson of same co. Reconveyance of a tract of land sold by sd. Colson to sd. Sharpe, as by Ind. dated Nov. 28, 1783, and release by sd. Colson of agreement therein made, etc., etc. Witnesses, Jno. Allen, O. Towles, Jas. Frazer. June 5, 1787.

Jany. 9, 1787. Lewis Pines, Sr., and Sarah, his wife, of Spots. Co. to Lewis Pines, jr., of same co. £3. 100 a. after the death of sd. Pines, Sr., and wife, etc., etc. Wm. Hall, Richd. x Brightwell, Thos. x Brightwell, James x Queir. June 5, 1787.

April 14, 1778. Thomas Colson and Frances, his wife, to James Frazer of same co. Whereas, sd. Colson has agreed to sell to the sd. Frazer the tract of land [whereon the court house stands] in Spots. Co. and to convey the sd. Frazer the estate in fee simple upon the payment of two sums, viz., £1100 and £550, and to secure the sd. payments the sd. Frazer mortgages to sd. Colson, a tract of 4 a. in Spots Co. called "Sligo," purchased of Dr. Chas. Mortimer, also several slaves, etc., etc. Witnesses, Jno. Allen, O. Towles, Thos. Sharpe. June 6, 1787.

July 3, 1787. Henry Pendleton of Spots. Co. to Jos. Herndon, Henry Pendleton, the younger; Jno. Pendleton, Philip Pendleton. In trust to pay several debts for which the sd. latter parties stand security, etc. Conveyance of 440 a. in Berkeley Par., Spots. Co., purchased of Jos. Tankersley and George Green Tankersley, also fourteen slaves, etc., etc. No witnesses. July 3, 1787.

Decr. 12, 1786. Jos. Herndon, Benja. Waller and Jonathan Clark, overseers of poor for Lower Dist. in Berkeley Par., Spots. Co., bind Sarah [bastard girl of Ann Middlebrooks], age 5 years, to John Greenhorn, of same par. and co., etc., etc. Witnesses, W. Clark, Edmd. Rogers. July 3, 1787.

June 28, 1787. Walter Colquhoun of Falmouth, Stafford Co., agt. and atto. for Wm. Cunningham & Co., Merchts., in Glasgow, formerly trading in Va., to Francis Meriwether of Spots. Co. £300 curr. 400 a. with tenement, storehouse, etc., known as New Market,* in St. Geo. Par., now Berkeley, Spots. Co., etc., etc. Jas. Blair, Jno. Sunderland, Robt. Grigg, R. Alexr. Sutherland. July 5, 1787.

May 16, 1787. Jno. Lewis and Mary Ann, his wife, of Fredksbg. to Henry Fitzhugh of Stafford Co. £653. 10 a. adj. upper end of town of Fredksbg., etc., etc. Wm. Wiatt, Zachary Lewis, Wm. Wells, Thornton Fitzhugh, Edwd. Wells. July 3, 1787.

June 13, 1787. Wm. Arnold and Judith, his wife, of Spots. Co. to James Edwards of same co. Whereas, John Butler of King Wm. Co., by deed of gift, dated July 20, 1727, did give to his granddaughter, Rosamond Roberts (wife of sd. James Edwards), and mother to the sd. Judith Arnold, certain slaves, descendants of which are claimed by the sd. Arnold and wife, and the sd. Arnold, etc., hath this day agreed to compromise the matter, the sd. Arnold and wife have agreed to release all interest, etc., in the above mentioned slaves, and the sd. Edwards, having this day lent unto sd. Arnold and wife, for the term of their natural lives, four negroes, which sd. four negroes, after the death of

*Ed. Note.—New Market is now known as Partlow.

sd. Arnold and wife, are to descend to Ann McGee, Austin Edwards Scuddy and Jno. Scuddy, children of sd. Judith Arnold and grandchildren of the sd. James Edwards, etc., etc. Witnesses, Jno. Graves, Peter x Arnold, Betsy x Arnold, Jno. C. Graves. July 3, 1787.

May 1, 1787. Thomas Fox, Wm. Fox and Joseph Fox, Gentlm., of Spots. Co. to Hawes Coleman of same co. £58 3s. 9d. curr. 33¼ a. in Berkeley Par., Spots. Co., etc., etc. Jas. Wiglesworth, jr.; Jas. Holladay, Osd. Smith. July 3, 1787.

Feby. 6, 1787. Thomas Colson and Frances, his wife, of Spots. Co. to Stapleton Crutchfield of same co. £311 specie. One moiety [240 a.] of a tract of 480 a. in Berkeley Par., Spots. Co., purchased by sd. Colson and Crutchfield, as by Ind. from Jno. Allen of Surrey Co., Esq., dated Octr. 8, 1785, etc., etc. No witnesses. Feby. 6, 1787.

July 13, 1787. Shadrach Moore and Ann, his wife, of Spots. Co. to Wm. Smith of Fredksbg. £190 2s. 6d. curr. 169 a. in St. Geo. Par., Spots. Co., etc., etc. James Smock, Jno. Richards, Jos. Ficklin, James Pettigrew, Jno. Steward, Saml. Roddey. Augt. 7, 1787.

Augt. 7, 1787. Charles Pemberton and Sarah, his wife, of Spots. Co., po. of atto. to Francis Coleman, of same co. Witnesses, Jno. Edwards, Wm. Graves, Edwd. Herndon. Augt. 7, 1787.

Augt. 7, 1787. Francis x King and Mary, his wife, of Maryland to Ezeriah King of Orange Co., Va. £95 curr. 290 a. in Spots. Co. No witnesses. Augt. 7, 1787.

March 21, 1787. Ambrose Dudley of Spots. Co. to Thomas Mastin of same county. £440. Bond to maintain the right in a certain tract of 175 a. in Spots. Co. to the sd. Mastin, which land was sold sd. Mastin by sd. Dudley, etc., etc. Witnesses, Benja. Stubblefield, Jas. Dudley. Augt. 7, 1787.

Augt. 8, 1787. Henry Head of Culpeper Co. to Alexander Spence Head of Spots. Co. £10, and in consideration of sd. A. S. Head being security on bond of the sd. Henry Head, etc., to indemnify the sd. A. S. Head, the sd. Henry deeds him lease of land held of Alexander Spotswood, Esq., known as Edings Springs, and containing 168¾ a. in Spots. Co., also horses, goods, cattle, etc., etc. Witnesses, Jno. Chew, G. Bell, Isaac Head. Augt. 8, 1787.

Augt. 8, 1787. Mary Champe of Culpeper Co., of first part; Francis Thornton of Spots. Co., of second part; Churchill Jones of Orange Co., of third part. Whereas, the sd. Mary is possessed of a large fee simple estate, as devisee of her late husband, Wm. Champe, as by his will recd. in Culpeper Co. will appear, and whereas, there is a marriage intended to be solemnized between the sd. Mary and the sd. Churchill Jones, and whereas, it is agreed between the sd. Churchill and Mary, that if the sd. marriage shall take effect then they are to hold and enjoy the sd. estate during their joint lives, and that it shall be lawful for the sd. Mary to dispose of any part of the sd. property, should she so desire by either deed or will, this Ind. therefore witnesseth, that the sd. Mary, with the consent of the sd. Churchill Jones, doth convey to the afsd. Francis Thornton, all the sd. property devised her by the will of her late husband, in trust for the sd. Mary, before the afsd. intended marriage and after the sd. marriage for the sd. Churchill Jones and the sd. Mary, as under the contract alluded to above, etc., etc., etc. Witnesses, G. Gray, Wm. Thompson, Sam Stephens. Augt. 8, 1787.

July 6, 1787. Ezekiel Haydon and Polly, his wife, of Spots. Co. to Henry Mitchell of Fredksbg. £133 18s. curr. 103 a. in Spots. Co. and purchased by Thos. Haydon [father of sd. Ezekiel] of Wm. Fitzhugh, Esqr., etc., etc. Witnesses, Jas. Somerville, Wm. Harvey, Jno. Miller, Jno. McFarlan. Septr. 4, 1787.

April 2, 1787. Jno. Chew, jr., of Spots. Co. to Thomas Towles of same co. To indemnify the sd. Towles who is security for the sd. Chew in several bonds, the sd. Chew deeds the sd. Towles 563 a. purchased of Col. Geo. Stubblefield and Mrs. Elizabeth Towles, in Berkeley Par., Spots. Co., also several slaves, etc., etc. Witnesses, Thos. Colson, Wm. Stanard, Nicho. Payne. Sept. 4, 1787.

—— ——, 1786. Jno. x Johnson and Ann, his wife, to Richard Carlton of Caroline Co. £25 curr. 25 a. in Spots. Co., bounded by lands of Spilsbe Coleman, David Lively, Wm. Coats and Wm. Durrett, etc., etc. Witnesses, Wm. Hewell, David Lively, Thos. Dodd, Henry Dodd. Sept. 4, 1787.

March ——, 1787. Nathaniel Sanders of Spots. Co. po. of atto. to Thomas Towles of same co. Witnesses, Saml. Sale, Wm. Winslow, Benj. Wharton, A. Simons. Sept. 4, 1787.

March ——, 1787. Sarah x Pattie, Executrix of her late husband, James Pattie, decd. of Spots. Co. po. of atto. to Thomas Towles of same co. Witnesses, Wm. Winslow, Benj. Wharton, Saml. Sale, A. Simons. Septr. 4, 1787.

Augt. 3, 1787. John Lewis of Fredksbg. to Wm. Stanard of Spots. Co. To indemnify the sd. Stanard who stands security for sd. Lewis, the sd. Lewis deeds the sd. Stanard, Lots 67, 68, 103, 104, 105 and 106 in town of Fredksbg., etc., etc. Thos. Towles, P. Temple, Jno. Smith, jr. Sept. 4, 1787.

May 1, 1787. Jno. Whitaker Willis and Ann, his wife, of Spots. Co. to Larkin Chew of same co. Whereas, sd. Jno. W. Willis and Ann, his wife, in right of the sd. Ann are seized and possessed of sundry tracts of land in Orange Co., and the sd. Ann, having consented to the sale thereof, etc., to make provision for the sd. Ann and their children begotten, etc., the sd. John W. Willis, deeds in trust to the sd. Chew, for the benefit of sd. Jno. W. Willis and Ann, his wife, during their natural lives, and then for any children begotten between them, 996 a. whereon the sd. Jno. W. and Ann Willis live, in Spots. Co., purchased by sd. Willis of Thos. Colson and Thos. Strachan, etc., etc. Witnesses, Geo. Stubblefield, Benj. Stubblefield, Hay Battaille. Septr. 4, 1787.

Novr. 1, 1786. Winslow Parker, Wm. Dawson and Lewis Holladay, Overseers of the Poor in Berkeley Par., Spots. Co., bind David and Harris Murphy, orphans, to Francis Coleman, house carpenter and joiner, of Spots. Co. No witnesses. Septr. 4, 1787.

March 6, 1787. Nathaniel Sanders and Sally, his wife, of Spots. Co. to Anthony Frazer of same co. £11 curr. 9¼ a. in Berkeley Par., Spots. Co., etc., etc. Thos. Crutcher, Danl. Branham, Jas. Frazer. Sept. 4, 1787.

June 13, 1787. James Edwards of Spots. Co. to his grandchildren, Ann McGee, Austin Edwards Scuddy and John Scuddy. Deed of Gift. 37 slaves, to be equally divided. Wm. McGee, jr., to act as trustee for the sd. A. E. and Jno. Scuddy until they are 14 yrs. old when they can choose their own guardian, etc., etc. [A. E. Scuddy being 12 yrs. old Oct. 15 next, and Jno. Scuddy, 8 yrs. old Decr. 4, next, etc.] Witnesses, Jno. Graves, Jno. C. Graves, Jno. Waller, Benja. Waller. Oct. 2, 1787.

July 23, 1787. Francis Meriwether of Spots. Co. and Mary, his wife, to Benja. Waller, Senr., of same co. £190 curr. 384 a. tract called New Market [purchased of Walter Colquhoun, agt. for Cunningham & Co.] in Spots. Co., etc., etc. Waller Lewis, Jno. Waller, Jas. Crawford, Joel Parrish, Theo. Wyatt, Jno. Parrish. Octr. 2, 1787.

July 23, 1787. Francis Meriwether and Mary, his wife, of Spots. Co. to Jno. Waller (Baptist). £100 curr. 150 a. part of New Market tract, etc., in Spots. Co., etc., etc. Waller Lewis, James Crawford, Benj Waller, Joel Parish, Theo. Wyatt, Jno. Parish. Oct. 2, 1787.

July 23, 1787. Francis Meriwether and Mary, his wife, of Spots. Co. to Waller Lewis of same co. £18 curr. 60 a. part of New Market tract, etc., in Spots. Co., etc., etc. Jno. Waller, Benja. Waller, Theo. Wyatt, Jas. Crawford, Joel Parrish, John Parrish. Octr. 2, 1787.

April 3, 1787. Jno. Carter of Orange Co. to son-in-law David Lively. For a horse the sd. Carter releases to sd. Lively all right, title, etc., in 1 negro slave, etc., etc. Waller Lewis, Benja. Waller, Jno. Waller. Oct. 2, 1787.

Septr. 30, 1787. John Edwards and Nancy, his wife, of Spots. Co. to Thomas Ball of Amelia Co. £130 curr. 130 a. adj. lands of Stokely Towles, Chas. Pemberton, Wm. Duvall, Wm. Holladay, Chas. Burridge, Edwd. Brasfield and Jno. Davenport, in Spots. Co., etc., etc. No witnesses. Oct. 2, 1787.

Octr. 2, 1787. Edwd. Brasfield and Anne, his wife, of Spots. Co. to Thomas Ball of Amelia Co. £330 curr. 365¼ a. in Berkeley Par., Spots. Co., etc., etc. No witnesses. Octr. 2, 1787.

Octr. 2, 1787. Wharton Schooler & Margaret, his wife, of Spots. Co. to Robt. Sales of same co. £50 curr. 127 a. in St. Geo. Par., Spots. Co., etc., etc. No witnesses. Octr. 2, 1787.

April 28, 1787. Joel Parrish of Spots. Co. to James Wilson of same co. £30 curr. 40 a. purchased of Jos. Temple, adj. lands of Jno. Partlow and Martin Davenport, in Spots. Co., etc., etc. Geo. Phillips, Saml. Luck, Waller Lewis. Octr. 2, 1787.

Octr. 2, 1787. Henry Terrell of Spots. Co. to Sharp Smith of same co. £70 10s. curr. 150 a. in Spots Co., etc., etc. No witnesses. Octr. 2, 1787.

Feby. 19, 1787. Wm. Hewell and Susannah, his wife, of Spots. Co. to George Mason of Caroline Co. £30 curr. 100 a. in Spots. Co., etc., etc. Richd. M. Owen, Ben. Johnson, Wm. Wiglesworth. Oct. 2, 1787.

Septr. 20, 1787. John Wiglesworth and Philadelphia, his wife, and Joseph Jones and Sarah, his wife, of Spots. Co. to David Blair of Fredksbg., Mercht. £250 curr. 154 a. (except 8½ a. lots, laid off for a town) in Spots. Co., etc., etc. Jos. Brock, Thos. Colson, Jos. Fox. Jno. Herndon, Ben. Stubblefield, Thos. Towles, Bevy. Stubblefield. Octr. 2, 1787.

Novr. 6, 1787. Jno. Gibson and Mildred, his wife, of Spots. Co. to Abram Simons of same co. £13 10s. curr. "All right, title, interest, claim, etc., that sd. Gibson and wife have of, in and to the tract of land whereon sd. Abram Simons now lives and which was devised among the children of Jno. Holladay, with whose widow sd. Abram intermarried," etc., etc. O. Towles, Larkin Stanard, Jos. Brock. Novr. 6, 1787.

Novr. 7, 1787. Jno. Wiglesworth and Philadelphia, his wife, of Spots. Co. to Thomas Megee of same county. £20 5s. curr. ¼ a. in Spots. Co., etc., etc. A. Frazer, J. Pierce, Jas. Pritchett, John Brock, jr.; Jno. Wiglesworth. Novr. 6, 1787.

May 11, 1787. Danl. Branham of Spots. Co. Deed of Gift to his children. To his eldest daughter, Sarah Branham, 1 slave, goods and chattels, etc., etc; to his son, Robt. Branham (when 21 yrs. old), 1 negro, goods and chattels; to his son, Richard Branham (when 21 yrs. old), 1 negro, goods and chattels; to his son, James Branham (when 21 yrs. old), 1 negro, goods and chattels. Witnesses, Tavener Branham, Jno. Brock, jr. Novr. 6, 1787.

Septr. 27, 1787. John Robinson and Benjamin Robinson, sons of Michael Robinson, late of Spots. Co., decd., to their sister Mary, wife of Thos. Magee of Spots. Co. Whereas, sd. Michael Robinson in and by his last will and testament dated Jany. 6, 1704, among other things mentioned his delivering to Richd. Young a land warrant for 15,246 a. to locate, etc., and desired the same should be divided and disposed of to his children and grandchildren, therein specially devised to some 1000, and to others 500 a. each, amounting to abt. 6000 a., the remainder of the warrant being abt. 9246 a. he devised in fee simple to sd. John and Benjamin, and whereas, Thomas Magee of same co. of Spots. having intermarried with Mary, dau. of the sd. testator and sister of the sd. John and Benjamin, and they knowing well that it was the full intent and desire of the sd. Michael, their father, to devise as well to his son-in-law, Thos. Magee, 1000 a. of the aforesaid tract, etc., in consequence of which the sd. John and Benjamin convey to the sd. Thos. Magee, 1000 a., a part of the sd. tract when surveyed and laid off, etc., etc. Witnesses, Henry Pemberton, Jas Smock, Thomas Pritchett. Novr. 6, 1787.

Septr. 23, 1787. Peter Stubblefield and Peggy, his wife, of Wilkes Co., Georgia, to John Cash of Spots. Co., Va. £90. 268 a. in Berkeley Par., Spots. Co., etc., etc. Benj. Stubblefield, Thos. Herndon, Benja, Alsop. Novr. 6, 1787.

April 17, 1787. Harry Bartlett and Sarah, his wife, of Spots. Co. to Jno. Chew, jr., and Anthony Frazer of same co. Sd. Bartlett to indemnify sd. Chew and Frazer who stand security for him, conveys them 258 a., whereon sd. Bartlett now lives, in Spots. Co., also several slaves, etc., etc. O. Towles, Jno. Herndon, Jas. Frazer. Novr. 6, 1787.

Novr. 8, 1787. Massey Thomas of Spots. Co. to his three sisters, Mildred, Peggy and Molly Thomas. Deed of Gift. Slaves. No witnesses. Novr. 8, 1787.

May 31, 1787. Thomas Strachan of Spots. Co. to Thos. Colson and Oliver Towles, executors of Wm. Daingerfield, decd., Matthew Maury and Thomas Walker, jr. To indemnify them, conveyance of certain negroes in trust, etc., etc. Jas. Lewis, Benja. Lewis. Novr. 9, 1787.

Octr. 10, 1787. Wharton Schooler and Margaret, his wife, of Spots. Co. to Edwd. Herndon and James Lewis, Executors of Jno. Herndon, decd. £120 10s. curr. 120½ a. in Spots. Co. in trust for widow and orphans of sd. Jno. Herndon, decd., as by articles in his will dated May 11, 1782, etc., etc. Thomas Strachan, J. Brock, Jno. Brock, jr.; Danl. Branham, Margaret Schooler. Novr. 9, 1787.

Octr. 17, 1787. Harry Bartlett and Sarah, his wife, of Spots. Co. to Jno. Chew, jr., and Anthony Frazer of same co. To indemnify the sd. Chew and Frazer, the sd. Bartlett conveys to them in trust, several slaves, etc., etc. Witnesses, Jas. Frazer, Wm. Frazer, Jno. Herndon. Decr. 4, 1787.

Decr. 4, 1787. Joseph Brock and John Lewis of Spots. Co., Court Commissioners, of first part; George Atkinson, of same co. of second part, to Jno. Herndon, son of Edward, of same co. of third part. Whereas, sd. Atkinson did mortgage certain property to Thos. Colson to secure payment of debt, and whereas, the sd. Atkinson failing in the payment thereof, the court directed sale of the mortgaged property and appt. sd. Brock and Lewis for that purpose, therefore the sd. Brock and Lewis, having sold the sd. 33 a. mentioned in the mortgage to the sd. Herndon for £50, etc., etc. No witnesses. Decr. 4, 1787.

May 18, 1787. Whitehead Coleman and Ann, his wife, of Essex Co. to Francis Coleman of Spots. Co. £105 curr. 520 a. in Spots. Co., pat. by Roger Tandy in 1727, and which Robt. S. Coleman, father of the sd. Whitehead Coleman died seized and possessed, etc., etc. Witnesses, Wm. Winslow, Ezekiel Haydon, Wm. Fortson, Thomas Winslow, Edwd. Hyde. Decr. 4, 1787.

Decr. 4, 1787. Jno. Lewis and Mary, his wife, of Fredksbg. to Wm. Lewis of same town. £250. Tract of land in Spots. Co. near town of Fredksbg., etc., etc. Eleazer Callender, Wm. Waddle, James Dix, French Gray. Decr. 4, 1787.

June 4, 1787. John Lewis and Mary Ann, his wife, of Fredksbg. to Eleazer Callender and David Henderson of same town. £306. 7 a. and 26 sq. poles in Spots. Co., etc., etc. Jno. Robinson, Wm. Waddle, Zachariah Lucas, Jno. Brown, French Gray, Jas. Dix. Decr. 4, 1787.

April 19, 1787. Eliazer Callender & Elizabeth, his wife, David Henderson and Mildred, his wife, of Fredksbg. to Samuel Stephens of same co. £94 8s. 8d. 38 sq. poles, in Spots. Co., part of land purchased of Jno. Lewis, etc., etc. Witnesses, Jas. Dix, French Gray, Wm. Waddle, Jas. Smith. Decr. 4, 1787.

Novr. 12, 1787. Thomas Carr, George Stubblefield and Sally, his wife, to Robert Young. £278 5s. curr. 456 a. in Berkeley Par., Spots. Co., etc., etc. W. Dawson, Benj. Stubblefield, Jas. Frazer. Decr. 4, 1787.

July 10, 1787. James Crawford, Senr.; Waller Lewis, Jno. Waller, Benj. Waller, Jno. Long, Anna Wyatt, Theophilus, Roxanna and Elizabeth Wyatt of one part and Thomas Towles, Gent., of other part. Whereas, Frans. Meriwether purchased of Messrs. Cunningham and Co., Merchts., before the late war with Gt. Britain began, a certain tract of land in Spots. Co. called New Market, cont. 720 a., etc., etc., and the sd. Lewis sold 316 a. thereof with the dwelling house to the sd. Thomas Towles, and gave him his bond for conveyance for same, the sd. Towles by verbal bargain sold the same to Fielding Woodroof and the sd. Woodroof verbally sold the same to Nicho. Lewis, the sd. Lewis becoming responsible to the sd. Towles for his payment of the property, and the sd. Lewis sold the sd. land out in parcels, etc., etc., etc. As the sd. land has been so frequently transferred in a verbal way the sd. Towles is apprehensive of danger in case he should deliver up the sd. Meriwether's bond, etc. The sd. parties of the first part of this contract, now the possessors of the sd. land through so many verbal interchanges, being desirious of indemnifying the sd. Towles from any future trouble, etc., in consideration of sd. Towles delivering them the sd. Meriwether's bond, each one of their lots to be mortgaged to the sd. Towles, etc., to be delivered up to him in case any person or persons hereafter make good a legal claim to sd. lots of land, etc., etc. Witnesses, Thos. Turner, Thomas Cason, James Crawford, Jas. Davenport, jr.; Robt. Hackney. Decr. 4, 1787.*

Augt. 7, 1787. Jos. Herndon, Benj. Waller and Jonathan Clarke, overseers of poor of Spots. Co., bind Avarilla Pinn Month, a Bastard, age 11 yrs. to Micajah Poole of Spots. Co. No witnesses. Decr. 4, 1787.

Decr. 31, 1787. Charles Steward of Spots. Co. to Wm. Duerson of same county. £112 10s. curr. 120 a. in Berkeley Par., Spots. Co., etc., etc. Wm. Trigg, Saml. Gibson. Jany. 1, 1788.

Jany 1, 1788. Mann Page of Spots. Co. to Roderick White of same co. Lease. 210 a. in St. Geo. Par., Spots. Co., etc., etc. 2100 lbs. tob. yearly, etc., etc. No witnesses. Jany. 1, 1788.

Jany 1, 1788. Harry Chew of Spots. Co. and Jno. Chew of same co. to Edwd Herndon, jr., of afsd. Co. £150. 202 a. in Spots. Co., mortgaged by sd. Harry Chew to Jno. Chew, the sd. Jno. agreeing to the sale thereof, etc., etc. No witnesses. Jany. 1, 1788.

Octr. 24, 1787. Benj. Perry and Mary, his wife, of Berkeley Par., Spots. Co., to Charles Beazley of same par. and co. £100. 100 a. in same par. and co., purchased of Jos. Willoughby, etc., etc. Witnesses, Jos. Pulliam, James McDonald, Benj. Mastin, Jno. Arnold, David Pulliam. Feby. 5, 1788.

Augt. 31, 1787. Christian Riffe and Elizabeth, his wife, of Spots. Co. to John True of same co. £120 curr. 78 a. in St. Geo. Par., Spots. Co., etc., etc. Jno. Crookshanks, Robt. True, Reuben Young. Feby. 5, 1788.

Octr. 13, 1787. Harry Bartlett of Spots. Co. to Priteyman Merry of Orange Co. Whereas, sd. Bartlett having purchased of sd. Merry 500 a. in Fayette Co., and being still due £100 to complete payment therefor,

*Ed. Note.—In the above conveyance is mentioned Jno. Wyatt, decd., and Anna, his wife, and their children, Theophilus, Roxanna and Elizabeth Wyatt.

the sd. Bartlett mortgages the sd. land to the sd. Merry, etc., etc. Witnesses, Geo. Alsop, Jas. Williams, Jas. Smith, Jno. Moore, Thos. Bartlett. Feby. 6, 1788.

Novr. 6, 1787. Thomas Fox, Wm. Fox and Joseph Fox of Spots. Co. to James Holladay of same co. £55 11s. 3d. curr. 31¼ a. in Spots. Co., etc., etc. Austin Sandidge, Jno. Smith, Jos. Holladay, jr. Feby. 5, 1788.

July 23, 1783. Francis Meriwether and Mary, his wife, of Spots. Co. to Anna Wyatt, Theophilus Wyatt, Roxanna Wyatt and Elizabeth Wyatt of same co. £60 curr. 50 a., part of New Market tract, etc., in Spots. Co., etc., etc. Waller Lewis, Jno. Waller, Jas. Crawford, Benj. Waller, Joel Parrish, Jno. Parrish. Feby. 5, 1788.

July 23, 1787. Francis Meriwether and Mary, his wife, of Spots. Co. to James Crawford, Senr., of same co. £30 curr. 70 a., part of the New Market tract, in Spots. Co., etc., etc. Waller Lewis, Benj. Waller, Jno. Waller, Joel Parrish, Theo. Wyatt, Jno. Parrish. Feby. 5, 1788.

Feby. 5, 1788. Wm. Coats and Sarah, his wife, of Spots. Co. to Wm. Durret of Caroline Co. £110 curr. 176 a. in St. Geo. Par., Spots. Co., etc., etc. No witnesses. Feby. 5, 1788.

Feby. 5, 1788. Jno. Hutcherson and Mary, his wife, of Spots. Co. to Wm. Plunkett of same co. £100 curr. 100 a. in Spots. Co., etc., etc. No witnesses. Feby. 5, 1788.

Augt. 14, 1787. Charles Benson of Culpeper Co. Deed of gift to his daughter Catherine, wife of Richard Bullard of Spots. Co. Slaves. Witnesses, Thomas Smith, Hezekiah x Fouracres. Feby. 5, 1788.

Jany. 12, 1787. Wm. Dawson and Mary, his wife, to Smith, Young and Hyde, Merchts. £25. Tract of land called the Handkerchief, purchased of Beverley Stubblefield in Spots. Co., etc., etc. Geo. Stubblefield, Wm. Frazer, Nicho. Payne, Edwd. Hyde. March 5, 1788.

March 1, 1788. Robert Young to Smith, Young and Hyde, Merchts. £300 curr. 456 a. in Berkeley Par., Spots. Co., etc., etc. Benj. Stubblefield, Stockley Towles, J. Dawson. March 5, 1788.

March 5, 1787. Wm. Willoughby and ——, his wife, and Chas x Burrage and ——, his wife, of Spots. Co., to Robert Scott of same Co. £90 curr. Tract of land in Spots. Co., leased by sd. Willoughby of Thomas Sharpe for 99 yrs., as by Ind. dat. Jany. 1, 1784, which sd. lease sd. Willoughby has since assigned to sd. Burrage, etc., etc. Witnesses, Edwd. Herndon, jr.; Wm. Frazer, Wm. Winslow. March 5, 1788.

March 1, 1787. Nathaniel Stevens and Sally, his wife, of Spots. Co. to Robert Scott of Fredksbg. £400. 207 a. in Spots. Co., etc., etc. Wm. Wiatt, Ben. Holladay, Jas. Julian. March 5, 1788.

May 18, 1787. Henry Fitzhugh of Stafford Co. to Wm. Thompson of Spots. Co. Lease. Part of lot No. 4 as in Tutts survey, in town of Fredksbg, on Caroline St., etc., etc. £16 yearly, etc., etc. Wm. Wiatt, Richd. Simcock, Jno. Brownlow, Jno. Legg, Thornton Fitzhugh. March 5, 1788.

Feby. 29, 1788. Jno. Bradley and Lucy, his wife, of Spots. Co. to John Nelson of same co. £45 curr. 200 a. in Spots. Co., etc., etc. Jno. White,

Benj. Davis, Peter Stevens, Francis Coleman, William Jinkins, Wm. Frazer. April 1, 1788.

Nov. 20, 1787. Jno. Wren of Spots. Co. to Robt. Hart of same co. £5 10s. 3¾ a. in Spots. Co., etc., etc. Wm. Smith, Benj. Haley, Jno. Lane, David Anderson. April 1, 1788.

Oct. 15, 1787. Chas. Pemberton and Sarah, his wife, of Spots. Co. to Zachariah Billingsly of same co. £150. 200 a. in Spots. Co., etc., etc. Wm. Smith, James King, Edwd. Herndon, Thos. Sharpe. April 1, 1788.

March 4, 1788. Wm. Rash and Elizabeth, his wife, to Thomas Towles. £50. 104 a. purchased of Humphries and Dillard in Spots. Co., etc., etc. No witnesses. April 1, 1788.

April 1, 1788. Abraham Simons and Mildred, his wife [which sd. Mildred was widow and relict of Jno. Holladay, Decd.], and Benja. Weeks and Agatha, his wife; Jno. Wood and Elizabeth, his wife; Norcut Slaven and Ann, his wife, and Sarah Holladay, a single woman [which sd. Agatha, Elizabeth, Ann and Sarah, are children of the afsd. Jno. Holladay, decd.], of Spots. Co. to Thomas Colson of same co., Gent. £50. Tract of land known as Holladay's Ordinary, purchased of Benjamin Johnston and Dorothy, his wife, in St. Geo. Par., Spots. Co., etc., etc. No witnesses. April 1, 1788.

——— ———, 1788. Danl. Baldwin and Anne, his wife, of Spots. Co. to Francis Coleman of same co. £35 curr. 236 a. in Spots. Co., etc., etc. Walter Chiles, Wm. Taylor, Jno. Day, Jno. Smith. April 1, 1788.

Decr. 31, 1787. Wm. Duerson and Mildred, his wife, of Spots. Co. to Samuel Gibson of same co. £112 10s. curr. 200 a. in Berkeley Par., Spots. Co., etc., etc. Wm. Trigg, Jeremiah Wilson, Chas. Steward. April 1, 1788.

Octr. 31, 1787. James Bartlett and Betsy Row Bartlett, his wife, of Spots. Co. to John White of same co. £100 curr. 300 a. adj. lands of Chas. Jenkins, Thomas Sharpe, Jno. Lambert, Benj. Dawson and David Cheves, in Spots. Co., etc., etc. Edmd. Bartlett, Frs. Crutcher, Jas. Barksdale, Jno. Berryman, Jno. Smith, Wm. Jenkins. April 1, 1788.

Oct. 24, 1787. Ann x Shackelford, Wm. Aill and Mary, his wife; Walker x Aill and Elizabeth, his wife, of Spots. Co. to Benja. Reynolds of Caroline Co. £212 curr. 250 a. in Spots. Co., etc., etc. Jona. Clark, Benj. Chapman, Rob. Reynolds, Jas. Crawford, Thos. Goodloe, Bernard Reynolds. April 1, 1788.

May 15, 1787. Whitehead Coleman and Ann, his wife, of Essex Co. to Wm. Plunkett of Spots. Co. £150 curr. 405 a. in upper Spots. Co., etc., etc. Wm. Mills, Martin Hawkins, Robt. E. Coleman, Frans. Coleman, Harry Parker. April 1, 1788.

April 1, 1788. Hugh Roy of Spots. Co. to George Goodloe of same co. £24 15s. curr. 22 a. in Spots. Co., etc., etc. No witnesses. April 1, 1788.

April 1, 1788. Alexander Johnston and Mary, his wife, of Spots. Co. to Benjamin Johnston of Caroline Co. £20. 147 a. in Spots. Co., etc., etc. No witnesses. April 1, 1788.

March 27, 1788. Jno. Shirley, Senr., to John Shirley, Junr., both of Spots. Co. £50 curr. 191 a. in Spots. Co., etc., etc. Thomas Shirley, Christopher Crawford, Dorothy Dood, Thos. Turner. April 1, 1788.

June 7, 1788. Samuel Allen, Executor of the last will and testament of Joseph Allen, late of Spots. Co., Decd., to John Carter of Spots. Co. £63 curr. 200 a. in Berkeley Par., Spots. Co., etc., etc. Zimri Tate, Jas. McAlister. April 1, 1788.

March 1, 1788. Beverley Winslow of Berkeley Par., Spots. Co., to his son, Thomas Winslow, of same par. and co. Deed of Gift. Tract of land purchased of Richd. Johnston in Berkeley Par., Spots. Co., etc., etc. No witnesses. April 1, 1788.

March 4, 1788. John Riadon of Spots. Co. to Nathan Hawkins, jr., of same co. £27 10s. curr. 80 a. in St. Geo. Par., Spots. Co., etc., etc. Ludlow Branham, Edwd. Collins, Rob. Frank. April 1, 1788.

April 1, 1788. Henry True and Jane, his wife, of Spots. Co. to Reubin Massey of same co. £20 10s. curr. 43 a. in Berkeley Par., Spots. Co., etc., etc. No witnesses. April 1, 1788.

Octr. 13, 1787. Richd. Kenny and Milley, his wife, of Spots. Co. to Richd. Garner of same co. £280 curr. 100 a. in St. Geo. Par., Spots. Co., etc., etc. Jno. Legg, Benj. Day, Wm. Harvey, Jas. Blair. April 1, 1788.

Octr. 29, 1787. Thomas Brown and Sarah, his wife, of Spots. Co. to Sarah Scott of same co. £5. 92 a. in Spots. Co., etc., etc. No witnesses. April 1, 1788.

April 1, 1788. Thomas Colson of Spots. Co. to Chas. Carter of same co. Lease. 80 a. in St. Geo. Par., Spots. Co., etc., etc. "Sd. Chas. Carter and Ann, his wife, and ——, their daughters," etc., etc. £5 specie. No witnesses. April 1, 1788.

Feby. 25, 1788. James Mercer of Fredksbg., Esq., to Samuel Selden of Stafford Co., Esq. To indemnify sd. Selden who was security for sd. Mercer, for certain estates purchased by him of Honble. Jno. Tayloe and George Washington, esqrs., then atto. for Col. Geo. Mercer (since decd.), then of London, etc., etc. The sd. Mercer deeds in trust to sd. Selden, 500 a. called "Retreat," in Spots. Co., purchased of Jno. Tayloe and others, trustees of Benj. Grymes, decd. Also 244 a., etc., etc., etc. Witnesses, Jno. Chew, jr.; Chs. Carter, J. Dawson, Jno. T. Brooke, Jas. Lilly, Jas. Pottinger, Fon. Maury. April 2, 1788.

Jany. 1, 1788. George Stubblefield and Sally, his wife, of Spots. Co. to Edwd. Herndon, jr., of same co. £84 16s. 336 a. in St. Geo. Par., Spots. Co., etc., etc. Thos. Herndon, Benj. Stubblefield, Harry Stubblefield. April 2, 1788.

Feby. 4, 1786. Wm. McWilliams of Fredksbg. and Dorothy Brayne, his wife, to Larkin Smith of King and Queen Co. £600 curr. 260 a. purchased of Wm. Miller Bledsoe, and adj. lands of Wm. Jackson, Chs. Dick, Wm. Porter and Ambrose Dudley, in Spots. Co., etc., etc. Jno. W. Willis, J. Dawson, Wm. Stanard. No date of Record.

Decr. 26, 1786. Wm. Plumer Thurston and Lucy Mary, his wife, of Spots. Co. to Garrett Minor of Louisa Co. £437 curr. 380 a. in Berkeley Par., Spots. Co., etc., etc. Aaron Fontaine, Martin Hawkins, Wm. Hawkins, Chas. Thomas. April 1, 1788.

Septr. 18, 1787. Wm. Thompson and Sarah, his wife, of Spots. Co. to Benjamin Day of Fredksbg. £108 curr. 108 a. in St. Geo. Par., Spots. Co., etc., etc. Jno. Legg, Wm. Waddle, Fontaine Maury, Henry Day, Thos. Goodwin. May 6, 1788.

May 6, 1788. Alexander Spotswood and Elizabeth, his wife, of Spots. Co. to John Brock of same co. £14 6s. curr. 74 a. in St. Geo. Par., Spots. Co., etc., etc. Geo. Burbridge, Danl. Branham, David Branham. May 6, 1788.

* Octr. 5, 1787. Mildred x Edwards [widow and relict of Uriah Edwards, Decd.] of Spots. Co. to Jno. Davenport of same co. £51 curr. 50 a. in Berkeley Par., Spots. Co., etc., etc. Wm. Duvall, Jeremiah Wilson, Jno. Cary. June 3, 1788.

Octr. 5, 1787. Thomas Minor of Spots. Co. to his granddaughter, Sarah Minor Woolfolk. Deed of Gift. 1 negro. No witnesses. June 3, 1788.

Feby. 11, 1788. Joseph Jones and Sarah, his wife, of Spots. Co. to Walter Payne of same co. £54 12s. curr. 91 a. in Spots. Co., etc., etc. Wm. Lewis, Jno. Benson, Wm. D. Spooner. June 3, 1788.

April 7, 1788. Thomas Crutcher and Martha, his wife, of Spots. Co. to Beverley Stubblefield of same co. £240 curr. 336 a. in Spots. Co., etc., etc. Thos. Colson, Thos. Megee, J. Brock, Jno. Chew, Lewis Holladay. June 3, 1788.

April 30, 1788. Joseph Brock, acting Execr. of Jno. Zachary Lewis, decd., and Geo. Stubblefield to Beverley Stubblefield of Spots. Co. £50 curr. 310 a. in Spots. Co. sold to the sd. Geo. Stubblefield out of the estate of the sd. Lewis, and the sd. Geo. having agreed for its conveyance to the sd. Beverley, joins in this indenture, etc., etc. Witnesses, Jno. Chew, Wm. Trigg, Larkin Chew. June 3, 1788.

March 24, 1788. Benjamin Robinson and Susannah, his wife, of Spots. Co. to John Brock of same co. Whereas, the sd. Robinson on Decr. 4, last, in consideration of a marriage then intended to be solemnized between him, the sd. Robinson and the sd. Susannah [which marriage did take place], deed to the sd. Brock, in trust for uses therein mentioned, a certain tract of land and sundry slaves, some of the negroes intended to be conveyed in the above mentioned Indenture were left out; now this Ind. witnesseth, the sd. Robinson and wife, in consideration of the premises and the fortune the sd. Robinson recd. with his wife, viz., 4 negroes and various sundry articles of household furniture, etc., they convey to the sd. Brock in trust, 400 a. purchased of Gawin Corbin, Gent., in Spots. Co. Also 13 slaves, etc., etc. Witnesses, Harry Chew, Jos. Brock, Benj. Stubblefield. June 3, 1788.

May 21, 1788. Jno. Chisum and Mary, his wife, of St. Geo. Par., Spots. Co., to Joseph Brock of same par. and co. £100 curr. 72 a. in afsd. Par. and Co., etc., etc. James Lewis, Thos. Strachan, Chas. Williams, Jos. Jones. June 3, 1788.

* Ed. Note.—This deed speaks of land sold by sd. Mildred to her son, Jno. Edwards, etc., etc.

April 24, 1788. Jno. W. Willis and Ann, his wife, of Spots. Co. to Thomas Colson of same co. Conveyance of several slaves to secure a debt due the sd. Colson, etc., etc. Witnesses, J. Dawson, O. Towles, Larkin Chew. June 3, 1788.

May 6, 1788. James Hutcherson and Peggy, his wife, of Spots. Co. to Henry Pemberton of same co. £150 curr. 121½ a. in St. Geo. Par., Spots. Co., etc., etc. Wm. Spindle, Benj. Chapman, Jas. Wiglesworth, jr. June 3, 1788.

April 4, 1788. Robt. Beverley Hutcherson and Phoebe, his wife, of Caroline Co. to Wm Lotspeich of Stafford Co. £47. 78 a. [devised the sd. R. B. Hutcherson by his decd. father, Wm. Hutcherson] in Berkeley Par., Spots. Co., etc., etc. Edwd. Thomas, Robt. E. Coleman, Asmond x Sorrell. June 3, 1788.

June 3, 1788. Jno. Wiglesworth and Philadelphia, his wife, of Spots. Co. to Edwd. Herndon and James Lewis, Executors of Jno. Herndon, decd. £20 curr. 20 a. in Spots. Co., etc., etc. No witnesses. June 3, 1788.

Decr. 3, 1787. Thomas Powell and Elizabeth, his wife, of Spots. Co. to Robert Hart of same co. £10 10s. 10½ a. of land, etc., etc. Henry Tolor, Francis Turnley, Harmon Anderson. June 3, 1788.

June 3, 1788. Jno. Wiglesworth and Philadelphia, his wife, and James Jones and Ann, his wife, of Spots. Co. to James Gillis of same co. £500 curr. 269½ a. in St. Geo. Par., Spots. Co., etc., etc. No witnesses. June 3, 1788.

June 3, 1788. Martin True and Elizabeth, his wife, of Spots. Co. to James Rains of same co. £12 curr. 53 a. in Berkeley Par., Spots. Co., held by the sd. True as heir at law of his father, Martin True, decd., etc., etc. Witnesses, Henry Gatewood, jr.; Jno. Pierce, Jno. Wood. June 3, 1788.

June 3, 1788. Stapleton Crutchfield and Sarah, his wife, of Spots. Co. to Jno. Crutchfield (son of the sd. Stapleton). In consideration of £101 5s. and the sd. Johns relinquishing to the sd. Stapleton 314 acres, 264 a., part thereof given the sd. Stapleton by John Durrett, and 50 a. purchased of Thomas Duerson, the sd. Stapleton conveys to the sd. John, 395 a. in Spots. Co., etc., etc. No witnesses. June 3, 1788.

March 20, 1788. John Carter to his brother, Chas. Carter. £45 curr. Right, title and interest of sd. Jno. Carter in the estate of their father, Henry Carter, Decd., "the sd. John being about to remove to Kentucky," etc., etc. Wm. Trigg, Wm. Stears, Wm. Henderson. June 3, 1788.

Jany. 26, 1788. Thomas Carr of Georgia, Geo. Stubblefield and Sally, his wife, of Spots. Co., Va., to Benjamin Hyde of Fredksbg. £25. 95 a. in Berkeley Par., Spots., etc., etc. Benja. Stubblefield, Thos. Herndon, O. Towles. June 3, 1788.

March 18, 1788. Dr. Elisha Hall and Coriolana, his wife, of Fredksbg. to Thomas Colson of Spots. Co. £365 curr. Lot No. 147 in Fredksbg., etc., etc. Jno. Lewis of Fredksbg., Esq., releases mortgage on the sd. lot, etc. Witnesses, Jos. Christy, J. Dawson, G. Heiskell, Wm. Smith, Stapleton Crutchfield, Elisha Dickerson, Thos. Cochran. July 1, 1788.

July 1, 1788. Thomas Colson and Frances, his wife, of Spots. Co. to Jno. Stewart of same co. £1200 curr. 574 a. in Berkeley Par., Spots. Co., etc., etc. Reubin Straugham conveys one acre, etc. No witnesses. July 1, 1788.

July 1, 1788. Jno. Steward and Lucy, his wife, of St. Geo. Par., Spots. Co., to Thomas Colson of same par. and co. £800 curr. 400 a. where sd. Steward lives, called "Silverton Hill," in St. Geo. Par., Spots. Co., etc., etc. No witnesses. July 1, 1788.

July 1, 1788. Agreement between Jas. Frazer and Thos. Colson about sale of some land. Mentions a place known as "Sligo," etc., etc. No witnesses. July 1, 1788.

July 1, 1788. Richd. Lowry of Caroline Co. to Daniel Lindsay of Spots. Co. £190 curr. 314 a. in Spots. Co., etc., etc. No witnesses. July 1, 1788.

April 18, 1788. Rice Curtis and Frances, his wife; Ann Curtis, John Curtis, Sarah Curtis and Elizabeth Curtis, to Wm. Carter of Spots. Co. £216 curr. 493 a. in Berkeley Par., Spots. Co., etc., etc. J. Brock, Jno. Crutchfield, Abraham Carter, Jane Carter. July 1, 1788.

Febry 23, 1788. Susannah x Bartlett of Spots. Co., po. of atto. to son-in-law, John Mitcham of same co., etc., etc. Witnesses, Thomas Waller, Wm. Robinson. July 1, 1788.

July 1, 1788. Wm. Jenkins of Fredksbg. to his daughter, Elizabeth Jenkins. Deed of Gift. Negro, goods and chattels, etc., etc. No witnesses. July 1, 1788.

July 1, 1788. Wm. Thompson and Sarah, his wife, of Spots. Co. to Thomas Posey of same co. £280. 188 a, purchased of Robt. Sharewood in Spots. Co., etc., etc. No witnesses. July 1, 1788.

April 23, 1788. Wm. Thompson of Spots. Co. to Jno. Lewis of same co. £132 9s. 6d. Mortgage. Land in Spots. Co., etc., etc. No witnesses. July 1, 1788.

March 5, 1788. John Frazer of Frederick Co. to James and Wm. Frazer of Spots. Co. To indemnify the sd. James and Wm. who are securities on a bond of the sd. Johns to Wm. Bradley of Culpeper Co. The sd. Jno. conveys to the sd. Jas. and Wm. 100 a., whereon sd. John lives in Frederick Co., also several slaves, etc., etc. Witnesses, Thos. Bartlett, Reubin Frazer, A. Frazer. July 1, 1788.

Augt. 8, 1787. Thomas Brown of Spots. Co. to Harry Bartlett of same co. To indemnify sd. Bartlett who is sd. Brown's security on a bond to Jos. Sutton of Caroline Co., the sd. Brown conveys 98½ a. assigned to Jos. Sutton of Caroline Co. by Capt. Jno. Carter's Executors and by him sold to sd. Brown, in Spots. Co., etc., etc. Jno. Wood, Wm. Rogers, Jas. Wood. July 1, 1788.

Septr. 2, 1788. Jno. Metcalf (son of Chas. Metcalf) aged 9 yrs. Jany. 12th last, apprenticed to John Wright of Spots. Co. No witnesses. Septr. 2, 1788.

Augt. 27, 1788. Jno. Waller and Elizabeth, his wife, of Spots. Co. to Ambrose Shackleford of same co. £45 curr. 93 a. purchased of Cain Acuff, and adj. lands of Henry Johnston, Thos. Towles, Elisha Dismukes and James Gimber, in Spots. Co., etc., etc. No witnesses. Septr. 2, 1788.

April 13, 1788. John Lewis and Mary Ann, his wife, of Fredksbg. to George French of same co. £130 curr. 130 a. in Spots. Co. purchased by Fielding Lewis, decd., of Richd. Pollard, etc., etc. Witnesses, Benja. Day, Jno. Legg, Jno. Richards. Septr. 2, 1788.

Feby. 29, 1787. John Bradley and Lucy, his wife, of Spots. Co. to Peter Staves of same co. £50 curr. 100 a. in Berkeley Par., Spots. Co., etc., etc. Francis Coleman, John White, Benj. Davis, Witham Jenkins, Wm. Frazer. Septr. 2, 1788.

March 8, 1788. Jno. Bradley and Lucy, his wife, of Spots. Co. to Joseph Williams of Orange Co. £20 curr. 100 a. in Berkeley Par., Spots. Co., etc., etc. Peter Stivers, Kenneth Southerlin, Thomas Clayton, Peter Mountague. Septr. 2, 1788.

May 6, 1788. Lewis Holladay, Wm. Bronaugh and Edwd. Herndon, Overseers of Poor in Dist. No. 2, Spots. Co., bind Wm. Garner, a poor orphan, aged 11 yrs. July 11 next, to John Peirce of Berkeley Par., Spots. Co., tailor, etc. Witnesses, Jno. Herndon, Thos. Sharpe, Bevy. Winslow, Jas. Holladay, Ben. Holladay. Septr. 2, 1788.

April 26, 1788. Jno. Whitaker Willis of Spots. Co. to Lewis Willis, Oliver Towles and Ann Willis, wife of the sd. Jno. Whitaker Willis, all of the same co. afsd. Whereas, the sd. Ann Willis did with the sd. Jno. W. Willis, her husband, by Ind. dated —— in the year afsd., convey to Matthew Maury for £800 a tract of land in Orange Co., being the inheritance of the sd. Ann, and by her the sd. Ann agreed to be sold for the express purpose of paying the sd. Jno. W. Willis' debts, in consideration of the sd. Ann's releasing her right, title, etc., in the sd. land to one Jonathan Coward, the sd. Jno. W. Willis doth grant, etc., convey, etc., to the sd. Lewis Willis and Oliver Towles, 30 slaves in trust for the sd. Ann during her life and then to the child or children of the body of the sd. Ann by the sd. Jno. W. Willis begotten, etc., etc. Witnesses, Jas. Frazer, Harry B. Towles, Ben. Johnston, Walter Payne. Septr. 2, 1788.

July 4, 1788. Peter Crawford and Betsy, his wife, of Louisa Co. to Eliezer Callender and David Henderson of Spots. Co. £40 curr. 200 a. in Spots. Co., etc., etc. Sherod Horn, Wm. Parker, Danl. Davis. Septr. 2, 1788.

Septr. 4, 1788. Beverley Stanard of Spots. Co. to Larkin Stanard of same Co. To indemnify the sd. Larkin who stands security for the sd. Beverley, the sd. Beverley conveys to the sd. Larkin, slaves, goods and chattels, cattle, etc., etc. Witnesses, Ben. Holladay, Thos. Sharpe, Baldwin M. Buckner, Lodowick Oneal. Octr. 7, 1788.

Septr. 3, 1788. Thomas Sharpe and Judith, his wife, of Spots. Co. to John Legg of same co. £65 curr. 130 a. in Spots. Co., etc., etc. No witnesses. Octr. 7, 1788.

Octr. 7, 1788. Nicholas x Curtis of St. Geo. Par., Spots. Co., binds himself to John Brock of same par. and co. No witnesses. Octr. 7, 1788.

Octr. 7, 1788. Thomas Henderson and Mary, his wife, of Spots. Co. to Charles Clarke of Caroline Co. £120 curr. 332 a. in Spots. Co., etc., etc. Benja. Massey, Thomas Cash, Nelly Lord. Octr. 7, 1788.

June 20, 1788. Charles Curtis of Spots. Co. to John Dawson of same co. £150 curr. 250 a. in St. Geo. Par., Spots. Co., etc., etc. Thomas Colson, John Brock, Charles Carter. Octr. 7, 1788.

April 16, 1788. Wm. Hewell of Spots. Co., po. of atto. to Thomas Towles, etc., etc. Witnesses, Thos. Davenport, Eliza. Towles, James Davenport, Wm. Davenport. Novr. 4, 1788.

June 13, 1788. Alex. Spence Head, release of mortgage held against property of Henry Head's, to James Pettigrove, etc. Witnesses, Jos. Brock, Danl. Branham, Ludlow Branham, Wm. Robinson, Thomas Allen. Novr. 4, 1788.

March 4, 1788. Thomas Goodloe and Dolly, his wife, to Thomas Towles. £132 specie. 141 a. in Spots. Co., etc., etc. Jona. Clark, Robt. Taylor, Geo. Stubblefield, Thos. Allen. Novr. 6, 1788.

Augt. 27, 1788. Thomas Colson and Frances, his wife, and Sarah Holladay, Spinister, of Spots. Co. to Abraham Simons of same co. £200 to sd. Colson and £15 to sd. Holladay, etc. Holladay's Ordinary in Spots. Co., etc., etc. Nicho. Payne, Benj. Stanard. Septr. 2, 1788.

April 1, 1788. Alexander Spotswood and Elizabeth, his wife, of Spots. Co.; James Gordon and Elizabeth, his wife, of Orange Co.; Wm. Pollock and ——, his wife, of Louisa Co. to Wm. Jones of Spots. Co. £600 curr. 300 a. in Spots. Co., etc., etc. No witnesses. April 1, 1788.

April 1, 1788. Alexander Spotswood and Elizabeth, his wife, of Spots. Co. to Wm. Jones of same co. £600 curr. 642 a. in Spots. Co., etc., etc. No witnesses. April 1, 1788.

DEED BOOK M

1788–1791

Oct. 15, 1788. Thomas Colson of Spts. Co., Gent., and Frances, his wife, to John Welsh of Fredksbg. £1600 curr. 722 a. in Spts. Co. Edwd. Herndon, Jos. Brock, Jas. Lewis, O. Towles. Dec. 2, 1788.

Oct. 15, 1788. Jno. Welch of Freksbg. and Nelly, his wife, to Thomas Colson of Spts. Co., Gent. £1600 curr. Lots in Fredksbg., etc. Jos. Brock, Edwd. Herndon, James Lewis, O. Towles. Decr. 2, 1788.

Oct. 16, 1788. John Welch of Fredksbg and Nelly, his wife, to Thomas Colson of Spts. Co. Mortgage. 722 a. in Spts. Co., formerly conveyed by sd. Thos. Colson, etc., also several slaves. Witnesses, Jos. Brock, Edwd. Herndon, James Lewis, O. Towles. Dec. 1, 1788.

Novr. 22, 1788. Wm. Fitzhugh of "Chatham," Stafford Co., Esq., and Anne, his wife, to Francis Thornton, jr., of Spts. Co., Esq. £253 10s. curr. Tract of land in Spts. Co. Mann Page, Thos. Posey, Thos. Moffatt, F. Thornton. Dec. 2, 1788.

Augt. 21, 1788. Benjamin McWilliams of Charles City Co. and Letitia, his wife, to Danl. Tiller of Spts. Co. £62 10s. 86¼ a. in St. Geo. Par., Spts. Co., part of a larger tract formerly conveyed by Wm. McWilliams to his son, Broadbent McWilliams, etc., etc. Jas. Bullock, Danl. Tiller, jr.; Jno. Bullock. Dec. 2, 1788.

Nov. 4, 1788. Hugh Roy of Spts. Co. and Elizabeth, his wife, and Ann Roy, his mother, to Benjamin Winn, Adms. of Aquilla Johnson, Decd. £97 curr. and £83 curr. 288 a. in Spts. Co., etc. Jos. Brock, Geo. Stubblefield, Richd. Long. Dec. 2, 1788.

April 19, 1788. John Lewis of Fredksbg. and Mary Ann, his wife, to Wm. Thompson of Spts. Co. £80 curr. 1⅓ a. adj. town of Fredksbg., etc. Z. Lucas, Tully Whithurst, Elijah Strother. Dec. 2, 1788.

April 19, 1788. John Lewis of Fredksbg. and Mary Ann, his wife, to Wm. Thompson of Spts. Co. £80. 1 a. near Fredksbg., etc. Z. Lucas, Tully Whithurst, Elijah Strother. Dec. 2, 1788.

Novr. 4, 1788. Thomas x Brooks and Judith, his wife, to James Young and Edward Hyde. £25. 100 a. Whereon sd. Thos. Brooks, etc., now lives and bequeathed him by his father, Wm. Brooks, Decd., etc. Witnesses, Benj. Holloday, Wm. Holloday, Wilson Brooks, Claiborne Chandler, John x Chandler, John Andrews, Joseph Triplet. Dec. 2, 1788.

April 6, 1788. Richard Coleman and Ann, his wife, of Spts. Co. to Spilsby Coleman of same county. £56 curr. 49 a. in Spts. Co., etc. Thomas Coleman, jr.; J. Childs, Richard Coleman. Dec. 2, 1788.

Oct. 7, 1788. Francis Coleman of Spts. Co. to Wm. King of same county. £40 specie. 100 a. in Spts. Co., etc. No witnesses. Decr. 2, 1788.

April 1, 1788. Thomas Fox and his two sons, Wm. and Jos. Fox, of Spts. Co. to Oswald Smith of same county. £50 15s. 29 a. in Spts. Co., etc. Lewis Young, Robt. Sale, Jno. Parish. Decr. 2, 1788.

June 20, 1788. James Frazer and Sarah, his wife, of Spts. Co. to Charles Curtis of same county. £150 curr. 112 a. in St. Geo. Par., Spts. Co., etc. Thos. Colson, Jos. Brock, Chas. Carter. Dec. 2, 1788.

Dec. 1, 1788. Michael Yates and Martha, his wife, of Caroline Co. to Wm. Ledwidch of Spts. Co. £60 specie. 250 a. in Spts. Co., etc. Wm. Yates, Marshall Yates, Geo. Shepherd, jr.; Jno. Bullock. Decr. 2, 1788.

Dec. 2, 1788. Jno. Coats and Ann (Nancy), his wife, to Ambrose Smith. £150 curr. 190 a. in Berkeley Par., Spts. Co., whereon sd. Coats now lives, etc. Wm. Fox, Gerard B. Berryman, Mathew Harris. Decr. 2, 1788.

Oct. 1, 1788. John Rogers of Spts. Co. and Caty, his wife, to Dr. Robert Wellford of Fredksbg. £724 6s. curr. 459 a. in Spts. Co., formerly conveyed by Lodowick Oneal and Susan, his wife, by deed dated May 15, 1783, to sd. Jno. Rogers, etc. Witnesses, Jno. W. Willis, James Lewis, Larkin Stanard, Thomas Strachan, O. Towles. Jany. 6, 1789.

Oct. 8, 1788. Bradley x Matthews of Spts. Co. and Rebecca, his wife, to Benjamin Waller of same county. £100 specie. 130 a. in Spts. Co., purchased of John Coats, etc. John Waller, William Aill, Jos. Woolfolk, Jno. Wiglesworth, —— Crawford, Edwd. Herndon, jr. Dec. 2, 1788.

Sept. 5, 1788. Thomas Bartlett and Mary, his wife, of Spts. Co. to Gerard Blackstone Berryman and Josias Beryman of same county. £260 curr. 300 a., whereon sd. Bartlett lives, and part of a tract purchased of John Sanders in Berkeley Par., Spts. Co., etc. Jos. Brock, Edwd. Herndon, A. Frazer, Jno. Crutcher. Decr. 2, 1788.

Jany. 6, 1789. Abram Simons of Spts. Co. and Mildred, his wife, and Sarah Holloday, Spinster, of same county, to Gabriel Long of Culpeper County. £280 to Simons and £15 to Holloday. 325 a. in St. Geo. Par., Spts. Co. No witnesses. Jany. 6, 1789.

Augt. 7, 1788. Wm. Riardon and Ann, his wife, of Spts. Co. to Thomas Haydon of same county. £30 curr. 100 a. in Spts. Co., etc. G. Bell, L. Branham, Thos. Whiting, Jno. McWhirt, Danl. Branham, Edwd. Leavell, James Lewis, Thomas Strachan. Jany. 6, 1789.

March 3, 1789. Edward Brasfield and Ann, his wife, of Spts. Co. to Jno. Humphries. £100. 262 a. in Spts. Co., formerly purchased by Henry Chiles of one G. Baylor, etc. No witnesses. March 3, 1789.

Jany. 23, 1789. Jno. Cooke and Catherine, his wife, of Berkeley Par., Spts. Co. to Saml. Sale, assignee of Abraham Darnall of Spts. Co. £100. 500 a. in Spts. Co., etc. Wm. Sale, Jno. Sale, Thos. Lane. March 4, 1789.

Oct. 1, 1788. Geo. Stubblefield of Spts. Co., Gent., and Sally, his wife, to Peter Rawlings of Caroline County. £337 8s. 241 a. in St. Geo. Par., Spts. Co., etc. Benja. Stubblefield, Richd. Loury, Peter Dudley. March 4, 1789.

July 1, 1788. Joseph Jones and Sarah, his wife, of Spts. Co. to Richard Loury of Caroline County. £243. 162 a. in St. Geo. Par., Spts. Co. Benj. Stubblefield, L. Stanard, Peter Dudley, A. Simons. March 5, 1789.

Sept. 3, 1788. Richard Loury of Caroline County, Gent., to George Stubblefield of Spts. Co., Gent. Mortgage. Whereas, sd. Loury is indebted to sd. Stubblefield in sum of £351 7s 10½d., and whereas, Wm. Loury, decd. (father of the sd. Richard), did by his will lend to his wife Rebecca, now Rebecca Jones, several slaves, etc., and after her death to be divide between his (the testator's) two daughters Martha and Sally, and his son, the sd. Richard, as by the sd. will recd. in Essex Co., etc., the sd. Richard conveys his reversion in the sd. slaves to the sd. Stubblefield, etc., also 162 a. in Spts. Co., etc. Witnesses, Benja. Stubblefield, Harry B. Towles, Thomas Herndon. March 5, 1789.

Decr. 13, 1788. John Lewis and Mary Ann, his wife, of Fredksbg. to Francis Thornton, Senr., of Spts. Co. Mortgage. £300. 5 a. in Spts. Co., etc. Wm. Lewis, Lawrence Lewis, Geo. Saunders. April 7, 1789.

Oct. 27, 1788. James Crawford, Senr., and John x Sherley, Senr., of Spts. Co. for "the natural love and affection they have for John Crawford and Phebe, his wife," of same county. Deed of Gift. 70 a. in Spts. Co. and two slaves, etc. Jno. Waller, Thos. Turner, Wm. x Arnold, Thomas Hicks, Jno. Sherley, jr.; James Crawford, jr. April 7, 1789.

Oct. ——, 1788. James Coleman Goodwin of Spts. Co., po. of atto., to friend Hawes Coleman of same county, to sell and convey 200 a. on Pamunkey River, Spts. Co., etc. Witnesses, Jos. Graves, Jas. Graves, Benja. Graves, Wm. Graves. April 7, 1789.

Jany 13, 1789. Samuel Bullock of North Carolina to James Bullock of Spts. Co., Va. £25. 136 a. in Spts. Co., etc. Geo. Shepherd, Jos. Bullock, Daniel Tiller, John Bullock. April 7, 1789.

—— ——, 1789. Thomas True and Mary, his wife, of Spts. Co. to Wm. Buchannan of same county. £20 curr. 50 a. in Berkeley Par., Spts. Co. No witnesses. April 7th, 1789.

Jany. 27, 1789. Edward Herndon and Edward Herndon, jr., to John Herndon, all of Spts. Co. Whereas, sd. Herndon, in 1783, did verbally give the sd. Herndon, jr., 450 a. on branches of East North East River in Spts. Co., purchased of Richd. Corbin, Esq., in 1764, and whereas, the sd. Herndon, jr., being so possessed in the year 1787, did sell the same to the sd. Jno. Herndon for the sum of £200 curr. then pd. This deed of conveyance in which sd. Herndon and Herndon, jr., join to the sd. Jno. Herndon, etc. No witnesses. April 7, 1789.

Decr. 1788. Wm. Pettus, Senr., and Susannah, his wife, of Spts. Co. to Wm. Pettus, jr., of same county. 5 shill. 100 a. in Spts. Co., etc. Robt. Dabney, Edward Eggleston, James Pettus, Thomas W. Pettus, Joseph Pettus. April 7, 1789.

Oct. 4, 1788. Thomas Fox and Wm. Fox of Spts. Co., Gentlemen, to Hawes Coleman of same county. £80 10s. 46 a. in Berkeley Par., Spts. Co., etc. George Stubblefield, Benj. Stubblefield, Beverley Stanard, John Frazer. April 7, 1789.

Oct. 2, 1788. Peter Rawlins of Caroline Co. to George Stubblefield of same county. £312 8s. specie. Mortgage. Tract of land in Spts. Co., conveyed by sd. Stubblefield to sd. Rawlins as by Indenture, Octr. 1, 1788, also several slaves, etc. Witnesses, Benjamin Stubblefield, Richard Loury, Peter Dudley. April 7, 1789.

April 7, 1789. Edwd. Herndon, Wm. Bronaugh and Lewis Holloday, overseers of the poor in Berkeley Par., Spts. Co., apprentice Mary Murphy to "Edward Coleman, house keeper of the Parish and County afsd., etc. No witnesses. April 7, 1789.

Novr. 3, 1788. Thomas Powell and Elizabeth, his wife, of Spts. Co. to James Stevens of same county. £5. 200 a. in Spts. Co., etc. Geo. Cammack, Jno. Carter, Micajah Poole. April 7, 1789.

March 12, 1789. Winslow Parker and Mary, his wife, of Orange County to Wm. Parker of Spts. County. £158 4s. curr. 113 a. on Terry's Run in Spts. Co., etc. Jos. Hawkins, jr.; Benj. Robinson, Richd. Parker, Jas. Powell, W. Daniel. April 7, 1789.

Feby. 5, 1789. John Cash and Elizabeth, his wife, to Thomas Cash. 5 shill. 100 a. in Spts. Co., etc. No witnesses. May 5, 1789.

Oct. 18, 1788. John Wiglesworth and Philadelphia, his wife, of Spts. Co. to Joseph Jones of same county. £243. 162 a. in St. Geo. Par., Spts. Co., etc. Benj. Stubblefield, Jno. Herndon, Thomas Towles. May 5, 1789.

April 23, 1789. John Wiglesworth and Philadelphia, his wife, of Spts. Co. to Richard Loury of Caroline Co. £80. 7 a. in St. Geo. Par., Spts. Co. Wm. Herndon, Peter Dudley, Benj. Stubblefield. May 5, 1789.

May 5, 1789. John Wiglesworth and Philadelphia, his wife, of Spts. Co. to David Blair of Fredksbg., Mercht. £30 curr. 6 a. in Spts. Co. Beverley Stubblefield, Willm. Frazer, Jno. Frazer. May 7, 1789.

May 15, 1789. Oliver Towles and Mary, his wife, of Spts. Co. to Charles Mortimer of Fredksbg. £400 specie. Mortgage. 633 a. in Spts. Co., whereon sd. Towes lives, etc. Jno. Chew, jr.; Wm. Lewis, Thomas Moffatt. June 2, 1789.

June 1, 1789. Jos. Brock of Spts. Co. and Mary Beverley, his wife, to Wm. Richards of Culpeper Co., Gent. £68 curr. 68 a. in Spts. Co., whereon Jno. Chisman lately lived, etc. Danl. Branham, Wm. Owen, Robt. Branham, Robt. Smith, Jno. Wiglesworth. June 2, 1789.

March 13, 1789. Wm. Parker of Spts. Co., Gent., to James Powell of same county. £257 curr. 217 a. in Spts. Co., etc. Wm. Daniel, Wm. Leavet, Benj. Robinson, Wm. Mills, Wm. Rice, Robt. Sp. Coleman, Winslow Parker. June 2, 1789.

May 12, 1789. Joseph Whitehead of Dinwiddie Co. to Stephen Johnston of Spts. Co. £50 curr. 200 a. in Spts. Co., adj. lands of Benj. Davis and a Mr. Jenkins, etc. Witnesses, James Holloday, P. B. Johnston, Philemon Davis. June 2, 1789.

March 19, 1788. Robt. Beverley Hutcherson of Caroline Co. to Francis Coleman of Spts. Co. £12 curr. Tract of land on Beverley Run in Berkeley Par., Spts. Co., devised by Wm. Hutcherson, decd., to his son, Charles Hutcherson, etc. Robt. E. Coleman, Elijah Carter, Robt. Sp. Coleman, Wm. Parker, jr. June 2, 1789.

Feby. 17, 1789. Dennis x Wright and Elinor, his wife, of Spts. Co. to Francis Coleman of Spts. Co. £60 curr. 370 a. in Spts. Co. Thos. Winslow, Robt. S. Coleman, Rowland Thomas, jr.; Richd. C. Webb. June 2, 1789.

June 11, 1789. James Marye of Spts. Co. to his sister, Elizabeth Marye. Deed of Gift. Slave. Witnesses, O. Towles, R. Wellford, Benj. Grayson. July 7, 1789.

May 23, 1789. James Marye of Spts. Co. to Elizabeth Marye of same county. Bill of Sale. Slaves. Witnesses, Gerard Banks, Elizabeth Bradwell, Elizabeth Marye. July 7, 1789.

March 7, 1788. Richd. Garner of Fredksbg. and Ann, his wife, to Charles Urquhart of Fredksbg. £425 curr. 90 a. sd. Garner purchased of Jno. Wiglesworth, as by deed dated Nov. 1, 1786, and 100 a. purchased of Richd. Kenny, as by deeds dated Oct. 13, 1787, etc. Robt. B. Chew, Jas. Dudley, Edwd. Herndon, jr.; Benj. Alsop, R. Frazer, Jno. Chew, jr. July 7, 1789.

July 7, 1789. Charles Beazley and Susannah, his wife, of Spts. Co. to John Long. £46 10s. 100 a. in Berkeley Par., Spts. Co., etc. No witnesses. July 7, 1789.

April 7, 1789. Dr. Charles Mortimer of Fredksbg and Sarah Griffin, his wife, to James Frazer of Spts. Co., Carpenter. £120. Lot No. 7 in town of Fredksbg., formerly purchased of the est. of Roger Dixon., Gent., Decd., etc. Thomas Colson, Edwd. Herndon, jr.; Daniel Branham, Wm. Bronaugh, Benj. Alsop. July 7, 1789.

April 20, 1789. Wm. Ficklin of Spts. Co. to George White of Stafford Co. £65 curr. 200 a. on Rappa. River, in Spts. Co., formerly leased of Wm. Fitzhugh, Esqr., etc. Danl. Branham, Jos. Brock, jr; Robt. Sale, Wm. Owen, George Burbridge, Benj. Edge, Bennett Rose, Ambrose Pitts. July 7, 1789.

July 7, 1789. Thomas Towles, Gent., late Sheriff·of Spts. Co., to Robt. Smith of same county, Gent. Whereas, Robt. Jardine of London, Gt. Britain, stood indebted to the sd. Towles in the sum of £3 3s. curr. for tax, etc., due on a tract of land in St. Geo. Par., Spts. Co., and the sd. Towles, acting under an act of the assembly, exposed the sd. land to sale when the sd. Smith became the purchaser for the amount of tax due, etc. Conveyance of sd. land to sd. Smith, etc. No witnesses. July 7, 1789.

June 26, 1789. Samuel Chiles and Sarah, his wife, and Catharine Rogers of Caroline Co. to John Rogers, now of Fayette County. Whereas, sd. Jno. Rogers did by his Indenture convey to Thomas Pollard of Fairfax Co., Gent., 645 a. in Spts. Co., and whereas, the sd. Samuel Chiles and Sarah, his wife, and Catherine Rogers (which sd. Sarah and Catharine are daughters of Wm. Rogers, late of Spts. Co., decd.), have a right to a part thereof, etc. Therefore the sd. Chiles and wife, and Catharine Rogers, for love and affection they bear, and the sum of £25 to each in hand paid, hereby convey their right thereto to the sd. John Rogers, etc. Witnesses, J. Chiles, Harry Sathworth (Southworth?), J. Sutton, Farish Coleman, Nancy x Mackdowel, Ann Coleman. July 7, 1789.

July 7, 1789. John Wood and Elizabeth, his wife, of Spts. Co. to Betty Slaven, eldest daughter of Northent Slaven and Ann, his wife, of Spts. Co. £40 curr. 40 a. in St. Geo. Par., Spts. Co. No witnesses. July 7, 1789.

Decr. 24, 1788. James Crane of Berkeley Par., Spts. Co., and Lucy, his wife, to Spilsbe Coleman of same county. £357. 504 a. in Berkeley Par., Spts. Co., etc. Jno. M. Herndon, Robt. S. Coleman, Thomas Coleman. Augt. 4, 1789.

May 6, 1789. Daniel Barkesdale of Spots. Co. to his daughter, Patty White. Bill of Sale. Slaves. Witnesses, Richard Coleman, Jos. Willoughby, Richard Finlenener. Augt. 7, 1789.

Jany. 29, 1789. Philip Lyscomb of Spts. Co. to John Crutchfield of same county. Bill of Sale. Slaves, goods and chattels, etc. £200. Jno. Shelton, Geo. Cammack, Wm. Duerson. Augt. 4, 1789.

Augt. 4, 1789. Joseph Herndon, Benjamin Waller and Jonathan Clarke, Overseers of the Poor, Dist. No. 1, Spts. Co., do bind Wm. Yates, orph. of Wm. Yates, late of Spts. Co., Decd., to Daniel Tiller of Spts. Co., planter. Augt. 6, 1789.

Augt. 14, 1789. Thomas Posey and Mary, his wife, of Spts. Co. to Fontaine Maury of Fredksbg. £282. 188 a. in Spts. Co., purchased of Wm. Thompson, etc. Witnesses, David Blair, Henry Mitchell, Jno. Legg, Thomas Goodwin. Sept. 1, 1789.

Augt. 4, 1789. Beverley Stanard of Spts. Co. and Thomas Magee and Mary, his wife, of same County, to James Marye of same county. Whereas, the sd. Magee in right of his wife, being seized of a tract of abt. 207 a. in Spts. Co., sold the same to Beverley Stanard, but before any conveyance thereof had been made the sd. Stanard agreed with the sd. Marye for the sale thereof to him for the sum of £500, etc. Conveyance to Marye, etc. Witnesses, Wm. Johnston, jr.; Jos. Brock, jr.; A. Parker, Jas. Lewis, Jno. Chew, Thomas Strachan. Sept. 1, 1789.

Jany. 6, 1789. John Sams and Mary, his wife, of Spts. Co. to Leonard Young of same county. £50 curr. 100 a. in Spts. Co., conveyed by Joseph Sams and wife to sd. John Sams, etc. Witnesses, Rice Vass, Reubin Arnold, James Buchanan, Joseph Sams, Thomas Coleman, John Carnahan. Sept. 1, 1789.

Jany. 30, 1789. David Sandige to James Sandige. 5 shill. 100 a. in Spts. Co., etc. Benj. Holloday, W. Bronaugh, David Sandidge, jr.; David Bronaugh, Zacharias Sandidge. Sept. 1, 1789.

Sept. 1, 1789. Thomas Coleman and Rebecca, his wife, of Spts. Co. to Jeremiah Wilson of same county. £30 curr. 18 a. in Spts. Co. and 9¼ a. in same county, etc. No witnesses. Sept. 1, 1789.

Sept. 1, 1789. Hawes Coleman of Spts. Co., attorney for James C. Goodwin, formerly of Spts. Co., now of the District of Kentucky, to Daniel Coleman of Caroline Co. Whereas, the sd. Goodwin was possessed of 200 a. in Spts. Co. and the sd. Hawes Coleman being security on bond of sd. Goodwin to James Edwards, and as the sd. Goodwin was abt. to move to Kentucky in order to indemnify the sd. Coleman, did execute a deed of trust to the sd. Coleman for the sd. land, and whereas, the sd.

Daniel Coleman having purchased for £200 the sd. tract of land, by which means the sd. Hawes Coleman is released from sd. securityship, the sd. Hawes Coleman conveys the afsd. tract of 200 a. to the sd. Danl. Coleman, etc., etc. No witnesses. Septr. 1, 1789.

April 8, 1789. James Frazer of Spts. Co., Carpenter, and Sarah, his wife, to Thomas Posey of same county. £400. Lot No. 7 near town of Fredksbg., purchased of Charles Mortimer, etc. Witnesses, Jno. Chew, jr.; Edwd. Herndon, Edwd. Herndon, jr.; John Jesse. Sept. 1, 1789.

Sept. 1, 1789. Wm. Carter of Spts. Co. to his son, John Carter. Deed of Gift. 216 a. in Berkeley Par., Spts. Co., etc. No witnesses. Sept. 1, 1789.

Augt. 6, 1789. John Whitaker Willis of Spts. Co., Gent., and Ann, his wife, to Lewis Willis, Larkin Chew, Oliver Towles of same county. Whereas, the sd. J. W. Willis and Ann, his wife, being seized and possessed of sundry tracts of land in her right (and as her inheritance is of very considerable value, greater than the same actually sold for, etc.), situate in Orange Co., and the sd. J. W. Willis is largely indebted to sundry persons, the sd. Ann consented to, and in order to relieve her sd. husband, etc., joined in conveyances of two tracts of land and sold the same for the sole purpose of applying the amounts therefrom realized, abt. £1560, to the paying of the sd. debts upon condition of the sd. J. W. Willis' conveying to the sd. Larkin Chew the tract of land in Spts. Co., whereon sd. Willis, etc., lived, in trust for the several purposes mentioned in Ind. dated May 1, 1787, and also on condition of his conveying to Lewis Willis and Oliver Towles, parties herein named, for the benefit of the sd. Ann and her children, 30 slaves for the purposes mentioned in an Ind. dated April 27, 1788, and whereas, the sd. Willis being still largely indebted, and the sd. Ann having consented to sell and dispose of another tract of land in Albermarle and Orange Counties and by Ind. dated this day, the sd. tract has been conveyed to the sd. Towles to be sold in consideration of the premises, etc., the sd. Willis does convey to the sd. Lewis Willis, Larkin Chew and Oliver Towles, all his right, title, interest, etc., in the sd. 30 slaves and the Spots. Co. lands as afsd. in trust for the benefit of the sd. Ann and her children begotten or to be begotten by the sd. Jno. W. Willis, etc., etc. Witnesses, Thos. Towles, Nicho. Payne, Thos. Garnett, A. Frazer, E. Herndon, Wm. Frazer. Octr. 6, 1789.

Oct. 6, 1789. John Woolfolk, Senr., of Spts. Co. and Elizabeth, his wife, and Joseph Woolfolk of same county (son of the sd. John) and Mary, his wife, to Benj. Waller, Senr., of same county. £152. 6s. curr. 125 a. in Spts. Co., whereon sd. Jos. Woolfolk now lives, etc. No witnesses. Oct. 6, 1789.

Feby. 12, 1789. Samuel Luck of Hanover Co., Executor of Saml. Luck of Spts. Co., Decd., to Jonathan Clark of Spts. Co. Whereas, sd. Saml. Luck, decd., by his last will and testament, did direct that his executor sell 209 a., whereon the sd. Luck then lived, which sd. tract the sd. Executor exposed to sale and the sd. Clark became the purchaser for the sum of £75 curr., etc. Witnesses, John Woolfolk, Sr.; Morton Davenport, Benj. Waller, Jno. Woolfolk, jr. Oct. 6, 1789.

May 17, 1789. David Partlow to his children, Henry Brock Partlow and Nancy Partlow. Deed of Gift. Slaves. Witnesses, Jno. Penny, Jno. Martin, Jos. Brock. Oct. 6, 1789.

May 2, 1789. Martin Hawkins of Spts. Co. to Wm. Mills, Benj. Robinson and Wm. Winslow. Mortgage, etc. Slaves, goods, chattels, etc. Witnesses, Richd. Dickerson, Jno. P. Thomas, Wm. Parker, Wm. Hawkins. Oct. 6, 1789.

Dec. 9, 1788. Wm. Plummer Thurston of Spts. Co. and Lucy Mary, his wife, to Joseph Hawkins, jr., son of John Hawkins, decd. £345 curr. 300 a. in upper end of Spts. County, etc. Winslow Parker, Rowland Thomas, jr.; Saml. Robinson, Wm. Hawkins, Benj. Robinson. April 7, 1789.

Novr. 12, 1789. John Wallace and Margaret, his wife, of Spts. Co. to Charles Yates of Fredksbg. £250 curr. Lot 212 in Fredksbg., etc. Edwd. Herndon, Jas. Frazer, Jno. Frazer, Jas. Pendleton, Wm. Oliffe. Dec. 1, 1789.

June 29, 1789. Benj. Holloday of Spts. Co. to his uncle, Joseph Holloday, etc. "My father, Jno. Holloday, decd. Deed for slaves, etc., etc. Witnesses, Lewis Holloday, Benj. Rawlings. Decr. 1, 1789.

Novr. 2, 1789. Wm. Chowning of Culpeper Co. to James King of Spts. Co. £30 curr. 100 a., part of a larger tract in Spts. Co., etc. Thos. Sharpe, Thomas Allen, Frederick Zimmerman, Absolem Bradley, Wm. Carter. Dec. 1, 1789.

Oct. 14, 1789. Thomas Bartlett of Berkeley Par., Spts. Co., and Mary, his wife, to Robert Scott of same par. and county. $143.00 specie. 143 a. in sd. par. and county, etc. J. Brock, Benj. Robinson, Jno. Davenport, Gerard B. Berryman, Wm. Burnett. Decr. 1, 1789.

May 10, 1789. John Herndon and Judith, his wife, of Spts. Co. to Anthony Frazer of same county. £225 curr. 450 a. in Berkeley Par., Spts. Co., purchased by Edwd. Herndon, Senr., of Richard Corbin, Esq., etc. Wm. Frazer, Philip Edge, Jno. Frazer. Dec. 1, 1789.

Augt. 29, 1789. David Simons and Catherine, his wife, of Fredksbg. to Wm. Jackson of Spts. Co., Stonemason. £200 curr. 158 a. known as "Chalkey Leavel" in Spts. Co., purchased of Jno. Benson and Eleanor, his wife, and Jno. Welch and Eleanor, his wife, etc. Thomas Colson, Thomas Strachan, Edward Herndon. Decr. 1, 1789.

June 8, 1789. Michael Yates to Mann Page. £700. 20 a., part of "Sligo," and 100 a. known as "Kennedy's Point," both in Spts. Co., etc. Thomas Hughes, Gwyn Page, Benj. Grymes of Orange. Jany. 5, 1790.

Feby. 17, 1789. Dennis x Wright and Eleanor, his wife, of Spts. Co. to Sarah Pollard of same county. £40 curr. 100 a. in Spts. Co., etc. Thomas Winslow, Robt. S. Coleman, Rowland Thomas, jr.; Francis Coleman. No date of Record.

Jany. 4, 1787. Henry Willis at present in Spts. Co., Va., "but intending soon to go to the State of Georgia," to John Whitaker Willis. Several Slaves, stock of Cattle, etc.; mentions tract of land, "Lamb's Creek," coming to him from Lewis Willis, Gent. To indemnify the sd. J. W. Willis who stands security of sd. Henry, and for the payment of debts, etc. Witnesses, Oliver Towles, Larkin Stanard, A. Dick, April 16, 1787. Edwd. Herndon (son of Joseph) of Spts. Co. standing with sd. Jno. W. Willis as security for the sd. Henry, the sd. John deeds him several slaves, etc. Witnesses, Wm. Daingerfield, Francis Bayle. Jany. 5, 1790.

July 14, 1789. Joel Parrish of Spts. Co. to Wm. Arnold of same county. £50 curr. 111 a. in Spts. Co. Jno. Waller, Benj. Waller, Absolem Waller, Aylett Waller. Feby. 2, 1790.

Jany. 6, 1790. Wm. Davenport of Spts. Co. to his son, James Davenport. Deed of Gift. 68½ a. in Spts. Co. Thomas Minor, Thomas Davenport, Jona. Clarke, Wm. Arnold, John Woolfolk, Senr. Feby. 2, 1790.

Oct. 22, 1789. John Wood and Elizabeth, his wife, of Spts. Co. and James Wood and Jenny, his wife, of County of —— to James Fuller of Caroline County. £94 curr. 224 a. in St. Geo. Par., Spts. Co., etc. Benj. Alsop, Jno. Carter, Wm. Spindle, Thomas Pritchett. Feby. 2, 1790.

Oct. 2, 1789. Alexander Spence Head and Sarah, his wife, to Benjamin Head, son of the sd. Alexander Spence Head. £150 curr. 331 a. in Berkeley Par., Spts. Co., whereon sd. A. S. Head lately lived, etc., and part of a tract purchased of John Holloday and bounded by lands of Capt. Stockley Towles, Wm. Smith, Gent., and David Head, etc. Witnesses, Joseph Head, David Head, Joel Fagg. Feby. 2, 1790.

Feby. 2, 1790. Elizabeth x Johnston, relict of Aquilla Johnston, decd., late of Spts. Co., "to my two sons, Wm. Fortson and Thomas Fortson. Deed of Gift. Slaves, goods and chattels, etc. Benjamin Fortson, Littleton Estes. Mallacai x Adkins, Feb. 2, 1790. Deed Delivered John Fortson, son of Wm. Fortson, etc.

*Feby. 1, 1790. Wm. Fortson of Spts. Co. to his daughter Ann and her husband, Littleton Estes. Deed of Gift. Slave, goods and chattels, etc. Witnesses, Benjamin Fortson, Malichi x Adkins. No date of Record.

July 23, 1789. Thomas Bartlett of Spts. Co. to Wm. Carter, Jno. Carter and Joseph Brock, Excrs. of John Carter, Gent., Decd. "£80 17s. 10d. due from Edward Bartlett to the Excrs. of the sd. Jno. Carter," etc., and to secure the sd. payment, etc. 900 a. whereon sd. Bartlett now lives (except 300 a. sold to Gerard Blackstone Berryman and Josias Berryman, except also 200 a. sold Jesse Bolin, etc.), etc. Witnesses, Benjamin Robinson, John Williams, Thomas Crutcher, John Bartlett, Beverley Stubblefield. Feby. 2, 1790.

Jany. 12, 1788. Wm. Dawson of Spts. Co. to John Rawlins, who saving Thomas Towles harmless, which sd. Towles stands security for the sd. Dawson, etc. A slave. Witnesses, Wm. Frazer, Abrah. Terry, John Frazer, Edwd. Roster, etc. No date of Record.

March 2, 1790. John Chew and Anthony Frazer of Spts. Co. to Thomas Duerson of same county. Whereas, Harry Bartlett, late of said county, by deed dated April 17, 1787, conveyed to sd. Chew and Frazer, abt. 500 a. in Spts. Co., and the sd. Bartlett impowered them to make sale thereof, the sd. Frazer and Chew convey the sd. land to the sd. Duerson for the sum of £96 12s. specie. Witnesses, R. B. Chew, Wm. Herndon, John Steward. March 2, 1790.

*Ed Note.—This deed is also signed by Mildred x Fortson, presumably wife of sd. Wm. Fortson, etc.

May 6, 1788. John W. Willis, Eleizer Callender and George French, overseers of the poor in District No. 3, St. Geo. Par., Spts. Co., bind two free mulatto boys, Daniel and Wm., children of a free mulatto woman, Milly Mann, to Thomas Herndon, house carpenter, of St. Geo. Par., Spts. Co. Witnesses, Edwd. Herndon, Jos. Brock, Jno. Anderson. March 2, 1790.

March 2, 1790. Charles Brown, son of Thomas Brown, late of Fredksbg., Decd., binds himself to Thomas Herndon, house carpenter, etc. No witnesses. March 2, 1790.

March 1, 1790. Thomas Olive of Spts. Ct. to James Kelly of Richmond County. Several negroes, also goods and chattels, etc., in trust, for support of sd. Thomas Olive and Elizabeth, his wife, and their children, Robert, Susanna, Lewis and Sarah, etc., etc. Witnesses, Joseph Brock, Joseph Brock, jr.; Wm. Ledwedge. March 2, 1790.

Oct. 26, 1789. Robert Cunningham of Spts. Co. to Edwd. Herndon, junr., of same county. £100 curr. Mortgage. 200 a. in Spts. Co., St. Geo. Par., purchased by James Cunningham, decd. (father of the sd. Robt.), of Wm. Fitzhugh, Esqr., etc. Witnesses, Joseph Jones, Jno. Herndon, jr.; Francis Simpson, jr.; Martin x True. March 2, 1790.

Dec. 7, 1789. Oliver Towles of Spts. Co., atto. at law, to Archibald Dick of Louisa Co., Mercht., and Oliver Towles, jr., "of the same county." Whereas, sundry persons stand as security for the sd. Towles for the payment of sundry debts, the sd. Towles to indemnify them, deeds the following named property to the sd. Dick and Towles, jr., giving them po. of atto. to act for him; the sd. property is as follows: Abt. 7000 a. in Kentucky, "the whole of his Military Bounty lands that he is entitled to," also all his the sd. Towles commutation pay in arrears and unpaid, due the sd. Towles "as an officer having served in the late Continental Army," also all debts, etc., due the sd. Towles, etc. Witnesses, Fanny Straughan, Eliza Towles, Mary Towles. March 2, 1790.

Dec. 7, 1789. Oliver Towles of Spts. Co. to Archibald Dick, jr., of Louisa Co., Merch. In consideration of sd. Dick and Molly, his wife, releasing all their right, title, etc., which they may have to any slaves under the will of Larkin Chew, Gent., grandfather of the sd. Molly Dick, etc., the sd. Towles deeds the sd. Dick and wife three slaves. Witnesses, Fanny Straughan, Eliza Towles, Mary Towles. March 2, 1790.

Decr. 7, 1789. Oliver Towles, atto. at law, of Spts. Co. to Archibald Dick of Louisa Co., Mercht., and Oliver Towles, jr., "of the last named county." Whereas, the sd. Oliver Towles is, amongst other things, possessed of two tracts of land in Spts. Co., the one whereon he lives, 600 a. called "Middlebrooke," and purchased of Thomas Carr, and the other tract, whereon Wm. Beasly, his overseer, now lives and contains parts of sundry tracts purchased of Saml. Moor and others, Larkin Stanard, Larkin Smith, and part of it called the Maidstoke Tract and adjacent to and remainder of all the land unconveyed to Ann, daughter of the sd. Thomas Towles, containing abt. 1400 a. The sd. Towles is seized and possessed of several slaves, also personal estate, goods and chattels, and having provided for the support of his daughter the sd. Ann Towles is also desirous of making provision for the rest of his family, viz., the sd. Oliver Towles daughter Molly, wife of sd. Archibald Dick, jr.; Oliver Towles, jr., and Harry Beverley Towles, sons of the sd. Oliver Towles, and the sd. Oliver Towles and Mary, his wife, etc. Therefore in consideration of the premises and the sum of £750 curr. the sd. Towles deeds to the sd. Dick and Towles, jr., the aforementioned property, nevertheless in trust that in case the lands in Western Country, etc., as deeded to the sd. Dick and Towles, jr., in a deed dated this same day, should prove insufficient to meet the demands therein referred to, then the lands, etc., herein conveyed to make up the deficiency, if any, subject, however, to the refunding the aforementioned £750 as herein acknowledged paid, and further that the sd. Dick and Towles, Jr., shall furnish a home and support for the sd. Oliver Towles and Mary, his wife, and the sd. Harry Beverley Towles, etc. To tract called "Middlebrooke" to the said Archibald Dick and Molly, his wife, and the 1400 a. tract, as before mentioned, to the sd. Oliver Towles, jr., etc., etc. Witnesses, Fanny Straughan, Eliza Towles, Mary Towles. March 2, 1790.

Decr. 1, 1789. Northent Slaven and Ann, his wife, of Fredksbg. to Isaac Head of Spts. Co. £25. 40 a. in St. Geo. Par., Spts. Co., etc. Henry Duerson, Henry Southworth, James Wilson. March 2, 1790.

March 2, 1790. Edwd. Herndon, Lewis Holloday and Wm. Bronaugh, Overseers of the Poor, Dist. No. 2, Spts. Co., do bind Nancy Atherton, daughter of Joseph Atherton, to John Pendleton, etc. Witnesses, Jno. Minor, A. Buchanan. March 4, 1790.

April 6, 1790. Benjamin Chapman of Spts. Co. and Elizabeth, his wife, to Benjamin Waller, jr., and his brother, John Nichodemus Waller. £75 curr. and £18 15s. curr. 150 a. in Spts. Co., etc. Thomas Towles, Merideth Anderson, Ambrose Smith, John Master. April 6, 1790.

Sept. 16, 1789. Elizabeth x Edwards of Spts. Co., Widow, to her son, James Arnold, of same county. In consideration of his paying the tax thereon, she has rented him ½ of the tract of 400 a. whereon she now lives, etc. Witnesses, Betsy x Reynolds, James Pettus, Wm. Arnold, Wm. Pettus, jr.; Jno. Arnold. April 6, 1790.

Jany. 25, 1790. John Estes and Ann, his wife, of Caroline Co. to Wm. Coleman of Spts. Co. £37 curr. 66½ a. in Spts. and Caroline Counties, whereon sd. Coleman now lives, etc. Hugh Roy, Fredk. Coghill, Wm. Waller. April 6, 1790.

Decr. 7, 1789. Wm. Lodspike of Stafford Co. to Elijah Carter of Spts. Co. £52 10s. 75 a. Witnesses, Edwd. Thomas, Samuel x Wharton, Robert E. Coleman.

Ocbr. 14, 1789. Thomas Bartlett and Mary, his wife, of Spts. Co. to Jessey Bowlin of same county. £115 curr. 200 a. in Berkeley Par., Spts. Co., etc. Benj. Robinson, Thomas Waller, James Ballard, Martin True, John Davenport, John Brock. April 6, 1790.

April 6, 1790. Michael x Blunt and Elizabeth, his wife, of Spts. Co. to Jonathan Johnston of same county. £41 9s. 9d. 78 a. in Berkeley Par., Spts. Co. No witnesses. April 6, 1790.

March 6, 1790. Thomas Turner, Benony Woodroof and Susanna Turner and Eliza. Woodroof, their wives, of Spts. Co. to Larkin Luck of same county. £50. 100 a. in Spts. County, etc. George Wilkerson, Thomas Turner, Clark Moorman. April 6, 1790.

Feby. 19, 1790. George Stubblefield, Gent., and Sally, his wife, of Spts. Co. to Thomas Colson of same county, Gent. £3000 curr. 1243 a. in Spts. Co., purchased of Dr. Thomas Powell, whereon sd. Colson now lives, conveyed by Identure dated April 8, 1782. 172½ a. purchased of Jos. and Edwd. Herndon, etc., and conveyed by Indenture dated April 17, 1783; 150 a. purchased of Abram Simons, etc., conveyed by Indenture dated Sept. 20, 1786; 107 a. purchased of Richd. Keown, all in Spts. County, etc. Geo. Lewis, Benja. Stubblefield, Oliver Towles, O. Towles. April 6, 1790.

Decr. 10, 1789. Lawrence Battaile of Caroline County to Thomas Colson of Spts. County. £860 curr. 860 a. in St. Geo. Par., Spts. County, etc. Wm. Hestot, Wm. Herndon, Wm. Lovell, Jno. Welch, Geo. Stubblefield. April 6, 1790.

Feby. 3, 1790. David Pullian. of Spts. Co. and Betty, his wife, to James Robbins of same county. £40 curr. 160 a. in Spts. Co., etc. Jos. Pulliam, Richd. Pulliam, Poley Pulliam. April 6, 1790.

April 6, 1790. Ambrose x Smith and Isabella Smith of Berkeley Par., Spts. Co. to our son, James Smith, of same par. and county. Deed of Gift. 50 a. whereon sd. James Smith now lives, etc. William Frazer, Benj. Chapman, Wm. Robinson. April 6, 1790.

Decr. 30, 1789. John Sorrel and Ashman Sorrel of Spts. Co. to Wm. Willoughby of Culpeper County. £50 curr. 100 a. in Spts. Co., etc. Joseph Willoughby, Wm. Fagg, Henry Willoughby, Larkin Stanard, Benjamin Waller. April 6, 1790.

April 6, 1790. Isaac Head of Spts. Co. and Rachael, his wife, to Benjamin Johnston of same county. £100. 40 a. in St. Geo. Par., Spts. Co. No witnesses. April 6, 1790.

Decr. 4, 1789. Robert Hill and Hannah, his wife, of St. Stephen's Par., King and Queen Co. to John Garlick of same Par. and same county. £5 curr. 413 a. in Berkeley Par., Spts. Co., etc. Thomas Minor, Jno. Woolfolk, Jno. Graves, Benj. Chapman, Wm. Croxton, Wm. Graves. April 6, 1790.

April 5, 1790. Jno. Woolfolk, Sr., of Spts. Co. and Elizabeth, his wife, to Jno. Woolfolk, jr., of same county. £100 curr. 125 a. in Spts. County, adjoining lands of Robt. Hill, Thomas Minor and Robt. Lewis, etc. No witnesses. April 6, 1790.

March 2, 1790. Thomas Colson of Spts. Co., Gent., and Frances, his wife, of first part; John Lewis of Fredksbg., Gent., and Mary, his wife, of second part; Dr. Elisha Hall of Fredksbg. of third part, to George Lewis of Spts. Co., Gent., of fourth part. Whereas, sd. Colson purchased 400 a. of John Steward, as by Indenture, July 1, 1788; he also purchased of Dr. Elisha Hall and Coriolana, his wife, and sd. Jno. Lewis, Lot No. 147 in town of Fredksbg. as by Indenture March 18, 1788; also purchased of the sd. Hall ½ a. lot in the sd. town, as by Indenture, March 28, 1789, the sd. Colson by this Indenture conveys the sd. above mentioned tracts to the sd. Geo. Lewis for the sum of £2500 curr.; the sd.

Hall and the sd. Lewis and wife, joining in the deed to make a full and complete relinquishment, etc., etc. Witnesses, O. Towles, F. Thornton, jr.; Wm. Glassell, Benja. Stubblefield, Walter Gregory, George Stubblefield, Charles Carter, jr.; Howell Lewis, Wm. Stanard, Larkin Chew. June 1, 1790.

March 9, 1790. Beverley Stubblefield of St. Geo. Par., Spts. Co., Gent., to David Sandidge of Berkeley Par., Spts. Co. £100 curr. 200 a. in Berkeley Par.; Spts. County, etc. Joseph Brock, jr.; Benj. Stubblefield, George Stubblefield. June 1, 1790.

May 4, 1790. Jno. Herndon of Spts. Co. [by virtue of a power of attorney to him from Abraham Simons and Mildred, his wife, late of Spots. Co.] to Larkin Stanard. £75 curr. 150 a. in Berkeley Par., Spts. Co., etc. Lewis Holloday, Joseph Holloday, Austin Sandidge, Thomas Magee. June 1, 1790.

Oct. 26, 1789. Sarah x Holloday to Joseph Holloday, jr. £40 curr. Two negroes. Mortgage. Jno. Scott, Austin Sandidge. June 1, 1790.

Decr. 12, 1789. Thomas Ball to Thomas Towles and Stockley Towles. Whereas, the sd. Towleses stand as securities on certain bonds, etc., the sd. Ball deeds them the following land, etc., to indemnify them, viz., 1 tract purchased of Edwd. Brasfield and Ann, his wife, as by Indenture dated Oct. 2, 1787, also 1 tract purchased of John Edwards and Nancey, his wife, as by Indenture dated Septr. 13, "in said year." Also several slaves, etc., also goods and chattels, etc. O. Towles, Wm. Duvall, Jno. Davenport. June 1st, 1790.

April 1, 1790. Alexander Spotswood of Spts. Co. to Edwd. Herndon, jr., of same county. Lease. 278 a. in St. Geo. Par., Spts. Co. "Sd. Edwd. Herndon, Elizabeth Herndon and George Herndon," etc. £3 5s curr. yearly. Chas. Urquhart, Wm. Richards, Richard Gaines. June 1, 1790.

April 1, 1790. Alexander Spotswood of Spts. Co. to Edwd. Herndon, jr., of same county. Lease. 325 a. in St. Geo. Par., Spts. Co. "Sd. Edwd. Herndon, Elizabeth Herndon and George Herndon," etc., 1077 lbs. tob. and 20s. specie, yearly. Wm. Richards, Chas. Urquhart, Richd. Gaines. June 1, 1790.

Nov. 2, 1789. Wm. Chewning and Jane, his wife, of Culpeper Co. to Thomas Sharpe of Spots. Co. £1000 curr. 100 a. in Berkeley Par., Spots. Co., etc. Thomas Allen, Fredk. Zimmerman, Absalem Bradley, Wm. Carter. June 2, 1790.

Octr. 31, 1789. Jno. Rawlings and Nancy, his wife, of Berkeley Par., Spots. Co., to Nathan Tally of Louisa Co. £65 curr. 200 a. in Berkeley Par., Spots. Co., formerly belonging to Benj. Holloday, decd., and assigned to the sd. Nancy, wife of sd. Jno. Rawlings, etc. Witnesses, Lewis Holloday, Beverley Winslow, Nicho. Payne. June 2, 1790.

Novr. 14, 1789. Richard Keowin and Elizabeth, his wife, of Spots. Co. to George Stubblefield of same co. £30. 100 a. in St. Geo. Par., Spots. Co., purchased from Nicho. Hawkins, jr., etc. Witnesses, Bevy. Stubblefield, Bevy. Stanard, T. F. Bayle, Bev. W. Stubblefield, Benj. Stubblefield. June 2, 1790.

May 22, 1789. "Jos. Brock, jr., of Spots. Co., but intending shortly to go to the State of South Carolina," po. of atto. to George Stubblefield of Spots. Co. to sell and convey 600 a. in Caroline Co., Va., etc. Witnesses, Wm. Fox, Jno. Herndon, jr.; Bev. W. Stubblefield, Wm. Herndon, etc. June 2, 1790.

June 1, 1790. Thomas Colson of Spots. Co. to James Wilson of same co. Lease. 337 a. in St. Geo. Par., Spots. Co., purchased of Jno. Taliaferro and Geo. Hensley, etc. "Sd. Jas. Wilson and Catherine, his wife," etc. £17 10s. specie, yearly. No witnesses. June 3, 1790.

Jany. 1, 1790. Nicholas Hawkins, Sr. Deed of gift to his son, Thos. Hawkins. 133 a. in Spots. Co. whereon sd. Nicho. Hawkins now lives, etc. Geo. Cammack, Henry Gatewood, Sr.; Richd. Todd. July 6, 1791.

Feby. 15, 1789. Jno. Baylor of Caroline Co., Esq., heir, devisee and surviving executor of his father, to Jno. Alcock. Sd. Baylor, heir, etc., having sold the within mentioned lands to Jno. Taylor, and given him his bond dated June 4, 1787, for the conveyance of same, and the sd. Taylor having disposed of same to the sd. Alcock, the sd. Baylor conveys the sd. two lots Nos. 2 and 5 in survey made by Winslow on occasion of Moore's Lottery, etc., containing 291 a. in Spots. Co., etc. Alexander Spotswood, Wm. Nelson, Edmund Pendleton, Jno. Minor, jr.; Abner Vernon. July 6, 1790.

March 2, 1790. Jos. Brock, only acting Execr. of Jno. Z. Lewis, decd., to Thomas Magee of Spots. Co. £61 16s. 61½ a., part of a larger tract in Spots. Co., etc. Richd. Lowry, W. Johnston, Jas. Weir. Wm. Frazer. Augt, 3, 1790.

Augt. 3, 1790. Thomas Colson of Spots. Co. to Richard Hulet of same co. Lease. 61 a. in St. Geo. Par., Spots. Co. "Sd. Richd. Hulet and Molly, his wife, and son Robinson," etc. £3 1s. etc. No witnesses. Augt. 3, 1790.

Augt. 3, 1790. Thomas Colson of Spots. Co. to Joseph Hulet of same co. Lease. 90 a. in St. Geo. Par., Spots. Co. "Sd. Jos. Hulet and Mary, his wife, and son Reubin," etc. £4 10s., etc. No witnesses. Augt. 3, 1790.

Augt. 3, 1790. Thomas Colson of Spots. Co. to Benjamin Hulet of Caroline Co. Lease. 110 a. in St. Geo. Par., Spots. Co. "Sd. Benj. Hulet and Ann, his wife, and son Wiatt," etc. £5 specie. No witnesses. Augt. 3, 1790.

Augt. 3, 1790. Thomas Colson of Spots. Co. to Williamson Jones of Caroline Co. Lease. 110 a. in St. Geo. Par., Spots. Co. "Sd. Williamson Jones and Sarah, his wife, and son Richard, etc. £5 10s., etc. No witnesses. Augt. 3, 1790.

Augt. 2, 1790. Jno. Dawson of City of Richmond to Thos. McKenny of Spots. Co. £280 curr. 323 a. in Berkeley Par., Spots. Co., part of a tract bought of Richd. Johnston by Mary Dawson, relict of Revd. Musgrove Dawson, etc. No witnesses. Augt. 3, 1790.

April 28, 1790. James Marye of Spots. Co. and Mildred, his wife, to Wm. Robinson of same co. £10 15s. 10¾ a. in St. Geo. Par., Spots. Co., etc. Jno. Levell, Jno. Mitcham, Henry Robinson, Jas. Lewis, Thomas Strachan. Augt. 3, 1790.

April 28, 1790. Wm. Robinson of Spots. Co. to James Marye of same co. £4. 4 a. in St. Geo. Par., Spots. Co., etc. Jno. Leavell, Jno. Mitcham, Henry Robinson. Augt. 3, 1790.

Augt. 3, 1790. Wm. Richards and Elizabeth, his wife, of Culpeper Co. to Joseph Jones of Spots. Co. £65 curr. 60 a. in Spots. Co. whereon Jno. Chishum lately lived, etc. No witnesses. Augt. 3, 1790.

Decr. 7, 1789. Oliver Towles of Spots. Co. to his daughter, Ann Towles. Deed of Gift. 550 a. in Spots. Co., also lands purchased by sd. Towles of Larkin Smith, etc.; also lands lying between the lands of Wm. Carter and the Tavern Houses, where Wm. Johnston keeps tavern, including the sd. Tavern, etc., etc. The sd. Ann Towles paying yearly unto the sd. Oliver Towles and Mary, his wife, during their lives, £15 curr., etc. Fanny Straughan, Eliza Towles, jr.; Mary Towles. Memorandum. On acc. of the recpt. of a complete and full sum the sd. Oliver Towles relinquishes forever the yearly sum of £15 for himself and heirs, etc. Augt. 3, 1790.

Dec. 7, 1789. Oliver Towles of Spots. Co. in consideration of sum of £216 14s. curr., pd. by his dau. Ann Towles, and in consideration of sd. Ann's releasing and giving up to sd. Oliver her right, title and interest in any slave or slaves by, from or under the will of her deceased grandfather, Larkin Chew (except a slave called Quashy), the sd. Oliver doth sell unto the sd. Ann, several slaves and goods and chattels, etc. Witnesses, Fanny Straughan, Eliza Towles, jr.; Mary Towles. Augt. 3, 1790.

March 2, 1790. Edward Carter and Sally, his wife, of Albemarle Co. to Charles Carter, jr., of Fredksbg. 5 shill. 430 a. in Spots. Co., etc. Geo. Stubblefield, Beverley Chew, Benj. Stubblefield. Augt. 3, 1790.

Decr. 14, 1789. John Knight of Stafford Co. and Winifred, his wife, to Ephraim Knight of Spots. Co. £60 curr. 79 a. in Spots. Co., etc. Zachariah Knight, Jas. Knight, Elizabeth Knight. Augt. 4, 1790.

Decr. 11, 1789. John Lewis and Mary, his wife, of Fredksbg. to Robert Brooke of Fredksbg. 5 shill. 317½ a. on Nassaponax, in St. Geo. Par., Spots. Co., purchased by sd. Jno. of his brother, Geo. Lewis, etc., part of two patents granted Jno. Quarles, Gent., decd., etc. Thomas Posey, Thomas Goodwin, Jas. Lewis. No date of record.

Augt. 24, 1790. Thomas Strachan, Gent., and Mary, his wife, of Spots. Co. of the first part; Mary Daingerfield, Executrix, and Oliver Towles one of the Executors of Wm. Daingerfield, Gent., Decd., and Thomas Walker, Gent., and Revd. Mathew Maury, Clerk, of the second part; Thomas Colson of Spots. Co., Gent., of the third part. Whereas, sd. Wm. Daingerfield, in his lifetime, with the sd. Walker and Maury, were securities for the sd. Strachan to the sd. Colson, in the sum of abt. £2000, including principal, interest, etc., and to indemnify the sd. Daingerfield, Walker and Maury, the sd Strachan did convey to them 237 a. whereon sd. Strachen now lives, also slaves, goods and chattels, for the purpose of meeting as far as possible the amnt. due the sd. Colson, the value of the sd. property is named at £535 10s.., etc. The sd. property is conveyed to the sd. Colson by the above named parties of the first and second parts and credited on the amnt. due by sd. Strachan to sd. Colson, etc., etc. Witnesses, Geo. Lewis, Beverley Stubblefield, Jno. Herndon, Benj. Alsop, Henry Pemberton, Wm. Stanard, Robt. Taylor. Novr. 3, 1790.

Augt. 7, 1790. Gerrard Blackstone Berryman and Josias Berryman of Spots. Co. to Wm. Fraser of same co. £260 curr. 300 a. in Spots. Co., whereon Willoughby N. Berryman now lives, and the same whereon Capt. Thomas Bartlett, late of this co., formerly lived, and conveyed by sd. Bartlett to the sd. Berrymans, as by deed of bargain, etc. A. Frazer, Hannah Frazer, Jno. Berryman, Jas. x Foreacres, Willoughby N. Berryman. Sept. 7, 1790.

Sept. 7, 1790. Larkin Stanard of Spots. Co. and wife Elizabeth, to James Mitcham of same co. £65 curr. 65 a. in Spots. Co., etc. Jos. Chew, Richd. Vass. Sept. 7, 1790.

Sept. 7, 1790. George Cunningham, with consent of Jno. Herndon, his guardian, apprentices himself to Richard Garner, Joiner and Carpenter, etc. No witnesses. Sept. 7, 1790.

Sept. 7, 1790. Charles McCalley apprentices himself to Richard Garner, Joiner and Carpenter, etc. No witnesses. Septr. 7, 1790.

Sept. 7, 1790. Thomas Colson of Spots. Co. to Wm. Keaton of same co. Lease. 100 a. in St. Geo. Par., Spots. Co. "Sd. Wm. Keaton and Mildred, his wife, and daughter Lucy." £5 specie, etc. No witnesses. Sept. 7, 1790.

Sept. 7, 1790. John Holladay and Martha, his wife, of Spotsylvania Co. to Robert Hart of same co. £100. 97½ a. in Berkeley Par., Spots. Co., part of the land lately belonging to the estate of Benj. Holladay, decd., and divided among his children, etc., etc. Witnesses, Lewis Holladay, Benj. Holladay, jr.; Wm. Fox, Wm. Holladay. Novr. 2, 1790.

Sept. 1, 1790. Joseph Holladay, Sr., of Berkeley Par., Spots. Co., to Benjamin Holladay, jr., of same par. and co. £30 curr. 84 a. in same Par. and co. Jno. Rawlins, Michael McDonald, Thomas Holladay, Wm. Holladay. Novr. 2, 1790.

Novr. 1, 1790. Ephriam Knight of Spots. Co. to his children, James Knight, Lewis Knight and Eliza Ann Knight of same co. Deed of Gift. To James Knight, 79 a. in Spots. Co., purchased of Jno. Knight; also cattle, goods and chattels, etc. To Lewis Knight, tract of land in same co., purchased of Abraham Darnall; also cattle, goods and chattels. To Eliza Ann Knight, stock, goods and chattels, etc. Witnesses, Zachariah Knight, Gibson Morris, Elijah Knight. Novr. 2, 1790.

May 14, 1790. Larkin Sandidge of Spots. Co., po. of atto. to his brother, Austin Sandidge, of same county, etc. Witnesses, Jas. Holladay, Jos. Holladay, David Bronaugh, Zachs. Sandidge, James Sandidge. Novr. 2, 1790.

April 7, 1788. Jno. Lewis and Mary, his wife, of Fredksbg., Spots. Co., to George Lewis of Frederick County. £440. 11 a. near town of Fredksbg. in Spots. Co., etc. Robt. Wellford, George French, Benja. Day, Philip Lipscomb. Novr. 2, 1790.

April 7, 1788. Jno. Lewis and Mary, his wife, of Fredksbg., Spots. Co., to George Lewis of Frederick Co. £40. 68 sq. poles in Spots. Co.

near Fredksbg., etc. George French, Robt. Wellford, Benj. Day, Philip Lipscomb. Novr. 2, 1790.

May 6, 1790. Richd. Lowry and Elizabeth, his wife, of Caroline Co. to James Pettus and Robert Sale. £165. 162 a. in St. Geo. Par., Spots. Co., etc. Edwd. Herndon, Bvy. Stubblefield, Geo. Burbridge, John Bond, Wm. Sale, jr. Novr. 2, 1790.

Oct. 16, 1790. Benjamin McWilliams and Letitia, his wife, of Charles City Co. to Danl. Tiller of St. Geo. Par., Spots. Co. £87 10s. curr. 146 a. in St. Geo. Par., Spots. Co., part of a tract conveyed by Wm. McWilliams to his son Broadbent McWilliams (both of Spots. Co.) during his life, and after his decease to his daughter Mary McWilliams, who dying without issue, the same descended to Wm. McWilliams, son of Wm. McWilliams, and by deed from him conveyed to Wm. McWilliams, son of Broadbent McWilliams, and by him conveyed to sd. Benja. McWilliams, and part thereof being part of tract given by Wm. McWilliams at his decease to his son Benj. McWilliams, etc., etc. Witnesses, Jas. Bullock, Jno. Bullock, Danl. Tiller, jr. Novr. 2, 1791.

Octr. 16, 1790. Benjamin McWilliams and Letitia, his wife, of Charles City Co. to Jno. Bullock of St. Geo. Par., Spots. Co. £123 curr. 205 a. in St. Geo. Par., Spots. Co., left by Wm. McWilliams, decd., to his son Benja. McWilliams, etc., etc. Witnesses, Jas. Bullock, Danl. Tiller, Sr.; Danl. Tiller, jr. Novr. 2, 1787.

—— ——, 1790. Benj. Johnston and Nancy, his wife, of Spots. Co. to Isaac Head of same co. In consideration of a tract of land whereon sd. Head now lives to the sd. Johnston, delivered, the sd. Johnston conveys to sd. Head, 147 a. in Spots. Co. Witness, Austin Sandadge. Novr. 2, 1790.

Jany. 4, 1790. Charles Beasley, Sr., and Susannah, his wife, of Spots. Co. to Chas. Beasley, jr., of same co. £50 curr. 165 a. in same co., etc., etc. David Partlow, Jno. P. Martin, Ann Clauton, Eliza Lollis. Novr. 3, 1790.

Nov. 2, 1790. Thomas Colson of Spots. Co. to James Pritchett of same co. Lease. 100 a. in Spots. Co., etc. "Sd. James Pritchett and Elizabeth, his wife, and James Pritchett, his son," etc., etc. 500 lbs. tob. yearly, etc. No witnesses. Novr. 3, 1790.

Novr. 6, 1788. An agreement in regard to a foreclosed mortgage agst. Jno. Wiglesworth in favor of Jos. Brock, Executor of Jno. Zachary Lewis, decd., to which Thomas Towles is a party, etc., etc. Witnesses, Edwd. Herndon, jr.; Jno. Brock, O. Towles. Novr. 3, 1790.

Novr. 3, 1790. Thomas Colson of Spots. Co. to Henry Goss of same co. Lease. 114 a. in St. Geo. Par., Spots. Co., etc. "Sd. Henry Goss and Elizabeth, his wife, and Joseph Goss, his son," etc., etc. £5 14s. specie. No witnesses. Novr. 3, 1790.

Novr. 3, 1790. Thomas Colson of Spots. Co. to James Ballard of same co. Lease. 104 a. in Spots. Co., etc. "Sd. Jas. Ballard and Isabella, his wife, and Sarah, his daughter," etc., etc. £5 specie. No witnesses. Novr. 3, 1790.

Decr. 7, 1790. Thomas Colson to George Shepperd. £75. 150 a. in Spots. Co., etc., etc. No witnesses. Decr. 7, 1790.

July 14, 1790. James Marye and Mildred, his wife, of Spots. Co. to Elizabeth Marye of same co. £408. 600 a. in St. Geo. Par., Spots. Co., whereon sd. Elizabeth now lives [abt. 220 a., part thereof assigned to the sd. Elizabeth for her dower in the tract of the endowment of her late husband, Revd. James Marye, Decd., etc., etc.] Witnesses, O. Towles, Wm. W. Henning, Wm. Robinson. Decr. 7, 1790.

Decr. 4, 1790. James Young and Edwd. Hyde to John Chandler. £30. 100 a. purchased of Thos. Brooks in Spots. Co., etc., etc. Wm. Fox, Tureman Lewis, Claibourn Chandler. Decr. 7, 1790.

Decr. 7, 1790. Thomas Colson of Spots. Co. to Wm. Spindle of same co. £112 curr. 112 a. in Spots. Co., etc. No witnesses. Decr. 7, 1790.

Decr. 7, 1790. Thomas Poole and Leah, his wife, of Spots. Co. to Jno. Greenhorn of same co. £22 curr. 100 a. in Spots. Co. No witnesses. Decr. 7, 1790.

July 5, 1790. Mary x Long of Spots. Co. to her two daughters, Martha Long and Aukey Long, of same co. Deed of Gift. Stock of Cattle, Hogs, Horses, etc., etc. Mentions "maintainance of my son Richard Long," etc., etc. Witnesses, Hugh Roy, Wm. Waller, M.D. Decr. 7, 1790.

Jany. 3, 1791. Skiller Harris and Frankey, his wife, of Albemarle Co. to Jno. Wiglesworth, jr., of Spots. Co. £120 curr. 100 a. in Spots. Co., etc., etc. Edwd. Hyde, Jas. Wiglesworth, Thos. Wiglesworth. Jany. 4, 1791.

Decr. 30, 1790. Larkin Smith of King and Queen Co. and Mary, his wife, to Larkin Stanard of Spots. Co. £120 curr. Lots. 151 and 152 in Town of Fredksbg., etc., etc. Robt. Brooke, Robt. B. Chew, Jno. McCaull, Jno. Chew. Jany. 4, 1791.

Feby. 1, 1791. James Mitcham of Spots. Co. to Ephriam Beasley of same co. £——. 40 a. purchased of Larkin Stanard in Spots. Co., etc., etc. No witnesses. Feby. 1, 1791.

Jany 17, 1791. Edward Carter of Fredksbg., Gent., to Chas. Carter, jr., and Francis Thornton, jr., Gentlm. Conveyance of several slaves in trust for the benefit of Jane Bradford, wife of Major Samuel K. Bradford, for and during her life and then for the benefit of her child or children, etc., etc. Witnesses, Jno. Chew, Beverley Chew. Feby. 1, 1791.

Jany. 7, 1791. Benj. Head of Spots. Co. to Edwd. Herndon of same co. £34 curr. 34 a., part of a tract purchased by sd. Benj. of his father, Alexr. Spence Head, in Spots. Co., etc., etc. No witnesses. Feby. 1, 1791.

Jany. 7, 1791. Edwd. Herndon of Spots. Co. to Benja. Head of same co. £23 10s. curr. 33 a., part of a tract purchased of Jos. Duerson in Spots. Co., etc., etc. No witnesses. Feby. 1, 1791.

Jany. 7, 1791. Lodowick Oneal of Spots. Co. to Lewis Proctor and Charles Procter, sons of Thomas Proctor and Susannah, his wife, of Spots. Co. For divers good reasons and also the sum of £100 curr. A slave each, etc., etc. In case of death of the sd. Lewis and Charles without heirs, then to Susannah Proctor, otherwise Sukey Proctor, wife of sd. Thomas Proctor, etc., etc. Witnesses, Wm. Proctor, Jno. McFarlin, Margaret McFarlin, Jean Proctor. Feby. 1, 1791.

March 1, 1791. Peter Rawlings and Ann, his wife, of Spots. Co. to Thomas Colson of same co. To secure the sd. Colson, to whom sd. Rawlings is justly indebted in the sum of £224 8s., the sd. Rawlings conveys to the sd. Colson, etc., tract of land purchased of Col. George Stubblefield, also several slaves, etc., etc. No witnesses. March 1, 1791.

Oct. 1, 1790. Geo. Stubblefield and Salley, his wife, of Spots. Co. to Samuel Alsop of same county. £250 curr. 203 a. in St. Geo. Par., Spots. Co., etc., etc. Jno. Wiglesworth; Peter Dudley, Robt. Crutchfield, Peter Rawlings, James Dudley. March 1, 1791.

Octr. 2, 1790. Thomas Brown of Spots. Co. to Wm. Brown of Caroline Co. £40 10s. 6d. Mortgage. 104 a. of land and crop of tobacco, etc., etc. O. Towles, Merideth Anderson, Jno. Long, O. Towles, jr.; Jno. Davenport, Isaac Head. March 1, 1791.

March 1, 1791. Moses x Wheeler of Spots. Co. to Jno. Mastin of same co. £50 curr. 150 a. in Berkeley Par., Spots. Co., etc., etc. No witnesses. March 1, 1791.

March 3, 1791. Thomas Colson of Spots. Co. to James Hutcherson of same co. £50. 100 a. in Spots. Co., and to secure the payment of the sd. £50, the sd. Hutcherson hereby mortgages to the sd. Colson the sd. land, also several slaves, goods and chattels, etc., etc. No witnesses. March 2, 1791.

Octr. 26, 1790. Wm. Ruffin and Margaret, his wife, of Spots. Co. to Daniel Stark of same Co. £200. 200 a. in Spots. Co., etc., etc. Thos. Colson, Wm. Stanard, Philip D. Redd, Jos. Bullock, James Starks. April 5, 1791.

Feby. 16, 1791. John x Overton of Spots. Co. to his son, Geo. Overton, of Orange Co. Deed of Gift. 150 a. in Spots. Co., etc., etc. Silvones Fisher, Robt. Humble, Jno. Overton. April 5, 1791.

April 5, 1791. Jno. Shirley, Sr., and Jno. Shirley, jr., and Frances, his wife, of Spots. Co. to James Wilson of same co. £45 curr. 60 a. adj. lands of Jas. Crawford, Waller Lewis, Jona. Clark, in Spots. Co., etc., etc. No witnesses. April 5, 1791.

April 1, 1791. Wm. Taliaferro (son of Walker Taliaferro, Decd.), of Caroline Co. and Elizabeth Hartwell, his wife, to Wm. Stanard of Spots. Co. £124 10s. curr. 166 a. in St. Geo. Par., Spots. Co., etc., etc. Geo. Buckner, Beverley Stanard, Larkin Chew. No date of record.

March 28, 1791. Alexander Spotswood and Elizabeth, his wife, of Spots. Co. to John Clayton of same co. £43 curr. 205 a. in St. Geo. Par., Spots. Co., etc., etc. Jas. Somerville, Jas. Lewis, Jno. Chew. April 5, 1791.

Jany. 26, 1791. Joseph Holladay of Spots. Co. and Agnes, his wife, to Robert Hart of same co. £120. 127 a., part of land lately belonging to Benj. Holladay, decd., and divided among his children . . . and allotted to the sd. Agnes, as her share of her father's land, etc., etc., in Spots. Co., etc., etc. Witnesses, Lewis Holladay, Benj. Holladay, H. C. Boggs. June 7, 1791.

Feby. 23, 1791. John Brock of Spots. Co. to indemnify Jos. Brock, conveys to him certain slaves, goods and chattels, etc., etc. Witnesses, Beverley Stubblefield, Jos. Brock. June 7, 1791.

Jany. 3, 1791. Joseph Rawlings of Spots. Co. to his brother, Benj. Rawlings of same co. £72. 196 a. on Pamunkey River, in Berkeley Par., Spots. Co., being an undivided moiety between the sd. Joseph and the sd. Benja. (who holds the other moiety under the will of his brother Thomas, unto whom it was devised by their father, James Rawlings) and devised the sd. Joseph by the will of his father, James Rawlings, Decd., etc., etc. Witnesses, Michael McDonald, Jas. Holladay, Wm. Tally, George Cason. June 7, 1791.

DEED BOOK N

1791–1794

July 5, 1791. Francis Meriwether and Mary, his wife, of Spots. Co. to George Tyler of Caroline Co. £900 curr. 814 a. in Spots. Co. No witnesses. July 5, 1791.

March 2, 1791. Edwd. Herndon, James Lewis and Thomas Strachan of Spots. Co., Gentlm., to Thomas Towles of same co. Whereas, by a decree in chancery obtained by Jos. Brock, execr. of Jno. Zachary Lewis, decd., against Thomas Towles, Executor of Robt. Lewis and Jno. Wiglesworth, it was decreed that sd. Herndon, Lewis and Strachan and Jno. Herndon and Wm. Stanard or any two commissioners named in sd. decree should sell a certain tract of land in occupation of sd. Wiglesworth, containing 784 a., for which the sd. Towles offered £573 4s. 1d., for which the sd. Herndon, Lewis and Strachan convey the sd. land to the sd. Towles. No witnesses. June 7, 1791.

March 2, 1791. Edward Herndon, James Lewis, Thos Strachan of Spots. Co. to Thomas Megee of same co. Under decree of court obtained by Jos. Brock, Exec. of Jno. Zachary Lewis, decd., against Thos. Towles, exec. of Robt. Lewis, and Jno. Wiglesworth, whereby it was decreed that sd. commissioners sell 50 a. belonging to sd. Wiglesworth, for which the sd. Megee offered £61 16s. curr., for which sum the sd. commissioners convey the sd. land to the sd. Megee, etc., etc. No witnesses. June 7, 1791.

June 6, 1791. Thomas James and Betty, his wife, of Fauqueir Co. to Michael Robinson of Spots. Co. £269 2s. curr. 207 a. left by Michael Robinson, Senr., to his daughter, the sd. Betty James, in Spots. Co., etc., etc. Jessee Haydon, Guy Bell, Saml. Hilldrup, Wm. Robinson, Thomas Montague. June 7, 1791.

Novr. 29, 1790. Nicholas Payne to Thos. Towles and Stockly Towles of Spots. Co. Whereas, sd. Payne stands indebted in a bond of £278 6s. 8d. to Sarah Jerdone, Executrix of Francis Jerdone, decd., with the sd. Towleses his securities, to indemnify the sd. Towleses, etc., the sd. Payne deeds them in trust 420 a. whereon he lives in Spots. Co., etc., etc. Witnesses, Wm. Trigg, Rice Vass, Thomas Spindle. June 7, 1791.

March 4, 1791. Wm. Welch of the State of Maryland and John Welch of Spots. Co., Va., to Thomas Towles of Spots. Co., Va. Whereas, the sd. Wm. Welch is indebted in a certain Sum, as by bond, to Abraham Van Bibber who assigned the same to the sd. Thomas Towles, on which sd. bond the sd. Jno. Welch stands as security, and whereas, the sd. Wm. and Jno. Welch being possessed of certain properties in the State of Virginia and being willing and anxious to secure the sd. debt to the sd. Towles, they, the sd. Welches, convey in trust to the sd. Towles the certain properties, etc., etc. Witnesses, Larkin Stanard, Stockly Towles, John Blaydes. June 7, 1791.

Novr. 3, 1790. Tureman Lewis and Mary, his wife, of first part; Thomas Henderson and Mary, his wife, of second part, to Stockley Towles of the third part. £150 curr. to the sd. Tureman Lewis in hand pd. the sd. Lewis conveys to the sd. Towles 253 a. whereon sd. Lewis formerly lived, and devised to him the sd. Lewis by Ignatius Tureman, Decd., etc., and the sd. Henderson for the sum of 50s. conveys to the sd. Towles a tract of land containing about 5 a. on s. side River Ta, etc., etc. Witnesses, Geo. Ball, Clement Borraighes, Jno. Pierce, Henry Gatewood, jr.; A. Frazer. June 7, 1791.

March 3, 1791. John Welch of Spots. Co., Va., to his son, Wm. Welch, of the state of Maryland. Whereas, Pearson Chapman, formerly of the Province of Maryland, Esqr., by Ind. dated May 9, 1768, did grant and farm lett unto Jno. Dalton and Elizabeth, his wife, and Walker Dalton, his son, ½ a. with houses, etc., in the town of Fredksbg., Va., and which has been in the occupation, etc., of Barbary Jones, widow, decd., and whereas, the sd. Dalton, by Ind. dated Oct. 9, 1779, did sell his right, title, etc., in the sd. lease to the sd. John Welch, and the sd. Welch in consideration of the sum of £600 assigns, hereby, the sd. lease to his son the sd. Wm. Welch, etc., etc. Subject to the original lease from sd. Chapman to sd. Dalton, etc., etc. Witnesses, A. Parker, W. Johnston, jr.; Geo. Cammack. June 7, 1791.

May 3, 1791. Wm. x. Moore and Elizabeth, his wife, to Thos. Gardner. £45 curr. 100 a. in Spots. Co., etc., etc. No witnesses. June 8, 1791.

April 19, 1791. John Welch and Nelly, his wife, of Spots. Co. to Thomas Colson of same co. £832 2s. 4d. 722 a. whereon sd. Welch resides, in Spots. Co., also several slaves, cattle, goods and chattels, etc., etc. Witnesses, Jno. W. Willis, O. Towles, Thomas Duerson. June 9, 1791.

Jany. 8, 1791. Wm. Henderson and Frances, his wife, of Spots. Co. to Wm. Duerson of same co. £20. 58 a. in Berkeley Par., Spots. Co., etc., etc. Rice Vass, Lend. Young, Thomas Spindle. July 5, 1791.

Jany. 26, 1791. John x Cammack and Ann, his wife, of Spots. Co. to John Long of same county. £30 curr. 140 a. whereon sd. Cammack lives, in Berkeley Par., Spots. Co., etc., etc. Jno. Davenport, Charles Burage, Jno. Ranes, Caty Burage. Augt. 2, 1791.

Feby. 10, 1791. Joseph Jones and Sarah, his wife, of Spots. Co. to James Pettigrew. £65 curr. 68 a. whereon Jno. Chisum lately lived, in Spots. Co., etc., etc. Edwd. Herndon, jr.; Jno. x Rose, Wm. Sale. Augt. 2, 1791.

Augt. 1, 1791. Jonathan Carpenter and Elizabeth, his wife, of Spots. Co. to Henry Duerson of same co. £155 curr. 162 a. in St. Geo. Par., Spots. Co., etc., etc. No witnesses. Augt. 2, 1791.

Jany. 12, 1791. Richd. Johnston of Spots. Co. to Moses Estes of same co. £11 1s. Mortgage. 1 negro slave, to indemnify sd. Estes who is security on a bond of sd. Johnston's to Wm. Stanard, etc., etc. Witnesses, Judith x Farish, Ann x Farish. Augt. 2, 1791.

Augt. 1, 1791. Thomas x Vaun [Vaughan] and Sarah, his wife, of Halifax Co. to Patrick Donally [Donnelly] of Spots. Co. Whereas, by Ind. dated Novr. 4, 1744, Bromfield Long conveyed to his son, Reubin Long, in fee simple, 118½ a. in Spots. Co., which sd. tract of land was afterwards conveyed by the sd. Broomfield Long to his daughters, Mary [the lower dividend] and Sarah [the upper dividend], now in consideration of the sum of £25 the sd. Thomas Vaun [who intermarried with the sd. Sarah, daughter of the sd. Broomfield Long] and Sarah, his wife, convey to the sd. Donally, the sd. tract of land in Spots. Co. afsd., given the sd. Sarah by her father, the sd. Broomfield Long, etc., etc. Witnesses, Jno. Frazer, Wm. Heslop, Reuben Straughan. Augt. 4, 1791.

March 25, 1791. James x Wilson and Fanny, his wife, to Martin Davenport of Spots. Co. £13 12s. 36¼ a. in Spots. Co., etc., etc. Edmund Clark, Jona. Clark, Elisha Dismukes, Thomas Turner. Septr. 6, 1791.

Septr. 6, 1791. Christopher Daniel and Mary, his wife, of Berkeley Par., Spots. Co. to Thomas Eves of par. and co. afsd. £12 curr. 119 a. purchased of Jno. Wildman and conveyed by Peter Rosell in Berkeley Par., Spots. Co., etc., etc. Wm. Eaves, Richd. Brightwell, Wm. x Eaves. Septr. 6, 1791.

Augt. 29, 1791. Zachariah Billingsley of Spots. Co. to Wm. Duval of same co. £150 curr. 200 a. purchased of Charles Pemberton in Spots. Co. No witnesses. Septr. 6, 1791.

Novr. 6, 1790. Agreement between Jane x Whitler, widow and relict of Jacob Whitler, late of Fredksbg., decd., and Edward Herndon and Wm. Herndon, who intermarried with Margaret and Isabella, daughters and co-heiresses of the sd. Jacob Whitler, who died intestate. The sd. Edwd. and Wm. Herndon allot to the sd. Jane Whitler, the blue house on Main street, lately occupied by Wm. Spooner, the yellow house where sd. Whitler last lived,. now used as a billiard room, and the kitchen adjoining, etc., on the lots of the sd. Whitler in Fredksbg., as the dower of sd. Jane in her late husband's estate, the sd. Jane accepting same and relinquishing all further claim whatsoever that she now hath or may hereafter have upon the sd. estate in any way, etc., etc. Witnesses, Wm. Carter, Thos. Duerson, Jno. Herndon, jr. Septr. 6, 1791.

Oct. 15, 1787. Larkine x Perry and Isbal, his wife, of Fayette Co. to James Jarrell of Spots. Co. £64 curr. 120 a. devised the sd. Perry by Nicho. Hawkins, jr., as will appear by deed dat. Augt. 15, 1782, in St. George Par., Spots. Co., etc., etc. Richd. Todd, Jno. Miller, Jno. x Daniel, Billey Gholson. Septr. 6, 1791.

March 3, 1791. Thomas Pritchett of Spots Co. to Wm. Waller, jr., of same co. £40 curr. 1 negro boy. Witnesses, Edwd. Herndon, jr.; John Herndon. Septr. 6, 1791.

March 4, 1791. Jessee Bowlin and Sarah, his wife, of Berkeley Par., Spots. Co. to Robert Scott of Par. and Co. afsd. £100. 139 a. in Par. and Co. afsd., etc., etc. Stockley Towles, James McDonald, Michael McDonald, jr.; Linefield Grady, John Pierce. Septr. 6, 1791.

May 10, 1791. John Shirley, jr., and Frances, his wife, of Spots. Co. to Jonathan Clark of same county. £22 10s. curr. 129 a. in Spots. Co., conveyed to sd. Jno. Shirley, jr., by his father, John Shirley, Senr., etc.,

etc. Witnesses, Thos. Turner, Edmund Clark, James Wilson, John Shirley, Senr.; Wm. Arnold. Sept. 6, 1791.

July 22, 1791. Wm. Arnold and Judith, his wife, of Spots. Co. to Jonathan Clark of same co. £55 10s. curr. 111 a. in Spots. Co., purchased of Joel Parrish, etc., etc. Witneses, Wm. x Arnold, Jno. Gwathmey, Edmd. Clark, John Shirley, jr.; Edwd. Herndon, jr.; John Dillard, Benj. Waller, Reuben Straughan, Thomas Davenport. Septr. 6, 1791.

Sept. 5, 1791. Anna Wyatt, Theophilus Wyatt, Roxana Wyatt and Elizabeth Wyatt of Spots. Co. to Edmund Clark of same co. £60. 50 a. called New Market [whereon they formerly lived] joining lands of Waller Lewis, Benj. Waller, Thomas Turner, James Crawford, Senr., in Spots. Co., etc., etc. Wm. Wiglesworth, John Shirley, jr.; Thomas Turner, Richd. Starke, Henry Dodd. Septr. 6, 1791.

Sept. 15, 1791. John Reed and Rachael, his wife, and Standish Forde of Philadelphia, Penna., to Wm. Lovell of Fredksbg., Va., Mercht. £750 curr. Lot 43 in town of Fredksbg., etc., etc. Elizabeth Glentworth, Clement Biddle, Chandl. Price. Novr. 1791.

Septr. 26, 1791. Austin Sandidge of Spots. Co. to Joseph Rawlings of same co. The sd. Austin Sandidge by virtue of po. of atto. given him by his brother, Larkin Sandidge, late of Spots. Co., dated May 14, 1790, conveys to sd. Rawlings for the sum of £110 curr., 150 a. in Berkeley Par., Spots. Co., etc., etc. Benja. Rawlings, David Bronaugh, Zachr. Sandidge, Wm. M. Estes. Novr. 1, 1791.

March 2, 1791. John Wiglesworth of Spots. Co. to Nathaniel Fox of Stafford Co. To indemnify sd. Fox who stands security for sd. Wiglesworth, etc., sd. Wiglesworth conveys to sd. Fox in trust, 200 a. purchased of Robt. Lewis, etc., in Spots. Co., etc., etc. Wm. Fox, Jos. Fox, Thomas Wiglesworth. Novr. 1, 1791.

Oct. 24, 1791. Richard Coleman of Berkeley Par., Spots. Co., to his son, Robt. Spilsby Coleman. Deed of Gift. 240 a. purchased of Danl. Lambert, adj. lands of Wm. Plunkett, John Corthorn, Robt. E. Coleman, Edwd. Collins, John Legg and Francis Coleman, in Berkeley Par., Spots. Co., etc., etc. Wm. Winslow, James Manning, Wm. Parker, jr. Novr. 1, 1791.

March 22, 1791. Robert Sale and Jenny, his wife, of Spots. Co. to Frances Jarvis, widow, of same county. £40. 128 a. in St. Geo. Par., Spots. Co., adj. lands of Alex. Spotswood, Mary Herndon, Wm. Bridges, Wm. Clayton, Henry Gatewood, jr., and purchased of Benj. Schooler, late of the sd. county, etc., etc. Witnesses, Wm. Vigar, Thos. Bridges, James Mason. Novr. 1, 1791.

Octr. 20, 1791. Thomas Lipscomb and Benjamin Waller, jr., of Spots. Co. to Granville Waller, son of sd. Benj. Waller and grandson of sd. Thomas Lipscomb. Deed of Gift. 2 negro girls, which sd. Lipscomb let his daughter Elizabeth Waller, decd., have, after she married the sd. Benja. Waller, jr., etc., etc. Witnesses, Elisha Dismukes, Jas. Wiglesworth, Jno. Waller, Thomas B. Waller. Novr. 1, 1791.

Octr. 24, 1791. Willis Hoard of Jefferson Co., Kentucky, to Beverley Stubblefield of Spots. Co., Va. £78 18s. curr. 313 a., part of which conveyed by the Executors of Jno. Battaley, decd., etc., by Ind. dated April

16, 1772, to Wm. Hoard, jr., and part sold by sheriff for Taxes, in Spots. Co., etc., etc. Wm. Waller, jr., Wm. Herndon, Adam Darby. March 6, 1792.

April 5, 1791. Wm. Davenport of Spots. Co. to Wm. Ashley of same county. £9 10s. curr. 9½ a., part of land on which lives James Davenport, son of the sd. Wm. Davenport, etc., in Spots. Co., etc., etc. John Minor, jr.; Wm. Winslow, Thomas Minor, John Parish, Lewis Partlow, Jno. Waller. Nov. 1, 1791.

July 2, 1791. John Washington of Spots. Co. to David Blair of Fredksbg. To secure the payment of certain sums due by sd. Washington to sd. Blair, the sd. Washington conveys to the sd. Blair several negroes, etc., etc. Witnesses, James Pettigrew, Wm. Sale, John Mullikin. Novr. 1, 1791.

Octr. 7, 1791. John Lewis of Spots. Co. to Robert Brooke of same county. To indemnify the sd. Brooke who stands bound as security for the sd. Lewis, etc., the sd. Lewis conveys to sd. Brooke, several negroes, etc., etc. Witnesses, B. Ball, John Robinson. Novr. 1, 1791.

Novr. 1, 1791. John Metcalfe binds himself to John Wright, etc., etc. No witnesses. Novr. 1, 1791.

July 7, 1791. Philip Lipscomb and Jane, his wife, of Fredksbg. to John Crutchfield of Spots. Co. To indemnify the sd. Crutchfield who stands bound as security for the sd. Lipscomb, etc., the sd. Lipscomb conveys to sd. Crutchfield Lot No. 81 in Fredksbg., etc., etc. Witnesses, Jno. Pilcher, Thomas Foster, Senr.; Jas. Frazer, Wm. Trigg, Wm. Duerson. Novr. 1, 1791.

Augt. 13, 1791. Joseph Jones of Spots. Co. to James Pettigrew of same co. £76. Mortgage. Tract of land leased by Gen. Alexander Spotswood to Henry Head, etc., etc. Witnesses, J. Brock, Edwd. Herndon, jr.; Robt. Branham. Novr. 1, 1791.

Augt. 18, 1791. Joseph Jones of Spots. Co. to James Pettigrew of same county. £150 curr. 4 negroes. Witnesses, J. Brock, Edwd. Herndon, jr.; Robert Branham. Novr. 1, 1791.

March 22, 1791. John Wiglesworth of Spots. Co. To indemnify Joseph Fox of same co., who stands bound as security for the sd. Wiglesworth to Neil McCoul, etc., the sd. Wiglesworth conveys to sd. Fox his household and kitchen furniture, several horses, cattle, etc., etc. Witnesses, Jno. Herndon, Geo. Cammack, Wm. Waller, jr. Novr. 1, 1791.

March 4, 1791. John Wiglesworth of Spots. Co. to Joseph Fox of same county. £170. Mortgage. Four negroes. Witnesses, Wm. Waller, jr.; Geo. Cammack, R. Frazer. Novr. 1, 1791.

Novr. 1, 1791. John Lewis of Spots. Co. to Thomas Colson of same co. To indemnify the sd. Colson [who with Col. George Stubblefield of Frederick Co.] stands bound as security for the sd. Lewis, the sd. Lewis conveys goods and chattles, horses, cattle, sheep, hogs and negroes, etc., etc. No witnesses. Novr. 1, 1791.

Novr. 2, 1791. John Wiglesworth and Philadelphia, his wife, of Spots. Co. to Charles Curtis of same co. Whereas, sd. Wiglesworth is possessed of a moiety of 16,000 a. in —— County, Kentucky, on Shelby's Creek, which is same land taken up in partnership with Richd. Young, etc., the sd. Wiglesworth, for the sum of £50, conveys 100 a. of the sd. moiety to the sd. Curtis, etc., etc. Witnesses, Thomas Montague, O. Towles, Wm. Robinson, Thomas Pritchett. Novr. 2, 1791.

Novr. 2, 1791. Charles Curtis and Susannah, his wife, of Spots. Co. to John Wiglesworth of same co. £50 curr. 112 a. in St. Geo. Par., Spots. Co., purchased of Richd. Stevens and Mary, his wife; Margaret Matthew and Lucy Carter, together, etc., etc. Witnesses, O. Towles, Wm. Robinson, Thomas Pritchett. Novr. 2, 1791.

Decr. 6, 1791. Sharp Smith and Agnes, his wife, of Spots. Co. to George Mason of Caroline Co. £70 curr. 150 a. purchased of Henry Terrell in Spots. Co., etc., etc. No witnesses. Decr. 6, 1791.

June 30, 1791. Alexander Parker of Spots. Co. to Larkin Stanard, Wm. Winslow and Jos. Chew of same co. Whereas, the sd. Parker by his po. of atto. authorized John Brownlow, late of Fredksbg., to sell and convey certain lands and tenements, property of him the sd. Parker, in the Kingdom of Gt. Britain, and whereas, the sd. Brownlow, having sold the same and recd. the monies therefor, etc., the sd. Parker doth direct the sd. Stanard, Winslow and Chew to receive the sd. monies from the sd. Brownlow and with them to satisfy the creditors of sd. Parker, and the sd. Trustees shall after the death of the sd. Parker, with the residue of the said sums of money, purchase in fee simple a tract or tracts of land, to be held in trust for the accommodation of the wife and children of the sd. Parker, etc., etc. Witnesses, Jos. Graham, John Buckner. Dec. 6, 1791.

June 30, 1791. Alexander Parker of Spots. Co., po. of atto. to Larkin Stanard of same co. Witnesses, Jos. Graham, Jno. C. Buckner. Decr. 6, 1791.

Septr. 22, 1791. Wm. Dawson of Westmoreland Co. to Saml. Sale and John Rawlings. Conveyance of 5 slaves, etc., etc. Witnesses, Benj. Rawlings, Austin Sandidge, Wm. Bronaugh, W. Dawson, jr. Decr. 6, 1791.

Jany. 24, 1791. Thomas Towles and Mary, his wife, of Spots. Co.. to John Shirley, jr., of same county. £145. 264 a. in Spots. Co., etc., etc. Witnesses, Nicho. Payne, Jas. Crawford, Jno. Coates, Benj. Waller, Thos. Shirley, Zachariah Billingsly. Decr. 6, 1791.

Jany. 3, 1792. Isaac Head and Rachel, his wife, of Spots. Co. to Lewis Johnson of same co. £30 curr. 147 a. adj. lands of Danl. Baulding, Jno. Smith and Alexander Johnson in Spots. Co., etc., etc. No witnesses. Jany. 3, 1792.

May 27, 1791. Joseph Fox and John Wiglesworth of Spots. Co. to Thomas Montgomerie of Dumfries, Prince Wm. Co. £38 3s. specie. Mortgage. 1 negro slave. Witnesses, John McCoull, James Johnston. Jany. 3, 1792.

Novr. 2, 1791. Edwd. x Ledwedge of Spots. Co. to Elizabeth Raines of same co. In consideration of sundry services heretofore rendered and hereafter to be rendered by sd. Elizabeth Raines and her husband, Isaac Raines, amting. to £60, the sd. Ledwedge doth hereby convey to sd. Eliza. Raines, 180½ a. in Spots. Co., also stocks of Hogs, cattle, horses, furniture, etc., etc. Witnesses, Wm. Ruffin, Jno. Duval, James Mills. Jany. 3, 1792.

Decr. 22, 1791. Thomas Fox of Spots. Co. and Delphia, his wife, and Wm. Fox, his son, to Stephen Johnson of same co. £187 10s. curr. 150 a. in Spots. Co., etc., etc. Thomas Strachan, Geo. Wm. Spooner, Jos. Brock. Jany. 3, 1792.

Jany. 2, 1792. Wm. Thompson and Sarah, his wife, of the first part; Wm. Fitzhugh, of the second part; Francis Thornton and Philip Rootes Thompson of the third part. Whereas, the sd. Wm. Thompson was indebted to the sd. Wm. Fitzhugh in the sum of £1910 19s. 1d., etc., and for securing the payment thereof did by Inds. dated May 4, 1789, and May 6, 1791, grant and convey to the sd. Fitzhugh, 240 a. in Spots. Co., a parcel of ground in Fredksbg. and a parcel near and adj. the sd. town, also numerous slaves, etc., and whereas, the sd. Thompson did pay the sd. Fitzhugh £500 on May 4, 1789, and on July 2, 1791, did release his right, etc., in and to sundry of the before conveyed slaves in consideration whereof the sd. Fitzhugh did grant an aquittance to the sd. Thompson for the sum of £529 10s. as a farther part of the sd. debt, which payments leave a bal. due of £1039 9s. 2d., etc., and whereas, the sd. Thompson and Fitzhugh to make a final settlement and it is the wish of the sd. Thompson that the residue of the lands and slaves as aforesd. conveyed, etc., if they should be found more than sufficient to pay the bal. due, should be applied to the discharge of a debt due his brother, Jno. Thompson of Culpeper, who stands bound as his security in several bonds, etc., and it is deemed expedient that the before mentioned lands and residue of the slaves, not heretofore made the absolute property of the sd. Fitzhugh, should be vested in the sd. Francis Thornton and Philip Rootes Thompson, as Trustees to sell and dispose thereof for the purposes aforesd. In witness whereof the sd. Wm. Thompson and Sarah, his wife, by this conveyance do make the same over accordingly, etc., etc. Witnesses, Fontaine Maury, Rt. Brooke, Mann Page, James Somerville, Robt. Mercer, R. Wellford, Jos. Brock, Clerk. Jany. 3, 1792.

Jany. 3, 1792. Edwd. Herndon, Lewis Holladay and Wm. Bronaugh, overseers of the poor in Dist. No. 2 in Spots. Co., do bind Zachariah Murphy, aged 16 yrs. Oct. 9 last, and Susanna Murphy, aged 14 yrs. June 7 last, orphans of John Murphy, Decd., to Stephen Smith Rice of Orange Co., Farmer and Planter, etc., etc. Witnesses, Stockley Towles, Jno. Herndon. Jany. 3, 1792.

Novr. 4, 1791. David Galloway and Margaret, his wife, of Frederick Co., Va., to Wm. Newton of Alexandria, Va., and Jno. Bronaugh of Fauquier Co., Va. £203 curr. 410 a. purchased of Aquilla Johnston, adj. lands of Gawin Corbin, Esq., and Richd. Todd in Spots. Co., to the sd. Newton and Bronaugh in trust to sell the same to satisfy a debt due by sd. Galloway to Williams, Cary & Co., Merchts., of Alexandria, etc., etc. Witnesses, James Gibbs, Edwd. Christian, Bushrod Taylor. Jany. 3, 1792.

Jany. 30, 1792. Alexander Spotswood, Senr., and Elizabeth, his wife, of St. Geo. Par., Spots. Co., to Edwd. Herndon, son of Joseph, of the Par. and County afsd. £135 curr. 445½ a. in Par. and Co. afsd., etc., etc.

Jas. Lewis, Edwd. Herndon, jr.; Benja. Lewis, Hezekiah Ellis, Jno. M. Herndon. Feby. 7, 1792.

Augt. 29, 1791. Alexander Spotswood and Elizabeth, his wife, of Spots. Co. to John Shelton of same co. £64 curr. 146 a. in Spots. Co., etc., etc. Edwd. Herndon, Benja. Lewis, Jas. Lewis, Edwd. Herndon, jr. Feby. 7, 1792.

Jany. 27, 1792. Thomas Coleman of Caroline Co. to his son, Thomas Coleman, of Spots. Co. Deed of Gift. 1000 a. whereon Thos. Coleman, the elder, formerly lived, in Spots. Co., also a smaller tract in Spots. Co., etc., etc. Saml. Coleman, Farish Coleman, Wm. Chandler, Jas. Coleman, Nathan Winston. Feby. 7, 1792.

Octr. 29, 1791. Joseph Rawlings to David Sandidge. £49 9s. 4d. Mortgage. 150 a. adj. lands of Jos. Eubauk, Wm. Estis, Hyde and Young and David Sandidge, in Berkeley Par., Spots. Co., etc., etc. Zachariah Sandidge, Winifred Sandidge, Elizabeth Sandidge, Edwd. Herndon, Jos. Holladay, jr.; Jno. Rawlings. Feby. 14, 1792.

Octr. 4, 1791. Edward Herndon of Spots. Co. to Ann Grayham Heslop. £42 specie. 1 negro woman. No witnesses. Feby. 7, 1792.

Jany. 13, 1792. Wm. Mills and Peggy, his wife, of Berkeley Par., Spots. Co. to Wm. Winslow of same par. and co. £500 curr. 350 a. in Berkeley Par., Spots. Co., whereon sd. Mills now lives; also a tract purchased of Wm. Dawson, etc., as by Ind. dated Decr. 11, 1784, containing 150 a. in same par. and co., etc., etc. Bevy. Winslow, Jas. Powell, Thomas Winslow. March 6, 1792.

Jany. 13, 1792. Wm. Winslow and Peggy, his wife, of Berkeley Par., Spots. Co., to Benjamin Robinson of same par. and co. £175 curr. 150 a, purchased of Wm. Mills, etc., in Par. and Co. afsd., etc., etc. Bevy. Winslow, Thomas Winslow, James Powell. March 6, 1792.

Jany. 13, 1792. Benjamin Robinson and Catherine, his wife, of Berkeley Par., Spots. Co., to Beverley Winslow of Par. and Co. afsd. £9 15s. curr. 6½ a. in Par. and Co. afsd., etc., etc. Thos Winslow, Jas. Powell, Wm. Winslow. March 6, 1792.

Jany. 13, 1792. Beverley Winslow of Berkeley Par., Spots. Co., to Benjamin Robinson of Par. and Co. afsd. £3 curr. 2 a. in Berkeley Par., Spots. Co., etc., etc. Thomas Winslow, Wm. Winslow, James Powell. March 6, 1792.

Jany. 13, 1792. Benjamin Robinson of Spots. Co. to James Powell of same co. To indemnify the sd. Powell who stands bound as security for the sd. Robinson, the sd. Robinson conveys the sd. Powell 150 a. in Spots. Co., together with 3 negroes, etc., etc. Witnesses, Wm. Winslow, Thomas Winslow, Bevy. Winslow. March 6, 1792.

Jany. 9, 1792. Rowland Thomas of Spots. Co. to Benjamin Winslow of Orange Co. £87 16s. curr. Slaves. Witnesses, Thomas Winslow, Wm. Winslow. March 6, 1792.

Novr. 4, 1791. Wm. Ruffin and Margaret, his wife, of Spots. Co. to James Somerville of Fredksbg., Mercht. £135 18s. 9d. curr. 181¼ a., part of a tract purchased of Alexander Spotswood in Spots Co., etc.,

etc. Wm. Waller, jr.; Daniel Grinnan, jr.; Thomas Simpson. March 6, 1792.

Decr. 12, 1788. John Lewis and Mary Ann, his wife, of Fredksbg. to Wm. Thompson of Spots. Co. £30 curr. Tract of land near town of Fredksbg., etc., etc. B. Ball, Chas. Carter, jr.; Fras. Thornton. March 6, 1792.

Feby. 5, 1791. Wm. Thompson and Sally, his wife, of Spots. Co. to Samuel K. Bradford of same co. £1000 specie. 100 a. called "Shere-wood," also 52½ a. in Spots. Co., etc., etc. Jos. Channon, James Starke, Jas. Clarke, Fontaine Maury, Elisha Hall, Thos. Strachan, J. Christy, Jas. Somerville, Chas. Croughton, Richd. S. Hackley, John Campbell. March 6, 1792.

July 18, 1791. Wm. Thompson and Sarah, his wife, of Spots. Co. to Charles Croughton of Fredksbg. £40 curr. 40 a. in Spots. Co., etc., etc. Charles Vowles, Jno. Campbell, Jas. Owens, Zeph. Turner, Archibald Ritchie, John Corbet, James Heath. March 6, 1792. Also conveyance of goods and chattels by sd. Thompson to sd. Croughton for the sum of £40, dated July 15, 1791, etc., etc. Same witnesses. Recd. March 6, 1792.

Octr. 21, 1791. John Arnold and Barbara, his wife, of Spots. Co. to James Arnold of same co. £40 curr. 400 a. in Spots. Co., etc., etc. Jno. Waller, Joel Trigg, Jona. Clark, John Wiglesworth, jr.; Wm. Buchanan. March 6, 1792.

March 6, 1792. Pursuant to the last will and testament of Thomas Burbridge, Decd., etc., Thomas Burbridge, Benjamin Robinson and Mildred, his wife; Henry Elley and Sarah, his wife; Tavener Branham and Elizabeth, his wife; Robt. Smith and Frances, his wife; Linsfield Burbridge and Nancy, his wife; Wm. Bullett [or Bullit] and Mary, his wife, and George Burbridge and Mary, his wife, to James Lewis of Spots. Co. £230. 200 a. whereon sd. Thos. Burbridge lived, adj. lands of James Lewis, Alexander Spotswood and others, etc., purchased of Wm. Fitzhugh, Esq., as by Ind. dated April 10, 1770, in Spots. Co., etc., etc. Witnesses, Richd. Jones, Frans. Simpson, Mathew Bridges, Richd. Branham. March 6, 1792.

March 8, 1792. Pursuant to the last will and testament of Thomas Burbridge, Decd., etc., Thomas Burbridge and others [same parties as of the first part in preceding deed] to Harmon Hanor, jr., of Spots. Co. £68. 100 a. adj. lands of Harmon Hanor, jr.; Jas. Lewis, Hezekiah Ellis, Alexander Spotswood, and is part of tract purchased of Wm. Fitzhugh, Esq., as by Ind. dated April 10, 1770, in Spots. Co., etc., etc. Witnesses, Thos. Strachan, Edwd. Herndon, Nicho. Payne, A. Frazer, Thos. Waller, Jos. Brock, Bevy. Stubblefield, Jas. Lewis, Danl. Branham, Jos. Jones, Jno. Mullikin, Richd. Jones, Francis Simpson, Mathew Bridges, Richd. Branham. March 8, 1792.

March 17, 1792. Mary Brock, widow and relict of Wm. Brock, decd.; Joseph Brock and Elizabeth, his wife, and Wm. Orril Brock of Berkeley Par., Spots. Co., to Thomas Duerson of same par. and county. £45 3s. curr. 83 a. in Berkeley Par., Spots. Co., etc., etc. Thomas Towles, Stockly Towles, Nicho. Payne, Edwd. Herndon, James Herndon. April 3, 1792.

March 17, 1792. Mary Brock, widow and relict of Wm. Brock, Decd.; Joseph Brock and Elizabeth, his wife, and Wm. Orril Brock of Berkeley Par., Spots. Co., to Joseph Duerson, jr., of same par. and co. £84 17s. curr. 156 a. in par. and co. afsd., etc., etc.

Feby. 3, 1792. Benjamin Robinson of Spots. Co. to Joseph Brock. £42 8s. 11d., etc. Mortgage. 4 negroes. Witness, Robt. Carter. April 3, 1792.

March 22, 1792. Wm. Pettus, Senr., and Susanna, his wife, and Wm. Pettus, jr., and Lucy Waters, his wife, of Spots. Co. to Larkin Reynolds of same co. £89. 119 a. in Spots. Co., etc., etc. Jos. Graves, Peter Arnold, Jos. Pettus, Saml. C. Pettus. April 3, 1792.

Septr. 30, 1791. Wm. Smith of Fredksbg. to Thomas Cochran of same town. £5 4s. 9d. 1 negro. Witnesses, Wm. Berry, Tully Whithurst. April 3, 1792.

Octr. 24, 1791. Clement x Montague of St. Geo. Par., Spots. Co., to James Ballard of same par. and co. 5s. Two negroes. Witnesses, Jno. Waller, Charles Carter, Ann x Carter. April 3, 1792.

Octr. 7, 1791. John Lewis of Spots. Co. to George Lewis of same co. To indemnify the sd. Geo. Lewis who stands bound as security for the sd. John Lewis, the sd. John conveys to him in trust, eight negroes, etc., etc. Witnesses, Robt. Mercer, Peter Garts. April 3, 1792.

Septr. 14, 1791. Wm. Glassell of Fredksbg. to John Minor, jr., of same town. The sd. Wm. Glassell by virtue of a po. of atto. from "John Glassell, Esq., late of Fredksburg., Va., but then of Co. Haddington in that part of Gt. Britain called Scotland," dated July 19, 1788, in consideration of £460, conveys to the sd. Jno. Minor, jr., a tract of land on Hazel Run in Spots. Co., containing 28 1-9 a. and 1200 sq. yds., etc., etc. Witnesses, Wm. Lewis, Richd. H. Young, Chas. Mortimer, Wm. Smock, Benja. Day, Alexander Roane. April 3, 1792.

June 1, 1792. Michael Blunt of Spots. Co. and Eliza., his wife, to Jonathan Johnston of same co. £100 curr. 112 a., residue of tract whereon sd. Blunt lives in Spots. Co., etc., etc. Benj. Tompkins, Alexr. Johnston, Jas. Arnold. June 5, 1792.

June 5, 1792. Steven White of Spots. Co., age 17 yrs. 6 mo., apprentices himself to John Whitlock of Caroline Co., Carpenter, etc., etc. No witnesses. June 5, 1792.

April 13, 1792. Nicholas Payne of Spots. Co., Gent., and Thomas Towles and Stockley Towles of Spots. Co., Gent., to Asariah King of Orange Co. Whereas, the sd. Payne, by Ind. dated Novr. 29, 1790, conveyed to the sd. Towleses, in trust, to indemnify them for securityship in a bond of the sd. Payne, a tract of 323 a. purchased by sd. Payne of the Executors of Jno. Z. Lewis, decd., in Spots. Co., and whereas, the sd. Towleses have pd. on the sd. bond the amnt. of £168 11s. 1d., etc., the sd. Payne, in order to repay the sd. Towlesses this advance, conveys to the sd. King the afsd. tract of land for the sum of £173 6s. curr., etc., etc. Witnesses, Zachariah Billingsley, John A. Billingsley, James King. June 5, 1792.

Decr. 2, 1791. John Rose, surviving executor of Robert Rose, Clerk, Deed. [will dated June, 1751], to Robert Brooke of Spots. Co. In con-

sideration of a bond for £125 curr. executed by sd. Brooke in favor of
sd. Jno. Rose, the sd. Jno. Rose conveys to sd. Brooke Lots 3, 3, 3 and
4, 4, 4, in that part of Fredksbg. known as Allen Town, and purchased
by the sd. Robt. Rose of Jno. Allen, etc., etc. Witnesses, Robt. Mercer,
F. Thornton, R. W. Peacock. June 6, 1792.

Jany. 3, 1792. Edwd. Herndon, Lewis Holladay and Wm. Bronaugh,
overseers of the poor in Dist. No. 2, Spots. Co., bind Garner Burge
(orphan of Leonard Burge, Decd.) aged 8 yrs. March 20th last, to Charles
Bennet of same co., Blacksmith, etc., etc. Witnesses, Thomas Towles,
Stockley Towles, June 6, 1792. Also by Ind. dated same day, the over-
seers bind Wm. Burge (orphan of Leonard Burge, decd.) aged 6 yrs.
Novr. 20th last, to John Steward of Spots. Co., etc., etc. Same witnesses.
Recd. June 6, 1792.

May 8, 1792. Alexander Spotswood and Elizabeth, his wife, to Han-
nah Montague. £77 10s. 310 a. in Spots. Co., etc., etc. Thomas Towles,
Edwd. Herndon, jr.; Danl. Grinnan, jr.; Jas. Lewis, Edwd. Herndon.
June 7, 1792.

May 8, 1792. Alexander Spotswood and Elizabeth, his wife, to Edwd.
Elley of Culpeper Co. £34 4s. 114 a. in Spots. Co., etc., etc. Same witnesses as previous deed. June 7, 1792.

May 8, 1792. Alexander Spotswood and Elizabeth, his wife, to John
Hord of Culpeper Co. £73 10s. curr. 210 a. in Spots. Co., etc., etc. Same
nesses as previous deed. June 7, 1792.

May 8, 1792. Alexander Spotswood and Elizabeth, his wife, to Richd.
Bullard of Spots. Co. £43 1s. 123 a. in Spots. Co., etc., etc. Same witnesses as previous deed. June 8, 1792.

March 25, 1791. Edmund Winder and Jane, his wife, of Fredksbg.
to Walter Young of Spots. Co. £130 curr. 158 a. known as Chalkey
Leavell, purchased by David Simons of Jno. Benson and Eleanor, his
wife, and John Welch and Eleanor, his wife, in Spots. Co., etc., etc. Jas.
Weir, Wm. Wiatt, Jas. Ross. June 7, 1792.

April 1, 1792. John Woolfolk, Senr., of Spots. Co. to his son, Elijah
Woolfolk. Deed of Gift. 125 a., part of tract sd. John lives on in Spots.
Co., etc., etc. No witnesses. July 3, 1792.

July 3, 1792. Thomas True and Mary, his wife, of Spots. Co. to Joshua
Long of same co. £46 curr. 130 a. in Berkeley Par., Spots. Co., etc., etc.
April 1, 1794.

June 29, 1792. John Chew of Fredksbg. to Edwd. Herndon, jr., of
Spots. Co. Whereas, Robt. Beverley Chew (now decd.) in his lifetime
did sell to the sd. Herndon for £41 5s. in hand paid, 33 a. in St. Geo.
Par., Spots. Co., but before any conveyance was thereof made the sd.
R. B. Chew departed this life, and by his last will and testament devised
all the residue [after several bequests] of his estate to his brother, the
sd. Jno. Chew, and thus the legal title being vested in him the sd. Jno.
Chew, he in consideration of the premises, etc., conveys the same to the
sd. Herndon, etc., etc. No witnesses. July 3, 1792.

June 2, 1792. Alexander Spotswood and Elizabeth, his wife, of "Not-
tingham," in Spots. Co., to Benjamin Wilcher [or Welcher] of same co.

£16 17s. 6d. 33¾ a. in Spots. Co., etc., etc. J. Posey, Chas. Carter, jr.; Edwd. Herndon, Fontaine Maury. July 3, 1792.

July 3, 1792. James Stevens and Mary Bird, his wife, of Spots. Co. to Robert Hart of same co. £38. 90 a. purchased of Dr. Thomas Powell in Berkeley Par., Spots. Co., etc., etc. Thos. Davenport, Jno. W. Buckner, Phil. B. Johnston. July 3, 1792.

July 2, 1792. Richard C. Noel and Mary, his wife, of Essex Co., of first part; Sarah Crutchfield, widow and relict of Stapleton Crutchfield, decd., of Spots. Co., of second part, and John and Stapleton Crutchfield of Spots. Co., of the third part. Whereas, Stapleton Crutchfield, decd., did by his last will and testament give to the sd. Mary Noel, his daughter, a slave and 1-5 part of all the estate and property that he lent to his sd. wife Sarah [party hereto] during her natural life, and whereas, sd. Richard Noel is seized of a tract of 250 a. in Essex Co., conveyed to him by his father, Rice Noel, and the sd. Richd. Noel being also possessed of a negro woman and her child, also a negro man, and the sd. Sarah Crutchfield being possessed of a negro woman, and the sd. Richd. Noel and Mary, his wife, and the sd. Sarah Crutchfield being desirous of making a reasonable and proper settlement of all the estate hereinbefore recited and so as to make provision as well for the children begotten as those that may be begotten between the sd. Noel and Mary, his wife, etc., etc., this Ind. witnesseth the sd. Noel and Mary, his wife, in consideration of £10 to them pd. by the sd. John and Stapleton Crutchfield afsd. and the sd. Sarah Crutchfield relinquishing the sd. female slave and her child, the sd. Noel and Mary, his wife, do grant unto the sd. Jno. and Stapleton Crutchfield, afsd., 250 a. in Essex Co., and also all right, title, etc., of the sd. Mary in or to any part of the Est. of her father, Stapleton Crutchfield, Decd., also 2 slaves in trust for the use of the sd. Mary Noel during her life, and after her death for the benefit of all the children of the sd. Mary by her sd. husband, Richd. Noel, etc., etc. "Sd. Sarah Crutchfield, mother of the sd. Mary Noel," etc., etc., relinquishes her right to the aforementioned 2 slaves, etc., etc. Witnesses, O. Towles, Jno. Pilcher, Jno. Frazer, Wm. Wilson, Lewis Young, Wm. Heslop, Thos. Foster, jr.; Ann Trigg. Augt. 7, 1792.

Decr. 31, 1791. Rice Vass of Spots. Co. to Thomas Coleman. To indemnify the sd. Coleman who stands bound as security for the sd. Vass, the sd. Vass conveys to him all of his stock, goods and chattels, etc., etc. Witnesses, Spilsbe Coleman, John Davenport, Farish Coleman. Augt. 7, 1792.

June 23, 1792. Peter Rawlings and Ann, his wife, of Spots. Co. to Samuel Alsop of same co. £20 1s. 3d. curr. 20 1-16 a. in Spots. Co., etc., etc. Peter Dudley, Benj. Alsop, Saml. Alsop. Augt. 7, 1792.

Jany. 5, 1792. Wm. Newton of Fairfax Co., and John Bronaugh of Fauqueir to Wm. Henry Washington of Fairfax Co. £246. 410 a. in Spots. Co., adj. lands of Gawin Corbin, Esq., and Richd. Todd, "which sd. tract of land the sd. Newton and Bronaugh have a po. of atto. to sell to discharge a debt due Wm. Carr & Co. (from David Galloway), etc., etc. Witnesses, Jno. Chew, Beverley Chew, W. S. Stone, Chas. Whiting, Wm. W. Hening, Alexander Roane. Augt. 7, 1792.

Decr. 12, 1791. Henry Goodloe, jr., of Spots. Co. to George Goodloe of Culpeper Co. £108 curr. 225 a. in Spots. Co., etc., etc. Hugh Roy, Bartlett Russell, Ambrose Holland. Novr. 6, 1792.

Decr. 27, 1791. Joseph Pulliam and Elizabeth, his wife, of Spots. Co. to Moses Wheeler of same co. £56 10s. curr. 113 a. in Berkeley Par., Spots. Co., etc., etc. John Mastin, Reuben Massey, Molley Massey. Augt. 7, 1792.

June 1, 1792. Rowland Thomas of Spots. Co. to Larkin Stanard of same co. £32 10s. Mortgage. Slaves. Witnesses, Will Winslow, Benj. Robinson, Martin Hawkins. Augt. 7, 1792.

March 16, 1792. Alexander Spotswood and Elizabeth, his wife, of Spots. Co. to Edward Herndon, jr., of same co. £150 curr. 570 a. in Spots. Co., etc., etc. Wm. Herndon, James Pottinger, Alex. E. Spotswood. Augt. 8, 1792.

Feby. 4, 1792. Wm. Fox of Spots. Co. to Wm. Bronaugh of same co. To indemnify sd. Bronaugh, etc. Two slaves. Witnesses, Austin Sandidge, Wm. Bronaugh, jr. Septr. 4, 1792.

June 13, 1792. Thomas Burbridge, Benjamin Robinson, Henry Ealey [Elley] and Tavenor Branham, all of the State of Kentucky, po. of atto. to friends Robert Smith, Linsfield Burbridge and Geo. Burbridge, to sell a tract of land in Spots. Co., Va., part of which is claimed by the parties of the first part as Legatees of Thos. Burbridge, decd., etc., etc. Witnesses, Mathew Bridges, Richd. Branham, Wm. Parker. Septr. 4, 1792.

Augt. 9, 1790. John Garlick and Ann, his wife, of St. Stephen's Par., King and Queen Co., to Sharpe Smith of St. Mary's Par.,* Spots. Co. £188 5s. curr. 125½ a. adj. lands of Wm. Blaydes, decd.; Wm. Pettus, Senr.; Larkin Reynolds and sd. Garlick in St. Mary's Par., Spots. Co., etc., etc. Saml. Hill, Wm. Cason, jr.; Humphrey Hill. Septr. 4, 1792.

April 19, 1792. Robert Hill and Hannah, his wife, of King and Queen Co., St. Stephen's Par., to Samuel Hill of same co. and Par. £500 curr. 515 a. in *St. Mary's Par., Spots. Co., etc., etc. Jno. Woolfolk, jr.; Wm. Cason, jr.; Sharp Smith, Wm. Cason. Septr. 4, 1792.

Septr. 4, 1792. Edwd. Herndon and Joseph Brock, acting executors of the last will and testament of Wm. Carr, Decd., late of Spots. Co., Va., po. of atto. to Walter Chiles of Spots. Co. to receive of Walter Chiles Carr of Fayette Co., Ky., etc., certain slaves, descendants of a Mulatto girl lent to Susanna, the wife of afsd. Wm. Carr, decd., by his will (during her natural life) which sd. Susannah is lately dead, etc., etc. No witnesses. Septr. 4, 1792.

Jany. 5, 1788. John Brock releases and relinquishes all right, title, etc., loaned him by his father, Joseph Brock, in Novr., 1784, etc., etc. Witnesses, Benj. Robinson, John Curtis, Joseph Brock, jr. Septr. 4, 1792.

Octr. 4, 1791. Joseph Pulliam and Elizabeth, his wife, of Spots. Co. to John Turnley of Orange Co. [assignee of Wm. Duvall of Spots. Co.]

* Ed. Note.—This is an error, there being no St. Mary's Parish in Spots. Co. It is probably intended for St. George's Parish.

£40 16s. curr. 136 a. in Berkeley Par., Spots. Co., etc., etc. Jno. Herndon, Nicho. Payne, Austin Sandidge. Septr. 4, 1792.

June 4, 1791. Oliver Towles, the elder, of Spots. Co., Attorney at Law, to Oliver Towles, jr. [his son], of the same co. Whereas, the sd. Towles, the Elder, by Ind. recd. in Spots. Co., Mar. 2, 1790, conveyed to Archibald Dick of Louisa Co., Mercht., and the sd. Oliver Towles, jr., all the sd. Oliver Towles, the Elder's, lands, etc., by warrant or surveys lying on the western waters commonly called Kentucky, supposed to contain upwards of 7000 a., and it was the whole military bounty lands that he was entitled to, etc., also all the sd. Oliver Towles, the Elder's, commutation, pay and wages that are any way in arrear and unpaid the sd. Towles, the Elder, as an officer in the late Continental Army, also all debts due the sd. Towles, the Elder, in trust for saving harmless and indemnifying sundry persons, securities for the sd. Towles, the Elder, and whereas, by Ind. dated Decr. 7, 1789, recd. March 2, 1790, the sd. Towles, the Elder, conveyed to the sd. Dick and Towles, the younger, sundry tracts of land and slaves therein described, in trust, in case the first conveyance was not sufficient for the purposes mentioned to be applied to complete the necessary amnt., and also to reimburse and repay the sd. Dick and Towles, jr., the sum of £750 pd. and advanced by them for the sd. Towles, the Elder, etc., etc., etc. Now this Ind. witnesseth, the sd. Oliver Towles, the Elder, in consideration of the sum of £1052 curr. [£750 of which to be applied toward paying sd. Dick and Towles, jr., the residue towards paying as in the first Ind. recited, etc.], in hand pd. by the sd. Oliver Towles, jr., the above mentioned [1440 a.] land in Spots. Co., also slaves, goods and chattels, etc., etc. [436 a., part of a patent granted Harry Beverley, Gent., Decd., grandfather to the sd. Mary, wife of the sd. Oliver Towles, the Elder, etc., etc.] Witnesses, Thomas Montague, Gabriel x Long, James Richards, Elizabeth Richards. Septr. 4, 1792.

—— ——, 1792. Wm. Frazer, Gent., and Philadelphia, his wife, of Beverley Par., Spots. Co., to Robert Scott of same par. and co., Gent. £57 curr. 57 a. in afsd. Par. and Co., etc., etc. Witness, John Crutcher. Septr. 4, 1792.

Novr. 3, 1792. Thomas Colson of Spots. Co. to Thomas Mastin. £114 curr. 114 a. in St. Geo. Par., Spots. Co., etc., etc. Wm. Keaton, Joseph Bullock, Fanny Straughan. Novr. 6, 1792.

July 13, 1792. John Woolfolk, Senr., and Sarah, his wife, of Spots. Co. to John Partlow. Deed of Gift. 40 a. adj. lands of Lewis Partlow, Widow Waller, Jonathan Clark and Martin Davenport in Spots. Co., and which is the land Jno. Partlow, Senr., decd., bequeathed by his last will and testament to his son the sd. John Partlow, reserving to his widow, Sarah Partlow, now wife of the sd. Jno. Woolfolk, Sr., use of the sd. land during her natural life, etc., etc. Witnesses, John Waller, Benj. Waller, J. C. Waller. Novr. 6, 1792.

June 7, 1792. John x Cammack and Ann, his wife, of Spots Co. to Charles Burrage of Spots. Co. £50 curr. 84 a. purchased of John Saunders and Jane, his wife; Uriah Edwards and Mildred, his wife, in separate tracts, adj. each other, in Berkeley Par., Spots. Co., etc., etc. Sherod Horn, Wm. Bowler, David Head. Novr. 6, 1792.

Novr. 3, 1792. George Carter, eldest son of Henry Carter, Decd., not desiring to take the land in Spots. Co. whereon his father lived on conditions in his will, relinquishes all right, title, etc., in same, except proportion of the value thereof, etc., etc. Witnesses, Edwd. Herndon, Wm. Herndon, Joseph Herndon. Novr. 6, 1792.

Octo. 15, 1792. James Monroe and Eliza, his wife, and John Taliaferro Brooke to Robert Mercer. Whereas, the sd. Monroe and Eliza, his wife, did sell unto the sd. Brooke, Lot 127 in Fredksbg., and the sd. Brooke, now for the sum of £435, conveys the same to the sd. Mercer, etc., etc. Witnesses, James Madison, jr.; John Minor, jr.; Jos. Jones. Novr. 8, 1792.

June 26, 1792, Patrick x Donally and Peggy, his wife, of Spots. Co., and Joshua Long of Spots. Co. to Mathew Carpenter of same co. Whereas, by Ind. dated Novr. 4, 1746, Broomfield Long gave to his son, Reuben Long, 118½ a. in Spots. Co., which sd. tract the sd. Reuben reconveyed to the sd. Broomfield and the sd. Broomfield Long afterwards conveyed the same by two indentures to his two daughters, Mary and Sarah, each an equal moiety, now for the sum of £37 9s. to the sd. Donally and Joshua Long in hand pd., convey "the afsd. tract of land," etc., etc. Witnesses, Jos. Graham, Jno. Chew Buckner, Geo. Goodloe, Thos. Oliver, Henry Beasley, James McKinney, Chas. Beasley. Decr. 4, 1792.

Decr. 4, 1792. David Head and Isabella, his wife, of Spots. Co. to James Frazer of same co. £63 curr. 88 a. given the sd. David Head by his father, Alexander Spence Head, as by Ind. dated July 15, 1779, in Berkeley Par., Spots. Co., etc., etc. No witnesses. Decr. 4, 1792.

May 8, 1792. Alexander Spotswood and Elizabeth, his wife, to James Skeggs. £54 curr. 72 a. in Spots. Co., etc., etc. Thomas Towles, Edwd. Herndon, jr.; Danl. Grinnan, jr.; Jas. Lewis, Edwd. Herndon. Decr. 1, 1792.

Decr. 23, 1792. Smith, Young & Hyde to Young & Hyde. £61 17s. 6d. One tract purchased of Thos. Carr and George Stubblefield, containing 170 a.; another tract of 5 a. purchased of Benj. Holladay in Spots. Co., etc., etc. Benj. Holladay, Arthur Clayton, John Andrew. Jany. 1, 1793.

Decr. 23, 1792. Smith, Young & Hyde to Edward Hyde & Co. £300 curr. 456 a. in Berkeley Par., Spots. Co., etc., etc. Benj. Holladay, Arthur Clayton, John Andrew. Jany. 1, 1793.

Decr. 23, 1792. Smith, Young & Hyde to Young & Hyde. £25. Tract of land purchased of Beverley Stubblefield in Spots. Co., etc., etc. Benj. Holladay, Arthur Clayton, John Andrew. Jany. 1, 1793.

Octr. 16, 1792. Charles Magill of town of Winchester, Va., to George Lewis, Esq. 5s. 1 negro girl. Witness, W. Daingerfield. Jany. 1, 1793.

Decr. 4, 1792. Wm. Carter, John Carter and Joseph Brock, acting executors of John Carter, Gent., Decd., to Henry Southard of Spots. Co. Whereas, Thomas Bartlett, late of Spots. Co., did by Ind. dated July 23, 1789, recd. Feby. 2, 1790, convey to the sd. Carters and Brock, 238 a. of land in Spots. Co., in trust to sell and convey the same, for the uses as stated in the Indenture, the sd. Carters and Brock for the sum of £77 15s. 4d. convey the sd. land to the sd. Southard, etc., etc. Witnesses, Jno. Herndon, Benj. Alsop, James Wilson, John Spindle. Jany. 1, 1793.

Augt. 1, 1791. Wm. Duval of Spots. Co. to Zachariah Billingsly of same co. Mortgage. 200 a. formerly purchased of sd. Billingsly in Spots. Co., etc., etc. Edwd. Herndon, Jos. Herndon. Jany. 1, 1793.

July 31, 1792. John Day of Hanover Co. to James Goodwin of same co. £420 curr. 900 a. in Spots. Co., etc., etc. Edmd. Taylor, Jno. M. Walker, Saml. Day, Wm. Day, Ro. Clough, Wilson Trevilian. Feby. 5, 1793.

April 25, 1791. Nicho. Payne, Gent., to Stockley Towles of same co. To indemnify the sd. Towles who stands bound as security for the sd. Payne, the sd. Payne deeds him in trust, 446 a. called Pennfield, etc., in Spots. Co., etc., etc. Jos. Duerson, Thos. Duerson, Leonard Young, Jno. Duerson. Feby. 5, 1793.

Jany. 17, 1793. Thomas Coleman of Caroline Co. to his son, Spilsby Coleman, of Spots. Co. 600 a. purchased of Thomas Payne in Spots. Co., etc., etc. J. Chiles, Saml. Coleman, Wm. Chandler, Farish Coleman. Feby. 5, 1793.

Jany. 8, 1793. Robert Scott and Jane, his wife, of Spots. Co. to Wm. Drummond and Adam Darby of Fredksbg. £1000 curr. 1580 a. in Spots. Co., etc., etc. Jos. Brock, Thomas Strachan, Lewis Hume, John Blanton, Edwd. x Ballenger. Feby. 5, 1793.

Decr. 26, 1791. Robert Smith and Frances, his wife, of Spots. Co. to Richard Todd of same county. £150 curr. 96 a. whereon Luke Mullineaux lives in Spots. Co., etc., etc. Josias Berryman, Robt. Throckmorton, Richard Todd. Feby. 5, 1793.

Jany. 18, 1793. John x True, Senr., to John True, the younger, son of Robt. True. Deed of Gift. 78 a. in St. Geo. Par., Spots. Co., etc., etc., in case of the death of John True, jr., without issue, then to Robt. True, jr., son of the afsd. Robt. True and brother of the sd. John True., jr., etc., etc. Witnesses, Beverley Chew, John Steward, Will. Welch. Feby. 5, 1793.

Jany. 23, 1793. Edwd. Hyde & Co. to Daniel Lane. £140 curr. 200 a., part of tract purchased of Robert Young in Berkeley Par., Spots. Co., etc., etc. John Andrew, John Purcell, Austin Sandidge. March 5, 1793.

Jany. 7, 1793. Nathan Tally and Julia, his wife, of Louisa Co. to Austin Sandidge of Spots. Co. £80. 200 a. in Spots. Co., etc., etc. Lewis Holladay, Jno. Rawlings, Wm. Tally, Wm. Trigg, Jno. Scott. March 5, 1793.

Jany. 25, 1792. Richard Luck and Frances, his wife, of Spots. Co. to Moses Bounsell and John Lehorn of same co. £36 curr. 90 a. in Spots. Co., etc., etc. Henry Johnson, Jos. Coleman, Ambrose Shackleford, Jno. Waller. March 5, 1793.

Feby. 8, 1793. Thomas Haydon of Spots. Co. to James Pettigrew of Fredksbg. 5s. 80 a. purchased of Nathan Hawkins, jr., etc., in Spots. Co., in trust to secure payment of a debt, etc., etc. Witnesses, Jno. Frazer, John Robinson, Michael Robinson, Thos. Sacrea. March 5, 1793.

—— ——, 1793. Edwd. Herndon, Lewis Holladay and Stephen Johnson, overseers of poor in Dist. No. 2, Spots. Co., bind Joseph Cooper, age 13 yrs., to Edward Ballenger of St. Geo. Par., Spots. Co., etc., etc. Witness, Beverley Stubblefield. March 5, 1793.

Novr. 3, 1792. Thomas Colson to Reuben Landram. £171 curr. 171 a. formerly leased Richd. and Benj. Hulet in Spots. Co., St. Geo. Par., etc., etc. No witnesses. March 5, 1793.

Novr. 6, 1792. Reuben Landram of Louisa Co. to Thomas Colson of Spots. Co. £121 curr. 171 a. in St. Geo., Spots. Co. Mortgage, etc., etc. No witnesses. March 5, 1793.

March 5, 1793. Wm. Pettus of Spots. Co. to Wm. Graves of Louisa Co. Po. of atto. Witnesses, Joseph Pettus, Larkin Reynolds. March 5, 1793.

March 6, 1793. Larkin Stanard and Elizabeth, his wife, of Spots. Co. to John Chew of Fredksbg. £132 curr. Lots 151 and 152 in town of Fredksbg., etc., etc. No witnesses. March 6, 1793.

May 14, 1792. James Thomson, Minister of the Gospel in Co. of Ayr in North Britain, eldest son and heir of Wm. Thomson of Poplar, near London, Shipmaster, Decd. Po. of atto. to Charles Mortimer, Esq., of Fredksbg., Va., to sell lot No. 251 in Fredksbg. purchased of Roger Dixon and Lucy, his wife, by the sd. Wm. Thomson, during his lifetime, etc., etc. Witnesses, Tho. Thompson, Tho. Thompson, jr. Oath of Mr. Thomas Thomson of Co. of Ayr, etc., M. G., and Thomas Thompson, his son, that they know James Thomson of Grivan, M. G., etc., as stated above, etc., etc. Witness, John McNeath, chief magistrate and Baillie of the burgh of Grivan. Recd. March 6, 1793.

Decr. 20, 1792. Chas. Mortimer of Fredksbg. to George Weedon of same town. By virtue of his po. of atto. from James Thomson [as above], sells and conveys to the sd. Weedon, Lot 251 in town of Fredksbg. for the sum of £100 curr. Witnesses, Benj. Day, David Henderson, Wm. Stanard, Robert Mercer, Jno. Chew, Jas. Somerville, Fontaine Maury. March 6, 1793.

Septr. 6, 1791. Beverley Stubblefield, Francis Thornton, jr., and James Lewis, Gentlm., overseers of poor, Dist. No. 4, Spots. Co., bind Moses Mulliken, aged 8 yrs. Novr. next, orph. of Burtin Mullikin, Decd., to John McWhirt, Sadler, etc., etc. Witnesses, Thos. Waller, Thos. Haydon, Thos. Strachan. March 8, 1793.

—— ——, 1793. Richard Bullard of Spots. Co., Va. Po. of atto. to Richard Cave of Fayette Co., Ky., etc., etc. Witnesses, Joseph Brock, Clk.; Robert Branham. April 2, 1793.

March 20, 1793. Henry Johnson of Spots. Co. to John Waller Johnson of Chesterfield Co. 14s. 121 23-40 a., part of tract sd. Henry Johnson lives on in Spots. Co., etc., etc. No witnesses. April 2, 1793.

Mar. 19, 1793. "Be it remembered that altho. my father, Henry Johnson has made me a deed for 121 23-40 a. of land, etc., etc., etc., he and my mother, Agnes Johnson," to have use of same during their lives, etc., etc. Signed, John W. Johnson. Recd. April 2, 1793.

Jany. 23, 1793. Benjamin McWilliams and Letitia, his wife, of Charles City Co. to James Bullock of Spots. Co. £192 curr. 320 a., part of tract given sd. Benj. by his father, Wm. McWilliams in Spots. Co., etc., etc. C. Holloway, Danl. Tiller, John Bullock, Frances Buckner. April 2, 1793.

Novr. 3, 1792. Wm. Durrett and Sarah, his wife, of Caroline Co. to Richard Carlton of Spots. Co. £25 curr. 95 a. purchased of Wm. Warren in Spots. Co., etc., etc. Henry Durrett, Sarah Durrett, Judith Durrett. April 2, 1793.

July 2, 1793. John Nelson, Senr., and Susanna, his wife, of Berkeley Par., Spots. Co., to Francis Coleman of same par. and co. £100. 102 a. purchased of Benj. Davis in par. and co. afsd., etc., etc. No witnesses. April 2, 1793.

April 1, 1793. Benjamin Nelson of Louisa Co. to John Nelson, Senr., of Spots. Co. £100 curr. 250 a. whereon sd. Jno. Nelson now lives in Berkeley Par., Spots. Co., etc., etc. Jos. Nelson, Jno. Carter, Sam. Gale, Jno. Sale. April 2, 1793.

Novr. 26, 1792. Ailce x Wilkerson, Nancy x Wilkerson and Jenny x Wilkerson of Spots. Co. to George Wilkerson of same co. Whereas, Robt. Wilkerson, Decd., by his last will and testament dated Decr. 20, 1778, did lend to his wife, Ailce Wilkerson, during her natural life, 200 a. in Spots. Co. whereon he lived, and at her death directed the sale thereof and the money arising from the sd. sale equally divided between his children, viz., Nancy, George and Jenny Wilkerson, parties to these presents, and they the sd. children being of lawful age with the consent of Ailce Wilkerson, their mother, have made a fair bargain for the land, etc., the sd. Ailce, Nancy and Jenny Wilkerson sell and convey unto the sd. George, 60 a. adj. lands of Benja. Waller, Sr., and Thomas Turner, Sr., the sd. George relinquishing all his right, title, etc., in the residue of the sd. tract, etc., etc. Witnesses, Jno. Waller, Benj. Waller, A. Waller, Sally x Hackney. April 2, 1793.

Decr. 26, 1792. Wm. Hewell of North Carolina to Wm. Herod. 150 a. in Spots. Co., sold to Jno. Harland who sold same to Wm. King, and the sd. King to the sd. Herod, but no conveyance ever having been made, etc., etc. Witnesses, O. Towles, jr.; Stockley Towles, Wm. King. April 2, 1793.

March 16, 1793. Robert Smith of Spots. Co., Va., removing to the State of Kentucky, po. of atto. to James Lewis, Gent., of Spots. Co., Va., Witnesses, Edwd. Herndon, jr.; Bevy. Stubblefield, Thomas Bartlett. April 1793.

July 2, 1793. Charles Clark and Phebe, his wife, of Caroline Co. to Catherine Smallwood, widow of James Smallwood, Decd., of Spots. Co. £60 curr., etc. 75 a. in Spots. Co., etc., etc. No witnesses. July 2, 1793.

June 4, 1793. Thomas Colson to Henry Dawson. £104 curr. 104 a. formerly leased by sd. Colson to James Ballard in St. Geo. Par., Spots. Co., etc., etc. Wm. Duerson, Jas. Hutcherson, Jno. M. Herndon. July 2, 1793.

March 13, 1793. Thomas Burbridge, Benj. Robinson and Mildred, his wife; Henry Eally and Sarah, his wife; Robert Smith and Frances, his wife; Tavener Branham and Elizabeth, his wife; Linsfield Burbridge and Ann, his wife; Wm. Bullet and Mary, his wife; George Burbridge and Mary, his wife, to Ann Hull. £180. 213 a. in Spots. Co., etc., etc. Lar. Stanard, Jno. Herndon, Edwd. Herndon, Bevy. Stubblefield, Edwd.

Herndon, jr.; Thomas Bartlett, Jas. Lewis, Hezk. Ellis, J. Chew. No date of Record.

Jany. 29, 1793. James Arnold and Nancy, his wife, of Spots. Co. to Thomas Shirley of same co. £22 8s. 9d. curr. 108 a., part of a tract conveyed by John Arnold to the sd. James in Spots. Co., etc., etc. Jno. C. Waller, Clement Boroughes, Jas. Wiglesworth, Jas. Wiglesworth, Sr.; Jos. Sams, Philip Young. July 2, 1793.

Decr. 21, 1792. Chas. x Burrage and Catherine, his wife, of Spots. Co. to Robert Scott of same co. £27 curr. 84 a. in Berkeley Par., Spots. Co., etc., etc. Harry Stubblefield, Archibald McFarland, Jesse Bowlin. July 2, 1793.

June 28, 1793. Stockley Towles and Elizabeth, his wife, of Spots. Co. to Gerard B. Berryman, of same co. £150 curr. 253 a. formerly sold by Henry Gatewood to Ignatius Tureman, and by the sd. Tureman given to Tureman Lewis, and by Lewis sold to the sd. Towles, in Spots. Co., etc., etc. Thos. Towles, Wm. Drake, Edwd. Herndon. July 2, 1793.

Decr. 8, 1792. Daniel Branham of Spots. Co. to Edwd. Herndon (son of Joseph), John Herndon and Edwd. Herndon, jr., who stand bound as security for the sd. Branham, the sd. Branham to indemnify them, conveys in trust, seven slaves and three horses, etc., etc. Bevy. Stubblefield, Wm. Waller. July 2, 1793.

July 2, 1793. James Bullock of Spots. Co. to John Etherton of Culpeper Co. £27, 136 a. in Spots. Co., etc., etc. No witnesses. July 2, 1793.

July 1, 1793. Joseph Herndon and Mary, his wife, of Spots. Co. to Robert Wellford of Fredksbg. £200 specie. 383 a. in Spots. Co., etc., etc. No witnesses. July 2, 1793.

Jany. 23, 1793. Benjamin McWilliams and Letitia, his wife, of Spots. Co. to Francis Buckner of Caroline Co. £192 curr. 320 a., part of tract given the sd. Benja. by his father, Wm. McWilliams, in Spots. Co., etc., etc. Septr. 3, 1793.

Septr, 3, 1793. Ephraim Knight and Sarah, his wife, and James Knight, their son, to John Billingsley. £60 curr. 79 a. purchased by sd. Ephraim of his brother, Jno. Knight, etc., etc., in Berkeley Par., Spots. Co., etc., etc. No witnesses. Septr. 3, 1793.

June 11, 1793. Wm. Parker of Berkeley Par., Spots. Co., to Francis Coleman of par. and co. afsd. £152 curr. 152 a. in same par. and co., etc., etc. Wm. Winslow, Robt. E. Coleman, Benja. Robinson, Thomas Winslow. Septr. 3, 1793.

Decr. 17, 1791. Jno. Proctor of Fayette Co., Va., heir at law of Wm. Proctor, Decd., of Spots. Co., Va., having brought suit as heir at law to recover the estate of the sd. decedent, etc., po. of atto. to George Mason of Caroline Co., Va. Witnesses, Jno. Shackleford, Moses Higgins, Micajah Mason. Septr. 3, 1793.

March 13, 1793. Robert Smith and Frances, his wife, of Spots. Co. to Edward Herndon, jr., of same co. £300 curr. 736 a. in St. Geo. Par., Spots. Co., etc., etc. Bevy. Stubblefield, Thomas Bartlett, Thos. Strachan, Edwd. Herndon, Larkin Stanard, Nimrod Branham. Septr. 3, 1793.

Feby. 22, 1793. Robert Cunningham of Spots. Co., po. of atto. to Edward Herndon, jr., etc. Witnesses, Nicho. Payne, Benj. Alsop, Jas. Frazer, Septr. 3, 1793.

July 27, 1793. James Arnold, jr., and Nancey, his wife, of Spots. Co. to Joel Fagg of same co. £30 curr. 128 a. in Spots. Co., etc., etc. Thomas Shirley, Austin Sandidge, Jno. A. Billingsley. Septr. 3, 1793.

March 29, 1793. Thomas Lipscomb of Spots. Co. to his son, Joel Lipscomb, of Edgefield Co., South Carolina. Deed of Gift. 2 negroes. Witness, Jos. Willoughby. Septr. 3, 1793.

May 20, 1793. Saml. Hawes of Caroline Co., Gent., to John Crawford of Spots. Co. £158 8s. curr. 198 a. in Spots. Co., etc., etc. John Carnohen, Stephen Humphries, Moroday Morriss, Jos. Carnehan. Septr. 3, 1793.

May 20, 1793. Saml. Hawes of Caroline Co., Gent., to John Carnohen of Spots. Co. £120 curr. 150 a. in Spots. Co., etc., etc. James Crawford Stephen Humphries, Moroday Morris, Stephen Carnehan. Septr. 3, 1793.

May 20, 1793. Saml. Hawes of Caroline Co., Gent., to James Crawford, jr., of Spots. Co. £17 12s. curr. 22 a. in Spots. Co., etc., etc. Jno. Carnehan, Moroday Morris, Stephen Humphries, Jos. Carnehan. Septr. 3, 1793.

April 23, 1793. Wm. Heslop of Spots. Co. to John Long of same co. £27 curr. 27 a. in Spots. Co., etc., etc. Benjamin Tompkins, Henry Beasley, Jno. Hart, Ephraim Beasley. Septr. 3, 1793.

Septr. 3, 1793. John Carnohan and Sally, his wife, of Spots. Co. to Joseph Duerson of same co. £80 curr. 75 a. in Spots. Co., etc., etc. O. Towles, Benja. Chapman, Philip Young. Septr. 3, 1793.

Feby. 6, 1793. "I, Wm. Threldkeld, do hereby agree to give from under my hand to Mrs. Mary Coleman that she should have and hold her property, etc., during her life, and at her death to dispose of as she thinks proper. I also agree . . . that I will never meddle nor concern with any of her property, etc., without her consent." Witnesses, Wm. Marshall Estes, Frankey x Wheeler. Septr. 3, 1793.

May 23, 1793. James Arnold, jr., and Nancy, his wife, and Elizabeth x Edwards, his mother, of Spots. Co. to Joseph Graves of same co. £200. 199 a. in Spots. Co., etc., etc. Geo. Tyler, Jos. Pettus, Larkin Reynolds, Peter Arnold. Septr. 3, 1793.

May 20, 1793. James Arnold, jr., and Nancy, his wife, of Spots. Co. to Larkin Reynolds of same co. £112 10s. curr. 190 a. (after death of Elizabeth Edwards, now living on the premises) in Spots. Co., etc., etc. Jos. Graves, Benj. Rennolds, Peter Arnold. Septr. 3, 1793.

—— ——, 1793. James Donalson, Lucy x Robins, Joanna x. Robins, Sarah x Robins of Scott Co., Kentucky, po. of atto. to James Robins of Spots. Co., Va., etc., etc. Jno. McEndree, Bartlet Collins. Septr. 3, 1793.

Decr. 3, 1793. Joseph Rawlings and Elizabeth, his wife, of Spots. Co. to John Andrews of same county. £26 10s. curr. 62 a. in Berkeley Par., Spots. Co., etc., etc. Jno. Lipscomb, Lewis Holladay. Decr. 3, 1793.

Octr. 28, 1793. John Waller and Elizabeth, his wife, of Spots. Co. to Benjamin Waller, Senr. £75 curr. 150 a., whereon Jno. Knight now lives, in Spots. Co., etc., etc. Jona. Clark, Lewis Holladay, Wm. Henderson, Absolem Waller, Wm. Duerson, Waller Lewis. Decr. 3, 1793.

Octr. 24, 1793. John Waller and Elizabeth, his wife, of Spots. Co. to Benja. Waller, Senr. £276 15s. curr. 369 a. whereon sd. Jno. Waller lives in Spots. Co., etc., etc. Jona. Clark, Lewis Holladay, Wm. Henderson, Absolem Waller, Wm. Duerson, Wm. Lewis. Decr. 3, 1793.

Septr. 21, 1793. John White and Mary, his wife, of Spots. Co. to Thomas Brightwell of same co. £130. 290 a. in Spots. Co., etc., etc. Jos. Willoughby, Thomas White, Archd. White. Decr. 3, 1793.

Septr. 7, 1793. John Mastin and Ellender, his wife; James x Wheeler and Mary, his wife; Moses x Wheeler and ——, his wife, of Spots. Co. to Richard Long of same co. Whereas, the sd. Moses Wheeler, as heir at law of his father, Jno. Wheeler, decd. (who died intestate), became entitled to a certain tract of land, and the sd. Moses being so entitled and possessed, sold a portion thereof to the sd. John Mastin and also a portion to the sd. James Wheeler, and whereas, the sd. James Wheeler and Jno. Mastin have agreed for the sale of their land to the sd. Long, and the sd. Moses Wheeler, willing that a good and sufficient title should be made the sd. Long, there having as yet been no conveyance to the sd. Jas. Wheeler and Jno. Mastin, this Ind. witnesseth, the sd. Moses Wheeler in consideration of the premises, the sd. Mastin in consideration of the sum of £60 curr., and the said Jas. Wheeler the sum of £19 4s. curr., convey to the sd. Long 190 a. in Berkeley Par., Spots. Co., etc., etc. Witnesses, Thomas Towles, Lewis Holladay, Robert Branham. Decr. 3, 1793.

Octr. 26, 1793. John Carter and Winifred, his wife, of Spots. Co. to John Nelson of same co. £20. 2 a. in Spots. Co., etc., etc. Saml. Sale, Wm. Nelson, Richard Nelson. Decr. 3, 1793.

Octr. 26, 1793. Joseph Nelson of Spots. Co. to John Nelson of same co. £20. 4 a. in Spots. Co., etc., etc. Saml. Sale, Richard Nelson, Wm. Nelson. Decr. 3, 1793.

Octr. 18, 1793. Alexander Spotswood and Elizabeth his wife, to Jonathan Carpenter. £100 curr. 200 a. in Spots. Co., etc., etc. Lawrence Brooke, Francis Taliaferro, Thomas Strachan, Edwd. Herndon, Bevy. Stubblefield. Decr. 3, 1793.

Decr. 3, 1793. James Frazer of Spots. Co. to Edwd. Herndon of same co. £70 curr. 88 a. purchased of David Head in Spots. Co., etc., etc. No witnesses. Decr. 3, 1793.

Octr. 23, 1793. Samuel Todd, Senr., of Spots. Co. to Joseph Chew of same co. £420 curr. 420 a. in St. Geo. Par., Spots. Co., etc., etc. Benja. Ballard, Richd. Todd, Reuben x Hudson, Edwd. Herndon, jr.; John Herndon, jr. Decr. 3, 1793.

April 17, 1792. Richard Coleman of Spots. Co. to Robt. S. Coleman of same co. The sd. Richd. Coleman conveys to the sd. Robt. S. Coleman "all the slaves and their increase which he [Richd. Coleman] got by marriage of his late wife," etc. The slaves in trust for the use of Fanny

Coleman, Thomas Wootten Coleman, Rice Coleman and Richard Coleman, children of Richard Coleman afsd. [all under 21 yrs. of age], etc., etc. Witnesses, Spilsbe Coleman, Mary x Aldiss. Decr. 3, 1793.

Jany. 1, 1793. James Marye of Spots. Co. to George Lewis of same co., father, etc., of Mary Willis Lewis. £350 curr. Mortgage. Negroes. Witnesses, Jno. Chew, W. Daingerfield. Decr. 3, 1793.

Novr. 7, 1793. Wm. Schooler to Larkin Smith of King and Queen Co. £200. Mortgage. 260 a. purchased of sd. Smith, adj. lands of Wm. Jackson's heirs, James Mercer, Wm. Porter and Wm. McWilliams in Spots. Co., etc., etc. Go. Lewis, Henry Daingerfield, Jno. Chew, Bev. Chew. Decr. 3, 1793.

Septr. 30, 1793. Larkin Smith and Mary Eleanor, his wife, of King and Queen Co. to Wm. Schooler (at present) of the same co. £260. 260 a. in Spots. Co., etc., etc. Thomas Towles, Jno. Chew, Robt. W. Peacock, Larkin Stanard, Bev. Chew. Decr. 3, 1793.

Novr. 14, 1793. "I, Archibald Mcfarland of Spots. Co. do appoint in my absence to manage my estate till I return, Wm. Wevar, Mercht., in Fredksbg., and James Darks and Lovel & Orchard, do. Mr. Benj. Robertson of Spots. Co.," etc., etc. No witnesses. A bond dated July 11, 1792. The obligation is such "that as soon as sd. Archd. Macfarland's bill of exchange for £200 drawn on Archd. McAusland of Greenock, dated this day, payable June 10, 1793, and his bond to Robt. Scott of £200, due October 1793, are pd., then the hereby bound Robt. Scott is to deed to Archd. Mcfarland 2 tracts of land on Gladyrun [Spots. Co.], containing 650 a., known by name of Scotts Quarter, etc., etc. Witnesses, Jno. Corbet, Jno. Mundell. Decr. 4, 1793.

Decr. 3, 1793. Wm. x King and Delilah, his wife, of Spots. Co. to Zachariah Knight of same co. £50 curr. 100 a. formerly the property of Richd. Coleman, and sold and conveyed to the sd. King by Francis Coleman, in Spots. Co., etc., etc. Elijah Knight, Ephraim Knight, Henry Pendleton, jr.; Robt. Hart, Lewis Holladay. Decr. 3, 1793.

Decr. 6, 1786. George Stubblefield, Gent., and Sally, his wife, of Spots. Co. to Charles Thornton of Caroline Co. £1818. 614 a. in Berkeley Par., Spots. Co., etc., etc. Benja. Stubblefield, Bevy. Stubblefield, Bevy. W. Stubblefield. Jany. 7, 1794.

Octr. 12, 1793. Ambrose Dudley and Ann, his wife, of Fayette Co., Kentucky, to Joseph Bullock of Spots. Co., Va. £218 15s. curr. 177 a., part of a tract purchased by Robt. Dudley, Decd., father of the sd. Ambrose Dudley, of a certain Mr. Goodloe, in St. Geo. Par., Spots. Co., etc., etc. Philip D. Redd, Peter Dudley, James Dudley, Thos. Colson. Jany. 7, 1794.

April 24, 1793. Beverley Stubblefield, John Herndon and Wm. Robinson, overseers of the poor in Dist. No. 4, Spots. Co., bind Mary Mullikin, age 5 yrs., orph. daughter of Burton Mulliken, Decd., to John Wallace of Spots. Co. No witnesses. Jany. 7, 1794.

Jany. 7, 1794. John Lewis of Spots. Co., Va., po. of atto. to Richard Terrell of town of Lexington, in Kentucky. No witnesses. Jany. 7, 1794.

May 20, 1793. James Stevens of Spots. Co. to Charles Carter of same co. £35. A negro. Witnesses, Willoughby N. Berryman, Reuben Straughan. Jany. 7, 1794.

Septr. 24, 1793. Thomas Wiglesworth of Spots. Co. to his daughter, Agnes Carr Wiglesworth, infant. Deed of Gift. "My sd. Daughter's grandfather, Henry Johnston," etc., etc. 1 negro girl slave, etc. Witnesses, George Penn, Jas. Wiglesworth, jr.; Betsey Webber. Jany. 7, 1794.

June 4, 1793. James King and Sukey, his wife, to Charles Bennett of Spots. Co. £35. Tract of land in Spots. Co., etc., etc. Jno. A. Billingsley, Wm. Waller, Benj. Alsop. Jany. 7, 1794.

Octr. 28, 1793. John Waller and Elizabeth, his wife, of Spots. Co. to Waller Lewis of same co. £60 curr. 105 a, adj. lands of Benj. Waller, jr.; Benj. Reynolds, Henry Johnston, James Gimbo and the sd. Lewis, in Spots. Co., etc., etc. Jona. Clark, Lewis Holladay, Wm. Henderson, Wm. Duerson, Absolem Waller, Benja. Waller. Jany. 7, 1794.

Jany. ——, 1794. Philemon Davis of Spots. Co. to Wm. Winslow of same co., po. of atto. to sell Kentucky lands, etc., etc. Witnesses, Robt. W. Peacock, Wm. Trigg. Jany. 7, 1794.

Jany. 7, 1794. Thomas Winslow of Spots. Co., Va., to Wm. Winslow of same county. Po. of atto. to sell lands in the Western Country or North Western Territory, etc., etc. Witnesses, Benjamin Robinson, John Nelson, jr.; Saml. Robinson. Jany. 7, 1794.

Novr. 27, 1793. Alexander Spotswood and Elizabeth, his wife, and Jonathan Carpenter and Elizabeth, his wife, of Spots. Co. to Edward Herndon (son of Joseph) of Spots. Co. £130 curr. pd. to sd. Carpenter. 230 a. in Spots. Co., purchased by sd. Carpenter of sd. Spotswood, but for which no legal conveyance having yet been made the sd. Spotswood becomes party to these presents, etc., etc. Witnesses, Alexr. E. Spotswood, Bevy. Stubblefield, Nimrod Branham, Wm. Herndon, Thos. Strachan. Jany. 7, 1794.

Jany. 6, 1794. Agreement between Barnett Mitcham, John Mitcham, Francis Jones, Ephraim Beazley, jr., and Reuben x Hudson, for himself and Dudley Mitcham, and also as trustee for Elijah Estes and Mary, his wife, legal representatives of Elizabeth Mitcham, lately decd., etc., etc. "No administration legally taken on the estate of the late husband of the sd. Elizabeth," etc., etc. Division of estate equally, etc. Witnesses, Jno. Herndon, David Scott. Jany. 7, 1794.

Feby. 4, 1794. Moses x Wheeler of Spots. Co. to Wm. Winslow of same county. Po. of atto. To sell land in Kentucky to which sd. Wheeler may be entitled as heir at law of John and Wm. Wheeler, as will appear by Pat. dated Novr. 18, 1785, etc., etc. Witnesses, Austin Sandidge, John Parrish, Jas. Frazer. Feby. 4, 1794.

Jany. 1, 1794. Edward Herndon, jr. [son of Edward], of Spots. Co. and Elizabeth, his wife, to Danl. Hyde of same co. £435 curr. 736 a. in St. Geo. Par., Spots. Co., etc., etc. Bevy. Stubblefield, Thomas Strachan, George Ellis. Feby. 4, 1794.

Decr. 21, 1793. Whereas, a marriage is intended to be solemnized between Molly x Mitcham and Elijah Estes of Spots. Co., etc., etc. The sd. Elijah being willing that the sd. Molly shall hold, possess and enjoy the right of disposing of any estate she may possess, etc. This Ind. witnesseth, that the sd. Molly, for the love and affection she beareth Reuben Hudson, all her personalty and her "proportion of Elizabeth Mitcham's Estate," etc., "for the use of the sd. Hudson and all his children he may have by my sister Nancy, with whom he intermarried," in trust, however, that should the sd. Molly have children by the sd. Elijah, then the before conveyed estates to descend to them, and for the sd. Elijah during his natural life, etc., etc. Witnesses, Jno. Herndon, Harry Chew, Bevy. Stubblefield, Wm. Robinson. Feby. 4, 1794.

Feby. 4, 1794. Edward Herndon and James Lewis, Executors of John Herndon, decd., to Jonathan Carpenter of Spots. Co. £140 curr. 120½ a. purchased by sd. Executors of Wharton Schooler for the est. of sd. Jno. Herndon, Decd., in Spots. Co., etc., etc. No witnesses. Feby. 4, 1794.

Feby. 1, 1794. Benjamin Head of Spots. Co. to his son, Theodoric Bland Head, of same co. Deed of Gift. "After the death of my wife, Mary Head," etc., etc. All of the sd. Benjamin's land, etc., etc. Witness, John Wiglesworth. Feby. 4, 1794.

Septr. 2, 1793. Richard S. Hackley of Spots. Co. to Charles McCauley of same co. Lease. 25 a. in St. Geo. Par., Spots. Co., etc., etc. "Sd. Chas. McCauley and Ann, his wife," etc., etc. £2 10s. curr. Witnesses, James Phillips, Reuben Daniel. Feby. 4, 1794.

July 10, 1793. Wm. Champe Carter and Maria, his wife, to Wm. Stanard. £345. 438½ a., which sd. land was a moiety devised by the last will and testament of Edward Carter, decd., of Fredksburg. to his wife during her natural life, and after her death to his son, the sd. Wm. Champe Carter, which sd. tract of land sd. Edwd. Carter formerly purchased of Wm. Champe, lying on Fall Hill, in Spots. Co., etc., etc. Witnesses, Robt. Patton, John W. Willis, Wm. Drummond, Peter Garts. Feby. 4, 1794.

Decr. 21, 1793. Benja. Head, to indemnify Joshua Long, who stands bound as security for sd. Head to Edwd. Herndon, the sd. Head conveys, in trust, to sd. Long, a negro, etc., etc. Witnesses, Thomas Towles, Thomas Pritchard. Feby. 4, 1794.

June 16, 1793. George Wilkinson and Martha, his wife, of Hanover Co. to Edmund Clark of same co. £45 curr. 60 a. formerly conveyed the sd. Geo. by Alcie, Nancy and Jane Wilkinson, as by deed dated Novr. 6, 1792, in Spots. Co., etc., etc. Jona. Clark, Wm. Clark, Bernard Dickinson, Absolem Waller, Jno. Shirley, jr.; George Mason. Feby. 4, 1794.

Novr. 4, 1793. Benjamin Waller, jr., and Joanna, his wife, of Spots. Co. to Edmund Clarke of Hanover Co. £70 curr. 140 a. in Spots. Co., etc., etc. Thomas Towles, Jona. Clark, James Arnold, Absolem Waller, Aylett Waller. Feby. 4, 1794.

Decr. 14, 1793. Wm. x King and Delilah, his wife, of Spots. Co. to Francis Coleman of same co. £40 curr. 100 a. on Pigeon Run in Berkeley Par., Spots. Co., etc., etc. Wm. Winslow, Benja. Robinson, Thomas Winslow, Wm. Parker, J. L. Hawkins. Feby. 4, 1794.

March 24, 1794. Wm. Smith and Ann, his wife, of Spots. Co., of first part; James Abbott and Mildred, his wife, of Orange Co., of second part, to George Maury of Fredksbg., of the third part. Whereas, Geddes and Abbott, Merchts. and partners, purchased part of the lot adj. Thos. Brown's lot [in Fredksbg.], of Wm. Smith and Ann, his wife, for £200 curr., and before any conveyance was therefor made, the sd. Geddis and Abbott, by their surviving and acting partner, Henry Geddis, directed the sale thereof by his agent, James Abbott, afsd., and at the sale thereof the sd. James Abbott became the purchaser thereof for the sum of £105 curr., and by this Ind. [the sd. Smith and wife entering in the deed there having been no former conveyance to the former purchasers] the sd. Abbott and Mildred, his wife, convey the sd. premises to the sd. Murray for the sum of £100 curr., etc., etc. Witnesses, Edwin Lee, Edward Herndon, James Lewis, Charles Julian. Recorded April 1, 1794.*

Novr. 14, 1793. Elisha Dismukes of Spots. Co. to John Shirley, jr., of same co. £50. 125 a. adj. lands of Thos. Dillard, Sarah Morris, Jas. Gimbo, Ambrose Shackleford, Jno. Shirley, jr.; Berryman Waller, in Spots. Co., etc., etc. Henry Dodd, Jno. Craivard, Garland Hill, Littleton Farres. April 1, 1794.

Decr. 23, 1793. Robert Hill and Hannah, his wife, of King and Queen Co. to Edward G. Hill [son of the sd. Robert Hill] of Spots. Co. Deed of Gift. 404 a. on East North East River in Spots. Co., etc., etc. Samuel Hill, Jno. Garlick, John Hill, jr.; Edwd. Lawrence. April 1, 1794.

March 19, 1794. Abel x Steers of Spots. Co. to Peter Pricket [or Picket] Nunley of same co. £160 curr. 100 a. on River Ta in Spots. Co. whereon the sd. Steers has dwelt for many years past, and purchased by sd. Steers of Benj. Arnold, etc., etc. And the sd. Nunley gives to the sd. Steers a deed of trust on the sd. property to secure several deferred payments, etc., etc. Witnesses, Jno. W. Willis, Oliver Towles, jr.; Stapleton Crutchfield, Charles Croughton. April 1, 1794.

Jany. 20, 1794. Wm. Heslop of Spots. Co. to Lewis Young of same co. £160 curr. 276 a., formerly property of Benj. Chapman and whereon sd. Heslop now dwells, in Spots. Co., etc., etc. O. Towles, Dan. Forward, Thomas Wiglesworth. April 1, 1794.

Jany. 3, 1794. Wm. Ruffin and Margaret, his wife, of Spots. Co. to James Somerville of Fredksburg., Mercht. £293 11s. 3d. curr. 533¾ a., part of a tract purchased of Genl. Alexander Spotswood, etc., as by Ind. dated April 5, 1789, in Spots. Co., etc., etc. Danl. Grinnan, jr.; Adam Darby, Wm. Herndon, Chas. Davis. April 1, 1794.

Mar. 1, 1794. James Dudley and Ann, his wife, of Spots. Co. to Joseph Steward of same co. £200 curr. 163 a. in St. Geo. Par., Spots. Co., etc., etc. Thomas Colson, James Purvis, Thomas Minor, Peter Dudley. April 1, 1794.

March 10, 1794. James Dudley and Ann, his wife, of Spots. Co. to Wm. McWilliams of same co. £12 curr. 15 a. in Spots. Co., etc., etc. Thomas Colson, Thomas Minor, James Purvis. April 1, 1794.

*Ed. Note.—Annexed to this indenture and recorded therewith are letters from the sd. Geddis, from Philadelphia and Newport, directed to the sd. James Abbott, also one from one John Legg, V. M., and the deposition of "Arthur Clayton of Louisa Co. of lawful age," that the extracts given are correct, etc., etc.

March 17, 1794. Joshua Long and Joana, his wife, of Spots. Co. to Wm. Spindle of same co. £70 curr. 130 a. in Berkeley Par., Spots. Co., etc., etc. Jno. Turnley, Reuben Landram, Thos. Fuller. April 1, 1794.

Feby. 4, 1794. Wm. Parker, jr., of Spots. Co. to Wm. Parker, Senr., of same co. £58 9s. 2d. curr. 1 negro woman, several horses, etc., etc. Philemon Davis, Archibald Terrell, Benj. Robinson. April 1, 1794.

March 20, 1794. Henry Johnston and Agnes, his wife, of Spots. Co. to John Shirley of same co. £158 8s. 280 a. adj. lands of Ambrose Smith, Jas. Smith, Elizabeth Towles, Benj. Reynolds, Waller Lewis, Jas. Gimbo, Ambrose Shackleford's Estate, Thomas Shirley and Waller Johnston in Spots. Co., etc., etc. Thomas Towles, Peter P. Nunly, John Duerson. April 1, 1794.

Novr. 4, 1793. Elisha Dismukes and Anna, his wife, of Spots. Co. to Sarah Morris of same co. £20 curr. 50 a. in Spots. Co., etc., etc. Jno. Shirley, jr.; Jas. Wiglesworth, Thomas Dillard, Jno. Sorrell. April 1, 1794.

March 20, 1794. James Wiglesworth, Senr., and Mary, his wife; James Wiglesworth, jr., and ——, his wife, and John Shirley and Frances, his wife, to Henry Johnston. Whereas, the sd. Wiglesworths sold to the sd. Shirley, 193 a. in Spots. Co., and before conveyance thereof the sd. Shirley sold the same to the sd. Johnston. This Ind. witnesseth, the sd. Wiglesworths in consideration of £144 15s. to them pd. by the sd. Shirley, and the sd. Shirley, in consideration of £144 15s. to him pd. by the sd. Johnston, they convey the sd. land to him the sd. Johnston, etc., etc. Witnesses, Thomas Towles, P. P. Nunly, Jno. Duerson. April 1, 1794.

Octr. 15, 1793. George Goodloe, jr., and Judith, his wife, to George Goodloe, Senr. £76 11s. curr. 74 a. of land, etc., etc. Claiburn Durrett, Hugh Roy, Benj. Tompkins, John Wright. April 1, 1794.

March 31, 1794. James Lewis and Elizabeth, his wife, of Spots. Co. to Michael Robinson of same co. £13 10s. 27 a. in Spots. Co., etc., etc. No witnesses. April 1, 1794.

Feby. 26, 1794. Thomas Turner and Thomas Hackney of Spots. Co. to John Turner of same county. £12 curr. 40 a. in Spots. Co., etc., etc. Wm. Arnold, Robert Knight, James Turner. April 1, 1794.

March 31, 1794. Thomas Haydon of Spots. Co. to Jno. Whitaker Willis of same co. £50 curr. 50 a. purchased of Nathan Hawkins, jr., in St. Geo. Par., Spots. Co., etc., etc. O. Towles, O. Towles, jr. April 1, 1794.

April 1, 1794. Edwd. Herndon, acting excr. of Stapleton Crutchfield, Decd., to Thos. Duerson of Spots. Co. £221 4s. 7d. curr. 287 a. known as the old house tract, belonging to est. of Stapleton Crutchfield, Decd., in Berkeley Par., Spots. Co., etc., etc. No witnesses. April 1, 1794.

July 1, 1793. Richd. Kenny and Milly, his wife, of Fredksbg. to Wm. Richards of Culpeper Co. £129 11s. Lot No. 78 in town of Fredksbg., sold by decree of Court to satisfy a debt due by the sd. Kenny, to Robt. Ralston and James Vanuxen, assignees of Tarrasson Bros. & Co., etc., etc. Witnesses, Wm. Smock, Jno. Mumford, David Oliver, Jas. Lilly, Thomas Goose, F. Thornton, jr. April 1, 1794.

June 3, 1794. John Wren of Spots. Co. to Edward Hyde of same co. £75. 106 a. in Spots. Co., etc., etc. Benj. Holladay, Thos. Goose, Jonathan Johnston. July 1, 1794.

July 1, 1794. Richard Todd and Margaret, his wife, of Spots. Co. to James Jarrel of same co. £36 curr. 117 a. in Spots. Co., etc., etc. No witnesses. July 1, 1794.

March 15, 1794. John Shirley, jr., and Frances, his wife, of Spots. Co. to Thomas Shirley of same co. £158 8s. curr. 243 a. whereon sd. Jno. Shirley lives in Spots. Co., etc., etc. Benj. Tompkins, Littleton Pharis, Wm. Aldress. July 1, 1794.

March 4, 1794. Henry Pemberton and Elizabeth, his wife, of Spots. Co. to Wm. Cason of same co. £50 curr. 121½ a. in Spots. Co., etc., etc. Jno. Herndon, Edwd. Herndon, John Crutchfield, Wm. Robinson. July 1, 1794.

Jany. 1, 1794. Thomas Shirley and Molly, his wife, of Spots. Co. to John Billingsley of same co. £100 curr. 70 a. of land, etc., etc. Thomas Towles, Stapleton Crutchfield, Robert Branham. July 1, 1794.

Jany. 2, 1793. Agreement between Henry Johnson of Spots. Co. and Jno. Waller Johnson of same co. The sd. Henry Johnson conveys to the sd. J. W. Johnson in trust, for the maintenance of the sd. Henry, viz., 402 a. whereon sd. Henry lives, also numerous slaves, cattle, sheep, hogs, goods and chattels, etc., etc., and whereas, the sd. Henry owes sundry debts, the sd. property, in trust, for the payment thereof and the over-plus for the benefit of sd. Henry, etc., etc., "sd. Henry Johnson and Agnes, his wife," etc., etc. Witnesses, Betsy Conner, John Somnell (?), Garland Hill. July 1, 1794.

March 25, 1794. Henry Pemberton and Elizabeth, his wife, of Spots. Co. to Larkin Pemberton of Culpeper Co. £80 curr. 171 a. in Spots. Co., etc., etc. Jno. W. Willis, Jno. Herndon, Clement Montague, James Long. July 1, 1794.

July 1, 1794. Articles of agreement between Dr. Robert Wellford of Fredksbg., etc., and Robert Brooke, atto. at law and Guardian of Wm. Thornton. The sd. Wm. Thornton is apprenticed to the sd. Wellford for the term of 6 yrs., to be instructed in practice of medicine and surgery, etc., etc. No witnesses. July 1, 1794.

July 1, 1794. John Scott of Spots. Co. and Mary, his mother, to Thomas Colson of same co. £150 curr. 220 a. in Spots. Co., etc., etc. No wit-nesses. July 1, 1794.

May 1, 1794. Capt. John Carter and Mary, his wife, of Spots. Co. and Margaret Marshall, widow, of Caroline Co. to Dr. Robt. Wellford of Fredksbg. Whereas, sd. Margaret Marshall is entitled to 1-7 part of a certain tract of land and the other 6 parts are vested in the afsd. Jno. Carter, who with the sd. Margaret Marshall have agreed to sell their respective parts to the sd. Wellford. This Ind. witnesseth, that sd. Carter and Marshall in consideration of the sum of £38 8s. to the sd. Carter, and £4 16s. to the sd. Marshall in hand pd. they convey to the sd. Wellford 28 a. in Spots. Co., etc., etc. Witnesses, Bennett Tompkins, Geo. G. Quarles, Jno. Tompkins, Jos. Brock, Wm. Carter, Reuben Straug-han. July 1, 1794.

June 23, 1794. Spencer Coleman and ——, his wife, of Spots. Co. from Robert Hill of King and Queen Co. and Hannah, his wife. £100 curr. 179 a. in Berkeley Par., Spots. Co., etc., etc. Saml. Hill, Jno. Hill, Waller Lewis, jr.; Richd. Hill, Edwd. Garlick. Septr. 2, 1794.

May 20, 1794. Wm. Reat and Ann, his wife, of Fredksbg. to Robert Pleasants and John Pleasants of Baltimore, Maryland, Merchts. Whereas, Jno. Dixon, atto. in fact for Roger Dixon and Lucy Dixon, did abt. June 26, 1789, assign and let over, for a certain consideration, to the sd. Reat a certain tract in the town of Fredksbg. on Caroline Street, etc., etc. And whereas, a certain James Heath and Susannah Heath of Fredksbg. did abt. Feby. 15, 1790, sell to the sd. Reat, Lot No. 20 in town of Fredksbg., etc., etc., and whereas, the sd. Reat stands justly indebted to the sd. Jno. Pleasants and Robt. Pleasants, afsd.; he the sd. Reat deeds the above named lots, in trust, to the sd. Pleasants, as security for the sd. debt, etc., etc. Witnesses, James McCormick, Jno. Jennings, jr. Septr. 2, 1794.

Feby. 20, 1794. Benj. Head to Joshua Long, who stands bound as security for the sd. Head. To indemnify him the sd. Head conveys him, the sd. Long, one negro wench, in trust, etc., etc. Witnesses, Thomas Towles, Wm. Drake. Septr. 2, 1794.

June 10, 1794. Edwd. Herndon and James Lewis, Execrs. of Jno. Herndon, Decd., and Mary Herndon, widow of sd. Jno. Herndon, Decd., to Revd. James Stevenson of Fredksbg. £300 curr. 277 a. in St. Geo. Par., Spots. Co., etc., etc. Robt. Hart, Lewis Holladay, Henry Daingerfield, Richd. Todd, Jno. Herndon, Jno. McWhirt, Thos. Strachan. Septr. 2, 1794.

May 12, 1794. Henry Chandler and Elizabeth, his wife, of Halifax Co. to Wm. Wiglesworth of Caroline Co. £50 curr. 100 a. adj. lands of sd. Wiglesworth, widow Wyatt and widow Newton, and purchased of Thomas Goodloe in Spots. Co., etc., etc. Jas Crawford, Jas. Crawford, jr.; Jas. Smith. Septr. 2, 1794.

April 14, 1794. James Skeggs and Catherine, his wife, to Wm. Drummond. £69 curr. 72 a. in Spots. Co., etc., etc. Robt. Patton, Wm. Lovell, Colin Ross, Rog. Coltart; Wm. Thomas. Septr. 2, 1794.

March 4, 1794. Thomas Ball and Mildred, his wife, of Spots. Co. to George Ball of same co. £120 curr. 133 a. purchased of Jno. Edwards, etc., as by deed dated Septr. 30, 1787; also 65 a., part of a tract purchased of Edward Brasfield, etc., as by deed dated Oct. 2, 1787, in Spots. Co., etc., etc. Wm. Bowlin, Anthony Arnold, Alexander x Moore. Septr. 2, 1794.

March 4, 1794. Thomas Ball of Spots. Co. to George Ball of same co. In trust 300 a. of land in Spots. Co. purchased of Edwd. Brasfield, etc., to be sold by the sd. Geo. Ball for the payment of certain debts due by sd. Thos. Ball, etc., etc. If any surplus is left after the payment of the sd. debts, then the same to be held in trust for the benefit of Mildred, the wife of sd. Thomas Ball, and Ann, Edward Portues, Mildred Downman, Mary Taylor, Thomas and Martha Taylor Ball, children of the afsd. Thomas Ball, etc., etc. Witnesses, Anthony Arnold, Wm. Bowlin, Alexander x Moore. Septr. 2, 1794.

Augt. 30, 1794. Gawin Corbin and Elizabeth, his wife, of Caroline Co. and Thomas Sthreshly and Patty, his wife, of King George Co. Exchange of Lands. Whereas, the sd. Corbin being seized in fee simple of 937 a. (part of a large tract) of land in Spots. Co., which he deeds to the sd. Sthreshly, the sd. Sthreshly deeding to the sd. Corbin, 312⅓ a. (purchased by sd. Sthreshly of Jno. Hipkins of Port Royal) in Westmoreland Co., which sd. Sthreshly holds in fee simple, etc., etc. Witnesses, Abner Harrison, James Knott, Sam Owens, James Nelson, Reuben Owens, Bathl. Jones, Jekyll Jones, Shelton Jones. Septr. 2, 1794.

Septr. 15, 1794. James Pettigrew and Mary, his wife, of Fredksbg. to James Clarke of Caroline Co. £40 curr. 60 a. whereon Jno. Chisum lately lived in Spots. Co., etc., etc. Ambrose Pitts, Wm. Sale, jr.; Richard Gouldman. Decr. 2, 1794.

Decr. 2d, 1794. Marriage agreement between James Frazer and Lucy Smith, "a marriage shortly intended to take place between them," etc., etc. Witnesses, Jno. Smith, James Smith, Richd. Long. Decr. 2, 1794.

Octr. 6, 1794. Jno. x Wilson of Washington Co. in the state or territory South of the Ohio River, po. of atto. to Thomas Dillard of Spots. Co., Va. To demand and receive of Saml. Luck of Hanover Co., Va., Executor of the last will and testament of Saml. Luck, late of Spots. Co., Decd., sums owing the sd. Wilson as a legacy under the will of the sd. Luck, Decd., etc., etc. Witnesses, Jno. Crawford, Thomas Dillard, Wm. Buckner, Booker Wilson, Jos. Wilson. Decr. 2, 1794.

Novr. 7, 1794. Thomas Colson of Spots. Co., Gent., from John Herndon [son of Edwd. Herndon] of same co., Gent. £960 curr. 549 a. whereon sd. Herndon lives in Spots. Co., etc., etc. Also several slaves, cattle, goods and chattels, etc., etc., and the sd. "Thomas Colson being desirous to make a reasonable settlement of the whole thereof and so as to make provision for his neice, Judith Herndon, wife of the sd. Jno. Herndon, etc., witnesseth that the sd. Colson gives to the sd. Jno. Herndon and Judith, his wife, and the children begotten or to begotten by them, the above mentioned lands, slaves, cattle, goods, etc., etc. Witnesses, Edwd. Herndon, Jas. Frazer, Edwd. Herndon, jr.; Wm. Stanard, Jas. Lewis, Jas. Stevenson, Tho. Minor. Decr. 2, 1794.

DEED BOOK O

1794–1797

*Septr. 1, 1795. James Clarke and Sally, his wife, of Essex Co., Va., to Wm. Strutton of Spots. Co. £55 curr. 60 a. purchased of James Pettigrew in Spots. Co., etc., etc. H. B. Brooke, Andw. Monroe, Henry Garnett. Septr. 1, 1795.

Novr. 4, 1794. Harmon Haner and Eleanor, his wife, of Spots. Co. to Lewis Holladay of same co. £100 curr. 220 a. in Spots. Co., etc., etc. Jno. M. Herndon, Edwd. Herndon, Jas. Lewis, Ephram Knight, Benja. Chapman. Decr. 2, 1794.

Septr. 26, 1794. Jno. White and Mary, his wife, of Spots. Co. to Lewis Holladay of same co. £250 curr. 550 a. in Spots. Co., etc., etc. Jo. Willoughby, Wm. Winslow, Thomas Winslow, Walter Chiles, Jos. Holladay, Thos. Lipscomb, Austin Sandidge. Decr. 2, 1794.

Septr. 26, 1794. Chas. x Jinkins and Elizabeth, his wife, of Spots. Co. to John White of same co. £3 curr. ½ a. in Spots. Co., etc., etc. Lewis Holladay, Quire Jinkins, Jno. x Smith, Robert x Gains. Decr. 2, 1794.

July 16, 1794. Benjamin Robinson to Wm. Drake, to indemnify the sd. Drake who stands bound as security for the sd. Robinson, the sd. Robinson conveys him a negro man, in trust, etc., etc. Witnesses, Wm. Burnett, R. Frazer. Decr. 2, 1794.

May 24, 1794. Samuel Partlow of Spots. Co. to his daughter, Ann Partlow. Deed of Gift. 2 negroes. Witnesses, John Penny, John Martin. Decr. 2, 1794.

Septr. 10, 1794. John Carter, jr., and Mary, his wife, of Spots. Co. to John Penny of same co. £20 curr. 20 a. in Berkeley Par., Spots. Co., etc., etc. No witnesses. Decr. 2, 1794.

July 2, 1794. James Stevens and Mary Bird, his wife, of Spots. Co. to Joseph Graham of same co. £35 0s. 4d. 110 a. adj. land whereon Dr. Thos. Powell lives in Spots. Co., etc., etc. Jas. Smith, Robt. Branham, Joel Fagg. Decr. 2, 1794.

—— ——, 1794. Samuel Partlow of Spots. Co. and Mary, his wife, to David Partlow of same co. £25 curr. 100 a. to be taken off tract whereon sd. Saml. lives in Spots. Co., etc., etc. No witnesses. Decr. 2, 1794.

Septr. 13, 1794. John x Shirley, Senr., of Spots. Co. to Wm. Anderson of Cumberland Co. £35. 1 negro after death of sd. Shirley, etc., etc. Jno. Shirley, jr.; Henry Dodd, Jas. Crawford. Decr. 2, 1794.

*Ed. Note.—This deed is recorded on an extra page at the commencement of the Deed Book.

Octr. 23, 1794. Clement Montague of Spots. Co. to John Herndon of same co. £11 4s. curr. 8 a., etc., in Spots. Co., etc., etc. No witnesses. Decr. 2, 1794.

Octr. 25, 1794. Henry Goodloe, jr., of Spots. Co. to James Stevens of same co. £50 curr. 54 a. in Spots. Co., etc., etc. Benj. Thompkins, Danl. Lindsay, Henry Durrett, George Goodloe, jr. Decr. 2, 1794.

Augt. 28, 1794. John Billingsley to Thomas Duerson, both of Spots. Co. 1 a. for mill purposes, etc., etc. No witnesses. Decr. 2, 1794.

Septr. 15, 1794. Wm. Carter of Spots. Co. to James Hume of same co. 4 slaves in trust for Wm. Lewis Hume (grandchild to sd. Wm. Carter and son to the sd. James Hume) when of age, etc., etc. Witnesses, Abraham Carter, Wm. Carter, junr.; Rice Carter. Decr. 2, 1794.

Novr. 4, 1794. Robert Scott and Janet, his wife, of Culpeper Co. to James Dykes of Fredksbg., Spots. Co. £375 curr. 639 a. in Spots. Co., in several tracts, etc., etc. Witnesses, Jno. Patton, Armistead Long, Wm. W. Thomas, Jno. Legg. Jany. 6, 1795.

Decr. 31, 1794. Henry Johnson and Agnes, his wife, and John Shirley, jr., and Frances, his wife. Exchange of lands. Sd. Johnson conveys to sd. Shirley, jr., 193 a. formerly purchased from sd. Shirley, James Wiglesworth, Sr. and Jr., etc., etc. The sd. Shirley conveys to sd. Johnson, 258 a. in Spots. Co., etc., etc. Witnesses, Thomas Towles, Richd. Shackleford, Mary Shackleford. Jany. 6, 1795.

Jany. 6, 1795. Wm. Estes and Frances, his wife, of Spots. Co. to Francis King of same co. £4 10s. 7½ a. in Berkeley Par., Spots. Co., etc., etc. No witnesses. Jany. 6, 1795.

Jany. 6, 1795. Thomas Lipscomb and Mary, his wife, of Spots. Co. to Francis King of same co. £74 10s. 100 a. in Berkeley Par., Spots. Co., etc., etc. No witnesses. Jany. 5, 1795.

Novr. 21, 1794. John Lewis of Spots. Co. to Wm. Fontaine of Hanover Co. and John Spotswood of Orange Co., Executors of Bowles Armistead, Decd., to indemnify them, conveys to them 2 negroes, etc., etc. Witnesses, Will. Frazer, R. Frazer. Jany. 6, 1795.

Jany. 4, 1795. Mann Page of Spots. Co. to Thomas Colson of same co. £1000 curr. Abt. 1180 a., part of a larger tract [from which several parcels have formerly been sold] in Spots. Co., etc., etc. Thos. Hughes, Littleton Goodwin, Jno. Baylor, Jas. Lewis, jr.; Robt. Mercer, Tho. Goodwin. Jany. 6, 1795.

Septr. 5, 1794. Thos. Posey and Mary, his wife, of Spots. Co. to John Lewis of same co. £1250 curr. 5 a. in Spots. Co. below the town of Fredksbg., and near to the same, purchased of Jas. Frazer and John Minor, and known as "Sligo," etc., etc. Witnesses, Gabriel Lewis, Jno. Scott, Reuben Straughan. Feby. 6, 1795.

Octr. 26, 1793. Elijah Woodfolk of Spots. Co. to John Woodfolk, Sr., of same co. £105 curr. 125 a., lately conveyed by the sd. John Woodfolk, Sr., to his son, the sd. Elijah Woodfolk in Spots. Co., etc., etc. Jno. Woodfolk, jr.; Thos. Hackett, Sally Woodfolk, Milly Cason. Feby. 3, 1795.

Jany. 28, 1795. Benjamin Ballard of Spots. Co. to his daughter, Pegg Ballard. Deed of Gift. A negro wench and her increase, etc., and should the sd. Pegg die unmarried or without leaving issue, then the sd. negro to my son Charles, etc., etc. No witnesses. Feby. 3, 1795.

Jany. 28, 1795. Benjamin Ballard of Spots. Co. to his son, Charles Ballard. Deed of Gift. A negro, etc., and should the sd. Charles die leaving no issue, then the sd. negro to my daughter Peggy, etc., etc. No witnesses. Feby. 3, 1795.

Jany. 21, 1795. Solomon Betton and Lucinda, his wife, of Loudoun Co. to Robert Brooke of the City of Richmond, Va. Whereas, the Honble. James Mercer, late of the town of Fredksbg., Esq., Decd., did by his last will, etc., devise unto his daughter, the sd. Lucinda (now the wife of the sd. Solomon Betton), £300 to be pd. to her on her marriage, also 100 guineas to be pd. her immediately on the death of the sd. James, her father, etc. This Ind. witnesseth, the sd. Solomon and Lucinda, his wife, in consideration of a tract of land sold the sd. Solomon Betton, in fee simple by the sd. Brooke and Mary, his wife, he, the sd. Solomon Betton and Lucinda, his wife, set over unto the sd. Brooke forever the sum of £440 the afsd. legacies devised the sd. Lucinda, etc., etc. Witnesses, Jno. T. Brooke, Jas. Mercer Garnett, Chas. Fenton Mercer. Feby. 3, 1795.

Jany. 21, 1795. Solomon Betton and Lucinda, his wife, of Loudoun Co. to Robt. Brooke of the City of Richmond. £420 curr. 360 a. on s. side road leading from Fredksbg. to Spots. C. H., in Spots. Co., etc., etc. Mortgage. Witnesses, Charles Fenton Mercer, Jas. Mercer Garnett, John T. Brooke. Feby. 3, 1795.

Feby. 2, 1795. Thomas Colson of Spots. Co., Gent., of first part; Jno. Whitaker Willis of same Co., Gent., of second part; Ann Willis, wife of sd. Jno. W. Willis, of same Co., of third part. Whereas, the sd. Jno. W. Willis being indebted to the sd. Colson in sum of £1000 and interest, to secure the payment of which, as far as it would go, the property hereinafter mentioned was conveyed and made over, besides some slaves, the whole of which was inadequate to meet the debt, and the sd. Colson hath agreed to give up a moiety of the sd. debt to the sd. Ann, provided she would in lieu thereof accept the property hereinafter mentioned, for the same, which she has agreed to do under the trusts, etc., etc. This Ind. therefore witnesseth, the sd. Colson in consideration of the premises, conveys to the sd. Ann Willis (with consent of sd. Jno. W. Willis) one mulatto wench slave, also goods and chattels, in trust for the sd. Ann Willis and her heirs, with power to dispose of the sd. slave, etc., etc., etc. Witnesses, Peter Dudley, O. Towles, Henry Daingerfield, Thomas Walden. Feby. 3, 1795.

May 1, 1792. Alexander Spotswood and Elizabeth, his wife, of Spots. Co. to Hezekiah Ellis of same co. £84 10s. curr. 130 a. in Spots. Co., etc., etc. Edwd. Herndon, Joseph Jones, Moses Estes. Feby. 3, 1795.

Feby. 3, 1794. John Lewis [heir at law and devisee of Colo. Fielding Lewis, Decd.] and Mary Ann, his wife, of Spots. Co., to Richard Dobson of the city of Richmond. Whereas, the sd. Fielding Lewis, Decd., during his lifetime did sell Lots 107 and 108 in Town of Fredksbg. to Geo. Washington, Esq., now Pres. of the U. S., etc., and the sd. Fielding Lewis in his lifetime meaning and intending to convey the afsd. lots to the sd. Washington, did in his lifetime execute a deed to the sd. Washington for two other lots, and which two other lots the sd. Fielding in his lifetime had sold to the late Judge Mercer, etc., etc., and the sd. Jno. Lewis, as heir and devisee of the sd. Fielding Lewis, hath since the death of sd. Fielding executed a deed for the same to the sd. Judge Mercer in his lifetime, and whereas, the sd. Washington is still deprived of a legal title to the lots 107 and 108 and hath sometime since sold the same to Charles Carter of Culpeper Co., Esq., who sold the same to the aforesd. Richard Dobson. Now this Ind. witnesseth, the sd. Jno. Lewis, in consideration of the premises and the sd. Washington agreeing to reconvey the afsd. lots sold, as afsd. to the sd. Judge Mercer during his lifetime, etc., the sd. Lewis hereby conveys to the sd. Dobson the afsd. lots Nos. 107 and 108 in Fredksbg., etc., etc. No witnesses. Feby. 3, 1795.

Octr. 20, 1794. Nathan Hawkins of Spots. Co., po. of atto. to Wm. Winslow of same co. Witnesses, Jno. Nelson, jr.; Benjamin Robinson. Feby. 3, 1795.

March 3, 1795. Wm. Chilton of Spots. Co. to Henry Gatewood, jr., and John Wallace, to indemnify them (they being bound as security for the sd. Chilton), conveys to them 5 slaves, two wagons, 8 horses, etc., etc., in trust, etc., etc. Witnesses, Jno. M. Herndon, Edward Herndon. April 7, 1795.

April 7, 1795. Thomas Towles and Mary, his wife, to John Humphries. £50. 104 a. purchased of Wm. Rash in Spots. Co., etc., etc. Robt. S. Chew, Elizabeth Towles, jr.; Mary B. Chew. April 7, 1795.

April 7, 1795. George Overton and Mary, his wife, of Spots. Co. to Benjamin Massey of same co. £20 curr. 70 a. in Berkeley Par., Spots. Co., etc., etc. No witnesses. April 7, 1795.

April 7, 1795. George Overton and Mary, his wife, of Spots. Co. to Thomas Moore of same co. £12 10s. curr. 57 a. in Spots. Co., etc., etc. No witnesses. April 7, 1795.

April 7, 1795. Daniel Lane and Ann, his wife, of Spots. Co. to Robert Hart of same county. £3 6s. 3d. 4 a. 67 poles in Spots. Co., etc., etc. Thomas Winslow, Jos. Chew, Thomas Minor. April 7, 1795.

Novr. 10, 1794. Saml. Todd, late of Spots. Co., po. of atto. to his brother, Richard Todd, and friend Edward Herndon, jr., both of Spots. Co., etc., etc. Witnesses, Jno. Herndon, Jos. Chew. April 7, 1795.

Decr. 30, 1794. James Arnold and Elizabeth, his wife, of Orange Co. to Wm. Willoughby of Spots. Co. £30 curr. 25 a. adj. lands of James Robins, Jonathan Johnson and sd. Willoughby in Spots Co., etc., etc. Jno. Sorrell, Jas. Ribias, Ashman Sorrell. April 7, 1795.

Novr. 14, 1793. Francis Coleman to John x Jinkins. Lease. 1000 a. on Pigeon Run in Spots. Co., etc., etc. "Sd. Jno. Jinkins and Sarah, his wife," etc. 500 lbs. tob. yearly, etc. Witnesses, Nicho. Fisher, Archbd. Terall. April 7, 1795.

Decr. 4, 1794. Alexander Spotswood of Spots. Co. to Henry Lee of Westmoreland Co. Lease. "All his vacant lands untenanted and being in Spots. Co. above falls of the Rappk. River," etc., etc. £900 specie, yearly, etc. No witnesses. April 7, 1795.

Decr. 3, 1788. Samuel Gibson and Milley, his wife, of Spots. Co. to Wm. Trigg of same county. £68 curr. 68 a. in Spots. Co., etc., etc. Jeremiah Wilson, Hezekiah Arnold, John Steward. April 7, 1795.

Octr. 6, 1794. John Waller and Elizabeth, his wife, to James Humphries. £60. 50 a. in Spots. Co., etc., etc. James Samuel, Jno. Shackelford, James Gimber. April 7, 1795.

March 2, 1795. Robert Hill and Hannah, his wife, of King and Queen Co. to Wm. Graves of Spots. Co. £30 7s. curr. 77 a. in Spots. Co., etc., etc. Saml. Hill, Jno. Garlick, Jno. Hill. April 7, 1795.

Feby. 25, 1795. Richard Long and Joseph Sams, both of Spots. Co. Sd. Long conveys to sd. Sams 5½ a. in Spots. Co., etc., etc.; sd. Sams conveys to sd. Long 15 a. in Spots. Co., etc., etc. Witnesses, Benj. Tompkins, Danl. Lindsay, Jno. Pulliam, Jas. Wray. April 7, 1795.

April 7, 1795. Charles Bennet and Patsy, his wife, of Spots. Co. to John Johnson of same co. £30. 100 a. in Spots. Co., etc., etc. Austin Sandidge, David Bronaugh, Rawlings Pulliam. April 7, 1795.

Octr. 1, 1794. Alexander Spotswood, Senr., Esq., and Elizabeth, his wife, of Spots. Co., to Edward Herndon [son of Joseph] of same county. £29 curr. 58 a. in Spots. Co., etc., etc. Edward Herndon, Jas. Hutcheson, Jas. Pritchett, Jno. M. Herndon. April 7, 1795.

May 1, 1790. Alexander Spotswood and Elizabeth, his wife, of Spots. Co. to Wm. Jones of same co. £30 curr. 100 a. in Spots. Co., etc., etc. No witnesses. April 7, 1795.

Septr. 27, 1794. John Graves of Spots. Co. to his son-in-law, Lewis Partlow. Deed of Gift. 2 negroes. Witnesses, Edwd. Cason, Wm. Graves, Elizabeth Graves. April 7, 1795.

Jany. 7, 1795. Benjamin Hyde and Mary, his wife, of Orange Co. to John Andrews of Spots. Co. £25. 95 a. in Berkeley Par., Spots. Co., etc., etc. Benj. Holladay, Jno. Lipscomb, Edwd. Hyde. April 7, 1795.

Septr. 23, 1794. Nathan Hawkins of Spots. Co. to James Ballard of same co. £23 curr. "All sd. Hawkins right, title, claim, etc., against the estate of Jarvis Haydon, Decd., exclusive of what sd. Hawkins hath now in his possession," etc., etc. Witnesses, Joseph Brock, Clerk; Richard Todd. April 7, 1795.

June 19, 1794. Benjamin Robinson to Jos. Brock. Whereas, March 24, 1788, sd. Robinson executed to Jno. Brock a deed of trust for the several uses, etc., therein stated, and among other things 5 negroes, which were to be held in trust for the sd. Benj. and Susannah, his wife, during their lives, etc., and after their deaths without issue, or being disposed of by the sd. Susannah, and she being since dead without issue, the sd. slaves will descend to her father, Joseph Brock, or his heirs, the sd. Robinson, in consideration of sd. Jos. Brock's giving up certain stock, slaves, etc., to the sd. Robinson, he conveys to sd. Brock the aforementioned 5 slaves, and 2 others, etc., etc. Witnesses, John Perry, James Underwood. April 8, 1795.

Feby. 16, 1795. Lewis Young and Elizabeth, his wife, and Wm. Heslop and Ann, his wife, of Spots. Co. to Wm. Carter of same co. £56 14s. curr.

63 a., part of a tract sold by sd. Heslop to sd. Young, in Spots. Co., etc., etc. Jno. M. Herndon, Jno. Crutchfield, Edmd. Foster. April 8, 1795.

Feby. 28, 1795. Lewis Young of Spots. Co. and Elizabeth, his wife, to Wm. Heslop of same co. £60 curr. 213 a. formerly purchased of sd. Heslop in Spots. Co., etc., etc. Edwd. Herndon, Wm. Carter, Stockley Towles, Robert Crutchfield. April 8, 1795.

Feby. 28, 1795. Wm. Heslop and Ann, his wife, of Spots. Co. to Wm. Carter of same co. To indemnify sd. Carter, etc., and for the benefit of Ann, wife of sd. Heslop, and any children begotten or to be begotten between them, the sd. Heslop conveys to sd. Carter in trust, 176 a. in Spots. Co., etc., etc., etc. Witnesses, Jno. Crutchfield, Robert Crutchfield, Edwd. Herndon, Stockley Towles. April 8, 1795.

April 7, 1795. Jno. Lewis and Mary, his wife, of Spots. Co. to Wm. Richards of Culpeper Co. £600. 15 a. on Rappk. River, Spots. Co., etc., etc. No witnesses. April 7, 1795.

Septr. 15, 1794. Thomas Sthreshly and Patty, his wife, of King Geo. Co. to Robert Wellford of Spots. Co. £190 curr. 227 a. in Spots. Co., etc., etc. Jas. Lilly, A. G. Beverley, Lar. Stanard, Bev. Chew, Wm. Thornton. July 7, 1795.

July 2, 1795. Thomas Pritchett and Ann, his wife, late the wife of Jno. Waller, Decd., to Wm. Waller, Bowker Waller, and James Jones and Ann, his wife. Whereas, Jno. Waller, late of Spots. Co., decd., father of the sd. Wm., Bowker and Ann, did on Feby. 25, 1775, by his deed then dated, sell unto Jno. Lewis, atto.-at-law, 914 a. in Spots. Co., in trust; 500 a. thereof, for the sd. Jno. Lewis, his heirs, etc., etc., and part of the price pd. for the sd. land to be applied to the payment of a certain debt, the residue to be laid out in slaves, to be held for the use of the sd. Ann Waller, for her lifetime, and after her death, in trust, for all the children of the sd. Jno. Waller and the sd. Ann, his wife, and the residue of the tract of land contg. 414 a. to be held in trust for the sd. Ann Waller during her life, and after her death, 150 a. (adj. the afsd. 500 a.) to be set apart for their son, Bowker Waller, and the residue of the tract, abt. 264 a., for the use of their son, Wm. Waller, and further in trust that sd. Ann Waller, out of the rents, profits, etc., should apply as much of them as should be necessary to the maintenance and education of the children of the sd. Jno. and Ann Waller during their respective minorities, and whereas, the sd. Wm. and Bowker Waller and the sd. Ann, Wife of James Jones, were not boarded, clothed, etc., etc., by the sd. Ann, agreeable to the trust, it is thought reasonable and just that they should receive a compensation for the same, witnesseth, that sd. Thos. Pritchett and Ann, his wife, in consideration of the premises, etc., release to the grantees in this indenture, all right, title, etc., in 2 slaves, goods and chattels, etc., etc. Witnesses, Jno. Herndon, Jas. Frazer. July 7, 1795.

Jany. 5, 1795. Wm. Burnett to Robt. Scott, to indemnify the sd. Scott, he being bound as security for the sd. Burnett, the sd. Burnett conveys to him several negroes, cattle, horses, etc., etc., in trust, etc. Witnesses, Danl. Grinnan, jr.; Jno. Mitchell. July 7, 1795.

March 1, 1795. Benj. Wharton of Spots. Co. to Thomas Alcock of Caroline Co. In consideration of a negro slave, one wagon and five horses, the sd. Wharton conveys to sd. Alcock, 400 a. adj. lands of David Chevis and Jno. White in Berkeley Par., Spots. Co., etc., etc. Jno. M. Herndon, Reubin Straughan, Joseph Pollard, jr.; Jas. Wilson. July 7, 1795.

Feby. 23, 1795. Geo. Goodloe, jr., and Judith, his wife, of Spots. Co. to Daniel Lindsay of same co. £200 curr. 167 a. in Spots. Co., etc., etc. Benj. Tompkins, Jno. Stevens, Richd. Johnson. July 7, 1795.

July 7, 1795. Edwd. Herndon, acting executor of Stapleton Crutchfield, decd., to Jno. Minor Herndon. £150 curr. 133 a. in Spots. Co., etc., etc. No witnesses. July 7, 1795.

July 7, 1795. Edwd. Herndon, acting executor of Stapleton Crutchfield, decd., to Joseph Herndon of Spots. Co. £150 curr. 299 a. in Spots. Co., etc., etc. No witnesses. July 7, 1795.

Decr. 10, 1794. Wm. Buchanan and Mary, his wife, of Spots. Co. to Charles Bennett of same co. £30. 60 a. in Berkeley Par., Spots. Co., etc., etc. Jos. Pulliam, Philip Young, Jno. Shirley, jr. July 7, 1795.

March 2, 1795. Jno. Chew Buckner to Larkin Stanard, both of Spots. Co. Whereas, by Ind. dated Sept. 18, 1794, the sd. Buckner mortgaged to the sd. Stanard, all the sd. Buckner's interest in the est. of his decd. father, Mordacai Buckner, in the hands of Wm. Stanard, Adms.. Now, in consideration of £200, the sd. Buckner conveys the sd. est. to the sd. Larkin Stanard, etc., etc. Witnesses, A. Parker, Betsy Turnley, Beverley Chew Stanard, Bev. Chew. July 7, 1795.

Feby. 3, 1795. Richard Young of Woodford Co., Kentucky, po. of atto. to John Robinson of Fredksbg., Va., to make sale of ⅓d part of 14,280 a., pat. by Jno. Robinson, Benj. Robinson and Richd. Young; ½ of 3121 a., pat. in names of Jno. Stewart and Richd. Young, also ½ of 1546 a., pat. by Wm. Richards and Richd. Young, etc., etc. No witnesses. July 7, 1795.

April 13, 1795. Joseph Chew and Mary, his wife, of Spots. Co. to George Cammack of same co. £96 9s. curr. 322½ a. in Spots. Co., etc., etc. Edwd. Herndon, Jno. Chew, Robert Cammack. July 7, 1795.

Jany. 3, 1795. Jeremiah Morton of Spots. Co. to Wm. Morton of Orange Co. £830 11s. Mortgage. Numerous slaves, etc., etc. Witnesses, Jas. Lewis, jr.; C. Davis, Wm. Herndon. July 7, 1795.

Feby. 2, 1795. Jno. Lewis and Mary Ann, his wife, of Spots. Co. to John Ferneyhough of Fredksbg. For considerations named, transfer of bonds, mortgages, etc., etc. 4½ a. and 30 sq. poles at "Sligo" (below Fredksbg.), bought by Gen. Thos. Posey of Jas. Frazer and Jno. Minor, and by the sd. Posey sold unto the sd. Lewis, in Spots. Co., etc., etc. Thos. Foster, R. Wellford, Jas. Frazer, Jas. Lewis, jr.; Wm. Herndon. July 7, 1795.

May 1, 1795. James Pritchett of Spots. Co. to Thomas Colson of same co. £28. Cattle, horses, goods and chattels, etc., etc. Witness, Jno. M. Herndon. July 7, 1795.

Augt. 14, 1795. Charles Thornton, in consideration of £60 curr. pd. him by Larkin Stanard for Jno. Wheeler, the sd. Thornton releases and emancipates a negro slave named Priscilla, purchased of Henry Fitzhugh, etc., etc. No witnesses. Augt. 4, 1795.

Septr. 1, 1795. Wm. Wiglesworth of Spots. Co. to James Crawford of same co. £23 14s. curr. 79 a. in Spots. Co., etc., etc. Septr. 1, 1795.

Jany. 4, 1795. John Arnold of Spots. Co. to his mother, Mary Arnold, of same co. and her children, viz., Sarah, Anthony, Mary, Rice, William Arnold and Isabella Mastin. Bond of £500 curr. to relinquish all his right, title, etc., in the est. of his father, Anthony Arnold, Decd. (except the land), to his (the sd. John's) brothers and sisters as afsd., the sd. Mary Arnold (his mother) conveying to him 1 negro wench, Nan, etc., etc. Witnesses, Edmd. Daniel, Jno. Millbank, Elizabeth Salmon. Septr. 1, 1795.

March 2, 1795. Thomas Ball and Mildred, his wife, and George Ball and Martha, his wife, of Spots. Co. to John Keegan of same co. £90. 180 a. in Spots. Co., etc., etc. Wm. Ludwidge, Patrick Keegan, Charles Burrage. Septr. 1, 1795.

Jany 12, 1795. Jno. x Shirley, Senr., of Berkeley Par., Spots. Co. to his daughter, Dorothy Dood, wife of Henry Dood. Deed of Gift. A negro girl, etc., etc. Witnesses, Thomas Shirley, Morady Morris, James Crawford. Septr. 1, 1795.

March 24, 1795. Joseph Brock and Mary Beverley, his wife, of Spots. Co. to Tilly Emerson of same co. £20 curr. 75 a. purchased of Genl. Alexr. Spotswood and Col. Gawin Corbin in Spots. Co., etc., etc. Witnesses, J. Brock, Nimrod Branham, Daniel Branham, Bevy. Stubblefield, Edwd. Herndon, Thos. Minor, O. Towles. Septr. 1, 1795.

June 18, 1795. John Lewis and Mary Ann, his wife, of Spots. Co. to Thomas Magee of same co. £125 curr. 250 a., part of a larger tract purchased of Major Thomas Sthreshley (late of King George Co.) in Spots. Co., etc., etc. Richd. S. Hackley, John T. Brooke, Wm. Herndon, Jno. Chew, Clement Montague, Wm. Stanard, Edwd. Herndon, Bevy. Stubblefield, Will. Frazer. Septr. 1, 1795.

July 18, 1795. Wm. Bronaugh and Mary Ann, his wife; Jos. Eubank and Nancy G., his wife, all of Spots. Co. to David Sandidge of same co. £137 4s. 196 a. in Spots. Co., etc., etc. Robert Hart, Lewis Holladay, Austin Sandidge, David Bronaugh. Septr. 1, 1795.

June 29, 1795. Oliver Towles of Spots. Co., of first part; Reubin Straughan of same co., of second part; Fanny Straughan of same co., of the third part. Whereas, by Ind. dated April 12, 1785, the sd. Reubin Straughan did convey to the sd. Towles, a tract of land and sundry goods and chattels, which among other purposes were conveyed to indemnify the sd. Towles on acc. of his standing bound as security for the sd. Straughan, and whereas, the sd. Towles is about to suffer on acc. thereof, and the sd. Towles had a sale on May 12 last, and did sell publicly all the property conveyed by aforementioned Ind., which goods and chattels were purchased by the afsd. Fanny Straughan for the sum of £80, this Ind. therefore witnesseth, conveyance of the sd. Articles to the afsd. Fanny Straughan, etc., etc. Witnesseth, Thos. Wiglesworth, Jno. Wiglesworth, jr.; Jas. Richards. Septr. 1, 1795.

April 1, 1794. Nathan Hawkins, jr,. of Spots. Co. to Benjamin Pritchett of same co. £100 curr. 146 a., part of a tract conveyed to sd. Hawkins by his father (as by deed recd. in Dist. Court of Fredksbg) in St. George

Par., Spots. Co., etc., etc. Jno. Herndon, Wm. Robinson, Benj. Scott, Wm. Alsop, Zachariah Shackleford. Septr. 1, 1795.

July 1, 1795. Edwd. Herndon and Margaret, his wife, of Spots. Co. to Fontaine Maury of Fredksbg. £175 10s. curr. 117 a. in Spots. Co., etc., etc. No witnesses. Septr. 1, 1795.

July 10, 1795. Robert Crutchfield of Spots. Co. to Edwd. Herndon, acting executor of Stapleton Crutchfield, Decd. Mortgage. 657 a. in Spots. Co., etc., etc. Jno. Mitcham, Jas. Lewis, Thomas Strachan, John M. Herndon. Septr. 1, 1795.

Feby. 28, 1795. Wm. Heslop and Ann, his wife, of Spots. Co. to John Crutchfield of same co. £25. 40 a. in Spots. Co., etc., etc. Edwd. Herndon, Stockley Towles, Robert Crutchfield. Septr. 1, 1795.

Decr. 1, 1795. Jno. Alcock and Patty, his wife, of Orange Co. to Wm. Quarles of Spots. Co. £100 curr. 88 a. formerly drawn in Col. Bernard Moore's Lottery, Lot No. 5, in Spots. Co., etc., etc. No witnesses. Decr. 1, 1795.

Octr. 5, 1795. James Sandidge and Patsy, his wife, to David Sandidge. £40. 100 a. in Spots. Co., etc., etc. Robt. Hart, Lewis Holladay, David Bronaugh, Austin Sandidge, Jno. x Johnson. Decr. 1, 1795.

Novr. 20, 1795. Account of running line and deciding boundaries between lands of Lawrence Battaille of Caroline Co. to Wm. Stanard of Spots. Co., etc., etc., and the sd. Battaille conveying to sd. Stanard 30 a. in Spots. Co., etc., etc. This Ind. speaks of an intended exchange of lands, etc., etc. Witnesses, Bevy. Stanard, Alexr. Burnett, Reuben Deane, Jesse x Rains, Jno. x Page. Decr. 1, 1795.

Novr. 20, 1795. Wm. Stanard of Spots. Co. to Lawrence Bataille of Caroline Co. £80 curr. 2 tracts of land in Spots. Co., etc., etc. Bevy. Stanard, Alexr. Burnet, Reubin Deane, Jno. x Page, Jesse x Rains. Decr. 1, 1795.

Octr. 29, 1795. Thomas Colson and Frances, his wife, of Spots. Co. to Betty Lewis of same co. £1000. 722 a. whereon sd. Thos. Colson formerly lived in Spots. Co., etc., etc. Jona. Harris, Bowker Waller, David C. Ker, Geo. Lewis, Wm. Stanard, Tho. Minor. Decr. 1, 1795.

Octr. 8, 1795. Edward Hyde of Spots. Co. to John Chandler of same co. £80. 106 a. in Spots. Co., etc., etc. Claiborn Chandler, Z. Lewis, Jas. Stevens. Decr. 1, 1795.

July 18, 1795. Wm. Bronaugh of Spots. Co. to his son, David Bronaugh, of same co. £100 curr. 168 a. whereon sd. David Bronaugh now lives in Spots. Co., etc., etc. Robt. Hart, Lewis Holladay, Austin Sandidge, Joseph Eubank. Decr. 1, 1795.

Octr. 25, 1793. Robert Sale and Jane, his wife, of Spots. Co and James Pitts and Patty, his wife, of Caroline Co. to James Clarke of Caroline Co. £162. 162 a. in St. Geo. Par., Spots. Co., etc., etc. Jno. McWhirt. Lewis Pitts, Jno. Sale. Decr. 1, 1795.

April 22, 1795. Edward Herndon, acting Executor of Stapleton Crutchfield, Decd., to Robert Crutchfield. £475 curr. 657 a. in Berkeley Par., Spots. Co., etc., etc. Jno. Mitcham, Jas. Lewis, Thomas Strachan, Jno. M. Herndon. Decr. 1, 1795.

June 4, 1795. Release from Thomas Towles to Wm. and John Welch of a mortgage, they having settled their bond, etc., etc. Witnesses, Thos. Whiting, Jno. Mullikin. Decr. 1, 1795.

May 27, 1795. Wm. Chilton of Spots. Co. to Stanton Slaughter of Culpeper Co. £150 curr., which sd. Chilton stands indebted to Robt. Slaughter of Culpeper, father of the sd. Stanton Slaughter, etc., etc. Mortgage. A life lease of land held by sd. Chilton of Alexr. Spotswood, several negroes, horses, etc., etc. Witnesses, Jos. Brock, Henry Gatewood, jr.; James Robb, John T. Thom. Decr. 1, 1795.

April 17, 1795. Robert Mercer of Fredksbg. to Charles Craughton, agt. for Thomas Southcomb. Mortgage. Lot in town of Fredksbg. whereon sd. Mercer lives, purchased of James Monroe and John T. Brooke, etc., etc. Witnesses, James Fisher, Nicholas Payne, James Pettigrew. Decr. 1, 1795.

Decr. 1, 1795. Benj. Waller and Jean, his wife, of Spots. Co. to James Smith. £90 curr. 150 a. whereon Jno. Knight lately lived in Spots. Co., etc., etc. Absolem Waller, Joseph Waller, Aylett Waller. Decr. 1, 1795.

April 23, 1794. Thomas x Adams and Amy, his wife, to Presley Thornton of Caroline Co. 5 shill. 149 a. in Spots. Co., etc., etc. Thomas Ellis, Robert Daniel, Richard Peatross. Decr. 1, 1795.

Septr. 10, 1795. Ann x Cammack, John Long and Ann, his wife, of Spots. Co. to Moses Perry of same co. £118 curr. 140 a. whereon sd. Ann Cammack, Jno. Long, etc., now live in Berkeley Par., Spots. Co., etc., etc. Sherod Horn, Chas. Burrage, Jas. McDonald, Edwd. Herndon, Stockley Towles. Decr. 1, 1795.

Augt. 11, 1795. Joseph McCann and Elizabeth, his wife; Edwd. Darnaby and Mildred, his wife; Oneal McCann and Sarah, his wife; Thomas Ellis and Hezekiah Ellis of Fayette County, Kentucky, to Edwd, Herndon of Spots. Co., Va. £60 curr. 96 a. in Spots. Co., etc., etc. Wm. Ellis, Benja. Welch, Jno. Parker, Robt. Smith. Feby. 1, 1795.

Decr. 1, 1795. Thomas Shirley and Polly, his wife, of Spots. Co. to Samuel Maxley of same co. £36 curr. 108 a., part of a tract conveyed to sd. Shirley by James Arnold, etc., etc. Decr. 1, 1795.

Decr. 27, 1794. John Waller Johnston of Nelson Co., Kentucky, po. of atto. to Benj. Childress of Amherst Co., Va., "to enter upon the agency which I have in trust on the est. of Henry Johnston of Spots. Co., as by Ind. there recorded, etc., etc. Witness, James Harden. Decr. 1, 1795.

Octr. 12, 1795. Jno. Knight of Spots. Co. to Thomas Turner of same co. £15 curr. 100 a. in Spots. Co., etc., etc. Jno. Turner, Larkin Luck, Thos. Turner, jr. July 6, 1796.

May 14, 1795. Saml. Hildrup and Kezia, his wife, of Spots. Co. to James Somerville of same co. Whereas, Wm. Fitzhugh did by Ind. dated May 22, 1773, grant unto Benja. Coyle, 100 a. in St. Geo. Par., Spots. Co., etc., for and during the natural lives of sd. Benj. Coyle, Kezia, his wife, and James Coyle, his son, etc., and whereas, the sd. Benj. Coyle, by his last will and testament dated Decr. 29, 1782, devised to his wife Kezia, all estate, real and personal, during her widowhood, and after her marriage or death to be divided amongst his children; to his dau. Kezia, the lot of land whereon he lived, and whereas, the sd. Saml. Hildrup and Kezia, his wife, will either upon the death or marriage of the sd. Kezia Coyle be entitled to the est. then to come, for and during the life of James Coyle, and whereas, the sd. Hildrup and Kezia, his wife, in consideration of the sum of £40, have sold the sd. interest to the sd. Somerville, etc., etc. Conveyance, etc. Witnesses, Thos. Moffatt, Danl. Grinnan, jr.; James Somerville, jr.; Thomas Seddon, jr.; Thomas Ware. Jany. 6, 1796.

Jany. 5, 1796. Ann Towles of Spots. Co., po. of atto. to her brother, Oliver Towles, jr., to lease 500 a. of land, of which she is possessed, in Berkeley Par., Spots. Co., etc., etc. Witnesses, Edwd. Herndon, O. Towles, Gabriel x Long. Jany. 5, 1796.

Jany. 4, 1796. Thomas Turner of Spots. Co. to Benjamin Massey of same co. £15 curr. 100 a. in Spots. Co., etc., etc. Jno. Turner, Larkin Luck, Thomas Turner, jr. Jany. 5, 1796.

Jany. 1, 1796. Thomas Colson and Frances, his wife, of Spots. Co. to James Smock of Fredksbg. £1000 curr. Part of lot in Town of Fredksbg. formerly part of the Church lot, formerly sold by act of assembly, etc., etc. Witnesses, Wm. Stanard, Tho. Minor, Wm. Landram. Jany. 5, 1796.

Jany. 1, 1796. Thomas Colson and Frances, his wife, of Spots. Co. to Charles Wardell of Fredksbg. £1000 curr. Part of lot in Town of Fredksbg. formerly part of the Church lot and formerly sold by act of assembly, etc., etc., etc. O. Towles, Peter Dudley, Geo. Shepherd, Wm. Stanard, Tho. Minor. Jany. 5, 1796.

Jany. 5, 1796. John Wallace of Spots. Co. to his son, John Wallace, jr. Deed of Gift. 1 negro boy, goods and chattels, cattle, etc., etc. No witnesses. Jany. 5, 1796.

Decr. 9, 1795. Agnes Robinson, widow and relict of Wm. Robinson, Esq., Decd.; Benjamin Robinson and Catherine, his wife, of Spots. Co. to Roger Tandy of same co. $288.00. 62 a., the tract whereon the sd. Wm. Robinson, Esq., Decd., lived at time of his demise in Spots. Co., etc., etc. Witnesses, Thomas Winslow, Philemon Davis, Edwd. Massey, Jos. Herndon. Jany. 5, 1796.

July 13, 1795. Richard Noell, formerly of Essex Co., at present of Spots. Co. to Robert Crutchfield of Spots. Co. Whereas, the sd. Noell is entitled to his choice of a moiety of 6000 a. in the State of Kentucky taken up and located, and as he expects, duly secured by and through the agency of Joseph Craig, and as acknowledged by his letter dated Sept. 21, 1793, etc., etc., and being desirous of making a reasonable settlement and provision of same for his creditors and children, this Ind. therefore witnesseth, that sd. Noell in consideration of the premises, etc., conveys to the sd. Crutchfield all right, title, etc., in the afsd. lands in trust, for children begotten or to be begotten between the sd. Richd. Noell and Mary, his present wife, ⅓ thereof; the remaining ⅔ds. to be sold, etc., etc. Witnesses, Robt. Lewis, Danl. Trigg, Stapleton Crutchfield, James x Ray, Thomas Crutchfield, Jos. Herndon, Z Shackleford, Thomas Foster. Letter dated Septr. 21, 1793, from Joseph Craig to Richd. Noel, Gt., in Essex Co. Recd. Jany. 5, 1796.

July 9, 1795. Benjamin Weeks and Aggy, his wife, of Stafford Co., Va.; John Gibson and Mildred, his wife; Norcut Slaven and Nancy, his wife, all of [Wilkes Co.], Georgia; Betsey Wood, widow of Jno. Wood, at present of Va., but intending immediately to remove to Georgia; also Lucy Holladay and Owen Holladay of the State of Georgia, to Gabriel Long of Spots. Co., Va. Whereas, Abram Simons and Mildred, his wife, and Sarah Holladay, by Ind. dated Jany. 6, 1789, did sell to the sd. Gabriel Long, 325 a. in Spots. Co., Va., and whereas, all the wives of the sd. parties hereto, as well as Betsy Wood, widow, and Lucy and Owen Holladay, are children and devisees of Jno. Holladay, late of Spots. Co., Decd., and each of them claim (under the sd. Holladay's will) 1-12 part of the land, etc., as afsd. conveyed by Abram Simons and Mildred, his wife, and Sarah Holladay, now Sarah Freeman, and whereas, the sd. several claimants having sold their respective parts to the sd. Long, and being willing and desirous of relinquishing the same, this Ind. therefore witnesseth, conveyance, etc., etc., etc. Witnesses, O. Towles, Jno. Welch. Jas. Hutcherson, Richard Long, Wm. Triplett, Jos. Reynolds, Benj. Reynolds. Recorded January 5th, 1796.

Feby. 2, 1796. Tilly Emmerson of Spots. Co. to Samuel Schoolar of same co. £20 curr. 75 a. purchased of Jos. Brock in Spots. Co., etc. No witnesses. Feby. 2, 1796.

Octr. 1, 1795. Richard S. Hackley and Ann, his wife, of Fredgsbg. to Wm. Jackson, mason, of St. Geo. Par., Spots. Co. £156 15s. curr. 104½ a. in St. Geo. Par., Spots. Co., etc., etc. Abraham Carter, Fielding Lucas, Jas. M. Garnett, Edwd. Herndon, Bevy. Stubblefield, Jas. Carmichael. Feby. 2, 1796.

Decr. 15, 1795. Joseph Chew and Mary, his wife, of Spots. Co. to John Lewis of same co. £420 curr. 420 a. in St. Geo. Par., Spots. Co., etc., etc. Edwd. Herndon, jr.; Richd. Todd, Jas. Newton, Wm. Waller. Feby. 2, 1796.

Feby. 2, 1796. Joseph Brock, acting executor of Jno. Z. Lewis, Decd., to Jonathan Clark of Spots. Co. £102 3s. 2d. curr. 90 a. adj. Azariah King in Spots. Co., etc., etc. No witnesses. Feby. 20, 1796.

Jany. 21, 1796. Agreement for sale of land by Augustin Woodfolk, guard. to Betsy Lewis and Jos. Brock, guard. to Jno. Z. Lewis, the interest of their respective wards in 200 a. set apart as dower to Elizabeth, relict of Jno. Z. Lewis, by his will, etc., etc. The sd. agreement made with Jonathan Clark, Gent. Witnesses, Thomas Towles, Bevy. Stubblefield, Benj. Waller, Edmund Clarke. Feby. 20, 1796.

Decr. 7, 1795. John Holladay of Wilkes Co., Georgia, one of the legatees of John Holladay, decd., late of Spots. Co., Va., to Gabriel Long of Spots. Co., Va. $40. 1-11th part of 325 a. in Spots. Co., conveyed to sd. Long by Abram Simons and Mildred, his wife (late Mildred Holladay), etc., etc. Witnesses, Wm. Triplett, Richd. Long, Jos. Reynolds, Benj. Reynolds. Feby. 20, 1796.

Septr. 14, 1795. James Clark and Sally, his wife, of Essex Co. to Philip Edge of Spots. Co. £162. 162 a. in St. Geo. Par., Spots. Co., etc., etc. H. B. Brooke, Henry Garnett, Andrew Monroe. Decr. 1, 1795.

April 3, 1796. Richard Carlton and Lettice, his wife, to Wm. Durrett. £25 curr. 25 a. adj. Spilsbe Coleman, David Lively and sd. Durrett in Spots. Co., etc., etc. Henry Durrett, Sarah Durrett, Judith Durrett. April 5, 1796.

March 18, 1796. Wm. Winslow of Fredksbg., Va., po. of atto. to Beverley Chew of Fredksbg. and Richard Terrell of Lexington, Kentucky, to sell lands in the State of Kentucky, etc., etc. No witnesses. April 5, 1796.

Decr. 29, 1795. James Arnold and Nancy, his wife, of Spots. Co. to Joel Fagg of same co. $127. 127 a. in Spots. Co., etc., etc. Overton H. Pettus, Joseph Graves, Wm. Graves. April 5, 1796.

—— ——, 1796. Walter Chiles and Phebe, his wife, of Spots. Co. to John Walters of Stafford Co. $758. 379 a. in Berkeley Par., Spots. Co., etc., etc. Wm. Herd, Thomas x Dunaway, Wm. Chiles. April 5, 1796.

March 11, 1796. John Rawlings and Nancy, his wife, of Spots. Co. to John Lipscomb of Spots. Co. £315 13s. 6d. curr. 209 a. in Berkeley Par., Spots. Co., etc., etc. Edwd. Hyde, Ben. Rawlings, Jno. Andrew, Thos. Towles, Rob. Hart, Austin Sandidge, Jas. Holladay. April 5, 1796.

Jany. 28, 1796. James Nelson of Louisa Co. to Joseph Nelson of Spots. Co. £50 curr. 50 a. in Spots. Co., etc., etc. John Carter, Zachariah x Wharton, Snelling x Johnston. April 5, 1796.

March 22, 1796. Jno. P. Pleasants and Robt. Pleasants, by Jno. P. Pleasants of Baltimore, Md., his atto., to Wm. Reat of Fredksbg., Va. Release of Mortgage, etc., etc. Witnesses, Geo. Salmon, Chas. C. Armistead. April 5, 1796.

Septr. 19, 1795. Geo. Penn of Spots. Co. to his sons, George and Wm. Penn. Deed of Gift. To sd. George Penn, 33 a. formerly laid off for Joshua Long on Honey Swamp, Spots. Co., etc.; remaining part of land to son Wm. Penn, etc. "Myself and wife Ann, to possess same during our natural lives," etc., etc. "My son John Penn," etc. Witnesses, Thomas Wiglesworth, James Wiglesworth, James Webber. April 5, 1796.

April 4, 1796. John x Fagg of Berkeley Par., Spots. Co. to his son, Joel Fagg, of same county and parish. Deed of Gift. 150 a. in Berkeley Par., Spots. Co., whereon he now lives, remainder of a tract purchased by sd. John Fagg of David Pulliam, after deducting 100 a. by him given to his son, Wm. Fagg, etc., etc. Witnesses, Nathaniel Pulliam, Moses x Wheeler, Robert x Pendleton. April 5, 1796.

Jany. 27, 1796. Robert Turnbull and Hannah, his wife, of Prince George Co. to Thomas Minor of Spots. Co. Whereas, Peter Minor, late of Brunswick Co., being possessed of a tract of land in Spots. Co., died so seized, having one child living, who hath since died intestate, in consequence whereof the sd. land hath descended to his mother, the sd. Hannah, who hath intermarried with the sd. Robt. Turnbull, who together with sd. Hannah, hath agreed for the sale of 141 a. (the afsd. tract) in Spots. Co., for £105 15s., etc., etc. Witnesses, Thomas C. Turnbull, Armistead Brown, Jno. Gholson. April 5, 1796.

Octr. 1, 1795. Thomas Winslow and Elizabeth, his wife, of Berkeley Par., Spots. Co., to Wm. Winslow of same par. and co. $1500.00. 400 a.

on Pigeon Run in Par. and Co. afsd., etc., etc. Adam Darby, Geo. W. B. Spooner, Jos. Chew. April 5, 1796.

April 5, 1796. Joseph Graham and Catherine, his wife, of Spots. Co. to Robert Hart of same co. £1 10s. 2 acres of land, etc., etc. No witnesses. April 5, 1796.

April 4, 1796. Wm. Winslow and Peggy, his wife, of Spots. Co. to Thomas Lipscomb of same co. $1680.00. 305 a. 64 poles in Berkeley Par., Spots. Co., etc., etc. Larkin Stanard, A. Parker. April 5, 1796.

Novr. 9, 1795. Jno. Knight and Winifred, his wife, of Stafford Co. to Elijah Knight of Spots. Co. £32 curr. 85 a., part of tract purchased by Ephriam Knight, decd., of Zachariah and Elijah Garton, in Spots. Co., etc., etc. Uriah Knight, Zachariah Knight, Wm. Knight. April 5, 1796.

March 25, 1796. Wm. A. Daingerfield of Spots. Co. to George Alsop of same co. Lease. 151 a. in Spots. Co., etc., etc. £24 curr. annually, etc., etc. Peter Dudley, Gawin Moore. April 5, 1796.

March 9, 1796. Jno. Lewis and Mary Ann, his wife, of Spots. Co. to David Oliver of same co. £420 curr. 420 a. in St. Geo. Par., Spots. Co., etc., etc. Jno. Legg, James Heath, Jno. Stewart, Thomas Goodwin, Wm. Drummond, Jno. Chew, Thomas Haydon, Wm. Winslow. April 5, 1796.

Jany. 16, 1797. Bathurst Daingerfield, po. of atto., to James Lewis, jr., of Fredksbg. Whereas, Wm. Allen Daingerfield having this day sold to the sd. Bathurst Daingerfield, 1 tract of land called "Snow Creek," in Spots. Co., containing 161 a., also a tract of 55¼ a. in same county, and whereas, the sd. Bathurst Daingerfield agreeing to pay at the rate of £5 per acre for the sd. land, and the sd. Bathurst having appt. Jno. Hoomes to sell and dispose of all the negroes the sd. Bathurst is entitled to under the will of his deceased father, Wm. Daingerfield, and the amount therefrom to be pd. the sd. Wm. A. Daingerfield, and also all bonds the sd. Bathurst being entitled to on acc. of sales of the property of his sd, decd. father, are also to be made over to the sd. Wm. A. Daingerfield, and after that the balance remaining due on the afsd. purchased land is to be secured by a mortgage of the sd. land to the sd. Wm. A. Daingerfield, by the sd. Jas. Lewis, jr., as atto. in fact for the sd. Bathurst Daingerfield, etc., etc. Witnesses, Thos. R. Rootes, Jno. Mercer, Fontaine Maury. April 6, 1796.

April 5, 1796. Wm. Allen Daingerfield of Fredksbg. to Bathurst Daingerfield. 5s. 161 a. called "Snow Creek," on s. side Rappk. River, in Spots. Co., also 55¼ a. in Spots. Co., etc., etc. No witnesses. April 5, 1796.

April 5, 1796. James Lewis, jr., atto. in fact for Bathurst Daingerfield, to Wm. Allan Daingerfield of Fredksbg. Mortgages the property as conveyed in the above deed to the sd. Wm. A. Daingerfield, to secure the payment of a balance due on the sd. purchase, etc., etc. No witnesses. April 5, 1796.

March 5, 1796. Archibald Dick, jr., of Caroline Co., of the first part; Oliver Towles, jr., and Agatha, his wife, of Spots. Co., of the second part, to Samuel Gibson of Spots. Co., of the third part. £56 curr. pd. sd. Dick, etc. 56 a., part of a larger tract of land purchased by sd. Dick of sd. Towles, jr., but before any conveyance was thereof made, the sd. Dick sold the above sd. 56 a., part to the sd. Gibson, in Spots. Co., etc., etc. The same parties under same conditions convey to Wm. Duerson of Spots. Co., 286 a., remaining part of the tract purchased by sd. Dick of sd. Towles, in consideration of the sum of £286 curr. pd. to sd. Dick, etc., etc. Witnesses to both Inds., Jeremiah Wilson, James Wilson, Wm. Steares. Recorded, Apr. 5, 1796.

Feby. 13, 1796. James Marye and Mildred, his wife, of Spots. Co. of the first part; Lawrence Slaughter and Susannah, his wife, of same co., of the second part; the Revd. James Stevenson of Spots. Co. and Baylor Banks of Culpeper Co., and the sd. James Marye of Spots. Co. as afsd., of the third part. Whereas, the sd. James Marye being indebted to the sd. Susannah Slaughter in the sum of £150, the amnt. of which to the sole and proper use of the sd. Susannah, and the sd. Susannah being desirous of making some provision for herself and her children, begotten or to be begotten, between the sd. Susannah and her husband, the afsd. Lawrence Slaughter, hath purchased of the sd. James Marye, for the afsd. sum of £150, a tract of land in Spots. Co. containing 148 acres, and it is hereby conveyed to the parties of the third part, in this Ind., in trust for the use of the sd. Susannah and the children as afsd., the fee simple estate therein being vested in her, and any disposition she should desire to make thereof is provided for herein, etc., etc. Witnesses, R. Wellford, Jas. Lewis, Thomas Strachan. July 5, 1796.

Jany. 27, 1796. Wm. Coleman of Spots. Co. to his son, Francis Wiley Coleman (Robt. Coleman his next friend and trustee). Deed of Gift. 67 a. whereon I now live in Spots. Co., and the part adjoining the same in Caroline Co. "To the afsd. Robt. Coleman during the minority of the sd. Francis Wiley Coleman, etc., etc. (excepting to Sarah Coleman, wife of the sd. Wm. Coleman, free use of the plantation for and during her natural life)," etc., etc. Witnesses, Hugh Roy, Wm. Waller, John Farish. July 5, 1796.

April 13, 1796. Thomas Powell of Spots. Co., Doctor of Physick, and Elizabeth, his wife, to Edward Powell, now of the town of Dumfries, Prince Wm. Co., sadler, and Thomas Powell, jr., of Spots. Co. £700 10s. 938 a. whereon sd. Powell and wife have lived for some years, and conveyed to him by Inds. from Messrs. Carr and Stubblefield, Richd. Loury and others in Berkeley Par., Spots. Co., etc., etc. Benj. Holladay, Jno. Andrew, Walter Chiles, Richd. Loury. July 5, 1796.

May 14, 1795. Thomas Powell of Spots. Co., Doctor of Physick, to Edward Digges Powell of Orange Co., Sadler. £647 curr. Slaves. Witnesses, Edmund Thomas, James Coleman, Thomas Coleman, jr. July 5, 1796.

July 5, 1796. Thomas Mastin and Mary, his wife, of Spots. Co. to Henry Mills of same co. In consideration of one mare, convey to sd. Mills 20¼ a., part of tract sd. Mastin lives on in Spots. Co. No witnesses. July 5, 1796.

Jany. 21, 1796. Henry Gatewood, jr., to Jno. Lewis. £135. Mortgage. Slaves. Witnesses, Harmon Haner, Jno. Carpenter, Richd. Vawter, Zaccheus Carpenter. July 5, 1796.

June 17, 1796. Agreement between Wm. Champe Carter of Va. and Wm. Stanard and Robert Patton of the sd. State, for sale of one undivided 8th part of 26,000 a. on Dan River, in North Carolina, devised by Francis Farley of Antiqua, to the late James Farley, and known by the name of Sama Towns, at the price of $2.00 pr, acre, etc., etc. Witnesses, Jno. Mercer, Howell Lewis, Go. Lewis. July 5, 1796.

Novr. 22, 1792. V. Long Wharton of Spots. Co., po. of atto. to his son, Benjamin Wharton of same co. Witnesses, Wm. Burnett, Gerard B. Berryman. July 6, 1796.

March 23, 1793. James Livingston and Thomas Livingston of Edgefield Co., South Carolina, po. of atto. to Benjamin Wharton of Spots. Co., Va. Witnesses, Walter Chiles, George Bronaugh. July 5, 1796.

April 16, 1796. Charles Clark, guard. to his nephew, Charles Smallwood (age 13 yrs. Dec. 6 next), apprentices the sd. Smallwood to Charles Bennet of Spots. Co., Blacksmith, etc., etc. Witnesses, Robert Spilsbe Coleman, Zachariah Shackelford. July 5, 1796.

May 30, 1796. Jno. Chew, executor of Robert B. Chew, Decd., emancipates Jamy, alias Jas. Gordon, a slave, etc. No witnesses. June 8, 1796.

Octr. 20, 1795. Robert Hill and Hannah, his wife, of King and Queen Co. to Edmund Clarke of Spots. Co. £100. 135 a. in Spots. Co., etc., etc. Benj. Gaines, Saml. Hill, John Hill, Humphrey Hill, Edwd. G. Hill. June 9, 1796. And Ind. of same date from same (grantors) to same (grantees). £100. 129½ a. in Spots. Co., etc., etc. Same witnesses. Recd. June 9, 1796.

Jany. 20, 1796. Augustine Lewis and Sarah, his wife, of Spots. Co.; Wm. Phillips and Ann, his wife, of Hanover Co. to Jonathan Clark of Spots. Co. £120 curr. Their right, title and interest in a tract of 310 a. in Spots. Co., devised by Jno. Zachary Lewis, decd., to his wife, Elizabeth, during her lifetime, then to his four children, the sd. Augustine, the sd. Ann (who hath since intermarried with the sd. Wm. Phillips), Betsy Lewis and John Zachary Lewis, and the sd. Elizabeth Lewis, the relict, having since departed this life, etc., etc. Witnesses, Joseph Brock, Thomas Towles, Bevy. Stubblefield, Benj. Waller, Edmund Clarke. Septr. 6, 1796.

May 3, 1792. Oliver Towles of Spots. Co., atto. at law, of first part; Archibald Dick of Louisa Co., Mercht., and Molly, his wife, of the second part, to Oliver Towles, jr., of Spots. Co. £500 curr. pd. to Oliver Towles, atto. at law, and 5s. to the sd. Dick, etc. 600 a. whereon sd. Oliver Towles [Sr.] now lives in Spots. Co., conveyed to him by Thomas Carr, as by Ind. dated Septr. 3, 1783, etc., etc. Witnesses, Wm. Fortson, Jno. Fortson, Jas. Richards, Wm. Duerson, Jeremiah Wilson, Jas. Wilson. Septr. 6, 1796.

Jany. 20, 1796. John Long to Thomas Towles and Oliver Towles, jr. £53 19s. 4½d. Mortgage. 110 a. on Glady Run, in Spots. Co., adj. lands of Jas. Arnold, Jno. Robins, Mary Arnold and Samuel Alsop, also 1 sorrel steed, etc., etc. Witnesses, Jno. Wiglesworth, Thos. Wiglesworth, John Towles. Septr. 6, 1796.

Septr. 3, 1796. Joseph Pulliam and Elizabeth, his wife; Susannah Garnett, Joseph Holladay and Mary Ann, his wife; Wm. Oliver and Sarah, his wife; Austin Sandidge and Mary, his wife, of Spots. Co. to Joseph Pulliam and Nathaniel Pulliam of same county, £140. To the sd. Jos. Pulliam and Nath. Pulliam (as executors of David Pulliam's estate, etc.), 214½ a. in Spots. Co., joining lands of Austin Sandidge, Wm. Oliver, Susannah Garnett, Jno. Edington, Wm. Bronaugh, Robert Hart and the dowry land of Mary Holladay, the land hereby conveyed is Lot No. 4 and is known by name of Molls Pines, being part of the land of Benj. Holladay, decd., allotted to Benj Holladay., jr., orphan, etc., etc. Witnesses, Robert Hart, Lewis Holladay, Waller Holladay, Wm. Holladay. Recd. Septr. 6, 1796.

March 16, 1796. Bond of Jno. Rawlings of Spots. Co. and Nancy, his wife, to convey to Joseph Pulliam, their right in a certain tract of land known as Molls Pines, which sd. land has fallen to the legatees of Benj. Holladay, Senr., decd., by the death of Benj. Holladay, jr., etc., etc., also bond dated Septr. 28, 1795, from John Holladay of Clarke Co., Kentucky, to the sd. Pulliam of Spots. Co., Va., for the same purpose, etc., etc. Recd. Septr. 6, 1796. Both bonds assigned to Nathaniel Pulliam for his proportion in the sd. tract, etc., etc.

July 18, 1796. Jno. Legg of Fredksbg. to John Carthorn of Spots. Co. £65 15s. curr. 131½ a. in Upper part of Spots. Co., etc., etc. Wm. Winslow, Thomas Corthorn, Wm. Sale, jr. Septr. 6, 1796.

March 31, 1795. James Maury of Liverpoole, County Lancaster, Kingdom of Great Britain, Mercht. and Consul of the U. S. of A., at the post of Liverpoole, afsd., po. of atto. to James Lewis of Spots. Co., Va., Gent., to receive from the hands of the executors of the last will and testament of Robert Armistead, late of Louisa Co., [Va.], father of my late wife Catherine, all and every legacy due from the est. of sd. Armistead, etc., etc. Witness, Jos. Lace, N. P. Liverpoole, etc. Recd. Spots. Co., Va. Septr. 6, 1796.

Augt. 15, 1796. John Chew of Fredksbg. to Harry Chew of Spots. Co. Whereas, Robt. B. Chew at his death being jointly entitled with sd. Harry Chew to 95 a. in Spots. Co., and by his will did (after bequeathing several specific legacies) bequeath to his brother, the afsd. Jno. Chew, "all my estate of what kind soever not hereinbefore particularly mentioned," etc. By virtue of which devise the sd. Jno. Chew hath become equally entitled with the sd. Harry Chew in the sd. land, now this Ind. witnesseth, the sd. Jno. Chew conveys to the sd. Harry, all the right, title, etc., of the sd. Jno. or his heirs in the afsd. tract, etc., etc. Witnesses, Edwd. Herndon, Robt. S. Chew, Jno. Chew, jr. Septr. 6, 1796.

Augt. 24, 1796. Harry Chew of Spots. Co. to Richard Todd of same co. £40 curr. 95 a. in Spots. Co., etc., etc. Jno. Herndon, Joseph Brock, Richd. Todd, jr. Septr. 6, 1796.

July 1, 1796. James Marye of Spots. Co. and Mildred, his wife, to James Smock of Fredksbg. £262 8s. and int. Mortgage. 1148 a. [purchased by the late Revd. James Marye of Jno. Smith and Mary, his wife, of Northumberland Co.; Martha Jacquelin of York Co., Spinster; Jacquelin Ambler of York Co., Gent.; Thomas Smith of Westmoreland Co., Clerk, and Mary, his wife; Sarah Smith of Westmoreland Co., Spinster; Wilson Miles Cary of town of Elizabeth City, Gent., and Robt. C. Nicholas, execr. of Ed. Ambler, Decd.], in Spots. Co., on River Ny, etc., etc. Tho. Goodwin, G. Heiskell, Go. Lewis. Septr. 6, 1796.

Septr. 1, 1796. John C. Blaydes and Polly B., his wife, of Spots. Co. to Wm. Cason of same co. £86 curr. 124 a. in Spots. Co., etc., etc. Edwd. Cason, Jacob Burruss, John Cason. Septr. 6, 1796.

June 5, 1796. Charles Clarke to James x Gordon. Lease. 20 a. of land. 40s. yearly rent. Witnesses, Harry Chew, Jos. Brock, Michl. Robinson, Benj. Head. Septr. 6, 1796.

Septr. 20, 1791. Richd. Todd and Peggy, his wife, of Spots. Co. to Henry Cammock of same co. Lease. 15 a. in Spots. Co., etc. £6 10s. yearly rent, etc. Witnesses, Joseph Brock, Clk.; Wm. Gholson, John Miller. Septr. 6, 1796.

July 2, 1796. Thomas Colson of Spots. Co. to John Scott of same co. £60 curr. Release of Mortgage, given July 1, 1794, etc., etc. No witnesses. Septr. 6, 1796.

July 4, 1796. Jno. Scott of Spots. Co. to Thomas Colson of same co. £62 10s. 40 a. in Spots. Co., etc., etc. No witnesses. Septr. 6, 1796.

Augt. 1, 1796. Thomas Pritchett and Ann, his wife, of Spots. Co. to Wm. Waller [son of the sd. Ann] of same co. Whereas, the sd. Ann Pritchett is entitled to 414 a. in Spots. Co. whereon the sd. Wm. Waller lives, for life, and the sd. Waller is seized in fee of a tract of 145 a. in Spots. Co. (whereon the afsd. Thos. Pritchett and Ann, his wife, now live), and also a negro slave, this Ind. witnesseth, the sd. Ann, with the sd. Thos. Pritchett, her husband, relinquishes all her right, title, etc., in the sd. 414 a. of land to the sd. Wm. Waller, and the sd. Waller conveys to the sd. Ann Pritchett the afsd. 145 a. in trust for the sd. Ann Pritchett during her lifetime, and the benefit of her five children, viz., Bird, Thomas, Parmenas, Henrietta and Lucy Pritchett, etc., etc. (children of sd. Ann, and her husband, Thomas Pritchett), etc., etc. Witnesses, Thomas Magee, Senr.; Wm. Magee, Thomas Robinson Magee. Septr. 6, 1796.

Septr. 6, 1796. Jno. Nelson and Susannah, his wife, of Spots. Co. to Richard Crittenden Webb of Orange Co. £375 curr. 300 a. on fork of Pamunkey River, in Spots. Co., etc., etc. Wm. Winslow, Thomas Winslow, George Bronaugh. Septr. 6, 1796.

Septr. 6, 1796. John Johnston and Orpha, his wife, of Spots. Co. to Thomas Johnston. £34 curr. 100 a. in Spots. Co., etc., etc. No witnesses. Septr. 6, 1796.

Augt. 1, 1796. John Pritchett of Albemarle Co., the elder son and heir of James Pritchett, late of Spots. Co., Decd., po. of atto. to Thomas Waller of Spots. Co., etc., etc. Clement Montague, Thomas Stanly Berry. Septr. 6, 1796.

Septr. 4, 1796. Merideth Anderson and Catherine Ammon Anderson, his wife, of Spots. Co. to Charles Bennett of Spots. Co. £140 curr. 77 a. in Spots. Co., etc., etc. No witnesses. Septr. 6, 1796.

Augt. 15, 1796. John Carter of Spots. Co. to David Lively of same co. £100 curr. 100 a. in Spots. Co., etc., etc. Merideth Anderson, Rich. C. Noel, Mary x Acres, Littleton Farish. Septr. 6, 1796.

Augt, 30, 1796. Sam'l. Moseley and H. Bassett of Borough of Norfolk, Va., his wife, to Francis T. Brooke. £825. 220 a. in Spots. Co., being 1-7 part of the tract called "Belvedeira," the estate of Wm. Daingerfield, decd., and allotted his dau. the sd. Bassett, wife of the sd. Moseley, by a decree of the High Court of Chancery, etc., etc. Witnesses, Daingerfield Starke, W. J. Starke, P. Kirby. Feby. 7, 1797.

Feby 7, 1796 (1797). Thomas Colson of Spots. Co. to Thomas Strachan and Mary, his wife. In consideration of securityship of James Lewis and Fontaine Maury, for sd. Strachan, to the sd. Colson, for the sum of £612 4s., etc., conveys to sd. Strachan and wife, 237 a. in Spots. Co., also slaves, goods and chattels, etc., etc. Witness, Wm. Stanard. Feby. 7, 1797.

—— ——, 1797. Thomas Colson of Spots. Co. to Wm. Steward of same co. £55 10s. 46¼ a., held by sd. Steward under lease from Jos. Hulett in Spots. Co., etc., etc. No witnesses. Feby. 7, 1797.

Feby. 6, 1797. Lewis Johnston and Barbara, his wife, of Spots. Co. to Saml. Parker of same co. £95 curr. 147 a. adj. lands of Robt. Scott, Danl. Baulding, Jno. Smith and Alexr. Johnston, in Spots. Co., etc., etc. Witness, Philip B. Johnston. Feby. 7, 1797.

Decr. 23, 1796. Thomas Hawkins of Spots. Co. to John Bledsoe of Orange Co. £130 curr. 190 a. in Spots. Co., etc., etc. Geo. Bledsoe, Moses Bledsoe, Roberson Spalding. Feby. 7, 1797.

Novr. 21, 1796. Thomas Lipscomb and Mary, his wife, of Spots. Co., Va., to Allen Billingsby of Maryland. £275 curr. 695 a. in Spots. Co., etc., etc. Will. Winslow, Antho. Arnold, Thos. Winslow, Lewis Holladay, Ben. Holladay, Jno. Lipscomb, Edwd. Hyde. Feby. 7, 1797.

Feby. 7, 1797. Jno. Keegan of Spots. Co. to Francis Brooke, of same co. 5 shill. 80 a. recovered by sd. Keegan by a suit in Chancery in Spots. Co. Court from Jack Raines and wife, in Spots. Co., etc., etc. No witnesses. Feby. 7, 1797.

Octr. 8, 1796. Joseph x Carter of Spots. Co. to his son, Elijah Carter, of same co. Deed of Gift. 2 negroes, goods and chattels, etc., etc. Jos. Carter, jr.; David Partlow, John Partlow. Feby. 7, 1797.

Jany. 17, 1796. John Shirley and Frances, his wife, of Spots. Co. to Thomas Dillard of same co. £40 curr. 115 a. in Spots. Co., etc., etc. Henry Dodd, Sarah Morriss, Mary Word. Feby. 7, 1797.

Novr. 12, 1796. Beverley Stubblefield of Spots. Co. to his daughter, Catharine Beverley Stubblefield. Deed of Gift. 7 negroes, etc., etc. Witnesses, Jos. Brock, Richd. Estes. Feby. 7, 1797.

Novr. 30, 1796. Mathew Harris and Nancy, his wife, of Amherst Co. to Wm. Cason of Spots. Co. £100 curr. 126 a. in Spots. Co., etc., etc. Philip B. Johnston, James Holladay, Jno. Cason, Benjamin Cason, Robt. Hart, Lewis Holladay. Feby. 7, 1797.

Augt. 3, 1796. Thomas Towles, Gent., late Sheriff of Spots. Co., to Edwd. Herndon, son of Edward, of same co. In pursuance of Revenue Act, etc., sale of 9 a. of land belonging to Robt. Jardine, late of Fredksbg. for taxes, to the sd. Herndon, etc., etc. Witnesses, O. Towles, jr.; Edwd. Herndon, Jno. M. Herndon, Jas. Herndon. Feby. 7, 1797.

Feby. 7, 1795. Edwd. Herndon, jr., and Elizabeth, his wife, of Spots. Co. to Richard Estes of same co. £200. 336 a. in Spots. Co., etc., etc. No witnesses. Feby. 7, 1797.

Septr. ——, 1796. Harmon Haner and Peggy, his wife, of Spots. Co. to Hezekiah Ellis of same co. £85 curr. 100 a. in Spots. Co., etc., etc. No witnesses. Feby. 7, 1797.

Augt. 6, 1796. Wm. Pettus of Spots. Co. to his children, Louisa Pettus, Hart Pettus, and Joseph Pettus. Deeds of Gift. A negro slave each, etc., etc. Witnesses, Robt. Dabney, Peter Arnold, Wm. Pettus, jr.; Overton H. Pettus, Larkin Reynolds, Jos. Pettus. Recorded Feby. 7, 1797.

Novr. 1, 1796. Thomas Colson of Spots. Co. to Joseph Chew of same co. Lease. 80 a. in St. Geo. Par., Spots. Co., etc., etc. "Sd. Jos. Chew and Mary, his wife, and Robt. B. Chew," etc. £5 specie yearly, rent, etc., etc. Witnesses, Jno. Herndon, Thomas Strachan, Wm. Robinson. Feby. 7, 1797.

Decr. 1, 1796. Jos. Hulet of Spots. Co. to Wm. Steward of same co. Lease. 46¼ a., leased of Thomas Colson by the sd. Hulet and with the sd. Colson's consent (the rentals being pd. him) released to the sd. Steward, in Spots. Co., etc., etc. Lease to the sd. Steward during the lives of sd. Jos. Hulet and Mary, his wife, and his son Reubin Hulet, etc., etc. 40s. 3d. specie, yearly rent, etc., etc. No witnesses. Feby. 7, 1797.

Augt. 28, 1796. Gawin Corbin and Elizabeth, his wife, to John Lewis. 5 shill. 449 a. in Spots. Co., etc., etc. Edwin Daingerfield, David T. Chevis, Chas. C. Robinson, Bowker Waller, Wm. Haner, Robt. Goodloe. Feby. 7, 1797.

Feby. 4, 1797. Jno. Lewis and Mary Ann, his wife, to Bowker Waller. 5 shill. 449 a. in Spots. Co., etc., etc. Wm. Stanard, Wm. Haner, Robert Goodloe. Feby. 7, 1797.

Decr. ——, 1796. Charles Bennett and Martha, his wife, of Spots. Co. to Wm. Spindle of same co. £40 curr. 60 a. in Berkeley Par., Spots. Co., etc., etc. Thomas Walden, James Wilson. Feby. 7, 1797.

Septr. 17, 1796. Daniel Coleman and Martha, his wife, of Caroline Co. to Jacob Reynolds of same co. £130. 200 a. in Spots. Co., etc., etc. Lewis Collins. Feby. 7, 1797.

Decr. 12, 1794. Robert Coleman of Spots. Co. to Thomas Coleman, jr., of same co. £400 curr. 750 a. whereon "sd. Coleman now lives," in Spots. Co., etc., etc. Daniel Trigg, Micajah Poole, Richd. Long, Wm. B. Coleman, Henry Dodd. Feby. 7, 1797.

April 21, 1796. Jno. Garlick and Ann, his wife, of King and Queen Co. to Edward Cason of Spots. Co. £287 10s. curr. 230 a. on East North East River, in Spots. Co., etc., etc. J. Hill, Charles Lewis, Edwd. G. Hill, H. Hill. Feby. 7, 1797.

Octr. 17, 1796. Wm. Phillips and Ann, his wife, of Hanover Co. to Reubin Cason of Spots. Co. £100 curr. 70 a. in Spots. Co., part of a tract divided by Spots. Co. Court among the orphans of John Zachary Lewis, decd., one of which was the sd. Ann Phillips, etc., etc. Witnesses, Jas. Wiglesworth, Benja. Waller, Thomas Wiglesworth, Joseph Fox, John Cason. Feby. 7, 1797.

Novr. 1, 1796. John Long and Ann, his wife, to Joshua Long. £60. 100 a. whereon sd. Jno. Long now lives. Wm. Ludwege, Nathaniel Pulliam, John Wiglesworth. Feby. 7, 1797.

July 11, 1796. Richard C. Noel of Spots. Co., po. of atto. to John Berryman of Spots. Co. "Mentions tract of land in Kentucky, a moiety of which is to be laid off to Joseph Craig, also mentions land heretofore deeded Robt. Crutchfield, etc., etc." Witnesses, Wm. Drake, Benj. Wharton, Thomas Olive, Gilson Berryman, Wm. Olive. Feby. 7, 1797.

April 4, 1797. Edward Cason to Wm. Cason, jr. £143. 115 a. on East North East River, in Spots. Co. No witnesses. April 4, 1797.

Octr. 10, 1796. James Hutcheson and Peggy, his wife, of Spots. Co. to James Hughes of Hanover Co. £127 curr. 130 a., part of which formerly property of Richd. Cowan, and part purchased of Thomas Colson. in Spots. Co., etc., etc. Jos. x Hulett, Jno. Hulett, Jas. Wilson, Wm. x Steward, Uriah Knight, Thomas Mastin. April 4, 1797.

Feby. 12, 1797. Jonathan Clark and Sarah, his wife, of Spots. Co. to Joseph Duerson of same co. £387 10s. "All the right of sd. Clark, in a tract of 310 a. formerly the property of Jno. Z. Lewis, decd. 90 a. thereof conveyed to sd. Clark as by Ind. dated Feby. 2, 1796, from Jos. Brock, Gent., Execr. of sd. Lewis, and the proportions in the afsd. tract conveyed sd. Clark by Ind. dated Jany. 20, 1796, from Augustine Lewis and Wm. Phillips and Ann, his wife, etc., etc. Witnesses, Benj. Waller, Larkin Stanard, Jno. Mercer, Austin Sandidge. April 4, 1797.

July 29, 1796. Benjamin Graves of Spots. Co. to Joseph Graves of same co. £101 15s. curr. 76 a. in Spots. Co., etc., etc. Spencer Coleman, Wm. Graves, Wm. Cason, Jno. C. Blaydes, Geo. Tyler. April 4, 1797.

March 24, 1797. Frances x Jarvis, widow, of Spots. Co. to James Gordon, jr., of Culpeper Co. £40. 128 a. adj. lands of Alexander Spotswood, Jonathan Carpenter (formerly Herndon), Wm. Bridges, Wm. Clayton, and Henry Gatewood, jr., in Spots. Co., St. Geo. Par., etc., etc. John Clayton, Wm. Bridges, Wm. Vigar, Armistead Gordon. April 4, 1797.

April 3, 1797. Sarah x Morris of Spots. Co. to Thomas Dillard of same co. £10 curr. 18 a. in Spots. Co., etc., etc. James Crawford, Thomas Malleara, Richd. Carlton. April 4, 1797.

Octr. 10, 1796. John Nelson, Senr., of Spots. Co. to Joseph Nelson of same co. £150 curr. Sale of Mill property in Spots. Co., Berkeley Par., etc. Witnesses, John Nelson, jr.; Geo. Bosley, Rial Thompson, Alvin x Ellet. April 4, 1797.

April 4, 1797. John Clayton and Elizabeth, his wife, of Spots. Co. to Wm. Jones of the Wilderness Run, same co. £125 curr. 253 a. in Spots. Co., etc., etc. James Gordon, jr.; Phil Grymes, Edwd. Herndon. April 4, 1797.

March 30, 1797. John Crawford and Phebe, his wife, of Spots. Co. to Thomas Mallery of Louisa Co. £70 curr. 80 a. in Spots. Co., etc., etc. Wm. Davenport, Benj. Tompkins, Richd. Carlton, Jas. Crawford, jr.; Thos. Dillard, Senr.; Jas. Crawford, Senr. April 4, 1797.

April 3, 1797. Henry True and Jane, his wife, of Spots. Co. to Wm. Spindle of same so. £9 12s. curr. 16 a. in Berkeley Par., Spots. Co., etc., etc. Benj. Alsop, Reubin Landrum, Wm. Spindle, jr. April 4, 1797.

April 3, 1797. Joseph Williams and Elizabeth, his wife, of Spots. Co.; Jno. x Adams and Ann, his wife, of Orange Co. to Jno. Richards of Prince

Wm. Co. £75 curr. 103 a. in Spots. Co., etc., etc. No witnesses. April 4, 1797.

Jany. 18, 1797. Ambrose x Smith of Spots. Co. to his children, James Smith, Frances Luck, Isabella Smith, Eliza Smith, John Smith, and George Smith, "and to the children of my daughter Eleanor Mastin." Deed of Gift. Negro slaves. No witnesses. April 4, 1797.

Octr. 11, 1796. Hawes Coleman and Nancy, his wife, of Amherst Co. to Spencer Coleman of Spots. Co. £304 curr. 304 a. in Spots. Co., etc., etc. Saml. Coleman, Jos. Graves, John C. Blaydes, Polly Graves, Jno. Coleman, Jos. Wiglesworth, Jos. Fleeman, Robt. Coleman, Geo. Coleman, Robt. Goodwin. April 4, 1797.

March 28, 1797. Thomas Johnson of Spots. Co. to Jonathan Johnson, of same co. £28 curr. 100 a. formerly part of Wm. Chewning's land in Spots. Co., etc., etc. Jno. Carter, Jos. Nelson, Jno. Long. April 4, 1797.

April 2, 1797. Benjamin Waller and Jean, his wife, of Spots. Co. to their son, Absolem Waller of same co. Deed of Gift. 124 a. in Spots. Co., etc., etc. Ay. Waller, Jos. Waller, Curtis Waller. April 4, 1797.

Augt. 8, 1796. John Nelson and Joseph Nelson, Execrs. of Benjamin Nelson, decd., and the sd. John Nelson, Jos. Nelson, James Nelson, Senr.; Susannah Cornelius Nelson, James Nelson, Abraham Darnall and Mary Ann, his wife (formerly Mary Ann Nelson), which sd. James Nelson, Senr., was father, and the sd. Jno., Jos., Susannah C., and Jas. Nelson and Mary Ann Darnall, are brother and sisters of Benjamin Nelson, decd., to Malcolm Hart. £310. 2 a. of land (one in Spots. Co. and one in Louisa Co.) with a mill, devised by Benj. Nelson, decd., as by his will dated June 17, 1780, and recorded in Louisa. Co., to his father and mother (being now dead) and brothers and sisters, and sold by decree of Louisa Co. Court, in a suit in Chancery, etc., etc. Witnesses, Ralph Quarles, Wm. Thompson, Wm. Collins, Benj. Robinson, Thos. Winslow, Saml. Sale, Tho. Lipscomb, Augustus Yancey, Thomas Cosby, Zachariah x Wharton. Feby. 13, 1797.

Septr. 15, 1796. John x Hackney, deed of trust to Jedediah Johnston, Thomas Hackney, Thomas Hackett and Jno. Sutton, to secure payment of all just claims, etc., after securing creditors, if negroes should remain unsold, then "to my son Thos. Hackney, 3 negroes; to my son Richard Hackney, 2 negroes; to my son Robert Hackney, 2 negroes; to my daughter Frances Johnston, 2 negroes." The sd. negroes subject to being hired out "for the support of myself and my wife Jane Hackney, during our natural lives," etc., etc. Witnesses, Martin Davenport, Stephen Hackney, Wm. Arnold. April 5, 1797.

April 28, 1797. George Cammack of Spots. Co. to Robert Cammack of same co. £200 curr. 328 a. in Spots. Co., etc., etc. No witnesses. May 2, 1797.

April 28, 1797. Robert Cammack of Spots. Co. to George Cammack of same co. £200 curr. 400 a. in Spots. Co., etc., etc. No witnesses. May 2, 1797.

May 2, 1797. John x Adams and Ann, his wife, of Orange Co. to John Richards of Prince Wm. Co. £57 18s. curr. 96½ a. in Upper end of Spots. Co. No witnesses. May 2, 1797.

July 4, 1797. Samuel Coleman and John Coleman of Caroline Co., guardians to our respective children, to-wit, Robert, Samuel, Clayton, Rebecah, Nancy, Frankey, and Nice Coleman, children of Saml. Coleman by his late wife, Sally Coleman, dau. of Robert Coleman of Spots. Co., and George, Lincey, John, and Hawes Coleman, children of John Coleman, by his late wife, Molly Coleman, dau. of sd. Robert Coleman of Spots. Co., and Elizabeth Coleman of Orange Co. for herself and as guardian for the orphans of James Coleman, decd., of Orange Co., the son of Robt. Coleman of Spots. Co., to-wit, Wilson, James, Elizabeth, Sally, Nancy, Polly, and Catharine Coleman and Thomas Coleman of Orange Co. (son of sd. James Coleman) for himself, being of age, po. of atto. to John Waller of South Carolina and John Coleman of Amherst Co., Va., to act for us as guardians and for ourselves as individuals, touching any interests we may have in the state of Georgia, * * * we may be entitled to of the estate of Reuben Coleman, decd., of the State of Georgia, etc., etc. Witnesses, Robert Coleman, Farish Coleman, jr.; Farish Coleman. Recd. July 4, 1797. "And it being proven to the Court that Robert, Samuel, Clayton, Rebecca, Nancey, Frankey and Nice Coleman are the children of Sally Coleman, who was the sister of Reuben Coleman, decd., and that George, Lindsay, Jno., and Hawes Coleman are the children of Molly Coleman, who was one of the sisters of Reuben Coleman, decd., and that Wilson, James, Elizabeth, Nancy, Sally, Polly, Catharine and Thomas Coleman are children of James Coleman, decd., one of the brothers of Robert Coleman, decd., and that Lindsay, Caleb, Joseph and Clayton Coleman are brothers of the sd. Reuben Coleman, decd., and heirs and heiresses of the sd. Reuben," etc., etc. Recd. July 4, 1797.

Novr. 30, 1796. James Carr and Hannah, his wife, of Westmoreland Co. to Lewis Johnston of Spots. Co. £40 curr. 100 a. in Spots. Co., etc., etc. Wm. Drake, James Faulconer, Rebekah Drake. July 4, 1797.

July 1, 1797. James Robins and Elizabeth, his wife, of Spots. Co. to Joshua Long of same co. £42 12s. 96 a. in Spots. Co., etc., etc. No witnesses. July 4, 1797.

May 1, 1791. Azaria King and Mary, his wife, to John Lansly. £100. 305 a. purchased of Francis King in Spots. Co., etc., etc. No witnesses. July 4, 1797.

March 10, 1797. Jonathan Clark and Sarah, his wife, of Spots. Co. to Zachariah Shackleford of same co. £117 curr. 117 a. in Spots. Co., etc., etc. Jno. M. Herndon, Jno. Wiglesworth, Wm. Arnold, Thomas Branan, Edmund Clark. July 4, 1797.

April 10, 1797. Richard Long and Fanny, his wife, of Spots. Co. to John Smith of same co. £140 curr. 198 a. purchased of Jno. Mastin, James Wheeler and Moses Wheeler, as by Ind. dated Septr. 7, 1793, in Spots. Co. No witnesses. July 4, 1797.

July 4, 1797. Rosamond Wright, Executrix; John Steward and Anthony Frazer, acting executors of the last will and testament of John Wright late of Spots. Co., decd., to Henry Southworth of same co. £26 19s. curr. 86½ a. in Berkeley Par., Spots. Co., part of land directed sold by the will of sd. Jno. Wright, decd., etc., etc. No witnesses. July 4, 1797.

July 4, 1797. Rosamond Wright, Executrix, and Jno. Steward and Anthony Frazer, acting executors of the last will and testament of John Wright, late of Spots. Co., decd., to Wm. Pritchett of same co. £38 5s. curr. 127½ a. in Berkeley Par., Spots. Co., part of land directed by the will of the sd. John Wright, decd., etc., etc. No witnesses. July 4, 1797.

Decr. 19, 1796. Wm. H. Washington and Elizabeth, his wife, of Fairfax Co. to John T. Washington of Westmoreland Co. £328 10s. 10d. 271 a. purchased of Saml. Donoho, in Spots. Co., etc., etc. No witnesses. July 4, 1797.

Feby. 17, 1797. Samuel Roddy and Mary, his wife, of Spots. Co. to James Cunningham of same co. £64 16s. curr. 108 a. conveyed to sd. Roddy by Ind. dated Novr. 9, 1782, by Edwd. Herndon and Jno. Wiglesworth and their wives, in St. Geo. Par., Spots. Co., etc., etc. Daniel Scrugham, John x Hannage, Robt. Cunningham, Thos. Haydon. July 4, 1797.

April 7, 1797. John Chew and Elizabeth, his wife, of Fredksbg. to Richard Long of Spots. Co. $2666.75. 563 a. purchased of Col. Geo. Stubblefield and Mrs. Elizabeth Towles, in Spots. Co., etc., etc. Tho. Minor, Jno. Chew, jr.; Robt. S. Chew, Zach. Lucas, Thos. Goodwin, W. Drummond. July 4, 1797.

Novr. 17, 1796. Thomas Crutcher of Nelson Co., Kentucky, conveys to Antho. Frazer, James Frazer, Wm. Frazer and Reubin Frazer, all of Spots. Co., Va., 300 a. whereon sd. Crutcher lives in Kentucky and co. of Nelson, to indemnify the sd. Frazers for standing bound as security for the sd. Crutcher, in trust, etc., etc. Witnesses, Thomas Magee, Thomas Olive, Robert Olive, Thomas Foster. July 4, 1797.

Augt. 26, 1797. David Blair, surviving partner of Heslop and Blair; Wm. Glassell, atto. in fact for John Glassell, and James Somerville, atto. in fact for McCall, Smillie & Co., po. of atto. to David Briggs of Stafford Co. to convey the lands that have been decreed by the County Court of Shenandoah to David Briggs, for Bland's Trustees, and Henry Mitchell for McCall, Smillie & Co., Wm., Glassell for Jno. Glassell, and David Blair, surviving partner of Heslop and Blair, etc., etc. Witnesses, Thos. Reade Rootes, Tho. Goodwin, Wm. Lovell, Geo. French, Fontaine Maury, Jno. Legg, Jno. Minor, jr. Septr. 5, 1797.

Septr. 1, 1797. James Redd and Lucy, his wife, of King and Queen Co. to Henry Wyatt of Spots. Co. £290 curr. 290 a. adj. lands of Thos. Minor, Thos. Colson, Peter Rawlings, decd., in St. Geo. Par., Spots. Co., which sd. land was given by James Redd, decd., to his son Mordacai Redd, and by the sd. Mordacai Redd to his son, the sd. James, etc., etc. Witnesses, Thos. Colson, Robert Wyatt, Tho. Minor. Septr. 5, 1797.

May 16, 1797. Wm. Brown Wallace, Execr. of Thomas Fox, decd., and Joseph Fox, devisee of sd. Thos. Fox, decd., and Philadelphia Fox, widow of sd. Thomas Fox, decd., to Spencer Coleman of Spots. Co. Whereas, the sd. Thos. Fox died, seized and possessed of a tract containing 337 a. in Spots. Co., and by his will devised 225 a. thereof to his son Jos. Fox, the remainder to be sold, etc., and the afsd. Philadelphia Fox being entitled to dower therein, therefore this Ind. witnesseth, the sd. Wallace, Fox and Philadelphia Fox, in consideration of £701 1s. pd. by the afsd.

Coleman convey to him the above sd. lands, etc., etc. Witnesses, Wm. Cason, Rebecca x Cason, Bradley x Matthews, Jno. N. Whitlock, Lee x Jones, Wm. Crop, Rhodr. Hord, Jno. Cason. Recd. Septr. 5, 1796.

Augt. 14, 1797. Wm. Forston of Spots. Co. to Elizabeth Johnson of same co., widow. £440 curr. Seven slaves, cattle, horses, etc., etc. O. Towles, Hugh Roy, George Durrett. Septr. 5, 1797.

Augt. 15, 1797. Elizabeth x Johnson (widow) of Spots. Co. to Wm. Fortson and Mildred, his wife; Lucy Fortson, John Fortson, Wm. Fortson, Marshall Fortson, James Fortson, Richard Fortson, John Durrett and Frances, his wife, children of sd. Wm. Fortson and Mildred, his wife, and grandchildren of the sd. Elizabeth Johnson. Deed of Gift. Slaves, etc., as conveyed to the sd. Elizabeth Johnson by Wm. Fortson in preceding deed, etc., etc. Witnesses, O. Towles, Hugh Roy, George Durrett. Septr. 5, 1797.

Augt. 14, 1797. Elizabeth x Johnson of Spots. Co. (widow). Deed of Gift to John Durrett of Caroline Co. 1 slave. Witnesses, O. Towles, Hugh Roy, George Durrett. Septr. 5, 1797.

Jany. 24, 1797. Christopher Crawford of Spots. Co. to John Partlow. £100 curr. Mortg. Horses, colt, oxen, cattle, etc., etc. Witnesses, Thomas Minor, Lewis Partlow, Elijah Partlow. Septr. 5, 1797.

June 29, 1797. James Newton of Spots. Co. to Jno. Newton of Fredksbg. £80 curr. Slaves. Witness, James Pettigrew. Septr. 5, 1797.

June 26, 1797. John Parish of Spots. Co. to Henry Hewlett of Caroline Co. £205. 301 a. in Spots. Co., etc., etc. Aylett Waller, Robert Coleman, Jeremiah Yarbrough. Septr. 3, 1797.

July 19, 1797. Kesia x Coyle (widow) of Spots. Co., of first part; James Coyle, Michael Coyle, Lucy Coyle, Wm. Coyle, Tully Whithurst and Saml. Hildrup and Kesia, his wife, of second part, to Wm. Richards of Culpeper Co. Whereas, Benj. Walden and Lucy, his wife, by Ind. dated May 15, 1777, did sell to Benj. Coyle (husband of sd. Kezia Coyle), 72 a. in Spots. Co., whereas, the sd. Benj. Coyle by his will dated Decr. 29, 1782, devised the sd. tract to his wife, the sd. Kesia, for life, the remainder to certain of his children. Whereas, the sd. Saml. Hildrup, in right of his wife (the afsd. Kezia Hildrup), hath set up a reversionary claim to the sd. land, and whereas, they, the sd. Saml. Hildrup and Kezia, his wife, together with Kezia Coyle, Jas. Coyle, Michael Coyle, Lucy Coyle, Wm. Coyle and Tully Whithurst (who intermarried with Polly Coyle, now decd., one of the daughters of the sd. Benj. Coyle, decd.), have agreed to sell the sd. tract to the afsd. Wm. Richards in consideration of the sum of 5 shillings to each, etc., etc. Conveyance. Witnesses, James Pettigrew, Tully Whithurst, Jno. Bogan. Septr. 5, 1797.

Septr. 1, 1797. Charles x Jinkins and Elizabeth, his wife, of Berkeley Par., Spots. Co. to Thomas Corthorn of same par. and county. £75. 112 a. in Berkeley Par., Spots. Co., conveyed to sd. Charles by Ind. dated March 2, 1767, from John Jenkins and Ann, his wife, etc., etc. No witnesses. Septr. 5, 1797.

Augt. 30, 1797. James Wiglesworth of Spots. Co. to Thomas Wiglesworth of same co. 5 shill. 215 a. whereon sd. Thos. now lives in Spots. Co., etc., etc. Betsy Penn, Geo. Penn, jr. Septr. 5, 1790.

Septr. 5, 1797. Jos. Brock, jr., now of Spots. Co. from my precarious situation in life, and being desirous of making the best provision . . . for my beloved wife Ann, convey to Jno. Chew, Jr., of Fredksbg. 1 negro, 1 phaeton, 2 horses, with undivided part or share of Est. of Capt. John Chew, decd. (father of sd. Ann), which I am or may be entitled to in right or behalf of my sd. wife Ann, in trust for the sole use of sd. Ann, etc., etc. Signed, "Jos. Brock of the Army." Witnesses, Jos. Brock, Edwd. Herndon, D. S. Septr. 5, 1797.

Jany. 30, 1797. John Partlow of South Carolina to Jonathan Clark of Spots. Co., Va. £62 curr. 62 a. devised to sd. Partlow by his father, Jno. Partlow, Decd., in Spots. Co., Va., etc., etc. Thos. Towles, Chris. Crawford, Jas. Crawford, Elijah Partlow, Lewis Partlow. Septr. 5, 1797.

DEED BOOK P

1797–1800

May 10, 1797. Richd. Coleman of Spots. Co. to Lucy Chiles of same co. £118 curr. 102 a. on Robinson Swamp, etc., etc. Benj. Tompkins, Spilsby Coleman, John Acres. Septr. 5, 1797.

March 17, 1797. Saml. Graves, John Graves and James Graves of Fayette Co., Kentucky, po. of atto. to Wm. Graves of Spots. Co., Va., to collect from and settle with the executor of our grandfather, Samuel McGee, Decd. Witnesses, Henry Garrett, jr.; Wm. Alsop. Septr. 5, 1797.

March 1, 1797. Saml. Newton of Caroline Co. to Wm. Wiglesworth of same co. £20 curr. 20 a. in Spots. Co., etc., etc. James Smith, Benjn. Tompkins, Woller [Waller] Stephens, Wm. Smith. Septr. 5, 1797.

July 3, 1797. Richard Long and Fanny, his wife, of Spots. Co. to Philip Young of same co. £222 18s. 8d. curr. 152 a. in Spots. Co., etc., etc. Jos. Herndon, jr.; Edwd. Clark, Hugh Roy, Jona. Clark. Septr. 5, 1797.

Augt. 31, 1797. Henry Lee, Esq., and Ann, his wife, of Westmoreland Co. to Richard Maury of Spots. Co., etc., etc. £66 19s. curr. 103 a., part of a tract purchased of Genl. Alexander Spotswood in Spots. Co., etc., etc. Edwd. Herndon, Abram Carter, Jas. Allan, jr.; Fontaine Maury, Jno. Minor, jr.; Geo. French, Wm. Payne. Septr. 5, 1797.

Augt. 31, 1797. Henry Lee of Westmoreland Co., Esq., to Richard Maury of Spots. Co. Lease. 323 a. in Spots. Co., etc. "Sd. Richd. Maury and Diana, his wife, and their son Jno. Minor," etc., etc. 1000 lbs. tob. yearly, etc., etc. Same witnesses as to preceding deed. Septr. 5, 1797.

May 10, 1797. John Lewis and Mary Ann, his wife, of Spots. Co. to Wm. Ledwedge of same co. £126 curr. 240 a., part of a tract formerly Gawin Corbin's, in Berkeley Par., Spots. Co., etc., etc. Wm. Frazer, Thos. Olive, Joel Fagg. Septr. 5, 1797.

Augt. 1, 1797. James Crawford of Spots. Co. to John Minor Herndon of same co. and Samuel Overton, jr., of Louisa Co. Mortgage. 400 a. whereon sd. Crawford lives in Spots. Co., purchased of Jno. Hall, adj. lands of Christopher Crawford, New Market tract, a tract purchased of Ann Wiatt, and Daniel Coleman, etc., etc. Witnesses, Thos. R. Rootes, Antho. Frazer, Wm. Frazer. Septr. 5, 1797.

Augt. 4, 1797. Wm. Estes and Fanny, his wife, of Spots. Co.; Joel Lewis and Lucy, his wife, of same co. to Joseph Holladay of same co. £160 curr. 177 a. adj. lands of Tuerman Lewis, David Sandidge, Jos. Rawlings, Jno. Andrews, Francis King and sd. Joel Lewis, in Spots. Co., etc., etc. Lewis Holladay, Jos. Rawlings, John Cash. Septr. 5, 1797.

Augt. 31, 1797. Henry Lee, Esq., and Ann, his wife, of Westmoreland Co. to Hezekiah Ellis of Spots. Co. £15 15s. curr. 35 a., part of a tract purchased of Gen. Alexander Spotswood in Spots. Co., etc., etc. Jno. Minor, jr.; Wm. Payne, Geo. French, Edwd. Herndon. Septr. 5, 1797.

Augt. 16, 1797. Elizabeth x Edwards of Spots. Co. to Wm. Graves and Susannah, his wife, of same co. £50 and love and affection the sd. Eliza. Edwards hath for her son-in-law, the sd. Wm. Graves, and her dau,, the sd. Susannah Graves, etc., etc. 200 a. of land, several negroes, horses, goods and chattels, the est. left her by her deceased husband, James Edwards, etc., etc. Witnesses, Jos. Graves, Edwd. Cason, Wm. Cason. Decr. 5, 1797.

Decr. 4, 1797. John Graves of Spots. Co. to his son, Wm. Graves, of same co. Deed of Gift. 50 a. in Spots. Co., etc., etc. Geo. Tyler, Jos. Graves, Edwd. Cason, Wm. Cason. Decr. 5, 1797.

Augt. 11, 1797. John Shelton and Sukey, his wife, of Spots. Co. to Thomas Shelton. £42 15s. 95 a. in Spots. Co., etc., etc. Jacob Stewart, Wm. Sharp, Wm. Shelton. Decr. 5, 1797.

Novr. 1, 1797. Henry Mills and Elizabeth, his wife, of Spots. Co. to Wm. Keaton of same co. £40. 20 a., part of tract Thos. Mastin lives on in Spots. Co., etc., etc. John Page, Thos. Mastin, John Mills. Decr. 5, 1797.

May 11, 1797. Richard Coleman of Spots. Co. to Wm. Trigg. Mortgage. Negroes, etc. Witnesses, Robt. Lindsay, Wm. x Alders. Decr. 5, 1797.

June 14, 1797. Joseph Nelson of Spots. Co. to Wm. T. Nelson and Benja. Massey. £320 curr. 7 negroes, cattle, horses, goods and chattels, etc., etc. Witnesses, Jno. D. Long, Jno. T. Nelson, Jas. Nelson. Decr. 5, 1797.

Novr. 9, 1797. John Whitaker Willis of Spots. Co., Gent. Being indebted to Thos. Colson of the same co., Gent., in a greater sum than he has secured to the sd. Colson, in consideration whereof he, the sd. Willis, conveys to sd. Colson, 1 negro man for the sum of £120 curr. to be applied towards sinking the sd. debt, and in case the sd. Willis fails in paying to sd. Colson the sd. sum of £120 with interest, then the sd. slave to remain the sd. Colson's, etc., etc. Witnesses, Tho. Minor, John Crutchfield, Thomas Towles. Recd. Decr. 5, 1797.

Octr. 12, 1797. Robert Hart of Spots. Co., Gent., and Mary, his wife, to Malcolm Hart of Louisa Co., Gent. £1100 curr. 167 a. and buildings in Spots. Co., etc., etc. O. Towles, James Scott, Archd. Dick, junr.; Jno. Lipscomb. Decr. 5, 1797.

July 28, 1797. Gabriel x Long and Lucy, his wife, of Spots. Co. to their son James Long. Deed of Gift. 325 a. in St. Geo. Par., Spots. Co., etc., etc. Jno. Nelson, Clement Montague, Reuben Daniel. Jany. 2, 1798.

Decr. 15, 1797. Augustin Lewis and Sally, his wife, of Spots. Co. to John Penn of same co. In consideration of 1 negro girl, the sd. Lewis conveys to sd. Penn, 100 a. in Spots. Co., which descended to sd. Augustin from his father, Jno. Zachary Lewis, decd., etc., etc. Witnesses, Lewis Holladay, Jas. Webber, Geo. Penn, jr.; Geo. Penn. Jany. 2, 1798.

Jany. 2, 1798. Zachariah Billingsly of Berkeley Par., Spots. Co., emancipates his slave Tom, commonly called Tom Butler, etc., etc. Witnesses, Tureman Lewis, Jno. A. Billingsly. Jany. 2, 1798.

Augt. 31, 1797. George Ball and Thomas Ball and Mildred, his wife, of Spots. Co. to Harry Towles of same co. £342. 347 a. in Spots. Co. adj. lands of Wm. Duvall, Wm. Holloday, Chas. Burrage, Mrs. Boling, Robt. Hoe, Jno. Hegans, Saml. Moxley, and John Davenport, etc., etc. Witnesses, Porteus Towles, Jno. Davenport, Joel Bowlin. Jany. 2, 1798.

Decr. 20, 1797. Benjamin Reynolds and Elizabeth, his wife, of Spots. Co. to Benja. Waller and Wm. Trigg as Trustees. £3. 4 a. for the use of Baptist Society in Spots. Co., etc., etc. A. Waller, Jno. A. Billingsly, Austin Sandidge, Joseph Waller. Feby. 6, 1798.

Feby. 2, 1798. Jacob Wray and John A. Stewart to James Purvis of Spots. Co. 5s. to sd. Wray and £50 curr. to sd. Stewart; Lot 225 in town of Fredksbg., purchased by afsd. Wray of Roger Dixon and wife, etc., etc. Witnesses, Jno. Purvis, Edwd. Darnaby. Feby. 6, 1798.

Feby. 6, 1798. John Long of Spots. Co. to Francis Turnley of same co. £11 4s. curr. 5½ a. in Spots. Co., etc., etc. No witnesses. Feby. 6, 1798.

May 23, 1797. Ephraim Beazley of Spots. Co. to Wm. Beazley of same co. £162 16s. curr. 148 a. in Spots. Co., etc., etc. Benjn. Tompkins, Jos. Perry, John Long, Henry Duerson. Feby. 6, 1798.

Feby. 6, 1798. Joseph Brock of Spots. Co. to his son, Jos. Brock, jr. Deed of Gift. 50 a. in Spots. Co. No witnesses. Feby. 6, 1798.

Feby. 6, 1798. Samuel Alsop and Sarah, his wife; George Alsop and Lucy, his wife, of Spots. Co. to Henry Neal of same co. £150. 162 a. and 27 a. in Spots. Co., etc., etc. No witnesses. Feby. 6, 1798.

Octr. 31, 1797. Richd. Loury of Caroline Co. to Daniel Lindsay of Spots. Co. £19 curr. 314 a. in Spots. Co., etc., etc. H. Anderson, Thomas Powell, Francis Turnley. Feby. 6, 1798.

Octr. 10, 1797. Joseph Willoughby of Spots. Co. to his son, Henry Willoughby. Mortgage. Goods and chattels. Witnesses, Edwd. Herndon, Jos. Herndon, jr.; Jno. Herndon. Feby. 6, 1798.

Decr. 5, 1797. Benjamin Day of Fredericksburg emancipates his slave Nannie. Witnesses, Sta. Crutchfield, Danl. Grinnan, Jr. Feby. 6, 1798.

Octr. 25, 1797. Gerard B. Berryman and Alice, his wife, of Spots. Co. to Martin Brent of Lancaster Co. £150 curr. 190 a. in Spots. Co. adj. lands of Jno. Carter, Jno. Penny, Moses Perry, Wm. Duvall and John Pierce, etc. Witnesses, Stockley Towles, John Pierce, John Berryman, Wm. Drake. Feby. 6, 1798.

Decr. 14, 1797. Gerard B. Berryman and Alice, his wife, of Spots. Co. to Jno. Pierce of same co. £26 curr. 80 a. adj. lands of Henry Gatewood, Wm. Duval and Martin Brent in Berkeley Par., Spots. Co., etc., etc. Martin Brent, Jno. Berryman, Wm. Duval, Sherod Horn. Feby. 6, 1798.

Feby. 6, 1798. Oliver Towles of Spots. Co. to Ann Towles of same co. £477 2s. 367 a. in Spots. Co. (as formerly conveyed the sd. Ann by sd. Oliver, as by Ind. dated Decr. 7, 1789, for 550 a. under certain conditions), etc., etc. Witnesses, Jos. Brock, W. Johnston, jr. Harry Chew. Feby. 6, 1798.

Feby. 10, 1795. Edmund Clark of Spots. Co. to Charles Young of the Borough of Norfolk. £600 curr. 50 a. purchased of Ann Wyatt in Spots. Co., etc., etc. Thos. Hackney, Jno. Gwathmey, Jona. Clark. Feby. 6, 1798.

Feby. 12, 1795. Edmund Clark of Spots. Co. to Charles Young of Borough of Norfolk. £60 curr. 60 a. in Spots. Co., etc., etc. Jno. Gwathmey, Thos. Hackney, Jona. Clark. Feby. 6, 1798.

Feby 12, 1795. Edmund Clark of Spots. Co. to Chas. Young of Borough of Norfolk. £100 curr. 45 a. purchased of Benj. Waller in Spots. Co., etc., etc. Thos. Hackney, Jno. Gwathmey, Jona. Clark. Feby. 6, 1798.

Feby. 6, 1795. Charles Clark and Phebe, his wife, of Spots. Co. to James Smith, Gent., of same co. £244 3s. curr. 257 a. purchased of Thomas Henderson in Berkeley Par., Spots. Co., etc., etc. No witnesses. Feby. 6, 1798.

Feby. 5, 1798. Stockley Towles of Spots. Co., of the first part; Oliver Towles and ——, his wife, of same co., of second part, to Wm. Glassell of Fredksbg., of the third part. Whereas, Nicho. Payne, Gent., by Ind. dated April 25, 1791, conveyed to sd. Stockley Towles (to indemnify him, he being sd. Payne's security), his, the sd. Payne's interest and title in a tract of 446 a. in Spots. Co., known as "Pennfield" (one moiety being claimed by the heirs of Wm. Reveley, decd., and the other by sd. Payne by virtue of their purchase), purchased of Oliver Towles, and the sd. Stockley Towles being forced to sell the same, and the sd. Oliver Towles never having conveyed the same as yet to the afsd. Payne, the sd. Oliver Towles joins in this conveyance. Witnesseth, the sd. Stockley Towles, in consideration of the sum of £71 curr. to be applied to indemnification of sd. Stockley, and pd. to him by the sd. Glassell, conveys to him the sd. Glassell, the right, title, etc., of the sd. Payne, in the above sd. tract, etc., etc. No witnesses. Feby. 6, 1798.

Augt. 30, 1796. Jonathan Clark of Spots. Co. and Sarah, his wife, to John Dillard of same co. £78 curr. 41 a. in Spots. Co., etc., etc. Thos. Hackney, John Crawford, Lewis Partlow, Jas. Crawford, jr. Feby. 6, 1798.

Augt. 30, 1796. Jonathan Clark and Sarah, his wife, of Spots. Co. to Christopher Crawford of same co. £38 10s. curr. 40 a. in Spots. Co., etc., etc. Jno. Crawford, Lewis Partlow, Thos. Hackney, Jas. Crawford, jr. Feby. 6, 1798.

Octr. 7, 1797. Wm. Bronaugh and Mary, his wife, of Spots. Co. to Tuerman Lewis of same co. £46 4s. 78 a. in Spots. Co., etc., etc. Lewis Holladay, Geo. Bronaugh, Zacherias Sandidge, Rich. C. Noel, David Bronaugh. Feby. 6, 1798.

April 3, 1798. Thomas Colson of Spots. Co. to Ann Rawlings, widow, and her two infant children, John and Peyton Rawlings, all of Spots. Co. Deed of Gift. 4 slaves, in trust for the sd. Ann Rawlings, until Nov. 1, 1810 (in case she shall so long live), and from and immediately after that period or after the death of sd. Ann, then to the afsd. John and Peyton Rawlings, etc., etc. Mentions "Jeremiah Rawlings, Sr., of Caroline Co., grandfather of sd. John and Peyton," etc., etc. No witnesses. May 1, 1798.

Decr. 11, 1797. Joseph Willoughby of Spots. Co. to his son, Henry Willoughby, of same co. Deed of Gift. 100 a. in Spots. Co., etc., etc. Ashman x Sorrel, Charles Burrage. May 1, 1798.

June 22, 1798. Peter Dudley of Spots. Co., Gent., of first part; Anna Rawlings, widow and relict of Peter Rawlings of same co., of second part, and Thomas Colson of same co., of third part. Whereas, there is a marriage intended shortly to be solemnized between the sd. Peter Dudley and Anna Rawlings, and they both being seized of property, and also both parties having children, sd. Peter, by his former wife, sundry sons and daughters, and sd. Anna, by her former husband, a dau. Nancy, married to Beckerton Winston, and two sons, John and Peyton, have come to an agreement previous to their marriage to settle and adjust their respective estates as is hereinafter mentioned and declared so as to make proper provision for themselves and the sd. children. Agreement with Thomas Colson as "trustee," etc., etc. Witnesses, George Shepherd, Joseph Bullock, Wm. Shepherd, Lucy D. Owen. July 3, 1798.

March 27, 1798. Francis T. Brooke and Mary, his wife, of Fredksbg. to Henry Mills of Sports Co. 5 shill. 80 a. purchased of Jno. Keegan in Spots. Co., etc., etc. Jno. Chew, Jno. Minor, jr.; Thos. R. Rootes. July 3, 1798.

Jany. 11, 1798. Elijah Estes, Richard Estes, Moses Estes, Fielding Estes, James Higgins and Nancy, his wife, to Jno. Hart. £323 18s. 4d. 460 a. in Spots. Co. whereon Abram Estes, decd., lived and devised by him to his wife, and directed by his will that after her death (which event hath taken place) that the same be sold and the profits arising therefrom divided between the sd. Elijah, Richd., Moses, and Fielding Estes and Nancy Estes, now wife of James Higgins, etc., etc. Witnesses, John Crump, John Harris, Robert Hart. July 3, 1798.

Decr. 23, 1797. Elijah Estes of Spots. Co. to Robt. Hart and Mary Long, wife of Leonard Long of same co. For love and affection which he beareth them, conveys to them all the property of which he the sd. Estes may die possessed, etc., etc. Witnesses, Jno. Hart, W. Johnston, jr.; Jos. Pollard, jr. July 3, 1798.

April 2, 1798. Thomas Winslow and Elizabeth, his wife, of Spots. Co. to John D. Long of same co. £73 17s. 3d. 134 a. in Spots. Co., etc., etc. Joshua Long, J. Willoughby, Benj. Robinson. July 3, 1798.

July 2, 1798. Spencer Coleman of Spots. Co. to Mary Ann Blaydes of same co. £50 curr. 8 a. in Spots. Co., etc., etc. No witnesses. July 3, 1798.

Jany. 29, 1798. Benja. Massey of Spots. Co. to Burgess Sullivan of same co. £50 curr. 70 a. in Spots. Co., etc., etc. Richd. C. Webb, Wm. Sullivan, James Faulconer, Jno. Overton, jr.; Edward Taylor, B. Hyde. July 3, 1798.

June 2, 1798. "Samuel Faulconer, Senr., of Spots. Co. to his eight children, Saml. and James Faulconer, Catherine Almond, Phebe Moore, Elizabeth, Jemima and Philadelphia Faulconer and Mary Underwood of same county." Deed of Gift. 150 a. of land, etc., etc. Witnesses, David Partlow, John Partlow, Benjamin Webb. July 3, 1798.

May 14, 1798. John Hall and Eliza Ann, his wife, of City of Philadelphia, Pennsylvania, to —— Towles of County of ——, in Va. $2700.00.
722 a. purchased of George Lewis and Catharine, his wife, as by Ind.
Octr. 12, 1797, in Spots. Co., Va., etc., etc. Witnesses, Bernard Webb, P.
Conway. July 3, 1798.

May 10, 1798. Edward Elley and Mary Ann, his wife, of Culpeper Co.
to Richard Bullard of Spots. Co. £44 16s. curr. 64 a. in Spots. Co., etc.,
etc. No witnesses. July 3, 1798.

April 9, 1798. Christopher Smith of Louisa Co. to Isaac Graves of
Orange Co. £183 curr. 203 a. in Spots. and Orange Counties, etc., etc.
Thos. Powell, Benjn. Robinson, Samuel Overton, jr.; James Powell, Fran-
cis Coleman, John Carter. July 3, 1798.

June 30, 1796. Edmund Clark of Spots. Co. to Jonathan Clark of same
co. £192 curr. 129½ a. on Arnold Run, in Spots. Co., etc., etc. Henry
Dodd, Benj. Rennolds, Jno. Wiglesworth. July 3, 1798.

June 30, 1798. Jonathan Clark and Sarah, his wife, of Spots. Co. to
James Wilson of same co. £30 15s. curr. 41 a. in Spots. Co., etc., etc.
Witness, Wm. Taylor. July 3, 1798.

Novr. 24, 1797. Robert Hart of Spots. Co. to Archibald Dick, jr., of
Caroline Co. £1583 (equal to 5276⅔ Spanish milled dollars). 1231 a.
purchased of Charles Gordon, of Henry Lewis, of Jos. Holladay, of John
Holladay, of Thomas Powell of John Wren, and of Danl. Lane in Spots.
Co., etc., etc. John Lipscomb, Thos. x Harris, Malcolm Hart. July 3,
1798.

May 5, 1798. Lewis Holladay, Execr. of Jos. Holladay, decd., of Spots.
Co. to Benjamin Holladay of same co. £180 curr. 80 a. in Spots. Co.,
etc., etc. Hugh C. Boggs, Thos. Towles, jr.; David Bronaugh, Austin
Sandidge, John Scott, John Lipscomb, A. Frazer. July 3, 1798.

May 1, 1798. Lewis Holladay, Execr. of Jos. Holladay, decd., of Spots.
Co. to James Holladay of same co. £135 curr. 100 a. in Spots. Co., etc.,
etc. David Bronaugh, Austin Sandidge, Jno. Scott, Jno. Lipscomb, A.
Frazer. July 3, 1798.

May 1, 1798. Lewis Holladay, Execr. of Jos. Holladay, decd., of Spots.
Co. to Wm. Holladay of same co. £357 15s. curr. 265 a. in Spots. Co.,
etc., etc. David Bronaugh, Austin Sandidge, John Scott, John Lipscomb,
A. Frazer. July 3, 1798.

March 1, 1798. Wm. McWilliams and Dorothea, his wife, of Spots.
Co. to Henry Goss of same co. £138 6s. 57⅝ a. in Spots. Co., etc., etc.
Geo. Shepherd, Jos. Bullock, Henry Mills. July 3, 1798.

Feby. 22, 1798. Wm. Willoughby, Ashmon x Sorrell and Thomas x
Sorrell (heirs of John Sorrell, Intestate) of Spots. Co. to James Robins
of same co. £3 10s. curr. 10 a. in Berkeley Par., Spots. Co., etc., etc.
Jno. Page, Thos. Fuller, Anthony Arnold. July 3, 1798.

Augt. 3, 1798. Jeremiah Morton and Mildred Garnett, his wife, to
Wm. Morton of Orange Co. Whereas, Jno. Jackson, surviving brother
of Wm. Jackson, the father of the afsd. Mildred, and Ann Hackley, wife
of Richd. S. Hackley, having been a resident in the Kingdom of Gt.
Britain for a considerable length of time, and this resulting from Mental

incapacity, and whereas, he possesses considerable property both real and personal in this State, but especially in Orange Co., and whereas, on acc. of the absence of the afsd. John Jackson and the circumstances attending him, he was supposed incompetent to the due presentation of the afsd. property, and whereas, the sd. Jeremiah Morton and Richd. S. Hackley who intermarried with the afsd. Mildred and Ann, only children of Wm. Jackson, who will, in case the sd. John Jackson should continue in his then and present incapacity, and thereby be unable to make any disposition of his estate, be claimants to his afsd. est. under the will of Robt. Jackson, father to the sd. Wm. and John, etc., and whereas, the sd. Jere. Morton and R. S. Hackley, upon making application, were apptd. curators or a committee of the afsd. property abt. the yr. 1794, by the Orange Co. Court, and the sd. Wm. Morton at that time became their security, etc., etc., to indemnify the afsd. Wm. Morton they, the sd. Jeremiah Morton and Mildred G., his wife, convey to him, viz., the moiety of the sd. Mildred G. in the estate of her father, Wm. Jackson, etc., etc. Witnesses, Jas. Lewis, jr.; Geo. Morton, jr.; Wm. Crooks, Edwd. Herndon, Jas. Lewis. Septr. 4, 1798.

Whereas, Elizabeth Towles, decd., did by her last will and testament, devise certain slaves to her grandchildren, Merryman Payne, Ann Payne, Elizabeth Payne, and Frances Payne, and whereas, Thomas Towles, Henry Towles, Stockley Towles, and Ann Reveley (children of the sd. Elizabeth Towles, decd.), are ready and willing to convey and release all right, title, etc., whatsoever, they may have to the sd. slaves, this Ind. therefore witnesseth, conveyance of the sd. slaves to Thos. Towles, in trust for the afsd. Paynes, etc., etc. Witnesses, Edwd. Herndon, Beverley Stubblefield, Thomas Winslow. Septr. 4, 1798.

April 14, 1798. John Duret Long of Spots. Co. to Charles Burrage of same co. £134. 134 a. and 58 poles in Spots. Co., etc., etc. No witnesses. Septr. 4, 1798.

Augt. 14, 1798. Charles Burrage and Katy, his wife, of Spots. Co. to John Duret Long of same co. £80. 130 a. in Spots. Co., etc., etc. No witnesses. Septr. 4, 1798.

May 30, 1798. Thomas Goodwin and Ann Maria, his wife, of Fredksbg. to Wm. Drummond of same town. £450 curr. Lot 133 in town of Fredksbg., purchased of Fontaine Maury and Betsy, his wife, as by Ind. dated March 23, 1793, etc., etc. Fontaine Maury, John Brownlow, James Ross, Leonard H. Maury. Septr. 4, 1798.

Augt. 6, 1798. Wm. Arnold, jr., and Nancy Arnold (children of Geo. Arnold, decd.) of Spots. Co., po. of atto. to Pomfrett Waller, jr., of Spots. Co., Va., etc., etc. Witnesses, Dabney Waller, Thos. Minor, jr.; Jacksill x Thacker. Septr. 4, 1798.

Augt. 22, 1798. Mary Daingerfield, Wm. Daingerfield, Henry Daingerfield, and Lewis Willis Daingerfield of Spots. Co. to John Steward of same co. £100. 100 a. in Spots. Co., etc., etc. Thomas Colson, Henry Duerson, Jno. M. Herndon, Thos. Walden. Septr. 4, 1798.

Augt. 22, 1798. Mary Daingerfield, Wm. Daingerfield, Henry Daingerfield, and Lewis Willis Daingerfield of Spots. Co. to John Coates of Louisa Co. £405. 405 a. in Spots. Co., etc., etc. Thos. Colson, Jno. M. Herndon, Henry Duerson, Thos. Walden. Septr. 4, 1798.

Augt. 25, 1798. Agreement of Wm. and Henry Daingerfield with their mother, Mary Daingerfield, and their brother Lewis Willis Daingerfield, concerning a certain tract of land, etc., etc. Witnesses, Thomas Walden, Henry Duerson, Thos. Colson. Septr. 4, 1798.

Feby. 21, 1798. Henry Gatewood, Senr., of Spots. Co. to John Pierce of same co. £25. 25 a. in Spots. Co., etc., etc. Jos. Anderson, jr.; John Carter, jr.; Martin Brent. Septr. 4, 1798.

May 14, 1798. Henry Gatewood, Senr., of Spots. Co. to John Carter, jr., of same co. £19. 23¾ a. in Spots. Co., etc., etc. Henry Towles, jr.; Reubin Herndon, Martin Brent. Septr. 4, 1798.

Septr. 3, 1798. Geo. French and Edwd. Herndon of Spots. Co. to Thomas Olive of same co. Lease. 89 a. in Spots. Co., etc., etc. £4 9s yearly rent, etc., etc. No witnesses. Septr. 4, 1798.

Septr. 3, 1798. Geo. French and Edwd. Herndon of Spots. Co. to Richard Todd of same co. Lease. 124 a. in Spots. Co., etc., etc. £6 4s. yearly rent, etc., etc. No witnesses. Septr. 4, 1798.

Septr. 4, 1798. Geo. French and Edwd. Herndon of Spots. Co. to Jessey Haydon, jr., of same co. Lease. 79 a. in Spots. Co., etc., etc. £3 19s. rent, etc. No witnesses. Septr. 4, 1798.

Septr. 3, 1798. Geo. French and Edwd. Herndon of Spots. Co. to Thomas Hawkins of same co. Lease. 60 a. in Spots. Co., etc., etc. £3 yearly rent, etc., etc. No witnesses. Septr. 4, 1798.

Augt. 9, 1798. Thomas Boxley of Spots. Co. to Wm. Quisenbury of Orange Co. $873.33⅓. 206 a. in fork of North Anna River, in Spots. Co., etc., etc. Thos. Winslow, Saml. Sale, Jno. Carter, Jas. Nelson, Wm. x Bickers. Septr. 4, 1798.

Augt. 4, 1796. Wm. Waller of Spots. Co. to Thos. Buckner of Caroline Co. In trust, one slave, for the use of Wm. Johnston and Ann, his wife, during their lives, etc., etc., and then to their children, etc., etc. Witnesses, Benj. Alsop, Jno. Bogan. Septr. 4, 1798.

Novr. 5, 1797. Joseph Duerson, jr., and Jennet, his wife, of Spots. Co. to John Clark of Fairfax Co. £120 curr. 156 a. in Berkeley Par., Spots. Co., etc., etc. Thos. Waller, Jno. Waller, Jno. Scott. Feby. 6, 1798.

Decr. 4, 1795. John Powell and Betsey Norment, his wife, of Spots. Co. to Wm. Powell of King Wm. Co. £470 curr. 435 a. whereon sd. Jno. Powell lives in Spots. Co. No witnesses. Decr. 4, 1798.

Jany. 24, 1798. Bathurst Jones of Hanover Co. to John Powell of King Wm. Co. £326 5s. 435 a. in Spots. Co., etc., etc. Jas. Legons, Wm. Manson, Benj. Oliver, jr. Decr. 4, 1798.

April 10, 1796. Joel Lewis and Lucy, his wife, of Spots. Co. to Ashmon Sorrel of same co. £40 curr. 80 a. in Berkeley Par., Spots. Co., etc., etc. Tureman Lewis.

Novr. 26, 1798. Susannah Garnett of Spots. Co. to Thomas Duerson of same co. £110 curr. 237 a. known as lot No. 3, of Benj. Holladay's Est. in Spots. Co., etc., etc. Geo. Shepherd, Wm. Shepherd, Henry Duerson. Decr. 4, 1798.

Decr. 1, 1798. Thomas Towles and Mary, his wife, of Spots. Co. to John Chewning of Caroline Co. £158 4s. curr. 113 a. n. of Robinson Run, Spots. Co. No witnesses. Decr. 4, 1798.

July 13, 1798. John W. Willis and Ann, his wife, to Chichester Curtis. Lease. Tract of land in Spots. Co., etc., etc. £3 yearly rent, etc., etc. Henry Daingerfield, W. Daingerfield. Decr. 4, 1798.

Septr. 27, 1798. Jos. Nelson and Lucy, his wife, of Spots. Co. to John Quarles of same co. £70 curr. (pd. by Francis Quarles, guard. of Jno. Quarles). 50 a. on Pamunkey River, in Spots. Co., etc., etc. Sam. Sale, Geo. Boxley, Joseph Duke. Decr. 4, 1798.

May 30, 1798. David Humphries and Elizabeth Moore, his wife, of Fayette Co., Kentucky; Charles Scott, jr., and Fanny, his wife, of Woodford Co., Kentucky (late Elizabeth and Fanny Cooke, daughters of Elizabeth Cooke, dau. of Jno. Roberson, decd.), to Samuel Sale of Spots. Co., Va. £100 curr. Convey ½ of a tract of 500 a. in Spots. Co., Va., being that tract of land bequeathed by Augustine Moore, decd., of Va., in his last will and testament, to the aforesd. Elizabeth Cooke and to Catherine Throgmorton, formerly Catherine Roberson, daughter of the afsd. Jno. Roberson, decd., and which half of the afsd. tract of land has been since conveyed by John Cooke, father of the afsd. Elizabeth Humphries and Fanny Scott, to the afsd. Saml. Sale, by deed dated Jany. 23, 178—. No witnesses. Decr. 4, 1798.

Augt. 16, 1798. Mary x Taylor of Spots. Co. to James Taylor of same co. £21. 1 bay mare. Witnesses, Geo. Bronaugh, John Humphreys. Decr. 4, 1798.

Novr. 21, 1798. Danl. Lane and Ann, his wife, of Spots. Co. to Thomas Porter of same co. $341.75. 205 a. in Spots. Co., etc., etc. Thos. Winslow, John Day, John Walters, Jonathan Johnson, Joseph Herndon, jr. Decr. 4, 1798.

Novr. 13, 1798. Elizabeth Carpenter, widow and relict of Jonathan Carpenter, late of Spots. Co., decd., to Edwd. Herndon (son of Joseph) of same county. Whereas, sd. Jonathan Carpenter, decd., did by his Ind. dated Nov. 27, 1793, convey to the afsd. Herndon, 230 a. in Spots. Co., and whereas, it was done with the consent of the sd. Elizabeth, but without her signature thereto, in consideration whereof she relinquishes her dower right therein, etc., etc. Witnesses, Jno. M. Herndon, Jos. Brock, Zacheus Carpenter, Wm. Bridges. Decr. 4, 1798.

Decr. 1, 1798. Lewis Holladay of Spots. Co. to Waller Holladay of same co. £37 10s. curr. 50 a. in Spots. Co., etc., etc. Austin Sandidge, Jno. Scott, Hugh C. Boggs. Jany. 1, 1799.

Jany. 1, 1799. Thos. Minor, Senr., of Spots. Co. to his son, Thomas Minor, jr. Deed of Gift. 141 a. purchased of Robert and Hannah Turnbull in Spots. Co., etc., etc. No witnesses. Feby. 5, 1799.

Feby. 5, 1799. Philip Garnett and Elizabeth, his wife, of Spots. Co. to Susannah Garnett of same co. £50. "All right, title, etc., which he, the sd. Philip Garnett has or may have under his, the sd. Philip's, deceased father's will to part of a certain tract of land in Spots. Co. joining lands of Mann Page, Esq.; Majr. Peter Dudley, and Mr. Joseph Bullock, and whereon the sd. Susanna Garnett now lives," etc. Witnesses, Thos. Colson, Tho. Minor, Phil. D. Redd, Peter Dudley. Feby. 5, 1799.

Feby. 4, 1799. Winslow Parker of the state of Kentucky, Thos. Winslow of Va., Susanna Parker, admx. of Wm. Parker, jr., decd., late of Va. The afsd. Winslow Parker, as atto. in fact; Henry Parker and Rowland Thomas and Mary, his wife, of the state of Kentucky; Wm. Stubblefield, atto. in fact for Robt. Stubblefield and Susanna, his wife; Richd. Parker and Thomas Parker, all of the State of Kentucky; Peter Dudley, atto. in fact for Ambrose Dudley of Kentucky, to James Powell and Benjamin Robinson of Spots. Co., Va. £443 8s. 9d. curr. 215 a. in Spots. Co., all that tract of land whereof Wm. Parker, the elder, of the sd. county, died, seized and possessed, bounded by Terry's Run and the land of sd. James Powell, Benj. Robinson, and Richard Dickerson, etc., etc. Witnesses, Jno. Nelson, Jno. Alcock, Jno. Day, Jno. Herndon, Isaac Graves. Feby. 5, 1799.

Jany. 3, 1799. Joel Lewis and Lucy, his wife, of Spots. Co. to Tureman Lewis of same co. £100 curr. 100 a. in Spots. Co., etc., etc. Lewis Holladay, Austin Sandidge, Jos. Holladay, Stockley Towles. Feby. 5, 1799.

Jany. 1, 1799. Richard Coleman to Robert S. Coleman. Whereas, sd. Richd. Coleman has enlisted as a soldier in the U. S. Army and the sd. Robt. S. Coleman having advanced sundry sums of money to him to enable him to procure proper clothes, etc., etc., in consideration whereof and £10 curr., the sd. Richd. Coleman conveys to the sd. R. S. Coleman, 3 slaves, etc., etc. Witnesses, Farish Coleman, Wm. Coleman, Jno. Whitlock. April 2, 1799.

Feby. 25, 1799. James Stevens and Mary Bird, his wife, of Spots. Co. to Spilsby Coleman of same co. £100. 54 a. in Spots. Co., etc., etc. Chas. Bennett, Thos. Trigg, James x Foreakers. April 2, 1799.

March 25, 1799. Henry Durrett and Dolly, his wife, to Paul Conner, both parties of Caroline Co. £20. 24 a. purchased of Thomas Towles in Spots. Co., etc., etc. Rowland Estes, Geo. Winn, Wm. Durrett. April 2, 1799.

Feby. 23, 1799. John Rains, heir of James Rains, decd., of Spots. Co. to Samuel Moxley of same co. £11 curr. 53 a., two-thirds thereof he, the sd. Jno. Rains, held as heir at law to his father, Jas. Rains, decd., the other fell to his mother, Sarah Rains, widow of sd. Jas. Rains, now wife of sd. Saml. Moxley, in Spots. Co., etc., etc. Witnesses, Jno. Pendleton, Robt. Pendleton, Elsandlr. More. April 2, 1799.

March 29, 1799. Wm. Durrett and Sarah, his wife, of Caroline Co. to Paul Conner of same co. £150. 301 a. in Spots. Co., etc., etc. No witnesses. April 2, 1799.

March 30, 1799. Samuel Moxley and Sarah, his wife, of Spots. Co. to Henry Willoughby of same co. £14. 27 a. in Spots. Co., etc., etc. Jos. Herndon, Bowker Waller, Jno. Nelson, Jos. Willoughby. April 2, 1799.

Jany. 14, 1799. Wm. Fagg, to indemnify Henry Willoughby, who stands security for sd. Fagg, to James Skinner of Md., on Bond of $100.00, the sd. Fagg conveys to sd. Willoughby goods and chattels, etc., etc. Witnesses, Jos. Willoughby, Jno. x May, Samuel Moxley. April 2, 1799.

March 28, 1799. John Gardner and Ann, his wife, to Thomas Gardner of Louisa Co. £130. 100 a. whereon sd. Jno. Gardner lives in Spots. Co., etc., etc. Jos. Willoughby, Saml. Sale, Thomas x Harris, April 2, 1799.

March 29, 1799. Henry Mills and Elizabeth, his wife, of Spots. Co. to Daniel Starke of sd. county. £46. 80 a. purchased of Francis Brooke in Spots. Co., etc., etc. Thos. Colson, James Starke, Jeremiah Starke. April 2, 1799.

March 29, 1799. Thomas Winslow and Elizabeth, his wife, to George Twyman, jr. £1760 11s. 582 a. in Spots. Co., etc., etc. Lewis Holladay, Benj. Robinson, Stockley Towles, James Powell, Jno. M. Herndon, Saml. Robinson. April 2, 1799.

May 12, 1798. Thomas Duvall and Jessee Carpenter of Fayette Co., Kentucky, po. of atto. to Zacheus Carpenter, to recover the equal parts, etc., of the sd. Duvall and Jessee Carpenter in the est. of Jonathan Carpenter, decd., in Spots. Co., Va. Witness, Thos. Bodley. April 2, 1799.

June 6, 1798. Nathan Hawkins and Frances, his wife, of Madison Co., Kentucky, to Thomas Waller of Spots. Co., Va. $110.00. 55 a. in Spots. Co., etc., etc. No witnesses. July 2, 1799.

May 27, 1799. Francis Coleman of Spots. Co., atto. in fact for John Nelson of Campbell Co., Kentucky, to Joseph Williams of Spots. Co. £75 curr. 176 a. on Plentiful Run. Spots. Co., etc., etc. Chas. Burrage, Thos. Olive, Wm. Burnett, Benj. Robinson, Saml. Robinson. July 2, 1799.

June 24, 1799. Michael Robinson, jr., and Nancy, his wife, and Henry Robinson and Elizabeth, his wife, to James Lewis, Sr. $490 to sd. Henry Robinson, in hand pd., etc. 98 a., part of a tract which sd. Michael and Henry Robinson are entitled to under the will of the grandfather, Michael Robinson, decd., in Spots. Co., etc., etc. Edwd. Herndon, Wm. Robinson, Dabney Herndon. July 2, 1799.

Octr. 29, 1796. Wm. Brock of Orange Co. to Jos. Brock of same co. £100 curr. "All my right, title, etc., in four negroes in possession of our father, Joseph Brock of Spots. Co., and are the same negroes and their increase which were lent our mother, Elizabeth, by her father, Jacob Clayton, Decd.," etc., etc. Witnesses, Edwd. Herndon, Jas. Lewis. July 2, 1799.

"1799, January 12th, Receivd. of Wm. McGehee the negroes left me by my grandfather, James Edwards," etc., etc. (Signed) John Scuddy. Witnesses, Geo. Pottie, John Toler, Jno. Waller. July 2, 1799.

July 1, 1799. Geo. W. B. Spooner of Fredksbg. to Geo. Wilson Spooner of Spots. Co. £200. 113½ a. purchased of heirs of Colo. Gaspee Stadler, in Spots. Co., etc., etc. Wm. Taylor, Eliza Spooner, Wm. Vass, James Lilly. July 2, 1799.

Decr. 25, 1798. Francis x King and Mary, his wife, of Spots. Co. to Reuben Moore of Culpeper Co. £107 curr. 107 a. in Spots. Co., etc., etc. Dabney Lipscomb, David Bronaugh, Edwd. Hyde. July 2, 1799.

March 15, 1799. Zachary Lewis and Ann, his wife, of Spots. county. James Holladay of same county. £277 10s. curr. 185 a. in Spots. Co., etc., etc. Richmond Lewis, Benjn. Rawlings, Lewis Holladay, Austin Sandidge. July 2, 1799.

——— ———, 1799. John Davenport and Elizabeth, his wife, of Spots. Co. to Samuel Moxley of same co. £6 curr. 6 a. in Berkeley Par., Spots. Co., etc., etc. Reuben Massey, Thomas Massey, Jas. Pulliam. July 2, 1799.

Decr. 31, 1798. James Weir of Spots. Co. to James Marye of same co. Whereas, the sd. Weir being possessed of sundry slaves which were seized and taken by virtue of an execution levied by the Sheriff of Spots. Co., to satisfy a large debt due by sd. Weir to Jas. Somerville, amnting. with interest to abt. £700, and whereas, the sd. slaves so seized being claimed by sd. James Marye, etc., etc., an agreement having been come to, viz., the sd. Marye would use no means to obstruct the payment of sd. Somerville's debt, and without molestation suffer as many of the sd. slaves to be sold as would be sufficient to meet the sd. debt, the sd. Weir conveying to sd. Marye all his right, title, etc., in and to remainder of sundry slaves in his possession, in trust for the uses, etc., and support of Lucy Mary Weir, wife of sd. James Weir, and sister of sd. James Marye and her children begotten or to be begotten, by this or any future marriage, etc., etc. This Ind. mentions Robert Weir, Sarah Marye Weir, Wm. James Weir, Elizabeth Letitia Ann Weir, the children of James Weir and Mary Ann, his wife, etc., etc. Witnesses, O. Towles, jr.; Law. Slaughter, O. Towles. July 2, 1799.

July 1, 1799. Geo. Wilson Spooner of Spots. Co. to Chas. Stewart of Fredksbg. £50. 100 a. leased by sd. Geo. Wilson Spooner in Spots. Co. for and during the lives of sd. Geo. W. Spooner and Sarah, his wife, and Geo. W. B. Spooner, his son, etc., etc. Witnesses, Jno. M. Herndon, Tureman Lewis, Robt. S. Coleman. July 2, 1799.

Jany. 8, 1799. Wm. Gholson and Mary, his wife, of Spots. Co. to John Bledsoe of Orange Co. £120 curr. 133 a. in Spots. Co., etc., etc. Moses Bledsoe, Jos. Johnson, Mary Johnson, Caleb Abell, Geo. Bledsoe. July 2, 1799.

July 2, 1799. Wm. Wilson to his brother, Jeremiah Wilson. Whereas, the sd. Jeremiah Wilson stood security for the sd. Wm. Wilson in his, the sd. Wm. Wilson's guardianhip of his, the sd. Williams' "first four children, viz., Polly, Betsy, Peggy, and Lucy." To indemnify the sd. Jeremiah and save him harmless, sd. Wm. conveys him two slaves, etc., etc. No witnesses. July 2, 1799.

Novr. 9, 1798. Larkin Reynolds and Elizabeth, his wife, of Spots. Co. to Wm. Graves of same co. £119 curr. 190 a. in Spots. Co. (with issue, profits, reversion, etc., after death of Elizabeth Edwards), etc., etc. Edwd. Cason, Benja. Waller, Jona. Clark. July 2, 1799.

April 4, 1799. Wm. Trigg and Ann, his wife, of Spots. Co. to Jeremiah Wilson of same co. £371 16s. 8d. curr. 224 a. in Spots. Co., etc., etc. John Tennent, Thomas Trigg, Spillsbe Coleman. July 2, 1799.

July 2, 1799. Wm. Trigg and Anne, his wife, of Spots. Co. to Robert Spilsbe Coleman, jr., of same co. £722 7s. 4d. curr. 302 a. in Spots. Co., etc., etc. No witnesses. July 2, 1799.

June 14, 1799. Thomas Duvall and Jessee Carpenter of Fayette Co., Kentucky, po. of atto. to Zacheus Carpenter of Spots. Co., Va., Gent., to ask, receive, etc., the estate of Jonathan Carpenter, decd., our parts of the estate, we being legatees of sd. decd., this is to say, Frances Carpenter,

Nancy Carpenter and Jonathan Carpenter, orphans, have chosen me, Thos. Duvall, their guardian, etc., etc. Septr. 3, 1799.

July 2, 1799. Thomas Strachan and Mary, his wife, of Spots. Co. to James Lewis and Fontaine Maury of same co. Mortgage to indemnify the grantees for their securityship, etc., etc. 237 a. in Spots. Co., goods and chattels, several negroes, formerly property of Revd. Jas. Marye, and also a slave formerly the property of Dr. Peter Strachan of the City of Richmond, etc., etc. Witnesses, Lucy Herndon, Richd. Maury, Edward Herndon. July 2, 1799.

Augt. 29, 1799. John Clark and Anna, his wife, of Spots. Co. to Joseph Herndon, jr., of same co. $130.00. 13 a., part of a tract purchased of Jos. Duerson, jr., in Berkeley Par., Spots. Co., etc., etc. Robt. Cammack, Wm. Duerson. Septr. 3, 1799.

Augt. 10, 1799. Hawes Coleman of Amherst Co. to Oswald Smith of Spots. Co. $1333.33. 220 a. (a line between sd. Hawes and his brother, Spencer Coleman) in Spots. Co., etc., etc. Joseph Graves, James Smith. Septr. 3, 1799.

Feby. 16, 1799. John Hart and Sarah, his wife, of Spots. Co. to Lewis Timberlake of Caroline Co. £93. 93½ a. in Spots. Co., etc., etc. Wm. Stanard, Jos. Pollard, jr.; Hugh Roy. Septr. 3, 1799.

May 5, 1799. Henry Lee, Esq., and Ann, his wife, and Alexander Spotswood, Esq., and Elizabeth, his wife, to Henry Robinson. £82 10s. 150 a. in Spots. Co. (on which sd. Spotswood holds a mortgage and hereby releases same), etc., etc. Jos. Brock, jr.; Stephen McFarlane, F. Thornton, Edwd. Herndon, Wm. Stanard, Thos. Strachan, Jno. M. Herndon, Wm. Herndon. Septr. 3, 1799.

March 19, 1799. Wm. Pettus, acting executor of Wm. Pettus, late of Spots. Co., Decd., to John C. Blaydes. £455 18s. curr. 376 a. whereon sd. Pettus, decd., lived in Spots. Co., etc., etc. Benj. Waller, Edwd. Cason, Jos. Graves, Jno. A. Billingsley, John Woolfolk. Septr. 3, 1799.

Octr. 26, 1798. Larkin Reynolds and Elizabeth, his wife, of Spots. Co. to Edward Cason of same co. £125 curr. 119 a. in Spots. Co., etc., etc. Geo. Tyler, Saml. Hill, Edwd. Hill, Elijah Partlow, Lewis Holladay, Jona. Clark. Septr. 3, 1799.

April 17, 1799. Thomas Coleman and Rebecca, his wife, of Spots. Co. to Leonard Young of same co. £50 curr. 43 a. in Spots. Co., etc., etc. Jno. Duerson, Wm. Henderson, Uriah Knight, Wm. Steers, Henry Lee. Septr. 3, 1799.

Septr. 3, 1799. Hugh Roy of Spots. Co. emancipates a slave called Lanney, etc., etc. No witnesses. Septr. 3, 1799.

Augt. 15, 1799. Richard Estes and Catherine, his wife; Wm. Beazley and Elizabeth, his wife, all of Spots. Co.; James Bates and Mary, his wife, of Fauqueir Co. to Ephraim Beazley, jr., of Spots. Co. Whereas, Ambrose Carlton by his last will and testament did lend to his wife, Lucy Carlton, his whole estate during her widowhood, and in case of her remarriage the whole estate to be divided into four equal parts, 1 part to his sd. wife and her heirs, and the other three parts to his daughters, the sd. Catherine, Elizabeth, and Lucy, parties hereto, as by the afsd. will recorded in Caroline Co., etc., etc. Sometime after the publishing of the sd. will, the sd. Lucy Carlton (widow of the testator) intermarried with James Mîtcham, and thereby became entitled to ¼ part of a certain tract of 280 a. in Spots. Co., and the sd. Lucy outliving her husband, the sd. James Mitcham, did by her will of record in Spots. Co., direct the sale thereof and the proceeds equally divided among her three daughters, the parties thereto. In consideration of the premises and of several sums to the grantors in hand paid, they conveyed to the sd. Ephraim Beazley, jr., the whole of the afsd. tract of 280 a. in Spots. Co., etc., etc. No witnesses. Septr. 3, 1799.

Septr. 3, 1799. Bowker Waller and Philadelphia, his wife, of Spots. Co. to John Chew, jr., of Fredksbg. $100.00. 33 a. in Spots. Co., being the sd. Waller and wife's share of the lands of Capt. Jno. Chew, decd., and known in a plot and division thereof as Lot. No. 5 (as by virtue of decree in Chancery in Spots. Co. Court, Augt. 9, 1798), etc., etc. No witnesses. Septr. 3, 1799.

May 25, 1799. Bathurst Jones of Hanover Co. to Wm. Grady of Orange Co. $2000.00. 450 a. in Spots. Co., etc., etc. Jno. Chew, jr.; Bowker Waller, John Blanton, Stewart Wallace. Septr. 3, 1799.

Augt. 29, 1799. Charles Thornton of Spots. Co. emancipates his slave Maria, etc., etc. Witnesses, Plummer Harris, Jas. McKenney. Septr. 3, 1799.

June 29, 1799. Robert Clough and Elizabeth, his wife, of Hanover Co. to Joseph Duerson of Spots. Co. £81 curr. 310 a. in Spots. Co., etc., etc. Jona. Clark, Lewis Holladay, Azariah King, E. Partlow, Robert Lewis, Thos. Hackney, Edmd. Clark. Septr. 3, 1799.

June 29, 1799. Robt. Clough and Elizabeth, his wife, of Hanover Co. to Azariah King of Spots. Co. £110 curr. 88 a. in Spots. Co., etc., etc. Jona. Clark, Lewis Holladay, Thomas Hackney, E. Partlow, Edm. Clark, Robt. Lewis, Jos. Duerson. Septr. 3, 1799.

April 2, 1799. Thomas Towles and Mary, his wife, of Spots. Co. to Wm. Durrett of Caroline Co. £120. 80 a. adj. land whereon sd. Durrett lives in both Spots. and Caroline Counties, etc., etc. Robert S. Coleman, Francis Coleman, Thos. R. Rootes. Septr. 3, 1799.

Augt. 1, 1799. Thomas Towles and Mary, his wife, of Spots. Co. to John Stevens Farish of same co. £1011 12s. curr. 515 a. in Spots. Co., etc., etc. O. Towles, Elizabeth Brock, Porteus Towles. Septr. 3, 1799.

July 27, 1799. Jeremiah Morton and Mildred Garnett, his wife, of Spots. Co. to Wm. Terrill, jr., of Orange Co. $1100.00. Lot in Fredksbg. known as the Brown Lot, leased by Wm. Jackson to James Brown, etc., etc. Witnesses, Edmond Leavill, John Minton, Wm. Crooks. Septr. 3, 1799.

July 10, 1799. John Mitchell and Susanna (his wife?) to Thomas Boxley. £462 13s. 956 a. purchased of Catherine Stubblefield and Henry Mitchell on Pamunkey River, in Spots. Co., etc., etc. Jos. Carter, Thomas Jones, Edwd. x Ballinger, John x Rains. Septr. 3, 1799.

"This is to certify that my desire is for my negro woman Betty to be free after living with Henry Newton, my niefue (nephew), as long as she shall think proper, and to serve no person only them she may chose (choose)." Signed, James Newton. Witness, Henry Newton. Recd. Septr. 3, 1799, at which time James Newton was dead.

April 5, 1785. Richard Coleman and Ann, his wife, of Spots. Co. to Spilsby Coleman of same co. £56 curr. 29 a. in Spots. Co., etc., etc. Benj. Tompkins, J. Chiles, Wm. Coleman, Thos. Coleman, Senr. Sept. 4, 1799.

July 3, 1799. Fontaine Maury of Fredksbg. to James Maury of Liverpoole, Eng. £2250 curr. 724½ a. purchased of Richd. S. Hackley in Spots. Co. and 303¾ a. purchased of Edwd. Vass in Spots. Co., etc., etc. Leon. H. Maury, Richd. Kenney, Thos. W. Maury. Decr. 3, 1799.

Decr. 3, 1799. Rice Vass and Peggy, his wife, of Spots. Co. to James King of same co. £6 curr. 4 a. in Spots. Co., etc., etc. Witness, Wm. Vass. Decr. 3, 1799.

Novr. 28, 1799. Benjamin Holladay of Spots. Co. to Lewis Holladay of same co. £160 curr. 80 a. in Spots. Co., etc., etc. Austin Sandidge, Benj. Rawlings, John Scott, Waller Holladay, Jno. Lipscomb, Wm. Holladay.

Novr. 28, 1799. Benj. Holladay of Spots. Co. to Jno. Lipscomb of same co. £136 10s. curr. 91 a. in Spots. Co., etc., etc. Austin Sandidge, Benj. Rawlings, John Scott, Waller Holladay, Lewis Holladay, Wm. Holladay. Decr. 3, 1799.

May 25, 1798. Joseph Nelson and Lucy, his wife, of Spots. Co. to Edwd. Massey of same co. $286.67. 86 a., part of tract sd. Nelson lives on in Spots. Co., etc., etc. Jos. Herndon, jr.; Geo. Bronaugh, Jno. D. Long, Francis Coleman, Wm. Winslow. Decr. 3, 1799.

Decr. 15, 1798. Thos. Minor and David Davenport, Executors of the late Wm. Davenport, decd., of Spots. Co. to Jonathan Clark of same co. £149 14s. 10d. 151 a. on East North East River, in Spots. Co., etc., etc. (the dower of Mary, widow of Wm. Davenport, decd., excepted). Witnesses, Edwd. G. Hill, Joseph Waller, James Crawford, Benj. Waller, Edward Clark. Decr. 3, 1799.

Novr. 28, 1799. Wm. McWilliams and Dorothea, his wife, of Spots. Co. to Thomas Colson of same co. £175 specie. 289 a. purchased of Ambrose and James Dudley in Spots. Co., etc., etc. Peter Dudley, Henry Goss, Alexander x McCloud. Decr. 3, 1799.

Decr. 3, 1799. Francis Coleman and Elizabeth, his wife, of Spots. Co. to John Penny of same co. $720.00. 360 a. in Spots. Co., etc., etc. Benj. Robinson, Thomas Winslow, Jos. Chew. Decr. 3, 1799.

Octr. 29, 1799. Richard Collins and Sarah, his wife, of Kentucky, by Henry Collins, their atto. in fact; Moses Quisenberry and Mary, his wife, of Orange Co., Va.; Wharton Schooler and Margaret, his wife, of Kentucky; John Edwards, by Wharton Schooler, his atto. in fact, and Henry Gatewood and Ann, his wife, of Spots. Co., Va. (heirs of Henry Gatewood, Senr., Decd.), to Martin Brent of Spots. Co., Va. £186 17s 6d. curr. 138 a. whereon sd. Henry Gatewood, Senr., decd., lately lived in Spots. Co., etc., etc. Henry Towles, Peter Hicks, John Pierce. Decr. 3, 1799.

June 13, 1799. Samuel Partlow of Spots. Co. to his daughter, Ann Partlow. Deed of Gift. Negro slave. Burgess x Sullivent, Luica x Sullivent, David Partlow. Decr. 3, 1799.

SHERIFFS OF SPOTSYLVANIA COUNTY

DEED BOOK A—1722–1729.

*Wm. Bledsoe, Gent. Com. dated July 9, 1722. Took the oath of office at the first court held for Spotsylvania County, August, 1722. (Page 16.)

WILL BOOK A—1722–1749.

Thomas Chew, Gent. Com. dated April 30, 1724. (Page 6.)
Thomas Chew, Gent. Com. dated April 5, 1725. (Page 31.)
Goodrich Lightfoot, Gent. Com. dated April 25, 1726. (Page 32.)
Goodrich Lightfoot, Gent. Com. dated April 1, 1727. (Page 48.)
Larkin Chew, Gent. Com. dated April 27, 1728. (Page 69.)
Edwin Hickman, Gent. Com. dated March 24, 1728–29. (Page 92.)
Edwin Hickman, Gent. Com. dated April 7, 1730. (Page 113.)
William Johnson, Gent. Com. dated May 5, 1731. (Page 134.)
Joseph Brock, Gent. Com. dated April 25, 1733. (Page 186.)
Joseph Thomas, Gent. Com. dated April 21, 1735. (Page 253.)
John Chew, Gent. Com. dated May 5, 1737. (Page 280.)
Larkin Chew, Gent. Com. dated June 13, 1739. (Page 303.)
John Taliaferro, Gent. Com. dated July 15, 1741. (Page 326.)
John Minor, Gent. Com. dated July 12, 1743. (Page 366.)
John Waller, Jr., Gent. Com. dated July 14, 1746. (Page 440.)
Richard Tutt, Gent. Com. dated August 31, 1748. (Page 474.)

WILL BOOK B—1749–1759.

John Thornton, Gent. Com. dated Sept. 1, 1750. (Page 52.)
John Thornton, Gent. Com. dated August 13, 1751. (Page 76.)
John Chew, Gent. Com. dated July 15, 1752. (Page 130.)
Larkin Chew, Gent. Com. dated July 17, 1754. (Page 214.)
Rice Curtis, Gent. Com. dated July 11, 1756. (Page 298.)
William Carr, Gent. Com. dated July 12, 1758. (Page 379.)
Robert Jackson, Gent. Com. dated August 25, 1760. (Page 489.)

WILL BOOK D—1761–1772.

Charles Dick, Gent. Com. dated August 10, 1762. (Page 32.)
Beverley Winslow, Gent. Com. dated October 15, 1764. (Page 158.)
Joseph Brock, Gent. Com. dated October 18, 1766. (Page 263.)
John Carter, Gent. Com. dated October 12, 1768. (Page 348.)
Robert Goodloe, Gent. Com. dated November 2, 1770. (Page 448.)

*First sheriff of the county.

WILL BOOK E—1772–1798.

John Crane, Gent. Com. dated October 26, 1772. (Page 25.)
William Smith, Gent. Com. dated October 25, 1774. (Page 83.)
Charles Yates, Gent. Com. dated November 6, 1776. (Page 164.)
Edward Herndon, Gent. Com. dated October 13, 1778. (Page 244.)
John Lewis, Gent. Com. dated November 8, 1780. (Page 370.)
George Stubblefield, Gent. Com. dated October 19, 1782. (Page 498.)

COLONIAL MILITIA

A list of the officers of the Colonial Militia of Spotsylvania County, who producing their commissions before the Court of His Majesty's Honourable Justices for the County aforesaid, took the oaths as directed by law.

ORDER BOOK—1724–1730.

Colonel John Robinson took the oath as Lieutenant of Spots. Co., August 5, 1729. (Page 331.)

Captain Thomas Chew and his officers, John Minor and Edward Franklyn; Captain William Johnson and his officers, Andrew Harrison and Thomas Warren, took ye oath August 5, 1729. (Page 332.)

Major Goodrich Lightfoot, Captain Robert Slaughter and his officers, Francis Kirkley and William Payton; Captain John Scott and his officers, Joseph Hawkins and John Lightfoot; Captain William Bledsoe and his officers, James Williams and George Home, took ye oath, September 2, 1729. (Page 342.)

Captain William Hansford and his officer, John Grayson, Jr., took ye oath, October 7, 1729. (Page 355.)

Henry Willis, Gent., before His Honor, William Gooch, Esq., Lt. Gov., etc. Commission to be Lieut.-Colonel of this county, took ye oath, August 4, 1730. (Page 405.)

ORDER BOOK—1730–1738.

Robert Green, Captain; Francis Slaughter, Lieut.; John Roberts, Ensign; Abraham Field, Captain; Henry Field, Lieut.; Francis Michall, Ensign of a company of foot, took the oath February 2, 1730–1. (Page 12.)

Benjamin Cave, Lieutenant to Captain John Scott, took the oath, February 2, 1730–1. (Page 13.)

John Taliaferro, Lieut.-Colonel; Francis Thornton, Jr., Major of the Horse; Francis Taliaferro, Captain of the Horse; Richard Tutt, his Lieutenant of Horse; Thomas Hill, Captain of a foot company, took ye oath, October 6, 1736. (Page 472.)

Richard Phillips, Gent., Lieutenant, and Edward Herndon, Jr., Gent., Cornet, produced their commissions and took the oath, etc., as officers to a troop of horse under Captain William Waller. November 1, 1737. (Page 523.)

ORDER BOOK—1738–1749.

Moseley Battaley, Gent., produced his commission to be Captain of a company of Foot in this county, and took the oath Apr., 1740. (Page 70.)

Thomas Duerson, Gent., commissioned to be Lieut. and George Green, Gent., commissioned to be Ensign of a company of Foot, under Capt. Battaley, and took the oath Apr. 1, 1740. (Page 70.)

Francis Thornton, Jr., Gent., commission as Lieut.-Colonel of this county; Francis Taliaferro, Gent., commissioned to be Major of the Horse; Richard ——, Gent., commissioned to be Captain of a company of Horse; Rice Curtis, Jr., Gent., commissioned to be Captain of a company of Horse; Joseph Hawkins, Gent., commissioned to be Captain of a company of Horse. The preceding took the oath Sept. 7, 1742. (Page 186.)

Edmund Waller commissioned to be Captain of a company of Foot; John Edwards, Gent., commissioned to be Captain of a company of Foot; Thomas Duerson, Gent., commissioned to be captain of a company of Foot. The preceding took the oath Dec. 8, 1742. (Page 192.)

William Robinson, Gent., commissioned to be Major of Militia in this county, took the oath Sept. 7, 1743. (Page 240.)

Joseph Collins, Gent., commissioned to be Lieutenant of a troop of Horse under Capt. Joseph Hawkins; George Carter, Gent., commissioned to be Cornet under the same. Henry Pendleton, Gent., commissioned to be Lieutenant of a company of Foot, under Capt. Edmund Waller; James Edwards, Gent., commissioned to be Ensign under the same. Dudley Gatewood, Gent., commissioned to be Ensign in a company of Foot, under Capt. Thomas Duerson. The preceding took the oath Dec. 6, 1743. (Page 246.)

Henry Brock, Gent., commissioned to be Lieutenant of a company of Foot, under Capt. Thomas Duerson, took the oath Feb. 7, 1743. (Page 251.)

John Taliaferro, Gent., commissioned to be Captain of a company of Foot; John Gordon, Gent., commissioned to be Lieutenant of a company of Foot, took the oath Dec. 4, 1744. (Page 289.)

Edward Herndon, Jr., Gent., commissioned to be Lieutenant of a troop of Horse, commanded by Capt. Richard Tutt, took the oath March 5, 1744. (Page 305.)

James Allan, commissioned to be Cornet of a troop of Horse, commanded by Capt. Richard Tutt, took the oath March 6, 1744. (Page 311.)

William Waller, Gent., commission to be Colonel of the Horse in this county, took the oath July 4, 1749. (Page 517.)

John Spotswood, Esq., commission to be Lieut.-Colonel of this county, took the oath Aug. 1, 1749. (Page 523.)

ORDER BOOK—1749-1755.

Rice Curtis, Jr., commission to be Major of the Horse; Richard Tutt, Gent., to be Major of the Foot, took the oath Apr. 3, 1750. (Page 55.)

Moseley Battaley, Gent., commission to be Captain of a troop of Horse, took the oath Sept. 4, 1750. (Page 88.)

Joseph Collins, Gent., commission to be Captain of a company of Foot, took the oath Nov. 6, 1750. (Page 100.)

Philemon Hawkins, Gent., commission to be Captain of a company of Foot, took the oath Feb. 5, 1750. (Page 109.)

John Spotswood, Esq., commission dated Nov. 18, last, as Lieut. and Chief Commanding Officer of the Militia in this county, took the oath Jan. 3, 1753. (Page 237.)

Francis Taliaferro as Colonel in this county; John Thornton as Colonel in this county; Richard Tutt as Major of Militia in this county, produced their commissions, all dated Nov. 18, 1752, and took the oath Feb. 6, 1753. (Page 240.)

Wm. Lynn, commission dated Jan. 26, 1753, as Captain of the Independent Company of Foot, composed of the Gentlemen Inhabitants of the Town of Fredericksburg, took the oath Feb. 7, 1753. (Page 246.)

John Dent, as Lieutenant and Humphrey Wallace as Ensign to Capt. William Lynn, Gent., Captain of the Independent Company of Foot, dated this day and took ye oath Feb. 7, 1753. (Page 247.)

George Washington, Esq., commission dated Dec. 13, 1752, to be Major and Adjutant of the Militia, Horse and Foot, in the counties of Princess Anne, Norfolk, Nansemond, Isle of Wight, Southampton, Surrey, Brunswick, Prince George, Dinwiddie, Chesterfield, Amelia, and Cumberland, and took the oath Feb. 10, 1753. (Page 284.)

Charles Lewis, William Miller, and Benjamin Pendleton, Gentlm., commissioned to be Captains of Foot, and Ambrose Bullard to be Lieutenant of Foot, took the oath Sept. 4, 1753. (Page 330.)

John Crane, Gent., commission dated Feb. the 11th, last, to be Captain of a troop of Horse, took the oath Nov. 6, 1754. (Page 504.)

Abraham Crittenden, William Jesse, Benjamin Whaley, Richard Harkless, James Low, Hugh Carpenter, and John Waller, came into Court and took the oath to the Government, and signed the test, etc., "soldiers," Dec. 3, 1754. (Page 509.)

* ORDER BOOK—1755–1765.

William Lynn, Gent., Major, commission dated July 29, 1755.

John Dent, Gent., Captain of Fredericksburg Company, commission dated July 22, 1755.

Philemon Hawkins, Gent., Captain of company of Foot, commission dated July 21, 1755.

Bushrod Fauntleroy, Gent., Captain of Company of Foot, commission dated July 21, 1755.

Lawrence Taliaferro, Gent., Lieut. of Company under Capt. Charles Lewis, commission dated July 21, 1755.

Moses Bledsoe, Lieutenant of company under Capt. William Miller, commission dated July 27, 1755.

Erasmus Withers Allen, Lieutenant of company under Capt. Philemon Hawkins, commission dated July 21, 1755.

Aaron Bledsoe, Lieutenant of company under Capt. Benjamin Pendleton, commission dated July 21, 1755.

John Herndon, Ensign of company under Capt. Miller, commission dated August 2, 1755.

The preceding took the oath August 5, 1755.

* The pages of subsequent Order Books are not numbered.

The following officers produced their commissions and took the oath and subscribed the test, as by law directed, at a Court held for Spotsylvania County, May 4, 1756:

Thomas Slaughter, Esq., commission dated Apr. 26, 1756, Lieut.-Colonel and Commander of the Forces from Culpeper against ye Indians above Winchester, on this expedition.

William Green, Gent., as Major under the said Slaughter, commission dated Apr. 29, 1756.

Francis Kirtley, Gent., Captain of a company of Foot, in the said forces, commission dated Apr. 29, 1756.

John Field, Gent., Captain of a company of Foot, in the said forces, commission dated Apr. 29, 1756.

William Stanton, Gent., as 1st Lieutenant in said expedition, commission dated May 4, 1756.

Lewis Willis, Gent., as Captain of Foot in Spots. County, under John Spotswood, Esq., commission dated Apr. 29, 1756.

Lawrence Taliaferro, Captain of Foot in Spots. County, commission dated March 4, 1756.

Aaron Bledsoe, Gent., Captain of Foot in Spots. County, commission dated Apr. 29, 1756.

James Cunningham, Gent., as 1st Lieutenant of company of Foot in Spots. County, commission dated May 4, 1756.

William Bell, Gent., 2nd Lieutenant of Foot in Spots. Co., commission dated May 4, 1756.

Beverley Winslow, Gent., as 1st Lieutenant of Foot in Spots. Co., commission dated May 4, 1756.

Robert Chew, Gent., 1st Lieutenant of Foot in Spots. Co., commission dated May 4, 1756.

James Tutt, Gent., as 1st Lieutenant of Foot in Spots. Co., commission dated May 4, 1756.

Zachary Lewis, Jr., Gent., 1st Lieutenant of Foot in Spots. Co., commission dated May 4, 1756.

Edward Herndon, Jr., 2nd Lieutenant of Foot in Spots. Co., commission dated May 4, 1756.

Humphrey Brooke, 2nd Lieutenant of Foot in Spots. Co., commission dated May 4, 1756.

John Robinson, 2nd Lieutenant of Foot in Spots. Co., commission dated May 4, 1756.

Spilsbe Coleman, 2nd Lieutenant of Foot in Spots. Co., commission dated May 4, 1756.

The following took the oath at a Court held May 5, 1756:

Benjamin Pendleton, Esq., Major of the Militia in Spots. Co., commission dated Apr. 29, 1756.

William Taliaferro, Esq., Lieut.-Colonel of Orange County, commission dated May 4, 1756.

Thomas Estes, as Ensign to Capt. Fauntleroy, commission dated July 21, 1755.

John Waller, the Younger, Gent., commission to be Lieutenant of a troop of Horse in Spots. Co., dated July 21, 1755, took the oath July 6, 1756.

Rice Curtis, Gent., commission as Colonel of Militia of Spots. Co., dated Apr. 26, 1756, took the oath July 7, 1756.

Thomas Estes, Gent., commission to be Captain of a company of Foot in this county, dated March 11, 1757, and John Herndon commission to be Ensign of a company of Foot, took the oath Apr. 5, 1757.

Charles Lewis, Gent., Major of the County of Spots., commission dated Oct. 4, 1757, took the oath Oct. 4, 1757.

Richard Tutt, Colonel in the Militia of Spots. Co., commission dated Aug. 27, 1756, took the oath Oct. 4, 1757.

Fielding Lewis, Esq., County Lieutenant of Spots. County, commission dated Oct. 15, took the oath Feb. 7, 1758.

Zachary Lewis, Jr., Gent., Captain of company of Foot in Spots. County, commission dated Feb. 17, 1758.

George Frazer, Gent., Captain of company of Foot, commission dated March 8, 1758.

Robert Duncanson, Gent., to be Lieutenant.

Hugh Lenox, Gent., to be Ensign.

The above took the oaths March 8, 1758.

Joseph Brock, Gent., commission dated Oct. 25, 1758, to be Captain of a company in this County.

Zachary Lewis, Gent., commission dated Oct. 25, 1758, to be Captain of a company in this County.

John Crane, Gent., commission dated Oct. 25, 1758, to be Major in this County.

John Carter, Gent., commission dated Oct. 25, 1758, to be Captain of a company in this county.

The preceding took the oaths Apr. 3, 1759.

Joseph Bledsoe, Gent., commission dated Apr. 8, 1759, to be Ensign of a company in the 14th Battalion, took the oath May 1, 1759.

Fielding Lewis, Esq., commission dated Oct. 25, 1758, to be County Lieutenant.

Beverley Winslow, Gent., commission dated Oct. 25, 1758, to be Captain of a company of Militia in this County.

The above took the oaths June 4, 1759.

Fielding Lewis, Esq., commission dated Nov. 12, 1761, as Commander in Chief of the Militia of this County.

John Crane, Gent., commission dated Nov. 12, 1761, to be Major of the Militia in this County.

Joseph Brock, commission dated Nov. 12, 1761, to be Captain of a company in this County.

The above took the oaths March 1, 1762.

Zachary Lewis, Gent., commission dated Nov. 12, 1761, to be Captain of a company in this County, took the oath Apr. 5, 1762.

John Waller, Esq., commission dated Apr. 4, 1764, to be Captain of a company of Foot.

John Beverley Roy, Gent., commission dated May 7, 1764, as a Lieutenant of a company of Foot.

The above took the oaths May 7, 1764.

John Lewis, Esq., commission to be Quarter Master of the Militia in this County, took the oath Aug. 1, 1763.

John Waller, Gent., commission dated July 11, 1763, to be Lieutenant of a company of Militia.

James Cunningham, commission dated July 27, 1763, to be Lieutenant of a company of Militia.

The above took the oaths Aug. 1, 1763.

George Weedon, Esq., commission dated March 1, 1764, to be Captain of a company of Militia, took the oath March 5, 1764.

Zachary Lewis, Jr., Esq., commission dated Apr. 30, 1764, to be Major in the Militia, took the oath Aug. 7, 1764.

Robert Chew, Esq., commission dated Sept. 3, 1764, to be Captain of a company of Militia, took the oath Sept. 4, 1764.

John Crane, Esq., commission dated Apr. 3, 1764, to be Colonel in the Militia in this County.

John Roan, commission dated March 5, 1765, to be Captain of a company of Militia.

The above took the oaths Apr. 2, 1765.

James Cunningham, commission dated Sept. 2, 1755, Ensign to Capt. Benjamin Pendleton, took the oath Sept. 3, 1755.

George Frazer, Gent., commission dated Aug. 23, 1755, as Lieutenant of a company in the Virginia Regiment, took the oath Dec. 4, 1755.

ORDER BOOK—1768–1774.

George Stubblefield, Gent., commission dated May 9, 1769, Capt. of a company of Militia, took the oath Nov. 6, 1769.

Henry Johnson, Gent., commission dated May 9, 1769, Lieutenant in the Militia of Spots. Co., took the oath Nov. 6, 1769.

ORDER BOOK—1774–1782.

The following proved their right to bounty lands granted by His Majesty the King to soldiers serving in defence of the Colony 1755 to 1760, etc.:

Thomas Collins, Decd., Sergt. and Capt. in Capt. Charles Lewis' company of a Virginia Regiment on the Frontier 1755.

Proved at a Court held for Spots. Co., Sept. 16, 1779.

Richard Johnston, Lieutenant in Col. William Byrd's Regiment in Cherokee Expedition in 1760.

Edward Ludwick (Ludwig or Ledwedge) served as a soldier in 1st Virginia Regiment, raised for the immediate defence of the Colony in 1756.

James Richards, served as a soldier in 1st Virginia Regiment, raised for immediate defence of the Colony in 1760.

Ezekiel Richardson served as Drum Major 1st Virginia Regiment, raised for immediate defence of the Colony, in 1758, also served as Drum Major in Regiment under command of Col. Adam Stephen in the year 1760.

Stephen Spicer, served as a soldier in the year 1758.

The above proved their services at a Court held for Spots. Co., Apr. 21, 1780.

George Stubblefield, Gent., served as a Cadet in the year 1762, in Regiment under the command of Adam Stephen.

Proved at a Court held for Spots. Co., June 15, 1780.

At a Court held for Spots. County, February 1780, the following proved their services in the Militia of the Colony 1755 to 1760, raised for the immediate defence thereof:

Edward Foley served as a soldier in 1st Va. Regiment.

Edward Sutton, soldier.

William Ross, soldier.

Charles —— as Sergt.

William Tins—— as soldier.

William Lampton as soldier.

Daniel Simpson as corp.

Edward Gold—— as Ensign in Col. Byrd's Regiment.

Nathaniel Gest (or Gist) deposeth and saith that he served in the office of Lieut. in Capt. Christopher Gest's company, raised in 1756, and served until the company was —— and also as a Captain in Col. George Washington's 1st Va. Regiment, raised in 1756, ———— continued as Captain until it was disbanded.

Nathaniel Gest, son and heir of Christopher Gest, Decd., deposeth and saith that the said Christopher Gest was Captain of a Company of Rangers, raised in 1756, for defence of the Frontier, and served until the said company was discharged in 1756.

Genl. George Weedon served as a Capt.-Lieut. in 1st Va. Regiment; also served as Captain in Col. Adam Stephen's Regiment.

Larkin Chew served as Ensign in Col. William Byrd's 2nd Va. Regiment, raised in 1758; served until disbanded, and also served in 1st Va. Regiment as a Lieut., at that time under command of Col. Byrd, served therein until it was disbanded, afterwards entered Regiment commanded by Col. Adam Stephen, and served as Lieut. until it was disbanded.

William Dangerfield served as Captain in 1st Va. Regiment till disbanded, afterwards in Regiment commanded by Col. Adam Stephen.

Richard Halbe——, soldier in Col. Byrd's and Col. Stephen's regiments.

Robert Saunders, Corp. in Frontier Battalion.

James Gimb—— as soldier in Col. Byrd's regiment.

John Conner as soldier in Col. Stephen's regiment.

Richard Br——, Serg. in Col. Byrd's Regiment, 1758.

Ludowick Oneal as soldier in Col. Byrd's regiment, 1758.

Joseph ——, Serg. 2nd Va. Regiment in 1758.

Richard F. A—— as soldier.

Francis —— as soldier.

William Tur—— as soldier in Byrd's regiment.

Richard Reynolds, soldier in Byrd's Regiment.

Benjamin Turner, Decd., soldier in Byrd's Regiment.

Joseph Bledsoe, Serg. in —— Va. Regiment, also served as Ensign in the ——er Battalion.

REVOLUTIONARY RECORDS

FROM ORDER BOOK, 1774–1782

Took oaths at Court, held for Spts. Co., Sept. 18, 1777.

James Tutt, Gent., Com. dat., Apr. 2, 1776, Captain of Co. Spts. Militia.
Wm. Mills,   "   "   "   Sept. 17, 1777, "   "   "   "   "
Jno. Carter,   "   "   "   "   18,   "   "   " " "   "
Jno. Meals,   "   —— ——, 1st Lieut. under Capt. Geo. Thornton.
Robt. Smith,   "   —— ——,   "   "   "   " Jno. Carter.
Thos. Miller,   "   —— ——,   "   "   of Co. Spts. Militia.
Robt. Yates,   "   —— ——, Com. 2nd Lt. in Spts. Militia.
Jas. Taylor,   "   —— ——,   "   "   "   "   "   "
Jno. Chew, jr,. "   —— ——,   "   "   "   "   "   "
Thos. Towles,   "   —— ——,   "   "   "   "   "   "
Jno. Chew,   "   —— ——,   "   "   "   "   "   "
Harry Bartlett, "   —— ——,   "   "   "   "   "   "
Jno. Legg,   "   —— ——,   " Ensign "   "   "
Thos. Clayton, "   —— ——,   "   "   "   "   "

At Court held Feby. 18, 1779.

Jas. Wiglesworth, Ensign in Compy. Militia, Spts. County.

At Court held Feby. 19, 1779.

Jno. Meals, Gent., Capt. in Spts. Militia in room of George Thornton, Gent.
Jas. Taylor,   Gent., 1st Lieut. Spts. Militia in same compy.
Benj. Johnston,   "   2nd   "   "   "   " • "   "
Jno. Hardia,   Ensign   "   "   "   "   "

At Court held June 15, 1780.

Jos. Brock, the younger, Ensign in Compy. Spts. Co. Militia.

At Court held Sept. 21, 1780.

Robt. Durrett, 2nd Lt. in Capt. Thos. Minor's Compy. in Spts. Militia.
J. Z. Lewis,   Ensign "   "   "   "   "   "   "   "
Jas. Taylor, Capt. Militia Compy. in Fredksbg.
Thos. Sharpe, 1st Lieut. in Capt. White's Militia Compy. in Spts. Militia.
J. Wright, 2nd Lieut. in Capt. White's Militia Compy. in Spts. Militia.
Wm. Wright, Ensign "   "   "   "   "   "   "   "

At Court held Oct. 19, 1780.

Wm. McWilliams, Capt. in Room of Chas. Washington, Gent., Spts. Militia.
Chas. Washington, Lt. Col. of Militia of this County.
Jno. Mason, Lieut. to Capt. Towles' Compy., Spts. Militia.
Thos. Sharpe, " " " White's " " "
Thos. Towles, Capt. of Compy., Spts. Co. Militia.
Beverley Winslow, Col. for Militia, this county.

At Court held Nov. 16, 1780.

Jno. Z. Lewis, Ensign, in Compy., Spts. Militia.
George Thornton, Major, in Spts. Militia.

At Court held Nov. 17, 1780.

Jno. McCalley, Capt. of Compy., Spts. Militia, formerly commanded by Jno. Tutt.
Bartlett Collins, 1st Lieut., Spts. Militia.
James Owens, 2d " " "
Peter Dudley, Ensign " "

At Court held Dec. 21, 1780.

Jas. Wiglesworth, 2nd Lt. in Capt. Stubblefield's Compy., Spts. Militia.
Jas. Holloday, Ensign, " " " " " "

At Court held May 17, 1781.

Jno. Legg, Capt. in room of Wm. McWilliams, Spts. Militia.

At Court held July 19, 1781.

Beverley Winslow, County Lieut., Qualified in Spts. Militia.
Mann Page, Esqr., Lieut. Col., " " " "
Wm. McWilliams, Major, " " " "
Francis Coleman, Capt. in room of Wm. Mills, resigned, Spts. Militia.
Jno. Tankersley, Capt. " " " Thos. Bartlett, " " "

At Court held Augt. 16, 1781.

Wm. McWilliams, Lt. Col. Militia in Spts. Co.
Thomas Towles, Major, " " " "

At Court held Feb. 20, 1783.

Thos. Minor, Capt. of Compy. Militia, Spts. Co., in room of Jno. McCalley, Decd.

At Court held April 17, 1783.

Agreeable to Act of Assembly concerning pensioners, the Court enquired into condition and state of bodily ability of following Pensioners and persons receiving annual allowance from the commonwealth, vizt., Lieut. Larkin Chew, disability by bad wound in his arm; Lieut. Jno. Chew, jr., same, by loss of left arm; Elijah Estes, by wound in left shoulder, causing his left arm to wither, etc.

From Order Book 1782–1786.

The following served as soldiers in the Continental Army and died in the service of the States:

Edmund Keeton and Wm. Keeton, sons of Jno. Keeton; John Keeton, jr., their heir.

Wm. Hensley, to whom Richardson Hensley, is heir.

Nathaniel and Wm. Dickenson were Sargeants, to whom Richd. Dickenson is heir.

Chas. Tutt, 1st Lieut., to whom Jas. Tutt is heir.

Wm. Knight, to whom Jno. Knight is heir.

Wm. Crutchfield, Sergt. 3 Regt. L. D. to whom Philadelphia Crutchfield is only daughter and heir.

James Bryant, to whom Jno. Bryant is heir.

The preceding proved at Courts held Feby. 19, Nov. 2, 1784.

At Courts held March 1, Nov. 1, 1785.

James Smith, to whom Jno. Smith, is heir.

Chas. Ficklin, to whom Thomas Ficklin is heir.

Francis Atherton, to whom Wm. Atherton, jr., is heir.

REVOLUTIONARY PENSIONERS

FROM ORDER BOOK 1829-1832, SPTS. CO., VA., COURT.

Declarations filed by residents of Spts. Co., who having rendered service in the Continental Army during the American Revolution, 1776–1783, were entitled to provision of an Act of Congress, passed June 7, 1838.

Augt. 7, 1832. John Pettis of Spts. Co., aged 78 years, entered service of U. S. 1779 or thereabouts, served under Philip Johnson, a captain; was drafted in Va. Militia in Caroline Co., marched thence to Williamsburg, where he remained 3 mos., and then marched home. Was again drafted in Caroline Co., and again marched to Williamsburg, under the same captain, and remained 40 days. Born Spts. Co., Va., abt. 1751. Was living in Caroline Co. when called into service and has since resided in Counties of Caroline, Orange, and Spotsylvania. Capt. James Nelson, Richard Richards, and Hezekiah Richards, my nearest neighbors. Died July 1, 1833. (Order Book, 1832–1838.)

Amendment to Declaration of John Pettis. John Pettis of Spts. Co., aged 78. Enlisted in Army of U. S. in 1780 with Saml. Coleman, and served in 1st Regt. Va. Line under Col. Samuel Hawes, Capt. Francis Cowherd, and General Green; lived in Co. of Caroline, when he entered the service; marched through States of North and South Carolina, was at Battle of Guilford C. H. and Eutaw Springs, and finally marched to Salisbury, and there discharged about Jany. ——, 1782, making tour of service 1 year, 6 months, etc.

Augt. 7, 1832. Harry Chew of Spts. Co. Born Septr. 23, 1758. Entered service of U. S. under the following officers and always as a volunteer: First entered service under Capt. Brock, at beginning of war, (John Pierce was with him), then a resident of Spts. Co., marched to Williamsburg. Secondly, under command of Capt. Beverley Winslow. Another company marched with them, believed to be Capt. John Craig, commanding, both companies under command of Major George Thornton, to Williamsburg, where our company was attached to Col. Thos. Matthews' Regiment (afterwards General Matthews). General Scott was at Williamsburg, left the station soon afterwards when the traitor Arnold aproached Wms'burg, and Col. Matthews retreated to Richmond, where Col. Samuel Temple of Caroline joined us. After Arnolds' retreat our Regt. ordered back to Wms'burg, did not reach there, got to Dimcastles, a tavern abt. 12 or 15 miles from Wms'burg, where Regt. was dismissed by Col Innes, who succeeded Col. Matthews. Said Chew volunteered as soldier in ranks, but during tour under Winslow was appt. quartermaster of Regt. under Col. Matthews and served as such until Regt. discharged. The next tour sd. applicant served under Capt. Wm. Mills;

marched to Wms'burg, were united to Col. Matthews Regt. The next
tour was a minute man under Capt. Francis Taliaferro; Henry Bartlett
was first Lieutenant, John Wiglesworth, 2d Lieut., and I, sd. Harry
Chew, ensign, and Thomas Towles, quarter-master. Rendevouzed at
Fredksbg., marched thence to Wms'burg., thence to Hampton; Maj.
Andrew Buchannan marching with us to Hampton. This tour lasted 3
mos.; we were regularly discharged by a relief commanded by Capt.
John Taliaferro of King George or Stafford.

Augt. 7, 1832. Henry Willoughby of Spots. Co., aged 73 years, enlisted
or joined the Army of the U. S. in 1779 with Capt. Tapley White, served
in 2d. Va. Regt. under Col. Saml. Hawes, Colo. Campbell, Colo. Williams,
and General Green; he lived in Spts.; marched through North and South
Carolina and parts of Ga. Was at Battles of Guilford C. H.; Cowpens and
Eutaw Springs and finally marched to Salisbury, and there discharged
about Jany. ——, 1784, by General Green, making his time of service
five years and six months.

Augt. 7, 1832. Francis Turnley of Spts. Co., aged 70 years, entered
Army of U. S. —— ——, 17——. Was drafted in Va. Militia in Spts. Co.
under Capt. Croucher in Octr., 1780. Marched from this Co. thro' Hanover, New Kent and James City and thence to Petersburg where he was
discharged, having served 3 mos. Returned home, was drafted under
Capt. Frank Coleman and marched to Culpeper and Fredksbg., remained
3 mos., again returned home and was drafted under Capt. Tankersley
and marched to the Seaboard thro' Hanover, James City and James River
country. Fought at Osborne's and was at Surrender at Yorktown. Discharged by original certificate of Major Wood Jones, Oct. 2, 1781; was
with Capt. Tankersley 4 months, making in all ten months. Was born
in 1762. Always lived in Spts. Co. Remembers Col. Hatch Richardson,
Col. Thos. Meriwether, Major Wood Jones and Captains Taylor and Carter. Died Decr. 18, 1836. (Order Book 1833–1838.)

Augt. 7, 1832. Richard Steers (or Stears) of Spts. Co., aged 70 years.
Drafted in Va. Militia June, 1779, under Capt. John White in Spts. Co.
Marched to Wms'burg. and the Seaboard of Va. Then under command
of Capt. Tankersley and then under Capt. Holloday. Cont'd. in service
until Octr. 1781, after battle of Yorktown. Philip Vass, now living, was
with him at Yorktown. He was born Septr., 1762. Always lived in Spts.
Co. Recollects Col. Meriwether, Major McWilliams, and Capt. Naylor.

Augt. 7, 1832. John Steers (or Stears) of Spts. Co., aged 75 years.
Enlisted in Army of U. S. in 1776 with Capt. Oliver Towles and served
in 7th Regt. Va. Line under Colo. Mordacai Buckner, Lt. Colo. Thomas
Aylett, Major James Hendricks, and Benjamin Alsop, Sergeant. Enlisted
in Spots. Co., marched to Fredksbg., from thence to Wms'burg., thence
to Hampton, returned to Wmsburg. and recd. orders to march to New
York. Taken sick and in consequence of ill health was discharged by
the surgeon. Enlisted Jany. 29, 1776, discharged Augt. 1776. Born 1755
or 1757. Benjamin Alsop, the sergeant, was with him and knows the
facts. Died Jany. 18, 1837. (Order Book, 1833–1838.)

Augt. 7, 1832. Abraham Wilson of Spts. Co., aged 72 years. Born in
Spts. Co., 1759. Lived at Culpeper when drafted and now lives in Spts.
Co. since the Revolution. Drafted in Culpeper Co., Feby., 1779. Officer,

Capt. Joseph Strother from Culpeper. Marched to Albemarle Barracks, continued 2 mos., was then marched to Fredksbg., and joined main army, continued down on Seaboard 2 mos. Returned home and in Oct., 1780, was drafted and marched under Capt. Frank Coleman thro' Hanover and James River country. Continued until after siege of Yorktown where he was present. Was in the service 18 mos.

Augt. 7, 1832. William Henderson of Spts. Co., aged 74 years. Enlisted in Army of U. S. in 1778 with Lieut. Samuel Potts; served under Colo. Frank Taylor of Orange and Major John Roberts of Culpeper. Was in Albemarle, Augusta and Frederick Counties with Burgoyne's prisoners, and also with them in Md. Discharged from service June, 1781. John Stewart of Spts. Co. served with him thro' the whole tour.

Augt. 7, 1832. John Stewart of Spts. Co., aged 71 years. Enlisted in Army of U. S. in 1778 with Capt. James Purvis. He then resided in Culpeper Co. Served under Colo. Frank Taylor of Orange, Major John Roberts of Culpeper and Capt. James Purvis. Left the service June, 1781. Stationed in Albemarle Co. with Burgoyne's prisoners, then marched with them to Augusta Co., was there abt. 3 weeks, then marched with them to Winchester; thence to Md., where was discharged June, 1781; then drafted in Va. Militia in Col. Meriwether's regiment and Capt. Nicholas Payne's Company, and marched thro' Hanover down the James River country to Yorktown where he was engaged in the siege until termination. Marched with Yorktown prisoners to Winchester and was discharged there abt. last of Novr., 1781. William Henderson of Spts. Co. with him during whole term.

Augt. 7, 1832. John Almond of Spts. Ct., aged 77 years. Enlisted under Capt. Gregory Smith in King and Queen Co. in 1775 as a soldier for 3 years. Marched under Capt. Smith to Wms'burg. and thence to Yorktown and Gloucester town and thence to Guin's Island agst. Lord Dunmore where he joined 7th Va. Regt., commanded by Colo. Daingerfield. Marched to the North and joined Gen. Washington's Army in 1776; in Battle at Brandywine, Sept. 11, 1776, and Germantown, Oct. 4; went into winter quarters at Valley Forge and discharged by orders of Genl. Washington. Refers to certificate of Wm. Campbell and Wm. Selden, R. L. Officers Va., accompanying this declaration.

Augt. 7, 1832. John Sorrell of Spts. Co., aged 72 years. Entered service of U. S. in 1775, served under Capt. Rob. Ware, Capt. Phillip Buckner, Capt. John Legg, and Capt. Coleman. Was a volunteer in Va. Militia, marched first under Capt. Philip Buckner from Caroline Co. to borders of the Potomac, afterwards returning to Caroline and discharged 1776. In April he again volunteered under Capt. Rob. Ware and marched from Caroline to Wms'burg. where he remained until last of Septr. On May 1, 1781, was drafted from Spts. Co., whither he had removed and marched as guard with eleven others under Sergt. Benj. Robinson to several prisoners taken somewhere at the South, some at Bottom's Bridge, and conveyed them to Winchester and Staunton, where they were confined in Jail. Retd. from Staunton to Fredksbg., and by Genl. Weedon's direction was employed in rolling tobacco that had been rolled to the River and concealed from the British, back to the Warehouses. In same year drafted in Spts. Co., and marched thence to Yorktown under Capt.

Coleman, where was taken ill and contd. so for some time. Says redoubts were stormed first on Sunday evening, and on following morning he asked permission of Dr. Tankard to allow himself fit for duty. The doctor having written on a paper "unfit for duty," he handed it to Col. Meriwether, who detailed him to carry it to his company officer. His Captain and others having returned home on acc. sickness, he handed the paper to Reuben Plunkett, his orderly sergeant. On next day Genl. Washington called for all able bodied men to be reported to him and he was reported at his instance as one by sd. Plunkett. Remained in works abt. 5 days and witnessed surrender of Lord Cornwallis. States the British at their surrender stacked their arms in front of American Army and marched into Yorktown to receive further orders. After the siege Col. Meriwether marched some of the prisoners towards Fredksbg. Was discharged by Colo. Meriwether at Yorktown. Born in Caroline Co. in or about 1760. Residing in Caroline Co. when first called into service, afterwards moved to Spts. where have resided ever since. First volunteered under Capts. Buckner and Ware, afterwards Drafted. Served under Genl. Mulenburg from Md., Marquis De Lafayette, and General Washington, and General Wayne. Was in General Stevens' Brigade. Now very infirm, confined to my house and lot for past eleven years. Can neither read or write. Refers to Major S. Chancellor, Mr. Geo. Chancellor, and Mr. Thomas Penn.

Septr. 3, 1832. Robert Layton of Spts. Co., aged 86 years. Enlisted in Army of U. S. 1776, about the fall of the year, with Turner Morehead and served in 3d Va. Regt. under the following officers: Capt. Turner Morehead, Major Chinn, Colo. Elias Edmunds, Genl. Charles Marshall, and Genl. Posey; at time of commencement of his service he held commission of a Lieut. Marched from Fauqueir Co., Va., in fall of 1776 under Capt. Morehead to Schuylkill, Penna., and there joined main army under Genl. Marshall; from Schuylkill marched to Germantown and was in engagement at that place, after this he was sent home to Fauqueir as recruiting officer; after about a month was ordered to Headquarters in neighborhood of Brandywine, and shortly after joining the army at Headquarters was promoted to Captain; the whole army under Genl. Marshall returned to the Schuylkill where they encamped several months, afterwards marched to near Philadelphia, where they were encamped several months; abt. this time Genl. Marshall went to Kentucky and Genl. Posey took the command. He then marched under Posey to Yorktown in Va., where he remained until after Cornwallis' surrender. Was ordered to Winchester with a guard over the prisoners where he remained until their exchange, then marching them to Md. line where they were received from him and he received his discharge about Jany., 1782. Mentions his ensign, John Morris, etc.

Sept. 3, 1832. James Ballard of Spts. Co., aged 69 years. Enlisted in Army of U. S. sometime in Novr., 1779, with Capt. Benjamin Robinson and served in regt. commanded by Col. Crocket under following named officers: Major George Slaughter, Capt. Mark Thomas, Lieutenant Thos. Slaughter, Lieut. Saunders, Ensigns Wm. Asher and Robt. Green, Genl. Geo. Rogers Clark, commanding. Left the service Decr., 1781, and entered it in Spts. Co., Va., where he then resided. Was in an engagement at Pecqua Town and was attacked by the Indians above Fort Jefferson. Passed thro' Va., part of Md., part of Penna., along the road called Braddocks, thence down the Monongalia River to Ft. Duquesne, from thence down the Ohio to Wheeling and from Wheeling to the falls of the Ohio which was the place of destination, from the falls to Ft. Jefferson below the mouth of the Ohio, thence up the Mississippi to Kuskuski and thence down the river tc Ft. Jefferson, thence up the Ohio to the falls.

Septr. 3, 1832. George Trible of Spts. Co., aged 76 years. Enlisted in Army of U. S. in 1776 with Capt. Vivion Minor of Caroline Co., Va., and served in Regt. of Va. line under the following officers: His enlistment was under sd. Minor in Col. Richard Johnston's Regt. as a minute man. Marched to Springfield below Wms'burg, where he joined battalion commanded by Maj. Andrew Buchannan, then marched to Hampton where he remained until discharged, etc.; served nine months, etc. Returned home and was shortly afterwards drafted in Va. Militia under Capt. Wm. Taliaferro and marched to Wms'burg and Jamestown. Served seven different tours at different times in Va. Militia, during which period was stationed at Port Royal, Va.; joined Lafayette in Culpeper Co., and thence marched to Charlottesville and Yorktown. At time of Cornwallis' surrender at Yorktown, was in a detachment reconoitering the adjacent Co. of Gloucester, etc.; was in but one engagement and that was in Gloucester, etc. Born in Caroline Co., 1757, whence he was called into service. Recollects officers as before stated and Col. Anthony Thornton and Col. Philip Johnson.

Septr. 3, 1832. Thomas Jones of Spts. Co., aged 75 years. Enlisted in the Army of the U. S. in 17— with Charles Bibbing and served under the following named officers: Capt. Charles Bibbing and Capt. Saml. Hawes. Enlisted for 12 mos. for purpose of performing any duty required of the company, and understood that the Co. to which he belonged was not to be attached to any regiment, but was to be kept in readiness to perform any service that might be required. Shortly after enlistment was marched to Bull Church in Caroline Co., where he then resided, under Capt. Bibbing, where he remained about 12 days, after which time the Company was discharged and he returned home. After a week or two he was again called into service by Capt. Hawes and served under him in Caroline Co., ten or eleven months, and was kept abt. Caroline C. H. and in that neighborhood waiting further orders. He was again discharged by Captn. Hawes to be called again when occasion should require. Shortly after his discharge he married and very soon thereafter was ordered into service again, when he hired George Hampton as his substitute, who performed the balance of his enlistment, etc.

Septr. 3, 1832. John Pierce of Spts. Co., aged 79 years. Volunteered in Spts. Co., where he was born and has always lived. In Augt., 1775, was in Colo. Joseph Brock's company who volunteered then as a Captain; marched through Caroline and Hanover Counties and James River Country to Wms'burg where he was put under command of Genl. Charles Scott and guarded the Capital and College landings, remained there abt. 50 days; returned home in Augt., 1777. Volunteered in Spts. Co. under command of Capt. Thomas Bartlett, marched to Wms'burg. and was placed under command of Colo. Thomas Nelson, etc.; remained in service at Wms'burg abt. 2 mos. and returned home. On Jany. 10, 1781, he was called out as militia man under Capt. Jno. Carter, marched as his orderly sergeant to Hanover C. H., where Gen. Geo. Weedon ordered the company to Fredksbg., he remained there more than 2 mos. and was then discharged, he returned home again and was called out in Sept., 1781, by Capt. Nicholas Payne, collected beeves all over the country and drove them with the company to Wms'burg. where they were delivered to Commissary Pierce; in this service he was engaged abt. 50 days. He was discharged 2 days before the surrender of Yorktown. He was born Decr. 20, 1752. Well recollects Colo. Towles, Colo. McWilliams, Colo. Mercer, Colo. Stubblefield, and Capt. Jno. Tankersley.

Octr. 1, 1832. Philip Pendleton of Spts. Co., aged 74 years. Enlisted in Continental Army, 1775, with Capt. George Stubblefield as a minute man for 12 mos.; the sd. Stubblefield enlisting in the regular army, he was then under Capt. Francis Taliaferro, under whom he marched to Hampton. The commanding officer was Maj. Buchannan. Having served in that tour he went as volunteer under Capt. J. Craig to Wms'burg and was out about 50 days. In next tour went as militia man under Capt. Harry Stubblefield, after which he served under Capt. Francis Coleman, and they were under Maj. McWilliams and Hardyman, a little before the close of the war, after which he went with a band of prisoners under Capt. Thomas Croutcher to Nolings Ferry. Was born April 6, 1758, in Spts. Co., where he has always lived.

Octr. 1, 1832. Enoch Breeden of Spts. Co., aged 73 years 8 mos. Was born in Maryland, Jany. ——, 1759. His father removed himself and his family to Va. when he was about 7 years old. Resided in Charles City Co. when the war commenced. His father having entered the Revolutionary War, from which he never returned, he and his mother removed to King Wm. Co., where two of his brothers resided. He entered the Va. militia in King Wm. Co. in summer of 1776, having been drafted and served a three months tour of duty. In this tour he served in Capt. Mordacai Abrahams company. Marched to Hampton where company remained until end of tour. Served several other short terms as volunteer and as substitute of his brothers, Moody and Caleb Breeden, who had families and had to take care of affiant's mother. Served on several missions in King Wm. Co., which was liable to the depredations of the enemy while their ships were in York River. While on these tours served under command of Colo. Hickman and Captains Mordacai Abraham, Christopher Tompkins, Mordacai Booth, and Harry Quarles. Militia service was performed by him at intervals as required until Jany., 1781. In that month was drafted and remained in the service performing his own tour and as substitute of his two brothers until the end of October in that year. In this service Capt. Drury was his first Captain; Capt. Booth commanded line part of time and Capt. Abraham the latter part of time. Company was in first Regiment commanded by Coll. Charles Dabney, and they joined Genl. Stevens at Four Mile Creek in Henrico Co., and from thence the troops retreated through Hanover and Spts. Counties into Culpeper, crossing the Rappk. River at Elleys Ford; the whole command under Genl. Lafayette. Shortly they recrossed the River at Raccoon Ford into Orange Co. and marched to Pogues Mills, thence to the Marquess New Road, and to Machunk Creek in lower end of Albemarle, thence marched towards Richmond and while on road were joined by Baron Steuben, and they marched into lower end of Hanover and were encamped for some time at Simms Neck on Pamunkey River, thence marched down country through New Kent to near Jamestown, where the affiant was detached to carry a parcel of broken down horses to King Wm. Co.; upon return was in Major Campbell's battalion. They crossed York River at White House Ferry in August, where they joined General Weedon's Army, marched thence to Ware Church in Gloucester Co. where they were joined by the "French horse" under Lauzan. They stood before the British in Gloucester Co. until the surrender. A few days before that event the three King Wm. Militia Companies to one of which affiant belonged, were sent up to their own County where they remained until their discharge. Shortly after the surrender the affiant removed to Spotsylvania Co. where he has since resided.

Ptolmey Powell of Spts. Co. The sd. Powell just before the surrender of Cornwallis at Yorktown, in 1781, being then about 14 years of age and a resident of King Wm. Co., having a brother in the militia of that County, then in service on Gloucester side of York River, went down to see his brother, and his brother wishing to see his family, the Capt., whose name was Abraham, agreed to receive the deponent as a substitute for his brother until his return. Deponent remained a fortnight and was in same command with Enoch Breeden. Maj. Campbell commanded Battalion.

Octr. 1, 1832. Edward Cason of Spts. Co., aged 80 years. Born in Spts. Co. in 1752, was living in Hanover Co. when called into the Continental Service; was drafted in 7th Division and marched under Capt. Price, his Colonel being Holt Richardson, to the South to oppose Cornwallis; was at Genl. Gates defeat and after having served 6 mos. was discharged; then removed to Spts. Co. where he was again drafted in same division, the next year after Gates defeat, under Capt. Legg and Colo. Tho. Meriwether and marched to the lower part of the State. Was again drafted to guard prisoners taken at Yorktown, under Capt. Croucher and Lieut. Branham and marched up to Nolins Ferry where he was discharged.

Died March 13, 1834. (Order Book, 1832–1838, p. 284.)

Octr. 1, 1832. Philip Smith of Spts. Co., aged 76 years. Drafted from Co. of King and Queen in 1776 in 7th Division of Militia under Capt. Tunstall Banks and marched to Gloucester-town and was discharged. Drafted in same Co. and same division in Jany. or Feby., 1777, and marched to Yorktown under Capt. Thomas Row and was discharged after having served 2 mos. Again drafted in like manner in Augt., 1777, and marched under Capt. Christopher Howard to Wms'burg where he was discharged after serving 2 mos. Again drafted in like manner in 1778, marched under Capt. Wm. Courtney to the Halfway House, between York and Hampton, thence to Newport News, where he was discharged after a service of 2 mos. Again drafted, in like manner, at close of same year or beginning of the next and marched under Capt. John Lines to Wms'burg, where he was discharged after service of 2 mos. Again drafted in fall of 1779 under Capt. Courtney and marched to Wms'burg, where he was again discharged after 2 mos. service, and in 1781 he was again drafted and marched about the country in various directions under

Capt. John Haskins, Colo. James Innes and Genl. Morgan; was finally discharged at Wms'burg. He was born in King and Queen Co. in 1757, where he was called into service; continued to live there until 1799 when he removed to Spts. Co.

Oct. 1, 1832. William Cason of Spts. Co., aged 72 years. Enlisted in Army of U. S. in 1776 in 2d Va. State Regt. under Colo. Thomas Minor, Capt. Quarles, Lieut. Benj. Edmondson. Served first under Genl. Putnam, afterwards under Muhlenburg; fought in Battle of Monmouth under Lafayette, and under Genl. Wayne at Storming of Stony Point. Lived in Spts. Co. where he entered the service in the year 1776 and enlisted for three years. In course of his service he marched through the States of Maryland, Penna., New Jersey, New York, and Virginia.

Harry Chew certifies as to Revolutionary Services of John Collins.

Nov. 6, 1832. Benjamin Alsop of Spts. Co., aged 74 years. About June 1, 1780, was ordered into service and was attached to company of militia under command of Capt. Thomas Minor, Lt. John Holloday, 2nd Lt. Lewis Holloday and Ensign Rob. Durrett, the Regiment under command of Col. Geo. Stubblefield, Lt. Col. Joseph Spencer, Maj. Wm. Moseley; marched from Spts. Co., where he resided, to Hillsborough, N. C., by way of Richmond and Petersburg. At Hillsborough he was appt. Quarter Master by Col. Stubblefield and continued to act in that capacity during that campaign; here they were organized with other regiments into a brigade under Genl. Edward Stevens of Culpeper, and from thence marched to Roughty Mills, S. C., where joined the main or Southern Army under General Gates, marched thence towards Camden and engaged British under Lord Cornwallis when Genl. Gates was defeated, Aug. 16, 1780. The Army partly united at Hillsborough and marched thence to New Garden, S. C., where affiant was discharged, his term of service not having quite expired as he was ordered in for 6 mos. Returned to Spts. Co., Va., and in May, 1781, was nominated by County Court of Spts. to the Governor of Va. for Lieut. in company of Militia then commanded by Capt. Thos. Bartlett; shortly after being commissioned as Lieut. was ordered into service and transferred from Capt. Bartlett's Co. to Capt. James Taylor's Company and joined Gen. Lafayette's Army as it passed through Spts. Co. to Raccoon Ford in Orange Co., regiment to which his command was attached was commanded by Col. James Meriwether, Majors Hardyman and McWilliams; he continued with this Army until abt. last of Sept., 1781, at which time he was discharged, then in the neighborhood of Wms'burg, having served in all rather more than 9 mos. Was. born in Spts. Co., March 17, 1758.

Feby. 4, 1833. Samuel Faulconer of Spts. Co., aged 76 years. Entered Army of U. S. under Capt. McWilliams, was drafted for 3 mos. tour and served his time, marched below Hanover C. H. on road to Wms'burg., but receiving orders they returned to Fredksbg. After this, volunteered under Capt. John Scott and marched to York at which place he served another 3 mos.; this was in the summer preceding siege of York, at which time Genl. Nelson commanded. Returned home and was immediately drafted for another 3 mos. service under Capt. Francis Coleman, and went to York where he remained during the siege, after which he was ordered to guard prisoners on march to Winchester; when he reached

Fredksbg., his term having expired, he was discharged. Was born in Orange Co., and is about 76 years of age. Served in the War from Spots. Co., and has resided in sd. County ever since.

Died April 9, 1833. (Page 89.)

June 3, 1833. Alexander Moore of Spts. Co., aged 73 years. Was drafted about the year 1780 in Spts. Co., under one Capt. Coleman. Marched thro' Fredksbg. to Wms'burg., down the Rappk. River. Was stationed at the Governor's palace. Served 2½ mos. on that tour. Enlisted under Serg. Maj. Tho. Hord and marched from Green Spring near Wmsburg, where he enlisted to the South to join Genl. Green, guarding baggage wagons. After staying there some time was ordered back by Gen. Green with same baggage. On this tour he was 5 mos. Cont'd about Wms'burg and did duty until the siege of York where he was present doing duty there for 5 mos., when he was discharged and returned home. Born Spts. Co., 1760. Called into service from Spts. Co. and has always lived in sd. county.

Died Feby. 4, 1834. (Order Book 1832–1838, p. 163.)

Augt. 6, 1833. Larkin Stanard of Spts. Co., aged 73 years. Entered service of the U. S. as a Cadet and served under Col. Mordacai Buckner, Lt. Col. Tho. Aylett, and Major James Hendricks, afterwards as a private under Capt. Joseph Brock, Capt. Thos. Bartlett, Capt. Winslow, Capt. Craig, and afterwards a purchasing commissary under Commissary Richard Young, etc. Entered service Jany. 1, 1776; the regiment lay about 4 miles below Wms'burg at the time of his joining. Cont'd with sd. regt. whilst it remained in Va., and with the sd. regt. marched to the North, and afterwards stationed at Amboy, from thence marched with his regt. to Woodbridge near New York, thence back to Amboy. He was the oldest Cadet and entitled to preferment in event of vacancy and one occurring, Colo. Buckner gave the appt'mt to his nephew, a junior Cadet, to him and others, in consequence whereof sd. Stanard with several others left the regt. and returned to Va. abt. early Decr., 1776; during this time, Jany. 1, 1776, to Dec., 1776, he ranked as an officer and messed with them. After his return to Va. he volunteered as private in Spts. Co., where he then resided, under Capt. Joseph Brock in 1777, and served a tour of 2 mos. and marched from Spts. to Wms'burg, passing through Hanover Co. After expiration of the two months he returned to Spts. Co. and again in the Spring of 1778 volunteered for another 2 mos. under Capt. Thos. Bartlett, again marched to Wms'burg, performing his tour, after which he returned home and in 1779 again volunteered for another 2 mos. under Capt. Winslow and again marched to Wms'burg, and at the expiration thereof was again discharged; he again volunteered for 2 mos. under Capt. Craig and again marched to Wms'burg, serving his tour he was again discharged, returning to Spts. Co. In 1780 he was appt. purchasing commissary by Richard Young in the month of August or thereabout, and served until December, a period of 4 mos., thus serving in all 1 yr. 11 mos., during the Revolutionary War. Born, Spts. Co., May, 1760.

John Marston, an officer in Revolutionary War, in Va. Line, died Oct., 1795. (Page 136.)

March 3, 1833.   Philip V. Vass of Spts. Co., aged 71 years.   In 1781 was drafted as a militia-man in Spts. Co., under Capt. Thos. Towles, in month of January and marched down to New Kent Co., was then called back to guard Fredksbg. under Gen. Weedon, was then discharged, having served 2 mos.   The next tour he was drafted in same Co., June, 1781, under Capt. Frank Coleman and marched down to Hanover C. H.; then retreated up country in what was called the Marquis Retreat, was in service 2 mos.   Was again in service and marched down to Yorktown where time being out he was discharged, having been on this tour 2 mos.   Born Spts. Co., Feby. 17, 1763.   In last tour affiant was substitute for Harry Chew.   Served under Col. Meriwether, Major Hardiman, and Capt. Frank Coleman.

Joseph Holloday was a Lieut. in the Va. line, Continental Army. (Page 179.)

George Tyler, an active and efficient officer in the Revolution, died Jany. 17, 1833.   (Page 180.)

Thomas Minor, a revolutionary officer, died July 21, 1834.   (Page 221.)

William Pritchett, decd., late of Spts. Co., was Sergeant in the Revolutionary War.   (May Court, 1835.)

Thomas Massey, formerly of Stafford Co., now of Orange Co., is only son and sole heir of Taliaferro Massey, Decd., who was reputed to have been a Revolutionary soldier.   (Page 286.)

Wm. Hutchinson, died July 12, 1835.   A revolutionary pensioner at the time of his death.   (Page 299.)

John Payne, a Revolutionary Pensioner, of the U. S., died Decr. 29. 1836.   (Page 492.)

INDEX

226, 246, 250, 267, 283, 385.

Bayn, George, 289; Richard, 60.

Baynham, G., 373; John, 274.

Baytop, James, 190.

Beadles, Dilly, 181, 229; Robert, 176, 180, 181, 229, 230.

B e a l e , Taverner, 173; T h o m a s, 103, 129; Thomas, Jr., 104.

Bean, John, 146.

B e a s l e y , B e a z l e y , Charles, 212, 215, 413, 426, 438, 456; Dorothy, 53; Elizabeth, 53, 509; Ephraim, 22, 219, 227, 232, 254, 310, 317, 355, 395, 403, 439, 499; Ephraim, Jr., 464, 509; John, 202, 212, 267; Susannah, 215, 426, 438; William, 53, 371, 499, 509; Winifred, 227.

Beattie, Beatty, Andrew, 59; Henry, 348.

Becket, John, 150.

Beckham, Stephen, 99, 106; William, 50.

Beckman, William, 97.

B e g n o l d , A n n e, 333; James, 333.

Belches, James, 145, 258; Judith, 235, 258; Patrick, 218, 235, 258, 268.

Belfield, John, 173; Mary, 173; Thomas Wright, 136, 174.

Bell, Ann, 88; Bathsheba, 173; Christopher, 90; David, 166, 173; Elizabeth, 110, 123; G., 46, 47, 231; Guy, 25, 220, 231, 442; Humphrey, 100, 147, 148, 154, 167, 174, 191, 197, 204, 211, 212, 216, 236, 266, 267; John, 31, 110; Joseph, 57; R., 123; Thomas, 291, 362; William, 149, 173, 185, 218, 306, 517; William, Jr., 192.

Ben, Benn, Antony, 252, 258.

Benger, Ann, 23, 76, 332; Betty, 25, 63, 76, 216, 258, 268, 286; Dorothea, 17, 58, 60, 204; Dorothea Brayne, 23, 76, 78, 353; Elliot, 4, 56, 57, 58, 60, 84, 105, 106, 123, 127, 131, 137, 139, 148, 177, 204, 248, 309; John, 17, 23, 28, 78, 202, 216, 229, 230, 239, 247, 248, 286, 291, 309, 353.

Bennet, Bennett, Charles, 452, 464, 475, 477, 486, 488, 490; Martha, 490; Patsy, 475.

Benson, Charles, 414; Eleanor, 403, 429, 452;

James, 272, 278, 280; John, 36, 357, 378, 390, 395, 403, 417, 429, 452; Sarah, 145; Thomas, 99, 109, 133, 145, 210, 234; William, 343.

Berch, Thomas, 112.

Berry, Henry, 115, 122; James, 384; Samuel, 39, 384; Thomas, 97; Thomas Stanly, 488; William, 451.

Berryman, Alice, 499; Benjamin, 112, 117, 124, 134; Cyrus, 80; Gerrard, 80; Gerard B., 423, 429, 430, 437, 460, 486, 499; Gilson, 16, 195, 491; John, 283, 415, 437, 491, 499; Josias, 423, 430, 437; Martha, 283; William, 80; Willoughby N., 437.

B e t t o n , Lucinda, 473; Solomon, 473.

Beverley, Agatha, 3, 4, 70, 85, 243, 254; Ann, 4, 85, 135; Catharine, 2, 4, 135, 168, 243; Chr., 95; Elizabeth, 391; Harry, 2, 3, 13, 15, 70, 89, 93, 94, 105, 158, 168, 178, 183, 190, 191, 193, 198, 205, 209, 232, 239, 243, 254, 305, 316, 386; Harry, Jr., 4; Harry Stanard, 50; Jane Wiley, 50, 386; Judith, 2, 84, 243; Margaret, 2, 84, 243; Mary, 2, 4, 84, 309; Robert, 2, 3, 89, 93, 118, 135, 183, 209, 309, 391; Robert Gains, 50, 391; Robert Hazlewood, 50; Susanna, 2, 84, 243; William, 3, 89, 132, 135, 149, 183.

Bibbing, Charles, 529.

Bickers, Elizabeth, 122; Robert, 122; William, 504.

Bicknell, William, 6.

Biddle, Clement, 404, 445; Owen, 404.

Bigbee, Rhodam, 355.

Bigers, Biggers, Bigger, John, 169; Meacon, 66; Peggy, 43; William, 66.

Billingsly, Allen, 489; John, 460, 468, 472; John A., 451, 499, 509; Zachariah, 358, 406, 415, 444, 451, 457, 499.

Bird, Byrd, John, 233; Mary, 44; Richard, 233; William, 520.

Birk, Edmund, 55.

Biscoe, Robert, 133, 134, 153.

Bishop, Richard, 326.

Black, Jane, 10; Margaret, 186; Sarah, 186; William, 171.

Blackaby, John, 137.

Blackburne, Robert, 5.

Blackgrove, Henry, 122.

Blackley, Edward, 134; John, 91, 93, 99, 106, 137, 164.

Blackwell, William, 57.

Blain, Ephraim, 404.

Blair, Alexander, 64, 311, 324, 339; David, 64, 260, 305, 309, 317, 322, 328, 339, 389, 404, 425, 446, 494; Elizabeth, 379; James, 332.

Blake, Elizabeth, 8, 177, 185; John, 8, 57, 85, 116, 148, 149, 154, 155, 158, 185; Mary, 8; Sarah, 10.

Blakey, George, 66, 180, 184, 283; Smith, 54, 66.

Bland, John, 122.

Blankenparker, Paultus, 4.

Blanton, Agnes, 383; Ann, 224; Elizabeth, 5; Hannah, 220; James, 214; Jane, 273, 334, 397; Joanna, 214, 233; John, 46, 57, 88, 89, 92, 110, 122, 510; Margaret, 110; Mary, 5; Priscilla, 5; Richard, 5, 188, 193, 214, 220, 228, 233, 261, 286; Richard, Jr., 5; Thomas, 5, 62, 208, 212, 224, 241, 261, 273, 304, 334, 343, 394, 397; William, 106, 110.

Blades, Blaydes, Clary, 49; Elizabeth, 49; John, 42, 49, 80, 369, 392, 443; John C., 488, 491, 509; Mary, 80, 319; Mary Ann, 42, 80, 380, 392, 501; Nancy, 80; Polly, 488; Sally, 49; Stephen, 49; Walker, 49; William, 42, 80, 275, 309, 319, 337, 356, 369, 376, 380, 392.

Blayle, Richard, 394.

Bledsoe, Aaron, 516, 517; Abraham, 55, 99, 100, 109, 117, 122; Elizabeth, 2, 87, 184, 214, 217, 237, 264, 336, 366, 375; George, 489, 508; Isaac, 2, 109; John, 489, 508; Joseph, 210, 214, 217, 232, 237, 260, 264, 309, 336, 375, 518, 521; Mary, 24; Miller, 24; Moses, 24, 61, 184, 209, 210, 214, 217, 227, 232, 254, 264, 349, 366, 489, 508, 516; Peachey, 349; Sarah, 122; William, 2, 89, 99, 100, 108, 110, 111, 112, 114, 121, 122, 132, 184, 210, 214, 217, 232, 264, 289, 349, 366, 512, 514; William Miller, 24, 375.